Change No. 1

ATP 3-21.8, C1

Headquarters
Department of the Army
Washington, DC, 23 August 2016

INFANTRY PLATOON AND SQUAD

1. Change 1 to ATP 3-21.8, 12 April 2016, updates the discussion and definitions of Casualty Operations, the duties of the combat medics and contents of combat lifesaver bags.
2. Modifies table A-2.
3. Modifies steps 3-b and 4-a Battle Drill 5: Knock out a Bunker (07-3-D9406).
4. Adds reference ATP 4-25.13, Casualty Evacuation, 15 February 2013.
5. A number sign (+) marks new and updated material.
6. ATP 3-21.8, 12 April 2016, is changed as following:

Remove Old Pages	**Insert New Pages**
Pages xv through xvi	Pages xv through xvi
Pages 1-23 through 1-24	Pages 1-23 through 1-24
Pages 1-27 through 1-28	Pages 1-27 through 1-28
Pages 1-49 through 1-50	Pages 1-49 through 1-50
Pages 6-17 through 6-20	Pages 6-17 through 6-20
Pages 7-3 through 7-4	Pages 7-3 through 7-4
Pages 7-11 through 7-12	Pages 7-11 through 7-12
Pages 7-21 through 7-28	Pages 7-21 through 7-28
Pages A-39 through A-40	Pages A-39 through A-40
Pages B-7 through B-10	Pages B-7 through B-10
Page D-43 through D-44	Page D-43 through D-44
Pages H-47 through H-48	Pages H-47 through H-48
Pages J-15 through J-16	Pages J-15 through J-16
References-1 through References-5	References-1 through References-5

7. File this transmittal sheet in front of the publication for reference purposes.

Distribution Restriction: Approved for public release; distribution is unlimited.

*Army Techniques Publication
No. 3-21.8

Infantry Platoon and Squad

Contents

		Page
	PREFACE	xxi
	INTRODUCTION	xxiii
Chapter 1	**ORGANIZATION**	1-1
	Section I – Operational Overview	1-1
	Operational Environment	1-1
	Unified Land Operations	1-5
	Law of Land Warfare	1-9
	Section II – Role of the Infantry Rifle Platoon and Squad	1-10
	Organization	1-10
	Duties and Responsibilities	1-14
	Habitual Attachments	1-23
	Capabilities	1-28
	Limitations	1-29
	Close Combat	1-29
	Employment Considerations	1-29
	Section III – Role of the Mechanized Infantry Platoon and Squad	1-30
	Organization	1-30
	Responsibilities	1-32
	Bradley Fighting Vehicle	1-38
	Capabilities	1-39
	Limitations	1-40

Distribution Restriction: Approved for public release; distribution is unlimited.

* This publication supersedes FM 3-21.8, The Infantry Rifle Platoon and Squad; ATTP 3-21.71, The Mechanized Infantry Platoon and Squad (Bradley); and ATTP 3-21.9, SBCT Infantry Rifle Platoon and Squad.

Contents

    Close Combat 1-40
    Employment Considerations 1-41
   Section IV – Role of the Stryker Infantry Platoon and Squad 1-41
    Mission 1-42
    Organization... 1-42
    Responsibilities 1-43
    Infantry Carrier Vehicle 1-51
    Employment Considerations 1-53
    Close Combat 1-53
   Section V – Company Organizations 1-54
    Infantry Rifle Company 1-54
    Mechanized Infantry and Armor Companies 1-54
    SBCT Infantry Rifle Company 1-56

Chapter 2 **OFFENSE** **2-1**
   Section I – Conduct of the Offense 2-1
    Characteristics of the Offense.. 2-1
    Offensive Tasks 2-3
    Forms of Maneuver 2-4
    Common Offensive Control Measures 2-10
    Sequence of the Offense 2-11
   Section II – Common Offensive Planning Considerations 2-11
    Mission Command 2-12
    Tactical Mission Tasks 2-12
    Movement and Maneuver 2-14
    Intelligence 2-14
    Fires 2-15
    Sustainment 2-15
    Protection.. 2-15
    Additional Planning Considerations 2-16
   Section III – Combat Formations 2-19
    Primary Formations.. 2-20
    Fire Team Formations.. 2-22
    Squad Formations 2-23
    Platoon Formations 2-27
   Section IV – Movement Techniques 2-43
    Squad Movement Techniques 2-44
    Platoon Movement Techniques... 2-47
    Mounted Movement Techniques 2-52
    Maneuver 2-56
   Section V – Actions on Contact 2-59
    Forms of Contact 2-59
    Five Steps of Actions on Contact 2-59

Section VI – Movement to Contact **2-62**
    Conduct of a Movement to Contact.. 2-62
    Organization of Forces 2-63
    Control Measures... 2-64
    Order of Events 2-65
    Plan 2-69
    Prepare 2-69
    Execute 2-70
    Assess 2-71
    Search and Attack.. 2-72
    Cordon and Search 2-76
Section VII – Attack... **2-83**
    Deliberate and Hasty Operations 2-83
    Organization of Forces 2-84
    Control Measures for an Attack... 2-85
    Order of Events 2-86
    Plan.. 2-87
    Prepare 2-89
    Execute 2-90
    Assess 2-94
    Special Purpose Attacks 2-95
Section VIII – Operation During Limited Visibility........................ **2-97**
Section IX – Battlefield Obscuration **2-99**
    Planning Considerations 2-100
    Employment Considerations 2-100
Section X – Transitions **2-100**
    Consolidation 2-100
    Reorganization 2-101
    Continuing Operations 2-101
    Transition to the Defense 2-102
    Transition to Stability... 2-102

Chapter 3   **DEFENSE** **3-1**
Section I – Basics of the Defense **3-1**
    Characteristics of the Defense 3-1
    Defensive Tasks... 3-3
    Order of Events 3-14
    Common Defensive Control Measures 3-17
    Sequence of the Defense... 3-20
    Priority of Work... 3-22
    Coordination... 3-26
    Security 3-27
    Remount Point 3-29

Contents

Section II – Common Defensive Planning Considerations.......... 3-30
Mission Command 3-30
Movement and Maneuver 3-31
Intelligence 3-37
Fires 3-38
Sustainment 3-38
Protection 3-39
Additional Planning Considerations 3-39

Section III – Forms of the Defense 3-41
Defense of a Linear Obstacle 3-41
Perimeter Defense 3-43
Reverse-Slope Defense 3-48

Section IV – Fighting Postions 3-51
Dismounted 3-52
Mounted 3-52

Section V – Engagement Area Development 3-55
Identify Likely Enemy Avenues of Approach 3-55
Determine the Enemy Scheme of Maneuver 3-56
Determine Where to Kill the Enemy 3-57
Plan and Integrate Obstacles 3-58
Emplace Weapon Systems 3-59
Plan and Integrate Indirect Fires 3-61
Rehearsals 3-62

Section VI – Transitions 3-63
Consolidation 3-63
Reorganization 3-63
Continuing Operations 3-64
Transition to the Offense 3-64
Transition to Stability 3-65

Chapter 4 STABILITY 4-1

Section I – Overview of Stability 4-1
Stability Framework 4-2
Stability Tasks 4-2

Section II – Planning Considerations 4-4
Mission Command 4-4
Movement and Maneuver 4-7
Intelligence 4-8
Fires 4-10
Sustainment 4-10
Protection 4-10

Section III – Unified Action Partners 4-12
Civil Affairs 4-12

	Human Terrain Teams	4-12
	Public Affairs	4-12
	Military Information Support Operations	4-13
	Host Nation Partners	4-14
	NonGovernmental Organizations	4-14
	Section IV – Tactical Actions and Tasks in Support of Stability	**4-15**
	Area Security	4-15
	Conduct Searches	4-16
	Tasks the Platoon Can Support for Other Forces	4-18
	Tasks the Platoon Monitors	4-19
	Section V – Transitions	**4-20**
	Transition to the Offense	4-21
	Transition to the Defense	4-21
	Transfer of Authority	4-21
	Transition to Civilian/Host-Nation Security Force Control	4-22
Chapter 5	**MOVEMENT**	**5-1**
	Section I – Troop Movement	**5-1**
	Methods of Troop Movement	5-1
	Administrative Movement	5-2
	Tactical Road Marches	5-3
	Approach March	5-7
	Section II – Route Selection and Navigation	**5-8**
	Navigation Aids	5-8
	Route Planning	5-9
	Types of Navigation	5-10
	Route Types	5-12
	Develop a Leg	5-12
	Execute the Route	5-13
	Section III – Actions at Danger Areas	**5-16**
	Crossing Danger Areas	5-17
	Crossing of Linear Danger Areas (Platoon)	5-18
	Actions at Danger Areas (Mounted)	5-20
	Ememy Contact at Danger Areas	5-23
	Section IV – Relief in Place	**5-24**
	Planning	5-24
	Coordination	5-25
	Conducting the Relief	5-26
	Section V – Passage of Lines	**5-27**
	Planning Considerations	5-27
	Forward Passage of Lines	5-27
	Rearward Passage of Lines	5-28

Contents

	Section VI – Linkup	**5-30**
	Control Measures	5-31
	Execution	5-31
	Phases of the Linkup	5-31
	Section VII – Movement with Combat Vehicles	**5-32**
	Combat Vehicles and Infantry Squad Formations	5-32
	Combat Vehicle and Infantry Platoon Formations	5-36
	Mounted Movement	5-38
	Convoys	5-41
	Section VIII – Security	**5-42**
	Enemy	5-42
	Terrain	5-43
	Camouflage, Noise, and Light Discipline	5-43
	Security Halts	5-43
	Section IX – Other Movement Situations	**5-47**
	Air Movement	5-47
	Movement by Water	5-47
	Movement During Limited Visibility	5-48
Chapter 6	**PATROLS AND PATROLLING**	**6-1**
	Section I – Overview	**6-1**
	Purpose of Patrolling	6-1
	Organization of Patrols	6-2
	Initial Planning and Coordination for Patrols	6-3
	Leader's Reconnaissance	6-4
	Completion of the Patrol Plan	6-6
	Departure From Friendly Lines or Fixed Base	6-8
	Patrol Base Activities	6-9
	Rally Points	6-13
	Mounted Patrols	6-15
	Section II – Patrol Preparations	**6-16**
	Orders, Briefings and Rehearsals	6-17
	Equipment	6-18
	Pre and Post Departure Preparation Activities	6-19
	Section III – Combat Patrols	**6-22**
	Raid	6-22
	Ambush	6-22
	Security Patrol	6-22
	Combat Patrol Planning	6-23
	Actions on the Objective – Raid	6-24
	Actions on the Objective – Ambush	6-26
	Security Patrols	6-41
	Section IV – Reconnaissance Patrols	**6-41**

	Area Reconnaissance Patrol	6-41
	Route Reconnaissance Patrol	6-43
	Zone Reconnaissance Patrol	6-43
	Control Measures	6-43
	Fundamentals of Reconnaissance	6-44
	Actions on the Reconnaissance Objective	6-47
	Area Reconnaissance Actions at Objective	6-50
	Route Reconnaissance Execution	6-51
	Zone Reconnaissance Methods	6-53
	Section V – Post Patrol Activities	**6-58**
	Accounting for Weapons and Equipment	6-58
	Debrief	6-59
	Patrol Report	6-59
Chapter 7	**SUSTAINMENT**	**7-1**
	Section I – Responsibilities	**7-1**
	Platoon Leader	7-1
	Platoon Sergeant	7-1
	Squad Leader	7-2
	Combat Lifesaver	7-3
	Section II – Soldier, Combat, and Unit Basic Loads	**7-3**
	Soldier Load	7-4
	Combat Loads	7-7
	Planning Consideration	7-8
	Section III – Functions of Sustainment	**7-9**
	Development of the Platoon Sustainment Plan	7-9
	Supply and Field Services	7-10
	Maintenance	7-19
	Human Resources	7-21
Appendix A	**PLANNING**	**A-1**
Appendix B	**DIRECT FIRE PLANNING AND CONTROL**	**B-1**
Appendix C	**INDIRECT FIRE SUPPORT PLANNING**	**C-1**
Appendix D	**SECURITY**	**D-1**
Appendix E	**VEHICLE EMPLOYMENT CONSIDERATIONS**	**E-1**
Appendix F	**MACHINE GUN EMPLOYMENT**	**F-1**
Appendix G	**SHOULDER-LAUNCHED MUNITIONS AND CLOSE COMBAT MISSILE SYSTEMS**	**G-1**
Appendix H	**OBSTACLE REDUCTION AND EMPLOYMENT**	**H-1**
Appendix I	**CBRN OPERATIONS**	**I-1**
Appendix J	**SELECTED BATTLE DRILLS/CREW DRILLS**	**J-1**

Contents

GLOSSARY Glossary-1
REFERENCES References-1
INDEX Index-1

Figures

Figure 1-1. Infantry rifle platoon and squads 1-11
Figure 1-2. Infantry fire team 1-12
Figure 1-3. Infantry squad 1-13
Figure 1-4. Infantry weapons squad 1-13
Figure 1-5. Attack aviation call for fire brief format 1-21
Figure 1-6. Indirect fire request format 1-24
Figure 1-7. Close air support 9-line request example 1-25
Figure 1-8. DD Form 1380, Tactical Combat Casualty Care (TCCC) Card 1-27
Figure 1-9. Bradley platoon organization 1-31
Figure 1-10. Stryker platoon organization 1-42
Figure 1-11. DD Form 1380, Tactical Combat Casualty Care (TCCC) Card 1-49
Figure 1-12. Infantry rifle company 1-54
Figure 1-13. Mechanized Infantry company 1-55
Figure 1-14. Armor company 1-56
Figure 1-15. SBCT Infantry rifle company 1-57
Figure 2-1. Envelopment 2-5
Figure 2-2. Turning movement 2-6
Figure 2-3. Frontal attack 2-7
Figure 2-4. Penetration 2-8
Figure 2-5. Infiltration 2-9
Figure 2-6. Flank attack 2-10
Figure 2-7. Fire team wedge 2-23
Figure 2-8. Fire team file 2-23
Figure 2-9. Squad column, fire teams in wedge 2-25
Figure 2-10. Squad line 2-26
Figure 2-11. Squad file 2-26
Figure 2-12. Platoon column 2-31

Contents

Figure 2-13. Platoon line, squads on line 2-32
Figure 2-14. Platoon line, squads in column 2-33
Figure 2-15. Platoon vee 2-34
Figure 2-16. Platoon wedge 2-35
Figure 2-17. Platoon file 2-36
Figure 2-18. Staggered column formation with dispersal for added
security 2-38
Figure 2-19. Wedge formation 2-39
Figure 2-20. Line formation 2-40
Figure 2-21. Echelon right formation 2-41
Figure 2-22. Coil formation 2-42
Figure 2-23. Herringbone formation 2-43
Figure 2-24. Squad traveling 2-44
Figure 2-25. Squad traveling overwatch 2-45
Figure 2-26. Squad bounding overwatch 2-46
Figure 2-27. Squad successive and alternate bounds 2-47
Figure 2-28. Platoon traveling 2-48
Figure 2-29. Platoon traveling overwatch 2-49
Figure 2-30. Platoon bounding overwatch 2-50
Figure 2-31. Example of platoon leader order for bounding
overwatch 2-52
Figure 2-32. Traveling, platoon mounted 2-53
Figure 2-33. Traveling overwatch 2-54
Figure 2-34. Bounding overwatch 2-55
Figure 2-35. Methods of bounding overwatch 2-56
Figure 2-36. Establishment of a cordon 2-80
Figure 3-1. Platoon defense in-depth 3-5
Figure 3-2. Platoon forward defense 3-6
Figure 3-3. Delay from alternate positions 3-10
Figure 3-4. Delay from subsequent positions 3-11
Figure 3-5. Types of withdrawals 3-12
Figure 3-6. Platoon unassisted withdrawal 3-13
Figure 3-7. Primary, alternate, supplementary and subsequent
battle positions 3-19
Figure 3-8. Platoon strongpoint battle position 3-19

Contents

Figure 3-9. Platoon defensive area of operation sketch 3-24
Figure 3-10. Stake the position 3-29
Figure 3-11. Protective wire obstacles 3-36
Figure 3-12. Platoon defense of a linear obstacle 3-42
Figure 3-13. Platoon perimeter defense 3-44
Figure 3-14. Y-shaped perimeter defense 3-46
Figure 3-15. Modified Y-shape perimeter defense 3-47
Figure 3-16. Platoon defense on a reverse slope 3-49
Figure 3-17. Developing deliberate fighting positions 3-53
Figure 3-18. Top view of Y-shaped fighting position 3-54
Figure 3-19. Likely enemy avenues of approach 3-56
Figure 3-20. Example of an enemy scheme of maneuver 3-57
Figure 3-21. Locations to kill enemy 3-58
Figure 3-22. Plans for and integration of obstacles 3-59
Figure 3-23. Emplacement of weapons systems 3-60
Figure 3-24. Integration of direct and indirect fires 3-62
Figure 5-1. Overlay with route control measures 5-4
Figure 5-2. Strip map 5-5
Figure 5-3. Example of sketching of legs 5-13
Figure 5-4. Crossing a linear danger area 5-18
Figure 5-5. Crossing a large open area 5-19
Figure 5-6. Crossing a small open area 5-20
Figure 5-7. Mounted traveling overwatch 5-21
Figure 5-8. Dismounting and clearing the area 5-22
Figure 5-9. Clearing a Defile 5-23
Figure 5-10. Forward passage of lines 5-28
Figure 5-11. Rearward passage of lines 5-29
Figure 5-12. Lead with Infantry squad 5-33
Figure 5-13. Lead with tanks 5-34
Figure 5-14. Lead with tanks and Infantry squad 5-36
Figure 5-15. Combat vehicle wedge, Infantry platoon diamond 5-37
Figure 5-16. Combat vehicle echelon right, Infantry platoon column .. 5-38
Figure 5-17. Lead vehicle moving by bounds 5-39
Figure 5-18. MRAP vehicle file/column or staggered formation 5-41
Figure 5-19. Movement to maneuver 5-43

Figure 5-20. Coil formation 5-44
Figure 5-21. Herringbone formation 5-45
Figure 5-22. Triangle Y formation.. 5-45
Figure 6-1. Five-point contingency plan 6-5
Figure 6-2. Leader's reconnaissance 6-6
Figure 6-3. Primary and alternate routes... 6-7
Figure 6-4. Objective rally point... 6-15
Figure 6-5. The five phases of a raid 6-25
Figure 6-6. Point and area ambush 6-27
Figure 6-7. Linear ambush 6-30
Figure 6-8. L-shaped ambush 6-31
Figure 6-9. V-shaped ambush 6-32
Figure 6-10. Security teams in position 6-33
Figure 6-11. Assault and support elements moving to the ambush site 6-35
Figure 6-12. Area ambush... 6-36
Figure 6-13. Anti-armor ambush 6-37
Figure 6-14. Organization of reconnaissance patrols 6-46
Figure 6-15. Forms of reconnaissance patrols..................................... 6-47
Figure 6-16. Route reconnaissance using fans.................................... 6-52
Figure 6-17. Fan method 6-54
Figure 6-18. Box method 6-55
Figure 6-19. Converging routes method... 6-56
Figure 6-20. Successive sector method 6-56
Figure 6-21. Zone reconnaissance using the stationary element technique... 6-57
Figure 6-22. Zone reconnaissance using multiple area reconnaissance.. 6-58
Figure 6-23. Patrol report example.. 6-60
Figure 7-1. Service station method 7-14
Figure 7-2. Tailgate resupply method.. 7-15
Figure 7-3. In-position resupply method 7-16
Figure 7-4a. DA Form 1156, Casualty Feeder Card (front)................... 7-27
Figure 7-4b. DA Form 1156, Casualty Feeder Card (back) 7-27
Figure A-1. Parallel planning A-2

Contents

Figure A-2. Troop leading procedures outline A-4
Figure A-3. Warning order format A-6
Figure A-4. Operations order format A-34
Figure B-1. Identifying probable enemy locations and determining enemy scheme of maneuver B-4
Figure B-2. Determining where and how to mass fires B-5
Figure B-3. Orienting forces to speed target acquisition B-6
Figure B-4. Constructed TRP markers example B-11
Figure B-5. Terrain-based quadrants example B-13
Figure B-6. Friendly-based quadrants example B-14
Figure B-7. Fire patterns examples B-22
Figure B-8. Target array examples B-23
Figure B-9. Example of a completed range card B-28
Figure B-10. Squad sector sketch B-30
Figure C-1. Defensive echelonment of fires C-4
Figure C-2. Offensive echelonment of fires C-5
Figure C-3. 81-mm mortars begin firing C-6
Figure C-4. 81-mm mortars shift, 60-mm mortars and supporting fires begin C-7
Figure C-5. 60-mm mortars shift C-8
Figure C-6. Supporting fire ceases C-9
Figure C-7. Company defense fire plan sketch C-10
Figure C-8. Platoon area of operation sketch C-12
Figure C-9. Squad sector of fire sketch C-13
Figure C-10. Comparison of lethal bursting radius of U.S. mortar rounds C-17
Figure C-11. Standing targets C-18
Figure C-12. Prone targets C-18
Figure C-13. Targets in open fighting positions C-19
Figure C-14. Targets beneath triple canopy jungle C-20
Figure D-1. Squad-sized stationary screen D-5
Figure D-2. On-line positioning of observation posts D-8
Figure D-3. In-depth positioning of observation posts D-9
Figure D-4. Selection of observation post location D-10
Figure D-5. Observation post area of operation sketch D-12

Figure D-6. Checkpoint sketch D-13
Figure D-7. Hasty checkpoint D-15
Figure D-8. Physical Layout D-16
Figure D-9. Controlling vehicle speed through obstacle placement
 and serpentine placement... D-18
Figure D-10. Convoy escort organization D-26
Figure D-11. Rear guard.. D-27
Figure D-12. Convoy escort actions toward ambush D-32
Figure D-13. Convoy continues to move D-32
Figure D-14. Escort suppresses ambush for reaction force attack D-33
Figure D-15. Infantry assaults ambush D-34
Figure D-16. Convoy escort overwatches an obstacle....................... D-35
Figure D-17. Platoon assembly area D-38
Figure D 18. Bradley and Stryker assembly area............................... D-39
Figure D-19. Detainee handling D-41
Figure D-20a. DD Form 2745, Enemy Prisoner of War Capture
 Tag (Part A)... D-43
Figure D-20b. DD Form 2745, Unit Record Card (Part B) D-44
Figure D-20c. DD Form 2745, Document/Special Equipment
 Weapons Card (Part C) D-44
Figure E-1. Reactive armor comparative levels of ballistic
 protection E-8
Figure E-2. M1A2 Abrams tank fields of fire on urban terrain E-10
Figure E-3. BFV 25-mm Infantry support E-12
Figure E-4. Mounting and riding arrangements on the outside of an
 M1-series Abrams tank E-23
Figure E-5. Seating diagram inside the M2A1 BFV E-24
Figure E-6. Seating diagram inside the M2A2/ODS and M2A3 BFV .. E-24
Figure E-7. Seating diagram inside the ICV E-25
Figure E-8. Seating diagram inside the Armament Carrier
 HMMWV.. E-25
Figure E-9. Seating diagram inside the MRAP MaxxPro Dash E-26
Figure E-10. M1-series Abrams tank danger zone E-31
Figure E-11. MGS danger zone E-32
Figure E-12. BFV danger zone.. E-33
Figure E-13. BFV TOW backblast danger zone E-34

Contents

Figure E-14. DA Form 2404 front page...E-41
Figure F-1. M249 light machine gun, bipod mode F-4
Figure F-2. M240B medium machine gun, bipod and tripod
 mounted..F-5
Figure F-3. M240L medium machine gun bipod mode F-6
Figure F-4. MK19, 40-mm grenade machine gun, MOD 3 ....F-7
Figure F-5. M2 .50-caliber heavy machine gun F-8
Figure F-6. M2A1 .50-caliber heavy machine gun...............................F-10
Figure F-7. Trajectory and maximum ordinate.....................................F-11
Figure F-8. Cone of fire and beaten zone F-12
Figure F-9. Surface danger zones for machine guns F-13
Figure F-10. Classes of fire with respect to the ground F-14
Figure F-11. Classes of fire with respect to the target F-16
Figure F-12. Frontal fire and flanking fire F-17
Figure F-13. Oblique fire and enfilade fire F-17
Figure F-14. Classes of fire with respect to the gun F-19
Figure F-15. Line of aim and placement of center of beaten zone
 on target..F-20
Figure F-16. March column with four machine guns............................F-21
Figure F-17. Application of gunner's rule F-24
Figure F-18. Application of leader's rule F-25
Figure F-19. Defilade positions F-25
Figure F-20. Observer adjusting fire F-26
Figure F-21. Arm-and-hand signals F-39
Figure G-1. M136 AT4 launcher and HEAT cartridge..........................G-4
Figure G-2. M136A1 AT4CS launcher and HEAT cartridge G-4
Figure G-3. M72A3 LAW..G-5
Figure G-4. M72A3 LAW 66-mm high-explosive antiarmor rocket G-6
Figure G-5. Improved M72A7 LAW with rocket G-7
Figure G-6. M141 bunker defeat munitions G-7
Figure G-7. M141 BDM high-explosive dual purpose assault rocket ...G-8
Figure G-8. Javelin close combat missile system G-9
Figure G-9. Javelin missile warhead G-12
Figure G-10. TOW 2B aero missile with identification G-16
Figure G-11. TOW bunker buster missile and identification G-17

Figure G-12. Armored vehicle weak points G-23
Figure G-13. Limited visibility of armored vehicles G-24
Figure G-14. Effects of SLM warheads on armor targets G-26
Figure G-15. SLM single firing G-29
Figure G-16. SLM sequence firing G-29
Figure G-17. SLM pair firing G-30
Figure G-18. SLM volley firing G-31
Figure G-19. Antiarmor ambush G-32
Figure G-20. TOW supporting offensive missions G-33
Figure G-21. M136 AT4 backblast danger area G-35
Figure G-22. Surface danger zones for firing M136 AT4 .... G-37
Figure G-23. Surface danger zones area F for firing M136 AT4 .... G-37
Figure G-24. M136A1 AT4CS backblast danger area G-38
Figure G-25. Surface danger zones area for firing M136A1 AT4CS ..G-38
Figure G-26. M72A2/3 LAW backblast area G-39
Figure G-27. Improved LAW backblast danger area G-39
Figure G-28. Surface danger zones for firing Improved LAW G-40
Figure G-29. M141 BDM backblast danger area G-40
Figure G-30. Surface danger zones for firing M141 BDM G-41
Figure G-31. Minimal dimensions of a confined space G-42
Figure G-32. Angle of launcher G-43
Figure G-33. Javelin back blast area and surface danger zones G-44
Figure G-34. TOW missile clearance requirements G-46
Figure G-35. Surface danger zones for firing basic TOW, TOW 2A, and TOW 2B missiles G-47
Figure G-36. M1121-mounted TOW firing angle limitations G-48
Figure H-1. Methods of activating mines H-3
Figure H-2a. Constructed wire and log obstacles H-5
Figure H-2b. Constructed wire and log obstacles H-6
Figure H-2c. Constructed wire and log obstacles H-6
Figure H-3. Urban obstacles H-7
Figure H-4. Reverse planning H-12
Figure H-5. AN/PSS-14 mine detector in operation H-15
Figure H-6. AN/PSS-12 mine detector H-15
Figure H-7. Bangalore torpedo H-17

Contents

Figure H-8. Antipersonnel obstacle breaching system H-18
Figure H-9. Man portable line charge H-19
Figure H-10. Tripod H-20
Figure H-11. Marking a footpath H-23
Figure H-12. Reducing wire obstacles with Bangalore torpedoes H-24
Figure H-13. Spiral firing pattern H-27
Figure H-14. Modular pack mine system H-40
Figure H-15. Antitank mines H-41
Figure H-16. Antipersonnel mines H-43
Figure H-17. M18A1 Claymore H-44
Figure H-18. Selectable lightweight attack munitions H-45
Figure H-19. M93 Hornet H-46
+Figure H-20. Example DD Form 3007 (Hasty Protective Row
    Minefield Record) H-48
Figure H-21. Triple standard concertina fence H-50
Figure H-22. Installing concertina H-50
Figure H-23. Joining concertina H-50
Figure H-24. Eleven-row anti-vehicular wire obstacle H-51
Figure H-25. Tanglefoot H-52
Figure J-1. Assuming nearest covered position J-2
Figure J-2. Control of the support element J-3
Figure J-3. Employing indirect fires to suppress enemy J-11
Figure J-4. Moving element occupies overwatch and engages
    enemy J-12
Figure J-5. Movement and fire technique J-12
Figure J-6. React to ambush (near) (dismounted) J-14
Figure J-7. Returning fire immediately J-14
Figure J-8. Assaulting through enemy positions J-15
Figure J-9. Clear a room, first two Soldiers enter simultaneously J-18
Figure J-10. Clear a room, third Soldier enters clearing his sector J-19
Figure J-11. Clear a room, third Soldier enters dominating his
    sector J-20
Figure J-12. Suppress, obscure, secure, reduce, and assault J-22
Figure J-13. Establishing a foothold J-23
Figure J-14. Securing assigned area J-24

Contents

Figure J-15. Isolating breach obstacle J-27
Figure J-16. BFV order of dismount J-35
Figure J-17. BFV order of dismount (continued) J-36
Figure J-18. ICV order of dismount J-37
Figure J-19. ICV order of dismount (continued) J-38
Figure J-20. BFV order of mount J-40
Figure J-21. BFV order of mount (continued) J-41
Figure J-22. ICV order of mount J-42
Figure J-23. ICV order of mount (continued) J-43
Figure J-24. Action right from line J-45
Figure J-25. Action right from wedge J-46
Figure J-26. Action right from column, wingman on left J-47
Figure J-27. Action right from column, wingman on right J-48
Figure J-28. Action left from a line J-49
Figure J-29. Action left from a wedge J-50
Figure J-30. Action left from a column, wingman on right J-51
Figure J-31. Action left from a column, wingman on left J-52

Tables

Table 2-1. Primary formations 2-21
Table 2-2. Comparison of fire team formations 2-22
Table 2-3. Comparison of squad formations 2-24
Table 2-4. Comparison of platoon formations 2-29
Table 2-5. Mounted formation characteristics 2-37
Table 2-6. Movement techniques and characteristics 2-44
Table 2-7. Consolidation and reorganization activities 2-68
Table 3-1. Advantages and disadvantages of delay techniques 3-9
Table 3-2. Obstacle effects 3-35
Table 5-1. Actions at rally point 5-16
Table 5-2. Stationary and passing unit responsibilities 5-30
Table 5-3. Actions at halts 5-46
Table 6-1. Actions by ambush elements 6-39
Table 6-2. Example infrared collection matrix 6-48

Contents

Table 7-1. Example of METT-TC Analysis 7-5
Table 7-2a. Example of 9-line Medical Evacuation Request Form (front) 7-24
Table 7-2b. 9-line Medical Evacuation Request Form Explanation (back) 7-25
Table A-1. Recommended enemy situation template items A-20
Table A-2. Precombat checks and precombat inspection checklist example A-40
Table B-1. Common fire control measures B-10
Table B-2. Weapons safety posture levels B-17
Table C-1. Indirect fire capabilities C-2
Table C-2. Normal final protective fires dimensions for each number of mortars C-14
Table C-3. Planning considerations C-15
Table C-4. Attack aviation call for fire capabilities C-25
Table D-1. Security fundamentals D-3
Table D-2. Active and passive security measures D-7
Table D-3. Task organization D-19
Table D-4. Road movement order format example D-29
Table E-1. Mobility characteristics of combat vehicles E-4
Table E-2. Weapons, ammunition, and targets E-6
Table E-3. Tasks of combat vehicles in Infantry operations E-20
Table E-4. Tasks of the Infantry in combat vehicle operations E-21
Table E-5. Dismounted rates of march (ideal terrain) E-21
Table E-6. Risk management matrix for tactical hazards E-29
Table E-7. Risk management matrix for accidental hazards E-30
Table E-8. Vehicle pre-execution checklist E-35
Table E-9. Classes of supply considerations for combat vehicles E-38
Table F-1. Machine gun specifications F-2
Table F-2. M249 light machine gun ballistic data F-4
Table F-3. M240B medium machine gun ammunition F-5
Table F-4. MK19 40-mm grenade machine gun ballistic data F-7
Table F-5. M2 .50-caliber heavy machine gun ballistic data F-9
Table F-6. Beaten zones of the M240B F-12
Table F-7. Weapons squad fire commands and actions F-31
Table F-8. Weapons squad equipment by position example F-40

Table F-9. Weapons squad duty positions and responsibilities F-42
Table F-10. M240-series rates of fire F-49
Table G-1. Shoulder-launched munitions G-2
Table G-2. Javelin capabilities and features G-9
Table G-3. Physical characteristics of the command launch unit........ G-10
Table G-4. Physical characteristics of the round G-11
Table G-5. Javelin capabilities and limitations G-13
Table G-6. Effects of the M141 BDM on field fortifications or bunkers G-20
Table G-7. Armored vehicle kills G-25
Table G-8. Effects of different munitions on vehicle types G-27
Table G-9. Missile selection priority chart G-31
Table G-10. Personnel duties G-34
Table G-11. AT4 Surface danger zones criteria in meters G-36
Table H-1. Relationship between breaching organization and breaching fundamentals H-11
Table H-2. Demolitions H-22
Table H-3. Charges H-33
Table H-4. Firing system components H-34
Table H-5. Mine delivery methods H-39
Table H-6. Characteristics of antitank mines H-42
Table H-7. Characteristics of antipersonnel mines H-43

Preface

ATP 3-21.8 provides the doctrinal framework for all Infantry platoons and squads. It provides techniques for employment of Infantry platoons and squads in conducting decisive actions.

The principle audiences for ATP 3-21.8 are commanders, staffs, and leaders who are responsible for planning, preparing, executing, and assessing operations of the Infantry platoon and squad. It serves as an authoritative reference for personnel developing doctrine materiel and force structure, institutional and unit training, and standard operating procedures (SOPs) for Infantry platoon and squad operations.

Commanders, staffs, and subordinates ensure their decisions and actions comply with principles and expectations of the Army Profession and any applicable U.S., international, and, in some cases, host-nation laws and regulations. Commanders at all levels ensure their Soldiers operate in accordance with the law of war and ROE. (Refer to FM 27-10 for more information.)

ATP 3-21.8 uses joint terms where applicable. Selected joint and Army terms and definitions appear in both the glossary and text. Terms for which ATP 3-21.8 is the proponent publication (the authority) are italicized in the text and are marked with an asterisk (*) in the glossary. Terms and definitions for which ATP 3-21.8 is the proponent publication are boldfaced in the text. For other definitions shown in the text, the term is italicized and the number of the proponent publication follows the definition. These doctrinal principles and procedures are intended as guides and are not to be considered prescriptive. This publication outlines the framework in which the Infantry platoon and squad will operate separately or as part of a combined arms team.

ATP 3-21.8 applies to the active Army, the U.S. Army National Guard, Army National Guard of the U.S., and the U.S. Army Reserve unless otherwise stated. It is designed for platoon, squad and company level chains of command, company grade officers, senior and junior noncommissioned officers (NCOs), U.S. Army Training and Doctrine Command (TRADOC) institutions and components, and the U.S. Army Special Operations Command.

The proponent and preparing agency of ATP 3-21.8 is the United States Army Maneuver Center of Excellence (MCoE). You may send comments and recommendations by any means—U.S. mail, e-mail, fax, or telephone—as long as you use or follow the format of Department of the Army (DA) Form 2028 (*Recommended Changes to Publications and Blank Forms*). Point of contact information follows:

- E-mail: usarmy.benning.mcoe.mbx.doctrine@mail.mil
- Phone: COM 706-545-7114 or DSN 835-7114
- Fax: COM 706-545-8511 or DSN 835-8511
- U.S. Mail: Commanding General, MCoE
  Directorate of Training and Doctrine
  Doctrine and Collective Training Division
  ATTN: ATZB-TDD
  Fort Benning, GA 31905-5410

Introduction

Army Techniques Publication (ATP) 3-21.8 encompasses techniques for the Infantry platoons and squads of the Infantry, Stryker, and Armored brigade combat teams (I, S, and ABCTs). It replaces Field Manual (FM) 3-21.8, published in March 2007, Army Tactics Techniques, and Procedures (ATTP) 3-21.71, published in November 2010, and ATTP 3-21.9, published in December 2010. ATP 3-21.8 provides doctrinal guidance; describes relationships within the platoon and squad; defines organizational roles and functions, capabilities, limitations; and lay outs the responsibilities for platoons and squads during unified land operations. The Infantry platoon and squad is an all-weather, all-terrain unit. Against this backdrop, the Infantry platoon and squad must be ready to adapt to various levels of conflict and peace in various environments. This requires bold, aggressive, resourceful, and adaptive leaders– leaders of character, competence and commitment - who are willing to accept known risks to accomplish the mission. Infantry leaders must use their initiative and make rapid decisions to take advantage of unexpected opportunities.

This publication addresses the significant changes in Army doctrinal terminology, concepts, and constructs and proven tactics, techniques, and procedures (TTPs). The following paragraphs provide a summary by chapter:

Chapter 1 – Organization:
- Provides a brief description of operational environments for Infantry platoons and squads. An overview of the Army's operational concept of unified land operations, operational structure, and law of war, rules of engagement (ROE), and combat power.
- Addresses the role and organizational characteristics the Infantry platoon and squad as trained to conduct offensive, defensive, and stability tasks.
- Addresses company team operations for the Stryker Infantry rife company, Infantry rifle company, and Armor and mechanized Infantry company.
- Describes task organization, mission, capabilities, and limitations the Infantry platoon and squad echelons within all three brigade combat teams (BCTs) as well as the duties and responsibilities of personnel within those echelons.

Chapter 2 – Offense:
- Addresses primary purpose of the offense—to decisively defeat, destroy, or neutralize the enemy force, or to seize key terrain.
- Discusses offensive actions to deceive or divert the enemy, deprive them of resources or decisive terrain, collect information, or fix the enemy in position.
- Describes offensive actions, during defensive missions, required to destroy an attacker and exploit success.
- Addresses the following keys to offensive missions—identify the enemy's decisive point; choose a form of maneuver avoiding the enemy's strength while exploiting

Chapter 1

the enemy's weakness; and ensure an operation massing overwhelming combat power.
- Discusses basics and sequence of the offense, planning considerations, and direct and indirect fire planning, which apply to all offensive actions.
- Concludes with synchronized attacks maximizing the Infantry's unique capabilities and planning considerations in transitioning to other operations.

Chapter 3 – Defense:
- Addresses primary purpose of the defense—to repel, to defeat, or to destroy an enemy attack and to gain the initiative for the offense.
- Discusses the basics, characteristics, and planning considerations and direct and indirect fire planning of defensive missions the Infantry platoon and squad performs.
- Describes the three defensive tasks—area defense, mobile defense, and retrograde operations.
- Addresses the five-step sequence of a defense during execution.
- Discusses three basic forms of the defense: defense of a linear obstacle, perimeter defense, or a reverse-slope defense.
- Addresses common defensive control measures.
- Concludes with a discussion of planning considerations in transitioning to other operations.

Chapter 4 – Stability:
- Discusses stability components of operations encompassing various military missions, tasks, and activities conducted outside the United States (U.S.) in coordination with other instruments of national power.
- Addresses BCT support to stability tasks, essential offensive and defensive tasks, and planning considerations.
- Describes conduct of mission command warfighting task—inform, influence and cyber/electromagnetic activities, replacement of the five Army information tasks (inform and influence, mission command warfare, information management, operations security (OPSEC), and military deception).
- Terms information engagement, command and control warfare, and information protection are rescinded.
- Provides discussion on transitioning from stability tasks to operations focused on offensive or defensive tasks.

Chapter 5 – Movement:
- Describes the different types of movements, administrative and tactical.
- Introduces the different types of movement formations and techniques.
- Discusses route selection, navigational aids, and route types.

- Provides techniques for crossing different types of danger areas and enemy contact at danger areas.
- Addresses movement with combat vehicles mounted and dismounted and security aspects going along with mission, enemy, terrain and weather, troops and support available, time available and civil considerations (METT-TC).
- Concludes with other movement situations, over water and under limited visibility.

Chapter 6 – Patrols and Patrolling:
- Provides an overview of patrolling, organization of patrols, planning, coordinating patrols, patrol plans, departure from friendly lines and rally points.
- Addresses combat patrols ambush, raid, and security, actions on objective, and combat patrol planning.
- Discusses reconnaissance patrols area, route and zone, control measures and actions on reconnaissance objective.
- Describes patrol preparations which include orders, briefings, rehearsals, and equipment.
- Identifies post-patrol activities, debriefs, equipment accountability, and patrol reports.

Chapter 7 – Sustainment:
- Addresses the sustainment challenges to ensure continuous operations during combat.
- Discusses sustainment of the Infantry platoon and squad (its Soldiers) to ensure maneuver and conduct of combat operation.
- Describes the process to continually anticipate Soldier needs and ensure the platoon and squad is properly sustained to conduct their mission.
- Addresses anticipation of future sustainment needs critical to operations and maintaining the momentum.
- Focuses platoon and squad sustainment operations, includes unit responsibilities, company trains operations, and functions of sustainment.

Ten appendixes complement the body of this publication addressing procedures performed at platoon and squad level. They are as follows:

- Appendix A describes the process of troop leading procedures (TLPs).
- Appendix B describes direct fire planning and control.
- Appendix C describes indirect fire support planning.
- Appendix D addresses security.
- Appendix E describes vehicle employment considerations.
- Appendix F addresses machine gun employment.
- Appendix G describes and addresses shoulder-launched munitions (SLMs) and close combat missile systems (CCMS).

Chapter 1

- Appendix H describes obstacle reduction and employment.
- Appendix I covers chemical, biological, radiological, and nuclear (CBRN) operations.
- Appendix J describes 14 selected battle drills for both the Bradley and Stryker.

Note. Unless otherwise stated, whenever the masculine gender is used, both male and female are implied.

Commentary

ATP 3-21.8 is truly the Bible for small unit operations. This publication is the doctrinal foundation for some of the more famous publications, such as the Ranger Handbook and Sapper Handbook. While reading, referencing, and studying this publication, we would like to encourage you to keep the appropriate mindset: Your small unit TTPs should not violate doctrine.

Too often in training we observe small units violate doctrine, and ultimately fail, because they "didn't have time" or because of their "TTPs."

Doctrine is the foundation upon which we build on and rise from. TTPs should improve upon doctrine, not detract from.

Chapter 1

Organization

The primary mission of the Infantry platoon and squad is to close with the enemy by means of fire and maneuver to destroy, capture, or repel an assault by fire, close combat, and counterattack. In order to succeed, Infantry platoons and squads are aggressive, physically fit, disciplined, and well-trained. The inherent strategic mobility of Infantry units dictates a need to be prepared for rapid deployment in response to situations in different operational environments. This chapter provides a brief discussion of operational environment and an operational overview of unified land operations, and the law of land warfare. It focuses on the role and organization, as well as the duties and responsibilities within the Infantry platoon and squad.

1-1. This section discusses in general terms, the Army's overarching guidance on unified land operations. Military operations occur in complex environments shaping their nature and affecting their outcomes. This requires an understanding of the operational environment in which the unit fights, how the Army fights, and the way small unit leaders lead their units and how Soldiers conduct themselves. (Refer to Army Doctrine Reference Publication [ADRP] 3-0 for more information.)

OPERATIONAL ENVIRONMENT

1-2. The operational environment for an Infantry platoon and squad is a composite of conditions, circumstances, and influences affecting the employment of that platoon or squad. It has a bearing on decisions made by the platoon leader and squad leader. As with Army leaders at all levels, platoon leaders and squad leaders use operational variables to analyze and understand the specific operational environment in which they conduct operations. They use mission variables to focus on specific elements of an operational environment during mission analysis. The operational environment for each operation is different and usually evolves as an operation progresses. It is critical that each platoon leader and squad leader understands his specific operational environment in order to plan, prepare, execute, and assess operations. (Refer to ADRP 5-0 for more information.)

OPERATIONAL VARIABLES

1-3. When Infantry forces are alerted for deployment, redeployment within a theater of operations, or assigned a mission, their assigned higher headquarters provides an analysis of the operational environment that affects operations at that higher level. From that

Chapter 1

higher-level operational environment analysis, a platoon leader or squad leader can draw any information relevant to his particular part of the higher headquarters operational environment. This allows him to use the limited resources available to collect and analyze additional information that applies only to his more specific operational environment. Analysis of operational environment at all levels of command uses the common framework of the eight operational variables and associated subvariables. The term PMESII-PT is used as a memory device. (Refer to JP 3-0 for more information.) The following is a list of the operational variables, their definitions, and examples (in parentheses) of questions a platoon leader or squad leader might need answered about each variable:

- *Political.* Describes the distribution of responsibility and power at all levels of governance—formally constituted authorities, as well as informal or covert political powers. (Who is the tribal leader in the village?)
- *Military.* Exposes the military and paramilitary capabilities of all relevant actors (enemy, friendly, and neutral) in a given operational environment. (Does the enemy in this neighborhood have antitank missiles?)
- *Economic.* Encompasses individual and group behaviors related to producing, distributing, and consuming resources. (Does the village have a high unemployment rate?)
- *Social.* Describes the cultural, religious, and ethnic makeup within an operational environment and the beliefs, values, customs, and behaviors of society members. (Who are the influential people in the village? For example, religious leaders, tribal leaders, warlords, criminal bosses, or prominent families.)
- *Information.* Describes the nature, scope, characteristics, and effects of individuals, organizations, and systems that collect, process, manipulate, disseminate, or act on information. (How much access does the local population have to news media or the Internet?)
- *Infrastructure.* Comprises the basic facilities, services, and installations needed for the functioning of a community or society. (Is the electrical generator in the village working?)
- *Physical environment.* Includes the geography and man-made structures as well as the climate and weather in the area of operations. (What types of terrain or weather conditions in this area of operation favor enemy operations?)
- *Time.* Describes the timing and duration of activities, events, or conditions within an operational environment, as well, as how the timing and duration are perceived by various actors in the operational environment. (For example, at what times are people likely to congest roads or conduct activities that provide cover for hostile operations?)

1-4. Upon receipt of a warning order (WARNORD) or mission, leaders filter relevant information categorized by the operational variables into the categories of the mission variables used during mission analysis. The mission variables consist of METT-TC.

1-5. Incorporating the analysis of operational variables into METT-TC ensures leaders consider the best available relevant information about conditions that pertain to the mission. Input from the operational variables often emphasizes the operational environment civil aspects. This emphasis is most obvious in civil considerations, but it affects the other mission variables of METT-TC as well. The platoon leader analyzes civil considerations in terms of, areas, structures, capabilities, organizations, people, and events (ASCOPE). (Refer to ATP 2-01.3 for more information.)

1-6. The Infantry platoon interacts with people at many levels. In general, the people in any area of operation can be categorized as a threat, an enemy, an adversary, a neutral, or a friend. One reason land operations are complex is all categories are intermixed, often with no easy means to distinguish one from another. Threat, enemy, adversary, and neutral are defined as—

- *Threat.* Any combination of actors, entities, or forces that have the capability and intent to harm U.S. forces, U.S. national interests, or the homeland. (Refer to ADRP 3-0.)
- *Enemy.* A party identified as hostile against which the use of force is authorized. (Refer to ADRP 3-0.) An enemy is a combatant and is treated as such under the law of war.
- *Adversary.* A party acknowledged as potentially hostile to a friendly party and against which the use of force may be envisaged. (Refer to JP 3-0.)
- *Neutral.* A party identified as neither supporting nor opposing friendly or enemy forces. (Refer to ADRP 3-0.)
- *Host Nation.* A nation which receives the forces and supplies of allied nations and NATO organizations to be located on, to operate in, or to transit through its territory.

THREAT

1-7. Threats may include individuals, groups of individuals (organized or not organized), paramilitary or military forces, nation-states, or national alliances. When threats execute their capability to do harm to the United States, they become enemies. Preparing for and managing these threats requires employing all instruments of national power: diplomatic, informational, military, and economic. (Refer to ADRP 2-0 for more information.)

1-8. The term hybrid threat has evolved to capture the seemingly increased complexity of operations, and the multiplicity of actors involved, and the blurring between traditional elements of conflict. A hybrid threat is the diverse and dynamic combination of regular forces, irregular forces, terrorist forces, or criminal elements unified to achieve mutually beneficial effects. Hybrid threats combine regular forces governed by international law, military tradition, and customs with irregular forces that act with no restrictions on violence or targets for violence. Such varied forces and capabilities enable hybrid threats to capitalize on perceived vulnerabilities, making them particularly effective. While the existence of innovative enemies is not new, hybrid threats demand the Infantry platoon and squad prepare for a range of possible threats simultaneously (Refer to ADRP 3-0 for more information.)

1-9. Incorporating civil considerations into mission analysis requires critical thinking, collaboration, continuous learning, and adaptation. It requires analyzing ASCOPE. In support of unified land operations, Army forces at every echelon must strive to obtain support from the indigenous population and institutions. Many social factors influence

Chapter 1

perceptions; these include language, culture, geography, history, education, beliefs, perceived objectives and motivation, communications media, and personal experience.

MISSION VARIABLES

1-10. Mission variables describe characteristics of the area of operation, focusing on how they might affect a mission. Incorporating the analysis of the operational variables into METT–TC ensures Army leaders consider the best available relevant information about conditions that pertain to the mission. Using the operational variables as a source of relevant information for the mission variables allows commanders to refine their situational understanding of their operational environment and to visualize, describe, direct, lead and assess operations. The mission variables are—

- *Mission.* Commanders and staffs view all of the mission variables in terms of their impact on mission accomplishment. The mission is the task, together with the purpose, that clearly indicates the action to be taken and the reason for the action. It is always the first variable commanders consider during decisionmaking. A mission statement contains the, who, what, when, where, and why of the operation.
- *Enemy.* The second variable to consider is the enemy dispositions (including organization, strength, location, and tactical mobility), doctrine, equipment, capabilities, vulnerabilities, and probable courses of action.
- *Terrain and weather.* Terrain and weather analysis are inseparable and directly influence each other's impact on military operations. Terrain includes natural features (such as rivers and mountains) and man-made features (such as cities, airfields, and bridges). Commanders analyze terrain using the five military aspects of terrain, observation and fields of fire, avenues of approach, key and decisive terrain, obstacles, cover and concealment (OAKOC). The military aspects of weather include visibility, wind, precipitation, cloud cover, temperature, and humidity.
- *Troops and support available.* This variable includes the number, type, capabilities, and condition of available friendly troops and support. This includes supplies, services, and support available from joint, host nation and unified action partners. They also include support from civilians and contractors employed by military organizations, such as the Defense Logistics Agency and the Army Materiel Command.
- *Time available.* Commanders assess the time available for planning, preparing, and executing tasks and operations. This includes the time required to assemble, deploy, and maneuver units in relationship to the enemy and conditions.
- *Civil considerations.* Civil considerations are the influence of manmade infrastructure, civilian institutions, and activities of the civilian leaders, populations, and organizations within an area of operation on the conduct of military operations. Civil considerations comprise six characteristics, expressed as ASCOPE: areas, structures, capabilities, organizations, people, and events.

UNIFIED LAND OPERATIONS

1-11. The Army's operational concept is unified land operations. It is based on the central idea that Army units seize, retain, and exploit the initiative, accepting prudent risk to gain a position of relative advantage over the enemy. This is accomplished through simultaneous combination of offensive, defensive, and stability-setting conditions for favorable conflict resolution.

1-12. Unified land operations describe the Army's approach to generating and applying combat power in campaigns and operations. Tactical action is a battle or engagement, employing lethal or nonlethal actions designed for a specific purpose relative to the enemy, the terrain, friendly forces, or another entity. Tactical actions include varied activities such as an attack to seize a piece of terrain or destroy an enemy unit, the defense of a population, and training other militaries as part of building partner capacity to assist security forces. Army unified land operations are characterized by flexibility, integration, lethality, adaptability, depth, and synchronization. (Refer to ADRP 3-0 for more information.)

FOUNDATIONS OF UNIFIED LAND OPERATIONS

1-13. The foundation of unified land operations is built upon initiative, decisive action, Army core competencies and mission command. By integrating the four foundations of unified land operations, leaders can achieve strategic success.

1-14. To seize, to retain, and to exploit the initiative, Army forces strike the enemy, lethal and nonlethal, in time, places, or manners for which the enemy is not prepared. To seize the initiative (setting and dictating the terms of action), Army forces degrade the enemy's ability to function as a coherent force. Leaders then prevent the enemy's recovery by retaining the initiative.

1-15. Army forces conduct decisive and sustainable land operations through the simultaneous combination of offense, defense, and stability (or defense support of civil authorities) appropriate to the mission and environment. Army forces conduct regular and irregular warfare against conventional and hybrid threats. (Refer to JP 3-27 for more information.) This includes:

- *Offensive tasks* are tasks conducted to defeat and destroy enemy forces, and seize terrain, resources, and population centers. They impose the leader's will on the enemy. (ADRP 3-0)
- *Defensive tasks* are tasks conducted to defeat an enemy attack, to gain time, to economize forces, and to develop conditions favorable for offensive or stability missions. Defense is aggressive, and platoon leaders use all available means to disrupt enemy forces. (ADRP 3-0)
- *Stability tasks* include various missions, tasks, and activities conducted outside the United States in coordination with other instruments of national power to maintain or reestablish a safe and secure environment, restore essential government services, and provide emergency infrastructure reconstruction and humanitarian relief. (ADRP 3-0)
- Defense Support of Civil Authorities represents the Department of Defense (DOD) support to U.S. civil authorities for domestic emergencies, law enforcement

Chapter 1

support, and other domestic activities, or from qualifying entities for special events. (Refer to ADRP 3-28 for more information.)
- Homeland defense is the protection of U.S. sovereignty, territory, domestic population, and critical defense infrastructure against external threats and aggression, or other threats as directed by the President. DOD leads the response, with other departments and agencies in support of the DOD efforts. (Refer to JP 3-27 for more information.)
- The philosophy of mission command—the exercise of authority and direction by the commander using mission orders to enable disciplined initiative within the commander's intent—guide leaders in the execution of unified land operations. Unified land operations begin and end with the exercise of collective and individual initiative to gain a position of advantage while degrading and defeating the enemy throughout the depth of enemy's organization. (Refer to ADRP 6-0 for more information.)

OPERATIONS STRUCTURE

1-16. The operations structure—operations process, warfighting functions, and operational framework—are the Army's common construct for operations. It allows Army leaders to rapidly organize efforts in a manner commonly understood across the Army. The operations process provides a broadly defined approach to developing and executing operations. The warfighting functions provide an intellectual organization for common critical functions. The operational framework provides Army leaders with basic conceptual options for visualizing and describing operations. (Refer to ADRP 5-0 for more information.)

Operations Process

1-17. The operations process is the Army's overarching framework to integrate processes and activities across the force by means of mission command. It consists of major mission command activities performed during operations, including:
- Planning is the process by which leaders translate the commander's visualization into a specific course of action (COA) for preparation and execution, focusing on the expected results. Planning to determine the relationship among the mission variables begins with the analysis and assessment of conditions in the operational environment, with particular emphasis on the enemy. It involves understanding and framing the problem and envisioning the set of conditions representing the desired end state.
- Preparation consists of activities performed by units to improve their ability to execute an operation. Preparation includes, but is not limited to, plan refinement, rehearsals, information collection and assessing, surveillance, and reconnaissance. This includes coordination, confirmation briefs and back briefs, inspections, and movement.
- Execution is putting a plan into action by applying combat power to accomplish the mission, and using situational understanding to assess progress and make execution and adjustment decisions.

Organization

- Assessment refers to the continuous monitoring and evaluation of the current situation and progress of an operation. Assessment precedes and guides every operations process activity and concludes each operation or phase of an operation. It involves a comparison of forecasted outcomes to actual events. (Refer to ADRP 6-0 for more information.)

1-18. TLPs are a dynamic process used by small-unit leaders within this framework to analyze a mission, develop a plan, and prepare for an operation. Small-unit leaders, company and below, lack formal staffs and use TLPs to maximize available planning time while developing plans and preparing their units for an operation. (Refer to appendix A of this publication for more information.)

Elements of Combat Power

1-19. Combat power is the total means of a unit's destructive, constructive, and information capabilities that can apply at a given time. Infantry platoons and squads generate combat power by converting potential into action. There are eight elements of combat power which include the six-warfighting functions (mission command, movement and maneuver, intelligence, fires, sustainment, and protection) plus leadership and information. (Refer to ADRP 3-0 for more information.)

1-20. Leadership is the multiplying and unifying element of combat power. The Army defines leadership as the process of influencing people by providing purpose, direction, and motivation, while operating to accomplish the mission and improve the organization. Army leaders of character, competence, and commitment understand the strategic implications of their decisions and actions. They motivate others to do what is right understanding that decisions and actions that are inconsistent with the Army profession are not tolerated and that any such act(s) can compromise the mission and have strategic implications contrary to the national interest. (Refer to ADRP 6-22 and ADRP 1 for more information.)

1-21. Information enables leaders at all levels to make informed decisions on how best to apply combat power. Ultimately, this creates opportunities to achieve decisive results. Required complementary tasks include:

- Information-related capabilities that developed synchronized multiple information-related capabilities in planning, coordination, synchronization, and assessment requirements in support of commander's objectives.
- Cyber electromagnetic activities to ensure information availability, protection, and delivery, as well as a means to deny, degrade, or disrupt the enemy's use of its mission command systems and other cyber capabilities.
- Knowledge management to make informed, timely decisions despite the uncertainty of operations and information management to make and disseminate decisions. (Refer to ADRP 3-0 for more information.)

Operational Framework

1-22. Army leaders are responsible for clearly articulating their concept of the operation in time, space, purpose, and resources. An established framework and associated

Chapter 1

vocabulary assist greatly in this task. Army leaders are not bound by any specific framework for conceptually organizing operations, but three operational frameworks have proven valuable in the past. Leaders often use these conceptual frameworks in combination. For example, a commander may use the deep-close-security framework to describe the operation in time and space, the decisive-shaping-sustaining framework to articulate the operation in terms of purpose, and the main and supporting efforts framework to designate the shifting prioritization of resources. These operational frameworks apply equally to tactical actions in the area of operation. (Refer to ADRP 3-0 for more information.)

1-23. Area of operation refers to areas assigned to Army units by higher headquarters. Within their area of operation, commanders integrate and synchronize maneuver, fires, and interdiction. To facilitate this integration and synchronization, commanders have the authority to designate targeting priorities and timing of fires.

1-24. Area of influence is a geographical area wherein a commander is directly capable of influencing operations by maneuver or fire support systems normally under the commander's command or control. (ADRP 3-0) The area of influence normally surrounds and includes the area of operation.

1-25. Area of interest is that area of concern to the commander, including the area of influence, adjacent areas, and areas extending into enemy territory. This area also includes areas occupied by enemy forces that could jeopardize the accomplishment of the mission. (Refer to ADRP 3-0 for more information.)

1-26. Deep-close-security framework that has been associated historically with a terrain orientation but can be applied to temporal and organizational orientations as well. Deep operations involve efforts to disrupt uncommitted enemy forces. Close operations involve efforts to have immediate effects with committed friendly forces, potentially in direct contact with enemy forces, to include enemy reserves available for immediate commitment. Security operations involve efforts to provide early and accurate warning of enemy operations, provide the force with time and maneuver space within which to react to the enemy, protect the force from surprise, and develop the situation so the commander can use the force.

1-27. Decisive-shaping-sustaining framework lends itself to a broad conceptual orientation. Decisive operations lead directly to the accomplishment of the mission. Commanders may combine the decisive-shaping-sustaining framework and the deep-close-security framework when this aids in visualizing and describing the operation. The decisive operation need not be a close operation. Shaping operations create and preserve conditions for the success of decisive operation. Commanders may designate more than one shaping operation. Sustaining operations enable the decisive operation or shaping operation by generating and maintaining combat power.

1-28. Main and supporting efforts are part of a framework, more simplistic than other organizing frameworks, focuses on prioritizing effort among subordinate units. Therefore, commanders can employ it with either the deep-close- security framework or the decisive-shaping-sustaining framework. The main effort is the designated subordinate unit whose mission at a given point in time is most critical to overall mission success. It is usually weighted with the preponderance of combat power. Typically, the main effort shifts one or more times during execution. Supporting efforts are designated subordinate units with missions that support the success of the main effort.

LAW OF LAND WARFARE

1-29. Leaders at all levels ensure their Soldiers operate according to the law of war. This also is called the law of armed conflict and is the body of international law that regulates the conduct of armed hostilities. The purposes of the law of war are to protect combatants and noncombatants from unnecessary suffering, make the transition to peace easier, and safeguard the rights of enemy prisoners of war (EPWs), detainees, the wounded and sick, and civilians.

1-30. Four important principles govern armed conflict: military necessity, distinction, proportionality, and unnecessary suffering. Military necessity permits combat forces to engage in those acts necessary to accomplish a legitimate military objective and not otherwise forbidden by the law of armed conflict. Distinction means discriminating between lawful combatant targets and noncombatant targets. The latter may include civilians, civilian property, EPW, and wounded personnel who are out of combat. Proportionality requires that the anticipated loss of life and damage to property incidental to attacks must not be excessive in relation to the concrete and direct military advantage expected to be gained. The principle of unnecessary suffering requires military forces to avoid inflicting gratuitous violence on the enemy. Soldiers consider these principles when planning and executing operations. (Refer to FM 27-10 for more information.)

1-31. ROE are directives issued by competent military authority that delineate the circumstances and limitations under which U.S. forces initiate or continue combat engagement with other forces encountered. (Refer to JP 1-04 for more information.) These directives may take the form of execute orders, deployment orders, memoranda of agreement, or plans. ROE always recognize a Soldier's inherent right of self-defense. These rules vary between operations and may change during an operation. Adherence to them ensures Soldiers act consistently with international law, national policy, and military regulations.

1-32. Soldiers use discipline when applying lethal and nonlethal action, a necessity for operations. Disciplined actions and decisions are a hallmark of our Army profession. In fact, the ethical, effective, and efficient accomplishment of our mission depends on the freedom to exercise disciplined initiative under mission command. Today's threats challenge the morals and ethics of Soldiers. Often an enemy feels no compulsion to respect international laws or conventions and commits atrocities simply to provoke retaliation. The enemy takes any loss of discipline on the part of Soldiers, distorts and exploits it in propaganda, and magnifies it through the media. The ethical challenge rests heavily on small-unit leaders who maintain discipline and ensure that Soldiers' conduct remains within moral and ethical boundaries that are in alignment with what is expected from the Army profession.

Chapter 1

1-33. The Soldier's Rules distill the essence of the law of war, outlining the ethical and lawful conduct required of Soldiers in operations. (Refer to Army Regulation [AR] 350-1 for more information.) Soldier's Rules are—
- Soldiers fight only enemy combatants.
- Soldiers do not harm enemies who surrender. They disarm them and turn them over to their superior.
- Soldiers do not kill or torture any personnel in their custody.
- Soldiers collect and care for the wounded, whether friend or enemy.
- Soldiers do not attack medical personnel, facilities, or equipment.
- Soldiers destroy no more than the mission requires.
- Soldiers treat civilians humanely.
- Soldiers respect private property and possessions.
- Soldiers should do their best to prevent violations of the law of war.
- Soldiers report all violations of the law of war to their superior.

SECTION II – ROLE OF THE INFANTRY RIFLE PLATOON AND SQUAD

1-34. Infantry rifle platoons and squads are optimized to conduct offensive, defensive, and stability or defense support of civil authorities' tasks. The Infantry rifle platoon and squad can deploy worldwide and conduct unified land operations.

ORGANIZATION

1-35. The Infantry rifle platoon and its squads can be task organized alone or as a combined arms force based upon METT-TC. (See figure 1-1.) Its effectiveness increases through the synergy of combined arms including tanks, Bradley fighting vehicles (BFVs) and Stryker Infantry carrier vehicles (ICVs), engineers, and other support elements. The Infantry rifle platoon and squad as a combined arms force can capitalize on the strengths of the team's elements while minimizing their limitations.

Organization

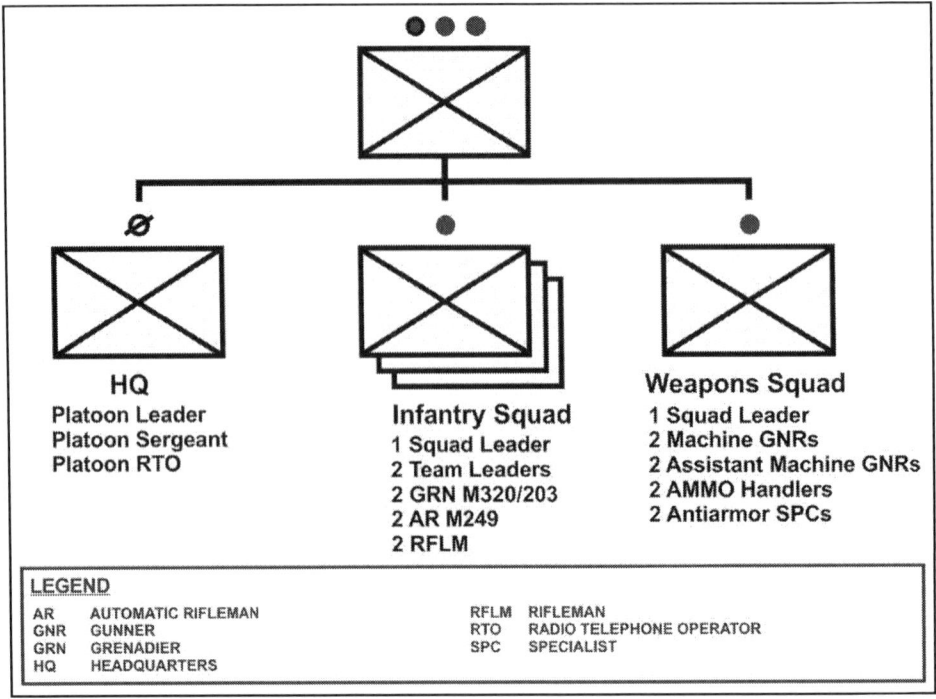

Figure 1-1. Infantry rifle platoon and squads

1-36. Infantry units can operate in all terrain and weather conditions. They might be the dominant force because of rapid strategic deployment. In such cases, they can take and gain the initiative early, seize and retain or control terrain, and mass fires to stop the enemy. Infantry units are particularly effective in urban terrain, where they can infiltrate and move rapidly to the rear of enemy positions. The leader can enhance their mobility by using helicopters and airlift.

1-37. The fundamental considerations for employing Infantry units result from the missions, types, equipment, capabilities, limitations, and organization of units. Other capabilities result from a unit's training program, leadership, morale, personnel strengths, and many other factors. These other capabilities constantly change based on the current situation.

INFANTRY SQUAD FIRE TEAM

1-38. The Infantry squad fire team is designed to fight as a team and is the fighting element within the Infantry platoon. Infantry platoons and squads succeed or fail based on the actions of their fire teams.

1-39. The Infantry squad fire team is designed as a self-contained team. (See figure 1-2, page 1-12.) The automatic rifleman provides an internal base of fire with the ability to deliver sustained suppressive small arms fire on area targets. The rifleman provides accurate, lethal direct fire for point targets. The rifleman may be issued an SLM. The

Chapter 1

grenadier provides high explosive (HE) indirect fires for both point and area targets. A team leader leads his team by example.

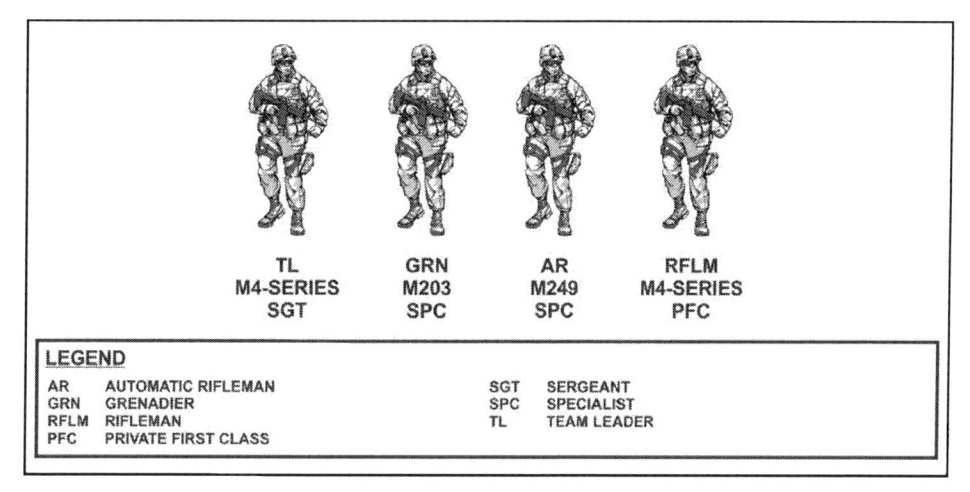

Figure 1-2. Infantry fire team

INFANTRY SQUAD

1-40. Currently, there is only one type of Infantry squad and its primary role is a maneuver or base-of-fire element. (See figure 1-3.) While the platoon's task organization may change, the Infantry squad's organization generally remains standard.

1-41. The Infantry squad is a model for all tactical task organizations. It is comprised of two fire teams and a squad leader. It can establish a base of fire, providing security for another element, or conducting fire and movement with one team providing a base of fire, while the other team moves to the next position of advantage or onto an objective. The squad leader has two subordinate leaders to lead the two teams, freeing him to control the entire squad.

> *Note.* The combat load for an SLM is two per rifle squad. Either two M72-series light antitank (AT) weapon, M136-series antitank (AT4), M141 bunker defeat munitions (BDMs), or a combination of are normally issued to the rifleman.

Organization

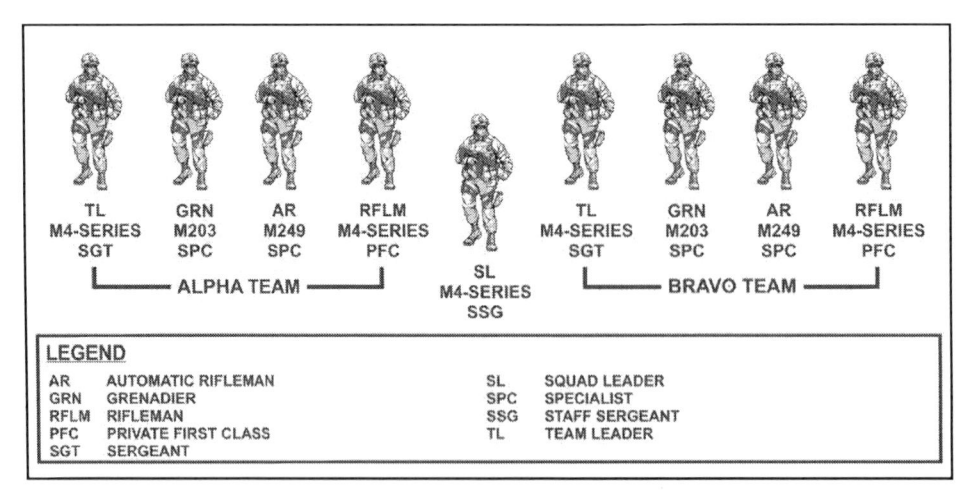

Figure 1-3. Infantry squad

INFANTRY WEAPONS SQUAD

1-42. The Infantry weapons squad provides the primary base of fire for the platoon's maneuver. It is comprised of two medium machine gun teams, two medium CCMS teams, and a weapons squad leader. (See figure 1-4.)

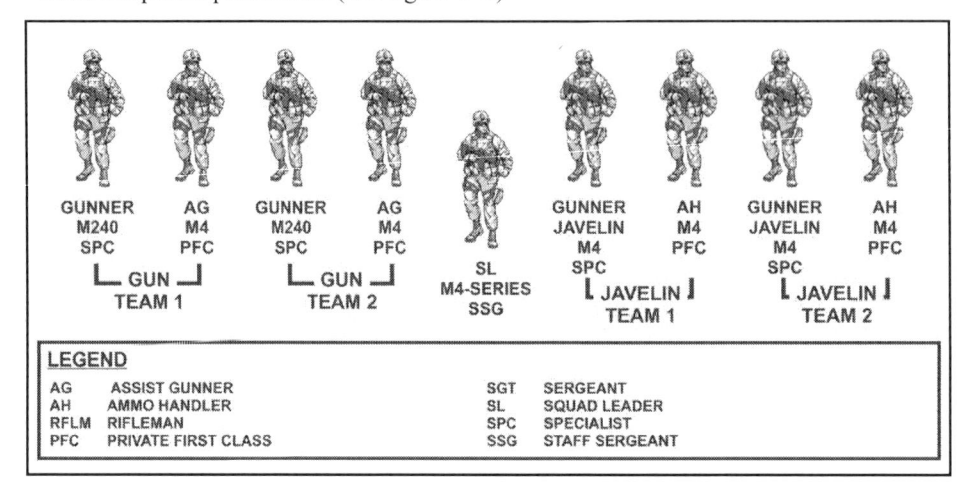

Figure 1-4. Infantry weapons squad

MEDIUM MACHINE GUN TEAM

1-43. The two-man medium machine gun team is comprised of a gunner and an assistant gunner. The weapon squad has two medium machine gun teams. These teams provide the platoon with medium-range area suppression at ranges up to 1100 meters during day, night, and adverse weather conditions.

Chapter 1

> *Note.* When referring to the medium machine gun in this manual, it refers to the M240-series machine gun. There are several variants of the M240. They are the M240, M240B, M240C, M240D, M240E, M240G, M240H and M240L, each supporting their specific platform. The M240B is the standard Infantry medium machine gun of the U.S. Army. The M240L machine gun is the next generation medium machine gun, currently being fielded to replace the M240B.

CLOSE COMBAT MISSILE TEAM

1-44. The two-man close combat missile team is comprised of a gunner and an ammunition handler. Currently, the team uses the Javelin missile system. The weapon squad has two close combat missile system teams. This system provides the platoon with an extremely lethal fire-and-forget, man-portable, direct- and top-attack capability to defeat enemy armored vehicles and destroy fortified positions at ranges up to 2000 meters. The Javelin has proven effective during day, night, and adverse weather conditions.

DUTIES AND RESPONSIBILITIES

1-45. This section describes the duties and responsibilities of personnel and habitual attachments in the Infantry rifle platoon and squad.

> *Note.* The duties and responsibilities of leadership and platoon members must be executed even in the absence of a particular leader to ensure mission accomplishment in accordance with the commander's intent.

PLATOON LEADER

1-46. The platoon leader leads his Soldiers by personal example and is responsible for all the platoon does or fails to do, having complete authority over his subordinates. This centralized authority enables him to maintain unit discipline, unity, and to act decisively. He must be prepared to exercise initiative within his company commander's intent and without specific guidance for every situation. The platoon leader knows his Soldiers, how to employ the platoon, its weapons, and its systems. Relying on the expertise of the platoon sergeant, the platoon leader regularly consults with him on all platoon matters. During operations, the platoon leader—

- Leads the platoon in supporting the higher headquarters missions. He bases his actions on his assigned mission and intent and concept of his higher commanders.
- Conducts troop leading procedures.
- Maneuvers squads and fighting elements.
- Synchronizes the efforts of squads.
- Looks ahead to the next "move" of the platoon.
- Requests, controls, and synchronizes supporting assets.
- Employs mission command systems available to the squads and platoon.

Organization

- Checks with squad leaders ensuring 360-degree, three-dimensional security is maintained.
- Checks with weapons squad leader controlling the emplacement of key weapon systems.
- Issues accurate and timely reports.
- Places himself where he is most needed to accomplish the mission.
- Assigns clear tasks and purposes to the squads.
- Understands the mission and commander's intent two levels up (company and battalion).
- Receives on-hand status reports from the platoon sergeant and squad leaders during planning.
- Coordinates and assists in the development of the obstacle plan.
- Oversees and is responsible for property management.

1-47. The platoon leader works to develop and maintain situational understanding. This is a product of four elements. First, the platoon leader attempts to know what is happening in present terms of friendly, enemy, neutral, and terrain situations. Second, he knows the end state representing mission accomplishment. Third, he determines the critical actions and events occurring to move his unit from the present to the end state. Finally, he assesses the risk throughout.

PLATOON SERGEANT

1-48. The platoon sergeant is the platoon's most experienced NCO and second-in-charge, accountable to the platoon leader for leadership, discipline, training, and welfare of the platoon's Soldiers. He sets the example in everything. He assists the platoon leader by upholding standards and platoon discipline. His expertise includes tactical maneuver, employment of weapons and systems, sustainment, administration, security, accountability, protection warfighting functions, and Soldier care. As the second-in-charge, the platoon sergeant assumes no formal duties except those prescribed by the platoon leader. However, the platoon sergeant traditionally—

- Ensures the platoon is prepared to accomplish its mission, which includes supervising precombat checks and inspections.
- Updates platoon leader on appropriate reports and forwards reports needed by higher headquarters.
- Prepares to assume the role and responsibilities of the platoon leader.
- Takes charge of task-organized elements in the platoon during tactical operations, which may include but is not limited to, quartering parties, support elements in raids or attacks, and security patrols.
- Monitors the morale, discipline, and health of the platoon.
- Positions where best needed to help the engagement (either in the base of fire or with the assault element).
- Receives squad leaders' administrative, logistical, and maintenance reports, and requests rations, water, fuel, and ammunition.

Chapter 1

- Requests logistical support from the higher headquarters, and usually coordinates with the company's first sergeant or executive officer.
- Ensures Soldiers maintain all equipment.
- Ensures ammunition and supplies are properly and evenly distributed after the platoon consolidates on the objective and while the platoon reorganizes.
- Manages the unit's combat load prior to operations, and monitors logistical status during operations.
- Establishes and operates the unit's casualty collection point (CCP). This includes directing the platoon medic and aid/litter teams in moving casualties, maintains platoon strength level information, consolidates and forwards the platoon's casualty reports, and receives and orients replacements.
- Employs the available digital mission command systems to the squads and platoon.
- Ensures Soldiers distribute supplies according to the platoon leader's guidance and direction.
- Accounts for Soldiers, equipment, and supplies.
- Coaches, counsels, and mentors Soldiers.
- Upholds standards and platoon discipline.
- Understands the mission and commander's intent two levels up (company and battalion).

WEAPONS SQUAD LEADER

1-49. The weapons squad leader leads his teams by personal example. He has complete authority over his subordinates and overall responsibility for those subordinates' actions. This centralized authority enables him to act decisively while maintaining troop discipline and unity. Under the fluid conditions of modern warfare, he accomplishes assigned missions using disciplined initiative without needing constant guidance from higher headquarters.

1-50. The weapons squad leader is usually the senior squad leader, second only to the platoon sergeant, and performs all the duties of the rifle squad leader. In addition, the weapons squad leader—

- Controls fires and establishes fire control measures.
- Recommends medium machine gun employment to the platoon leader.
- Coordinates directly with the platoon leader for medium machine gun base-of-fire effect, and plans accordingly.
- Monitors ammunition expenditure.
- Coordinates directly with the platoon leader in placement of the Javelin-CCMS to best cover armored avenues of approach in the defense and overwatch positions in the attack.
- Employs mission command systems available to the squad and platoon.
- Performs the role of the platoon sergeant as required.
- Conducts troop leading procedures.
- Understands the mission two levels up (platoon and company).

Organization

SQUAD LEADER

1-51. The squad leader directs team leaders and leads by personal example. He has authority over his subordinates and overall responsibility of those subordinates' actions. Centralized authority enables him to act decisively while maintaining troop discipline and unity. Under the fluid conditions of close combat, the squad leader accomplishes assigned missions without constant guidance from higher headquarters.

1-52. The squad leader is the senior Infantry Soldier in the squad and is responsible for everything the squad does or fails to do. He is responsible for the care of the squad's Soldiers, weapons, and equipment, and leads the squad through two team leaders. During operations, the squad leader—

- Is the subject matter expert on all battle and individual drills.
- Is the subject matter expert for the squad's organic weapons employment, and employment of supporting assets.
- Knows weapon effects, surface danger zones, and risk estimate distances for all munitions.
- Uses control measures for direct fire, indirect fire, and tactical movement effectively.
- Controls the movement of the squad and its rate and distribution of fire (including call for and adjust fire).
- Fights the close fight by fire and movement with two fire teams and available supporting weapons.
- Selects the fire team's general location and temporary sector of fires in the defense.
- Communicates timely and accurate situation reports (SITREPs) and status reports including—
  - Size, activity, location, unit, time, and equipment (SALUTE) spot reports (SPOTREPs).
  - Status to the platoon leader (including squad location and progress, enemy situation, enemy killed in action [KIA], and security posture).
  - Status of ammunition, casualties, and equipment to the platoon sergeant.
- Employs digital mission command systems available to the squad and platoon.
- Operates in all environments to include the urban environment.
- Conducts troop leading procedures.
- Assumes duties as the platoon sergeant or platoon leader as required.
- Understands the mission and commander's intent two levels up (platoon and company).

TEAM LEADER

1-53. The team leader leads his team members by personal example and has authority over his subordinates and overall responsibility of their actions. Centralized authority enables him to maintain troop discipline and unity and to act decisively. Under the fluid conditions of close combat, he accomplishes assigned missions using initiative without needing constant guidance from higher headquarters.

Chapter 1

1-54. The team leader's position on the battlefield requires immediacy and accuracy in all of his actions and is a fighting leader who leads by example. He is responsible for all his team does or fails to do, and is responsible for caring of the team's Soldiers, weapons, and equipment. During operations, the team leader—

- Is the subject matter expert for all the team's weapons and duty positions and all squad battle drills.
- Leads his team in fire and movement.
- Controls the movement of his team and its rate and distribution of fire.
- Employs digital mission command systems available to the squad and platoon.
- Ensures security of the team's area of operations.
- Assists the squad leader as required.
- Is prepared to assume the duties of squad leader and platoon sergeant.
- Enforces field discipline and preventive medicine measures.
- Determines his team's combat load and manages its available classes of supply as required.
- Understands the mission two levels up (squad and platoon).

1-55. When maneuvering the team, the team fights using one of three techniques. This includes:

- Individual movement techniques. This is the lowest level of movement.
- Buddy team fire and movement.
- Fire team fire and movement (maneuver).

1-56. Determining a suitable technique is based on the effectiveness of the enemy's fire and available cover and concealment. The more effective the enemy's fire, the lower the level of movement. Because the team leader leads his team, he is able to make this assessment firsthand. Other leaders must be sensitive to his decision on movement.

GRENADIER

1-57. The grenadier currently is equipped with an M203/M320 weapon system consisting of an M16-series or M4-series rifle/carbine and an attached 40-mm grenade launcher. He provides the fire team with a high trajectory and an HE capability out to 350 meters. His fire enables the fire team to achieve complementary effects with high trajectory, HE munitions, and flat trajectory ball ammunition from the team's weapons. The grenade launcher allows the grenadier to perform three functions: suppress and destroy enemy Infantry and lightly armored vehicles with HE or high explosive dual purpose (HEDP); provide obscurants to screen and cover his squad's fire and movement; and employ illumination rounds to increase his squad's visibility and mark enemy positions. The grenadier—

- Accomplishes all tasks of the rifleman.
- Engages targets with appropriate type of rounds both day and night.
- Identifies 40-mm rounds by shape and color. He must know how to employ each type of round and know its minimum safety constraints.
- Knows the maximum ranges for each type of target of the grenade launcher.

Organization

- Knows the leaf sight increments without seeing the markings.
- Knows how to make an adjustment from the first round fired so a second-round hit can be attained.
- Loads the grenade launcher quickly in all firing positions and while running.
- Is prepared to assume the duties of the automatic rifleman and team leader.
- Understands the mission two levels up (squad and platoon).

AUTOMATIC RIFLEMAN

1-58. The automatic rifleman's primary weapon is currently the 5.56-mm M249 light machine gun. The automatic rifleman provides the unit with a high volume of sustained suppressive direct fires of area targets. The automatic rifleman employs his weapon system to suppress enemy Infantry and bunkers, destroy enemy automatic rifle and AT teams, and enable the movement of other teams and squads. He is normally the senior Soldier of the fire team and must—

- Be able to accomplish all tasks of the rifleman and grenadier.
- Be prepared to assume the duties of team leader and squad leader.
- Be able to engage groups of enemy personnel, thin-skinned vehicles, bunker doors or apertures, and suspected enemy locations with automatic fire.
- Be able to provide suppressive fire on these targets so his teammates can close with and destroy the enemy.
- Be familiar with field expedient firing aids to enhance the effectiveness of his weapon: an example is aiming stakes.
- Be able to engage targets from the prone, kneeling, and standing positions with and without night observation devices, and understands the mission two levels up (squad and platoon).

RIFLEMAN

1-59. The rifleman provides the baseline standard for all Infantry Soldiers and is an integral part of the fire team. The rifleman is an expert in handling and employing the weapon and placing well-aimed fire on the enemy. Additionally, the rifleman must—

- Be an expert on his weapon system, his rifle, its optics, and its laser-aiming device, and is effective with this weapon system day or night.
- Be capable of engaging all targets with well-aimed shots.
- Employ all weapons of the squad, as well as common munitions.
- Construct and occupy a hasty firing position and know how to fire from it. He must know how to occupy covered and concealed positions in all environments and what protection they provide from direct fire weapons, and is competent in the performance of these tasks while using night vision devices.
- Fight as part of his unit, which includes proficiency in his individual tasks and drills.
- Know the duties of his teammates and is prepared to fill in with their weapons, if needed.

Chapter 1

- Contribute as a member of special teams, including detainee search, aid/litter, demolitions and. wire/mine breach teams.
- Inform his team leader of everything he hears and sees when in a tactical situation.
- Perform individual preventive medical measures.
- Administer buddy aid as required.
- Manage his food, water, and ammunition during operations.
- Be prepared to assume the duties of the automatic rifleman and team leader.
- Understand the mission two levels up (squad and platoon).

PLATOON RADIOTELEPHONE OPERATOR

1-60. The platoon radiotelephone operator (RTO) primarily is responsible for communication with its controlling headquarters (usually the company). During operations, the RTO—

- Has communications at all times. If communication with the platoon's next higher element is lost, the radiotelephone operator immediately informs the platoon leader or platoon sergeant and reestablishes communication.
- Conducts radio checks with higher according to unit standard operating procedures when in a static position. If radio contact cannot be made as required, he informs the platoon sergeant or platoon leader.
- Is an expert in radio procedures and report formats such as close combat attack (see figure 1-5), call for indirect fire (see figure 1-6, page 1-24), or medical evacuation (see table 7-1, page 7-5). Plus is an expert on types of field expedient antennas.
- Has the frequencies and call signs on his person in a location known to all Soldiers in the platoon.
- Assists the platoon leader with information management.
- Assists the platoon leader and platoon sergeant employing digital mission command systems with the squads and platoon.
- Determines his combat load prior to operations and manages battery utilization during operations.

Organization

FORMAT 12. Attack Aviation Call for Fire Briefing-Ground to Air (5-Line)

1. Observer/Warning Order
" _____ , this is _____ , Fire Mission, Over"
   (Aircraft Call Sign)   (Observer Call Sign)
 	
2. Friendly Location/Mark
"My position _____ **, marked by** _____ "
         (TRP, Grid, etc.)   (Strobe, Beacon, IR Strobe, etc.)
 	
3. Target Location
"Target Location _____ "
      (Bearing [magnetic] and Range [meters], TRP, Grid, etc.)
 	
4. Target Description/Mark
" _____ , **marked by** _____ "
   (Target Description)   (IR Pointer, Tracer, etc.)
 	
5. Remarks (Threats, Danger Close Clearance, Restriction, At My Command, etc.)
"Over"

AS REQUIRED: 1. Clearance: Transmission of the 5-Line Attack Aviation Call for Fire Brief is clearance to fire (unless danger close). For closer fire, the observer/commander must accept responsibility for increased risk. State "Cleared Danger Close" in line 5. This clearance may be preplanned. 2. At My Command: For positive control of the aircraft, state **"At My Command"** on line 5. The aircraft will call **"Ready for Fire"** when ready.
LEGEND IR   INFRARED   TRP   TARGET REFERENCE POINT

Figure 1-5. Attack aviation call for fire brief format

SQUAD-DESIGNATED MARKSMAN

1-61. The squad-designated marksman employs an optically enhanced general-purpose weapon. He also receives training available within the unit's resources to improve the squad's precision engagement capabilities at short and medium ranges.

1-62. A rifleman may be assigned as the squad-designated marksman. He is chosen for his demonstrated shooting ability, maturity, reliability, good judgment, and experience. He must be able to execute the entire range of individual and collective rifleman tasks within the squad. (Refer to FM 3-22.9 for more information.)

Chapter 1

1-63. The squad designated marksman is not the squad sniper, he is a fully integrated member of the rifle squad and provides an improved capability for the rifle squad. He does not operate as a semi-autonomous element on the battlefield as a sniper, nor does he routinely engage targets at the extreme ranges common to snipers.

MACHINE GUNNER

1-64. The gunner is normally the senior member of the medium machine gun team. During operations, the gunner—
- Is responsible for his assistant gunner and all the gun equipment.
- Is responsible for putting the gun in and out of action.
- Is the subject matter expert for information contained in FM 3-22.68.
- When attached to a rifle squad, is the subject matter expert for employment of the medium machine gun, and advises the rifle squad leader of the best way to employ the medium machine gun.
- Enforces field discipline while the gun team is employed tactically.
- Knows the ballistic effects of the weapon on all types of targets.
- Assists the weapons squad leader and is prepared to assume his responsibilities.
- Understands the mission two levels up (squad and platoon).

ASSISTANT MACHINE GUNNER

1-65. The assistant gunner is the second member of the gun team. He is prepared to assume the gunner's role in any situation. During operations, the assistant gunner—
- Provides a supply of ammunition to the gun when employed.
- Spots rounds and reports recommended corrections to the gunner.
- Constantly updates the weapons squad leader on the round count and serviceability of the medium machine gun.
- Watches for Soldiers to the flanks of the target area or between the gun and target.
- Obtains ammunition from other Soldiers who are carrying 7.62-mm machine gun ammunition.
- Immediately assumes the role of gunner if the gunner is unable to continue his duties.
- Understands the mission two levels up (squad and platoon).

COMBAT LIFESAVER

1-66. The combat lifesaver (CLS) is a nonmedical Soldier trained to provide enhanced first aid/lifesaving procedures beyond the level of self-aid or buddy aid. The CLS is not intended to take the place of medical personnel. Using specialized training, the CLS can slow deterioration of a wounded Soldier's condition until treatment by medical personnel is possible. Each certified CLS is issued a CLS aid bag. Whenever possible, the platoon leader ensures each fire team includes at least one CLS.

Organization

1-67. The CLS—
- Ensures that the squad CLS bags and litters are properly packed and stored.
- Identifies Class VIII shortages to the platoon medic.
- + Provides enhanced first aid for injuries and participates in all litter-carry drills.
- Uses enhanced first-aid skills in the field until casualties can be evacuated.
- Knows the location of the casualty collection point and the tactical standard operating procedure (TACSOP) for establishing it.

HABITUAL ATTACHMENTS

1-68. Fire support team and combat medics normally are attached anytime the platoon deploys.

FORWARD OBSERVER

1-69. The forward observer (FO), along with his RTO, is the platoon subject matter expert on indirect planning and execution. He advises the platoon leadership on the employment and execution for all fire support assets, including company mortars (if assigned), battalion mortars, field artillery, and other allocated fire support assets. He is responsible for locating targets, and calling and adjusting indirect fires. The fire support team also knows the mission and concept of operation, specifically the platoon's scheme of maneuver and concept of fires, and is the platoon leader's indirect fire expert. The forward observer also—
- Informs the fire support team of the platoon situation, location, and indirect fire support requirements.
- Prepares and uses maps, overlays, and terrain sketches.
- Calls for and adjusts indirect fires. (See figure 1-6, page 1-24.)
- Operates as a team with the fire support radiotelephone operator.
- Selects targets to support the platoon's mission.
- Selects observation posts and movement routes to and from selected targets.
- Operates digital message devices and maintains communication with the company and battalion fire support officer (FSO).
- Maintains grid coordinates of his location.
- Prepares to employ close air support (CAS) assets. (See figure 1-7, page 1-25.)

Chapter 1

INDIRECT FIRE REQUEST FORMAT

1. **OBSERVERS IDENTIFICATION**
   - Call signs

2. **WARNING ORDER**
   - Adjust fire
   - Fire for effect
   - Suppress
   - Immediate suppression/immediate smoke

3. **LOCATION OF TARGET**
   - Grid coordinate
   - Shift from a known point
   - Polar plot

4. **DESCRIPTION OF TARGET**
   - Type
   - Activity
   - Number
   - Degree of protection
   - Size and shape (length/width or radius)

5. **METHOD OF ENGAGEMENT**
   - Type of adjustment
   - Danger close
   - Mark
   - Ammunition
   - Distribution

6. **METHOD OF FIRE AND CONTROL**
   - Method of fire
   - Method of control

Figure 1-6. Indirect fire request format

Organization

Format 15. Close Air Support 9-Line Briefing

Do not transmit line numbers. Units of measure are standard unless briefed. Lines 4, 6 and restrictions are mandatory readback (*). JTAC may request additional readback.

JTAC: "_____ this is _____"
       (Aircraft Call Sign)   (JTAC Call Sign)

"Type _____ (1, 2, or 3) Control"

1. IP/BP: "_____"
2. Heading: "_____"
   (Degrees Magnetic, IP/BP-to-Target)
   Offset: "_____"
   (Left / Right, when required)
3. Distance: "_____"
   (IP-to-Target in nautical miles/BP-to-Target in meters)
4.* Target Elevation: "_____"
   (In feet MSL)
5. Target Description: "_____"
6.* Target Location: "_____"
   (Lat/Long or grid to include map datum offsets or visual)
7. Type Mark: "_____" Code: "_____"
   (WP, Laser, IR, Beacon)   (Actual Laser Code)
8. Location of Friendlies: "_____"
   (From target, cardinal directions and distance in meters)
   Position marked by: "_____"
9. "Egress: _____"

Remarks (as appropriate): "_____"
(Restrictions*, Ordnance Delivery, threats, final attack heading, hazards, ACAs, weather, target information, SEAD, LTL/GTL (degrees magnetic), night vision, danger close [with commander's initials])

Time on Target: "_____" or
Time to Target: "_____"

"Stand by _____ plus _____ ready, ready HACK"
            (minutes) (seconds)

NOTE: When identifying position coordinates for joint operations, include map data. Grid coordinates must include 100,000-meter grid identification.

IP: Identifiable Geographical Point	**IR:** Infrared
BP: Battle Position	**WP:** White Phosphorous
Deg: Degree	**FAH:** Final Attack Heading
MSL: Mean Sea Level	**ACA:** Airspace Coordination Area
Lat: Latitude	**SEAD:** Suppression of Enemy Air Defenses
Long: Longitude	**Tgt:** Target
JTAC: Joint Terminal Attack Controller	**LTL:** Laser Target Line
	GTL: Gun Target Line

Figure 1-7. Close air support 9-line request example

Chapter 1

PLATOON MEDIC

1-70. Combat medics are assigned to the medical platoon and are tasked to support the Infantry battalion. Combat medics are allocated to the Infantry companies on the basis of one combat medic per platoon, and one senior combat medic per company. The platoon combat medic or the company senior combat medic goes to the casualty's location, or the casualty is brought to the combat medic at the CCP. The CCP combat medic makes his assessment, administers initial medical care, initiates a DD Form 1380 (*Tactical Combat Casualty Care [TCCC] Card*) (see figure 1-8) then, requests evacuation or returns the individual to duty. (Refer to AR 40-66 for details and instructions on completing the form.)

Organization

TACTICAL COMBAT CASUALTY CARE (TCCC) CARD

BATTLE ROSTER #: Do2270

EVAC: ☒ Urgent ☐ Priority ☐ Routine

NAME (Last, First): DOE, LARRY **LAST 4:** 2270

GENDER: ☒ M ☐ F **DATE** (DD-MMM-YY): 18 NOV 15 **TIME:** 1345

SERVICE: ARMY **UNIT:** 2-327th INF BN **ALLERGIES:** PCN

Mechanism of Injury: (X all that apply)
☐ Artillery ☐ Blunt ☐ Burn ☐ Fall ☐ Grenade ☒ GSW ☐ IED
☐ Landmine ☐ MVC ☐ RPG ☐ Other: _____

Injury: (Mark injuries with an **X**)

TQ: R Arm	TQ: L Arm
TYPE: IMPROV	TYPE:
TIME: 1400	TIME:

TQ: R Leg	TQ: L Leg
TYPE:	TYPE:
TIME:	TIME:

Signs & Symptoms: (Fill in the blank)

Time	1400	1415		
Pulse (Rate & Location)	116	118		
Blood Pressure	112 / 76	108 / 70	/	/
Respiratory Rate	20	20		
Pulse Ox % O2 Sat	98	98		
AVPU	A - Alert	A - Alert		
Pain Scale (0-10)	6 Intense	5 Very		

DD Form 1380, JUN 2014   TCCC CARD

Figure 1-8. DD Form 1380, Tactical Combat Casualty Care (TCCC) Card

Chapter 1

1-71. The Infantry platoon combat medic usually locates with, or near, the platoon sergeant. When the platoon moves on foot in the platoon column formation, the combat medic positions himself near the platoon sergeant. If the platoon is mounted, the combat medic usually rides in the same vehicle as the platoon sergeant. + Emergency medical treatment (EMT) procedures performed by the combat medic may include opening an airway, starting intravenous (IV) fluids, controlling hemorrhage, preventing or treating for shock, splinting fractures or suspected fractures, and providing relief for pain.

1-72. The Infantry platoon combat medic is trained under the supervision of the battalion surgeon or physician's assistant and medical platoon leader. The platoon combat medic is responsible for—

- Triaging injured, wounded, or ill friendly and enemy personnel for priority of treatment.
- Conducting sick call screening.
- Assisting in the evacuation of sick, injured, or wounded personnel under the direction of the platoon sergeant.
- Assisting in the training of the platoon's combat lifesavers in enhanced first-aid procedures.
- Requisitioning Class VIII supplies from the battalion aid station (BAS) for the platoon according to the tactical SOPs.
- Recommending locations for platoon casualty collection point.
- Providing guidance to the platoon's combat lifesavers as required.

CAPABILITIES

1-73. The following lists capabilities of the Infantry rifle platoon and squad:

- Conduct offensive and defensive tasks in all types of environments, day and night.
- Seize, secure, occupy, and retain terrain.
- Destroy, neutralize, suppress, interdict, disrupt, block, canalize, and fix enemy forces.
- Breach enemy obstacles.
- Feint and demonstrate to deceive the enemy.
- Screen friendly units.
- Reconnoiter, deny, bypass, clear, contain, and isolate. These tasks might be oriented on both terrain and enemy.
- Conduct small-unit operations.
- Participate in air assault operations.
- Participate in airborne operations (airborne only).
- Operate in conjunction with mounted forces.
- Operate in conjunction with special operations forces.
- Participate in amphibious operations.

LIMITATIONS

1-74. The Infantry rifle platoon and squad has the following limitations:
- Limited close combat and sustainment assets.
- Limited vehicle mobility, the foot speed of organic elements may establish the pace of operations.
- Vulnerable to enemy armor, artillery, and air assets when employed in open terrain.
- Vulnerable to enemy CBRN attacks with limited decontamination capability.

CLOSE COMBAT

1-75. Infantry platoons and squads normally operate as part of a larger force. They habitually benefit from the support of organic mortars, artillery, close air support, Army attack aviation, air defense, and engineers. They may additionally receive support from elements of armored or Stryker formations. They provide their own suppressive fires either to repel enemy assaults or to support their own maneuver. During close combat, platoon leaders determine how to employ their squads by considering the following objectives:
- Support the rifle squads with direct fires.
- Suppress or neutralize enemy elements or positions using indirect fires, Army attack aviation, or close air support.
- Destroy enemy armored vehicles with Javelin fires.

1-76. Success in operations requires seamless coordination of platoons and rifle squads in close combat. It depends on their ability to react to contact; employ suppressive direct and indirect fires; maneuver to a position of reletive advantage; and assault to defeat, destroy, or capture an enemy. For success the Infantry platoon relies on the ability of leaders and Soldiers to—
- Maximize the use of restricted and complex terrain to achieve a position of advantage while mitigating the Infantry platoons lack of inherent protection.
- Use limited visibility to their advantage to maximize the effect of surprise complemented with aggressive maneuver.
- Operate their weapons with accuracy and deadly effect.
- Outthink, outmaneuver, and outfight the enemy.

EMPLOYMENT CONSIDERATIONS

1-77. Infantry units can operate in all terrain and weather conditions. They might be the dominant force because of rapid strategic deployment. In such cases, they can take and gain the initiative early, seize and retain or control terrain, and mass fires to stop the enemy. Infantry units are particularly effective in restricted or urban terrain, where they can infiltrate and move rapidly to the rear of enemy positions. The leader can enhance their mobility by using helicopters and airlift.

1-78. Squads and platoons fight through enemy contact at the lowest possible level. Upon enemy contact, all Soldiers and leaders must act at once. Battle drills are the standard procedures that help the platoon take immediate action.

Chapter 1

1-79. Before they can maneuver, squads or platoons in contact must establish effective suppressive fires and gain fire superiority. If the platoon or squad cannot move under its own fires, the leader must request support from the commander. Once fire superiority is achieved, they maneuver against an enemy position. Infantry platoons and squads must optimize the use of terrain to its greatest advantage masking avenues of approach to maximize surprise and shock during the assault.

SECTION III – ROLE OF THE MECHANIZED INFANTRY PLATOON AND SQUAD

1-80. Bradley Infantry platoon and squads are a versatile force that can fight mounted, dismounted while being supported by the BFVs, or dismounted and independent of the fighting vehicles. The BFV is an extremely powerful and robust weapon system that enables the mechanized Infantry to find and destroy the enemy at long ranges while the dismounted Infantrymen, supported by the BFV, can destroy the enemy in close combat.

ORGANIZATION

1-81. The mechanized Infantry platoon is equipped with four BFVs and is divided into two elements: mounted and dismounted. Figure 1-9 (page 1-30) depicts the BFV-equipped mechanized Infantry platoon organization. The platoon can fight as two mutually supporting maneuver elements or as two distinct maneuver elements—one mounted and one dismounted. The platoon must prepare to fight in a variety of operational environments. Once the rifle squads have dismounted, the mounted element can provide a base of fire for the rifle squads as they close with and destroy the enemy.

Organization

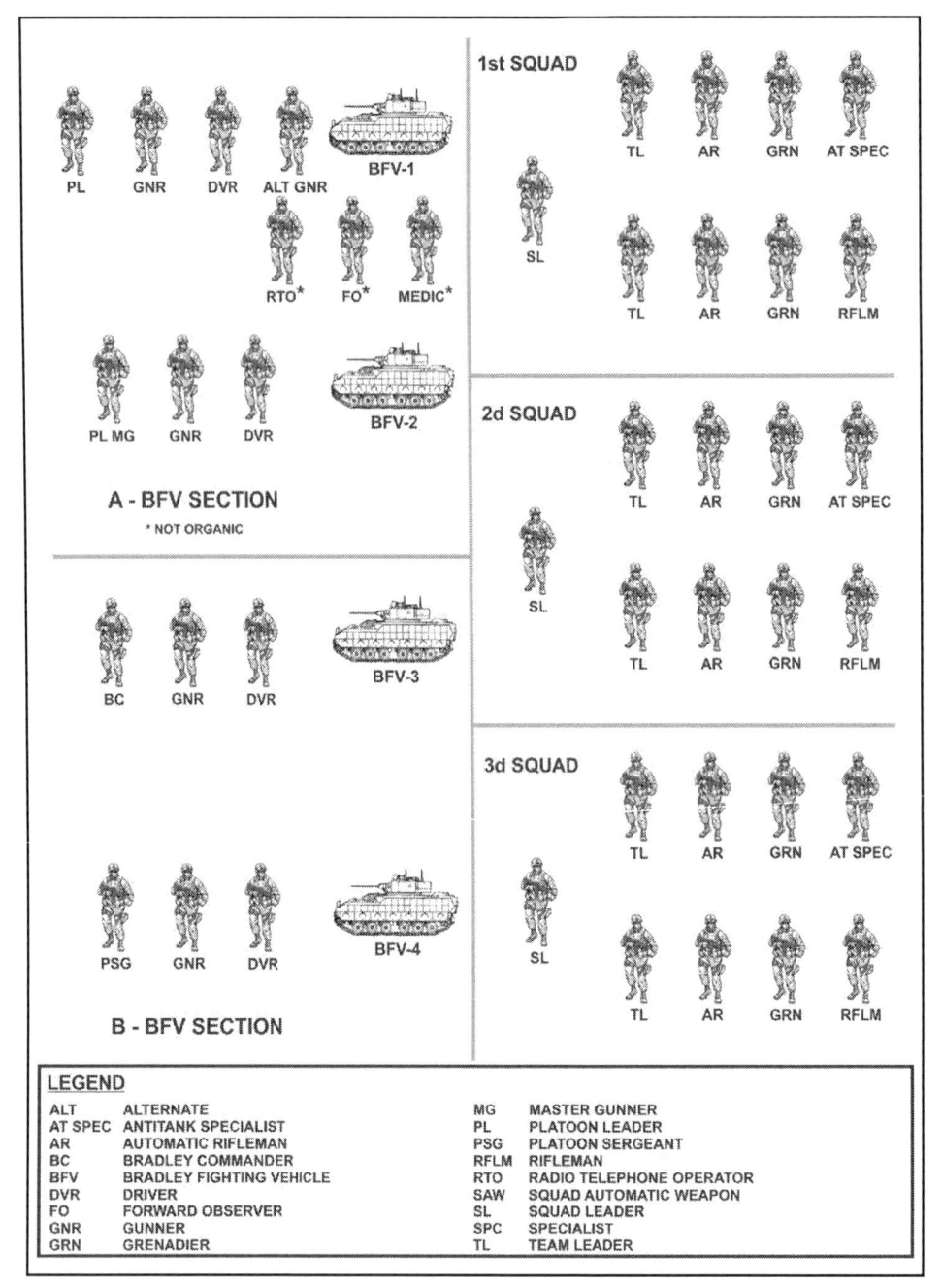

Figure 1-9. Bradley platoon organization

Chapter 1

MOUNTED ELEMENT

1-82. The mounted element comprises four BFVs that are organized into the following two sections:
- The A section with the platoon leader as the section leader and the second BFV as his wingman.
- The B section with the platoon sergeant as the section leader and the second BFV as his wingman.

DISMOUNTED ELEMENT

1-83. Three, nine-man rifle squads make up the platoon's dismounted element. The rifle squads are organized as follows:
- The rifle squad has two, four-man fire teams and a squad leader.
- Each fire team is comprised of a —
  - Fire team leader.
  - Squad automatic weapon (SAW) gunner.
  - Grenadier.
  - Rifleman.
- One of the riflemen in the fire team is designated and trained as the antiarmor specialist and fires the Javelin close combat munitions.
- The other rifleman in the squad is the squad's designated marksman.

1-84. Based on the mission, the squad can carry the Javelin command launch unit and missiles as well as an M240B medium machine gun.

RESPONSIBILITIES

1-85. The employment of the BFV by well-trained and proficient Soldiers enhances the platoon's capabilities to conduct operations with greater lethality, survivability, mission command, and mobility.

PLATOON LEADER

1-86. The platoon leader leads his Soldiers by personal example and is responsible for all the platoon does or fails to do, having complete authority over his subordinates. This centralized authority enables him to maintain unit discipline, unity, and to act decisively. He must be prepared to exercise initiative within his company commander's intent and without specific guidance for every situation. The platoon leader knows his Soldiers, how to employ the platoon, its weapons, and its systems. Relying on the expertise of the platoon sergeant, the platoon leader regularly consults with him on all platoon matters. During operations, the platoon leader—
- Leads the platoon in supporting the higher headquarters missions. He bases his actions on his assigned mission and intent and concept of his higher commanders.
- Conducts troop leading procedures.

Organization

- Maneuvers squads and fighting elements.
- Synchronizes the efforts of squads.
- Looks ahead to the next "move" of the platoon.
- Requests, controls, and synchronizes supporting assets.
- Employs mission command systems available to the squads and platoon.
- Checks with squad leaders ensuring 360-degree, three-dimensional security is maintained.
- Checks with weapons squad leader controlling the emplacement of key weapon systems.
- Issues accurate and timely reports.
- Places himself where he is most needed to accomplish the mission.
- Assigns clear tasks and purposes to the squads.
- Understands the mission and commander's intent two levels up (company and battalion).
- Normally dismounts when the situation causes the platoon to dismount.
- Serves as Bradley commander when mounted.
- Receives on-hand status reports from the platoon sergeant, section leaders, and squad leaders during planning.
- Develops the fires with the platoon sergeant, section leaders, and squad leaders.
- Coordinates and assists in the development of the obstacle plan.
- Oversees and is responsible for property management.

1-87. The platoon leader works to develop and maintain situational understanding. This is a product of four elements. First, the platoon leader attempts to know what is happening in present terms of friendly, enemy, neutral, and terrain situations. Second, he knows the end state representing mission accomplishment. Third, he determines the critical actions and events occurring to move his unit from the present to the end state. Finally, he assesses the risk throughout.

PLATOON SERGEANT

1-88. The platoon leader should consider the platoon sergeant a fighter by trade and place him in the tactical plan either dismounted or maneuvering the mounted element. The platoon sergeant is the senior NCO and most experienced Soldier in the platoon. He assists and advises the platoon leader. In the platoon leader's absence, he leads the platoon. He supervises the platoon's administration, logistics, and maintenance. He handles individual training management and the professional development of his Soldiers. He advises the platoon leader on appointments, promotions and reductions, assignments, and discipline of NCOs and enlisted Soldiers in the platoon. His tactical expertise in platoon operations includes maneuver of the platoon and employment of all weapons.

1-89. The platoon sergeant—
- Controls the mounted element when the platoon leader dismounts; or, dismounts with, commands, and controls the platoon when necessary (METT-TC dependent).

Chapter 1

- Updates the platoon leader on appropriate reports, and forwards reports needed by higher headquarters.
- Takes charge of task-organized elements in the platoon during tactical operations, which may include, but are not limited to, quartering parties, support elements in raids or attacks, and security patrols.
- Serves as a Bradley commander when the platoon operates mounted.
- Monitors the morale, discipline, and health of platoon members.
- Ensures Soldiers maintain all equipment.
- Coordinates and supervises company directed platoon resupply operations.
- Collects, prepares, and forwards logistical status updates and requests to the company headquarters.
- Ensures ammunition and supplies are properly and evenly distributed after the platoon consolidates on the objective and while the platoon reorganizes.
- Directs the platoon's casualty evacuation process during mounted or dismounted operations.
- Maintains platoon strength information, consolidates and forwards the platoon's casualty reports, and receives and orients replacements.
- Receives section and squad leaders' administrative, logistical, and maintenance reports and requests for rations, water, fuel, and ammunition.
- Ensures Soldiers distribute supplies according to the platoon leader's guidance and direction.
- Accounts for Soldiers, equipment, and supplies.
- Coaches, counsels, and mentors Soldiers.
- Upholds standards and platoon discipline.

PLATOON MASTER GUNNER

1-90. The platoon master gunner serves as the technical expert on gunnery and turret weapon systems. He serves as section leader for Alpha section.

1-91. During combat or field exercises, the platoon master gunner—
- Advises the platoon leader and platoon sergeant concerning BFV weapons effects, capabilities, and safety.
- Advises the platoon leader about fire control measures and preparation.
- Serves as the lead technical trainer for the mounted element under the routine supervision of the platoon sergeant.
- Helps the platoon leader set up the gunnery task for training.
- Performs services on the 25-mm Bushmaster chain gun.

BRADLEY COMMANDER

1-92. The platoon leader, platoon sergeant, and the two section leaders serve as the Bradley commander for their BFVs. In the platoon leader's absence, the gunner assumes the responsibilities of the Bradley commander.

Organization

1-93. The Bradley commander—
- Acquires targets.
- Commands the vehicle.
- Controls vehicle fires.
- Ensures the welfare of the crew.
- Holds the vehicle's position in platoon formations.
- Issues fire commands.
- Lays the gun for deflection.
- Maintains the BFV hull and turret.
- Maintains the BFV weapon systems.
- Monitors the commander's tactical display for vehicle position, digital overlays, and digital reports.
- Navigates correctly, with or without precision navigation system.
- Sends SITREPs as requested or when the vehicle makes contact.
- Trains Soldiers to use weapons.

SECTION LEADER

1-94. While mounted, the platoon leader and platoon sergeant are the section leaders. However, in the event that the platoon leader or platoon sergeant must dismount, the senior Bradley commander within each section becomes the section leader, assisting and advising the platoon leader in the employment of the mounted section. The section leader handles—
- Tactically employing and maintaining the BFVs within the section and individual training of the section's personnel.
- Monitoring his vehicle and section position on the platoon formation, digital overlays, and digital reports.
- Navigating correctly, with or without precision navigation system.
- Sending SPOTREPs as requested or when the section makes contact.

BRADLEY GUNNER

1-95. The gunner observes the battlefield to detect enemy targets. The gunner handles—
- Operating the turret weapons as directed by the Bradley commander to engage and destroy targets.
- Serving as Bradley commander when only two men remain in the BFV.
- Bearing the responsibility for performing unit-level maintenance on the turret and its weapons systems.
- Helping with navigation and with radio operation.

BRADLEY DRIVER

1-96. The driver operates the vehicle under the Bradley commander's control. The driver—
- Follows terrain-driving procedures and tries to select hull-down positions.

Chapter 1

- Helps detect targets and observe rounds fired.
- Helps with navigation by monitoring odometer readings and observing terrain.
- Bears the main responsibility for maintaining the vehicle's automotive (hull) systems.

SQUAD LEADER

1-97. The squad leader is the senior Infantry Soldier in the squad and is responsible for everything the squad does or fails to do. He is responsible for the care of the squad's Soldiers, weapons, and equipment, and leads the squad through two team leaders. The senior dismounted squad leader is responsible for the employment of the dismount element until the platoon leader or platoon sergeant arrives. During operations, the squad leader—

- Is the subject matter expert on all battle and individual drills.
- Is the subject matter expert for the squad's organic weapons employment, and employment of supporting assets.
- Knows weapons effects, surface danger zones, and risk estimate distances for all munitions.
- Uses control measures for direct fire, indirect fire, and tactical movement effectively.
- Controls the movement of the squad and its rate and distribution of fire (including call for and adjust fire).
- Fights the close fight by fire and movement with two fire teams and available supporting weapons.
- Selects the fire team's general location and temporary sector of fires in the defense.
- Communicates timely and accurate SITREPs and status reports, including—
  - SALUTE SPOTREPs.
  - Status to the platoon leader (including squad location and progress, enemy situation, enemy KIA, and security posture).
  - Status of ammunition, casualties, and equipment to the platoon sergeant.
- Employs digital mission command systems available to the squad and platoon.
- Operates in all environments to include the urban environment.
- Conducts troop leading procedures.
- Assumes duties as the platoon sergeant or platoon leader as required.
- Understands the mission and commander's intent two levels up (platoon and company).

TEAM LEADER

1-98. The team leader leads his team members by personal example and has authority over his subordinates and overall responsibility of their actions. Centralized authority enables him to maintain troop discipline and unity and to act decisively. Under the fluid conditions of close combat, he accomplishes assigned missions using initiative without needing constant guidance from higher headquarters.

Organization

1-99. The team leader's position on the battlefield requires immediacy and accuracy in all of his actions and is a fighting leader who leads by example. He is responsible for all his team does or fails to do, and is responsible for caring of the team's Soldiers, weapons, and equipment. During operations, the team leader—

- Is the subject matter expert for all the team's weapons and duty positions and all squad battle drills.
- Leads his team in fire and movement.
- Controls the movement of his team and its rate and distribution of fire.
- Employs digital mission command systems available to the squad and platoon.
- Ensures security of the team's area of operations.
- Assists the squad leader as required.
- Is prepared to assume the duties of squad leader and platoon sergeant.
- Enforces field discipline and preventive medicine measures.
- Determines his team's combat load and manages its available classes of supply as required.
- Team members provide local security as needed. They provide maintenance support for the BFV. Each team member is equally responsible for the welfare of the squad.
- Understands the mission two levels up (squad and platoon).

1-100. When maneuvering the team, the team fights using one of three techniques. This includes—

- Individual movement techniques. This is the lowest level of movement.
- Buddy team fire and movement.
- Fire team fire and movement (maneuver).
- Determining a suitable technique is based on the effectiveness of the enemy's fire and available cover and concealment. The more effective the enemy's fire, the lower the level of movement. The team leader leads his team; therefore, he is able to make this assessment firsthand. Other leaders must be sensitive to his decision on movement.

RIFLEMAN

1-101. Each rifle squad has two riflemen. Each rifleman is either designated as the antiarmor specialist or designated marksman.

Antiarmor Specialist

1-102. The designated antiarmor specialist has a Javelin AT missile system. This weapon system gives the squad, platoon, and company a lethal fire-and-forget, man-portable, top attack antiarmor capability. With it, they can defeat enemy main battle tanks up to 2000 meters during day, night, and in adverse weather conditions. If required, the squad antiarmor specialist destroys enemy armor threats that might impede the squad or platoon's progress.

Designated Marksman

1-103. The designated marksman acts as a member of the squad under the direction of the squad leader or as designated by the platoon leader. Although normally functioning as a rifleman within one of the fire teams in a rifle squad, the designated marksman is armed with a modified rifle. He is employed at the direction of the fire team leader or squad leader. He is trained to eliminate high-payoff enemy personnel targets (such as enemy automatic rifle teams, AT teams, and snipers) with precision fires.

GRENADIER

1-104. Each squad has two grenadiers with an M320/203 weapon system, which comprises a carbine with an attached 40-mm grenade launcher. The M320/203 can be used in two ways. It can be attached to the M16 assault rifle and the M4 carbine, attaching under the barrel forward of the magazine, or it can be used dismounted with a stock attached as a standalone model.

AUTOMATIC RIFLEMAN

1-105. Each rifle squad has two automatic weapons. The automatic rifleman mainly uses the M249 SAW.

COMBAT LIFESAVER

1-106. The CLS is a nonmedical Soldier trained to provide enhanced first aid/lifesaving procedures beyond the level of self-aid or buddy aid. The CLS is not intended to take the place of medical personnel. Using specialized training, the CLS can slow deterioration of a wounded Soldier's condition until treatment by medical personnel is possible. Each certified CLS is issued a CLS aid bag. Whenever possible, the platoon leader ensures each fire team includes at least one CLS.

1-107. The CLS—
- Ensures that the squad CLS bag and litters are properly packed and stored.
- Identifies Class VIII shortages to the platoon medic.
- Participates in all casualty treatment and litter-carry drills.
- Uses enhanced first-aid skills in the field until casualties can be evacuated.
- Knows the location of the casualty collection point and the TACSOP for establishing it.

BRADLEY FIGHTING VEHICLE

1-108. The BFV enhances the platoon's capabilities to conduct operations with greater lethality, survivability, sustainability, and mobility. The information systems enhance the crew's communication during operations. Because the BFV platoon can transfer more information at every level, leaders and Soldiers must work together to manage the information. (Refer to TM 9-2350-252-10-1/2 for more information on capabilities and equipment.)

Organization

WEAPON SYSTEMS

1-109. The BFV's four weapon systems include the 25-mm automatic gun, the 7.62-mm coaxial machine gun, the tube-launched, optically tracked, wire-guided (TOW) missile-launcher system, and two smoke-grenade launchers.

LETHALITY

1-110. The BFV features an improved Bradley acquisition system, which adds an improved target acquisition subsystem and missile control subsystem. The improvements include a second-generation, forward-looking infrared thermal sight; a target-designation function; dual-target tracking; an eye-safe laser range finder; an automatic gun-target adjustment; automatic optical alignment; and "hunter-killer" capability. Second-generation forward-looking infrared thermal sight allows the Bradley commander or gunner to identify and acquire targets beyond the range of the vehicle's weapon systems. The improved Bradley acquisition system enables the user to acquire, recognize, identify, and automatically track two targets within the same field of view and selected magnification, day or night. The M2A3 BFV can use the 25-mm cannon or 7.62-mm machine gun to engage either of two targets appearing in the same field of view and any aspect, and the TOW while stationary.

SURVIVABILITY

1-111. Equipment on the BFV that helps ensure survivability includes—
- Roof fragmentation protection.
- Mounting capability for reactive armor tiles.
- Aluminum structure with steel appliqué spaced laminate, steel armor, or both.
- Titanium roof armor.
- 10-Soldier gas particulate filter unit.
- Halon fixed fire suppression systems in engine and personnel compartments.
- Portable carbon dioxide fire extinguishers.
- Bradley urban survivability kits.

CAPABILITIES

1-112. In accomplishing its assigned missions, the platoon employs close combat forces and sustainment assets within its capabilities. The platoon's effectiveness depends on the synergy of its subordinate elements, to include its BFVs and the rifle squads. To employ the platoon effectively, the platoon leader capitalizes on its strengths. The BFV-equipped mechanized Infantry platoon can—
- Assault enemy positions.
- Assault with small arms and indirect fires to deliver rifle squads to tactical positions of advantage.
- Use 25-mm cannon and 7.62-mm machine gun fire to effectively suppress or destroy the enemy's Infantry.

Chapter 1

- Block dismounted avenues of approach.
- Seize and retain key and decisive terrain.
- Clear danger areas and prepare positions for mounted elements.
- Conduct mounted or dismounted patrols and operations in support of security operations.
- Develop the situation through reconnaissance and close combat.
- Establish strong points to deny the enemy important terrain or flank positions.
- Infiltrate enemy positions.
- Overwatch and secure tactical obstacles.
- Repel enemy attacks through close combat.
- Participate in air assault operations.
- Destroy light armor vehicles using direct fire from the BFV.
- Employ 25-mm cannon fire to fix, suppress, or disrupt the movement of fighting vehicles and antiarmor systems up to 2500 meters.
- Use TOW fires to destroy tanks and fighting vehicles out to 3750 meters.
- Use Javelin fires to destroy tanks and fighting vehicles out to 2000 meters.
- Operate in a CBRN environment.
- Conduct stability tasks.
- Participate in Defense Support of Civil Authorities operations.

LIMITATIONS

1-113. The platoon leader must understand the limitations of the BFV-equipped mechanized Infantry platoon to effectively employ the platoon. These limitations include the following:

- BFVs are vulnerable to enemy antiarmor fires, attack helicopters, mines, AT guided missiles, and close attack aircraft.
- Rifle squads are vulnerable to small arms, improvised explosive device (IED), and indirect fires when not mounted.
- The foot speed of the dismounted Soldiers may establish the pace of operations.
- The BFV poses a variety of challenges in water-crossing operations. Between other things, the platoon could have difficulty finding adequate fording sites or a bridge with a sufficient weight classification.
- Radio communications may be significantly degraded in built-up areas and other restricted terrain.
- Noise generated by BFVs may prevent them from arriving in an area undetected.

CLOSE COMBAT

1-114. BFV-equipped Infantry platoons and rifle squads normally operate as part of a larger force. They benefit from the support of armor, artillery, mortars, close air support, close combat attack, air defense, and engineers. They provide their own suppressive fires either to repel enemy assaults or to support their own maneuver. During close combat,

platoon leaders determine how to employ the BFVs by considering the following objectives:
- Support the rifle squads with direct fires.
- Provide mobile protection to transport rifle squads to the critical point on the battlefield.
- Suppress or destroy enemy vehicles and other lightly armored vehicles.
- Destroy enemy armor with TOW fires.

1-115. Success in operations hinges on the actions of platoons, sections, and rifle squads in close combat. It depends on their ability to react to contact; employ suppressive fires; maneuver to an enemy's vulnerable flank; and fight through to defeat, destroy, or capture an enemy. For success, the BFV-equipped Infantry platoon relies on the ability of leaders and Soldiers to—
- Use the potential of both the rifle squads and the BFV.
- Operate their weapons with accuracy and deadly effect.
- Outthink, outmaneuver, and outfight the enemy.
- Use terrain to their advantage.

EMPLOYMENT CONSIDERATIONS

1-116. Leaders must consider the following guidelines when employing mechanized Infantry during decisive operations:
- Squads and platoons fight through enemy contact at the lowest possible level. Upon enemy contact, all Soldiers and leaders must act at once and follow up. Battle drills are standard procedures that help the platoon take immediate action.
- Before they can maneuver, squads or platoons in contact must establish effective suppressive fires and gain fire superiority. If the platoon or squad cannot move under its own fires, the leader must request support from the commander. Once they gain fire superiority, they maneuver against an enemy position. The BFVs suppress the enemy, move to a dismount location (if caught in the open), and dismount the rifle squads. The BFVs quickly build a base of fire for the rifle squads to maneuver.

SECTION IV – ROLE OF THE STRYKER INFANTRY PLATOON AND SQUAD

1-117. Stryker Infantry platoon and squads are a versatile force that can fight mounted, dismounted while being supported by the Stryker vehicle, or dismounted and independent of the vehicles. The Stryker is a highly mobile vehicle that enables the Stryker Infantry to close with and destroy a lightly armored enemy with the Remote Weapon Station (RWS) weapon system while the dismounted Infantrymen, supported by the Stryker, can destroy the enemy in close combat.

Chapter 1

MISSION

1-118. Stryker Infantry platoons and squads share their company's primary mission, which is to close with and destroy the enemy through fire and maneuver; to destroy or capture the enemy; and to repel the enemy assault by fire, close combat, and counterattack.

ORGANIZATION

1-119. The platoon must prepare to fight in a variety of operational environments. Once the rifle squads have dismounted, the mounted element can provide a base of fire for the rifle squads as they close with and destroy the enemy. Figure 1-10 (page 1-42) depicts the platoon headquarters, the mounted elements, and the Infantry squads. The platoon can fight as in multiple mutually supporting maneuver elements to include—

- Squad leader controls two dismounted teams and mounted Stryker vehicle.
- The squads fight dismounted while the Stryker vehicles move in vehicle sections.
- The platoon fights in sections with mounted and dismounted elements supporting one another.
- The platoon fights with dismounted squads and Stryker vehicles or as two distinct maneuver elements one mounted and one dismounted.

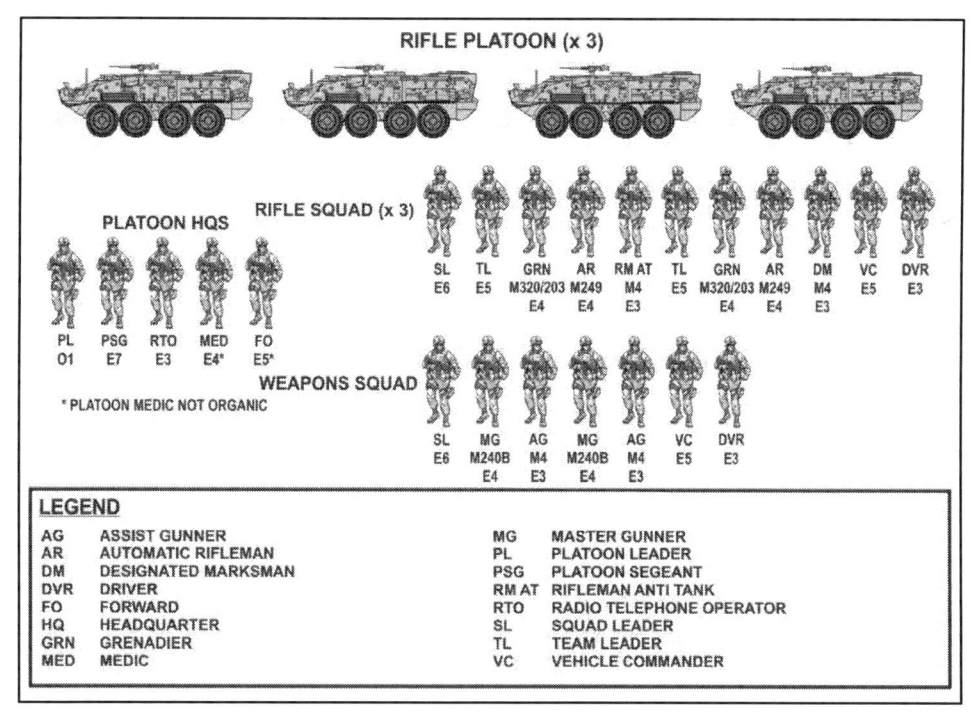

Figure 1-10. Stryker platoon organization

PLATOON HEADQUARTERS

1-120. The platoon headquarters consists of the platoon leader, platoon sergeant, RTO, and attached fire support team and platoon combat medic. The platoon leader responsibilities include the employment of the platoon and all the platoon's systems. The platoon sergeant is the senior NCO in the platoon. He is second in succession of command and leads the platoon's mounted element when the platoon leader dismounts with the Infantry squads. He assists and advises the platoon leader and leads the platoon in the platoon leader's absence.

STRYKER INFANTRY RIFLE SQUAD

1-121. Each of the three rifle squads consists of a rifle squad leader and ten Soldiers. The rifle squad leader is the senior tactical leader of the squad and controls the squad's movement and fires. He conducts squad training and maintains the squad's ability to conduct successful tactical missions.

1-122. Each Infantry squad is further organized into three teams, two four-man teams consisting of a team leader, a grenadier, and an automatic rifleman. The fourth member within each fire team is a rifleman with the added duties of being either the squad's antitank specialist or the squad's designated marksman. The third team consists of the vehicle commander and the vehicle driver.

1-123. The fire team leader is a fighting leader and leads his team by example. He controls the movement of his team and the placement of fires against enemy soldiers and assists the squad leader as required.

1-124. The vehicle commander is responsible for the overall employment of the ICV when the squad leader is not mounted and operates the ICV's defensive armaments. The vehicle driver operates the vehicle during all conditions. At the vehicle commander's direction, the driver negotiates the vehicle through all terrain and obstacles to safely deliver the Infantry rifle squad to the point of employment on the battlefield.

WEAPONS SQUAD

1-125. The weapons squad consists of a squad leader, two two-man machine gun teams and a vehicle team. The weapons squad provides the primary base of fire for the maneuver of the platoon's rifle squads with accurate fires against enemy personnel and equipment. The two machine gun teams consist of the gunner and assistant gunner. Each team is currently equipped with the M240B 7.62-mm medium machine gun with an effective range of over 800 meters. The platoon leader may want to consider providing additional security for the weapons squad if their base of fire is otherwise protected from enemy units. The vehicle team organization is the same as above.

RESPONSIBILITIES

1-126. The increased complexity of the ICV-equipped Infantry platoon requires highly trained Soldiers and leaders. The increase of equipment in the platoon requires more cross training to ensure Soldiers can fill vacancies or shortfalls in critical positions. Increases in the amount and complexity of equipment and the transfer of increased information at every level require platoon members to work closer than ever before.

PLATOON LEADER

1-127. The platoon leader leads his Soldiers by personal example and is responsible for all the platoon does or fails to do, having complete authority over his subordinates. This centralized authority enables him to maintain unit discipline, unity, and to act decisively. He must be prepared to exercise initiative within his company commander's intent and without specific guidance for every situation. The platoon leader knows his Soldiers, how to employ the platoon, its weapons, and its systems. Relying on the expertise of the platoon sergeant, the platoon leader regularly consults with him on all platoon matters. During operations, the platoon leader—

- Leads the platoon in supporting the higher headquarters missions. He bases his actions on his assigned mission and intent and concept of his higher commanders.
- Conducts troop leading procedures.
- Maneuvers squads and fighting elements.
- Synchronizes the efforts of squads.
- Looks ahead to the next "move" of the platoon.
- Requests, controls, and synchronizes supporting assets.
- Employs mission command systems available to the squads and platoon.
- Checks with squad leaders ensuring 360-degree, three-dimensional security is maintained.
- Checks with weapons squad leader controlling the emplacement of key weapon systems.
- Issues accurate and timely reports.
- Places himself where he is most needed to accomplish the mission.
- Assigns clear tasks and purposes to the squads.
- Understands the mission and commander's intent two levels up (company and battalion).
- Normally dismounts when the situation causes the platoon to dismount.
- As leader of Section A, keeps his crew and wingman informed.
- Receives on-hand status reports from the platoon sergeant, section leaders and squad leaders during planning.
- Develops the fires with the platoon sergeant, section leaders, and squad leaders.
- Coordinates and assists in the development of the obstacle plan.
- Oversees and is responsible for property management.

1-128. The platoon leader works to develop and maintain situational understanding. This is a product of four elements. First, the platoon leader attempts to know what is happening in present terms of friendly, enemy, neutral, and terrain situations. Second, he knows the end state representing mission accomplishment. Third, he determines the critical actions and events occurring to move his unit from the present to the end state. Finally, he assesses the risk throughout.

Organization

PLATOON SERGEANT

1-129. The platoon sergeant is the platoon's most experienced NCO and second-in-charge, accountable to the platoon leader for leadership, discipline, training, and welfare of the platoon's Soldiers. He sets the example in everything. He assists the Platoon Leader by upholding standards and platoon discipline. His expertise includes tactical maneuver, employment of weapons and systems, sustainment, administration, security, accountability, protection warfighting functions, and Soldier care. As the second-in-charge, the platoon sergeant assumes no formal duties except those prescribed by the platoon leader. However, the platoon sergeant traditionally—

- Ensures the platoon is prepared to accomplish its mission, which includes supervising precombat checks and inspections.
- Updates platoon leader on appropriate reports and forwards reports needed by higher headquarters.
- Prepares to assume the role and responsibilities of the platoon leader.
- Takes charge of task-organized elements in the platoon during tactical operations, which may include, but is not limited to, quartering parties, support elements in raids or attacks, and security patrols.
- Monitors the morale, discipline, and health of the platoon.
- Positions where best needed to help the engagement (either in the base of fire or with the assault element).
- Receives squad leaders' administrative, logistical, and maintenance reports, and requests rations, water, fuel, and ammunition.
- Requests logistical support from the higher headquarters, and usually coordinates with the company's first sergeant or executive officer.
- Ensures Soldiers maintain all equipment.

    Ensures ammunition and supplies are properly and evenly distributed after the platoon consolidates on the objective and while the platoon reorganizes.
- Manages the unit's combat load prior to operations, and monitors logistical status during operations.

    Establishes and operates the unit's CCP. This includes directing the platoon medic and aid/litter teams in moving casualties, maintains platoon strength level information, consolidates and forwards the platoon's casualty reports, and receives and orients replacements.
- Employs the available digital mission command systems to the squads and platoon.
- Ensures Soldiers distribute supplies according to the platoon leader's guidance and direction.
- Accounts for Soldiers, equipment, and supplies.
- Coaches, counsels, and mentors Soldiers.
- Upholds standards and platoon discipline.
- Understands the mission and commander's intent two levels up (company and battalion).

Chapter 1

RIFLE SQUAD LEADER

1-130. The squad leader directs team leaders and leads by personal example. He has authority over his subordinates and overall responsibility of those subordinates' actions. Centralized authority enables him to act decisively while maintaining troop discipline and unity. Under the fluid conditions of close combat, the squad leader accomplishes assigned missions without constant guidance from higher headquarters.

1-131. The squad leader is the senior Infantry Soldier in the squad and is responsible for everything the squad does or fails to do. He is responsible for the care of the squad's Soldiers, weapons, and equipment, and leads the squad through two team leaders. During operations, the squad leader—

- Is the subject matter expert on all battle and individual drills.
- Is the subject matter expert for the squad's organic weapons employment, and employment of supporting assets.
- Knows weapon effects, surface danger zones, and risk estimate distances for all munitions.
- Uses control measures for direct fire, indirect fire, and tactical movement effectively.
- Controls the movement of the squad and its rate and distribution of fire (including call for and adjust fire).
- Fights the close fight by fire and movement with two fire teams and available supporting weapons.
- Selects the fire team's general location and temporary sector of fires in the defense.
- Communicates timely and accurate SITREPs and status reports, including—
  - SALUTE SPOTREPs.
  - Status to the platoon leader (including squad location and progress, enemy situation, enemy KIA, and security posture).
  - Status of ammunition, casualties, and equipment to the platoon sergeant.
- Employs digital mission command systems available to the squad and platoon.
- Operates in all environments to include the urban environment.
- Conducts troop leading procedures.
- Assumes duties as the platoon sergeant or platoon leader as required.
- Understands the mission and commander's intent two levels up (platoon and company).
- Assists the vehicle commander in maintaining the ICV.

WEAPONS SQUAD LEADER

1-132. The weapons squad leader leads his teams by personal example. He has complete authority over his subordinates and overall responsibility for those subordinates' actions. This centralized authority enables him to act decisively while maintaining troop discipline and unity. Under the fluid conditions of modern warfare, he accomplishes assigned missions using initiative without needing constant guidance from higher headquarters.

Organization

1-133. The weapons squad leader is usually the senior squad leader, second only to the platoon sergeant, and performs all the duties of the rifle squad leader. In addition, the weapons squad leader—

- Controls fires and establishes fire control measures.
- Recommends medium machine gun employment to the platoon leader.
- Coordinates directly with the platoon leader for medium machine gun base-of-fire effects, and plans accordingly.
- Monitors ammunition expenditure.
- Coordinates directly with the platoon leader in placement of the Javelin-CCMS to best cover armored avenues of approach in the defense and overwatch positions in the attack.
- As the senior squad leader, becomes the alternate platoon sergeant on the ground if the platoon sergeant does not dismount.
- Employs mission command systems available to the squad and platoon.
- Trains his squad on individual and collective tasks required to sustain combat effectiveness.
- Manages the logistical and administrative needs of his squad, such as requesting and issuing ammunition, water, rations, and special equipment.
- Maintains accountability of Soldiers and equipment.
- Conducts troop leading procedures.
- Assists the vehicle commander in maintaining the ICV.
- Assumes control of the vehicle in absents of the platoon sergeant and platoon leader.
- Understands the mission two levels up (platoon and company).

TEAM LEADER

1-134. Two fire team leaders lead by example and control the movement and fires of the fire team. They assist the squad leader in tactical control of the squad and in training team members on individual and collective tasks and battle drills. Team leaders provide the necessary local security and maintenance support for the ICV and are responsible for the welfare of their teams. They control fires and distribution of fires for the team by designating and marking targets.

VEHICLE COMMANDER

1-135. The vehicle commander is responsible for the employment and maintenance of the ICV. He acquires targets, issues fire commands, and controls vehicle fires. The vehicle commander is primarily responsible for the overall maintenance of the ICV weapon systems and the automotive portion of the vehicle. He is responsible for the weapons training and welfare of the crew. He sends digital SITREPs as requested or when the vehicle makes contact. He navigates, assisted by the Precision Navigation System, and ensures his vehicle maintains position in platoon formations.

Chapter 1

VEHICLE DRIVER

1-136. The driver drives the vehicle under the vehicle commander's control. He follows terrain-driving procedures and tries to select hull-down positions. He also aids in detecting targets and observing rounds fired. He assists in navigation by monitoring odometer readings and observing terrain. The driver is primarily responsible for operator maintenance of vehicle automotive systems.

GRENADIER

1-137. The grenadier is equipped with an M320/M203 Weapon System consisting of an M4/M16 rifle and an attached 40-mm grenade launcher. The M320/M203 allows him to fire HE rounds to suppress and destroy enemy Infantry and lightly armored vehicles. He also can employ smoke to designate targets or screen his squad's movement, fire, and maneuver. During night and adverse weather conditions, the grenadier also may employ illumination rounds to increase his squad's visibility and mark enemy or friendly positions.

AUTOMATIC RIFLEMAN

1-138. The automatic rifleman's primary weapon is the M249 SAW. Each Infantry squad has two automatic weapons. The M249 provides the squad with a high volume of sustained long-range suppressive and lethal fires beyond the effective range of the M16/M4 rifle. The automatic rifleman employs the SAW to suppress enemy Infantry and bunkers, destroy enemy automatic rifle and antitank teams, and enable maneuver of other teams and squads. (Refer to appendix B for more information on the employment of the M249 SAW.)

SQUAD DESIGNATED MARKSMAN

1-139. The designated marksman acts as a member of the squad under the direction of the squad leader or as designated by the platoon leader. Although normally functioning as a rifleman within one of the fire teams in a rifle squad, the designated marksman is armed with a modified rifle. He is trained to eliminate high-payoff enemy personnel targets (such as enemy automatic rifle teams, antitank teams, and snipers) with precision fires.

COMBAT LIFESAVER

1-140. The CLS is a nonmedical Soldier trained to provide enhanced first aid/lifesaving procedures beyond the level of self-aid or buddy aid. The CLS is not intended to take the place of medical personnel. Using specialized training, the CLS can slow deterioration of a wounded Soldier's condition until treatment by medical personnel is possible. Each certified CLS is issued a CLS aid bag. Whenever possible, the platoon leader ensures each fire team includes at least one CLS.

1-141. The CLS—
- Ensures that the squad CLS and litters are properly packed and stored.
- Identifies Class VIII shortages to the platoon medic.

Organization

- + Provides enhanced first aid for injuries and participates in all litter-carry drills.
- Uses enhanced first-aid skills in the field until casualties can be evacuated.
- Knows the location of the casualty collection point and the TACSOP for establishing it.

PLATOON MEDIC

1-142. Platoon combat medics are assigned to the medical platoon and are tasked to support the Infantry battalion. Combat medics are allocated to the Infantry companies on the basis of one combat medic per platoon, and one senior combat medic per company. The location of the combat medic is of extreme importance for rapid medical treatment of casualties.

1-143. The company senior combat medic collocates with the company trains. When a casualty occurs, the CLS renders first aid, or first aid is provided through self-aid or buddy aid. The platoon combat medic or the company senior combat medic goes to the casualty's location, or the casualty is brought to the combat medic at the CCP. The CCP combat medic makes his assessment, administers initial medical care, initiates a DD Form 1380 (see figure 1-11) then requests evacuation or returns the individual to duty. (Refer to AR 40-66 for details and instructions on completing the form.)

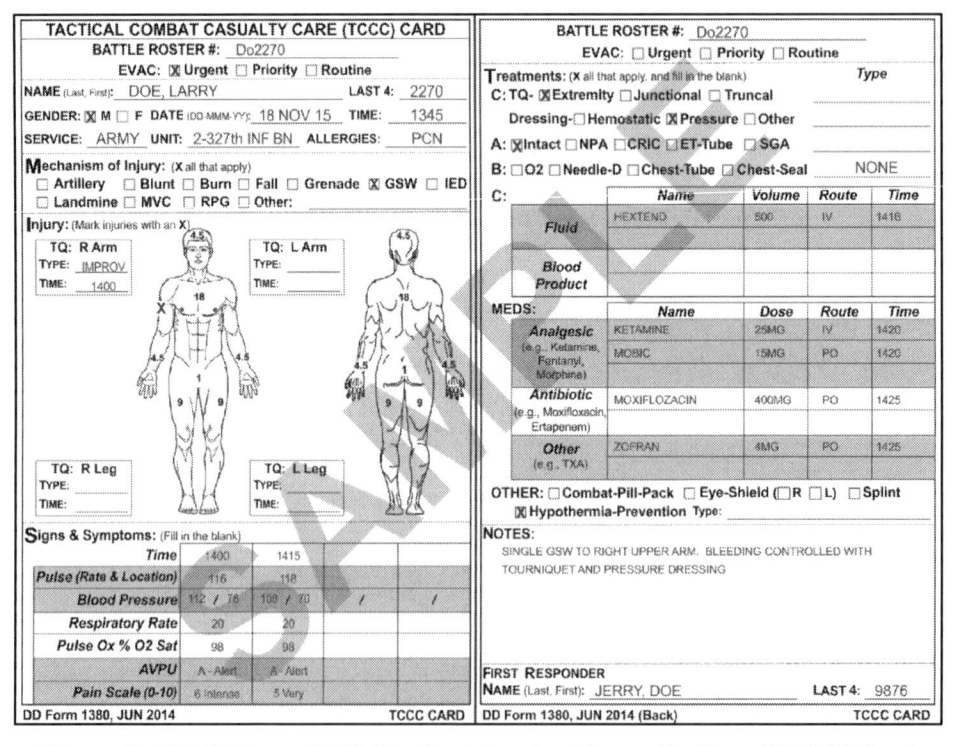

Figure 1-11. DD Form 1380, Tactical Combat Casualty Care (TCCC) Card

Chapter 1

1-144. The Infantry platoon combat medic usually locates with, or near, the platoon sergeant. When the platoon moves on foot in the platoon column formation, the combat medic positions himself near the platoon sergeant. If the platoon is mounted, the combat medic usually rides in the same vehicle as the platoon sergeant. + EMT procedures performed by the combat medic may include opening an airway, starting IV fluids, controlling hemorrhage, preventing or treating for shock, splinting fractures or suspected fractures, and providing relief for pain.

1-145. The Infantry platoon combat medic is trained under the supervision of the battalion surgeon or physician's assistant and medical platoon leader. The platoon combat medic is responsible for—

- Triaging injured, wounded, or ill friendly and enemy personnel for priority of treatment.
- Conducting sick call screening.
- Assisting in the evacuation of sick, injured, or wounded personnel under the direction of the platoon sergeant.
- Assisting in the training of the platoon's combat lifesavers in enhanced first-aid procedures.
- Requisitioning Class VIII supplies from the BAS for the platoon according to the TACSOP.
- Recommending locations for platoon casualty collection point.
- Providing guidance to the platoon's combat lifesavers, as required.

FORWARD OBSERVER

1-146. The fire support team is the platoon's expert on indirect fire planning and execution. The fire support team is the primary observer for all fire support assets to include company and battalion mortars, field artillery, and any other allocated fire support assets. He is responsible for locating targets and calling and adjusting indirect fires. He must know the mission and the concept of operation, specifically the platoon's scheme of maneuver and concept of fires. He works directly for the platoon leader and interacts with the company fire support team. The fire support team must also—

- Inform the fire support team headquarters of the platoon situation, location, and fire support requirements.
- Prepare and use maps, overlays, and terrain sketches.
- Call for and adjust indirect fires.
- Select targets to support the platoon's mission.
- Select observation post(s) and movement routes to and from selected targets.
- Operate digital message devices and maintain communication with the battalion and company FSO.
- Maintain grid coordinates of his location.
- Be prepared to back up the platoon leader's radio on the higher headquarters net if needed.

Organization

- Be prepared to employ close air support assets and Army aviation during close combat attacks.

INFANTRY CARRIER VEHICLE

1-147. The ICV is an eight-wheeled armored vehicle. It is a four-wheeled drive vehicle with selectable eight-wheeled drive and has—

- A sprint capability of 50 meters in 9 seconds.
- A sustained maximum speed of greater than 60 miles per hour (mph).
- A cruising range, at 40 mph, for 330 or more miles.
- Central Tire Inflation System.
- Run-flat tires.

PROTECTION

1-148. The Stryker ICV has several levels of protection depending on what armor and systems have been added. Furthermore, it's reduced audible and thermal signature, speed provide significant additional protection. Future modifications may include reactive and active armor systems. Currently, the ICV has the following protection features:

- The basic steel body armor protects against 7.62-mm fire.
- A spall liner protects Soldiers and equipment from fragments of the inner hull breaking off when hit by a projectile.
- The ceramic appliqué armor, applied to the basic steel body, protects against 14.5-mm machine gun and 152-mm artillery fragmentation.

REMOTE WEAPONS STATION

1-149. The RWS provides the ICV and other Stryker variants with an accurate and lethal weapon and is operated under armor. It provides the squad and platoon with close in security and enables the ICV to be used in a support or attack by fire mission.

Description

1-150. The Remote Weapon Station-Improved (RWS-I M151E2) is a weapon mount turret on which an M2HB .50-caliber machine gun or MK19 40-mm grenade machine gun can be mounted. It is remotely operated from inside the vehicle compartment, providing complete armored protection from direct enemy fire. The remote operation of the RWS–I M151E2 is carried through the computerized fire control unit and a joystick. This enables the part of the weapon station above vehicle deck, remote controlled elevation and depression of the weapon mount and 360 degrees unrestricted traverse rotation. The system also has remote weapon charging capability as well as firing. A stabilization system enables the operator to track and engage targets while on the move. The tracking and control capabilities of the RWS-I M151E2 provide a high first-round hit probability against stationary and moving targets.

Chapter 1

Characteristics

1-151. The RWS M151E1 is mounted to the top right side of the vehicle and is operated and controlled from the interior of the chassis. The RWS M151E1 can accept either the M2 or the MK19 40-mm grenade machine guns. It has the following characteristics:
- Both day and night operation modes.
- Traversing a full 360 degrees under power.
- Powered traverse and elevation at a rate of 80 degrees per second.
- Maximum elevation of +60 degrees.
- Maximum depression of –20 degrees.
- Foldable for transportability.
- Integrated fire control unit color display for operator interface.
- Smoke grenade launchers for local protection capable of firing four banks of four grenades each.
- Thermal imaging module: Provides visual images for both day and night operations.
- Video imaging module: Provides a color day camera for clear and easier target identification.
- A Small, Tactical, Optical, Rifle-Mounted (STORM), Micro-laser Rangefinder is mounted above the thermal imaging module and allows for accurately determining the range to a target. It also provides visible aiming lasers, and an infrared aiming laser. Although the STORM laser range finder is capable of much more, only these features are utilized when mounted on the RWS M151E1.

Armament

1-152. The RWS M151E1 is capable of mounting either the M2HB .50-caliber machine gun or the MK19 40-mm grenade machine gun. Because of stabilization, the machine guns have different maximum effective ranges than when ground mounted.

M2HB .50-Caliber Machine Gun: 1 ea.
- Maximum range (approx): 5000 meters.
- Maximum effective range (approx): 2000 meters.
- Cyclic rage of fire: 450-550 rounds/min.

MK19 40-mm Grenade Machine Gun: 1 ea.
- Maximum range: 2200 meters.
- Maximum effective range: 1500 meters.
- Cyclic rate of fire: 325-375 rounds/min.

Note. The MK19 40-mm grenade machine gun's range is reduced when used on a Stryker RWS compared to ground mounting due to limitations imposed by the maximum range of movement of the Sight Servo Assembly in relation to the weapon station platform's elevation angle.

Organization

M6 Smoke Grenade Launchers
- M6 smoke grenade launchers. Each with four smoke grenade tubes.
- Total of smoke grenade tubes: 16 ea.
- Detonating Range: 32.8 yards (30 m).
- Obscuration clouds: 6.6 to 7.7 yards (6 to 7 m) high.
- Covering arc: 6o 45" (120 mils) per launcher.

EMPLOYMENT CONSIDERATIONS

1-153. Leaders must consider the following guidelines when employing Stryker Infantry during decisive operations:
- Squads and platoons fight through enemy contact at the lowest possible level. Upon enemy contact, all Soldiers and leaders must act at once and follow up. Battle drills are standard procedures that help the platoon take immediate action.
- Before they can maneuver, squads or platoons in contact must establish effective suppressive fires and gain fire superiority. If the platoon or squad cannot move under its own fires, the leader must request support from the commander. Once they gain fire superiority, they maneuver against an enemy position. The Stryker ICV can suppress the enemy, move to a dismount location (if caught in the open), and dismount the rifle squads. The ICVs quickly build a base of fire for the rifle squads to maneuver.

CLOSE COMBAT

1-154. ICV-equipped Infantry platoons and rifle squads normally operate as part of a larger force. They benefit from the support of armor, artillery, mortars, close air support, close combat attack, air defense, and engineers. They provide their own suppressive fires either to repel enemy assaults or to support their own maneuver. During close combat, platoon leaders determine how to employ the ICVs by considering the following objective:
- Support the rifle squads with direct fires.
- Provide mobile protection to transport rifle squads to the critical point on the battlefield.
- Suppress or destroy enemy personnel and other soft targets with a .50-cal machine gun or an MK19.

1-155. Success in operations hinges on the actions of platoons, sections, and rifle squads in close combat. It depends on their ability to react to contact; employ suppressive fires; maneuver to an enemy's vulnerable flank; and fight through to defeat, destroy, or capture an enemy. For success, the ICV-equipped Infantry platoon relies on the ability of leaders and Soldiers to—
- Use the potential of both the rifle squads and the ICV.
- Operate their weapons with accuracy and deadly effect.
- Outthink, outmaneuver, and outfight the enemy.
- Use terrain to their advantage.

Chapter 1

SECTION V – COMPANY ORGANIZATIONS

1-156. This section discusses the organizational characteristics and capabilities of the Stryker Brigade Combat Team (SBCT) Infantry rifle companies and the ABCT mechanized Infantry and Armor companies. The SBCT Infantry rifle platoon may be task organized as part of a company team with the Infantry rifle company, the mechanized Infantry company, or the Armor company.

INFANTRY RIFLE COMPANY

1-157. The Infantry rifle company can deploy rapidly and be sustained by a support structure. (See figure 1-12, page 1-54.) The platoon's composition and training uniquely equip it to conduct missions against conventional and hybrid threats in all types of terrain and climate conditions. In addition to the Infantry rifle platoon's primary warfighting mission, it performs platoon level tasks in support of stability and defense support of civil authorities' tasks, semi-independently or as an integral part of a larger force.

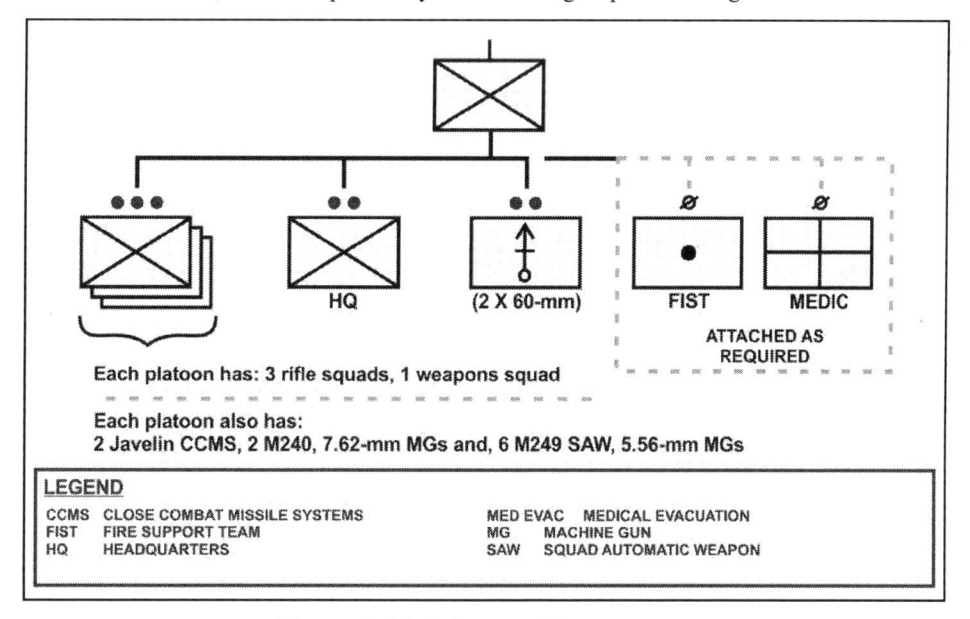

Each platoon has: 3 rifle squads, 1 weapons squad

Each platoon also has:
2 Javelin CCMS, 2 M240, 7.62-mm MGs and, 6 M249 SAW, 5.56-mm MGs

LEGEND
CCMS   CLOSE COMBAT MISSILE SYSTEMS
FIST   FIRE SUPPORT TEAM
HQ   HEADQUARTERS
MED EVAC   MEDICAL EVACUATION
MG   MACHINE GUN
SAW   SQUAD AUTOMATIC WEAPON

Figure 1-12. Infantry rifle company

MECHANIZED INFANTRY AND ARMOR COMPANIES

1-158. The combined arms battalion has two mechanized Infantry companies and two Armor companies. Application of Armor and mechanized Infantry companies as a combined arms team can capitalize on the strengths the company elements while minimizing their limitations. (Refer to ATP 3-90.1 for more information.)

MECHANIZED INFANTRY COMPANY

1-159. The mechanized Infantry company is organized, equipped, and trained to fight with organic assets or as a task-organized company team. The mechanized Infantry company consists of a headquarters and three BFV platoons. Figure 1-13 illustrates the organization of a mechanized Infantry company.

1-160. The company maneuvers in various types of terrain, climate, and visibility conditions. It capitalizes on all forms of mobility, to include helicopters and tactical airlift. The inherent versatility of Infantry makes it well suited for employment against asymmetrical threats. Unlike the Infantry and Stryker rifle companies, it has no organic mortars.

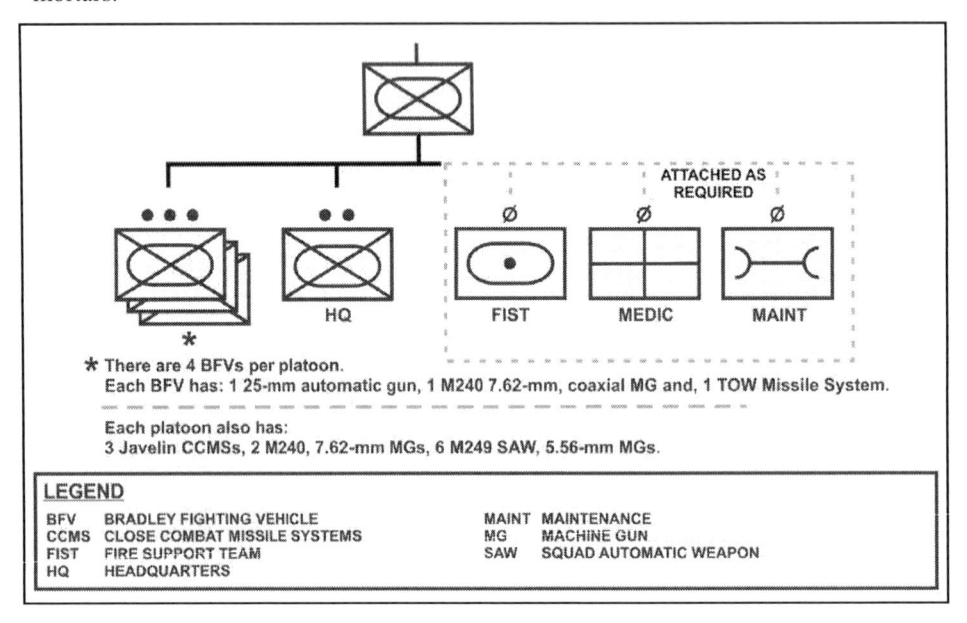

Figure 1-13. Mechanized Infantry company

ARMOR COMPANY

1-161. The Armor company is organized, equipped, and trained to fight pure or as a task organized company team. The Armor company comprises a headquarters and three tank platoons. The company headquarters comprises the commanding officer, executive officer, first sergeant, and supply section. The company headquarters is equipped with two tanks, a M113A2/A3 armored personnel carrier, and wheeled vehicles for mission command and sustainment. A maintenance section from the forward support company is normally attached to the Armor company. The ambulance squad in the combined arms battalion may deploy and attach an armored medical evacuation vehicle to an Armor company with its assigned crew of one emergency care sergeant with two ambulance drivers/crew. (See figure 1-14, page 1-56.)

Chapter 1

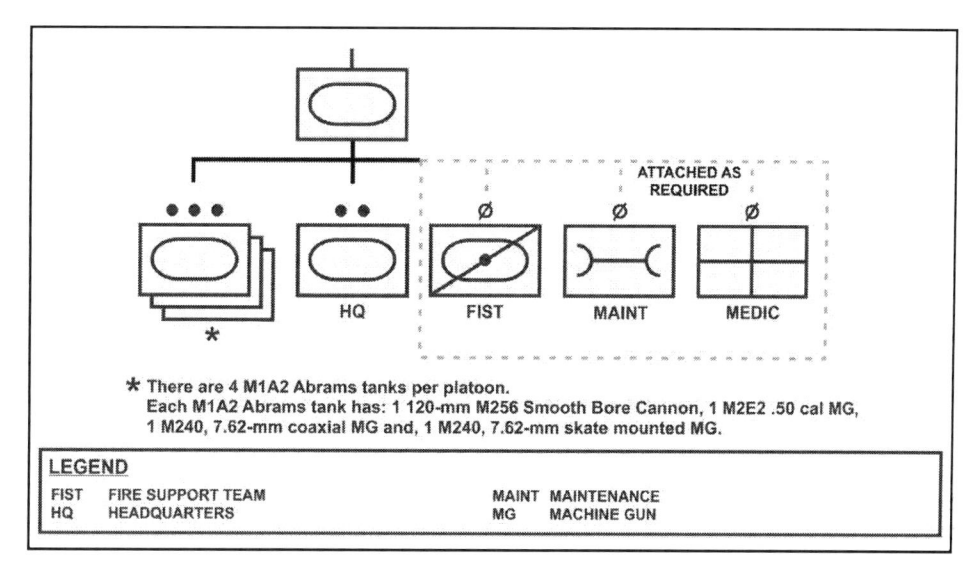

Figure 1-14. Armor company

SBCT INFANTRY RIFLE COMPANY

1-162. The SBCT Infantry battalion has three Infantry companies with three Infantry platoons each. The SBCT Infantry rifle company can be task organized based upon METT-TC. Its effectiveness increases through the synergy of combined arms including Infantry, engineers, and other support elements. The SBCT Infantry rifle company as a combined arms force can capitalize on the strengths the company's elements while minimizing their respective limitations. SBCT units can operate in most terrain and weather conditions. They might be the dominant arm in fast-breaking operations because of rapid strategic deployment, and mobility capabilities. In such cases, they can take and gain the initiative early, seize and hold ground, and mass fires to stop the enemy. Figure 1-15 illustrates the organization of a SBCT Infantry rifle company. (Refer to ATP 3-21.11 for more information.)

Organization

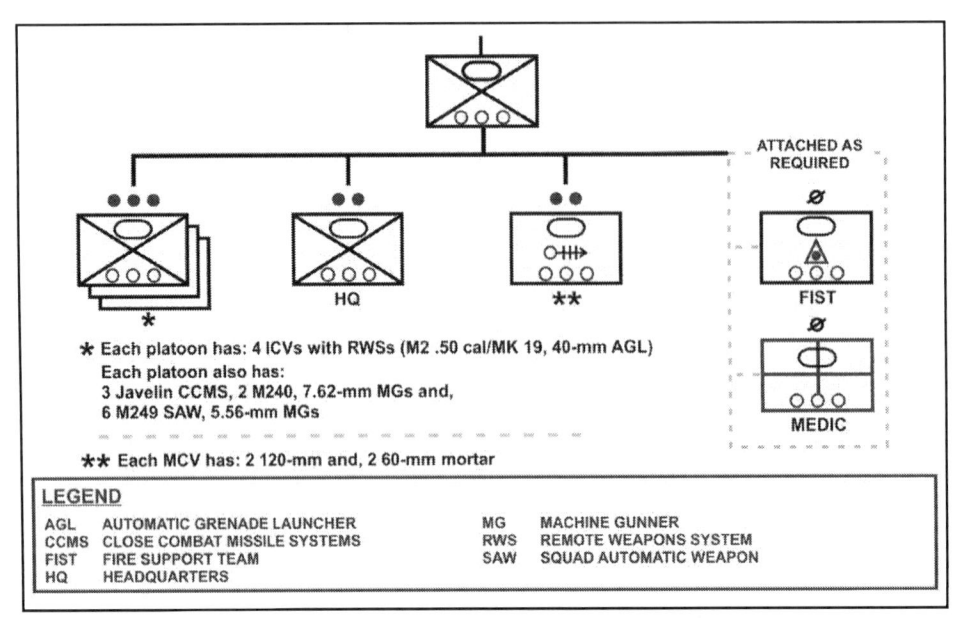

* Each platoon has: 4 ICVs with RWSs (M2 .50 cal/MK 19, 40-mm AGL)
  Each platoon also has:
  3 Javelin CCMS, 2 M240, 7.62-mm MGs and,
  6 M249 SAW, 5.56-mm MGs

** Each MCV has: 2 120-mm and, 2 60-mm mortar

LEGEND
AGL	AUTOMATIC GRENADE LAUNCHER	MG	MACHINE GUNNER
CCMS	CLOSE COMBAT MISSILE SYSTEMS	RWS	REMOTE WEAPONS SYSTEM
FIST	FIRE SUPPORT TEAM	SAW	SQUAD AUTOMATIC WEAPON
HQ	HEADQUARTERS		

Figure 1-15. SBCT Infantry rifle company

This page intentionally left blank.

Chapter 2
Offense

Platoon leaders and squad leaders must understand the principles and TTP associated with the offense. They must comprehend their role when operating within a larger organization's operations, and when operating independently. Leaders must recognize the complementary and reinforcing effects of other maneuver elements and supporting elements with their own capabilities, and understand the impact of open or restrictive terrain on their operations. The platoon conducts the offense to deprive the enemy of resources, seize decisive terrain, deceive or divert the enemy, develop intelligence, or hold an enemy in position. This chapter covers the basic principles of the offense, common offensive planning considerations, actions on contact, movement to contact attack, and transitions.

SECTION I – CONDUCT OF THE OFFENSE

2-1. The leader seizes, retains, and exploits the initiative when conducting offensive tasks. Even when conducting primarily defensive tasks, taking the initiative from the enemy requires offensive tasks that are force- or terrain-oriented. Force-oriented tasks focus on the enemy. Terrain-oriented tasks focus on seizing and retaining control of terrain and facilities. (Refer to FM 3-90-1 for more information.)

CHARACTERISTICS OF THE OFFENSE

2-2. The Infantry platoon and squad gains, maintains the initiative and keeps constant pressure on the enemy throughout its area of operation. Success in the offense greatly depends upon the proper application of the characteristics of the offense discussed in the following paragraphs.

AUDACITY

2-3. Audacity is a simple plan of action, boldly executed. Audacity inspires Soldiers to overcome adversity and danger. It is a key component of all offensive actions, increasing the chance for surprise. Audacity depends upon the leader's ability to see opportunities for action, decide in enough time to seize opportunities, and accept prudent risks. Leaders understand when and where to take risks, plan, and execute boldly.

Chapter 2

CONCENTRATION

2-4. Concentration is the massing of overwhelming effects of combat power to achieve a single purpose. Leaders balance the necessity for concentrating forces to mass effects against the need to disperse forces in order to avoid creating lucrative targets. Advances in ground, air mobility, target acquisition, and long-range precision fires enable attackers to concentrate effects. Mission command systems provide reliable, relevant information that assist commanders in determining when to concentrate forces to mass effects. The Infantry platoon and squad achieves concentration through—

- Careful planning and coordination based on a thorough terrain and enemy analysis, plus accurate reconnaissance.
- Designation of a main effort and allocation of resources to support it.
- Continuous information flow.
- Massing firepower using long-range precision fires and maneuver.

SURPRISE

2-5. In the offense, surprise is achieved by attacking the enemy at a time or place they do not expect or in a manner for which they are unprepared. Estimating the enemy commander's intent and denying the ability to gain thorough and timely situational understanding are necessary to achieve surprise. Unpredictability and boldness help gain surprise. The direction, timing, and force of attack also help achieve surprise. Surprise delays enemy reactions, overloads and confuse his command and control systems, induces psychological shock in enemy soldiers and leaders, and reduces the coherence of defensive missions. By diminishing enemy combat power, surprise enables the attackers to exploit enemy paralysis and hesitancy. The Infantry platoon and squad achieve surprise by—

- Gaining and maintaining information dominance by conducting thorough information collection and counterreconnaissance efforts.
- Striking the enemy from an unexpected direction, at an unexpected time, and by unique combinations of movement with units that cross all types of terrain.
- Quickly changing the tempo of operations.
- Being unpredictable.

TEMPO

2-6. Tempo is the relative speed and rhythm of military operations over time with respect to the enemy. Controlling or altering tempo is necessary to retain the initiative. A faster tempo allows attackers to quickly penetrate barriers and defenses, and destroy enemy forces in-depth before they can react. Leaders adjust tempo as tactical situations, sustainment necessity, or operational opportunities allow. This ensures synchronization and proper coordination, but not at the expense of losing opportunities, that defeats the enemy. Rapid tempo demands quick decisions. It denies the enemy the chance to rest while continually creating offensive opportunities.

Offense

OFFENSIVE TASKS

2-7. The four offensive tasks are movement to contact, attack, exploitation, and pursuit. Each is explained below.

MOVEMENT TO CONTACT

2-8. Movement to contact is an offensive task designed to develop the situation and establish or regain contact. (Refer to FM 3-90-1 for more information.) It creates favorable conditions for subsequent tactical actions. The leader conducts a movement to contact when the enemy situation is vague or not specific enough to conduct an attack. Forces executing this task seek to make contact with the smallest friendly force possible. A movement to contact may result in a meeting engagement, which is a combat action occurring when a moving force engages an enemy at an unexpected time and place. Once making contact with an enemy force, the leader has five options: attack, defend, bypass, delay, or withdraw. Two movement to contact techniques are search and attack, and cordon and search.

ATTACK

2-9. An attack destroys or defeats enemy forces, seizes and secures terrain, or both. (Refer to FM 3-90-1 for more information.) Attacks incorporate coordinated movement supported by direct and indirect fires. They may be decisive or shaping operations and hasty or deliberate, depending upon the time available for assessing the situation, planning, and preparing. However, based on METT-TC, the leader may decide to conduct an attack using only fires. An attack differs from a movement to contact because enemy main body dispositions are at least partially known, allowing the leader to achieve greater synchronization. This enables the massing effects of attacking forces combat power more effective in an attack than in a movement to contact.

EXPLOITATION

2-10. Exploitation follows an attack and disorganizes the enemy in-depth (Refer to FM 3-90-1 for more information.) Exploitations seek to disintegrate enemy forces to the point where they have no alternative but surrender or retreat. Exploitation take advantage of tactical opportunities, foreseen or unforeseen. Division and higher headquarters normally plan site exploitations as branches or sequels plans. However, the Infantry platoon and squad may participate as part of the fixing force or striking force.

PURSUIT

2-11. A pursuit is an offensive task designed to catch or cut off a hostile force attempting to escape, with the aim of destroying them. (Refer to FM 3-90-1 for more information.) A pursuit normally follows exploitation. Transition into a pursuit can occur if it is apparent enemy resistance has broken down entirely and the enemy is fleeing the area of operation. Pursuits entail rapid movement, decentralized control and clear commanders' intent to facilitate control.

Chapter 2

FORMS OF MANEUVER

2-12. Leaders select the form of maneuver based on METT-TC. The leader then synchronizes the contributions of all warfighting functions to the selected form of maneuver. An operation may contain several forms of offensive maneuver, such as frontal attack to clear enemy security forces, followed by a penetration to create a gap in enemy defenses, which in turn is followed by an envelopment to destroy a counterattacking force. While Infantry platoons and squads do not have the combat power to conduct all forms of maneuver on its own, they will participate as part of a larger organization. The six forms of maneuver are—

- Envelopment.
- Turning movement.
- Frontal attack.
- Penetration.
- Infiltration.
- Flank attack.

ENVELOPMENT

2-13. Envelopment is a form of maneuver in which an attacking force seeks to avoid the principal enemy defenses by seizing objectives behind those defenses allowing the targeted enemy force to be destroyed in their current positions. BCTs and above normally plan and conduct envelopments. At the tactical level, envelopments focus on seizing terrain, destroying specific enemy forces, and interdicting enemy withdrawal routes. The leader's decisive operation focuses on attacking an assailable flank. It avoids the enemy's strength at the front where the effects of fires and obstacles are greatest. Generally, the leader prefers to conduct envelopment instead of a penetration or frontal attack because the attacking force tends to suffer fewer casualties while having the most opportunities to destroy the enemy. Envelopment also produces great psychological shock on the enemy. If no assailable flank is available, the attacking force creates one. The four varieties of envelopment are single envelopment, double envelopment, encirclement, and vertical envelopment. (See figure 2-1.)

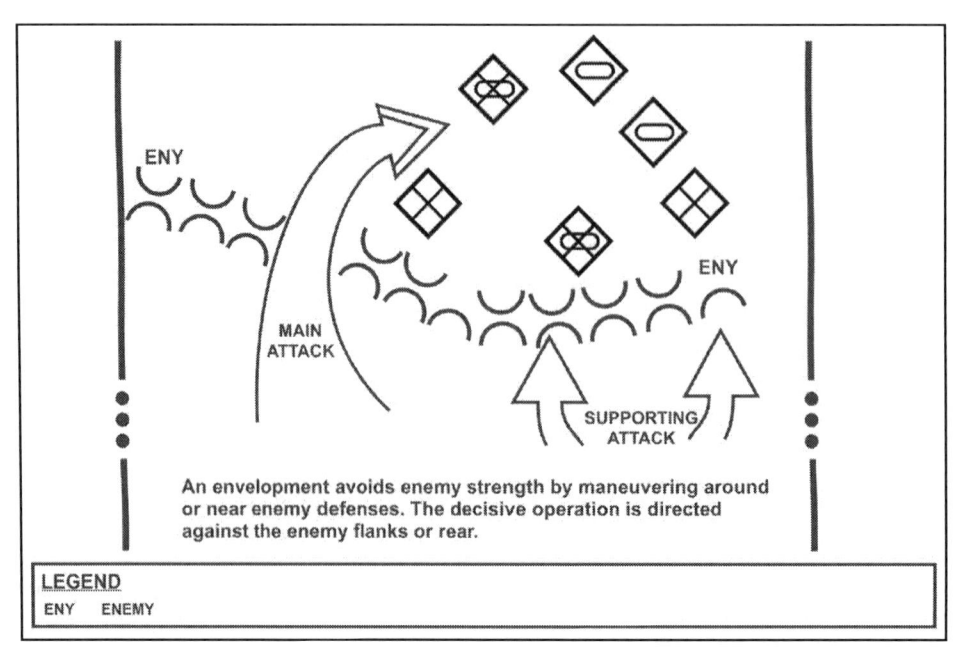

Offense

![Figure 2-1. Envelopment - An envelopment avoids enemy strength by maneuvering around or near enemy defenses. The decisive operation is directed against the enemy flanks or rear. LEGEND: ENY ENEMY]

Figure 2-1. Envelopment

TURNING MOVEMENT

2-14. A turning movement is a form of maneuver in which the attacking force seeks to avoid the enemy's principle defensive positions by seizing objectives behind the enemy's current position. This causes the enemy forces to move out of their current positions or divert major forces to meet the threat. The leader uses this form of offensive maneuver to seize vital areas in the enemy's support area before the main enemy force can withdraw or receive reinforcements. This form of offensive maneuver transitions from an attack into a site exploitation or pursuit. A turning movement seeks to make the enemy force displace from their current locations, whereas an enveloping force seeks to engage the enemy in their current locations from an unexpected direction. Divisions normally execute turning movements. (See figure 2-2, page 2-6.)

Chapter 2

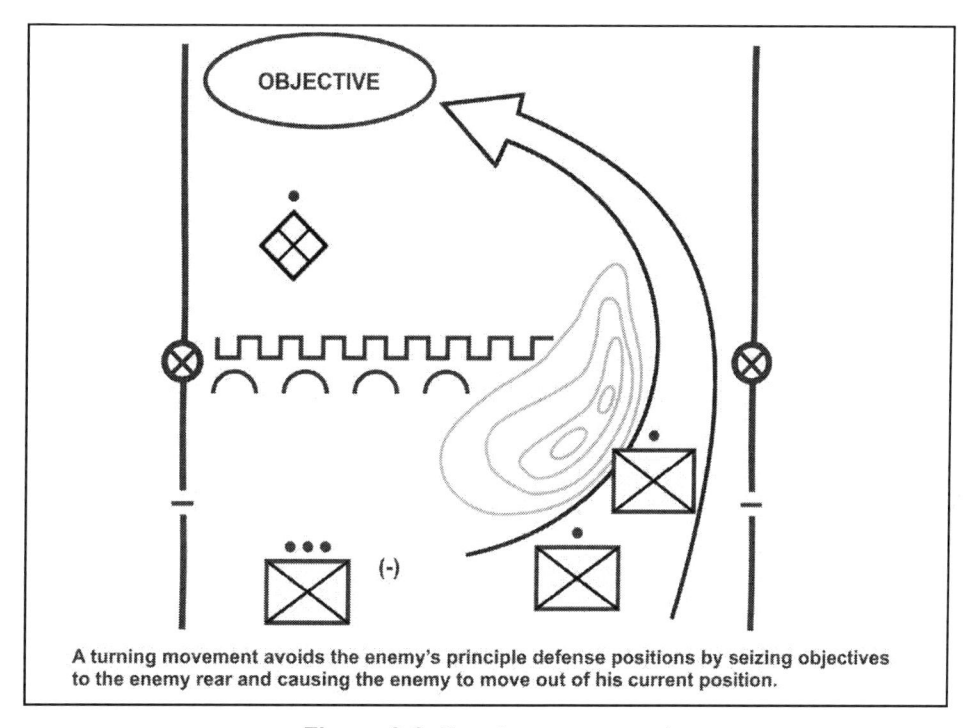

Figure 2-2. Turning movement

A turning movement avoids the enemy's principle defense positions by seizing objectives to the enemy rear and causing the enemy to move out of his current position.

FRONTAL ATTACK

2-15. A frontal attack is a form of maneuver where an attacking force seeks to destroy a weaker enemy force, or fix a larger enemy in place over a broad front. An attacking force can use a frontal attack to overrun a weak enemy force. The leader commonly uses a frontal attack as a shaping operation in conjunction with other forms of maneuver. (See figure 2-3.)

Offense

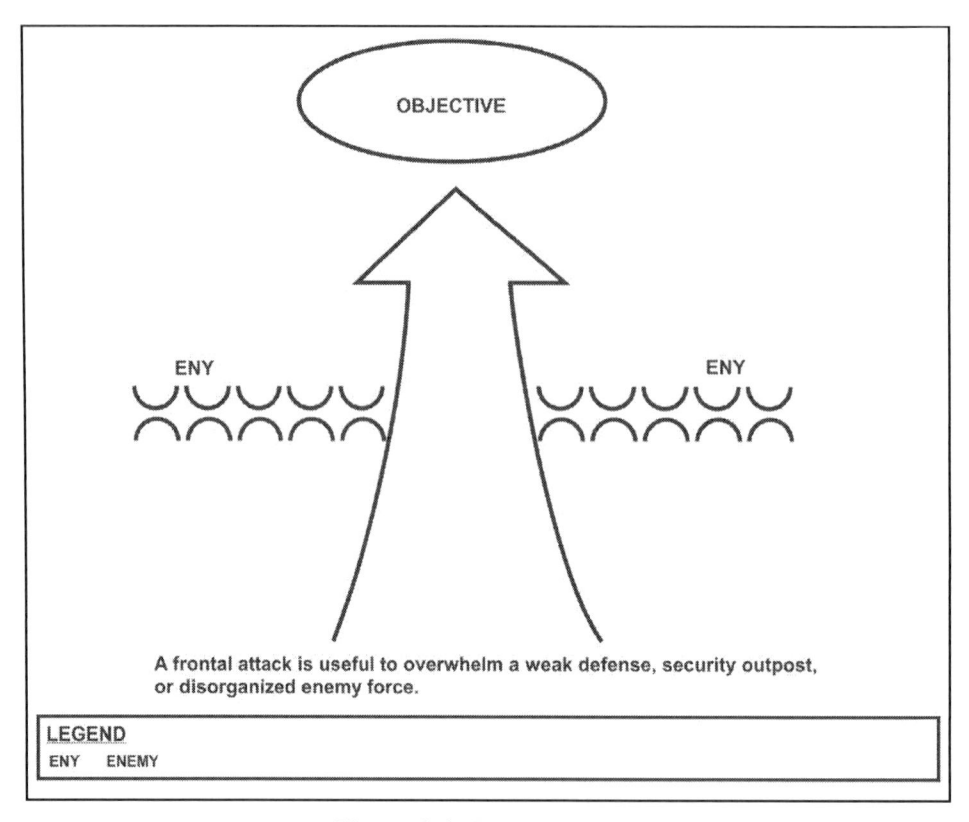

Figure 2-3. Frontal attack

PENETRATION

2-16. A penetration is a form of maneuver where an attacking force seeks to rupture enemy defenses in a narrow front to disrupt the defensive system. Destroying the continuity of defense allows the enemy's subsequent isolation and defeat in detail by exploiting friendly forces. The penetration extends from the enemy's security area through main defensive positions into the enemy support area. The leader employs a penetration when there is no assailable flank, enemy defenses are overextended and weak spots are detected in the enemy's positions, or time pressures do not permit envelopment. (See figure 2-4, page 2-8.)

Chapter 2

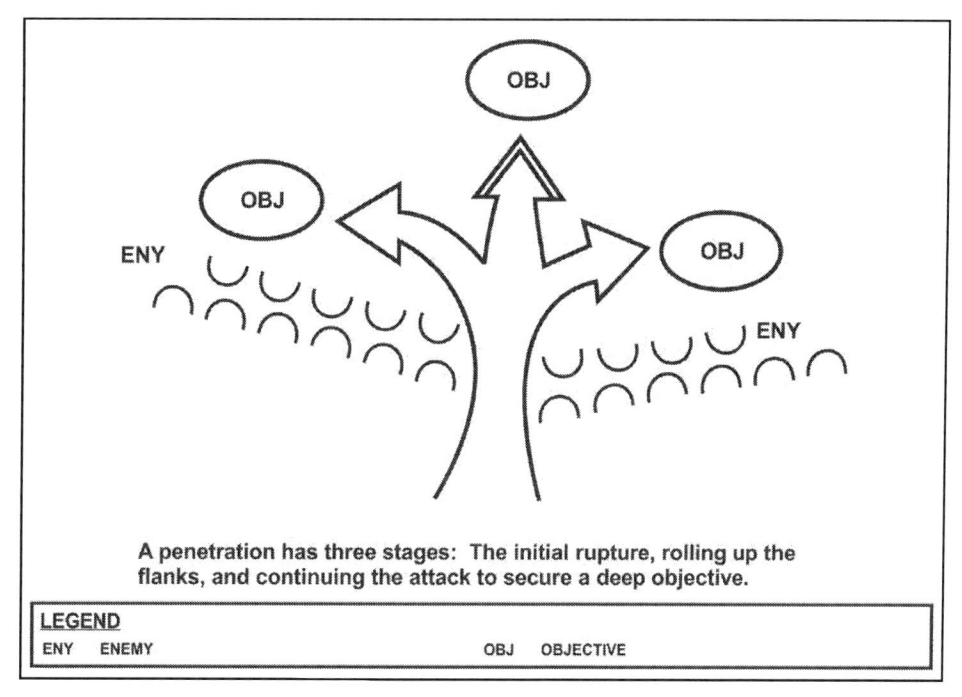

Figure 2-4. Penetration

INFILTRATION

2-17. An infiltration is a form of maneuver where an attacking force conducts undetected movement through or into an area controlled by enemy forces. The goal is to occupy a position of advantage behind enemy positions while exposing only small friendly elements to their defensive fires. Infiltration occurs by land, water, air, or a combination of means. Moving and assembling forces covertly through enemy positions takes a considerable amount of time. To infiltrate, the force avoids detection and engagement. Since this requirement limits the size and strength of the infiltrating force, and infiltrated forces alone rarely can defeat an enemy, infiltration normally is used in conjunction with and in support for other forms of maneuver. (See figure 2-5.)

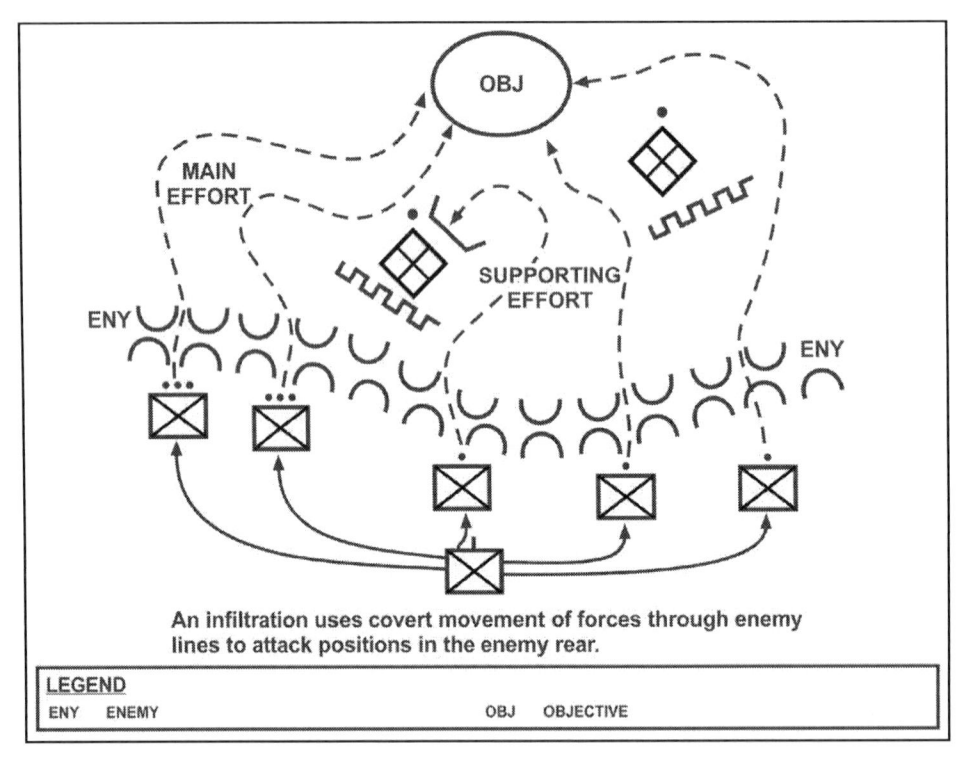

Figure 2-5. Infiltration

FLANK ATTACK

2-18. A flanking attack is a form of offensive maneuver directed at the flank of an enemy force as illustrated in figure 2-6, page 2-10. A flank is the right or left side of a military formation and is not oriented toward the enemy. It is usually not as strong in terms of forces or fires as is the front of a military formation. A flank may be created by the attacker with fires or by a successful penetration. A flanking attack is similar to envelopment but generally conducted on a shallower axis. It is designed to defeat the enemy force while minimizing the effect of the enemy's frontally-oriented combat power. Flanking attacks normally are conducted with the main effort directed at the flank of the enemy. Usually, a supporting effort engages the enemy's front by fire and maneuver while the main effort maneuvers to attack the enemy's flank. This supporting effort diverts the enemy's attention from the threatened flank. Corps and divisions are the most likely echelons to conduct turning movements. It often is used for a hasty operation or meeting engagement where speed and simplicity are paramount to maintaining battle tempo and, ultimately, the initiative.

Chapter 2

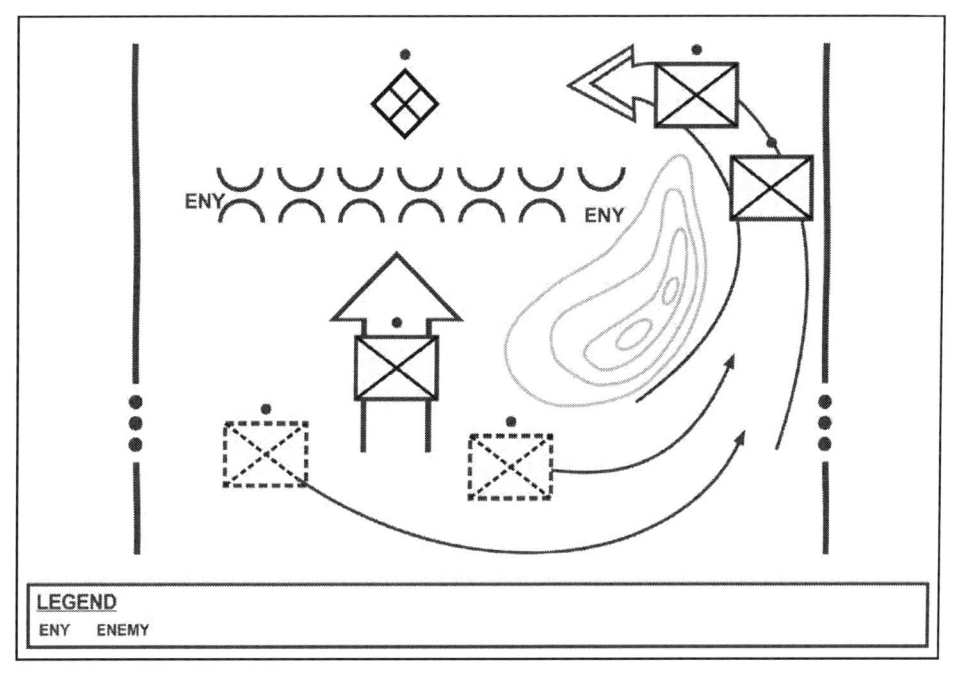

Figure 2-6. Flank attack

COMMON OFFENSIVE CONTROL MEASURES

2-19. The higher commander defines the commander's intent and establishes control measures allowing for decentralized execution and platoon leader initiative to the greatest extent. Common control measures for the offense are the—

- Assault position.
- Assault time.
- Attack by fire position.
- Attack position.
- Axis of advance.
- Battle handover line.
- Direction of attack.
- Final coordination line.
- Limit of advance.
- Line of departure.
- Objective.
- Point of departure.
- Probable line of deployment.
- Rally point.

- Support of fire position.
- Time of attack.

2-20. An area of operation defines the location where the subordinate units conduct their offensive. One technique breaks the battalion and company area of operation into many named smaller area of operation. Units remain in designated area of operation as they conduct their missions. Battalion and higher reconnaissance assets might be used to observe area of operation with no platoons in them, while platoons or companies provide their own reconnaissance in the area of operation. This technique, along with target reference points (TRPs), help avoid fratricide in noncontiguous environments. A TRP facilitates the responsiveness of fixing and finishing elements once the reconnaissance element detects the enemy. Objectives and checkpoints guide the movement of subordinates and help leaders control their organizations. Contact points help coordination among the units operating in adjacent areas.

2-21. When looking for terrain features to use as control measures, leaders consider three types: contiguous; point; and area. Contiguous features follow major natural and man-made features such as ridgelines, valleys, trails, streams, power lines, and streets. Point features can be identified by a specific feature or a grid coordinate including, hilltops and prominent buildings. Area features are significantly larger than point features and require a combination of grid coordinates and terrain orientation.

SEQUENCE OF THE OFFENSE

2-22. Offensive tasks are typically executed in a five-step sequence. This sequence is for discussion purposes only and is not the only way of conducting offensive tasks. These sequences overlap during the conduct of the offense. Normally the first three steps are shaping operations, while the maneuver step is the decisive operation. Follow through is usually a sequel or branch to the plan based upon the situation. The five-step sequence of the offense during execution is—
- Gain and maintain enemy contact.
- Disrupt the enemy.
- Fix the enemy.
- Maneuver.
- Follow through.

SECTION II – COMMON OFFENSIVE PLANNING CONSIDERATIONS

2-23. The warfighting functions are critical activities leaders use to plan, to prepare, and to execute. Synchronization and coordination among the warfighting functions is critical for success. This section discusses warfighting functions and other planning considerations.

MISSION COMMAND

2-24. In the Infantry platoon, the platoon leader is the central figure in mission command and is essential to integrating the capabilities of the warfighting functions. Mission command invokes the greatest possible freedom of action to his subordinates, facilitating their abilities to develop the situation, adapt, and act decisively through disciplined initiative within the platoon leader's intent. It focuses on empowering subordinate leaders and sharing information to facilitate decentralized execution.

2-25. Mission command conveys the leader's intent, and an appreciation of METT-TC, with special emphasis on—
- Enemy positions, strengths, and capabilities.
- Missions and objectives, including task and purpose, for each subordinate element.
- Commander's intent.
- Areas of operations for use of each subordinate element with associated control graphics.
- Time the operation is to begin.
- Scheme of maneuver.
- Special tasks required to accomplish the mission.
- Risk.
- Options for accomplishing the mission.

2-26. In addition to mission command warfighting function tasks, five additional tasks reside within the mission command warfighting function. These tasks are—
- Conduct military deception.
- Conduct civil affairs operations.
- Install, operate, and maintain the network.
- Conduct airspace control.
- Conduct information protection.

2-27. The planning and coordination requirements and procedures for offensive tasks are the same for both mechanized and Stryker Infantry units. The mechanized and Stryker platoon leader, however, must consider the following:
- The speed of the BFV versus speed of the dismounted Infantryman.
- The increased firepower of the BFV and Stryker and supporting weapons.
- The ability to rapidly bring combat power to bear at the decisive point with enhanced communication and coordination capabilities.

TACTICAL MISSION TASKS

2-28. Tactical mission tasks describe the results or effects the commander wants to achieve—the what and why of a mission statement. The "what" is an effect that is normally measurable. The "why" of a mission statement provides the mission's purpose.

2-29. The following paragraphs are select tactical mission tasks that a platoon may receive that are typically associated with offensive tasks. Each are described below.

> *Note.* The situations used in this section are examples only. For the complete list, refer to FM 3-90-1. They are not applicable in every tactical operation, nor intended to prescribe specific method for achieving the purpose of the operation.

BREACH

2-30. A platoon may conduct a breach during an attack to break through or secure a passage through an enemy defense, obstacle, minefield, or fortification. A platoon can participate in a hasty breach or participate as part of a larger unit during the conduct of a deliberate breach. A deliberate breach requires a synchronized combined arms operation.

DEFEAT

2-31. A platoon defeats an enemy force when the enemy force has temporarily or permanently lost the physical means or the will to fight. During a defeat, the defeated force's leader is unwilling or unable to pursue his adopted course of action, thereby yielding to the friendly commander's will. Also, he can no longer interfere with the actions of friendly forces to a significant degree.

DESTROY

2-32. A platoon destroys an enemy force when it physically renders an enemy force combat-ineffective until it is reconstituted. A platoon can destroy an enemy force by—
- Executing an ambush where the entire enemy element is in the kill zone.
- Using surprise direct and indirect fire into an engagement area.
- Coordinating direct and indirect fires onto an objective.
- Massing indirect fires onto an unprepared enemy.

SEIZE

2-33. A platoon has seized an objective when it physically occupies it and the enemy can no longer place direct fire on it. A platoon may seize during either offensive or defensive tasks. Examples include:
- A platoon seizes the far side of an obstacle as part of a company team breach.
- A platoon seizes a portion of an enemy defense as part of a company team deliberate attack.
- A platoon seizes key terrain to prevent its use by the enemy.

SUPPRESS

2-34. A platoon or squad has suppressed an enemy when the enemy cannot prevent our forces from accomplishing their mission. It is a temporary measure. The platoon can use direct fire or call in indirect and obscuring fires. Units in support and attack by fire

Chapter 2

positions often use suppressive fires to accomplish their mission. It is often used by the platoon during an attack to—
- Allow further movement of friendly forces.
- Isolate an objective by suppressing enemy units in mutually supporting positions.
- Cover the dismounted assault element from the line of departure (LD) to the objective.

MOVEMENT AND MANEUVER

2-35. The platoon leader conducts maneuver to avoid enemy strengths and create opportunities that increase the effects of combat power. Surprise is achieved by making unexpected maneuvers, rapidly changing the tempo of ongoing operations, avoiding observation, and using deceptive techniques and procedures. The platoon leader seeks to overwhelm the enemy with one or more unexpected actions before it has time to react in an organized fashion. This occurs when the attacking force is able to engage the defending enemy force from positions of advantage with respect to the enemy, such as engaging from a flanking position.

2-36. The platoon leader maneuvers the platoon to close with and destroy the enemy by close combat and shock effect. Close combat is direct-fire and movement warfare carried out on land and supported by direct-, indirect-, and air-delivered fires. (Refer to ADRP 3-0 for more information.) Close combat defeats or destroys enemy forces, or seizes and retains ground.

2-37. The movement and maneuver warfighting function includes the following tasks:
- Deploy.
- Move.
- Maneuver.
- Employ direct fires.
- Occupy an area.
- Conduct mobility and countermobility operations.
- Conduct reconnaissance and surveillance.
- Employ battlefield obscuration.

INTELLIGENCE

2-38. Leaders use threat event templates, the situation template, the likely threat COA, the most dangerous threat COA, civil consideration products, terrain products, and other intelligence products. The platoon leader may need to request information through the company intelligence support team (CoIST) company intelligence analyst from the battalion staff to answer platoon information requirements. (Refer to FM 3-21.10 for more information.)

2-39. By studying the terrain, the leader tries to determine the principal enemy heavy and light avenues of approach to the objective. Leaders also try to determine the most advantageous area the enemy's main defense might occupy, routes the enemy may use to conduct counterattacks, and other factors such as OAKOC. The attacking unit continuously conducts information collection during the battle because it is unlikely the leader has complete knowledge of the enemy's intentions and actual actions.

FIRES

2-40. The platoon leader must have a good, indirect fire plan for his route to cover anticipated places of contact. These targets are a product of the platoon leader's analysis of the factors of METT-TC and must be incorporated into the company's indirect fire plan.

2-41. Leaders conduct fires planning concurrently with maneuver planning at all levels. BCTs and battalions typically use top-down fire support planning, with bottom-up refinement of plans. As part of the top-down fire planning system, the company commander refines the fire plan from higher headquarters to meet mission requirements, ensuring these refinements are incorporated into the higher headquarters plan.

2-42. A clearly defined concept of the operation enables the platoon leader and FO to articulate precisely how they want indirect fires to affect the enemy during the different phases of the operation. In turn, this allows the company FSO to facilitate the development of fires supporting accomplishment of the company's mission down to the squad level. (Refer to ADRP 3-09 for more information.)

SUSTAINMENT

2-43. The objective of sustainment in the offense is to assist the platoon in maintaining the momentum. The platoon leader wants to take advantage of windows of opportunity and launch offensive tasks with minimum advance warning time. Platoon sergeant and squad leaders must anticipate these events and maintain flexibility to support the offensive plan accordingly.

2-44. A key to an offense is the ability to anticipate the requirement to push support forward, specifically in regard to ammunition, fuel, and water. This anticipation helps maintain the momentum of attack by delivering supplies as far forward as possible. Leaders use throughput distribution, and preplanned, preconfigured packages of essential items to help maintain offensive momentum and tempo.

PROTECTION

2-45. The rapid tempo and changing nature of the offense presents challenges to the protection of friendly assets. The forward movement of subordinate units is critical if the leader is to maintain the initiative necessary for offensive tasks. Denying the enemy a chance to plan, prepare, and execute a response to the friendly offense by maintaining a high operational tempo is a vital means the leader employs to ensure the survivability of his force. Using multiple routes, dispersion, highly mobile forces, piecemeal destruction of isolated enemy forces, scheduled rotation and relief of forces before they culminate, and wise use of terrain are techniques for maintaining a high tempo of offense. The exact techniques employed in a specific situation reflect METT-TC.

Chapter 2

2-46. The leader protects subordinate forces to deny the enemy the capability to interfere with their ongoing operations. Protection also meets the leader's legal and moral obligations to the organization's Soldiers. Some protection assets may need to be requested from higher. (Refer to ADRP 3-37 for more information.) To help preserve the force, the leader constantly assesses and ensures the following doctrinal protection tasks are addressed during the platoon's planning, preparation, and execution:

- Conduct operational area security.
- Employ safety techniques (including fratricide avoidance).
- Implement operation security.
- Provide intelligence support to protection.
- Implement physical security procedures.
- Apply antitank measures.
- Conduct survivability operations.
- Conduct CBRN operations.
- Provide support for EOD.
- Coordinate air and missile defense.

ADDITIONAL PLANNING CONSIDERATIONS

2-47. Additional offensive planning considerations include air assault operations, urban terrain, and operations in mountainous terrain.

AIR ASSAULT OPERATIONS

2-48. Air assaults are high-risk, high-payoff missions. When properly planned and vigorously executed, these missions allow leaders to generate combat power and apply warfighting functions. An air assault can provide leadership the means to control the tempo of operations, enabling rapid execution of operations to retain or exploit the initiative.

2-49. An air assault task force is most effective in environments where limited lines of communications are available to the enemy, who also lacks air superiority and effective air defense systems. It should not be employed in roles requiring deliberate operations over an extended period, and is best employed in situations providing a calculated advantage due to surprise, terrain, threat, or mobility. In particular, an air assault task force is employed in missions requiring:

- Massing or shifting combat power quickly.
- Using surprise.
- Using flexibility, mobility, and speed.
- Gaining and maintaining the initiative.

2-50. FM 3-99 addresses the following basic considerations for planning and execution of air assaults:

- Air assault operations are best conducted at night or during weather conditions allowing aircraft operations that obscure enemy observation. This facilitates deception and surprise.

- Indirect fire support planning provides suppressive fires along air routes and in the vicinity of landing zones. Priority for fires should be to the suppression of enemy air defense systems.
- Infantry unit operations are not changed fundamentally by integrating with aviation units. However, tempo and distance are changed dramatically.
- Ground and aerial reconnaissance units should be employed as early as possible to conduct reconnaissance and surveillance activities to shape the operational area for execution.

URBAN TERRAIN

2-51. Offensive tasks in urban terrain are designed to impose the leader's will on the enemy. Offensive missions in an urban environment aim to destroy, defeat, or neutralize an enemy force. However, the purpose may be to achieve some effect relating to the population or infrastructure of the urban area. Leaders should use a combined arms approach for offensive urban operations.

2-52. Offensive missions in urban areas are based on offensive doctrine applied to urban terrain. Urban terrain imposes a number of demands different from ordinary field conditions, such as problems with troop requirements, maneuver, and use of equipment. As with all offensive missions, the leader must retain his ability to maneuver against enemy positions. (Refer to ATTP 3-06.11 for more information.)

SUBTERRANEAN ENVIRONMENTS

2-53. In cities, subterranean features include underground garages, passages, subway lines, utility tunnels, sewers, and storm drains. Most allow troop movement. In smaller towns, sewers and storm drains may permit Soldiers to move beneath the fighting to surface behind the enemy. Knowledge of nature and location of underground facilities is of great value to both the urban attacker and defender. Subterranean routes can grant attackers use of both surface and subterranean avenues of approach, enabling them to place a smaller force behind enemy defenses. Depending upon strength and depth of the aboveground defense, attackers along the subterranean avenue of approach can become the main attack. If subterranean efforts are not immediately successful, it forces defenders to fight on two levels and to extend his resources to more than just street-level fighting. (Refer to ATTP 3-06.11 for more information).

2-54. The presence of subterranean passages forces defenders to cover urban areas above and below ground with observation and fire. Subterranean passages are more a disadvantage to defenders than the attackers are. However, given the confining, dark environment of these passages, they do offer some advantages when thoroughly reconnoitered and controlled by the defender. A small group of determined Soldiers in a prepared defensive position can defeat a numerically superior force. Subterranean passages—
- Provide covered and concealed routes to move reinforcements or to launch counterattacks.

Chapter 2

- Can be used as lines of communications, for movement of supplies, evacuation of casualties, and to cache supplies for forward companies.
- Offer defenders a ready-made conduit for communications wire, protecting it from tracked vehicles and indirect fires.
- Afford attackers little cover and concealment other than darkness and any man-made barriers.

OPERATIONS IN MOUNTAINOUS TERRAIN

2-55. Combat in mountainous areas present units with complicated hazards, difficulties, opportunities, and risks. Mountainous combat operations call for high levels of physical fitness, mental toughness, endurance, and tactical and technical proficiency on the part of all individuals.

2-56. A disciplined and prepared Infantry platoon and squad is task-organized with and supported by other members of the combined arms team, which are crucial to small-unit mountain operations. Units fighting in mountainous areas, overcome difficulties, measures risks, and exploit opportunities to close with and defeat the enemy. Prepared leaders anticipate, understand, and adapt to physical demands of mountainous environments. They face and overcome challenges of fighting in areas where technological supremacy can be negated by crude and nontechnical enemy actions. Unit leaders who know what to expect during mountainous operations create situations allowing their units to adapt to challenges and achieve victory in all environments.

2-57. Infantry units conducting operations in mountainous terrain are able to adapt and skillfully use environmental challenges to their advantage. (Refer to ATTP 3-21.50 for more information.) The landscape and climatic conditions create a unique set of mountainous operations characterized by—

- Close fights with dismounted Infantry. Mountainous combat often is close in nature as opposing forces meet on rugged terrain. Though engaging targets near limits of direct fire weapons occurs in mountainous engagements, intervening crests, hills, ridges, gullies, depressions, and other terrain features often limit long-range battles with the enemy. Upper levels of mountainous terrain are characterized by lack of trafficable roads. Use of vehicles often is restricted, forcing dismounted operations.
- Decentralized small unit operations. Conflicts in mountainous environments are often fought on platoon and squad level, as terrain commonly does not support movement and maneuver of large units. Compartmentalization of mountainous terrain can separate brigades from battalions, battalions from companies, and companies from platoons for long periods. As altitude increases in mountainous environments, terrain generally becomes more rugged and restrictive, which drives the need for decentralized execution of missions by dismounted platoons and squads.
- Degraded mobility and increased movement times. Ruggedness of mountainous terrain often restricts mobility to foot movements using file-type formations on roads and trails. A relatively short distance from point to point may be an arduous movement over steep, rocky, uneven terrain with multiple trail switchbacks increasing distance traveled and tremendous energy expenditure.

Offense

- Unique sustainment solutions. Sustainment in mountainous environments is challenging and time-consuming. Terrain and weather complicate virtually all sustainment operations including logistics resupply, medical evacuation, casualty evacuation, and Soldier health and hygiene. Network of restrictive mountainous roads often does not support resupply vehicles with large turning radius, or permit two-way traffic. Movement of supplies often involves a combination of movement types including air, vehicle, foot, and animal, with each technique having its own challenges in mountainous environments.
- Operations in thinly populated areas. Populace in typical mountainous environments mostly live in small villages in valleys, with some scattered villages in upper mountainous areas. Although farmers and animal herders make up a large majority of the indigenous population and may work higher up in altitude, the vast majority of mountainous terrain remains unpopulated.

TUNNELS AND CAVES

2-58. Tunnels, caves, and dry wells have historically been used for hiding places, food and weapons caches, headquarters complexes, protection against air strikes and artillery fire. Enemy personnel use these areas for both offensive and defensive actions. An extensive tunnel system containing rooms for storage and hiding as well as passages to interconnected fighting points may be encountered. Tunnels and caves are not only dangerous obstacles but can be an outstanding source of enemy information. Presence of a tunnel complex within or near an area of operations poses a continuing threat to all personnel in the area and no area containing tunnel complexes should ever be considered completely cleared.

2-59. Since tunnel complexes are carefully concealed and camouflaged, search and destroy operations should provide adequate time for thorough searches of an area to locate all tunnels and caves. Using of local nationals and host-nation scouts can be of great assistance in locating caves, tunnels, defensive positions, and likely ambush sites. Caves, trenches, spider holes, and tunnels are well incorporated into mountainous terrain and enemy operations and may be used as a deception to draw friendly forces into a cave or tunnel system rigged with booby traps or set with an ambush. (Refer to ATTP 3-21.50 for more information.)

SECTION III – COMBAT FORMATIONS

2-60. This section discusses combat formations of Infantry fire team, squad, platoon and mounted platoon. The platoon leader uses formations for several purposes: to relate one squad to another on the ground; to position firepower to support the direct-fire plan; to establish responsibilities for area of operation security among squads; or to aid in the execution of battle drills. Just as he does with movement techniques, the platoon leader plans formations based on where he expects enemy contact, and on the company commander's plans to react to contact. The platoon leader evaluates the situation and decides which formation best suits the mission and situation.

Chapter 2

2-61. Every squad and Soldier has a standard position. Soldiers can see their team leaders. Fire team leaders can see their squad leaders. Leaders control their units using arm-and-hand signals and intra-squad/team communications.

2-62. Formations also provide 360-degree security and allow units to give the majority of their firepower to the flanks or front in anticipation of enemy contact.

2-63. Formations do not demand parade-ground precision. Platoons and squads must retain the flexibility needed to vary their formations to the situation. Using formations allows Soldiers to execute battle drills quickly and gives them the assurance their leaders and buddy team members are in the expected positions and performing the right tasks.

2-64. Sometimes platoon and company formations differ due to METT-TC. For example, the platoons could move in wedge formations within a company vee. It is not necessary for platoon formations to be the same as the company formation unless directed by the company commander. However, the platoon leader coordinates his formation with other elements moving in the main body team's formation.

Note. Formation illustrations shown in this chapter are examples only. They might not depict actual situation or circumstances. Leaders must be prepared to adapt their choice of formation to the specific situation. Leaders always should position themselves where they can best control their formations.

PRIMARY FORMATIONS

2-65. Combat formations are composed of two variables: lateral frontage, represented by the line formation; and depth, represented by the column formation. The advantages attributed to one of these variables are disadvantages to the other. Leaders combine the elements of lateral frontage and depth to determine the best formation for their situation. In addition to the line and column/file, the other five types of formations—box, vee, wedge, diamond, and echelon—combine these elements into varying degrees. Each does so with different degrees of emphasis resulting in unique advantages and disadvantages

2-66. The seven combat formations can be grouped into two categories: formations with one lead element, and formations with more than one lead element. The formations with more than one lead element, as a general rule, are better for achieving fire superiority to the front, but are more difficult to control. Conversely, the formations with only one lead element are easier to control but are not as useful for achieving fire superiority to the front.

2-67. Leaders attempt to maintain flexibility in their formations. Doing so enables them to react when unexpected enemy actions occur. The line, echelon, and column formations are the least flexible of the seven formations. The line mass to the front has vulnerable flanks. The echelon is optimized for a flank threat, something units want to avoid. The column has difficulty reinforcing an element in contact. Leaders using these formations should consider ways to reduce the risks associated with their general lack of flexibility. (See table 2-1.)

Offense

Table 2-1. Primary formations

NAME / FORMATION / SIGNAL (IF APPLICABLE)	CHARACTERISTICS	ADVANTAGES	DISADVANTAGES
Line Formation	- All elements arranged in a row - Majority of observation and direct fires oriented forward; minimal to the flanks - Each subordinate unit on the line must clear its own path forward - One subordinate designated as base on which the other subordinates cue their movement	Ability to: - Generate fire superiority to the front - Clear a large area - Disperse - Transition to bounding overwatch, base of fire, or assault	- Control difficulty increases during limited visibility and in restrictive or close terrain - Difficult to designate a maneuver element - Vulnerable assailable flanks - Potentially slow - Large signature
Column/File Formation	- One lead element - Majority of observation and direct fires oriented to the flanks; minimal to the front - One route means unit only influenced by obstacles on that one route	- Easiest formation to control (as long as leader can communicate with lead element) - Ability to generate a maneuver element - Secure flanks - Speed	- Reduced ability to achieve fire superiority to the front - Clears a limited area and concentrates the unit - Transitions poorly to bounding overwatch, base of fire, and assault - Column's depth makes it a good target for close air attacks and machine gun beaten zone
Vee Formation	- Two lead elements - Trail elements move between the two lead elements - Used when contact to the front is expected - "Reverse wedge" - Unit required to two lanes/routes forward	The ability to: - Generate fire superiority to the front - Generate a maneuver element - Secure flanks - Disperse - Transition to bounding overwatch, base of fire, or assault	- Control difficulty increases during limited visibility and in restrictive or close terrain - Potentially slow
Box Formation	- Two lead elements - Trail elements follow lead elements - All-around security	Same as vee formation advantages	Same as vee formation disadvantages
Wedge Formation	- One lead element - Trail elements paired off abreast of each other on the flanks - Used when the situation is uncertain	The ability to: - Control, even during limited visibility, in restrictive terrain, or in close terrain - Transition trail elements to base of fire or assault - Secure the front and flanks - Easy transition to line and column	- Trail elements are required to clear their path forward - Frequent need to transition to column in restrictive, close terrain
Diamond Formation	- Similar to the wedge formation - Fourth element follows the lead element	Same as wedge formation advantages	Same as wedge formation disadvantages
Echelon Formation	- Elements deployed diagonally left and right - Observation and fire to both the front and one flank - Each subordinate unit on the line clears its own path forward	- Ability to assign sectors that encompass both the front and flank	- Difficult to maintain proper relationship between subordinates - Vulnerable to the opposite flanks

Chapter 2

FIRE TEAM FORMATIONS

2-68. The term fire team formation refers to the Soldiers' relative positions within the fire team. Fire team formations include the fire team wedge and fire teams file. (See table 2-2.) Both formations have advantages and disadvantages. Regardless of which formation the team employs, each Soldier must know his location in the formation relative to the other fire team members and team leader. Each Soldier covers a set area of responsibility for observation and direct fire as the team is moving. To provide the unit with all-around protection, these areas interlock. Team leaders are constantly aware of their teams' sectors of fire and correct them as required.

Table 2-2. Comparison of fire team formations

MOVEMENT FORMATION	WHEN MOST OFTEN USED	Movement Characteristics			
		CONTROL	FLEXIBILITY	FIRE CAPABILITIES AND RESTRICTIONS	SECURITY
Fire team wedge	Basic fire team formation	Easy	Good	Allows immediate fires in all directions	All-round
Fire team file	Close terrain, limited visibility, dense vegetation	Easiest	Less flexible than the wedge	Allows immediate fires to the flanks, masks most fires to the rear	Least

2-69. The team leader adjusts the team's formation as necessary while the team is moving. The distance between Soldiers will be determined by the mission, the nature of the threat, the closeness of the terrain, and by the visibility. As a general rule, the unit should be dispersed up to the limit of control. This allows for a wide area to be covered, makes the team's movement difficult to detect, and makes it less vulnerable to enemy ground and air attack. Fire teams rarely act independently. However, in the event they do, when halted, they use a perimeter defense to ensure all-around security.

FIRE TEAM WEDGE

2-70. The wedge (see figure 2-7) is the basic formation of the fire team. The interval between Soldiers in the wedge formation is normally 10 meters. The wedge expands and contracts depending on the terrain. Fire teams modify the wedge when rough terrain, poor visibility, or other factors make control of the wedge difficult. The normal interval is reduced so all team members still can see their team leader and all team leaders still can see their squad leader. The sides of the wedge can contract to the point where the wedge resembles a single file. Soldiers expand or resume their original positions when moving in less rugged terrain where control is easier.

Offense

2-71. In this formation the fire team leader is in the lead position with his men echeloned to the right and left behind him. The positions for all but the leader may vary. This simple formation permits the fire team leader to lead by example. The leader's standing order to his Soldiers is, "Follow me and do as I do." When he moves to the right, his Soldiers should move to the right. When he fires, his Soldiers fire. When using the lead-by-example technique, it is essential for all Soldiers to maintain visual contact with their leader.

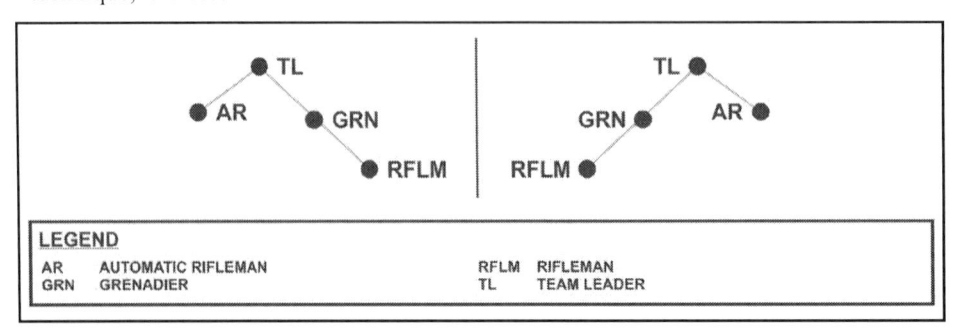

Figure 2-7. Fire team wedge

FIRE TEAM FILE

2-72. Team leaders use the file when employing the wedge is impractical. This formation most often is used in severely restrictive terrain, like inside a building; dense vegetation; limited visibility; and so forth. The distance between Soldiers in the column changes due to constraints of the situation, particularly when in urban operations. (See figure 2-8.)

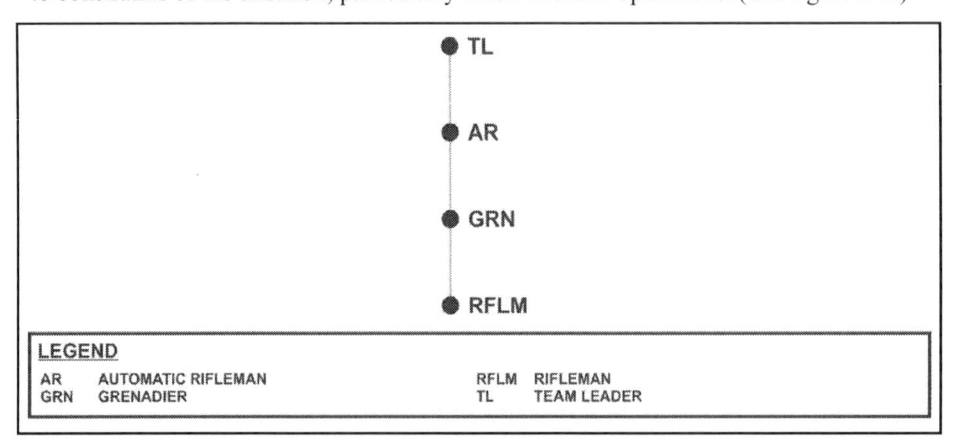

Figure 2-8. Fire team file

SQUAD FORMATIONS

2-73. The term squad formation refers to the relative locations of the fire teams. Squad formations include the squad column, the squad line, and squad file. Table 2-3, page 2-24 compares squad formations.

Chapter 2

Table 2-3. Comparison of squad formations

MOVEMENT FORMATION	WHEN MOST OFTEN USED	Movement Characteristics			
		CONTROL	FLEXIBILITY	FIRE CAPABILITIES AND RESTRICTIONS	SECURITY
Squad column	The main squad formation	Good	Aids maneuver, good dispersion laterally and in depth	Allows large volume of fire to the flanks but only limited volume to the front	All-round
Squad line	Fore maximum firepower to the front	Not as good as the column	Limited maneuver capability (both fire teams committed)	Allows maximum immediate fire to the front	Good to the front, little to the flank and rear
Squad fire	Close terrain, dense vegetation, limited visibility conditions	Easiest	Most difficult formation to maneuver from	Allows immediate fire to the flanks, masks most fire to the front and rear	Least

2-74. The squad leader adjusts the squad's formation as necessary while moving, primarily through the three movement techniques. The squad leader exercises mission command primarily through the two team leaders and moves in the formation where he can best achieve this. The squad leader is responsible for 360-degree security, for ensuring the team's sectors of fire are mutually supporting, and for being able to rapidly transition the squad upon contact.

2-75. The squad leader designates one of the fire teams as the base fire team. The squad leader controls the squad's speed and direction of movement through the base fire team while the other team and attachments cue their movement off the base fire team. This concept applies when not in contact and when in contact with the enemy.

2-76. Weapons from the weapons squad (a medium machine gun or a Javelin) may be attached to the squad for movement or throughout the operation. These high value assets need to be positioned so they are protected and can be quickly brought into the engagement when required. Ideally, these weapons should be positioned so they are between the two fire teams.

SQUAD COLUMN

2-77. The squad column is the squad's main formation for movement unless preparing for an assault. (See figure 2-9.) It provides good dispersion both laterally and in-depth without sacrificing control. It also facilitates maneuver. The lead fire team is the base fire team. Squads can move in either a column wedge or a modified column wedge. Rough terrain, poor visibility, and other factors can require the squad to modify the wedge into a file for control purposes. As the terrain becomes less rugged and control becomes easier, the Soldiers resume their original positions.

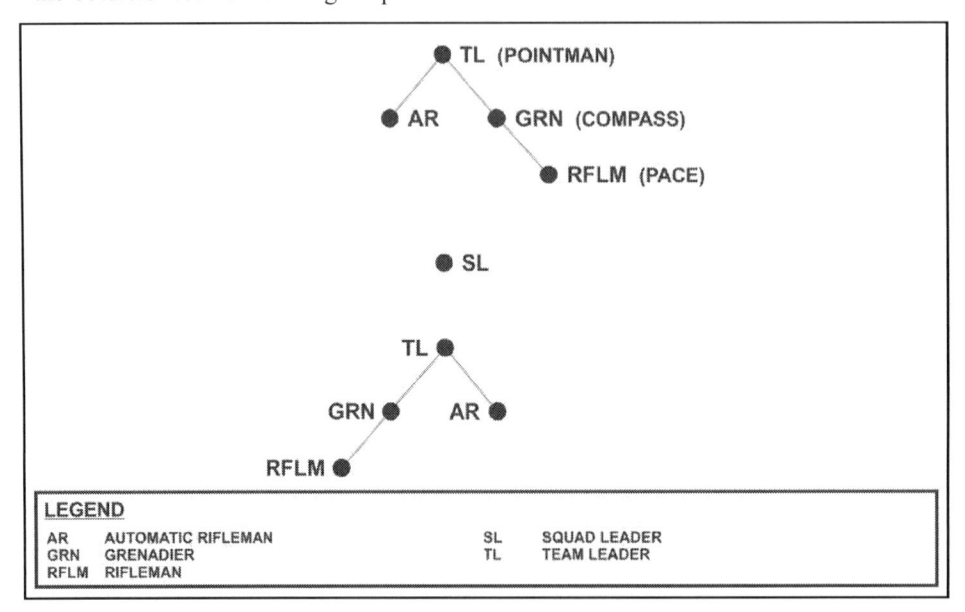

Figure 2-9. Squad column, fire teams in wedge

SQUAD LINE

2-78. The squad line provides maximum firepower to the front and is used to assault or as a pre-assault formation. (See figure 2-10, page 2-26.) To execute the squad line, the squad leader designates one of the teams as the base team. The other team cues its movement off the base team. This applies when the squad is in close combat as well. From this formation, the squad leader can employ any of the three movement techniques or conduct fire and movement.

Chapter 2

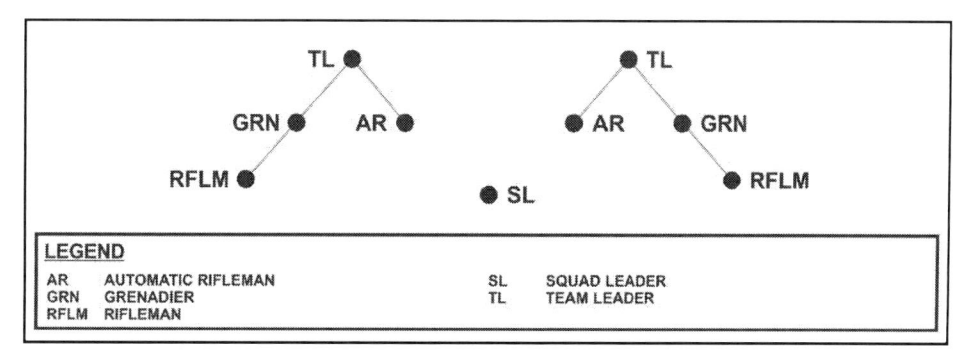

Figure 2-10. Squad line

SQUAD FILE

2-79. The squad file has the same characteristics as the fire team file. (See figure 2-11.) In the event the terrain is severely restrictive or extremely close, teams within the squad file also may be in file. This disposition is not optimal for enemy contact, but provides the squad leader with maximum control. He increases control over the formation moving forward to the first or second position. Moving forward enables him to exert greater morale presence by leading from the front, and to be immediately available to make vital decisions. Moving a team leader to the last position can provide additional control over the rear of the formation.

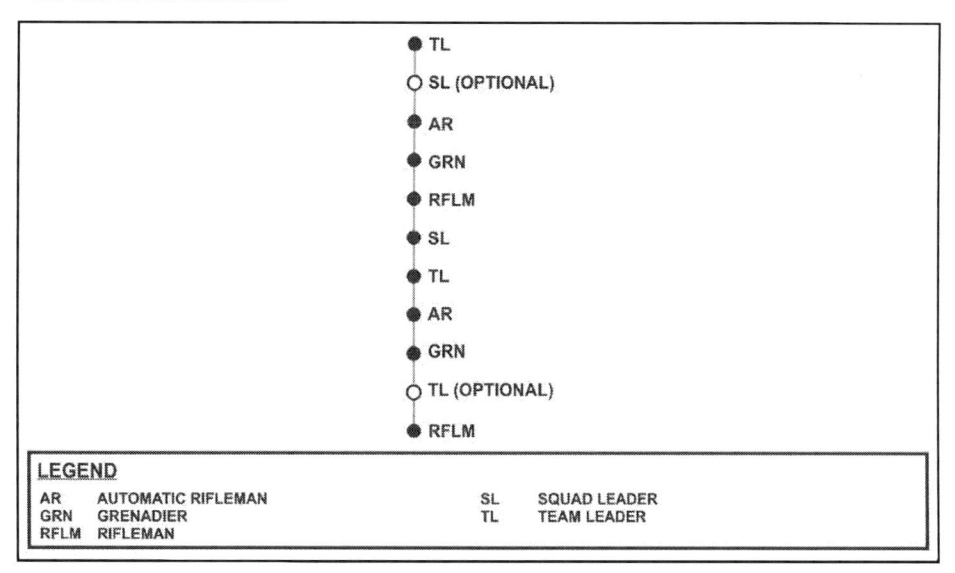

Figure 2-11. Squad file

WEAPONS SQUAD FORMATION

2-80. The weapons squad is not a rifle squad and should not be treated as such. During tactical movement the platoon leader has one of two options when it comes to positioning the weapons squad. The weapons squad can either travel as a separate entity, or can be broken up and distributed throughout the formation. The advantage to keeping the weapons squad together is the ability to quickly generate a support by fire and gain fire superiority under the direction of the weapons squad leader. The disadvantage to this approach is the lack of redundancy throughout the formation. The advantage to distributing the weapons squad throughout the rifle squads is the coverage afforded to the entire formation. The disadvantage is losing the weapons squad leader as a single mission command element and time required reassembling the weapons squad if needed.

2-81. When the weapons squad travels dispersed, it can either be attached to squads or attached to the essential leaders like the platoon leader, platoon sergeant, and weapons squad leader. There is no standard method for its employment. Rather, the platoon leader places the weapons using two criteria: ability to quickly generate fire superiority, and protection for high value assets.

2-82. Like the rifle squad, the weapon squad, when traveling as a squad, uses either a column or line formation. Within these formations, the two sections can be in column or line formation.

PLATOON FORMATIONS

2-83. The actual number of useful combinations of squad and fire team combat formations within the platoon combat formations is numerous, creating a significant training requirement for the unit. Add to the requirement to modify formations with movement techniques, immediate action drills, and other techniques, and it is readily apparent what the platoon leader needs a few simple methods. These methods should be detailed in the unit SOP.

PLATOON LEADER RESPONSIBILITIES

2-84. Like the squad leader, the platoon leader exercises mission command primarily through his subordinates and moves in the formation where he can best achieve this. The squad leader and team leader execute the combat formations and movement techniques within their capabilities based on the platoon leader's guidance.

2-85. The platoon leader is responsible for 360-degree security, for ensuring each subordinate unit's sectors of fire are mutually supporting, and for being able to rapidly transition the platoon upon contact. He adjusts the platoon's formation as necessary while moving, primarily through the three movement techniques. Like the squad and team, this determination is a result of the task, the nature of the threat, the closeness of terrain, and visibility.

2-86. The platoon leader also is responsible for ensuring his squads can perform their required actions. He does this through training before combat and rehearsals during combat. Well-trained squads are able to employ combat formations, movement techniques, actions on contact, and stationary formations.

PLATOON HEADQUARTERS

2-87. The platoon leader also has to decide how to disperse the platoon headquarters elements (himself, his RTO, his interpreter, forward observer, platoon sergeant, and medic). These elements do not have fixed positions in the formations. Rather, they should be positioned where they can best accomplish their tasks. The platoon leader's element should be where he conducts actions on contact, where he can supervise navigation, and where he can communicate with higher. The forward observer's element should be where he can best see the battlefield and where he can communicate with the platoon leader and battalion fire support officer. This is normally in close proximity to the platoon leader. The platoon sergeant's element should be wherever the platoon leader is not. Typically, this means the platoon leader is toward the front of the formation, while the platoon sergeant is toward the rear of the formation. Because of the platoon sergeant's experience, he should be given the freedom to assess the situation and advise the platoon leader accordingly.

BASE SQUAD

2-88. The platoon leader designates one of the squads as the base squad. He controls the platoon's speed and direction of movement through the base squad, while the other squads and attachments cue their movement off of the base squad.

MOVING AS A PART OF A LARGER UNIT

2-89. Infantry platoons and squads often move as part of a larger unit's movement. The next higher commander assigns the platoon a position within the formation. The platoon leader assigns his subordinates an appropriate formation based on the situation, and uses the appropriate movement technique. Regardless of the platoon's position within the formation, it must be ready to make contact or to support the other elements by movement, by fire, or by both.

2-90. When moving in a company formation, the company commander normally designates a base platoon to facilitate control. The other platoons cue their speed and direction on the base platoon. This permits quick changes and lets the commander control the movement of the entire company by controlling only the base platoon. The company commander normally locates himself within the formation where he can best see and direct the movement of the base platoon. The base platoon's center squad is usually its base squad. When the platoon is not acting as the base platoon, its base squad is its flank squad nearest the base platoon.

PRIMARY PLATOON FORMATIONS

2-91. Platoon formations include the column, the line (squads on line or in column), the vee, the wedge, and the file. The leader should weigh these carefully to select the best formation based on his mission and on METT-TC analysis. Comparisons of the different formations are in table 2-4. The figures below are examples and do not dictate the location of the platoon leader or platoon sergeant.

Table 2-4. Comparison of platoon formations

MOVEMENT FORMATION	WHEN MOST OFTEN USED	Movement Characteristics			
		CONTROL	FLEXIBILITY	FIRE CAPABILITIES AND RESTRICTIONS	SECURITY	MOVEMENT
Platoon column	Platoon primary movement formation	Good for maneuver (fire and movement)	Provides good dispersion laterally and in depth	Allows limited firepower to the front and rear, but high volume to the flanks	Extremely limited overall security	Good
Platoon line, squads on line	When the leaders wants all Soldiers forward for maximum firepower to the front and the enemy situation is known	Difficult	Minimal	Allows maximum firepower to the front, little to flanks and rear	Less secure than other formations because of the lack of depth, but provides excellent security for the higher formations in the direction of the echelon	Slow
Platoon line, squads in column	May be used when the leaders does not want everyone on line; but wants to be prepared for contact: when crossing a line of departure near an objective	Easier than platoon column, squads on line, but less than platoon line, squads on line	Greater than platoon column, squads on line, but less than platoon line, squads on one	Good firepower to the front and rear, minimum fires to the flanks; not as good as platoon column, better than platoon line	Good security all around	Slower than platoon column, faster than platoon line, squads on line

Table 2-4. Comparison of platoon formations (continued)

MOVEMENT FORMATION	WHEN MOST OFFEN USED	Movement Characteristics					
		CONTROL	FLEXIBILITY	FIRE CAPABILITIES AND RESTRICTIONS	SECURITY	MOVEMENT
Platoon vee	When the enemy situation is vague, but contact is expected from the front	Difficult	Provides two squads up front for immediate firepower and one squad to the rear to the rear for movement (fire and movement) upon contact from the flank	Immediate heavy volume of firepower to the front or flanks, but minimum fires to the rear	Good security to the front	Slow
Platoon wedge	When the enemy situation is vague, but contact is not expected	Difficult but better than platoon vee and platoon line, squads in line	Enables leader to make a small element and still have two squads to maneuver	Provides heavy volume of firepower to the front or flanks	Good security to the flanks	Slow, but faster than platoon vee
Platoon file	When visibility is poor due to terrain, vegetation, or light	Easiest	Most difficult formation from which to maneuver	Allows immediate fires to the flanks, masks most fires to front and rear	Extremely limited overall security	Fastest for dismounted movement

Offense

Platoon Column

2-92. In the platoon column formation, the lead squad is the base squad. (See figure 2-12.) It normally is used for traveling only.

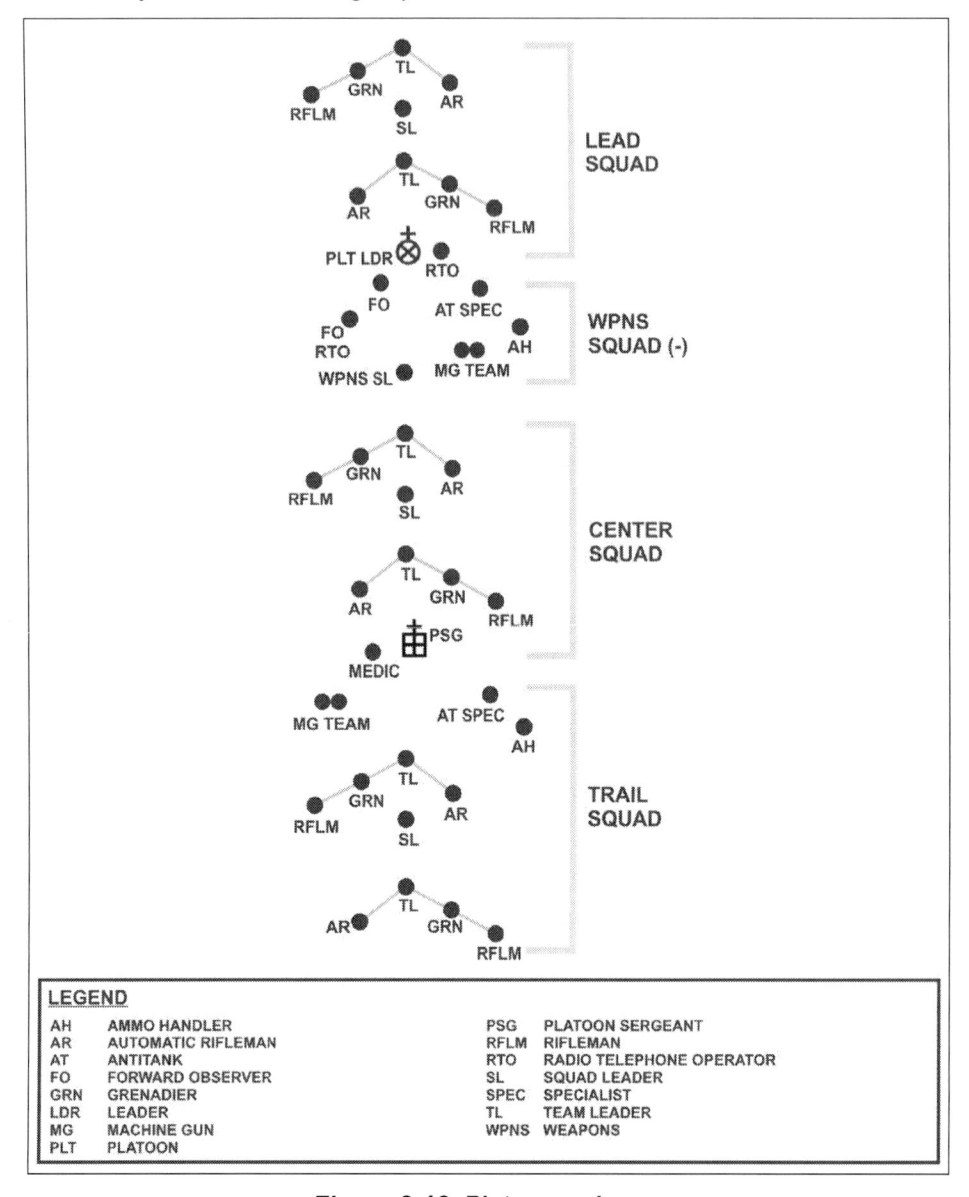

Figure 2-12. Platoon column

Chapter 2

> *Note.* METT-TC considerations determine where the weapons squad or medium machine gun teams locate in the platoon formation.

Platoon Line, Squads on Line

2-93. In the platoon line, squads on line formation, or when two or more platoons are attacking, the company commander chooses one of them as the base platoon. The base platoon's center squad is its base squad. When the platoon is not acting as the base platoon, its base squad is its flank squad nearest the base platoon. The weapons squad may move with the platoon or it can provide the support-by-fire position. This is the basic platoon assault formation. (See figure 2-13.)

2-94. The platoon line with squads on line is the most difficult formation from which to make the transition to other formations.

2-95. It may be used in the assault to maximize the firepower and shock effect of the platoon. This normally is done when there is no intervening terrain between the unit and the enemy when antitank systems is suppressed, or when the unit is exposed to artillery fire and must move rapidly.

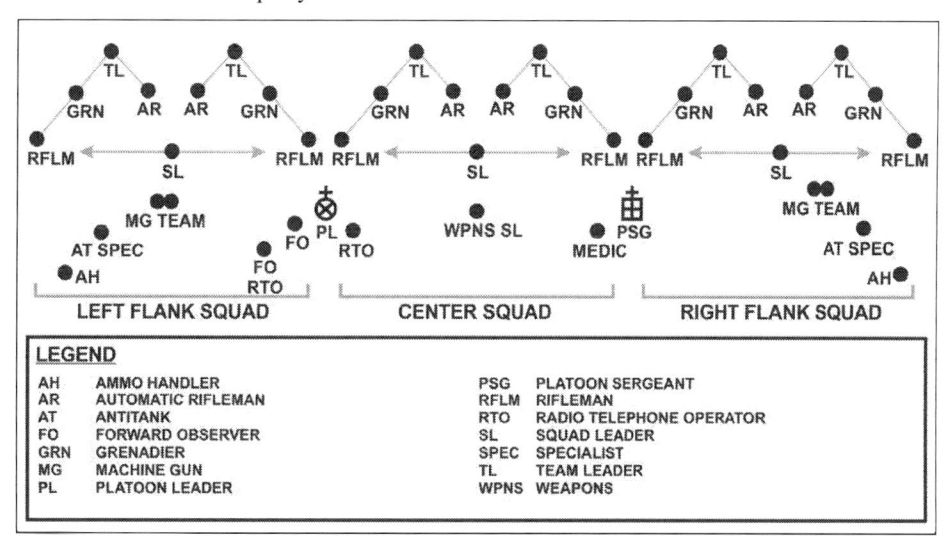

Figure 2-13. Platoon line, squads on line

Platoon Line, Squads in Column

2-96. When two or more platoons are moving, the company commander chooses one of them as the base platoon. The base platoon's center squad is its base squad. When the platoon is not the base platoon, its base squad is its flank squad nearest the base platoon. (See figure 2-14.) The platoon line with squads in column formation is difficult to transition to other formations.

Offense

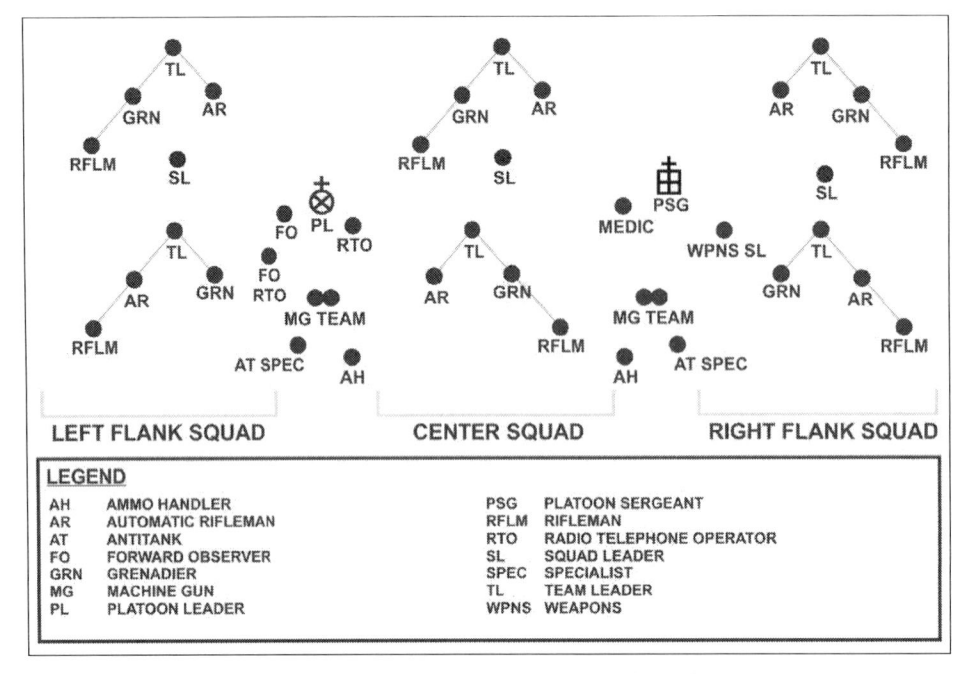

Figure 2-14. Platoon line, squads in column

Platoon Vee

2-97. This formation has two squads up front to provide a heavy volume of fire on contact. (See figure 2-15, page 2-34.) It also has one squad in the rear either overwatching or trailing the other squads. The platoon leader designates one of the front squads as the platoon's base squad.

Chapter 2

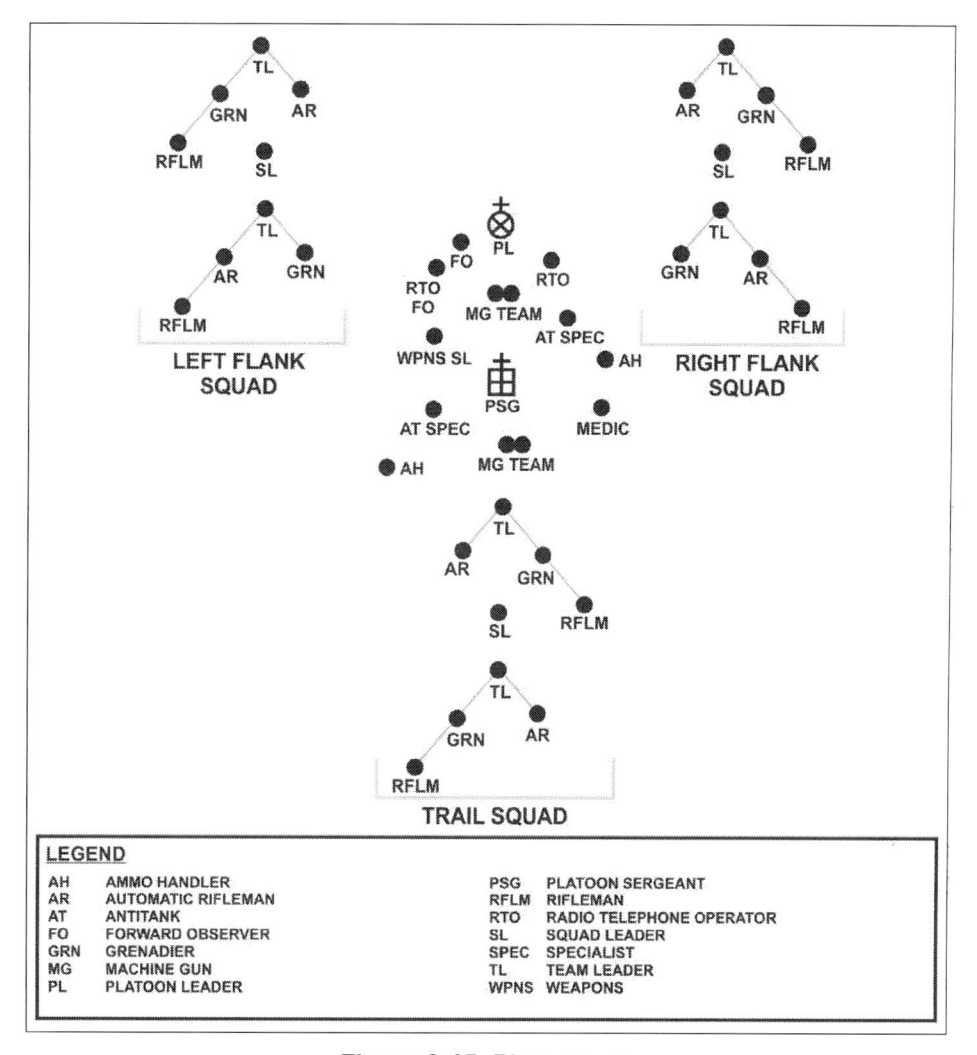

Figure 2-15. Platoon vee

Platoon Wedge

2-98. This formation has two squads in the rear overwatching or trailing the lead squad. (See figure 2-16.) The lead squad is the base squad. The wedge formation—
- Can be used with the traveling and traveling overwatch techniques.
- Allows rapid transition to bounding overwatch.

Offense

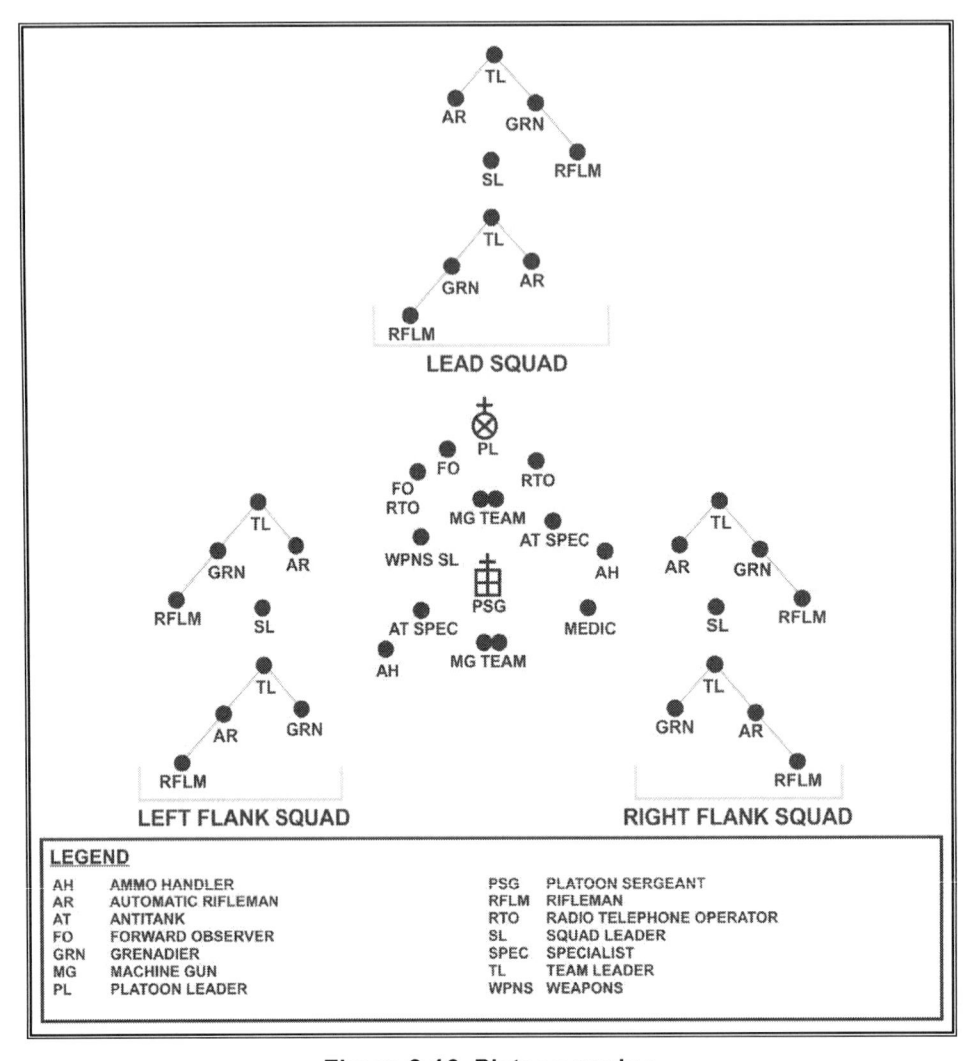

Figure 2-16. Platoon wedge

Platoon File

2-99. This formation may be set up in several methods. (See figure 2-17, page 2-36.) One method is to have three-squad files follow one another using one of the movement techniques. Another method is to have a single platoon file with a front security element (point) and flank security elements. The distance between Soldiers is less than normal to allow communication by passing messages up and down the file. The platoon file has the same characteristics as the fire team and squad files. It normally is used for traveling only.

Chapter 2

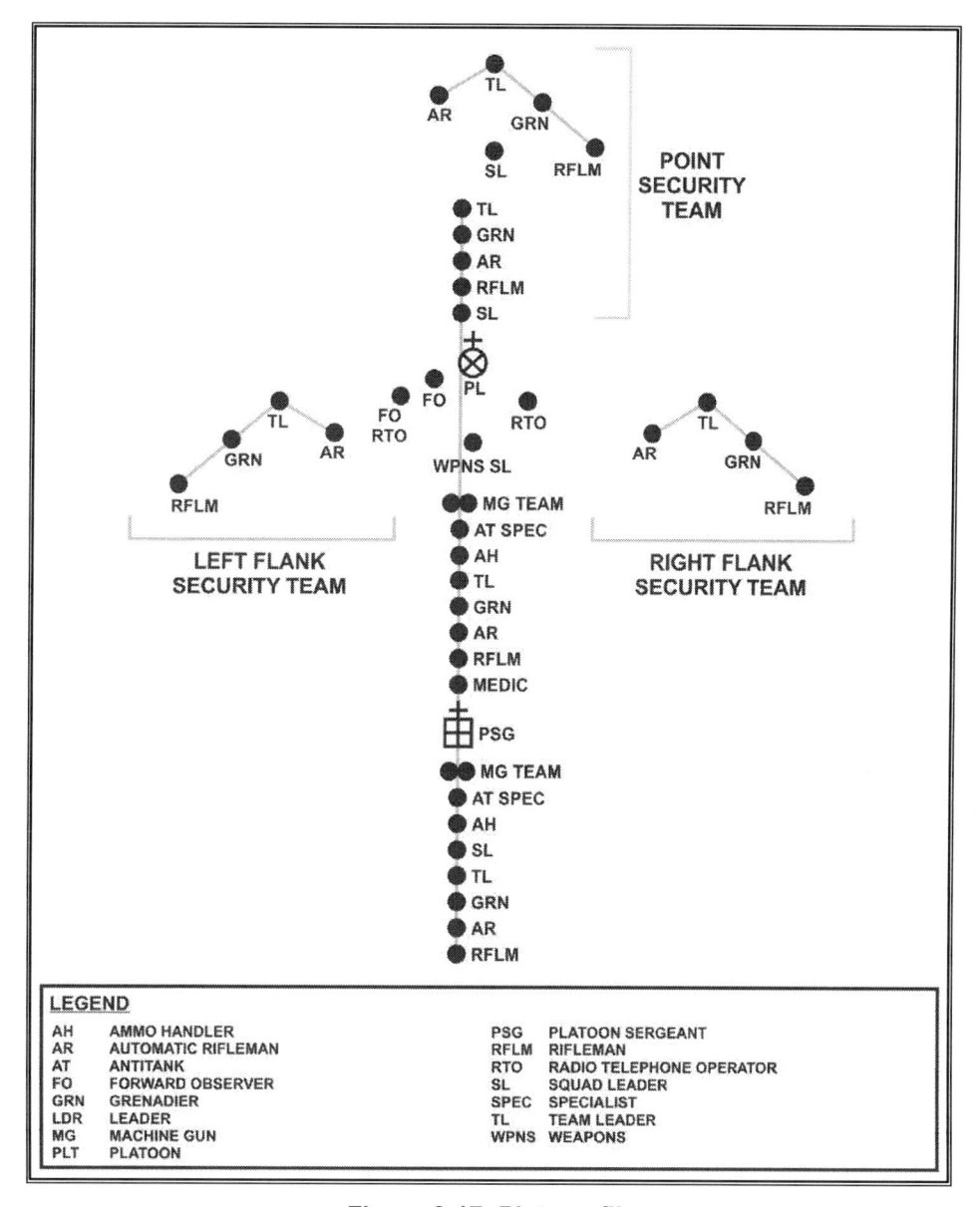

Figure 2-17. Platoon file

MOUNTED MOVEMENT FORMATIONS

2-100. The platoon leader uses formations to relate one vehicle or squad to another on the ground and to position firepower to support the direct fire plan. He uses them to establish responsibilities for security between vehicles or squads and to aid in the execution of battle drills and directed course of action.

2-101. When mounted, the platoon uses the column, wedge, line, echelon, coil, and herringbone formations (based on METT-TC variables). The platoon leader tracks his platoon's formation and movement in conjunction with the company's formation. Table 2-5 shows characteristics, advantages, and disadvantages of each type of standard mounted formations.

Table 2-5. Mounted formation characteristics

Formation	Control	Fires Front/Rear	Fires Flank	Security
Column	Easy	Limited	Excellent	Overall Limited
Staggered Column	Easy	Good	Good	Overall Good
Wedge	Easy	Excellent	Good	Good, especially for flanks
Line	Difficult	Excellent	Poor	Least secure
Echelon	Difficult	Excellent	Excellent for echeloned side	Good for echeloned side

Column

2-102. The platoon uses the column when moving fast, when moving through restricted terrain on a specific route, or when it does not expect enemy contact. Each vehicle normally follows directly behind the vehicle in front of it. However, if the situation dictates, vehicles can disperse laterally to enhance security. This is sometimes referred to as a staggered column.

Staggered Column

2-103. The staggered column formation is a modified column formation with one section leading, and one section trailing to provide overwatch. The staggered column permits good fire to the front and flanks. It is used when speed is critical, when there is a limited area for lateral dispersion, or when enemy contact is possible. Figure 2-18 (page 2-38) shows this type of column movement.

Chapter 2

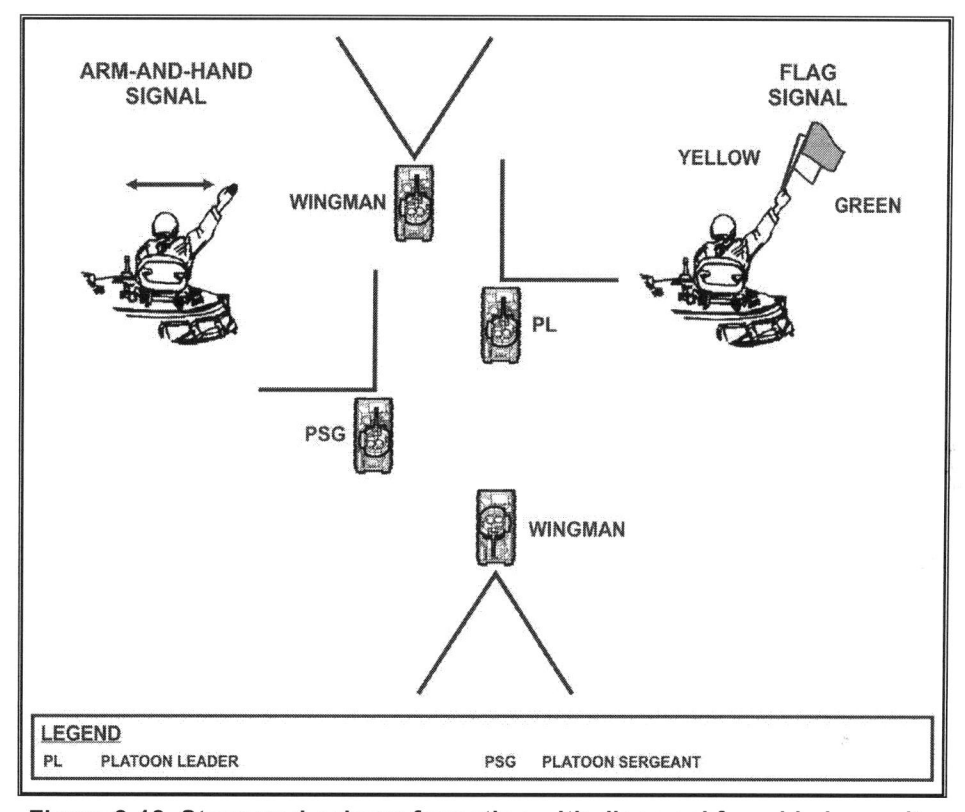

Figure 2-18. Staggered column formation with dispersal for added security

Wedge

2-104. The wedge formation (see figure 2-19), permits excellent firepower to the front and good fire to each flank. The platoon leader can easily control all vehicles and deploy rapidly into other formations. The wedge formation is often used when the enemy situation is vague. The orientation of the pairs is left and right. The platoon leader and platoon sergeant control the other vehicle (wingman) of their pair by directing it to follow to the outside and to orient its weapons toward the flanks.

2-105. When the platoon leader's vehicle is slightly forward one flank has more firepower. Depending on METT-TC, the platoon leader makes the adjustment to which side needs the most fire power.

Offense

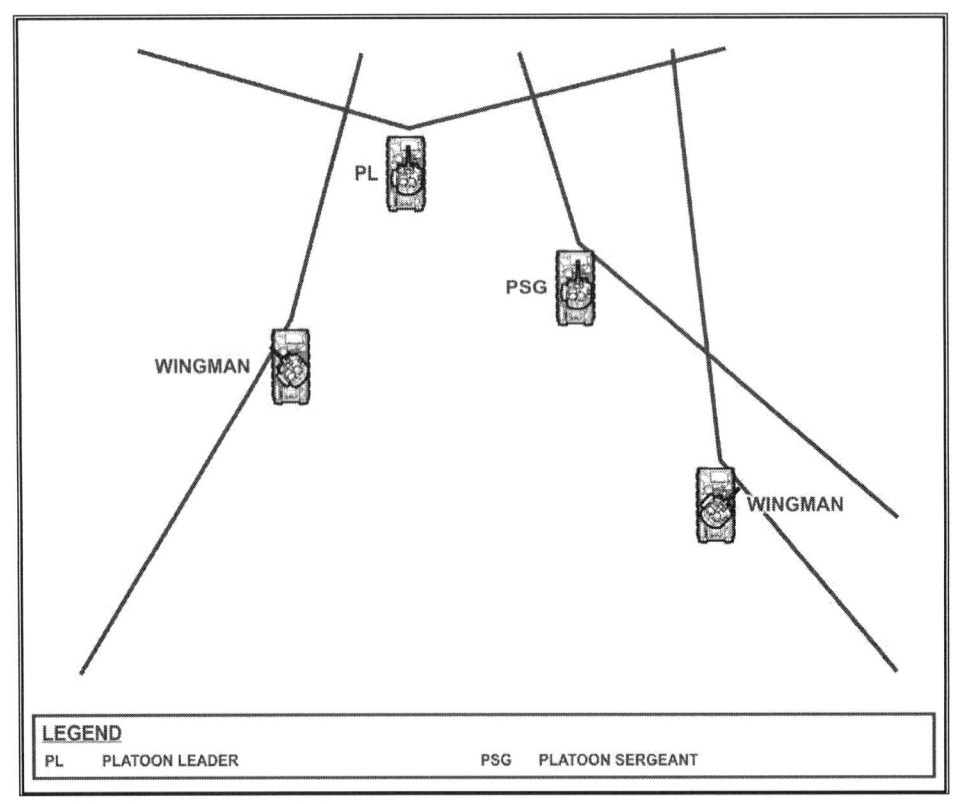

Figure 2-19. Wedge formation

Line

2-106. When assaulting a weakly defended objective, crossing open areas, or occupying a support-by-fire position, the platoon mainly uses the line formation shown in figure 2-20, page 2-40. The platoon can use the line formation in the assault to maximize the platoon's firepower and shock effect. The platoon normally uses the line formation when no terrain remains between it and the enemy, when the platoon has suppressed the enemy's AT weapons, or when the platoon is vulnerable to artillery fire and must move fast.

Chapter 2

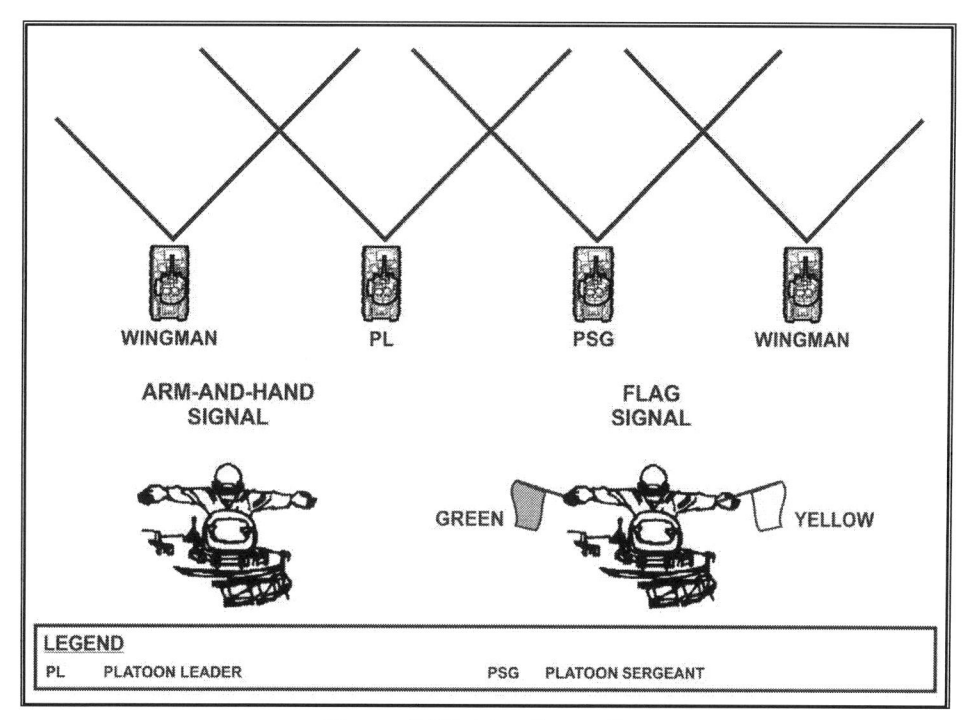

Figure 2-20. Line formation

Echelon

2-107. When the company team wants to maintain security or observation of one flank, and when the platoon does not expect enemy contact, the platoon uses the echelon formation shown in figure 2-21.

Note. The echelon formation can be used either left or right.

Offense

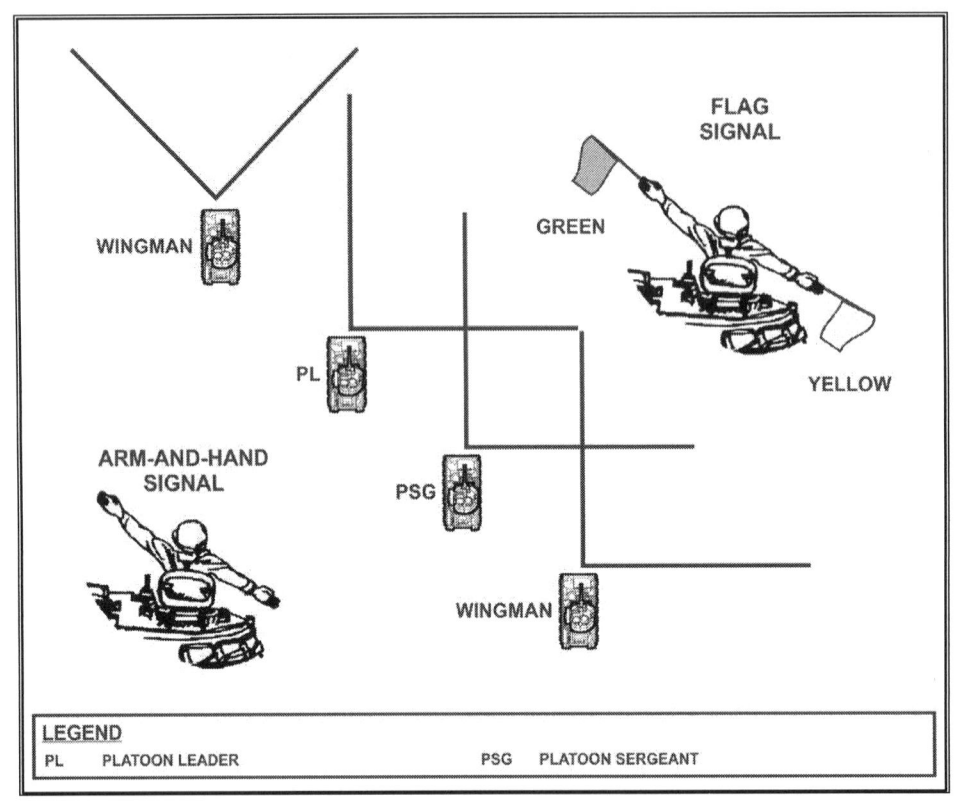

Figure 2-21. Echelon right formation

Coil and Herringbone

2-108. The coil and herringbone are platoon-level formations employed when elements of the company team are stationary and must maintain 360-degree security.

Coil

2-109. The coil (see figure 2-22, page 2-42) provides all-round security and observation when the platoon is stationary. It is useful for tactical refueling, resupply, and issuing platoon orders. Security is posted to include air guards and dismounted fire teams. The vehicle turrets are manned.

Chapter 2

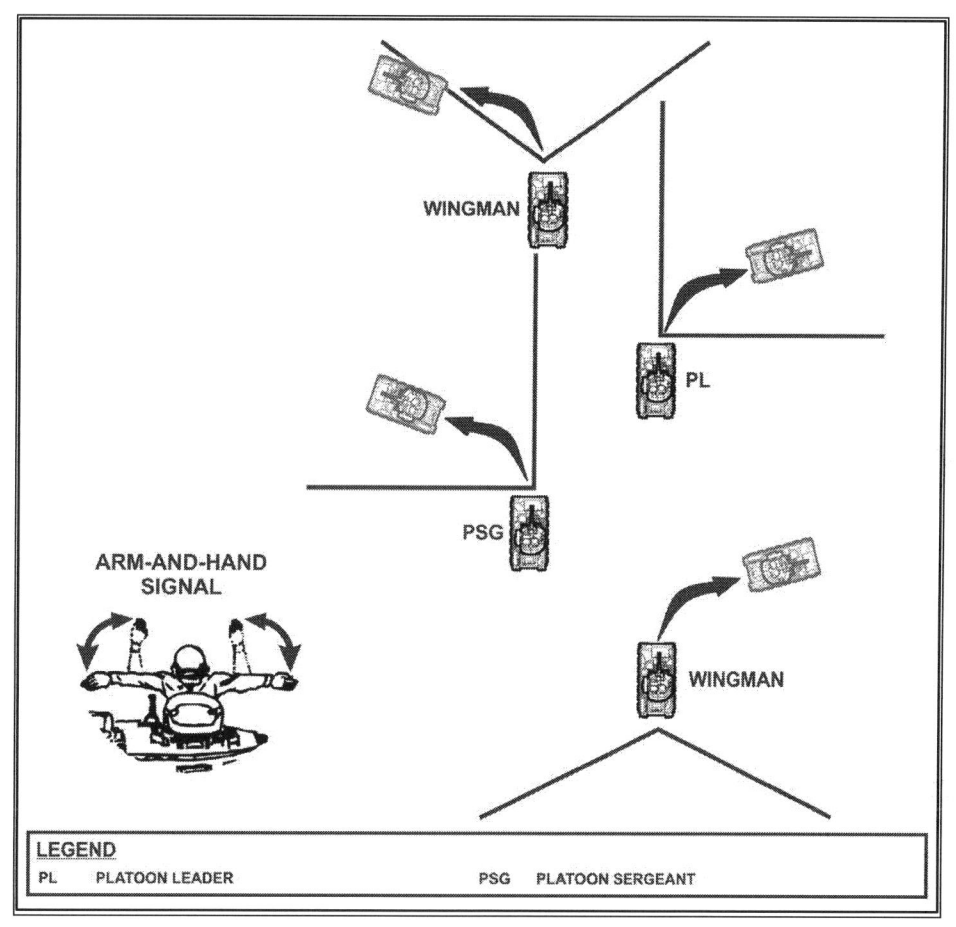

Figure 2-22. Coil formation

Herringbone

2-110. The platoon uses the herringbone to disperse when traveling in column formation (see figure 2-23). They can use it during air attacks or when they must stop during movement. It lets them move to covered and concealed positions off a road or from an open area and set up all-round security without detailed instructions. They reposition the vehicles as needed to take advantage of the best cover, concealment, and fields of fire. Fire team members dismount and establish security.

Offense

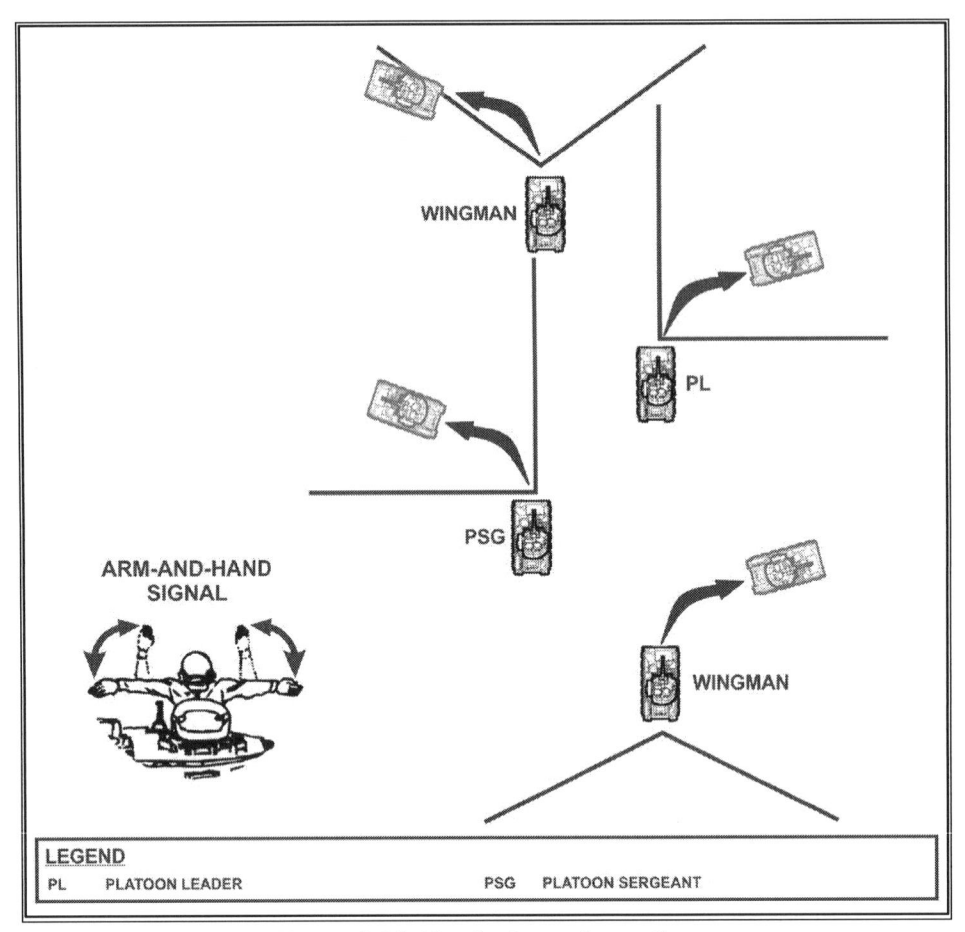

Figure 2-23. Herringbone formation

SECTION IV – MOVEMENT TECHNIQUES

2-111. Movement techniques are not fixed formations. They refer to the distances between Soldiers, teams, and squads vary based on mission, enemy, terrain, visibility, and other factors affecting control. There are three movement techniques: traveling; traveling overwatch; and bounding overwatch. The selection of a movement technique is based on the likelihood of enemy contact and need for speed. Factors to consider for each technique are control, dispersion, speed, and security. (See table 2-6, page 2-44.) Individual movement techniques include high and low crawl, and three to five second rushes from one covered position to another.

Chapter 2

Table 2-6. Movement techniques and characteristics

MOVEMENT TECHNIQUES	WHEN NORMALLY USED	CHARACTERISTICS			
		CONTROL	DISPERSION	SPEED	SECURITY
Traveling	Contact not likely	More	Less	Fastest	Least
Traveling overwatch	Contact possible	Less	More	Slower	More
Bounding overwatch	Contact expected	Most	Most	Slowest	Most

SQUAD MOVEMENT TECHNIQUES

2-112. The platoon leader determines and directs which movement technique the squad will use.

SQUAD TRAVELING

2-113. Traveling is used when contact with the enemy is not likely and speed is needed. (See figure 2-24.)

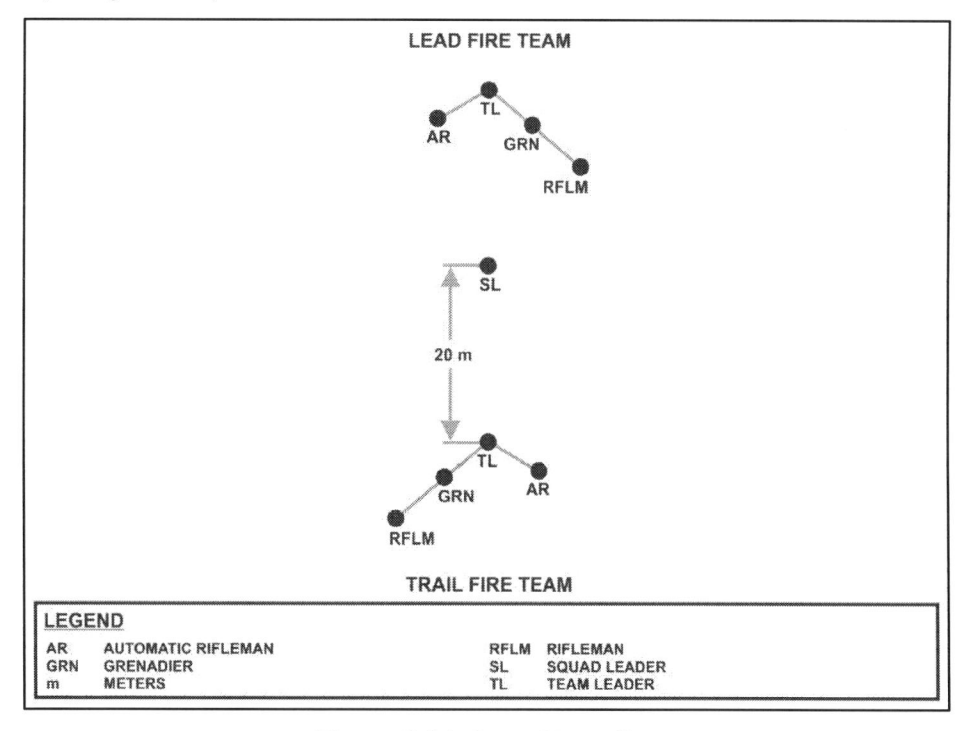

Figure 2-24. Squad traveling

Offense

SQUAD TRAVELING OVERWATCH

2-114. Traveling overwatch is used when contact is possible. Attached weapons move near and under the control of the squad leader so they can employ quickly. Rifle squads normally move in column or wedge formation. (See figure 2-25.) Ideally, the lead team moves at least 50 meters in front of the rest of the element.

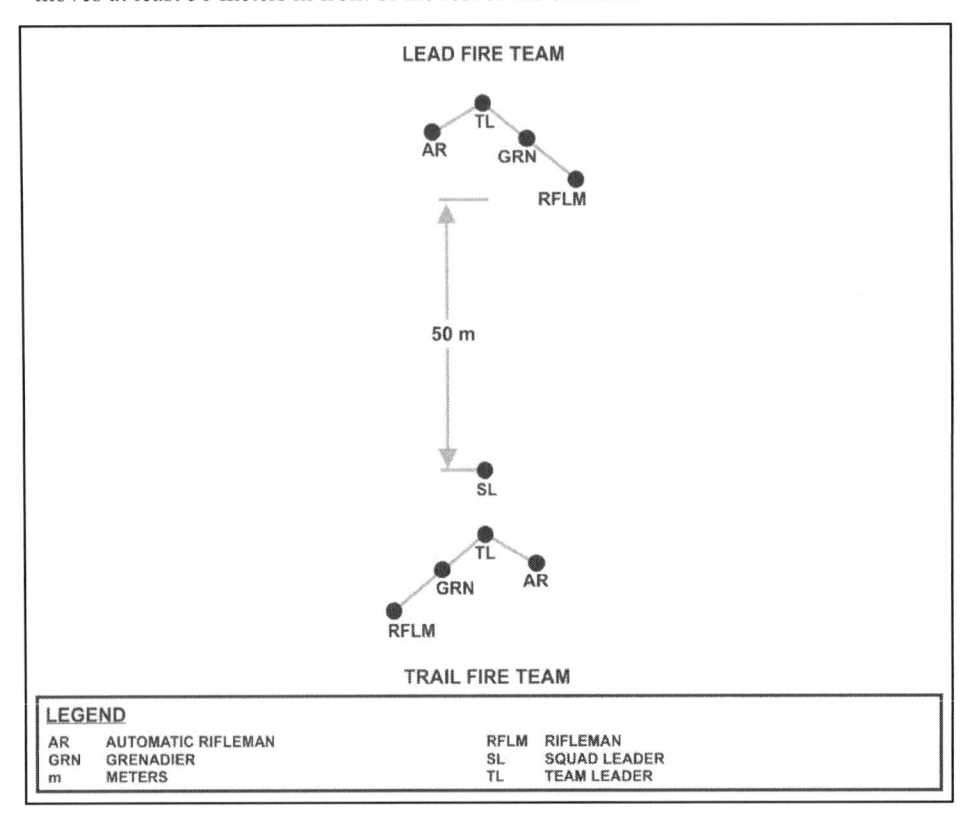

Figure 2-25. Squad traveling overwatch

SQUAD BOUNDING OVERWATCH

2-115. Bounding overwatch is used when contact is expected, the squad leader feels the enemy is near (based upon movement, noise, reflection, trash, fresh tracks, or even a hunch), or a large open danger area must be crossed. The lead fire team overwatches first. Soldiers in the overwatch team scan for enemy positions. The squad leader usually stays with the overwatch team. The trail fire team bounds and signals the squad leader when his team completes its bound and is prepared to overwatch the movement of the other team.

2-116. Both team leaders must know with which team the squad leader will be. The overwatching team leader must know the route and destination of the bounding team. The bounding team leader must know his team's destination and route, possible enemy locations, and actions to take when he arrives there. He also must know where the

Chapter 2

overwatching team will be and how he will receive his instructions. (See figure 2-26.) The cover and concealment on the bounding team's route dictates how its Soldiers move.

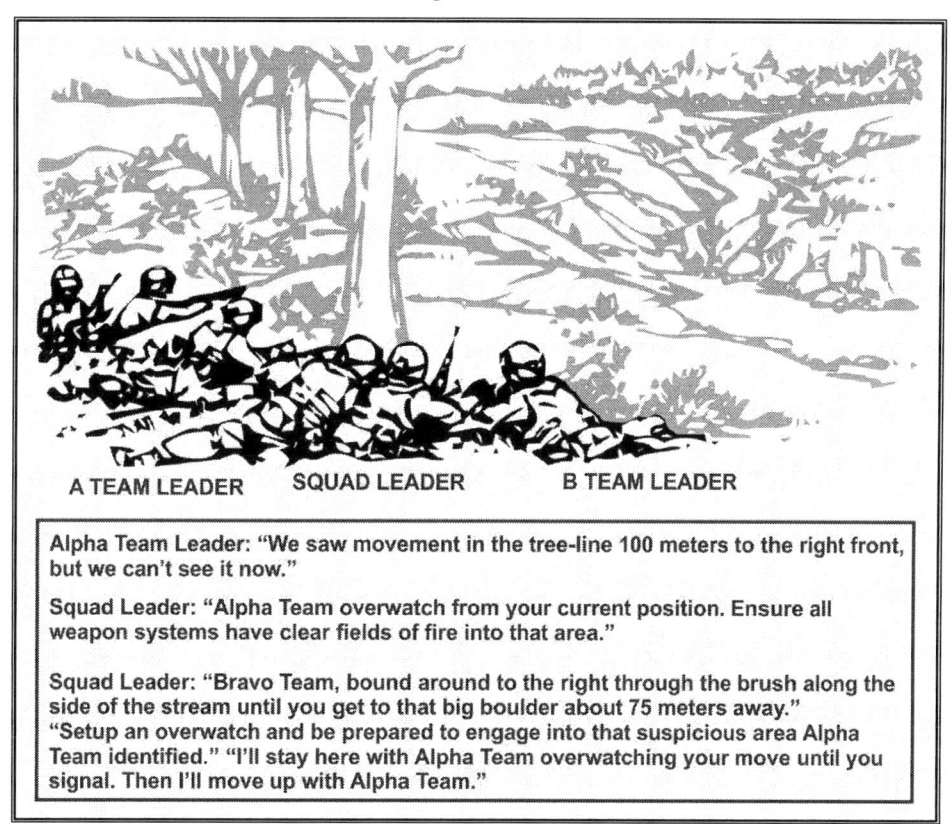

Figure 2-26. Squad bounding overwatch

2-117. Teams can bound successively or alternately. Successive bounds are easier to control; alternate bounds can be faster. (See figure 2-27.)

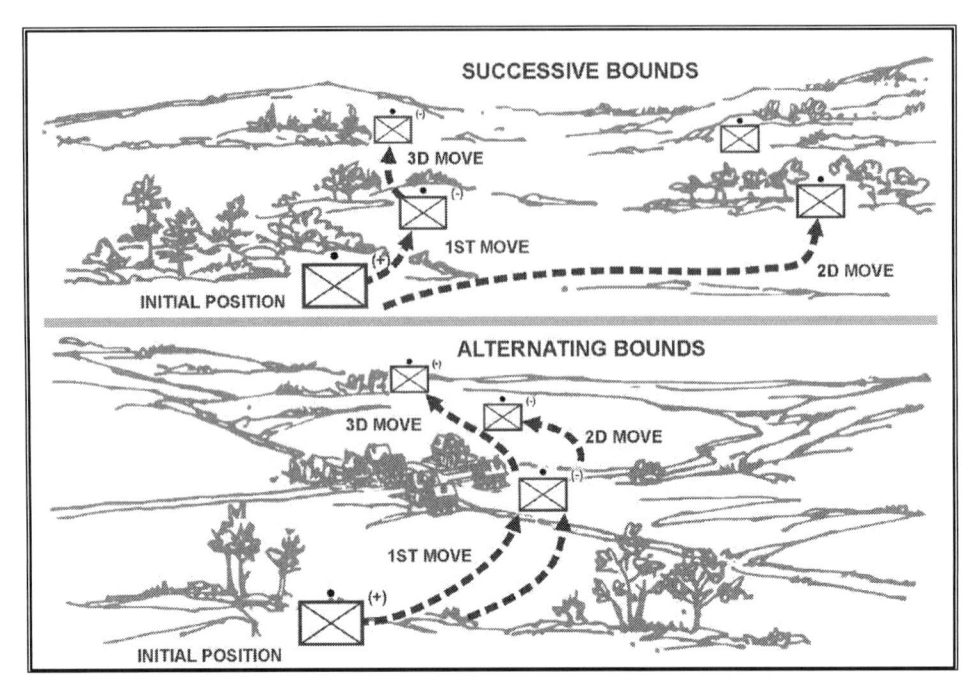

Figure 2-27. Squad successive and alternate bounds

PLATOON MOVEMENT TECHNIQUES

2-118. The platoon leader determines and directs which movement technique the platoon uses. While moving, leaders typically separate their unit into two groups: a security element and main body. In most scenarios, the Infantry platoon and squad are not large enough to separate its forces into separate security forces and main body forces. However, it is able to accomplish these security functions by employing movement techniques. A movement technique is the manner a platoon uses to traverse terrain

2-119. As the probability of enemy contact increases, the platoon leader adjusts the movement technique to provide greater security. The essential factor to consider is the trail unit's ability to provide mutual support to the lead element. Soldiers must be able to see their fire team leader. The squad leader must be able to see his fire team leaders. The platoon leader should be able to see his lead squad leader.

TRAVELING

2-120. The platoons often use the traveling technique when contact is unlikely and speed is needed. (See figure 2-28, page 2-48.) When using the traveling technique, all unit elements move continuously. In continuous movement, all Soldiers travel at a moderate rate of speed, with all personnel alert. During traveling, formations are essentially not altered except for effects of terrain.

Chapter 2

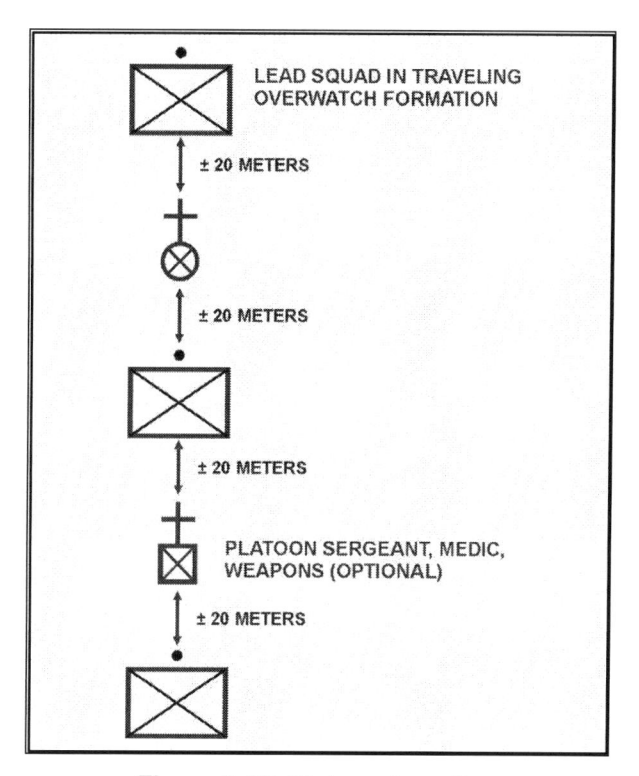

Figure 2-28. Platoon traveling

TRAVELING OVERWATCH

2-121. Traveling overwatch is an extended form of traveling in which the lead element moves continuously but trailing elements move at varying speeds, sometimes pausing to overwatch movement of the lead element. (See figure 2-29.) Traveling overwatch is used when enemy contact is possible but not expected. Caution is justified but speed is desirable.

2-122. The trail element maintains dispersion based on its ability to provide immediate suppressive fires in support of the lead element. The intent is to maintain in-depth, provide flexibility, and sustain movement in case the lead element is engaged. The trailing elements cue their movement to the terrain, overwatching from a position where they can support the lead element if needed. Trailing elements overwatch from positions and at distances that do not prevent them from firing or moving to support the lead element. The idea is to put enough distance between the lead units and trail units so that if the lead unit comes into contact, the trail units will be out of contact but have the ability to maneuver on the enemy.

2-123. Traveling overwatch requires the leader to control his subordinate's spacing to ensure mutual support. This involves a constant process of concentrating (close it up) and dispersion (spread it out). The primary factor is mutual support, with its two critical

Offense

variables being weapon ranges and terrain. Infantry platoons' and squads' weapon range limitations dictate units generally should not get separated by more than 300 meters. In compartmentalized terrain this distance is closer, but in open terrain this distance is greater.

Figure 2-29. Platoon traveling overwatch

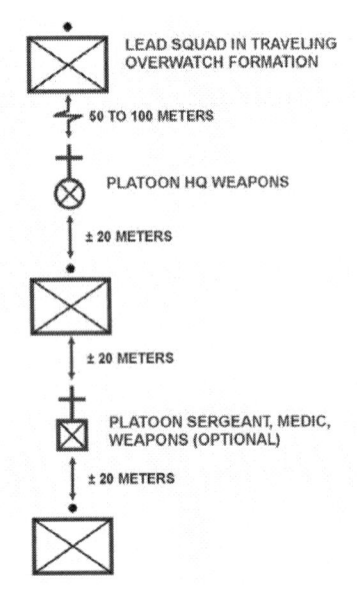

```
        ▪
      ┌───┐  LEAD SQUAD IN TRAVELING
      │ X │  OVERWATCH FORMATION
      └───┘
        ↕  50 TO 100 METERS
        
        ⊗  PLATOON HQ WEAPONS
        ↕  ± 20 METERS
        ▪
      ┌───┐
      │ X │
      └───┘
        ↕  ± 20 METERS
      ┌───┐  PLATOON SERGEANT, MEDIC,
      │ X │  WEAPONS (OPTIONAL)
      └───┘
        ↕  ± 20 METERS
        ▪
      ┌───┐
      │ X │
      └───┘
```

BOUNDING OVERWATCH

2-124. Bounding overwatch is similar to fire and movement in which one unit overwatches the movement of another. (See figure 2-30, page 2-50.) The difference is there is no actual enemy contact. Bounding overwatch is used when the leader expects contact. The key to this technique is the proper use of terrain.

Commentary

One difficulty with doctrine is making it "actionable." For planning and executing movements, it is best to use a synchronization matrix like the one below to ensure you are implementing all of the various doctrinal principles in your patrol. Poor movement planning and execution is a very common mistake made by small units.

Check point	Grid	Terrain	Distance	Direction (Azimuth)	OOM	Movement Technique	Formation
SP							
CP 1							
CP 2							
CP 3							
Long Halt							
ORP							

Chapter 2

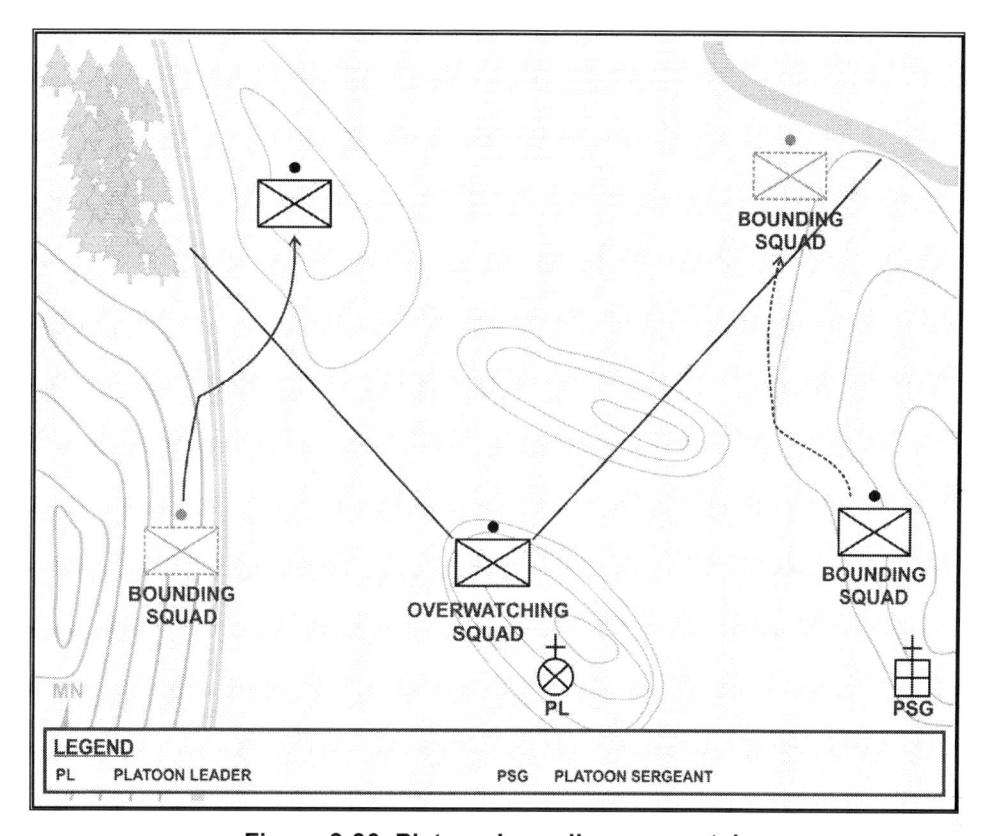

Figure 2-30. Platoon bounding overwatch

One Squad Bounding

2-125. One squad bounds forward to a chosen position; it then becomes the overwatching element unless contact is made en route. The bounding squad can use traveling overwatch, bounding overwatch, or individual movement techniques (low and high crawl, and three- to five-second rushes by the fire team or buddy teams).

2-126. METT-TC dictates the length of the bounds. However, the bounding squads never should move beyond the range at which the base-of-fire squads can suppress known, likely, or suspected enemy positions. In severely restrictive terrain, the bounding squad's makes shorter bounds than it would in more open areas. The destination of the bounding element is based on the suitability of the next location as an overwatch position. When deciding where to send his bounding squad, a platoon leader considers—

- The requirements of the mission.
- Where the enemy is likely to be.
- The routes to the next overwatch position.
- The ability of an overwatching element's weapons to cover the bound.
- The responsiveness of the rest of the platoon.

2-50　　　　　　　　　　ATP 3-21.8　　　　　　　　　　12 April 2016

One Squad Overwatching

2-127. One squad overwatches the bounding squad from covered positions and from where it can see and suppress likely enemy positions. The platoon leader remains with the overwatching squad. Normally, the platoon's medium machine guns are located with the overwatching squad.

One Squad Awaiting Orders

2-128. Based on the situation, one squad is uncommitted and ready for employment as directed by the platoon leader. The platoon sergeant and leader of the squad awaiting orders position themselves close to the platoon leader. On contact, this unit should be prepared to support the overwatching element, move to assist the bounding squad, or move to another location based on the platoon leader's assessment.

Weapons Squad

2-129. Medium machine guns normally are employed in one of two ways—
- Attached to the overwatch squad or the weapons squad supporting the overwatching element.
- Awaiting orders to move (with the platoon sergeant) or as part of a bounding element.

Mission Command of the Bounding Element

2-130. Ideally, the overwatch element maintains visual contact with the bounding element. However, the leader of the overwatch element may have the ability to digitally track the location of the bounding element without maintaining visual contact. This provides the bounding element further freedom in selecting covered and concealed routes to its next location. Before a bound, the platoon leader gives an order to his squad leaders from the overwatch position. (See figure 2-31, page 2-52.) He tells and shows them the following:
- The direction or location of the enemy (if known).
- The positions of the overwatching squad.
- The next overwatch position.
- The route of the bounding squad.
- What to do after the bounding squad reaches the next position.
- What signal the bounding squad will use to announce it is prepared to overwatch.
- How the squad will receive its next orders.

Chapter 2

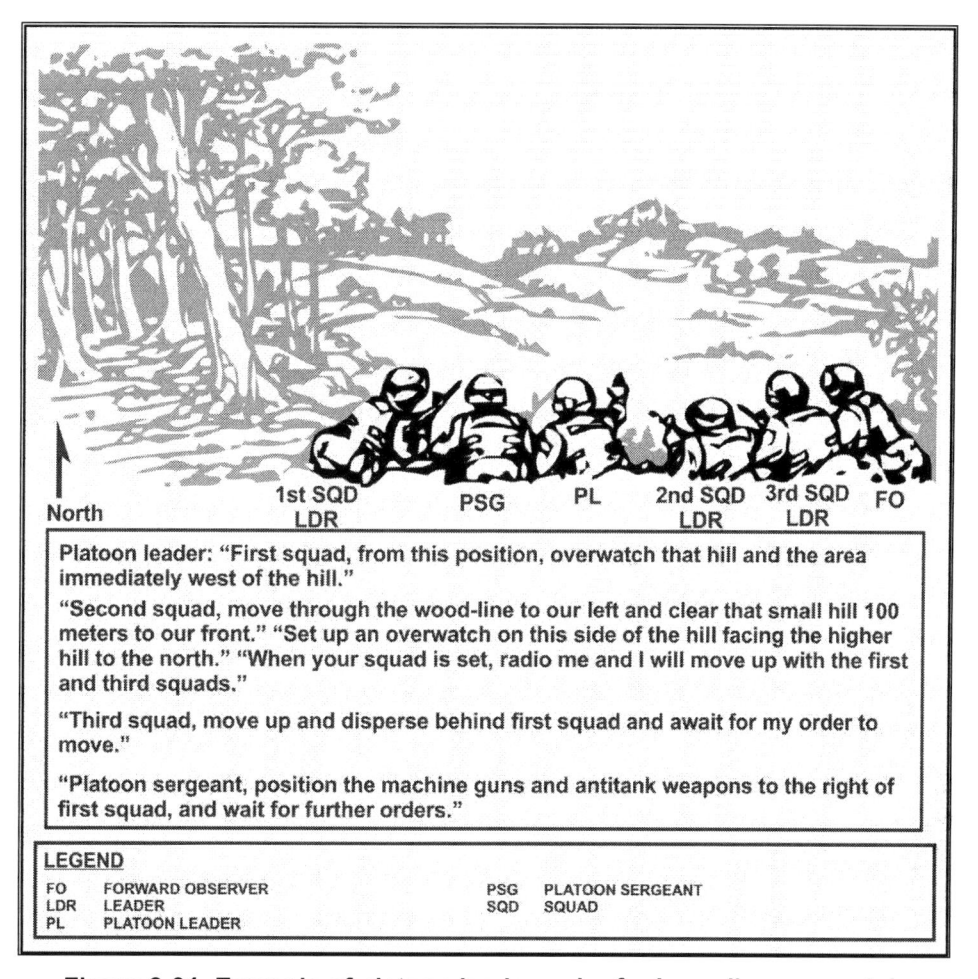

Platoon leader: "First squad, from this position, overwatch that hill and the area immediately west of the hill."

"Second squad, move through the wood-line to our left and clear that small hill 100 meters to our front." "Set up an overwatch on this side of the hill facing the higher hill to the north." "When your squad is set, radio me and I will move up with the first and third squads."

"Third squad, move up and disperse behind first squad and await for my order to move."

"Platoon sergeant, position the machine guns and antitank weapons to the right of first squad, and wait for further orders."

LEGEND
FO   FORWARD OBSERVER   PSG   PLATOON SERGEANT
LDR LEADER   SQD   SQUAD
PL   PLATOON LEADER

Figure 2-31. Example of platoon leader order for bounding overwatch

MOUNTED MOVEMENT TECHNIQUES

2-131. The movement techniques while mounted are traveling, traveling overwatch, and bounding overwatch.

TRAVELING

2-132. The platoon travels mounted when contact with the enemy is not likely and speed is desired. (See figure 2-32.) The leader analyzes the latest intelligence on the enemy and determines if contact with the enemy is unlikely. Because units generally move faster when traveling mounted, leaders must remember the increased potential for a break in contact. Should a break in contact occur—

- The leader or detached element uses global positioning system (GPS) aids to reestablish contact with the main body.

- The platoon's main body can use an infrared or thermal source to regain visual contact with the element and link it back to the main body.

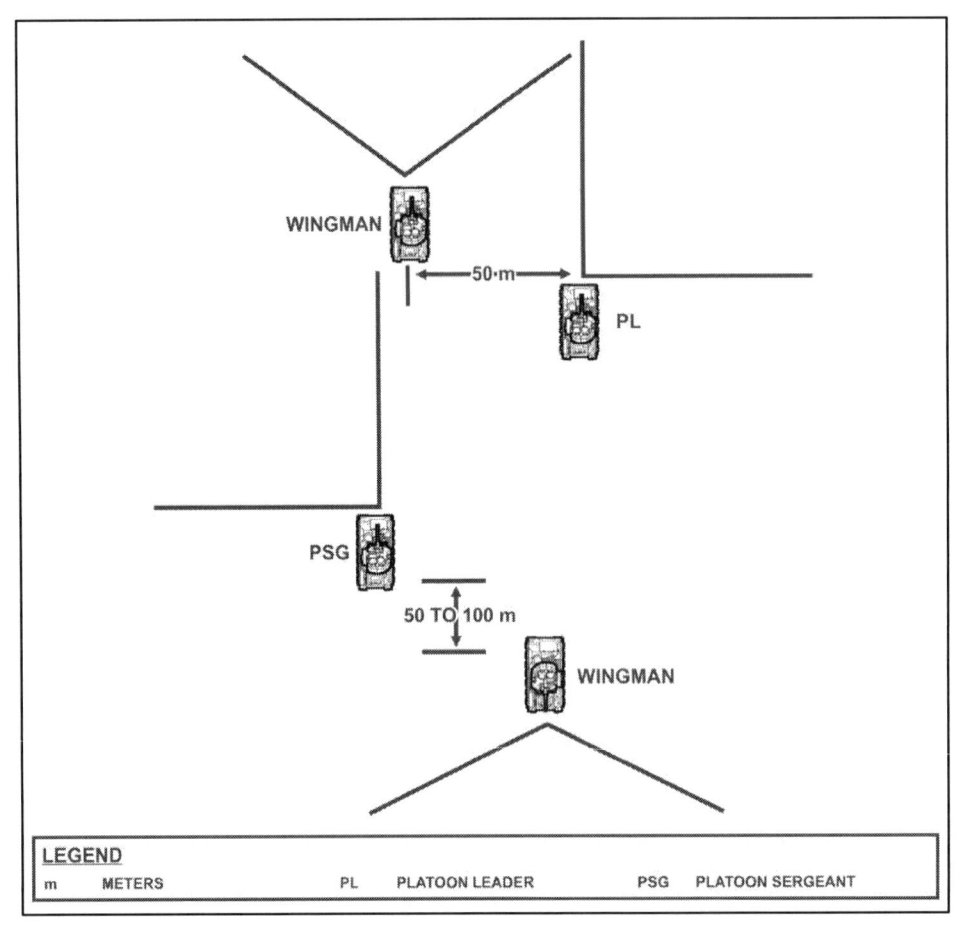

Figure 2-32. Traveling, platoon mounted

TRAVELING OVERWATCH

2-133. The platoon leader uses traveling overwatch when he thinks contact could occur. (See figure 2-33, page 2-54.) He designates one of his subordinate elements to provide security forward of the main body. In some cases, the improved awareness might prompt the security element to increase these distances. Leaders track the movement of forward security elements. They get position updates to ensure the forward security element remains on azimuth and within range of supporting direct fires.

Chapter 2

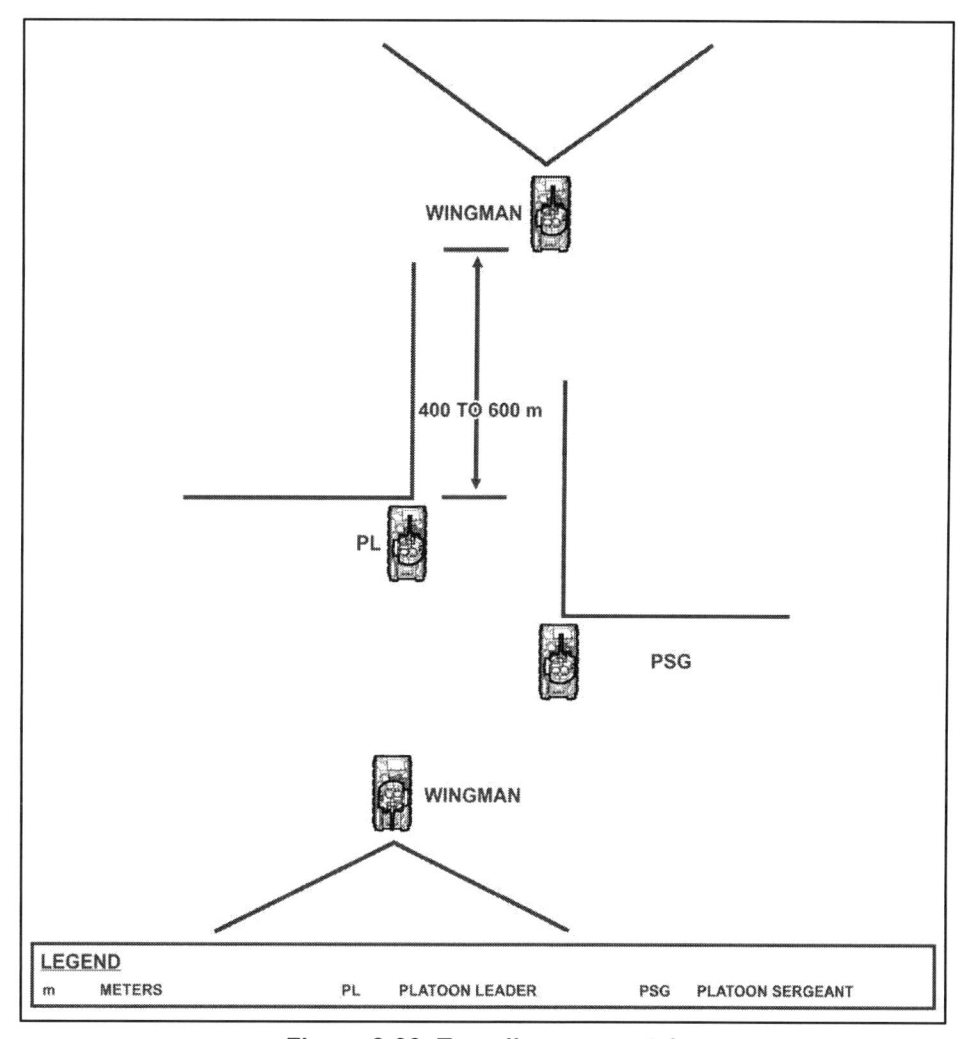

Figure 2-33. Traveling overwatch

BOUNDING OVERWATCH

2-134. When the platoon leader expects enemy contact, he uses bounding overwatch. He initiates it based on planning reports received earlier about the enemy situation and on SITREPs received during movement. He bounds elements using successive or alternate bounds. (See figure 2-34.)

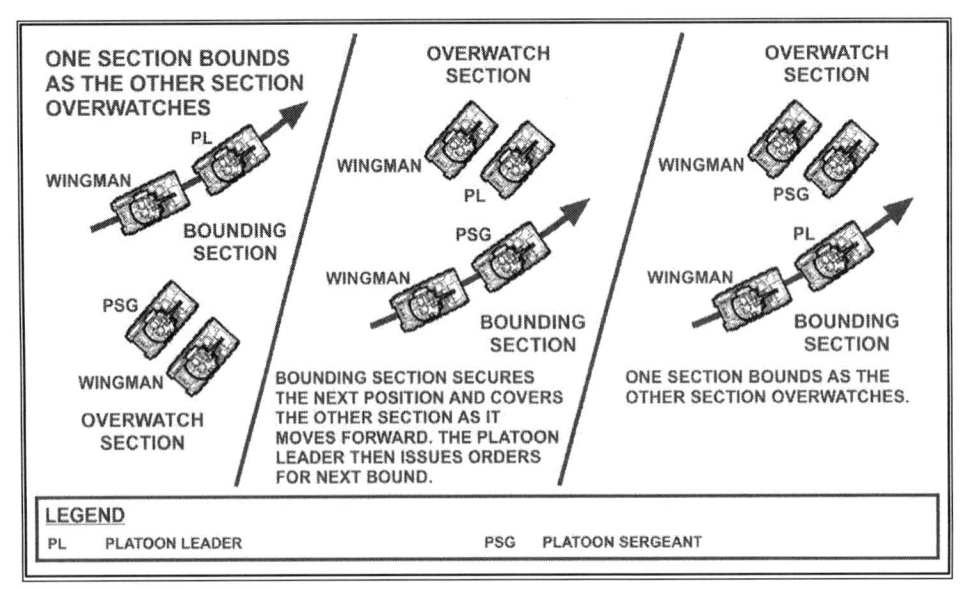

Figure 2-34. Bounding overwatch

2-135. Before bounding, the leader shows the bounding element the location of the next overwatch position. Ideally, the overwatch element keeps the bounding element in sight. Once the bounding element reaches its overwatch position, it signals READY by voice or visual means to the element that overwatched it's bound. (See figure 2-35, page 2-56.) The platoon leader makes sure the bounding element stays within two-thirds of the weapons range of the overwatch element.

Chapter 2

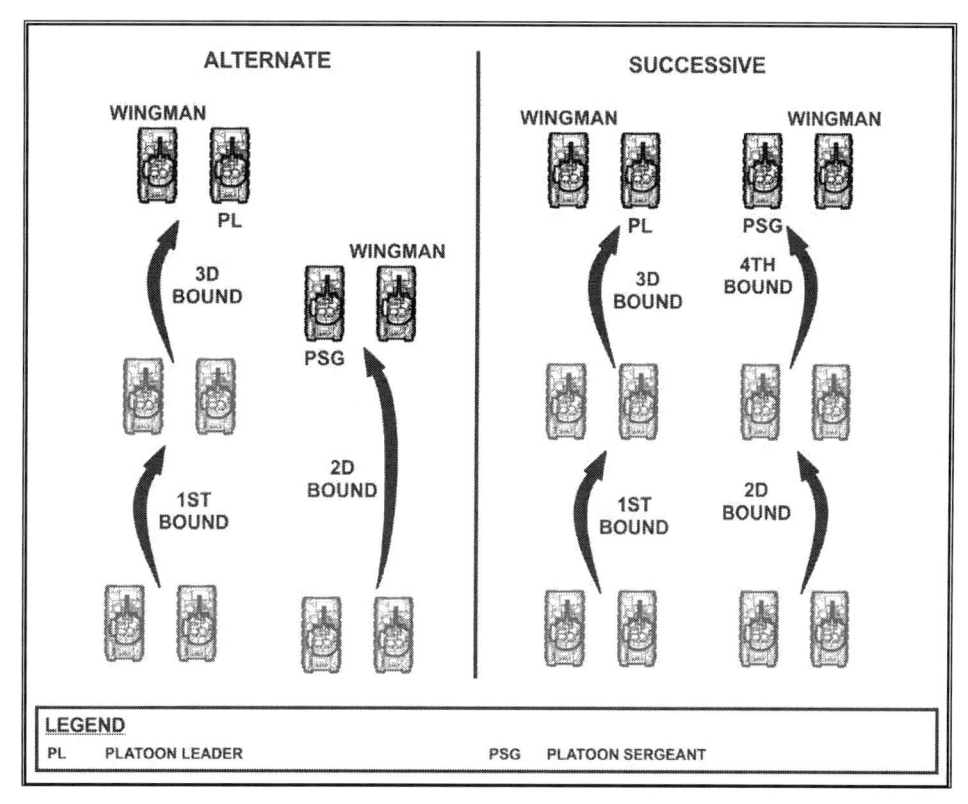

Figure 2-35. Methods of bounding overwatch

MANEUVER

2-136. Maneuver begins once a unit has made contact with the enemy. Direct fire is inherent in maneuver, as is close combat. At the mounted platoon level, maneuver forms the heart of every tactical operation and task. It combines maneuver, direct and indirect fire, and other combat power. The platoon leader maneuvers his mounted element and dismounted squads to close with, gain positional advantage over, and ultimately destroy the enemy.

BASE-OF-FIRE ELEMENT

2-137. Combining fire and movement requires a base of fire. Some platoon elements (usually a section, the weapons squad, and the BFVs or Stryker) remain stationary to provide protection for bounding elements by suppressing or destroying enemy elements. The dismounted mechanized platoon can maneuver while protected by the BFVs in a base-of-fire position and then establish another base of fire with the weapons or a rifle squad.

2-138. Because maneuver is decentralized in nature, the platoon leader determines from his terrain analysis where and when he wants to establish a base of fire. During actions on contact, he adjusts maneuver plans as needed. Making maneuver decisions normally falls to the leader on the ground, who knows what enemy elements can engage the maneuvering element and what friendly forces can provide the base of fire.

2-139. The base-of-fire element occupies positions that afford the best possible cover and concealment, a clear view, and clear fields of fire. The platoon leader normally designates a general location for the base of fire, and the element leader selects the exact location. Once in position, the base-of-fire element suppresses known, likely, or suspected enemy elements while aggressively scanning its assigned area of operation. It identifies previously unknown elements and then suppresses them with direct and indirect fires. The base-of-fire element allows the bounding unit to keep maneuvering so it can retain the initiative even when the enemy can see and fire on it. While maneuvering to or in position, the base-of-fire element leader is constantly looking for other locations that may provide better support for the maneuvering element.

BOUNDING ELEMENT

2-140. Maneuver is inherently dangerous. Enemy weapons, unknown terrain, and other operational factors all increase the danger. When maneuvering, the platoon leader considers the following:

- The bounding element must take full advantage of whatever cover and concealment the terrain offers.
- Squad members must maintain all-round security at all times and continuously scan their assigned area of operations.
- METT-TC variables dictate the length of the bounds. However, the bounding element should never move beyond the range at which the base-of-fire element can effectively suppress known, likely, or suspected enemy positions. General practice is to limit movement to no more than two-thirds the effective range of the supporting weapon system.
- In severely restricted terrain, the bounding element makes shorter bounds than it would in more open areas.
- The bounding element must focus on its ultimate goal—gaining a positional advantage. Once achieved, the element uses this advantage to destroy the enemy with direct fires and dismounted infantrymen assault.

DISMOUNTING INFANTRY

2-141. When to dismount Infantry during maneuver is a critical decision for the platoon leader. He must balance the vulnerability of his mounted element, the speed and vulnerability of his dismounted infantrymen, and the effectiveness of the enemy's fire. The platoon leader can use successive bounds with his dismounted infantrymen moving along covered and concealed routes to secure the next base-of-fire position.

2-142. Considerations for remaining mounted include:
- Open terrain.
- Good covered and concealed mounted routes.

Chapter 2

- Ineffective antiarmor fires.
- Maneuver distance.

2-143. Considerations for dismounting include:
- Good covered and concealed terrain for Infantry.
- Effective antiarmor fire.
- Restricted terrain and obstacles for mounted movement.

2-144. Stryker units plan dismount points in a cover and concealed position out of the maximum effective range of the enemy weapon systems or audible range based on the last known enemy point of contact or suspected position.

DIRECT FIRE SUPPORT

2-145. The Bradley companies are routinely task organized within the combined arms battalion. Bradley companies will routinely have a tank platoon attached or a Bradley platoon can be routinely attached to a tank company. The Bradley platoon may therefore have a tank platoon as a base of fire or become the base of fire while the tank platoon bounds.

2-146. Other units within or outside the ABCT can be available as a base of fire or bounding element. Today's modular force can be rapidly tailored and task organized to meet tactical requirements. This means that mechanized units can be attached to other BCTs for operations. Therefore, the mechanized platoon leader has to be prepared to operate with tanks, Stryker antitank guided missile (ATGM) carriers, ATGM units mounted on high-mobility multipurpose wheeled vehicles, and so on.

PLATOON AS THE RESERVE

2-147. The designation of a reserve allows the commander to retain flexibility during the attack. The commander should be prepared to commit his reserve to exploit success and to continue the attack. The reserve may repulse counterattacks during consolidation and reorganization. The reserve is normally under the commander's control and positioned where it can best exploit the success of the attack. The reserve should not be so close that it loses flexibility during the assault.

2-148. During the attack, the mechanized platoon may be designated the company or battalion reserve. It may be an on-order or be-prepared mission. The company or battalion commander commits the reserve platoon to reinforce the decisive operation and to maintain the attack's momentum. To exploit the success of the other attacking units, the reserve should attack the enemy from a new direction. Because of the many missions the platoon may be assigned, the platoon leader has to maintain situational awareness, know the missions and tactical plans of the other units, and be familiar with the terrain and enemy situation in the whole area of operation. It must react quickly and decisively when committed.

Offense

2-149. The reserve platoon may be assigned one or more of the following missions:
- Protect the flank and rear of the unit.
- Conduct a counterattack or establish a blocking position.
- Maintain contact with adjacent units.
- Clear a position that has been overrun or bypassed by another unit.
- Establish a support-by-fire position.
- Assume the mission of an attacking unit.
- Attack from a new direction.
- Protect or assist in the consolidation and reorganization on the objective.

SECTION V – ACTIONS ON CONTACT

2-150. Actions on contact are a series of combat actions, often conducted simultaneously, taken upon contact with the enemy to develop the situation. (Refer to ADRP 3-90 for more information.) Leaders analyze the enemy throughout TLP to identify all likely contact situations that may occur during an operation. This process should not be confused with battle drills such as Battle Drill "React to Contact." Battle drills are the actions of individual Soldiers and small units when they meet the enemy. Through planning and rehearsals conducted during TLP, leaders and Soldiers develop and refine COA to deal with the probable enemy actions. The COA becomes the foundation schemes of maneuver. (Refer to FM 3-90-1 for more information.)

FORMS OF CONTACT

2-151. In offensive and defensive tasks, contact occurs when a member of the Infantry unit encounters a situation requiring a lethal or nonlethal response to the enemy. These situations may entail one or more forms of contact:
- Direct.
- Indirect.
- Non-hostile civilian contact.
- Obstacles.
- CBRN or CBRNE.
- Aerial.
- Visual.
- Electronic warfare.

FIVE STEPS OF ACTIONS ON CONTACT

2-152. The Infantry unit should execute actions on contact using a logical, well-organized process of decisionmaking and action entailing these five steps:
- Deploy and report.
- Evaluate and develop the situation.
- Choose a course of action.

Chapter 2

- Execute the selected course of action.
- Recommend a course of action to the higher commander.

2-153. This five-step process is not intended to generate a rigid, lockstep response to the enemy. Rather, the goal is to provide an orderly framework enabling the company and its platoons and squads to survive the initial contact, and apply sound decisionmaking and timely actions to complete the operation. Ideally, the unit sees the enemy (visual contact) before being seen by the enemy; it then can initiate direct contact on its own terms by executing the designated COA.

2-154. Once the lead elements of a force conducting movement to contact encounter the enemy, they conduct actions on contact. The unit treats obstacles like enemy contact, assuming the obstacles are covered by fire. The unit's security force gains tactical advantage over an enemy by using tempo and initiative to conduct these actions, allowing it to gain and maintain contact without becoming decisively engaged. How quickly the unit develops the situation is directly related to its security, and the tempo is directly related to the unit's use of well-rehearsed SOP and drills.

2-155. Leaders understand properly executed actions on contact require time at the squad and platoon levels. To develop the situation, a platoon or company may have to execute flanking movements, conduct reconnaissance by fire, or call for and adjust indirect fires. Each of these activities requires time, and the leader balances the time required for subordinate elements to conduct actions on contact with the need for the company or battalion to maintain momentum. (Refer to FM 3-90-1 for more information.)

DEPLOY AND REPORT

2-156. If the leader expects contact based upon reports, through reconnaissance, or other means, the company or platoon is deployed by transitioning to the bounding overwatch movement technique. If the company or platoon is alert to the likely presence of the enemy, it has a better chance of establishing the first visual and physical contact on its own terms. This contact usually is made by an overwatching or bounding platoon, which initiates the companies or platoons' actions on contact. In a worst-case scenario, a previously undetected (but expected) enemy element may engage the platoon or squad. The platoon or squad in contact then conducts a battle drill for its own survival and initiates actions on contact.

2-157. In some cases, the platoon or squad makes unexpected contact with the enemy while using traveling or traveling overwatch. The element in contact or, if necessary, the entire platoon or squad may deploy using battle drills to survive the initial contact. When making unexpected contact, the platoon or squad in contact immediately sends a contact report. The most efficient way the battalion intelligence staff officer (S-2) provides situational understanding and the common operational picture (COP) to the battalion is through digital reports sent by those in contact. The Infantry company platoons and squads develop SOP utilizing the capabilities of digital reports while destroying the enemy force and protecting the unit.

EVALUATE AND DEVELOP THE SITUATION

2-158. While the Infantry unit deploys, the leader evaluates and continues to develop the situation. The leader quickly gathers as much information as possible, either visually or, more often, through reports of the platoons or squad s in contact and analyzes the information to determine critical operational considerations, including the—

- Size of enemy element.
- Location, composition, activity, and orientation of enemy force.
- Impact of obstacles and terrain.
- Enemy capabilities.
- Probable enemy intentions.
- Method of gaining positional advantage over the enemy.
- Friendly situation (location, strength, and capabilities).
- Possible friendly courses of action to achieve the specified end state.

2-159. Once the leader determines the size of enemy force encountered by the Infantry unit, a report is sent to the platoon or company. However, after evaluating the situation, the leader may discover there is not enough information to identify the necessary operational considerations. To make this determination, the leader further develops the situation according to the commander's intent, using a combination of techniques such as—

- Surveillance, employing Infantry squads, unmanned aircraft systems, and snipers using binoculars and other optical aids.
- Maneuver, including flanking maneuvers to gain additional information by viewing the enemy from another perspective.
- Indirect fire.
- Reconnaissance by fire.

CHOOSE A COURSE OF ACTION

2-160. After developing the situation and determining he has enough information to make a decision, the leader selects a COA meeting the requirements of the commander's intent that is within the unit's capabilities.

EXECUTE THE SELECTED COURSE OF ACTION

2-161. In executing a COA, the Infantry unit transitions to maneuver. It then continues to maneuver throughout execution as part of a tactical task, or to advance while in contact to reach the point on the battlefield from which it executes its tactical task. The unit can employ a number of tactical tasks as COA, which may be preceded or followed by additional maneuver. Some of these tasks are—

- Attack by fire.
- Breach.
- Bypass.
- Clear.

Chapter 2

- Control.
- Counterreconnaissance.
- Disengagement.
- Exfiltrate.
- Follow and assume.
- Follow and support.
- Occupy.
- Retain.
- Secure.
- Seize.
- Support by fire.

2-162.   As execution continues, more information becomes available to the leader. Based upon the emerging details of the enemy situation, the leader may have to alter his COA during execution. For example, as the Infantry platoon maneuvers to destroy what appears to be a dismounted squad, it discovers two additional squads in prepared positions. The leader analyzes and develops the new situation. He then selects an alternate COA, such as establishing a support-by-fire position to support another platoon's maneuver against the newly discovered enemy force.

RECOMMEND A COURSE OF ACTION TO THE HIGHER COMMANDER

2-163.   Once the platoon leader selects a COA, keeping in mind the commander's intent, the company commander is informed, and he has the option of approving or disapproving it based upon its impact on the overall mission. To avoid delay, a unit SOP may provide automatic approval of certain actions.

SECTION VI – MOVEMENT TO CONTACT

2-164.   Movement to contact is an offensive task designed to develop the situation and establish or regain contact. It ends when enemy contact is made. When necessary, the Infantry platoon conducts this task regardless of which decisive action element is currently predominate: offense, defense, or stability... The platoon usually conducts movement to contact as part of an Infantry company or larger element. Based upon METT-TC, the platoon may conduct the operation independently. Search and attack, and cordon and search are techniques of movement to contact.

CONDUCT OF A MOVEMENT TO CONTACT

2-165.   Purposeful and aggressive movement, decentralized control, and hasty deployment of formations from the march to conduct offensive, defensive, or stability tasks characterize the movement to contact. The fundamentals of movement to contact—

- Focus all efforts on finding the enemy.
- Make initial contact with the smallest force possible, consistent with protecting the force.

Offense

- Make initial contact with small, mobile, self-contained forces to avoid decisive engagement of the main body on ground chosen by the enemy. This allows the leader maximum flexibility to develop the situation.
- Task-organizes the force and uses movement formations to deploy and attack rapidly in all directions.
- Keep subordinate forces within supporting distances to facilitate a flexible response.
- Maintains contact regardless of the course of action adopted once contact is gained.

ORGANIZATION OF FORCES

2-166. Movement to contact is organized with a forward security force, either a covering force or an advance guard, and a main body as a minimum. A portion of the main body composes the leader's sustaining base. Based on METT-TC, the leader may increase the unit's security by resourcing an offensive covering force and an advance guard for each column, as well as flank and rear security. This is normally a screen or guard.

SECURITY FORCES

2-167. The primary attribute to this organization is the early and accurate reporting it provides on the enemy and terrain. Depth is essential for providing early warning and reaction time to leaders at the platoon, company, and battalion levels. It enables leaders to conduct actions on contact, preserving the parent unit's freedom of movement and maneuver.

ADVANCE GUARD

2-168. When the platoon serves as the advance guard, its purpose is to protect the main body from surprise attack, and develop the situation to protect the deployment of the main body when it is committed to action. These responsibilities include—

- Providing security and early warning for the main body and facilitating its uninterrupted advance.
- Conducting reconnaissance to locate enemy forces along the battalion's axis of advance.
- Conducting actions on contact to retain freedom of maneuver for the battalion.
- Calling for indirect fires to impede or harass the enemy.
- Destroying enemy reconnaissance elements.
- Finding, fixing, defeating, destroying, or containing enemy security forces to retain freedom of maneuver for the battalion.
- Bypassing and reporting obstacles, or act as the battalion support or breach force during breaching operations.

2-169. Composition of the advance guard depends upon METT-TC. In open terrain, it may move mounted; but in restricted, close, complex, or urban terrain, dismounted movement with vehicles in the overwatch may be a better choice. Engineers, tank, or Infantry company platoons may be attached to the advance guard. The mortar platoon or a mortar section may also support the advance guard.

Chapter 2

2-170. The advance guard is the battalion commander's main effort until the main body is committed; then the priority of fires shifts to the main body. In planning the movement to contact, each decision point should be based on the actions of the advance guard.

FLANK GUARD

2-171. To provide flank guard, platoon-size elements from one of the companies in the battalion's main body provide a moving flank screen under company control. These elements remain at a distance from the main body, allowing the battalion time and space to maneuver to either flank. Flank security elements also operate far enough out to prevent the enemy from surprising the main body with direct fires. Indirect fires are planned on major flank approaches to enhance security.

REAR GUARD

2-172. One platoon pulled from the main body may provide rear security, but combat forces are not normally available to perform this mission. The battalion provides its own rear security, assisted by rapid forward movement, which gives the enemy less opportunity to react or reposition forces to attack.

MAIN BODY

2-173. The combat elements of the main body are prepared to deploy and maneuver rapidly to a decisive point on the battlefield to destroy the enemy. The main body focuses its movement to the advance guard. The main body, remaining attuned to the advance guard's situation, provides responsive support when the advance guard is committed.

2-174. Tasks the company or platoon can perform within the main body include—
- Find, fix, defeat, destroy, or contain the enemy's fixing force followed by the enemy assault force or site exploitation force, to retain freedom of maneuver for the remainder of the BCT.
- Execute a course of action to defeat or destroy a designated enemy main body element.

2-175. The use of standard formations and battle drills allows the battalion commander, to shift combat power rapidly. Platoons and squads employ the appropriate movement techniques within the company formation. Company commanders, based on their knowledge of commander's intent and their own situational awareness, anticipate the battalion commander's decisions for commitment of the main body and plan accordingly.

CONTROL MEASURES

2-176. Execution of this task usually starts from a LD at the time specified in the operation order (OPORD). The leader controls the movement to contact by using phase lines, contact points, and checkpoints as required. The leader controls the depth of movement to contact by using a limit of advance (LOA) or a forward boundary. The leader could designate one or more objectives to limit the extent of movement to contact and orient the force. However, these are often terrain-oriented and used only to guide movement. Although movement to contact may result in taking a terrain objective, the primary focus should be on the enemy force. If the leader has enough information to locate significant enemy forces, then the leader should plan some other type of offensive action.

2-177. Leaders use positive control over maneuver units, coupled with battle drills and formation discipline. Normally platoons are not assigned their own area of operation during a movement to contact.

2-178. The leader can designate a series of phase lines successively becoming the new rear boundary of forward security elements as force advances. Each rear boundary becomes the forward boundary of the main body and shifts as the security force moves forward. The rear boundary of the main body designates the limit of responsibility of the rear security element. This line also shifts as the main body moves forward. (Refer to FM 3-90-1 for more information.)

ORDER OF EVENTS

2-179. As the platoon leader plans for a movement to contact, the following considerations apply to most, but not all, offensive tasks:

- Assembly area (AA).
- Reconnaissance.
- Movement to the LD.
- Maneuver.
- Deployment.
- Assault.
- Consolidation and reorganization.

ASSEMBLY AREA

2-180. The AA is the area a unit occupies to prepare for an operation. To prepare the platoon for upcoming battles, the platoon leader plans, directs, and supervises mission preparations in the AA. This time allows the platoon and squads to conduct precombat checks and inspections, rehearsals, and sustainment activities. The platoon typically conducts these preparations within a company AA, as it rarely occupies its own AA.

RECONNAISSANCE

2-181. All leaders should aggressively seek information about the terrain and enemy. Because the enemy situation and available planning time may limit a unit's reconnaissance, the platoon usually conducts reconnaissance to answer the company commander's critical information requirements (CCIRs). The use of CCIRs cover friendly forces information requirements (FFIRs), priority intelligence requirements (PIRs), and essential elements of friendly information (EEFI) when dictated by the commander. An example is reconnoitering and timing routes from the AA to the LD. The platoon also may augment the efforts of the battalion reconnaissance platoon to answer the CCIRs. Other forms of reconnaissance include maps and terrain software/databases. Updates from reconnaissance can occur at any time while the platoon and squad are planning for,

Chapter 2

preparing for, or executing the mission. As a result, the leader must be prepared to adjust his plans.

MOVEMENT TO THE LINE OF DEPARTURE

2-182. The platoon and squad typically move from the AA to the LD as part of the company movement plan. This plan may direct the platoon or squad to move to an attack position and await orders to cross the LD. If so, the platoon leader reconnoiters, times, and rehearses the route to the attack position. Section leaders and squad leader know where they are to locate within the assigned attack position, which is the last position an attacking element occupies or passes through before crossing the LD. The company commander may order all platoons to move within a company formation from the AA directly to the point of departure at the LD. The point of departure is the point where the unit crosses the LD and begins moving along a direction or axis of advance. If one point of departure is used, it is important the lead platoon and trail platoons reconnoiter, time, and rehearse the route to it. This allows the company commander to maintain synchronization. To maintain flexibility and to maintain synchronization, a point of departure along the LD may be designated for each platoon.

MANEUVER

2-183. The platoon leader plans the approach to the movement to contact, ensuring synchronization, security, speed, and flexibility by selecting the platoon's routes, movement techniques, formations, and methods of movement. He must recognize this portion of the battle as a fight, not as a movement. He must be prepared to make contact with the enemy. He must plan accordingly to reinforce the commander's needs for synchronization, security, speed, and flexibility. During execution, the platoon leader may display disciplined initiative and alter his platoon's formation, technique, or speed to maintain synchronization with the other platoons and squads. This retains flexibility for the company commander.

DEPLOYMENT

2-184. As the platoon deploys and moves on its movement to contact it minimizes delay and confusion by analyzing what movement technique to use, traveling, traveling overwatch, or bounding overwatch. These movements allow the platoon to move in the best tactical posture before encountering the enemy. Movement should be as rapid as the terrain, unit mobility, and enemy situation permits. A common control measure is the probable line of deployment (PLD), which is used most often under conditions of limited visibility. The PLD is a phase line the leader designates as a location where he intends to deploy his unit into an assault formation before beginning the assault.

ASSAULT

2-185. During an offensive task, the platoon's objective may be terrain-oriented or force-oriented. Terrain-oriented objectives may require the platoon to seize a designated area, and often requires fighting through enemy forces. If the objective is force-oriented, an objective may be assigned for orientation while the platoon's efforts are focused on the enemy's actual location. Actions on the objective begin when the company or platoon begins placing direct and indirect fires on the objective. This may occur while the platoon is still moving toward the objective from the assault position or PLD.

CONSOLIDATION AND REORGANIZATION

2-186. The platoon and squads consolidate and reorganize as required by the situation and mission. Consolidation is the process of organizing and strengthening a newly captured position so it can be defended. Reorganization is the action taken to shift internal resources within a degraded unit to increase its level of combat effectiveness. Reorganization actions can include cross-leveling ammunition, and ensuring essential weapons systems are manned and vital leadership positions are filled if the operators/crew became casualties. The platoon executes follow-on missions as directed by the company commander. A likely mission may be to continue the attack against the enemy within the area of operation. Regardless of the situation, the platoon and squads posture and prepare for continued offensive missions. Table 2-7 (page 2-68) contains common consolidation and reorganization activities.

Chapter 2

Table 2-7. Consolidation and reorganization activities

CONSOLIDATION ACTIVITIES	REORGANIZATION ACTIVITIES

• Security Measures include:
   ▪ Stabling 360-degree local security.
   ▪ Using security patrols.
   ▪ Using observation posts/outposts.
   ▪ Emplacing early warning devices.
   ▪ Establishing and registering final protective fires.
   ▪ Seeking out and eliminated enemy resistance (on and off the objective).
• Automatic weapons (man, position, and assign principal direction of fire (PDFs) to Soldiers manning automatic weapons).
• Fields of fire (establish sectors of fire and other direct fire control measures for each subunit/Soldier).
• Entrenchment (provide guidance on protection requirements such as diffing/building fighting positions).
	• Reestablishing the chain of command.
	• Manning key weapon systems.
	• Maintaining communications and reports, to include:
	   ▪ Restoring communication with any unit temporarily out of communication.
	   ▪ Sending unit situation report.
	   ▪ Sending SITREPSs (at a minimum, subordinates report status of mission accomplishment).
	   ▪ Identifying and requesting resupply of critical shortages.
	• Resupplying and redistributing ammunition and other critical supplies.
	• Performing special team actions such as—
	   ▪ Consolidating and evacuating causalities, EPWs, enemy weapons, noncombatants/refugees and damaged equipment (not necessarily in the same location).
	   ▪ Treating and evacuating wounded personnel.
	   ▪ Evacuating friendly killed in action (KIA).
	   ▪ Treating and processing enemy prisoners of war (EPWs).
	   ▪ Segregating and safeguarding noncombatants/refugees.
	   ▪ Searching and marking positions to indicate to other friendly forces that they have been cleared.

2-187. Purposeful and aggressive movement, decentralized control, and hasty deployment of combined arms formations from the march to attack or defend characterize the movement to contact. The fundamentals of a movement to contact—

- Focus all efforts on finding the enemy.
- Make initial contact with the smallest force possible, consistent with protecting the force.
- Make initial contact with small, mobile, self-contained forces to avoid decisive engagement of the main body on ground chosen by the enemy. This allows the leader maximum flexibility to develop the situation.
- Task-organize the force and use movement formations to deploy and attack rapidly in all directions.

PLAN

2-188. Movement to contact is one of the most difficult missions to plan. The goal is preventing a meeting engagement with the enemy. (Refer to FM 3-90-1 for more information.) Planning movement to contact allows for flexibility and promoting subordinate initiative. Planning begins by developing the concept of the operation with a focus on ultimate control of the objective, and conducting a reverse planning sequence from the objective to the LD. This is accomplished by issuing a clear commander's intent, developing a simple concept of the operation and developing a series of decision point to execute likely maneuver options. Increased emphasis is placed on developing an aggressive and flexible reconnaissance effort linking to the commander's PIRs, which normally focuses on locating and gathering information about the enemy's strength, disposition, and activities.

2-189. The Infantry leader conducts information collection to determine the enemy's location and intent while conducting security operations to protect the main body. This includes the use of available manned and unmanned aircraft assets, allowing the main body to focus on planning and preparation. This includes rehearsals on the conduct of hasty operations, bypass maneuvers, and hasty defenses. The plan addresses actions anticipated by the leader based on available information and intelligence and the conduct of meeting engagements and other anticipated battle drills.

PREPARE

2-190. Preparation actions are performed by the platoon to improve its ability to execute an operation. The platoon's success during missions depend as much on preparation as planning. Activities specific to preparation include:

- Revising and refining the plan.
- Rehearsals.
- Troop movements.
- Precombat checks and inspections.
- Sustainment preparations.
- Subordinate confirmation briefs and back briefs.

REHEARSALS

2-191. The platoon uses rehearsals to help understand their roles in upcoming operations, practice complicated tasks, and ensure equipment and weapons function properly. Following the last company rehearsal, the platoon should conduct a final rehearsal of its own to incorporate adjustments to the company scheme of maneuver. (Refer to FM 6-0 for more information.) The platoon rehearsal should cover the following subjects:

- Movement from current positions.
- Routes (to include passage points, contact points, checkpoints, and CCP).

INSPECTIONS

2-192. A precombat inspection (PCI) is a formal, time-intensive inspection that is done before the mission. Its goal is to make sure Soldiers and vehicles are fully prepared to execute the upcoming mission. In general, PCIs enable the platoon leader to check the platoon's operational readiness.

2-193. A precombat check (PCC) is less formal and more mission-specific than a PCI. Precombat checks emphasize areas, missions, or tasks required for upcoming missions. The squad and section leaders perform the PCC. It is essential that the entire platoon chain of command know how to conduct PCCs and PCIs.

2-194. The platoon leader or platoon sergeant should observe each squad and mounted crew during preparation for combat. They should conduct the inspection once the mounted section and squad leaders report that they are prepared.

EXECUTE

2-195. Each element of the force synchronizes its actions with adjacent and supporting units, maintaining contact and coordination as prescribed in orders and unit SOP. The following paragraphs discuss executing movement to contact using the sequence of the offense mentioned earlier in this chapter.

GAIN AND MAINTAIN ENEMY CONTACT

2-196. All reconnaissance assets focus on determining the enemy's dispositions and providing the Infantry leader with current intelligence and relevant combat information. This ensures friendly forces are committed under optimal conditions. The leader uses all available sources of combat information to find the enemy's location and dispositions. The platoon and squad leaders ensure that the platoon makes enemy contact with the smallest friendly element possible in order to preserve combat power and conceal the size and capabilities of the platoon.

DISRUPT THE ENEMY

2-197. Once contact is made, the main body brings overwhelming fires onto the enemy to prevent them from conducting a spoiling attack or organizing a coherent defense. The security force maneuvers as quickly as possible to find gaps in the enemy's defenses. The leader gathers as much information as possible about the enemy's dispositions, strengths, capabilities, and intentions. As more intelligence becomes available, the main body attacks to destroy or disrupt enemy command and control centers, fire control nodes, and communication nets.

FIX THE ENEMY

2-198. Infantry leaders initiate maneuvers at a tempo the enemy cannot match, since success in a meeting engagement depends upon actions on contact. The security force does not allow the enemy to maneuver against the main body. The organization, size, and

Offense

combat power of the security force are major factors determining the size of the enemy force it can defeat without deploying the main body. The techniques the leader employs to fix the enemy when both forces are moving are different from those employed when the enemy force is stationary during the meeting engagement. In both situations, when the security force cannot overrun the enemy by conducting a hasty frontal attack, a portion of the main body is deployed. When this occurs, the unit is no longer conducting movement to contact but an attack. (Refer to ADRP 3-90 for more information.)

MANEUVER

2-199. If the security force cannot overrun the enemy with a frontal attack, the leader quickly maneuvers the main body to conduct a penetration or envelopment that overwhelms the enemy force before it can react or reinforce. The leader attempts to defeat the enemy in detail while still maintaining the momentum of advance. After an attack, the main body leader resumes the movement to contact. If the enemy is not defeated, there are three main options: bypass, transition to a more deliberate operation, or conduct some type of defense.

2-200. Main body elements deploy rapidly to the vicinity of contact if the leader initiates a frontal attack. Maneuvering unit leaders coordinate forward passage through friendly forces in contact as required. The intent is to deliver the assault before the enemy can deploy or reinforce his engaged forces. The leader may order an attack from a march column for one of the main body's columns, while the rest of the main body deploys. The leader also can wait to attack until bringing the bulk of the main body forward. This avoids piecemeal commitment except when rapidity of action is essential, combat superiority at the vital point is present, can be maintained throughout the attack, or when compartmentalized terrain forces a COA. When trying to conduct envelopment, the leader focuses on attacking the enemy's flanks and rear before preparing to counter these actions. The leader uses the security force to fix the enemy while the main body maneuvers to look for an assailable flank. The main body also can be used to fix the enemy while the security force finds the assailable flank. (Refer to ADRP 3-90 for more information.)

FOLLOW THROUGH

2-201. If the enemy is defeated, the unit transitions back into movement to contact and continue to advance. The movement to contact terminates when the unit reaches the final objective or LOA, or transitions to a more deliberate operation, defense, or retrograde.

ASSESS

2-202. Assessment is the continuous monitoring and evaluation of a current situation, and the progress of an operation. It involves deliberately comparing forecasted outcomes to actual events in order to determine the overall effectiveness of force employment. Assessment allows the leader to maintain accurate situational understanding, and amend his visualization, which helps the commander make timely and accurate decisions. Assessment of effects is determining how friendly actions have succeeded against the

Chapter 2

enemy. Effects typically are assessed by measure of performance and measure of effectiveness.

SITUATION

2-203. Every combat situation is unique. Leaders do their best to accurately assess the situation and make good decisions about employing their units. The environment of combat, application of military principles, and the desired end state of Army operations culminate with the close fight of Infantry platoons and squads. Leaders should understand the larger military purpose and how their actions and decisions might affect the outcome of the larger operation.

RISK ASSESSMENT

2-204. Risk assessment is the process leaders use to assess and to control risk. There are two types of risk associated with combat actions: tactical hazards resulting from the presence of the enemy and accidental hazards resulting from the conduct of operations. All combat incurs both risks. The objective is to minimize them to acceptable levels. The leader identifies risk to the unit and mission by—

- Defining the enemy action.
- Identifying friendly combat power shortfall.
- Identifying available combat multipliers, if any, to mitigate risk.
- Considering the risks are acceptable or unacceptable.

METT-TC ASSESSMENT

2-205. Infantry platoon leaders and squad leaders use METT-TC to understand and describe the operational environment. These six widely known and used factors are categories for cataloging and analyzing information. Leaders and Soldiers constantly observe and assess their environment.

TERRAIN ASSESSMENT

2-206. The leader assesses the terrain in his proposed area of operation. In addition to the standard Army map, the leader may have aerial photographs and terrain analysis overlays from the parent unit, or he may talk with someone familiar with the area.

SEARCH AND ATTACK

2-207. Search and attack is a technique for conducting movement to contact sharing many of the same characteristics of an area security mission. (Refer to ADRP 3-90 for more information.) Conducted primarily by Infantry forces and often supported by armored forces, the leader employs this form of movement to contact when the enemy is operating as a small, dispersed element, or when the task is to deny the enemy the ability to move within a given area. Maneuver battalions and companies normally conduct search and attack.

ORGANIZATION OF FORCES FOR A SEARCH AND ATTACK

2-208. Commanders task-organize subordinate units (platoons and squads) into reconnaissance, fixing, and finishing forces, each with a specific purpose and task. The size of the reconnaissance force is based upon the available combat information and intelligence about the size of enemy forces in the area of operation. The nature of the operational environment sometimes requires an Infantry platoon to conduct a search and attack while operating in a noncontiguous area of operation. The Infantry leader primarily employs ground forces, often supported by armored or wheeled forces if available, when the enemy is operating with small, dispersed elements or when the task is to deny the enemy the ability to move within a given area.

Reconnaissance

2-209. The reconnaissance force conducts a zone reconnaissance to reconnoiter identified named areas of interest. The reconnaissance force is small enough to achieve stealth, but large enough to provide adequate self-defense until the fixing and finishing forces arrive.

Fixing

2-210. The fixing force develops the situation and executes one of two options based upon the commander's guidance and METT-TC. The first option is to block identified routes the detected enemy can use to escape or reinforce. The fixing force maintains contact with the enemy and positions its forces to isolate and fix him before the finishing force attacks. The second option is to conduct an attack to fix the enemy in his current positions until the finishing force arrives. The fixing force can be a combination of mounted and dismounted forces with enough combat power to isolate the enemy after the reconnaissance force finds him. The fixing force attacks if action meets the commander's intent and can generate sufficient combat power against the enemy.

Finishing

2-211. The finishing force is used to destroy the detected and fixed enemy during a search and attack. This is accomplished by conducting hasty or deliberate operations, maneuvering to block enemy escape routes while another unit conducts the attack, or employing indirect fire or CAS. The leader may have his finishing force establish an area ambush and use his reconnaissance and fixing forces to drive the enemy into the ambushes. The finishing force must have enough combat power to destroy those enemy forces expected in the platoon area of operation.

CONTROL MEASURES FOR A SEARCH AND ATTACK

2-212. The leader establishes control measures allowing for decentralized actions and small-unit initiative to the greatest extent possible. The minimum control measures for a search and attack are an area of operation, TRP, objectives, checkpoints, and contact points. The use of TRP facilitates responsive fire support once the reconnaissance force makes contact with the enemy. The leader uses objectives and checkpoints to guide the movement of subordinate elements. Coordination points indicate a specific location for coordinating fires and movement between adjacent units. The leader uses other control measures such as phase lines, as necessary.

PLANNING A SEARCH AND ATTACK

2-213. Applying all of the warfighting functions, the leader conducts a search and attack to—

- Destroy the enemy and render enemy units in the areas of operations combat-ineffective.
- Deny the area and prevent the enemy from operating unhindered in a given area.
- Protect the force and prevent the enemy from massing to disrupt or destroy friendly military or civilian operations, equipment, property, and essential facilities.
- Collect information and gain information about the enemy and terrain to confirm the enemy COA predicted because of the intelligence preparation of the battlefield (IPB) process.

2-214. The search and attack plan places the finishing force where it can best maneuver to destroy enemy forces or essential facilities located by reconnaissance assets. Typically, the finishing force occupies a central location in the area of operation. However, METT-TC may allow the leader to position the finishing force outside the search and attack area. The leader weights the finishing force by using priority of fires and assigning priorities of support to available combat multipliers such as engineer elements and helicopter lift support. The leader establishes control measures as necessary to consolidate units and concentrate the combat power of the force before the attack. Once the reconnaissance force locates the enemy, the fixing and finishing forces can fix and destroy it. The leader also develops a contingency plan in the event the reconnaissance force is compromised.

PREPARING FOR A SEARCH AND ATTACK

2-215. The preparations for conducting a search and attack are the same as those for an attack. See the appropriate paragraph with the attack section in this chapter for additional information.

EXECUTION OF THE SEARCH AND ATTACK

2-216. Each subordinate element operating in its own area of operation is tasked with destroying the enemy to the best of its capability. The leader should have established control measures and communications means between all closing elements to prevent fratricide and friendly fire. The reconnaissance force conducts a zone reconnaissance to reconnoiter identified named areas of interest.

Gain and Maintain Enemy Contact

2-217. Once the information collection effort locates the enemy, the fixing force develops the situation and executes one of two options based on the leader's guidance and

METT-TC. The first option is to block identified routes the detected enemy can use to escape or bring in reinforcements. The fixing force maintains contact with the enemy and positions its forces to isolate and fix him before the finishing force attacks. The second option is to conduct an attack to fix the enemy in his current positions until the finishing force arrives. The fixing force attacks if this action meets the commander's intent and it can generate sufficient combat power against the detected enemy. Depending on the enemy's mobility and likelihood of the reconnaissance force being compromised, the leader may need to position the fixing force before the reconnaissance force enters the area of operation.

Disrupt the Enemy

2-218. The leader uses the finishing force to destroy the detected and fixed enemy during a search and attack by conducting hasty or deliberate operations, maneuvering to block enemy escape routes while another unit conducts the attack, or employing indirect fire or CAS to destroy the enemy.

Fix the Enemy

2-219. If conditions are not right to use the finishing force/main body to attack the detected enemy, the reconnaissance or fixing forces can continue to conduct reconnaissance and surveillance activities to develop the situation. Whenever this occurs, the force maintaining surveillance is careful to avoid detection and possible enemy ambushes.

Maneuver

2-220. The finishing force may move behind the reconnaissance and fixing forces, or locate at a pickup zone and air assault into a landing zone near the enemy once he is located. The finishing force/main body must be responsive enough to engage the enemy before he can break contact with the reconnaissance force or the fixing force. The battalion intelligence staff provides the leader with a time estimate for the enemy to displace from his detected locations. The leader provides additional mobility assets so the finishing force/main body can respond within the timeframe.

2-221. The leader may have the finishing force/main body establish an area ambush and use the reconnaissance and fixing forces to drive the enemy into the ambushes.

Follow Through

2-222. The leader uses the finishing force to destroy the detected and fixed enemy during a search and attack by conducting hasty or deliberate operations, maneuvering to block enemy escape routes while another unit conducts the attack, or employing indirect fire or CAS to destroy the enemy.

CORDON AND SEARCH

Note. The Infantry platoon usually does not have the resources to conduct an independent cordon and search. However, the platoon may conduct it as part of a larger force as the cordon or search element in whole or in part. Each element's function may be assigned to a platoon that can be broken down into teams.

2-223. The most common tactical task during stability is a cordon and search. This involves two potentially inflammatory processes: limiting freedom of movement and searching dwellings. These two actions have a clear potential for negative consequences. Therefore, organizing cordon and search elements requires extensive mission tailoring and Infantry leaders always are prepared for a civil disturbance.

2-224. Searches are an important aspect of populace and resource control. The need to conduct a search operation or to employ search procedures is a continuous requirement. A search conducted by civil police and Soldiers can orient on people, materiel, buildings, or terrain. Searches may be enabled by biometric or forensic exploitation.

2-225. Cordon and search involves isolating the target area and searching suspected buildings to capture or destroy possible insurgents and contraband. It involves the emplacement of a cordon, or security perimeter, to prevent traffic in and out of the area. The cordon permits the search element to operate unimpeded within the secured area. The purpose of cordon and search is to obtain weapon caches, materiel or information, persons of interest, or a specific high-value target.

2-226. There are two cordon and search methods and the method selected to accomplish the mission depends on a number of factors. The primary consideration is to capture the designated personnel, site, or equipment but additional factors such as the enemy threat, local populace support, and host-nation security force capabilities are taken into account during planning this task.

2-227. The cordon and kick method is used to maintain speed, surprise, and timeliness in entry to the target within the objective. In this instance, considerations of population perceptions and integration of host-nation security force are less important than accomplishing the task of capturing the target individual, site, or equipment.

2-228. If the mission is focused on increasing the legitimacy of the host-nation government and security forces, it may be necessary to sacrifice a degree of surprise and timeliness to achieve its goal by conducting a cordon and knock/ask. In this instance, the unit focuses on maintaining a presence and control of an area by incorporating local authorities into the mission. (Refer to ATP 3-06.20 for more information.)

ORGANIZATION OF FORCES FOR A CORDON AND SEARCH

2-229. A cordon and search requires a command, security, search and support element to perform the major tasks. The security element sets up the cordon, which usually consists of an outer cordon "ring" and an inner cordon "ring." The search element clears and searches suspected buildings to capture or destroy insurgents and contraband. This is the main effort. The support element may be the reserve, provide support by fire, and be prepared to perform the other cordon and search tasks.

Note. The United States Marine Corps uses the term "search/assault element instead of "search element" for the United States Army. (Refer to ATP 3-06.20 for more information.)

Command Element

2-230. The command element is the headquarters executing mission command for cordon and search. There may be several combat multipliers attached. Frequently, the leader is given a variety of assets to assist him in accomplishing his mission. Ideally, the leader task-organizes his assets in order to maintain control of three to five elements.

2-231. The location of the command element provides the ability to control the subordinate teams and supporting assets of cordon and search mission. The ability to observe the search element generally causes the command element to collocate with the inner cordon. Visibility and communication capability are deciding factors in identifying the best location for the command element during the actual mission.

2-232. The composition of the command element may be as small as the leader and an RTO, or may include security vehicles, interpreters, host-nation officials and local authorities. The command element remains mobile and able to move to all points within the cordon and search operation, ensuring coordination of all elements and supporting assets. When host-nation forces or authorities are involved in the mission, the command element coordinates with them and integrates them as identified during the planning phase of the operation. Operation and communication security are guiding principles when conducting integrated operations with host-nation forces.

2-233. The command element is the single point of coordination for supporting assets and status reporting to higher headquarters. As a critical component of cordon and search operations, the command element designates a backup team in the event it becomes combat ineffective. It ensures all actions are documented as required, and rules of evidence are followed where necessary. In the event a person is detained, the command element monitors the documentation, security, and transport of detainees. It also ensures damage caused during the cordon and search is documented to identify legitimate future claims by the occupants of the target.

Security Element

2-234. The primary task of the security element is total isolation of the target area, either physically or by fire. The security element limits enemy or civilian influence in the objective area and prevents targets from escaping the cordon. It may have to use multiple avenues of approach and operate decentralized to accomplish its mission. It also may have to establish multiple blocking positions and observation posts and conduct patrols in order to isolate the target area. The security element may include the—
- Vehicle-mounted sections or platoons.
- Interpreters.

Chapter 2

- Detainee teams.
- Crowd control teams.
- Observation posts.
- Traffic control post or blocking positions.
- Host-nation security force (military or police).
- Integrated aviation assets.
- Dismounted squads or platoons.
- Female search teams.

2-235. The execution of outer cordon missions is an integral part of the security element in all cordon and search missions. The outer cordon isolates the objective area and prevents enemy or civilian influence. This requires detailed planning, coordination, integration, and synchronization to achieve the lethal and nonlethal combined arms effects required for mission execution. Some considerations for outer cordon include—

- Vehicles for traffic control post and blocking positions.
- Operational environment fire planning and coordination.
- Overwatch positions.
- Aviation assets to observe the target area and inform the outer cordon if vehicles or persons leave the target area. Constant communication between the aviation element and outer cordon better facilitates the isolation of the target area.
- An initial detainee collection point for receipt and temporary holding of detainees.
- An initial materiel collection point for consolidation of captured materiel.

2-236. Each outer cordon element traffic control point blocking position has a designated leader, and a clear task and purpose. Weapon systems to consider for outer cordon positions are wheeled or tracked vehicles with weapons systems, crew-served weapons, Javelin with the command launch unit (CLU), and snipers or designated marksman.

2-237. The leader of the outer cordon element develops and maintains situational awareness of his area of responsibility and the areas of inner cordon and search elements. This enables him to anticipate threat activity, control direct and indirect fires, and facilitate the achievement of the outer cordon's task and purpose. Aviation assets, communications systems, and reporting procedures are implemented to facilitate situational awareness for the entire element.

Search Element

2-238. The search element's mission is to clear, and search the target in order to capture, kill, or destroy the targeted individuals and materiel. The search element initiates action once the outer and inner cordons are in place. The element accomplishes its mission by gaining a foothold on or in the target to clear all enemy and noncombatant personnel, and by conducting a systematic search of the target. These areas may be searched selectively (only specific rooms/buildings/blocks) or systematically (everything within a given area). Due to the split-second decisions made, it is imperative this element not only understands but also complies with the ROE.

2-239. To accomplish its mission, the search element has three primary tasks: securing, clearing, and searching the target. The search element may be task-organized into search, security, and support teams in order to facilitate mission accomplishment. All these teams understand and are prepared to assume the role of other teams in the search element.

Support Element

2-240. The support element reinforces, and is capable of accomplishing, the task and purpose of the unit's main effort. In addition, the leader may direct the support element to accomplish priority-planning tasks. This means the support element leader is intimately familiar with all aspects of cordon and search missions from planning through its completion.

2-241. The leader identifies the tasks the support element may be required to execute. These tasks are prioritized and given to the support element leader to plan and rehearse these actions according to the commander's plan. Probable tasks assigned to the support element during a cordon and search operation are (but are not limited to)—

- Reinforce outer/inner cordon.
- Clear buildings.
- Search buildings.
- Biometric and forensic enabled collections. (Refer to ATP 2-22.85 for more information.)
- Document and media exploitation. (Refer to ATP 2-91.8 for more information.)
- Secure, safeguard, and escort civilians or detainees.
- Secure and safeguard captured materiel or equipment.

2-242. Commitment criteria is a guide to assist the leader on when to commit the support element, but is not intended to be a trigger for employment. (See figure 2-36, page 2-80.) Possible commitment criteria can be—

- A hostile crowd forming around the inner cordon.
- Loss of main effort.
- Numerous rooms in the building being searched.
- More than a specified number of detainees.
- The enemy engages the inner cordon.

Chapter 2

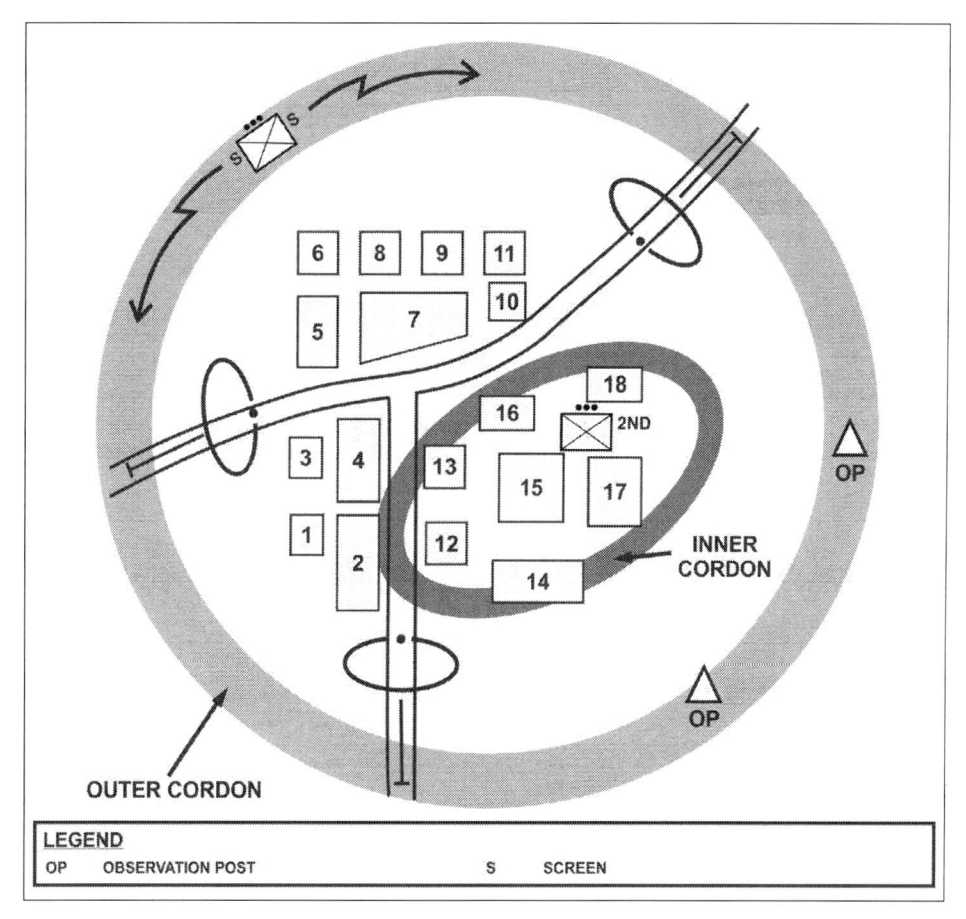

Figure 2-36. Establishment of a cordon

CONTROL MEASURES FOR A CORDON AND SEARCH

2-243. The use of standard tactical control measures is essential to mission command over forces approaching and conducting cordon and search operations. This includes—

- Assembly areas. Due to the relative safety, size, and location, base camp or combat outposts are the most convenient areas for staging a cordon and search operation. However, leaders assume all friendly positions are under constant observation. If possible, position AA in remote or separate areas, or use multiple AA in order to minimize all enemy surveillance efforts.
- Checkpoints. Checkpoints leading to the target and in the objective area are essential for ensuring all units arrive at the target in the proper order and on time.
- Rally points. Rally points to and from the objective area allow for cordon and search elements to reorganize if units become engaged, lost, have vehicle trouble, or lose communications during ingress and egress from the target.

- Phase lines. Phase lines are helpful in controlling cordon and search elements approaching the target from different directions or at different times.
- Restrictive fire lines (RFLs). RFL prohibit fires and their effects between converging friendly forces.

2-244. Vital tips for cordon and search success includes—
- Positioning vital leaders so they can see and control all subordinate elements.
- Positioning essential assets such as crew-served weapons and interpreters at the critical locations.
- Being prepared to move leadership and support assets from one location to another during mission execution or as necessary.
- Positioning vehicles and personnel to be searched so the security element's sectors of fire face to the outside of the friendly element and away from noncombatants when executing searches.
- Keeping the bulk of forces within the perimeter so if the situation escalates they are essentially in a battle or support-by-fire position.
- Ensuring all personnel understand direct fire and contingency plans. For example:
  - What actions to take in the event a vehicle penetrates a traffic control point from outside the established perimeter?
  - Who engages and with what weapons systems?
  - Engage crew-served weapons or should they use only M4?
  - When to cease fire, and what signal to use for cease-fire?

PLANNING A CORDON AND SEARCH

2-245. Leaders consider numerous factors when planning and preparing for a cordon and search mission. Leaders apply the same steps used in TLP, applying the warfighting functions. When the objective of cordon and search operation is a high payoff target, planning time can be extremely limited between first receiving the mission and executing it. Given the complexity of the mission and the assets task-organized to support it, planning time may require immediate collaboration with vital leaders of all the elements, and accelerated TLP. The "civilian" part of METT-TC should be considered specifically, and interpreters added as required.

2-246. The cordon and search operation is uniquely vulnerable to time. Planning time may be short due to the urgency of conducting the operation to exploit a fleeting opportunity. While time in the objective area may be considerably longer than planned, if the search yields significant items or results in intelligence which results in follow-on searches in the immediate area. Additional time issues are those associated with the lead times necessary to request assets, such as aviation, and acquire intelligence from various agencies.

PREPARING A CORDON AND SEARCH

2-247. A search can orient on people, materiel, buildings, or terrain, and involve civil police and Soldiers. Authority for search is carefully reviewed. Military personnel perform searches only in areas of military jurisdiction or where they are otherwise lawful.

2-248. Soldiers record and maintain the chain of custody for the seizure of contraband, evidence, captured enemy or detainee documents, weapons, and materiel, supplies, or other items for the seizure to be of legal value. Search teams have detailed instructions for handling controlled items. Lists of prohibited or controlled-distribution items should be widely disseminated and on-hand during a search. The unit contacts military or civil police, who work with the populace and resource control program before the search begins. Units also consider the effect of early warning on their mission, and have required interpreters provided.

2-249. A unit conducts the search at a methodical pace to help ensure success, but rapidly enough to prevent the enemy from reacting. Soldiers use only the force necessary to eliminate all encountered resistance. There should be plans for securing the search area (establishing a cordon) and handling detained personnel.

EXECUTING A CORDON AND SEARCH

2-250. Cordon and search missions involve isolating the target area and searching suspected buildings to capture or destroy possible insurgents and contraband. A cordon is critical to the success of the search effort. It is designed to prevent persons of interest from escaping and insurgents from reinforcing while protecting the forces conducting the operation. Based on METT-TC, the Infantry platoon can establish an inner cordon and an outer cordon. A mounted platoon is best suited to provide the outer cordon given its mobility and armaments. Both cordon elements must focus inward and outward for security purposes.

2-251. The outer cordon's composition and capabilities should be based on METT-TC, and its mission is providing containment to prevent a high-value target from escaping the objective area. The outer cordon may have to accomplish this task by being more terrain-oriented, focusing on the most probable avenues of approach into and out of the objective area. It also can be tasked to obstruct specific locations to prevent escape from inside and block interference from the outside. A mounted platoon is best suited to provide the outer cordon due to its mobility and armaments.

2-252. The mission of the inner cordon is containing the immediate vicinity of the target to prevent escape and providing security to the search element. If the cordon and search is opposed by a hostile force, the inner cordon provides support by fire and direct fires to suppress the enemy force and allow maneuver of the search element to the objective.

2-253. Due to the congested nature of urban environments, direct fire control measures can be complicated. One proven TTP is for units to number buildings, letter building corners, and number floors. Then a request for immediate direct fire suppression can be specific and the risk of collateral damage, fratricide, and friendly fire is reduced. The fire command can be, "Immediate suppression, two personnel with weapons, building 23, side

A-B, second floor, second window, fire when ready." Due to the condensed and compressed nature of the physical area, fires are precise and accurate, as opposed to high volume.

CIVILIAN CONSIDERATIONS

2-254. All operations across the spectrum of warfare must take into account civilian considerations in terms of their presence in the battlefield/operational environment, infrastructure damage, injury to civilians, and so forth. Considering the likely operating environments in which a cordon and search would be conducted, civilian considerations represent a significant planning aspect for the commander. (Refer to ATP 3-06.20 for more information.)

SECTION VII – ATTACK

2-255. An attack is a primary offensive task that destroys or defeats enemy forces, seizes and secures terrain, or both. When the Infantry leader decides to attack, or the opportunity to attack occurs during combat operations, the execution of an attack masses the effects of overwhelming combat power against selected portions of the enemy force with a tempo and intensity that cannot be matched by the enemy. The resulting combat should not be a contest between near equals. Attackers are determined to seek decisions on the ground of their choosing through the deliberate synchronization and employment of the combined arms team.

DELIBERATE AND HASTY OPERATIONS

2-256. The primary difference between a deliberate operation and hasty operation is the extent of planning and preparation the attacking force conducts. At one end of the continuum, an Infantry unit launches hasty operation as a continuation of an engagement that exploits a combat power advantage and preempts enemy actions. At the other end of the continuum, an Infantry unit conducts a deliberate operation from a reserve position or AA with detailed knowledge of the enemy, a task organization designed specifically for attacking, and a fully rehearsed plan. Most attacks fall somewhere between the two extremes.

2-257. A deliberate operation normally is conducted when enemy positions are too strong to be overcome by a hasty operation. It is a fully synchronized operation employing every available asset against the enemy defense, and are characterized by a high volume of planned fires, use of major supporting attacks, forward positioning of the resources needed to maintain momentum, and operations throughout the depth of enemy positions. Deliberate operations follow a preparatory period that includes planning, reconnaissance, coordination, positioning of follow-on forces and reserves, preparation of troops and equipment, rehearsals, and operational refinement.

2-258. A hasty operation is conducted during movement to contact, as part of a defense, or when the enemy is in a vulnerable position and can be defeated quickly with available resources. This type of operation may cause the attacking force to lose a degree of synchronization. To minimize this risk, the leader maximizes use of standard formations and well-rehearsed, thoroughly understood battle drills and SOPs. A hasty operation often is the preferred option during continuous operations, enabling the leader to maintain momentum while denying the enemy time for defense preparations.

ORGANIZATION OF FORCES

2-259. Once the scheme of maneuver is determined, the Infantry leader task-organizes the force to ensure he has enough combat power to accomplish the mission. The leader normally organizes a security force, main body, and a reserve, which are all supported by some type of sustainment organization. The leader should complete all changes in task organization on time to allow units to conduct rehearsals with their attached and supporting elements.

SECURITY FORCES

2-260. Under normal circumstances, the leader resources dedicated security forces during an attack only if the attack uncovers one or more flanks, or the rear of the attacking force as it advances. In this case, the leader designates a flank or rear security force and assigns it a guard or screen mission, depending on METT-TC. Normally an attacking unit does not need extensive forward security forces as most attacks are launched from positions in contact with the enemy, which reduces the usefulness of a separate forward security force. The exception occurs when the attacking unit is transitioning from defense to attack and had previously established a security area as part of the defense.

MAIN BODY

2-261. The Infantry leader organizes the main body into combined arms formations to conduct the decisive operation and necessary shaping operations. The leader aims the decisive operation toward the immediate and decisive destruction of the enemy force and will to resist, seizure of a terrain objective, or the defeat of the enemy's plan. The maneuver scheme identifies the focus of the main effort. All forces' available resources operate in concert to assure the success of the main effort. The subordinate unit or units designated to conduct the decisive operation can change during the course of attack. The leader designates an assault, breach, and support force, if he expects to conduct a breach operation during the attack.

2-262. If it is impractical to initially determine when or where the echelon's main effort will be, such as during a hasty operation, the leader retains flexibility by arranging forces in-depth, holding out strong reserves, and maintaining centralized control of long-range indirect fire support systems. As soon as the tactical situation develops enough to allow the leader to designate the decisive point, the leader focuses available resources to support the main efforts achievement of its objective.

RESERVE

2-263. The leader uses the reserve to exploit success, defeat enemy counterattacks, or restore momentum to a stalled attack. For a company mission this usually is a squad size force. For a battalion mission it is usually a platoon-size element. Once committed, the reserve's actions normally become or reinforce the echelon's decisive operation. The Infantry leader makes every effort to reconstitute another reserve from units made available by the revised situation. Often the leader's most difficult and important decision concerns the time, place, and circumstances for committing the reserve. The reserve is not a committed force and is not used as a follow-and-support force, or a follow-and-assumes force.

2-264. In the attack, the combat power allocated to the reserve depends primarily on the level of uncertainty about the enemy, especially the strength of all expected enemy counterattacks. The leader only needs to resource a small reserve to respond to unanticipated enemy reactions when detailed information about the enemy exists. When the situation is relatively clear and enemy capabilities are limited, the reserve may consist of a small fraction of the command. When the situation is vague, the reserve initially may contain the majority of the Infantry leader's combat power.

SUSTAINMENT ORGANIZATION

2-265. Leaders' resource sustaining operations to support the attacking force. A maneuver battalion commander organizes the supporting sustainment and other logistics assets into combat and field trains. In an Infantry Brigade Combat Team (IBCT), a forward support company (FSC) is part of the Infantry battalion. It is responsible for sustainment of the Infantry battalion. The IBCT sustainment organization is different in structure from the ABCT and SBCT. Higher echelon commanders appoint someone to control sustaining operations within their echelon support areas.

CONTROL MEASURES FOR AN ATTACK

2-266. Units conducting offensive tasks operate within an assigned area of operation. Regardless of whether the attack takes place in a contiguous or noncontiguous environment, the commander of this area of operation normally designates control measures such as the—

- Areas of operation for subordinate units of battalion size or larger.
- Phase line as the line of departure, which also may be the line of contact (LC).
- Time to initiate the operation.
- Objective.

2-267. Infantry leaders use all other control measures necessary to control the attack. Short of the LD or LC, the leader may designate AA and attack positions where the unit prepares for the offense or waits for the establishment of required conditions to initiate the attack. Beyond the LD or LC, leaders may designate checkpoints, phase lines, PLD, assault positions, and direct and indirect fire support coordination measures. Between the PLD and objective, a final coordination line, assault positions, support by fire and attack by fire positions, and time of assault to better control the final stage of attack can be used. Beyond the objective, the Infantry leader can impose a LOA if an exploitation or pursuit is not conducted. (Refer to FM 3-90-1 for more information.)

ORDER OF EVENTS

2-268. As the platoon leader plans for an attack, the order of events typically follow the sequence described in the paragraphs below.

MOVING FROM THE ASSEMBLY AREA TO THE LINE OF DEPARTURE

2-269. The tactical situation and order in which the leader wants his subordinate units to arrive at their attack positions govern the march formation.

MANEUVERING FROM THE LINE OF DEPARTURE TO THE PROBABLE LINE OF DEPLOYMENT

2-270. Units move rapidly through their attack positions and across the LD, which should be controlled by friendly forces. The leader considers METT-TC when choosing the combat formation which best balances firepower, tempo, security, and control.

ACTIONS AT THE PROBABLE LINE OF DEPLOYMENT, ASSAULT POSITION

2-271. The attacking unit splits into one or more assault and support forces as it reaches the PLD, if not already accomplished. All forces supporting the assault should be set in their support-by-fire position before the assault force crosses the LD. The assault force maneuvers against or around the enemy to take advantage of support force's efforts to suppress targeted enemy positions.

CONDUCTING THE BREACH

2-272. As necessary, the platoon conducts a combined arms breach. The preferred method of fighting through a defended obstacle is to employ an in-stride breach. However, the leader must be prepared to conduct a deliberate breach. (Refer to appendix H for more information on breaching.)

ASSAULTING THE OBJECTIVE

2-273. The leader employs all means of direct and indirect fire support to destroy and to suppress the enemy, and to sustain the momentum of attack. Attacking units move as quickly as possible onto and through the objective. Depending on the size and preparation of enemy forces, it may be necessary to isolate and destroy portions of the enemy in sequence.

CONSOLIDATING ON THE OBJECTIVE

2-274. Immediately after an assault, the attacking unit seeks to exploit its success. It may be necessary, though, to consolidate its gains. Consolidation can vary from repositioning force and security elements on the objective, to reorganization the attacking force, to the organization and detailed improvement of the position for defensive missions.

TRANSITION

2-275. After seizing the objective, the unit typically transitions to some other type of task. This operation could be the site exploitation or pursuit, or perhaps a defense. Transitions (through branches and sequels) are addressed and planned prior to undertaking the offensive task. Transitions are discussed in section VI of this chapter.

PLAN

2-276. In an attack, friendly forces seek to place the enemy in a position where the enemy can be defeated or destroyed easily. The leader seeks to keep the enemy off-balance while continually reducing the enemy's options. In an attack, the leader focuses movement and maneuver effects, supported by the other warfighting functions, on those enemy forces seeking to prevent the unit from accomplishing its mission and seizing its objective. Planning helps the leader synchronize the effects of combat power through TLP. (Refer to appendix A for more information.)

MISSION COMMAND

2-277. The leader states the desired effect of fires on the enemy weapon systems, such as suppression or destruction, as part of his planning process. The leader assigns subordinate units their missions and imposes those control measures necessary to synchronize and maintain control over the operation.

2-278. Using the enemy situational and weapons templates previously developed, the leader determines the probable LC and enemy trigger lines. As the leader arrays subordinate elements to shape the battlefield, friendly weapon systems are matched against the enemy has to determine the PLD. Once the leader determines the PLD, the leader establishes how long it takes subordinates to move from the LD to the PLD and all support-by-fire positions the attack requires. The leader establishes when and where the force must maneuver into enemy direct-fire range.

2-279. In addition to accomplishing the mission, every attack plan must contain provisions for exploiting success or all advantages may arise during the operation. The leader exploits success by aggressively executing the plan, promoting subordinate leader initiative, and using units that can rapidly execute battle drills.

MOVEMENT AND MANEUVER

2-280. In the plan of attack, the Infantry leader seeks to surprise the enemy by choosing an unexpected direction, time, type, or strength for attacking and by exploiting the success of military deception operations. Surprise delays enemy reactions, overloads and confuses enemy command and control, induces psychological shock in the enemy, and reduces the coherence of the enemy's defensive operations. The leader achieves tactical surprise by attacking in bad weather and over seemingly impassable terrain, conducting feints and demonstrations, maintaining a high tempo, destroying enemy forces, and employing sound OPSEC. The leader may plan different attack times for decisive and shaping operations to mislead the enemy and allow the shifting of supporting fires to successive attacking

Chapter 2

echelons. However, simultaneous attacks provide a means to maximize the effects of mass in the initial assault. They also prevent the enemy from concentrating defensive fires against successive attacks.

2-281. The platoon leader often will find himself as the observer (and executor) of company and battalion level fires. Understanding the concept of echelon fires is critical for indirect fire plan to be synchronized with the maneuver plan. The purpose of echeloning fires is to maintain constant fires on a target while using the optimum delivery system up to the point of its risk-estimate distance in combat operations or minimum safe distance (MSD) in training. Echeloning fires provides protection for friendly forces as they move to and assault an objective, allowing them to close with minimal casualties. It prevents the enemy from observing and engaging the assault by forcing the enemy to take cover, allowing the friendly force to continue the advance unimpeded.

2-282. In planning Infantry leaders focus on the routes, formations, and navigational aids they will use to traverse the ground from the LD or PD to the objective. Some terrain locations may require the attacking unit to change its combat formation, direction of movement, or movement technique when it reaches those locations. The unit can post guides at these critical locations to ensure maintaining control over the movement.

INTELLIGENCE

2-283. To employ the proper capabilities and tactics, leader and subordinate leaders must have detailed knowledge of the enemy's organization, equipment, and tactics. They must understand enemy's strengths and weaknesses. The platoon leader may need to request information through the CoIST, from the battalion staff to answer platoon information requirements. (Refer to FM 3-21.10 for more information.)

2-284. Generally, if the leader does not have good intelligence and does not know where the overwhelming majority of the enemy's units and systems are located, the leader cannot conduct a deliberate operation. The attacking unit must conduct a movement to contact, conduct a hasty operation, or collect more combat information.

FIRES

2-285. The planning process synchronizes the unit's scheme of maneuver with the indirect fire support plan. It must identify critical times and places where the Infantry leader needs the maximum effects from fire-support assets. Leaders combine maneuver with fires to mass effects, achieve surprise, destroy enemy forces, and obtain decisive results.

2-286. The goal of Infantry leader's attack criteria is to focus fires on seizing the initiative. The leader emphasizes simple and rapidly integrated direct and indirect fire support plans. This is done using quick-fire planning techniques and good SOPs. Leader integrates fire assets as far forward as possible in the movement formation to facilitate early emplacement. Fires concentrate (mass) on forward enemy elements to enable maneuver efforts to close with the enemy positions.

SUSTAINMENT

2-287. The leader and subordinate unit leaders must plan to provide support and services to ensure freedom of action, extend operational reach, and prolong endurance. Sustainment is the provision of logistics, personnel services, and health service support (HSS) necessary to maintain operations until mission accomplishment.

PROTECTION

2-288. Protection facilitates the Infantry leader's ability to maintain force integrity and combat power. Protection determines the degree to which potential threats can disrupt operations and counters or mitigates those threats. Emphasis on protection increases during preparation and continues throughout execution. Protection is a continuing activity; it integrates all protection capabilities to safeguard bases, secure routes, and protect forces.

PREPARE

2-289. Even in fluid situations, attacks are best organized and coordinated in AA. If the leader decides rapid action is essential to retain a tactical advantage, he may opt not to use an AA. Detailed advance planning, combined with digital communications, SOP, and battle drills, may reduce negative impacts of such a decision.

2-290. Unless already in an AA, the attacking unit moves into one during the preparation phase. The unit moves with as much secrecy as possible, normally at night and along routes preventing or degrading the enemy's capabilities to visually observe or otherwise detect the movement. It avoids congesting its AA and occupies it minimal possible time. While in the AA, each unit is responsible for its own protection activities, such as local security.

2-291. The attacking unit should continue its TLP and priorities of work to the extent the situation and mission allow before moving to attack positions. These preparations include but are not necessarily limited to:

- Protecting the force.
- Conducting task organization.
- Performing reconnaissance.
- Refining the plan.
- Briefing the troops.
- Conducting rehearsals, to include test firing of weapons.
- Moving logistics and medical support forward.
- Promoting adequate rest for both leaders and Soldiers.
- Positioning the force for subsequent action.

2-292. As part of TLP, leaders at all levels should conduct a personal reconnaissance of the actual terrain when this will not compromise operational security or result in excessive risk to the unit leadership. Modern information systems can enable leaders to conduct a virtual reconnaissance when a physical reconnaissance is not practical. If a limited-visibility attack is planned, they also should reconnoiter the terrain at night.

EXECUTE

2-293. Executing an attack is a series of advances and assaults by attacking units until they secure the final objective characterizes the attack. Leaders at all levels must use their initiative to shift their main effort between units as necessary to take advantage of opportunities and momentum to ensure the enemy's rapid destruction. Attacking units move as quickly as possible, following reconnaissance elements or probes through gaps in the enemy's defenses. They shift their strength to reinforce success and carry the battle deep into the enemy's rear. The leader does not delay the attack to preserve the alignment of subordinate units or to adhere closely to the preconceived plan of attack.

2-294. The leader avoids becoming so committed to the initial plan that opportunities are neglected, and is mentally prepared to abandon failed attacks in order to exploit all unanticipated successes or enemy errors. This is achieved by designating another unit to conduct the decisive operation in response to the changing situation.

2-295. The following sequence is used to execute an attack:
- Gain and maintain enemy contact.
- Disrupt the enemy.
- Fix the enemy.
- Maneuver.
- Follow through.

GAIN AND MAINTAIN ENEMY CONTACT

2-296. Gaining and maintaining contact with the enemy when he is determined to break contact is vital to the success of the offense. A defending enemy generally establishes a security area around his forces to make early contact with the attacking forces. This helps determine their capabilities, intent, chosen COA, and delays their approach. The enemy commander wants to use his security area to strip away friendly reconnaissance forces and hide his dispositions, capabilities, and intent. The goal is to compel the attacking force to conduct movement to contact against his defending force while knowing the exact location of the attacking forces.

DISRUPT THE ENEMY

2-297. Disrupting one or more parts of the enemy weakens the entire force and allows the friendly leader to attack the remaining enemy force in an asymmetrical manner. The assessment and decisions regarding what to disrupt, when to disrupt, and to what end are critical.

2-298. Once all types of contact, even sensor contact is made with the enemy, the leader wants to use the element of surprise to conduct shaping operations striking at the enemy and disrupt both the enemy's combined arms team and his ability to plan and control his forces. Once this disruption process begins, it continues throughout the attack.

FIX THE ENEMY

2-299. A primary purpose in fixing the enemy is to isolate the objective of the force conducting the echelons decisive operation to prevent the enemy from maneuvering to reinforce the unit targeted for destruction. The Infantry leader does everything possible to limit the options available to his opponent. Fixing an enemy into a given position or a COA and controlling his movements limit his options and reduce the amount of uncertainty on the battlefield.

2-300. Fixing the enemy is done with the minimum amount of force. The Infantry leader normally allocates the bulk of his combat power to the force conducting his decisive operation. Fixing operations are, by necessity, shaping operations illustrating economy of force as a principle of war. Therefore, the leader must carefully consider which enemy elements to fix and target only those he can significantly affect the outcome of the fight.

MANEUVER

2-301. The Infantry leader maneuvers his forces to gain positional advantage to seize, retain, and exploit the initiative while avoiding the enemy's defensive strength. He employs tactics defeating the enemy by attacking through a point of relative weakness, such as a flank or the rear. The key for success is to strike hard and fast, overwhelm a portion of the enemy force, and quickly transition to the next objective or phase, thus maintaining the momentum of attack without reducing the pressure. Examples of maneuver include—

Movement From the Line of Departure to the Probable Line of Deployment

2-302. The unit transitions from troop movement to maneuver once it crosses the LD. It moves aggressively and as quickly as the terrain and enemy situation allow. It moves forward using appropriate movement techniques assisted by the fires of supporting units. Fire and movement are integrated and coordinated closely. Suppressive fires facilitate friendly movement, and friendly movement facilitates more fires. Whenever possible, the attacking unit uses avenues of approach avoiding strong enemy defensive positions, takes advantage of all available cover and concealment, and places the unit on the flanks and rear of the defending enemy. Where cover and concealment are not available, the unit uses obscurants to conceal its movement.

Actions at the Probable Line of Deployment, Assault Position, or Final Coordination Line

2-303. The attacking unit maintains the pace of its advance as it approaches its probable line of deployment. The attacking unit splits into one or more assault and support forces once it reaches the PLD if not previously completed. All forces supporting the assault force should be set in their support-by-fire positions before the assault force crosses the probable line of deployment. The leader synchronizes the occupation of support-by-fire positions with the maneuver of the supported attacking unit to limit the vulnerability of forces occupying these positions. Leaders use unit tactical SOPs, battle drills, prearranged

Chapter 2

signals, engagement area, and TRP to control direct fires from these supporting positions and normally employs RFL between converging forces.

Breaching Operations

2-304. To conduct breaching operations successfully, the platoon applies the breaching fundamentals of suppress, obscure, secure, reduce, and assault (SOSRA). The support force sets the conditions, the breach force reduces, clears, and marks the required number of lanes through the enemy's tactical obstacles to support the maneuver of the assault force. The leader must clearly identify the conditions allowing the breach force to proceed to avoid confusion. From the PLD, the assault force maneuvers against or around the enemy to take advantage of support force's efforts to suppress the targeted enemy positions. (Refer to appendix H, section II of this publication for a more detailed explanation.)

Actions on the Objective

2-305. The effects of overwhelming and simultaneous application of fire, movement, and shock action characterize the final assault. This violent assault destroys or defeats and drives the enemy from the objective area. Small units conduct the final assault while operating under the control of the appropriate echelon command post.

2-306. Mounted forces have the option of conducting this final assault in either a mounted or dismounted configuration.

2-307. The platoon leader and company commander must decide whether or not the assault element will assault the objective mounted or dismounted. Generally, if the enemy is in restrictive terrain and poses a significant antiarmor threat, the platoon assaults the objective dismounted. If the objective is on unrestrictive terrain and the enemy's antiarmor threat is minimal, the assault element may assault mounted.

- Mounted assault. If the platoon leader decides to assault mounted, then as soon as the BFVs assault across the objective, the rifle squads dismount to clear the objective of enemy forces
- Dismounted assault. If the platoon leader decides to assault the objective dismounted, the platoon dismounts its rifle squads to assault the objective, and the vehicles move to support-by-fire positions. If possible, the platoon dismounts in an area that offers some cover and concealment from enemy observation and direct fire, which allows the platoon to assemble and orient appropriately. The dismount point must be close enough to the objective that the rifle squads do not become excessively fatigued while moving to the objective.

2-308. Whether assaulting mounted or dismounted, the platoon leader or company team commander designates the dismount point based on the following factors:
- Short of the objective (near or at the assault position).
- On the objective.
- Beyond the objective.

Short of the Objective

2-309. The advantages of dismounting the rifle squads before reaching the objective include: protection for the squad members while dismounting; better control at the dismount point; and an ability to suppress the enemy with indirect fires without endangering the platoon. The disadvantages include: exposure of the rifle squads to indirect and direct fires as the move toward the objective; and the enemy may target possible dismount points with indirect fires.

On the Objective

2-310. The advantages of dismounting the rifle squads on the objective include: better platoon speed toward the objective; protection for the rifle squads and the platoon maneuvers toward the objective. The disadvantages include: difficult to orient the rifle squads on specific locations or objectives while riding in the vehicle; difficult to control at the dismount point; and the vehicles are vulnerable to short-range, handheld antiarmor systems while dismounting the rifle squads.

Beyond the Objective

2-311. Dismounting beyond the objective has several potential advantages: effective control at the dismount point; easier to orient the rifle squads to the terrain and the objective; and confused or disoriented enemy are forced to fight in an unexpected direction. Significant disadvantages remain the platoon is vulnerable to attack from enemy defensive positions in-depth; the platoon is vulnerable to attack by enemy reserve forces; the vehicles are vulnerable to short-range, handheld antiarmor systems; and it is difficult to control direct fires, increasing the risk of fratricide.

2-312. Ideally, the platoon's assault element occupies the assault position without the enemy detecting the platoon's elements. Preparations in the assault position may include preparing Bangalore, other breaching equipment, or demolitions; fixing bayonets; lifting or shifting direct fires; or preparing smoke pots.

2-313. If the platoon is detected as it nears its assault position, indirect fire suppression is required on the objective and the support element increases its volume of fire. If the platoon needs to make last-minute preparations, then it occupies the assault position. If the platoon does not need to stop, it passes through the assault position, treating it as a PLD and assaults the objective. Sometimes, a platoon must halt to complete preparation and to ensure synchronization of friendly forces. Once the assault element moves forward of the assault position, the assault continues. If the assault element stops or turns back, the element could sustain excessive casualties.

2-314. Infantry leaders employ all direct and indirect fire support means to destroy and suppress the enemy and sustain the momentum of attack. By carefully synchronizing the effects of indirect-fire systems and available CAS, leaders improve the likelihood of success. Fires are planned in series or groups to support maneuver against enemy forces on or near the geographical objective. As the leader shifts artillery fires and obscurants from the objective to other targets, the assault element moves rapidly across the objective. The support element must not allow its suppressive fires to lapse. These fires isolate the

Chapter 2

objective and prevent the enemy from reinforcing or counterattacking. They also destroy escaping enemy forces and systems.

FOLLOW THROUGH

2-315. After seizing the objective, the Infantry force has two alternatives: exploit success and continue the attack or terminate the offensive mission. After seizing an objective, the most likely on-order mission is to continue the attack. During consolidation, the unit continues TLP in preparation for all on-order missions assigned by a higher headquarters.

ASSESS

2-316. Assessment refers to the continuous monitoring and evaluation of current situation, particularly the enemy, and progress of an operation. Assessment precedes and guides every operations process activity and concludes each operation or phase of an operation. It involves a comparison of forecasted outcomes to actual events. Assessment entails three tasks:

- Continuously assessing the enemy's reactions and vulnerabilities.
- Continuously monitoring the situation and progress of operation towards the commander's desired end state.
- Evaluating the operation against measures of effectiveness and measures of performance.

INITIAL ASSESSMENT

2-317. Upon receiving the mission, leaders perform an initial assessment of the situation and METT-TC, focusing on the unit's role in the larger operation, and allocating time for planning and preparing. The two most important products from this initial assessment should be at least a partial restated mission, and a timeline. Leaders issue their initial WARNORD on this first assessment and time allocation.

INTELLIGENCE ASSESSMENT

2-318. Army forces conduct (plan, prepare, execute, and assess) operations based on the all-source intelligence assessment developed by the intelligence section. The all-source intelligence assessment is expressed as part of the intelligence estimate. They are continuous and occur throughout the operations process and intelligence process. Most products resulting from all-source intelligence are initially developed during planning, and updated as needed throughout preparation and execution based on information gained from continuous assessment.

EXECUTION ASSESSMENT

2-319. During execution, assessment of risk assists the leader in making informed decisions on changing task organization, shifting priorities of effort and support, and shaping future operations. Effectiveness entails making accurate assessments and good decisions about how to fight the enemy. Mission complements command by using the most efficient means available. Vital supporting concepts are TLP, actions on contact, and risk management. Leaders use the assessment process to generate combat power.

SPECIAL PURPOSE ATTACKS

2-320. Special purpose attacks are ambush, counterattack, demonstration, feint, raid, and spoiling attack. (Refer to ADRP 3-90 for more information.) The commander's intent and METT-TC determine which special purpose attacks to employ. Each attack can be conducted as either a hasty or a deliberate operation. The commander's intent and METT-TC determine the specific attack form. As subordinate attack tasks, they share many of the planning, preparation, and execution considerations of attack. Demonstrations and feints, while forms of attack, also are associated with military deception operations. (Refer to FM 3-13 for more information.)

AMBUSH

2-321. An ambush is an assault by fire or other destructive means from concealed positions on a moving or temporarily halted enemy. An ambush stops, denies, or destroys enemy forces by maximizing the element of surprise. Ambushes can employ direct fire systems as well as other destructive means, such as command-detonated mines, indirect fires, and supporting nonlethal effects. They may include an assault to close with and destroy enemy forces. In an ambush, ground objectives do not have to be seized and held.

2-322. The three forms of ambush are point, area, and antiarmor ambush. In a point ambush, a unit deploys to attack a single kill zone. In an area ambush, a unit deploys into two or more related point ambushes. Units smaller than a platoon normally do not conduct an area ambush.

2-323. A typical ambush is organized into three elements: assault, support, and security. The assault element fires into the kill zone. Its goal is to destroy the enemy force. When used, the assault force attacks into and clears the kill zone. It also may be assigned additional tasks, to include searching for items of intelligence value, capturing prisoners, photographing new types of equipment and when unable to take enemy equipment, completing the destruction of enemy equipment to avoid its immediate reuse. The support element supports the assault element by firing into and around the kill zone, and it provides the ambush's primary killing power. The support element attempts to destroy the majority of enemy combat power before the assault element moves into the objective or kill zone. The security element isolates the kill zone, provides early warning of arrival of all enemy relief forces, and provides security for the assault and support elements. It secures the objective rally point (ORP) and blocks enemy avenues of approach into and out of the ambush site, which prevents the enemy from entering or leaving. (Refer to chapter 6 this publication for detailed discussion.)

COUNTERATTACK

2-324. A counterattack is an attack by part or all of a defending force against an enemy attacking force, for such specific purposes as regaining ground lost or cutting off or destroying enemy advance units. The general objective is to deny the enemy his goal in attacking. The leader directs a counterattack normally conducted from a defensive posture, to defeat or destroy enemy forces, exploit an enemy weakness such as an exposed flank, or to regain control of terrain and facilities after an enemy success. A unit conducts a counterattack to seize the initiative from the enemy through offensive action. A counterattacking force maneuvers to isolate and destroy a designated enemy force. It can be an assault by fire into an engagement area to defeat or destroy an enemy force, restore the original position, or block an enemy penetration. Once launched, the counterattack normally becomes a decisive operation for the leader conducting the counterattack.

2-325. To be decisive, the counterattack occurs when the enemy is overextended, dispersed, and disorganized during his attack. All counterattacks should be rehearsed in the same conditions they will be conducted. Careful consideration is given to the event triggering the counterattack. Once committed, the counterattack force conducts the decisive operation.

DEMONSTRATIONS

2-326. In military deception, a demonstration is a show of force in an area where a decision is not sought but made to deceive a threat. It is similar to a feint, but no actual contact with the threat is intended.

FEINTS

2-327. A feint is an attack used to deceive the enemy as to the location or time of the actual decisive operation. Forces conducting a feint seek direct fire contact with the enemy but avoid decisive engagement. As in the demonstration, leader use feints in conjunction with other military deception activities.

RAID

2-328. A raid is a limited-objective, deliberate operation entailing swift penetration of hostile terrain. A raid is not intended to hold territory; and it requires detailed intelligence, preparation, and planning. The Infantry platoon and squad conducts raids as part of a larger force to accomplish a number of missions, including the following:

- Capture prisoners, installations, or enemy materiel.
- Capture or destroy specific enemy command and control locations.
- Destroy enemy materiel or installations.
- Obtain information concerning enemy locations, dispositions, strength, intentions, or methods of operation.
- Confuse the enemy or disrupt his plans.
- Liberate friendly personnel.

SPOILING ATTACK

2-329. A spoiling attack is a tactical maneuver employed to impair a hostile attack while the enemy is in the process of forming or assembling for an attack. The spoiling attack usually employs heavy, attack helicopter, or fire support elements to attack on enemy assembly positions in front of a main line of resistance or battle position.

2-330. The objective of a spoiling attack is to disrupt the enemy's offensive capabilities and timelines while destroying targeted enemy personnel and equipment, not to secure terrain and other physical objectives. Two conditions must be met to conduct a survivable spoiling attack:

- The spoiling attack's objective must be obtainable before the enemy being able to respond to the attack in a synchronized and coordinated manner.
- The force conducting the spoiling attack must be prevented from becoming over extended.

2-331. Infantry forces conduct a spoiling attack whenever possible during friendly defensive missions to strike an enemy force while it is in AA or attack positions preparing for its own offensive mission or is stopped temporarily.

ELECTRONIC WARFARE

2-332. Army electronic warfare operations seek to enable the land force commander to support unified land operations through decisive action. Decisive action consists of the simultaneous combination of offense, defense, and stability or defense support of civil authorities appropriate to the mission and environment. The central idea of unified land operations is to seize, retain, and exploit the initiative to gain and maintain a position of relative advantage in sustained land operations in order to create the conditions for favorable conflict resolution.

2-333. The foundation of unified land operations is built on initiative, decisive action, and mission command—linked and nested through purposeful and simultaneous execution of both combined arms maneuver and wide area security—to achieve the commander's intent and desired end state. Appropriately applied, electronic warfare enables successful unified land operations. Commanders and staffs determine which resident and joint force electronic warfare capabilities to use in support of each element of decisive action. As they apply the appropriate level of electronic warfare effort to support these elements, commanders can seize, retain, and exploit the initiative within the electromagnetic environment.

2-334. Once a commander can seize, retain, and exploit the initiative within the electromagnetic environment, then control becomes possible. Commanders plan, prepare, execute, and assess electronic warfare operations to control the electromagnetic spectrum.

2-335. To exercise electromagnetic spectrum control commanders effectively apply and integrate electronic warfare operations across the warfighting functions: mission command, movement and maneuver, intelligence, fires, sustainment, and protection.

SECTION VIII – OPERATION DURING LIMITED VISIBILITY

2-336. Effective use of advanced optical sights and equipment during limited visibility attacks enhances the ability of squads and platoons to achieve surprise, hit targets, and cause panic in a lesser-equipped enemy. Advanced optics and equipment allow the

Chapter 2

Infantry Soldier to see farther and with greater clarity. They provide an advantage over the enemy. Infantry platoons and squads have—

- Night vision equipment mounted on the helmet of each Soldier.
- Weapon-mounted and handheld devices to identify and designate targets.
- Vision devices and thermal imagers on the BFV for both the driver and the vehicle commander manning the turret.

2-337. Night vision devices provide good visibility in all but pitch-black conditions but do somewhat limit the Soldier's field of view. Since they do not transmit a light source, the enemy detection devices cannot detect them.

2-338. The BFV is as effective at night as during the day. It can be driven and its weapon systems can be fired during limited visibility. The driver has an enhanced vision capability, and the vehicle commander has both an enhanced vision and thermal imaging capability. The BFV is capable of accurately identifying its current location with the onboard GPS. The common operational picture allows leaders to locate their subordinate units at all times.

2-339. Infantry leaders and Soldiers have an increased ability to designate and control fires during limited visibility. There are three types of advanced optics and equipment for use in fire control:

- *Target designators.* Leaders can designate targets with greater precision using infrared laser pointers that place an infrared light to designate targets and sectors of fire and to concentrate fire. The leader lazes a target on which he directs his Soldiers to place their fires. The Soldiers then use their weapon's aiming lights to engage the target.
- *Aiming lights.* Soldiers with aiming lights have greater accuracy of fires during limited visibility. Each Soldier in the Infantry platoon is equipped with an aiming light for his individual weapon. Aiming lights work with the individual Soldier's helmet-mounted night vision goggles. It puts an infrared light on the target at the point of aim.
- *Target illuminators.* Leaders can designate larger targets using target illuminators. Target illuminators are essentially infrared light sources that light the target, making it easier to acquire effectively. Leaders and Soldiers use the infrared devices to identify enemy or friendly personnel and then engage targets using their aiming lights.

2-340. Illuminating rounds fired to burn on the ground can mark objectives. This helps the platoon orient on the objective, but may adversely affect night vision devices.

2-341. Leaders plan but may not use illumination during limited visibility attacks. Battalion commanders normally control conventional illumination, but may authorize the company team commander to do so. If the commander decides to use conventional illumination, he should not call for it until the assault is initiated or the attack is detected. It should be placed on several locations over a wide area to confuse the enemy as to the exact place of the attack. It should be placed beyond the objective to help assaulting Soldiers see and fire at withdrawing or counterattacking enemy Soldiers.

2-342. The platoon leader, squad leaders, and vehicle commanders must develop TACSOPs and sound COAs to synchronize the employment of infrared illumination devices, target designators, and aiming lights during their assault on the objective. These include using luminous tape or chemical lights to mark personnel and using weapons control restrictions.

2-343. The platoon leader may use the following techniques to increase control during the assault:

- Use no flares, grenades, or smoke on the objective.
- Use only certain personnel with night vision devices to engage targets on the objective.
- Use a magnetic azimuth for maintaining direction.
- Use mortar or artillery rounds to orient attacking units.
- Use a base squad or fire team to pace and guide others.
- Reduce intervals between Soldiers and squads.

2-344. Like a daylight attack, indirect and direct fires are planned for a limited visibility attack, but are not executed unless the platoon is detected or is ready to assault. Some weapons may fire before the attack and maintain a pattern to deceive the enemy or to help cover noise made by the platoon's movement. This is not done if it will disclose the attack.

2-345. Smoke further reduces the enemy's visibility, particularly if he has night vision devices. The forward observer fires smoke rounds close to or on enemy positions so it does not restrict friendly movement or hinder the reduction of obstacles. Employing smoke on the objective during the assault may make it hard for assaulting Soldiers to find enemy fighting positions. If enough thermal sights are available, smoke on the objective may provide a decisive advantage for a well-trained platoon.

Note. If the enemy is equipped with night vision devices, leaders must evaluate the risk of using each technique and ensure the mission is not compromised by the enemy's ability to detect infrared light sources.

SECTION IX – BATTLEFIELD OBSCURATION

2-346. Obscuration mission planning and execution can occur during both the offense and the defense and can be very effective. Firing smoke on enemy positions can degrade the vision of gunners and known or suspected observation posts, preventing them from seeing or tracking targets and, thereby, reducing their effectiveness. When employed against an attacking force, white phosphorus (WP) can cause confusion and disorientation by degrading the enemy's mission command capabilities; while friendly units retain the ability to engage the enemy using thermal sights and range cards. Enemy vehicles become silhouetted as they emerge from the smoke. If smoke employment is planned and executed correctly, this occurs as the enemy reaches the trigger line.

PLANNING CONSIDERATIONS

2-347. Obscuration missions are important functions for mortars. Smoke missions must be planned well in advance so that the mortar carriers are loaded with a sufficient number of smoke rounds.

2-348. Atmospheric stability, wind velocity, and wind direction are the most important factors when planning target effects for smoke and WP mortar rounds. The effects of atmospheric stability can determine whether mortar smoke is effective at all or, if effective, how much ammunition is needed. The considerations are—

- During unstable conditions, mortar smoke and WP rounds are almost ineffective—the smoke does not spread but often climbs straight up and quickly dissipates.
- Under moderately unstable atmospheric conditions, base-ejecting smoke rounds are more effective than BFV bursting WP rounds.
- Under stable conditions, both red phosphorous and WP rounds are effective.
- The higher the humidity, the better the screening effects of mortar rounds.

2-349. The terrain in the target area affects smoke and WP rounds. If the terrain in the target area is swampy, rain-soaked, or snow-covered, then burning smoke rounds may not be effective. These rounds produce smoke by ejecting felt wedges soaked in phosphorus. These wedges then burn on the ground, producing a dense, long-lasting cloud. If the wedges fall into mud, water, or snow, they can extinguish. Shallow water can reduce the smoke produced by these rounds by as much as 50 percent. The terrain in the target area affects BFV bursting WP rounds little, except that deep snow and cold temperatures can reduce the smoke cloud by about 25 percent.

EMPLOYMENT CONSIDERATIONS

2-350. The vehicle smoke grenade launchers can provide a screening, incendiary, marking, and casualty-producing effect. It produces a localized, instantaneous smoke cloud by scattering burning WP particles. The 120-mm heavy mortar and 81-mm medium mortar WP and red phosphorus rounds produce a long-lasting and wide area smoke screen and can be used for incendiary effects, marking, obscuring, screening, and casualty producing. The 60-mm lightweight company mortar WP round can be used as a screening, signaling, and incendiary agent. All mortar smoke rounds can be used as an aid in target location and navigation.

SECTION X – TRANSITIONS

2-351. The Infantry leader halts an offensive task when he accomplishes his mission, culminates, or receives a change in mission from higher headquarters.

CONSOLIDATION

2-352. Consolidation is the process of organizing and strengthening a newly captured position so it can be defended. Normally, the attacking unit tries to exploit its success regardless the type of assault. In some situations, however, the unit may have to consolidate its gains. Consolidation may vary from a rapid repositioning of forces and security elements on the objective, to a reorganization of the attacking force, to the organization and detailed improvement of positions for defensive missions.

2-353. Consolidation consists of actions taken to secure the objective and defend against an enemy counterattack. Leaders use TLP to plan and prepare for this phase of operation. They ensure the unit is ready to conduct the following actions that usually are part of consolidation:

- Eliminate enemy resistance on the objective.
- Establish security beyond the objective by securing areas that may be the source of enemy direct fires or enemy artillery observation.
- Establish additional security measures such as observation posts and patrols.
- Prepare for and assist the passage of follow-on forces (if required).
- Continue to improve security by conducting other necessary defensive actions. These defensive actions include engagement area development, direct fire planning, and battle position preparation.
- Adjust final protective fires and register targets along likely mounted and dismounted avenues of approach.
- Protect the obstacle reduction effort.
- Secure enemy detainees.
- Prepare for enemy counterattack.

REORGANIZATION

2-354. Reorganization usually is conducted concurrently with consolidation. It consists of actions taken to prepare units for follow-on operations. As with consolidation, unit leaders plan and prepare for reorganization as they conduct TLP. Unit leaders ensure the following actions are conducted:

- Provide essential medical treatment and evacuate casualties as necessary.
- Treat and evacuate wounded detainees and process the remainder of detainees.
- Cross-level personnel and adjust task organization as required to support the next phase or mission.
- Conducts resupply operations, including rearming and refueling.
- Redistribute ammunition.
- Conduct required maintenance.
- Continue improvement of defensive positions as necessary.

CONTINUING OPERATIONS

2-355. For all attacks, Infantry units should and must plan to exploit success. However, at the conclusion of an engagement, the unit leader may be forced to defend. For short defenses, units make use of existing terrain to enhance their survivability. If a longer defense is envisioned, engineer assets immediately should refocus their efforts on providing survivability support (fighting positions and similar activities). Engineer assets should do this even as they sustain mobility and integrate countermobility into the planned defensive mission. The Infantry leader considers the higher commander's concept of the operation, friendly capabilities, and enemy situation when making the decision to defend or continuing the offense.

TRANSITION TO THE DEFENSE

2-356. As offensive tasks approach a culmination point, the unit leader could order a transition to defensive tasks. The leader can use two basic techniques when he transitions to the defense. The first technique is leading elements to commit forces and push forward to claim enough ground to establish a security area anchored on defensible terrain. The second technique is to establish a security area generally along the unit's final positions, moving the main body rearward to defensible terrain.

2-357. The Infantry leader anticipating the termination of unit offensive tasks prepares orders including the time or circumstances under which the current offensive task transitions to a defensive-focused mission, the missions and locations of subordinate units, and mission command measures. As the unit transitions from an offensive to a defensive focus, the leader takes the following actions:

- Maintains contact and surveillance of the enemy, using a combination of reconnaissance units and surveillance assets to develop the information required to plan future actions.
- Establishes a security area and local security measures.
- Redeploys indirect fire assets to ensure the support of security forces.
- Redeploys forces based on probable future employment.
- Maintains or regains contact with adjacent units in a contiguous area of operations and ensures units remain capable of mutual support in a noncontiguous area of operations.
- Request engineer assets to shift the emphasis from mobility to countermobility and survivability.
- Consolidates and reorganizes.

TRANSITION TO STABILITY

2-358. As an offensive task approaches a culmination, or upon order from higher headquarters, the Infantry leader could order a transition to stability focused mission. These tasks establish a safe, secure environment facilitating reconciliation among local or regional threat. Stability tasks aim to establish conditions supporting the transition to legitimate host-nation governance, a functioning civil society, and a viable market economy.

2-359. For the Infantry platoon the platoon leader must ensure contingencies are planned to transition quickly from offense to stability and vice versa. For example, it may be tactically wise for him to plan a defensive contingency with on-order offensive missions or stability tasks could deteriorate.

2-360. Subordinate leaders must be fully trained to recognize activities initiating this transition. Actions in one unit's area of operation can affect whatever type operation an adjacent unit is conducting. For example, an offensive task may cause noncombatants to be displaced to another section of the city creating a humanitarian assistance mission for the unit in the area of operation.

This page intentionally left blank.

Chapter 3

Defense

A defensive task is a task conducted to defeat an enemy attack, gain time, economize forces, and develop conditions favorable for offensive or stability tasks. (Refer to ADRP 3-90 for more information.) Normally, the defense alone cannot achieve a decision. However, it can set conditions for a counteroffensive or counterattack that enables Army forces to regain the initiative. Other reasons for conducting defensive tasks include, retain decisive terrain or deny a vital area to the enemy, attrition or fix the enemy as a prelude to the offense, counter surprise action by the enemy, or to increase the enemy's vulnerability by forcing the enemy commander to concentrate subordinate forces. This chapter covers basics of the defense, common defensive planning considerations, forms of the defense engagement area development, and transitions.

SECTION I – BASICS OF THE DEFENSE

3-1. The Infantry platoon and squad uses the defense to occupy and prepare positions and mass the effects of direct fires on likely avenues of approach or mobility corridors. While the offense is the most decisive type of combat operation, the defense is the stronger type. The following paragraphs discuss the basics of the defense.

Note. METT-TC considerations determine the characteristics, placement, movement and maneuver of defensive positions.

CHARACTERISTICS OF THE DEFENSE

3-2. The defense shares the following characteristics: preparation, security, disruption, mass and concentration, flexibility, maneuver, and operations in-depth. (Refer to ADRP 3-90 for more information.)

PREPARATION

3-3. The defense has inherent strengths. The defender arrives in the area of operation before the attacker and uses the available time to prepare. These preparations multiply the defense's effectiveness. Preparations end only when the defenders retrograde or begin to fight. Until then, preparations are continuous. Preparations in-depth continues, even as the close fight begins.

Chapter 3

SECURITY

3-4. Security helps deceive the enemy as to friendly locations, strengths, and weaknesses. It also inhibits or defeat enemy reconnaissance. Security measures provide early warning and disrupt enemy attacks early and continuously.

DISRUPTION

3-5. Defenders disrupt attackers' tempo and synchronization with actions designed to prevent them from massing combat power. Disruptive actions attempt to unhinge the enemy's preparations and, ultimately, his attacks. Methods include defeating or misdirecting enemy reconnaissance forces, breaking up his formations, isolating his units, and attacking or disrupting his systems.

MASS AND CONCENTRATION

3-6. Defenders seek to mass the effects of overwhelming combat power where they choose and shift it to support the decisive operation. To obtain an advantage at decisive points, defenders economize and accept risk in some areas; retain and, when necessary, reconstitute a reserve; and maneuver to gain local superiority at the point of decision. Unit leaders accept risk in some areas to mass effects elsewhere. Obstacles, security forces, and fires can assist in reducing risk.

FLEXIBILITY

3-7. The defense requires flexible plans. Planning focuses on preparation in-depth, use of reserves, and ability to shift the main effort. Leaders add flexibility by designating supplementary positions, designing counterattack plans, and preparing to counterattack.

MANEUVER

3-8. Maneuver allows the defender to take full advantage of area of operation and to mass and concentrate when desirable. Maneuver, through movement in combination with fire, allows the defender to achieve a position of advantage over the enemy to accomplish the mission. It also encompasses defensive actions such as security and support area operations.

OPERATION IN-DEPTH

3-9. Simultaneous application of combat power throughout the area of operation improves the chances for success while minimizing friendly casualties. Quick, violent, and simultaneous action throughout the depth of the defender's area of operation can hurt, confuse, and even paralyze an enemy force just as it is most exposed and vulnerable. Such actions weaken the enemy's will and do not allow all early enemy successes to build the confidence of the enemy's Soldiers and leaders. In-depth planning prevents the enemy from gaining momentum in the attack. Synchronization of decisive, shaping, and sustaining operations facilitates mission success.

DEFENSIVE TASKS

3-10. There are three basic defensive tasks: area defense, mobile, and retrograde. Each contains elements of the others, and usually contains both static and dynamic aspects. Infantry platoons serve as the primary maneuver element, or terrain-controlling units for the Infantry company. They can defend area of operation, positions; serve as a security force or reserve as part of the Infantry company's coordinated defense. (Refer to FM 3-90-1 for more information.)

3-11. As part of a defense, the Infantry platoon can defend, delay, withdraw, counterattack, and perform security tasks. The Infantry platoon usually defends, as part of the Infantry company's defense in the main battle area. It conducts the defense to achieve one or more of the following:
- Gain time.
- Retain essential terrain.
- Support other operations.
- Preoccupy the enemy in one area while friendly forces attack in another.
- Wear down enemy forces at a rapid rate while reinforcing friendly operations.

AREA DEFENSE

3-12. An area defense concentrates on denying enemy forces access to designated terrain for a specific time rather than destroying the enemy outright. The focus is on retaining terrain where the bulk of the defending force positions itself in mutually supporting positions and controls the terrain between positions. The defeat mechanism is fires into engagement area, which reserve units can supplement. The leader uses the reserve force to reinforce fires, add depth, block penetrations, restore positions, counterattack to destroy enemy forces, and seize the initiative.

Organization of Forces

3-13. The leader organizes the defending force to accomplish information collection, reconnaissance operations; security; main battle area; reserve; and sustainment missions. The leader has the option of defending forward or defending in-depth. When the leader defends forward within an area of operation, the force is organized so most of available combat power is committed early in the defensive effort. To accomplish this, the leader may deploy forces forward or plan counterattacks well forward in the main battle area or even beyond the main battle area. If the leader has the option of conducting a defense in-depth, security forces and forward main battle area elements are used to identify, define, and control the depth of the enemy's main effort while holding off secondary thrusts. This allows the leader to conserve combat power, strengthen the reserve, and better resource the counterattack.

Security

3-14. The leader balances the need to create a strong security force to shape the battle with the resulting diversion of combat power from the main body's decisive operation.

Chapter 3

The leader usually allocates security forces to provide early warning and protect those forces, systems, and locations necessary to conduct the decisive operation from unexpected enemy contact.

Main Battle Area

3-15. The leader builds the decisive operation around identified decisive points, such as key terrain or high-payoff targets. The leader positions the echelon main body within the main battle area where the leader wants to conduct the decisive operation. The leader organizes the main body to halt, defeat, and ultimately destroy attacking enemy forces. The majority of the main body deploys into prepared defensive positions within the main battle area.

Reserve

3-16. The reserve is not a committed force. The leader can assign it a wide variety of tasks on its commitment, and it must be prepared to perform other missions. In certain situations, it may become necessary to commit the reserve to restore the integrity of the defense by blocking an enemy penetration or reinforcing fires into an engagement area.

Sustainment

3-17. The sustainment mission in an area defense requires a careful balance between establishing forward supply stocks of petroleum, oil, and lubricants (POL); barrier materiel; and ammunition in adequate amounts to support defending units and having too many supplies located in forward locations that they cannot be rapidly moved in reacting to enemy advances. All suitable POL, barrier materiel, construction equipment, and laborers can be lawfully obtained from the civil infrastructure reducing the defending unit's transportation requirements. Likewise, maintenance and medical support with their associated repair parts and medical supplies also must be forward deployed.

Forms of Defensive Maneuver

3-18. Two forms of defensive maneuver within an area defense are defense in-depth and forward defense. The Infantry platoon is expected to be able to do both. While the Infantry company commander usually selects the type of area defense to use, the higher commander often defines the general defensive scheme for the Infantry company. The specific mission may impose constraints such as time, security, and retention of certain areas that are significant factors in determining how the Infantry company will defend.

Defense In-Depth

3-19. Defense in-depth reduces the risk of the attacking enemy quickly penetrating the defense. The enemy is unable to exploit a penetration because of additional defensive positions employed in-depth. (See figure 3-1.) The in-depth defense provides more space and time to defeat the enemy attack.

Defense

3-20. The Infantry platoon uses a defense in-depth when—
- The mission allows the Infantry platoon to fight throughout the depth of the areas of operations.
- The terrain does not favor a defense well forward, and better defensible terrain is available deeper in the areas of operations.
- Sufficient depth is available in the areas operations.
- Cover and concealment forward in the areas of operations is limited.
- Weapons of mass destruction may be used.

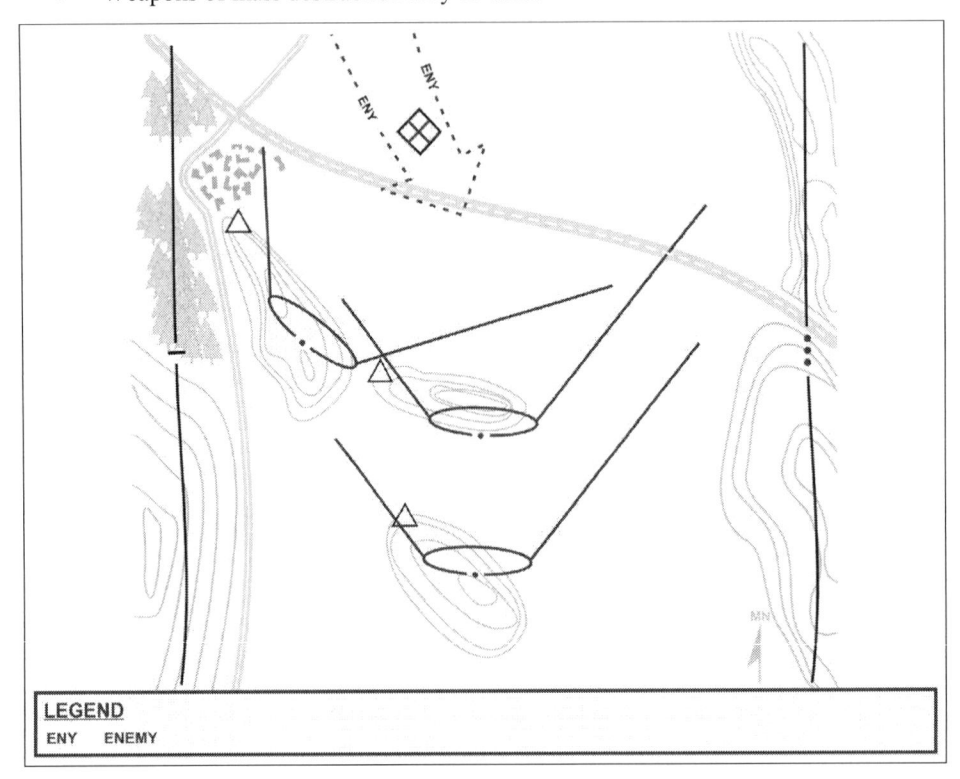

Figure 3-1. Platoon defense in-depth

Forward Defense

3-21. The intent of a forward defense is to prevent enemy penetration of the defense. (See figure 3-2, page 3-6.) Due to lack of depth, a forward defense is least preferred. The Infantry platoon deploys the majority of its combat power into forward defensive positions near the forward edge of the battle area. While the Infantry company may lack depth, the platoon and squads must build depth into the defense at their levels. The leader fights to retain the forward position, and may conduct counterattacks against enemy penetrations, or to destroy enemy forces in forward engagement area. Often, counterattacks are planned forward of the forward edge of the battle area to defeat the enemy.

Chapter 3

3-22. The Infantry platoon uses a forward defense when—
- Terrain forward in the areas of operations favors the defense.
- Strong existing natural or man-made obstacles, such as river or a rail lines, are located forward in areas of operations.
- The assigned area of operations lacks depth due to location of the area or facility to be protected.
- Cover and concealment in rear portions of the areas of operations is limited.
- Directed by higher headquarters to retain or initially control forward terrain.

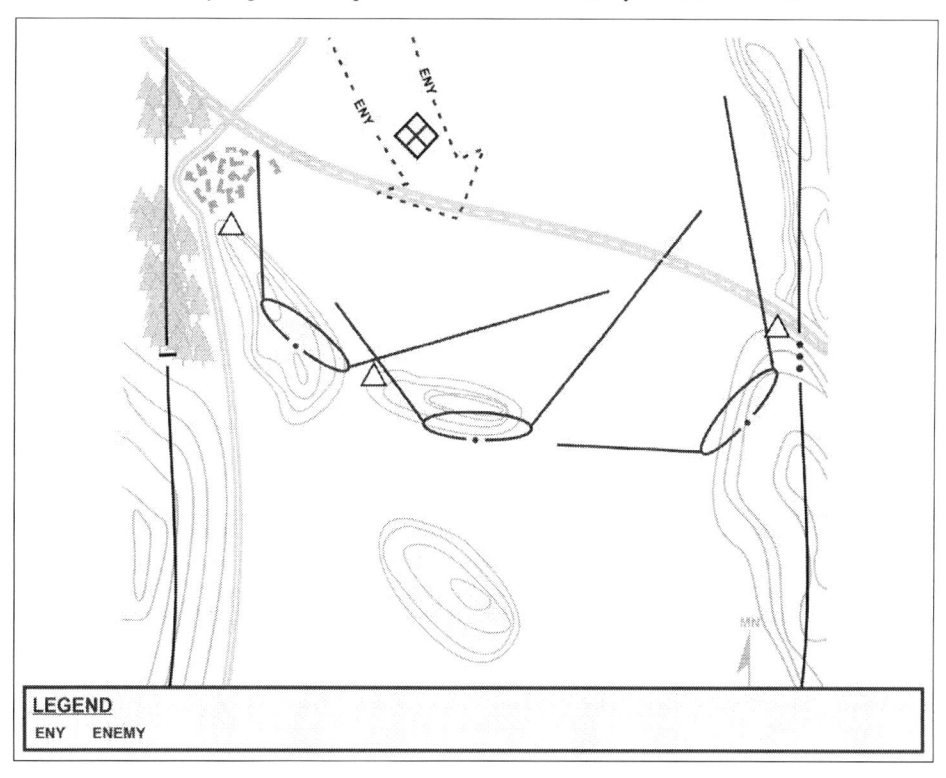

Figure 3-2. Platoon forward defense

MOBILE DEFENSE

3-23. Mobile defense is a defensive task that concentrates on destruction or defeat of the enemy through a decisive attack by a striking force. Mobile defenses focus on defeating or destroying the enemy by allowing enemy forces to advance to a point where they are exposed to a decisive counterattack by the striking force. The leader uses the fixing force to hold attacking enemy in position, to help channel attacking enemy forces into ambush areas, to retain areas from which to launch the striking force. Mobile defenses require an area of operation of considerable depth. The leader must able to shape the battlefield, causing an enemy to overextend its lines of communication, expose its flanks, and dissipate its combat power. Likewise, the leader must be able to move friendly forces around and behind the enemy force targeted to cut off and destroyed. Divisions or larger formations normally execute mobile defenses. However, the platoon may participate as part of the fixing force or the striking force.

> *Note.* Units smaller than a division usually do not conduct a mobile defense because of inability to fight multiple engagements throughout the width, depth, and height of their area of operation, while simultaneously resourcing the striking, fixing, and reserve forces. Typically, the striking force in a mobile defense consists of one-half to two-thirds of the defender's combat power.

3-24. Infantry platoons' missions in a mobile defense are similar to missions in area defense and offensive missions. They are either a part of the fixing force or part of the striking force, not both. As part of the fixing force, platoons defend within their assigned area of operation, although the area of operation might be larger than usual. As part of the striking force, Infantry platoons plan, rehearse, and execute offensive tasks.

3-25. Platoons use the term "striking force" rather than the term "reserve" because "reserve" indicates an uncommitted force. The striking force is a committed force that has the resources to conduct a decisive counterattack as part of the mobile defense. The striking force decisively engages the enemy as it becomes exposed in attempts to overcome the fixing force. The striking force normally attacks a moving enemy force, normally armor heavy.

RETROGRADE

3-26. Retrograde is a defensive task involving organized movement away from the enemy. The enemy may force a retrograde or the leader may execute it voluntarily. In either case, the higher commander of the force executing the operation must approve retrograding.

3-27. Retrogrades are conducted to improve a tactical situation or preventing a worse situation from developing. Platoons usually conduct retrogrades as part of a larger force but may conduct independent retrogrades (withdrawal) as required. Retrograde operations can accomplish the following:

- Resist, exhaust, and defeat enemy forces.
- Draw the enemy into an unfavorable situation.
- Avoid contact in undesirable conditions.
- Gain time.
- Disengage a force from battle for use elsewhere for other missions.
- Reposition forces, shorten lines of communication, or conform to movements of other friendly units.
- Secure favorable terrain.

3-28. The three forms of retrograde are—
- Delay.
- Withdrawal.

Chapter 3

- Retirement.

Delay

3-29. Delays allow units to trade space for time, avoiding decisive engagement and safeguard its forces. Ability of a force to trade space for time requires depth within the area of operation assigned to the delaying force. The amount of depth required depends on several factors, including the—

- Amount of time to be gained.
- Relative combat power of friendly and enemy forces.
- Relative mobility of forces.
- Nature of terrain.
- Ability to shape areas of operations with obstacles and fires.
- Degree of acceptable risk.

3-30. Delays succeed by forcing the enemy to concentrate forces to fight through a series of defensive positions. Delays must offer a continued threat of serious opposition, forcing the enemy to repeatedly deploy and maneuver. Delaying forces displace to subsequent positions before the enemy is able to concentrate sufficient resources to decisively engage and defeat delaying forces in current positions. The length of time a force can remain in position without facing danger of becoming decisively engaged is primarily a function of relative combat power, METT-TC and weather. Delays gain time to—

- Allow friendly forces to establish a defense.
- Cover withdrawing forces.
- Protect friendly force's flanks.
- Allow friendly forces to counterattack.

Parameters of the Delay

3-31. Parameters of the delay are specified in the order for a delay mission. First, leaders direct one of two alternatives: delay within the area of operation or delay forward of a specified line or terrain feature for a specified time. The second parameter in the order must specify acceptable risk. Acceptable risk ranges from accepting decisive engagement in an attempt to hold terrain for a given time maintaining integrity of the delaying force. The order must specify whether the delaying force may use the entire area of operation or must delay from specific battle positions. A delay using the entire area of operation is preferable, but a delay from specific positions may be required to coordinate two or more units.

Alternate or Successive Positions

3-32. Leaders normally assign subordinate units contiguous area of operation that are deeper than they are wide. Leaders use obstacles, fires, and movement throughout the depth of assigned area of operation. If the leader plans the delay to only last a short time or the area of operation's depth is limited, delaying units may be forced to fight from a single set of positions. If the leader expects the delay to last for longer periods, or sufficient depth is available, delaying units may delay from either alternate or successive positions.

3-33. In both techniques, delaying forces normally reconnoiter subsequent positions before occupying them if possible, and post guides on one or two subsequent positions. Additionally, in executing both techniques, it is critical the delaying force maintains contact with the enemy between delay positions. Advantages and disadvantages of the two techniques are summarized in table 3-1.

Table 3-1. Advantages and disadvantages of delay techniques

METHOD OF DELAY	USE WHEN	ADVANTAGES	DISADVANTAGES
Delay from Subsequent Positions	• Area of operation is wide. • Forces available do not allow themselves to be split.	• Masses fires of all available combat elements.	• Limited depth to the delay positions. • Less available time to prepare each position. • Less flexibility.
Delay from Alternate Positions	• Area of operation is narrow. • Forces are adequate to be split between different positions.	• Allows positioning in-depth. • Provides best security on most dangerous avenue of approach. • Allows more time for equipment and Soldier maintenance. • Increases flexibility.	• Requires more forces. • Requires continuous maneuver coordination. • Requires passage of lines. • Engages only part of the force at one time. • Risk losing contact with enemy between delay positions.

3-34. The alternate position technique normally is preferred when adequate forces are available and areas of operation have sufficient depth. Delays from alternate positions, two or more units in a single area of operation occupy delaying positions in-depth. (See figure 3-3, page 3-10.) As the first unit engages the enemy, the second occupies the next position in-depth and prepares to assume responsibility for the operation. The first force disengages and passes around or through the second force. It then moves to the next position and prepares to re-engage the enemy while the second force takes up the fight.

Chapter 3

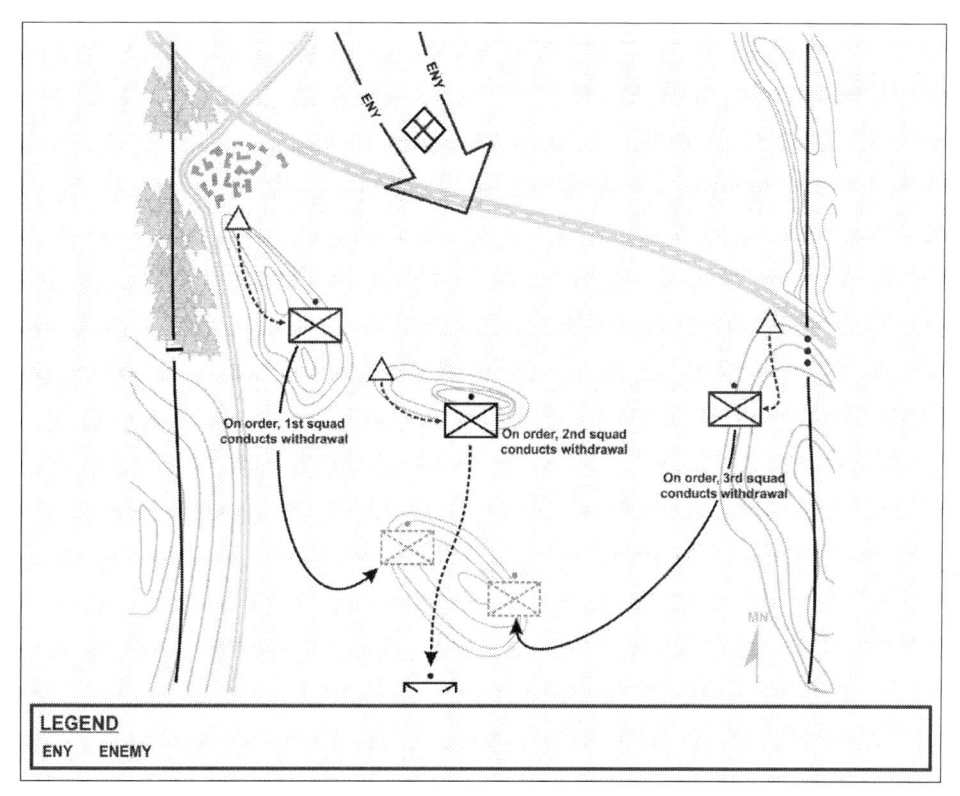

Figure 3-3. Delay from alternate positions

3-35. Delays from subsequent positions are used when assigned area of operation are so wide available forces cannot occupy more than a single tier of positions. (See figure 3-4.) Delays from subsequent positions must ensure all delaying units are committed to each of the series of battle positions or across the area of operation on the same phase line. Most of the delaying force is located well forward. Mission dictates the delay from one battle position or phase line to the next. Delaying unit movement is staggered so not all forces are moving at the same time.

Defense

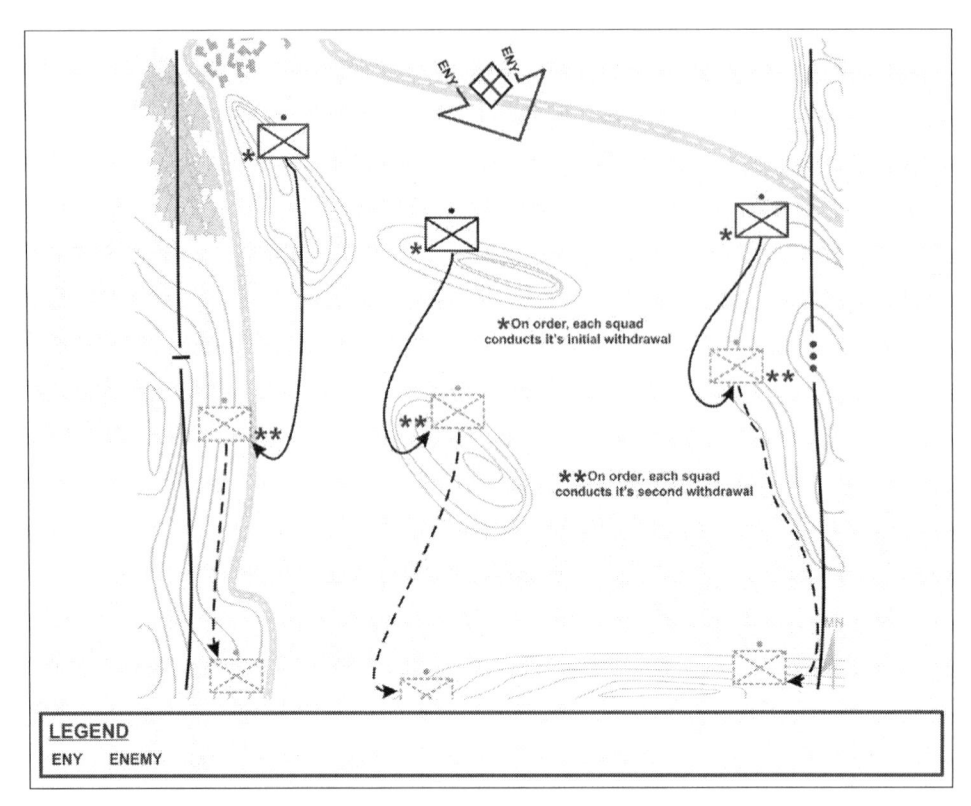

Figure 3-4. Delay from subsequent positions

Withdrawal

3-36. Withdrawal is a planned retrograde operation, which a force in contact disengages from an enemy force, and moves in a direction away from the enemy. Although the leader avoids withdrawing from action under enemy pressure, it is not always possible. Withdrawal is used to preserve the force or release it for a new mission.

3-37. Withdrawals are inherently dangerous. They involve moving units to the rear and away from what is usually a stronger enemy force. The heavier the previous fighting and closer the contact with the enemy, the more difficult the withdrawal. Units usually confine rearward movement to times and conditions when the advancing enemy force cannot observe the activity or easily detect the operation. OPSEC is extremely important, especially crucial during the initial stages of a delay when most of the functional and sustainment forces displace.

Planning a Withdrawal

3-38. The leader plans and coordinates a withdrawal in the same manner as a delay. METT-TC applies differently because of differences between a delay and withdrawal. A withdrawal always begins under the threat of enemy interference. Because the force is

Chapter 3

most vulnerable when the enemy attacks, the leader plans for a withdrawal under pressure. The leader then develops contingencies for a withdrawal without pressure. In both cases, the leaders main considerations are to—
- Plan a deliberate break from the enemy.
- Displace the main body rapidly, free of enemy interference.
- Safeguard withdrawal routes.
- Retain sufficient maneuver, functional/multifunctional support and sustainment capabilities throughout the operation supporting forces in contact with the enemy.

Assisted or Unassisted

3-39. Withdrawals may be assisted or unassisted. They may or may not take place under enemy pressure. These two factors combined produce four variations. (See figure 3-5.) The figure below depicts the mission graphic for a withdrawal and withdrawal under enemy pressure. The withdrawal plan considers which variation the force currently faces.

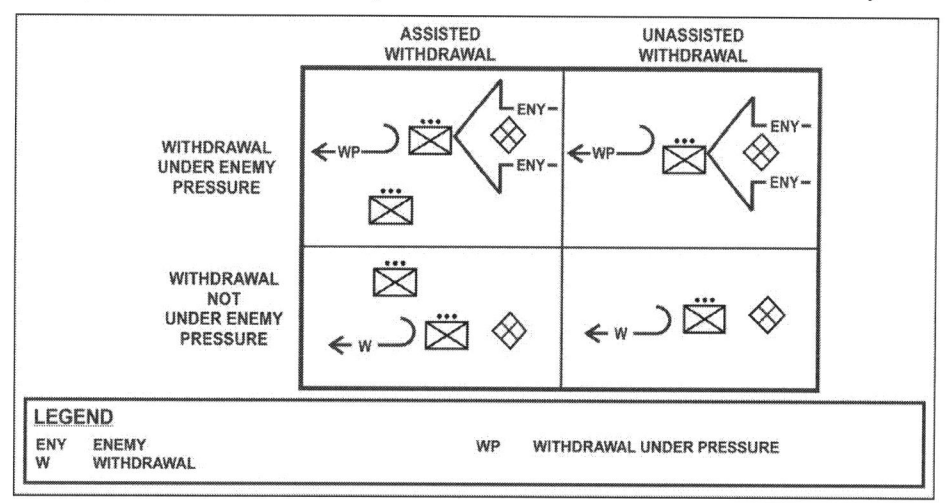

Figure 3-5. Types of withdrawals

3-40. Leaders prefer to conduct a withdrawal while not under enemy pressure and without assistance. Actions by the enemy, as well as additional coordination needed because of presence of an assisting unit, complicate the operation.

3-41. During an assisted withdrawal, the assisting force occupies positions to the rear of the withdrawing unit and prepares to accept control of the situation. Both forces closely coordinate the withdrawal. A withdrawing force can receive assistance from another force in the form of—
- Additional security for the area through which the withdrawing force will pass.
- Information concerning withdrawal routes (reconnaissance and maintenance).
- Forces to secure choke points or key terrain along withdrawal routes.
- Elements to assist in movement control, such as traffic control post.

Defense

- Required maneuver, direct fire support and sustainment, which can involve conducting a counterattack to assist the withdrawing unit in disengaging from the enemy.

3-42. During an unassisted withdrawal, the withdrawing unit establishes routes and develops plans for the withdrawal. It establishes the security force as a rear guard while the main body withdraws. Sustainment and protection forces usually withdraw first, followed by combat forces. As the unit withdraws, the detachment left in contact (DLIC) disengages from the enemy and follows the main body to its final destination.

3-43. In an unassisted platoon withdrawal, the platoon leader may designate one squad to execute the DLIC mission for the platoon, or constitute the DLIC using elements from the remaining rifle squads with the platoon sergeant as the DLIC leader. Figure 3-6 shows an example of an unassisted withdrawal.

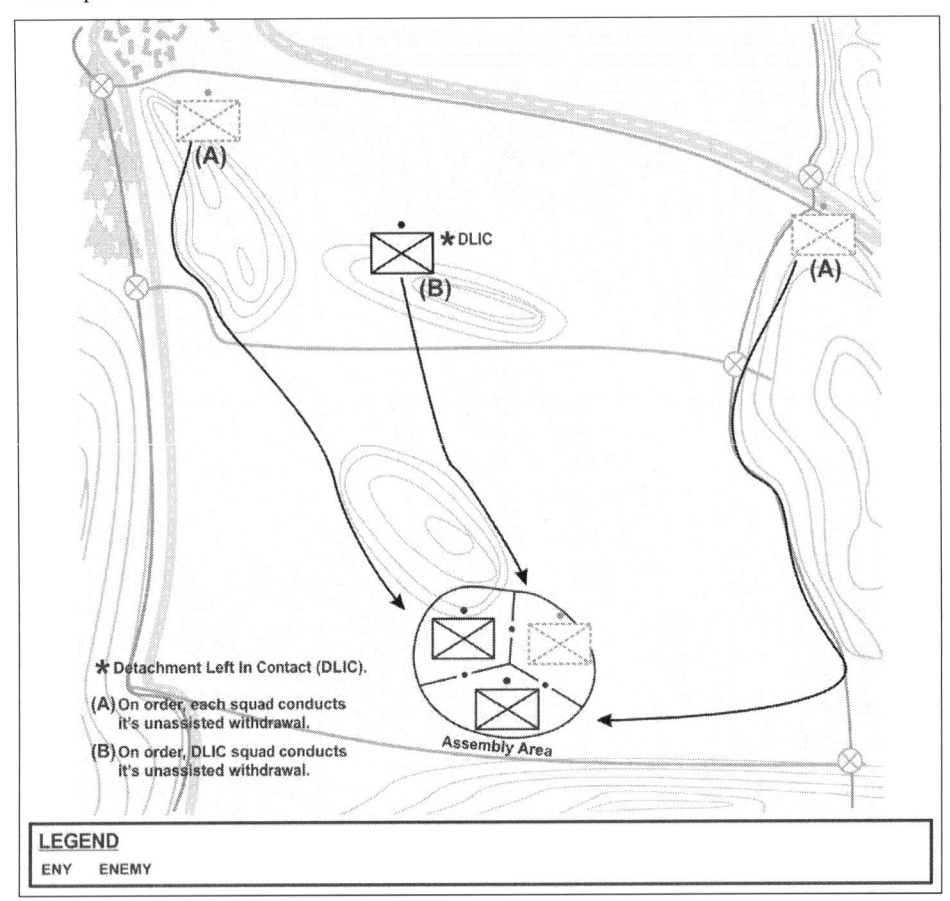

Figure 3-6. Platoon unassisted withdrawal

3-44. In a withdrawal under enemy pressure, all units withdraw simultaneously when available routes allow, using delaying tactics to fight their way to the rear. When

simultaneous withdrawal of all forces is not practical, the leader decides the order of withdrawal. Several factors influence this decision:
- Subsequent missions.
- Availability of transportation assets and routes.
- Disposition of friendly and enemy forces.
- Level and nature of enemy pressure.
- Degree of urgency associated with the withdrawal.

Retirement

3-45. Retirement is a task employing to move a force not in contact to the rear. Retirement is a form of retrograde, which a force not in contact with the enemy moves away from the enemy. A retiring unit organizes for combat but does not anticipate interference by enemy ground forces. Typically, another unit's security force covers the movement of one formation as the unit conducts a retirement. However, mobile enemy forces, unconventional forces, air strikes, air assaults, or long-range fires may attempt to interdict the retiring unit. The leader plans for enemy actions and organizes the unit to fight in self-defense. The leader usually conducts retirement to reposition his forces for future operations or to accommodate the current concept of the operation. Units conduct retirements such as tactical road marches where security and speed are the most important considerations. (Refer to chapter 5 of this publication for more information.)

ORDER OF EVENTS

3-46. Usually, as part of a larger element, the Infantry platoon conducts the defense performing several integrated and overlapping activities. The following paragraphs focus on the tactical considerations and procedures involved in each activity. This discussion shows an attacking enemy that uses depth in its operations, but there will be situations where a platoon must defend against an enemy that does not have a doctrinal operational foundation. The platoon must be prepared to defend against such threats. This unconventional (insurgent or terrorist force) enemy situation requires a more flexible plan that allows for more responsive and decentralized control of combat power rather than spreading it evenly throughout the platoon's area of operation. The platoon also may conduct 'base-camp' (Refer to FM 3-21.10 for more information.) or perimeter defense along with offense and patrolling against terrorist and insurgent forces. (Refer to chapter 6 of this publication for a discussion on patrol base activities.)

3-47. As the platoon leader plans his defense, he generally follows this order of events:
- Reconnaissance and surveillance (R&S) operations and enemy preparatory fires.
- Occupation and preparation.
- Approach of the enemy main attack.
- Enemy assault.
- Counterattack.
- Consolidation and reorganization.

Reconnaissance and Security Operations and Enemy Preparatory Fires

3-48. Security forces must protect friendly main battle area forces in order to allow them to prepare their defense. These security forces work in conjunction with and complement company and battalion security operations. The enemy will try to discover the defensive scheme of maneuver using reconnaissance elements and attacks by forward detachments and disruption elements. It also tries to breach the platoon's tactical obstacles.

Security Force

3-49. The security force's goals normally include providing early warning, destroying enemy reconnaissance units, and impeding and harassing enemy assault elements. The security force continues its mission until directed to displace. The commander also may use security forces in his deception effort to give the illusion of strength in one area while establishing the main defense in another. While conducting this type of security operation, the Infantry platoon may simultaneously have to prepare battle positions, creating a challenging time-management problem for the commander and his subordinate leaders.

Guides

3-50. During this activity, the Infantry platoon might be required to provide guides to pass the security force and might be tasked to close the passage lanes. The platoon also may play a role in shaping the battlefield. The platoon leader may position the platoon to deny likely enemy attack corridors to enhance flexibility and force enemy elements into friendly engagement area. When it is not conducting security or preparation tasks, the platoon normally occupies hide positions to avoid possible CBRN strikes or enemy artillery preparation.

Occupation and Preparation

3-51. A leader's reconnaissance is critical during this time in order for the platoon to conduct occupation without hesitation and begin the priorities of work. The participants in the reconnaissance are the platoon leader, platoon sergeant, and selected squad leaders, forward observer, RTO, and a security element. The goals are, but not limited to, identification of enemy avenues of approach, engagement area, sectors of fire, the tentative obstacle plan, indirect fire plan, observation post, rally point and command post locations. Operational security is critical during the occupation to ensure the platoon avoids detection and maintains combat power for the actual defense. Soldiers, at all levels of the platoon, must thoroughly understand their duties and responsibilities related to the occupation; they must be able to execute the occupation quickly and efficiently to maximize the time available for planning and preparation of the defense.

Approach of the Enemy Main Attack

3-52. The platoon engages the enemy at a time and place where direct and indirect fire systems are maximized to achieve success within his designated area of operation. If available, as the enemy's assault force approaches the engagement area, the platoon may

Chapter 3

initiate CAS to weaken the enemy. Friendly forces occupy their actual defensive positions before the enemy reaches direct fire range and may shift positions in response to enemy actions or other tactical factors.

Note. Long-range fires might be withheld in accordance with a higher commander's intent.

ENEMY ASSAULT

3-53. During an assault, the enemy deploys to achieve mass at a designated point, normally employing assault and support forces. This may leave him vulnerable to the combined effects of indirect and direct fires and integrated obstacles. The enemy may employ additional forces to fix friendly elements and prevent their repositioning. Friendly counterattack forces might be committed against the enemy flank or rear, while other friendly forces may displace to alternate, supplementary, or subsequent positions in support of the commander's scheme of maneuver. All friendly forces should be prepared for the enemy to maximize employment of combat multipliers to create vulnerabilities. The enemy also is likely to use artillery, CAS, and CBRN weapons to set the conditions for the assault.

3-54. The platoon engages the enemy. Squad leaders and team leaders control their Soldiers' direct fires. Destroyed vital positions are reoccupied. Soldiers move to alternate positions if the primary positions become untenable. Casualties are evacuated. Mines, indirect fires to include mortars are fired. Javelins and other direct fire weapons target the enemy's support positions.

3-55. Under limited visibility, selected mortars and field artillery units initially may fire infrared illumination if the enemy has not identified the defenders' positions. Once the platoon engages the enemy from its primary positions, regular illumination is used. If the platoon has overhead cover and the enemy penetrates the tactical wire, fires may include variable timed fuzed HE.

3-56. When required, final protective fires are initiated. Indirect fire systems to include field artillery and heavy mortars; join in firing their final protective fires concentrations until ordered to cease-fire or have exhausted their ammunition. Medium machine guns fire along their final protective lines (FPL). Soldiers fire to the flank to provide mutual support. Soldiers are resupplied with ammunition, and casualties evacuated.

COUNTERATTACK

3-57. As the enemy's momentum slows or stops, friendly forces may conduct a counterattack. The counterattack might be for offensive purposes to seize the initiative from the enemy. In some cases, the purpose of the counterattack is mainly defensive such as reestablishing a position or restoring control of the sector. The Infantry platoon may participate in the counterattack as a base-of-fire element—providing support by fire for the counterattack force—or as the actual counterattack force.

CONSOLIDATION AND REORGANIZATION

3-58. The platoon secures its defensive area by repositioning forces, destroying remaining enemy elements, processing EPW, and reestablishing obstacles. The platoon conducts all necessary sustainment functions as it prepares to continue the defense. Even when enemy forces are not actively engaging it, the platoon maintains awareness of the tactical situation and local security at all times. The platoon prepares itself for possible follow-on missions.

COMMON DEFENSIVE CONTROL MEASURES

3-59. The leader controls defensive tasks by using control measures to provide the flexibility needed to respond to changes in the situation and allow the defending leader to concentrate combat power at the decisive point. Defensive control measures within the leader's area of operation include designating the security area, the battle handover line (BHL), the main battle area with its associated forward edge of the battle area, and echelon support area. The leader can use battle positions and additional direct fire control and fire support coordination measures in addition to those control measures to synchronize the employment of combat power. The leader designates disengagement lines to trigger the displacement of subordinate forces.

BATTLE HANDOVER LINE

3-60. The BHL is a designated phase line on the ground where responsibility transitions from the stationary force to the moving force and vice versa.

BATTLE POSITIONS

3-61. A battle position is a defensive location oriented on a likely enemy avenue of approach. Units as large as battalion task forces and as small as squads or sections use battle positions. They may occupy the topographical crest of a hill, a forward slope, a reverse slope, or a combination of all areas. The leader selects his positions based on terrain, enemy capabilities, and friendly capabilities. A leader can assign all or some subordinates battle positions within the area of operation. The types of battle positions are—

- Primary.
- Alternate.
- Supplementary.
- Subsequent.
- Strongpoint.

Primary Position

3-62. Primary positions cover the enemy's most likely avenue of approach into the area. (See figure 3-7, page 3-19.)

Alternate Position

3-63. Alternate positions are those assigned when the primary position becomes untenable or unsuitable for carrying out the assigned task. (See figure 3-7.) These positions allow the defender to carry out his original task. The following considerations apply for an alternate battle position:
- It covers the same avenue of approach or sector of fire as the primary battle position.
- It is located slightly to the front, flank, or rear of the primary battle position.
- It may be positioned forward of the primary battle position during limited visibility operations.
- It is employed to supplement or support positions with weapons of limited range, such as dismounted positions.

Supplementary Position

3-64. A supplementary position is a defensive position located within a unit's assigned area of operation providing sectors of fire and defensible terrain along an avenue of approach not the enemy's expected avenue of attack. (See figure 3-7.) For example, an avenue of approach into a company's area of operation from one of its flanks could require the company to direct its platoons to establish supplementary positions to allow the platoons to engage enemy forces traveling along an avenue. The platoon leader formally assigns supplementary positions when the platoon must cover more than one avenue of approach.

Subsequent Position

3-65. Subsequent positions are those to which the unit expects to move during the course of the battle. A defending unit may have a series of subsequent positions. (See figure 3-7.) Subsequent positions also can have primary, alternate, and supplementary positions associated with them.

Strong Point

3-66. A strongpoint is a heavily fortified battle position tied to a natural or reinforcing obstacle to create an anchor for the defense or to deny the enemy decisive or key terrain. (See figure 3-8.) The mission to create and defend a strongpoint implies retention of terrain to stop or redirect enemy formations. Strongpoints require extensive time, engineer support, and Class IV resources to construct. A strongpoint also is used to—
- *Canalize enemy forces.* Canalize is a mission task in which the leader restricts enemy movement to a narrow zone by exploiting terrain coupled with the use of obstacles, fires, or friendly maneuver.
- *Contain enemy forces.* Contain is a mission task requiring the leader to stop, to hold, or to surround enemy forces or to cause them to center their activity on a given front and prevent them from withdrawing any part of forces for use elsewhere.

Defense

Note. A minimally effective strongpoint typically requires a one-day effort from an engineer unit the same size as the unit defending the strong point. (Refer to ADRP 3-90 for more information.)

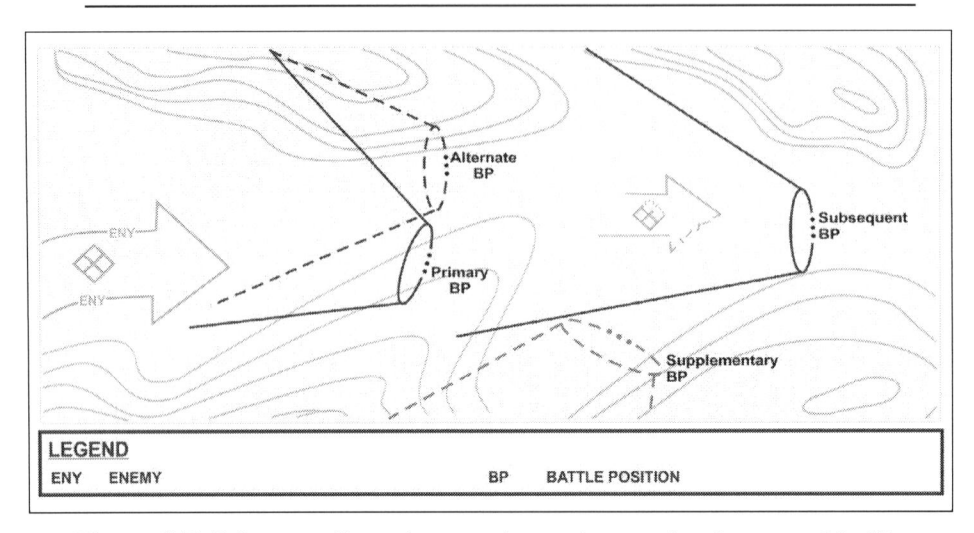

Figure 3-7. Primary, alternate, supplementary and subsequent battle positions

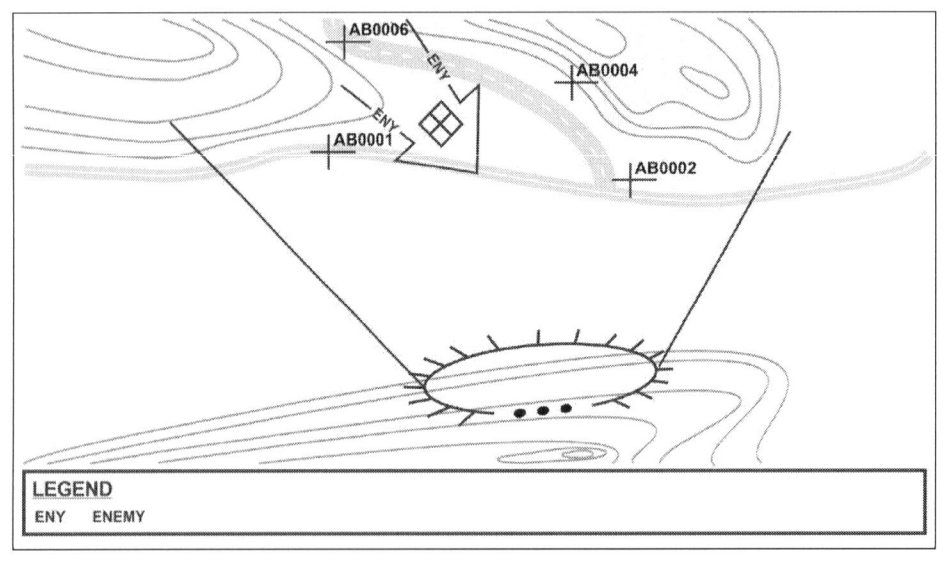

Figure 3-8. Platoon strongpoint battle position

FORWARD EDGE OF THE BATTLE AREA

3-67. The forward edge of the battle area is the foremost limits of a series of areas in which ground combat units are deployed, excluding the areas in which the covering or screening forces are operating, designated to coordinate fire support, the positioning of forces, or the maneuver of units.

MAIN BATTLE AREA

3-68. The main battle area is the area in a defense where the leader intends to deploy the bulk of the unit's combat power and conduct decisive operations to defeat an attacking enemy. The defending leader's major advantage is the ability to select the ground on which the battle takes place. The defender positions subordinate forces in mutually supporting positions in-depth to absorb enemy penetrations or canalize them into prepared engagement area, defeating the enemy's attack by concentrating the effects of overwhelming combat power. The natural defensive strength of positions determines the distribution of forces in relation to both frontage and depth. In addition, defending units typically employ field fortifications and obstacles to improve the terrain's natural defensive strength. The main battle area also includes the area where the defending force creates an opportunity to deliver a decisive counterattack to defeat or destroy the enemy.

SEQUENCE OF THE DEFENSE

3-69. Usually as part of a larger force, the Infantry platoon conducts the defense performing several integrated and overlapping activities.

3-70. As in the offense, this section divides execution into five steps for discussion purposes. These steps are—
- Gain and maintain enemy contact.
- Disrupt the enemy.
- Fix the enemy.
- Maneuver.
- Follow through/counterattack.

3-71. These steps may not occur sequentially; they may occur simultaneously. The first three steps are usually shaping operations and depending on the circumstances, either of the last two steps may be the decisive operation. (Refer to FM 3-90-1 for more information.)

GAIN AND MAINTAIN ENEMY CONTACT

3-72. Gaining and maintaining enemy contact in the face of the enemy's determined efforts to destroy friendly reconnaissance assets is vital to the success of the defense. As the enemy's attack begins, the defending unit's first concerns are to identify committed enemy units' positions and capabilities, determine the enemy's intent and direction of attack, and gain time to react. The platoon leader uses the information available to him, in conjunction with military judgment, to determine the point at which the enemy commits to a COA.

3-73. Early detection of the enemy's decisive operation provides the leader with reaction time to adjust the fixing force's positions and shape the enemy penetration, which, in turn, provides the time necessary to commit the striking force. The striking force leader requires as close to real-time updates of enemy situation as possible to ensure the striking force engages the enemy at the right location and time.

DISRUPT THE ENEMY

3-74. The leader executes shaping operations to disrupt the enemy regardless of enemy's location within the area of operation. After making contact with the enemy, the leader seeks to disrupt the enemy's plan, ability to control forces, and the combined arms team. Ideally, the results of leader's shaping operations should force a disorganized enemy, whose ability to synchronize its elements has been degraded, to conduct movement to contact against prepared defenses. Once the process of disrupting the attacking enemy begins, it continues throughout the defense.

3-75. Whenever possible the leader sequences these shaping operations, to include enemy command and control warfare, so the impact of effects coincides with the commitment of the striking force. Generating a tempo temporarily paralyzes enemy command and control, the intensity of these shaping operations may increase dramatically on the commitment of the striking force. The leader continues to conduct shaping operations once the striking force commits to prevent enemy forces from outside the operational area from interfering with executing the decisive counterattack.

FIX THE ENEMY

3-76. When conducting an area defense, the leader does everything possible to limit the options available to the enemy. In addition to disrupting the enemy, the leader conducts shaping operations to constrain the enemy into a specific COA, control enemy movements, or fix the enemy in a given location. These actions limit the enemy's options. While executing these operations, the leader continues to find, and to delay or to eliminate enemy follow-on reserve forces to keep them from entering the main battle area.

3-77. The leader has several options to help fix an attacking enemy force. The leader can design shaping operations, such as securing the flanks and point of a penetration, to fix the enemy and to allow friendly forces to execute decisive maneuver elsewhere.

3-78. The leader uses obstacles covered by fire to fix, to turn, to block, or to disrupt to limit the enemy's available options. Properly executed obstacles are a result of synthesis of top-down and bottom-up obstacle planning and emplacement. Blocking forces also can affect enemy movement. A blocking force may achieve its mission from a variety of positions depending on METT-TC.

Chapter 3

MANEUVER

3-79. During the defense, the decisive operation occurs in the main battle area. This is where the effects of shaping operations, coupled with sustaining operations, combine with the decisive operations of the main battle area force to defeat the enemy. The leader's goal is to prevent the enemy's increased advance through a combination of fires from prepared positions, obstacles, and possible counterattack.

3-80. Situational understanding is critical in establishing the conditions initiating the striking force's movement and in determining the general area serving as a focus for counterattacking. It includes identifying those points in time and space where the counterattack proves decisive. A force-oriented objective or an engagement area usually indicates the decisive point.

FOLLOW THROUGH

3-81. The purpose of the defense is to retain terrain and create conditions for a counteroffensive regaining the initiative. The area defense does this by causing the enemy to sustain unacceptable losses short of all decisive objectives. An area defense allows the leader transition to an attack. An area defense also could result in a stalemate with both forces left in contact with each other. Finally, it could result in the defender being overcome by the enemy attack and needing to transition to a retrograde. All decisions to withdraw must take into account the current situation in adjacent defensive areas. Only the leader who ordered the defense can designate a new forward edge of the battle area or authorize a retrograde.

3-82. The intent of the defense is creating the opportunity to transition to the offense. In a mobile defense, a transitional opportunity generally results from the success of the striking force's attack. The leader exploits success and attempts to establish conditions for a pursuit if the result of the leader's assessment of the striking force's attack shows there are opportunities for future offensive missions. If the conduct of the mobile defense is unsuccessful and enemy retains the initiative, the leader must either reestablish a viable defense or conduct a retrograde.

PRIORITY OF WORK

3-83. Priority of work is a set method of controlling the preparation and conduct of a defense. Tactical SOPs should describe priority of work including individual duties. The platoon leader changes priorities based on the situation. All leaders in the platoon should have a specific priority of work for their duty position. Although listed in sequence, several tasks are performed at the same time. An example priority of work sequence is as follows:
- Post local security.
- Position and assign sectors of fire for each BFV or ICV.
- Establish the platoons reconnaissance and surveillance.
- Position Javelins, machine guns, and Soldiers; assign sectors of fire.
- Position other assets (platoon command post).
- Designate final protective lines and final protective fires.

- Clear fields of fire and prepare range cards and area of operations sketches.
- Adjust indirect fire final protective fires. The firing unit fire direction center should provide a safety box clearing of all friendly units before firing adjusting rounds.
- Prepare fighting positions.
- Install wire communications, if applicable.
- Emplace obstacles and mines.
- Mark (or improve marking for) target reference points and direct fire-control measures.
- Improve primary fighting positions such as overhead cover.
- Prepare alternate and supplementary positions.
- Establish sleep and rest plan.
- Reconnoiter movements.
- Rehearse engagements and disengagements or displacements.
- Adjust positions and control measures as required.
- Stockpile ammunition, food, and water.
- Dig trenches between positions.
- Reconnoiter routes.
- Continue to improve positions.

PLATOON LEADER

3-84. Many duties can be delegated to subordinates, but the platoon leader ensures they are done. This includes:

- Ensuring local security and assigning observation post responsibility.
- Conducting a leader's reconnaissance with the platoon sergeant and selected personnel.
- Confirming or denying significant deductions or assumptions from the mission analysis.
- Confirming the direct fire plan, to include engagement area, sectors of fire, position essential weapons, and fire control measures.
- Designating primary, alternate, supplementary, and subsequent positions supporting the direct fire plan, for platoons, sections, and supporting elements.
- Requiring squads to conduct coordination. Integrating indirect fire plan and obstacles to support the direct fire plan.
- Designating the general platoon command post location, and positioning essential weapons.
- Checking the platoon command post and briefing the platoon sergeant on the situation and logistics requirements.
- Upon receipt of the squads' area of operations sketches, makes two copies of the platoon defensive area of operations sketch and fire plan, retaining one copy and forwarding the other copy to the company. (See figure 3-9, page 3-24.)

Chapter 3

- Confirming the direct fire plan and squad positions before digging starts. Coordinating with the left and right units.
- Checking with the company commander for all changes or updates in the orders.
- Finishing the security, deception, counterattack, and obstacle plans.
- Walking the platoon positions after they are dug.
- Confirming clear fields of fire and complete coverage of the platoon's entire area of operations by all essential weapons.
- Looking at the defensive plan from an enemy point of view, conceptually and physically.
- Checking dissemination of information, interlocking fires, and dead space.
- Ensuring immediate correction of deficiencies.
- Ensuring rehearsals are conducted and obstacle locations reported.

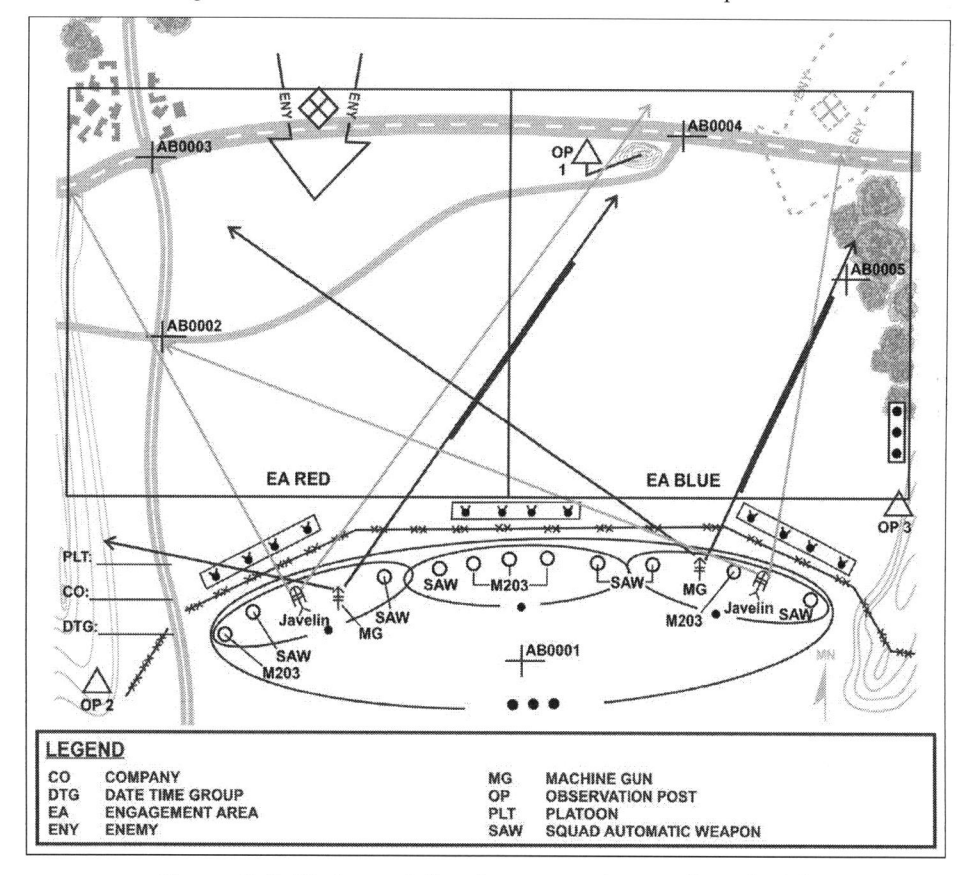

Figure 3-9. Platoon defensive area of operation sketch

Defense

PLATOON SERGEANT

3-85. Duties and responsibilities include:
- Establishing the platoon command post and ensures wire communications link the platoon, squads, and attached elements, if applicable.
- Establishing casualty collection points, platoon logistics release points, and detainee collection points, and locating company level points.
- Briefing squad leaders on the platoon command post location, logistics plan, and routes between positions.
- Assisting the platoon leader with the sector of fire and area of operations sketch.
- Requesting and allocating pioneer tools, barrier materiel, rations, water, and ammunition.
- Walking the positions with the platoon leader. Supervising emplacement of squads, essential weapons, check range cards, and area of operations sketches.
- Establishing routine security or alert plans, radio watch, and rest plans and briefing the platoon leader.
- Supervising continuously and assisting the platoon leader with other duties as assigned.
- Selecting slit trench location and ensuring it is properly marked.

SQUAD LEADERS

3-86. The squad leader—
- Emplaces local security.
- Confirms positioning and assigned sectors of fire for his squad.
- Confirms positioning and assigned sectors of fire for the CCMS and medium machine gun teams.
- Positions and assigns sectors of fire for automatic rifleman, grenadiers, and riflemen.
- Establishes command post and wire communications.
- Confirms designate FPL and final protective fires.
- Clears fields of fire and prepares range cards.
- Prepares squad range card and area of operations sketches.
- Digs fighting positions.
- Establishes communication and coordination within the platoon, and adjacent units.
- Coordinates with adjacent units. Reviews sector of fire and area of operations sketches.
- Emplaces antitank and Claymores, then wire and other obstacles.
- Marks or improves marking for target reference points and other fire control measures.
- Improves primary fighting positions and adds overhead cover (stage 2).
- Prepares supplementary and alternate positions (same procedure as the primary position).

Chapter 3

- Establishes sleep and rest plans.
- Distributes and stockpiles ammunition, food, and water.
- Digs trenches to connect positions.
- Continues to improve positions, construct revetments, replace camouflage, and add to overhead cover.

FORWARD OBSERVER

3-87. The FO—
- Assists the platoon leader in planning the indirect fires to support defensive missions.
- Advises the platoon leader on the status of all firing units, and on the use of obscurants or illumination.
- Coordinates with the Infantry company fire support officer, firing units, and squad leaders to ensure the fire plan is synchronized and fully understood.
- Ensures the indirect fire plan is rehearsed and understood by all.
- Ensures all final protective fires are adjusted as soon as possible.
- Develops an observation plan.
- Coordinates and rehearses all repositioning of observers within the platoon area of operations to ensure they can observe targets or areas of responsibility.
- Develops triggers.
- Reports information collection activities.
- Ensures redundancy in communications.

ADJACENT UNIT COORDINATION

3-88. The ultimate goal of adjacent unit coordination is to ensure unity of effort in accomplishment of the Infantry mission. Items adjacent units coordinate include—
- Unit positions, including locations of vital leaders' call signs and frequencies.
- Locations of observation posts and patrols.
- Overlapping fires (to ensure direct fire responsibility is clearly defined).
- Target reference points).
- Alternate, supplementary, and subsequent battle positions.
- Indirect fire information.
- Obstacles (location and type).
- Air defense considerations, if applicable.
- Routes to be used during occupation and repositioning.
- Sustainment considerations.

COORDINATION

3-89. In the defense, coordination ensures that units provide mutual support and interlocking fires. In most circumstances, the platoon leader conducts face-to-face

Defense

coordination to facilitate understanding and to resolve issues effectively. However, when time is extremely limited, digital coordination may be the only means of sending and receiving this information. The platoon leader should send and receive the following information using his radio or mission command system before conducting face-to-face coordination:

- Location of leaders.
- Location of fighting positions.
- Location of observations posts and withdrawal routes.
- Location and types of obstacles.
- Location, activities, and passage plan for scouts and other units forward of the platoon's position.
- Platoon's digital sector sketch.
- Location of all Soldiers and units operating in and around the platoon's area of operation.

3-90. Current techniques for coordination hold true for units that are digitally equipped. If a digitized and a nondigitized unit are conducting adjacent unit coordination, face-to-face is the preferred method. The leader of the digitized unit has the option to enter pertinent information about the nondigitized unit into mission command systems for later reference. The digitally equipped platoon leader should show the adjacent unit leader his digital sector sketch. If face-to-face coordination is not possible, leaders share pertinent information by radio.

SECURITY

3-91. Security in the defense includes all active and passive measures taken to avoid detection by the enemy, deceive the enemy, and deny enemy reconnaissance elements accurate information on friendly positions. The two primary tools available to the platoon leader are observation posts and patrols. In planning for the security in the defense, the platoon leader considers the military aspects of terrain: observation and fields of fire, avenues of approach, key terrain, obstacles and cover, and concealment. He uses his map to identify terrain that will protect the platoon from enemy observation and fires, while providing observation and fires into the engagement area. He uses intelligence updates to increase his situational understanding, reducing the possibility of the enemy striking at a time or in a place for which the platoon is unprepared.

3-92. Current mission commands systems allow mechanized squads to digitally transmit enemy situation and observation reports. This simplifies the reporting process without compromising security. Dismounted observation posts still render reports by frequency modulation radio transmission.

OBSERVATION POSTS

3-93. An observation post provides the primary security in the defense. Observation posts provide early warning of impending enemy contact by reporting direction, distance, and size. It detects the enemy early and sends accurate reports to the platoon. The platoon leader establishes observation posts along the most likely enemy avenues of approach into

Chapter 3

the position or into the area of operation. Leaders ensure that observation posts (mounted or dismounted) have communication with the platoon.

3-94. Early detection reduces the risk of the enemy overrunning the observation post. Observation post may be equipped with a Javelin command launch unit; class 1 unmanned aircraft system; seismic, acoustic, or frequency detecting sensors to increase its ability to detect the enemy. They may receive infrared trip flares, infrared parachute flares, infrared M203 or M320 rounds, and even infrared mortar round support to illuminate the enemy. The platoon leader weighs the advantages and disadvantages of using infrared illumination when the enemy is known to have night vision devices that detect infrared light. Although infrared and thermal equipment within the platoon enables the platoon to see the observation post at a greater distance, the observation post should not be positioned outside the range of the platoon's small-arms weapons.

3-95. To further reduce the risk of fratricide, observation posts use GPS to navigate to the exit and entry point in the platoon's position. The platoon leader ensures he submits an observation post location to the company team commander to ensure a no fire area is established around each observation post position.

PATROLS

3-96. Platoons actively patrol in the defense. Patrols enhance the platoon's ability to fill gaps in security between observation posts. The platoon leader forwards his tentative patrol route to the commander to ensure they do not conflict with other elements within the company team. The commander forwards the entire company team's patrol routes to the task force. This allows the operations and intelligence staff officers to ensure all routes are coordinated for fratricide prevention and no gaps are present. The patrol leader may use a GPS to enhance his basic land navigational skills as he tracks his patrol's location on a map, compass, and pace count or odometer reading.

VEHICULAR FIRING POSITION

3-97. After a range card is completed, the position should be marked with ground stakes. This enables the vehicle or a replacement vehicle to reoccupy the position and to use the range card data. The steps in marking a vehicle position are staking the position and moving into position. Each are described below.

Stake the Position

3-98. Before the vehicle is moved, the position should be staked. Three stakes must effectively mark the position as shown in figure 3-10.

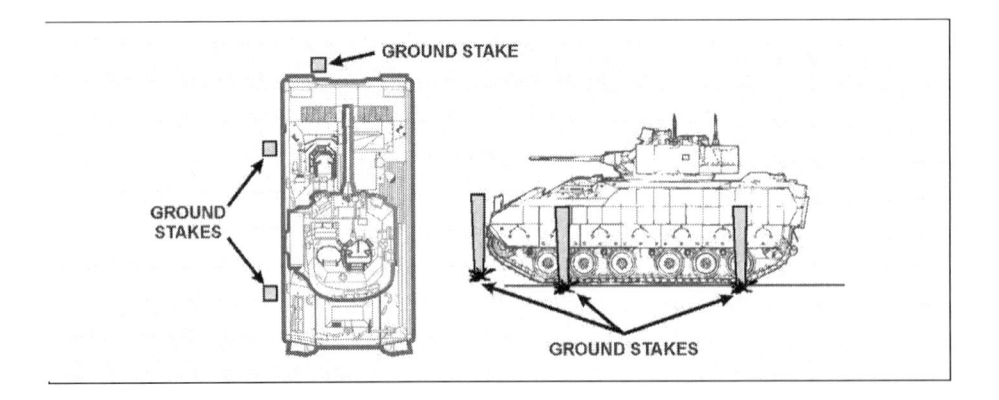

Figure 3-10. Stake the position

3-99. One stake is placed in front of the vehicle, centered on the driver's station and just touching the hull. The stake should be long enough for the driver to see it when in position. The other two stakes are placed parallel to the left track and lined up with the hub on the front and rear wheels. The stakes should be placed close to the vehicle with only enough clearance to move the vehicle into position.

3-100. The stakes should be driven firmly into the ground. Engineer tape or luminous tape can be placed on the friendly side of the stakes so that the driver can see them. A rock is placed at each of the front two corners of the vehicle to assist in reoccupation if the stakes are lost.

Move into Position

3-101. If the situation permits, a ground guide can be used to assist the driver. If a ground guide cannot be used, the driver moves the vehicle in, parallel to the side stakes, with the front stake centered on the driver's station. Once the vehicle is in position, the gunner should index the range and azimuth for one of the TRPs on the range card. If the sight is aligned on the TRP, the vehicle is correctly positioned. If the sight is not aligned on the TRP, the gunner should tell the driver which way to move the vehicle to align the sight on the target. Only minor adjustments should be necessary. If the stakes are lost and the position is not otherwise marked, the vehicle is moved to the approximate location. The vehicle commander or gunner can use a compass to find the left and right limits. The vehicle should be moved if time allows until it is within 6 to 8 inches of exact position.

REMOUNT POINT

3-102. The platoon leader selects a remount point that permits the rapid loading of the dismounted element into vehicles, while minimizing both the dismounted Soldier's and vehicles exposure to enemy fire. He tries to locate the remount point as close as possible to his dismounted element. Squad leaders ensure that their Soldiers know the remount point location. When moving to the vehicles, the dismounted element ensures that they do not mask the BFV or ICV fields of fire.

Chapter 3

3-103. Three remount point locations exist: near the dismounted element, near the mounted element, or between the two. Positioning the remount point near the dismounted element is preferred if it does not unnecessarily expose the vehicles to enemy fire. Based on the situation however, the platoon leader may have to accept risk and expose his BFVs or ICVs to remount his platoon. Locating the remount point near the vehicle is preferred if the area around or the mounted route to the dismounted element is exposed to enemy fire, and include a covered dismounted route back to the vehicles. The platoon leader selects a remount point between the two elements when both can reach it without unnecessarily exposing themselves to enemy fire.

SECTION II – COMMON DEFENSIVE PLANNING CONSIDERATIONS

3-104. Planning a defensive task is a complex effort requiring detailed planning and extensive coordination. In the defense, synchronizing the effects of the Infantry platoons and squads combat and supporting systems enables the platoon leader to apply overwhelming combat power against selected advancing enemy forces. This unhinges the enemy commander's plan and destroys his combined arms team. As an operation evolves, the Infantry leader knows a shift to decisive and shaping operations is a probability to press the fight and keep the enemy off balance. Warfighting functions provide the Infantry leader a means and structure for planning, preparing, and executing the defense. The following paragraphs discuss the synchronization and coordination of activities within each warfighting function critical to the success of the Infantry platoon and squad. This section also discusses urban and mountainous defensive planning considerations.

Note. To avoid redundancy, the six warfighting functions for the offense are similar to the six-warfighting functions for the defense. Commander's intent and METT-TC determines how they are applied.

MISSION COMMAND

3-105. The first step is the expression of the leader's vision of anticipated enemy actions integrated with the Infantry companies IPB. The Infantry battalion and company IPB should not differ significantly, giving the Infantry platoon and squad a clear understanding of how the Infantry battalion and company commanders envision the enemy fight and plan for the operation. The Infantry company commander and CoIST refine the IPB to focus on the details of the operation in the company area of operation. The platoon leader refines his IPB to focus on the details of the mission in the Infantry platoon and squad area of operation. The Infantry battalion commander usually defines where and how the Infantry battalion will defeat or destroy the enemy. The Infantry company commander and platoon leader then defines how they envision how their units will execute their portion of the battalion fight.

MOVEMENT AND MANEUVER

3-106. Maneuver considerations employ direct fire weapons on the battlefield. In the defense, weapons positioning is critical to the Infantry platoon's and squad's success. Weapons positioning enables the platoon to mass fires at critical points on the battlefield and shift fires as necessary. The platoon leader exploits the strengths of his weapons systems while minimizing the platoon's exposure to enemy observation and fires.

3-107. If the platoon, or squad are designated in a reserve role positioning the reserve in a location where it can react to several contingency plans is vital to success. The platoon leader considers terrain, traffic of roads, potential engagement area, probable points of enemy penetrations, and commitment time. The Infantry battalion commander can have a single reserve under battalion control, or, if the terrain dictates, the Infantry company can designate its own reserves. The reserve should be positioned in a covered and concealed position. Information concerning the reserve may be considered EEFI and protected from enemy reconnaissance. The commander might choose to position his reserve forward initially to deceive the enemy, or to move the reserve occasionally to prevent it from being targeted by enemy indirect fires.

DEPTH AND DISPERSION

3-108. Dispersing positions laterally and in-depth helps to protect the force from enemy observation and fires. The positions are established in-depth, allowing sufficient maneuver space within each position to establish in-depth placement of weapons systems, and Infantry elements. Engagement areas are established to provide for the massing of fires at critical points on the battlefield. Sectors of fire are established to distribute and shift fires throughout the extent of the engagement area. Once the direct fire plan is determined, fighting positions are constructed in a manner to support the fire plan.

FLANK POSITIONS

3-109. Flank positions enable a defending force to fire on an attacking force moving parallel to the defender's forces. A flank position provides the defender with a larger and more vulnerable target while leaving the attacker unsure of the defense location. Major considerations for employment of a flank position are the defender's ability to secure the flank and his ability to achieve surprise by remaining undetected. Fire control and fratricide avoidance measures are critical considerations in the employment of flank positions. (See appendix B of this publication for more information.)

DISPLACEMENT PLANNING

3-110. Disengagement and displacement allow the platoon to retain its flexibility and tactical agility in the defense. The ultimate goals of disengagement and displacement are to enable the platoon to avoid being fixed or decisively engaged by the enemy. The overarching factor in a displacement is to maintain a mobility advantage over the enemy. The platoon leader must consider several important factors in displacement planning. These factors include, among others:

Chapter 3

- The enemy situation, for example, an enemy attack with one company-size enemy unit might prevent the platoon from disengaging.
- Disengagement criteria.
- Availability of direct fire suppression that can support disengagement by suppressing or disrupting the enemy.
- Availability of cover and concealment, indirect fires, and obscurants to assist disengagement.
- Obstacle integration, including situational obstacles.
- Positioning of forces on terrain that provides an advantage to the disengaging elements such as linear obstacles.
- Identification of displacement routes and times when disengagement or displacement will take place. Routes and times are rehearsed.
- The size of the friendly force that must be available to engage the enemy in support of the displacing unit.

3-111. While disengagement and displacement are valuable tactical tools, they can be extremely difficult to execute in the face of a rapidly moving enemy force. In fact, displacement in contact poses such great problems that the platoon leader thoroughly plans for it and rehearses displacement before conducting the defense. He then carefully evaluates the situation when displacement in contact becomes necessary to ensure it is feasible and does not result in unacceptable personnel or equipment losses.

DISENGAGEMENT CRITERIA

3-112. Disengagement criteria dictate to subordinate elements the circumstances, in which they will displace to alternate, supplementary, or subsequent positions. The criteria are tied to an enemy action, such as an enemy unit advancing past a certain phase line. They also are linked to the friendly situation. For example, the criteria might depend on whether artillery or an overwatch element can engage the enemy. Unique disengagement criteria are developed during the planning process for each specific situation.

DIRECT FIRE SUPPRESSION

3-113. The attacking enemy force must not be allowed to bring direct and indirect fires to bear on a disengaging friendly force. Direct fires from the base-of-fire element, employed to suppress or disrupt the enemy, are the most effective way to facilitate disengagement. The platoon may receive base of direct fire support from another element in the company, but in most cases, the platoon establishes its own base-of-fire element. Having an internal base of fire requires the platoon leader to sequence the displacement of his forces.

COVER AND CONCEALMENT

3-114. The platoon and subordinate squads use covered and concealed routes when moving to alternate, supplementary, or subsequent positions. Regardless of the degree of protection the route itself affords, the platoon and squads try to rehearse the movement

Defense

prior to contact. Rehearsals increase the speed at which they can conduct the move and provide an added measure of security. The platoon leader makes a concerted effort to allocate available time to rehearse movement in limited visibility and degraded conditions.

INDIRECT FIRES AND OBSCURANTS

3-115. Artillery or mortar fires assist the platoon during disengagement. Suppressive fires slow the enemy and cause him to seek cover. Smoke obscures the enemy's vision, slows his progress, or screens the defender's movement out of the battle position or along his displacement route.

OBSTACLE INTEGRATION

3-116. Obstacles are integrated with direct and indirect fires. By slowing and disrupting enemy movement, obstacles provide the defender with the time necessary for displacement and allow friendly forces to employ direct and indirect fires against the enemy. The Modular Pack Mine System (MOPMS) also can be employed in support of the disengagement, to either block a key displacement route once the displacing unit has passed through it or close a lane through a tactical obstacle. The location of obstacles in support of disengagement depends on METT-TC. Ideally, an obstacle should be positioned far enough away from the defender that enemy elements could be engaged on the far side of the obstacle while keeping the defender out of range of the enemy's massed direct fires.

MOBILITY

3-117. Mobility operations in the defense ensure the ability to reposition forces, delay, and counterattack. Initially during defensive preparations, mobility operations focus on the ability to resupply, reposition, and conduct rearward and forward passage of forces, materiel, and equipment. Once defensive preparations are complete, the focus normally shifts to supporting the platoon reserve, local counterattacks, and the higher headquarters counterattack or reserve. Priorities set by the company may specify routes for improvement in support of such missions. Normally, most engineer assets go to survivability and countermobility. At a set time or trigger, engineers disengage from obstacle and survivability position construction and start preparing for focused mobility missions. The platoon leader analyzes the scheme of maneuver, obstacle plan, and terrain to determine mobility requirements. Critical considerations may include:

- Lanes and gaps in the obstacle plan.
- Lane closure plan and subunit responsibility.
- Route reconnaissance, improvement, and maintenance.

COUNTERMOBILITY

3-118. To succeed in the defense, the platoon leader integrates individual obstacles into direct and indirect fire plans, considering the intent for each obstacle group. (Refer to ATTP 3-90.4 for more information on countermobility in the defense.) Obstacles are normally constructed by engineers with help from the platoon. In the defense, the platoon or squad uses obstacles to:

Chapter 3

- Slow the enemy's advance to give the platoon or squad more time to mass fires on him.
- Protect defending units.
- Canalize the enemy into places where he can easily be engaged.
- Separate the enemy's tanks from his infantry.
- Strengthen areas that are lightly defended.

3-119. Obstacle intent includes the target and desired effect (clear task and purpose) and the relative location of the obstacle group. The purpose influences many aspects of the operation, from selecting and designing obstacle sites to conducting the defense. Normally, the company commander designates the purpose of an obstacle group. When employing obstacles, the leader considers the following principles:

- *Support the tactical plan.* Obstacles supplement combat power, decrease the mobility of the enemy, and provide security for the platoon. While considering enemy avenues of approach, he also considers his own movement requirements, such as routes for resupply, withdrawal, counterattacks, patrols, and observation posts.
- *Tie in.* He ties in his reinforcing obstacles with existing obstacles. He must also tie in the obstacle plan with his plans for fires.
- *Covered by observation and fire.* He ensures that all obstacles are covered by observation and fire. This reduces the enemy's ability to remove or breach the obstacles and increases the possibilities of placing fire on the enemy when he encounters the obstacle.
- *Constructed in-depth.* He emplaces obstacles so that each new obstacle encountered by the enemy attrites the enemy force and causes a desired and controlled reaction. Proper use of obstacles in-depth wears the enemy down and significantly increases the overall effect.
- *Employed for surprise.* An obvious pattern of obstacles would divulge locations of units and weapons. Friendly forces must avoid readily discernable, repetitive patterns.

Tactical Obstacles

3-120. The company commander assigns obstacle groups, and tells the platoon leaders and engineers what he wants to do to the enemy, and then he resources the groups accordingly. Obstacle intent includes these elements:

- The target, which is the enemy force that the commander wants to affect with fires and tactical obstacles. The commander identifies the target's size, type, echelon, avenues of approach, or any combination of these.
- The obstacle effect describes how the commander wants to attack enemy maneuver with obstacles and fires. Tactical obstacles block, turn, fix, or disrupt. Obstacle effect integrates the obstacles with direct and indirect fires.
- The relative location is where the commander wants the obstacle effect to occur against the targeted enemy force. The commander initiates the obstacle integration

Defense

process after identifying where on the terrain the obstacle will most decisively affect the enemy.
- For example, the company commander might say, "Deny the enemy access to our flank by turning the northern, mechanized Infantry battalion into our engagement area. Allow companies B and C to mass their fires to destroy the enemy." Scatterable minefield systems and submunitions are the main means of constructing tactical obstacles. These systems, with their self- and command-destruct capabilities, are flexible, and they aid in rapid transitions between offensive and defensive tasks. They do this better than other constructed obstacles. The force constructs conventional minefields and obstacles only for a deliberate, long-term defense. In those cases, the company and platoons usually are augmented with assets from a divisional engineer battalion. Table 3-2 shows the symbols for each obstacle effect, and it describes the purpose and characteristics of each.

Table 3-2. Obstacle effects

OBSTACLE EFFECT	PURPOSE	FIRES AND OBSTACLES MUST:	OBSTACLE CHARACTERISTICS
DISRUPT	• Break up enemy formations. • Interrupt enemy's timetable and C2. • Cause premature commitment of breach assets. • Cause the enemy to piecemeal his attack.	• Cause the enemy to deploy early. • Slow part of his formation while allowing part to advance unimpeded.	• Do not require extensive resources. • Ensure obstacles are difficult to detect at long range.
FIX	• Slow an attacker within an area so he can be destroyed. • Generate the time necessary for the friendly force to disengage.	• Cause the enemy to deploy into attack formation before encountering the obstacles. • Allow the enemy to advance slowly in an EA or AO. • Make the enemy fight in multiple directions once he is in the EA or AO.	• Array obstacles in depth. • Span the entire width of the avenues of approach. • Avoid making the terrain appear impenetrable.
TURN	• Force the enemy to move in the direction desired by the friendly commander.	• Prevent the enemy from bypassing or breaching the obstacle belt. • Maintain pressure on the enemy force throughout the turn. • Mass direct and indirect fires at the anchor point of the turn.	• Tie into impassable terrain at the anchor point. • Use obstacles in depth. • Provide a subtle orientation relative to the enemy's approach.
BLOCK	• Stop an attacker along a specific avenue of approach. • Prevent an attacker from passing through an AO or EA. • Stop the enemy from using an avenue of approach and force him to use another avenue of approach.	• Prevent the enemy from bypassing or penetrating through the belt. • Stop the enemy's advance. • Destroy all enemy breach efforts.	• Tie into impassable terrain. • Use complex obstacles. • Defeat the enemy's mounted and dismounted breaching effort.

AO   area of operations   EA   engagement area
C2   command & control

Protective Obstacles

3-121. Infantry platoons plan and construct their own protective obstacles. For best effect, protective obstacles are tied into existing or tactical reinforcing obstacles. The platoon can use mines and wire, or it might receive additional materiel from company,

Class IV or V supply point. The platoon also might conduct any other required coordination, such as needed in a relief in place, to recover or destroy the obstacle:

- In planning protective obstacles, the platoon leader evaluates the potential threat to the platoon's position. Then, employs the best system for that threat.
- Protective obstacles usually are located beyond hand grenade distance (40 to 100 meters) from the Soldier's fighting position, and may extend out 300 to 500 meters to tie into tactical obstacles and existing restricted terrain. As with tactical obstacles, the platoon leader should plan protective obstacles in-depth and try to maximize the range of his weapons.
- When planning protective obstacles, the platoon leader considers preparation time, the burden on the logistical system, the Soldiers' loads, and the risk of loss of surprise.

3-122. The three types of wire obstacles (see figure 3-11) are protective, tactical, and supplementary:

- *Protective wire* can be a complex obstacle providing all-around protection of a platoon perimeter. It also might be a simple wire obstacle on the likely dismounted avenue of approach into a squad ambush position. Command-detonated M18 Claymores can be integrated into the protective wire or used separately.
- *Tactical wire* is positioned to increase the effectiveness of the platoon's fires. Usually, it is positioned along the friendly side of the medium machine gun FPL. Tactical minefields also may be integrated into these wire obstacles or used separately.
- *Supplementary wire* obstacles can break up the line of tactical wire. This helps prevent the enemy from locating friendly weapons (particularly the medium machine guns) by following the tactical wire.

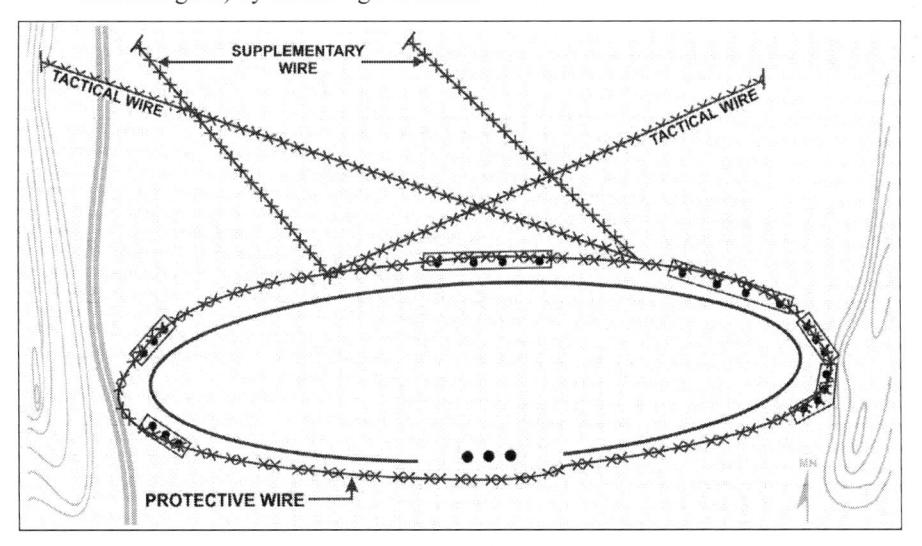

Figure 3-11. Protective wire obstacles

Obstacle Lanes

3-123. The platoon might be responsible for actions related to lanes through obstacles. These duties can include marking lanes in an obstacle, reporting locations of the start and ends of each lane, operating contact points, providing guides for elements passing through the obstacle, and closing the lane.

Situational Obstacle

3-124. A situational obstacle is planned and possibly prepared before a mission, but it executes only if specific criteria are met. It gives the platoon leader the flexibility to emplace tactical obstacles based on battlefield development—

- The platoon leader anticipates situations that require maneuver and fire plan modifications to defeat the threat, and considers the use of situational obstacles to support these modifications.
- By their very nature, situational obstacles must be quickly installable, but still achieve the desired effect. Therefore, scatterable mines (SCATMINEs) such as MOPMS, Hornets, and Volcanoes are the most common versions used at the platoon level. However, situational obstacles can consist of any type of individual obstacle.
- The platoon leader considers where he can employ situational obstacles. He ensures the combination of fires and obstacles are enough to achieve the obstacle effect.
- The platoon leader identifies execution triggers; situational obstacles are triggered based on friendly actions, enemy actions, or a combination of both.
- Finally, the platoon leader withholds execution of a situational obstacle until the obstacle effect is required. Once committed, those assets are no longer available to support any other mission. The platoon leader also considers that SCATMINEs have a self-destruct time. Emplacing an obstacle too soon can cause the mines to self-destruct before the enemy arrives.

INTELLIGENCE

3-125. The Infantry platoon leader never has all the information needed about the enemy. Therefore, the platoon leader obtains or develops the best possible IPB products, conducts continuous reconnaissance, and integrates new and updated intelligence throughout the operation. He may need to request information through the CoIST from the battalion staff to answer platoon information requirements. (Refer to FM 3-21.10 for more information.)

3-126. As with all tactical planning, IPB is a critical part of defensive planning. It helps the platoon leader define where to concentrate combat power, where to accept risk, and where to plan potential decisive operations. To aid in the development of a flexible defensive plan, the IPB must present all feasible enemy courses of action. The essential areas of focus are—

- Analyze terrain and weather.
- Determine enemy force size and likely courses of action with associated decision points.

- Determine enemy vulnerabilities and high value targets.
- Impact of civilian population on the defense.

3-127. The platoon leader, in coordination with the CoIST, base determinations of how and where to defeat the enemy on potential future enemy locations, the terrain, and forces available. The Infantry company may define a defeat mechanism including the use of single or multiple counterattacks to achieve success. The platoon leader analyzes the platoon's role in the Infantry company fight and determines how to achieve success.

FIRES

3-128. For indirect fire plan to be effective in the defense, the Infantry platoon plans and executes fires in a manner, which achieves the intended task and purpose of each target. Indirect fires serve a variety of purposes in the defense, including the following:
- Slow and disrupt enemy movement.
- Prevent the enemy from executing breaching operations.
- Destroy or delay enemy forces at obstacles using massed fires or precision munitions.
- Disrupt enemy support-by-fire elements.
- Defeat attacks along avenues of approach with the use of final protective fires.
- Disrupt the enemy to enable friendly elements to disengage or conduct counterattacks.
- Obscure enemy observation or screen friendly movement during disengagement and counterattacks.
- Provide obscurants screens to separate enemy echelons or to silhouette enemy formations to facilitate direct fire engagement.
- Provide illumination as necessary.
- Execute suppression of enemy air defense missions to support aviation operations.

3-129. In developing the fire plan, the platoon leader evaluates the indirect fire systems available to provide support. Considerations when developing the plan include tactical capabilities, weapons ranges, and available munitions. These factors help the platoon leader and forward observer determine the best method for achieving the task and purpose for each target in the fire plan. The Infantry company fire support personnel contribute significantly to the platoon fight. Positioning is critical. The platoon leader, in coordination with the company fire support officer, selects positions providing his forward observer with unobstructed observation of the area of operation, ensuring survivability.

SUSTAINMENT

3-130. In addition to the sustainment functions required for all missions, the platoon leader's planning process includes pre-positioning of ammunition caches, identifying the positioning of company trains, and Class IV and V supply points and mine dumps.

3-131. The platoon leader's mission analysis may reveal the platoon's ammunition requirements during an upcoming mission exceed its basic load. This requires the platoon to coordinate with the company to preposition ammunition caches. The platoon usually positions ammunition caches at alternate or subsequent positions. The platoon also may dig in these caches and guard them to prevent their capture or destruction by the enemy.

3-132. The Infantry company trains usually operate 500 to 1000 meters or one terrain feature to the rear of the company to provide immediate recovery and medical support. The company trains conduct evacuation (of those wounded in action [WIA], weapons, and equipment) and resupply as required. The company trains are located in covered and concealed positions close enough to the company to provide responsive support, but out of enemy direct fire. The company first sergeant or executive officer positions the trains and supervises sustainment operations with the platoon. It is the Infantry company commander's responsibility to ensure all subordinate units know the locations of battalion combat and field trains as well as the company CCP, BAS, and medical and casualty evacuation procedures. The platoon leader's analysis determines the measures for every mission.

PROTECTION

3-133. Air and missile defense support to the platoon may be limited. Units should expect to use their organic weapons systems for self-defense against enemy air threats. Plan for CBRN reconnaissance at likely locations for enemy employment of CBRN agents and hazards. Use obscurants to support disengagement or movement of forces. Assign sectors of fire to prevent fratricide and friendly fire.

3-134. Survivability construction includes fighting positions, protective positions, and hardening. These are prepared to protect vehicles, personnel and weapons systems. Positions can be constructed and reinforced with overhead cover to increase the survivability of dismounts and crew-served weapons against shrapnel from airbursts. Vehicle fighting positions can be constructed with both hull and turret-defilade observation positions. In addition, the Infantry platoon and squad may use digging assets for ammunition caches at alternate, supplementary, or subsequent positions. All leaders must understand survivability plans and priorities. Typically, at platoon level the engineer platoon leader creates a leader's card, which enables the platoon leader to track the survivability effort. One person in the platoon, usually the platoon sergeant is designated to enforce the plan and priorities, and ensure the completion status is reported accurately, tracked, and disseminated down to subordinate squads and attachments.

ADDITIONAL PLANNING CONSIDERATIONS

3-135. Additional defensive planning considerations for missions in urban and mountainous environments include urban terrain, subterranean threats, mountainous terrain and tunnel and cave complexes. Each of these are described below.

URBAN TERRAIN

3-136. Infantry forces defend urban areas to defeat an attack, gain time, economize forces, protect infrastructure, protect a populace, and shape conditions for offensive or stability urban operations. Usually two or more purposes apply to urban defense tasks in

Chapter 3

urban terrain. Defensive urban operations provide leaders opportunities to turn the environment's characteristics to the advantage of Army forces. Urban areas are ideal for the defense and enhance the combat power of defending units.

3-137. In a built-up area, the defender takes advantage of inherent cover and concealment afforded by urban terrain. Restrictions to the attacker's ability to maneuver and observe are taken into consideration. By using the terrain and fighting from well-prepared and mutually supporting positions, a defending force can delay, block, fix, turn, disrupt, or destroy a much larger attacking force. The defense of a built-up area is organized around key terrain features, buildings, and areas that preserves the integrity of the defense and provide the defender ease of movement. The defender organizes and plans defensive missions by considering OAKOC, fire hazards, and communications restrictions. (Refer to ATTP 3-06.11 for more information.)

SUBTERRANEAN THREATS

3-138. The enemy will likely use tunnels and may have the advantage of marked routes and detailed reconnaissance. Because he is able to select ambush positions and withdrawal routes, the defender typically has the element of surprise. A defended position in an underground facility can be very effective in countering enemy subterranean operations. The best underground defensive positions are well protected and canalize the enemy into a killing zone to inflict maximum casualties.

3-139. When moving through tunnels, take great care to avoid booby traps. These are normally deployed near junctions and are often operated by tripwires. Standing water in tunnels provides excellent camouflage for antipersonnel mines and booby traps scattered on likely routes. With the battle above continuing, flooding and cave-ins are highly possible due to the likelihood of artillery barrages and the use of demolitions. Thus, identifying escape routes is essential.

3-140. Chemical defense is a constant concern for Soldiers conducting subterranean operations. In tunnels, Soldiers may encounter chemical warfare agents as well as industrial chemicals in dense concentrations. A chemical agent alarm system, carried by the point man, provides instantaneous warning of the presence of chemical warfare agents. M8 and M9 detection papers also test for the presence of chemical agents. (Refer to ATTP 3-06.11 for more information.)

MOUNTAINOUS TERRAIN

3-141. Defensive tasks in mountainous areas are conducted to resist, defeat, or destroy an enemy attack to support subsequent offensive tasks. Infantry leaders use the defense to withstand an enemy attack while preparing to seize the initiative and develop conditions favorable for transitioning to the offense. During the defense, friendly forces withstand enemy attacks and hold the enemy while preparing to seize the initiative and transition to an attack or to conduct stability tasks. A thorough understanding of the commander's intent is especially critical in the defense, which demands precise integration of all combat power.

Defense

3-142. Forces operating in mountainous terrain often possess weapons and equipment more advanced in technology than the enemy does. Knowing this, enemy offensive tactics commonly involve short violent engagements followed by a hasty withdrawal through preplanned routes. They often strike quickly and fight only as long as the advantage of initial surprise is in their favor. Attacks may include direct fires, indirect fires, or IEDs and may be against stationary or moving forces. (Refer to ATTP 3-21.50 for more information.)

TUNNEL AND CAVE COMPLEXES

3-143. Tunnel and complexes may be interconnected with other tunnels and caves, concealed by trapdoors or blocked dirt passages that are up to three or four feet thick. Secret passages are usually known only to selected personnel and are used mainly in emergencies. Tunnels and caves may be interconnected by much longer passages through which relatively large bodies of men may be transferred from one area to another. The connectivity of these systems often allows the enemy to move unnoticed from one area to another, eluding friendly forces.

3-144. Characteristic of a typical tunnel or cave complex is normally superb camouflage, conceal entrances, exits and camouflage bunkers. Within the tunnel and cave complex itself, side tunnels may be concealed, trapdoors are often hidden and dead-end tunnels or caves are used to confuse the attackers. Airshafts are usually spaced at intervals throughout a tunnel or cave system. In many instances, the first indication of a tunnel or cave complex comes from direct fire received from a concealed bunker. Spoils from the tunnel or cave system may be distributed over a wide area, giving clues to its existence. (Refer to ATTP 3-21.50 for more information.)

SECTION III – FORMS OF THE DEFENSE

3-145. The Infantry platoon usually defends using one of three forms of defense: defense of a linear obstacle, perimeter defense, and reverse slope. The platoon also can defend using a combination of these forms. (Refer to FM 3-90-1 for more information.)

DEFENSE OF A LINEAR OBSTACLE

3-146. A platoon leader may conduct either an area or mobile defense along or behind a linear obstacle. The Infantry leader normally prefers an area defense because it accepts less risk by not allowing the enemy to cross the obstacle. Linear obstacles such as mountain ranges or river lines generally favor a forward defense. It is extremely difficult to deploy in strength along the entire length of a linear obstacle. The defending leader must conduct economy of force measures in some areas.

3-147. Within an area defense, the leader's use of a defense in-depth accepts the possibility the enemy may force a crossing at a given point. The depth of the defense should prevent the enemy from rapidly exploiting its success. It also defuses the enemy's combat power by forcing the enemy to contain bypassed friendly defensive positions in addition to continuing to attack positions in greater depth.

Chapter 3

3-148. This form of defense may be used when defensible terrain is available in the forward portion of the platoon's area of operation, or to take advantage of a major linear natural obstacle. It also is used when the enemy is mainly Infantry; the platoon conducts a security mission such as counter infiltration, or as directed by company. This technique allows interlocking and overlapping observation and fields of fire across the platoon's front. (See figure 3-12.) The bulk of the platoon's combat power is well forward. Sufficient resources must be available to provide adequate combat power to detect and stop an attack. The platoon relies on fighting from well-prepared mutually supporting positions. It uses a high volume of direct and indirect fires to stop the attacks. The main concern when fighting this form of defense is the lack of flexibility and the difficulty of both seizing the initiative and seeking out enemy weaknesses. Obstacles, indirect fires, and contingency plans are vital to this maneuver. The platoon depends upon surprise, well-prepared positions, and deadly accurate fires to defeat the enemy. The reserve is usually small, perhaps a squad.

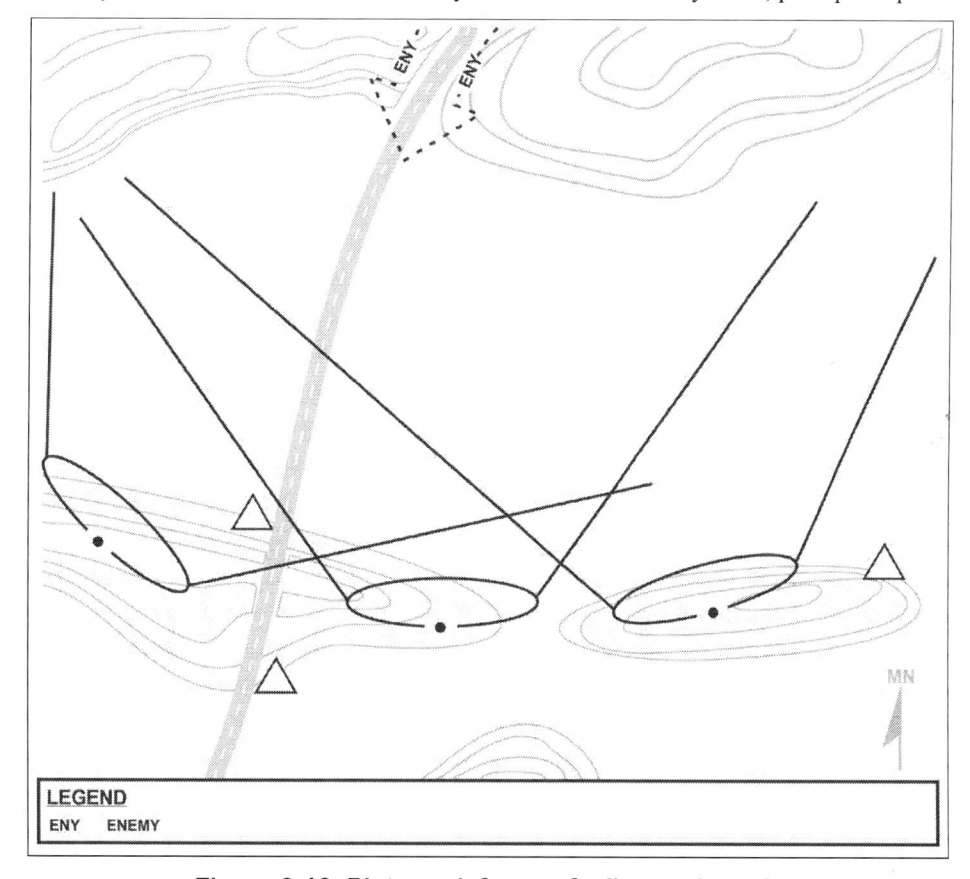

Figure 3-12. Platoon defense of a linear obstacle

3-149. Minefields and other obstacles are positioned and covered by fire to slow the enemy and inflict casualties. Engaging the enemy at long range by supporting fires (CAS, attack helicopters, and field artillery) disrupts the momentum of his the attack. Use fires from mortars, machine guns, and small arms as he comes into range. If the defense is penetrated, block the advance with the reserve and shift fire from the forward squads onto the enemy flanks. Then, counterattack with the platoon reserve or the least committed squad with intense fires. The purpose is to destroy isolated or weakened enemy forces and regain key terrain.

3-150. The counterreconnaissance effort is critical when fighting to deny the enemy the locations of the platoon's forward positions. If the enemy locates the forward positions, he will concentrate combat power where he desires while fixing the rest of the platoon to prevent their maneuver to disrupt his attack. This effort might be enhanced by initially occupying and fighting from alternate positions forward of the primary positions. This tactic enhances the security mission and deceives the enemy reconnaissance that may get through the security force.

PERIMETER DEFENSE

3-151. The platoon leader can employ the perimeter defense as an option when conducting an area or mobile defense. A perimeter defense is a defense oriented in all directions. (See figure 3-13, page 3-44.) The Infantry platoon uses it for self-security, and to protect other units located within the perimeter. The platoon can employ a perimeter defense in urban or woodland terrain. The platoon might be called upon to execute the perimeter defense under a variety of conditions, including:

- When it must secure itself against terrorist or insurgent attacks in an urban area.
- This technique also may apply if the platoon must conserve or build combat power in order to execute offensive tasks or patrolling missions.
- When it must hold critical terrain in areas where the defense is not tied in with adjacent units.
- When it has been bypassed and isolated by the enemy and must defend in place.
- When it conducts occupation of an independent assembly area or reserve position.
- When it begins preparation of a strongpoint.
- When it is directed to concentrate fires into two or more adjacent avenues of approach.

Chapter 3

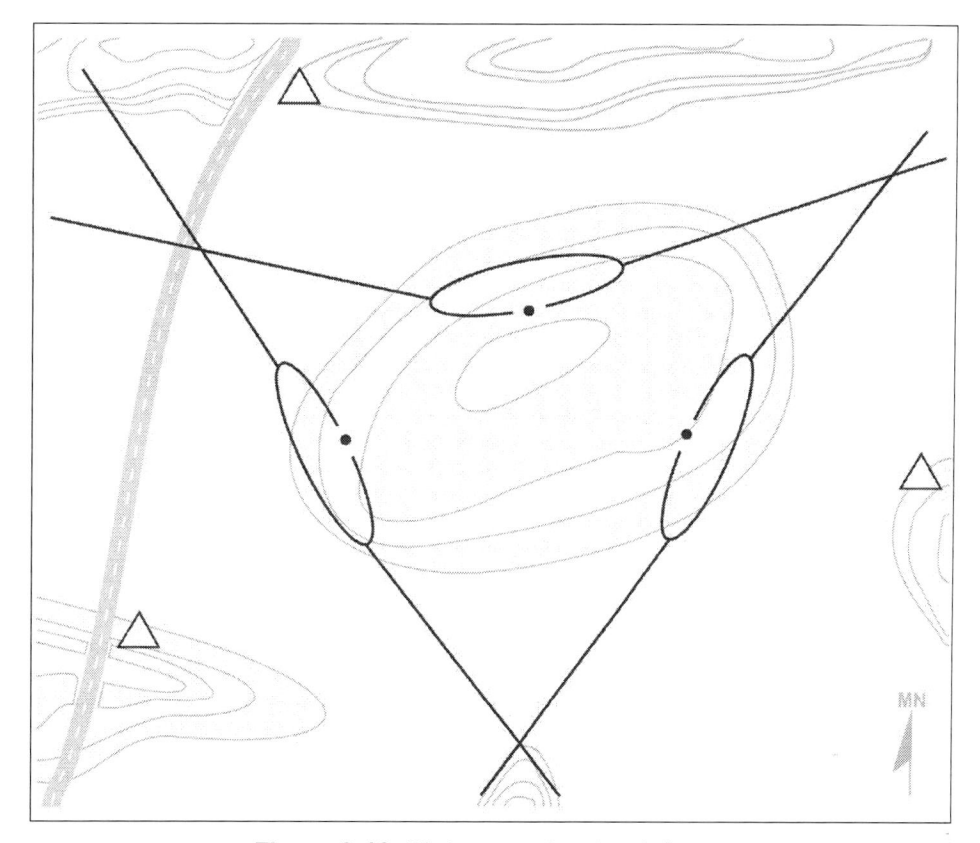

Figure 3-13. Platoon perimeter defense

PREPARATIONS

3-152. The Infantry platoon prepares a perimeter defense when there are no friendly units adjacent to it. A perimeter defense might be used in a reserve position, in an AA or patrol base, on a follow-on decentralized platoon operation during resupply or when the platoon is isolated. The following actions constitute setting up a perimeter defense:

- Preparing a perimeter defense is like preparing any other position defense, but the platoon must disperse in a circular configuration for all-round security. (The actual shape depends on the terrain.) The platoon must be prepared to defend in all directions.
- The platoon leader assigns squads to cover the most likely approach, and prepares alternate and supplementary positions within the perimeter.
- Javelins cover likely armor approaches.
- They may use hide positions and move forward to fire as the enemy appears. The platoon leader assigns several firing positions. If there are few positions for them, they are assigned a primary position and are dug in.

- Snipers or designated marksman should cover likely or suspected enemy positions or observation posts.
- Snipers and designated marksmen also should be used to observe or overwatch areas where civilians congregate.
- Keep attached mortars near the center of the perimeter so their minimum range does not restrict their ability to fire in any direction.
- They should dig in and have covered ammunition storage bunkers.
- If possible, hold one or more rifle team in reserve.
- The platoon leader assigns a primary position to the rear of the platoon, covering the most dangerous avenues of approach, and may assign the rifle squad supplementary positions since the platoon is prepared to fight in all directions.
- Prepare obstacles in-depth around the perimeter.
- Plan direct and indirect fire as for any type of defense.
- Plan and use direct and indirect fire support from outside the perimeter when available.
- Counter enemy probing attacks by area fire weapons (artillery, mortars, claymores, and grenade launchers) to avoid revealing the locations of fighting positions (rules of engagement-dependent).
- If the enemy penetrates the perimeter, the reserve destroys, and then blocks the penetration.
    - It also covers friendly Soldiers during movement to alternate, supplementary, or subsequent positions.
    - Even though the platoon's counterattack ability is limited, it must strive to restore its perimeter.
- Sustainment elements may support from within the perimeter or from another position.
- Supply and evacuation might be by air. Consider the availability of landing zones and drop zones (protected from enemy observation and fire) when selecting and preparing the position.

Y-Shape Variation

3-153. The Y-shaped perimeter defense is a variation of the perimeter defense that uses the terrain effectively. This defense is used when the terrain, cover and concealment, or fields of fire do not support the physical positioning of the squads in a circular manner. The Y-shaped perimeter defense is so named because the squad's battle positions are positioned on three different axes radiating from one central point. (See figure 3-14, page 3-46.) It is still a perimeter defense because it is effective against an attack from any direction. The Y-shaped defense provides all-round perimeter fires without having to position Soldiers on the perimeter. It is likely to be most effective in mountainous terrain, but it also may be used in a dense jungle environment due to limited fields of fire. All of the fundamentals of a perimeter defense previously discussed apply, with the following adjustments and special considerations:

Chapter 3

- Although each squad battle position has a primary orientation for its fires, each squad must be prepared to reorient to mass fires into the engagement areas to its rear.
- When no most likely enemy approach is identified, or in limited visibility, each squad may have half its Soldiers oriented into the engagement areas to the front and half into the engagement areas to the rear. Ideally, supplementary individual fighting positions are prepared, allowing Soldiers to reposition when required to mass fires into one engagement area.

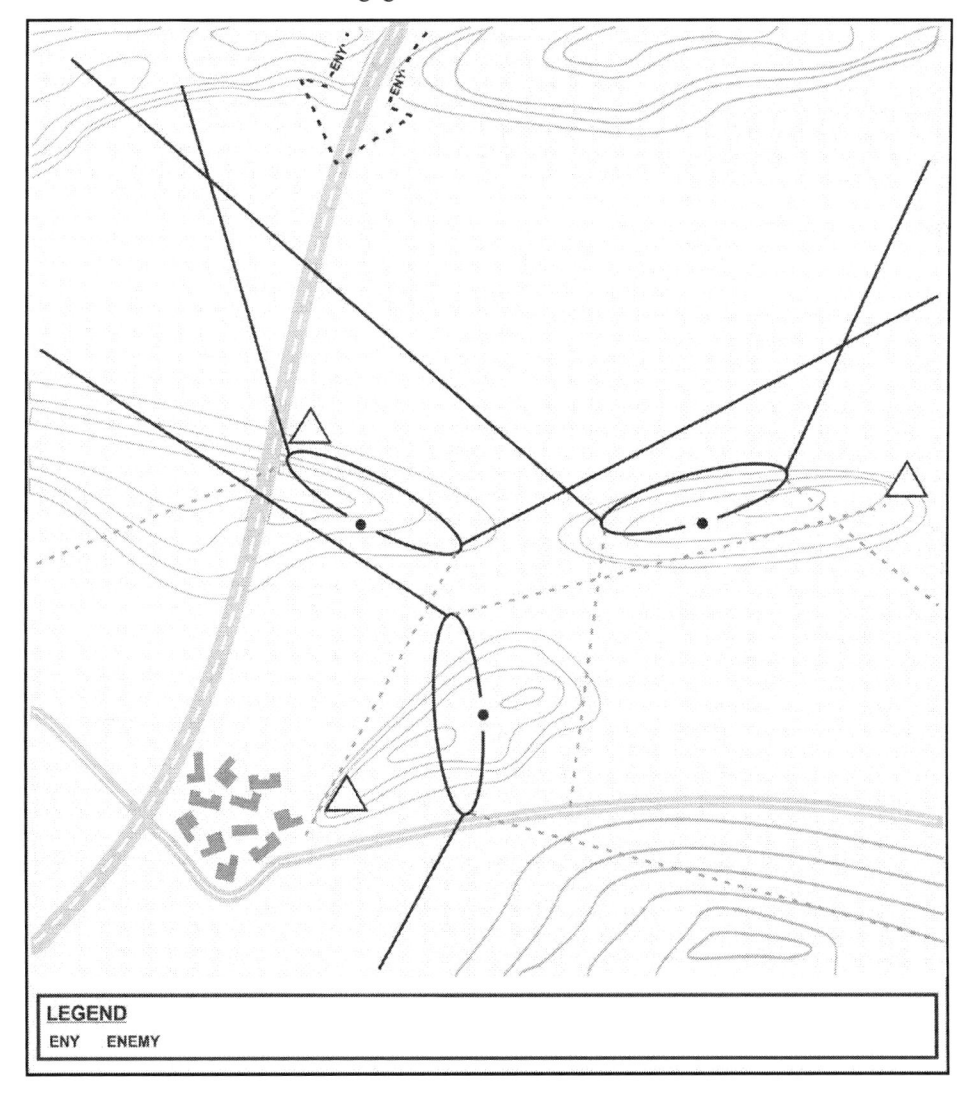

Figure 3-14. Y-shaped perimeter defense

Defense

- When a most likely enemy avenue of approach is identified, the platoon leader may adjust the normal platoon orientations to concentrate fires (see figure 3-15) for the following reasons:
  - This entails accepting risk in another area of the perimeter.
  - The platoon security plan should compensate for this with additional observation posts, patrols, or other measures.
- The positioning of the platoon command post, reserve, or any sustainment assets is much more difficult due to a lack of depth within the perimeter.

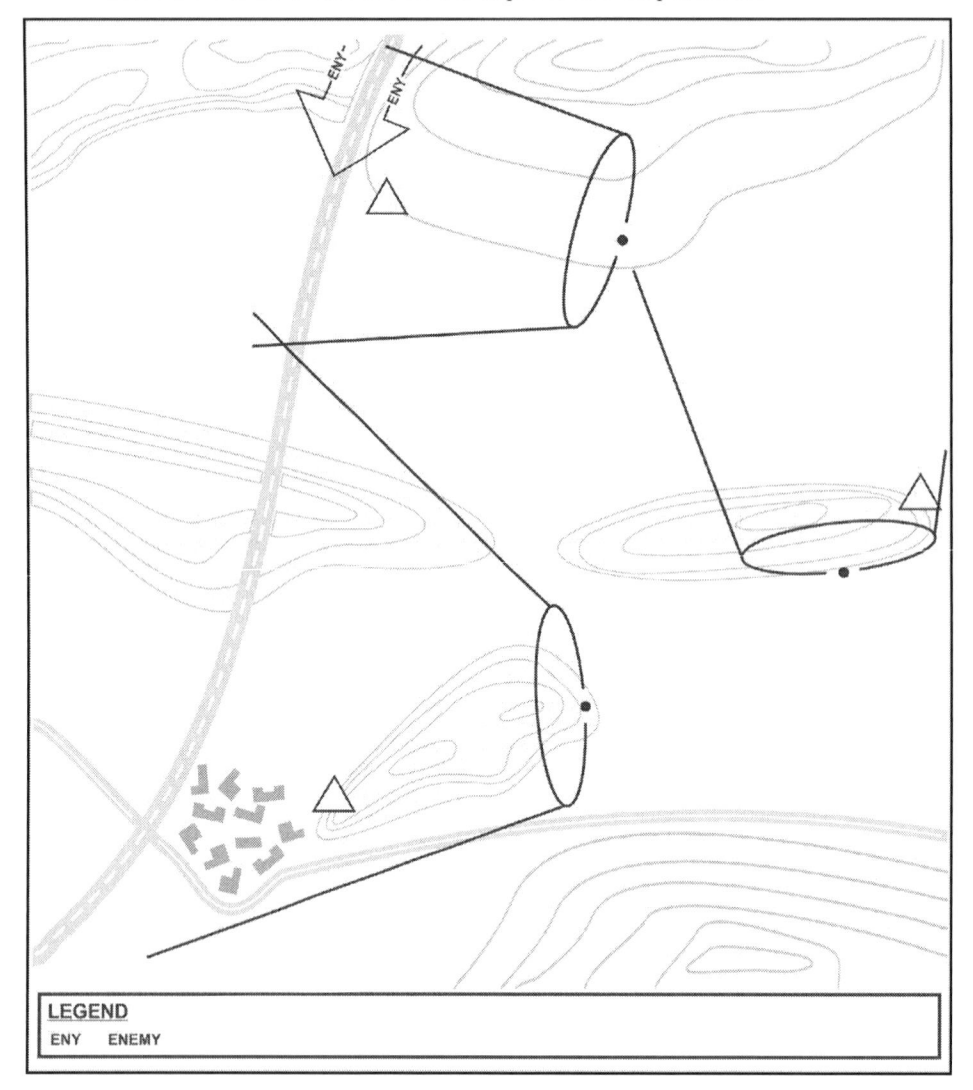

Figure 3-15. Modified Y-shape perimeter defense

Chapter 3

3-154. The most difficult aspect of the Y-shape perimeter defense is the fire control measures required. To fight this defense without casualties from friendly fire, the leaders must ensure the limits of fire for each weapon do not allow fires into the adjacent squad positions. In a mountainous environment, firing downward into the engagement area may make this simpler. Some measures to consider include:

- Position medium machine guns near the apex of the "Y" to allow a final protective line that covers the platoon front while firing away from the adjacent units.
- Cover the areas of the engagement areas closest to the apex with Claymores, non-persistent mines, or obstacles to reduce the need for direct fires in these areas.
- Identify those positions at most risk to friendly fires and prepare the fighting position to protect the Soldier from fires in this direction.
- The loss of one squad position may threaten the loss of the entire platoon. To prevent this, plan and rehearse immediate counterattacks with a reserve or the least committed platoon.
- Consider allowing the enemy to penetrate well into the engagement areas and destroy him as in an ambush.
- Be aware that if a Y-shape defense is established on the prominent terrain feature and the enemy has the ability to mass fires, he may fix the platoon with direct fires and destroy it with massed indirect fires.

REVERSE-SLOPE DEFENSE

3-155. An alternative to defending on the forward slope of a hill or a ridge is to defend on a reverse slope. (See figure 3-16.) In such a defense, the Infantry platoon is deployed on terrain that is masked from enemy direct fire and ground observation by the crest of a hill. Although some units and weapons might be positioned on the forward slope, the crest, or the counter-slope (a forward slope of a hill to the rear of a reverse slope), most forces are on the reverse slope. The key to this defense is control the crest by direct fire.

Defense

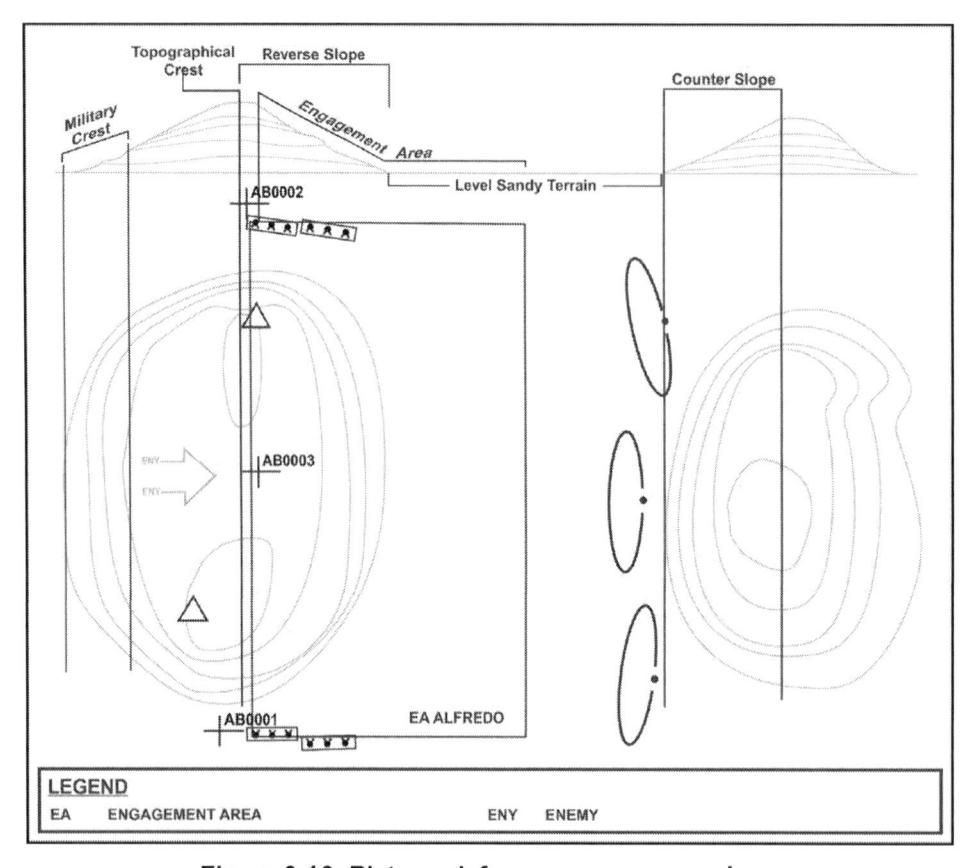

Figure 3-16. Platoon defense on a reverse slope

FUNDAMENTALS

3-156. Planning fundamentals to a defense on a reverse slope include:
- Positioning forward squads so they block enemy approaches and exploit existing obstacles. Plans should—
  - Permit surprise fire on the crest and on the approaches around the crest.
  - Have rear and overhead cover to protect friendly Soldiers from fratricide while in forward fighting positions.
- Positioning observation posts, on the crest or the forward slope of the defended hill. Plans should—
  - Increase observation posts and patrols to prevent infiltration at night.
  - Consider attaching medium machine guns to observation posts.
- Positioning the squad in-depth or reserve where it can provide the most flexibility, support the forward squads by fire, protect the flanks and the rear of the platoon, and counterattack, if necessary. It might be positioned on the counterslope to the

rear of the forward squad if that position allows it to fire and hit the enemy when he reaches the crest of the defended hill.
- Positioning the platoon command post to the rear where it will not interfere with the reserve or supporting units. Plans should consider that—
  - The platoon leader may have an observation post on the forward slope or crest and another on the reverse slope or counterslope.
  - The observation post is used on the forward slope or crest before the battle starts when the platoon leader is determining the enemy's intentions.
  - During the fight, he moves the observation post on the reverse slope or counterslope.
- Planning indirect fire well forward of, on, and to the flanks of the forward slope, crest, reverse slope, and counterslope.
- Planning direct final protective fires on the crest of the hill to control the crest and stop assaults.
- Reinforcing existing obstacles.
- Knowing that protective obstacles on the reverse slope—just down from the crest where it can be covered by fire—can slow the enemy's advance and hold him under friendly fire.
- Knowing that the platoon leader normally plans for counterattacks and plans to drive the enemy off the crest by fire, if possible.
- Knowing that the platoon leader is prepared to drive the enemy off by fire and movement.

EMPLOYMENT

3-157. The Infantry leader can adopt a reverse slope position when—
- Enemy fire makes the forward slope untenable.
- Lack of cover and concealment on the forward slope makes it untenable.
- The forward slope has been lost or not yet been gained.
- The forward slope is exposed to enemy direct fire weapons fired from beyond the effective range of the defender's weapons. Moving to the reverse slope removes the attacker's standoff advantage.
- The terrain on the reverse slope provides better fields of fire than the forward slope.
- Surprising and deceiving the enemy as to the true location of the Infantry platoon's defensive positions is essential.
- Enemy weapons systems have overmatch in range and lethality.

3-158. When executing a reverse slope defense, the leader places special emphasis on—
- A direct and indirect fire support plan to prevent the enemy's occupation and using crest of the hill.
- The use of observation posts or reconnaissance elements on the forward slope to provide observation across the entire front and security to the main battle positions.
- A counterattack plan specifying measures necessary to clear the crest or regain it from the enemy.

- Direct and indirect fire support to destroy disrupt, and attrition of enemy forces on the forward slope.

3-159. The forward edge of positions should be within small arms range of the crest. It should be far enough from the crest, which fields of fire, allow the defender time to place well-aimed fire on the enemy before he reaches friendly positions. The platoon establishes observation posts on or forward of the topographical crest. This allows long-range observation over the entire front and indirect fire coverage of forward obstacles. Observation posts usually are provided by the unit owning the terrain being observed, and may vary in size from a few Soldiers to a reinforced squad. They should include forward observers. At night, their number should be increased to improve security.

SPECIAL CONSIDERATIONS

3-160. These are some considerations leaders may apply when defending on a reverse slope:
- Observation of the enemy is more difficult.
- Soldiers in this position see forward no farther than the crest. This makes it hard to determine exactly where the enemy is as he advances, especially when visibility is poor.
- Observation posts must be placed forward of the topographic crest for early warning and long-range observation.
- Egress from the position might be more difficult.
- Fields of fire are usually short.
- Obstacles on the forward slope can be covered only with indirect fire or by units on the flanks of the company unless some weapons systems are placed forward initially.
- If the enemy gains the crest, he can assault downhill. This may give him a psychological advantage.
- If observation posts are insufficient or improperly placed, the defenders might have to fight an enemy who suddenly appears in strength at close range.
- A reverse slope engagement is decisive resulting in one or both forces being severely attritted. Very difficult to break contact.
- Placing the vehicles at the bottom of the hill and the Infantry on counter slope allows the platoon to maximize its firepower into the engagement area as the enemy crests the slope.
- The defender often has the opportunity to take the first shot at the attacker.

SECTION IV – FIGHTING POSTIONS

3-161. The defensive plan normally requires building fighting positions. The mechanized platoon uses fighting positions for its dismounted Infantrymen and for its BFV.

DISMOUNTED

3-162. Fighting positions protect Soldiers by providing cover from direct and indirect fires and concealment through positioning and proper camouflage. Because the battlefield conditions confronting Soldiers are never standard, no single standard fighting position design fits all tactical situations.

3-163. Refer to Training Circular (TC) 3-21.75 for details on the construction of—
- Hasty fighting positions.
- Fighting positions for crew-served weapons, to include machine guns and Javelins.
- Fighting positions for one, two, and three men.
- Shoulder-launched munitions positions.

MOUNTED

3-164. Vehicles use natural cover and concealment in hide positions initially to increase survivability. As time, assets, and situations permit, positions are prepared using organic excavation equipment or engineer support. Priority is given to those vehicles containing essential equipment or supplies. Crews use these fighting positions for individual protection as well.

3-165. Parapets positioned at the front of or around major weapon systems provide improved protection from direct fire and from blast and fragments of indirect fire, artillery, mortar, and rocket shells. At its base, the parapet should be at least 8 feet thick. The parapet functions as a standoff barrier for impact-detonating direct fire high explosive antitank and ATGM projectiles. The parapet should cause the fuzes to activate, thereby increasing survivability for the protected vehicles. If the enemy uses kinetic energy, direct fire armor-piercing, or hypervelocity projectiles, it is impractical to construct parapets thick enough for protection. To protect against these projectiles, deep-cut, hull defilade, or turret defilade positions are prepared. Fighting and protective positions for essential vehicles should be constructed no larger than needed.

3-166. Success in the area of operation requires maneuver between fighting positions between main gun firings. Maximum use of terrain is required to conceal fighting vehicles maneuvering between fighting positions. After a major weapon system fires its main gun, the vehicle should move concealed to another position before firing again. If the major weapon system immediately reappears in the old position, the enemy knows where to fire his next round.

HASTY

3-167. Hasty fighting positions for combat vehicles, to include armored personnel carriers and mortar carriers, take advantage of natural terrain features. These positions are prepared with at least construction effort. A frontal parapet, as high as practical without interfering with the vehicle's weapon systems, shields the position from frontal attack and provides limited concealment if properly camouflaged. Protection is improved if the position is made deeper and the parapet extended around the vehicle's sides. Parapets provide a false sense of security against kinetic energy and hypervelocity projectiles; therefore, hasty vehicle fighting positions with parapets are not recommended for vehicles

Hasty fighting positions offer protection from HE antitank projectiles and provide limited concealment if properly camouflaged. As the tactical situation permits, hasty positions are improved to deliberate positions.

DELIBERATE

3-168. Deliberate fighting positions must protect a vehicle from kinetic energy and hypervelocity projectiles. The position is constructed in four parts: hull defilade, concealed access ramp or route, hide location, and turret defilade. (See figure 3-17 and figure 3-18, page 3-54.)

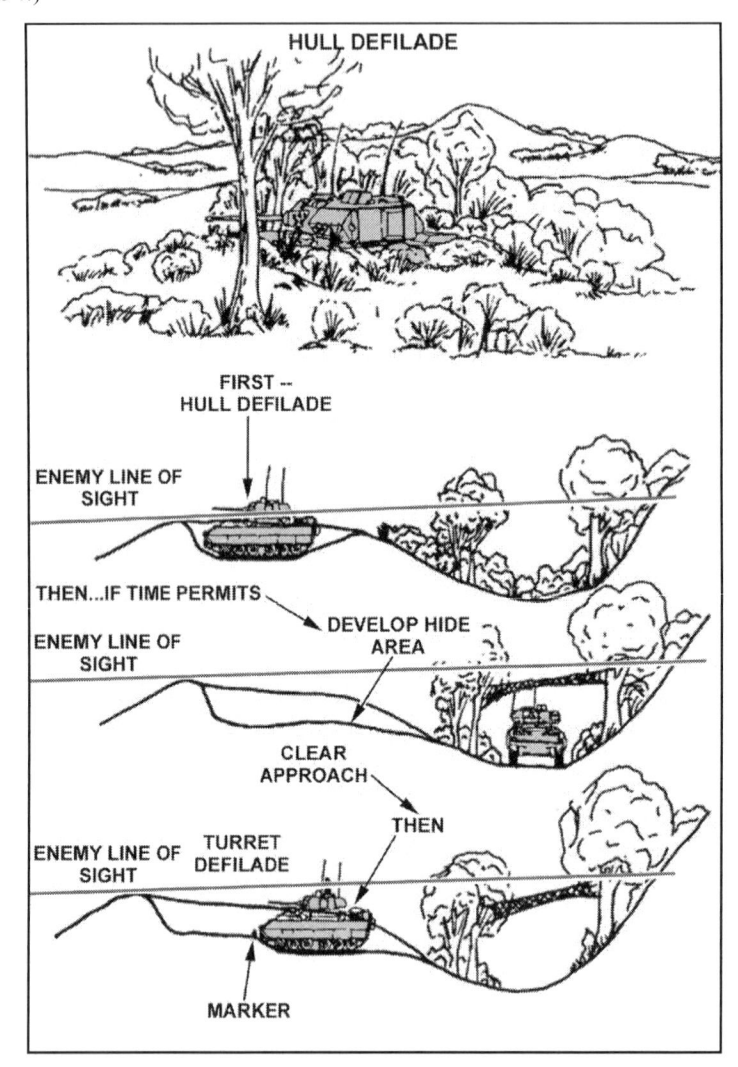

Figure 3-17. Developing deliberate fighting positions

Chapter 3

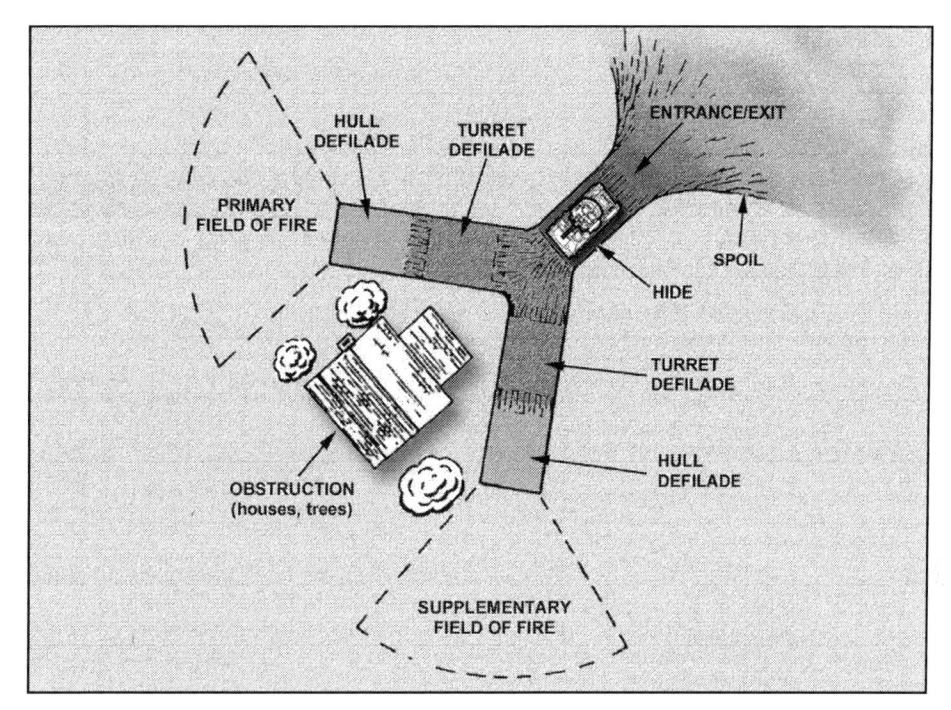

Figure 3-18. Top view of Y-shaped fighting position

POSITIONS FORMED BY NATURAL TERRAIN

3-169. Positions formed by natural terrain are usually best because they are easy to modify. If preparation is necessary, extensive engineer support is required. Each position is camouflaged with either natural vegetation or a camouflage net, and the spoil is flattened out or hauled away. All fighting positions for fighting vehicles (tanks and BFVs) are planned as deliberate positions. Since the lack of time usually does not allow full construction of a deliberate position, only some parts of the position are prepared. For example, the complete fighting position for a BFV requires the construction of a hull defilade, turret defilade, concealed access ramp or route, and hides location all within the same position. The maneuver team commander uses organic and engineer earthmoving assets and usually constructs part of the fighting position.

3-170. Digging hide locations and concealed routes between fighting positions is normally not practical due to the lack of engineer assets and time. Engineer assets are used to dig the hull and turret defilade positions. The ramps and concealed routes require only partial clearing and leveling with blade tanks or engineer equipment because natural concealed routes and hide locations are used. If time permits, the commander expands the fighting position to all four parts, to include a hide and turret defilade location. The access ramp from the hide location to the hull defilade position usually provides turret defilade for a vehicle at some point on the ramp. This location can be marked with engineer tape and a chemical light so the driver knows when to stop.

Defense

SECTION V – ENGAGEMENT AREA DEVELOPMENT

3-171. The engagement area is where the Infantry leader intends to engage and destroy an enemy force using the massed fires of all available weapons. Leaders combine natural and man-made obstacles to canalize the attacking force into engagement area. The success of engagements depends on how the leader can integrate the obstacle plan, indirect fire plan, and direct fire plan within the engagement area to achieve the Infantry platoon's and squads' tactical purposes.

3-172. At the platoon level, engagement area development is a complex function demanding parallel planning and preparation if the Infantry platoon and squad are to accomplish the myriad tasks for which it is responsible. Despite this complexity, engagement area development resembles a drill, and the platoon leader and his subordinate leaders use an orderly, standard set of procedures. The steps of engagement area development are not a rigid sequential process. Some steps may occur simultaneously to ensure the synergy of combined arms. Beginning with evaluation of METT-TC, the development process—

- Identifies all likely enemy avenues of approach.
- Determines likely enemy schemes of maneuver.
- Determines where to kill the enemy.
- Plans and integrates obstacles.
- Emplaces weapon systems.
- Plans and integrates indirect fires.
- Rehearses the execution of operations in the engagement area.

IDENTIFY LIKELY ENEMY AVENUES OF APPROACH

3-173. Procedures and considerations when identifying the enemy's likely avenues of approach (see figure 3-19, page 3-56) include:
- Conducting initial reconnaissance. If possible, do this from the enemy's perspective along each avenue of approach into the area of operations or engagement area.
- Identifying key and decisive terrain. This includes locations affording positions of advantage over the enemy, as well as natural obstacles and choke points restricting forward movement.
- Determining which avenues provide cover and concealment for the enemy while allowing him to maintain his tempo.
- Determining what terrain the enemy is likely to use to support each avenue.
- Evaluating lateral routes adjoining each avenue of approach.

Chapter 3

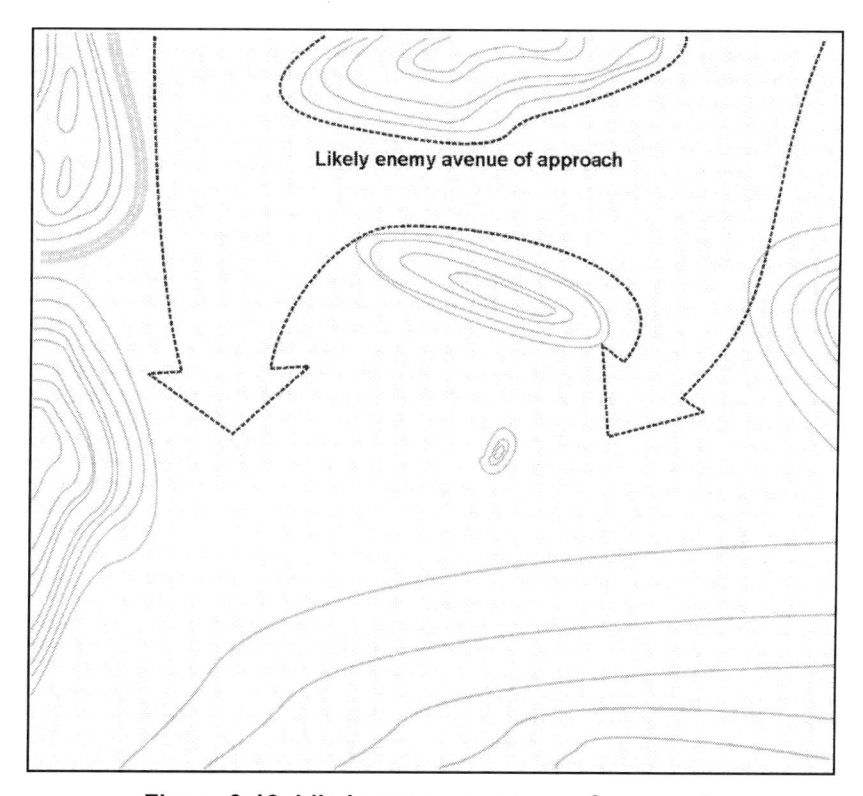

Figure 3-19. Likely enemy avenues of approach

DETERMINE THE ENEMY SCHEME OF MANEUVER

3-174. Procedures and considerations in determining the enemy's scheme of maneuver (see figure 3-20) include:
- Determining how the enemy will structure the attack.
- Determining how the enemy will use his reconnaissance assets. Will he attempt to infiltrate friendly positions?
- Determining where and when the enemy will change formations and establish support-by-fire positions.
- Determining where, when, and how the enemy will conduct his assault or breaching operations.
- Determining where and when he will commit follow-on forces.
- Determining the enemy's expected rates of movement.
- Assessing the effects of his combat multipliers and anticipated locations/areas of employment.
- Determining what reactions the enemy is likely to have in response to projected friendly actions.

Defense

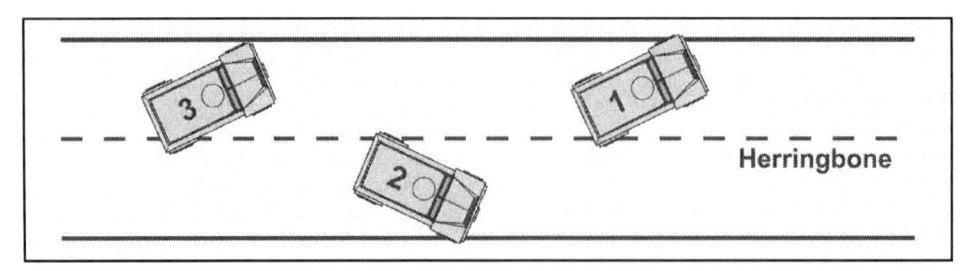

Figure 3-20. Example of an enemy scheme of maneuver

DETERMINE WHERE TO KILL THE ENEMY

3-175. The following steps apply in identifying and marking where the enemy engagement (see figure 3-21, page 3-58) is to occur:
- Identify target registration points matching the enemy's scheme of maneuver allowing the Infantry platoon and squad to identify where it will engage enemy forces through the depth of the area of operations.
- Identify and record the exact location of each target registration point.
  - In marking target registration points, use thermal sights to ensure visibility at the appropriate range under varying conditions, including daylight and limited visibility (darkness, smoke, dust, or other obscurants).
- Determine how many weapon systems will focus fires on each target registration point to achieve the desired end state.
- Determine which element will mass fires on each target registration point.
- Establish engagement areas around target registration points.
- Develop the direct fire planning measures necessary to focus fires at each target registration point.

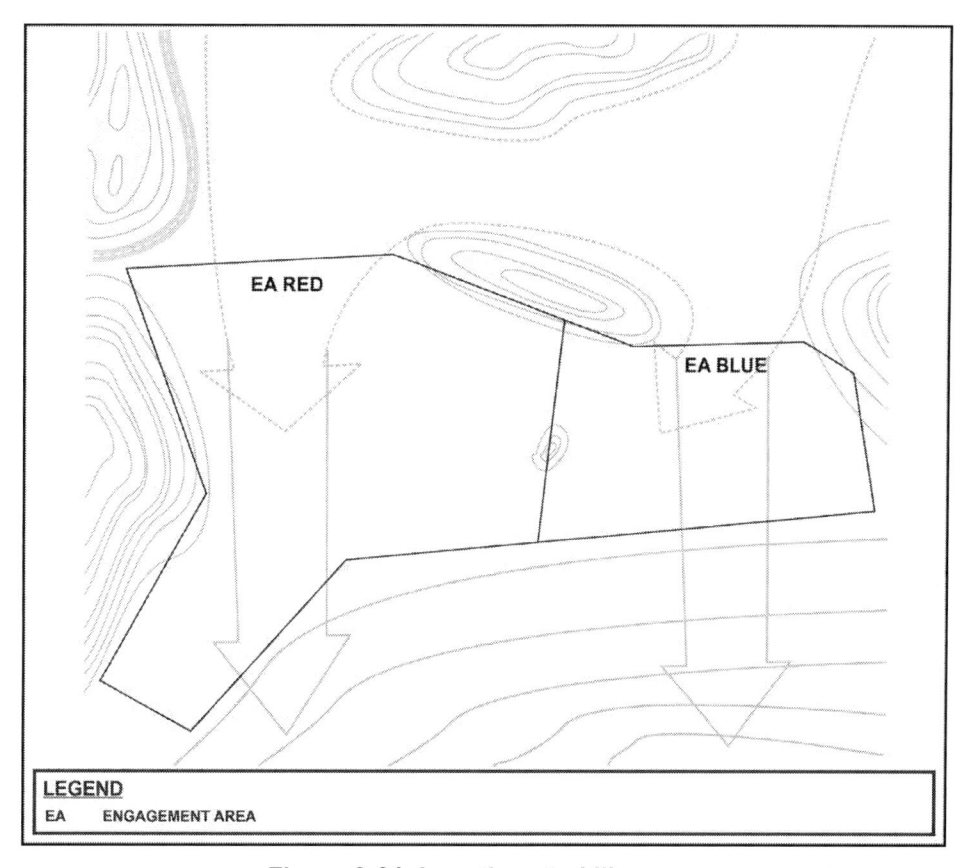

Figure 3-21. Locations to kill enemy

PLAN AND INTEGRATE OBSTACLES

3-176. The following steps apply in planning and integrating obstacles (see figure 3-22) during defensive missions:
- Determine the obstacle group intent with the engineer platoon leader confirming the target, relative location, and effect. Ensure intent supports the task force scheme of maneuver.
- In conjunction with the engineer platoon leader, identify, site, and mark the obstacles within the obstacle group.
- Integrate protective obstacle types and locations within Infantry platoon defensive perimeter.
- Ensure coverage of all obstacles with direct fires and or indirect fires.
- Assign responsibility for guides and lane closure as required.
- According to METT-TC, assist engineer platoons in emplacing obstacles, securing Class IV/V point, and securing obstacle work sites.

Defense

- Coordinate engineer disengagement criteria, actions on contact, and security requirements with the engineer platoon leader at the obstacle work site.

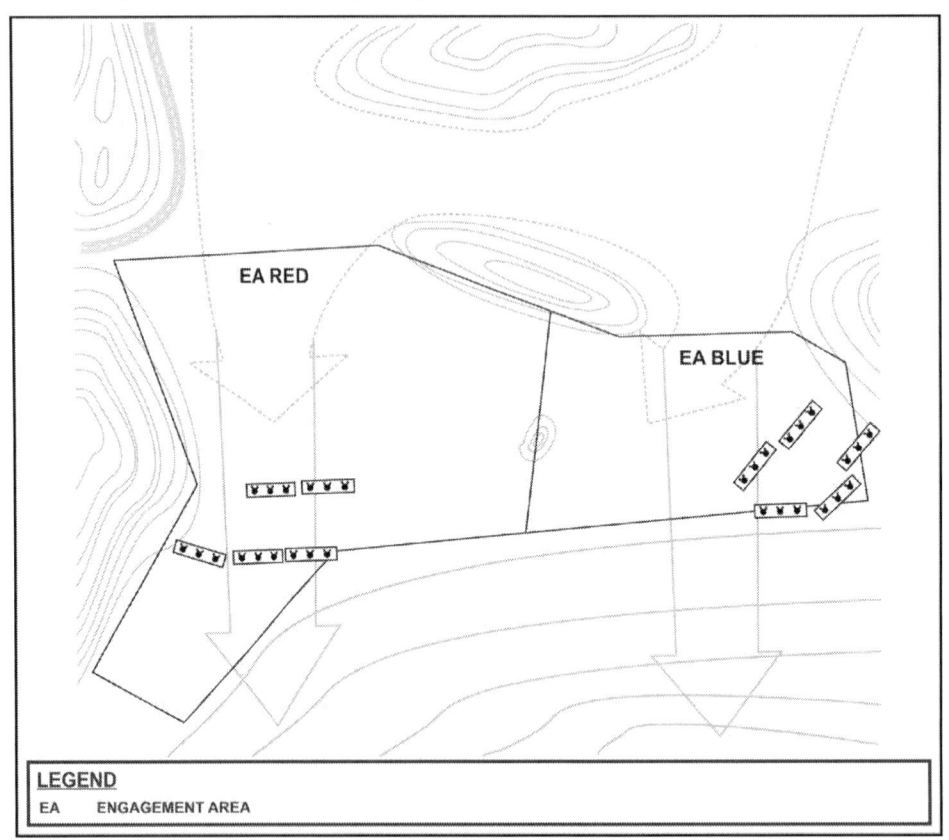

Figure 3-22. Plans for and integration of obstacles

EMPLACE WEAPON SYSTEMS

3-177. The following steps apply in selecting and improving battle positions and emplacing the Infantry platoon and squad vehicles, crew-served weapon systems, (see figure 3-23, page 3-60) and dismounted Infantry positions:
- Select tentative platoon/squad battle positions.

Note. When possible, select battle positions while moving in the engagement area. Using the enemy's perspective enables the Infantry leader to assess survivability of positions.

- Conduct a leader's reconnaissance of the tentative battle positions.
- Drive the engagement area to confirm selected positions are tactically advantageous.

Chapter 3

- Confirm and mark the selected battle positions.
- Ensure battle positions do not conflict with those of adjacent units and are tied in with adjacent positions.
- Select primary, alternate, and supplementary fighting positions to achieve the desired effect for each target registration point.
- Ensure platoon sergeants, vehicle commanders, or dismounted Infantry squad leaders position weapon systems so each target registration point is covered by the required number of weapons, vehicles, and squads.
- Ensure positions allow vehicle commanders, loaders, and gunners (as applicable for each vehicle or weapons system) to observe the engagement area and engage enemy forces from the hull down position.
- Stake vehicle or weapons system positions according to unit SOPs so engineers can dig in the positions while vehicle crews perform other tasks.
- Confirm all vehicle or weapons system positions.

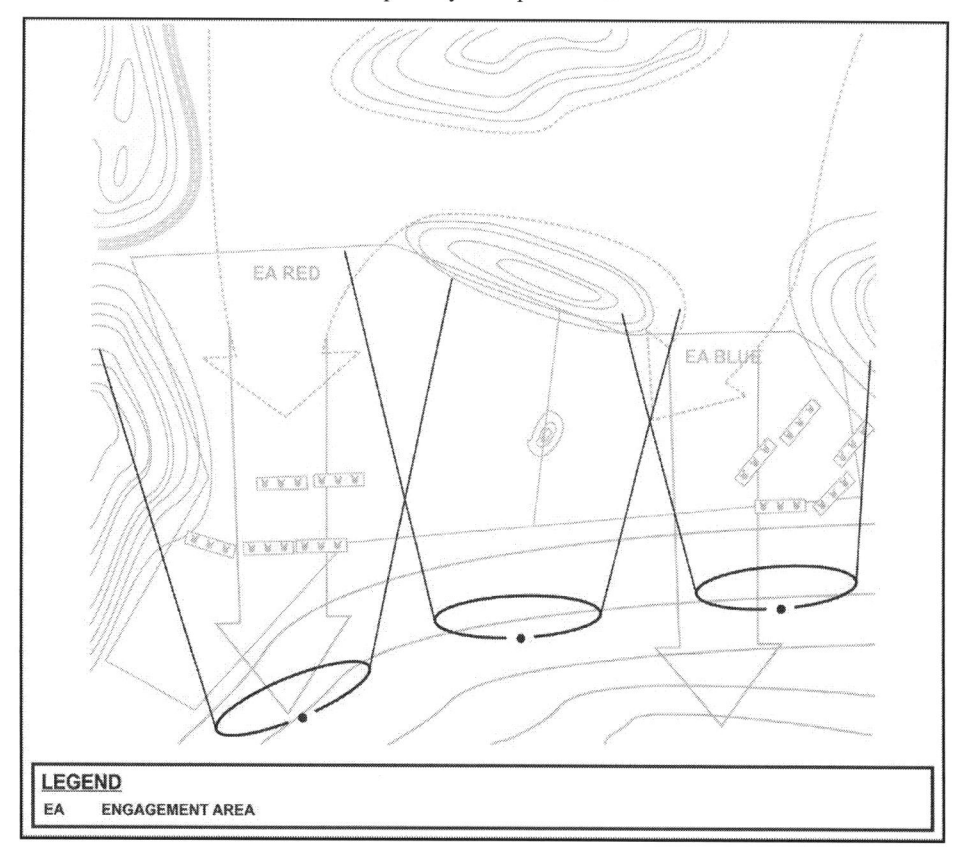

Figure 3-23. Emplacement of weapons systems

PLAN AND INTEGRATE INDIRECT FIRES

3-178. The following steps apply in planning and integrating indirect fires (See figure 3-24, page 3-62.):
- Determine the purpose of fires.
- Determine where purpose will best be achieved.
- Establish the observation plan that includes—
  - Redundancy for each target.
  - Observers who will include the fire support team, as well as members of maneuver elements with direct fire support execution responsibilities.
- Establish triggers based on enemy movement rates.
- Obtain accurate target locations using organic target location devices or survey/navigational equipment.
- Refine target locations to ensure coverage of obstacles.
- Plan final protection fire.
- Request critical friendly zone for protection of maneuver elements and no-fire areas for protection of observation posts and forward positions.

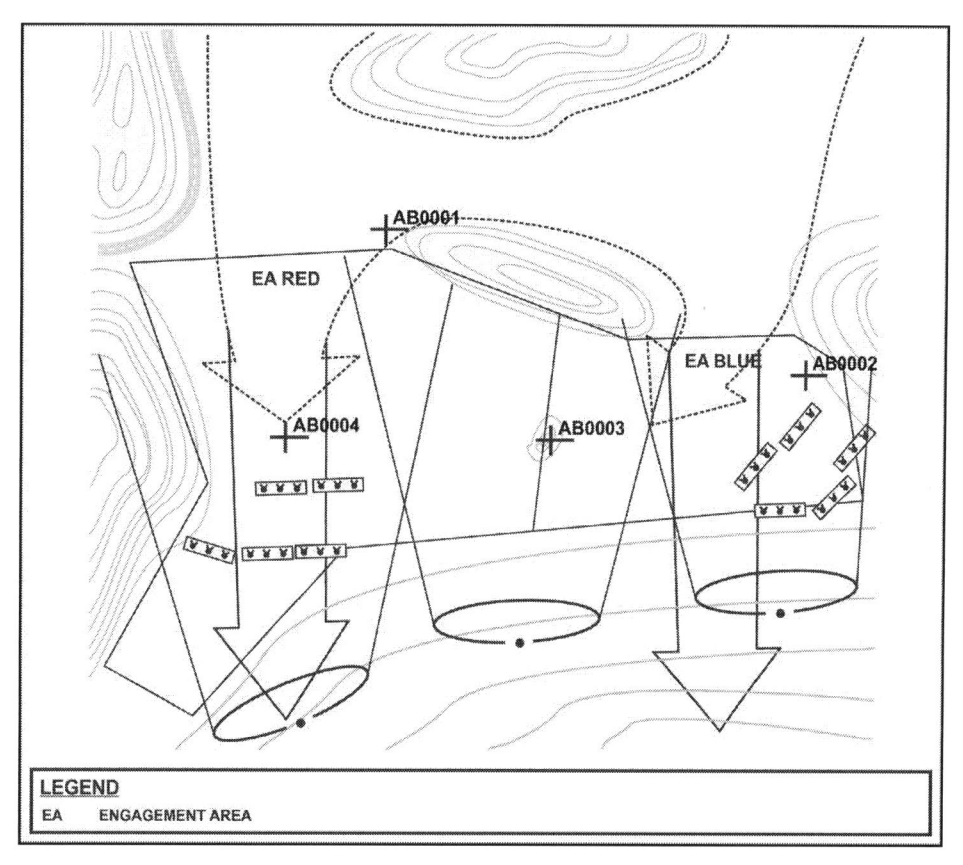

Figure 3-24. Integration of direct and indirect fires

REHEARSALS

3-179. The purpose of rehearsals is to ensure every leader and Soldier understands the plan and elements are prepared to cover their assigned areas with direct and indirect fires. The rehearsal should cover—
- Rearward passage of security forces (as required).
- Closure of lanes (as required).
- Movement from the hide position to the battle position.
- Use of fire commands, triggers, and maximum engagement lines (MELs) to initiate direct and indirect fires.
- Shifting of fires to refocus and redistribute fire effects.
- Disengagement criteria.
- Identification of displacement routes and times.
- Location of remount points, the times remount operations will take place, and movement considerations for conduct of a remount in contact.

Defense

- Preparation and transmission of critical reports using radio and digital systems, as applicable.
- Assessment of the effects of enemy weapon systems.
- Displacement to alternate, supplementary, or subsequent battle positions.
- Cross-leveling or resupply of Class V.
- Evacuation of casualties.

3-180. The platoon leader should coordinate rehearsals with higher headquarters to ensure there are no conflicts with other units. Coordination leads to efficient use of planning and preparation time for all units involved with the operation. It eliminates dangers of misidentifying friendly forces in the rehearsal area, which could result in fratricide.

SECTION VI – TRANSITIONS

3-181. During the planning for operations, the Infantry leader must discern from the higher headquarters OPORD what the potential follow-on missions are and begin to plan how they intend to achieve them. During this planning, the leader determines the possible timeline and location for consolidation and reorganization best facilities future operations and provides adequate protection.

CONSOLIDATION

3-182. Small unit leaders plan and prepare for consolidation during TLP. The following actions are usually a part of consolidation:

- Eliminate enemy resistance on the objective.
- Establish security beyond the objective by securing areas that may be the source of enemy direct fires or enemy artillery observation.
- Establish additional security measures such as observation posts and patrols.
- Prepare for and assist the passage of follow-on forces, if required.
- Continue to improve security by conducting other necessary defensive actions. These defensive actions include engagement area development, direct fire planning, and battle position preparation.
- Adjust final protective fires and register targets along likely mounted and dismounted avenues of approach.
- Protect the obstacle reduction effort.
- Secure detainees.
- Prepare for enemy counterattack.

REORGANIZATION

3-183. Reorganization usually is conducted concurrently with consolidation. It consists of actions taken to prepare the unit for follow-on tasks. As with consolidation, small unit leaders plan and prepare for reorganization during TLP. During reorganization, the small unit leader ensures the following actions are taken:

Chapter 3

- Provide essential medical treatment and evacuate casualties as necessary.
- Treat and evacuate wounded detainees and process the remainder of detainees.
- Cross-level personnel and adjust task organization as required to support the next phase or mission.
- Conducts resupply operations, including rearming and refueling.
- Redistribute ammunition.
- Conduct required maintenance.
- Continue improving defensive positions as necessary.

CONTINUING OPERATIONS

3-184. At the conclusion of an engagement, the Infantry platoon may continue the defense, or if ordered, transition to the offense or stability. The platoon leader considers the higher commander's concept of the operation, friendly capabilities, and enemy situation when making this decision. All missions should include plans for exploiting success or assuming a defensive posture.

3-185. A defending unit may transitions from defensive tasks to the retrograde as a part of continuing operations. A retrograde usually involves a combination of a delay, withdrawal, and retirement that may occur simultaneously or sequentially. As in other missions, the leader's concept of the operation and intent drive planning for the retrograde. Each form of retrograde has its unique planning considerations, but considerations common to all retrogrades are risk, the need for synchronization and security.

TRANSITION TO THE OFFENSE

3-186. A company commander may order a defending Infantry platoon to conduct a hasty operation or participate in a movement to contact. As part of a reserve force, the Infantry platoon and squad may execute a counterattack to destroy exposed enemy elements and free decisively engaged friendly elements. A base-of-fire element suppresses or fixes the enemy force while the counterattack (maneuver) element moves on a concealed route to firing positions from which it can engage the enemy in the flank and rear. The counterattack element must maneuver rapidly to its firing position, often fighting through enemy flank security elements, to complete the counterattack before the enemy can bring follow-on forces forward to influence the fight.

3-187. Execution of the counterattack is similar to an assault by fire. Planning and preparation considerations for counterattack vary depending on the purpose and location of the operation. For example, the counterattack may be conducted forward of friendly positions, requiring the reserve force to move around friendly elements and through their protective and tactical obstacles. In other situations, the Infantry leader may use a counterassault by fire to block, fix, or contain a penetration. In any case, the reserve force conducts the counterattack as an enemy-oriented task.

TRANSITION TO STABILITY

3-188. It may be tactically wise for the leader to plan a defensive contingency with on-order offensive tasks for operations focused on stability tasks. Subordinate leaders must be fully trained to recognize activities, which initiate this transition. Leaders and Soldiers must be aware that elements of the BCT could be conducting offensive, defensive, and stability missions simultaneously within a small radius of each other. Actions in one unit's area of operation can affect a change in whatever type task an adjacent unit is conducting. For example, an engagement with an enemy force may have caused noncombatants to be displaced to another section of the city leaving the area of operation open to theft, looting, and vandalism by belligerents.

This page intentionally left blank.

Chapter 4
Stability

Stability components of an operation leverage the coercive and constructive capabilities of the military force to establish a safe and secure environment, facilitate reconciliation between local or regional adversaries; establish political, legal, social, and economic institutions; and facilitate the transition of responsibility to a legitimate civil authority. This chapter discusses Infantry platoon and squad support to stability tasks; it addresses tactical actions and tasks in support of stability, planning considerations and transitions. (Refer to ADRP 3-07 for more information.)

SECTION I – OVERVIEW OF STABILITY

4-1. Unified land operations require continuous, simultaneous combinations of offensive, defensive, and stability tasks. *Stabilization* is the process by which underlying tensions that might lead to resurgence in violence and a breakdown in law and order are managed and reduced, while efforts are made to support preconditions for successful long-term development. (FM 3-07) *Stability operations* encompass various military missions, tasks, and activities conducted outside the United States in coordination with other instruments of national power to maintain or reestablish a safe and secure environment; provide essential governmental services, emergency infrastructure reconstruction, and humanitarian relief. (JP 3-0)

4-2. As combat operations culminate, part of the force secures critical infrastructure and populated areas. Protecting or preventing further harm to the civilian population are legal obligations of military forces during operations. However, if a unit is decisively engaged in conducting combat tasks, it should not divert from mission accomplishment to perform stability tasks, until the situation permits. If unable to perform minimum essential stability tasks, the unit should inform higher headquarters and continue with its mission as assigned. (Refer to ADP 3-07 for more information.)

4-3. Leaders plan to minimize the effects of combat on the populace. Properly focused, executed stability tasks prevent population centers from degenerating into civil unrest and becoming recruiting areas for opposition movements or insurgencies.

4-4. Infantry platoons and squads are not capable of achieving the desired end state of stability tasks independently. They support stability tasks by performing platoon and squad-level missions, tasks, and activities supporting the stability tasks of its higher headquarters often partnered and working closely with other unified action partners.

STABILITY FRAMEWORK

4-5. A stability framework based on conditions within the area of operations of initial response, transformation, and fostering stability, helps the unit determine the required training and task organization of forces prior to initial deployment, and serves as a guide to actions in an operation focused on stability tasks. (Refer to ATP 3-07.5 for more information.) Stability tasks occur in three phases described in the following paragraphs. These phases facilitate identifying lead responsibilities and determining priorities and describe the conditions on the operational environment.

INITIAL RESPONSE PHASE

4-6. These actions generally reflect activity executed to stabilize a crisis state in the area of operations. Army conventional force units typically perform initial response actions during, or directly after, a conflict or disaster in which the security situation prohibits the introduction of civilian personnel. Initial response actions aim to provide a secure environment that allows relief forces to attend to the immediate humanitarian needs of the local population. They reduce the level of violence and human suffering while creating conditions that enable other actors to participate safely in relief efforts.

TRANSFORMATION PHASE

4-7. Stabilization, reconstruction, and capacity-building are transformation phase actions that are performed in a relatively secure environment. Transformation phase actions take place in either crisis or vulnerable states. There is the presence of a legitimate authority either interim or established as well as indigenous host nation security forces. These actions aim to build host-nation capacity across multiple sectors. Transformation phase actions are essential to the continuing stability of the environment. These actions are essential to fostering stability within the area.

FOSTERING SUSTAINABILITY PHASE

4-8. These are actions that encompass long-term efforts, which capitalize on capacity building and reconstruction activities. Successful accomplishment of these actions establishes conditions that enable sustainable development. Usually military forces perform fostering sustainability phase actions only when the security environment is stable enough to support efforts to implement the long-term programs that commit to the viability of the institutions and economy of the host nation. Often military forces conduct these long-term efforts to support broader, civilian-led efforts.

STABILITY TASKS

4-9. Army forces conduct the following five primary stability tasks: civil security, civil control, restore essential services, support to governance, and support to economic and infrastructure development. At brigade level and below, the primary stability tasks are too broad to focus effort appropriately; at lower tactical echelons, lines of effort are best designed using standard mission-essential tasks. Lines of effort may focus on specific aspects of the local situation, such as the restoration of essential civil services. There, activities of military forces often are shaped using lines of effort based on (sewage, water, electricity, academics, trash, medical, security, and other considerations) while addressing the need to provide food aid and shelter.

ESTABLISH CIVIL SECURITY

4-10. Establishing civil security involves providing for safety of the host nation and its population, including protection from internal and external threats; it is essential to providing a safe and secure environment. Civil security includes a diverse set of activities. These range from enforcing peace agreements to conducting disarmament, demobilization, reintegration, and includes biometric identity data collection to identify criminal elements, known and suspected terrorists, and other irregular forces.

4-11. Subordinate platoons of the Infantry company execute stability tasks for the Infantry battalion. Until a legitimate civil government can assume responsibility for the security, military forces perform the tasks associated with civil security. At the same time, they help develop host nation security and police forces. Normally, the responsibility for establishing and maintaining civil security belongs to military forces from the onset of operations through transition, when host nation security and police forces assume this role.

ESTABLISH CIVIL CONTROL

4-12. Establishing civil control is an initial step toward instituting rule of law and stable governance. Although establishing civil security is the first responsibility of military forces in stability, this can only be accomplished by also restoring civil control. Internal threats may manifest themselves as an insurgency, subversive elements within the population, organized crime, or general lawlessness.

4-13. Civil control regulates selected behavior and activities of individuals and groups. This control reduces risk to individuals or groups and promotes security. Curfews and traffic checkpoints, together with biometric identity data collection, are examples of civil control.

RESTORE ESSENTIAL SERVICES

4-14. The Infantry platoon and squad is capable of providing only the most essential services. Normally, the military force supports other government, intergovernmental, and host-nation agencies improving essential services. Essential services include the following:
- Emergency medical care and rescue.
- Providing food and water.
- Providing emergency shelter.

SUPPORT TO GOVERNANCE

4-15. Stability tasks establish conditions enabling interagency and host nation actions to succeed. Military forces focus on transferring control to a legitimate civil authority according to the desired end state. At the platoon and squad level, supports to governance tasks are dependent on those of the Infantry battalion and IBCT. Those tasks focus primarily on continuing civil security and civil control operations to provide a safe and secure environment. As in other stability tasks, leader and Soldier engagement with local officials and the population are ongoing.

4-16. Company level and below tasks commonly support external agencies along specific themes nested with higher efforts. Targeted civil reconnaissance, and in some cases surveillance of the population, groups, and institutions, is ongoing to monitor the efficacy of programs, policies, and procedures established by a transitional or civil authority. Early identification of developing problems provides a means to focus additional tasks and available resources to support the appropriate authority before becoming a source of instability and dissent among the populace.

SUPPORT TO ECONOMIC AND INFRASTRUCTURE DEVELOPMENT

4-17. Support to economic and infrastructure development helps a host nation develop capability and capacity in these areas. It may involve direct and indirect military assistance to local, regional, and national entities. At the platoon and squad level, support to economic and infrastructure development focuses primarily on continuing civil security and civil control operations in order to provide a safe and secure environment that allows external agencies to leverage their capabilities.

4-18. As in other stability tasks, leader and Soldier engagement with local officials and the population are ongoing. At the company and below these efforts are commonly in coordination with external agencies in order to identify the economic and infrastructure development needs at the local level and match those needs with available programs and funding sources.

SECTION II – PLANNING CONSIDERATIONS

4-19. The small unit leader plans for stability in a manner similar to the offense and defense. The planning process is continuous, constantly adapting as the conditions of the operational environment are shaped by activities, both natural and human. Often planning for the next mission begins simultaneously as assessing the previous mission during stability. The leader must be aware of more than the accomplishment of the mission but also the manner in which it was conducted and the sentiment the population had during its execution. The resultant plan must foster flexibility, initiative, and adaptability in the face of unforeseen events. The following warfighting functions discuss planning considerations and activities critical for mission success.

MISSION COMMAND

4-20. Stability tasks tend to be decentralized in nature, over extended distances. As such, Infantry unit activities will consist largely of independent small-unit operations conducted across an assigned area of operation. Units must conduct these operations with consistency, impartiality, and discipline to encourage cooperation from unified action partners for a cohesive effort.

4-21. Stability tasks, more so than offensive and defensive tasks, present a unique challenge. Where offense and defense typically focuses on the defeat of an enemy force, stability focuses on the people. In setting the tone for planning, the Infantry leader provides—
- Understanding.
- The intent and planning guidance.
- Concept of operation.

4-22. The platoon leader must clearly understand mission, situation, commander's intent and he must ensure his subordinate units understand as well. He must plan for continuous operations, and, as with offense and defense, planning and preparation time is often limited. The plan must facilitate adjustment based upon changes in the situation. Additional considerations and activities include:
- Civil-military operations (CMO).
- Civil affairs operations.
- Military information support operations (MISO).
- Rules of engagement. (Refer to chapter 1, section I of this publication for more information.)
- Rules of interaction, which include:
  - Persuasion.
  - Negotiation.
  - Communication skills.
- Task organization, which includes:
  - Augmentation. Required individual augmentees and augmentation cells to support force-tailoring requirements and personnel shortfalls. Augmentation supports coordination with the media, government agencies, nongovernmental organizations, international organizations, other multinational forces, and civil-military elements. Analyses of METT-TC drive augmentation.
  - Liaison. Task-organized small liaison teams to deal with situations that develop with the local population. Depending the situation requirements, unit ministry, engineers, MISO, civil affairs, counterintelligence, linguistics, and logistics personnel may be task-organized to make up these liaison teams. These teams can free up maneuver elements (may require security from platoon) and facilitate negotiation. Negotiation teams must have linguists and the personnel who have the authority to negotiate.
  - Operations with outside agencies. Includes other U.S. armed services or government agencies as well as international organizations (including nongovernmental organizations, coalition, and United Nation military forces or agencies). Coordination and integration of civilian and military activities must take place at every level. Coordinating centers such as the civil-military operations center are designed to accomplish this task. These operations centers should include representatives from as many agencies as required.
- Media. Soldiers must be aware of current media reports from about the area and be willing to work with journalists in efforts to promote good relationship and combat

Chapter 4

false information. Involvement with media should be coordinated under public affairs guidance.

IMPORTANCE OF UNDERSTANDING CULTURE

4-23. Soldiers derive their effectiveness from their ability to understand and work with foreign counterparts from another culture. They need to understand enough of their own culture and their counterpart's culture to accurately convey ideas, concepts, and purpose without causing counterproductive consequences. Soldiers need to be aware of aspects of the local culture and history that influence behavior in their operational environment. Soldiers need to understand the reasons and motivations underlying personal interaction and practice patience when working with their counterparts. Group norms guide individual behavior, and Soldiers need to understand how individuals in a society tend to interact as members of a group, whether a race, ethnic, or kinship group. Cultural understanding is not derived from demographic information provided to the military through country briefs prior to deployment. It is gained from studying, interacting, and understanding the people, religion, history, customs, and social and political structures within an area. For true understanding, it is necessary to live among the people, gradually understanding the subtleties and nuances of their culture. Leaders in the Infantry company ensure that Soldiers understand that the actions of one can have a positive or negative effect in the way that the entire unit is viewed by the local population. (Refer to ATP 3-07.10 for more information.)

THEMES, MESSAGES, AND ACTIONS

4-24. Leaders use their own themes and messages to support their narratives. Narratives are tied to actions in their operational environments and area of operations. A narrative is a brief description of a leader's story used to visualize effects the leader wants to achieve in the information environment to support and shape their operational environments. An effective leader's theme supports overarching U.S. Government and higher headquarters themes, has details, and is tailored to environmental conditions in their area of operations.

Themes Explain Mission

4-25. Themes are planning tools that guide development of the narrative, messages, and other information products (talking points, MISO objectives, and public affairs guidance). Themes represent broad ideas the leader wants to convey to selected audiences. Themes are not communicated to selected audiences, messages are. Themes are broad and enduring, and as such, they do not change frequently.

Messages Support Themes

4-26. They can be verbal, written, gestured, or electronic communications supporting a theme focused on an audience. They support a specific action or objective. Messages are tailored to specific audiences. Leaders use messages to communicate clear information and, if necessary, elicit a response or change in behavior. Messages are situation and mission dependent. Command information messages convey local leaders' policies and intent to their subordinates.

4-27. The public affairs officer develops command information and public information messages. Army public information is information of a military nature, the dissemination of which is consistent with security and the DOD principles of information. Command information is communication from the commander to help members of the command understand organizational goals, operations, and significant developments. (Refer to FM 3-61 for more information.)

4-28. Psychological messages convey specific information to selected foreign audiences to influence their perceptions, attitudes, beliefs, and behavior. The military information support planner or unit develops these messages. MISO messages and actions support themes established in the approved MISO program for that particular mission. (Refer to JP 3-13.2 and ADRP 3-05 for detailed information on MISO.)

Actions Reinforce Messages

4-29. Leaders consider perceptions and ramifications of their actions to gain and maintain support of populations in conflict areas. Leaders first understand host-nation laws and cultures, enabling them to operate effectively in the information environment. Second, leaders determine how to inform audiences at home, gain support abroad, and generate support or empathy for missions in their area of operations.

4-30. Leaders use information to marginalize or defeat adversary or enemy information efforts by shaping attitudes and behaviors of foreign audiences residing in area of operations. Synchronized themes, messages, and actions support the leader's operational goals by integrating words, images, and deeds to avoid confusion or information fratricide.

LINES OF EFFORT

4-31. All activities in the information environment communicate in some way. They serve to make an impression on minds of those that observe or hear those communications. Leaders and staffs distinguish the two lines of effort by intention of the communicator and the message. Sometimes, a communication intended merely to inform might eventually lead to a changed opinion or behavior. A communication designed to influence may not achieve the desired outcome. (Refer to FM 3-13 for more information.)

MOVEMENT AND MANEUVER

4-32. Movement and maneuver stability tasks are similar to the offense and defense with extensive emphasis on security and engagement skills (negotiation, rapport building, cultural awareness, and critical language phrases). The intent is to create a stable environment allowing peace to take hold while ensuring the force is protected.

4-33. Movement and maneuver often is decentralized to the small unit level. At company level, the commander works stability problems collectively with subordinate platoon leaders who own the ground in the area of operation, sharing understanding and exploring possible solutions. Once leaders understand the situation, seeking consensus helps subordinates understand the commander's intent. Subordinates exercise initiative and act

Chapter 4

based on the commander's intent informed by whatever situational awareness they have developed.

4-34. Leaders must be prepared to rely on direct and indirect fire support, protection, and sustainment elements to assist movement and maneuver. When new requirements develop, these same elements must be ready to shift priorities.

4-35. Establishing the force's presence in the area of operation is often the first requirement of the platoon's stability mission. Being on the ground establishes links with the local populace. Through Soldier engagement, the populace begins to trust and relate to friendly forces. Driving around in an armored convoy may degrade situational awareness. It can make Soldiers targets and often is more dangerous than moving on foot and remaining close to the populace.

4-36. Upon arrival in the area of operation, it may not be advisable to go straight for the main aggressor stronghold or to try to take on villages that support criminals and criminal networks or other hostile actors. Start from secure areas and work gradually outward. Extend influence through local networks. First, win the confidence of a few villages, and then work with those with whom they trade, intermarry, or do business. This tactic develops local allies, a mobilized populace, and trusted networks.

4-37. Seek a victory early during stability to demonstrate dominance of the area of operation. This does not require a combat victory. Often victories can be attained by building relationships rather than by combat. Early combat without accurate situational understanding may create unnecessary collateral damage and ill will. Instead, victories may involve using leader engagement to resolve a long-standing issue or co-opt a key local leader. Achieving even a small early victory can set the tone for the mission and help commanders seize the initiative.

4-38. The platoon may be tasked to establish a quick reaction force for the security of checkpoints, outposts, observation post, and work sites, and to support patrols, meetings, and convoys in the area of operation. Planning should provide a force of the appropriate size for a quick reaction force to separate local hostile parties before potential violent situations grow out of control. The force must have the ability to respond anywhere in the area of operation, and be rapidly reinforced by augmentation and maneuver elements.

4-39. Mobility, countermobility, survivability, and general engineering capabilities support critical tasks applied through the movement and maneuver warfighting function. These capabilities provide a major role in protecting positions, headquarters, support facilities, base camps, and highly vulnerable assets.

INTELLIGENCE

4-40. Intelligence plays an important role in the accomplishment of any stability task. The small unit leader uses all available information collection to help accomplish the mission. Every member of the platoon plays a role in gathering information to support higher echelon planning. The company commander uses his CoIST to produce intelligence for his subordinate unit. The CoIST manages the information collection effort to ensure every member of the company headquarters and its subordinate units understands the operational

Stability

environment and plays an active role in the development of the common operational picture. (Refer to FM 3-21.10 for more information.)

4-41. During stability, threats must be identified and decisive points defined. Leaders focus information collection activities to identify sources of instability. Platoon tasks will have different requirements, time frames, ROE, and other differences influencing what information collection is required in order to provide recommendations or decisions for platoon and higher echelon planning. Predictive assessment contributes to future planning and force disposition the end state and its defining conditions for every task. (Refer to FM 3-55 for more information.)

4-42. Collaboration and interaction with local populace is essential. Once the platoon occupies an area of operation, its next task is to build trust and relationships with the local populace. Relationships are built with community leaders and local security forces. Over time, these relationships may lead to partnership and collaboration in support with stability tasks.

4-43. Threat mitigation during stability is intelligence driven. The platoon often develops much of its own intelligence in relation to the amount they receive from higher headquarters. Small unit leaders organize their assets to collect local information unavailable to higher sources of intelligence. Linguists are important in the collection of local information, but like any other scarce resource, must be allocated and utilized effectively. Biometrics collections and its use prior to conducting essential tasks or activities enhance protection. Soldiers utilizing the biometrically enabled watchlist (BEWL) loaded on handheld devices or other biometrics collect/match systems can identify individuals via prior biometric enrollments so that regardless of who they say they are their identities are known with certainty. Social network analysis and other analytical tools can be useful for promoting situational understanding of the operational environment for stability tasks as well as counterinsurgency. (Refer to FM 3-24.2 for more information.)

4-44. Civil reconnaissance (Refer to chapter 6, section III of this publication) focuses specifically on the civil component, the elements of which may best be represented by ASCOPE. Civil reconnaissance can be conducted by civil affairs personnel or by other forces, as required. It differs from other reconnaissance in that it usually is not targeted at a specific enemy; instead, it focuses on answering information requirements for civil situation awareness. (Refer to JP 3-57 for more information.)

FIRES

4-45. Although indirect fire support planning for stability is the same as for offense and defense, the use of indirect fire support may be very restricted and limited. (Refer to appendix C of this publication for more information.) The Infantry leader integrates indirect fire support into his plan considering the ROE. The ROE may impose restrictions on the use of certain munitions and detail release authority/strike approval authorization. Special considerations include the following:

- Procedures for rapid clearance of fires.
- Close communication and coordination with host country officials.
- Increased security for indirect firing positions.
- Restricted use of certain munitions such as dual purpose improved conventional munitions, area denial artillery munitions, or remote antiarmor mine.

SUSTAINMENT

4-46. The operational environment the Infantry platoon and squad operates in during stability may be very austere, creating special sustainment considerations. (Refer to chapter 7 of this publication for more information.) These factors include, but are not limited to, the following:

- Reliance on local procurement of certain items.
- Shortages of various critical items, including repair parts, Class IV supply materials, and lubricants.
- Special Class V supply requirements.
- Reliance on bottled water.
- Class IV supplies for construction of fixed observation posts and checkpoints.
- Use of existing facilities or new construction for quarters; water, sewer, and power utilities; reinforced hardstand areas for maintenance.
- Barriers or berms to protect ammunition and fuel.
- Use of female Soldiers to assist with searching host-nation female suspects.
- Class IX items.

PROTECTION

4-47. Protection of the force during stability is essential for success at all levels. Infantry leaders continually balance protection needs between military forces and civil populations. Frequent interaction between U.S. forces and local population make protection planning difficult and essential. Threats often blend in with the local populace during stability and are difficult to identify, making heightened levels of awareness the norm. The close proximity of civilians and Soldiers also can promote health issues (such as communicable disease) through close contact with local civilians, detainees, or local foods.

4-48. The protection of civil institutions, processes, and systems required to reach the end state conditions of stability strategy often can be the most decisive factor in stability because its accomplishment is essential for long-term success. Civil areas typically contain structured and prepared routes, roadways, and avenues canalizing traffic. This can lead to predictable friendly movement patterns that maybe exploited by the enemy. An additional planning consideration during stability tasks is to protect the force while using the minimum force consistent with the approved ROE. Additional protection considerations during stability include:

- Reducing the unexploded ordnance and mine threat in the area of operations.
- Fratricide and friendly fire prevention and minimizing escalation of force (EOF) incidents through combat, civilian, and coalition identification measures.
- Developing rapid and efficient personnel recovery techniques and drills.
- Clear operations security procedures account for close proximity of civilians, nongovernmental organizations, and contractors.
- Disciplined information management techniques to preserve access to computer networks.
- Containment of toxic industrial materiel is present in the civilian environment.
- Survivability requirements for static facilities, positions, or outposts.

4-49. Small unit leaders must implement appropriate security measures to protect the force. Establishment of checkpoints, base camp security procedures, and aggressive patrolling are examples of protecting the force. Protecting the force requires special considerations in stability tasks. This is because threats may be different and, in some cases, opposing forces seek to kill or wound U.S. Soldiers, or destroy or damage property for political purposes.

4-50. Leaders must always consider the aspects of protection and how they relate to the ROE. Some examples of protective measures are—

- Secure the inside perimeter if the host nation secures the outside perimeter.
- Avoid becoming an easy target and do not become predictable.
- Include security in each plan, SOP, operations order, and movement order.
- Develop specific security programs such as threat awareness and operational security.
- Restrict access of unassigned personnel to the unit's location.
- Constantly maintain an image of professionalism and readiness.
- Base the degree of security established on a continuous threat assessment.

4-51. The Army protects human and automated decisionmaking in peacetime and in conflict using OPSEC. It's a leader's responsibility supported by Soldiers, supporting civilian staff members and operators. OPSEC enhances mission success by preserving advantages of secrecy and surprise. OPSEC is a force multiplier. It includes reducing predictability and eliminating indicators of operations. Leaders use OPSEC countermeasures to deny adversaries knowledge of friendly operations. This requires adversaries to expend more resources to obtain critical information needed to make decisions. (Refer to ADRP 3-37 for more information on OPSEC.)

SECTION III – UNIFIED ACTION PARTNERS

4-52. Unified action partners are military forces, governmental and nongovernmental organizations, and elements of the private sector with whom Army forces plan, coordinate, synchronize, and integrate during the conduct of operations. Unified action partners can include joint forces and components, multinational forces, and U.S. government agencies and departments.

CIVIL AFFAIRS

4-53. Civil affairs forces support leaders by engaging civil component (interagency, indigenous population and institutions, host nation, intergovernmental organizations or private sector) of an operational environment conducting civil affairs operations and support to the commander's civil-military operations. Civil affairs forces ensure sustained legitimacy of the mission and transparency and credibility of the military force before, during, or after other military missions. This support involves applying specialty skills (normally responsibility of a local, regional, or national government) to enhance conduct of civil-military operations. As they relate to information related capabilities civil affairs operations and civil-military operations differ in purpose, focus, and specialization. Civil-military operations are a leader's activities establishing, maintaining, influencing, or exploiting relations among military forces, governmental, nongovernmental civilian organizations, authorities, and civilians.

HUMAN TERRAIN TEAMS

4-54. Human terrain teams fully integrate into unit staffs and conduct field research among the local population. Human terrain teams consist of five or six military and civilian personnel, and include one team leader, one or two social scientists, one research manager, and one or two analysts with specific local knowledge. Human terrain teams are considered subject matter experts in the local area and culture and are primarily involved with non-lethal unit activities. These teams maintain social and political networks and can be an invaluable resource to a leader to build general situational awareness. When possible, teams deploy with at least one female to facilitate access to the often inaccessible female population. Often a platoon or squad is detailed to transport, provide security, or other support to these teams.

PUBLIC AFFAIRS

4-55. Public affairs operations fulfill the Army's obligation to keep the American people and Army informed. They help to establish conditions leading to confidence in the Army and its readiness to conduct unified land operations. Public affairs operations strive to enhance public understanding and garner American, as well as global, support for the Army by engaging with both domestic and foreign media entities. (Refer to FM 3-61 for more information.)

Mission and Operations

4-56. Public affairs Soldiers accomplish their mission through public information, command information, and public engagement. Public information focuses on informing external audiences. It primarily engages media and key audiences to convey Army and command themes and messages to global and American audiences. Command information focuses on internal audiences—Soldiers, civilians, and family members—who recognize that an informed force is a more ready, reliable, and resilient force. Public engagement places special emphasis on two-way communication with identified publics and communities surrounding military installations. It recognizes a positive rapport between the Army and its host communities is mutually beneficial, supporting the Army as an institution as well as its individual Soldiers.

4-57. Integrating public affairs with other information-related capabilities helps leaders shape the information environment, provides valuable media assessment, and counters enemy propaganda and disinformation. Public affairs operations support the leader's development of themes and messages and collaborate with other information-related capabilities to protect OPSEC and avoid information fratricide.

4-58. Public affairs Soldiers participate in information-related capability and information integration process in the information operations element by continually assessing media information environment to determine the degree and nature of media coverage. They take steps to correct misinformation and propaganda. They also seek to leverage other information-related capabilities—such as combat camera or civil affairs operations—to provide greater accuracy, context, and characterization while informing. Additionally, public affairs operations provide reinforcing messaging for other information-related capabilities actions and the overarching strategic communication.

Media Considerations

4-59. The presence of the media is a reality that confronts every Soldier involved in all operations. All leaders and Soldiers must know how to deal effectively with broadcast and print reporters and photographers. This should include an understanding of subjects they are authorized to discuss and subjects the public affairs officer must address.

4-60. The objective of the Infantry battalion commander in dealing with the media is to ensure that operations are presented to the public in proper context. All leaders and soldiers must know how to deal effectively with reporters and photographers. They should understand which subjects they are authorized to discuss and which ones they must refer to the public affairs officer.

MILITARY INFORMATION SUPPORT OPERATIONS

4-61. Military information support operations are the leader's primary capability to inform and influence foreign populations in areas of operations. Military information support Soldiers conduct operations to induce or reinforce specific attitudes and behaviors favorable to U.S. military objectives. (Refer to FM 3-53 for more information.)

INFORMATION OPERATIONS

4-62. Military information support Soldiers provide subject matter expertise in the information operations. As primary members of the information operations working group, they advise, plan, provide operations oversight, and assess messages and actions having potential or actual psychological effects. Military information support units also provide analysis, development, production, distribution, and dissemination capabilities for MISO and are the primary executors for purposes of informing and influencing target audiences. Military information support Soldiers, provide dedicated intelligence support can also provide post-delivery measures of performance and measures of effectiveness. The information operations element utilizes military information support analyses of audiences and their environments. The information operations element also assesses adversary information and capability, including information for effects, misinformation, disinformation, and propaganda.

4-63. Military information support planners and attached military information support units help leaders in executing Soldier and leader engagement efforts in areas of operations. Military information support Soldiers are trained, educated, equipped, and organized to plan, monitor, and assess engagement with foreign populations and select audiences. This engagement includes planning engagements with foreign populations, leaders, key communicators, and others with specific intent to influence to support leader objectives. Military information support planners plan, manage, and assess Soldier and leader engagement efforts. They support the leader's larger engagement strategy.

COMBAT CAMERA

4-64. Combat camera video specialists provide leaders with still and video imagery capabilities to support operational and planning requirements. These forces use video documentation capabilities ranging from aerial to underwater photography. They access areas and events inaccessible to other personnel or media. Furthermore, combat camera teams have a technological capability to transmit real-time images in turn serve to reinforce other information-related capability efforts. Likewise, their documentation of operations provides imagery support countering misinformation or propaganda. (Refer to ATP 3-55.12 for more information on combat camera.)

HOST NATION PARTNERS

4-65. Host-nation partners may include military, police, border, intelligence, paramilitary, and other security elements such as militias or private security companies. Other potential partners may include host-nation government representatives and agencies, tribal leaders, and influential private citizens.

NONGOVERNMENTAL ORGANIZATIONS

4-66. If present in the host nation, intergovernmental organizations such as the United Nations, African Union, European Union, and others can be valuable partners for stabilization and reconstruction because of their knowledge of the local situation, ties, and experience. They may have military or nonmilitary components and will operate under their own mandates and direction. Their forces may be best suited for a relatively benign peacekeeping role and less militarily capable than U.S. Army units, but they are generally perceived as legitimate by a wide range of actors. By maintaining a safe and secure environment, nonmilitary organizations—such as the United Nations World Food Program and World Health Organization—often prove vital in providing humanitarian assistance and development. Enabling such organizations may be one of the most important stability objectives. Although U.S. forces often view nongovernmental organizations as partners to be integrated, most nongovernmental organizations prefer a clearly neutral posture and avoid being associated with any military force.

SECTION IV – TACTICAL ACTIONS AND TASKS IN SUPPORT OF STABILITY

4-67. During stability, the Infantry platoon and squad provide support to facilitate the execution of tasks for which the host nation normally is responsible. Typically, these tasks have a security component ideally performed by military forces. However, military forces sometimes provide logistic, medical, or administrative support to enable the success of civilian agencies and organizations. Tasks the Infantry platoon and squad performs generally will fall into one of three categories, representing the collective effort associated with a stability task:

- Tasks for which the platoon retains primary responsibility.
- Tasks the platoon supports other forces.
- Tasks the platoon monitors.

AREA SECURITY

4-68. Established to preserve freedom of movement to; position fire support assets, conduct mission command operations, provide for sustainment operations, prevent threat ground reconnaissance, and prevent threat ground maneuver forces from penetrating defensive perimeters established by the platoon leader. (See appendix D, section I of this publication for more information.) Area security missions require a significant amount of time and normally operate from outposts such as a base camp or combat outposts. Like an AA or defensive strongpoint, the base camp also provides some protection because it requires all-round security. (Refer to FM 3-21.10 for more information.)

4-69. To add security, aid in information gathering and provide for a strong presence in an operation area. Security patrols and civil reconnaissance usually occur in urban areas and leaders must be aware of the ROE and the purpose of the patrol. (Refer to chapter 6 of this publication for more information.)

4-70. Establish observation posts are created for a specified time and purpose. Some observation posts are overt (clearly visible) and deliberately constructed. Others are covert and designed to observe an area or target without the knowledge of the local population. Each type of observation post must be integrated into supporting direct and indirect fire plans and into the overall observation plan. (Refer to appendix D, section II of this publication for more information.)

4-71. Checkpoints are another technique used to provide area security and gain information. To establish a checkpoint to achieve one or more of the following: control movement, obtain information, disrupt enemy movement or actions. (Refer to appendix D, section III of this publication for more information.)

4-72. Convoy escort is a task to provide close-in protection from direct fire while on the move. Infantry forces must be augmented with additional transportation assets to carry out this mission. (Refer to appendix D, section IV of this publication for more information.)

CONDUCT SEARCHES

4-73. To conduct search operations or to employ search procedures is a continuous requirement. A search can orient on people, materiel, buildings, or terrain. (Refer to chapter 6 of this publication for more information.) Techniques include Search and Attach and Cordon and Search. Often during these tasks, site exploitation is conducted.

SITE EXPLOITATION

4-74. *Site exploitation* is the synchronized and integrated application of scientific and technological capabilities and enablers to answer information requirements, facilitate subsequent operations, and support host-nation rule of law. (ATP 3-90.15) Site exploitation is guided by the unit's information collection plan. (Refer to JP 2-0 and FM 3-55 on doctrine pertaining to information collection and collection planning.) The information collection plan enables the commander to focus assets on collecting information to answer specific information requirements. (ATP 3-90.15)

4-75. Primarily, site exploitation is a means of gaining information supporting the intelligence process. Site exploitation missions doctrine emphasizes three purposes:
- To answer information requirements (usually the commander's critical information requirements).
- To facilitate subsequent missions (already planned or not yet anticipated).
- To facilitate criminal prosecution by host nation, coalition, or international authorities (related to war crimes).

4-76. Site exploitation missions may focus on one fundamental purpose or involve all three simultaneously. The purpose of the site exploitation should be considered throughout TLP. The development of intelligence, through immediate analysis or off site processing can enable the leader to target additional objectives. At the platoon level, many of the site exploitation related activities answer higher headquarters information requirements.

4-77. Site exploitation forces provide critical data for inclusion in the intelligence process, which subsequently supports operations already planned or not yet anticipated. They identify information, materiel, and persons of interest, collect and preserve these items, and, after the mission is completed, debriefed by appropriate intelligence representatives, usually the S-2 or CoIST. The information (in any medium or form), materiel, and persons collected are processed by the appropriate agencies and analyzed to produce intelligence supporting ongoing or subsequent operations.

4-78. During stability tasks, units can use site exploitation to gain information supporting criminal prosecution by host nation authorities. Clearly documenting the details surrounding the initial detention, preserving evidence, and maintaining chain of custody are critical and aid in determining if further detention is warranted, in classifying the detainee, in developing intelligence, and in prosecuting detainees suspected of committing criminal acts. Documentation should be detailed and answer the six Ws—who, what, when, where, why, and witnesses. Record these details on the DD Form 2745 (*Enemy Prisoner of War (EPW) Capture Tag*), DA Form 2823 (*Sworn Statement)*, DA Form 4137 (*Evidence/Property Custody Document*), and locally developed forms if necessary. (Refer to ATP 3-90.15 for more information.)

PROTECT CRITICAL SITES AND PERSONNEL

4-79. Certain locations within the area of operation may be identified as critical and require protection. This may be a facility or infrastructure providing important civil services to the population or a facility or asset where the loss of which would increase destabilization and hostilities among belligerents. To provide security for key personnel may be in the form of a personal security detachment or security escorts when they must circulate through the local area. (Refer to appendix D, section I of this publication for more information.)

NEGOTIATIONS

4-80. The Infantry platoon and squad may face a number of situations in which leaders need to conduct negotiations. There are two general types of negotiations, situational and planned. Units conduct situational negotiations in response to a requirement for on-the-spot discussion and resolution of a specific issue or problem. For example, a unit is patrolling its area of operation when a local official approaches it; the local official wishes to discuss an assault that occurred in the area. Units conduct planned negotiations when they foresee a problem, or identify a situation that must be resolved through advanced planning and coordination. For example, the platoon leader conducts a coordination meeting, otherwise known as key leader engagement, between leaders of two belligerent groups to determine route clearance responsibilities.

4-81. At the Infantry platoon and squad level, situational negotiations are far more common than the planned type. In fact, stability operations require the leader, his subordinate leaders, and other Soldiers to conduct some form of negotiations almost daily. This requires them to have a thorough understanding of the ROE.

4-82. Infantry platoon and squad members apply this working knowledge to the process of discussing and, whenever possible, resolving issues or problems that may arise between opposing parties, including the platoon itself. A critical aspect of this knowledge is the negotiator's ability to recognize that the options under the ROE and rules of interaction are exhausted and turns the discussion over to a higher authority. Negotiations continue at progressive levels of authority until the issue is resolved.

Chapter 4

TASKS THE PLATOON CAN SUPPORT FOR OTHER FORCES

4-83. The Infantry platoon can support other forces by providing security force assistance, focus on IED defeat, and support to civil affairs operations. Each are describe below.

SECURITY FORCES ASSISTANCE

4-84. *Security force assistance* is defined as—the Department of Defense activities that contribute to unified action by the United States Government to support the development of the capacity and capability of foreign security forces and their supporting institutions. (JP 3-22) Consistent with DOD policy for security force assistance, the Army develops, maintains, and institutionalizes the capabilities of its personnel to support DOD efforts to organize, train, equip, and advise foreign security forces and relevant supporting institutions.

4-85. *Security forces* are duly constituted military, paramilitary, police, and constabulary forces of a state. (JP 3-22) When directed to do so in accordance with appropriate legal authorities, Army forces conduct security force assistance activities in support of combatant commanders' campaign plans and national objectives.

4-86. Military personnel should avoid confusing security force assistance and security assistance. Security assistance is a set of programs, authorized by law, that allow the United States to transfer defense articles, training, and services to partner nations. Security force assistance often works in conjunction with security assistance programs, but the focus of security force assistance is on building of the capacity and capability of foreign security forces and their supporting institutions. Security force assistance encompasses various activities related to the organizing, training, advising, equipping, and assessing of foreign security forces and their supporting institutions, from tactical to ministerial levels.

4-87. These activities contribute to unified action to generate, employ, and sustain foreign security forces. *Foreign security forces* are forces, including but not limited to, military, paramilitary, police, and intelligence forces; border police, coast guard, and customs officials; and prison guards and correctional personnel, that provide security for a host nation and its relevant population or support a regional security organization's mission. (FM 3-22) Security force assistance activities are conducted primarily to assist host nations build the capacity to defend against internal, external, and transnational threats to stability. However, DOD may also conduct security force assistance to assist host nations to defend against external threats; contribute to multinational operations; or organize, train, equip, and advise a nation's security forces or supporting institutions.

4-88. It is DOD policy that security force assistance is a subset of DOD overall security cooperation initiatives and that security force assistance activities directly increase the capacity or capability of foreign security forces or their supporting institutions. Security force assistance consists of those security cooperation activities tied directly to the security capability and capacity of foreign security forces. Security assistance programs, with their associated resources and authorities, can provide a means to conduct some security force assistance tasks.

4-89. Other forms of security force assistance—specifically, advising in a hostile environment and other activities geared toward assisting a partner nation engaged in conflict—are performed by U.S. forces using resources and authorities specially provided to DOD for employment in support of combat operations. Global train-and-equip funding to support the missions in Iraq and Afghanistan is a good example. (Refer to FM 3-22 for more information.)

Note. Soldiers should be trained and would benefit the unit if they receive training on cultural, local customs, and courtesies.

CIVIL AFFAIRS OPERATIONS

4-90. These activities occur in a friendly, neutral, or hostile area of operations to facilitate military operations in an effort to influence and support U.S. national objectives. Civil affairs operations and civil-military operations involve direct interaction with indigenous populations and institutions. Both civil-military operations and civil affairs operations focus on the indigenous population and institutions to create a favorable civil environment for military operations.

TASKS THE PLATOON MONITORS

4-91. The platoon can monitor and assist in civil-military operations and other enablers performing CMO, that include MISO, Special Operations Forces, legal support, public affairs, engineer, transportation, health service support, military police, security forces, and maneuver units. (Refer to FM 3-57 for more information.)

CIVIL-MILITARY OPERATIONS

4-92. Tactical-level CMO include support of stakeholders at local levels, and promoting the legitimacy and effectiveness of U.S. presence and operations among locals, while minimizing friction between the military and the civilian organizations in the field. These may include local security operations, processing and movement of displaced civilians, project management and project nomination, civil reconnaissance, and basic HSS. (Refer to JP 3-57 for further information.)

4-93. Civil affairs operations are those military operations planned, supported, or executed by civil affairs forces that—
- Enhance the relationship between military forces and civil authorities in localities where military forces are present.
- Require coordination with other interagency organizations, intergovernmental organizations, nongovernmental organizations, indigenous populations and institutions, and the private sector.
- Involve application of functional specialty skills that normally are the responsibility of civil government to enhance the conduct of CMO. They involve application of civil affairs functional specialty skills, in areas usually the responsibility of civil government. These activities are fundamental to executing stability tasks.

Chapter 4

4-94. Stability emphasizes nonlethal, constructive actions by Soldiers working among noncombatants. In stability, civil affairs forces work with and through host-nation agencies and other civilian organizations to enhance the host-nation government's legitimacy. Often, civil affairs teams work with or alongside the Infantry platoon and squad during stability. A framework for evaluating civil considerations is ASCOPE. (Refer to ADRP 6-0 for further information.) Each consideration is described as follows:

- *Structures*. Describe the man-made structures in which the people live and work; determine those having cultural, religious, and economic significance.
- *Capabilities*. Determine the ability of various groups to influence the area of operations and the rest of the population relative to their possible intent to do so- determine economic and military potential given the areas and infrastructure.
- *Organizations*. Determine what informal and formal social, religious, familial or political organizations exist and their intentions, purposes, and resources.
- *People*. Determine how the population aligns with organizations and one another; determine if they are likely to be supportive, detrimental, or neutral to the unit's mission.
- *Events*. Create significant population event template and determine if future activity can be predicted based on pattern analysis.

OTHER

4-95. Monitor compliance with an agreement involves observing belligerents and working with them to ensure they meet the conditions of one or more applicable agreements. (See section II of this chapter for more information.) Expeditionary forensic collection missions. Involves tasked support to the collection and analysis of materials in an area of operation, applies to both IED and non-IED events. Includes collecting, identifying, and labeling portable items for future exploitation, and the collection of fingerprints, DNA, and other biometric data from nontransportable items at a scene, such as a bomb maker's table and chairs. (Refer to ATP 2-22.82 for more information.)

4-96. Support relief operations in a foreign country using the Army to respond with a wide array of capabilities and services to aid authorities in the following types of actions: protecting public health, restoring public order, assisting in disaster recovery, alleviating large-scale suffering, and protecting critical infrastructure. (Refer to chapter 4 of this publication for more information.)

SECTION V – TRANSITIONS

4-97. Transitions mark a change of focus between phases or between the ongoing operation and execution of a branch or sequel. Shifting priorities between the elements of unified land operations, such as from offense to stability, also involves a transition. Transitions require planning and preparation well before their execution to maintain the momentum and tempo of operations. The force is naturally more vulnerable during transitions, thus requiring leaders to establish clear conditions for their execution. Transitions may create unexpected opportunities; they also may make forces vulnerable to enemy threats.

TRANSITION TO THE OFFENSE

4-98. During stability operations, there may be instances where units must transition quickly back to the offense against irregular forces or defense to defeat counterattacks.

4-99. Under unified land operations, forces conduct simultaneous offensive, defensive, and stability tasks. Offensive and defensive tasks focus on defeating enemy forces. Stability tasks focus on the establishment of a safe and secure environment to facilitate the transition of responsibility to a legitimate civil authority.

4-100. Security components of an operation, including area security, pertain to actions taken to protect the force. They are associated with the offense and defense. Civil security and civil control are stability tasks. Army leaders expect a mission of protecting and providing security for a population to be expressed in terms of civil security or civil control.

TRANSITION TO THE DEFENSE

4-101. Leaders must ensure transitions from defensive to stability tasks and vice versa are planned. For example, it may be tactically wise for leaders to plan a defensive contingency with on-order offensive missions if certain stability conditions could deteriorate. Leaders within the platoon must be fully trained to recognize activities, which would initiate this transition. Indicators to transition include:

- Increased insurgent activity, strength, and combat power.
- Increased insurgent movements.
- An increase in civilian attacks.
- Upcoming key host nation events.
- Concentration of insurgent activities in local or adjoining areas of operations.

TRANSFER OF AUTHORITY

4-102. Often during stability, a relief in place is referred to as a transfer of authority. In addition to the normal responsibilities of a relief, leaders and Soldiers also must deal with civilians or coalition partners. During stability, units generally know whether they will be relieved at the end of their tour. Planning for a transfer of authority begins as soon as the unit occupies the area of operation.

4-103. Before the transfer of authority, the departing unit develops a continuity book with the necessary information on the area of operation. The book should include lessons learned, details about the populace, village and patrol reports, updated maps, and photographs; anything helping the incoming unit master the outgoing unit's operational environment. Computerized databases are suitable. Leaders should ensure these continuity books are updated during the unit's tour of duty. This extensive effort reduces casualties and increase the current and succeeding units' efficiency and knowledge of operations.

4-104. A consistent theme from recent operations is the importance of the transition training (right seat/left seat rides) with incoming Soldiers during a transfer of authority. A detailed and programmed transfer of authority allows Soldiers to learn the culture and work

Chapter 4

with host nation personnel during the deployment. Typical training during the relief includes:

- Use of theater-unique equipment not available before the transfer of authority.
- Enemy tactics, techniques and procedures for improvised explosive devices specific to the area of operations.
- Personal meetings with nongovernmental organizations, contractors, interpreters, informants, and local police operating in the unit area of operations.
- Negotiation techniques with local tribal, religious and government officials.
- Operations and intelligence handover of databases, plans, products, and briefings.
- Information collection procedures, processes and policies.

TRANSITION TO CIVILIAN/HOST-NATION SECURITY FORCE CONTROL

4-105. During long-term security force assistance, conditions determine the rotation of in-theater units. Time is not the only governing factor. The overall authority for handoff and subsequent transfer of authority lies with the leader ordering the change. The authority for determining the handoff process lies with the incoming leader assuming responsibility for the mission. This changeover process may affect conditions under which the mission will continue. (Refer to ADRP 3-07 and FM 3-22 for more information.)

4-106. Changes in the operational environment may require reshaping force packages as situations change. In addition, internal administrative concerns might prompt or support the leader's decision to rotate units. Regardless, mission handoff is necessary and defined as the process of passing an ongoing mission from one unit to another with no discernible loss of continuity.

4-107. Although intended for a direct handoff between U.S. units, Infantry leaders must make specific considerations along with METT-TC when making a handoff to a multinational force. For units relieved of a function by a government agency, procedures typically entail longer handoff times and more complex coordination. However, the other areas of consideration still apply and may in fact be a greater issue for an agency. Outgoing units that have past, present, or future projects planned with agencies prepare to transfer these projects to responsible agents in the incoming unit.

Chapter 5

Movement

Tactical movement involves movement of a unit assigned a mission under combat conditions when not in direct ground contact with the enemy. Tactical movement is based on the anticipation of early ground contact with the enemy, either en route or shortly after arrival at the destination. Movement ends when ground contact is made or the unit reaches its destination. Movement is not maneuver. Maneuver happens once a unit has made contact with the enemy and combines movement with direct fires to gain a position of advantage over the enemy. Because tactical movement shares many of the characteristics of an offensive action, the area of operation is organized in a manner similar to other offensive actions. This chapter discusses troop movement, the basics and formations of tactical movement.

SECTION I – TROOP MOVEMENT

5-1. *Troop movement* is the movement of troops from one place to another by any available means. (ADRP 3-90) The ability to posture the force for a decisive or shaping operation depends on the capability to conduct rapid and orderly movement to concentrate the effects of combat power at decisive points and times. Movement places troops and equipment at their destination at the proper time, ready for combat. The three types of troop movement are administrative movement, tactical road march, and approach march.

METHODS OF TROOP MOVEMENT

5-2. Troop movements are made by dismounted and mounted marches using organic combat vehicles and motor transport, air, rail, and water means in various combinations. The method employed depends on the situation, size and composition of the moving unit, distance unit must cover urgency of execution, and condition of the troops. It also depends on the availability, suitability, and capacity of the different means of transportation. Troop movements over extended distances have extensive sustainment considerations. Dismounted and mounted marches can be hurried when necessary by conducting a forced march.

5-3. *Dismounted marches,* also called foot marches, are movements of troops and equipment, mainly by foot, with limited support from vehicles. They are conducted when stealth is required, the distance to travel is short, transport or fuel is limited, or the situation precludes using a large number of vehicles. (Refer to FM 21.18 for more information.) Advantages and disadvantages include:

Chapter 5

- Combat readiness—can immediately respond to enemy attack without the need to dismount, ease of control, adaptability to terrain, and independence from the existing road network.
- Limitations—slow movement rate and increased personnel fatigue, carrying heavy loads over long distances, changes in elevation. A unit conducts a dismounted march when the situation requires stealth, the distance to travel is short, transport or fuel is limited, or the situation or terrain precludes using a large number of vehicles.

5-4. *Mounted march* is the movement of troops and equipment by combat and tactical vehicles. (FM 3-90-2) The speed of the march and the increased amounts of supplies that can accompany the unit characterize this march method. The Infantry platoon is not equipped with organic truck assets and will need augmentation from transportation elements to conduct mounted marches. Considerations for mounted marches over extended distances include:

- Route network to support the numbers, sizes, and weights of the combat vehicles assigned to or supporting the unit making the move.
- Refueling and maintenance sites and crew-rest areas.
- Recovery and evacuation assets.
- Spill kits, personal protective equipment, and spill cleanup waste disposal equipment.

5-5. *Air movements* are operations involving the use of utility and cargo rotary-wing assets for missions other than air assaults. Air movements are conducted to move troops and equipment, to emplace systems, and to transport ammunition, fuel, and other high-value supplies. Air movements have the same planning considerations as air assault operations. (Refer to FM 3-04.113 or FM 3-99 for more information.)

5-6. *Rail and water movements* are used to conduct troop movement if they are available within an area of operations. (Refer to ATP 4-15 for more information.)

5-7. *Forced marches* in cases of tactical necessity can accelerate the rate of movement so as to arrive at its destination quickly. Forced marches require a combination of speed, exertion, and an increase in the number of hours marched or traveled by vehicles each day beyond normal standards. Soldiers cannot sustain forced marches for more than a short period. During a forced march, a unit may not halt as often or for as long as recommended for maintenance, rest, feeding, and fuel. The leader must understand that immediately following a long and fast march, Soldiers and combat vehicles experience a temporary deterioration in their condition. The combat effectiveness and cohesion of the unit also decreases temporarily. The forced march plan must accommodate the presence of stragglers and address increased maintenance failures.

ADMINISTRATIVE MOVEMENT

5-8. Administrative movement is a movement in which troops and vehicles are arranged to expedite their movement and conserve time and energy when no enemy ground interference, except by air, is anticipated. (Refer to FM 3-90-2 for more information.) Administrative movements only are conducted in secure areas. They include rail and

Movement

highway movement within the continental United States. Once deployed into theater of war, administrative movements normally are not conducted.

TACTICAL ROAD MARCHES

5-9. A *tactical road march* is a rapid movement used to relocate units within area of operation to prepare for combat operations. Units maintain security against enemy air attack and prepare to take immediate action against an enemy ambush, although they do not expect contact with significant enemy ground forces. (If the moving unit anticipates making contact with significant enemy ground forces then it will use a mix of combat formations and movement techniques.)

5-10. The primary consideration of the tactical road march is rapid movement. However, the moving force employs security measures, even when contact with enemy ground forces is not expected. Units conducting road marches may or may not be organized into a combined arms formation. During a tactical road march, the unit always is prepared to take immediate action if the enemy attacks. (Refer to FM 21.18 for more information.)

ORGANIZATION FOR A TACTICAL ROAD MARCH

5-11. The organization for a tactical road march is the march column. A *march column* consists of all elements using the same route for a single movement under control of a single commander. The four elements of a march column include, reconnaissance, quartering/advance party, main body, and trail party.

5-12. A brigade conducting a tactical road march is an example of a march column. The subordinate elements of a march column are a march serial and a march unit. A *march serial* is a major subdivision of a march column that is organized under one commander who plans, regulates, and controls the serial. An example is a battalion serial formed from a brigade-size march column. A *march unit* is a subdivision of a march serial. It moves and halts under the control of a single commander who uses voice and visual signals. An example of a march unit is a company from a battalion-size march serial.

5-13. A march column provides excellent speed, control, and flexibility, but sacrifices flank security. It provides the ability to deploy forces to the front of the column. A march column is utilized when speed is essential and enemy contact is unlikely. However, functional and multifunctional support elements, such as air defense and engineers, are spaced throughout the column to protect and support the movement. (Refer to FM 3-90-2 for more information.)

GRAPHIC CONTROL MEASURES

5-14. An overlay or strip map often is used to graphically depict critical information about a tactical road march route to subordinates. The overlay (see figure 5-1, page 5-4) or strip map (see figure 5-2, page 5-5) typically shows the route of march, start points, release points, checkpoints, critical points (such as bridges), light line, and traffic control post. Other graphic control measures include AA and phase lines. The terms are defined below:

Chapter 5

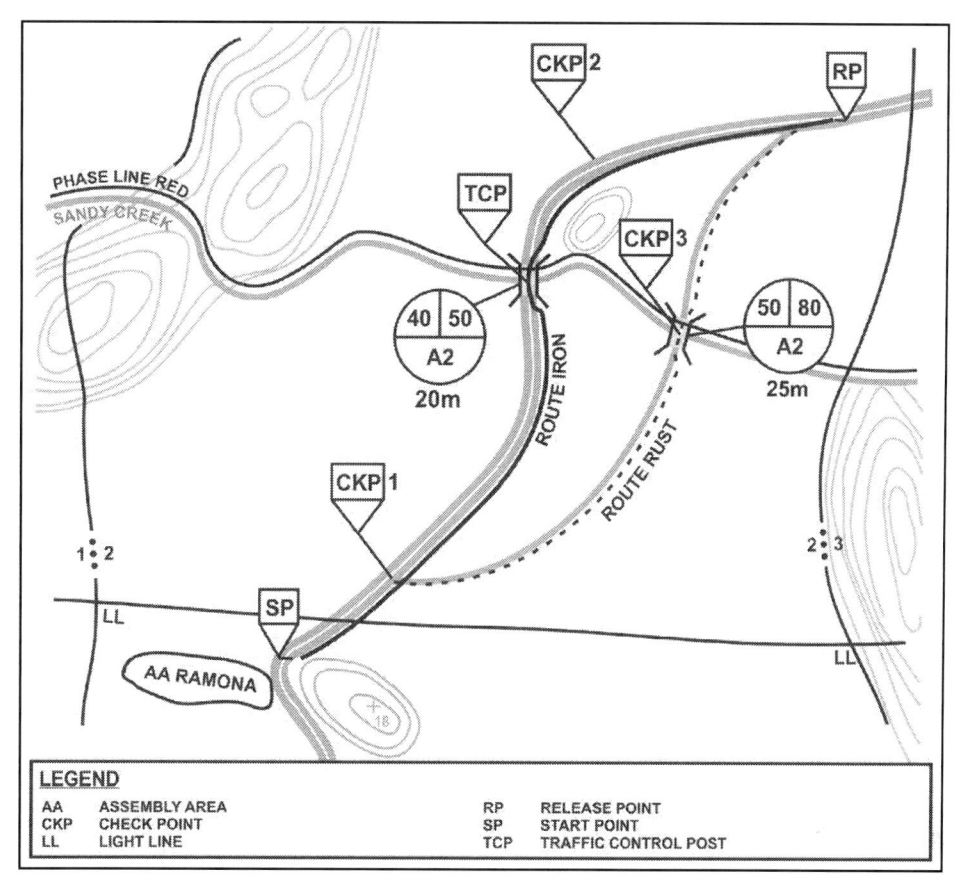

Figure 5-1. Overlay with route control measures

Movement

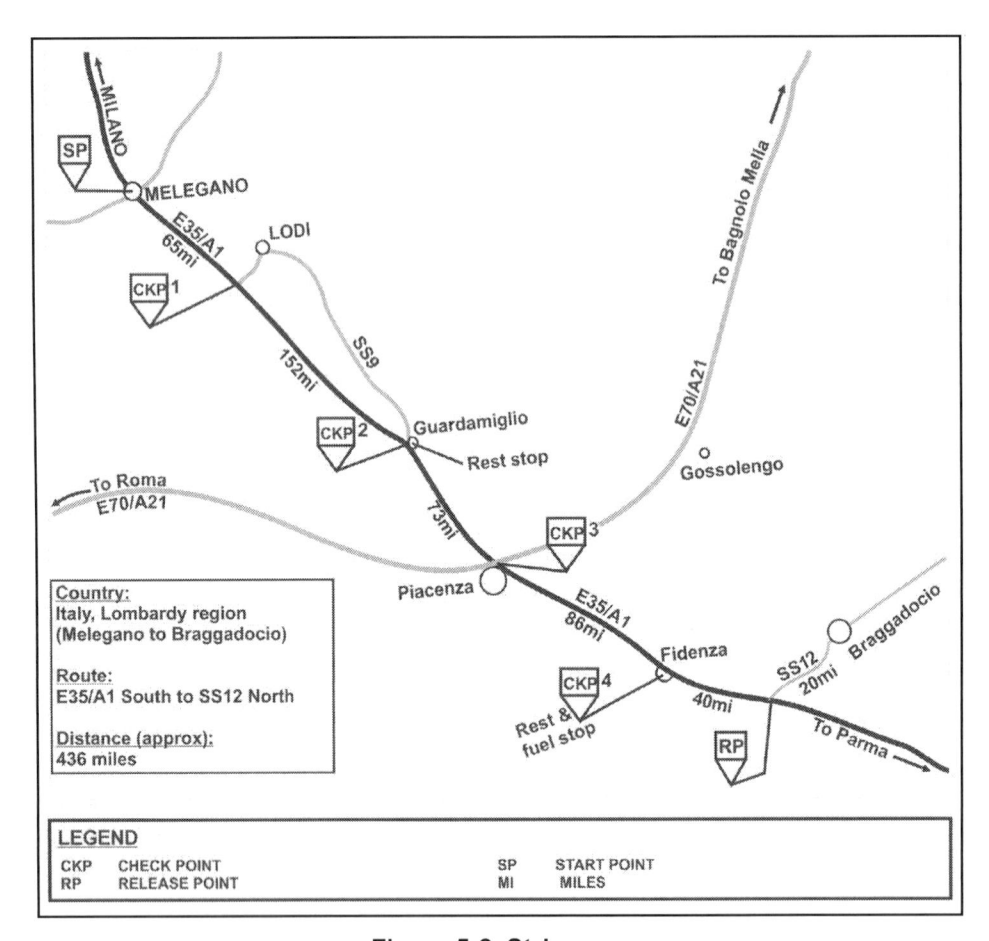

Figure 5-2. Strip map

- Start point is a location on a route where the marching elements fall under the control of a designated march commander.
- Release point is a location on a route where marching elements are released from centralized control.
- Checkpoint is a point designated along the route to assist marching units in complying with the timetable.
- Critical point is a point that identifies where interference with movement might occur.
- Light line is a designated phase line, forward of which vehicles are required to use blackout lights during limited visibility.
- Traffic control post are positioned along the route to prevent congestion and confusion. Points may be manned by military police or unit personnel. These Soldiers report to the appropriate area movement control organization when each convoy, march column, and march serial arrives at and completes passage of their location.

- Movement corridor is a designated area; established to protect and enable ground movement along a route, establish a movement corridor to set the conditions to protect and enable movement of traffic along a designated surface route.

TACTICAL MARCH TECHNIQUES

5-15. Tactical road marches are employed using three tactical march techniques: open column, close column, and infiltration. Each of these techniques uses scheduled halts to control and sustain the road march. METT-TC requires adjustments in the standard distances between vehicles and dismounts.

5-16. During movement, elements within a column may encounter many different types of routes and obstacles simultaneously. Consequently, parts of the column may be moving at different speeds, which can produce an undesirable accordion-like effect. The movement order establishes the order of march, rate of march, interval or time gaps between units, column gap, and maximum catch-up speed. Unless the commander directs them not to do so for security reasons, march units report when they have crossed each control measure. Throughout the move, air and ground security are maintained.

Open Column

5-17. The open column is the most common tactical march technique because it offers the most security while still providing a reasonable degree of control. It normally is used during daylight but also may be used at night with infrared lights, blackout lights, or passive night-vision equipment. Using an open column roughly doubles the column's length and thereby doubles the time it takes to clear a point when compared to a close column moving at the same speed.

5-18. Vehicle distance varies from 50 to 100 meters, and may be greater if required. The distance between dismounted Soldiers varies from two to five meters to allow for dispersion and space for marching comfort. Any distance that exceeds five meters between dismounted Soldiers increases the length of the column and hinders control. In an open column, vehicle density varies from 15 to 20 vehicles per kilometer. A single Infantry company, with intervals between its platoons, occupies roughly a kilometer of road or trail.

Close Column

5-19. A close column normally is employed for marches during darkness under blackout driving conditions or for marches in restricted terrain. This march technique takes maximum advantage of the traffic capacity of a route but provides little dispersion. Distance between vehicles varies from 20 to 25 meters. At night, vehicles are spaced so each driver can see the two lights in the blackout marker of the vehicle ahead. Normally, vehicle density is from 40 to 50 vehicles per kilometer along the route in a close column.

5-20. The dismounted equivalent to the close column is a limited-visibility march. The distance between individual Soldiers is reduced to one to three meters to help maintain contact and facilitate control. Limited-visibility marches are characterized by close formations, difficult mission command and reconnaissance, a slow rate of march, and good concealment from enemy observation and air attack.

Infiltration

5-21. Infiltration provides the best possible passive defense against enemy observation and attack. It is suited when time, space, security, deception, and dispersion are necessary. During infiltration, vehicles are dispatched in small groups, or at irregular intervals, at a rate that keeps the traffic density low and prevents undue massing of vehicles during the movement.

5-22. The disadvantages of an infiltration are that more time is required to complete the move, column control is nearly impossible, and recovery of broken-down vehicles by the trail party is more protracted when compared to vehicle recovery in close and open columns. Additionally, unit integrity is not restored until the last vehicle arrives at the destination, complicating the unit's onward deployment. *Infiltration during troop movement should not be confused with infiltration as a form of maneuver as discussed in chapter 2 of this publication.*

5-23. During extended road marches, halts are necessary to rest personnel, service vehicles, and adjust movement schedules. The march order or unit SOP regulates when to take halts, and addresses actions for various tapes of halts, such as maintenance, security, and unexpected halts. During halts, each unit normally clears the march route and moves to a previously selected AA to prevent route congestion and avoid being a lucrative target. Units establish security and take other measures to protect the force.

5-24. In motor movements, short halts are scheduled every two to three hours of movement and halts may last up to an hour. Long halts occur on marches that exceed 24 hours and last no more than two hours. Long halts are not scheduled at night, which allows maximum time for night movement. Unit leaders promptly notify commanders of the time and approximate length of unscheduled halts.

APPROACH MARCH

5-25. An *approach march* is the advance of a combat unit when direct contact with the enemy is intended. However, it emphasizes speed over tactical deployment. The approach march is employed when the enemy's approximate location is known, since it allows the force to move with greater speed and less physical security or dispersion. In an approach march, units are task-organized to allow them to transition to an on-order or a be-prepared mission without making major organizational adjustments. The approach march terminates in a march objective, such as an attack position, AA, or assault position, or it can be used to transition to an attack.

5-26. The key to movement involves selecting the best combination of combat formation and movement technique for each situation. Leaders consider METT-TC in selecting the best route and appropriate formation and movement technique. The leader's selection must allow the moving unit to—

- Maintain cohesion.
- Maintain communication.
- Maintain momentum.
- Provide maximum security.

- Make enemy contact in a manner allowing them to transition smoothly to offensive or defensive action.

5-27. Careless movement usually results in contact with the enemy at a time and place of the enemy's choosing. To avoid this, leaders must understand the constantly-changing interrelationship between unit movement, terrain, and weapon systems within their area of operation. This understanding is the basis for employing combat formations, movement techniques, route selection and navigation, crossing danger areas, and security.

SECTION II – ROUTE SELECTION AND NAVIGATION

5-28. During planning and preparation for tactical movement, leaders analyze the terrain from two perspectives. First, they analyze the terrain to see how it can provide tactical advantage to friendly and enemy forces. Second, they look at the terrain to determine how it can aid navigation. Leaders identify areas or terrain features dominating their avenue of approach. These areas can become possible intermediate and final objectives.

5-29. Leaders identify good ground along the route that facilitates navigation and the destruction of enemy forces in the event that contact is occurs. If the leader wants to avoid contact, he chooses terrain that hides the unit. If the leader wants to make contact, he chooses terrain from where he can easily scan and observe the enemy. On other occasions, the leader may require terrain allowing stealth or speed. Regardless of the requirement, the leader must ensure most of the terrain along his route provides some tactical advantage.

5-30. Route selection and navigation are made easier with the aid of technology. The latest Mission Command Systems enhance the Infantry platoon's and squad's ability to ensure they are in the right place at the right time, and to determine the location of adjacent units.

Note. Soldiers should be proficient in land navigation. They shouldn't always rely on technology alone.

NAVIGATION AIDS

5-31. There are two categories of navigational aids: linear; and point. Linear navigational aids are terrain features such as trails, streams, ridgelines, wood lines, power lines, streets, and contour lines. Point terrain features include hilltops, and prominent buildings. Navigation aids usually are assigned control measures to facilitate communication during the movement. Typically, linear features are labeled as phase lines while point features are labeled as checkpoints (or rally points). There are three primary categories of navigation aids: catching features; handrails; and navigational attack points.

CATCHING FEATURES

5-32. Catching features are obvious terrain features which go beyond a waypoint or control measure and can be either linear or point. The general idea is if the unit moves past the objective, LOA, or checkpoint the catching feature will alert it that it has traveled too far.

Movement

The Offset-Compass Metheod

5-33. If there is the possibility of missing a particular point along the route (such as the endpoint or a navigational attack point), it is sometimes preferable to deliberately aim the leg to the left or right of the end point toward a prominent catching feature. Once reached, the unit simply turns the appropriate direction and moves to the desired endpoint. This method is especially helpful when the catching feature is linear.

Boxing-In the Route

5-34. One of the techniques leaders can use to prevent themselves from making navigational errors is to "box in" the leg or the entire route. This method uses catching features, handrails, and navigational attack points to form boundaries. Creating a box around the leg or route assists in easily recognizing and correcting deviation from the planned leg or route.

HANDRAILS

5-35. Handrails are linear features parallel to the proposed route. The general idea is to use the handrail to keep the unit oriented in the right direction. Guiding off of a handrail can increase the unit's speed while also acting as a catching feature.

NAVIGATIONAL ATTACK POINTS

5-36. Navigational attack points are an obvious landmark near the objective, LOA, or checkpoint that can be found easily. Upon arriving at the navigational attack point, the unit transitions from rough navigation (terrain association or general azimuth navigation) to point navigation (dead reckoning). Navigational attack points typically are labeled as checkpoints.

ROUTE PLANNING

5-37. Route planning must take into account enabling tasks specific to tactical movement. These tasks facilitate the overall operation. Tactical movement normally contains some or all of the following enabling tasks:

- Planning movement with global positioning system waypoints or checkpoints utilizing navigation skills.
- Movement to and passage of friendly lines.
- Movement to an objective rally point.
- Movement to a phase line of deployment.
- Movement to a limit of advance.
- Linkup with another unit.
- Movement to a patrol base or assembly area.
- Movement back to and reentry of friendly lines.

5-38. Leaders first identify where they want to end up (the objective or LOA). Then, working back to their current location, they identify all of the critical information and

Chapter 5

actions required as they relate to the route. For example, navigational aids, tactical positions, known and templated enemy positions, and friendly control measures. Using this information, they break up their route in manageable parts called legs. Finally, they capture their information and draw a sketch on a route chart. There are three decisions leaders make during route planning:

- The type of (or combination of) navigation to use.
- The type of route during each leg.
- The start point and end point of each leg.

5-39. The leader assesses the terrain in his proposed area of operation. In addition to the standard Army map, the leader may have aerial photographs and terrain analysis overlays from the parent unit, or he may talk with someone familiar with the area.

5-40. To control movement, a leader uses axis of advance, directions of attack, infiltration lanes, phase lines, PLD, checkpoints (waypoints), final coordination line, rally points, AA, and routes.

TYPES OF NAVIGATION

5-41. There are three types of navigation: terrain association, general azimuth method, and point navigation. Leaders use whichever type or combination best suits the situation.

TERRAIN ASSOCIATION

5-42. Terrain association is the ability to identify terrain features on the ground by the contour intervals depicted on the map. The leader analyzes the terrain using the factors of OAKOC, and identifies major terrain features, contour changes, and man-made structures along his axis of advance. As the unit moves, he uses these features to orient the unit and to associate ground positions with map locations. The major advantage of terrain association is it forces the leader to continually assess the terrain. This leads to identifying tactically-advantageous terrain and using terrain to the unit's advantage.

GENERAL AZIMUTH METHOD

5-43. For this method, the leader selects linear terrain features; then while maintaining map orientation and a general azimuth, he guides on the terrain feature. An advantage the general azimuth method has is it speeds movement, avoids fatigue, and often simplifies navigation because the unit follows the terrain feature. The disadvantage is it usually puts the unit on a natural line of drift. This method should end like terrain association, with the unit reaching a catching feature or a navigational attack point, then switching to point navigation.

POINT NAVIGATION

5-44. Point navigation, also called dead reckoning, is done by starting from a known point and strictly following a predetermined azimuth and distance. This form of navigation requires a high level of leader control because even a slight deviation over the course of a movement can cause navigation errors. This method uses the dismounted compass and a distance from the pace man (or a vehicle's odometer when mounted) to follow a prescribed route. Point navigation requires the leader to follow these steps:

- Use the compass to maintain direction.
- Use the pace man's pace or a vehicle odometer to measure the distance traveled for each leg or part.
- Review the written description of the route plan to help prevent navigational errors.

Note. Do not take compass reading from inside vehicles. Move away from vehicles when using lensatic compass.

5-45. When performed correctly, point navigation is very reliable, but time-consuming. It is best used when the need for navigational accuracy outweighs the importance of using terrain. Point navigation is particularly useful when recognizable terrain features do not exist or are too far away to be helpful. For example, deserts, swamps, and thick forest make terrain association difficult. Using point navigation early on in a long movement can stress the compass man and it may be advisable to switch him. One of the problems with point navigation is negotiating severely restrictive terrain or danger areas.

COMBINATION

5-46. Leaders can benefit from combining the three types of navigation. Terrain association and general azimuth method enable leaders to set a rough compass bearing and move as quickly as the situation allows toward a catching feature or a navigational attack point. Once reached, leaders switch to point navigation by paying close attention to detail, taking as much time as necessary to analyze the situation and find their point. Terrain association and general azimuth method allow for some flexibility in the movement, and do not require the same level of control as point navigation. Point navigation, on the other hand, enables leaders to precisely locate their objective or point.

MOUNTED LAND NAVIGATION

5-47. The principles of land navigation while mounted are basically the same as while dismounted. The major difference is the speed of travel. To be effective at mounted land navigation, the travel speed must be considered. When preparing to move, the effects of terrain on navigating mounted vehicles must be determined. You will cover great distances very quickly, and you must develop the ability to estimate the distance you have traveled. Using the odometer on the vehicle can assists with distance traveled but can be misleading on a map due to turns and going up and down hills for instance. Having a mobility advantage helps while navigating. Mobility makes it much easier if you get disoriented to move to a point where you can reorient yourself. When determining a route to be used when mounted, consider the capabilities of the vehicles to be used. Most military vehicles are limited in the degree of slope they can climb and the type of terrain they can negotiate. Swamps, thickly wooded areas, or deep streams may present no problems to dismounted soldiers, but the same terrain may completely stop mounted soldiers.

Chapter 5

STABILIZED TURRET ALIGNMENT NAVIGATION

5-48. Another method, if you have a vehicle with a stabilized turret, is to align the turret on the azimuth you wish to travel, then switch the turret stabilization system on. The gun tube remains pointed at your destination no matter which way you turn the vehicle. This technique has been proven; it works. It is not harmful to the stabilization system. It is subject to stabilization drift, so use it for no more than 5000 meters before resetting.

ROUTE TYPES

5-49. There are three types of routes leaders can choose from: those which follow linear terrain features; those which follow a designated contour interval; and those which go cross compartment. Terrain association can be used with all three route types. The general azimuth method is used with the contour and terrain feature method. Point navigation is used primarily with cross compartment.

TERRAIN FEATURE

5-50. Following a terrain feature is nothing more than moving along linear features such as ridges, valleys, and streets. The advantage of this method is the unit is moving with the terrain. This is normally the least physically taxing of the methods. The disadvantage is following terrain features also means following natural lines of drift, which leads to a higher probability of chance contact with the enemy.

CONTOURING

5-51. Contouring (remaining at the same height the entire leg) follows the imaginary contour line around a hill or along a ridgeline. Contouring has two advantages. First, it prevents undue climbing or descending. Second, following the contour acts as handrail or catching feature. The disadvantage of contouring is it can be physically taxing.

CROSS COMPARTMENT

5-52. Cross compartment means following a predetermined azimuth and usually means moving against the terrain. The advantage of this method is it provides the most direct route from the start point to the end point of the leg or route. There are two primary disadvantages to this type of route. First, this method can be physically taxing. Second, the unit might expose itself to enemy observation.

DEVELOP A LEG

5-53. The best way to manage a route is to divide it into segments called "legs." By breaking the overall route into several smaller segments, the leader is able to plan in detail. Legs typically have only one distance and direction. A change in direction usually ends the leg and begins a new one.

5-54. A leg must have a definite beginning and ending, marked with a control measure such as a checkpoint or phase line. (When using GPS, these are captured as waypoints.)

Movement

When possible, the start point and end point should correspond to a navigational aid (catching feature or navigational attack point).

5-55. To develop a leg, leaders first determine the type of navigation and route best suiting the situation. Once these two decisions are made, the leader determines the distance and direction from the start point to the end point. He then identifies critical METT-TC information as it relates to the specific leg. Finally, leaders capture this information and draw a sketch on a route chart. (See figure 5-3.)

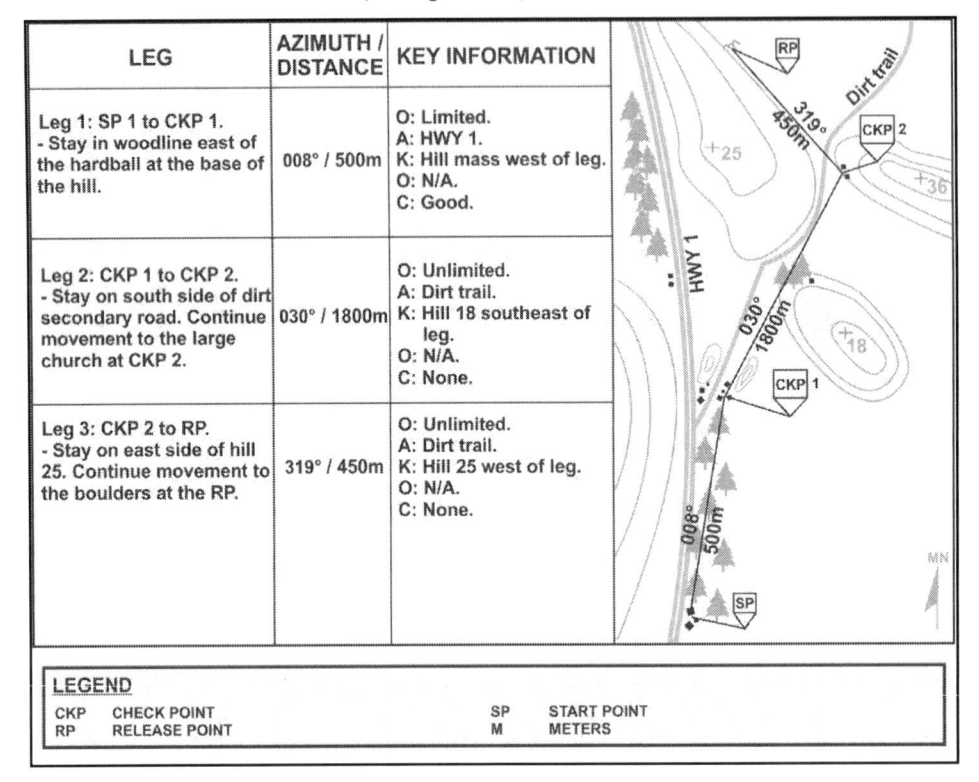

LEG	AZIMUTH / DISTANCE	KEY INFORMATION
Leg 1: SP 1 to CKP 1. - Stay in woodline east of the hardball at the base of the hill.	008° / 500m	O: Limited. A: HWY 1. K: Hill mass west of leg. O: N/A. C: Good.
Leg 2: CKP 1 to CKP 2. - Stay on south side of dirt secondary road. Continue movement to the large church at CKP 2.	030° / 1800m	O: Unlimited. A: Dirt trail. K: Hill 18 southeast of leg. O: N/A. C: None.
Leg 3: CKP 2 to RP. - Stay on east side of hill 25. Continue movement to the boulders at the RP.	319° / 450m	O: Unlimited. A: Dirt trail. K: Hill 25 west of leg. O: N/A. C: None.

LEGEND
CKP   CHECK POINT   SP   START POINT
RP   RELEASE POINT   M   METERS

Figure 5-3. Example of sketching of legs

EXECUTE THE ROUTE

5-56. Using decisions about the route and navigation made during planning and preparation, leaders execute their route and direct their subordinates. In addition to executing the plan, leaders—

- Determine and maintain accurate location.
- Designate rally points.

Chapter 5

DETERMINE LOCATION

5-57. A leader always must know his unit's location during movement. Without accurate location, the unit cannot expect to receive help from supporting arms, integrate reserve forces, or accomplish their mission. To ensure accurate location, a leader uses many techniques, including:

- Executing common skills.
- Designating a compass man and pace man.
- Using Mission Command Systems.

Common Skills

5-58. All Infantry Soldiers, particularly leaders, must be experts in land navigation. Important navigation tasks common to all include:

- Locating a point using grid coordinates. Using a compass (day/night).
- Determining location using resection, intersection, or modified resection.
- Interpreting terrain features.
- Measuring distance and elevation.
- Employing Mission Command Systems.

Compass Man

5-59. The compass man assists in navigation by ensuring the lead fire team leader remains on course at all times. The compass man should be thoroughly briefed. His instructions must include an initial azimuth with subsequent azimuths provided as necessary. The platoon leader or squad leader also should designate an alternate compass man. The leader should validate the patrol's navigation with GPS devices.

Pace Man

5-60. The pace man maintains an accurate pace at all times. The platoon leader or squad leader should designate how often the pace man reports the pace. The pace man also should report the pace at the end of each leg. The platoon leader or squad leader should designate an alternate pace man.

Global Positioning Systems

5-61. GPSs receive signals from satellites or land-based transmitters. They calculate and display the position of the user in military grid coordinates as well as in degrees of latitude and longitude. During planning, leaders enter their waypoints into the GPS. Once entered, the GPS can display information such as distance and direction from waypoint to waypoint. During execution, leaders use the GPS to establish their exact location.

Movement

> *Note.* Leaders need to remember GPS and digital displays are not the only navigational tools they can use. The best use of GPS or digital displays is for confirming the unit's location during movement. Terrain association and map-reading skills still are necessary, especially for point navigation. Over reliance of GPS and digital displays can cause leaders to ignore the effects of terrain, travel faster than conditions allow, miss opportunities, or fail to modify routes when necessary.

DESIGNATE RALLY POINTS

5-62. A rally point is a place designated by the leader where the unit moves to reassemble and reorganize if it becomes dispersed. It also can be a place for a temporarily halt to reorganize and prepare for actions at the objective, to depart from friendly lines, or to reenter friendly lines. (Refer to ADRP 1-02 for more information.) Planned and unplanned rally points are common control measures used during tactical movement. Planned ORP, initial rally points (IRP), and reentry rally points (RRP). Unplanned rally points are en route rally points, near side rally points, and far side rally points. Despite the different types of rally points, the actions occurring are generally the same.

5-63. Prior to departing, leaders designate tentative rally points and determine what actions will occur there. When occupying a rally point, leaders use a perimeter defense to ensure all-around security. Those rally points used to reassemble the unit after an event are likely to be chaotic scenes and will require immediate actions by whatever Soldiers happen to arrive. These actions and other considerations are listed in table 5-1 (page 5-16).

Chapter 5

Table 5-1. Actions at rally point

RALLY POINTS	SOLDIER ACTIONS at an RP	OTHER CONSIDERATIONS
Select a rally point that— • Is easily recognized. • Is large enough for the unit to assemble. • Is defensible for a short time. • Is away from normal movement routes and natural lines of drift. • Designate a rally point by one of the following three ways: • Physically occupy it for a short period. • Use hand-and-arm signals (either pass by at a distance or walk through). • Radio communication.	• Establish security. • Reestablish the chain of command. • Account for personnel and equipment status. • Determine how long to wait until continuing the unit's mission or linkup at a follow-on rally point. • Complete last instructions.	• Travel time and distance. • Maneuver room needed. • Adjacent unit coordination requirements. • Line of sight and range requirements for communication equipment. • Trafficability and load bearing capacity of the soil (especially when mounted). • Ability to prevent being surprised by the enemy. • Energy expenditure of Soldiers and condition they will be in at the end of the movement.

SECTION III – ACTIONS AT DANGER AREAS

5-64. When analyzing the terrain through METT-TC during the TLP, the platoon leader may identify danger areas. When planning the route, he marks the danger areas on his overlay. The term *danger area* refers to areas on the route where the terrain could expose the platoon to enemy observation, fire, or both. If possible, the platoon leader plans to avoid danger areas, but sometimes he cannot. When the unit must cross a danger area, it does so as quickly and carefully as possible. During planning, the leader designates near-side and far-side rally points. If the platoon encounters an unexpected danger area, it uses the en route rally points closest to the danger area as far-side and near-side rally points. Examples of danger areas include:

- *Open areas.* Conceal the platoon on the near side and observe the area. Post security to give early warning. Send an element across to clear the far side. When cleared, cross the remainder of the platoon at the shortest exposed distance and as quickly as possible.
- *Roads and trails.* Cross roads or trails at or near a bend, a narrow spot, or on low ground.
- *Villages.* Pass villages on the downwind side and well away from them. Avoid animals, especially dogs, which might reveal the platoon's presence.
- *Enemy positions.* Pass on the downwind side. (The enemy might have scout dogs.) Be alert for trip wires and warning devices.
- *Minefields.* Bypass minefields if at all possible, even if it requires changing the route by a great distance. Clear a path through minefields only if necessary.

- *Streams.* Select a narrow spot in the stream offering concealment on both banks. Observe the far side carefully. Emplace near- and far-side security for early warning. Clear the far side and cross rapidly but quietly.
- *Wire obstacles.* Avoid wire obstacles. (The enemy covers obstacles with observation and fire.)

CROSSING DANGER AREAS

5-65. Regardless of the type of danger area, when the platoon must cross one independently, or as the lead element of a larger force, it must perform the following:
- When the lead team signals "danger area" (relayed throughout the platoon), the platoon halts.
- The platoon leader moves forward, confirms the danger area, and determines what technique the platoon will use to cross. The platoon sergeant also moves forward to the platoon leader.
- The platoon leader informs all squad leaders of the situation, the near-side and far-side rally points.
- The platoon sergeant directs positioning of the near-side security (usually conducted by the trail squad). These two security teams may follow him forward when the platoon halts and a danger area signal is passed back.
- The platoon leader reconnoiters the danger area and selects the crossing point providing the best cover and concealment.
- Near-side security observes to the flanks and overwatches the crossing.
- When the near-side security is in place, the platoon leader directs the far-side security team to cross the danger area.
- The far-side security team clears the far side.
- The far-side security team leader establishes an observation post forward of the cleared area.
- The far-side security team signals to the squad leader the area is clear. The squad leader relays the message to the platoon leader.
- The platoon leader selects the method the platoon will use to cross the danger area.
- The platoon quickly and quietly crosses the danger area.
- Once across the danger area, the main body begins moving slowly on the required azimuth.
- The near-side security element, controlled by the platoon sergeant, crosses the danger area where the platoon crossed. They may attempt to cover tracks left by the platoon.
- The platoon sergeant ensures everyone crosses and sends up the report.
- The platoon leader ensures accountability and resumes movement at normal speed.

Note. Same principles stated above are used when crossing a smaller unit (such as a squad) across a danger area.

Chapter 5

5-66. The platoon leader or squad leader decides how the unit will cross based on the time he has, size of the unit, size of the danger area, fields of fire into the area, and amount of security he can post. An Infantry platoon or squad may cross all at once, in buddy teams, or one Soldier at a time. A large unit normally crosses its elements one at a time. As each element crosses, it moves to an overwatch position or to the far-side rally point until told to continue movement.

CROSSING OF LINEAR DANGER AREAS (PLATOON)

5-67. A linear danger area is an area where the platoon's flanks are exposed along a relatively narrow field of fire. Examples include streets, roads, trails, and streams. The platoon crosses a linear danger area in the formation and location specified by the platoon leader. (See figure 5-4.)

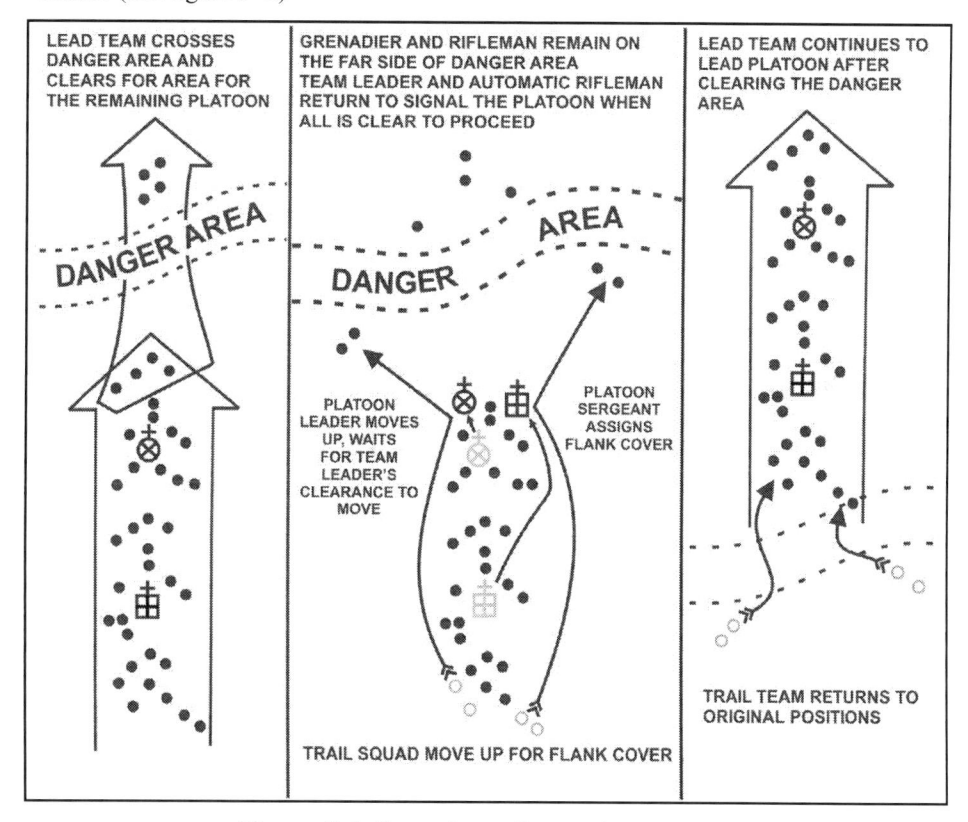

Figure 5-4. Crossing a linear danger area

CROSSING OF LARGE OPEN AREAS

5-68. If the large open area is so large the platoon cannot bypass it due to the time needed to accomplish the mission, a combination of traveling overwatch and bounding overwatch is used to cross the large open area. (See figure 5-5.) The traveling overwatch technique is used to save time. The squad or platoon moves using the bounding overwatch technique any point in the open area where enemy contact may be expected. The technique also may be used once the squad or platoon comes within range of enemy small-arms fire from the far side (about 250 meters). Once beyond the open area, the squad or platoon re-forms and continues the mission.

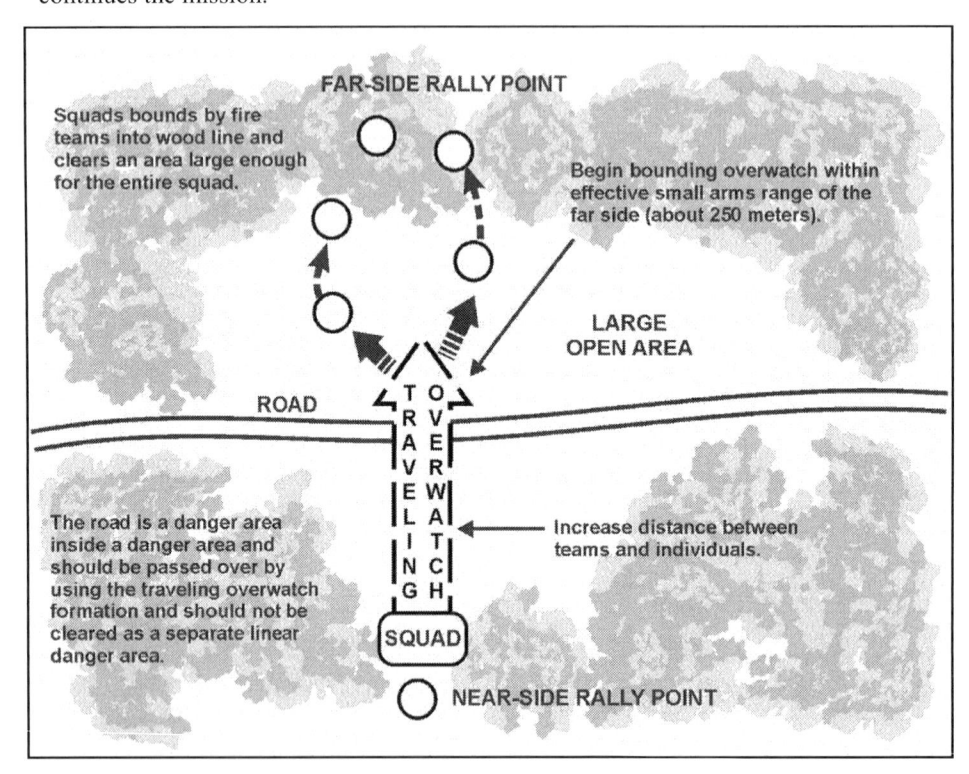

Figure 5-5. Crossing a large open area

CROSSING OF SMALL OPEN AREAS

5-69. Small open areas are small enough to bypass in the time allowed for the mission. Two techniques can be used. (See figure 5-6, page 5-20.)

Contouring Around the Open Area

5-70. The leader designates a rally point on the far side with the movement azimuth. He then decides which side of the open area to contour around (after considering the distance, terrain, cover and concealment), and moves around the open area. He uses the wood line and vegetation for cover and concealment. When the squad or platoon arrives at the rally point on the far side, the leader reassumes the azimuth to the objective area and continues the mission. (See figure 5-6, page 5-20.)

Chapter 5

Detour Bypass Method

5-71. The squad or platoon turns 90 degrees to the right or left around the open area and moves in the direction of travel. Once the squad or platoon has passed the danger area, the unit completes the box with another 90-degree turn and arrives at the far-side rally point, then continues the mission. The pace counts of the offset and return legs is not added to the distance of the planned route. (See figure 5-6.)

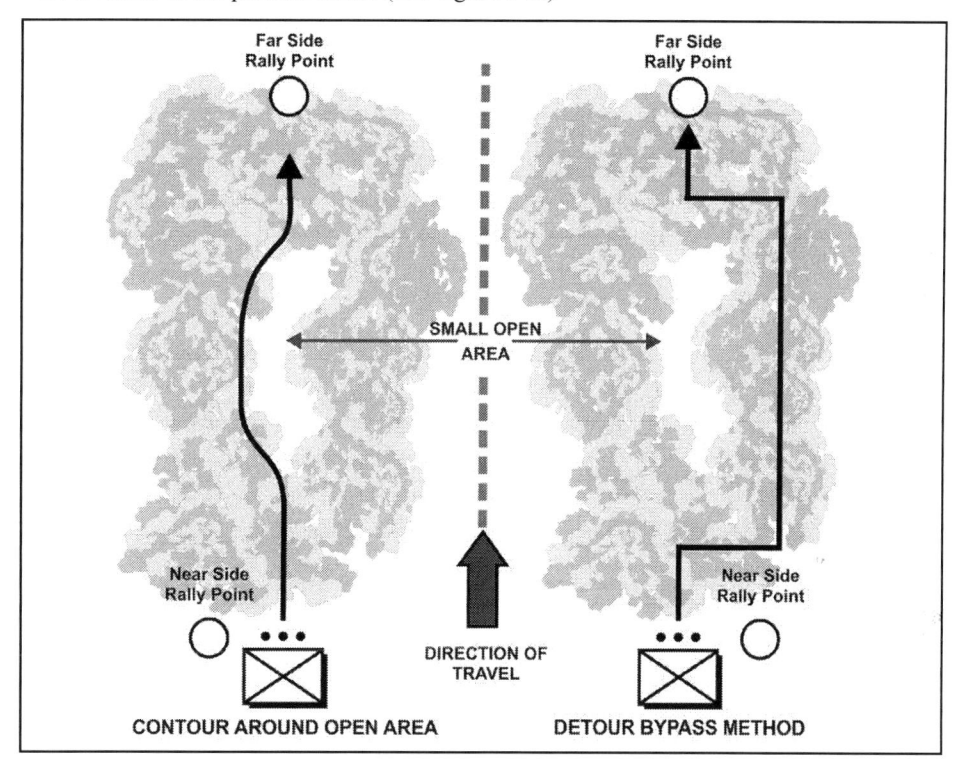

Figure 5-6. Crossing a small open area

ACTIONS AT DANGER AREAS (MOUNTED)

5-72. Infantry platoons and squads must be prepared to negotiate danger areas when mounted. The discussion of leader and unit action are deliberately generic because of the wide variety of scenarios in which leaders might find themselves.

5-73. When moving mounted, units normally travel on roads, trails, and in unrestrictive terrain. Mounted units are typically vulnerable in the type of terrain favored by Infantry such as restrictive and close terrain. In addition, areas such as bridges, road junctions, defiles, and curves (denying observation beyond the turn) are also considered danger areas. When leaders identify a danger area, they determine the appropriate movement technique to employ (traveling, traveling overwatch, or bounding overwatch). They then dismount their Infantry squads and clear the area or do a combination of both.

Movement

5-74. If time and terrain permit, the unit should either bypass a danger area or dismount Infantry to reconnoiter and clear it. However, the distances between covered and concealed positions may make this impractical. If time constraints prevent these options, the unit uses a combination of traveling overwatch and bounding overwatch to negotiate the danger area. As with dismounted actions at a danger area, the leader must be prepared to quickly transition to maneuver in case the unit makes contact with the enemy.

MOUNTED TRAVELING OVERWATCH

5-75. The lead element moves continuously along the covered and concealed routes giving it the best available protection from possible enemy observation and direct fire. (See figure 5-7.) The trail element moves at variable speeds providing continuous overwatch, keeping contact with the lead element, and stopping periodically to get a better look. The trail element stays close enough to ensure mutual support of the lead element. However, it must stay far enough to the rear to retain freedom of maneuver in case an enemy force engages the lead element.

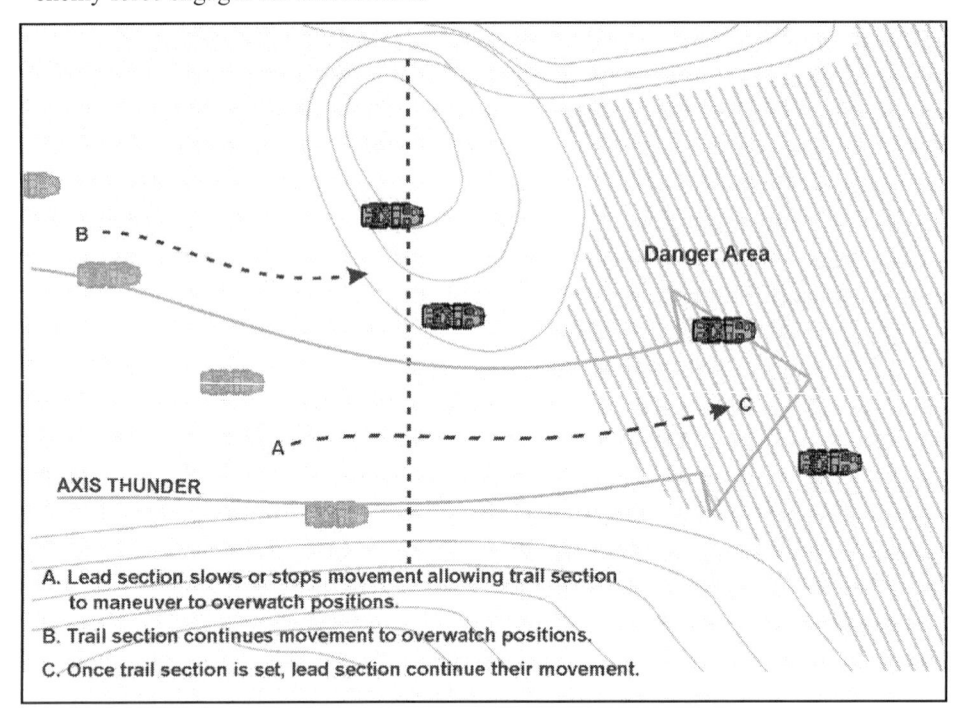

Figure 5-7. Mounted traveling overwatch

MOUNTED BOUNDING OVERWATCH

5-76. With bounding overwatch, one section always is stopped to provide overwatching fire. The unit executing bounding overwatch uses either the successive or alternate bounding method.

Chapter 5

DISMOUNTING AND CLEARING THE AREA

5-77. The commander of the lead vehicle immediately notifies the platoon leader when he encounters an obstacle or other danger area. If needed, Soldiers dismount and take advantage of available cover and concealment to investigate these areas. (See figure 5-8.) If possible, the vehicle is moved off the road into a covered or concealed position. Weapons from the vehicle cover the advance of the dismounted element. Designated Soldiers reconnoiter these places under cover of the weapons in the vehicle. Obstacles are marked and bypassed, if possible. When they cannot be bypassed, they are removed cautiously.

5-78. Side roads intersecting the route of advance are investigated. Soldiers from one vehicle secure the road junction. One or two vehicles investigate the side road. The amount of reconnaissance on side roads is determined by the leader's knowledge of the situation. Soldiers investigating side roads do not move past supporting distance of the main body.

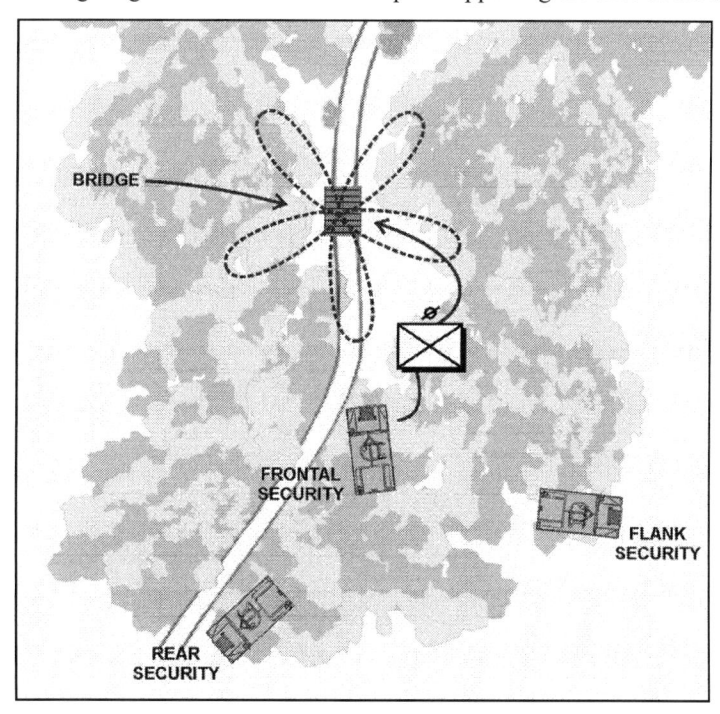

Figure 5-8. Dismounting and clearing the area

DEFILE

5-79. A defile is a narrow passage that constricts the movement of Soldiers. It is the ideal ambush site. If a defile is encountered that forces the platoon to move in single vehicle file for a significant distance the platoon leader might choose to lead with dismounted Infantry. (See figure 5-9.) Common defiles for mechanized platoons are roads or trails across streams, though swamps or heavy forests, or narrow valleys in rolling or mountainous

Movement

terrain. When clearing a defile, the dismount element clears each side far enough from the choke point to make sure that there are no ambushes. It also checks the surface for evidence of mines or IEDs. Because contact should be expected at defiles, the leading squad should use bounding overwatch.

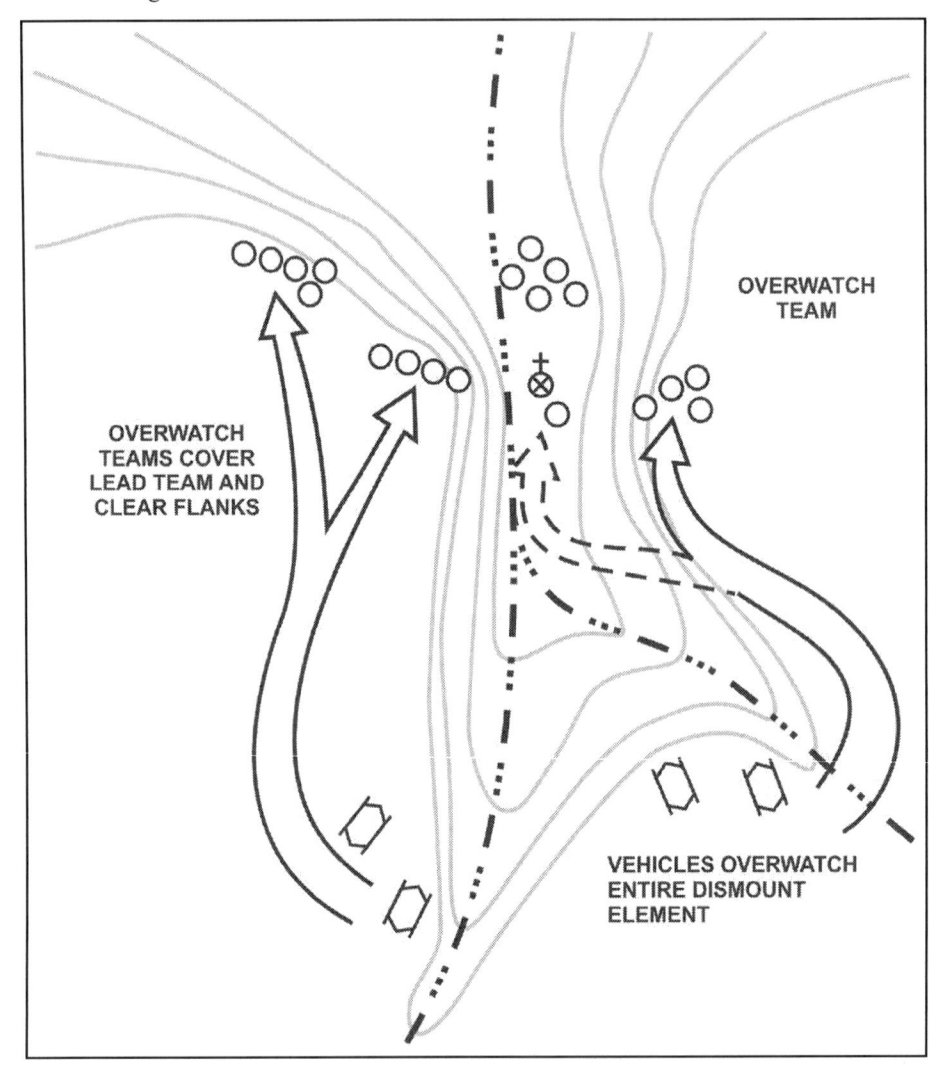

Figure 5-9. Clearing a Defile

EMEMY CONTACT AT DANGER AREAS

5-80. An increased awareness of the situation helps the platoon leader control the platoon when it makes contact with the enemy. If the platoon makes contact in or near the danger area, it moves to the designated rally points. Based on the direction of enemy contact, the leader designates the far- or near-side rally point. During limited visibility, he also can use

Chapter 5

his laser systems to point out the rally points at a distance. If the platoon has a difficult time linking up at the rally point, the first element to arrive should mark the rally point with an infrared light source. This helps direct the rest of the platoon to the location. During movement to the rally point, position updates allow separated elements to identify each other's locations. These updates help them linkup at the rally point by identifying friends and foes.

SECTION IV – RELIEF IN PLACE

5-81. A relief in place is a tactical enabling task in which all or part of a unit is replaced in an area by the incoming unit. The responsibilities of the replaced elements for mission and assigned area of operation are transferred to the incoming unit. The incoming unit continues the operations as ordered. (Refer to FM 3-90-2 for more information.) There are three techniques for conducting a relief: sequentially, simultaneously, or staggered, which are described as the following:

- A sequential relief occurs when each element within the relieved unit is relieved in succession, from right to left or left to right, depending on how it is deployed.
- A simultaneous relief occurs when all elements are relieved at the same time.
- A staggered relief occurs when the leader relieves each element in a sequence determined by the tactical situation, not its geographical orientation.

5-82. Simultaneous relief takes the least time to execute, but is more easily detected by the enemy. Sequential or staggered reliefs can take place over a significant amount of time. These three relief techniques can occur regardless of the range of military operations in which the unit is participating.

5-83. A relief also can be characterized as either deliberate or hasty, depending on the amount of planning and preparations associated with the relief. The major differences are the depth and detail of planning and, potentially, the execution time. Detailed planning generally facilitates shorter execution time by determining exactly what the leader believes needs to be done and resources needed to accomplish the mission. Deliberate planning allows the commander and staff to identify, develop, and coordinate solutions to most potential problems before they occur and to ensure the availability of resources when and where they are needed.

PLANNING

5-84. Once ordered to conduct a relief in place, the leader of the relieving unit contacts the leader of the unit to be relieved. The collocation of unit command posts also helps achieve the level of coordination required. If the relieved unit's forward elements can defend the area of operation, the relieving unit executes the relief in place from the rear to the front. This facilitates movement and terrain management.

5-85. When planning for a relief in place, the Infantry platoon leader takes the following actions:

- Issues an order immediately.

- Sends himself or key leader with platoon advance party to conduct detailed reconnaissance and coordination.
- As the relieving unit, adopts the outgoing unit's normal pattern of activity as much as possible.
- As the relieving unit, determines when the platoon will assume responsibility for outgoing unit's position.
- As the relieving unit, collocates with the relieved unit's headquarters.
- Maximizes operations security to prevent the enemy from detecting the relief operation.

Note. When possible, conduct the relief at night or under other limited visibility conditions.

- Plans for relief of sustainment elements after combat elements are relieved.
- As the unit being relieved, plans for transfer of excess ammunition, wire, petroleum, oil, and lubricants, and other materiel of tactical value to the incoming unit.
- Controls movement by reconnoitering, designating, and marking routes, and providing guides.

COORDINATION

5-86. The incoming and outgoing unit leaders meet to exchange tactical information, conduct a joint reconnaissance of the area, and complete other required coordination. The two leaders carefully address passage of command and jointly develop contingency actions to deal with enemy contact during the relief. This process usually includes coordination of the following information:

- Location of vehicle and individual fighting positions (to include hide, alternate, and supplementary positions). Leaders should verify fighting positions both by conventional map and using the latest Mission Command Systems available.
- The enemy situation.
- The outgoing unit's tactical plan, including graphics, company and platoon fire plans, and individual vehicles' area of operations sketches.
- Direct and indirect fire support coordination, including indirect fire plans and time of relief for supporting artillery and mortar units.
- Types of weapons systems being replaced.
- Time, sequence, and method of relief.
- Location and disposition of obstacles, and time when the leaders will transfer responsibility.
- Supplies and equipment to be transferred.
- Movement control, route priority, and placement of guides.
- Command and signal information.

Chapter 5

> *Note.* Units conduct relief on the radio nets of the outgoing unit to facilitate control during the relief.

- Maintenance and logistical support for disabled vehicles.
- Visibility considerations.

CONDUCTING THE RELIEF

5-87. When conducting the relief, the outgoing leader retains responsibility of the area of operation and mission. He exercises operational control over all subordinate elements of the incoming unit having completed their portion of the relief. Responsibility passes to the incoming leader when all elements of the outgoing unit are relieved and adequate communications are established.

SEQUENTIAL RELIEF

5-88. Sequential relief is the most time-consuming relief method. The relieving unit moves to an AA to the rear of the unit to be relieved. Subordinate elements are relieved one at a time. This can occur in any order, with the relief following this general sequence:

- The outgoing and incoming unit's collocates their headquarters and trains elements to facilitate mission command and transfer of equipment, ammunition, fuel, water, and medical supplies.
- The first element being relieved (such as a platoon) moves to its alternate fighting positions or battle positions while the relieving element moves into the outgoing element's primary fighting positions. The incoming element occupies vehicle and individual fighting positions as appropriate.
- Incoming and outgoing elements complete the transfer of equipment and supplies.
- The relieved element moves to the designated assembly area behind its position.
- Once each outgoing element clears the rally point en route to its assembly area, the next relieving element moves forward.

SIMULTANEOUS RELIEF

5-89. Simultaneous relief is the fastest, but least secure, method. All outgoing elements are relieved at once, with the incoming unit usually occupying existing positions, including battle positions, and vehicle and individual fighting positions. The relief takes place in this general sequence:

- Outgoing elements move to their alternate battle positions or vehicle and individual positions.
- Incoming elements move along designated routes to the outgoing elements' primary fighting positions.
- The units complete the transfer of equipment and supplies.
- Relieved elements move to the designated unit assembly area.

SECTION V – PASSAGE OF LINES

5-90. Passage of lines is a tactical-enabling task in which a force moves forward or rearward through another unit's positions with the intent of moving into or out of contact with the enemy. A passage may be designated as a forward or rearward passage of lines. Units usually conduct passage of lines when at least one METT-TC factor does not permit the bypass of a friendly unit. A passage of lines is a complex operation requiring close supervision and detailed planning, coordination, and synchronization between the leaders of the unit conducting the passage and unit being passed. The primary purpose of a passage of lines is to transfer responsibility (forward or rearward) for an area from one unit to another.

5-91. Passage of lines occur under two basic conditions. A forward passage of lines occurs when a unit passes through another unit's positions while moving toward the enemy. A rearward passage of lines occurs when a unit passes through another unit's positions while moving away from the enemy.

PLANNING CONSIDERATIONS

5-92. The controlling Infantry company is responsible for planning and coordinating a passage of lines involving the Infantry platoon and squad. In some situations, such as the company using multiple passage routes for example, a separate route for each platoon, the company commander takes responsibility for planning and coordinating each phase of the operation.

5-93. When planning a passage of lines, the following tactical factors and procedures are considered: passage lanes, use of deception, battle handover, obstacles, air defense, sustainment responsibilities, mission command, reconnaissance and coordination, forward passage of lines, and rearward passage of lines.

FORWARD PASSAGE OF LINES

5-94. In a forward passage, the passing unit first moves to an AA or an attack position behind the stationary unit. Designated liaison personnel move forward to linkup with guides and confirm coordination information with the stationary unit. Guides then lead the passing elements through the passage lane.

5-95. The Infantry unit conducts a forward passage by employing tactical movement. It moves quickly, using appropriate dispersal and formations whenever possible, and keeping radio traffic to a minimum. It bypasses disabled vehicles as necessary. The unit holds its fire until it passes the BHL or the designated fire control measure, unless the leader has coordinated fire control with the stationary unit. Once clear of passage lane restrictions, the unit consolidates at a rally point or attack position, and conducts tactical movement according to its orders. (See figure 5-10, page 5-28.)

Chapter 5

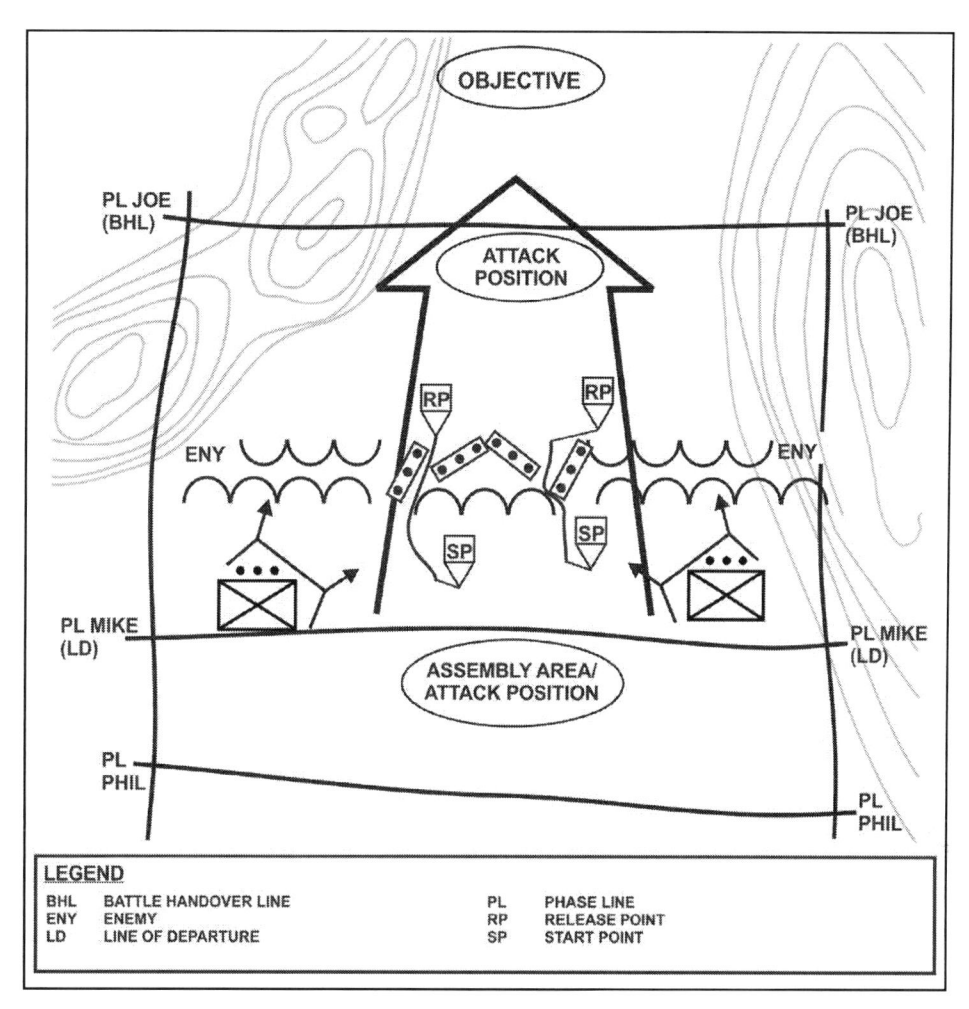

Figure 5-10. Forward passage of lines

REARWARD PASSAGE OF LINES

5-96. Because of the increased chance of fratricide and friendly fire during a rearward passage, coordination of recognition signals and direct fire restrictions is critical. Rehearsals and training can help reduce fratricide and friendly fire. The passing unit contacts the stationary unit while it is still beyond direct fire range and conducts coordination as discussed previously. Near recognition signals and location of the BHL are emphasized. Both passing and stationary unit can employ additional fire control measures, such as RFL, to minimize the risk of fratricide and friendly fire. (See figure 5-11.)

Movement

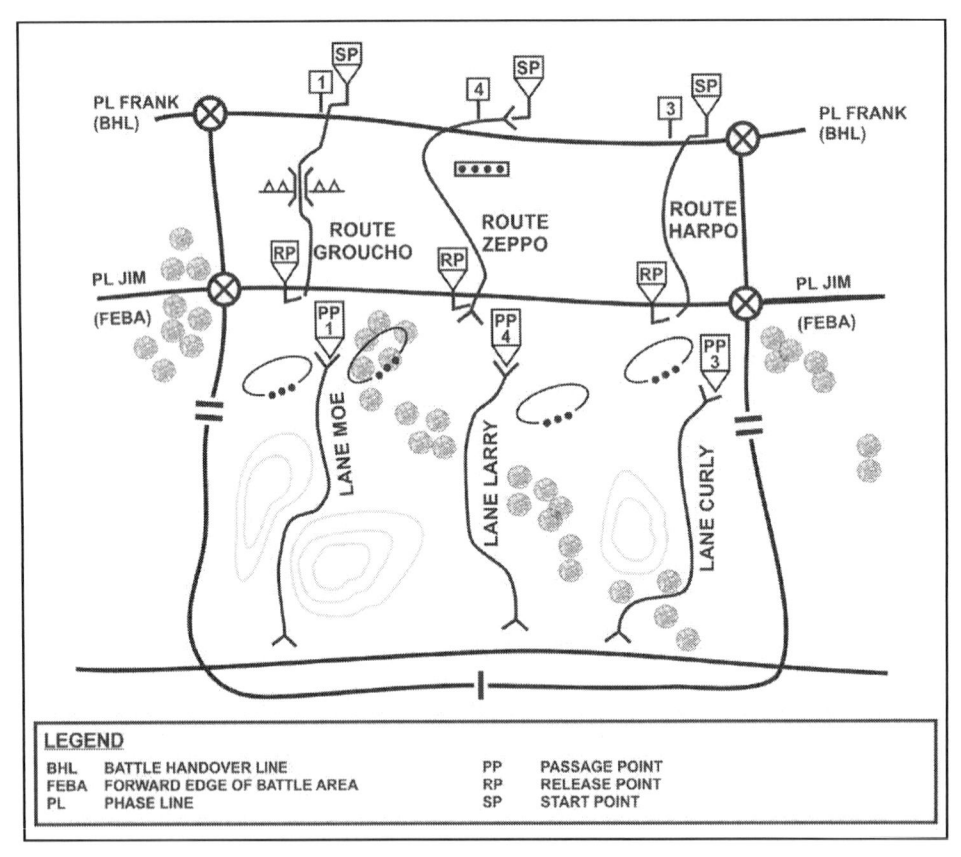

Figure 5-11. Rearward passage of lines

5-97. Following coordination, the passing unit continues tactical movement toward the passage lane. The passing unit is responsible for its security until it passes the BHL. If the stationary unit provides guides, the passing unit can conduct a short halt to linkup and coordinate with them. The passing unit moves quickly through the passage lane to a designated location behind the stationary unit.

5-98. Stationary unit and passing unit responsibilities. (See table 5-2, page 5-30.)

Table 5-2. Stationary and passing unit responsibilities

STATIONARY UNIT	PASSING UNIT
Clears lanes or reduces obstacles along routes.	May assist with reducing obstacles.
Provides obstacle and friendly units' locations.	Provides order of movement and scheme of maneuver.
Clears and maintains routes up to the battle handover line (BHL).	May assist with maintaining routes.
Provides traffic control for use of routes and lanes.	Augments the traffic control capability of the stationary unit as required
Provides security for passage up to the BHL.	Maintains protection measures
Identifies locations for the passing unit to use as assembly area (AA) and attack positions.	Reconnoiters from its current location to its designated AA and attack positions
Provides the passing unit previously coordinated or emergency logistics assistance within its capability.	Assumes full responsibility for its own sustainment support forward of the BHL.
Controls all fires in support of the passage.	Positions artillery to support the passage

SECTION VI – LINKUP

5-99. A linkup is a meeting of friendly ground forces, which occurs in a variety of circumstances. It happens when an advancing force reaches an objective area previously seized by an airborne or air assault; when an encircled element breaks out to rejoin friendly forces or a force comes to the relief of an encircled force; and when converging maneuver forces meet. Both forces may be moving toward each other, or one may be stationary. Whenever possible, joining forces exchange as much information as possible before starting an operation.

5-100. The headquarters ordering the linkup establishes—
- A common operational picture.
- Command relationship and responsibilities of each force before, during, and after linkup.
- Coordination of direct and indirect fire support before, during, and after linkup, including control measures.
- Linkup method.
- Recognition signals and communication procedures to use, including pyrotechnics, armbands, vehicle markings, gun-tube orientation, panels, colored smoke, lights, and challenge and passwords.
- Operations to conduct following linkup.

CONTROL MEASURES

5-101. The leader who orders the linkup establishes control measures for units conducting the linkup—
- Assigns each unit an area of operations defined by left and right boundaries and a restrictive fire line also acts as a limit of advance.
- Establishes a no fires area around one or both units and establishes a coordinated fire line beyond the area where the unit's linkup.
- Establishes a no fires area to ensure unclear air-delivered munitions or indirect fires do not cross either the restrictive fire line or a boundary and impact friendly forces.

5-102. The coordinated fire line allows available fires to quickly attack enemy targets approaching the area where the linkup is to occur. The linkup forces use the linkup points established by the leader to make physical contact with each other. The leader designates alternate linkup points, since enemy action may interfere with the primary linkup points. Control measures are adjusted during the operation to provide for freedom of action as well as positive control.

EXECUTION

5-103. There are two linkup methods. The preferred method is when the moving force has an assigned LOA near the other force and conducts the linkup at predetermined contact points. Units then coordinate additional operations. The leader uses the other method during highly fluid mobile operations when the enemy force escapes from a potential encirclement, or when one of the linkup forces is at risk and requires immediate reinforcement. In this method, the moving force continues to move and conduct long-range recognition via radio or other measures, stopping only when it makes physical contact with the other force.

PHASES OF THE LINKUP

5-104. The Infantry platoon and squad conducts linkup activities independently or as part of a larger force. Within a larger unit, the platoon may lead the linkup force. The linkup consists of three phases. The following actions are critical to the execution of a linkup.

PHASE 1 – FAR RECOGNITION SIGNAL

5-105. During this phase, the forces conducting a linkup establish both radio and digital communications before reaching direct fire range. The lead element of each linkup force should monitor the radio frequency of the other friendly force.

PHASE 2 – COORDINATION

5-106. Before initiating movement to the linkup point, the forces must coordinate necessary tactical information including the following:
- The known enemy situation.

Chapter 5

- Mission Command Systems, if equipped, filter setting and address book commonality.
- Type and number of friendly vehicles and number of vehicles equipped with Mission Command Systems.
- Disposition of stationary forces (if either unit is stationary).
- Routes to the linkup point and rally point, if any.
- Direct and indirect fire control measures.
- Near recognition signals.
- Communications information.
- Sustainment responsibilities and procedures.
- Finalized location of the linkup point and rally points, if any.
- Special coordination, such as those covering maneuver instructions or requests for medical support.

PHASE 3 – MOVEMENT TO THE LINKUP POINT AND LINKUP

5-107. All units or elements involved in the linkup enforce strict fire control measures to help prevent fratricide and friendly fire. Moving or converging forces must easily recognize linkup points and RFL. Linkup elements take the following actions:

- Conduct far recognition using radios or Mission Command Systems, if equipped.
- Conduct short-range (near) recognition using the designated signal.
- Complete movement to the linkup point.
- Establish local security at the linkup point.
- Conduct additional coordination and linkup activities, as necessary.

SECTION VII – MOVEMENT WITH COMBAT VEHICLES

5-108. There are several options available to the platoon leader when augmented with vehicles. The platoon leader should employ the vehicles in conjunction with the rifle squads so each complements the other. Some options include—

- Employ them to support the Infantry rifle squads.
- Employ them separately to provide heavy direct fires or antiarmor fires.
- Leave in hide positions.
- Displace them to a secure location.

COMBAT VEHICLES AND INFANTRY SQUAD FORMATIONS

5-109. The principles of METT-TC guide the leader in selecting formations for combat vehicles and Infantry. The same principles for selecting combat formations with Infantry Soldiers apply when selecting combat formations for combat vehicles moving with Infantry Soldiers. The platoon leader can employ the fundamental column, line, echelon, vee, and wedge formations for combat vehicles to meet the needs of his mission. The

Movement

column, line, echelon, vee, and wedge are fundamental combat formations for combat vehicles. After the leader combines the mounted and Infantry elements into one combat formation, it is his responsibility to ensure proper communication and fire control measures are implemented to maximize lethality and prevent fratricide.

5-110. After selecting the combat formations for combat vehicles and Infantry, the leader can decide whether to lead with combat vehicles, Infantry Soldiers, or a combination of the two. The default technique is to lead with Infantry Soldiers.

LEAD WITH INFANTRY

5-111. Infantry Soldiers are better suited for leading combat formations (see figure 5-12) when—
- A route leads through restrictive urban or rural terrain
- Stealth is desired.
- Enemy antitank minefields are templated.
- Enemy antitank teams are templated.

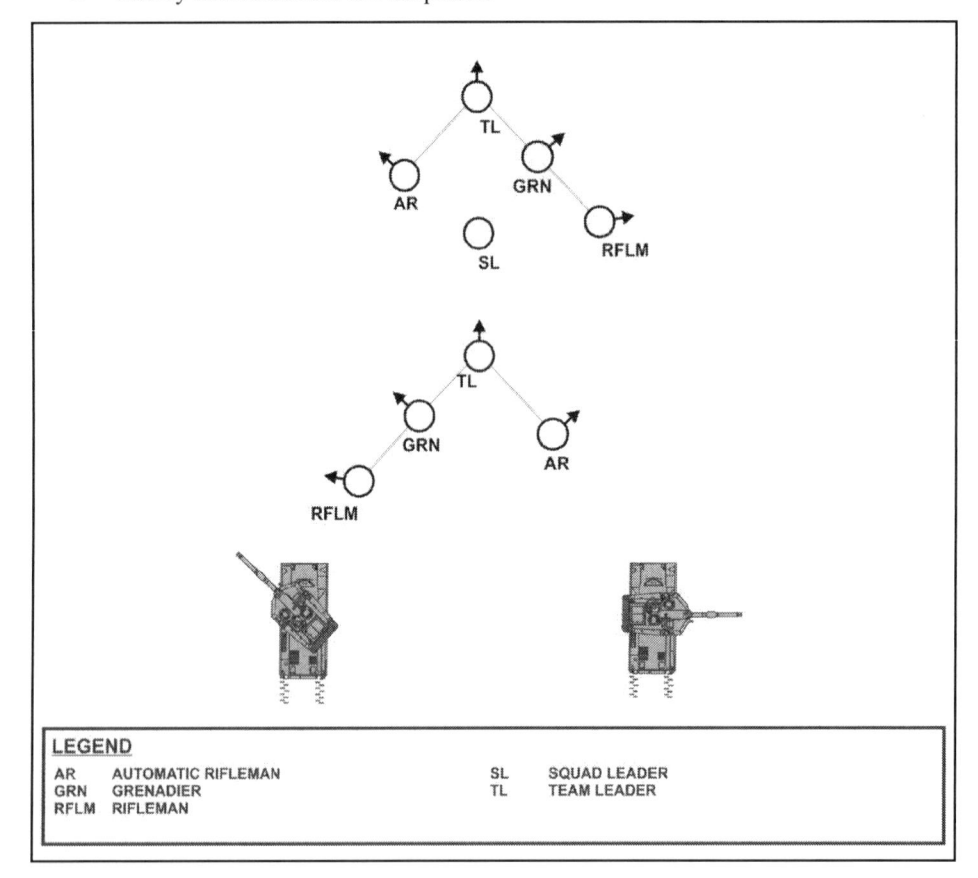

Figure 5-12. Lead with Infantry squad

Chapter 5

> *Note.* Tanks fire high-velocity, armor-piercing, discarding sabot rounds that pose hazards to Infantry. Dismounted Soldiers should be at 300 meters to the left or right of the line of fire and at least 1300 meters to the front of a firing tank. Any Infantry within this danger area must have adequate cover as defined in Department of the Army Pamphlet 385-63 from the rear.

LEAD WITH TANKS

5-112. Infantry leaders may choose to lead with tanks (see figure 5-13) when—
- There is an armored or tank threat.
- Moving through open terrain with limited cover or concealment.
- There is a confirmed enemy location/direction.
- There are templated enemy antipersonnel minefields.

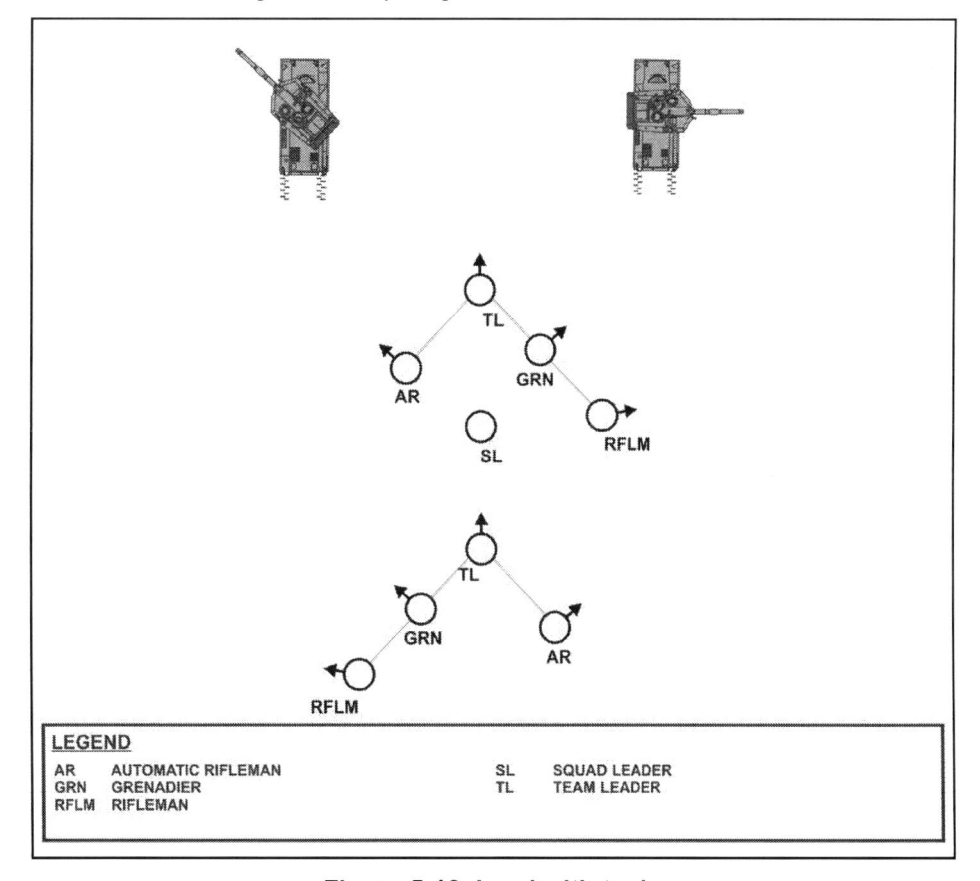

Figure 5-13. Lead with tanks

> *Note.* The exhaust from an M1-series tank may reach more than 1700 degrees. Dismounted Soldiers following behind the tank must position themselves either to the side of the exhaust grill or, if they are directly behind the vehicle, at a safe distance away. Exhaust shield will overcome this problem. The shield is a critical element in tanks recovering other tanks, so they should be readily available in the tank platoons. Consideration should be given to fabricating enough for all tanks as a leader will not know when he will be working with the Infantry

LEAD WITH BOTH TANKS AND INFANTRY SQUAD

5-113. Infantry leaders may choose to centrally locate the tanks in their formation (see figure 5-14, page 5-36) when—
- Flexibility is desired.
- The enemy location is unknown.
- There is a high threat of dismounted enemy antitank teams.
- The ability to mass the fires of the combat vehicles quickly in all directions is desired.

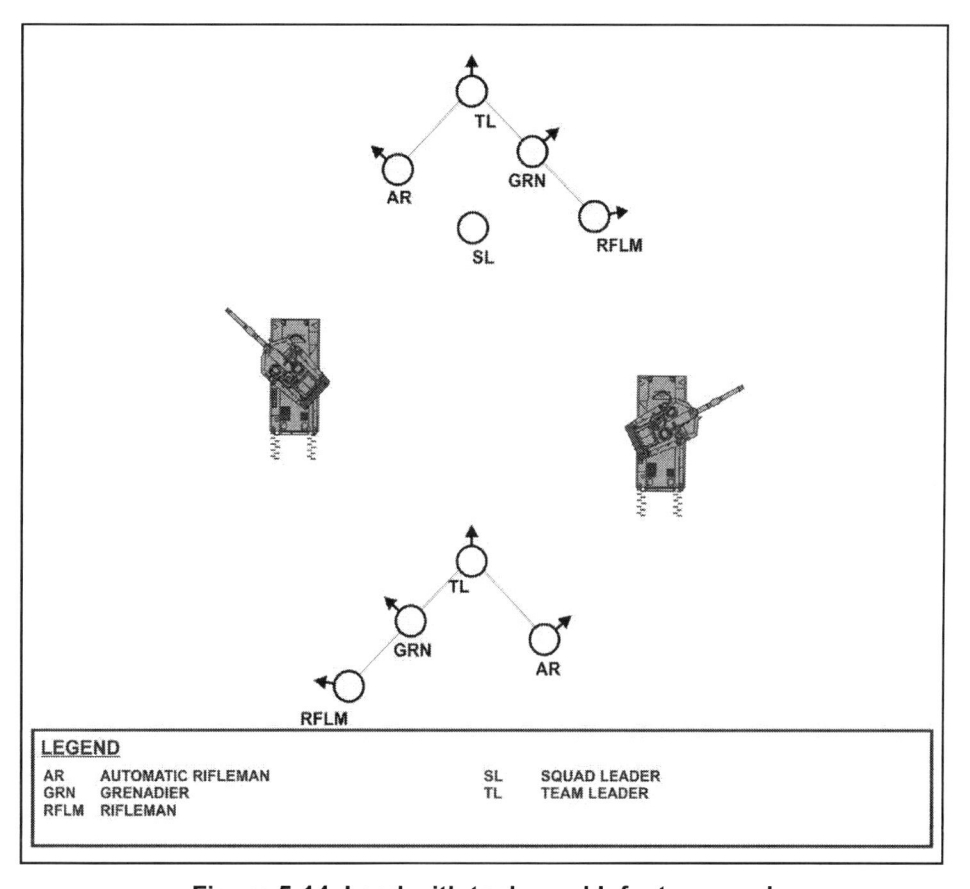

Figure 5-14. Lead with tanks and Infantry squad

COMBAT VEHICLE AND INFANTRY PLATOON FORMATIONS

5-114. Infantry platoons also can incorporate their formations with those of combat vehicular units. The principles for choosing platoon combat formations are the same as squad combat formations. The Infantry platoon can conduct tactical movement with a platoon of combat vehicles (normally four) or a section of combat vehicles (normally two). Figure 5-15 and figure 5-16 (page 5-38) detail some basic Infantry platoon formations with combat vehicle platoon formations.

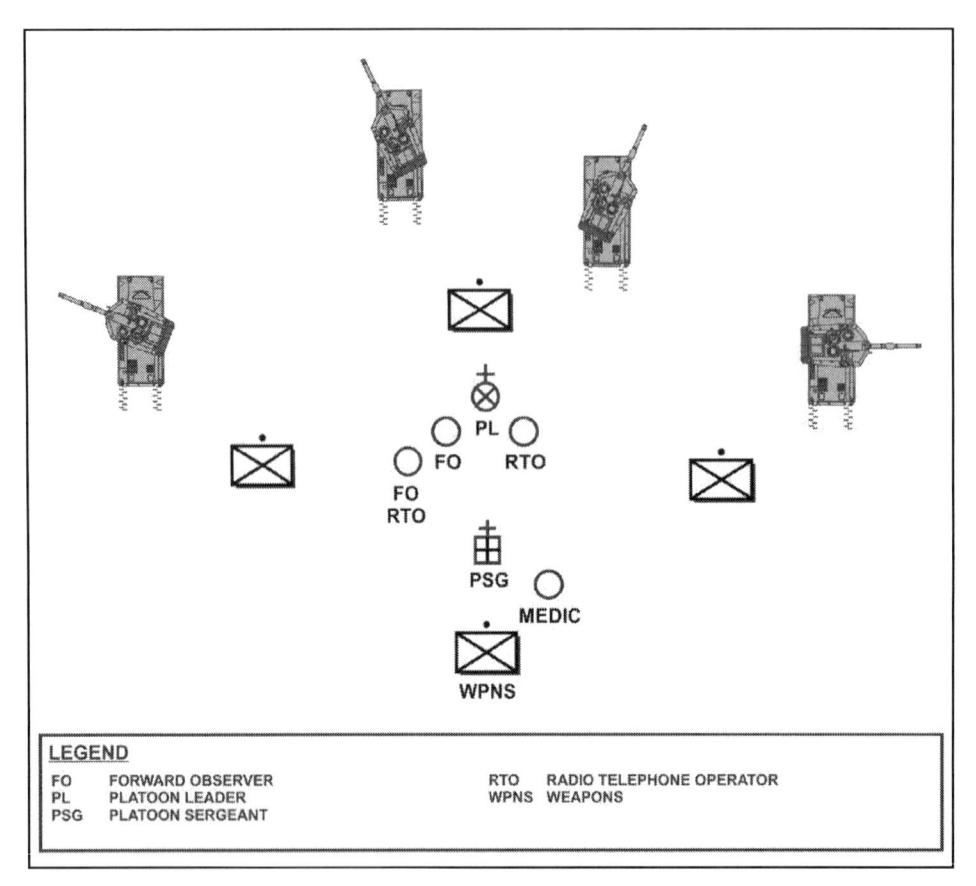

Figure 5-15. Combat vehicle wedge, Infantry platoon diamond

Chapter 5

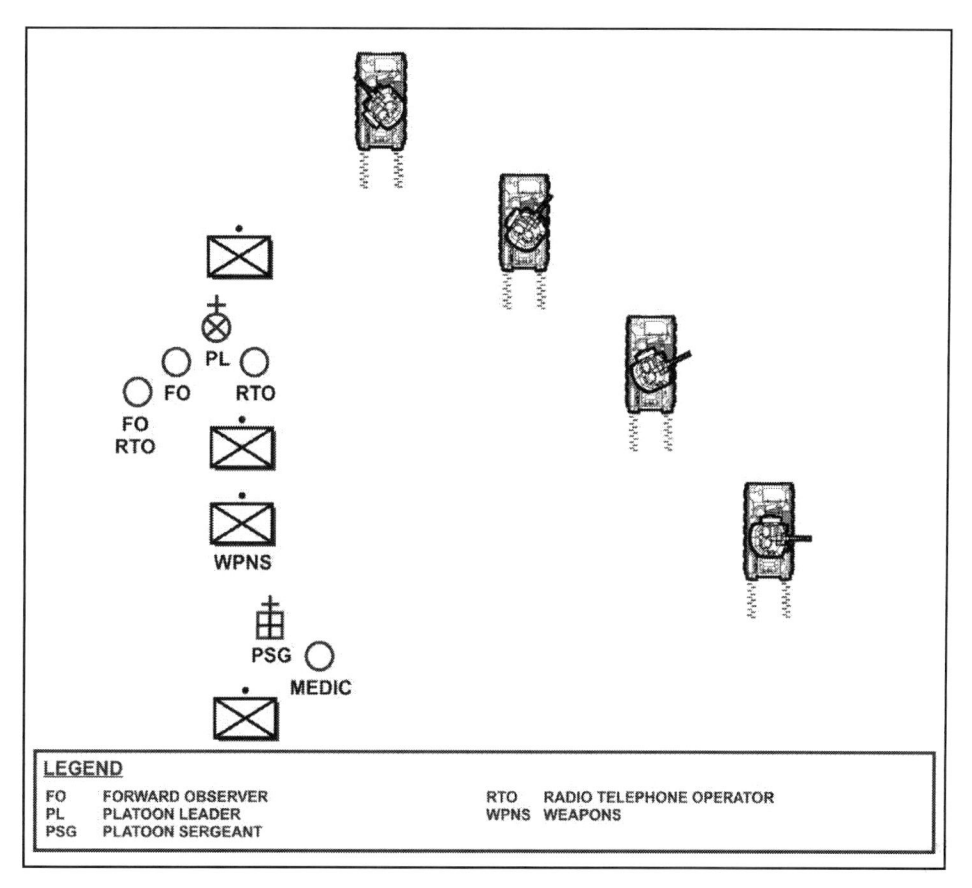

Figure 5-16. Combat vehicle echelon right, Infantry platoon column

MOUNTED MOVEMENT

5-115. Mounted movement is similar to dismounted movement. Depending on the vehicle type, a platoon may have a squad in multiple vehicles. Units with more than four vehicles should consider splitting the vehicles into two or more sections and control these sections much the same way squads control their teams.

5-116. Units augmented with four or more vehicles can use any of the seven formations. They use them within the context of the three movement techniques (See chapter 2, section IV for more information.) and should be prepared to execute immediate action drills when transitioning to maneuver. When the mounted unit stops, they use the coil and herringbone formations to ensure security.

5-117. In mounted successive bounds, vehicles keep their relative positions in the column. The first and second vehicles operate as a section in moving from one observation point to another. The second vehicle is placed in a concealed position, occupants dismounting if necessary, to cover movement of the first vehicle to an observation point.

Movement

On reaching this point, occupants of the first vehicle observe and reconnoiter, dismounting if necessary. When the area is determined to be clear, the second vehicle is signaled forward to join the first vehicle.

5-118. The commander of the first vehicle observes the terrain to the front for signs of enemy forces and selects the next stopping point. The first vehicle then moves out and the process is repeated. Movement distance of the lead vehicle does not exceed the limit of observation or the range of direct fire support from the second vehicle. The lead vehicle and personnel are replaced frequently to ensure constant alertness. The other vehicles in the column move by bounds from one concealed position to another. Each vehicle maintains visual contact with the vehicle ahead but avoids closing up. (See figure 5-17.) However, as a rule, vehicles always work in pairs and should never be placed in a situation where one vehicle is not able to be supported by the second.

5-119. In mounted alternate bounds, all except the first two vehicles keep their relative places in the column. The first two vehicles alternate as lead vehicles on each bound. Each covers the bound of the other. This method provides a more rapid advance than movement by successive bounds, but is less secure. Security is obtained by the vehicle commander who assigns each Soldier a direction of observation (to the front, flank[s], or rear). This provides each vehicle with some security against surprise fire from every direction, and provides visual contact with vehicles to the front and rear.

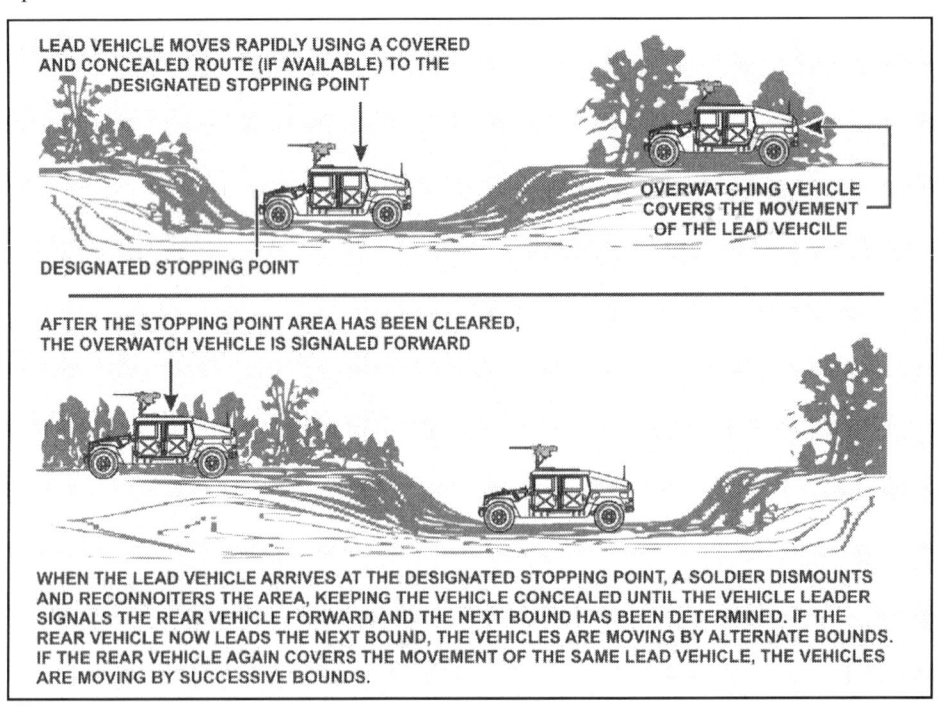

Figure 5-17. Lead vehicle moving by bounds

Chapter 5

MINE RESISTANT AMBUSH PROTECTED VEHICLE MISSION AND PURPOSE

5-120. The mine resistant ambush protected (MRAP) vehicle's mission role is similar to the Stryker in many respects. MRAP provides small units with protected mobility and mounted firepower. Squads and platoons use MRAP vehicles to conduct and support both mounted and dismounted missions.

5-121. MRAP is designed for distinct purpose of increasing the protection of Soldiers against small-arms fire and detonation of mines or IEDs employed singularly or in combination. With increased protection, an MRAP vehicle can increase its standoff to potential threats or move through potential danger areas when METT-TC dictates the increased risk.

MINE RESISTANT AMBUSH PROTECTED VEHICLE CAPABILITIES AND LIMITATIONS

5-122. Units employ MRAP vehicles by understanding the vehicle's capabilities and limitations while integrating protection with training to standard, detailed planning, smart tactics, and well-rehearsed drills, MRAP vehicles operate under the full spectrum of weather and terrain conditions, to include off-road operation across firm soil that supports the weight of the vehicle.

5-123. Exiting the vehicle in response to an ambush and loading or unloading equipment and casualties are difficult due to the steps and back ramp on some MRAP variants. Units must train and rehearse individuals and teams to streamline the process for mounting and dismounting operations under various conditions, especially in an emergency.

5-124. The field of view from the armored windows is limited for Soldiers, which results in blind spots and overall poor visibility.

> **WARNING**
>
> Operating on single-lane or steeply crowned rural roads with no shoulders, roads with soft shoulders or washouts around culverts, especially road bordering water (such as canal, irrigation ditch, or pond) requires extreme caution. The majority of MRAP vehicle rollovers are due to road, shoulder or bridge approaches giving way under the MRAP vehicle's weight and high center of gravity.

5-125. Trafficability studies/products must be available to the leaders and Soldiers operating MRAP vehicles. They can factor area of operation-specific trafficability and terrain limitations into their risk management and combat planning processes. (Refer to ADRP 3-37 for more information.)

5-126. Figure 5-18 shows possible mounted movement with MRAP vehicles both file/column or staggered. The leader based on information and intelligence, commander's intent and METT-TC makes the determination which mounted maneuvering technique will be used.

Note. Refer to TC 7-31 for more information on the MRAP family of vehicles.

Vehicle Transit Formations

COLUMN/FILE Formation

STAGGERED COLUMN Formation

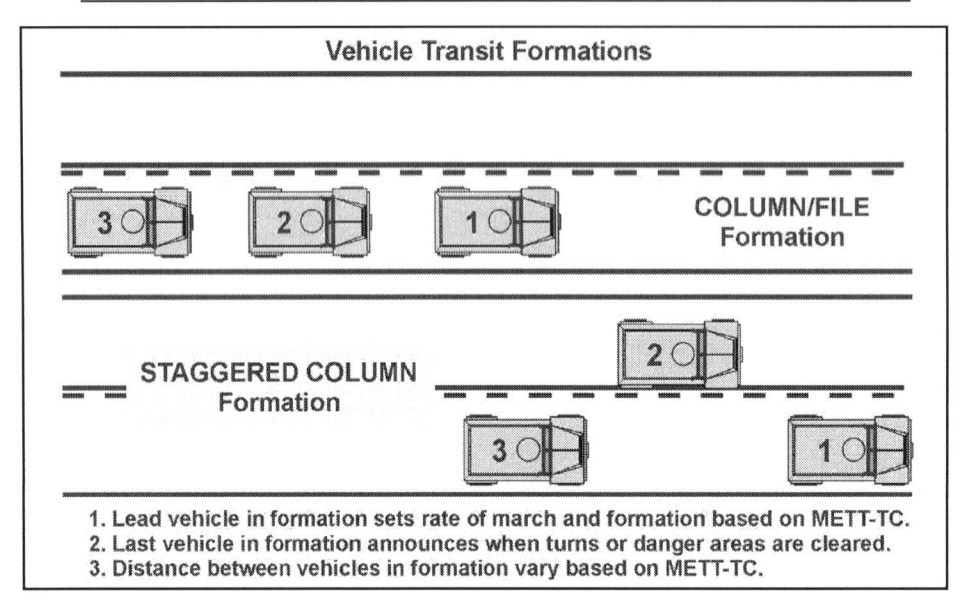

1. Lead vehicle in formation sets rate of march and formation based on METT-TC.
2. Last vehicle in formation announces when turns or danger areas are cleared.
3. Distance between vehicles in formation vary based on METT-TC.

Figure 5-18. MRAP vehicle file/column or staggered formation

CONVOYS

5-127. A convoy is a group of vehicles organized for purposes of control and orderly movement with or without escort protection moving over the same route at the same time under one commander. (Refer to ADRP 1-02 for more information.)

5-128. The platoon conducts motor marches, usually in trucks or armored protected vehicles. Some of the special considerations may include:

- *Protection.* Sandbag the bottom of non-mine protected trucks to protect from mines. Ensure crew-served weapons are manned with qualified gunners.
- *Observation.* Ensure Soldiers sit facing outward and remove bows and canvas to allow 360-degree observation and rapid dismount.
- *Inspection.* Inspect vehicles and drivers to ensure they are ready. Perform before, during, and after preventive maintenance checks and services (PMCS). Ensure drivers' knowledge of the route, speed, and convoy distance.
- *Loading.* Keep fire team, squad, and platoon integrity when loading vehicles. Fire teams and squads are kept intact on the same vehicle. Platoon vehicles are together

Chapter 5

in the same march serial. Key weapons and equipment are cross loaded with platoon leader and platoon sergeant in different vehicles.

- *Rehearsals.* Rehearse immediate action to enemy contact (near and far ambushes, air attack). Ensure drivers know what to do.
- *Air Guards.* Post air guards for each vehicle, with special consideration on the placement of crew-served weapons.

SECTION VIII – SECURITY

5-129. Maintaining security is a constant theme of tactical movement. Security can prevent enemy surprise. Security requires everyone to concentrate on the enemy. Though this seems simple enough, in practice, it is not. This means leaders and Soldiers must be proficient in the basics of tactical movement. Failure to attain proficiency diverts attention away from the enemy, thereby directly reducing the unit's ability to fight.

5-130. Platoons and squads enhance their own security during movement through the use of covered and concealed terrain; the use of the appropriate combat formation and movement technique; the actions taken to secure danger areas during crossing; the enforcement of noise, light, and radiotelephone discipline; and use of proper individual camouflage techniques.

5-131. During planning and preparation for movement, leaders analyze the enemy situation, determine known and likely enemy positions, and develop possible enemy courses of action. After first considering the enemy, leaders determine what security measures to emplace during tactical movement.

ENEMY

5-132. Leaders have to decide whether they are going to move aggressively to make contact, or stealthily to avoid contact. Either way, leaders have to anticipate enemy contact throughout. If possible, leaders should avoid routes with obvious danger areas such as built-up areas, roads, trails, and known enemy positions. If these places cannot be avoided, risk management should be conducted to develop ways to reduce danger to the unit. If stealth is desired, the route should avoid contact with local inhabitants, built-up areas, and natural lines of drift.

5-133. Movement techniques help the leader manage the amount of security his unit has during movement. Traveling is the least secure and used when contact is unlikely. Traveling overwatch is used when contact is likely but not imminent. Bounding overwatch is used when contact is imminent. The leader establishes the PLD to indicate where the transition from traveling overwatch to bounding overwatch should occur. When in contact with the enemy, the unit transitions from movement to maneuver (fire and movement) while the leader conducts actions on contact. (See figure 5-19.)

Movement

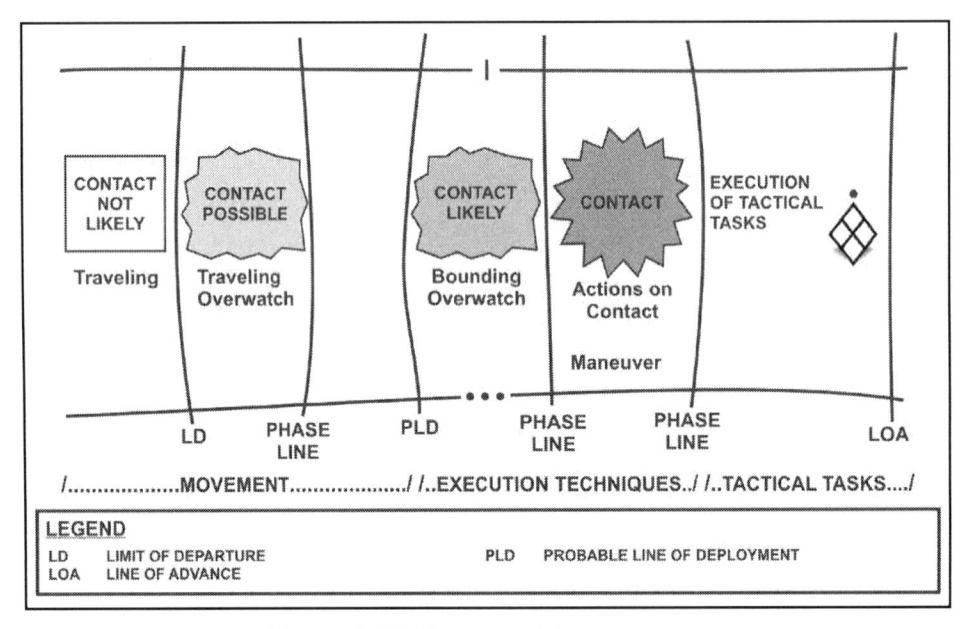

Figure 5-19. Movement to maneuver

TERRAIN

5-134. When planning movements, the leader must consider how terrain affects security while simultaneously considering METT-TC. Some missions may require the unit to move on other than covered and concealed routes. While the leader may not be able to prevent the unit's detection, he can ensure it moves on the battlefield in a time and place for which the enemy is unprepared. Particularly when moving in the open, the leader must avoid predictability and continue to use terrain to his advantage.

CAMOUFLAGE, NOISE, AND LIGHT DISCIPLINE

5-135. Leaders must ensure camouflage used by their Soldiers is appropriate to the terrain and season. Platoon SOPs specify elements of noise and light discipline.

5-136. If Soldiers need more illumination than an image intensifier can provide in infrared mode during movement, they should use additional infrared light sources. The combination should provide the light needed with the least risk of enemy detection. When using infrared light, leaders must consider the enemy's night vision and infrared capabilities. For instance, an enemy with night vision capability can send infrared light signals, and he can concentrate direct and indirect fire on a platoon using infrared light.

SECURITY HALTS

5-137. Units conducting tactical movement frequently make temporary halts. These halts range from brief to extended periods. For short halts, platoons use a cigar-shaped perimeter

Chapter 5

intended to protect the force while maintaining the ability to continue movement. When the platoon leader decides not to immediately resume tactical movement, he transitions the platoon to a perimeter defense. The perimeter defense is used for longer halts or during lulls in combat.

CIGAR–SHAPED PERIMETER

5-138. When the unit halts, if terrain permits, Soldiers should move off the route and face out to cover the same sectors of fire they were assigned while moving, allowing passage through the center of the formation. This results in a cigar-shaped perimeter. Actions by subordinate leaders and their Soldiers occur without an order from the leader. Soldiers are repositioned as necessary to take advantage of the best cover, concealment, and fields of fire.

PERIMETER DEFENSE

5-139. When operating independently, the platoon uses a perimeter defense during extended halts, resupply, and issuing platoon orders or lulls in combat. Normally the unit first occupies a short halt formation. Then after conducting a leader's reconnaissance of the position and establishing security, the unit moves into the perimeter defense.

MOUNTED SECURITY HALT

5-140. The platoon employs the coil, herringbone, and triangle "Y" formations to maintain 360-degree security when stationary

5-141. The coil provides all-round security and observation when the platoon is stationary. The patrol also uses the coil for tactical refueling, resupply, and issuing patrol orders. When in a coil, leaders post security. (See figure 5-20.)

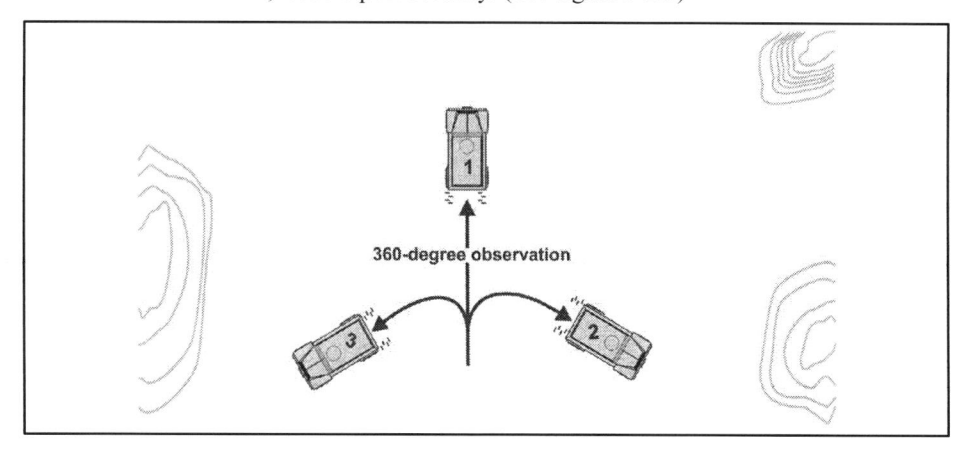

Figure 5-20. Coil formation

5-142. The patrol leader uses the herringbone and triangle during temporary halts or when getting off a road to allow another unit to pass. It lets the patrol move to covered and concealed positions off a road or from an open area and establishes all-round security without issued detailed instructions. The truck commander repositions their vehicles as necessary to take advantage of the best cover, concealment, and fields of fire. Fire team members dismount and establish security. (See figures 5-21 and 5-22.)

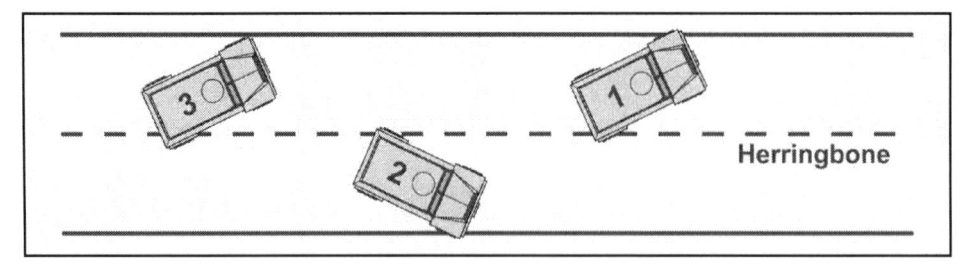

Figure 5-21. Herringbone formation

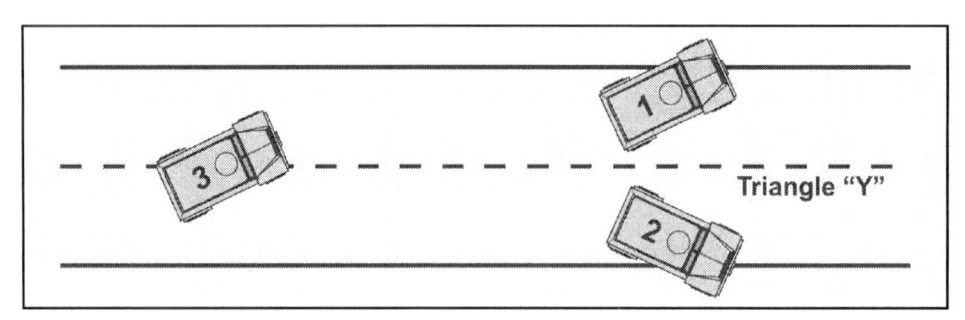

Figure 5-22. Triangle Y formation

ACTIONS AT HALTS

5-143. Table 5-3 (page 5-46) lists the standard actions taken at halts by the Soldier, squad leader, and platoon leader.

Table 5-3. Actions at halts

SOLDIER (OR VEHICLE) ACTIONS*	SQUAD LEADER (OR SECTION LEADER) ACTIONS	PLATOON LEADER ACTIONS
• Moves to as much of a covered and concealed position as available. • Visually inspects and physically clears his immediate surroundings (a roughly 5- to 25-meter radius around his position). • Establishes a sector of fire for his assigned weapon (using 12 o'clock as the direction the Soldier is facing, the Soldier's sector of fire ranges from 10 o'clock to 2 o'clock). • Determines his observation and field of fire. Identifies dead space in his field of fire. • Identifies obstacles and determines enemy avenues of approach (both mounted and dismounted). • Identifies the dominant ground in his immediate surroundings. • Coordinates his actions with the Soldiers (or vehicles) on his left and right. (*These actions occur without leader prompting.)	• Adjusts his perimeter: 　▪ If operating independently, the squad leader establishes 360-degree, three-dimensional security. 　▪ Attempts to find terrain that anchors his position. 　▪ If operating as part of a platoon, the squad leader arrays his teams to best fit into the platoon leader's defensive scheme, based on the platoon leader's guidance. • Visually inspects and physically clears (if required) the squad's immediate surrounding (about 35 meters, the distance within hand grenade range). • Ensures his squad's individual sectors of fire overlap with each other, creating a seamless perimeter with no gaps of fire coverage. • Identifies his dead space and adjusts his M203 grenadiers accordingly. • Identifies obstacles and the likely enemy avenue of approach (mounted and dismounted). • Identifies the dominant ground in his area of operation. • Coordinates responsibilities and sectors with the units on his left and right.	• Adjusts his perimeter: 　▪ If operating independently, he establishes 360-degree, three-dimensional security. 　▪ If operation as part of another organization, he arrays his squads to best fist into the controlling commander's defensive scheme. 　▪ Supervises the emplacement of the weapons squad's weapon systems. • Dispatches an element (usually a fire team) to visually inspect and physically clear the platoon's immediate surrounding (an area out to small arms range, roughly 100-300 meters depending on terrain). • Ensures his squads' sectors of fire overlap with each other, creating a seamless perimeter with no gaps of fire coverage. • Identifies his dead space not covered and requests indirect fire support to overwatch dead space in the area of operation. • Identifies obstacles and the likely enemy avenue of approach (mounted and dismounted). • Identifies the dominant ground in his area of operation. • Coordinates with the units on his left and right.

SECTION IX – OTHER MOVEMENT SITUATIONS

5-144. Movement operations are conducted to reposition units, personnel, supplies, equipment, and other critical combat elements in support of current or future operations. Other movement forms may include air movement, movement by water, and movement during limited visibility.

AIR MOVEMENT

5-145. Air movement operations include both airdrops and air landings. Planning for air movements is similar to other missions. In addition to the normal planning process, however, air movement planning must cover specific requirements for air infiltration and exfiltration:

- Coordinate with the supporting aviation units.
- Plan and rehearse with the supporting aviation unit before the mission if possible. If armed escort accompanies the operation, the platoon leader and company commander, as well as the assault or general support aviation unit, should ensure aircrews are included in the planning and rehearsals.
- Gather as much information as possible, such as the enemy situation, in preparation of the mission.
- Plan and coordinate joint suppression of enemy air defense.

5-146. The unit also should plan different ingress and egress routes, covering the following:

- Planned insertion and extraction points.
- Emergency extraction rally points.
- Lost communications extraction points.

5-147. Planned extraction points and emergency extraction rally points require communications to verify the preplanned pickup time or coordinate an emergency pickup time window. Planning must include details for extraction when communications between higher headquarters and unit are lost. The lost communications extraction point involves infiltration teams moving to the emergency extraction point after two consecutive missed communications windows and waiting up to 24 hours for pickup. (Refer to FM 3-04.113 for more information.)

MOVEMENT BY WATER

5-148. Platoons avoid crossing water obstacles when possible. Before crossing, however, leaders should identify weak or nonswimmers and pair them with good swimmers in their squads.

5-149. When platoons or squads must move into, through, or out of rivers, lakes, streams, or other bodies of water, they treat the water obstacle as a danger area. While on the water, the platoon is exposed and vulnerable. To offset the disadvantages, the platoon—

Chapter 5

- Moves during limited visibility.
- Disperses.
- Moves near the shore to reduce the chances of detection.

5-150. When moving in more than one boat, the platoon—
- Maintains tactical integrity and self-sufficiency.
- Cross loads essential Soldiers and equipment.
- Ensures the radio is with the leader.

5-151. If boats are not available, several other techniques can be used such as—
- Swimming.
- Poncho rafts.
- Air mattresses.
- Waterproof bags.
- A 7/16-inch rope used as a semisubmersible, one-rope bridge, or safety line.
- Water wings (made from a set of trousers).

MOVEMENT DURING LIMITED VISIBILITY

5-152. At night or when visibility is poor, a platoon must be able to function in the same way as during daylight. It must be able to control, navigate, and maintain security, move, and stalk at night or during limited visibility.

CONTROL

5-153. When visibility is poor, the following methods aid in control—
- Use of night vision devices.
- Infrared chemical lights.
- Leaders move closer to the front.
- The platoon reduces speed.
- Soldiers use two small strips of luminous tape on the rear of their helmet, allowing Soldiers behind them to see them from the rear.
- Leaders reduce the interval between Soldiers and units to make sure they can see each other.
- Leaders conduct headcounts at regular intervals and after each halt to ensure personnel accountability.

NAVIGATION

5-154. To assist in navigation during limited visibility, leaders use—
- Terrain association (general direction of travel coupled with recognition of prominent map and ground features).
- Dead reckoning, compass direction and specific distances or legs. (At the end of each leg, leaders should verify their location.)

- Movement routes that parallel identifiable terrain features.
- Guides or marked routes.
- Mission Command Systems.

SECURITY AT NIGHT

5-155. For stealth and security in night moves, squads and platoons—
- Designate a point man to maintain alertness, the lead team leader to navigate, and a pace man to count the distance traveled. Alternate compass and pace men are designated.
- Ensure good noise and light discipline.
- Use radio-listening silence.
- Camouflage Soldiers and equipment.
- Use terrain to avoid detection by enemy surveillance or night vision devices.
- Make frequent listening halts.
- Mask the sounds of movement with artillery fires.

This page intentionally left blank.

Chapter 6

Patrols and Patrolling

A *patrol* is a detachment sent out by a larger unit to conduct a specific mission that operates semi-independently and return to the main body upon completion of mission. Patrolling fulfills the Infantry's primary function of finding the enemy to engage him or report his disposition, location, and actions. Patrols act as ground sensors or early warnings for larger units and the planned action determines the type of patrol. This chapter provides an overview on patrolling by the Infantry platoon and squad and discusses in detail; combat and reconnaissance patrols.

SECTION I – OVERVIEW

6-1. If a patrol is made up of a single unit, such as a rifle squad sent out on a reconnaissance patrol, the squad leader is responsible. If a patrol is made up of mixed elements from several units, then the senior officer or NCO is designated as the patrol leader. This temporary title defines his role and responsibilities during the mission. The patrol leader may designate an assistant, normally the next senior man in the patrol, and subordinate element leaders he requires.

6-2. A patrol can consist of a unit as small as a fire team but are usually squad and platoon-sized. For larger combat tasks such as for a raid, the patrol is sometimes a company. The planned action determines if the patrols are combat and reconnaissance. Regardless of the type of patrol, the unit needs a clear task and purpose.

6-3. The leader of any patrol, regardless of the type or the tactical task assigned, has an inherent responsibility to prepare and plan for possible enemy contact while on the mission. Patrols always are assigned a tactical mission. On his return to the main body, the patrol leader reports to the commander and describes the patrol's actions, observations, and condition.

PURPOSE OF PATROLLING

6-4. There are several specific purposes which can be accomplished by patrolling—
- Gathering information on the enemy, on the terrain, or on the populace.
- Regaining contact with the enemy or with adjacent friendly forces.
- Engaging the enemy in combat to destroy him or inflict losses.
- Reassuring or gaining the trust of a local population.
- Preventing public disorder.
- Deterring and disrupting insurgent or criminal activity.

Chapter 6

- Providing unit security.
- Protecting essential infrastructure or bases.

ORGANIZATION OF PATROLS

6-5. A patrol is organized to perform specific tasks. It must be prepared to secure itself, navigate accurately, identify and cross danger areas, and reconnoiter the patrol objective. If it is a combat patrol, it must be prepared to breach obstacles, assault the objective, and support those assaults by fire. Additionally, a patrol must be able to conduct detailed searches as well as deal with casualties and detainees.

6-6. The leader identifies those tasks that must be or will likely be conducted during the patrol and decides which elements will perform which tasks. Where possible, he should maintain squad and fire team integrity. Squads and fire teams may perform more than one task during the time a patrol is away from the main body or it may be responsible for only one task. The leader must plan carefully to ensure he has identified and assigned all required tasks in the most efficient way.

6-7. Elements and teams for platoons conducting patrols include the common and specific elements for each type of patrol. The following elements are common to all patrols.

HEADQUARTERS ELEMENT

6-8. The headquarters element normally consists of the platoon leader and his RTO. The platoon sergeant may be designated as the assistant patrol leader. Combat patrols may include a forward observer, perhaps his RTO and a medic.

> *Note.* In this chapter the patrol leader is the person in charge of the patrol. In a platoon-size element that person would most likely be the platoon leader. The assistant patrol leader is the second person in charge of the patrol. In a platoon-size element that person most likely is the platoon sergeant.

AID AND LITTER TEAMS

6-9. Aid and litter teams are responsible for locating, treating, and evacuating casualties.

DETAINEE TEAMS

6-10. Detainee teams are responsible for processing detainees, according to the five Ss (search, silence, segregate, speed, safeguard) and leader's guidance. These teams also may be responsible for accounting for and controlling recovered personnel.

SURVEILLANCE TEAMS

6-11. Surveillance teams are used to establish and maintain covert observation of an objective for as long as it takes to complete the patrol's mission.

EN ROUTE RECORDER

6-12. An en route recorder can be designated to record all information collected during the mission.

COMPASS AND PACE MAN

6-13. If the patrol does not have access to GPSs, or if it is operating in a location where there is no satellite reception, it may be necessary to navigate using terrain association, dead reckoning, or a combination of both. This is accomplished with a compass man and a pace man.

ASSAULT TEAMS

6-14. Combat patrols designate assault teams to close with the enemy on the objective or to clear the ambush kill zone.

SUPPORT TEAMS

6-15. Combat patrols designate teams to provide direct fire in support of the breach and assault teams.

BREACH TEAMS

6-16. Combat patrols have breach teams to assist the assault team in getting to the objective.

SEARCH TEAMS

6-17. Search teams are designated to conduct a cursory or detailed search of the objective area.

INITIAL PLANNING AND COORDINATION FOR PATROLS

6-18. Leaders plan and prepare for patrols using TLP. They must identify required actions on the objective, plan backward to the departure from friendly lines, then forward to the reentry of friendly lines.

6-19. The patrol leader normally will receive the OPORD in the battalion or company command post where communications are good and vital personnel are available for coordination. Because patrols act semi-independently, move beyond the supporting range of the parent unit, and often operate forward of friendly units, coordination must be thorough and detailed.

6-20. Patrol leaders may routinely coordinate with elements of the battalion staff directly. Unit leaders should develop tactical SOPs beyond what is found in ATP 3-90.90 with detailed checklists to preclude omitting items vital to the mission accomplishment.

Chapter 6

6-21. Items coordinated between the leader and battalion staff, company commander or CoIST include:
- Changes or updates in the enemy situation.
- Best use of terrain for routes, rally points, and patrol bases.
- Light and weather data.
- Changes in the friendly situation.
- The attachment of Soldiers with special skills or equipment (engineers, sniper teams, military working dog teams, forward observers, or interpreters).
- Use and location of landing or pickup zones.
- Departure and reentry of friendly lines.
- Direct and indirect fire support on the objective and along the planned routes, including alternate routes.
- Rehearsal areas and times. The terrain for rehearsal should be similar to the objective, to include buildings and fortifications if necessary. Coordination for rehearsals includes security of the area, use of blanks, pyrotechnics, and live ammunition.
- Special equipment and ammunition requirements.
- Transportation support, including transportation to and from rehearsal sites.
- Signal plan, call signs frequencies, code words, pyrotechnics, and challenge and password.

6-22. The leader coordinates with the unit through which his platoon or squad conducts its forward and rearward passage of lines. The leader also coordinates patrol activities with the leaders of other units patrolling in adjacent areas at the same time.

LEADER'S RECONNAISSANCE

6-23. The leader's reconnaissance reconnoiters the objective just before an attack or prior to sending elements forward to locations where they will support by fire. It confirms the condition of the objective, gives each subordinate leader a clear picture of the terrain where he will move, and identifies parts of the objective he must seize or suppress. The leader's reconnaissance patrol can consist of the unit leader or representative, the leaders of major subordinate elements, and (sometimes) security personnel and unit guides. It gets back to the main body as quickly as possible. The leader can use the aid in (see figure 6-1) to help in remembering the five-point contingency plan which is used when a leader or other individuals separate from the main body.

> G: Going – where is the leader going?
>
> O: Others – are others are going with the leader and who?
>
> T: Time (duration) – how long will the element be gone?
>
> W: What procedures do we take if the leader fails to return?
>
> A: Actions – what actions does the departing element and main body plan to execute on enemy contact?

Figure 6-1. Five-point contingency plan

6-24. A patrol leader should conduct a leader's reconnaissance when time or the situation allows. The plan includes a leader's reconnaissance of the objective once the platoon or squad establishes the ORP. During his reconnaissance, the leader pinpoints the objective, selects positions for his squads, teams and adjusts his plan based upon his observation of the objective. Each type of patrol requires different tasks during the leader's reconnaissance, and the leader takes different elements depending upon the patrol's mission. The leader ensures the objective remains under continuous observation once deciding to return to the ORP. The leader designates a rally point and plans for adequate time to return to the ORP, complete his plan, disseminate information, issue orders and instructions, and allow his squads to make additional preparations. (See figure 6-2, page 6-6.)

Chapter 6

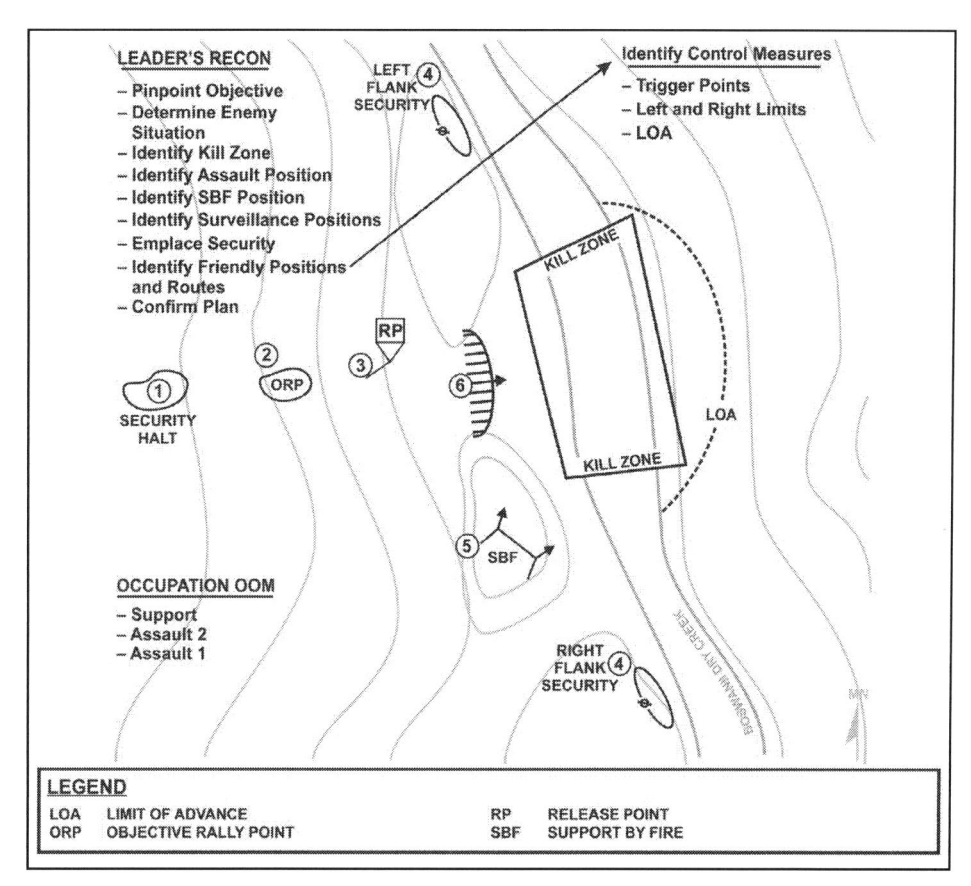

Figure 6-2. Leader's reconnaissance

Note. A leader's reconnaissance may alert the enemy a patrol is in the area by evidence of movement or noise, before the patrol begins its mission.

COMPLETION OF THE PATROL PLAN

6-25. As the patrol leader completes his plan, the following elements are considered.

ESSENTIAL AND SUPPORTING TASKS

6-26. The leader ensures all essential tasks have been assigned to be performed on the objective, at rally points, at danger areas, at security or observation locations, along the routes, and at passage lanes.

KEY TRAVEL AND EXECUTION TIMES

6-27. The leader estimates time requirements for movement to the objective, leader's reconnaissance of the objective, establishment of security and surveillance, compaction of all assigned tasks on the objective, movement to an ORP to debrief the platoon, and return through friendly lines.

PRIMARY AND ALTERNATE ROUTES

6-28. The leader selects primary and alternate routes to and from the objective. (See figure 6-3.) Return routes should differ from routes to the objective.

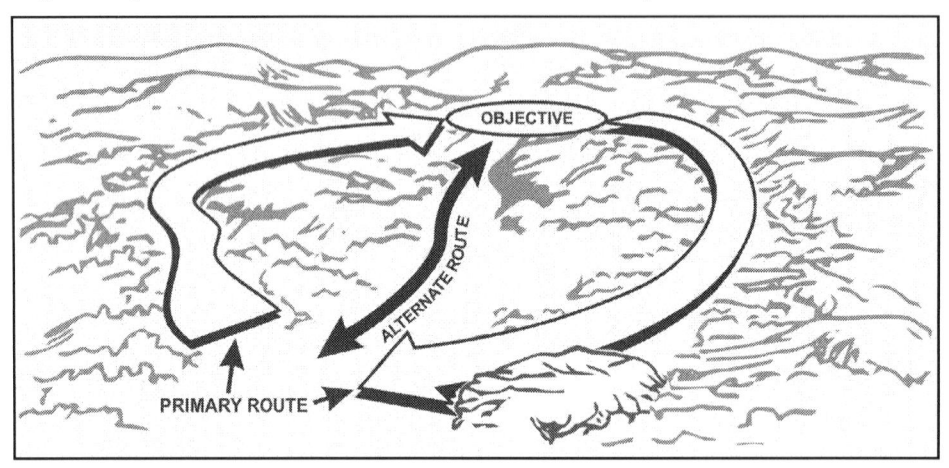

Figure 6-3. Primary and alternate routes

SIGNALS

6-29. The leader should consider the use of special signals. These include hand-and-arm signals, flares, pyrotechnics, voice, whistles, radios, and visible or nonvisible lasers. All signals are rehearsed to ensure all patrol members understand what they mean.

CHALLENGE AND PASSWORD OUTSIDE OF FRIENDLY LINES

6-30. The challenge and password from the signal operating instructions must not be used when the patrol is outside friendly lines. The unit's tactical SOP should state the procedure for establishing a patrol challenge and password as well as other combat identification features and patrol markings. Two methods for establishing a challenge and password are the odd number system and running password.

Odd Number System

6-31. The leader specifies an odd number. The challenge can be any number less than the specified number. The password will be the number that must be added to it to equal the specified number, for example, the number is 9, the challenge is 4, and the password is 5.

Chapter 6

Running Password

6-32. Signal operating instructions also may designate a running password. This code word alerts a unit that friendly are approaching in a less than organized manner and possibly under pressure. The number of friendly approaching follows the running password. For example, if the running password is *"eagle,"* and seven friendly are approaching, they would say *"eagle seven."*

LOCATION OF LEADERS

6-33. The leader considers where he, the platoon sergeant or assistant patrol leader, and other essential leaders should be located for each phase of the patrol mission. The platoon sergeant or assistant patrol leader normally is with the following elements for each type of patrol:

- On a raid or ambush, he normally controls the support element.
- On an area reconnaissance, he normally supervises security in the objective rally point.
- On a zone reconnaissance, he normally moves with the reconnaissance element setting up the linkup point.

ACTIONS ON ENEMY CONTACT

6-34. The leader's plan must address actions on chance contact at each phase of the patrol mission:

- The plan must address the handling of seriously WIA and KIA personnel.
- The plan must address actions required to recover isolated Soldiers.
- The plan must address the handling of prisoners captured as a result of chance contact who are not part of the planned mission.

DEPARTURE FROM FRIENDLY LINES OR FIXED BASE

6-35. The departure from friendly lines, or from a fixed base, must be thoroughly planned and coordinated.

COORDINATION

6-36. The platoon leader must coordinate with the commander of the forward unit and leaders of other units patrolling in the same or adjacent areas. The coordination includes automated network control device information, signal plan, fire plan, running passwords, procedures for departure and reentry of lines, planned dismount points, IRPs, actions at departure and reentry points, and information about the enemy:

- The platoon leader provides the forward unit leader with the unit identification, size of the patrol, departure, return times, and area of operation.
- The forward unit leader provides the platoon leader with the following:
    - Additional information on terrain just outside the friendly unit lines.
    - Known or suspected enemy positions in the near vicinity.

- Likely enemy ambush sites.
- Latest enemy activity.
- Detailed information on friendly positions, obstacles, and observation posts.
- Friendly unit fire plan.
- Support the unit can provide (direct and indirect fire support, litter teams, guides, communications, and reaction force).

PLANNING

6-37. In planning for departure of friendly lines, the leader should consider the following sequence of actions:
- Making contact with friendly guides at the contact point.
- Moving to a coordinated initial rally point just inside friendly lines.
- Completing final coordination.
- Moving to and through the passage point.
- Establishing a security-listening halt beyond the friendly unit's final protective fires.

PATROL BASE ACTIVITIES

6-38. A patrol base is a security perimeter which is set up when a squad or platoon conducting a patrol halts for an extended period. A patrol base should not be occupied for more than a 24-hour period (except in emergency). A patrol never uses the same patrol base twice. The following activities at a minimum should be taken into consideration:
- Use.
- Site selection.
- Planning consideration.
- Security measures.
- Occupation.
- Priorities of work.

USE

6-39. Patrol bases typically are used—
- To avoid detection by eliminating movement.
- To hide a unit during a long detailed reconnaissance.
- To perform maintenance on weapons, equipment, eat and rest.
- To plan and issue orders.
- To reorganize after infiltrating an enemy area.
- To establish a base from which to execute several consecutive or concurrent operations.

Chapter 6

SITE SELECTION

6-40. The leader selects the tentative site from a map or by aerial reconnaissance. The site's suitability must be confirmed and secured before the unit moves into it. Plans to establish a patrol base must include selecting an alternate patrol base site. The alternate site is used if the first site is unsuitable or if the patrol must unexpectedly evacuate the first patrol base.

PLANNING CONSIDERATIONS

6-41. Leaders planning for a patrol base must consider the mission, passive and active security measures. A patrol base must be located so it allows the unit to accomplish its mission:
- Observation posts and communication with observation posts.
- Patrol or platoon fire plan.
- Alert plan.
- Withdrawal plan from the patrol base to include withdrawal routes and a rally point, rendezvous point, or alternate patrol base.
- A security system that makes sure specific individuals are awake at all times.
- Enforcement of camouflage, noise, and light discipline.
- The conduct of required activities with minimum movement and noise.
- Priorities of work.

SECURITY MEASURES

6-42. The following security measures should be taken into consideration as a minimum:
- Select terrain the enemy probably would consider of little tactical value.
- Select terrain off main lines of drift.
- Select difficult terrain impeding foot movement, such as an area of dense vegetation, preferably bushes and trees spreading close to the ground.
- Select terrain near a source of water.
- Select terrain defendable for a short period and offers good cover and concealment.
- Avoid known or suspected enemy positions.
- Avoid built up areas.
- Avoid ridges and hilltops, except as needed for maintaining communications.
- Avoid small valleys.
- Avoid roads and trails.

OCCUPATION

6-43. A patrol base is reconnoitered and occupied in the same manner as an ORP, with the exception the platoon will typically plan to enter at a 90-degree turn. The leader leaves a two-Soldier observation post at the turn; the patrol covers tracks from the turn to the patrol base.

6-44. The platoon moves into the patrol base. Squad-sized patrols generally will occupy a cigar shaped perimeter; platoon-sized patrols generally will occupy a triangle shaped perimeter.

6-45. The leader inspects and adjusts the entire perimeter, as necessary.

6-46. After the leader has checked each squad's portion of the perimeter, each squad leader sends a two-Soldier R&S team to the leader at the patrol's command post. The leader issues the three R&S teams a contingency plan, reconnaissance method, and detailed guidance on what to look for (enemy, water, built up areas or human habitat, roads, trails, or possible rally points).

6-47. Where each R&S team departs is based on the leader's guidance. The R&S team moves a prescribed distance and direction, and reenters where the leader dictates:
- R&S teams will prepare a sketch of the area to the squad front if possible.
- The patrol remains at 100 percent alert during this recon.
- If the leader feels the patrol was tracked or followed, he may elect to wait in silence at 100 percent alert before sending out R&S teams.
- The R&S teams may use reconnaissance methods such as a box or fan discussed later in this chapter. Regardless of the method chosen; the R&S team must be able to provide the leader with the same information.
- Upon completion of the information collection by the R&S teams, the platoon leaders makes a decision to either stay in the current patrol base and begin priorities of work or move the patrol base to an alternate location.

PRIORITIES OF WORK

6-48. Once the leader is briefed by the R&S teams and determines the area is suitable for a patrol base, the leader establishes or modifies defensive work priorities in order to establish the defensive posture of the patrol base. Priorities of work are not a laundry list of tasks to be completed, priorities of work must consist of a task, a given time, and a measurable performance standard. For each priority of work, a clear standard must be issued to guide the element in the accomplishment of each task. It also must be designated whether the work will be controlled in a centralized or decentralized manner. Priorities of work are determined in accordance with METT-TC. Priorities of work may include the tasks described below, but are not limited to them.

Continuous Security

6-49. Prepare to use all passive and active measures to cover the entire perimeter all of the time, regardless of the percentage of weapons used to cover all the terrain. Employ all elements, weapons, and personnel to meet conditions of the terrain, enemy, or situation.

Withdraw Plan

6-50. The leader designates the signal for withdrawal, order of withdrawal, platoon rendezvous point, and alternate patrol base.

Chapter 6

Continuous Communication

6-51. Communications must be maintained with higher headquarters, observation posts, and within the unit. Other Soldiers within the patrol may rotate duties with the platoon's RTO allowing accomplishment of continuous radio monitoring, radio maintenance, act as runners for leader, or conduct other priorities of work.

Mission Preparation and Planning

6-52. The leader uses the patrol base to plan, issue orders, rehearse, inspect, and prepare for future missions.

Weapons and Equipment Maintenance

6-53. The leader ensures medium machine guns, weapon systems, communications equipment, and night vision devices (as well as other equipment) are maintained. No more than one-third of any given type of system carried by the patrol should be disassembled for preventative checks and services at any one time. As a general rule weapons should not be disassembled for routine maintenance at night. If one of the patrol's medium machine guns is down for maintenance, then security levels for all remaining systems are raised.

Water Resupply

6-54. The platoon sergeant or assistant patrol leader organizes watering parties as necessary. The watering party carries canteens in an empty rucksack or duffel bag, and must have communications and contingency plans related to their making enemy contact en route or returning from the water point or if the patrol base has to displace during their absence prior to their departure from the patrol base.

Mess Plan

6-55. At a minimum, security and weapons maintenance are performed prior to mess. Normally no more than half the platoon eats at one time. Soldiers typically eat one to three meters behind their fighting positions to avoid distracting those Soldiers providing security.

Rest and Sleep Plan Management

6-56. All leaders within the platoon must understand the problems associated with sleep deprivation and the consequences of not following the unit rest and sleep plan. The body needs regular rest to restore physical and mental vigor. When a Soldier is tired, his bodily functions are sluggish, and his ability to react is slower than normal, which makes him more susceptible to sickness, and to making errors that could endanger him or other members of the platoon. For the best health, you should get six to eight hours of uninterrupted sleep each day. As that is seldom possible in combat, use rest periods and off-duty time to rest or sleep.

6-57. The platoon leader must develop and enforce the unit sleep plan that provides Soldiers with a minimum of 4 hours of uninterrupted sleep in a 24-hour period. If sleep is interrupted, then 5 hours should be given. During continuous operations when uninterrupted sleep is not possible, blocks of sleep which add up to 6 hours in a 24-hour period are adequate for most people. Remember, 4 hours each 24-hour period is far from ideal. Do not go with only 4 hours sleep each 24 hours for more than two weeks before paying back sleep debt. Recovery time should be approximately 8 to 10 hours sleep each 24 hours over a 5- to 7-day period.

Alert Plan and "Stand To"

6-58. The leader states the alert posture and stand to time. He develops the plan to ensure all positions are checked periodically, observation posts are relieved periodically, and at least one leader always is alert. The patrol typically conducts stand to at a time specified by unit SOP such as 30 minutes before and after the begin morning nautical twilight (BMNT) or the end of evening nautical twilight (EENT).

Resupply

6-59. Distribute or cross load ammunition, meals, equipment, and so on.

Sanitation and Personal Hygiene

6-60. The platoon sergeant or assistant patrol leader and medic ensure a slit trench is prepared and marked. All Soldiers will brush their teeth, wash their face, shave, and wash their hands, armpits, groin, and feet. The patrol will not leave trash behind. METT-TC always is taken in consideration prior to executing sanitation and personal hygiene.

RALLY POINTS

6-61. The leader considers the use and locations of rally points. A rally point is a place designated by the leader where the platoon moves to reassemble and reorganize if it becomes dispersed.

SELECTION OF RALLY POINTS

6-62. The leader physically reconnoiters routes to select rally points whenever possible. He selects tentative points if he only can conduct a map reconnaissance. Routes are confirmed by the leader through actual inspection as the platoon moves through them. Rally points must—
- Be easy to recognize on the ground.
- Have cover and concealment.
- Be away from natural lines of drift.
- Be defendable for short periods.

TYPES OF RALLY POINTS

6-63. The most common types of rally points are initial, en route, objective, reentry, near- and far-side. Soldiers must know which rally point to move to at each phase of the patrol mission. They should know what actions are required there and how long they are to wait at each rally point before moving to another. The following are descriptions of these five rally points:

- *Initial rally point.* An IRP is a place inside of friendly lines where a unit may assemble and reorganize if it makes enemy contact during the departure of friendly lines or before reaching the first en route rally point. It is normally selected by the commander of the friendly unit.
- *Enroute rally point.* The leader designates en route rally points based on the terrain, vegetation, and visibility.
- *Objective rally point.* ORP is a point out of sight, sound, and small-arms range of the objective area. It normally is located in the direction the platoon plans to move after completing its actions on the objective. The ORP is tentative until the objective is pinpointed. (See figure 6-4.) Actions at or from the ORP include—
  - Issuing a final fragmentary order (FRAGORD).
  - Disseminating information from reconnaissance if contact was not made.
  - Making final preparations before continuing operations.
  - Accounting for Soldiers and equipment after actions at the objective are complete.
  - Reestablishing the chain of command after actions at the objective is complete.

Note. Isolated Soldiers still able to function on their own will make an attempt to move to the objective rally point, or a rally point designated in the patrol plan.

- *Reentry rally point.* The RRP is located out of sight, sound, and small-arms weapons range of the friendly unit through which the platoon will return. This also means the RRP should be outside the FPFs of the friendly unit. The platoon occupies the RRP as a security perimeter.
- *Near-and far-side rally points.* These rally points are on the near and far side of danger areas. If the platoon makes contact while crossing the danger area and control is lost, Soldiers on either side move to the rally point nearest them. They establish security, reestablish the chain of command, determine their personnel and equipment status, continue the patrol mission, and linkup at the ORP.

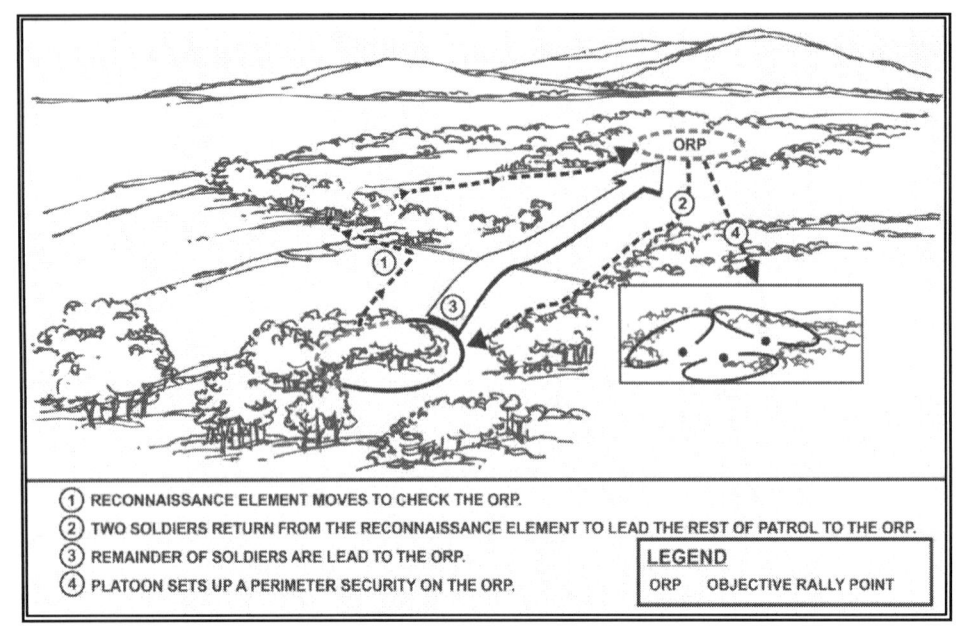

Figure 6-4. Objective rally point

MOUNTED PATROLS

6-64. An analysis of the METT-TC variables determines whether the patrol is mounted or dismounted. The planning and coordination required for both types of patrols is the same. Some factors to consider when determining which mode to use include—

- Mission, especially where distance and speed are factors.
- Onboard visibility, navigation, and communication.
- Firepower and protection.
- Stealth and surprise.
- Terrain.

CONSIDERATIONS

6-65. Mechanized and Stryker Infantry units frequently conduct mounted patrols. The same considerations that apply to dismounted patrol apply to vehicle mounted patrols. The platoon leader should additionally consider the following:

- Organize and orient vehicle gunners and vehicle commanders to maintain all-round security and, for urban areas, high-low security. Carefully consider leader locations in each vehicle and within the convoy.
- Rehearse mounted battle drills, reaction to contact, roll over drills, and mounting and dismounting in contact. If water hazards are present include evacuation of the vehicle from the top hatches. Include drivers in all rehearsals.
- Plan alternate routes to avoid civilian traffic and roadblocks.

Chapter 6

- Remember that four is generally the minimum number of vehicles to conduct an operation. If one vehicle is disabled or destroyed, it can be recovered while the others provide security. Unit TACSOPs determine the number of vehicles required.
- Plan for actions required if a vehicle breaks down and has to be repaired or recovered. Review self-recovery procedures. Plan actions in case a vehicle gets stuck and cannot be recovered. Plan actions for catch-ups and breaks in contact.
- Establish alternative communications plans.
- Secure external gear to prevent theft.
- Plan for heavy civilian vehicle and pedestrian traffic.
- Conduct a map reconnaissance and identify likely chokepoints, ambush sites (intersections), and overpasses.
- Plan primary and alternate routes to avoid potential hazards.
- Drive offensively, unpredictably, but within ROE restrictions.
- Avoid stopping; it can create a potential kill zone.
- Learn the characteristics of the vehicle, to include how high a vehicle can clear curbs and other obstacles, its turning radius, its high-speed maneuverability, and its estimated width (especially with slat armor).

PATROLS WITH MOUNTED AND DISMOUNTED PHASES

6-66. The mounted patrol normally moves to a dismount point (often the designated objective rally point) and conducts the same actions on the objective as a dismounted patrol. If possible, the vehicles establish a support-by-fire position to cover the objective, establish blocking positions, provide security, or otherwise support the actions of the dismounted element. The dismounted element conducts its required part of the mission and returns to the vehicles, remounts, and continues mission. Types of combat patrols that are especially suited for mounted movement include antiarmor ambushes, reconnaissance patrols covering long distances and security patrols.

SECTION II – PATROL PREPARATIONS

6-67. Units send out patrols under many and varied conditions on the battlefield. The specific actions taken in preparing for a patrol, while conducting the mission, and after returning to the main body will vary depending on the tactical situation. The principles, however, will remain the same. During high-intensity combat, some of the actions described below may be abbreviated. Those same actions may be executed in greater detail and specificity during stability or during support to civil authority. In general, patrol activities are more closely documented during operations in other than high-intensity combat. Patrol operations require considerable preparation before a patrol departs. The commander or platoon leader should brief the patrol leader and give him clear orders before sending him away from the main body. Patrol members should depart on patrol confident of the patrol's capabilities. This can be understood through detailed knowledge of the mission's task and purpose, the threats which may be encountered during the patrol, and good situational awareness.

ORDERS, BRIEFINGS AND REHEARSALS

6-68. Patrol orders, pre-patrol briefings, and rehearsals should cover—

- *Environment, local situation and possible threats.* The patrol leader should coordinate an intelligence briefing covering the operational environment, local civil situation, terrain and weather which might affect the patrol's mission, general and specific threats to the patrol, suspect persons, and vehicles and locations known to be in the patrol's area.
- *Mine and IED threat.* The patrol leader should make a mine and IED risk assessment based on the latest information available. This will determine many of the actions of the patrol. Patrol members must be informed of the latest mine and IED threats and restrictions to the unit's tactical SOPs.
- *Operations update.* The patrol leader should coordinate for an up-to-date briefing on the location and intentions of other friendly patrols and units in the patrol's area. This briefing should include the existing fire and maneuver control measures in effect, no-go or restricted areas, special effects of the patrol's area, and all other operational issues affecting the patrol and its mission.
- *Mission and tasks.* Every patrol leader should be given a specific task and purpose to accomplish with his patrol. Accordingly, each patrol member knows the mission and is aware of his responsibilities.
- *Locations and route.* The patrol leader must brief his patrol on all pertinent locations and routes. Locations and routes may include drop-off points, pick-up points, planned routes; rally points, exit and re-entry points, and alternates for each should be covered in detail.
- *Posture.* This is a vital consideration during a civil reconnaissance patrol. (Refer to FM 3-57 for more information.) The patrol leader should not depart until he is sure he completely understands what posture or attitude the leader wishes the patrol to present to the populace it encounters. The posture may be soft or hard depending on the situation and environment. The patrol posture may change several times during a patrol.
- *Biometric enrollments/BEWL.* An additional consideration during civil reconnaissance may be the number of biometric enrollments accomplished as well as how many people were identified with organic biometric devices as Tier/Level 1-6 Targets on the BEWL.
- *Personnel recovery.* Operations that focuses on recovering isolated or missing personnel before becoming detained or captured and extracting those detained or captured personnel through coordinated and well-planned operations.
- *Actions on contact and actions at the scene of an incident.* These are likely to be part of the unit's tactical SOPs but should be covered especially if there are local variations or new patrol members.
- *Rules of engagement, rules of interaction, and rules for escalation of force.* Each patrol member must know and understand these rules.
- *Communications plan/Lost communications plan.* Every patrol member should know the means in which the patrol plans to communicate, to whom, how, and when it should report. The patrol leader must ensure he has considered what actions the

patrol will take in the event it loses communications. The unit may have established these actions in its tactical SOP, but all patrol members should be briefed on the communication plan and be given the appropriate frequencies, contact numbers, and passwords in effect.

- *Electronic warfare countermeasures plan.* This is especially important if the IED threat level is high. The patrol leader should clearly explain to all patrol members which electronic warfare devices are being employed and their significant characteristics. These issues may be covered by the unit's tactical SOP, but all patrol members should be briefed on the electronic warfare plan in effect during the patrol.
- *Standard and special uniforms and equipment.* Equipment should be distributed evenly among the patrol members. The location of essential or unique equipment should be known by all members of the patrol. SOPs should be developed to stipulate what uniform is to be worn for various types of patrols. The dress state will be linked to threats and posture of the patrol, so patrol members should be briefed in sufficient time to enable proper preparations. All patrols must have a day and night capability regardless of the expected duration of the patrol.
- *+ Medical.* Every Soldier should carry their own individual improved first aid kit per unit tactical SOP. The leader should ensure that every patrol has a medic and one CLS qualified Soldier with a CLS bag. All patrol members must know who is responsible for carrying the pack and know how to use its contents.
- *Attachments.* The patrol leader must ensure all personnel attached to the patrol are introduced to the other patrol members and briefed thoroughly on the tactical SOP; all patrol special orders; and existing chain of command. The following personnel may be attached to a unit going out on patrol:
    - Interpreters
    - Host-nation police, military police or local security forces.
    - Explosive ordnance disposal teams.
    - Female Soldiers specifically designated and trained to search local women.
    - Military working dog teams.
    - Foreign security forces.
    - Host-nation forces.
    - Provincial reconstruction teams.

EQUIPMENT

6-69. Equipment carried by the patrol will be environment- and task-specific and should cover—

- *Radios and electronic warfare equipment.* Radios and electronic warfare equipment should be checked prior to every patrol ensuring it is serviceable and operates correctly. Batteries must be taken for expected duration of the patrol plus some extra for backup. Patrol members must be trained in the operation of all electronic warfare and radio equipment. It is the patrol leader's responsibility to ensure radios and electronic warfare equipment is switched on and working and communication checks are conducted prior to leaving the base location.

Chapter 6

- *Weapons.* All weapons must be prepared for firing prior to departure from the larger unit. Slings should be used to ensure weapons do not become separated from Soldiers who became incapacitated. This also ensures a weapon cannot be snatched away from a distracted Soldier while he is speaking with locals and used against him.
- *Ammunition.* Sufficient ammunition, signal pyrotechnics, obscurants, and nonlethal munitions must be carried to enable the patrol to conduct its mission. The amount a patrol carries may be established by the unit's tactical SOP or by the patrol leader based upon an evaluation of the situation the patrol faces.
- *Load-carrying equipment.* Patrol members should carry sufficient team and personal equipment to enable them to accomplish other missions such as reassignment to a cordon position before returning to the larger unit for resupply. The unit's tactical SOP should establish the standard amount of equipment and supplies to be carried. The leader carefully considers the burden being placed on Soldiers going on a foot patrol, especially in extreme weather conditions or rugged terrain.
- *Documentation.* Team leaders are responsible to the patrol leader for ensuring appropriate documentation is carried by individuals for conducting the mission. Under normal circumstances, Soldiers should carry just their identification card and tags. The unit tactical SOP may prohibit or require the carrying of other appropriate theater specific documentation such as cards with rules on EOF or ROE.

6-70. A number of equipment checks should be conducted prior to the patrol departing. These checks can include the following:

- *Individual equipment check.* It is the responsibility of every patrol member to check their individual equipment. Soldiers should ensure all loose items of carried equipment are secured.
- *Team leader's equipment check.* Leaders must ensure individual team members limit what they carry to which is required for the patrol. Team equipment must be checked for serviceability.
- *Patrol leader's equipment check.* Patrol leaders should check individual and team equipment from each team prior to deploying, paying particular attention to the serviceability of mission specific equipment.

PRE AND POST DEPARTURE PREPARATION ACTIVITIES

6-71. Patrol preparation activities prior to departure and after departure include:
- Rehearsals.
- Communication checks.
- Patrol manifest.
- Departure report.
- Weapons status.
- Exiting and entering a fixed base.

- Security checks while on patrol.
- Five and twenty five meter checks.

REHEARSALS

6-72. Patrols should rehearse all specific tactical actions or drills for situations the patrol leader anticipates encountering.

COMMUNICATIONS CHECKS

6-73. Communications checks should be conducted with the unit headquarters or command post before every patrol. Patrols should not leave the vicinity of the main body until all communication systems are operating correctly.

PATROL MANIFEST

6-74. When the situation allows, the patrol leader should submit a written patrol manifest to the commander or to command post personnel prior to departing the main body. Regardless of the situation, whenever the unit sends out a patrol there should be a specific list of the patrol members made before it departs. The unit tactical SOP may establish a specific format for this manifest, but generally it should contain the following information:

- Patrol number or call sign designation.
- Unit designation of unit sending the patrol out.
- Patrol task and purpose (mission).
- Names and rank of patrol leader and all subordinate leaders.
- Estimated date-time-group out.
- Estimated date-time-group in.
- Brief description of the patrol's intended route.
- Complete names, rank, and unit of all members of the patrol, including attachments.
- Number, nomenclature, and serial number of all weapons with the patrol.
- Number, nomenclature, and serial number of all electronic warfare devices, radios, and other special or sensitive equipment with the patrol.
- Vehicle type and registration number, if appropriate.

6-75. The purpose of the manifest is to allow the higher headquarters to keep track of all the patrols which are out and those having returned. If the patrol engages the enemy or fails to return on time without reporting, the headquarters has information on the size, capability and intentions of the patrol that it may need. If the patrol suffers casualties or has a vehicle disabled, this manifest can be used to check that all personnel, weapons and sensitive items were recovered.

DEPARTURE REPORT

6-76. The patrol leader should render a departure report just as the patrol departs the main body location or the base. Depending on the procedure established by the unit's tactical

SOP, this might include a detailed listing of the patrol's composition. It also may simply state the patrol's call sign or patrol number and report its departure.

WEAPONS STATUS

6-77. Immediately upon leaving an established base or the main body position, the patrol leader, vehicle commanders, and team leaders should ensure all the patrol weapons are loaded and prepared for in accordance with ROE. Electronic warfare equipment should be checked to ensure it is turned on if appropriate and all radio frequency settings should be confirmed.

6-78. When the patrol returns to the base, each Soldier should clear his weapon immediately after entering the protected area. The unit's tactical SOP normally will establish precise procedures for this clearing. Patrol leaders should ensure all individual and crew-served weapons are unloaded.

EXITING AND ENTERING A FIXED BASE

6-79. Exiting and entering a fixed operating base is a high risk activity due to the way troops are channeled through narrow entry or exit points. Insurgents are known to monitor patrols leaving and entering base locations to identify and exploit patterns and areas of weakness. Patrols leaving and entering a base reduce the risks of attack by varying the points used to exit and enter the base, and routes used to transit the immediate area around the base. If this is not possible, extreme caution should be used in the vicinity of the exit and entry points. Patrol leaders ensure their patrols do not become complacent. Units should ensure close coordination between patrol leaders and guards at the entry point while the patrol is transiting the gate.

SECURITY CHECKS WHILE ON PATROL

6-80. Patrol members assist their patrol leader by consistently applying basic patrolling techniques. This gives the team leader more time to concentrate on assisting the patrol leader in the conduct of the patrol. Team members should concentrate on maintaining spacing, formation, alertness, conducting 5- and 25-meter checks and taking up fire positions without supervision.

FIVE- AND TWENTY FIVE-METER CHECKS

6-81. Every time a patrol stops, it should use a fundamental security technique known as the 5- and 25-meter check. The technique involves every patrol member requiring him to make detailed, focused examinations of the area immediately around him, and looking for anything out of the ordinary which might be dangerous or significant. Five-meter checks should be conducted every time a patrol member stops. Twenty-five-meter checks should be conducted when a patrol halts for more than a few minutes.

6-82. Soldiers should conduct a visual check using their unaided vision, and by using the optics on their weapons and binoculars. They should check for anything suspicious, and anything out of the ordinary. This might be as minor as bricks missing from walls, new string or wire run across a path, mounds of fresh soil, or other suspicious signs. Check the area at ground level through to above head height.

6-83. When the patrol makes a planned halt, the patrol leader identifies an area for occupation and stops 50 meters short of it. While the remainder of the patrol provides security, the patrol leader carries out a visual check using binoculars. After moving the patrol forward 20 meters from the position, the patrol leader conducts a visual check using optics on the weapon or with unaided vision.

6-84. Before actually occupying the position, each Soldier conducts a thorough visual and physical check for a radius of five meters. Each Soldier must be systematic, take time and show curiosity. Use touch and, at night, white light if appropriate.

6-85. Obstacles must be physically checked for command wires. Fences, walls, wires, posts and ground immediately underneath must be carefully felt by hand, without gloves.

SECTION III – COMBAT PATROLS

6-86. A *combat patrol* provides security and harasses, destroys, or captures enemy troops, equipment, or installations. When the commander gives a unit the mission to send out a combat patrol, he intends the patrol to make contact with the enemy and engage in close combat. A combat patrol always tries to remain undetected while moving, but when it discloses its location to the enemy it is with a sudden and violent attack. For this reason, the patrol normally carries a significant amount of weapons and ammunition. It may carry specialized munitions. A combat patrol collects and reports information gathered during the mission, whether related to the combat task or not. The three types of combat patrols are raid, ambush, and security patrol.

RAID

6-87. Raids are surprise attacks against a position or installation for a specific purpose other than seizing and holding the terrain. It is conducted to destroy a position or installation, to destroy or capture enemy soldiers or equipment, or to free prisoners. A raid patrol retains terrain just long enough to accomplish the intent of the raid. A raid always ends with a planned withdrawal off the objective and a return to the main body.

AMBUSH

6-88. An ambush is a surprise attack from a concealed position on a moving or temporarily halted target. An ambush patrol does not need to seize or hold terrain. It can include an assault to close with and destroy the target, or an attack by fire only.

SECURITY PATROL

6-89. A security patrol is sent out from a unit location when the unit is stationary or during a halt to search the local area, detect enemy forces near the main body, and to engage and destroy the enemy within the capability of the patrol. This form of combat patrol normally is sent out by units operating in close terrain with limited fields of observation and fire.

Although this form of combat patrol seeks to make direct enemy contact and to destroy enemy forces within its capability, it should try to avoid decisive engagement. A security patrol detects and disrupts enemy forces conducting reconnaissance of the main body or massing to conduct an attack. Security patrols normally are away from the main body of the unit for limited periods, returning frequently to coordinate and rest. They do not operate beyond the range of communications and supporting fires from the main body, especially mortar fires.

COMBAT PATROL PLANNING

6-90. There are three essential elements for a combat patrol: security; support; and assault. Assault elements accomplish the mission during actions on the objective. Support elements suppress or destroy enemy on the objective in support of the assault element. Security elements assist in isolating the objective by preventing enemy from entering and leaving the objective area as well as by ensuring the patrol's withdrawal route remains open. The size of each element is based on the situation and leader's analysis of METT-TC.

ASSAULT ELEMENT

6-91. The assault element is the combat patrol's main effort. Its task is to conduct actions on the objective. In most cases, the assault element will accomplish the overall purpose. This element must be capable (through inherent capabilities or positioning relative to the enemy) of destroying or seizing the target of the combat patrol. Tasks typically associated with the assault element include:

- Conduct of assault across the objective to destroy enemy equipment, capture or kill enemy, and clearing of key terrain and enemy positions.
- Maneuver close enough to the objective to conduct an immediate assault if detected.
- Being prepared to support itself if the support element cannot suppress the enemy.
- Providing support to a breach element in reduction of obstacles, if required.
- Planning detailed fire control and distribution.
- Conducting controlled withdrawal from the objective.

6-92. Analysis of METT-TC, particularly for a raid, may result in the requirement to organize a separate breach force. At times this may include reducing an obstacle. Additional tasks/special purpose teams assigned may include:

- Search teams. To find and collect documents, equipment and information which can be used to produce intelligence.
- Detainee teams. To capture, secure, and document detainees.
- Demolition teams. To plan and execute the destruction of obstacles and when necessary enemy equipment.
- Breach team. To create lanes in protective obstacles to facilitate the completion of the patrol's primary task.
- Aid and litter teams. To identify, collect, render immediate aid and coordinate casualty evacuation.

Support Element

6-93. The support element suppresses the enemy on the objective using direct and indirect fires. The support element is a shaping effort setting conditions for mission's main effort. This element must be capable of supporting the assault element. The support force can be divided up into two or more elements if required.

6-94. The support element is organized to address a threat of enemy interference with the assault elements. The support force suppresses, fixes, or destroys elements on the objective. The support force's primary responsibility is to suppress enemy to prevent reposition against main effort. The support force—
- Initiates fires and gains fire superiority with crew-served weapons and indirect fires.
- Controls rates and distribution of fires.
- Shifts/ceases fire on signal.
- Supports the withdrawal of the assault element.

Security Element

6-95. The security element is a shaping force having three roles. The first is to isolate the objective from enemy personnel and vehicles attempting to enter the objective area. These actions range from simply providing early warning, to blocking enemy movement. This element may require several different forces located in various positions. The patrol leader is careful to consider enemy reserves or response forces that will be alerted once the engagement begins. The second role is to prevent enemy from escaping the objective area. The third role is to secure the patrol's withdrawal route.

6-96. There is a subtle yet important distinction to the security element. All elements of the patrol are responsible for their own local security. What distinguishes the security element is they are protecting the entire patrol. Their positions must be such they can, in accordance with their engagement criteria, provide early warning of approaching enemy.

6-97. The security element is organized to address the primary threat to the patrol, being discovered and defeated by security forces prior to execution of actions on the objective. To facilitate the success of the assault element, the security element must fix or block (or at a minimum screen) all enemy security or response forces located on parts of the battlefield away from the raid.

Leader Locations

6-98. Leaders locate where they can best influence the situation, which is usually with either the support element or assault element. The second-in-charge normally locates at the opposite location of the leader.

ACTIONS ON THE OBJECTIVE – RAID

6-99. A raid is a surprise attack against a position or installation for a specific purpose *other than* seizing and holding the terrain. It is conducted to destroy a position or installation, destroy or capture enemy soldiers or equipment, or free prisoners. A raid

Patrols and Patrolling

patrol retains terrain just long enough to accomplish the intent of the raid. A raid always ends with a planned withdrawal off the objective and a return to the main body.

6-100. Raids are characterized by the following:
- Destruction of essential systems or facilities (command and control nodes, logistical areas, other high value areas).
- Provide or deny critical information.
- Securing of hostages or prisoners.
- Confusing the enemy or disrupting his plans.
- Detailed information collection (significant collection assets committed).
- Mission command from the higher headquarters to synchronize the operation.
- Creating a window of opportunity.

6-101. Raids normally are conducted in five phases—(See figure 6-5, page 6-26.)
1) Approach the objective.
2) Isolate the objective area.
3) Set conditions for the assault element.
4) Assault the objective.
5) Tactical movement away from the objective area.

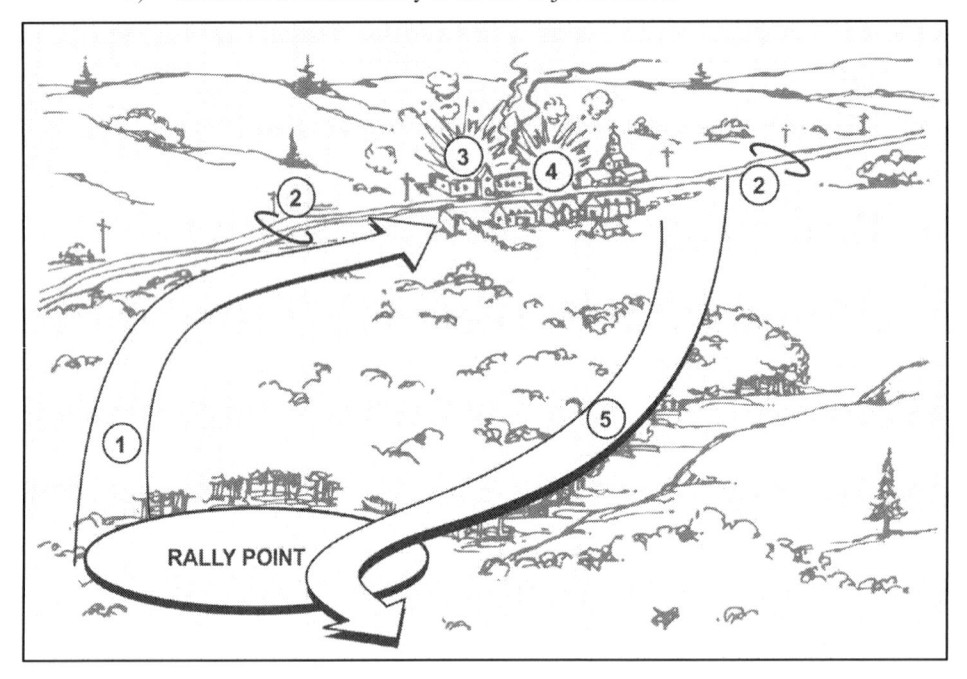

Figure 6-5. The five phases of a raid

Chapter 6

ACTIONS ON THE OBJECTIVE – AMBUSH

6-102. An ambush is a surprise attack from a concealed position on a moving or temporarily halted target. It can include an assault to close with and destroy the target or an assault by fire. An ambush need not seize or hold ground. The purpose of an ambush is to destroy or to harass enemy forces. The ambush combines the advantages of the defense with the advantages of the offense, allowing a smaller force with limited means the ability to destroy a much larger force. Ambushes are enemy-oriented. Terrain is held only long enough to conduct the ambush, and then the force withdraws. Ambushes range from simple to complex and synchronized; short duration of minutes to long duration of hours; and within hand grenade range, to maximum standoff. Ambushes employ direct fire systems as well as other destructive means, such as command-detonated mines and explosives, and indirect fires on the enemy force. The attack may include an assault to close with and destroy the enemy or may just be a harassing assault by fire. Ambushes may be conducted as independent operations or as part of a larger operation.

6-103. There are countless ways for leaders to develop an ambush. To assist the leader he clarifies what he wants, he develops the ambush based on its purpose, form, time, and formation.

6-104. The purpose of an ambush is either harassment or destruction. A harassing ambush is one in which attack is by fire only (meaning there is no assault element). A destruction ambush includes assault to close with and destroy the enemy.

6-105. The three forms of ambushes are point, area, and antiarmor. In a point ambush, Soldiers deploy to attack a single kill zone. In an area ambush, Soldiers deploy as two or more related point ambushes. These ambushes at separate sites are related by their purpose. (See figure 6-6.) A unit smaller than a platoon normally does not conduct an area ambush. Antiarmor ambushes focus on moving or temporarily halted enemy armored vehicles

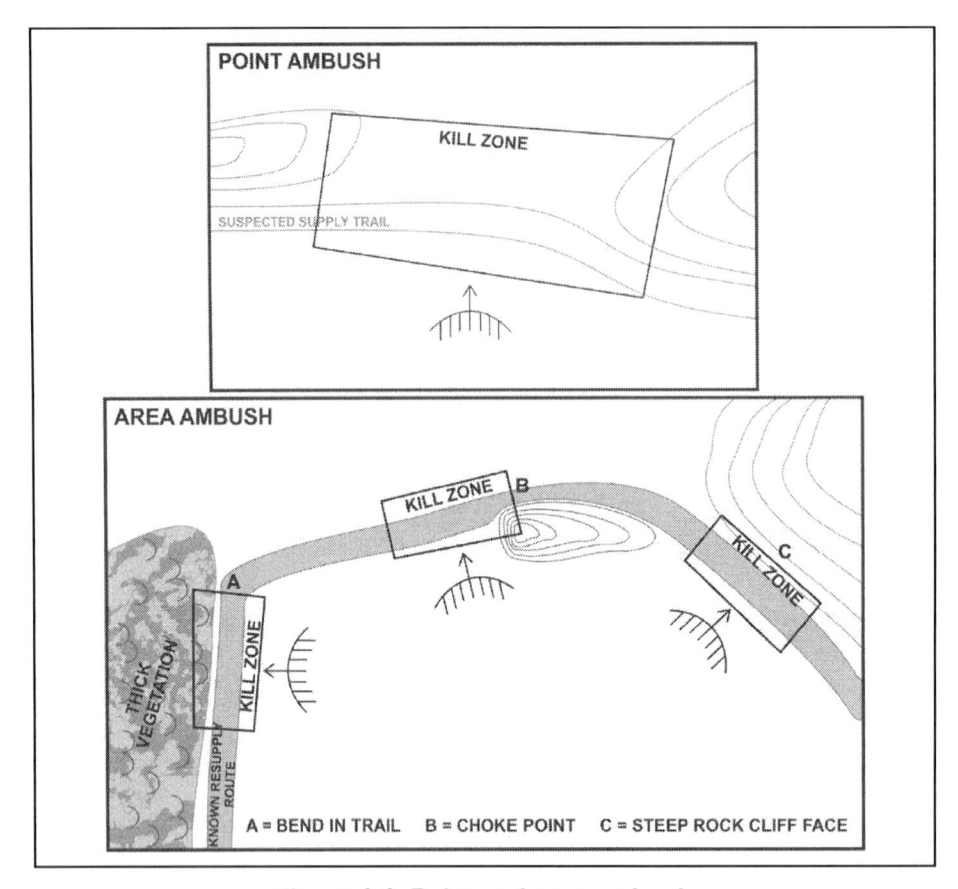

Figure 6-6. Point and area ambush

6-106. Based on the amount of time available to set an ambush, ambushes are hasty and deliberate. A hasty ambush is conducted based on an unanticipated opportunity. It is used when a patrol sees the enemy before the enemy sees it, and the patrol has time to act. The leader gives the prearranged signal to start the action and all Soldiers move to concealed firing positions, prepared to engage the enemy. Depending on the mission, the patrol may allow the enemy to pass if the enemy does not detect the patrol.

6-107. A deliberate ambush is conducted against a specific target at a location chosen based on intelligence. With a deliberate ambush, leaders plan and prepare based on detailed information allowing them to anticipate enemy actions and enemy locations. Detailed information includes: type and size of target, organization or formation, routes and direction of movement, time the force will reach or pass certain points on its route, and weapons and equipment carried.

TERMINOLOGY

6-108. During terrain analysis, leaders identify at least four different locations: the ambush site, the kill zone, security positions, and rally points. As far as possible, so-called "ideal" ambush sites should be avoided because alert enemies avoid them if possible and increase their vigilance and security when they must be entered. Therefore, surprise is difficult to achieve. Instead, unlikely sites should be chosen when possible. Following are characteristics of these four ideal positions.

Ambush Site

6-109. The ambush site is the terrain on which a point ambush is established. The ambush site consists of a support-by-fire position for the support element and an assault position for the assault element. An ideal ambush site—
- Has a good field of fire into the kill zone.
- Has good cover and concealment.
- Has a protective obstacle.
- Has a covered and concealed withdrawal route.
- Makes it difficult for the enemy to conduct a flank attack.

Kill Zone

6-110. The kill zone is the part of an ambush site where fire is concentrated to isolate or destroy the enemy. An ideal kill zone has the following characteristics:
- Enemy forces are likely to enter it.
- It has natural tactical obstacles.
- Large enough to observe and engage the anticipated enemy force.

6-111. A near ambush is a point ambush with the assault element within reasonable assaulting distance of the kill zone (less than 50 meters). Close terrain, such as an urban area or heavy woods, may require this positioning. It also may be appropriate in open terrain in a "rise from the ground" ambush.

6-112. A far ambush is a point ambush with the assault element beyond reasonable assaulting distance of the kill zone (beyond 50 meters). This location may be appropriate in open terrain offering good fields of fire or when attack is by fire for a harassing ambush.

Security Positions

6-113. An ideal security position—
- Does not mask fires of the main body.
- Provides timely information to the main body. (Gives the leader enough time to act on information provided.)
- Can provide a support-by-fire position.

Rally Points

6-114. The platoon leader considers the use and locations of rally points. The rally point is a place designated by the leader where the platoon moves to reassemble and reorganize if it becomes dispersed.

6-115. The leader physically reconnoiters routes to select rally points whenever possible. He selects tentative points if he can only conduct a map reconnaissance. He confirms them by actual inspection as the platoon moves through them. Rally points must—
- Be easy to find.
- Have cover and concealment.
- Be away from natural lines of drift.
- Be defendable for short periods.

FORMATIONS

6-116. Many ambush formations exist. This section only discusses the linear, L-shaped, and V-shaped (see figures 6-7 through 6-9, pages 6-30 through 6-32.) All of these formations require leaders to exercise strict direct fire control. Leaders need to understand strengths and weaknesses of their units and plan accordingly. The formation selected is based on the following: terrain, visibility, Soldiers available, weapons and equipment, ease of control, and target to be attacked.

Linear Ambush

6-117. In an ambush using a linear formation, the assault and support elements parallel the target's route. This positions the assault and support elements on the long axis of the kill zone and subjects the target to flanking fire. (See figure 6-7.) Only a target that can be covered with a full volume of fire can be engaged in the kill zone. A dispersed target might be too large for the kill zone. This is the disadvantage of linear formations.

6-118. The linear formation is good in close terrain restricting the target's maneuver, and in open terrain where one flank is blocked by natural obstacles or can be blocked by other means such as Claymores. Claymores or explosives can be placed between the assault and support elements and kill zone to protect the unit from counter-ambush actions.

6-119. When the ambushing unit deploys this way, it leaves access lanes through the obstacles so it can assault the target. An advantage of the linear formation is the relative ease by which it can be controlled under all visibility conditions.

Chapter 6

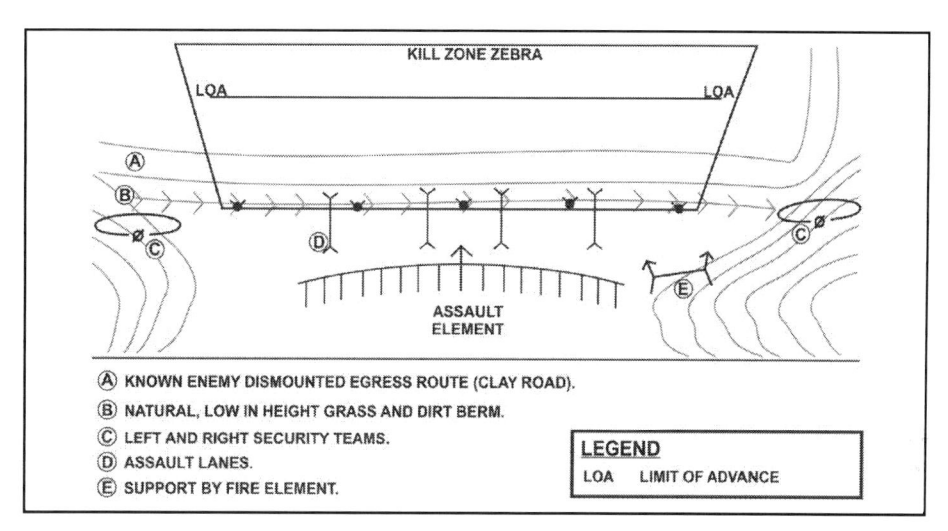

Figure 6-7. Linear ambush

L-Shaped Ambush

6-120. An ambush in the L-shaped formation (see figure 6-8) is a variation of the linear formation. The long leg of the L (assault element) is parallel to the kill zone. This leg provides flanking fire. The short leg (support element) is at the end of and at a right angle to the kill zone. This leg provides enfilade fire working with fire from the other leg. The L-shaped formation can be used at a sharp bend in a trail, road, or stream.

Patrols and Patrolling

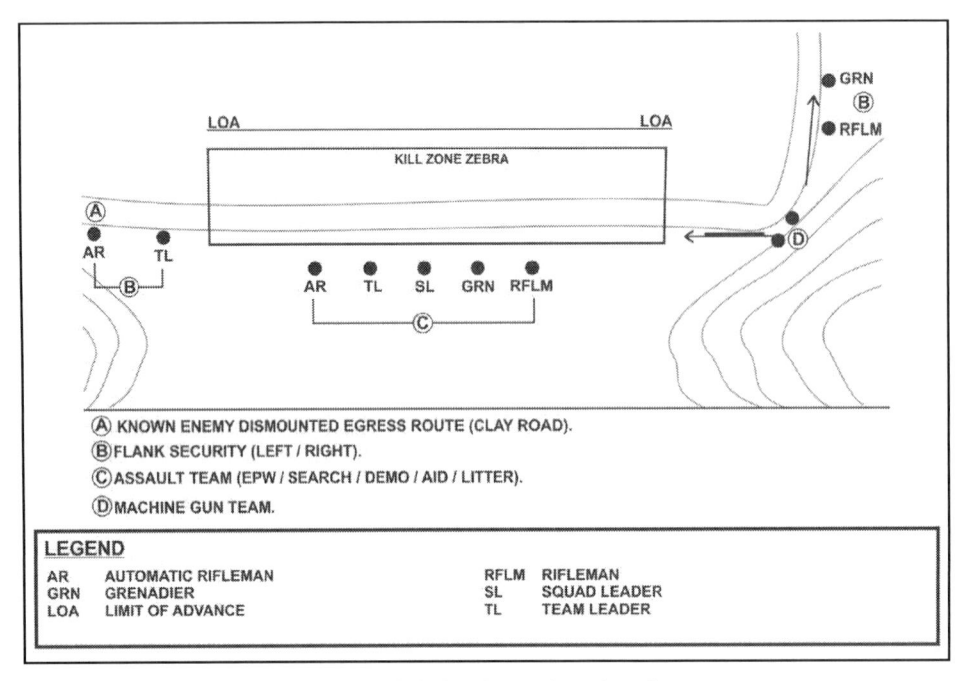

Figure 6-8. L-shaped ambush

6-121.   The V-shaped ambush assault elements (see figure 6-9, page 6-32) are placed along both sides of the enemy route so they form a V. Take extreme care to ensure neither group fires into the other. This formation subjects the enemy to both enfilading and interlocking fire.

6-122.   When performed in dense terrain, the legs of the V close in as the lead elements of the enemy force approach the point of the V. The legs then open fire from close range. Here, even more than in open terrain, all movement and fire is carefully coordinated and controlled to avoid fratricide.

6-123.   A wider separation of the elements makes this formation difficult to control, and fewer sites favor its use. Its main advantage, it is difficult for the enemy to detect the ambush until well into the kill zone.

Chapter 6

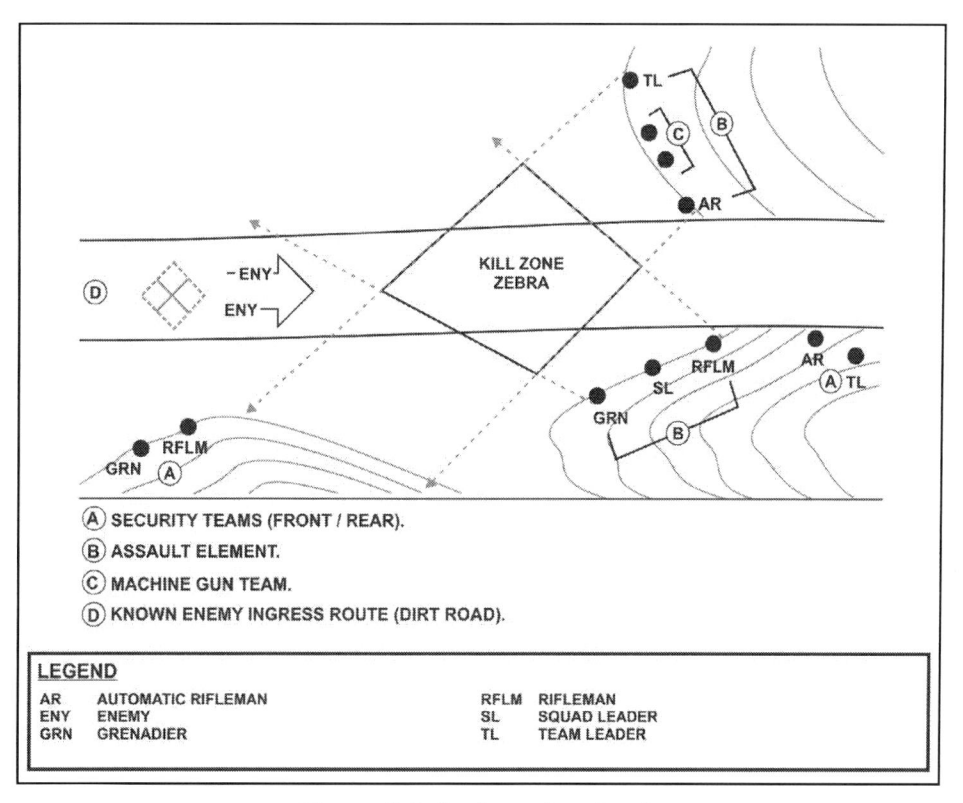

Figure 6-9. V-shaped ambush

FINAL PREPARATIONS

6-124. Final preparations begin with the unit occupying an ORP and end with the main body prepared to depart for the ambush site. The unit halts at the ORP and establishes security. When ready, the leader conducts his reconnaissance to confirm the plan, positions the security element, and returns to the ORP. The security element leaves the ORP first. Teams of the security element move to positions from which they can secure the ORP and flanks of the ambush site. (See figure 6-10.)

Note. Security elements should use a release point if there is a large distance between the ORP and objective.

Patrols and Patrolling

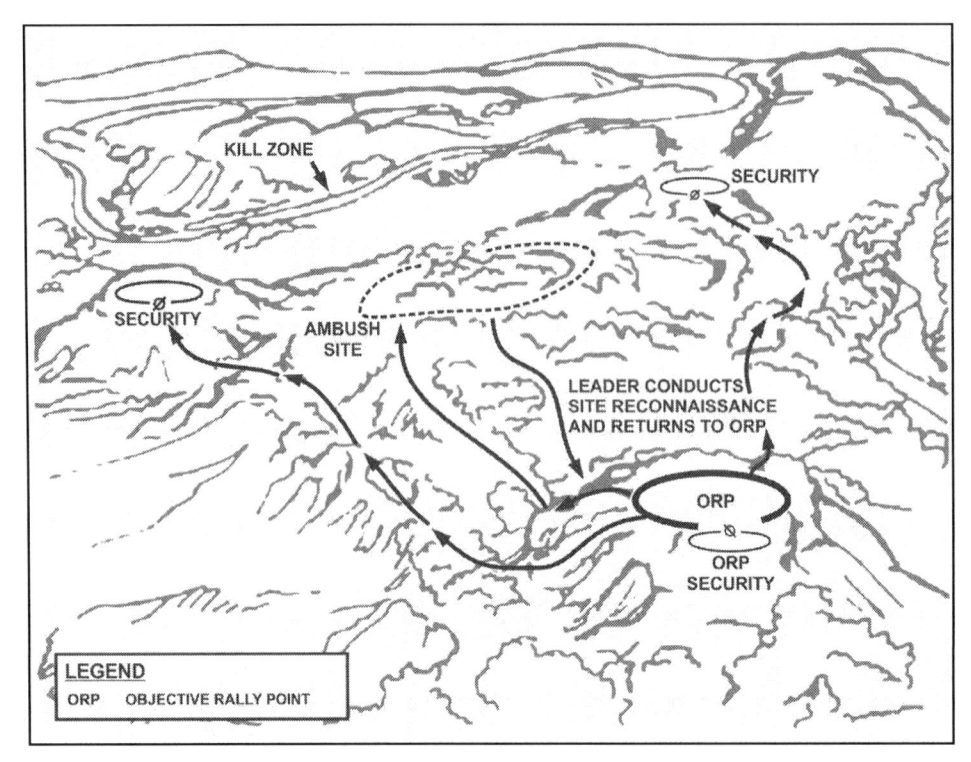

Figure 6-10. Security teams in position

OCCUPY THE SITE AND CONDUCT AMBUSH

6-125. Occupying the site and conducting the ambush begins with main body movement out of the ORP, and ends when the leader initiates a withdrawal. Common control measures include:
- Kill zone.
- Limit of advance.
- Assault by fire/ support-by-fire position.
- Assault position.
- Target registration point.

Time of Occupation

6-126. As a rule, the ambush force occupies the ambush site at the latest possible time permitted by the tactical situation and amount of site preparation required. This reduces the risk of discovery and time Soldiers must remain still and quiet in position.

Occupying the Site

6-127. Security elements are positioned first to prevent surprise while the ambush is being established. When the security teams are in position, the support and assault elements leave the ORP and occupy their positions. If there is a suitable position, the support element can overwatch the assault element's move to the ambush site. If not, both elements leave the ORP at the same time. (See figure 6-11.)

6-128. The main body moves into the ambush site from the rear. Ideally, the leader emplaces the most casualty-producing weapons first, ensuring they have line of sight (LOS) along the entire kill zone. Once in place, the leader locates his subordinate units to complement and reinforce the vital positions. The leader then selects his location where he can best initiate and control the action. Once on the objective, movement is kept to a minimum in order to enhance security measures.

Positions

6-129. Each Soldier must be hidden from the target and have LOS into the kill zone. At the ambush site, positions are prepared with minimal change in the natural appearance of the site. Soldiers conceal debris resulting from preparation of positions.

Confirming the Direct Fire Plan

6-130. Claymores, explosives, and grenade launchers may be used to cover dead space left by automatic weapons. All weapons are assigned sectors of fire to provide mutual support. The unit leader sets a time by which positions must be prepared.

Movement in the Kill Zone

6-131. Kill zone is not entered if entry can be avoided. When emplacing tactical obstacles, care is taken to remove tracks or signs which might alert the enemy and compromise the ambush. If claymores or explosives are placed on the far side, or if the appearance of the site might cause the enemy to check it, a wide detour around the kill zone should be made. Here, too, care is taken to remove all traces which might reveal the ambush. An alternate route from the ambush site also is planned.

Patrols and Patrolling

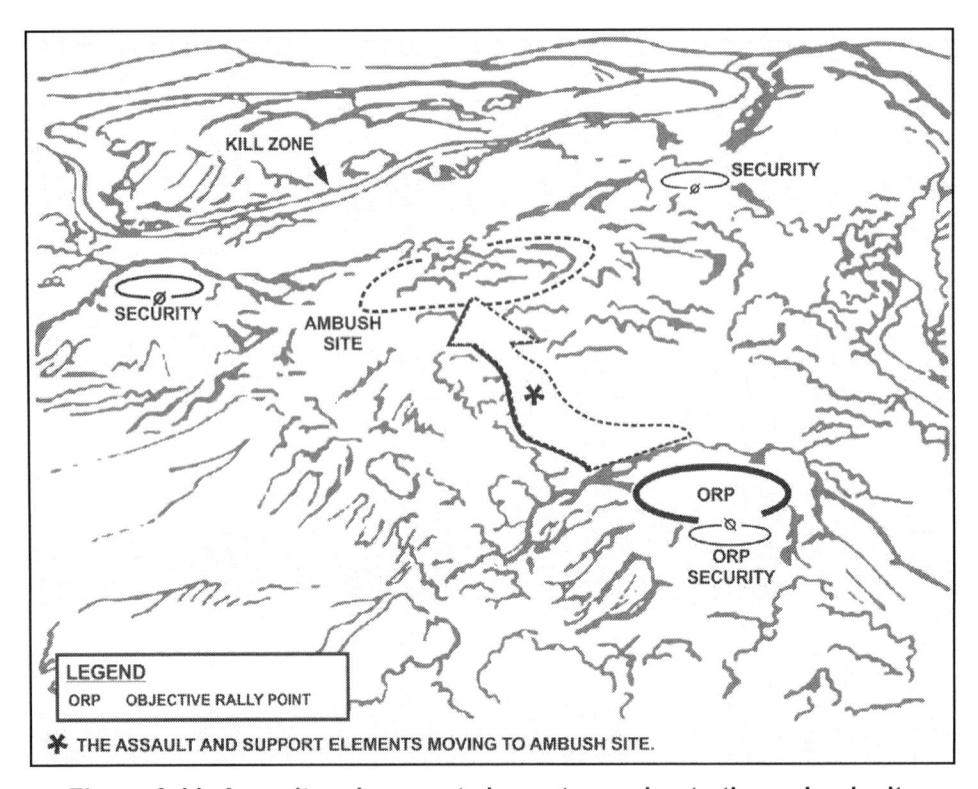

Figure 6-11. Assault and support elements moving to the ambush site

Initiating the Ambush

6-132. Once all friendly elements are in position, the unit waits for enemy targets. When the target approaches, the security team spots it and alerts the ambush leader. The security team reports the target's direction of movement, size, and special weapons or equipment. Upon receipt of the report, the leader alerts the other elements.

6-133. When most of the enemy force is in the kill zone, the leader initiates the ambush with the most casualty-producing weapon, medium machine gun fire, or the detonation of mines or explosives. The detonation of explosives can cause a pause in the initiation of fires due to the obscuration created by the explosion. Once conditions are set, cease or shift fires. The assault element may conduct an assault through the kill zone to the LOA. If the assault element must assault the kill zone, the leader signals to cease or shift fire. This also signals the start of the assault. Besides destruction of the enemy force, other kill zone tasks can include searching for items of intelligence value, capturing prisoners, and completing the destruction of enemy equipment. When the assault element has finished its mission in the kill zone, the leader gives the signal to withdraw to the ORP.

6-134. Fire discipline is critical during an ambush. Soldiers do not fire until the signal is given. Then it must be delivered at once in the heaviest, most accurate volume possible. Well-trained gunners and well-aimed fire help achieve surprise and destruction of the

Chapter 6

target. When the target is to be assaulted, the ceasing or shifting of fire also must be precise. If it is not, the assault is delayed, and the target has a chance to react. Sector stakes should be used if possible.

Withdrawal

6-135. The withdrawal begins once the assault element completes its actions on the objective and ends with consolidation/reorganization at a designated rally point. On signal, the unit withdraws to the ORP, reorganizes, and continues its mission. At a set terrain feature, the unit halts and disseminates information. If the ambush fails and enemy pursues, the unit withdraws by bounds. Units should use obscurants to help conceal the withdrawal. Obstacles already set along the withdrawal routes can help stop the pursuit.

CONDUCTING AN AREA AMBUSH

6-136. In an area ambush, Soldiers deploy in two or more related point ambushes. The platoon may conduct an area ambush as part of a company offensive or defensive plan, or it may conduct a point ambush as part of a company area ambush.

6-137. The platoon is the smallest level to conduct an area ambush. Platoons conduct area ambushes (see figure 6-12) where enemy movement is largely restricted to trails or streams.

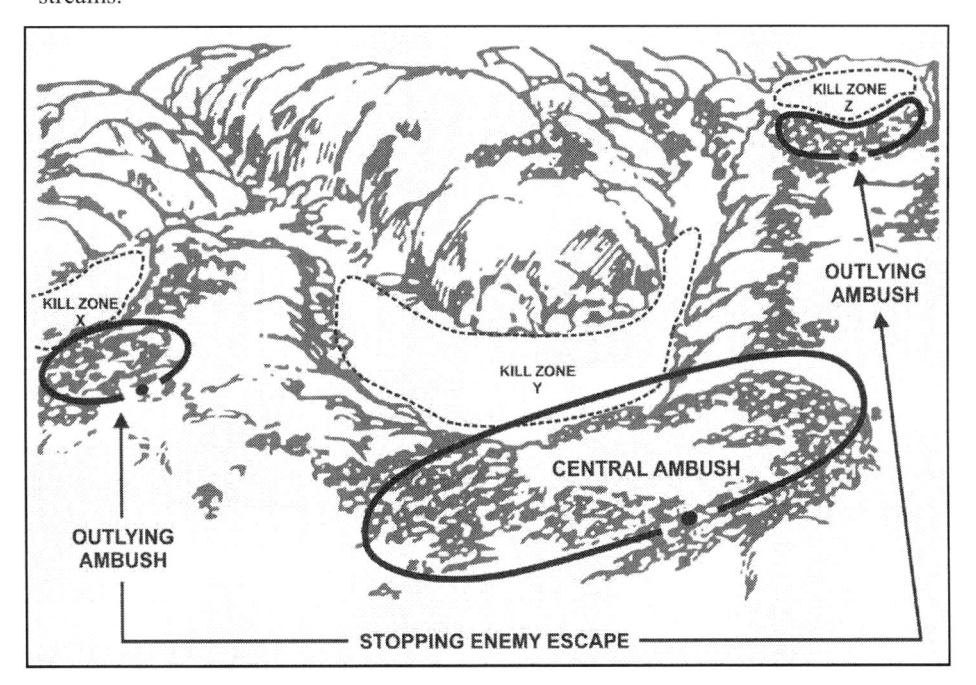

Figure 6-12. Area ambush

6-138. The platoon leader (or company commander) selects one principal ambush site around which he organizes outlying ambushes. These secondary sites are located along the enemy's most likely avenue of approach and escape routes from the principal ambush site. Squads normally are responsible for each ambush site.

6-139. The platoon leader considers METT-TC to determine the best employment of the weapons squad. He normally locates the medium machine guns with the support element in the principal ambush site.

6-140. Squads or sections responsible for outlying ambushes do not initiate their ambushes until the principal one has been initiated. They then engage to prevent enemy forces from escaping the principal ambush or reinforcing the ambushed force.

CONDUCTING AN ANTIARMOR AMBUSH

6-141. Platoons and squads conduct antiarmor ambushes (see figure 6-13) to destroy armored vehicles. The antiarmor ambush may be part of an area ambush. The antiarmor ambush consists of the assault element (armor-killer element) and support-security element.

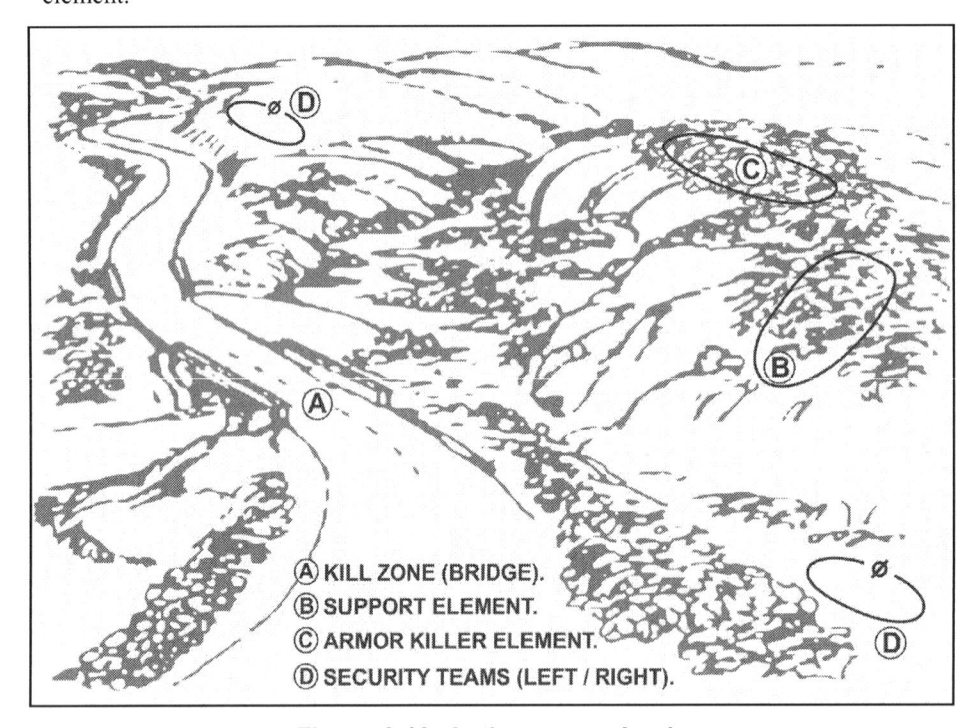

Figure 6-13. Anti-armor ambush

6-142. The armor-killer element is built around the CCMSs. (See appendix G of this publication for information about employment of the Javelin.) The leader should consider additional SLMs available to supplement the CCMS fires. The leader considers the mission variables of METT-TC to position all antiarmor weapons to take advantage of their best engagement aspect (rear, flank, or top). The remainder of the platoon must function as support-security elements in the same manner as the other forms of ambushes to cover dismounted enemy avenues of approach into the ambush site.

6-143. In a platoon antiarmor ambush, the company commander selects the general site of the ambush with the platoon leader finding a specific site restricting the movement of enemy armored vehicles out of the designated kill zone. The platoon leader should emplace his weapons so an obstacle is between the platoon and the kill zone. In a squad antiarmor ambush, the platoon leader selects the general site of the ambush and the squad leader then finds a site restricting the movement of enemy armored vehicles out of the kill zone.

6-144. The leader should consider the method for initiating the antiarmor ambush. The preferred method should be a mass casualty-producing signal initiated by a reliable weapon system or explosive, such as a main gun round from a tank or infantry carrier, the detonation of mines or explosives, or other direct fire crew-served weapons that fire from a closed bolt. The Javelin can be used to initiate the ambush, but even with its limited signature, it may be less desirable than an antitank mine.

6-145. The armor-killer team destroys the first and last vehicle in the enemy formation, if possible. All other weapons begin firing once the ambush has been initiated.

6-146. The leader must determine how the presence of dismounted enemy soldiers with armored vehicles will affect the success of the ambush. The leader's choices include:

- Initiate the ambush as planned.
- Withdraw without initiating the ambush.
- Initiate the ambush with medium machine guns without firing antiarmor weapons.

6-147. Because of the speed enemy armored forces can reinforce the ambushed enemy with, the leader should plan to keep the engagement short and have a quick withdrawal planned. The platoon, based on METT-TC, may not clear the kill zone as in other forms of ambushes.

CONDUCTING A POINT AMBUSH

6-148. In a point ambush, Soldiers deploy to attack an enemy in a single kill zone. The platoon leader is the leader of the assault element. The platoon sergeant or assistant patrol leader probably will locate with the platoon leader in the assault element.

6-149. The security or surveillance teams should be positioned first. The support element should then be emplaced before the assault element moves forward. The support element must overwatch the movement of the assault element into position.

6-150. The platoon leader must check each Soldier once he emplaces. The platoon leader signals the surveillance team to rejoin the assault element if it is positioned away from the assault location. Actions of the assault element, support element, and security element are shown in table 6-1.

Patrols and Patrolling

Table 6-1. Actions by ambush elements

ASSAULT ELEMENT	SUPPORT ELEMENT	SECURITY ELEMENT
• Identify individual sectors of fire assigned by the platoon leader; emplace aiming stakes. • Emplace claymores and other protective obstacles. • Emplace claymores, mines, or other explosives in dead space within the kill zone. • Camouflage positions. • Take weapons off safe when directed by the platoon leader.	• Identify sectors of fire for all weapons, especially medium machine guns. • Emplace limiting stakes to prevent friendly fires from hitting the assault element in an L-shaped ambush. • Emplace claymores and other protective obstacles. • Camouflage positions.	• Identify sectors of fire for all weapons; emplace aiming stakes. • Emplace claymores and other protective obstacles. • Camouflage positions. Secure the objective rally point (ORP). • Secure a route to the ORP, as required.

6-151. The platoon leader instructs the security element (or teams) to notify him of the enemy's approach into the kill zone using the SALUTE reporting format. The security element also must keep the platoon leader informed if additional enemy forces are following the lead enemy force. This will allow the platoon leader to know if the enemy force meets the engagement criteria directed by the company commander. The platoon leader must be prepared to give free passage to enemy forces too large or do not meet the engagement criteria. He must report to the company commander or CoIST enemy forces passing through the ambush unengaged.

6-152. The platoon leader initiates the ambush with the greatest casualty-producing weapon, typically a command-detonated Claymore. He also must plan a back-up method, typically a medium machine gun, to initiate the ambush should the primary means fail. All Soldiers in the ambush must know the primary and back-up methods. The platoon should rehearse with both methods to avoid confusion and loss of surprise during execution of the ambush.

6-153. The platoon leader must include a plan for engaging the enemy during limited visibility. Based on the company commander's guidance, the platoon leader should consider the use and mix of tracers and employment of illumination, night vision devices, and thermal weapon sights. For example, if Javelins are not used during the ambush, the platoon leader still may employ the CLU with its thermal sights in the security or support element to observe enemy forces.

6-154. The platoon leader also may include the employment of indirect fire support in his plan. Based upon the company commander's guidance, the platoon leader may employ indirect fires to cover flanks of the kill zone. This isolates an enemy force or assists the platoon's disengagement if the ambush is compromised or the platoon departs the ambush site under pressure.

Chapter 6

6-155. The platoon leader has a good plan (day and night) that signals the advance of the assault element into the kill zone to begin its search and collection activities. He should take into consideration the existing environmental factors. For example, obscurants may not be visible to the support element because of limited visibility or the lay of the terrain. Soldiers must know and practice relaying the signal during rehearsals to avoid the potential of fratricide.

6-156. The assault element must be prepared to move across the kill zone using individual movement techniques if there is return fire once they begin to search. Otherwise, the assault element moves across by bounding fire teams.

6-157. The assault element collects and secures all EPWs and moves them out of the kill zone to an established location before searching dead enemy bodies. The EPW collection point should provide cover and should not be easily found by enemy forces following the ambush. The friendly assault element searches from the far side of the kill zone to the near side.

6-158. Once the bodies have been thoroughly searched, search teams continue in this manner until all enemy personnel in and near the kill zone have been searched. Enemy bodies should be marked once searched; for example, folded arms over the chest and legs crossed to ensure thoroughness and speed and to avoid duplication of effort.

6-159. The platoon identifies and collects equipment to be carried back and prepares it for transport. Enemy weapon chambers are cleared and put on safe. The platoon also identifies and collects at a central point the enemy equipment to be destroyed. The demolition team prepares the fuse and awaits the signal to initiate. This is normally the last action performed before departing the ambush site. The flank security element returns to the ORP after the demolition team completes its task.

6-160. The flank security teams also may emplace antiarmor mines after the ambush has been initiated if the enemy is known to have armored vehicles which can quickly reinforce the ambushed enemy force. If a flank security team makes enemy contact, it fights as long as possible without becoming decisively engaged. It uses prearranged signals to inform the platoon leader it is breaking contact. The platoon leader may direct a portion of the support element to assist the security element in breaking contact.

6-161. The platoon leader must plan the withdrawal of the platoon from the ambush site. The planning process should include the following:
- Elements normally are withdrawn in the reverse order they established their positions.
- Elements may return to the release point, then to the ORP, depending on the distance between the elements.
- The security element at the ORP must be alert to assist the platoon's return. It maintains security of the ORP while the remainder of the platoon prepares to depart.

6-162. Actions back at the ORP include, but are not limited to, accounting for personnel and equipment, stowing captured equipment, and first aid (as necessary). Upon return personnel within the patrol are reorganized as required and ammunition and equipment redistributed for movement out of the ORP.

SECURITY PATROLS

6-163. Security patrols prevent surprise of the main body by screening to the front, flank, and rear of the main body and detecting and destroying enemy forces in the local area. Security patrols do not operate beyond the range of communication and supporting fires from the main body; especially mortar fires, because they normally operate for limited periods, and are combat-oriented.

6-164. Security patrols are employed both when the main body is stationary and when it is moving. When the main body is stationary, the security patrol prevents enemy infiltration, reconnaissance, or attacks. When the main body is moving, the security patrol prevents the unit from being ambushed or coming into surprise chance contact.

SECTION IV – RECONNAISSANCE PATROLS

6-165. A *reconnaissance patrol* collects information or confirms or disproves the accuracy of information previously gained. The intent for this type of patrol is to avoid enemy contact and accomplish its tactical task without engaging in close combat. With one exception (reconnaissance in force patrol), reconnaissance patrols always try to accomplish their mission without being detected or observed. Because detection cannot always be avoided, a reconnaissance patrol carries the necessary arms and equipment to protect itself and break contact with the enemy.

6-166. A reconnaissance patrol normally travels light, with as few personnel and as little arms, ammunition, and equipment as possible. This increases stealth and cross-country mobility in close terrain. Regardless of how the patrol is armed and equipped, the leader always plans for direct-fire contact with a hostile force. Leaders must anticipate where they may possibly be observed and control the hazard by emplacing measures to lessen their risk. If detected or unanticipated opportunities arise, reconnaissance patrols must be able to rapidly transition to combat. The three types of reconnaissance patrols normally conducted by an Infantry platoon and squad are—

- Area reconnaissance patrol.
- Route reconnaissance patrol.
- Zone reconnaissance patrol.

AREA RECONNAISSANCE PATROL

6-167. Area reconnaissance patrols focus on obtaining detailed information about the enemy activity, terrain, or specific civil considerations within a prescribed area. This area may include a town, a neighborhood, a ridgeline, woods, an airhead, or any other feature critical to operations. The area may consist of a single point (such as a bridge or an installation). Areas are normally smaller than zones and not usually contiguous to other friendly areas targeted for reconnaissance. Because the area is smaller, units conduct an area reconnaissance quicker than a zone reconnaissance. Other unique techniques falling under an area reconnaissance patrol include:

- Point.
- Contact.

Chapter 6

- Civil.
- Tracking.

POINT RECONNAISSANCE

6-168. Point reconnaissance patrol goes straight to a specific location and determines the situation there. As soon as it does so, it either reports the information by radio or returns to the larger unit to report. This patrol can obtain, verify, confirm, or deny extremely specific information for the platoon leader or commander.

CONTACT RECONNAISSANCE

6-169. Contact reconnaissance patrol is a special type of reconnaissance patrol sent from one unit to physically contact and coordinate with another. Modern technology has reduced, but not eliminated, the need for contact patrols. They most often are used today when a U.S. force must contact a non-U.S. coalition partner who lacks compatible communications or position-reporting equipment. Contact patrols may either go to the other unit's position, or the units can meet at a designated contact point. The leader of a contact patrol provides the other unit with information about the location, situation, and intentions of his own unit, and obtains and reports the same information about the contacted unit back to his unit. The contact patrol also observes and reports pertinent information about the area between the two units.

CIVIL RECONNAISSANCE

6-170. Civil reconnaissance patrol is a targeted, planned, and coordinated observation and evaluation of specific civil aspects of the environment. Civil reconnaissance focuses on the civil component, the elements of which are best represented by ASCOPE. Priority information requirements focus on civil reconnaissance for purposes of collecting civil information to enhance situational understanding and facilitate decisionmaking. (Refer to FM 3-57 for more information.) Potential sources of civil information which a coordinated civil reconnaissance plan considers include:
- Ongoing ASCOPE assessments of the area of operations.
- Identified unknowns in civil information:
  - Gaps identified during collation and analysis.
  - Gaps remaining in the area study and area assessment.
- Civil affairs interaction, including but not limited to:
  - Host-nation government officials.
  - Religious leaders.
  - Tribal or clan leaders.
  - Dislocated civilian camp leadership.
  - Dislocated civilians on the move.
  - Infrastructure managers and workers.
  - Local industry personnel.
  - Medical and educational personnel.

TRACKING RECONNAISSANCE

6-171. Tracking reconnaissance patrol is normally a squad-size, possibly smaller, element. It is tasked to follow the trail of a specific enemy unit in order to determine its composition, final destination, and actions en route. Patrol members look for subtle signs left by the enemy as he moves. As they track, they gather information about the enemy unit, the route it took, and surrounding terrain. Normally, a tracking patrol avoids direct fire contact with the tracked unit. Tracking patrols often use tracker dog teams to help them maintain the track.

ROUTE RECONNAISSANCE PATROL

6-172. Obtains detailed information about a specified route and terrain where the enemy could influence movement along a route. Route reconnaissance focuses along a specific line of communications (such as a road, railway, or cross-country mobility corridor). It provides new or updated information on route conditions (such as obstacles and bridge classifications, and enemy and civilian activity along the route). A route reconnaissance includes not only the route itself, but also all terrain along the route from which the enemy could influence the friendly force's movement. The commander normally assigns this mission to use a specific route for friendly movement.

ZONE RECONNAISSANCE PATROL

6-173. Zone reconnaissance involves a directed effort to obtain detailed information on all routes, obstacles, terrain, enemy forces, or specific civil considerations within a zone defined by boundaries. Obstacles include both existing and reinforcing, as well as areas CBRN contamination. Commanders assign zone reconnaissance missions when they need additional information on a zone before committing other forces in the zone. Zone reconnaissance missions are appropriate when the enemy situation is vague, existing knowledge of the terrain is limited, or combat operations have altered the terrain. A zone reconnaissance may include several route or area reconnaissance missions assigned to subordinate units.

6-174. A zone reconnaissance is normally a deliberate, time-consuming process. It takes more time than any other reconnaissance mission, so the commander must allow adequate time to conduct it. A zone reconnaissance is normally conducted over an extended distance and starts from a line of departure. It requires all ground elements executing the zone reconnaissance to be employed abreast of each other. However, when the reconnaissance objective is the enemy force, a commander may forgo a detailed reconnaissance of the zone and focus assets on those named areas of interest that would reveal enemy dispositions and intentions. A reconnaissance unit cannot disregard terrain when focusing on the enemy. However, it minimizes its terrain reconnaissance to that which may influence a named areas of interest.

CONTROL MEASURES

6-175. Control measures help leaders anticipate being detected. They include:

- Rendezvous point: a location designated for an arranged meeting from which to begin an action or phase of an operation or to return to after an operation. This term generally is synonymous with linkup point.
- Release point: a location on a route where marching elements are released from centralized control. (Refer to FM 3-90-1 for more information.) The release point also is used after departing the objective rally point.
- Linkup point: a point where two infiltrating elements in the same or different infiltration lanes are scheduled to consolidate before proceeding with their missions. (Refer to FM 3-90-1 for more information.)

FUNDAMENTALS OF RECONNAISSANCE

6-176. Leaders use the seven fundamentals of reconnaissance to organize their patrols into two forces: a reconnaissance element, and a security element. The seven fundamentals are—
- Ensure continuous reconnaissance.
- Do not keep reconnaissance assets in reserve.
- Orient on the reconnaissance objective.
- Report information rapidly and accurately.
- Retain freedom of maneuver.
- Gain and maintain enemy contact.
- Develop the situation rapidly.

RECONNAISSANCE ELEMENTS

6-177. The reconnaissance element's task is to obtain information requirements for the purposes of facilitating tactical decisionmaking. The primary means is R&S enabled by tactical movement and continuous, accurate reporting. The reconnaissance patrol leader decides how in-depth the reconnaissance will be. A thorough and accurate reconnaissance is important. However, avoiding detection is equally important.

6-178. Below are some of the additional tasks normally associated with a reconnaissance element:
- Reconnoiter all terrain within the assigned area, route, or zone.
- Determine trafficability routes or potential avenues of approach (based on the personnel or vehicles to be used on the route).
  - Inspect and classify all bridges, overpasses, underpasses, and culverts on the route.
  - Locate fords or crossing sites near bridges on the route.
- Determine the time it takes to traverse the route.
- Reconnoiter to the limit of direct fire range.
  - Terrain influencing the area, route, or zone.
  - Built-up areas.
  - Lateral routes.

- Within capabilities, reconnoiter natural and man-made obstacles to ensure mobility along the route. Locate a bypass or reduce/breach, clear, and mark—
  - Lanes.
  - Defiles and other restrictive/severely restrictive terrain.
  - Minefields.
  - Contaminated areas.
  - Log obstacles such as abatis, log cribs, stumps, and posts.
  - AT ditches.
  - Wire entanglements.
  - Fills, such as a raised railroad track.
  - Other obstacles along the route.
- Determine the size, location, and composition of society/human demographics.
- Identify essential infrastructure influencing military operations, including the following:
  - Political, government, and religious organizations and agencies.
  - Physical facilities and utilities (such as power generation, transportation, and communications networks).
- Find all threat forces influencing movement along the area, route, or zone.
- Report information.

Note. Infantry platoons and squads typically do not have the expertise to complete a full technical inspection of bridges, roads, and culverts; this task normally requires Engineer augmentation. Infantry platoons and squads do, however; have the ability to conduct a general assessment.

SECURITY ELEMENTS

6-179. The security element has two tasks: provide early warning of approaching enemy; and provide support by fire to the reconnaissance elements if they come in contact with the enemy. The security element's purpose is to protect the reconnaissance element, thereby allowing it to obtain the information requirement. Security elements tasked to provide early warning must be able to observe avenues of approach into and out of the objective area. If the reconnaissance element is compromised, the security element must be able to quickly support it. It does so by occupying positions enabling it to observe the objective as well as cover the reconnaissance element. Soldiers in these positions must be able to engage the enemy with direct and indirect fire. They also must be able to facilitate communication to higher as well as all supporting assets. This worst-case scenario must be well rehearsed and well thought out.

6-180. Regardless of how the R&S elements are organized, each element always maintains responsibility for its own local security. In a small reconnaissance patrol, the patrol headquarters may form a part of one of the subordinate elements rather than being a separate element. The number and size of the various teams and elements must be

Chapter 6

determined through the leader's METT-TC analysis. There are three ways to organize the R&S elements. (See figure 6-14.)

6-181. The first technique is to organize the reconnaissance elements separate from security elements. This technique is used when the security element is able to support the reconnaissance element from one location. This requires the reconnaissance objective to be defined clearly and area to be fairly open.

6-182. The second technique is to organize the reconnaissance elements and security elements together into R&S teams. This technique is used when the reconnaissance objective is not defined clearly or the teams are not mutually supporting and each reconnaissance element potentially needs its own security force. Within the R&S team, the reconnaissance can be done by one or two individuals while the rest of the element provides security. The number of Soldiers in an R&S team varies depending on the mission. Usually a fire team (three to four Soldiers) is required for an adequate reconnaissance and still provide local security.

6-183. The third technique is to establish R&S teams with an additional, separate security element. The separate security element also-can act as a reserve or as a quick reaction force.

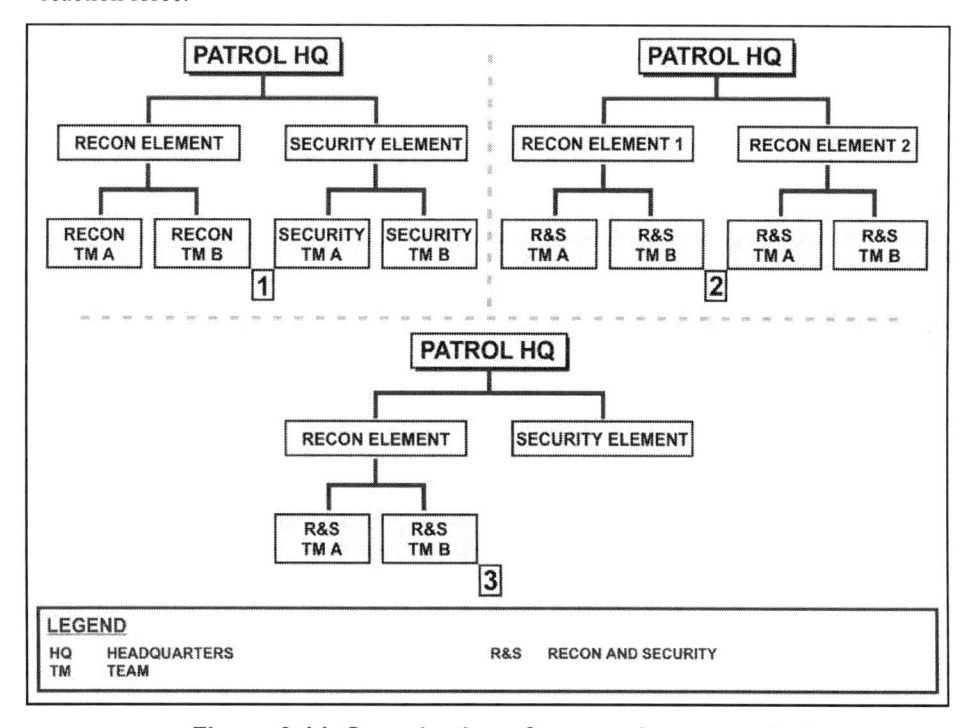

Figure 6-14. Organization of reconnaissance patrols

ACTIONS ON THE RECONNAISSANCE OBJECTIVE

6-184. The actual reconnaissance begins at the designated transition point and ends with a follow-on transition to tactical movement away from the reconnaissance objective. Leaders mark the follow-on transition point with a control measure similar to the first transition point, using a linkup point, rendezvous point, a LOA, or a phase line. During this phase, leaders execute one of the three forms of reconnaissance (area, zone, or route). These forms of reconnaissance are distinguished by the scope of the reconnaissance objective. The forms of reconnaissance patrols Infantry units conduct are area, zone, and route. (See figure 6-15.)

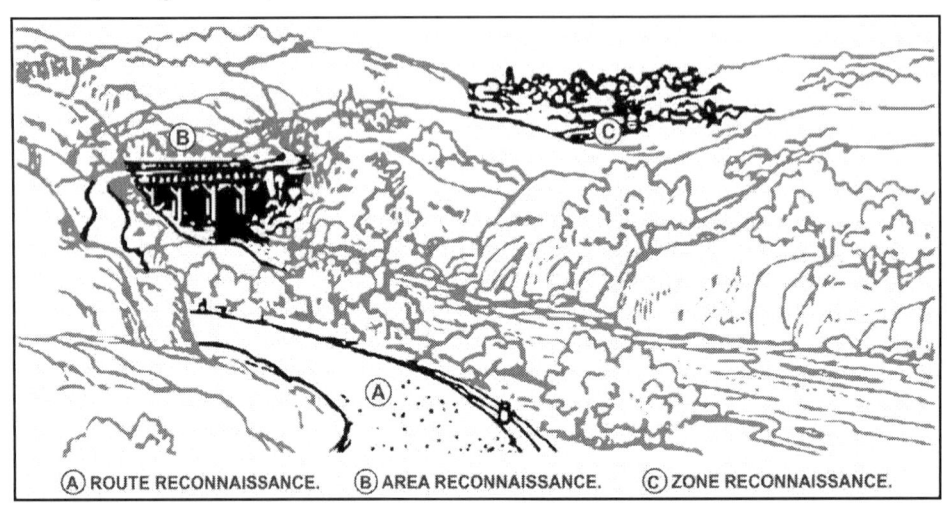

Figure 6-15. Forms of reconnaissance patrols

6-185. To plan for a reconnaissance, use the reverse-planning process. The leader first determines the reconnaissance objective, an information requirement corresponding to the terrain or enemy in a specific area, route, or zone; it may be designated by a control measure such as named areas of interest, checkpoints, objective, route, phase lines, or boundaries. Once the leader has clarified the reconnaissance objective, he determines the observation plan enabling the patrol to obtain the information required. After determining the observation plan, the leader determines the tactical movement necessary to position the patrol to achieve his observation plan.

INFORMATION REQUIREMENTS

6-186. Information requirements are the basis for the development of the CCIRs, the answers to which are needed to allow commanders to make tactical decisions. The controlling headquarters must clearly define the information requirements it wants the patrol to determine. The patrol leader must clarify these information requirements prior to conducting the mission. Table 6-2 (page 6-48) illustrates an example matrix used to capture the information requirements for the headquarters' collection plan.

Chapter 6

Table 6-2. Example infrared collection matrix

INFORMATION REQUIREMENT	LOCATION/ DESCRIPTION	TIME	PURPOSE
Enemy forces within small arms range of intersection	NV 12349875 road intersection	From: 20 1700 Nov To: 21 0600 Nov	Facilitate the platoon's passage through the area

6-187. Information requirement can be enemy-oriented, terrain-oriented, civil-oriented, or a combination. It is important the leader clarifies the requirement prior to conducting the reconnaissance. Knowing this orientation enables the leader to demonstrate the initiative required to meet the higher leader's information requirement.

6-188. Terrain-oriented information requirements focus on determining information on the terrain of a particular area, route, or zone. While the unit looks for enemy presence, the overall intent is to determine the terrain's usefulness for friendly purposes. For example, the company commander may send out a squad-sized reconnaissance patrol to identify a location for the company's future AA. The patrol leader may send out a squad-sized reconnaissance patrol to obtain information about a bridge on a proposed infiltration route.

6-189. Enemy-oriented information requirements focus on finding a particular enemy force. The purpose of enemy-oriented reconnaissance is to confirm or deny planning assumptions. While the unit may be given a terrain feature as a reference point, the overall intent is to find the enemy. This means if the enemy is not in the location referenced, the leader must demonstrate the initiative to find the enemy force within his given parameters.

6-190. Civil-oriented information requirements focus on determining information on the human environment in a particular area, route, or zone. A civil-oriented information requirement is a larger, vaguer category requiring more clarification than the other two categories. Examples of civil-oriented information requirements are the physical infrastructures; service infrastructures such as sewer, water, electric, and trash; the political situation; demographics; and dislocated civilians.

OBSERVATION PLAN

6-191. Once the patrol leader understands the information requirement, he then determines how he will obtain it by developing an observation plan. The leader captures the observation plan as part of the patrol leader's COA sketch. This is done by asking two basic questions:
- What is the best location to obtain the information required?
- What is the best way to obtain the information without compromising the patrol?

6-192. The answer to the first question is: all vantage points and observation posts from which the patrol can best obtain the required information. A vantage point is a temporary position enabling observation of the enemy. It is meant to be occupied only until the enemy activity is confirmed or denied. The answer to the second question is: use the routes and number of teams necessary to occupy the vantage points and observation posts. An observation post is a position where military observations can be made, and fire can be directed and adjusted. Observation posts must possess appropriate communications. The observation post can be short-term (12 hours or less) or long-term, depending upon guidance from higher. Unlike a vantage point, the observation post normally is occupied and surveillance is conducted for a specified period.

6-193. The patrol views the reconnaissance objective from as many perspectives as possible, using whatever combinations of observation posts and vantage points are necessary. The leader selects the tentative locations for patrol's vantage points, observation posts, and movement after analyzing METT-TC. These locations are proposed and are confirmed and adjusted as necessary by the actual leader on the ground. From his analysis, the leader determines how many vantage points and observation posts he must establish and where to position them. Once he decides on these general locations, he designs the routes for necessary movement between these and other control measures (such as the release points and linkup points). Positions should have the following characteristics:

- Covered and concealed routes to and from each position.
- Unobstructed observation of the assigned area, route, or zone. Ideally, the fields of observation of adjacent positions overlap to ensure full coverage.
- Cover and concealment. Leaders select positions with cover and concealment to reduce their vulnerability on the battlefield. Leaders may need to pass up a position with favorable observation capability but no cover and concealment to select a position affording better survivability.
- A location not attracting attention. Positions should not be sited in such locations as a water tower, an isolated grove of trees, or a lone building or tree. These positions draw enemy attention and may be used as enemy artillery target registration posts.
- A location not skylining the observers. Avoid hilltops. Locate positions farther down the slope of the hill or on the side, provided there are covered and concealed routes into and out of the position.

6-194. The locations selected by the patrol are either long range or short range. Long-range positions must be far enough from the objective to be outside enemy's small-arms weapons, sensors, and other local security measures. Long-range positions are the most desirable method for executing a reconnaissance because the patrol does not come in close enough to be detected. If detected, the patrol is able to employ direct and indirect fires. Therefore, it is used whenever METT-TC permits the required information to be gathered from a distance. Security must be maintained by—

- Selecting covered and concealed observation posts.
- Using covered and concealed routes in and around the operations area.
- Deploying security elements, including sensors, to give early warning, and providing covering fire if required.

6-195. Short-range positions are within the range of enemy local security measures and small-arms fire. When information required cannot be obtained by a long-range position, reconnaissance elements move closer to the objective. The vantage points and routes used during short-range observation should be planned carefully and verified prior to using them. Doing so prevents detection by the enemy or friendly units from stumbling into one another or covering ground already passed over by another element.

AREA RECONNAISSANCE ACTIONS AT OBJECTIVE

6-196. Area reconnaissance is a directed effort to obtain detailed information concerning the terrain or enemy activity within a prescribed area. The area may be given as a grid coordinate, an objective, on an overlay. In an area reconnaissance, the patrol uses vantage points or observation posts around the objective to observe it and surrounding area.

6-197. Actions at the objective for an area reconnaissance begin with the patrol in the ORP, and end with a dissemination of information after a linkup of the patrol's subordinate units. The critical actions include:
- Actions from the objective rally point.
- Execute the observation plan.
- Linkup and continue the mission.

ACTIONS FROM THE OBJECTIVE RALLY POINT

6-198. The patrol occupies the ORP and conducts associated priorities of work. While the patrol establishes security and prepares for the mission, the patrol leader and selected personnel conduct a leader's reconnaissance. The leader must accomplish three things during this reconnaissance: pin point the objective and establish surveillance, identify a release point and follow-on linkup point (if required), and confirm the observation plan.

OBSERVATION PLAN FOR AN AREA RECONNAISSANCE

6-199. Upon returning from the leader's reconnaissance, the patrol leader disseminates information and FRAGORDs as required. Once ready, the patrol departs. The leader first establishes security. Once security is in position, the reconnaissance element moves along the specified routes to the observation posts and vantage points in accordance with the observation plan.

SHORT RANGE

6-200. On nearing the objective, the patrol leader should establish a forward release point. It should be sited so it is well-hidden, no closer than 200 meters from known enemy patrol routes, observation posts, or sentry positions. The forward release point provides the patrol leader with a temporary location close to the objective from which he can operate. While the close reconnaissance is in progress, it should be manned by the patrol second in charge and RTO. Only vital transmissions should be made while in the forward release point. The volume setting should be as low as possible on the radio, and if available, the operator should use an earphone.

6-201. The close reconnaissance team should make its final preparation in the forward release point. Movement from the forward release point must be slow and deliberate. Leaders should allow sufficient time for the team to obtain the information. If time is limited, the team should only be required to obtain essential information. If the enemy position is large, or time is limited, the leader may employ more than one close reconnaissance team. If this occurs, each patrol must have clearly defined routes for movement to and from the forward release point. They also must have clearly defined areas in which to conduct their reconnaissance in order to avoid clashes.

6-202. The close reconnaissance team normally consists of one to two observers and two security men. The security men should be close enough to provide protection to the observer, but far enough away so his position is not compromised. When moving in areas close to the enemy position, only one man should move at one time. Accordingly, bounds should be short.

6-203. Once in position, the patrol observes and listens to acquire the needed information. No eating, no talking, and no unnecessary movement occurs at this time. If the reconnaissance element cannot acquire the information needed from its initial position, it retraces the route and repeats the process. This method of reconnaissance is extremely risky. The reconnaissance element must remember the closer it moves to an objective, the greater the risk of being detected.

MULTIPLE RECONNAISSANCE AND SURVEILLANCE TEAMS

6-204. When information cannot be gathered from just one observation post or vantage point, successive points may be used. Once determined, the leader decides how his patrol will actually occupy them. The critical decision is determining the number of teams in the reconnaissance element. The advantages of a single team are the leader's ability to control the team, and a decreased probability of enemy detection. The disadvantages of a single team are the lack of redundancy, and the objective area is observed with just one team. The advantages of using multiple teams include providing the leader redundancy in accomplishing his mission, and ability to look at the objective area from more than one perspective. The disadvantages include the increased probability of being detected by the enemy, and increased difficulty in controlling the teams.

6-205. The leader may include a surveillance team in his reconnaissance of the objective from the ORP. He positions these surveillance teams while on the reconnaissance. He may move them on one route, posting them as they move, or he may direct them to move on separate routes to their assigned locations.

SECURITY ELEMENT

6-206. The subordinate leader responsible for security establishes security at the ORP and positions other security teams as required on likely enemy avenues of approach into the objective area.

ROUTE RECONNAISSANCE EXECUTION

6-207. A route reconnaissance is conducted to obtain detailed information about one route and all its adjacent terrain, or to locate sites for emplacing obstacles. Route reconnaissance is oriented on a road, a narrow axis such as an infiltration lane, or on a general direction of attack. Patrols conducting route reconnaissance operations attempt to view the route from both the friendly and enemy perspective. Infantry platoons and squads require augmentation with technical expertise for a complete detailed route

Chapter 6

reconnaissance. However, platoons are capable of conducting hasty route reconnaissance or area reconnaissance of selected route areas.

CONDUCT

6-208. Route reconnaissance is conducted to obtain and locate the following:
- Detailed information about trafficability on the route and all adjacent terrain.
- Detailed information about an enemy activity or enemy force moving along a route.
- Sites for emplacing hasty obstacles to slow enemy movement.
- Obstacles, chemical, biological, radiological and nuclear contamination, and so forth.

6-209. The Infantry platoon and squad also can be tasked to survey a route in a planned infiltration lane. After being briefed on the proposed infiltration, the patrol leader conducts a thorough map reconnaissance and plans a series of fans along the route. (See figure 6-16.) The coverage must reconnoiter all intersecting routes for a distance greater than the range at which enemy direct-fire weapons could influence the infiltrating forces.

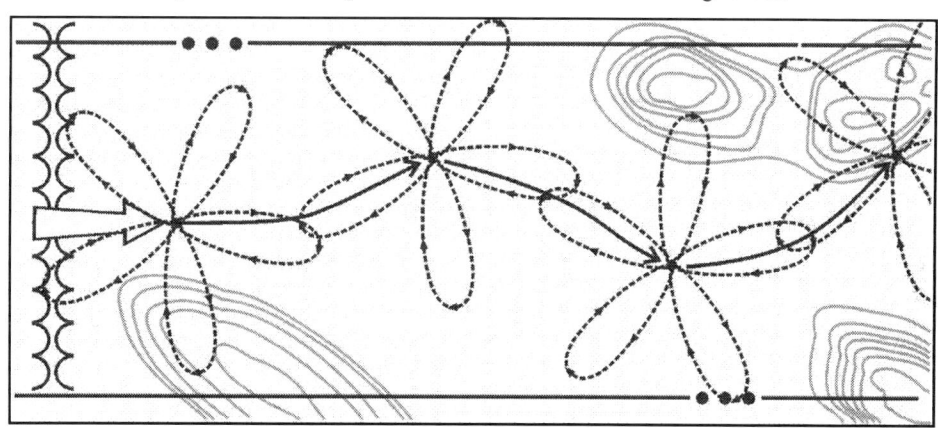

Figure 6-16. Route reconnaissance using fans

6-210. The platoon reports conditions likely to affect friendly movement. These conditions include:
- Presence of the enemy.
- Terrain information.
- Location and condition of bypasses, fords, and obstacles.
- Choke points.
- Route and bridge conditions.

6-211. If all or part of the proposed route is a road, the leader must treat the road as a danger area. The platoon moves parallel to the road, using a covered and concealed route. When required, R&S teams move close to the road to reconnoiter important areas. The platoon plans a different route for its return.

CONTROL MEASURES

6-212. Control measures for a route reconnaissance create an area of operation for the unit conducting the reconnaissance. (Refer to ATP 3-20.98 for more information.) The leader should submit the patrol report in an overlay format including:

- Two grid references (required).
- Magnetic north arrow (required).
- Route drawn to scale (required).
- Title block (required).
- Route classification formula (required).
- Road curves with a radius of less than 45 degrees.
- Steep grades and maximum gradients.
- Road width of constrictions such as bridges and tunnels, with the widths and lengths of the traveled ways (in meters).
- Underpass limitations with limiting heights and widths.
- Bridge bypasses classified as easy, hard, or impossible.
- Civil or military road numbers or other designations.
- Locations of fords, ferries, and tunnels with limiting information.
- Causeways, snow sheds, or galleries if they are in the way. Data about clearance and load-carrying capacity should be included to permit an evaluation to decide whether to strengthen or remove them.

ZONE RECONNAISSANCE METHODS

6-213. A zone reconnaissance is conducted to obtain information on enemy, terrain, and routes within a specified zone. Zone reconnaissance techniques include the use of moving elements, stationary teams, or multiple area reconnaissance actions.

MOVING ELEMENT TECHNIQUES

6-214. When moving elements are used, the elements (squads or fire teams) move along multiple routes to cover the whole zone. When the mission requires a unit to saturate an area, the unit uses one of the following techniques: the fan; the box; converging routes; or successive sectors.

Fan Method

6-215. When using the fan method, the leader first selects a series of ORPs throughout the zone to operate from. The patrol establishes security at the first ORP. Upon confirming the ORP location, the leader confirms reconnaissance routes out from and back to the ORP. These routes form a fan-shaped pattern around the ORP. The routes must overlap to ensure the entire area is reconnoitered. Once the routes are confirmed, the leader sends out R&S teams along the routes. When all R&S teams have returned to the ORP, the platoon collects and disseminates all information to every Soldier before moving on to the next ORP.

Chapter 6

6-216. Each R&S team moves from the ORP along a different fan-shaped route overlapping with others to ensure reconnaissance of the entire area. (See figure 6-17.) These routes should be adjacent to each other. Adjacent routes prevent the patrol from potentially making contact in two different directions. The leader maintains a reserve at the ORP.

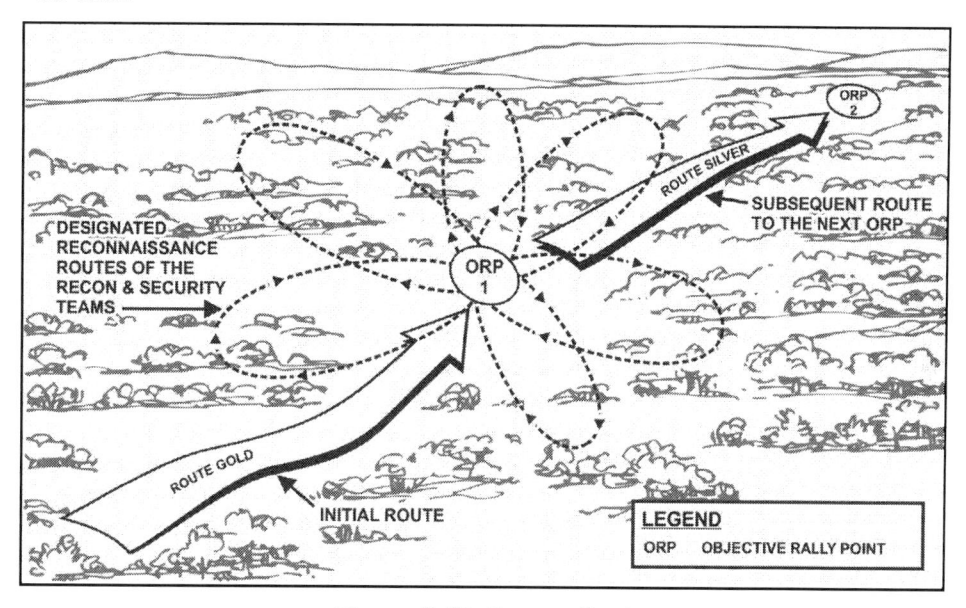

Figure 6-17. Fan method

Box Method

6-217. When using the box method, the leader sends his R&S teams from the ORP along routes forming a boxed-in area. He sends other teams along routes through the area within the box. (See figure 6-18.) All teams meet at a linkup point at the far side of the box from the ORP.

Patrols and Patrolling

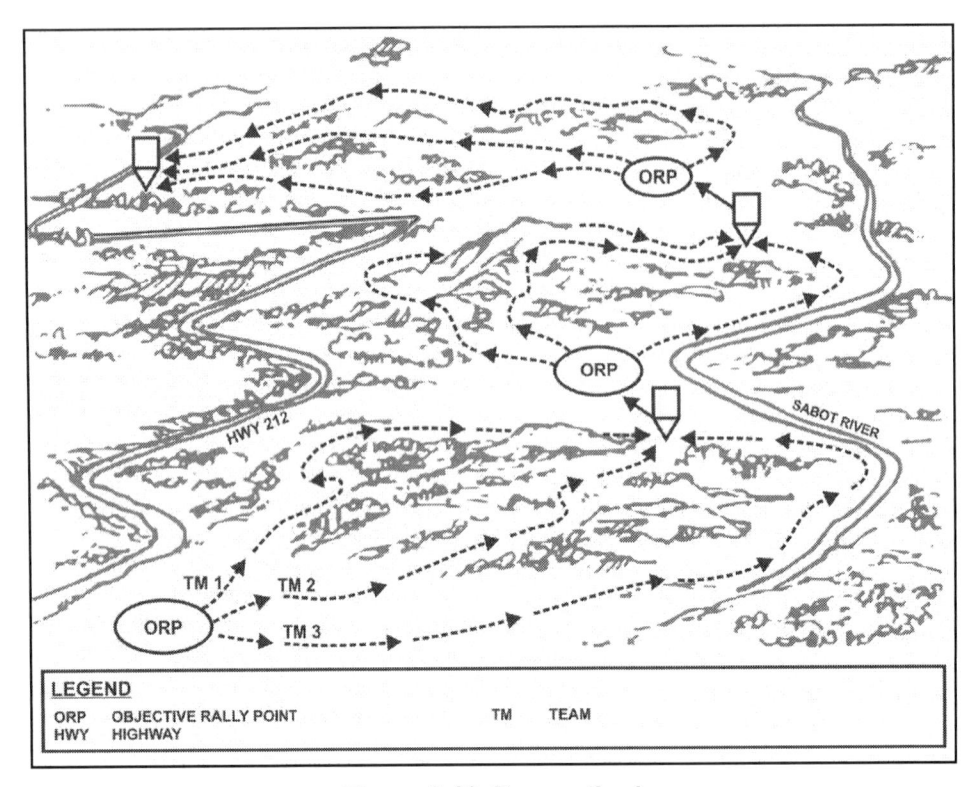

Figure 6-18. Box method

Converging Routes Method

6-218. When using the converging routes method, the leader selects routes from the ORP through the zone to a rendezvous point at the far side of the zone from the ORP. Each R&S team moves along a specified route and uses the fan method to reconnoiter the area between routes. (See figure 6-19, page 6-56.) The leader designates a time for all teams to linkup. Once the unit arrives at the rendezvous point, it halts and establishes security.

Chapter 6

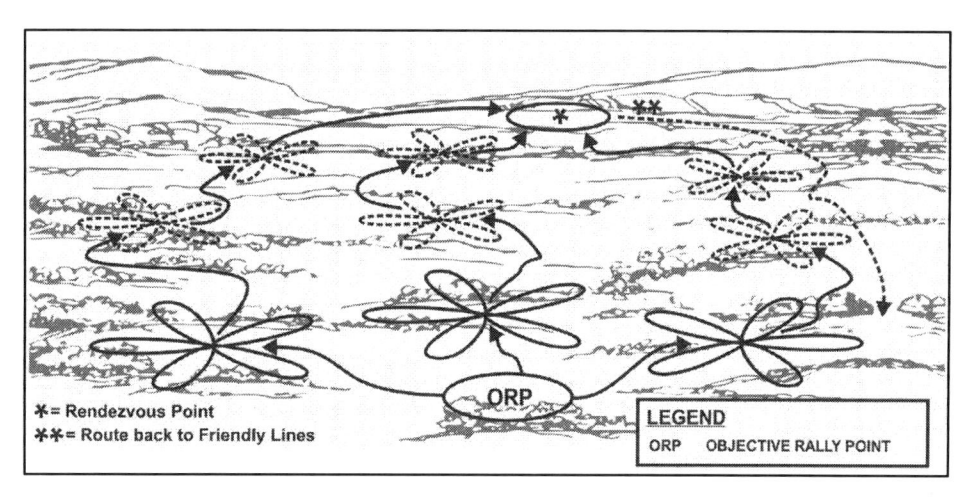

Figure 6-19. Converging routes method

Successive Sector Method

6-219. The successive sector method is a continuation of the converging routes method. (See figure 6-20.) The leader divides the zone into a series of sectors. The platoon uses the converging routes within each sector to reconnoiter to an intermediate linkup point where it collects and disseminates the information gathered to that point. It then reconnoiters to the next sector. Using this method, the leader selects an ORP, a series of reconnaissance routes, and linkup points. The actions from each ORP to each linkup point are the same as in the converging routes method. Each linkup point becomes the ORP for the next phase. Upon linkup at a linkup point, the leader again confirms or selects reconnaissance routes, a linkup time, and next linkup point. This action continues until the entire zone has been reconnoitered. Once the reconnaissance is completed, the unit returns to friendly lines.

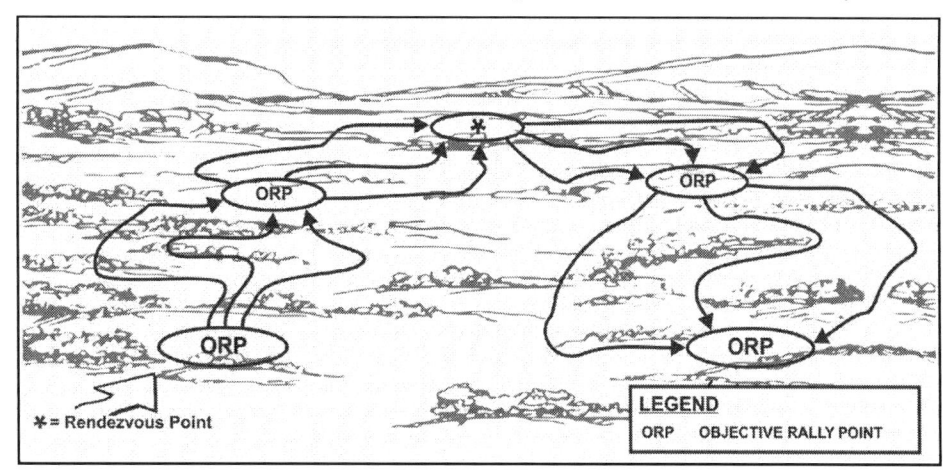

Figure 6-20. Successive sector method

STATIONARY ELEMENT TECHNIQUES

6-220. Using the stationary element technique, the leader positions R&S teams in locations where they can collectively observe the entire zone for long-term, continuous information gathering. (See figure 6-21.) The leader considers sustainment requirements when developing his Soldiers' load plans.

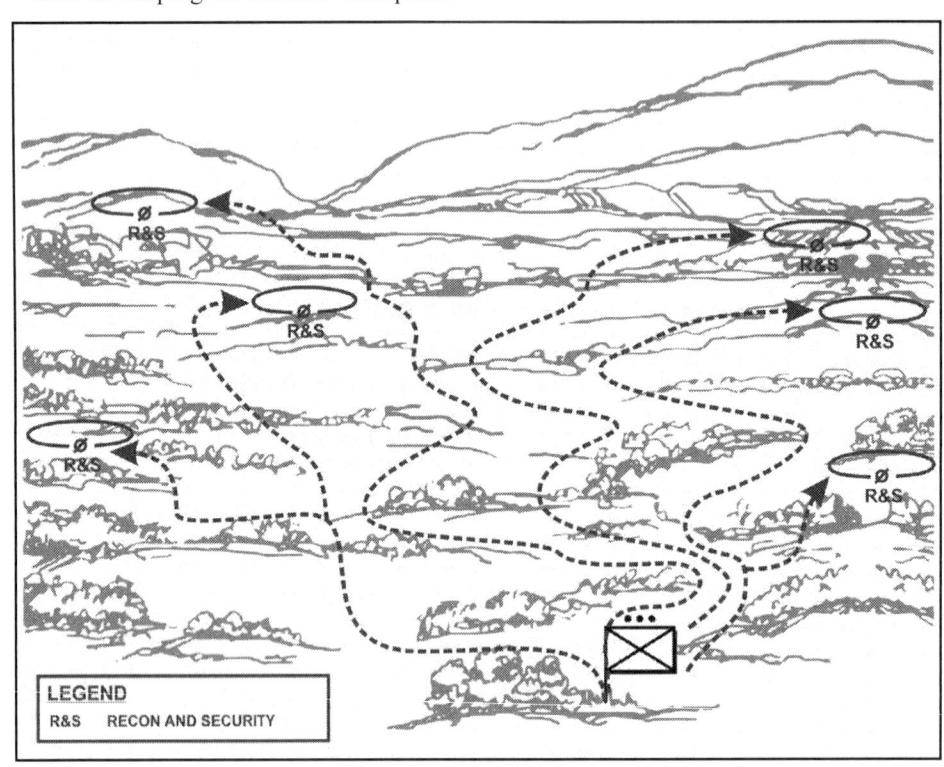

Figure 6-21. Zone reconnaissance using the stationary element technique

MULTIPLE AREA RECONNAISSANCE

6-221. When using multiple area reconnaissance the leader tasks each of his subordinate units to conduct a series of area reconnaissance actions within the zone. (See figure 6-22, page 6-58.)

Chapter 6

Commentary

Below are line wire diagrams for the task organization of a Raid and Ambush. They should help you visualize the way to organize your forces.

Generic Ambush Task ORG

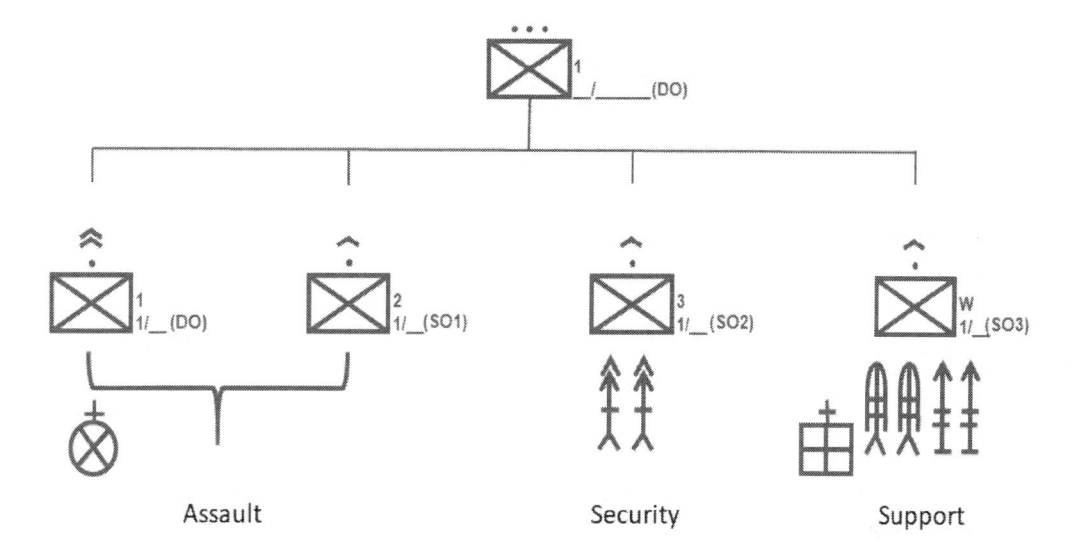

Command element (DO)

- **Assault** — 1/__(DO) and 2/__(SO1)
- **Security** — 3/__(SO2)
- **Support** — W 1/__(SO3)

Generic Raid Task ORG

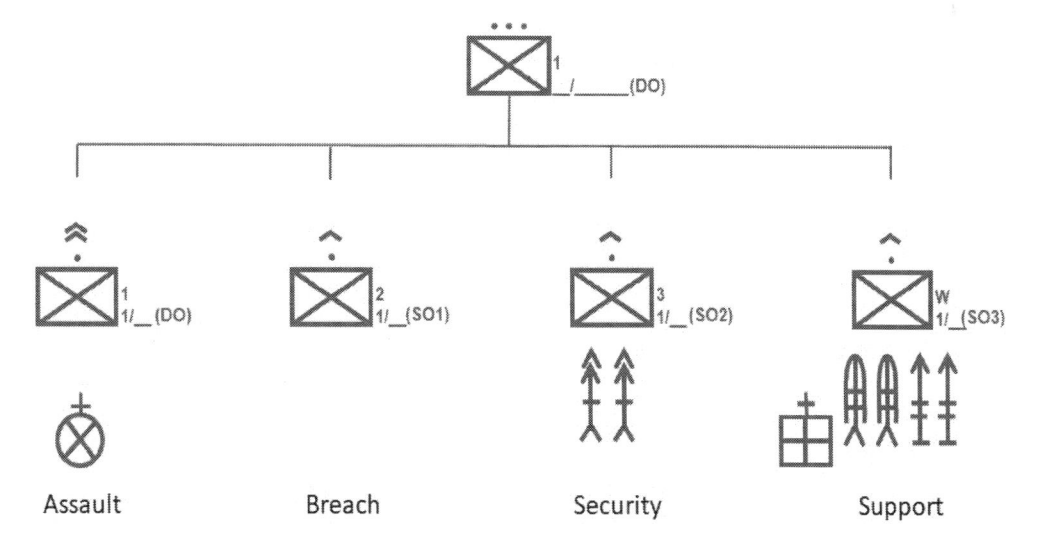

Command element (DO)

- **Assault** — 1/__(DO)
- **Breach** — 2/__(SO1)
- **Security** — 3/__(SO2)
- **Support** — W 1/__(SO3)

ATP 3-21.8   12 April 2016

This page intentionally left blank.

Chapter 6

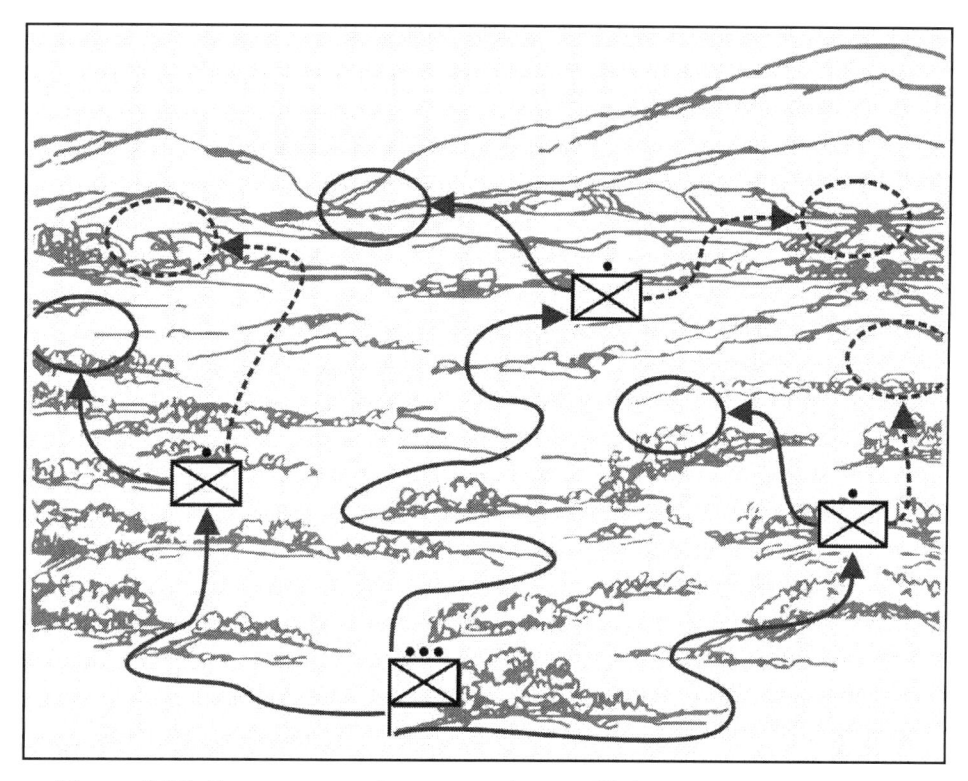

Figure 6-22. Zone reconnaissance using multiple area reconnaissance

SECTION V – POST PATROL ACTIVITIES

6-222. Immediately on reentering the secure base or rejoining the unit, the patrol leader should positively verify all members of the patrol and attachments, prisoners, or detainees are accounted for. The patrol leader should check in with the company or battalion command post as soon as possible after entering the base location or rejoining the unit. Additional post patrol activities will include:
- Account for weapons and equipment.
- Debrief.
- Patrol report.

ACCOUNTING FOR WEAPONS AND EQUIPMENT

6-223. The patrol leader is responsible for verifying all the patrol's weapons, ammunition, munitions and equipment are properly accounted for and reporting the status to the commander or the operations center. Lost or missing equipment must be reported immediately. The patrol may be ordered to return to the area where it was lost, if it is assessed safe to do so, and try to find the item.

DEBRIEF

6-224. The patrol leader should conduct a "debrief" with the entire patrol as soon as possible after entering the base or rejoining the main body. This allows him to capture low-level information while the Soldiers' memories are fresh and information relevant. He should go over the notes taken by the patrol scribe chronologically to facilitate the discussion. Every patrol member should participate. If there was an interpreter or other attachments with the patrol, they should be debriefed as a source of human intelligence by allowing them to pass on information they obtained during the patrol. The patrol leader includes significant information necessary during the debriefing of his patrol report to the commander.

6-225. Normally the debriefing is oral. Sometimes a written report is required. Information on the written report should include:

- Size and composition of the unit conducting the patrol.
- Mission of the platoon such as type of patrol, location, and purpose.
- Departure and return times.
- Routes. Use checkpoints, grid coordinates for each leg or include an overlay.
- Detailed description of terrain and enemy positions identified.
- Results of contact with the enemy.
- Unit status at the conclusion of the patrol mission, including the disposition of dead or wounded Soldiers.
- Number of isolated Soldiers platoon/squad unable to recover during execution of the mission.
- Conclusions or recommendations.

PATROL REPORT

6-226. The patrol leader is responsible for the patrol report, and may be assisted by his assistant patrol leader and specialist personnel attached to the patrol. Immediately after the debriefing, the patrol leader should render his patrol report to the commander. This report may be verbal or written, simple, or elaborate depending on the situation and commander's requirements.

6-227. The commander may have the patrol leader render his report to the battalion intelligence officer or to the duty officer at the battalion command post, especially during stability. The patrol report (see figure 6-23, page 6-60) should include a description of the actual route taken by the patrol (as opposed to the planned route), including halt locations. If the unit uses digital mission command systems automatically tracking and displaying the patrol's route, the information is known already. If not, the patrol leader reports it.

6-228. When GPS devices are used by the patrol, gathering route information is easier and faster. The actual route the patrol took is important for planning future patrol routes and actions. Enemy intelligence operations attempt to identify pattern settings by U.S. and coalition patrols, including the locations of halts. This may result in attack against locations regularly used by security forces.

Chapter 6

6-229. Additional information may include the number of biometric enrollments and identification on the BEWL; was anyone detained according to the instructions on the BEWL; and what is the status?

Patrol Report (Example)

To: (Commander of unit ordering the patrol)
From: (Rank and name of the patrol leader)
Title: PATROL SITREP for Patrol # (Patrol designation or number per unit tactical SOP)
DTG Patrol Departed and DTG Patrol Returned: (All dates and times per the unit tactical SOP)

Mission: (Restatement of original mission, including any modifications or FRAGORDs receive during the patrol's duration)

Friendly forces: (Only specify details on patrol composition that have changed.)

Situation: (The patrol leader's evaluation of the mission accomplishment with a general description of any significant sightings)

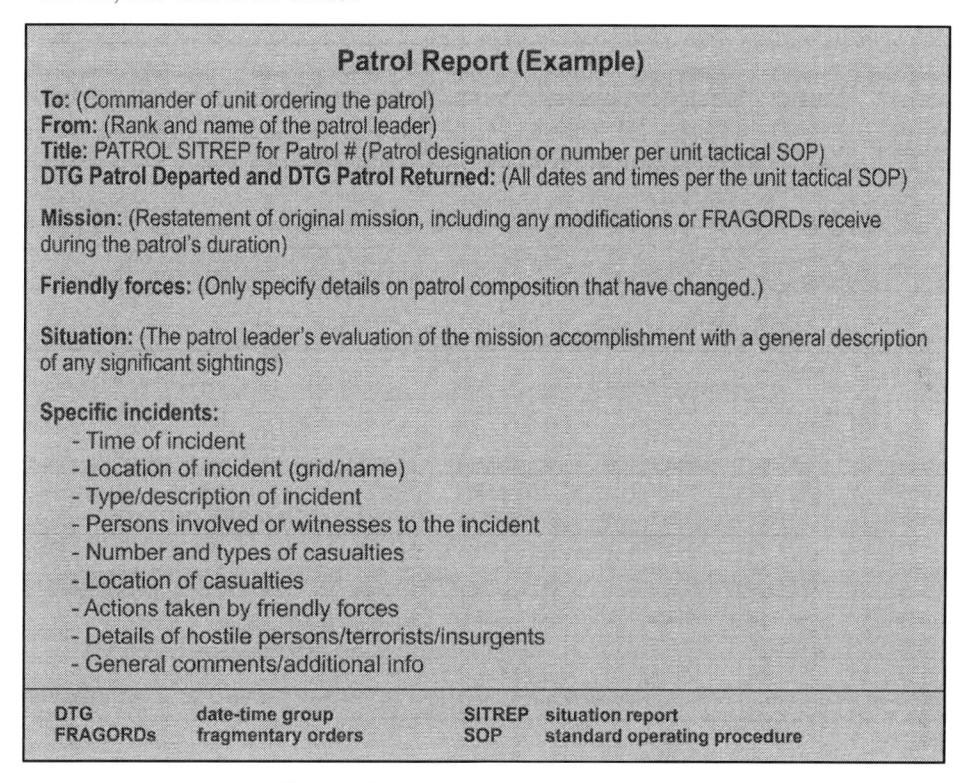

Specific incidents:
- Time of incident
- Location of incident (grid/name)
- Type/description of incident
- Persons involved or witnesses to the incident
- Number and types of casualties
- Location of casualties
- Actions taken by friendly forces
- Details of hostile persons/terrorists/insurgents
- General comments/additional info

DTG	date-time group	SITREP	situation report
FRAGORDs	fragmentary orders	SOP	standard operating procedure

Figure 6-23. Patrol report example

Chapter 7
Sustainment

Sustainment is the provision of logistics, personnel services, and HSS necessary to maintain operations until successful mission completion. In the Infantry platoon, the BFV platoon, and the Stryker platoon, the platoon leader handles sustainment; the platoon sergeant and squad leader have the ultimate responsibility for sustainment. The platoon sergeant is the platoon's primary sustainment operator; he works closely with the company executive officer and first sergeant to ensure he receives the required support for the platoon's assigned missions. Sustainment responsibilities and procedures in the platoon remain basically the same. The company normally forecasts supplies and "pushes" rather than "pulls" them to the platoon. This chapter covers: responsibilities, unit combat and basic loads, trains, and functions of sustainment.

SECTION I – RESPONSIBILITIES

7-1. The Infantry platoon and squad must plan, prepare, and execute its portion of the Infantry company sustainment plan. Concurrent with other operational planning, the platoon develops its sustainment plan during the mission analysis and refines it in the war-gaming portion of the TLP. Rehearsals normally are conducted at each echelon to ensure the smooth, continuous flow of materiel and services.

7-2. Sustainment responsibilities for the Infantry platoon and squad include—report and request support requirements through the company and ensure sustainment operations are properly executed when support elements arrive in the platoon area. The platoon sergeant is normally in charge of these functions, with guidance and oversight provided by the platoon leader. The platoon sergeant must submit accurate personnel and logistical reports, along with other necessary information and requests.

PLATOON LEADER

7-3. The platoon leader is responsible for his platoon's execution of the sustainment plan at platoon level. He plans and relays support requirements for mission accomplishment to the company headquarters where it is consolidated and passed on.

PLATOON SERGEANT

7-4. The platoon sergeant is the platoon's primary sustainment planner, coordinator, and operator; reporting directly to the platoon leader. He executes the platoon's logistical plan,

Chapter 7

relying heavily on platoon and company SOPs. The platoon sergeant directly supervises and controls the platoon's assets. During preparations of the mission, he works closely with the platoon leader and squad leaders to determine specific support requirements of the tactical plan. He then ensures proper arrangements are made to provide those support requirements. The platoon sergeant also performs these logistical functions:

- Determines the location of the platoon's resupply point based on data developed during planning and war-gaming process.
- Compiles DA Form 2404 (*Equipment Inspection and Maintenance Worksheet*) or DA Form 5988-E (*Equipment Maintenance and Inspection Worksheet*), from the squad leaders and provides updates to the platoon leader as required.
- Ensures the platoon executes sustainment operations according to the company's sustainment plan.
- Leads the sustainment rehearsal in coordination with squad leaders to ensure integration into the platoon's rehearsal.
- Assists the platoon leader in developing sustainment priorities and guidance according to the Infantry company's concept of support, and enforces those priorities.
- Conducts close coordination with the company executive officer and first sergeant for planning and to resource platoon missions.
- Coordinates and synchronizes human resources support with the company first sergeant. This includes personnel accountability reports, casualty reports, replacement operations, personnel readiness management, mail operations, essential personnel services, and other administrative or personnel requirements.
- Meets the logistics package (LOGPAC) at the company logistics release point (LRP); guides it to the Infantry platoon resupply point and supervises resupply operations.
- Provides an Infantry platoon orientation for new personnel and, in consultation with the platoon leader makes recommendations on replacements to the platoon's leadership.
- Directs and supervises evacuation of casualties, detainees, and damaged equipment.
- Directs and supervises the collection, initial identification, and evacuation of human remains to the mortuary affairs collection point.
- Maintains the Infantry platoon manning roster.
- Cross-leveling supplies and equipment throughout the platoon.
- Coordinating logistics/personnel requirements with attached or operational control units.

SQUAD LEADER

7-5. Squad leader sustainment duties include:
- Ensuring Soldiers perform proper maintenance on all assigned equipment.
- Ensuring Soldiers maintain personal hygiene.
- Compiling personnel and logistics reports of the platoon and submitting them to the platoon sergeant as directed or in accordance with unit SOP.

Sustainment

- Obtaining supplies, equipment (except Class VIII), and mail from the platoon sergeant and ensuring proper distribution.
- Cross-leveling supplies and equipment throughout the squad.

> *Note.* It is vital the squad leader ensures all squad members carry their own improved first aid kit to sustain survivability.

COMBAT LIFESAVER

7-6. CLS is a nonmedical Soldier trained to provide advanced first aid and lifesaving procedures beyond the level of self-aid or buddy aid. The CLS is not intended to take the place of platoon combat medic or medical personnel. His specialized training can slow deterioration of a wounded Soldier's condition until treatment by medical personnel is possible. + Each certified CLS is issued a CLS aid bag. Whenever possible, the platoon leader or platoon sergeant ensures there is at least one CLS qualified Soldier in each fire team.

TRAINING

7-7. + Because combat lifesavers are an organic capability, the platoon should make the Combat Lifesaver Program a training priority.

DUTIES

7-8. + The CLS ensures the squad CLS bag and litters are properly packed. Identifies Class VIII shortages to the platoon medic, and participates in all + CLS and litter-carry drills. His advanced first-aid skills are called upon in the field until casualties can be evacuated or medical personnel arrive. The CLS knows the location of the CCP and SOP for establishing it.

> *Note.* The CLS should have a laminated quick reference nine-line medical evacuation card.

SECTION II – SOLDIER, COMBAT, AND UNIT BASIC LOADS

7-9. Determining the Soldier's load is a critical leader task. The Soldier's load is always METT-TC dependent and must be closely monitored. Soldiers cannot afford to carry unnecessary equipment into battle. The primary consideration is not "how" much a Soldier can carry, but how much can he carry "without" impairing his combat effectiveness. While Leaders cannot be prepared for all contingencies, they must learn to prepare for the most likely based on available information. (Refer to FM 21.18 for detailed information.)

Chapter 7

SOLDIER LOAD

7-10. The Soldier's load is a main concern of the leader. How much is carried, how far, and in what configuration are important mission considerations. Commanders and leaders must balance the risk to their soldiers from the enemy against the risk to mission accomplishment due to excess loads, soldier exhaustion, and injury. Leaders must ensure that soldiers travel as light as possible. Commanders and leaders must be willing to accept calculated risks to reduce the soldier's load and they should base load limits on well thought out METT-TC analysis.

7-11. Personal protection equipment constitutes the largest weight category of Soldiers load. The greatest PPE weight is body armor that additionally limits the Soldier's ability to maintain body core temperature and, to varying degrees, regulate breathing due to constriction of the torso. Depending on mission variables and environmental conditions, commanders and leaders may adjust the level of body armor protection or even remove body armor balancing an increased risk to individual soldiers to improve the likelihood of mission accomplishment.

7-12. Equipment and ammunition loads must be tailored to mission requirements and the likely enemy threat. For example, if the enemy threat does not include armor formations, leaders may not include the Javelin CCMS. In certain circumstances, it may be appropriate for units to carry additional small arms ammunition due to sustainment constraints. In other circumstances, based on the enemy threat and historical analysis it may be necessary to carry mine detectors but not ECM equipment.

7-13. The platoon's planning and preparation processes will include detailed load planning and calculation. This assists leaders and Soldiers in organizing tactical loads to manage energy expenditure and combat effectiveness. (See table 7-1.)

Table 7-1. Example of METT-TC Analysis

MISSION	ENEMY	TIME	TROOPS	TERRAIN	CIVIL CONSIDERATIONS	LOAD ANALYSIS
Platoon (as a part of a company) clears by conducting a movement to contact to defeat enemy forces in the area of operation (AO)	Dismounted Infantry platoon with small arms	Expected duration is 24 to 48 hours	3 squads plus weapons squad	Severely restricted terrain, rolling hills, dense vegetation, high humidity, high temperature	None	Approach march load without body armor, only light antitank (AT)/bunker defeat munitions (BDM) weapons, 2x stripped meals ready to eat (MRE)
Platoon (as a part of a company) raids to seize an objective to capture or kill enemy elements	Dismounted Infantry reinforced squad	Expected duration is less than 24 hours	3 squads plus weapons squad	Severely restricted urban terrain, limited visibility, moderately high temperature	Non-combatants present in vicinity the target objective	Fighting load, body armor with front/back/side plates
Platoon (as a part of a company) attacks to seize an enemy objective	Dismounted Infantry platoon with small arms and light AT weapons in a prepared defense	Expected duration is 24 to 48 hours	3 squads plus weapons squad	Severely restricted terrain, rolling steep hills, dense vegetation, freezing temperature/ snow fall	None	Approach march load, cold weather uniforms, extra silks, fleece, socks, body armor with front/back plates, only light AT/BDM weapons, 2x stripped MRE

Chapter 7

Table 7-1. Example of METT-TC analysis (continued)

MISSION	ENEMY	TIME	TROOPS	TERRAIN	CIVIL CONSIDERATIONS	LOAD ANALYSIS
Stryker platoon (as a part of a company) attacks to seize an enemy objective	Mechanized Infantry defending in vicinity a small village, Former Soviet Union (FSU) Armored Infantry Combat Vehicle (BMP1)-FSU Armored Personnel Carrier (BTR) mix	Expected duration is less than 24 hours	3 squads plus weapons squad	Restricted terrain, moderate vegetation, moderate temperature	Non-combatants present in vicinity the target objective	Fighting load, body armor with front/back plates, Javelin combat missile systems (CCMS) with 2x additional rounds

7-14. Maximum effort should be placed on echeloning excess loads. Leaders must resist the mindset that we must carry everything to be prepared for every eventuality. Leaders at the lowest levels must enforce load discipline to ensure that soldiers do not voluntarily carry excess weight. Additionally, leaders must rely on the chain of command to deliver equipment forward for subsequent operations.

Note. The ability of an Infantry Soldier to fight is directly related to the load he must carry.

7-15. An excessive load reduces energy and agility. A Soldier carrying an excessive load is at a disadvantage when he must react to enemy contact. Conversely, if the load is tailored to be light, leaders may make a decision to leave behind mission-essential or crucial equipment to balance the load. Sometimes a Soldier must carry more than the recommended combat load. However, leaders must realize how this will affect the unit's overall effectiveness. (FM 21.18 provides additional information on a Soldier's load.)

7-16. Infantry forces are designed to be flexible and responsive in all types of terrain and environments, and for this reason, they consist mainly of foot-mobile fighters. Their success depends on the ability of Infantry Soldiers to deliver the appropriate weapon systems and materiel, to the decisive place on the battlefield in a timely manner; while at the same time, maintaining the ability to defeat the enemy and survive. The Soldier's load

Sustainment

is managed at the company and platoon level; however, standards are established at the battalion level using planning considerations to ensure Soldiers are properly equipped, and mentally and physically ready for combat.

COMBAT LOADS

7-17. A combat load is determined by the mission leader and consists of only what is necessary to fight and survive immediate combat operations. The levels of combat loads are—

- Fighting loads.
- Approach march loads
- Emergency approach march loads.

FIGHTING LOAD

7-18. A fighting load is the essential items the Soldier needs to fight, such as, weapon, UBL of ammo and grenades, night vision goggles, and protective mask. Items can be added or removed based on METT-TC and other factors. Excessive combat loads of assaulting troops must be configured so the excess can be redistributed or shed (leaving only the fighting load) before or upon contact with the enemy.

APPROACH MARCH LOAD

7-19. An approach march load contains those operational essential equipment that are needed for extended operations, in addition to the fighting load. These items are dropped in an assault position, ORP, or other rally point, before or upon contact with the enemy. Soldiers must carry enough equipment and munitions to fight and exist until a planned resupply can take place.

EMERGENCY APPROACH MARCH LOAD

7-20. Circumstances could require Soldiers to carry excess loads (greater than 45 percent of body weight) such as approach marches through terrain impassable to vehicles or where ground and air transportation resources are not available. (Refer to FM 21.18 for detailed information.)

7-21. These emergency approach march loads can be carried by well-conditioned Soldiers. Although loads of up to 70 percent or more of an individual body weight are feasible, the Soldier will become fatigued or possibly injured. If possible, contact with the enemy should be avoided since march speeds will be slowed tremendously

UNIT BASIC LOAD

7-22. The platoon's combat load varies by mission and includes the supplies physically carried into the fight. The leader may direct minimum requirements or be specific for composition of the combat load. Often, the unit SOP or the platoon leader specifies most items. The unit basic load includes supplies kept by the platoon for use in combat. The

Chapter 7

quantity of most unit basic load supply items depends on how many days in combat the platoon might have to sustain itself without resupply. For Class V ammunition, the higher commander or SOP specifies the platoon's basic load.

SUSTAINMENT LOAD

7-23. A sustainment load consists of the equipment required by the company commander for sustained operations. This equipment usually is stored by the company supply section in the field trains and brought forward when needed. A sustainment load can include rucksacks, squad duffel bags, and sleeping bags. In combat, protective items for specific threats may be stored in preconfigured unit loads.

PLANNING CONSIDERATION

7-24. Planning sustainment operations is primarily a company- and battalion-level operation. While the company commander and executive officer plan the operation, the platoon leader is responsible for execution at platoon level.

7-25. Sustainment at the Infantry platoon level is characterized by the following:
- Responsiveness.
- Economy.
- Flexibility.
- Integration.
- Survivability.

RESPONSIVENESS

7-26. To be effective sustainment needs to be responsive. This requires users to provide timely requests for supplies and support while requiring providers to anticipate user needs in advance.

ECONOMY

7-27. To be efficient, sustainment providers and users exercise conservation. Because resources always are limited, it is in the best interest of everyone to use only what is needed. The principle of economy necessitates that Soldiers, leaders, and their units conserve resources whenever possible. This also ensures other Soldiers and units will have the supplies they need.

FLEXIBILITY

7-28. The principle of flexibility embodies the chaotic nature of combat. Providers and users alike remain aware that, despite the best efforts of all involved, things seldom go as planned; shipments are delayed, convoys are attacked, and supplies are destroyed. Supporting the needs of both the individual unit and the rest of the units on the battlefield requires both the user and provider to know what they need, when they need it and possible substitutes.

INTEGRATION

7-29. To function properly, sustainment considerations must be integrated into every aspect of an operation. Sustainment is not branch or rank specific— it is an essential part of all operations at all levels by all Soldiers. Again, without sustainment units cannot accomplish their mission.

SURVIVABILITY

7-30. On the whole, sustainment assets are necessary yet finite resources that are easily destroyed. Units without their classes of supply cannot fight. Accordingly, survivability of sustainment assets is a high priority for everyone. This affects the platoon in two ways. First, units may be required to conduct security missions for sustainment assets, such as convoy security, base security, and response force activities. Second, units must ensure the survivability of their own supplies and any asset that might be under their charge by properly safeguarding them.

7-31. Sustainment for mounted platoons are additionally characterized by the following:
- Anticipation.
- Simplicity.
- Continuity.
- Improvisation.

SECTION III – FUNCTIONS OF SUSTAINMENT

7-32. Sustainment planning is fully integrated into all operational planning. The company SOP should be the basis for sustainment operations, with planning conducted to determine specific requirements and to prepare for contingencies. The platoon order should address specific support matters of the mission. Deviations from the sustainment SOPs should be covered early in the planning process. In some situations, sustainment planning begins before receipt of the mission, as part of the ongoing process of refining the sustainment plan.

DEVELOPMENT OF THE PLATOON SUSTAINMENT PLAN

7-33. The Infantry platoon leader develops his sustainment plan by determining exactly what he has on hand to accurately estimate his support requirements. It is critical for the company to know what the platoon has on hand for designated critical supplies. This process is important not only in confirming the validity of the sustainment plan but also in ensuring the platoon's support requests are submitted as early as possible. The platoon leader can formulate his sustainment execution plan and submit support requests based on the results of his maneuver plan.

Chapter 7

7-34. The sustainment plan should provide answers to operational questions such as the following:
- *Types of support.* Based on the nature of the operation and specific tactical factors, what types of support will the platoon need?
- *Quantities.* In what quantities will this support be required?
  - Will emergency resupply (Class III and V) be required during the battle?
  - Does this operation require prestocked supplies?
- *Threat.* What are the composition, disposition, and capabilities of the expected enemy threat? How will these affect sustainment plan during execution?
  - Where and when will the expected contact occur?
  - What are the platoon's expected casualties and vehicle losses based on the nature and location of expected contact?
  - What impact will the enemy's special weapons capabilities (such as CBRN) have on the battle and on expected sustainment requirements?
  - How many EPWs are expected, and where?
- *Terrain and weather.* How will terrain and weather affect sustainment plan during the battle?
  - What ground will provide the best security for maintenance and CCPs?
  - What are the platoon's vehicle and casualty evacuation routes?
  - What are the company's dirty routes for evacuating contaminated personnel, vehicles, and equipment?
- *Time and location.* When and where will the platoon need sustainment?
  - Based on the nature and location of expected contact, what are the best sites for the CCP?
  - Where will the EPW collection points be located?
- *Requirements.* What are the support requirements, by element and type of support?
  - Which section has priority for emergency Class III resupply?
  - Which section or squad has priority for emergency Class V resupply?
- *Risk.* Will lulls in the battle permit support elements to conduct resupply operations in relative safety?
- *Resupply techniques.* Based on information developed during the sustainment planning process, which resupply technique should the platoon use?

SUPPLY AND FIELD SERVICES

7-35. The general classes of resupply operations are routine, emergency, or prestock. The Infantry platoon and squad SOP specifies cues and procedures for each method, which the platoon and squad rehearse during training exercises. The actual method selected for resupply in the field depends on METT-TC.

Sustainment

7-36. Supplies are divided into 10 major categories, which are referred to as classes. They are:
- Class I – Food, rations and water.
- Class II – Clothing.
- Class III – Petroleum, oil, and lubricants.
- Class IV– Fortification and barrier materiels.
- Class V – Ammunition.
- Class VI – Personal items.
- Class VII – Major end items.
- + Class VIII – Medical materiel and supplies (including blood, blood products, and repair parts for medical items).
- Class IX – Repair parts.
- Class X – Miscellaneous supplies.

7-37. Resupply operations fall into one of three classifications: routine, emergency, or prestock. The platoon and company SOP specifies cues for each method. The platoon should rehearse or conduct resupply operations every time they conduct field training. The actual method selected for resupply in the field depends on METT-TC.

COMPANY TRAINS

7-38. The company trains provide sustainment for subordinate platoons of the Infantry company during combat operations. Company trains usually include the first sergeant; supply sergeant, armorer. Casualty evacuation team's maybe collocated in the trains based on the situation. Usually, the FSC provides a field maintenance team, with capabilities for maintenance, recovery, and limited combat spares. The supply sergeant can collocate in the combat trains, if it facilitates LOGPAC operations. The 1SG usually directs movement and employment of the company trains; although the company commander may assign the responsibility to the company XO. Generally, company trains are located between 500 and 1000 meters or a major terrain feature away from the company's combat operations. By placing at least one terrain feature between it and the enemy, company trains will be out of the enemy's direct fire weapons.

> *Note.* METT-TC ultimately dictates the actual distance at which the company trains operates.

ROUTINE RESUPPLY

7-39. Routine resupply operations cover items in Classes I, III, V, and IX as well as mail and other items the Infantry platoon and squad requests. Whenever possible, the Infantry company should conduct routine resupply daily, ideally during limited visibility. BFVs and other large combat vehicles use large amounts of fuel, so the platoon must resupply Class III at every opportunity.

Chapter 7

Logistics Package

7-40. The LOGPAC technique is a simple, efficient way to accomplish routine resupply operations. The key feature is a centrally organized resupply convoy originating at the unit trains. It carries all items needed to sustain the Infantry platoon and squad for a specific period, usually 24 hours or until the next scheduled LOGPAC. Infantry company and Infantry battalion SOPs specify the exact composition and march order of the LOGPAC.

Preparation

7-41. The Infantry platoon must provide supply requests to the company in order to receive supplies. Based on the requests, he then assembles the LOGPAC under the supervision of the FSC or the headquarters company (HHC) or FSC commander. He obtains the following:
- Class I, Class III (bulk and packaged products), and Class V supplies from the forward support company. This usually entails employment of one or two fuel heavy expanded mobility tactical trucks (HEMTT) and one or two cargo HEMTT.
- Class II, Class IV (basic load resupply only), Class VI, and Class VII supplies from Infantry battalion S-4 personnel in the field trains.
- Routine Class IX supplies and maintenance documents (as required) from the prescribed load list section in the field trains.
- Replacement personnel and Soldiers returning from a medical treatment facility.
- Vehicles returning to the company area from maintenance.
- Mail and personnel action documents (including awards and finance and legal documents) from the battalion S-1 section.

7-42. When LOGPAC preparations are completed, the supply sergeant initiates tactical movement to the LRP under the supervision of the FSC, support platoon leader. The supply sergeant and LOGPAC linkup with the company element (company XO, 1SG or security element from a platoon) at the LRP.

Actions at the Logistics Release Point

7-43. When the company representative arrives at the LRP to pick up the Infantry company LOGPAC, he updates all personnel and logistical reports and is briefed by the field trains officer in charge on changes to the tactical or support situation. He then escorts the convoy to the company resupply point, providing security during movement from the LRP.

Resupply Procedures

7-44. The time required for resupply is an important planning factor. Units must conduct resupply as quickly and efficiently as possible to ensure operational effectiveness, and to allow the Infantry company LOGPAC to return to the LRP on time.

7-45. Once the unit completes resupply operations, the unit prepares the LOGPAC vehicles for the return trip. The Infantry company vehicles requiring recovery for maintenance or salvage are lined up and prepared for towing. Cargo trucks, fuel trucks, or damaged vehicles transport those KIA and detainees ride in the cargo trucks, and are guarded by capable friendly wounded or other capable company personnel. All supply requests, human resources actions, and outgoing mail are consolidated for forwarding to the field trains, where the appropriate staff section processes them for the next LOGPAC.

7-46. The company representative leads the LOGPAC back to the LRP, where he links up with the FSC, support platoon leader. Whenever possible, the reunited task force LOGPAC convoy returns to the field trains together. When METT-TC dictates or when the LOGPAC arrives too late to rejoin the larger convoy, the Infantry company vehicles must return to the field trains on their own. Because only minimal security assets are available, this situation should be avoided.

Resupply Methods

7-47. As directed by the commander or executive officer, the first sergeant establishes the Infantry company's resupply point using the service station method or the tailgate method or in-position method. He briefs each LOGPAC driver on which method or methods to use. When the resupply point is ready, the first sergeant informs the commander, who in turn directs each platoon or element to conduct resupply based on the tactical situation. The platoon sergeant can resupply the squads the same way the first sergeant resupplies the platoons.

Service Station Method

7-48. Allows the squads to move individually to a centrally located resupply point. (See figure 7-1, page 7-14.) This method requires the Soldiers to leave their fighting positions. Depending on the tactical situation, a squad moves out of its position, conducts resupply operations, and moves back into position. The squads rotate individually to eat; pick up mail, Class IX supplies, and other supplies and sundries; and refill or exchange water. This process continues until the entire platoon has received its supplies. The technique is used when contact is unlikely and for resupply of one or several classes of supplies.

7-49. With the service station method, vehicles move individually or in small groups to a centrally located resupply point. Depending on the tactical situation, one vehicle or section or even an entire platoon moves out of its position, conducts resupply operations, and moves back into position. This process continues until the entire Infantry company or platoons have been resupplied.

7-50. When using this method, vehicles enter the resupply point following a one-way traffic flow; only vehicles requiring immediate maintenance stop at the maintenance holding area. Vehicles move through each supply location, with crews rotating individually to eat, pick up mail and sundries, and refill or exchange water cans. When all platoon vehicles and crews have completed resupply, they move to a holding area, where, time permitting, the platoon leader and platoon sergeant conduct a PCI. The company command group (company commander, executive officer and first sergeant) also can take this opportunity to conduct PCIs of each platoon as it passes through the resupply point.

Chapter 7

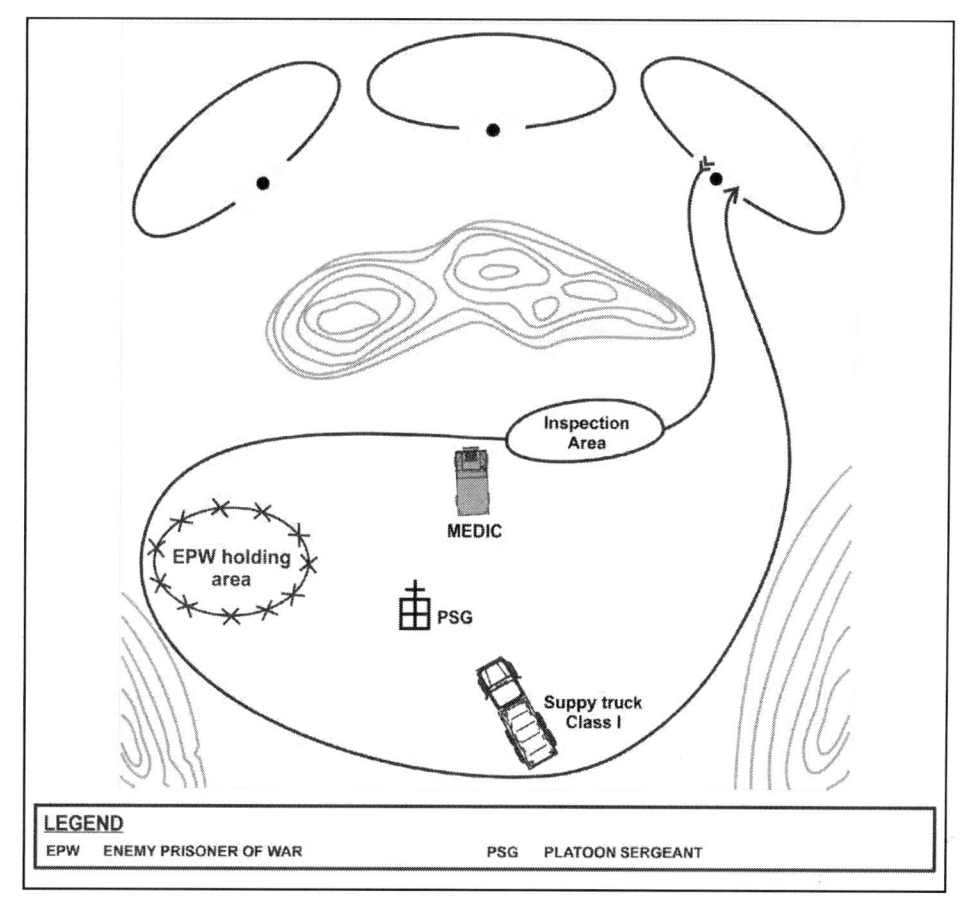

Figure 7-1. Service station method

Note. The platoon order should state the sequence for moving squads or Soldiers out of position. Companies may vary the technique by establishing a resupply point for each platoon or squad and moving the supplies to that point.

Tailgate Resupply

7-51. The first sergeant or platoon sergeant normally uses the tailgate method in the AA. (See figure 7-2.) Individual Soldiers rotate through the feeding area. While there, they pick up mail and sundries and refill or exchange water cans. They centralize and guard EPW. They take Soldiers KIA and their personal effects to the holding area (normally a location downwind and out of sight of the platoon/company), where the first sergeant assumes responsibility of them.

7-52. Tailgate resupply usually requires significantly more time than do service station operations. Usually, units use the tailgate method only when the tactical situation allows or dictates. Combat vehicles remain in their vehicle positions or back out a short distance

Sustainment

to allow trucks carrying Class III and Class V supplies to reach them. Individual crewmembers rotate through the feeding area, pick up mail and sundries, and fill or exchange water cans. Detainees are centralized and guarded. Soldiers KIA and their personal effects are brought to the holding area, where the first sergeant takes charge of them.

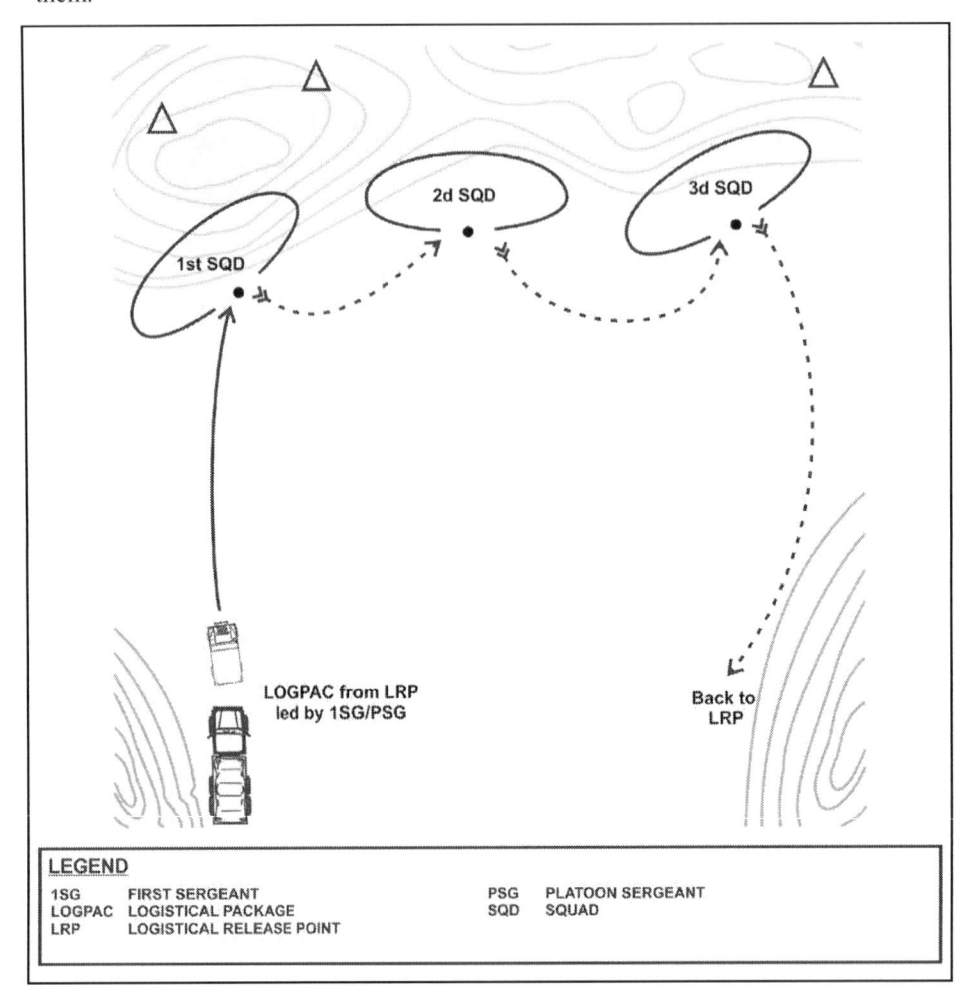

Figure 7-2. Tailgate resupply method

Combination of Service Station and Tailgate Resupply

7-53. The Infantry company or platoon may select to employ the tailgate resupply method, but selected platoons may have to use the service station resupply method. Selected platoons may use the service station resupply method and some sections may have to use the tailgate resupply method.

Chapter 7

In-Position Resupply

7-54. In-position resupply is used during operations when contact with the enemy is imminent; the in-position resupply method (see figure 7-3) may be required to ensure adequate supplies are available to the squads. This method requires the company to bring forward supplies, equipment, or both to individual fighting positions. The platoon normally provides a guide to ensure the supplies are distributed to the most critical position first. This method:

- Is used when an immediate need exists.
- Is used to resupply single classes of supply.
- Enables leaders to keep squad members in their fighting positions.

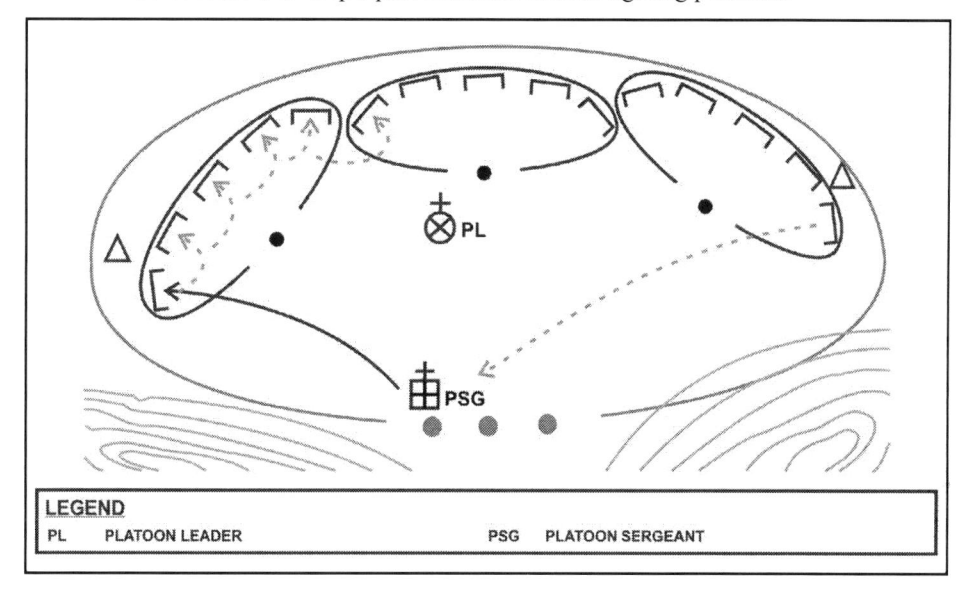

Figure 7-3. In-position resupply method

Note. If resupply vehicles cannot move near platoon positions, platoon Soldiers may need to help resupply personnel, move supplies and equipment forward.

EMERGENCY RESUPPLY

7-55. Occasionally (usually during combat operations), platoons have such an urgent need for resupply it cannot wait for a routine LOGPAC. Emergency resupply may involve Classes III, V, and VIII, as well as CBRN equipment and, on rare occasions, Class I. The battalion usually uses the FSC's supply and transportation platoon, and medical assets located in the Infantry battalion combat trains to conduct emergency resupply of the element.

7-56. Emergency resupply can be conducted using either the service station or tailgate method although procedures may have to be adjusted when the platoon, squad and companies are in contact with the enemy. In the service station method, individual vehicles pull back during a lull in combat on order of the commander or platoon leader; they conduct resupply and return to the fight. With tailgate resupply, the Infantry company brings limited supplies forward to the closest concealed position behind each vehicle or element.

PRE-POSITIONED SUPPLIES

7-57. In defensive operations, or other times as appropriate, the platoons will most likely need prestocked supplies, also known as pre-positioned or "cached" resupply. Normally, the platoon only pre-positions Class IV and V items, but they can pre-position Class III supplies. However, they must refuel platoon vehicles before they move into fighting positions, while first occupying the battle position, or while moving out of their fighting position to refuel.

7-58. All levels must carefully plan and execute prestock operations. All leaders, down to the squad leader level, must know the exact locations of prestock sites. They verify these locations during reconnaissance or rehearsals. The platoon takes steps to ensure the survivability of the prestock supplies. These measures include selecting covered and concealed positions and digging in the prestock positions. The platoon leader must have a removal and destruction plan to prevent the enemy from capturing prepositioned supplies.

7-59. During the offense, the company or platoon can preposition supplies on trucks well forward on the battlefield. This works well if the company or platoon expects to use a large volume of fire, with corresponding ammunition requirements. It allows the platoons to quickly resupply during consolidation or during lulls.

AERIAL SUSTAINMENT

7-60. Aerial sustainment is an aviation mission consisting of moving personnel, equipment, materiel, and supplies by utility, cargo, and fixed-wing assets for use in operations. Overland resupply might not work due to terrain, distance, or the existing enemy threat. The platoon must initiate a request for resupply and must push it through company to battalion. The platoon must prepare to receive the supplies at the specified time and location.

7-61. An aerial sustainment with speed balls is a technique with preconfigured loads to resupply Infantry platoons and squads in urban areas. Sustainment personnel prepackage supplies in aviation kit bags, duffle bags, or other suitable containers. Helicopters fly as close to the drop point as possible, reduce speed, drop supplies, and leave the area quickly. Supplies should be packaged in bubble wrap or other shock-absorbing material to minimize damage.

7-62. When employing aerial delivery, the following should be considered:
- The use of aerial delivery requires the coordination of the Infantry battalion staff, BCT S-3, S-4, and air defense airspace management/brigade aviation element sections. Special focus must be placed on the enemy air defense capability.

Chapter 7

- The FSC must be prepared to both receive and package bulk supplies by sling-load operations or joint precision airdrop system. To conduct these operations, sling load trained personnel are required in the FSC's distribution platoon.
- Receiving unit must know how to select landing zone/drop zone to receive aerial resupply. The delivered supplies immediately are transported away from the landing zone/drop zone.
- Units should return the sling or air delivery equipment to its owning unit.

Planning

7-63. Planning for aerial resupply requires close coordination, with elements reviewing the entire mission and resolving all limitations and problem areas. If a resupply item poses a problem it cannot resolve, leaders should consider another mode of transport. Planning factors include the following:

- Priorities of cargo/unit resupply.
- Integration of the resupply operation into the tactical plan.
- Selection, identification, and marking of the pickup zone or landing zone.
- Type/amount of cargo.
- Helicopter assets available.
- Requirements for slings, cargo nets, and cargo containers.
- Ground crew training requirements; such as those for ground guides and hookup personnel.
- Pickup zone and landing zone security.
- Flight routes.

7-64. The selection of a usable pickup zone or landing zone is extremely important. The platoon leader or company commander analyzes logistical and tactical considerations taking into account pickup zone or landing zone positioning is at the right place to support the ground unit. The area also must be accessible to the aircraft involved in the resupply operation. The air mission commander, the pilot in command, an aviation liaison officer (ALO), or a Pathfinder-qualified officer or NCO make the final decision on pickup zone or landing zone selection and acceptance.

7-65. The Infantry platoon or squad receiving the supplies is responsible for preparing the pickup zone or landing zone. In addition to the general pickup zone and landing zone responsibilities, Soldiers in the platoon or company perform the following specific tasks for aerial resupply:

- Recover and assemble equipment and supplies.
- Train available ground crews in guiding the aircraft during approach, landing, unloading/loading, departure, and derigging the load.
- Train hookup personnel.
- Coordinate with the sending unit for control and return of the unit's transport equipment, such as slings and A-22 bags.
- Prepare, coordinate, and inspect backloads (such as slings and A-22 bags) and have them ready for hookup or loading when the aircraft arrives.

MAINTENANCE

7-66. The maintenance of weapons and equipment is continuous. Every Soldier must know how to maintain his weapon and equipment according to the related technical manual. The platoon leader, platoon sergeant, and squad leaders must understand maintenance for every piece of equipment in the platoon.

7-67. Maintenance includes inspecting, testing, servicing, repairing, requisitioning, recovering, and evacuating vehicles and equipment. Maintenance at the platoon and squad level comprises thorough preventive maintenance checks and services and accurate reporting of maintenance problems to the company.

7-68. Maintenance and the early identification of problems prevent equipment down-time and the reduction of combat effectiveness. The result of good PMCS is a properly completed equipment inspection and maintenance forms. These forms (DA Form 2404 or DA Form 5988-E) are the primary means through which the platoon and squads obtain maintenance support or repair parts. The forms follow a pathway from crew level to the brigade support area and back. Per unit SOP, the company executive officer or 1SG supervises the flow of these critical maintenance documents and parts. The flow of reporting and repairing equipment includes the following:

- The squad leaders or vehicle commanders collect the maintenance forms and send them via Force XXI Battle Command Brigade and Below or give them to the platoon sergeant, who consolidates the forms for the platoon.
- The platoon sergeant forwards an electronic version or gives a hard copy of the forms to the executive officer or 1SG, who reviews and verifies problems and deficiencies and requests parts needed for maintenance and repairs.
- The electronic versions of the forms are consolidated at company level and then transmitted to the battalion and it's supporting combat repair team.
- During the next LOGPAC operation, the completed hard copy forms are returned to the combat repair team to document completion of the repair.
- In the brigade support area, required repair parts are packaged for delivery during the next scheduled resupply or through emergency resupply means.
- If the repair or installation of the part requires higher skills and equipment than the operator, a combat repair team is dispatched to assess the repair and to install the part on site.
- The operator conducts initial maintenance, repair, and recovery actions on site. Once it is determined that the crew cannot repair or recover the vehicle or equipment, the platoon contacts the executive officer or 1SG. If additional assistance is needed, the combat repair team assesses the damaged or broken equipment and makes necessary repairs to return the piece of equipment to fully mission-capable or mission-capable status, if appropriate.

7-69. The unit SOP should detail when maintenance is performed, to what standards, and who inspects it. The squad leader is most often the one who inspects maintenance work, with the platoon sergeant and platoon leader conducting spot-checks. Besides operator maintenance, selected Soldiers are trained to perform limited maintenance on damaged weapons and battle damage assessment and repair.

Chapter 7

7-70. Inoperative equipment is fixed as far forward as possible. When a piece of equipment is damaged, it should be inspected to see if it can be repaired on the spot. If equipment cannot be repaired forward, it is evacuated immediately or returned with a LOGPAC. Even if the item cannot be evacuated at once, the maintenance system is alerted to prepare for repair or replacement. If a replacement is available (from an evacuated Soldier or inoperative equipment), it is sent forward. If not, the leader must work around it by prioritizing remaining equipment. For example, using a squad radio for the company command net if the platoon radio is broken.

SCHEDULED SERVICES

7-71. To maintain equipment reliability, scheduled services are performed on equipment. Equipment services are specified maintenance actions performed when required where equipment, components, and systems are routinely checked, adjusted, lubed, and so on, according to engineer specifications. Maintenance personnel use scheduled services to replace faulty items and avoid projected component failures based on analysis and engineering documentation.

LEVELS OF MAINTENANCE

7-72. The Army employs the field and sustainment levels of maintenance as described in the following paragraphs.

Field Maintenance

7-73. Field maintenance is on-system maintenance, and mainly involves preventive maintenance and replacement of defective parts. The goal of field maintenance is to repair and return equipment to the Soldier. It covers tasks previously assigned to operator/crew, organization/unit, and direct support maintenance levels. It includes some off-system maintenance critical to mission readiness.

7-74. Platoon leaders ensure vehicles (if equipped) crews and equipment operators perform PMCS. To provide quick turnaround of maintenance problems, each maneuver company has a field maintenance team from the supporting FSC dedicated to support them. These field maintenance teams have forward repair systems and mechanics trained in the company's and platoon's equipment.

Sustainment Maintenance

7-75. Sustainment maintenance consists of repairing components off the user's platform. To maximize unit combat readiness, maintenance personnel must repair and return the equipment to the user as quickly as possible. (See appendix E of this publication for more information.)

Vehicle Recovery

7-76. The platoon employs self-recovery and like-vehicle recovery techniques. If the unit is unable to perform the recovery mission, it reports the need for recovery to the company.

Sustainment

A recovery team is dispatched to perform recovery operations at the breakdown site or from an intermediate coordinated location within the area of operation. The recovery section accomplishes its mission by performing damage assessment and initial damage classification and recovering battle damaged equipment.

HUMAN RESOURCES

7-77. Human resources supports all functions affecting the Soldier's status, readiness, and welfare. It includes casualty operations, which comprises production, dissemination, coordination, validation and synchronization of information regarding each casualty. Human resources teams are responsible for casualty reporting, casualty notification, casualty assistance, line-of-duty determination, disposition of remains, and disposition of personal effects, military burial honors, and casualty mail coordination.

+ Casualty Operations

7-78. Casualty operations include production, dissemination, coordination, validation and synchronization of information regarding each casualty. This information includes casualty reporting, casualty notification, casualty assistance, line-of-duty determination, disposition of remains, and disposition of personal effects, military burial honors, and casualty mail coordination.

7-79. Unit SOPs and OPORDs must address + first aid procedures and casualty evacuation in detail + to include aid for chemical casualties with particular emphasis on lifesaving tasks. They should cover the duties and responsibilities of essential personnel, the evacuation of CBRN contaminated casualties (on routes separate from noncontaminated casualties), and priority for manning essential weapons and positions. They should specify preferred and alternate methods of evacuation and make provisions for retrieving and safeguarding the weapons, ammunition, and equipment of casualties. Slightly wounded personnel are treated + at the appropriate role of care and returned to duty + as soon as possible. Platoon medics evaluate sick Soldiers and either treat or evacuate them as necessary. Medical and casualty evacuations should be rehearsed like other critical part of an operation.

7-80. + Specific procedures should be followed +when providing aid, evacuation, and reporting of combat casualties.

+ Casualty Care

7-81. When combat begins and casualties occur, the platoon first must provide + aid to those WIA. + Casualty care is provided by combat medics who are assisted by nonmedical personnel performing first aid procedures to alleviate potential life-threatening situations and ensure maximum survivability on the battlefield. + This support is most commonly provided by enlisted personnel and includes first aid (self-aid/buddy aid), enhanced first aid (by the CLS), and EMT (platoon medic). Casualties are cared for at the point of injury or under nearby cover and concealment.

7-82. The tactical situation will determine how quickly fellow Soldiers can + provide aid for wounded Soldiers. Understandably, fewer casualties occur if Soldiers focus on destroying or neutralizing the enemy causing the casualties. This is a critical situation discussed and rehearsed by the squads and platoons prior to executing a mission.

7-83. During the fight, casualties should remain under cover. As soon as the situation allows, squad leaders arrange for casualty evacuation to the platoon CCP. The platoon normally sets up the CCP in a covered and concealed location to the rear of the platoon position. At the CCP, the platoon medic conducts triage on all casualties, takes steps to stabilize their conditions, and starts the process of moving them to the rear for advanced treatment.

7-84. Before the platoon evacuates casualties to the CCP or beyond, leaders should remove all essential operational items and equipment from each person. Removal should include an automated network control device, GPS maps, position-locating devices, and laser pointers. Every unit should establish an SOP for handling the weapons and ammunition of its WIA.

MOVEMENT

7-85. Timely movement of casualties from the battlefield is important not only for safety and care for the wounded, but also for troop morale. Squad leaders are responsible for casualty evacuation from the battlefield to the platoon CCP. At the CCP, the senior medic assists the platoon sergeant and first sergeant in arranging evacuation by ground or air ambulance or by nonstandard means. Leaders must minimize the number of Soldiers required to evacuate casualties.

7-86. Casualties with minor wounds can walk or even assist with carrying the more seriously wounded. Soldiers can make field-expedient litters by cutting small trees and putting the poles through the sleeves of zippered Army combat uniform blouses or ponchos. A travois, or skid, may be used for casualty evacuation. This is a type of litter on which wounded can be strapped; it can be pulled by one person. It can be fabricated locally from durable, plastic rolls on which tie-down straps are fastened. In rough terrain (or on patrols), casualties may be evacuated all the way to the BAS by litter teams. From there they can be carried with the unit until transportation can reach them, or left at a position and picked up later.

7-87. From the platoon area, casualties normally are evacuated to the company CCP and back to the BAS. The company first sergeant, with the assistance of the platoon sergeant, normally is responsible for movement of the casualties from the platoon CCP to the company CCP. The unit SOP should address this activity, including the marking of casualties during limited visibility operations. Small, standard, or infrared chemical lights work well for this purpose. Once the casualties are collected, evaluated, and treated, they are sent to company CCP. Once they arrive, the above process is repeated while awaiting their evacuation back to the BAS.

7-88. When the company is widely dispersed, the casualties may be evacuated directly from the platoon CCP by vehicle or helicopter. Helicopter evacuation may be restricted due to the enemy air defense artillery or small arms/rocket-propelled grenade (RPG) threat.

Sustainment

In some cases, casualties must be moved to the company CCP or battalion combat trains before helicopter evacuation. When there are not enough battalion organic ambulances to move the wounded, unit leaders may direct supply vehicles to "backhaul" casualties to the BAS after supplies are delivered. Normally, urgent casualties will move by ambulance. Less seriously hurt Soldiers are moved by other means. If no ambulance is available, the most critical casualties must get to the BAS as quickly as possible. In some cases, the platoon sergeant may direct platoon litter teams to carry casualties to the rear.

7-89. The senior military person present determines whether to request medical or casualty evacuations and assigns precedence. These decisions are based on the advice of the senior medical person at the scene, the patient's condition, and tactical situation. Casualties will be picked up as soon as possible, consistent with available resources and pending missions. Following are priority categories of precedence and criteria used in their assignment:

- Priority I-Urgent—assigned to emergency cases being evacuated as soon as possible and within a maximum of one hour in order to save life, limb, or eyesight; to prevent complications of serious illness; or to avoid permanent disability.
- Priority IA-Urgent-Surgical—assigned to patients who must receive far forward surgical intervention to save their lives and stabilize them for further evacuation.
- Priority II-Priority—assigned to sick and wounded personnel requiring prompt medical care. The precedence is used when special treatment is not available locally; the individual will suffer unnecessary pain or disability (becoming URGENT precedence) if not evacuated within four hours.
- Priority III-Routine—assigned to sick and wounded personnel requiring evacuation but whose condition is not expected to deteriorate significantly. The sick and wounded in this category should be evacuated within 24 hours.
- Priority IV-Convenience—assigned to patients for whom evacuation by medical vehicle is a matter of medical convenience rather than necessity.

MEDICAL EVACUATION

7-90. Medical evacuation is the term used to refer to movement of casualties by air or ground utilizing medical vehicles or aircraft. Medical evacuation operations normally involve the initial movement of wounded or injured Soldiers to the nearest medical treatment facility. Medical evacuation includes the provision of en route medical care, whereas casualty evacuations might not provide medical care during movement. (Refer to ATP 4-02.5 and ATP 4-02.2 for more information.) (See table 7-2a, page 7-24, and table 7-2b, page 7-25 on the 9-line request for medical evacuation procedures.

7-91. When possible, medical platoon ambulances provide evacuation and en route care from the Soldier's point of injury or the platoon's or company's CCP to the BAS. The ambulance team supporting the company works in coordination with the senior + combat medic supporting the platoons. In mass casualty situations, nonmedical vehicles may be used to assist in casualty evacuation as directed by the Infantry company commander or leader. However, plans for use of nonmedical vehicles to perform casualty evacuations should be included in the unit SOP.

Chapter 7

Table 7-2a. +GTA 08-01-004 (front)

LINE	ITEM	EVACUATION REQUEST MESSAGE
	MEDEVAC REQUEST CARD	GTA 08-01-004
1	Location of Pickup Site.	
2	Radio Frequ., Call Sign, & Suffix.	
3	No. of Patients by Precedence.	
4	Special Equipment Required.	
5	Number of Patients by Type.	
6	Security of Pickup Site (Wartime).	
6	Number and Type of Wound, Injury, or Illness (Peacetime).	
7	Method of Marking Pickup Site.	
8	Patient Nationality and Status.	
9	NBC Contamination (Wartime).	
9	Terrain Description (Peacetime).	

This publication contains technical or operational information that is for official Government use only. Distribution is limited to U.S. Government agencies. Requests from outside U.S Government agencies for release of this publication under the Freedom of Information Act or the Foreign Military Sales Program must be made to Commander USATSC, ATTN: GTA Program Manager ATIC-ITST-T, Fort Eustis, VA 23064-5166. DESTRUCTION NOTICE: Destroy by any method that will prevent disclosure of contents or reconstruction of document.

August 2016　Use of previous version authorized until exhausted

Distributed by atsc

DISTRIBUTION: US ARMY TRAINING SUPPORT CENTERS (TSCs), HEADQUARTERS, DEPARTMENT OF THE ARMY, ATTN: ATIC-SAA, GTA Program, Fort Eustis, VA 23604-5166

Sustainment

Table 7-2b. +GTA 08-01-004 (back)

LINE ITEM	EXPLANATION
1. Location of Pickup Site.	Encrypt grid coordinates. When using *DRYAD Numeral Cipher*, the same SET line will be used to encrypt grid zone letters and coordinates. To preclude misunderstanding, a statement is made that grid zone letters are included in the message (unless unit SOP specifies its use at all times).
2. Radio Frequency, Call Sign, Suffix.	Encrypt the frequency of the radio at the pickup site, *not* a relay frequency. The call sign (and suffix if used) of person to be contacted at the pickup site may be transmitted in the clear.
3. No. of Patients by Precedence.	Report only applicable info & encrypt brevity codes. A = Urgent, B = Urgent-Surg, C = Priority, D = Routine, E = Convenience. (If 2 or more categories reported in same request, insert the word "break" btwn. each category.)
4. Spec Equipment.	Encrypt applicable brevity codes. A = None, B = Hoist, C = Extraction equipment, D = Ventilator.
5. No. of Patients by Type.	Report only applicable information and encrypt brevity code. If requesting MEDEVAC for both types, insert the word "break" between the litter entry and ambulatory entry: L + # of Pnt -Litter; A + # of Pnt - Ambul (sitting).
6. Security Pickup Site (Wartime).	N = No enemy troops in area, P = Possibly enemy troops in area (approach with caution), E = Enemy troops in area (approach with caution), X = Enemy troops in area (armed escort required).
6. Number and type of Wound, Injury, Illness (Peacetime).	Specific information regarding patient wounds by type (gunshot or shrapnel). Report serious bleeding, along with patient blood type, if known.
7. Method of Marking Pickup Site.	Encrypt the brevity codes. A = Panels, B = Pyrotechnic signal, C = Smoke Signal, D = None, E = Other.
8. Patient Nationality and Status.	Number of patients in each category need not be transmitted. Encrypt only applicable brevity codes. A = US military, B = US civilian, C = Non-US mil, D = Non-US civilian, E = EPW.
9. NBC Contamination, (Wartime).	Include this line only when applicable. Encrypt the applicable brevity codes. N = nuclear, B = biological, C = chemical.
9. Terrain Description (Peacetime).	Include details of terrain features in and around proposed landing site. If possible, describe the relationship of site to a prominent terrain feature (lake, mountain, tower).

Reference: ATP 4-02.2, *Medical Evacuation*.

CASUALTY EVACUATION

7-92. Casualty evacuation is a term used to refer to the movement of casualties aboard nonmedical vehicles or aircraft.

WARNING

Casualties transported in this manner may not receive proper en route medical care or be transported to the appropriate medical treatment facility to address the patient's medical condition. If the casualty's medical condition deteriorates during transport, or the casualty is not transported to the appropriate medical treatment facility, an adverse impact on his prognosis and long-term disability or death may result.

Chapter 7

7-93. If dedicated medical evacuation platforms (ground and air) are available, casualties should be evacuated on these conveyances to ensure they receive proper en route medical care.

7-94. Since casualty evacuation operations can reduce combat power and degrade the efficiency of the Army health system (AHS), units should only use casualty evacuation to move Soldiers with less severe injuries when medical evacuation assets are overwhelmed. Planners should ensure casualty evacuations operations are addressed in the operation plan (OPLAN)/OPORD as a separate operation, as these operations require preplanning, coordination, synchronization, and rehearsals. The casualty evacuation plan should ensure casualties with severe or life threatening injuries are prioritized for evacuation and are evacuated on dedicated medical evacuation platforms.

7-95. When possible, nonmedical vehicles/aircraft transporting casualties should be augmented with a + combat medic or CLS. (On nonmedical aircraft, sufficient space may not be available to permit a caregiver to accompany the casualties.) + (Refer to ATP 4-25.13 for more information.) The type of en route monitoring and medical care/first aid provided is limited by the following factors:

- Skill level of the individual providing care. (The combat medic is military occupational specialty [MOS]-qualified [MOS 68W] to provide EMT; the CLS is trained to provide enhanced first aid). The combat medic can provide emergency medical intervention, whereas the CLS only can monitor the casualty and ensure the basic lifesaving first-aid tasks are accomplished.
- Medical equipment available.
- Number of casualties being transported.
- Accessibility of casualties—if nonstandard evacuation vehicle is loaded with the maximum number of casualties, the combat medic or CLS may not be able to attend to the casualties while the vehicle is moving. If the condition of a casualty deteriorates and emergency measures are required, the vehicle will have to be stopped to permit care to be given.

UNIT REPORTING

7-96. As casualties occur, the nearest observer informs the platoon sergeant who then informs the first sergeant via the most expedient method available; for example, free text within Mission Command Systems, radio voice. The first sergeant submits a personnel status report to the Infantry battalion S-1 section. This report documents duty status changes on all casualties. Casualties are taken to CCP for classification of injury type (routine, urgent, return to duty), evacuation, and integration into the medical treatment system.

7-97. A casualty report is filled out when a casualty occurs, or as soon as the tactical situation permits. This usually is done by the Soldier's squad leader and turned in to the platoon sergeant, who forwards it to the first sergeant. A brief description of how the casualty occurred (including the place, time, and activity being performed) and who or what inflicted the wound is included. If the squad leader does not have personal knowledge of how the casualty occurred, he gets this information from Soldiers who have the knowledge.

7-98. DA Form 1156, *Casualty Feeder Card* (see figure 7-4a and figure 7-4b), are used to report those Soldiers who have been killed and recovered, and those who have been wounded. This form also is used to report KIA Soldiers who are missing, captured, or not recovered. The Soldier with the most knowledge of the incident should complete the witness statement. This information is used to inform the Soldier's next of kin and to provide a statistical base for analysis of friendly or enemy tactics. Once the casualty's medical condition has stabilized, the company commander may write a letter to the Soldier's next of kin. During lulls in the battle, the platoon forwards casualty information to the company headquarters. The first sergeant ensures a completed DA Form 1156 is forwarded to the Infantry battalion S-1, who then enters the data into the defense casualty information processing system.

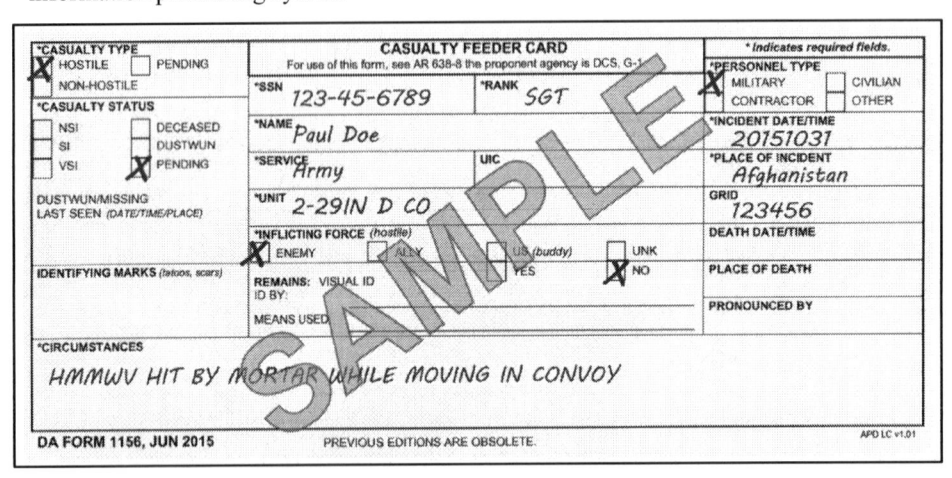

Figure 7-4a. DA Form 1156, Casualty Feeder Card (front)

Chapter 7

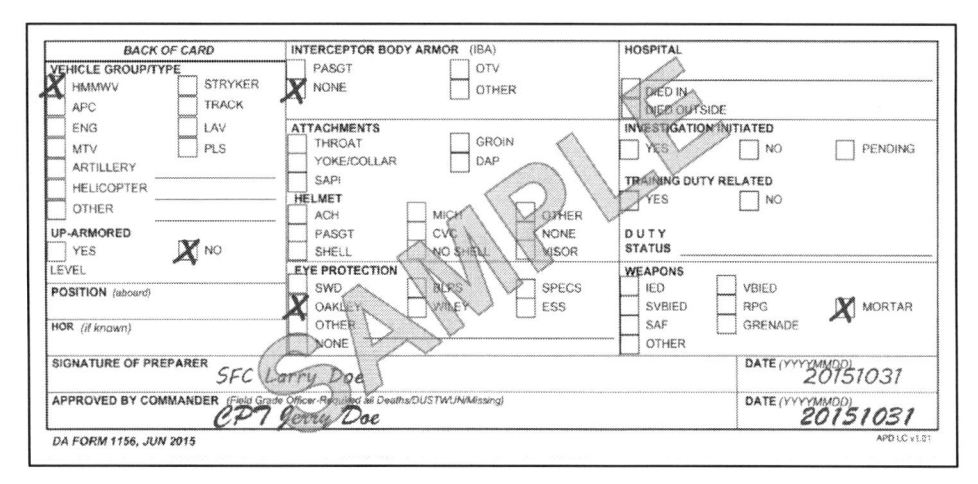

Figure 7-4b. DA Form 1156, Casualty Feeder Card (back)

KILLED IN ACTION

7-99. The platoon leader designates a location of the collection of KIAs. All personal effects remain with the body. However, squad leaders remove and safeguard equipment and issue items. They keep these until they can turn the equipment and issue items over to the platoon sergeant. The platoon sergeant turns over the KIA to the first sergeant. As a rule, the platoon should not transport KIA remains on the same vehicle as wounded Soldiers. KIAs normally are transported to the rear on empty resupply trucks, but this depends on unit SOP.

7-100. Commanders and first sergeants must establish procedures to ensure the Soldier's next of kin are notified properly and according to procedure. The potential for unofficial communications exist with KIA and casualty operations. The use of cell phones and computers in proximity to the area of operation enables many Soldiers to contact their home station regarding the casualty. Such communication is unofficial and unacceptable. The next of kin for Soldiers WIA or KIA should not receive notification through unofficial means. There usually is a communication blackout until the next of kin is notified. No internet or phone calls home are permitted.

MEDICAL/PERSONNEL ACCOUNTING

7-101. When a Soldier becomes a casualty, the platoon combat medic or senior combat medic records the medical treatment the Soldier receives on the Soldier's DD Form 1380. The BAS and brigade support medical company read the Soldier's DD Form 1380 when they treat the Soldier. The Infantry battalion S-1 should electronically receive a notification message to update the Soldier's patient tracking status. In turn, this message should be forwarded to the company. In this manner, a casualty's location can be determined and Soldiers properly accounted for by the company.

Appendix A
Planning

Troop leading procedures provide small unit leaders a framework for planning and preparing for operations. Smaller units, company and below lack formal staffs and use TLP to plan and prepare for operations. This places the responsibility for planning primarily on the small-unit leader.

SECTION I – PLANNING CONSIDERATIONS

A-1. Planning is the process by which the small-unit leader translates his visualization into a specific COA for preparation and execution, focusing on the expected results. Planning to determine the relationship among METT-TC begins with the analysis and assessment of the conditions in the operational environment, with particular emphasis on the enemy. It involves understanding and framing the problem and envisioning the set of conditions representing the desired end state. Based on the higher commander's guidance, the platoon leader's planning includes formulating one or more suitable COA to accomplish the mission. Planning continues as necessary during preparation and execution. The platoon leader relies on intuitive decisionmaking and direct contact with subordinate leaders to integrate activities when circumstances are not suited for TLP.

A-2. Preparation consists of activities performed by units to improve their ability to execute an operation. Preparation includes, but is not limited to, plan refinement; rehearsals; information collection; coordination; inspections; and movement.

A-3. Execution is putting a plan into action by applying combat power to accomplish the mission and using situational understanding to assess progress and make execution and adjustment decision.

A-4. Assessment refers to the continuous monitoring and evaluation of the current situation, particularly the enemy, and progress of an operation. Assessment precedes and guides every operations process activity and concludes each operation or phase of an operation. It involves a comparison of forecasted outcomes to actual events. Assessment entails three tasks:
- Continuously assessing the enemy's reactions and vulnerabilities.
- Continuously monitoring the situation and progress of the operation towards the leader's desired end state.
- Evaluating the operation against measures of effectiveness and measures of performance.

A-5. Leaders use TLP when working alone or with a small group to solve tactical problems. For example, a platoon leader may use the platoon sergeant, squad leaders, and the forward observer to assist during TLP. The type, amount, and timeliness of information

Appendix A

passed from higher to lower directly impact the lower unit leader's TLP. (Refer to FM 6-0 for more information.)

A-6. Parallel planning occurs when two or more echelons plan the same operation at about the same time. Parallel planning is easiest when the higher unit continuously shares information on future operations with subordinate units. Rather than waiting until company commander finishes planning, the platoon leader starts to develop his unit's missions as information is received, and fleshes out his missions as more information becomes available.

A-7. The platoon leader starts by identifying his unit's missions, stating his intent, and ensuring his intent reflects the operational concepts of his higher and second higher command. He chooses the tasks most likely to be assigned to his unit, and develops mission statements based on the information received. At all levels, developing and describing the vision of leaders requires time, explanation, and ongoing clarification. All leaders understand that their next higher commander's concept of the operation continues to mature, and continue parallel planning as it does so, up until execution. Figure A-1 illustrates the parallel sequences of the MDMP of a battalion, TLP of a company with the TLP of its platoons.

Battalion MDMP	Company TLP	Platoon TLP
Receive Mission	Receive Mission	Receive Mission
Mission Analysis	Issue WARNORD	Issue WARNORD
COA Development	Make a Tentative Plan	Make a Tentative Plan
COA Analysis	Initiate Movement	Initiate Movement
COA Comparison	Conduct Reconnaissance	Conduct Reconnaissance
COA Approval	Complete the Plan	Complete the Plan
Order Production	Issue OPORD	Issue OPORD
	Supervise and Refine	Supervise and Refine

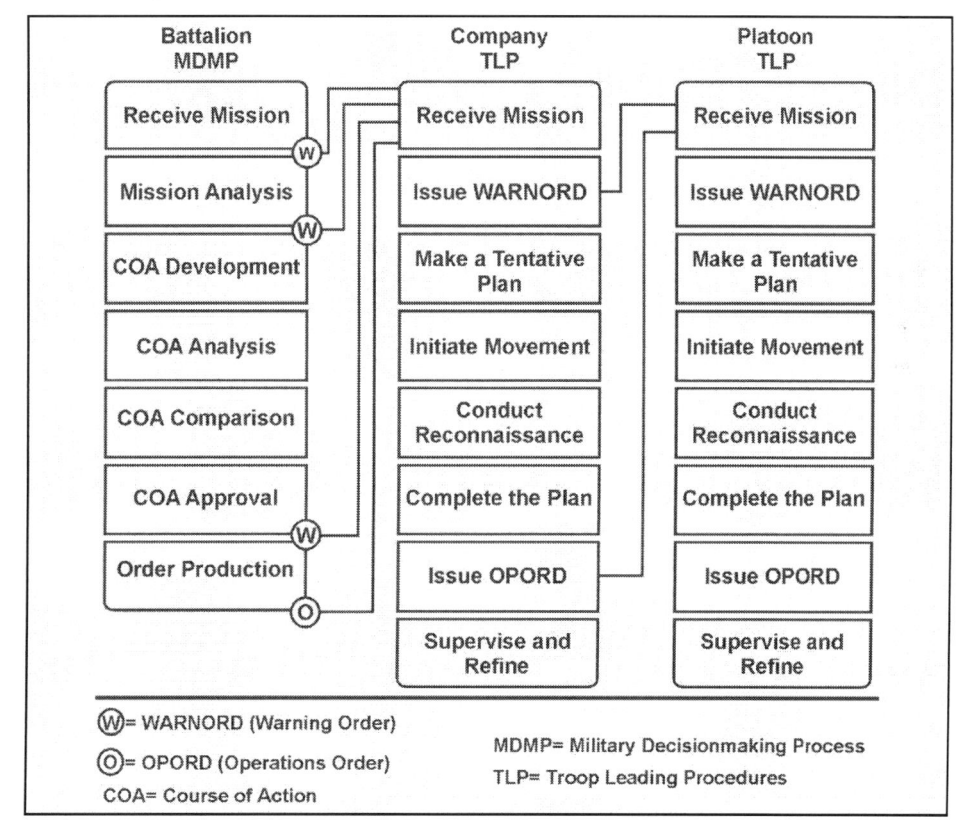

(W) = WARNORD (Warning Order)
(O) = OPORD (Operations Order)
COA = Course of Action
MDMP = Military Decisionmaking Process
TLP = Troop Leading Procedures

Figure A-1. Parallel planning

A-8. Normally, the first three steps (receive the mission, issue a WARNORD, and make a tentative plan) of TLP occur in order. However, the sequence of subsequent steps is based on the situation. The tasks involved in some steps example, initiate movement and conduct reconnaissance may occur several times. The last step, supervise and refine, occurs throughout.

A-9. A tension exists between executing current operations and planning for future operations. The small unit leader must balance both. If engaged in a current operation, there is less time for TLP. If in a lull, transition, or an AA, leaders have more time to use TLP thoroughly. In some situations, time constraints or other factors may prevent leaders from performing each step of TLP as thoroughly as they would like. For example during the step, make a tentative plan; small-unit leaders often develop only one acceptable COA vice multiple COA. If time permits, leaders may develop, compare, and analyze several COA before arriving at a decision on which one to execute.

A-10. The platoon leader begins TLP when he receives the initial WARNORD or receives a new mission. As each subsequent order arrives, he modifies his assessments, updates tentative plans, and continues to supervise and assess preparations. In some situations the platoon leader may not receive or issue the full sequence of WARNORDs; security considerations or tempo may make it impractical. Leaders carefully consider decisions to eliminate WARNORDs. Subordinates always need to have enough information to plan and prepare for their mission. In other cases, TLP are started before receiving a WARNORD based on existing plans and orders (contingency plans or be-prepared missions) and on subordinate leader's understanding of the situation.

A-11. Parallel planning hinges on distributing information as it is received or developed. Subordinate leaders cannot complete their plans until they receive their unit mission. If each successive WARNORD contains enough information, the higher command's final order will confirm what subordinate leaders have already analyzed and put into their tentative plans. In other cases, the higher command's order may change or modify the subordinates' tasks enough additional planning and reconnaissance are required.

SECTION II – STEPS OF TROOP LEADING PROCEDURES

A-12. TLP provide small-unit leaders a framework for planning and preparing for operations. TLP begin when the platoon leader receives the first indication of an upcoming mission and continues throughout the operational process (plan, prepare, execute, and assess). The TLP comprise a sequence of actions helping the leader use available time effectively and efficiently to issue orders and execute operations.

A-13. TLP are not a hard and fast set of rules. Some actions may be performed simultaneously or in an order different than shown in figure A-2 (page A-4). They are a guide being applied consistent with the situation and experience of the platoon leader and his subordinate leaders. The tasks involved in some actions (such as initiate movement, issue the WARNORD, and conduct reconnaissance) may recur several times during the process.

A-14. The last action (activities associated with supervising and refining the plan) occurs continuously throughout TLP and execution of the operation. The following information

Appendix A

concerning TLP assumes the small unit leader will plan in a time-constrained environment. All steps should be done, even if in abbreviated fashion. As such, the suggested techniques are oriented to help a leader quickly develop and issue a combat order. (Refer to FM 6-0 for more information.)

Troop-Leading Procedures Outline

1. **Receive the Mission**
   Initial time line, possible mission
2. **Issue the WARNORD**
   6 paragraph format (min info)
3. **Make a Tentative Plan**
   a. Mission analysis
   b. COA development
   c. COA analysis
   d. COA comparison
   e. COA selection
4. **Initiate Movement**
   XO, 1SG
5. **Conduct Reconnaissance**
6. **Complete the Plan**
   Orders production
7. **Issue the Order**
   Verbal, terrain model, paper
8. **Supervise**
   Confirm briefs
   Back-briefs
   Rehearsals
   PCC-1 up = check equipment
   PCC-2 up = company, mission

- Type of operation
- General location of operation
- Initial operational time line
- Reconnaissance to initiate
- Movement to initiate
- Planning and preparation instructions
  - To include planning time line
- Information requirements (IR and CCIR)

METT-TC
- Summary of mission analysis
  - Restated mission
  - Initial risk assessment (tactical and accidental)
  - Tentative decisive point
  - Initial commanders's intent

- Analysis relative combat power
- Generate operations
- Array forces
- Develop concept operations
- Assign responsibilities (2-5)
- Prepare COA statement and sketch

COA Screening Criteria at end of COA Dev
COA must be:
- Suitable
- Acceptable
- Distinguishable
- Complete
- Feasible

COA Analysis (war-game)
[Action - Reaction - Counteraction]
- Methods
  - Box
  - Belt
  - Avenue in depth

Mission
- Mission, intent, concept
  - 1 up and 2 up
- Purpose
- Tasks
  Specified
  Implied
  Essential
- Constraints (require/limit action)
- Restated mission
- Significant conclusions

Terrain
- AO
- AI
- Terrain
  - Obstacles
  - Avenues of approach
  - Key terrain
  - Observation & fields of fire
  - Cover and concealment
- Weather
  - Wind
  - Precipitation
  - Visibility
  - Cloud coverage
  - Temp/humidity
- Significant conclusions

- Purpose of the operation
- Form of maneuver of defensive technique
- Decisive point and why
- Risk and mitigation
- Decisive operation with task and purpose
- Shaping operations with task and purpose
- Concept of supporting fires/assets
- End state

Time
- Battalion times
- Hard times
- Company TLPs
- Light data
- Enemy data
- 1/3, 2/3 rule
- Significant conclusions

Enemy
- General situation
- Disposition
- Composition
- Strength
- Vulnerabilities
- Capabilities by WFF
- MPCOA & MDCOA
- Significant conclusions
- High value target list
- High pay-off target list

Troops
- Leadership
- Morale
- Training and experience
- Capabilities by WFF elements
- Significant conclusions

Civil Considerations
- Areas
- Structure
- Capabilities
- Organizations
- People
- Events
- Significant conclusions

LEGEND

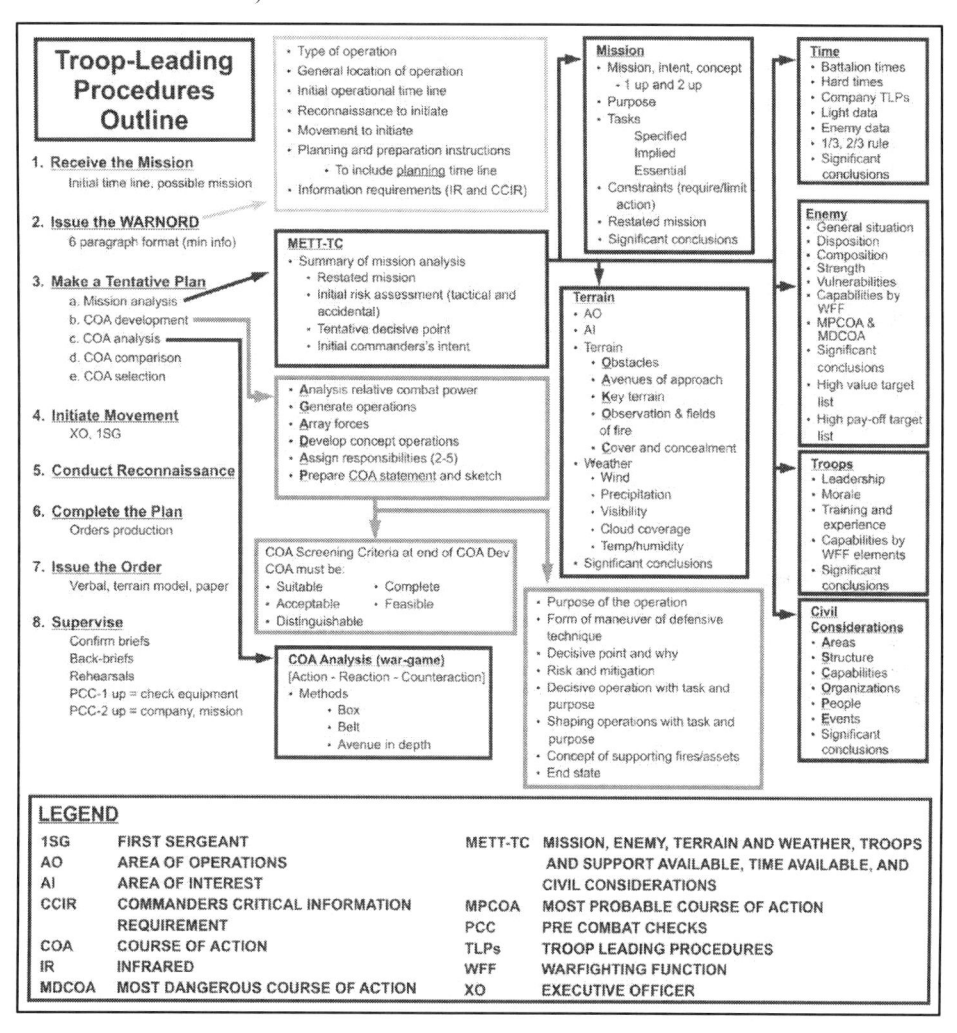

1SG	FIRST SERGEANT	METT-TC	MISSION, ENEMY, TERRAIN AND WEATHER, TROOPS AND SUPPORT AVAILABLE, TIME AVAILABLE, AND CIVIL CONSIDERATIONS
AO	AREA OF OPERATIONS		
AI	AREA OF INTEREST		
CCIR	COMMANDERS CRITICAL INFORMATION REQUIREMENT	MPCOA	MOST PROBABLE COURSE OF ACTION
		PCC	PRE COMBAT CHECKS
COA	COURSE OF ACTION	TLPs	TROOP LEADING PROCEDURES
IR	INFRARED	WFF	WARFIGHTING FUNCTION
MDCOA	MOST DANGEROUS COURSE OF ACTION	XO	EXECUTIVE OFFICER

Figure A-2. Troop leading procedures outline

STEP 1 – RECEIVE THE MISSION

A-15. In Step 1 of TLP, leaders *determine their units' missions* and *assess the time available to accomplish them.* They can conduct an initial (light) analysis of the order using METT-TC. They conduct detailed METT-TC analyses only *after* they issue the first WARNORD (Step 2). Rarely will they receive their missions until after higher command issues the third WARNORDs or the OPORDs themselves. However, in the course of parallel planning, small-unit leaders already will have deduced their tentative missions.

A-16. Leaders can receive their missions in several ways. They can get them in the form of WARNORDs or, if higher chooses to wait for more information, an actual OPORD. Sometimes higher chooses not to send WARNORDs, opting instead to wait and send a full OPORD. Worst case, leaders receive new missions due to situational changes occurring during the execution of a prior mission. In addition to receiving (or deducing) their missions during this step, the leaders must also—

- Assess the time available to prepare for and execute the mission.
- Prepare an initial timeline for planning and executing the mission.
- Conduct an initial planning-time analysis.
- Determine the total amount of time to plan and prepare.
- As planning continues, use the initial planning-time analysis to conduct a detailed time analysis.
- Analyze the time his unit has available.
- Prepare an initial timeline.

A-17. The most important element of the leader's WARNORD is the initial timeline for planning. They also may convey other instructions or information they think will help their subordinates prepare for the upcoming mission.

STEP 2 – ISSUE WARNING ORDER

A-18. A WARNORD is a preliminary notice of an order or action to follow. (Refer to ADRP 1-02 for more information.) Though less detailed than a complete OPORD, a WARNORD aids in parallel planning. After the leaders receive new missions and assess the time available for planning, preparing, and executing the mission, they immediately issue WARNORDs to their subordinates. By issuing the initial WARNORDs as quickly as possible, they enable subordinates to begin their own planning and preparation (parallel planning) while they begin to develop the OPORDs. When they obtain more information, they issue updated WARNORDs, giving subordinates as much as they know.

A-19. Leaders can issue WARNORDs to their subordinates right after they receive higher command's initial WARNORDs. In their own initial WARNORDs, they include the same elements given in their higher headquarters' initial WARNORDs. If practical, leaders brief their subordinate leaders face-to-face, on the ground. Otherwise, they use a terrain model, sketch, or map. (See figure A-3, page A-6 for an example of a warning order format.)

Appendix A

```
1. SITUATION
    • Area of Interest
    • Area of Operations
    • Enemy Forces
    • Attachments and Detachments

2. MISSION
    • Who
    • What
    • When
    • Where
    • Why

3. EXECUTION
    • Concept of Operations
    • Tasks to Subordinate Units
    • Coordinating Instructions

4. SUSTAINMENT
    • Logistics
    • Personnel Services Support
    • Army Health Systems Support

5. COMMAND AND SIGNAL
    • Command
    • Control
    • Signal
```

Figure A-3. Warning order format

WARNING ORDER

A-20. The WARNORD follows the five-paragraph OPORD format and includes the following items, at a minimum:

- Type of operation.
- General location of operation.
- Initial operational timeline.
- Reconnaissance to initiate.
- Movement to initiate.
- Planning and preparation instructions (to include planning timeline).
- Information requirements.
- Commander's critical information requirements.

STEP 3 – MAKE A TENTATIVE PLAN

A-21. In a time-constrained environment, a platoon leader typically develops only one COA. However, as time permits, he can develop as many COA, for comparison purposes, as time allows. He begins TLP Step 3 after he issues his own WARNORD, and after he has received company's third WARNORD, or until he has enough information to proceed. He need not wait for a complete OPORD before starting to develop his own tentative plan.

MISSION ANALYSIS

A-22. The platoon leader begins mission analysis when receiving the mission. During mission analysis, the platoon leader—
- Restates the mission.
- Conducts an initial risk assessment.
- Identifies a tentative decisive point.
- Defines his own intent.

A-23. He conducts mission analysis to help him start developing his vision, and to confirm what he must do to accomplish his mission. At the lower levels, leaders conduct their mission analyses by evaluating METT-TC. He makes significant deductions about the terrain, enemy, and own forces affecting operations. These significant deductions drive the planning process and execution of operations. A leader must convey to his subordinates the importance of these deductions, and effect they will have on the units operations. In the end, the usefulness of mission analysis lies in recognizing and capitalizing on opportunities. The answers to the following questions become inputs into developing a COA. Mission analysis has no time standard. A leader may take as much time as needed, while still adhering to the one-third/two-thirds rule. Mission analysis answers the four questions of the leader's visualization:
- What is my mission?
- What is the current situation?
- How do we accomplish the mission?
- What are the risks?

METT-TC

A-24. Analyzing METT-TC is a continuous process. Leaders constantly receive information, from the time they begin planning through execution. During execution, their continuous analyses enable them to issue well-developed FRAGORDs. They must assess if the new information affects their missions and plans. If so, then they must decide how to adjust their plans to meet these new situations. They need not analyze METT-TC in a particular order. How and when they do so depends on when they receive information as well as on their experience and preferences. One technique is to parallel the TLP based on the products received from higher. Using this technique, they would, but need not, analyze mission first; followed by terrain and weather; enemy; troops and support available; time available; and finally civil considerations.

Analysis of Mission

A-25. A mission is task and purpose clearly indicating the action to be taken and reason for the action. In common usage, especially when applied to lower military units, a mission is a duty or task assigned to an individual or unit. The mission is always the first factor leaders consider and most basic question: What have I been told to do, and why?

A-26. Leaders at every echelon must understand the mission, intent, and operational concept one and two levels higher. This understanding makes it possible to exercise

Appendix A

disciplined initiative. Leaders capture their understanding of what their units are to accomplish in their revised mission statements. They take five steps to fully analyze their assigned mission as directed from —
- Higher headquarters' (two levels up) mission, intent, and concept.
- Immediate higher headquarters' (one level up) mission, intent, and concept.
- Unit's purpose.
- Constraints.
- Specified, implied, and essential tasks.
- Restated mission.

Higher Headquarters' (Two Levels Up) Mission, Intent, and Concept

A-27. Leaders understand their second higher up concepts of the operation. They identify the tasks and purposes, and how their immediate higher up are contributing to the fight. They also must understand leaders' intent (two levels up).

Immediate Higher Headquarters' (One Level Up) Mission, Intent, and Concept

A-28. Leaders understand their immediate headquarters' concept of the operation. They identify their headquarters' tasks and purposes as well as their own contributions to this fight. They must clearly understand their immediate higher up intent from the OPORD. Also, they identify the tasks, purposes, and dispositions for all adjacent maneuver elements under headquarters' control.

Unit's Purpose

A-29. Leaders find their units' purposes in the concepts of the operation in the immediate higher headquarters' OPORDs. The operation's purpose usually matches or achieves the purpose of the immediate higher headquarters. Similarly, shaping operation purposes must relate directly to those of the decisive operation. Sustaining operation purposes relate directly to those of the decisive and shaping operations. Leaders must understand how their units' purposes relate to higher. They must understand why their leaders one level up assigned their unit's particular purposes. Then, they determine how those fit into their superior's concepts of the operation.

Constraints

A-30. Constraints either prohibit or require an action. Leaders identify all constraints the OPORD places on their units' ability to execute their missions. The two types of constraints are proscriptive (required; mandates action) and prohibitive (not allowed; limits action).

Tasks

A-31. Leaders must identify and understand tasks required to accomplish a given mission. The three types of tasks are specified, implied, and essential.

A-32. **Specified Tasks.** Specified tasks are specifically assigned to a unit by a higher headquarters and are found throughout the OPORD. Specified tasks also may be found in

Planning

annexes and overlays; for example—*"Seize OBJ FOX.;" "Reconnoiter route BLUE;" "Assist the forward passage of 1st platoon, B Company." "Send two Soldiers to assist in the loading of ammunition."*

A-33. **Implied Tasks.** Implied tasks are those being performed to accomplish a specified task, but that are not stated in a higher headquarters' order. Implied tasks derive from a detailed analysis of higher up orders, from the enemy situation and COA, from the terrain, and from knowledge of doctrine and history. Analyzing the unit's current location in relation to future area of operation as well as the doctrinal requirements for each specified task might reveal the implied tasks. Only those requiring resources should be used. For example, if the specified task is "*Seize Objective Fox*," and new intelligence has OBJ FOX surrounded by reinforcing obstacles, this intelligence would drive the implied task of "*Breach reinforcing obstacles vicinity Objective Fox*."

A-34. **Essential Task.** The essential task is the mission task—it accomplishes the assigned purpose. It, along with the platoon's purpose, is usually assigned by the higher headquarters' OPORD in *concept of the operation* or *Tasks to Maneuver Units*. For decisive operations, since the purposes are the same (nested concept) the essential task also accomplishes the higher headquarters' purpose. For shaping operations, it accomplishes the assigned purpose, which shapes the decisive operation. For sustaining operations, it accomplishes the assigned purpose, which enables both the shaping and decisive operation (again, nested concept).

Restated Mission

A-35. Leaders conclude their mission analyses by restating their missions. To do this, they answer the five Ws:
- Who (the unit).
- What (the unit's essential task and type of operation).
- When (this is the time given in the company OPORD).
- Where (the objective or location stated in company OPORD), and.
- Why (the units purpose, taken from the companies concept of the operation).

Analysis of Terrain and Weather

A-36. When analyzing terrain, leaders consider manmade features and effects on natural terrain features and climate. Leaders also consider the effects of manmade and natural terrain in conjunction with the weather on friendly and enemy operations. In general, terrain and weather do not favor one side over the other unless one is better prepared to operate in the environment or is more familiar with it. The terrain, however, may favor defending or attacking. Analysis of terrain answers the question: *What is the terrain's effect on the operation?* Leaders analyze terrain using the categories of OAKOC.

A-37. From the modified combined obstacle overlay (MCOO) developed by higher headquarters, leaders already appreciate the general nature of the ground and effects of weather. However, they must conduct their own detailed analyses to determine how terrain and weather uniquely affects their units' missions and the enemy. They must go beyond merely passing along the MCOO to their subordinate leaders and making general

Appendix A

observations of the terrain such as "*This is high ground*," or "*This is a stream.*" They must determine how the terrain and weather will affect the enemy and their units. Additionally, they apply these conclusions when they develop COA for both enemy forces and their units. At company level and below, leaders develop a graphic terrain analysis overlay. This product is similar to the MCOO in it shows the critical military aspects of terrain. Not only does it facilitate planning, but it also aids in briefing subordinates.

Defined Operational Environment

A-38. Leaders to have *starting points* for terrain analysis must first define their operational environment. They must know their areas of operation and areas of interest:

- Areas of operation. Higher commanders use boundaries to define their platoons' and companies' areas of operations. Assigning areas of operations to subordinates lets the subordinates use their initiative and supports decentralized execution.
- Area of interest. An area of interest is a geographical area, usually larger than the leader's area of operation. The area of interest includes threat forces or other elements characterizing the operational environment and greatly influencing the accomplishment of the mission.

Prioritization of Terrain Analysis

A-39. Limited planning time forces leaders to prioritize their terrain analyses. For example, in the conduct of attacks, leaders might prioritize the areas immediately around their objective for analysis, followed by the platoon's specific axis leading to the objective. Given more time, they might analyze the remainder of their platoons area of operation and area of interest.

Visual Aids

A-40. Leaders prepare a graphic depiction of terrain to help explain their findings about the effects of terrain and weather on the mission. The graphic depiction of terrain can be a photograph, overlay for a map sheet, or a terrain model. In it, leaders show terrain mobility classifications, key terrain, intervisibility lines, known obstacles, avenues of approach, and mobility corridors.

OAKOC

A-41. Military aspects of terrain OAKOC are used to analyze the ground. The sequence can vary. The leader determines the effects of each aspect of terrain on both friendly and enemy forces. These effects translate directly into conclusions applying to friendly or enemy COA. Even if time is tight, the leader should allocate as much time as possible to factor, starting at the objective area, and analyzing other aspects of key terrain. Terrain and weather are the most important aspects. Conclusions include at least the following:

- Template of enemy forces and essential weapon systems.
- Positioning of own assets.
- Understanding of time and space relationships of events, leading to thorough contingency plans.

Planning

- Echeloning and identifying of enemy observation and indirect fires.
- Selecting of movement techniques and formations, to include when to transition to tactical maneuver.

Obstacles

A-42. Leaders identify existing (inherent to terrain and either natural or man-made) and reinforcing (tactical or protective) obstacles limiting mobility in his area of operation. Reinforcing obstacles are constructed, emplaced, or detonated by military force:
- Existing obstacles, natural include rivers; forests; mountains; ravines; gaps and ditches more than three meters wide; tree stumps and large rocks more than 18 inches high; forests with trees eight inches or more in diameter, with less than four meters between trees.
- Existing obstacles, man-made include towns; canals; railroad embankments; buildings; power lines; telephone lines.
- Reinforcing obstacles, tactical—tactical (reinforcing) obstacles inhibit the ability of the opposing force to move, mass, and reinforce. Examples include mine fields (conventional and situational); antitank ditches; wire obstacles.
- Reinforcing obstacles, protective (reinforcing) obstacles offer close-in protection and are important to survivability.
- Offensive considerations when analyzing obstacles and restricted terrain:
  - How is the enemy using obstacles and restricted terrain features?
  - What is the composition of the enemy's reinforcing obstacles?
  - How will obstacles and terrain affect the movement or maneuver of the unit?
  - If necessary, how can I avoid such features?
  - How do I detect and, if desired, bypass the obstacles?
  - Where has the enemy positioned weapons to cover the obstacles, and what type of weapons is he using?
  - If I must support a breach, where is the expected breach site and where will the enemy be overwatching the obstacle?
  - How will the terrain affect the employment of mortars, medium machine guns, and Javelin missiles?
- Defensive considerations when analyzing obstacles and restricted terrain:
  - Where does the enemy want to go? Where can I kill him? How do I get him to go there?
  - How will existing obstacles and restricted terrain affect the enemy?
  - How can I use these features to force the enemy into its engagement area, deny him an avenue, or disrupt his movement?
  - How will the terrain affect the employment of mortars, medium machine guns, and Javelin missiles?
- Categories of terrain, unrestricted—terrain free of restrictions to movement, so no actions are needed to enhance mobility. For armored forces, unrestricted terrain typically is flat or moderately sloped, with scattered or widely spaced obstacles such

Appendix A

as trees or rocks. This terrain generally allows wide maneuver and offers unlimited travel over well-developed road networks. It allows the platoon and squads to move with little hindrance.

- Categories of terrain, restricted—terrain hindering movement somewhat. Little effort is needed to enhance mobility, but units might have to zigzag or make frequent detours. They could have a hard time maintaining optimum speed, moving in some types of combat formations, or transitioning from one formation to another. For armored forces, restricted terrain typically means moderate to steep slopes or moderate to dense spacing of obstacles such as trees, rocks, or buildings. Swamps and rugged ground are two examples of restricted terrain for Infantry forces. Poorly developed road systems may hamper logistical or rear area movement.
- Categories of terrain, severely restricted—terrain which severely hinders or slows movement in combat formations unless some effort is made to enhance mobility. Engineer forces might be needed to improve mobility or platoon and squads might have to deviate from doctrinal tactics. For example, they might have to move in columns rather than in lines. Or, they might have to move much more slowly than they would like. For armored forces, steep slopes, densely spaced obstacles, and absence of a developed road system characterize severely restricted terrain.

Avenues of Approach

A-43. An avenue of approach is an air or ground route of an attacking force leading to an objective or key terrain. Avenues of approach are classified by type (mounted, dismounted, air, or subterranean), formation, and speed of the largest unit traveling on it.

A-44. The leader groups mutually supporting mobility corridors to form an avenue of approach. If he has no mutually supporting mobility corridors, then a single mobility corridor might become an avenue of approach. Avenues of approach are classified the same as mobility corridors. After identifying these avenues, the leader evaluates each and determines its importance.

A-45. Offensive considerations the leader can include in his evaluation of avenues of approach:
- How can I use each avenue of approach to support my movement and maneuver?
- How will each avenue support movement techniques, formations and, once we make enemy contact, maneuver?
- Will variations in trafficability force changes in formations or movement techniques, or require clearance of restricted terrain?
- What are the advantages and disadvantages of each avenue?
- What are the enemy's likely counterattack routes?
- What lateral routes could we use to shift to other axes, and which could the enemy use to threaten our flanks?
- How will each avenue of approach affect the rate of movement of each type force?

A-46. Defensive considerations the leader can include in his evaluation of avenues of approach:
- What are all likely enemy avenues into my area of operations?

- How can the enemy use each avenue of approach?
- What lateral routes could the enemy use to threaten our flanks?
- What avenues would support a friendly counterattack or repositioning of forces?

Key Terrain

A-47. Key terrain is locations or areas whose seizure, retention, or control gives a marked advantage to either combatant. It is a conclusion, usually arrived at after enemy analysis and COA development, rather than an observation.

A-48. A prominent hilltop overlooking an avenue of approach might or might not be key terrain. Even if it offers clear observation and fields of fire, it offers nothing if the enemy can easily bypass it, or if the selected course of action involves maneuver on a different avenue of approach. However, if it offers cover and concealment, observation, and good fields of fire on multiple avenues of approach, or on the *only* avenue of approach, then it offers a definite advantage to whoever controls it.

A-49. The leader must assess what terrain is essential to mission accomplishment. Another example of essential terrain for a platoon and squad in the attack is high ground overlooking the enemy's reverse-slope defense. Controlling this area could prove critical in establishing a support-by-fire position to protect a breach force.

A-50. Decisive terrain. Leaders also must determine if terrain is decisive. This is key terrain which seizure, retention, or control is necessary for mission accomplishment. Some situations have no decisive terrain. If a leader identifies terrain as decisive, this means he recognizes seizing or retaining it is necessary to accomplish the mission.

A-51. Tactical considerations in analyzing key terrain. Terrain is important for friendly observation, both for commanding and controlling and for calling for fire? What terrain is important to the enemy and why? Is it important to me? What terrain has higher headquarters named as key? Is this terrain also important to the enemy? Is the enemy controlling this key terrain? How do I gain or maintain control of key terrain? What terrain is essential for communications nodes dictating the employment of digital communications equipment?

Observation and Fields of Fire

A-52. The leader identifies locations along each avenue of approach providing clear observation and fields of fire for both the attacker and defender. He analyzes the area surrounding key terrain, objectives, engagement area, and obstacles. He locates intervisibility lines (ridges or horizons which can hide equipment or personnel from observation). He assesses the ability of the attacking force to overwatch or support movement (with direct fire). An intervisibility line analysis enables the leader to visualize the profile view of terrain when only a topographic product (map) is provided.

A-53. In analyzing fields of fire, he considers the friendly and enemy potential to cover avenues of approach and key terrain, in particular, with direct fires. He also identifies positions where artillery observers can call for indirect fire. The observer must observe both the impact and effects of indirect fires. He analyzes if vegetation will affect the

Appendix A

employment or trajectory of the Javelin, or 60-mm mortars. It can do this by masking the target or by reducing overhead clearance. When possible, the observer conducts a ground reconnaissance from both enemy and friendly perspectives. He might do it personally, by map, or with his subordinate units, or he can use the assets and information provided by the battalion reconnaissance platoon. This reconnaissance helps him to see the ground objectively and to see how it will affect both forces.

A-54. Offensive considerations in analyzing observation and fields of fire include:
- Are clear observation and fields of fire available on or near the objective for enemy observers and weapon systems?
- Where can the enemy concentrate fires?
- Where will the enemy be unable to concentrate fires?
- Where is the enemy vulnerable?
- Where can I support the movement of a friendly force with mortar, medium machine gun, or Javelin?
- Where can friendly forces conduct support by fire or assault by fire?
- Where are the natural target registration points?
- Where do I position indirect fire observers?

A-55. Defensive considerations in analyzing observation and fields of fire:
- What locations have clear observation and fields of fire along enemy avenues of approach?
- Where will the enemy establish firing lines or support-by-fire positions?
- Where will I be unable to mass fires?
- Where is the dead space in my area of operations? Where am I vulnerable?
- Where are the natural target registration points?
- Where can I destroy the enemy? Can I observe and fire on his location with at least two-thirds of my combat power?
- How obvious are these positions to the enemy?
- Where do I position indirect fire observers?

Cover and Concealment

A-56. Leaders look at the terrain, foliage, structures, and other features along avenues of approach (and on objectives or key terrain) to identify sites offering cover (protection from the effects of direct and indirect fire) and concealment (protection from observation). In the defense, weapon positions must be both lethal to the enemy and survivable to the Soldier. Cover and concealment is just as vital as clear fields of fire. Cover and concealment can be either part of the environment or something brought in by the unit to create the desired effect. Both offensive and defensive considerations must be made:
- Offensive considerations include:
    - What axes afford both clear fields of fire and cover and concealment?
    - Which terrain provides bounding elements with cover and concealment while increasing lethality?

- Defensive considerations include:
  - What locations afford cover and concealment as well as good observation and fields of fire?
  - How can friendly and enemy forces use the available cover and concealment?

CONCLUSIONS FROM TERRAIN ANALYSIS

A-57. Terrain analysis should produce several specific conclusions:
- Battle, support by fire, and assault by fire positions.
- Engagement areas and ambush sites.
- Immediate and intermediate objectives.
- Asset locations such as enemy command posts or ammunition caches.
- Assembly areas.
- Observation posts.
- Artillery firing positions.
- Air defense artillery system positions.
- Reconnaissance, surveillance, and target-acquisition positions.
- Forward area arming and refueling points.
- Landing and drop zones.
- Breach locations.
- Infiltration lanes.

FIVE MILITARY ASPECTS OF WEATHER

A-58. The five military aspects of weather are visibility; winds; precipitation; cloud cover; and temperature and humidity. Consideration of the weather's effects is an essential part of the leader's mission analysis. The leader goes past observing to application. He determines how the weather will affect the visibility, mobility, and survivability of his unit and that of the enemy. He reviews his commander's conclusions and identifies his own. He applies the results to the friendly and enemy COA he develops.

Visibility

A-59. The leader identifies critical conclusions about visibility factors such as light data, fog, and smog; and about battlefield obscurants such as smoke and dust. He considers light data and identifies critical conclusions about BMNT, sunrise, sunset, EENT, moonrise, moonset, and percentage of illumination. Some additional visibility considerations include:
- Will the sun rise behind my attack or in my eyes? Will I attack toward the sunrise?
- How can I take advantage of the limited illumination?
- How will this affect friendly and enemy target acquisition?
- Will the current weather favor the use of smoke to obscure during breaching?
- When are night vision devices effective?

Appendix A

Winds

A-60. Winds of sufficient speed can reduce the combat effectiveness of a force downwind as the result of blowing dust, obscurants, sand, or precipitation. The upwind force usually has better visibility. CBRN operations usually favor the upwind force. Windblown sand, dust, rain, or snow can reduce the effectiveness of radar and other communication systems. Strong winds also can hamper the efficiency of directional antenna systems by inducing antenna wobble. Strong winds and wind turbulence limit airborne, air assault, and aviation operations.

A-61. Evaluation of weather in support of these operations requires information on the wind at the surface as well as at varying altitudes. Near the ground, high winds increase turbulence and may inhibit maneuver. At greater altitudes, it can increase or reduce fuel consumption. Wind always is described as "*from...to*" as in "*winds are from the east moving to the west.*" The leader must answer these questions:
- Will wind speed cause obscurants to dissipate quickly?
- Will wind speed and direction favor enemy use of obscurants?
- Will wind speed and direction affect the employment of available mortars?
- What is the potential for chemical, biological, radiological and nuclear contamination?

Precipitation

A-62. Precipitation affects soil trafficability, visibility, and functioning of many electro-optical systems. Heavy precipitation can reduce the quality of supplies in storage. Heavy snow cover can reduce the efficiency of many communication systems as well as degrade the effects of many munitions and air operations. The leader identifies critical factors such as type, amount, and duration of precipitation. Some precipitation questions to answer include:
- How will precipitation (or lack of it) affect the mobility of the unit or of enemy forces?
- How can precipitation (or lack of it) add to the unit achieving surprise?

Cloud Cover

A-63. Cloud cover affects ground operations by limiting illumination and solar heating of targets. Heavy cloud cover can degrade many target acquisition systems, infrared guided munitions, and general aviation operations. Heavy cloud cover often canalizes aircraft within air avenues of approach and on the final approach to the target. Partial cloud cover can cause glare, a condition attacking aircraft might use to conceal their approach to the target. Some types of clouds reduce the effectiveness of radar systems. The leader identifies critical factors about cloud cover, including limits on illumination and solar heating of targets. Some cloud cover questions include?
- How will cloud cover affect unit operations at night? How will it affect the enemy?
- How will cloud cover affect the target acquisition of the command launch unit?
- How will cloud cover affect helicopter and close air support?

Temperature and Humidity

A-64. Extremes of temperature and humidity reduce personnel and equipment capabilities and may require the use of special shelter or equipment. Air density decreases as temperature and humidity increase. This can require reduced aircraft payloads. Temperature crossovers, which occur when target and background temperatures are nearly equal, degrade thermal target acquisition systems. The length of crossover time depends on air temperature, soil and vegetation types, amount of cloud cover, and other factors. The leader identifies critical factors about temperature, including high and low temperatures, infrared crossover times, and effects of obscurants and CBRN. Some temperature considerations include:

- How will temperature and humidity affect the unit's rate of march?
- How will temperature and humidity affect the Soldiers and equipment?
- Will temperatures and humidity favor the use of nonpersistent chemical, biological, radiological and nuclear?

ANALYSIS OF ENEMY

A-65. The second mission variable to consider is the enemy. Leaders analyze the enemy's dispositions, compositions, strengths, doctrine, equipment, capabilities, vulnerabilities, and probable COA. The line between enemy combatants and civilian noncombatants is sometimes unclear. This requires the leader to understand the laws of war, the ROE, and local situation.

Questions

A-66. Analyzing the enemy answers the question, "*What is the enemy doing and why?*" Leaders also answer—
- What is the composition and strength of the enemy force?
- What are the capabilities of his weapons? Other systems?
- What is the location of current and probable enemy positions?
- What is the enemy's most probable course of action? (DRAW-D [defends, reinforce, attack, withdraw, or delay]).

Assumptions

A-67. Leaders must understand assumption the battalion S-2 uses to portray the enemy's COA. Furthermore, their own assumptions about the enemy must be consistent with those of their higher commander. Leaders must continually improve their situational understanding of the enemy and update their enemy templates as new information or trends become available. Deviations or significant conclusions reached during their enemy analysis could positively or negatively affect the battalion's and company's plan should be shared immediately with the battalion, company commander and S-2.

A-68. In analyzing the enemy, the leader must understand the IPB. Although he usually does not prepare IPB products for his subordinates, he must be able to use the products of the higher headquarters' IPB.

Appendix A

Doctrinal Analysis (How Enemy Will Fight)

A-69. Leaders must know more than just the number and types of vehicles, Soldiers, and weapons the enemy has. The leader must thoroughly understand when, where, and how the enemy prefers or tends to use his assets. A situation template is a visual illustration of how the enemy force might look and act without the effects of weather and terrain. The leader looks at specific enemy actions during a given operation and uses the appropriate situation template to gain insights into how the enemy may fight. Likewise, he must understand enemy doctrinal objectives. In doctrinal terms, he asks—"Is the enemy oriented on the terrain, example, a reconnaissance force, his own force (assault force, terrorists, or insurgent forces), civilian forces or critical infrastructure (terrorist or insurgent forces, sabotage), or other supporting or adjacent friendly forces (as in a disruption zone)? What effect will this have on the way the enemy fights?"

A-70. However, as the global situation changes, the possibility of fighting threat who lack a structured doctrine increases. In such a situation, a leader must rely on information provided by battalion or higher echelon R&S assets and, most importantly, his and his higher headquarters' pattern analysis and deductions about the enemy in his area of operation. He also may make sound assumptions about the enemy, human nature, and local culture.

Composition

A-71. Leader's analysis must determine the types of vehicles, Soldiers, and equipment the enemy could use against his unit. He should be familiar with the basic characteristics of the units and platforms identified.

Disposition

A-72. Higher headquarters' information, he determines how the enemy is (or might be) arrayed. If the information is available, he determines the echelon force where the enemy originated. He determines the disposition of the next two higher enemy elements. From this analysis, he might be able to determine patterns in the enemy's employment or troops and equipment.

Strength

A-73. Identifies the enemy's strength by unit. He can obtain this information by translating percentages given from higher headquarters to the actual numbers in each enemy element or from information provided the COP.

Capabilities

A-74. Based on the S-2's assessment and enemy's doctrine and current location, the leader must determine the enemy's capabilities. This includes studying the maximum effective range for each weapon system, the doctrinal rates of march, and timelines associated with the performance of certain tasks. One technique is to use the warfighting functions as a checklist to address every significant element the enemy brings to the fight. The leader also determines the capabilities of the next higher enemy element. These capabilities should include reasonable assets the next higher element, or other higher enemy headquarters, may provide. This should include at least the employment of reserves, CBRN weapons, artillery or mortar locations and ranges, and reconnaissance assets.

Recent Activities

A-75. Gaining complete understanding of the enemy's intentions can be difficult when his situation templates, composition, and disposition are unclear. In all cases, the enemy's recent activities must be understood, because they can provide insight into his future activities and intentions. If time permits, the leader might be able to conduct a pattern analysis of the enemy's actions to predict future actions. In the operational environment, this might be the most important analysis the leader conducts and is likely to yield the most useful information to the leader.

Enemy Situation Template

A-76. Identifies how the enemy may potentially fight; the leader weighs the result of his analysis of terrain and weather against the higher headquarters' situation template. The refined product is a platoon situation template, a graphic showing how he believes the enemy will fight under specific operational conditions. This situation template is portrayed one echelon lower than developed by the higher headquarters' S-2. For example, if a battalion situation template identifies a platoon-size enemy element on the company's objective and squad-size enemy elements on the platoon's objective, the leader, using his knowledge of both the enemy's doctrine and terrain, develops a situation template positioning squad-size battle positions, crew-served weapons positions, or defensive trenches.

A-77. He includes in this situation template the likely sectors of fire of the enemy weapons and tactical and protective obstacles, either identified or merely templated, which support defensive tasks. Table A-1 (page A-20) shows recommended situation template items. (Refer to ATP 2-01.3 for more information.)

Appendix A

Table A-1. Recommended enemy situation template items

DEFENSE	OFFENSE
Primary, alternate, subsequent positions	Attack formations
Engagement area	Axes of advance
Individual vehicles	Firing lines
Crew-served weapons	Objectives
Tactical and protective obstacles	Reserve force commitment
Trenches	Planned indirect-fire targets
Planned indirect-fire targets	Situational obstacles
Observation posts	Reconnaissance objectives
Command and control positions	Reconnaissance force routes
Final protective fires and FPL	Phase lines
Locations of reserves	Planned point of penetration
Routes for reserve commitment	
Travel time for reserve commitment	
Battle positions, strongpoint, area of operation	
Sectors of fire	

A-78. The leader must avoid developing his situation template independently of the higher commander's guidance and S-2's product. The product must reflect the results of reconnaissance and shared information. Differences between the situation templates must be resolved before the leader can continue analyzing the enemy. Finally, given the scale with which the leader often develops his situation template, on a 1:50,000 maps, the situation template should be transferred to a graphic depiction of terrain for briefing purposes, as the situation allows. This is not for analysis, but to show subordinates the details of the anticipated enemy COA. Once he briefs the enemy analysis to his subordinates, he must ensure they understand differences between what he knows, what he suspects, and what he just templates (estimates). Unless given the benefit of information collection, his situation template is only an estimate of how the enemy might be disposed. He must not take these as facts. This is why the leader must develop a tactically sound and flexible plan. It is also why he must clearly explain his intent to his subordinates. This allows them to exercise initiative and judgment to accomplish the unit's purpose. Reconnaissance is critical in developing the best possible enemy scenario.

Information Requirements

A-79. The CCIRs identify and filter information needed by leaders to support their vision and to make critical decisions, especially to determine or validate COA. CCIRs also helps focus the efforts of subordinates and aids in the allocation of resources. Commanders should limit their CCIRs to essential information. The two key elements are friendly forces information and priority intelligence requirements.

A-80. Priority intelligence requirements are information a leader needs to know about terrain or enemy to make a critical decision. PIR are best expressed in a question being answered yes or no.

A-81. Friendly forces information requirements include information leaders need to know about their units or about adjacent units to make critical decisions.

A-82. Although EEFIs are not part of the CCIRs, they still become priorities when the leader states them. EEFI are the critical aspects of a friendly operation if known by the enemy, that subsequently would compromise or lead to failure of the operation. Consequently, this information must be protected from identification by the enemy.

ANALYSIS OF TROOPS AND SUPPORT AVAILABLE

A-83. Leaders study their task organization to determine the number, type, capabilities, and condition of available friendly troops and other support. Analysis of troops follows the same logic as analyzing the enemy by identifying capabilities, vulnerabilities and strengths. Leaders should know the disposition, composition, strength, and capabilities of their forces one and two levels down. This information can be maintained in a checkbook-style matrix for use during COA development (specifically array forces). They maintain understanding of subordinates' readiness, including maintenance, training, strengths and weaknesses, leaders, and logistic status. Analysis of troops and support answers the question: What assets are available to accomplish the mission? Leaders also answer these questions:
- What are the strengths and weaknesses of subordinate leaders?
- What is the supply status of ammunition, water, fuel (if required), and other necessary items?
- What is the present physical condition of Soldiers (morale, sleep)?
- What is the condition of equipment?
- What is the unit's training status and experience relative to the mission?
- What additional Soldiers or units will accompany?
- What additional assets are required to accomplish the mission?

A-84. Perhaps the most critical aspect of mission analysis is determining the combat potential of one's own force. The leader must realistically and unemotionally determine all available resources and new limitations based on level of training or recent fighting. This includes troops who are either attached to or in direct support of his unit. It also includes understanding the full array of assets in support of the unit. He must know, how much indirect fire, by type, is available and when it will become available.

A-85. Because of the uncertainty always present in operations at the small unit level, leaders cannot be expected to think of everything during their analysis. This fact forces leaders to determine how to get assistance when the situation exceeds their capabilities. Therefore, a secondary product of analysis of troops and support available should be an answer to the question, how do I get help?

Appendix A

ANALYSIS OF TIME AVAILABLE

A-86. The fifth mission variable of METT-TC is time available. Time refers to many factors during the operations process (plan, prepare, execute, and assess). The four categories the leader considers include:
- Planning and preparation.
- Operations.
- Next higher echelon's timeline.
- Enemy timeline.

A-87. During all phases, leaders consider critical times, unusable time, the time it takes to accomplish activities, the time it takes to move, priorities of work, and tempo of operations. Other critical conditions to consider include visibility and weather data, and events such as higher headquarters tasks and required rehearsals. Implied in the analysis of time is leader prioritization of events and sequencing of activities.

A-88. As addressed in step 1 of the TLP, time analysis is a critical aspect to planning, preparation, and execution. Time analysis is often the first thing a leader does. The leader must not only appreciate how much time is available, but he also must be able to appreciate the time/space aspects of preparing, moving, fighting, and sustaining. He must be able to see his own tasks and enemy actions in relation to time. Most importantly, as events occur, he must adjust the time available to him and assess its impact on what he wants to accomplish. Finally, he must update previous timelines for his subordinates, listing all events affecting the platoon and its subordinate elements.

ANALYSIS OF CIVIL CONSIDERATIONS

A-89. Civil considerations include the influences of manmade infrastructure, civilian institutions, and attitudes, activities of civilian leaders, populations, and organizations within an area of operation, with regard to the conduct of military operations. Civil considerations generally focus on the immediate impact of civilians on operations in progress. Civil considerations of the environment can either help or hinder friendly or enemy forces; the difference lies in which leader has taken time to learn the situation and its possible effects on the operation. Analysis of civil considerations answers three critical questions:
- How do civilian considerations affect the operation?
- How does the operation affect the civilians?
- How do our forces build national will in our area of operations?

A-90. Higher headquarters provides the leader with civil considerations affecting the next echelon's mission. The memory aid the higher headquarters may use to analyze and describe these civil considerations is ASCOPE. (Refer to ATP 2-01.3 for more information.)

Areas

A-91. The population within a prescribed area of operation comprises several different groups, both ethnically and politically. Leaders must understand each group's perceptions about the United States, the Army, and specific units operating within that area. Population statuses overlays can best describe groups and define what feelings the group has toward American forces. This is extremely important in understanding when and where to commit combat power, what relationships can be reinforced with certain groups versus what relationships need to start or cease, and ultimately what second and third order effects our actions will have in the area of operation. Information related capabilities also can be properly focused with a healthy understanding of the perceptions of the civilian population.

A-92. This characteristic addresses terrain analysis from a civilian perspective. Analyze how vital civilian areas affect the missions of respective forces and how military operations affect these areas. Factors to consider include political boundaries, locations of government centers, by-type enclaves, special regions such as mining or agricultural, trade routes, and possible settlement sites.

Structures

A-93. Include traditional high-payoff targets, protected cultural sites, and facilities with practical applications. The analysis is a comparison of how a structure's location, functions, and capabilities as compared to costs and consequences of such use.

Capabilities

A-94. Assess capabilities in terms of those required to save, sustain, or enhance life, in that order. Capabilities can refer to the ability of local authorities to provide essential functions and services. These can include areas needed after combat operations and contracted resources and services.

Organizations

Consider all nonmilitary groups or institutions in the area of operation. These may be indigenous, come from a third country or U.S. agencies. They influence and interact with the populace, force, and each other. Current activities, capabilities, and limitations are some of the information necessary to build situational understanding. This often becomes a union of resources and specialized capabilities.

People

A-95. People is a general term describing all nonmilitary personnel military forces encountered in the area of operation. This includes those personnel outside the area of operation whose actions, opinions, or political influence can affect the mission. Identify the essential communicators and formal and informal processes used to influence people. In addition, consider how historical, cultural, and social factors shape public perceptions beliefs, goals, and expectations.

Appendix A

Events

A-96. Routine, cyclical, planned, or spontaneous activities which significantly affect organizations, people, and military operations, including seasons, festivals, holidays, funerals, political rallies, and agricultural crop/livestock and market cycles and paydays. Other events, such as disasters and those precipitated by military forces, stress and affect the attitudes and activities of the populace and include a moral responsibility to protect displaced civilians. Template events and analyze them for their political, economic, psychological, environmental, and legal implications.

A-97. The leader also must identify civil considerations affecting his mission. Civil considerations are important when conducting operations against terrorist or insurgent forces in urban areas. Most terrorists and insurgents depend on the support or neutrality of the civilian population to camouflage them. Leaders must understand impact of their actions—as well as their subordinate's actions—on the civilian population, and effects they will have on current and future operations. Considerations may include:

- Ethnic dynamics.
- Organizations of influence.
- Patterns.
- Leaders and influencers.
- Economic environment.

A-98. Ethnic dynamics include religion, cultural mores, gender roles, customs, superstitions, and values certain ethnic groups hold dear which differ from other groups. Leaders who analyze the ethnic dynamics of their area of operation can best apply combat power, shape maneuver with information related capabilities, and ultimately find the common denominator all ethnic varieties have in common and focus unit efforts at it. Gaining local support can best be accomplished by the leader who demonstrates dignity and respect to the civilian population he is charged to protect and train.

A-99. Organizations of influence force the leader to look beyond preexisting civilian hierarchical arrangements. By defining organizations within the community, leaders can understand what groups have power and influence over their own smaller communities and what groups can assist our forces. After these groups have been defined, analyzing them and determining their contributions or resistance to friendly operations is easier. Many Eastern cultures rely upon religious organizations as their centers of power and influence, whereas Western culture's power comes from political institutions by elected officials. Defining other influential organizations or groups of influence allows for information collection.

A-100. Every culture, every group of people, has patterns of behavior. Whether it is set times for prayer, shopping or commuting, people follow patterns. Understanding these patterns helps leaders plan and execute information collection, combat operations, and logistical resupply. Also, unit leaders who study the history of civic culture can better understand and explain to others how and why the people have fought previous wars and conflicts. Starting with a baseline pattern and keeping a mission analysis on how the population is responding or have responded in the past under similar circumstances will assist leaders in using patterns to the unit's advantage.

A-101. Know who is in charge and who can influence and enable unit leaders to exercise governance and monitor security within a prescribed area. Many times, the spiritual leader is not necessarily the decision maker for a community, but the spiritual leader must approve the decision maker's actions. Commanders and staff officers who make link-diagrams of leadership including religious, political, and criminal personnel allow focused planning and decentralized execution which bolsters legitimacy within the population. Using the targeting methodology of D3A (decide, detect, deliver, and assess) may prove useful in determining whether a leader or influencer would best facilitate an operation, when to engage them, and what to expect.

A-102. Money and resources drive prosperity and stability. Leaders who identify the economic production base of their area of operation can execute civil-military campaigns within their area of operation bolstering the economic welfare of the people. These campaigns include infrastructure rebuild projects, creation of labor opportunities, and education. By focusing on the motivations for civilian labor and creating essential services and prosperity where there was none, unit leaders/commanders can win the support of the civilian who now can feed and clothe his family and now has clean running water. This aspect of civil considerations reinforces the security of the community against poverty and other enablers to instability.

RISK ASSESSMENT

A-103. Risk assessment is the identification and assessment of hazards allowing a leader to implement measures to control hazards. Leaders assess risk to protect the force and aid in mission accomplishment. The leader must consider two kinds of risk: tactical and accident. Tactical risk is associated with hazards existing due to the enemy's presence. The consequences of tactical risk take two major forms:

- Enemy action where the leader has accepted risk such as an enemy attack where the friendly leader has chosen to conduct an economy of force.
- Lost opportunity, such as movement across terrain severely restricts the speed of traverse. This then would restrict the unit's ability to mass the effects of combat power.

A-104. Accident risk includes all operational risk other than tactical risk and can include hazards concerning friendly personnel, equipment readiness, and environment. Fratricide is an example of an accident risk.

A-105. The leader must identify risks based on the results of his mission analysis. Once identified, risk must be reduced through controls. For example, fratricide is a hazard categorized as an accident risk; surface danger zones and risk estimate distance are used to identify the controls, such as TRP and phase lines, to reduce this accidental risk. When the leader decides what risks he is willing to accept, he also must decide in his COA how to reduce risk to an acceptable level.

IDENTIFY TENTATIVE DECISIVE POINTS

A-106. Identifying a tentative decisive point and verifying it during COA development is the most important aspect of the TLP. Visualizing a valid decisive point is how the leader

Appendix A

determines how to achieve success and accomplish his purpose. The leader develops his entire COA from the decisive point. Without determining a valid decisive point, the leader cannot begin to develop a valid or tactically sound COA. The leader, based on his initial analysis of METT-TC, his situational awareness, his vision, and insight into how such factors can affect the unit's mission, should visualize where, when, and how his unit's ability to generate combat power (firepower, protection, maneuver, leadership, and information) can overwhelm the enemy's abilities to generate combat power. The decisive point might orient on terrain, enemy, time, or a combination of these. The decisive point might be where or how, or from where, the unit will combine the effects of combat power against the enemy. The decisive point might be the event or action (with respect to terrain, enemy, or time, and generation of combat power) will ultimately and irreversibly lead to the unit achieving its purpose.

A-107. The decisive point does not simply restate the unit's essential task or purpose; it defines how, where, or when the unit will accomplish its purpose. The unit's decisive operation always focuses at the decisive point, and always accomplishes the unit's purpose. Designating a decisive point is critical to the leader's vision of how he will use combat power to achieve the purpose, how he will task-organize his unit and how his shaping operations will support the decisive operation, and how the decisive operation will accomplish the unit's purpose. This tentative decisive point forms the basis of his planning and COA development; it also forms the basis of communicating the COA to his subordinates. The leader should clearly explain what the decisive point is to his subordinate leaders and why it is decisive; this objective, in conjunction with his commander's intent, facilitates subordinate initiative. A valid decisive point enables the leader to clearly and logically link how the application of combat power elements with respect to terrain, enemy, and time allows the unit to accomplish its purpose. If the leader determines his tentative decisive point is not valid during COA development or analysis, then he must determine another decisive point and restart COA development.

COURSE OF ACTION DEVELOPMENT

A-108. From developing a strategy to analyzing, refining, and rehearsing the plan, a leader should be knowledgeable in the following areas detailed under this subheading to construct a solid COA. The purpose of COA development is to determine one or more ways to accomplish the mission consistent with the immediate higher commander's intent. A COA describes how the unit might generate the effects of overwhelming combat power against the enemy at the decisive point with the least friendly casualties. Each COA the leader develops must be detailed enough to clearly describe how he envisions using all of his assets and combat multipliers to achieve the unit's mission-essential task and purpose.

A-109. To develop a COA, he focuses on the actions the unit must take at the decisive point and works backward to his start point. The leader should focus his efforts to develop at least one well-synchronized COA; if time permits, he should develop several. The result of the COA development process is paragraph 3 of the OPORD. A COA should position the unit for future operations and provide flexibility to meet unforeseen events during execution. It also should give subordinates the maximum latitude for initiative.

SCREENING CRITERIA

A-110. A COA should be suitable, feasible, acceptable, distinguishable, and complete:
- Suitable. If executed, the COA accomplishes the mission consistent with the higher commander's concept and intent.
- Feasible. The unit has the technical and tactical skills and resources to accomplish the COA, with available time, space, and resources.
- Acceptable. The military advantage gained by executing the COA must justify the cost in resources, especially casualties. This assessment is largely subjective.
- Distinguishable. If more than one COA is developed, it must be sufficiently different from the others to justify full development and consideration.
- Complete. The COA covers the operational factors of who, what, when, where, and how, and must show from start to finish how the unit will accomplish the mission. The COA must address the doctrinal aspects of the mission. For example, in an attack against a defending enemy, the COA must address the movement to, deployment against, assault of, and consolidation upon the objective.

Note. Leaders assess risk continuously throughout COA development.

ACTIONS

A-111. Next, the leader analyzes relative combat power, generates options, arrays his forces, develops a concept of the operation, assigns responsibility, and prepares a COA statement and sketch.

Analyze Relative Combat Power

A-112. During the first step of COA development, analyzing relative combat power, leaders compare and contrast friendly combat power with the enemy. There four goals include:
- Identify an enemy weakness to exploit.
- Identify friendly strengths to exploit the enemy weakness.
- Identify enemy strengths to mitigate.
- Identify friendly weaknesses to protect.

A-113. The purpose of this step is to compare the combat power of friendly and enemy forces. It is not merely a calculation and comparison of friendly and enemy weapons numbers or units with the aim of gaining a numerical advantage. Using the results of all previous analyses done during mission analysis, the leader compares his unit's combat power strengths and weaknesses with those of the enemy. He seeks to calculate the time and manner in which his force (and enemy) can maximize the effects of maneuver, firepower, protection, leadership, and information in relation to the specific terrain, disposition, and composition of each force. The leader also determines how to avoid enemy strengths or advantages in combat power. In short, he strives to determine where, when, and how his unit's combat power (the effects of maneuver, firepower, protection, leadership, and information) can overwhelm the enemy's ability to generate combat power.

Appendix A

An analysis of the ability to generate combat power will help the leader confirm or deny his tentative decisive point.

Generate Options

A-114. Most missions and tasks can be accomplished in more than one way. The goal of this step, generating options, is to determine one or more of those ways quickly. First, leaders consider TTP from doctrine, unit SOPs, history, or other resources to determine if a solution to a similar tactical problem exists already. If it does, the leader's job is to take the existing solution and modify it to his unique situation. If a solution does not exist, the leader must develop one. Second, leaders confirm the mission's decisive point. Then, using doctrinal requirements as a guide, the leader assigns purposes and tasks to decisive, and shaping, and sustaining operations.

A-115. This doctrinal requirement provides a framework for the leader to develop a COA. For example, a breach requires an assault element, support element, breach element, security element, and possibly a reserve. Beginning with the decisive point identified during mission analysis, the leader identifies the decisive operation's purpose and purposes of his shaping and sustaining operations. The decisive operation's purpose is nested to his unit's overall purpose and is achieved at his decisive point. The shaping operation's purposes are nested to the decisive operation's purpose by setting the conditions for success of the decisive operation. The sustaining operation's purposes are nested to the decisive and shaping operation's purposes by providing sustainment, operational area security, movement control, terrain management, and infrastructure. The leader then determines the tactical mission tasks for the decisive, shaping, and sustaining operations. These tasks must be accomplished to achieve the subordinate unit's purpose.

Array Forces

A-116. Using the product from generating options, the leader then determines what combinations of Soldiers, weapons, and other systems are needed to accomplish each task. This is known as "*arraying forces*" or "*assigning troops to task*." This judgment call is unique to the specific METT-TC conditions the leader faces. He then must task organize his forces specific to the respective essential tactical tasks and purposes assigned to his subordinate elements. He determines the specific quantity of squads, weapons (by type), and fire support necessary to accomplish each task against the enemy array of forces. He allocates resources required for the decisive operation's success first and determines the resources needed for shaping operations in descending order of importance.

Develop a Concept of Operations

A-117. The concept of the operation describes how the leader envisions the operation unfolding, from its start to its conclusion or end state. Operations/actions consist of numerous activities, events, and tasks. The concept of the operation describes the relationships between activities, events, and tasks, and explains how the tasks will lead to accomplishing the mission. The concept of the operation is a framework to assist leaders, not a script. The normal cycle for an offensive mission is tactical movement, actions on the objective, and consolidation and reorganization. The normal cycle for defensive missions is engagement area development and preparation of the battle positions, actions in the engagement area, counterattack, and consolidation and reorganization. In developing the concept of the operation, the leader clarifies in his mind the best ways to use the available terrain and to employ the unit's strengths against the enemy's weaknesses. He includes the requirements of indirect fire to support the maneuver. He then develops the maneuver control measures necessary to convey his intent, enhance the understanding of the schemes of maneuver, prevent fratricide, and clarify the tasks and purposes of the decisive shaping, and sustaining operations. He also determines the sustainment aspects of the COA.

Assign Responsibilities

A-118.   Leaders assign responsibility for each task to a subordinate. Whenever possible and depending on the existing chain of command, they avoid fracturing unit integrity. They try to keep their span of control between two to five subordinate elements. The leader ensures every unit in his command is employed, every asset is attached and adequate mission command is provided for each element. The leader must avoid unnecessary complicated mission command structures and maintain unit integrity where feasible.

Prepare a Course of Action Statement and Sketch

A-119.   Leaders in small units primarily use the COA statement and COA sketch to describe the concept of the operation. These two products are the basis for paragraph three of the OPORD. The COA statement specifies how the unit will accomplish the mission. The first three steps of COA development provide the bulk of the COA statement. The COA statement details how the unit's operation supports the next higher leader's operation, the decisive point and why it is decisive, the form of maneuver or type of defensive mission, and operational framework. The COA sketch is a drawing or series of drawings to assist the leader in describing how the operation will unfold. The sketch provides a picture of the maneuver aspects of the concept. Leaders use tactical mission task graphics and control measures (Refer to ADRP 1-02 for more information.) to convey the operation in a doctrinal context. Both the COA statement and sketch focus at the decisive point. The COA statement should identify—

- Decisive point and what makes it decisive.
- Form of maneuver or type of defensive mission.
- Tasks and purposes of the decisive, shaping, and sustaining operations.
- Reserve planning priorities.
- Purposes of critical warfighting functions elements.
- The end state.

A-120.   The COA sketch should identify how the unit intends to focus the effects of overwhelming combat power at the decisive point. When integrated with terrain, the refined product becomes the unit's operations overlay.

Appendix A

COURSE OF ACTION ANALYSIS

A-121. COA analysis begins with both friendly and enemy COA and, using a method of action-reaction-counteraction war game, results in a synchronized friendly plan, identified strengths and weaknesses, and updated risk assessment. After developing the COA, the leader analyzes it to determine its strengths and weaknesses, visualizes the flow of the battle, identifies the conditions or requirements necessary to enhance synchronization, and gains insights into actions at the decisive point of the mission. If he has developed more than one COA, he applies this same analysis to each COA developed. He does this analysis through war gaming or "*fighting*" the COA against at least one enemy COA. For each COA, the leader thinks the operation from start to finish. He compares their COA with the enemy's most probable COA. At small-unit level, the enemy's most probable COA is what the enemy is most likely to do. During the war game, the leader visualizes a set of enemy and friendly actions and reactions. War gaming is the process of determining "*what if?*" factors of the overall operations. The object is to determine what can go wrong and what decision the leader likely will have to make as a result. COA analysis allows the leader to synchronize his assets, identify potential hazards, and develop a better understanding of the upcoming operation. It enables him—

- To determine how to maximize the effects of combat power while protecting friendly forces and minimizing collateral damage.
- To anticipate events within the area of operations.
- To determine conditions and resources required for success.
- To identify additional control requirements.
- To identify friendly coordination requirements.

A-122. COA analysis (war gaming) brings together friendly and enemy forces on the actual terrain to visualize how the operation will unfold. It is a continuous cycle of action, reaction, and counteraction. This process highlights critical tasks, stimulates ideas, and provides insights rarely gained through mission analysis and COA development alone. War gaming is a critical step in the planning process and should be allocated more time than the other steps. War gaming helps the leader fully synchronize friendly actions, while considering the likely reactions of the enemy. The product of this process is the synchronization matrix. War gaming, depending on how much time is devoted to planning, provides—

- An appreciation for time, space, and triggers needed to integrate direct and indirect fire support, obscurants, engineers, air defense artillery, and chemical, biological, radiological, nuclear with maneuver platoons (Infantry, antiarmor, or tank) to support unit tasks and purposes identified in the scheme of maneuver.
- Flexibility built into the plan by gaining insights into possible branches to the basic plan.
- The need for control measures, such as checkpoints, contact points, and target registration points, aid in control, flexibility, and synchronization.
- Coordinating instructions to enhance execution and unity of effort, and to ease confusion between subordinate elements.
- Information needed to complete paragraphs three, four, and five of the OPORD. Assessments regarding on-order and be-prepared missions.

Planning

- Projected sustainment expenditures, friendly casualties, and resulting medical requirements.

COURSE OF ACTION COMPARISON AND SELECTION

A-123. If the leader has developed more than one COA, he must compare them by weighing the specific advantages, disadvantages, strengths, and weaknesses of each as noted during the war game. These attributes may pertain to the accomplishment of the unit purpose, the use of terrain, the destruction of the enemy or other aspect of the operation he believes is important. He uses these factors, gained from his relational combat power analysis matrix, as his frame of reference in tentatively selecting the best COA. He makes the final selection of a COA based on his own judgment, the start time of the operation, the area of operation, the scheme of maneuver, and subordinate unit tasks and purposes.

STEP 4 – INITIATE MOVEMENT

A-124. Leaders initiate movements necessary to continue mission preparation or to posture the unit for starting the mission. This step can be executed anytime throughout the sequence of the TLP. It can include movement to an AA, battle position, or new area of operation, or the movement of guides or quartering parties.

STEP 5 – CONDUCT RECONNAISSANCE

A-125. To exploit the principles of speed and surprise, leaders should weigh the advantages of reconnoitering personally against the combat multiplier in the form of supplied information from battalion information systems. They realistically consider the dangers of reconnoitering personally, and time required to conduct them. Leaders might be able to plan their operations using the unprecedented amount of combat information provided by the higher echelon information collection assets. However, if time permits, leaders should verify higher headquarters' intelligence by reconnoitering visually. They should seek to confirm the PIR supporting their tentative plans. These PIR usually consists of assumptions or critical facts about the enemy. This can include strength and location, especially at templated positions. It also can include information about the terrain. For example, verification of a tentative support-by-fire position can suppress the enemy, or an avenue of approach is useable.

A-126. If possible, leaders should include their subordinate leaders in their reconnaissance efforts. This allows the subordinates to see as much of the terrain and enemy as possible. The reconnaissance also helps subordinate leaders gain insight into the leaders' visions of the operation.

A-127. The leaders' recons might include moving to or beyond the LD, reconnaissance of an area of operation, or walking from the forward edge of the battle area back to and through the platoon area of operation or battle position along likely enemy avenues of approach. If possible, leaders should select vantage points with the best possible view of the decisive point. In addition to the leaders' reconnaissance efforts, units can conduct additional reconnaissance operations. Examples include surveillance of an area by subordinate elements, patrols to determine enemy locations, and establishment of

Appendix A

observation posts to gain additional information. Leaders also can incorporate Javelin CLUs as surveillance tools (day or night), based on an analysis of METT-TC.

A-128. The nature of the reconnaissance, including what it covers and how long it lasts, depends on the tactical situation and time available. The leader should use the results of the COA development process to identify information and security requirements of the unit's reconnaissance operations.

A-129. The leader must include disseminating results and conclusions arrived from reconnaissance into his time analysis. He also must consider how to communicate changes in the COA to his subordinates and how these changes affect his plans, actions of the subordinates, and other supporting elements.

STEP 6 – COMPLETE THE PLAN

A-130. During this step, leaders expand their selected (or refined) COA into complete OPORD. They prepare overlays, refine the indirect fire list, complete sustainment and mission command requirements and, of course, update the tentative plan based on the latest reconnaissance or information. They prepare briefing sites and other briefing materials they might need to present the OPORD directly to their subordinates.

A-131. Using the five-paragraph OPORD format helps them to explain all aspects of the operation: terrain, enemy, higher and adjacent friendly units, unit mission, execution, support, and mission command. The format also serves as a checklist to ensure they cover all relevant details of the operation. It also gives subordinates a smooth flow of information from beginning to end.

STEP 7 – ISSUE OPERATIONS ORDER

A-132. The OPORD precisely and concisely explains both the leader's intent and concept of how he envisions the unit accomplishing the mission. The order does not contain unnecessary information. The OPORD is delivered quickly and in a manner allowing subordinates to concentrate on understanding the leader's vision and not just copying what he says verbatim. The leader must prepare adequately and deliver the OPORD confidently and quickly to build and sustain confidence in his subordinates.

A-133. When issuing the OPORD, the leader must ensure his subordinates understand and share his vision of what must be done and when and how it must be done. They must understand how all the platoon elements work together to accomplish the mission. They also must understand how the platoon mission supports the intentions of the immediate higher commander. When the leader has finished issuing the order, subordinate leaders should leave with a clear understanding of what the leader expects their elements to do. The leader is responsible for ensuring his subordinates understand.

A-134. In many respects more importantly, the leader must issue the order in a manner instilling subordinates with confidence in the plan and a commitment to do their best to achieve the plan. Whenever possible, he must issue the order in person. He looks into the eyes of his subordinate leaders to ensure each one understands the mission and what the element must achieve.

A-135. Complete the order with a confirmation brief. At a minimum, each subordinate leader should be able to back brief the unit mission and intent, the immediate higher commander's intent, his own tasks and purpose, and time he will issue his unit's OPORD. Each subordinate should confirm he understands the commander's vision and how the mission is accomplished with respect to the decisive point. This confirmation brief provides an opportunity to highlight issues or concerns.

A-136. The five-paragraph OPORD format (see figure A-4, page A-34), helps the leader paint a picture of all aspects of the operation, from the terrain to the enemy, and finally to the unit's own actions from higher to lower. The format helps him decide what relevant details he must include and in providing subordinates with a smooth flow of information from beginning to end. At the same time, the leader must ensure the order is not only clear and complete but also as brief as possible. If he has already addressed an item adequately in a previous WARNORD, he can simply state "*No change*," or provide necessary updates. The leader is free to brief the OPORD in the most effective manner to convey information to his subordinates.

Appendix A

1. **SITUATION**
    - Area of Interest
    - Area of Operations
        - Terrain
        - Weather
    - Enemy Forces
        - Latest Intelligence
    - Friendly Forces
        - Two Levels up
        - One Level up
        - Adjacent Units
    - Attachments and Detachments
        - Who / Why

2. **MISSION**
    - Who
    - What
    - When
    - Where
    - Why

3. **EXECUTION**
    - Commander's Intent
    - Concept of Operations
    - Scheme of Movement and Maneuver
        - Explain from Start to Finish
    - Tasks to Subordinate Units
    - Coordinating Instructions
        - Time Schedule
        - CCIR, PIR, FFIR, EEFI
        - Risk Reduction Control Measures
        - ROE
        - Environment Considerations
        - Force Protection

4. **SUSTAINMENT**
    - Logistic
        - Maintenance
        - Transportation
        - field Services
    - Personnel Services Support
        - Handling of EPW
    - Army Health Systems Support
        - Medical / Casualty Evacuations
        - Preventive Medicine

5. **COMMAND AND SIGNAL**
    - Command
        - Location of Leaders
    - Control
        - Command Post Location
    - Signal
        - Radio Frequencies
        - Passwords / Running Passwords
        - Pyrotechnic Signals

Figure A-4. Operations order format

STEP 8 – SUPERVISE AND REFINE

A-137. This final step of the TLP is crucial. After issuing the OPORD, the leader and his subordinate leaders must ensure the required activities and tasks are completed in a timely manner prior to mission execution. Supervision is the primary responsibility of all leadership. Both officers and NCOs must check everything important for mission accomplishment. This includes, but is not limited to—

- Conducting numerous back briefs on all aspects of the platoon and subordinate unit operations.
- Ensuring the second in command in each element is prepared to execute in his leaders' absence.
- Listening to subordinates' OPORD.
- Observing rehearsals of subordinate units.
- Checking load plans to ensure they are carrying only what is necessary for the mission or what the OPORD specified.
- Checking the status and serviceability of weapons.
- Checking on maintenance activities of subordinate units.
- Ensuring local security is maintained.

REHEARSALS

A-138. Rehearsals are practice sessions conducted to prepare units for an upcoming operation or event. They are essential in ensuring thorough preparation, coordination, and understanding of the commander's plan and intent. Leaders should never underestimate the value of rehearsals.

A-139. Rehearsals require leaders and, when time permits, other platoon Soldiers to perform required tasks, ideally under conditions as close as possible to those expected for the actual operation. At their best, rehearsals are interactive; participants maneuver their actual vehicles or use vehicle models or simulations while verbalizing their elements' actions. During every rehearsal, the focus is on the how element, allowing subordinates to practice the actions called for in their individual scheme of maneuver.

Note. Rehearsals are different from a discussion of what is supposed to happen during the actual event. Leaders can test subordinates understanding of the plan by ensuring they push the rehearsal forward rather than waiting to dictate each step of the operation.

A-140. The leader uses well-planned, efficiently run rehearsals to accomplish the following:

- Reinforce training and increase proficiency in critical tasks.
- Reveal weaknesses or problems in the plan, leading to more refinement of the plan or development of additional branch plans.
- Integrate the actions of subordinate elements.
- Confirm coordination requirements between the platoon and adjacent units.

Appendix A

- Improve each Soldier's understanding of the concept of the operation, the direct fire plan, anticipated contingencies, and possible actions and reactions for various situations may arise during the operation.
- Ensure seconds-in-command are prepared to execute in their leaders' absence.

REHEARSAL TYPES

A-141. Leaders may use several types of rehearsals, which include:
- Backbrief.
- Combined arms rehearsal.
- Support rehearsal.
- Battle drill or standard operating procedure rehearsal.

Backbrief

A-142. A backbrief is a briefing by subordinates to the commander to review how subordinates intend to accomplish their mission. Normally, subordinates perform backbriefs throughout preparation. These briefs allow commanders to clarify the commander's intent early in subordinate planning. Commanders use the backbrief to identify problems in the concept of the operation.

Combined Arms Rehearsal

A-143. A combined arms rehearsal is a rehearsal in which subordinate units synchronize their plans with each other. A maneuver unit headquarters normally executes a combined arms rehearsal after subordinate units issue their operation order. This rehearsal type helps ensure subordinate commanders' plans achieve the higher commander's intent.

Support Rehearsal

A-144. The support rehearsal helps synchronize each warfighting function with the overall operation. This rehearsal supports the operation so units can accomplish their missions. Throughout preparation, units conduct support rehearsals within the framework of a single or limited number of warfighting functions. These rehearsals typically involve coordination and procedure drills for aviation, fires, engineer support, or casualty evacuation. Support rehearsals and combined arms rehearsals complement preparations for the operation. Units may conduct rehearsals separately and combine them into full-dress rehearsals. Although these rehearsals differ slightly by warfighting function, they achieve similar results.

Battle Drill or Standard Operating Procedure Rehearsal

A-145. A battle drill or SOP rehearsal ensures all participants understand a technique or a specific set of procedures. Throughout preparation, units and staffs rehearse battle drills and SOPs. These rehearsals do not need a completed order from higher headquarters. Leaders place priority on those drills or actions they anticipate occurring during the

Planning

operation. All echelons use these rehearsal types; however, they are most common for platoons, squads, and sections. They are conducted throughout preparation and are not limited to published battle drills.

METHODS OF REHEARSALS

A-146. Rehearsals should follow the crawl-walk-run training methodology whenever possible. This prepares the platoons and subordinate elements for increasingly difficult conditions. (Refer to FM 6-0 for more information).Units can conduct these forms of rehearsals if mission variables permit—

- Full-dress rehearsal.
- Reduced-force rehearsal.
- Terrain-model rehearsal.
- Digital terrain-model rehearsal.
- Sketch-map rehearsal.
- Map rehearsal.
- Network rehearsal.

Full-Dress Rehearsal

A-147. A full-dress rehearsal produces the most detailed understanding of the operation. It includes every participating Soldier and system. Leaders rehearse their subordinates on terrain similar to area of operation, initially under good light conditions, and then in limited visibility. Leaders repeat small unit actions until executed to standard. Full-dress rehearsals help Soldiers clearly understand what commanders expect of them. It helps them gain confidence in their ability to accomplish the mission. Supporting elements, such as aviation crews, meet and rehearse with Soldiers to synchronize the operation.

Reduced-Force Rehearsal

A-148. Circumstances may prohibit a rehearsal with all members of the unit. A reduced-force rehearsal involves only key leaders of the organization and subordinate units. It normally takes fewer resources than a full-dress rehearsal. Terrain requirements mirror those of a full-dress rehearsal, even though fewer Soldiers participate. The commander first decides the level of leader involvement. Then selected leaders rehearse the plan while traversing actual or similar terrain. Often commanders use this technique to rehearse fire control measures for an engagement area during defensive operations. Commanders often use a reduced-force rehearsal to prepare key leaders for a full-dress rehearsal. It may require developing a rehearsal plan mirroring the actual plan but fits the rehearsal terrain.

Terrain-Model Rehearsal

A-149. The terrain-model rehearsal is the most popular rehearsal technique. It takes less time and fewer resources than a full-dress or reduced-force rehearsal. (A terrain-model rehearsal takes a platoon between one to two hours to execute to standard.) An accurately

Appendix A

constructed terrain model helps subordinate leaders visualize the commander's intent and concept of the operation. When possible, commanders place the terrain model where it overlooks the actual terrain of the area of operation. However, if the situation requires more security, they place the terrain model on a reverse slope within walking distance of a point overlooking the area of operation. The model's orientation coincides with the terrain. The size of the terrain model can vary from small (using markers to represent units) to large (on which the participants can walk). A large model helps reinforce the participants' perception of unit positions on the terrain.

Digital Terrain-Model Rehearsal

A-150. With today's digital capabilities, users can construct terrain models in virtual space. Units drape high-resolution imagery over elevation data thereby creating a fly-through or walk-through. Holographic imagery produces views in three dimensions. Often, the model hot links graphics, detailed information, unmanned aircraft systems, and ground imagery to key points providing accurate insight to the plan. Digital terrain models reduce the operations security risk because they do not use real terrain. The unit geospatial engineers or imagery analysts can assist in digital model creation. Detailed city models exist for many world cities.

Sketch-Map Rehearsal

A-151. Commanders can use the sketch-map technique almost anywhere, day or night. The procedures are similar to a terrain-model rehearsal except the commander uses a sketch map in place of a terrain model. Large sketches ensure all participants can see as each participant walks through execution of the operation. Participants move markers on the sketch to represent unit locations and maneuvers. Sketch-map rehearsals take less *time* than terrain-model rehearsals and more time than map rehearsals.

Map Rehearsal

A-152. A map rehearsal is similar to a sketch-map rehearsal except the commander uses a map and operation overlay of the same scale used to plan the operation. The map rehearsal itself consumes the most time. A map rehearsal is normally the easiest technique to set up since it requires only maps and graphics for current operations. Units gear a map rehearsal's operation overlay to the echelon conducting the rehearsal. Multi-echelon rehearsals using this technique are difficult. This rehearsal can present operations security risks if the area around the rehearsal site is not secured. This technique requires the least terrain of all rehearsals. A good site ensures participants can easily find it yet stay concealed from the enemy. An optimal location overlooks the terrain where the unit will execute the operation.

Network Rehearsal

A-153. Units conduct network rehearsals over wide-area networks or local area networks. Commanders and staffs practice these rehearsals by talking through critical portions of the operation over communications networks in a sequence the commander establishes. The organization rehearses only critical parts of the operation. These

Planning

rehearsals require all information systems needed to execute portions of the operation. All participants require working information systems, operation order, and overlays. Command posts can rehearse battle tracking during network rehearsals.

PRECOMBAT CHECKS AND INSPECTIONS

A-154. PCCs and PCIs are critical to the success of missions. These checks and inspections are leader tasks and cannot be delegated below the team leader level. They ensure the Soldier is prepared to execute the required individual and collective tasks supporting the mission. Checks and inspections are part of the TLP protecting against shortfalls endangering Soldiers' lives and jeopardize the execution of a mission.

A-155. PCCs and PCIs must be tailored to the specific unit and mission requirements. Each mission and each patrol may require a separate set of checklists. Each element will have its own established set of PCCs and PCIs, but each platoon within its element should have identical checklists. Weapons squads will have a different checklist than line squads, but each weapon squad within an organization should be the same.

A-156. One of the best ways to ensure PCCs and PCIs are complete and thorough is with full-dress rehearsals. These rehearsals, run at combat speed with communication and full battle-equipment, allow the leader to envision minute details, as they will occur in the area of operation. If the operation is to be conducted at night, Soldiers should conduct full-dress rehearsals at night as well. PCCs and PCIs should include back briefs on the mission, the task and purpose of the mission, and how the Soldiers' role fits into the scheme of maneuver. The Soldiers should know the latest intelligence updates, ROE, be versed in medical and casualty evacuation procedures and sustainment requirements.

A-157. Table A-2 (page A-40) lists sensitive items, high dollar value items, issued pieces of equipment, and supplies. This table should spur thought it's not a final list. Follow your own unit SOP guidelines.

Appendix A

Table A-2. Precombat checks and precombat inspection checklist example

ID card/ID tags	T&E mechanisms	Grappling hook
Canteens/MOLLE hydration bladder	Spare barrels	Sling sets
Ammunition/magazines	Spare barrel bags	Pick-up zone marking kit
Individual weapons	Extraction tools	Radio's
Protective mask	Asbestos gloves	GPS/Laser range finder
All clothing items in packing list	Barrel changing handles	Handheld microphones
Flashlights	Headspace and timing gauges	Night vision devices
Radios and backup communications	VS-17 panel	Batteries and spare batteries
Call for fire procedures	Vehicle tools (if applicable)	Improved outer tactical vest
9- line medical evacuation procedures	Binoculars	MOLLE ruck/assault pack systems
Night vision goggles mounting plate	Earplugs	Knee and elbow pads
Poncho	Weapons cleaning kit	Ballistic spectacles
Improved rain suit top and bottom	Meals/food	Insect repellent
Litter	Flexi cuffs	Infrared Strobe
Protractor/map	Visual/language translator card	Advanced combat helmet
Bayonet and scabbard	Water purification tablets	Chemical lights
Lensatic compass	Watch	Combat boots
Notebook/pen/pencil	Lip balm/sunscreen	Entrenching tool
Tripods	Concertina wire gloves	Weapon tie downs
Pintles	Equipment packed according to SOP	+ Combat Lifesaver bags
Counter-radio electronic warfare device	Camouflage stick	Pocket mirror

Appendix B
Direct Fire Planning and Control

Suppressing or destroying the enemy with direct fires is fundamental to success in close combat. Direct fire is inherent in maneuver, as is close combat. Small-unit leaders of the Infantry platoon must plan to focus, distribute, and shift the overwhelming mass of the platoon's direct fire capability at critical locations and times to succeed in combat. Efficient and effective fire control means the platoon acquires the enemy and masses the effects of direct fires to achieve decisive results in the close fight. This appendix covers: principles of direct fire control, fire control process, direct fire planning, and direct fire control. (Refer to TC 3-20.31-4 for more information.)

SECTION I – PRINCIPLES OF DIRECT FIRE CONTROL

B-1. Fire control requires a unit to acquire the enemy and mass the effects of fires rapidly to achieve decisive results in the close fight. When planning and executing direct fires, the platoon leader and subordinate leaders must know how to apply several fundamental principles. The purpose of the principles of direct fire is not to restrict the actions of subordinates. Applied correctly, they help the platoon to accomplish its primary goal in direct fire engagements both to acquire first and shoot first. These principles give subordinates the freedom to act quickly upon acquisition of the enemy. This discussion focuses on the following principles:

- Mass the effects of fire.
- Destroy the greatest threat first.
- Avoid target overkill.
- Employ the best weapon for specific target.
- Minimize friendly exposure and avoid fratricide.
- Plan for limited visibility conditions.
- Develop contingencies

MASS THE EFFECTS OF FIRE

B-2. The Infantry platoon must mass its fires to achieve decisive results. Massing entails focusing fires at critical points and distributing the effects. Random application of fires is unlikely to have a decisive effect. For example, concentrating the platoon's fires at a single target may ensure its destruction or suppression; however, fire control technique probably will not achieve a decisive effect on the enemy formation or position.

Appendix B

DESTROY THE GREATEST THREAT FIRST

B-3. The order in which the platoon engages enemy forces is in direct relation to the danger they present. The threat posed by the enemy depends on his weapons, range, and positioning. Presented with multiple targets, a unit will, in almost all situations, initially concentrate fires to destroy the greatest threat first, and distribute fires over the remainder of the enemy force.

AVOID TARGET OVERKILL

B-4. Use only the amount of fire required to achieve necessary effects. Target overkill wastes ammunition and ties up weapons better employed acquiring and engaging other targets. The idea of having every weapon engage a different target, however, must be tempered by the requirement to destroy the greatest threats first.

EMPLOY THE BEST WEAPON FOR SPECIFIC TARGET

B-5. Using the appropriate weapon increases the probability of rapid enemy destruction or suppression; at the same time, it saves ammunition. The platoon and squad have many weapons with which to engage the enemy. Target type, range, and exposure are vital factors in determining the weapon and ammunition being employed, as are weapons and ammunition availability and desired targets effects. Additionally, a leader should consider individual crew capabilities when deciding on the employment of weapons. The platoon leader arrays his forces based on the terrain, enemy, and desired effects of fires. As an example, when he expects an enemy dismounted assault in restricted terrain, the platoon leader would employ his squads, taking advantage of their ability to best engage numerous fast-moving targets.

MINIMIZE FRIENDLY EXPOSURE AND AVOID FRATRICIDE

B-6. Units increase their survivability by exposing themselves to the enemy only to the extent necessary to engage him. Natural or man-made defilade provides the best cover from lethal direct fire munitions. Infantry Soldiers minimize their exposure by constantly seeking available cover, attempting to engage the enemy from the flank, remaining dispersed, firing from multiple positions, and limiting engagement times.

B-7. The platoon leader and subordinate leaders must be proactive in reducing the risk of fratricide, friendly fire and noncombatant casualties. They have several tools to assist them in this effort: identification training for combat vehicles and aircraft, the unit's weapons safety posture, the weapons control status, recognition markings, and a COP to include range cards, area of operation sketches, and rehearsals. Knowledge and employment of applicable ROE are the primary means of preventing noncombatant casualties.

> *Note.* Because it's difficult to distinguish between friendly and enemy dismounted Soldiers, small-unit leaders must constantly monitor positions of friendly squads.

PLAN FOR LIMITED VISIBILITY CONDITIONS

B-8. At night, limited visibility fire control equipment enables the platoon to engage enemy forces at nearly the same ranges are applicable during the day. Obscurants such as dense fog, heavy smoke, and blowing sand, however, can reduce the capabilities of thermal and infrared equipment. Leaders should develop contingency plans for such extreme limited visibility conditions. Although decreased acquisition capabilities have minimal effect on area fire, point target engagements likely will occur at decreased ranges. Typically, firing positions, whether offensive or defensive, must be adjusted closer to the area or point where the platoon leader intends to focus fires. Another alternative is the use of visual or infrared illumination when there is insufficient ambient light for passive light intensification devices.

> *Note.* Vehicles equipped with thermal sights can assist squads in detecting and engaging enemy Infantry forces in conditions such as heavy obscurants and low illumination.

DEVELOP CONTINGENCIES

B-9. Leaders initially develop plans based on their units' maximum capabilities; they make backup plans for implementation in the event of casualties or weapon damage or failure. While leaders cannot anticipate or plan for every situation, they should develop plans for what they view as the most probable occurrences. Building redundancy into these plans, such as having two systems observe the same area of operation, is an invaluable asset when the situation (and number of available systems) permits. Designating alternate sectors of fire provides a means of shifting fires if adjacent elements are knocked out of action.

SECTION II – FIRE CONTROL PROCESS

B-10. To bring direct fires against an enemy force, leaders must continuously apply the steps of the fire control process. At the heart of this process are two critical actions: rapid, accurate target acquisition and massing of fire to achieve decisive effects on the target. Target acquisition is the detection, identification, and location of a target in sufficient detail to permit the employment of weapons. Massing entails focusing fires at critical points and distributing the fires for optimum effect.

B-11. The following discussion examines target acquisition and massing of fires using these basic steps of the fire control process:
- Identify probable enemy locations and determine the enemy scheme of maneuver.
- Determine where and how to mass fires.

Appendix B

- Orient forces to speed target acquisition.
- Shift fires to refocus or redistribute.

IDENTIFY PROBABLE ENEMY LOCATIONS AND DETERMINE THE ENEMY SCHEME OF MANEUVER

B-12. Leaders plan and execute direct fires based on their mission analysis. An essential part of this plan is the analysis of the terrain and enemy force, which aids the leader in visualizing how the enemy will attack or defend a particular piece of terrain. A defending enemy's defensive positions or an attacking enemy's support positions are normally driven by intervisibility. Typically, there are limited points on a piece of terrain providing both good fields of fire and adequate cover for a defender. Similarly, an attacking enemy will have only a limited selection of avenues of approach providing adequate cover and concealment.

B-13. Coupled with available intelligence, an understanding of the effects of a specific piece of terrain on maneuver, figure B-1 will assist the leader in identifying probable enemy locations and likely avenues of approach both before and during the fight. The leader may use all of the following products or techniques in developing and updating the analysis:

- An enemy situation template based on the analysis of terrain and enemy.
- A spot or contact report on enemy locations and activities.
- Information collection within the areas of operations.

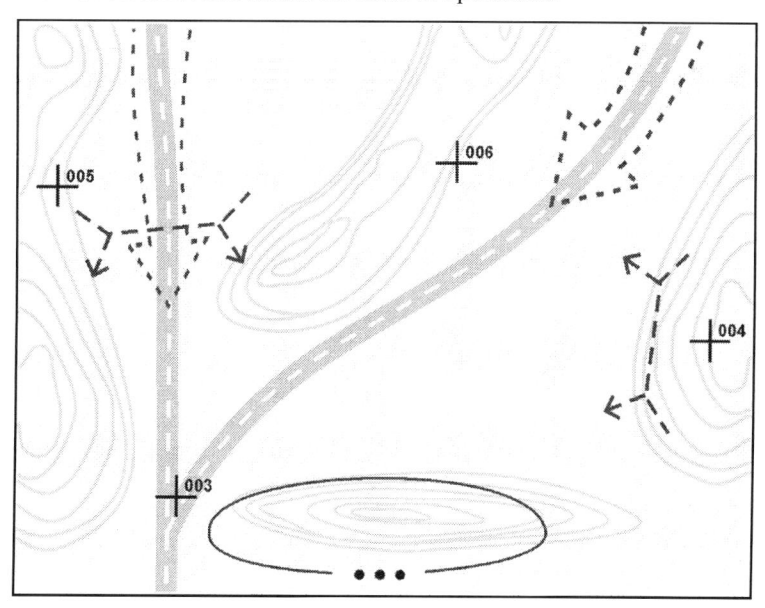

Figure B-1. Identifying probable enemy locations and determining enemy scheme of maneuver

Direct Fire Planning and Control

DETERMINE WHERE AND HOW TO MASS FIRES

B-14. To achieve decisive effects, friendly forces must mass their fires. (See figure B-2.) Massing requires the leader both to focus the fires of subordinate elements and to distribute the effects of the fires. Based on his mission analysis and his concept of the operation, the leader identifies points where he wants to, or must, focus the unit's fires. Most often, these are locations he has identified as probable enemy positions or points along likely avenues of approach where the unit can mass fires. Because subordinate elements may not initially be oriented on the point where the leader wants to mass fires, he may issue a fire command to focus the fires. At the same time, the leader must use direct fire control measures to distribute the fires of his elements, which now are focused on the same point.

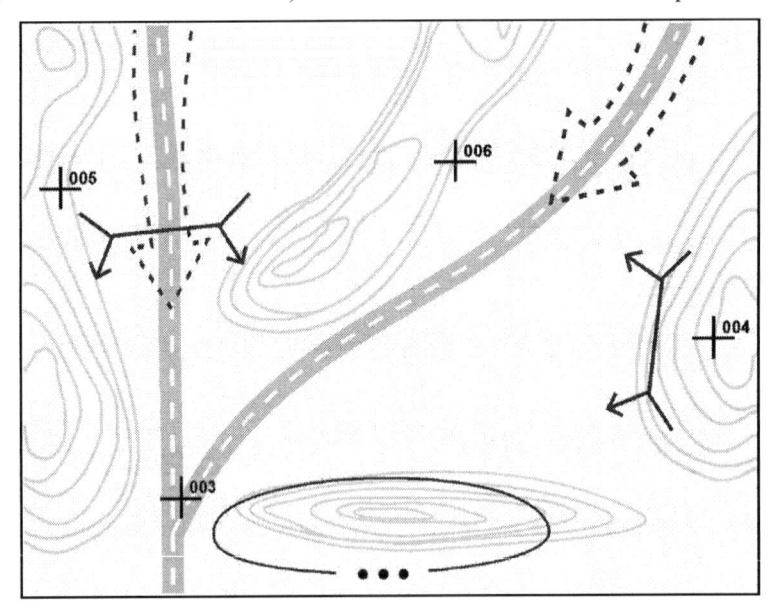

Figure B-2. Determining where and how to mass fires

ORIENT FORCES TO SPEED TARGET ACQUISITION

B-15. To engage the enemy with direct fires, friendly forces must rapidly and accurately acquire enemy elements. (See figure B-3, page B-6.) Orienting friendly forces on probable enemy locations and on likely avenues of approach will speed target acquisition. Conversely, failure to orient subordinate elements will result in slower acquisition; this greatly increases the likelihood enemy forces will be able to engage first. The clock direction orientation method, which is prescribed in most unit SOPs, is good for achieving all-around security; however, it does not ensure friendly forces are most oriented to detect the enemy. To achieve this critical orientation, the leader typically designates TRP on or near probable enemy locations and avenues of approach; he orients his subordinate elements using directions of fire or sectors of fire. Normally, the gunners on crew-served weapons scan the designated direction, sector, or area while other crewmembers observe alternate sectors or areas to provide all-around security.

Appendix B

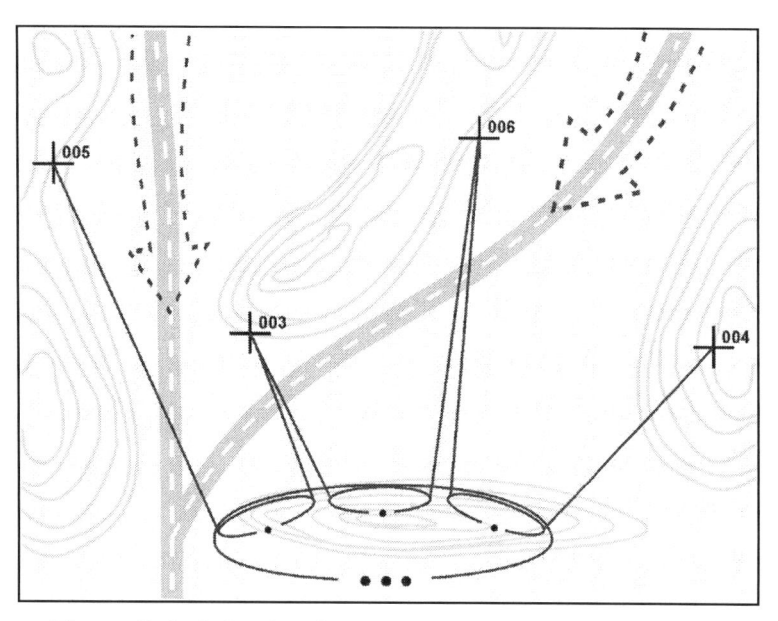

Figure B-3. Orienting forces to speed target acquisition

SHIFT FIRES TO REFOCUS AND REDISTRIBUTE

B-16. As the engagement proceeds, leaders must shift fires to refocus and redistribute the effects based on their evolving mission analysis. Situational awareness becomes an essential part of the fire control process at this point. Leaders apply the same techniques and considerations, including fire control measures they used earlier to focus and distribute fires. A variety of situations will dictate shifting of fires, including the following:
- Appearance of an enemy force posing a greater threat than the one currently being engaged.
- Extensive attrition of the enemy force being engaged, creating the possibility of target overkill.
- Attrition of friendly elements engaging the enemy force.
- Change in the ammunition status of the friendly elements engaging the enemy force.
- Maneuver of enemy or friendly forces resulting in terrain masking.
- Increased fratricide and friendly fire risk as a maneuvering friendly element closes with the enemy force being engaged.

SECTION III – DIRECT FIRE PLANNING

B-17. The platoon leader plans direct fires as part of the TLP. Determining where and how the platoon can and will mass fires is an essential step as the platoon leader develops his concept of the operation.

LEADER PLANNING

Direct Fire Planning and Control

B-18. Leaders plan direct fires in order to be able to distribute and control their fire. Determining where and how leaders can mass fires is an essential step in this process.

B-19. Based on where and how they want to focus and distribute fires, leaders can establish the weapons ready postures of their elements as well as triggers for initiating fires. During mission preparation, leaders plan and conduct rehearsals of direct fires (and of the fire control process) based on METT-TC.

B-20. The platoon leader plans direct fires in conjunction with development of his mission analysis and completion of the plan. Determining where and how the platoon can and will mass fires are also essential steps as the platoon leader develops his concept of the operation.

B-21. The platoon leader plans direct fires in conjunction with development of his mission analysis and completion of the plan. Determining where and how the platoon can and will mass fires are also essential steps as the platoon leader develops his concept of the operation.

B-22. After identifying probable enemy locations, the platoon leader determines points or areas where he can focus combat power. His visualization of where and how the enemy will attack or defend assists him in determining the volume of fires he must focus at particular points to have a decisive effect. In addition, if he intends to mass the fires of more than one subordinate element, the platoon leader must establish the means for distributing fires.

B-23. Based on where and how they want to focus and distribute fires, the platoon leader and subordinate leaders can then establish the weapons ready postures for platoon elements as well as triggers for initiating fires. Additionally, they must evaluate the risk of fratricide, friendly fire and establish controls to prevent it; these measures include the designation of recognition markings, weapons control status, and weapons safety posture.

B-24. After determining where and how they will mass and distribute fires, the platoon leader and subordinate leaders then must orient elements so they can rapidly and accurately acquire the enemy. They also can war-game the selected COA or concept of the operation to determine probable requirements for refocusing and redistributing fires and to establish other required controls. Also during mission preparation, the platoon leader plans and conducts rehearsals of direct fires (and of the fire control process) based on his mission analysis.

B-25. The platoon leader and his subordinate leaders must continue to apply planning procedures and considerations throughout execution. They must be able to adjust direct fires based on a continuously updated mission analysis, combining situational awareness with the latest available intelligence. When necessary, they also must apply direct fire SOPs, which are covered in the following discussion.

STANDARD OPERATING PROCEDURES

B-26. A well-rehearsed direct fire SOP ensures quick, predictable actions by all members of the platoon. The platoon leader bases the various elements of the SOP on the capabilities

Appendix B

of his force and on anticipated conditions and situations. SOP elements should include standing means for focusing fires, distributing their effects, orienting forces, and preventing fratricide and friendly fire. The platoon leader should adjust the direct fire SOP whenever changes to anticipated and actual METT-TC become apparent.

B-27. If the platoon leader does not issue other instructions, the squads begin the engagement using the SOP. Subsequently, the platoon leader can use a fire command to refocus or redistribute fires. The following paragraphs discuss specific SOP provisions for focusing fires, distributing fires, orienting forces, and preventing fratricide and friendly fire.

FOCUSING FIRES

B-28. TRP are a common means of focusing fires. One technique is to establish a standard respective position for TRP in relation to friendly elements and to consistently number the TRP, such as from left to right. This allows leaders to quickly determine and communicate the location of the TRP.

DISTRIBUTING FIRES

B-29. Two useful means of distributing the platoon's fires are engagement priorities and target array. One technique is to assign an engagement priority, by type of enemy vehicle or weapon, for each type of friendly weapons system. The target array technique can assist in distribution by assigning specific friendly elements to engage enemy elements of approximately similar capabilities.

ORIENTING FORCES

B-30. A standard means of orienting friendly forces is to assign a principal direction of fire (PDF), using a TRP, to orient each element on a probable enemy position or likely avenue of approach. To provide all-around security, the SOP can supplement the PDF with sectors using a friendly-based quadrant. The following example SOP elements illustrate the use of these techniques:

- The center (front) squad's PDF is TRP 2 (center) until otherwise specified; the squad is responsible for the front two quadrants.
- The left flank squad's PDF is TRP 1 (left) until otherwise specified; the squad is responsible for the left two friendly quadrants (overlapping with the center squad).
- The right flank squad's PDF is TRP 3 (right) until otherwise specified; the squad is responsible for the right two friendly quadrants (overlapping with the center squad).

AVOIDING FRATRICIDE AND FRIENDLY FIRE

B-31. A primary means of minimizing fratricide and friendly fire risk is to establish a standing weapons control status of WEAPONS TIGHT, which requires positive enemy identification before engagement. +The SOP also must dictate ways of identifying friendly rifle squads and other dismounted elements; techniques include using arm bands, glint tape, or an infrared light source or detonating a smoke grenade of a designated color at the appropriate time. Minimizing the risk of fratricide in the platoon can be accomplished through Mission Command Systems (if equipped); however, this does not supplant the platoon leader's responsibility to plan for fratricide and friendly fire avoidance.

B-32. Finally, the SOP must address the most critical requirement of fratricide and friendly fire prevention maintaining situational awareness. It must direct subordinate leaders to inform the platoon leader, adjacent elements, and subordinates whenever a friendly force is moving or preparing to move.

SECTION IV – DIRECT FIRE CONTROL

B-33. The small unit leader communicates to his subordinates the manner, method, and time to initiate, shift, and mass fires, and when to disengage by using direct fire control measures. The leader should control his unit's fires so he can direct the engagement of enemy systems to gain the greatest effect. The leader uses IPB and information collection to determine the most advantageous way to use direct fire control measures to mass the effects on the enemy and reduce fratricide and friendly fire from direct fire systems. (Refer to ATP 2-01.3 and FM 3-55 for more information.)

FIRE CONTROL MEASURES

B-34. Fire control measures are the means by which the platoon leader or subordinate leaders control fires. Application of these concepts, procedures, and techniques assists the unit in acquiring the enemy, focusing fires on him, distributing the effects of the fires, and preventing fratricide and friendly fire. At the same time, no single measure is sufficient to control fires. At the platoon level, fire control measures will be effective only if the entire unit has a common understanding of what they mean and how to employ them. The following discussion focuses on the various fire control measures employed by the Infantry platoon. Table B-1 (page B-10) lists the control measures; it is organized by whether they are terrain-based or threat-based.

Appendix B

Table B-1. Common fire control measures

TERRAIN-BASED FIRE CONTROL MEASURES	THREAT-BASED FIRE CONTROL MEASURES
TRP	ROE
Engagement area	Weapons ready posture
Sector of fire	Weapons safety posture
Direction of fire	Weapons control status
Terrain-based quadrant	Engagement priorities
Friendly-based quadrant	Trigger
MEL; RFL; FPL	Engagement techniques; fire patterns; target array
LEGEND FPL – final protective line; MEL – maximum engagement line; RFL – restrictive fire line; ROE – rules of engagement; TRP – target reference point	

TERRAIN-BASED FIRE CONTROL MEASURES

B-35. Leaders use terrain-based fire control measures to focus and control fires on a particular point, line, or area rather than on a specific enemy element. The following paragraphs describe the TTP associated with this type of control measure.

Target Reference Point

B-36. A TRP is a recognizable point on the ground leaders use to orient friendly forces, and to focus and control direct fires. In addition, when leaders designate TRP as indirect fire targets, they can use the TRP when calling for and adjusting indirect fires. Leaders designate TRP at probable enemy locations and along likely avenues of approach. These points can be natural or man-made. A TRP can be an established site. For example, a hill or a building, or an impromptu feature such as a burning enemy vehicle or obscurants generated by an artillery round can be designated as a TRP. Friendly units also can construct markers to serve as TRP. (See figure B-4.) Ideally, TRP should be visible in three observation modes (unaided, passive-infrared, and thermal) so all forces can see them. Examples of TRP include the following features and objects:

- Prominent hill mass.
- Distinctive building.
- Observable enemy position.
- Destroyed vehicle.
- Ground-burst illumination.
- Obscurants round for immediate engagements only; this is the least preferred method.

Direct Fire Planning and Control

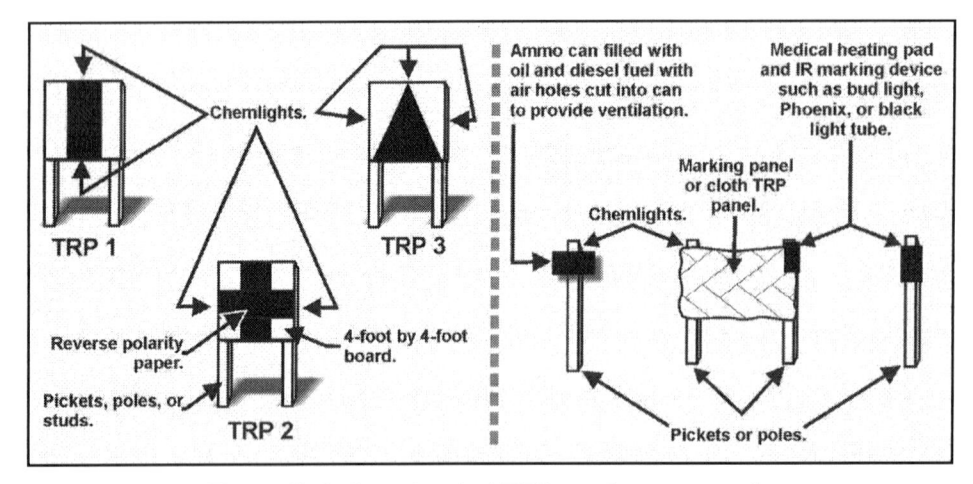

Figure B-4. Constructed TRP markers example

Engagement Area

B-37. This fire control measure is an area along an enemy avenue of approach where the leader intends to mass the fires of available weapons to destroy an enemy force. The size and shape of the engagement area is determined by the degree of relatively unobstructed intervisibility available to the unit's weapons systems in their firing positions and by the maximum range of those weapons. Typically, the platoon leader delineates responsibility within the engagement area by assigning each squad a sector of fire or direction of fire.

Sector of Fire

B-38. A sector of fire is a defined area being covered by direct fire. Leaders assign sectors of fire to subordinate elements, crew-served weapons, and individual Soldiers to ensure coverage of sectors; they also may limit the sector of fire of an element or weapon to prevent accidental engagement of an adjacent unit. In assigning sectors of fire, platoon leader and subordinate leaders consider the number and types of weapons available. In addition, they must consider acquisition system type and field of view in determining the width of a sector of fire. For example, while unaided vision has a wide field of view, its ability to detect and identify targets at range and in limited visibility conditions is restricted. Conversely, most fire control acquisitions systems have greater detection and identification ranges than the unaided eye, but their field of view is narrow. Means of designating sectors of fire include the following:

- Target registration points.
- Clock direction.
- Terrain-based quadrants.
- Friendly-based quadrants.
- Azimuth or cardinal direction.

Appendix B

Direction of Fire

B-39. A direction of fire is an orientation or point used to assign responsibility for a particular area on the battlefield being covered by direct fire. Leaders designate directions of fire for purposes of acquisition or engagement by subordinate elements, crew-served weapons, or individual Soldiers. Direction of fire is most commonly employed when assigning sectors of fire would be difficult or impossible because of limited time or insufficient reference points. Means of designating a direction of fire include the following:

- Closest target registration point.
- Clock direction.
- Azimuth or cardinal direction.
- Tracer on target.
- Infrared laser pointer.
- M203 smoke round.

Quadrants

B-40. Quadrants are subdivisions of an area created by superimposing an imaginary pair of perpendicular axes over the terrain to create four separate areas or sectors. Establish quadrants on the terrain, friendly forces, or on the enemy formation.

> *Note.* Techniques in which quadrants are based on enemy formations usually are referred to as target array; it is covered in discussion of threat-based fire control measures.

B-41. The method of quadrant numbering is established in the unit SOP; however, care must be taken to avoid confusion when quadrants based on terrain, friendly forces, and enemy formations are used simultaneously.

Terrain-Based Quadrant

B-42. A terrain-based quadrant entails use of a TRP, either existing or constructed, to designate the center point of the axes dividing the area into four quadrants. This technique can be employed in both the offense and defense. In the offense, the platoon leader designates the center of the quadrant using an existing feature or by creating a reference point. For example, using a ground burst illumination round, an obscurant marking round, or a fire ignited by incendiary or tracer rounds. The axes delineating the quadrants run parallel and perpendicular to the direction of movement. In the defense, the platoon leader designates the center of the quadrant using an existing or constructed TRP.

B-43. In examples shown in figure B-5, quadrants are marked using the letter "Q" and a number (Q1 to Q4); quadrant numbers are in the same relative positions as on military map sheets (from Q1 as the upper left-hand quadrant clockwise to Q4 as the lower left-hand quadrant).

Direct Fire Planning and Control

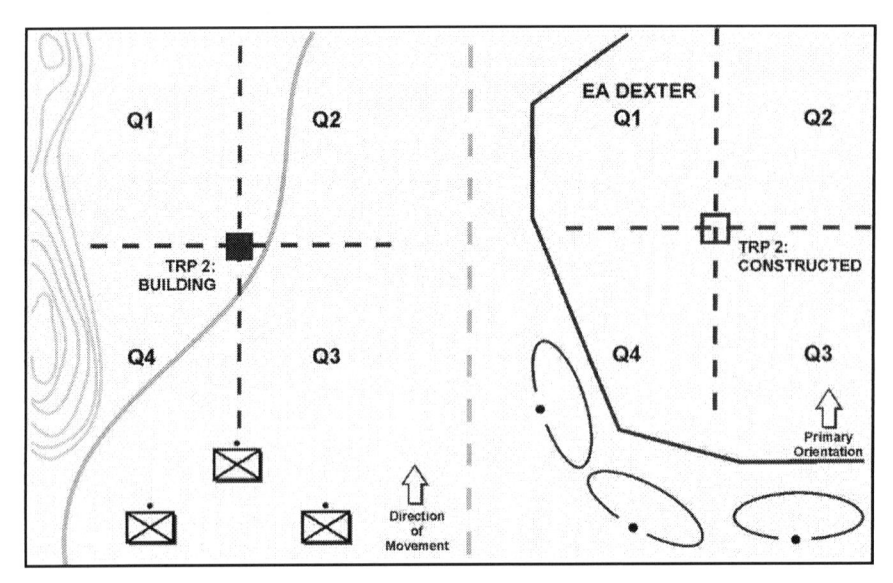

Figure B-5. Terrain-based quadrants example

Friendly-Based Quadrant

B-44. The friendly-based quadrant technique entails superimposing quadrants over the unit's formation. The center point is based on the center of the formation, and axes run parallel and perpendicular to the general direction of travel. For rapid orientation, the friendly quadrant technique may be better than the clock direction method; because different elements of a large formation rarely are oriented in the same exact direction and the relative dispersion of friendly forces causes parallax to the target. Figure B-6 (page B-14) illustrates use of friendly-based quadrants.

Appendix B

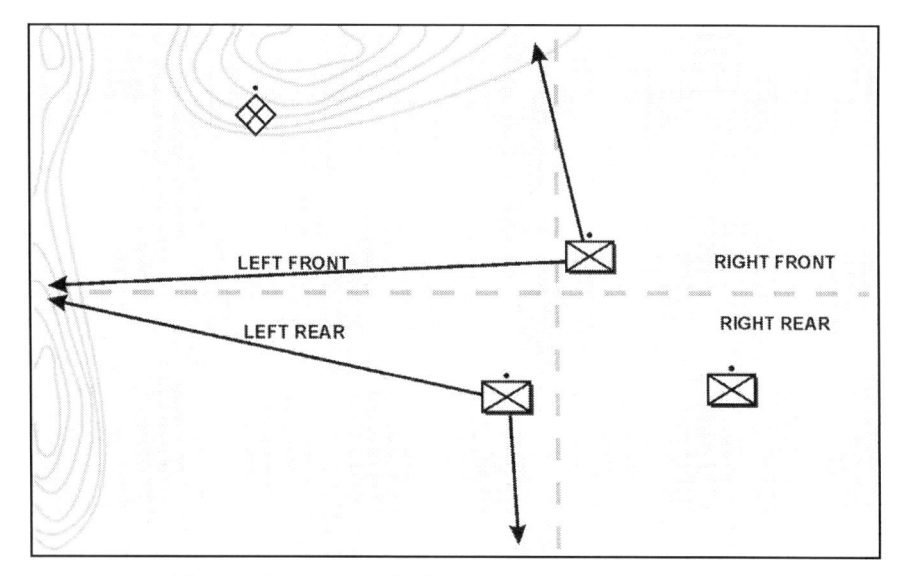

Figure B-6. Friendly-based quadrants example

Maximum Engagement Line

B-45. MEL is the linear depiction of the farthest limit of effective fire for a weapon or unit. This line is determined by both the weapons, unit's maximum effective range and by the effects of terrain. For example, slope, vegetation, structures, and other features provide cover and concealment preventing the weapon from engaging to the maximum effective range. A MEL serves several purposes. The platoon leader can use it to prevent crews from engaging beyond the maximum effective range, to define criteria of the establishment of triggers, and to delineate the maximum extent of sectors on the area of operation sketch.

Restrictive Fire Line

B-46. An RFL is a linear fire control measure beyond which engagement is prohibited without coordination. In the offense, the platoon leader can designate an RFL to prevent a base-of-fire element from firing into the area where an assaulting element is maneuvering. This technique is particularly important when armored vehicles support the maneuver of rifle squads. In the defense, the platoon leader may establish a RFL to prevent the unit from engaging a friendly rifle squad positioned in restricted terrain on the flank of an avenue of approach.

Final Protective Line

B-47. FPL is a line of fire established where an enemy assault is to be checked by the interlocking fires of all available weapons. The unit reinforces this line with protective obstacles and with final protective fires whenever possible. Initiation of the final protective fires is the signal for elements, crews, and individual Soldiers to shift fires to their assigned portion of the FPL. They spare no ammunition in repelling the enemy assault, a particular concern for medium machine guns and other automatic weapons.

THREAT-BASED FIRE CONTROL MEASURES

B-48. The platoon leader uses threat-based fire control measures to focus and control fires by directing the unit to engage a specific enemy element rather than to fire on a point or area. The following paragraphs describe the TTP associated with this type of control measure.

Rules of Engagement

B-49. ROE specify the circumstances and limitations under which forces may engage; they include definitions of combatant and noncombatant elements and prescribe the treatment of noncombatants. Factors influencing ROE are national command policy, mission, commander's intent, the operational environment, and the law of war. ROE always recognize a Soldier's right of self-defense; while at the same time, they clearly define circumstances in which he may fire.

B-50. For example, during a cordon and search mission, the command may establish a weapons control status of WEAPONS TIGHT for antiarmor weapons. The commander does this because higher command directives explicitly restrict the use of antiarmor weapons as an explosive breach technique.

Weapons Ready Posture

B-51. Weapons ready posture is the selected ammunition and range for individual and crew-served weapons in rifle squads. It is a means by which leaders use their mission analysis to specify the ammunition and range of the most probable anticipated engagement. Ammunition selection depends on the target type, but the leader may adjust it based on engagement priorities, desired effects, and effective range. Range selection depends on the anticipated engagement range; it is affected by terrain intervisibility, weather, and light conditions. Within the platoon, weapons ready posture affects the types and quantities of ammunition loaded in ready boxes, stowed in ready racks, and carried by rifle squads. The following considerations apply:

B-52. Examples of weapons ready posture include:
- An M203/M320 GRN, whose, most likely engagement is to cover dead space at 200 meters from his position, might load high-explosive dual purpose ammunition and set 200 meters on his quadrant sight.
- To prepare for an engagement in a wooded area where engagement ranges are extremely short, an antiarmor specialist might dismount with an M136 AT4-series, instead of a Javelin.

Weapons Safety Posture

B-53. Weapons safety posture is an ammunition handling instruction enabling the platoon leader to control the safety of his unit's weapons precisely. Leaders' supervision of the weapons safety posture, as well as Soldiers' adherence to it, minimizes the risk of accidental discharge and fratricide and friendly fire. Table B-2 outlines procedures and

Appendix B

considerations for the platoon when using the four weapons safety postures, listed in ascending order of restrictiveness—
- AMMUNITION LOADED.
- AMMUNITION LOCKED.
- AMMUNITION PREPARED.
- WEAPONS CLEARED.

B-54. When setting and adjusting the weapons safety posture, the platoon leader must weigh the desire to prevent accidental discharges against the requirement for immediate action based on the enemy threat. If the threat of direct contact is high, the platoon leader could establish the weapons safety posture as AMMUNITION LOADED. If the requirement for action is less immediate, he might lower the posture to AMMUNITION LOCKED or AMMUNITION PREPARED. Additionally, the platoon leader can designate different weapons safety postures for different elements of the unit.

Direct Fire Planning and Control

Table B-2. Weapons safety posture levels

ELEMENT SAFETY POSTURE	BFV WEAPONS AND AMMUNITION	INFANTRY SQUAD WEAPONS AND AMMUNITION	ICV WEAPONS AND AMMUNITION
Ammunition Loaded	25-mm rounds cycled to bolt. Coax rounds on feed tray; bolt locked to rear. Tube-launched, optically tracked, wire-guided (TOW) missiles in launchers. Smoke grenades in launchers. Weapons on electrical safe.	Rifle rounds chambered. Machine gun and squad automatic weapon ammunition on feed tray; bolt locked to rear. Grenade launcher loaded. Weapons on manual safe.	Fire on Weapon Control Station. Round in chamber bolt forward (M2). Weapon charged-open bolt (MK-19). Smoke grenades in launchers.
Ammunition Locked	25-mm rounds loaded into feeder, but not cycled to bolt. TOW missiles in launchers. Smoke grenades in launchers. Weapons on electrical safe.	Magazines locked into rifles. Machine gun and squad automatic weapon ammunition on feed tray; bolt locked forward. Grenade launcher unloaded.	On safe Weapon control station. Round in chamber and bolt forward (M2). Weapon charged-open bolt (MK-19). Smoke grenades in launchers.
Ammunition Prepared	25-mm ready boxes filled. Coax ammunition boxes filled. TOW missiles in launchers. Smoke grenades in launchers.	Magazines, ammunition boxes, launcher grenades, and hand grenades prepared but stowed in pouches/vests.	No round chambered. On Safe from Weapon control station. Bolt forward (M2 only). Rounds in tray. Smoke grenades in launchers.
Weapons Cleared	25-mm feeder removed; feeder and chamber cleared. Coax bolt group removed and chamber cleared.	Magazine, ammunition boxes, and launcher grenades removed; weapons cleared.	MK-19/M2 ammunition cleared from feed tray. On safe on weapon control station. Ammo stowed.

Weapons Control Status

B-55. The three levels of weapons control status outline the conditions, based on target identification criteria, under which friendly elements can engage. The platoon leader sets and adjusts the weapons control status based on friendly and enemy disposition, and clarity of the situation. Generally speaking, the higher the probability of fratricide and friendly

Appendix B

fire, the more restrictive the weapons control status. The three levels, in descending order of restrictiveness, are—
- WEAPONS HOLD. Engage only if engaged or ordered to engage.
- WEAPONS TIGHT. Engage only targets positively identified as enemy.
- WEAPONS FREE. Engage targets not positively identified as friendly.

B-56. As an example, the platoon leader may establish the weapons control status as WEAPONS HOLD when friendly forces are conducting a passage of lines. By maintaining situational understanding of his own elements and adjacent friendly forces, however, he may be able to lower the weapons control status. In such a case, the platoon leader may be able to set a WEAPONS FREE status when he knows there are no friendly elements in the vicinity of the engagement. This permits his elements to engage targets at extended ranges even though it is difficult to distinguish targets accurately at ranges beyond 2000 meters under battlefield conditions. Another consideration is the weapons control status are extremely important for forces using combat identification systems. Establishing the weapons control status as WEAPONS FREE permits leaders to engage an unknown target when they fail to get a friendly response.

Engagement Priorities

B-57. Engagement priorities, which entail the sequential ordering of targets to be engaged, can serve one or more of the following critical fire control functions:
- Prioritize high-payoff targets. In concert with his concept of the operation, the platoon leader determines which target types provide the greatest payoff; he then can set these as a unit engagement priority. For example, he may decide destroying enemy engineer assets is the best way to prevent the enemy from reducing an obstacle.
- Employ the best weapons to the target. Establishing engagement priorities for specific friendly systems increases the effectiveness with which the unit employs its weapons. For example, the engagement priority of the Javelin could be enemy tanks first, then enemy personnel carriers; this would decrease the chance the platoon's lighter systems will have to engage enemy armored vehicles.
- Distribute the unit's fires. Establishing different priorities for similar friendly systems helps to prevent overkill and achieve distribution of fires. For example, the platoon leader may designate the enemy's tanks as the initial priority for the weapons squad, while making the enemy's personnel carriers the priority for one of his rifle squads. This would decrease the chances of units launching multiple tube launched, optically tracked, wire guided missiles (TOW) against two enemy tanks, while ignoring the dangers posed by the personnel carriers.

Trigger

B-58. A trigger is a specific set of conditions dictating initiation of fires. Often referred to as engagement criteria, a trigger specifies the circumstances in which subordinate elements should engage. The circumstances can be based on a friendly or enemy event. For example, the trigger for a friendly platoon to initiate engagement could be three or more enemy combat vehicles passing or crossing a given point or line. This line can be natural or man-made linear feature, such as a road, ridge line, or stream. It also may be a line perpendicular to the unit's orientation, delineated by one or more reference points.

Engagement Techniques

B-59. Engagement techniques are effects-oriented fire distribution measures. The following engagement techniques are common in platoon operations:
- Point fire.
- Area fire.
- Simultaneous.
- Alternating fire.
- Observed fire.
- Sequential fire.
- Time of suppression.
- Reconnaissance by fire.

Point Fire

B-60. Entails concentrating the effects of a unit's fire against a specific, identified target such as a vehicle, machine gun bunker, or ATGM position. When leaders direct point fire, all of the unit's weapons engage the target, firing until it is destroyed or the required time of suppression has expired. Employing converging fires from dispersed positions makes point fire more effective because the target is engaged from multiple directions. The unit may initiate an engagement using point fire against the most dangerous threat, and revert to area fire against other, less threatening point targets.

Note. Use of point fire is fairly rare because a unit seldom encounters a single, clearly identified enemy weapon.

Area Fire

B-61. Involves distributing the effects of a unit's fire over an area in which enemy positions are numerous or are not obvious. If the area is large, leaders assign sectors of fire to subordinate elements using a terrain-based distribution method such as the quadrant technique. Typically, the primary purpose of the area fire is suppression; however, sustaining suppression requires judicious control of the rate of fire.

Simultaneous Fire

B-62. To rapidly mass the effects of their fires or to gain fire superiority. For example, a unit may initiate a support-by-fire operation with simultaneous fire, then, revert to alternating or sequential fire to maintain suppression. Simultaneous fire also is employed to negate the low probability of the hit and kill of certain antiarmor weapons. For example, a rifle squad may employ simultaneous fire with its M136 AT4 series to ensure rapid destruction of an enemy armored fighting vehicle engaging a friendly position.

Appendix B

Alternating Fire

B-63. Pairs of elements continuously engage the same point or area target one at a time. For example, an Infantry company may alternate fires of two platoons; an Infantry platoon may alternate the fires of its squads; or an Infantry platoon may alternate the fires of a pair of medium machine guns. Alternating fire permits the unit to maintain suppression for a longer duration than does volley fire; it also forces the enemy to acquire and engage alternating points of fire.

Observed Fire

B-64. Usually is used when the platoon is in protected defensive positions with engagement ranges in excess of 2500 meters for stabilized systems and 1500 meters for unstabilized systems. It can be employed between elements of the platoon, such as the squad lasing and observing while the weapons squad engages. The platoon leader directs one squad to engage. The remaining squads observe fires and prepare to engage on order in case the engaging element consistently misses its targets, experiences a malfunction, or runs low on ammunition. Observed fire allows for mutual observation and assistance while protecting the location of the observing elements.

Sequential Fire

B-65. Entails the subordinate elements of a unit engaging the same point or area target one after another in an arranged sequence. Sequential fire also can help to prevent the waste of ammunition, as when a platoon waits to see the effects of the first Javelin before firing another. Additionally, sequential fire permits elements already have fired to pass on information they have learned from the engagement. An example would be a Soldier who missed an enemy armored fighting vehicle with M136 AT4 series fires passing range and lead information to the next Soldier preparing to engage the enemy armored fighting vehicle with an M136 AT4 series.

Time of Suppression

B-66. Is the period, specified by the platoon leader, during which an enemy position or force is required to be suppressed. Suppression time is typically dependent on the time it will take a supported element to maneuver. Usually, a unit suppresses an enemy position using the sustained rate of fire of its automatic weapons. In planning for sustained suppression, a leader must consider several factors: the estimated time of suppression, the size of the area being suppressed, the type of enemy force to be suppressed, range to the target, rates of fire, and available ammunition quantities.

Reconnaissance by Fire

B-67. Is the process of engaging possible enemy locations to elicit a tactical response, such as return fire or movement? This response permits the platoon leader and subordinate leaders to make target acquisition and to mass fires against the enemy element. Typically, the platoon leader directs a subordinate element to conduct the reconnaissance by fire. For example, he may direct an overwatching squad to conduct the reconnaissance by fire against a probable enemy position before initiating movement by a bounding element.

Fire Patterns

B-68. Fire patterns are a threat-based measure designed to distribute the fires of a unit simultaneously among multiple, similar targets. Platoons use those most often to distribute fires across an enemy formation. Leaders designate and adjust fire patterns based on terrain and anticipated enemy formation. The basic fire patterns, illustrated in figure B-7 (page B-22), include:

- Frontal fires.
- Cross fires.
- Depth fires.

B-69. Leaders may initiate frontal fire when targets are arrayed in front of the unit in a lateral configuration. Weapons systems engage targets to their respective fronts. For example, the left flank weapon engages the left-most target; the right flank weapon engages the right-most target. As weapons systems destroy targets, weapons shift fires toward the center of the enemy formation from near too far.

B-70. Leaders initiate cross fire when targets are arrayed laterally across the unit's front in a manner permitting diagonal fires at the enemy's flank, or when obstructions prevent unit weapons from firing frontally. Right flank weapons engage the left-most targets; left flank weapons engage the right-most targets. Firing diagonally across an engagement area provides more flank shots, thus increasing the chance of kills; it also reduces the possibility of the enemy detecting friendly elements should the enemy continue to move forward. As friendly elements destroy targets, weapons shift fires toward the center of the enemy formation.

B-71. Leaders initiate depth fire when enemy targets disperse in-depth, perpendicular to the unit. Center weapons engage the closest targets; flank weapons engage deeper targets. As the unit destroys targets, weapons shift fires toward the center of the enemy formation.

Appendix B

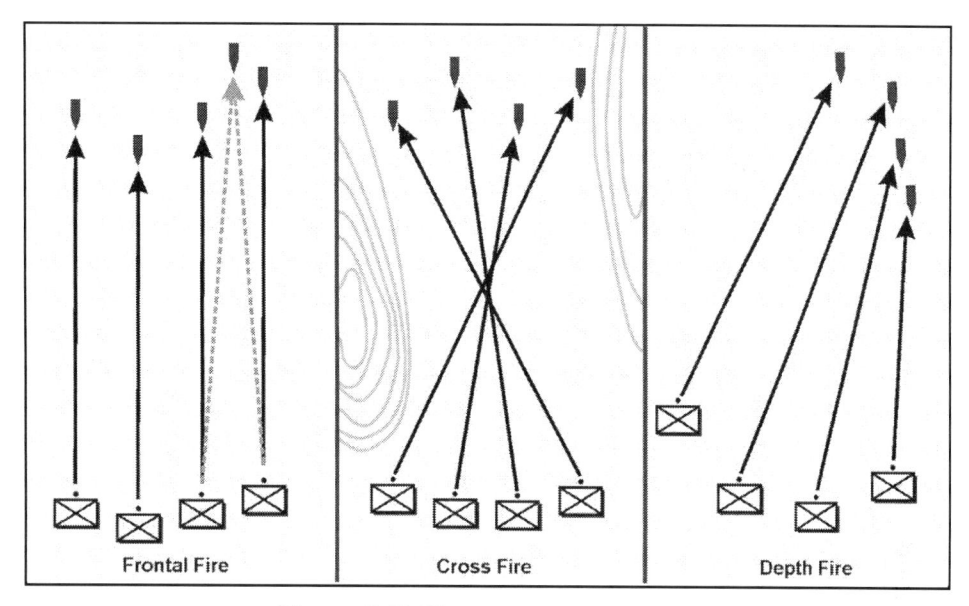

Figure B-7. Fire patterns examples

Target Array

B-72. Target array enables the leader to distribute fires when the enemy force is concentrated and terrain-based controls are inadequate. Forces create this threat-based distribution measure by superimposing a quadrant pattern on the enemy formation. Soldiers center the pattern the enemy formation, with the axes running parallel and perpendicular to the enemy's direction of travel. The target array fire control measure is effective against an enemy with a well-structured organization and standardized doctrine. However, it may prove less effective against an enemy presenting few organized formations, or does not follow strict prescribed tactics. Leaders describe quadrants using the quadrants' relative locations. The examples in figure B-8 illustrate the target array technique.

Direct Fire Planning and Control

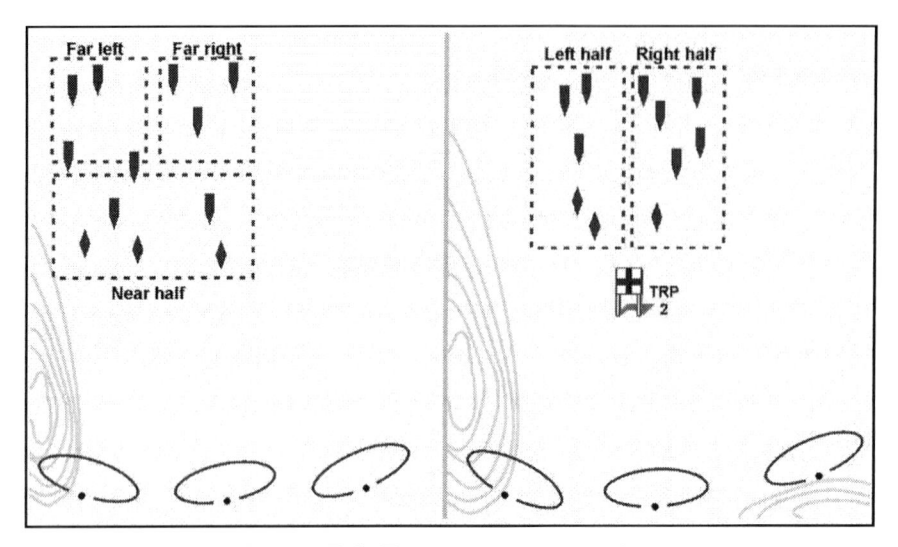

Figure B-8. Target array examples

FIRE COMMANDS

B-73. Fire commands are oral orders issued by leaders to focus and distribute fires as required achieving decisive effects against the enemy. They allow leaders to rapidly and concisely articulate their firing instructions using a standard format (Refer to TC 3-20.31-4 for more information). Unit fire commands include these elements, which are discussed in the following paragraphs:

- Alert.
- Weapon or ammunition (optional).
- Target description.
- Direction.
- Range (optional).
- Method.
- Control (optional).
- Execution.
- Termination

ALERT

B-74. The alert specifies the elements directed to fire. It does not require the leader initiating the command to identify him. Examples of the alert element (call signs and code words based on unit SOP) include the following:

- "GUIDONS" (all subordinate elements).
- "RED" (1st platoon only).

Appendix B

WEAPON OR AMMUNITION (OPTIONAL)

B-75. This element identifies the weapon and ammunition to be employed by the alerted elements. Leaders may designate the type and number of rounds to limit expenditure of ammunition. Examples of this element include the following::
- "TOW."
- "TWO ROUNDS SABOT."

TARGET DESCRIPTION

B-76. Target description designates which enemy elements are to be engaged. Leaders may use the description to focus fires or achieve distribution. Examples of target description include the following:
- "TROOPS IN TRENCH."
- "BUNKER."
- "PCs."

DIRECTION

B-77. This element identifies the location of the target. There are several ways to designate the location of target, including the following:
- Closest TRP. Example: "TRP 13."
- Clock direction. Example: "ONE O'CLOCK."
- Terrain quadrant. Example: "QUADRANT ONE."
- Friendly quadrant. Example: "LEFT FRONT."
- Target array. Example: "FRONT HALF."
- Tracer on target. Example: "ON MY TRACER."
- Laser pointer. Example: "ON MY POINTER."

RANGE (OPTIONAL)

B-78. The range element identifies the distance to the target. Announcing range is not necessary for systems ranging finder-equipped or employing command-guided or self-guided munitions. For systems requiring manual range settings, leaders have a variety of means for determining range, including the following—
- Predetermined ranges to target registration points or phase lines.
- Handheld range finders.
- Range stadia.
- Mil reticle.

METHOD

B-79. Method describes to the firer the way or method the target(s) are engaged. Leaders use this element when presented with multiple targets to identify which target to engage

Direct Fire Planning and Control

first. For collective fire commands, this can also indicate the fire pattern used to engage the threats. Multiple methods may be used in one fire command.

CONTROL (OPTIONAL)

B-80. The platoon leader may use this optional element to direct desired target effects, distribution methods, or engagement techniques. Subordinate leaders may include the control element to supplement the platoon leader's instructions and achieve distribution. Examples of information specified in the control element include the following:

- Target array. Example: "FRONT HALF."
- Fire pattern. Example: "FRONTAL."
- Terrain quadrant. Example: "QUADRANT ONE."
- Engagement priorities. Example: "M203/M320 ENGAGE BUNKERS; MACHINE GUNS ENGAGE TROOPS."
- Engagement technique. Example: "VOLLEY."
- Target effect. Example: "AREA."

EXECUTION

B-81. The execution element specifies when fires will be initiated. The platoon leader may wish to engage immediately, delay initiation, or delegate authority to engage. Examples of this element include the following:

- "FIRE."
- "AT MY COMMAND."
- "AT YOUR COMMAND."
- "AT PHASE LINE ORANGE."

TERMINATION

B-82. Termination is the ninth element of the fire command. It informs the Soldiers to stop firing all weapons and systems in their control. All fire commands are terminated. This command may be given by any Soldier or crewmember for any reason, typically safety.

B-83. The leader that issued the fire command is required to terminate the fire command at the completion of every engagement, regardless if another Soldier or crewmember announced it. All fire commands, regardless of type or who issued them, are terminated by the announcement of, CEASE FIRE.

SECTION V – RANGE CARD AND SECTOR SKETCHES

B-84. Range cards are used to record firing data for individual or crew-served weapons and sector sketches are used to record a unit's positioning of its weapons and direct fire control measures.

RANGE CARDS

Appendix B

B-85. A range card (DA Form 5517, *Standard Range Card*) is a sketch of the assigned area for a direct fire weapon system on a given sector of fire. (Refer to TC 3-21.75 for more information.) A range card aids in planning and controlling fires and aids the crews and squad gunners in acquiring targets during limited visibility. Range cards show possible target areas and terrain features plotted with a firing position. The process of walking and sketching the terrain to create a range card allows the individual Soldier or gunner to become more familiar with his area of operation. He should continually assess the area and, if necessary, update his range card. The range card is an aid for replacement personnel or platoons or squads to move into the position and orient on their area of operation. The individual Soldier or BFV gunner should make the range card so that he becomes more familiar with the terrain in his area of operation. To prepare a range card, the individual Soldier or BFV gunner must know the following information:

- **Sectors of fire.** A sector of fire is a piece of the battlefield for which a gunner is responsible.
- **Target reference points.** Leaders designate natural or man-made features as reference points. A Soldier uses these reference points for target acquisition and range determination.
- **Dead space.** Dead space is an area that cannot be observed or covered by direct-fire systems within the sector of fire.
- **Maximum engagement line.** The maximum engagement line is the depth of the area and is normally limited to the maximum effective engagement range of the weapons systems.
- **Weapons reference point.** The weapons reference point is an easily recognizable terrain feature on the map used to assist leaders in plotting the vehicle, squad, or weapon position.

B-86. The individual Soldier or gunner prepares two copies of the range card. If alternate and supplementary firing positions are assigned, two copies are required for these as well. A copy is kept with the vehicle or weapons position, and the other given to the section leader for his sketch. The Soldier or gunner prepares the range card according to TC 3-21.75.

B-87. An example range card for a BFV is shown in figure B-9 (page B-28). It incorporates all of the standard components of a range card but with more detail for the maximum engagement line and data section.

MAXIMUM ENGAGEMENT LINE

B-88. Although the maximum engagement line is typically limited to the maximum effective engagement range of the weapons systems, it can be less if objects prevent the Soldier from engaging targets at maximum effective ranges of his assigned weapon. The BFV's range card includes three different weapons and their maximum engagement line: the 25-mm, the TOW, and the 7.62-mm co-axial machine gun.

DATA SECTION

B-89. The gunner completes the position identification, date, weapon, and circle value according to TC 3-21.75. The table information is as follows:

- **Number.** Start with left and right limits, then list TRPs and reference points in numerical order.
- **Direction and Deflection.** The direction is in degrees and taken from a lensatic compass. The most accurate technique is to have the gunner aim at the terrain feature, and to have the driver dismount and align himself with the gun barrel and the terrain feature to measure the azimuth. To achieve correct deflection and elevation readings of the terrain feature, select TOW. Show the deflection reading taken from the BFV's azimuth indicator in the deflection block next to the magnetic azimuth.
- **Elevation.** Show the gun elevation reading in tens or hundreds of mils. The smallest increment of measure on the elevation scale is tens of mils. Any number other than "0" is preceded by a "plus" or "minus" symbol to show whether the gun needs to be elevated or depressed. Ammunition and range must be indexed to have an accurate elevation reading.
- **Range.** This is the distance, in meters, from vehicle position to L and R limits and TRPs and reference points.
- **Ammunition.** List types of ammunition used.
- **Description.** List the name of the object.
- **Remarks.** Enter the weapons reference point data. As a minimum, weapons reference point data include a description of what the weapons reference point is, a six-digit or eight-digit grid coordinate of the weapons reference point, the magnetic azimuth and the distance from the weapons reference point to the vehicle position.

Appendix B

STANDARD RANGE CARD
For use of this form see ATP 3-21.8; the proponent agency is TRADOC.

SQD **A22**
PLT **2**
CO **C**

May be used for all types of direct fire weapons.

MAGNETIC NORTH

DATA SECTION

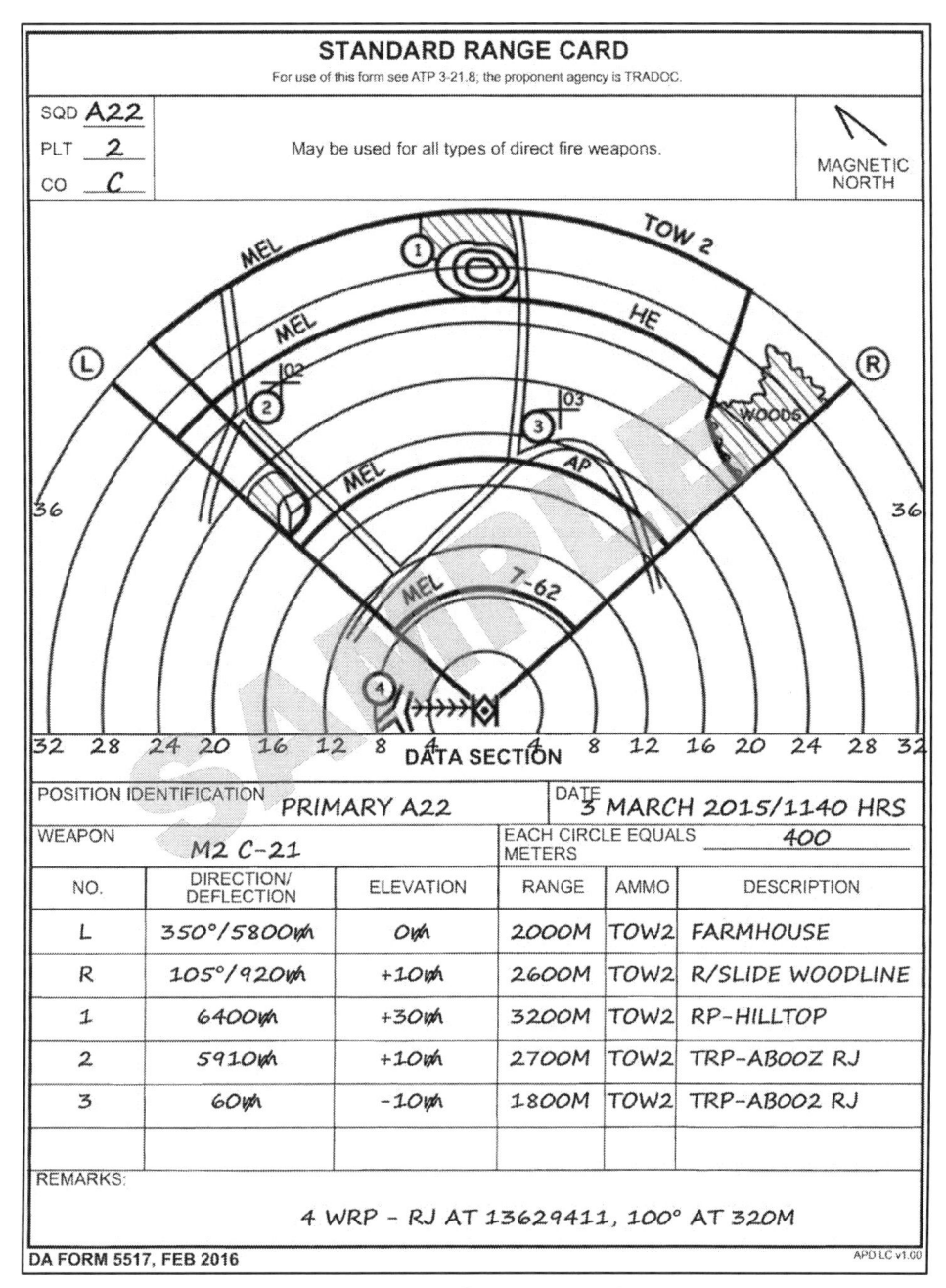

POSITION IDENTIFICATION	PRIMARY A22	DATE 3 MARCH 2015/1140 HRS
WEAPON	M2 C-21	EACH CIRCLE EQUALS 400 METERS

NO.	DIRECTION/ DEFLECTION	ELEVATION	RANGE	AMMO	DESCRIPTION
L	350°/5800↺	0↺	2000M	TOW2	FARMHOUSE
R	105°/920↺	+10↺	2600M	TOW2	R/SLIDE WOODLINE
1	6400↺	+30↺	3200M	TOW2	RP-HILLTOP
2	5910↺	+10↺	2700M	TOW2	TRP-AB00Z RJ
3	60↺	-10↺	1800M	TOW2	TRP-AB002 RJ

REMARKS:
4 WRP - RJ AT 13629411, 100° AT 320M

DA FORM 5517, FEB 2016

Figure B-9. Example of a completed range card

SECTOR SKETCHES

B-90. Individual Soldiers in squads and BFV gunners prepare range cards. Squad and platoon leaders prepare sector sketches. Section leaders may have to prepare sector sketches if they are assigned separate positions. The platoon leader reviews his squad's, and if applicable section's, sector sketches and ensures the sketches are accurate and meet his requirements. If he finds gaps or other flaws, the platoon leader adjusts weapons locations within the area of operation. Once the platoon leader approves the squad and section sector sketches, he prepares a consolidated report for the company team commander and incorporates this into a consolidated platoon sector sketch. The platoon leader or platoon sergeant physically prepares the platoon sector sketch. The sector sketch can be on acetate taped to a map or it can be a hand drawn sketch. Accurate and detailed sketches aid in direct fire planning, and in direct fire control and distribution.

SQUAD SECTOR SKETCH

B-91. The squad leaders and section leaders make two copies of their sector sketches; one copy goes to the platoon leader, the other remains at the position. The squad leaders and section leaders draw sector sketches (see figure B-10, page B-30) as close to scale as possible, showing—

- Main terrain features in the area of operation and the range to each.
- Each primary position.
- Engagement area or primary and secondary sectors of fire covering each position.
- M240B machine gun final protective line or principle direction of fire.
- M249 SAW final protective lines or principle direction of fires.
- Type of weapon in each position.
- Reference points and TRPs in the area of operation.
- Observation post locations.
- Dead space.
- Obstacles.
- Maximum engagement lines for all BFV weapon systems.
- Maximum engagement lines for Javelin (if applicable) and AT4s.
- Indirect fire targets.

Appendix B

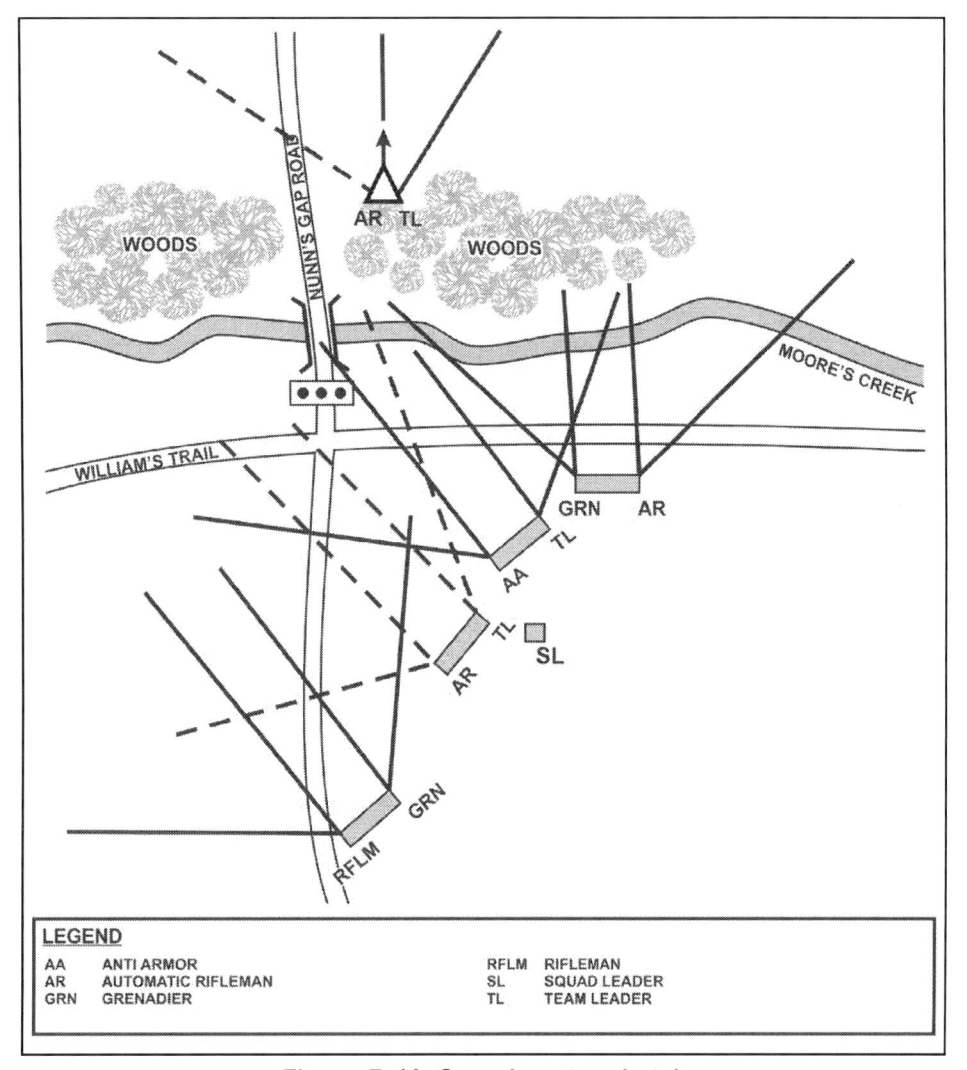

Figure B-10. Squad sector sketch

PLATOON SECTOR SKETCH

B-92. Squad leaders and section leaders prepare their sketches and submit them to the platoon leader. The platoon leader combines all sector sketches (and possibly separate range cards) to prepare a platoon sector sketch, which is drawn as close to scale as possible and includes a target list for direct and indirect fires. One copy is submitted to the company team commander, one copy is given to the platoon sergeant (controlling the mounted element), and one copy is given to the leader of the dismounted element (usually the platoon leader). As a minimum, the platoon sector sketch should show—

- Primary and secondary sectors of fire or engagement areas.

Direct Fire Planning and Control

- Primary, alternate, and supplementary BFV and squad positions.
- Remount points.
- Javelin, M240B, and M249 positions with primary directions of fire.
- M240B and M249 final protective lines or principle direction of fires.
- Maximum engagement lines for 25-mm, M240C, and TOW.
- Observation posts.
- TRPs.
- Mines and other obstacles.
- Indirect fire target locations and final protective fire location (if applicable).
- Position and area of flanking unit vehicles.
- Priority engagement by weapon system and crew.

COORDINATION WITH ADJACENT UNITS

B-93. Platoon leaders coordinate with adjacent platoons. Squad leaders coordinate with adjacent squads so that all positions and all platoon and squads are mutually supporting. The platoon leader must ensure that this coordination take place. Coordination is usually initiated from left to right. Gaps between positions are covered by fire as a minimum. Contact points are established to ensure friendly forces meet at some specific point on the ground to tie in their flanks. In many cases, the exchange of sector sketches will accomplish most of this. Typical information that is exchanged includes—

- Locations of primary, alternate, and supplementary positions; sectors of fire for BFVs, M240Bs, and Javelins.
- Location of dead space between platoons and how it is to be covered.
- Location of observation posts.
- Location and types of obstacles and how to cover them.
- Patrols (size, type, time of departure and return, and routes).

This page intentionally left blank.

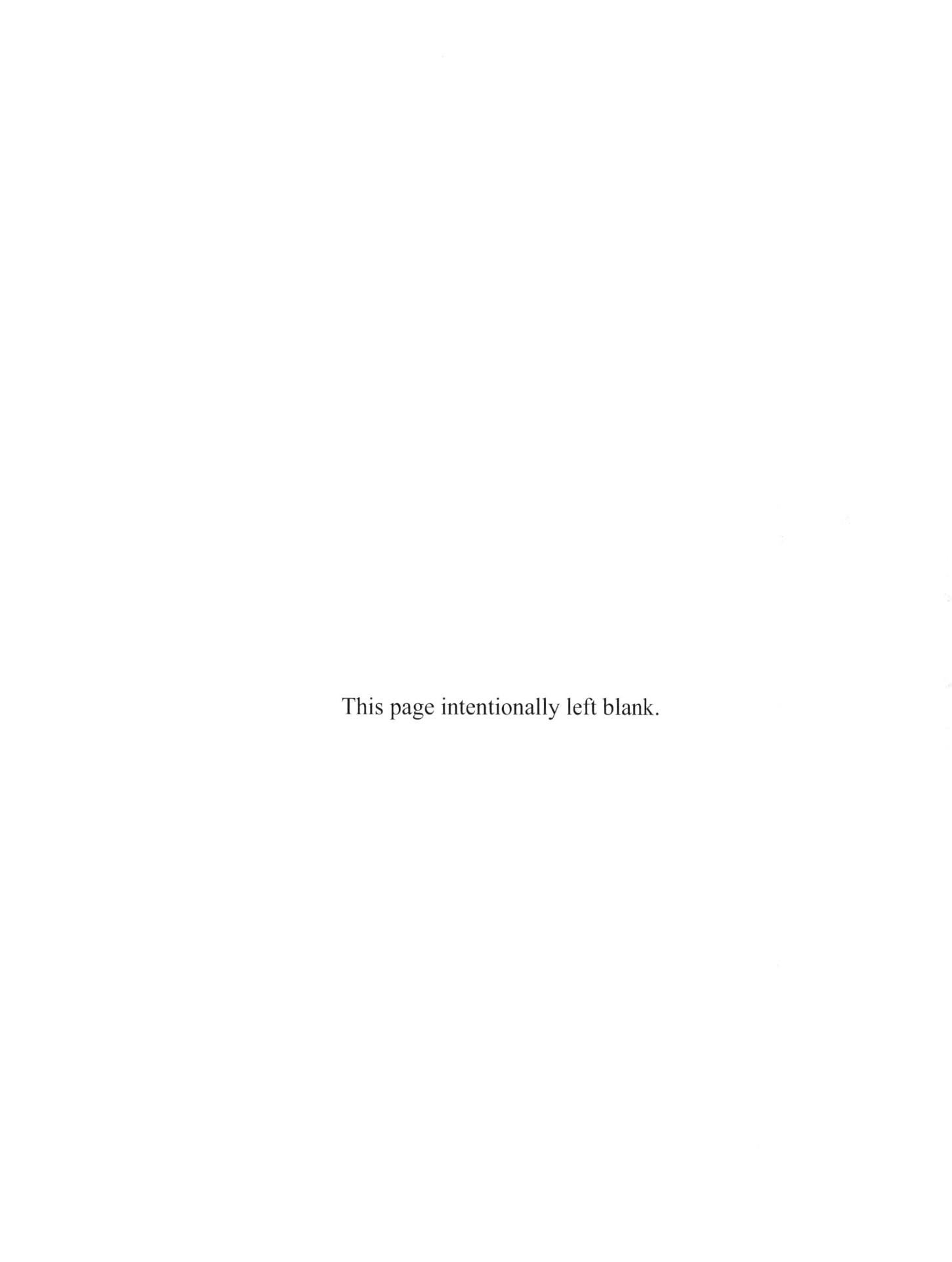

Appendix C
Indirect Fire Support Planning

Fire planning is the continual process of selecting targets on which fires are prearranged to support a phase of the concept of the operation. Fire planning is accomplished concurrently with maneuver planning at all levels. Leaders conduct fire planning to suppress, isolate, obscure, neutralize, destroy, deceive, or disrupt known, likely, or suspected targets, and to support the actions of the maneuver element. Fires are planned for all phases of an operation. (Refer to ADRP 3-09 for more information).

SECTION I – INDIRECT FIRE PLANNING

C-1. Fire planning starts as soon as the leader gets a mission. Once begun, fire planning continues through the operation's completion. The primary aim of fire planning is to develop how fire is to be massed, distributed and controlled to best support the leader's concept of the operation. (See table C-1, page C-2, for capabilities of indirect fire support.)

C-2. Fires are either targets of opportunity, or planned targets. Targets of opportunity are not planned in advance, but are engaged as they present themselves in accordance with established engagement criteria and ROE. Planned targets are ones on which fires are prearranged, although the degree of this prearrangement may vary. The degree of prearrangement influences the time it takes to receive fires. The greater the prearrangement, the faster the reaction time. The subject of this section is planned fires.

C-3. Planned targets are categorized as *scheduled,* or *on-call.* Scheduled fires are fired in accordance with a pre-established time schedule and sequence. On-call targets are fired in response to a request for fires. Priority targets are a special type of on-call target. Priority targets have quick reaction times because the firing unit has guns set on a specific target when not engaged in other fire missions.

C-4. Fires must be integrated and synchronized in time, space, and purpose over the entire concept of the operation. Integration means all available assets are planned and used throughout an operation. Synchronization means these assets are sequenced in time, space, and purpose in an optimal manner, producing complementary and reinforcing effects of the maneuver element.

Appendix C

Table C-1. Indirect fire capabilities

CAPABILITIES OF THE INDIRECT FIRE SYSTEM						
CALIBER	60-mm	81-mm	120-mm	105-mm	155-mm	155-mm
MODEL	M224	M252	M285	M119	M198/M777-series	M109A6
MAX RANGE (HE)(m)	3,490	5,608	7,000	14,000 w/ charge 8	30,000	18,600 w/M23A1
PLANNING RANGE (m)	(2/3 max)	(2/3 max)	(2/3 max)	11,500 2/3 max range of the largest powder and projectile lots of the appropriate type of shells at the firing unit	2/3 max range of the largest powder and projectile lots of the appropriate type shells available at the firing unit	2/3 max range of the largest powder and projectile lots of the appropriate type shells at the firing unit
PROJECTILE	HE, WP, Illum, RP, IR Illum	HE, WP, Illum, RP, IR Illum	HE, SMK, Illum, IR Illum	HE M760, Illum, RAP, APICM, HEP-T	HE, WP, Illum, SMK, RAP, FASCAM, CPHD, Excalibur, APICM, RAP	HE, WP, Illum, SMK, RAP, FASCAM, CPHD, Excalibur, APICM, DPICM
MAX RATE OF FIRE	30 RPM for 2 min	30 RPM for 2 min	16 RPM for 1 min	8 RPM for 3 min	8 RPM for 3 min	4 RPM for 3 min
SUSTAINED RATE OF FIRE (rd/min)	20	15	4	3 for 30 minutes	3 for 30 minutes	1
MINIMUM RANGE (m)	70	83	200	Direct fire	Direct fire	Direct fire
FUZES	PD, VT, time, dly, MO	PD, VT, time, dly, MO	PD, VT, time, dly, MO	PD, VT, CP, MT, MTSQ, dly	PD, VT, CP, MT, MTSQ, dly	PD, VT, CP, MT, MTSQ, dly

APICM   antipersonnel improved conventional munitions
CP   concrete piercing
CPHD   copperhead
dly   delay
DPICM   dual purpose improved conventional munitions
FASCAM family of scatterable mines
HE   high explosive
HEP-T   high explosive plastic-tracer
Illum   illumination
IR   infrared
min   minute
MO   multi option (VT, PD, dly)
MT   mechanical time
MTSQ   mechanical time super quick
PD   point detonating
RAP   rocket assisted projectile
rd   round
RP   red phosphorous
RPM   rounds per minute
SMK   smoke
time   adjustable time delay
VT   variable time
WP   white phosphorous

INDIRECT FIRE PLANNING PROCESS

C-5. Fire planning begins with the concept of fires. This essential component of the concept of the operation complements the leader's scheme of maneuver detailing the leader's plan for direct and indirect preparatory and supporting fires. Fire planning requires a detailed knowledge of weapon characteristics and logistical capabilities of those providing the support. Although leaders may be augmented with personnel to assist in planning and controlling attached or supporting assets, the responsibility for planning and execution of fires lies with the leader. Leaders do not wait to receive the higher headquarters' plan to begin their own fire planning, but, begins as soon as possible to integrate fires into concept of the operation and concept of the operation of the higher headquarters.

C-6. Additional assets are allocated in either a command or support relationship. An example of a command relationship would be an attachment of a section from the weapons company. The leader relies on the senior representative from the organization to provide expertise when planning. An example of a support relationship would be direct support from the artillery battalion or from an attack aviation company. When planning fires or

CAS from a supporting unit, the leader normally receives someone from that organization to assist them. Attached fire support team and Joint Terminal Attack Controllers are examples. Developing the concept of fire should be fairly straight forward during deliberate operations because of the ability to conduct reconnaissance, planning, and preparation. However, during hasty operations the unit may have to rely on its internal SOPs and more hands on control by the leader.

TACTICAL USES OF PLANNED INDIRECT FIRES

C-7. Fires are used for many different tactical reasons. They include:
- Preparatory fire, delivered before an attack to weaken the enemy position (Refer to ADRP 3-90 for more information.)
- Supporting fires (covering fires). Supporting fires enable the friendly maneuver element to move by destroying, neutralizing, or suppressing enemy fires, positions, and observers.
- Final protective fires are an immediately available prearranged barrier of fire designed to impede enemy movement across defensive lines or areas.
- Suppression.
- Obscuration.
- Counterfire (indirect fires only). Counterfire is fire to destroy or neutralize enemy artillery/mortars.
  - These missions normally are controlled at higher level headquarters.
  - Direct support artillery moves with supported units and aviation may be used to destroy enemy direct and indirect fire support means, essential enemy units and facilities.
  - Counterfire radars are positioned to maintain radar coverage to ensure continuous coverage during rapid movement forward.
- Harassing fire is observed or predicted (unobserved) fire intended to disrupt enemy troop and vehicle movement, disturb their rest, and lower their morale.
- Illumination.

ECHELONMENT OF INDIRECT FIRE

C-8. Echelonment of fires is the schedule of fire ranging from the highest caliber munitions to the lowest caliber munitions. The purpose of echeloning fires is to maintain constant fires on the enemy while using the optimum delivery system. Leaders use risk estimate distance, surface danger zones, and MSD to manage associated risks. In the defense, triggers are tied to the progress of the enemy as it moves through the area of operation, enabling the leader to engage the enemy throughout the depth of the area of operation. In the offense, triggers are tied to the progress of the maneuver element as it moves toward the objective protecting the force and facilitating momentum up to the objective.

Appendix C

DEFENSIVE ECHELONMENT

C-9. In defensive missions, echeloning fires are scheduled based on their optimum ranges to maintain continuous fires on the enemy, disrupting his formation and maneuver. Echelonment of fires in the defense places the enemy under increasing volumes of fire as he approaches a defensive position. Aircraft and long-range indirect fire rockets and artillery deliver deep supporting fires. Close supporting fires such as final protective fires are integrated closely with direct fire weapons such as Infantry weapons, tank support, and antiarmor weapons systems. Figure C-1 illustrates an example of defensive echelonment.

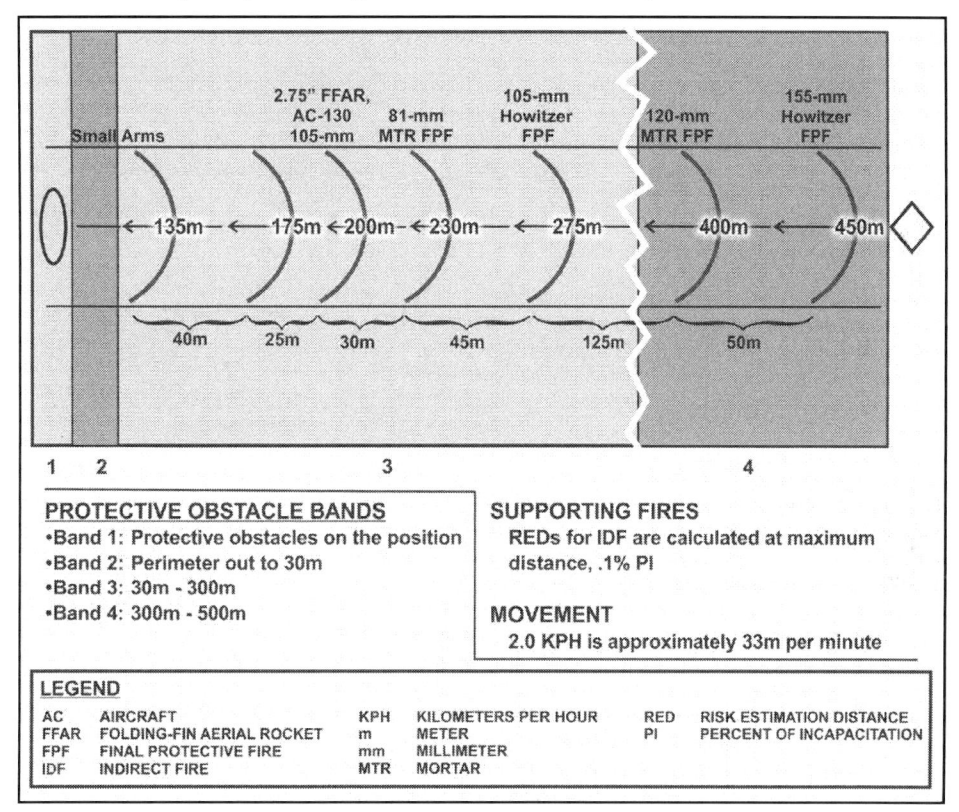

Figure C-1. Defensive echelonment of fires

OFFENSIVE ECHELONMENT

C-10. In the offense, weapons are scheduled based on the point of a predetermined safe distance away from maneuvering friendly troops. When scheduled, fires provide protection for friendly forces as they move to and assault an objective. They also allow friendly forces to get in close with minimal casualties and prevent the defending enemy from observing and engaging the assault by forcing him to take cover. The overall objective of offensive scheduled fires is to allow the friendly force to continue the advance unimpeded. (See figure C-2, page C-5.)

Indirect Fire Support Planning

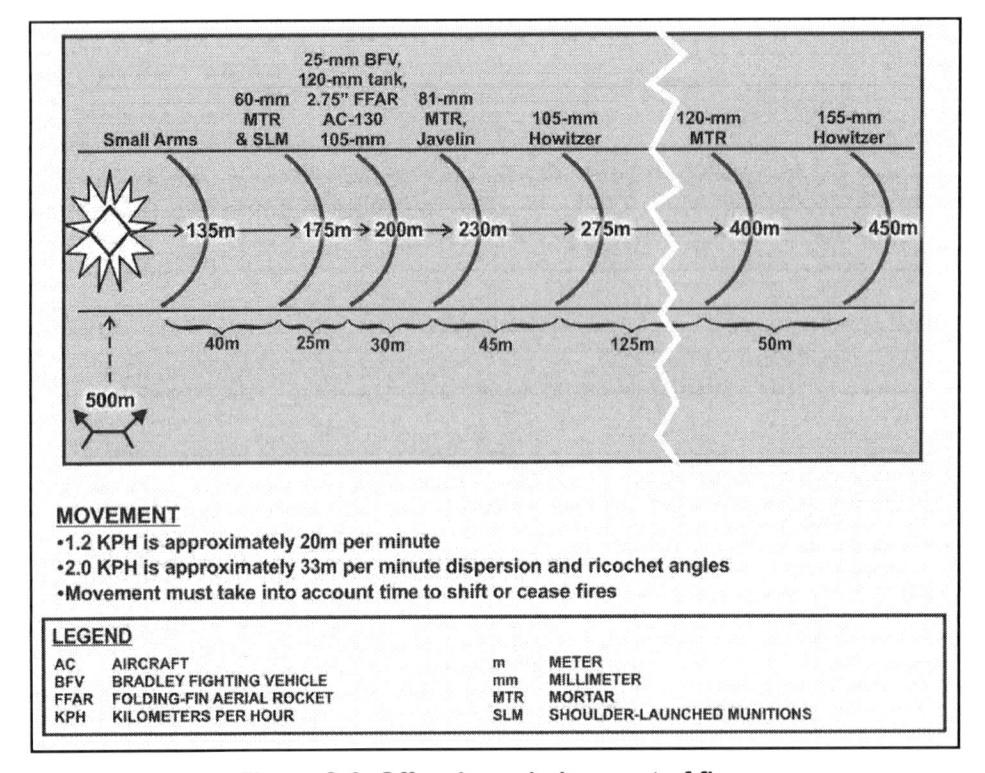

Figure C-2. Offensive echelonment of fires

C-11. As an example of echelonment of fires use during the conduct of a mission, consider an operation in which a platoon assaults an enemy position. (See figures C-3 through C-6, pages C-6 through C-9.) As the lead elements of the unit approach the designated phase line enroute to the objective, the leader orders the fire support officer to begin the preparation. Observers track friendly movement rates and confirm them. Other fire support officers in the chain of command may need to adjust the plan during execution based on unforeseen changes to anticipated friendly movement rates.

C-12. As the unit continues its movement toward the objective, the first weapon system engages its targets. It maintains fires on the targets until the unit crosses the next phase line corresponding to the risk estimate distance of the weapon system being fired.

C-13. To maintain constant fires on the targets, the next weapon system begins firing before the previous weapon system ceases or shifts. This ensures no break in fires, enabling the friendly forces' approach to continue unimpeded. However, if the unit rate of march changes, the indirect fire support system must remain flexible to the changes.

C-14. The fire support officer shifts and engages with each delivery system at the prescribed triggers, initiating the fires from the system with the largest risk estimate distance to the smallest. Once the maneuver element reaches the final phase line, the fire support officer ceases the final indirect fire system or shifts to targets beyond the objective

Appendix C

to cease all fires on the objective. Direct fire assets in the form of supporting fires also are maintained until the final assault, then ceased or shifted to targets beyond the objective.

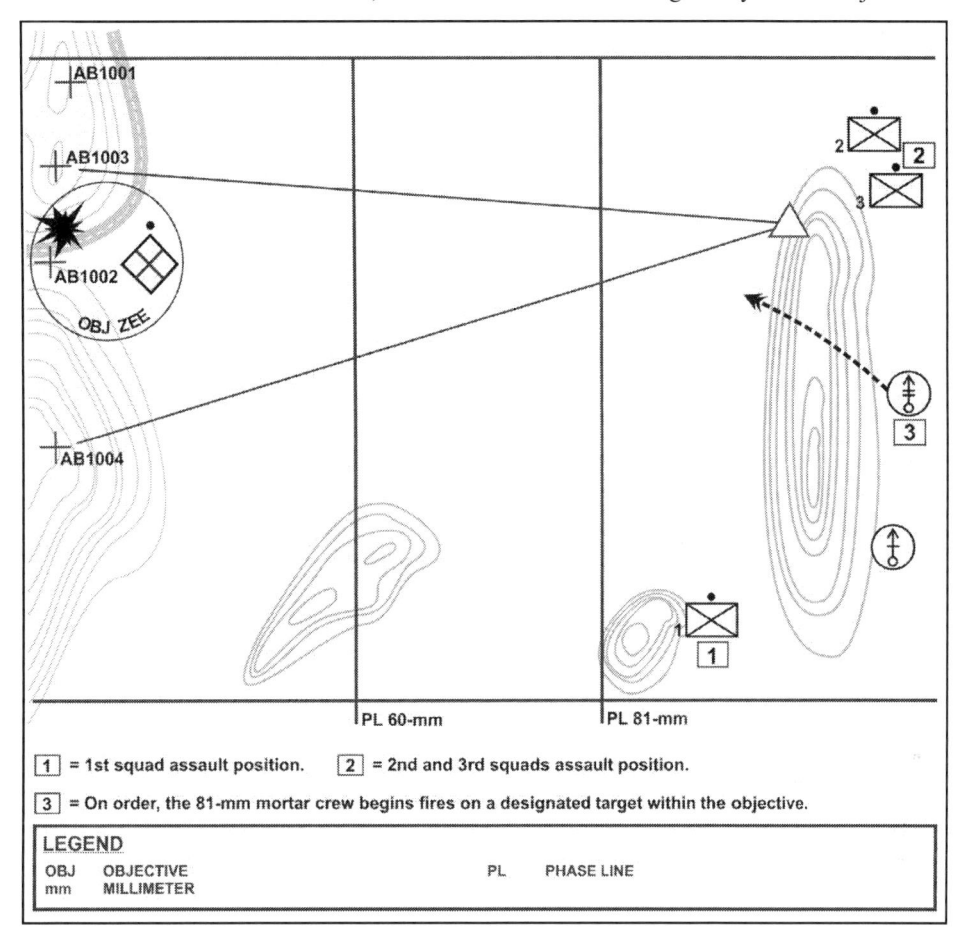

Figure C-3. 81-mm mortars begin firing

Indirect Fire Support Planning

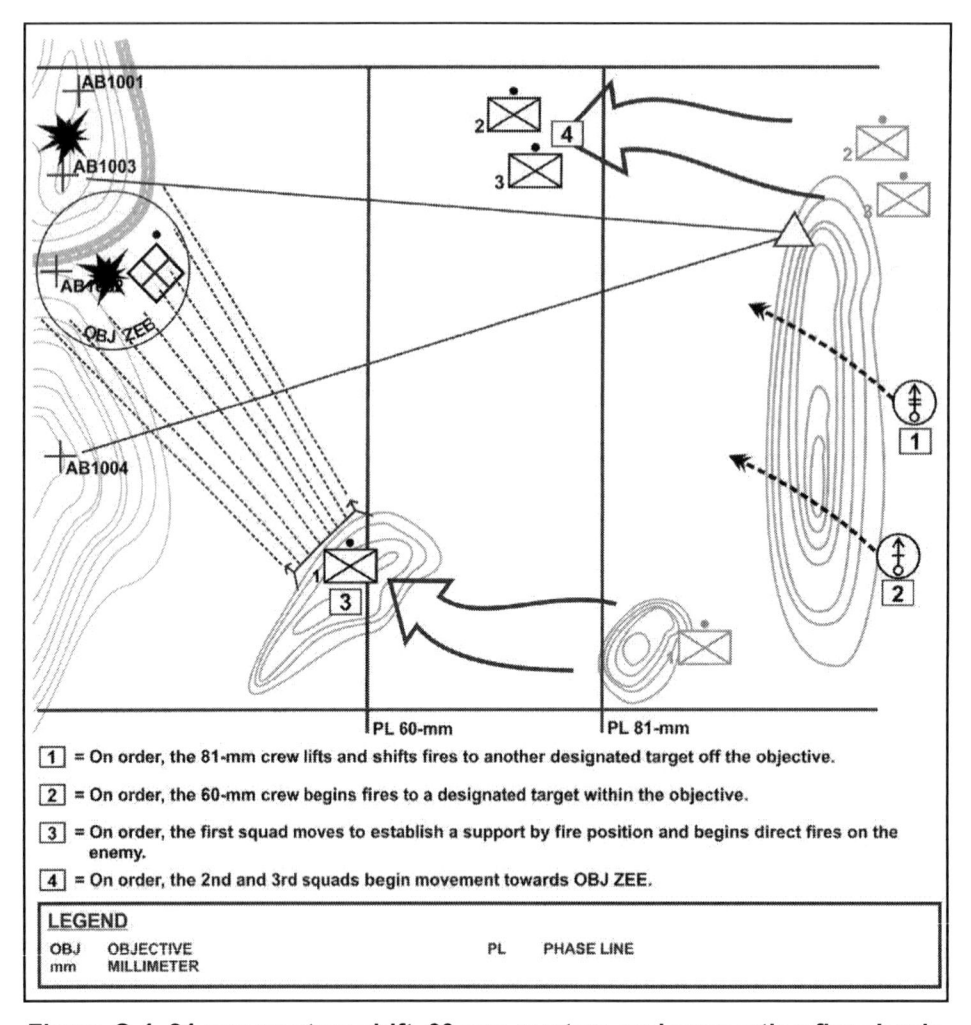

Figure C-4. 81-mm mortars shift, 60-mm mortars and supporting fires begin

1 = On order, the 81-mm crew lifts and shifts fires to another designated target off the objective.

2 = On order, the 60-mm crew begins fires to a designated target within the objective.

3 = On order, the first squad moves to establish a support by fire position and begins direct fires on the enemy.

4 = On order, the 2nd and 3rd squads begin movement towards OBJ ZEE.

LEGEND
OBJ   OBJECTIVE
mm   MILLIMETER
PL   PHASE LINE

Appendix C

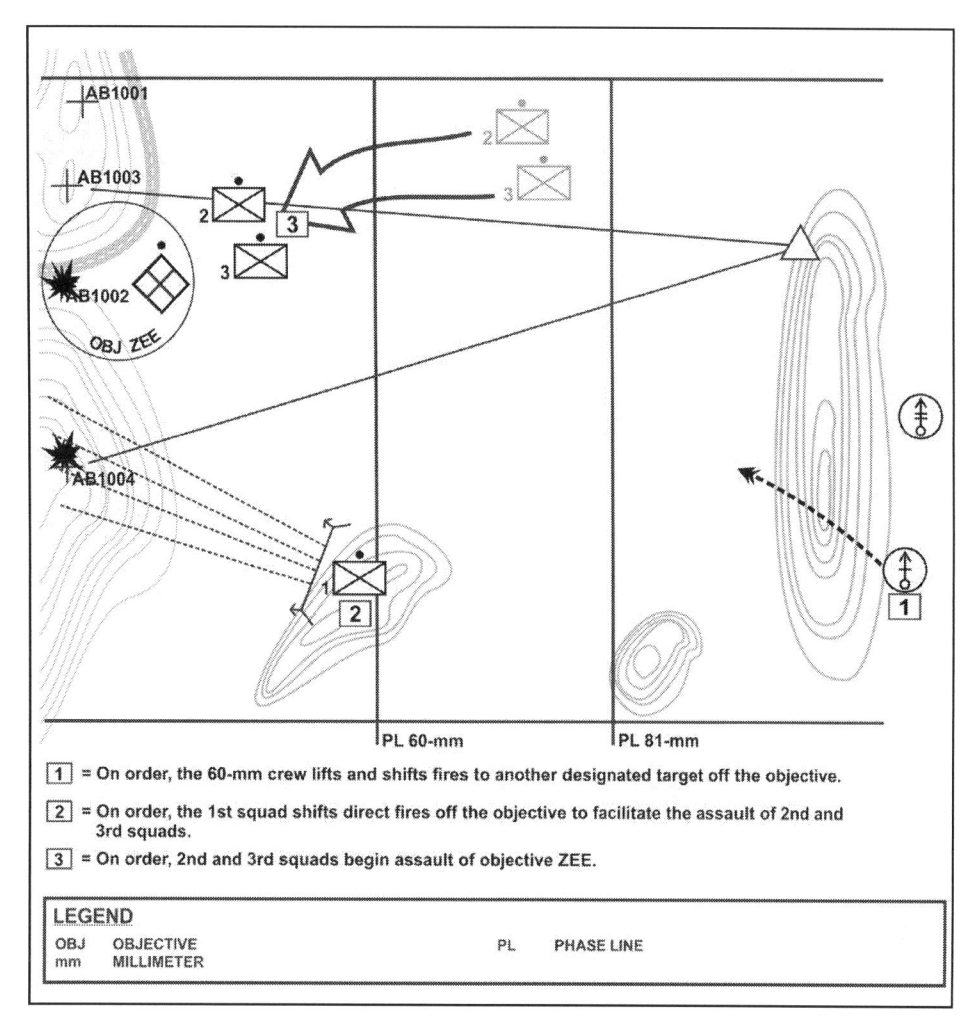

☐ 1 = On order, the 60-mm crew lifts and shifts fires to another designated target off the objective.
☐ 2 = On order, the 1st squad shifts direct fires off the objective to facilitate the assault of 2nd and 3rd squads.
☐ 3 = On order, 2nd and 3rd squads begin assault of objective ZEE.

LEGEND
OBJ   OBJECTIVE   PL   PHASE LINE
mm   MILLIMETER

Figure C-5. 60-mm mortars shift

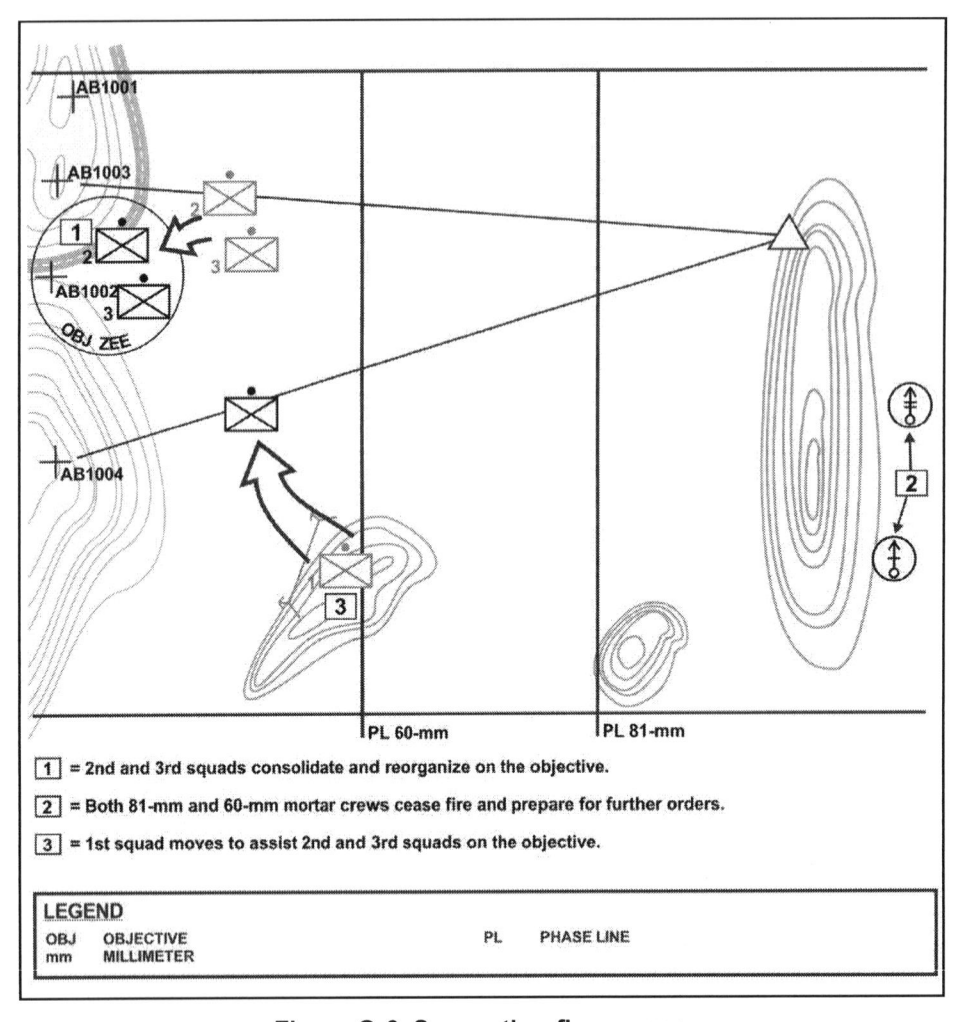

Figure C-6. Supporting fire ceases

FIRE PLANNING THE DEFENSE

C-15. To develop a defensive fire plan, the leader—
- Assigns primary and secondary sectors from primary and alternate position to each subordinate.
- Designates unit point or area targets and other control measures, such as target registration points, to coordinate the fire when more than one subordinate is firing into the same engagement area or area of operations.
- Receives target information from subordinates (normally provided on areas of operations sketches or individual weapon range cards). The leader reviews this

Appendix C

target information to ensure fire is equally distributed across the entire unit's area of operations and sufficient control measures are established.
- Completes the unit's fire plan and gives a sketch to his higher headquarters.

C-16. In defensive missions, fires are planned in three locations – in front of the unit's position, on the position final protective fires, and behind the position. Figure C-7 shows fires massed in front of a company-sized position. Fire plans are best developed using the seven steps of engagement area development technique:

(1) Identify likely enemy avenues of approach.
(2) Identify the enemy scheme of maneuver.
(3) Determine where to kill the enemy.
(4) Emplace weapon systems.
(5) Plan and integrate obstacles.
(6) Plan and integrate indirect fires
(7) Conduct rehearsals.

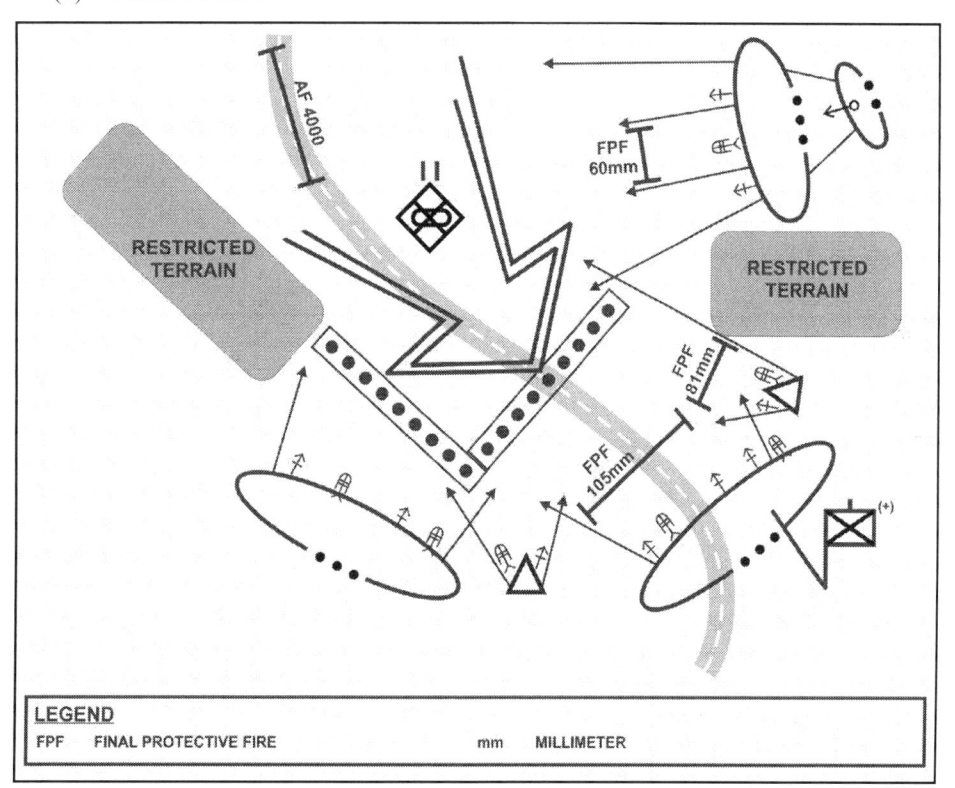

Figure C-7. Company defense fire plan sketch

C-17. The engagement area is the place where the leader intends to destroy an enemy force using the massed fires of all available weapons. The success of engagements depends on how the leader can integrate the obstacle and indirect fire plans with his direct fire plan in the engagement area to achieve the unit's purpose. Completing the steps of engagement area development is not a lengthy process. Particularly at the Infantry platoon level, engagement area development can occur rapidly without an elaborate decisionmaking process.

PLATOON FIRE PLANNING

C-18. Squad leaders prepare their sketches and submit them to the platoon leader. The platoon leader combines all sectors of fire and area of operation sketches (and possibly separate range cards) to prepare a platoon sector of fire and area of operation sketch. A platoon area of operation sketch is drawn as close to scale as possible including a target list for direct and indirect fires. One copy is submitted to the company commander, one copy is given to the platoon sergeant, and one copy is maintained by the platoon leader. As a minimum, the platoon area of operation sketch should show the elements contained in figure C-8 (page C-12).

This page intentionally left blank.

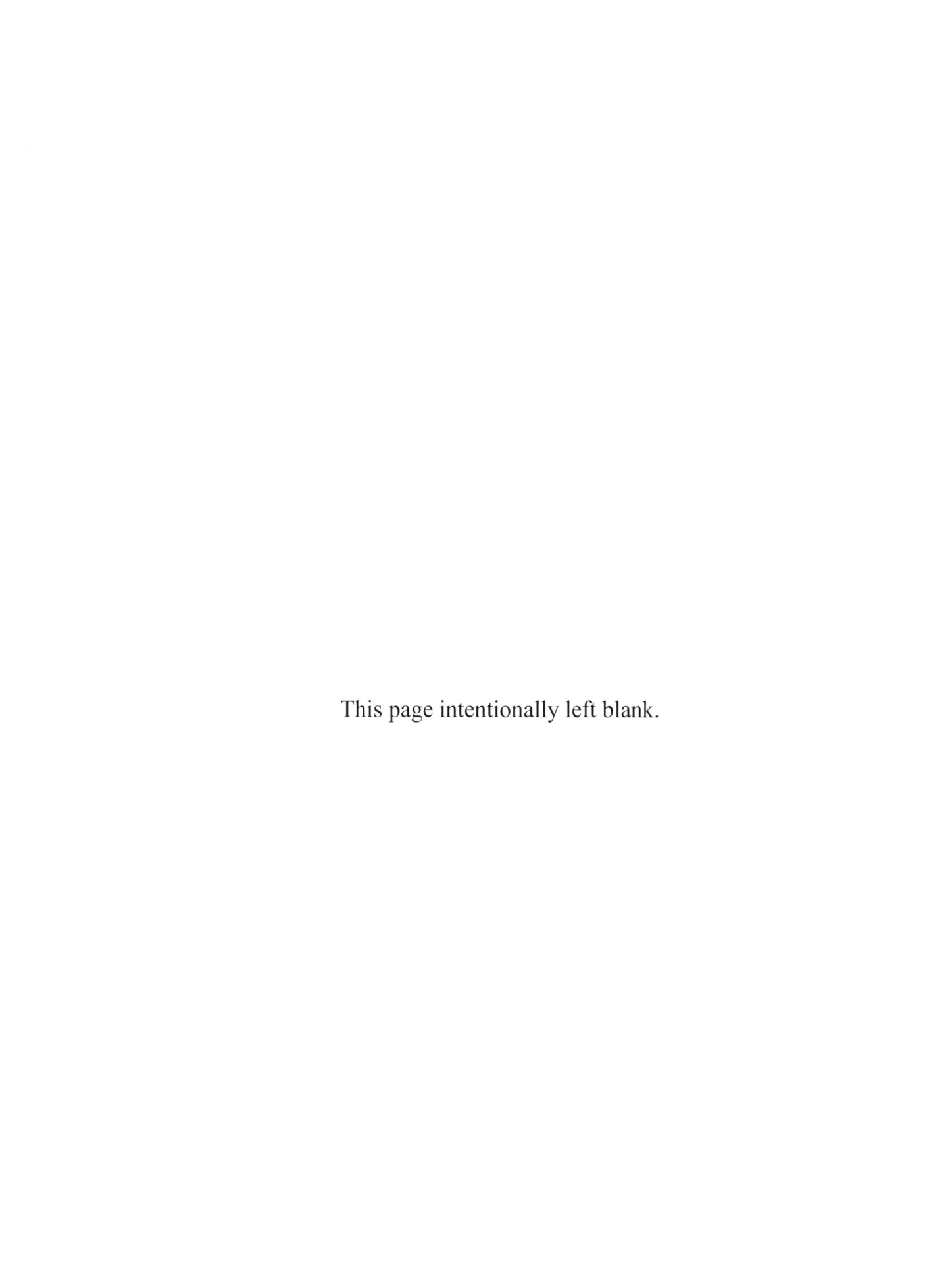

Indirect Fire Support Planning

in the engagement area to achieve the unit's purpose. Completing the steps of engagement area development is not a lengthy process. Particularly at the Infantry platoon level, engagement area development can occur rapidly without an elaborate decisionmaking process.

PLATOON FIRE PLANNING

C-18. Squad leaders prepare their sketches and submit them to the platoon leader. The platoon leader combines all sectors of fire and area of operation sketches (and possibly separate range cards) to prepare a platoon sector of fire and area of operation sketch. A platoon area of operation sketch is drawn as close to scale as possible including a target list for direct and indirect fires. One copy is submitted to the company commander, one copy is given to the platoon sergeant, and one copy is maintained by the platoon leader. As a minimum, the platoon area of operation sketch should show the elements contained in figure C-8 (page C-12).

Commentary

The above reference to a "target list" is a bit obscure. Typically, the target list is created as a TTLODAC table. Below you can find an example. This table also explains each part of the TTLODAC in more detail.

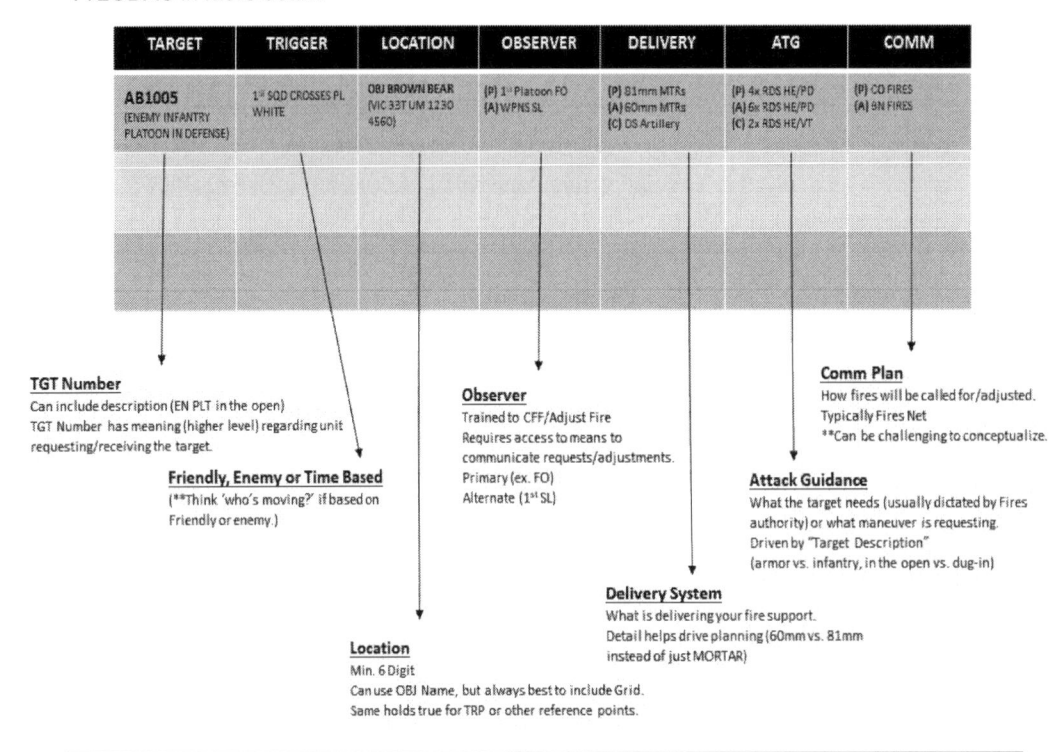

TARGET	TRIGGER	LOCATION	OBSERVER	DELIVERY	ATG	COMM
AB1005 (ENEMY INFANTRY PLATOON IN DEFENSE)	1st SQD CROSSES PL WHITE	OBJ BROWN BEAR (VIC 33T UM 1230 4560)	(P) 1st Platoon FO (A) WPNS SL	(P) 81mm MTRs (A) 60mm MTRs (C) DS Artillery	(P) 4x RDS HE/PD (A) 6x RDS HE/PD (C) 2x RDS HE/VT	(P) CO FIRES (A) BN FIRES

TGT Number
Can include description (EN PLT in the open)
TGT Number has meaning (higher level) regarding unit requesting/receiving the target.

Friendly, Enemy or Time Based
(**Think 'who's moving?' if based on Friendly or enemy.)

Location
Min. 6 Digit
Can use OBJ Name, but always best to include Grid.
Same holds true for TRP or other reference points.

Observer
Trained to CFF/Adjust Fire
Requires access to means to communicate requests/adjustments.
Primary (ex. FO)
Alternate (1st SL)

Delivery System
What is delivering your fire support.
Detail helps drive planning (60mm vs. 81mm instead of just MORTAR)

Attack Guidance
What the target needs (usually dictated by Fires authority) or what maneuver is requesting.
Driven by "Target Description" (armor vs. infantry, in the open vs. dug-in)

Comm Plan
How fires will be called for/adjusted.
Typically Fires Net
**Can be challenging to conceptualize.

Appendix C

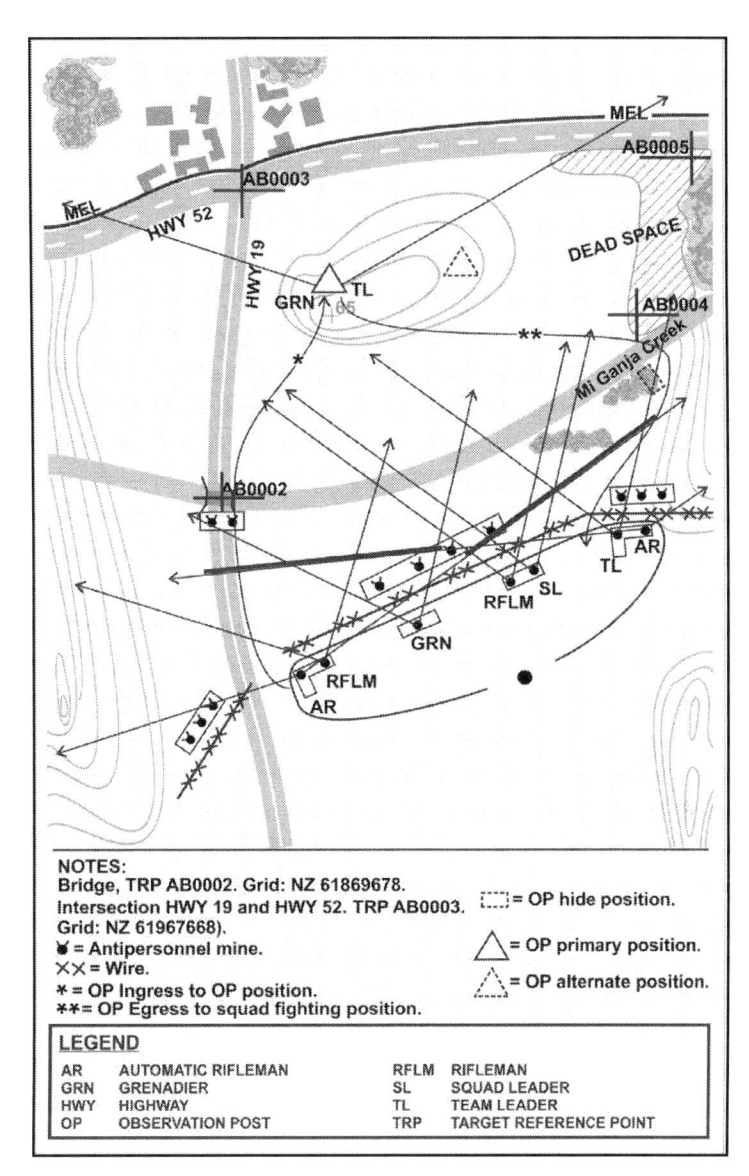

Figure C-8. Platoon area of operation sketch

SQUAD FIRE PLANNING

C-19. The squad leaders make two copies of their sector of fire sketches. One copy goes to the platoon leader; the other remains at the position. The squad leaders draw sector of fire sketches as close to scale as possible, showing the elements contained in figure C-9.

Indirect Fire Support Planning

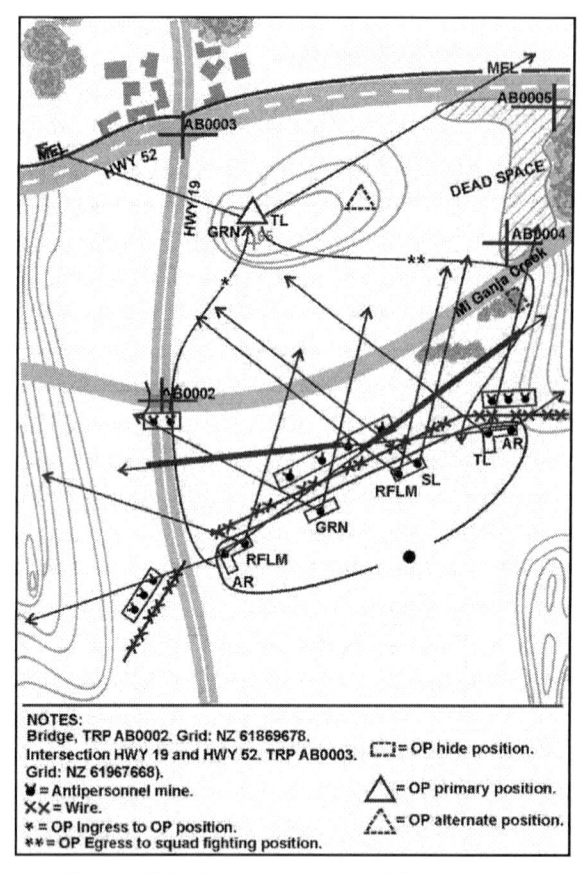

Figure C-9. Squad sector of fire sketch

FINAL PROTECTIVE LINE

C-20. FPL is a line of fire selected where an enemy assault is to be checked by interlocking fire from all available weapons and obstacles. (Refer to ADRP 1-02 for more information.) The FPL consists of all available measures, to include protective obstacles, direct fires, and indirect fires. The final protective fires targets the highest type of priority targets and takes precedence over all other fire targets. The final protective fires differs from a standard priority target in that fire is conducted at the maximum rate until the mortars are ordered to stop, or until ammunition is depleted. If possible, the final protective fires should be registered.

C-21. If Soldiers are in well-prepared defensive positions with overhead cover, A final protective fires can be adjusted close to the friendly positions, just beyond bursting range. If required, the leader can even call for artillery fires right on the unit's position using proximity or time fuzes for airbursts. Table C-2 (page C-14) shows indirect fire mortar weapon system characteristics being used when planning the FPF.

Appendix C

Table C-2. Normal final protective fires dimensions for each number of mortars

WEAPON	NUMBER OF TUBES	WIDTH (METERS)	DEPTH (METERS)	RISK ESTIMATED DISTANCE, .1% PI	RISK ESTIMATED DISTANCE, 10% PI
MORTARS					
120 mm	4	300	75	400 m	100 m
120 mm	2	150	75		
81 mm	4	150	50	230 m	80 m
81 mm	2	75	50		
60 mm	2	60	30	175 m	65 m
LEGEND m – meters; mm – millimeters					

FIRE PLANNING THE OFFENSE

C-22. Offensive fire planning follows the same methodology as defensive fire planning within constraints of the situation. The main difference is offensive fire planning always includes the synchronization between the base of fire and maneuver element. Inevitably, the leader's plan will not be as detailed as the defensive plan, but the presence of a maneuver element requires a baseline of planning and control to ensure indirect fire support is effective and efficient.

C-23. The leader must plan how he will engage known or suspected enemy targets, where friendly suppressive fire may be needed, and how he will control the unit's fires against both planned targets and targets of opportunity. Fire planning should include a thorough analysis of the type of threat expected. This will aid the supporting friendly element in tailoring the weapon and ammunition requirements to suit the situation.

C-24. Offensive fire planning supports four phases: planning and preparation, approach to the objective, actions on the objective, and follow-through. The degree of completeness and centralization of offensive fire planning depends on the time available to prepare the offensive. Fires are planned in four locations on the battlefield short of the LD/LC, LD/LC to the objective, on the objective, and behind the objective. Table C-3 lists planning considerations for each of the four locations.

Table C-3. Planning considerations

PHASE	PLAN FIRES TO:
1) Planning and Preparation (Short of the LD/LC)	• Support unit in AA. • Support unit's movement to the LD/LC. • Disrupt enemy reconnaissance forces. • Disrupt enemy defensive preparations. • Disrupt enemy spoiling attacks.
2) Approach to the Objective (LD/LC to the Objective)	• Begin echeloning fires for maneuver units. • Suppress and obscure for friendly breaching operations. • Suppress and obscure enemy security forces throughout movement. • Provide priority of fires to lead element. • Screen/guard exposed flanks.
3) Actions on the Objective (On the Objective)	• Fires to block enemy reinforcements. • Fires to suppress enemy direct fire weapons. • Suppress and obscure point of penetration. • Suppress and obscure enemy observation of friendly forces.
4) Follow Through (Beyond the Objective)	• Disrupt movement of enemy reinforcements during the assault. • Block avenues of enemy approach. • Disrupt enemy withdraw. • Screen friendly forces from enemy counterattacks during the assault. • Consolidate objective after the assault.
LEGEND AA – assembly area; LC – line of contact; LD – line of departure	

C-25. Offensive fire planning is divided into two categories — preparatory and supporting fires. The concept of fires has artillery and mortars in support of an attack to gain and maintain fire superiority on the objective until the last possible moment. When this indirect fire ceases, the enemy should be stunned and ineffective for a few moments. Take full advantage of this period by executing any or all of the following:

- Combat vehicles. Vehicles used in the attack, or as direct fire support, continue to give close support.
- Maintaining fire superiority. Small-arms fire from local and internal support by fire is continued as long as possible.
- Maneuver elements. Assaulting troops must try to fire as they advance. Troops must observe fire discipline, as in many cases fire control orders will not be possible. They must not arrive at the objective without ammunition.

Appendix C

- Audacity. Where the ground and vegetation do not prohibit movement, leading sections should move quickly over the last 30 or 40 meters to the enemy positions to minimize exposure.

C-26. When planning fires for the offense, leaders verify the fire element's task organization and ensure their plans coordinate measures for the attack, site exploitation, pursuit, and contingency plans. Leaders develop or confirm with the responsible level authority supporting systems are positioned and repositioned to ensure continuous fires throughout the operation. Mutual support of fire systems promotes responsive support and provides the commanders of maneuver units freedom of action during each critical event of the engagement or battle

C-27. There exists a diverse variety of munitions and weapon systems, direct and indirect, to support close offensive missions. To integrate direct and indirect fire support, the leader must understand the mission, commander's intent, concept of the operation, and critical tasks to be accomplished. The leader plans fires to focus on enemy capabilities and systems being neutralized. Critical tasks include:

- Continuous in-depth support (accomplished by proper positioning of systems).
- Isolating enemy forces.
- Softening enemy defenses by delivering preparatory fires.
- Suppressing and obscuring enemy weapon systems to reduce enemy standoff capabilities.
- Interdicting enemy counterattack forces, isolating the defending force, and preventing its reinforcement and resupply.

SECTION II – TARGET EFFECTS PLANNING

C-28. Not only must indirect fire support planners determine what enemy targets to hit, and when, but also must decide how to attack each enemy target. Leaders should consider all the aspects of target effects when planning fires. Although this section is specific to mortars, the following concepts generally apply to most indirect fires. (Refer to ATP 3-09.32 for more information.)

HIGH-EXPLOSIVE AMMUNITION

C-29. When mortar rounds impact they throw fragments in a pattern never truly circular, and may even travel irregular, based on the round's angle of fall, the slope of the terrain, and type soil. However, for planning purposes, each mortar HE round is considered to have a circular lethal bursting area. Figure C-10 shows a scale representation of the lethal bursting areas of mortar rounds.

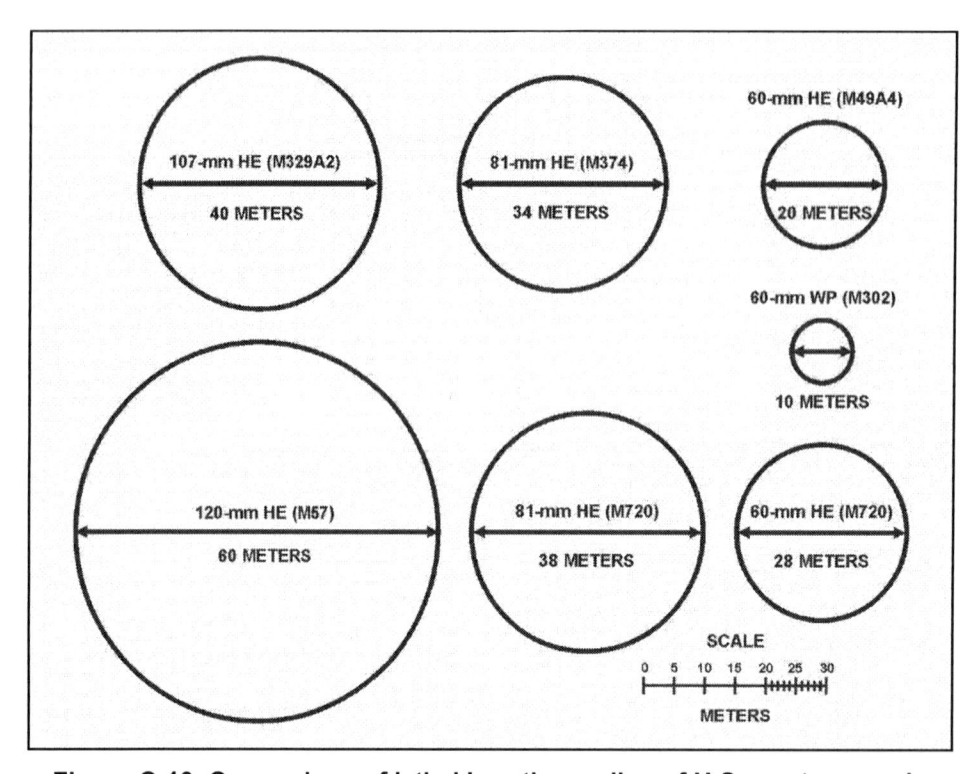

Figure C-10. Comparison of lethal bursting radius of U.S. mortar rounds

FUZE SETTING

C-30. The decision concerning what fuze setting to use depends on the position of the enemy.

C-31. Exposed enemy troops standing up are best engaged with impact or near surface burst fuze settings. The round explodes on, or near, the ground. Shell fragments travel outward perpendicular to the long axis of the standing target. (See figure C-11, page C-18.)

Appendix C

Figure C-11. Standing targets

C-32. If exposed enemy troops are lying prone, the proximity fuze setting is most effective. The rounds explode high above the ground, and fragments coming downward are traveling once again perpendicular to the long axis of the targets. (See figure C-12.)

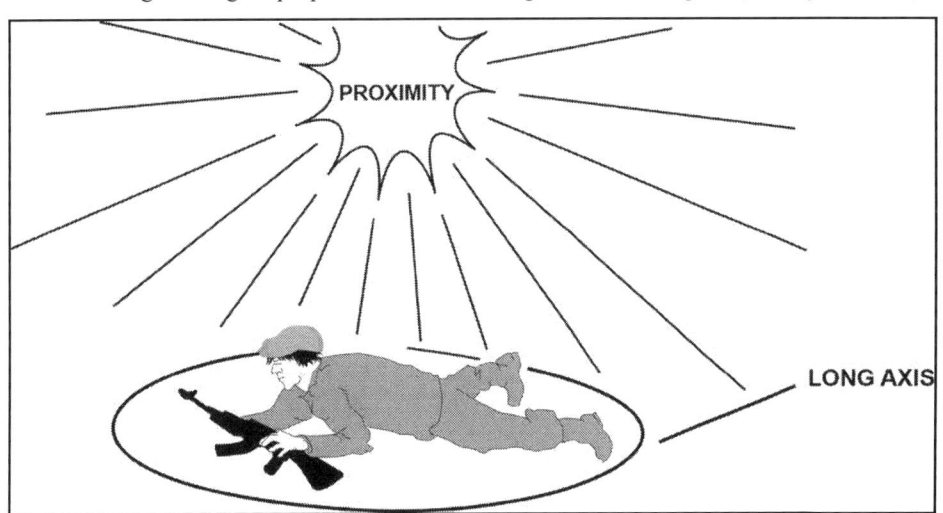

Figure C-12. Prone targets

C-33. The proximity setting is the most effective if the enemy is in open fighting positions without overhead cover. Even proximity settings will not always produce effects if the positions are deep. (See figure C-13.)

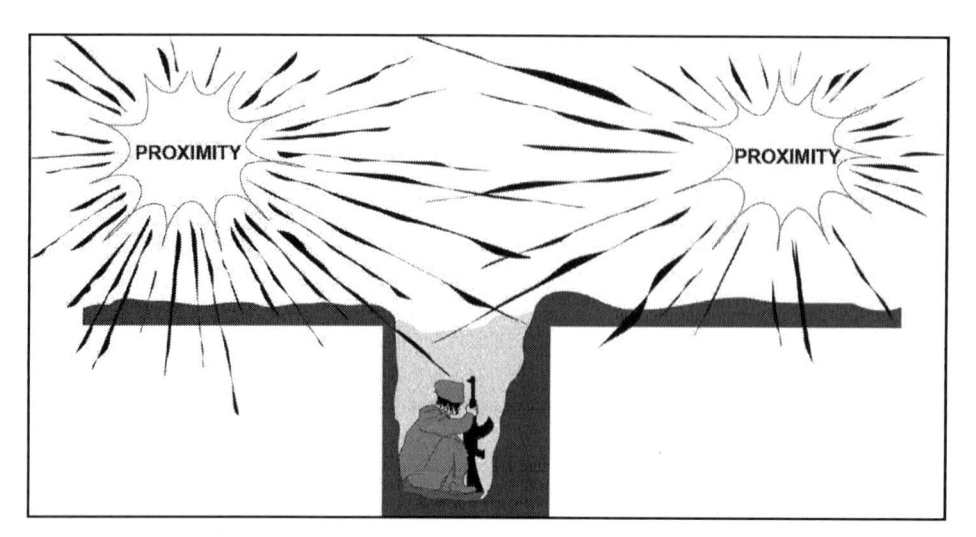

Figure C-13. Targets in open fighting positions

C-34. The delay fuze setting is most effective when the enemy is below triple canopy jungle or in fighting positions with overhead cover. Light mortars will have little effect against overhead cover. Even medium mortars have limited effect. Heavy mortars can destroy a bunker or enemy troops beneath jungle canopy with a hit or near-miss. (See figure C-14, page C-20.)

Appendix C

Figure C-14. Targets beneath triple canopy jungle

EFFECTS OF COVER ON HIGH-EXPLOSIVE ROUNDS

C-35. Enemy forces normally will be either standing or prone. They maybe in the open or protected by varying degrees of cover. Each of these changes the target effects of mortar fire.

C-36. Surprise mortar fire is always more effective than fire against an enemy being warned and seeks cover. Recent studies have shown a high casualty rate can be achieved with only two rounds against an enemy platoon standing in the open. The same studies required 10 to 15 rounds to duplicate the casualty rate when the platoon was warned by adjusting rounds and sought cover. If the enemy soldiers merely lay prone, they significantly reduce the effects of mortar fire. Mortar fire against standing enemy forces is almost twice as effective as fire against prone targets.

C-37. Proximity fire is usually more effective than surface-burst rounds against targets in the open. The effectiveness of mortar fire against a prone enemy is increased by about 40 percent by firing proximity-fuzed rounds rather than surface-burst rounds.

C-38. If the enemy is in open fighting positions without overhead cover, proximity-fuzed mortar rounds are about five times as effective as impact-fuzed rounds. When fired against troops in open fighting positions, proximity-fuzed rounds are only 10 percent as effective as they would be against an enemy in the open. The greatest effectiveness against troops

Indirect Fire Support Planning

in open fighting positions, the charge with the lowest angle of fall should be chosen. It produces almost two times as much effect as the same round falling with the steepest angle.

C-39. If the enemy has prepared fighting positions with overhead cover, only impact-fuzed and delay-fuzed rounds will have much effect. Proximity-fuzed rounds can restrict the enemy's ability to move from position to position, but they will cause few, if any, casualties. Impact-fuzed rounds cause some blast and suppressive effect. Delay-fuzed rounds can penetrate and destroy a position but must achieve a direct hit. Only the 120-mm mortar with a delay-fuze setting can damage a Soviet-style strongpoint defense. Heavy bunkers cannot be destroyed by light or medium mortar rounds.

SUPPRESSIVE EFFECTS OF HIGH-EXPLOSIVE MORTAR ROUNDS

C-40. Suppression from mortar is not as easy to measure as the target effect. It is the psychological effect produced in the mind of the enemy preventing him from returning fire or carrying on his duties. Inexperienced or surprised Soldiers are more easily suppressed than experienced, warned Soldiers. Soldiers in the open are much more easily suppressed than those with overhead cover. Suppression is most effective when mortar fires first fall; as they continue, their suppressive effects lessen. HE rounds are the most suppressive, but bursting WP mixed with HE has a great psychological effect on the enemy:

- If a 60-mm mortar round lands within 20 meters of a target, the target probably will be suppressed, if not hit.
- If a 60-mm mortar round lands within 35 meters of a target, there is a 50 percent chance it will be suppressed. Beyond 50 meters, little suppression takes place.
- If an 81-mm mortar round lands within 30 meters of a target, the target probably will be suppressed, if not hit.
- If an 81-mm mortar round lands within 75 meters of a target, there is a 50 percent chance the target will be suppressed. Beyond 125 meters, little suppression takes place.
- If a heavy mortar round (proximity-fuzed) lands within 65 meters of target, the target probably will be suppressed, if not hit.
- If a heavy mortar round (proximity-fuzed) lands within 125 meters of a target, there is a 50 percent chance the target will be suppressed. Beyond 200 meters, little suppression takes place. The 120-mm mortar round is better for suppression than the 107-mm, but both are excellent suppressive rounds.

ILLUMINATION, OBSCURANTS, AND WHITE PHOSPHORUS

C-41. Illumination and obscuration missions are important functions for mortar platoons or sections. Atmospheric stability, wind velocity, and wind direction are the most important factors when planning target effects for obscurants and WP mortar rounds. The terrain in the target area also affects obscurants and WP rounds.

Appendix C

C-42. The bursting WP round provides a screening, incendiary, marking, and casualty-producing effect. It produces a localized, instantaneous obscurants cloud by scattering burning WP particles.

C-43. The WP round is used mainly to produce immediate, close point obscuration. It can be used to screen the enemy's field of fire for short periods, which allows troops to maneuver against him. The 60-mm WP round is not sufficient to produce a long-lasting, wide-area obscurants screen, but the much larger WP round from the heavy mortar is.

C-44. WP rounds generally should not be used solely to produce casualties due to the law of war principle of unnecessary suffering. Unnecessary suffering would be implicated because of the persistent burning WP causes in the wounds it produces and the availability of a superior round for producing casualties, the HE round. While the bursting WP round can produce casualties among exposed enemy troops the casualty-producing radius of the WP round is much less than that of the HE round. Generally, more casualties can be produced by firing HE ammunition than by firing WP. A few WP rounds mixed into a fire mission of HE rounds for a valid purpose (that is target marking) may increase the suppressive effect of the fire because of the significant psychological effect a WP burst may have on exposed troops.

C-45. When WP is used for its incendiary and casualty-producing effects it should not be used against the civilian population, or civilian objects. The Law of Armed Conflict also prohibits the use of incendiary weapons against military objectives located in "concentrations of civilians," unless the military objective is separated sufficiently from civilians and civilian objects to prevent collateral damage.

C-46. The WP rounds can be used to mark targets, especially for attack by aircraft. Base-ejecting obscurants rounds, such as the 81-mm M819 red phosphorous round, produce a dispersed obscurants cloud, normally too indistinct for marking targets.

C-47. The effects of atmospheric stability can determine whether mortar obscurants is effective at all or, if effective, how much ammunition will be needed:
- During unstable conditions, mortar obscurants and white phosphorous rounds are almost ineffective the obscurant does not spread but often climbs straight up and quickly dissipates.
- Under moderately unstable atmospheric conditions, base-ejecting obscurants' rounds are more effective than bursting white phosphorous rounds. The M819 red phosphorous round of the M252 mortar screens for over 2 and a half minutes.
- Under stable conditions, both red phosphorous and white phosphorous rounds are effective.
- The higher the humidity, the better the screening effects of mortar rounds.

C-48. The M819 red phosphorous round loses up to 35 percent of its screening ability if the ground in the target area is covered with water or deep snow. During extremely cold and dry conditions over snow, up to four times the number of obscurant's rounds than expected may be needed to create an adequate screen. The higher the wind velocity, the more bursting WP rounds are, and less effective burning obscurant's rounds become.

C-49. If the terrain in the target area is swampy, rain-soaked, or snow-covered, then burning obscurant's rounds may not be effective. These rounds produce obscurants by ejecting felt wedges soaked in red phosphorus. These wedges then burn on the ground, producing a dense, long-lasting cloud. If the wedges fall into mud, water, or snow, they can be extinguished. Shallow water can reduce the obscurants produced by these rounds by as much as 50 percent. Bursting WP rounds are affected little by the terrain in the target area, except deep snow and cold temperatures which can reduce the obscurants cloud by about 25 percent.

C-50. Although bursting WP rounds are not designed to cause casualties, the fragments of the shell casing and bits of burning WP can cause injuries. Burning obscurant rounds do not cause casualties and have little suppressive effect.

ILLUMINATION

C-51. Illumination rounds can be used to disclose enemy formations, to signal, or to mark targets. There are illumination rounds available for all mortars.

C-52. The 60-mm illumination round available now is the standard cartridge, illuminating, M83A3. This round has a fixed time of delay between firing and start of the illumination. The illumination lasts for about 25 seconds, providing moderate light over a square kilometer.

C-53. The 60-mm illumination round does not provide the same degree of illumination as do the rounds of the heavier mortars and field artillery. However, it is sufficient for local, point illumination. The small size of the round can be an advantage where illumination is desired in an area but adjacent friendly forces to not want to be seen. The 60-mm illumination round can be used without degrading the night vision devices of adjacent units.

C-54. The medium and heavy mortars can provide excellent illumination over wide areas. The 120-mm mortar illumination round provides one million candlepower for 60 seconds.

C-55. The M203/M320 40-mm grenades, as well as all mortars have the capability to deliver infrared illumination rounds in addition to the more common white light.

SPECIAL ILLUMINATION TECHNIQUES

C-56. Following are three special illumination techniques mortars have used.

C-57. An illumination round fired extremely high over a general area will not always alert an enemy force that it is being observed. However, it will provide enough illumination to optimize the use of image intensification (starlight) scopes such as the AN/PVS-14.

C-58. An illumination round fired to burn on the ground will prevent observation beyond the flare into the shadow. This is one method of countering enemy use of image intensification devices. A friendly force could move behind the flare with greater security.

C-59. An illumination round fired to burn on the ground can be used to mark targets during day or night. Illumination rounds have an advantage over WP as target markers during

Appendix C

high winds. The obscurants cloud from a WP round will be blown quickly downwind. The obscurants from the burning illumination round will continue to originate from the same point, regardless of the wind.

CONSIDERATIONS WHEN USING THERMAL SIGHTS

C-60. Although illumination rounds may aid target acquisition when friendly forces are using image intensification devices (such as night vision devices), this is not so when thermal sights are used. As the illumination flares burn out and land on the ground, they remain as a distinct hot spot seen through thermal sights for several minutes. This may cause confusion, especially if the flare canisters are between the enemy and friendly forces. WP rounds also can cause these hot spots which can make target identification difficult for gunners using thermal sights (tanks, BFV, TOW, or Javelin).

SECTION III – ARMY ATTACK AVIATION

C-61. Army attack aviation uses maneuver to concentrate and sustain combat power at critical times and places to find, fix, and destroy enemy forces. Aviation units design, tailor, and configure their assets for specific operational support based on mission guidance and specific theater in which the units operate. (See chapter 1, figure 1-6 of this publication for information on a 5-line attack aviation call for fire briefing ground to air).

ATTACK AVIATION CALL FOR FIRE

C-62. When the Infantry platoon or squad engages in in the area of operation, it may request Army aviation support. Attack aviation call for fire is a hasty or deliberate operation by Army aviation in support of units engaged in close combat. The hasty operation in the close fight typically lacks detailed coordination between air and ground elements. Coordination between ground maneuver units and attack aviation maximizes the capabilities of the combined arms team while minimizing the risk of fratricide and friendly fire. To ensure adequate air-ground integration, the following major problem areas should be addressed:

- Ensure aircrews understand ground tactical plan and unit commander's intent.
- Ensure adequate common control measures are used to allow both air and ground unit's maximum freedom of fire and maneuver.
- Ensure aircrews and ground forces understand methods of differentiating between enemy and friendly forces on the ground.

EMPLOYMENT CONSIDERATIONS

C-63. Mission success in attack aviation call for fire employment depends on leaders conducting detailed planning and coordination between the aerial attack team and ground unit already engaged in close combat. Once execution begins, there must be integration of the fires and movement of both maneuver and aerial elements. (See table C-4 for attack aviation call for fire capabilities.)

Table C-4. Attack aviation call for fire capabilities

AIRCRAFT	ORDNANCE	DATALINK	SENSORS AND MARKING	FREQUENCY BAND	FREQUENCY HOPPING
AH-1W/Z	TOW 1, Hellfire, B/K/N/M, 2.75"/5" Rockets, 20mm Cannon, APKWS		NTS2 (W only), TSS2 (Z only)	UHF-AM, VHF-AM//FM, FMV	HQ II, SINCGARS
AH-6	7.62 MG, .50 cal MG, Hellfire, 2.75" Rockets		FLIR, IR Pointer	VHF-AM/FM x 2, UHF-AM/FM SATCOM	HQ II, SINCGARS
AH-64D	Hellfire (Laser or RF), 2.75" Rockets, 30mm Cannon		FLIR (LTD3), MMW, Radar, DTV, IZLID	UHF-AM, VHF-FM x 2, VHF-AM, SATCOM VMF/BFT	HQ I/II, SINCGARS
HH-60G4	.50 cal MG, 7.76mm MG	SADL	FLIR, IR Pointer	VHF-AM/FM x 2, UHF-AM, SATCOM, LARS	HQ II, SINCGARS
HH-60H	M240, GAU-17, GAU-16, Hellfire	BFT	AN/AAS-44 (V) IZLID	VHF-AM/FM, UHF-AM/FM, SATCOM	
MH-60L DAP	7.62mm MG, 30mm Cannon, 2.75" Hellfire		FLIR (LTD), IR Pointer	VHF-AM/FM x 2, UHF-AM/FM, SATCOM	HQ II, SINCGARS
MH-60R	M240, GAU-21, Hellfire	Link 16, Hawklink	AN/AAS-44C (V)2, LTM, PEQ, Pulsed Doppler Radar	VHF-AM/FM, UHF-AM/FM, SATCOM/J-Voice x 2	HQ II, SINCGARS
MH-60S	M240, GAU-21, Hellfire	Link 16	AN/AAS-44C (V)2	VHF-AM/FM, UHF-AM/FM, SATCOM/J-Voice x 2	
OH-58D	Hellfire, 2.75" Rockets, 50 cal MG	BFT, VMF	FLIR (LTD), TVS, Smoke Grenades, IR Pointer	UHF-AM, VHF-FM x 2, VHF-AM, SATCOM BFT/VMF	HQ I/II, SINCGARS
SH-60B	M60 MG, GAU-16, Hellfire	Hawklink	AN/AAS-44, PEQ, Pulsed Radar	VHF-AM/FM, UHF-AM/FM	
Tiger	30mm Cannon, 2.75" Rockets, Hellfire		FLIR (LTD)	UHF-VHF	
UH-1N/Y	7.62 MG, .50 cal MG, 2.75" Rockets, APKWS		BRITE STAR (Block II)	UHF, VHF-AM/FM SATCOM	HQ II, SINCGARS

NOTES:
1. AH-1W.
2. The AH-1W can designate codes 1111-1788.
3. The AH-64 can designate codes 1XXX-8XXX.
4. The HH-60G crew train to the Attack Aviation Call for Fire/AC-130 5-Line attack briefing.

AM	amplitude modulation	LTD	laser target designator
ANDVT	advanced narrowband digital voice terminal	MG	machine gun
APKWS	advanced precision kill weapon system	mm	millimeter
BFT	blue force tracking	MMW	millimeter wave
cal	caliber	NTS	night targeting system
COMSEC	communications security	RF	radio frequency
DAP	direct action penetrator	TOW	tube-launched, optically tracked, wire-guided missile
DTV	day television	TSS	target sight system
FM	frequency modulation	TVS	television system
FLIR	forward looking infrared	SADL	situational awareness data link
FMV	full motion video	SATCOM	satellite communication
HQ I	have quick I	SINCGARS	single-channel ground and airborne radio system
HQ II	have quick II	UHF	ultra high frequency
IR	infrared	VMF	variable message format
IZLID	infrared zoom laser illuminator designator	VHF	very high frequency
LARS	lightweight airborne recovery system		

C-64. Planning for attack reconnaissance helicopter support usually begins at battalion level or above. The battalion provides the aviation brigade or Infantry battalion with information on locations, routes, and communications before the attack team's departure from its AA. As part of this effort, the Infantry platoons usually provide information for attack aviation call for fire employment. All platoon Soldiers should familiarize themselves with the procedures used to call for attack reconnaissance helicopter support. If attack reconnaissance helicopter assets are working for their battalion, the platoon and

Appendix C

company provides suppressive fires on any known or suspected threat air defense artillery locations.

C-65. Critical elements of the planning process are the procedures and resources used in marking and identifying targets and friendly positions. Leaders consider these factors thoroughly, regardless of the time available to the ground and air commanders.

C-66. The aerial attack team coordinates directly with the lowest-level unit in contact on the Infantry platoon and company radio command net. Whenever practicable, before the attack team launches the attack aviation call for fire operation, the leader or commander conducts final coordination with the attack reconnaissance helicopters in a concealed position known as the aerial holding area. The holding area is a point in space within the supported unit's area of operation oriented toward the threat; it allows the attack team to receive requests for immediate attack aviation call for fire and expedite the attack. The aerial holding area could be an alternate battle position positioned out of range of the threat's direct fire and indirect fire weapons ranges.

C-67. Final coordination between the ground and helicopter units must include agreement on methods of identifying and marking friendly and threat positions. This should take advantage of the equipment and capabilities of the attack team, including the forward-looking infrared system, the thermal imaging system, and night vision devices.

C-68. Coordination also should cover the battle position, and assault by fire, or support-by-fire positions used by the attack reconnaissance helicopters. The leader should offset these positions from the ground maneuver unit to maximize the effects of the attack team's weapons and to minimize the risk of fratricide and friendly fire. To prevent indirect fires within the area of operation or zone from posing a danger to the helicopters, the commander informs direct support artillery and organic mortars of the aerial positions. (Refer to ATP 3-09.32 for more information.)

Appendix D
Security

Security is the measures taken by the platoon or squad to protect it against all acts designed to impair its effectiveness. Security measures are an inherent aspect of all military operations and can be moving or stationary.

SECTION I – SECURITY TASKS

D-1. Infantry platoons and squads conduct security tasks independently or part of a larger force. Security tasks are screen, guard, cover, area security, and local security. These tasks are executed in the larger unit's security zone (advance, flank, or rear of the main body). Leaders given these tasks or participating in the task of a larger unit must, at a minimum, understand their engagement criteria and whether or not to become decisively engaged. (Refer to FM 3-90-2 for more information.) Security tasks include the following options:

- Screen. Screen is a security task that primarily provides early warning to the protected force. (Refer to FM 3-90-2 for more information.) A screen at platoon level may consist of a combination of observation post and security patrols.
- Guard. Guard is a term with a dual meaning; the difference is the size of the element. When used to refer to individuals, a guard is the individual responsible to keep watch over, protect, shield, defend, warn, or duties prescribed by general orders or special orders. Guards also are referred to as a sentinels, sentries, or lookouts. When used in reference to units, a guard is a security task to protect the main force by fighting to gain time while also observing and reporting information and preventing enemy ground observation of and direct fire against the main body. Units conducting a guard mission cannot operate independently because they rely upon fires and functional and multifunctional support assets of the main body. (Refer to FM 3-90-2 for more information.) A platoon participating in a guard tasks may conduct a combination of observation posts, battle positions, combat patrols, reconnaissance patrols, or movement to contact for protection.
- Cover. Cover is a security task to protect the main body by fighting to gain time while also observing and reporting information and preventing the enemy ground observation and direct fire against the main body for an extended period of time. (Refer to FM 3-90-2 for more information.) Ordinarily only brigade -sized and larger elements have the assets necessary to conduct this type of security operation.
- Area security. Area security is a security task conducted to protect friendly forces, installations, routes, and actions within a specific area. (Refer to FM 3-90-2 for more information.) During conventional operations area security refers the security measures used in friendly controlled areas. Many of the tasks traditionally associated with stability and small scale contingencies fall within the scope of area

Appendix D

security. These include road blocks, traffic control post, route security, convoy security, and searches.
- Local security. Local security is a security task that includes low-level security activities conducted near a unit to prevent surprise by the enemy. (ADRP 3-90) Local security measures are the same as those outlined for *exterior guards* in FM 22-6.

D-2. The screen, guard, and cover are the security measures used primarily by battalion-sized units to secure themselves from conventional enemy units. These measures, respectively, contain increasing levels of combat power and provide increasing levels of security of the main body. Along with the increase of combat power, there is an increase in the unit's requirement to fight for time, space, and information on the enemy. Conceptually, the measures serve the same purpose as the local security measures by smaller units. For example, a battalion will employ a screen for early warning while a platoon or squad will emplace an observation post. The purpose is the same, early warning, only the degree and scale are different.

D-3. Local and area security are related since they both focus on the enemy threat within a specified area. Again, the difference is one of degree and scale. Local security is concerned with protecting the unit from enemy in the immediate area, whereas area security is concerned with enemy anywhere in the leader's area of operation.

SECURITY FUNDAMENTALS

D-4. The techniques employed to secure a larger unit are generally the same as those of the offense and defense. It is the application of those techniques that differ. Table D-1 lists the most common techniques used, information required executing the operation, and principles used to employ them.

Security

Table D-1. Security fundamentals

FUNDAMENTALS OF SECURITY OPERATIONS	TECHNIQUES USED TO PERFORM SECURITY OPERATIONS	INFORMATION REQUIRED FROM CONTROLLING HEADQUARTERS
Provide early and accurate warning. Provide reaction time and maneuver space. Orient on the force, area, or facility to be protected. Perform continuous reconnaissance. Maintain enemy contact.	Observation post. Combat outpost. Battle position. Patrols. Combat formations. Movement techniques. Infiltration. Movement to contact. Dismounted, mounted, and air insertion. Roadblocks. Checkpoints. Convoy and route security. Searches.	Trace of the security area (front, sides, and rear boundaries), and initial position within the area. Time security is to be established. Main body size and location. Mission, purpose, and commander's intent of the controlling headquarters. Counterreconnaissance and engagement criteria. Method of movement to occupy the area (reconnaissance or security patrol; infiltration; tactical; mounted, dismounted, or air insertion). Trigger for displacement and method of control when displacing. Possible follow-on missions.

SCREEN

D-5. A screen primarily provides early warning to the main body. A unit performing a screen observes, identifies, and reports enemy actions. Screen is defensive in nature but not passive in execution. It is employed to cover gaps between forces, exposed flanks, or the rear of stationary or moving forces. Generally, a screening force fights in a limited engagement where it can quickly destroy an enemy element without revealing its own position or engages high payoff targets the severely degrades the enemies capabilities. However, it may engage enemy reconnaissance elements within its capability (counterreconnaissance). A screen provides the least amount of protection of all security missions. It does not have the combat power to develop the situation. It is used when the likelihood of enemy contact is remote, the expected enemy force is small, or the friendly main body needs only a minimum amount of time once it is warned to react

D-6. Screen tasks are to—
- Allow no enemy ground element to pass through the screen undetected and unreported.

Appendix D

- Maintain continuous surveillance of all avenues of approach larger than a designated size into the area under all visibility conditions.
- Destroy or repel all enemy reconnaissance patrols within its capabilities.
- Locate the lead elements of each enemy advance guard and determine its direction of movement in a defensive screen.
- Maintain contact with enemy forces and report all activities in the area of operations.
- Maintain contact with the main body and security forces operating on its flanks.
- Impede and harass the enemy within its capabilities while displacing.

STATIONARY SCREEN

D-7. When tasked to conduct a stationary screen (see figure D-1), the leader first determines likely avenues of approach into the main body's perimeter. The leader determines the location of potential observation posts along these avenues of approach. Ideally, the leader assigns observation posts in-depth if he has the assets available. If necessary, he identifies additional control measures (named areas of interest, phase lines, TRP, or checkpoints) to assist in controlling observation, tracking of the enemy, and movement of his own forces. The unit conducts mounted and foot patrols to cover ground not being observed from observation posts. Once the enemy is detected from an observation post, the screening force may engage him with indirect fires. This prevents the enemy from penetrating the screen line and does not compromise the location of the observation post. If enemy pressure threatens the security of the screening force, the unit reports the situation to the controlling headquarters and requests permission to displace to a subsequent screen line or follow-on mission.

Security

Figure D-1. Squad-sized stationary screen

MOVING SCREEN

D-8. Platoons may conduct a moving screen to the flanks or rear of the main body force. The movement of the screen is tied to time and distance factors associated with the movement of the friendly main body.

D-9. Responsibilities for a moving flank screen begin at the front of the main body's lead combat element and end at the rear of the protected force. In conducting a moving flank screen, the unit either occupies a series of temporary observation posts along a designated screen line to overwatch the main body, or if the main body is moving too fast, continues to move while maintaining surveillance. The screening force uses one or more of the three basic movement techniques to control movement along the screened flank (traveling, traveling overwatch, and bounding overwatch).

GUARD

D-10. A guard differs from a screen in a guard force contains sufficient combat power to defeat, cause the withdrawal of, or fix the lead elements of an enemy ground force before it can engage the main body with direct fires. A guard force uses all means at its disposal, including decisive engagement, to prevent the enemy from penetrating the security zone. It operates within the range of the main body's indirect fire weapons, deploying over a narrower front than a comparable-size screening force to permit concentrating combat power. The three types of guard operations are: advance; flank; and rear guard.

Appendix D

D-11. Platoons as part of a company can be assigned a guard mission conduct all of the measures associated with a screen. Additionally they—
- Destroy the enemy advance guard.
- Cause the enemy main body to deploy, report its disposition, composition, strength, and capabilities.

COVER

D-12. The covering force, or portions of it, often becomes decisively engaged with enemy forces. Therefore, the covering force must have substantial combat power to engage the enemy and accomplish its mission. The platoon along with the company team may participate in covering force operations but does not conduct them on its own. The covering force develops the situation earlier than a screen or a guard force. It fights longer and more often and defeats larger enemy forces.

AREA SECURITY

D-13. Area security is used by units to secure their area of operation from smaller enemy units (special purpose forces, guerrillas).

D-14. During area security operations civilians will be present. Therefore, leaders must ensure Soldiers understand current ROE. However, leaders always are responsible for protecting their forces and consider this responsibility when applying the ROE. Restrictions on conducting operations and using force must be explained clearly and understood by everyone. Soldiers must understand their actions, no matter how minor, may have far-reaching positive or negative effects. They must realize both friendly or hostile media and adversary information activities quickly can exploit their actions, especially the manner in which they treat the civilian population.

D-15. Leaders executing area security measures in a densely populated area must assess the effect of imposing a degree of control on both traffic and pedestrians carefully. For instance, during the rush hour period, however efficient the traffic control point, a crowd of impatient civilians or cars and trucks can quickly build-up and precipitate the very situation the traffic control point leader is trying to avoid.

D-16. Population and resource control operations cause inconvenience and disruption to all aspects of community life. Therefore, it is important members of the civil community appreciate the purpose of such operations. In particular, they must understand control measures are protective and not punitive. All personnel involved in operations designed to ensure security must be thoroughly conversant with their duties and responsibilities. They must be able to work quickly and methodically to prevent delay and disruption to legitimate activities. They also must work to avoid unnecessary damage to personnel, vehicles, and property. To achieve their purpose they must be thorough. Leaders, at all levels, must ensure adequate security is in place to counter all assessed risks

LOCAL SECURITY

D-17. Local security prevents a unit from being surprised and is an important part of maintaining the initiative. Local security includes local measure taken by units against enemy actions. It involves avoiding detection by the enemy or deceiving the enemy about friendly positions and intentions. It also includes finding any enemy forces in the immediate vicinity and knowing as much about their positions and intentions as possible. The requirement for maintaining local security is an inherent part of all operations. Table D-2 lists a sample of active and passive local security measures.

Table D-2. Active and passive security measures

	ACTIVE AND PASSIVE SECURITY MEASURES
Active Measures (moving)	Combat formations, movement techniques, movement to contact, spoiling attacks. Moving as fast as conditions allow preventing enemy detection and adaptation. Skillful use of terrain.

Active Measures (stationary)	Outside the perimeter:
	    Observation posts, security patrols.
	    Battle positions, combat patrols, and reconnaissance patrols.
	    Employing early warning devices.
	    Establishing roadblocks / checkpoints.
	 Inside the perimeter:
	    Establishing access points (entrance and exits).
	    Establishing the number and types of positions to be manned.
	    Establishing readiness control levels.
	    Designating a reserve/response force.
	    Establishing stand-to measures.

Passive Measures	Camouflage, cover and concealment, and deception measures. Signal security. Noise and light discipline.

SECTION II – OBSERVATION POSTS

D-18. The observation post, the primary means of maintaining surveillance of an assigned avenue or named areas of interest, is a position from where units observe the enemy and direct and adjust indirect fires against him. From the observation post, platoons or squads send SALUTE reports to their controlling headquarters when observing enemy activity.

TYPES OF OBSERVATION POSTS

D-19. Observation posts can be executed either mounted or dismounted. As they are complementary, if possible they should be used in combination.

D-20. The main advantage of a dismounted observation post is it provides maximum stealth hopefully preventing the enemy from detecting it. The two main disadvantages are

Appendix D

it has limited flexibility, taking time to displace and limited firepower to protect itself if detected.

D-21. The main advantages of a mounted observation post are the flexibility coming from vehicle mobility as well as the additional combat power resident in the vehicle's optics, communications, weapons, and protection. The main disadvantage is vehicles inherently are easier to detect and can prevent the unit from accomplishing its mission.

POSITIONING OF OBSERVATION POSTS

D-22. Based on METT-TC, leaders may array observation posts on-line or in-depth. (See figures D-2 and D-3.) Depth is the preferred technique for maintaining contact with a moving enemy along a particular avenue of approach. On-line placement is optimal when there is no clear avenue of approach or the enemy is not moving.

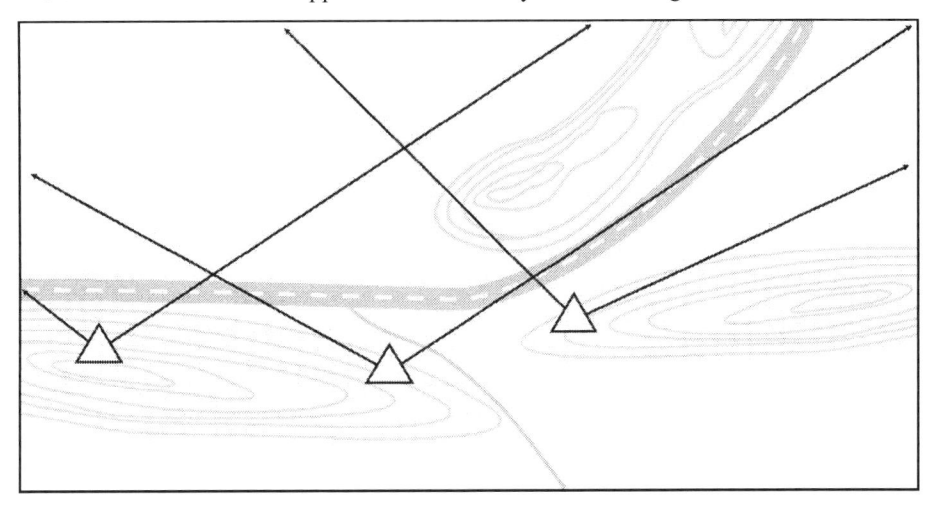

Figure D-2. On-line positioning of observation posts

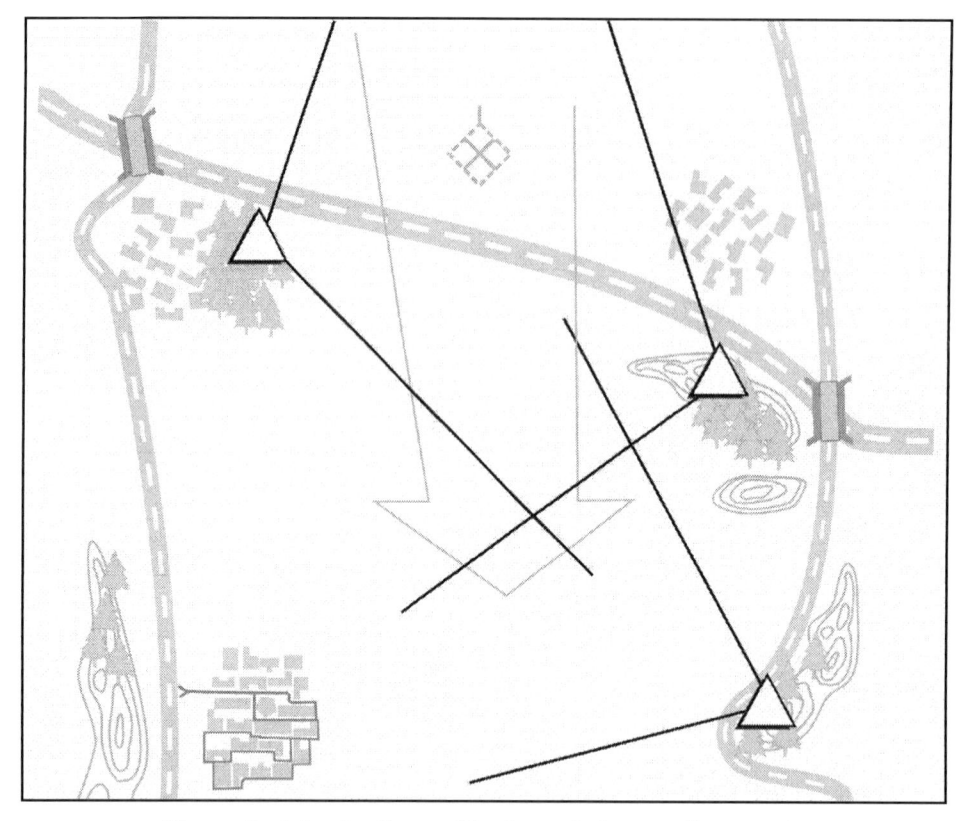

Figure D-3. In-depth positioning of observation posts

SELECTION AND SECURING THE OBSERVATION POST

D-23. Based on guidance from the controlling headquarters, the leader selects the general location of the unit's observation posts after conducting METT-TC. From his analysis, he determines how many observation posts he must establish. He also decides where they must be positioned to allow long-range observation along the avenues exact position when they get on the actual ground. Figure D-4 (page D-10) shows an example of observation post selection in urban terrain. Observation posts should have the following characteristics:

- Covered and concealed routes to and from the observation post. Soldiers must be able to enter and leave their observation post without being seen by the enemy.
- Unobstructed observation of the assigned area or sector. Ideally, the fields of observation of adjacent observation post overlap to ensure full coverage of the sector.
- Cover and concealment. Leaders select positions with cover and concealment to reduce their vulnerability on the battlefield. Leaders may need to pass up a position with favorable observation capability but with no cover and concealment to select

Appendix D

a position affording better survivability. This position should not attract attention or skyline the observer.

- Observation posts should be placed no further than half maximum effective range of the weapon system overwatching them assuming a clear line of fire. If the line of fire is less than the maximum effective range then it should be no further than half the distance than the farthest visible point.

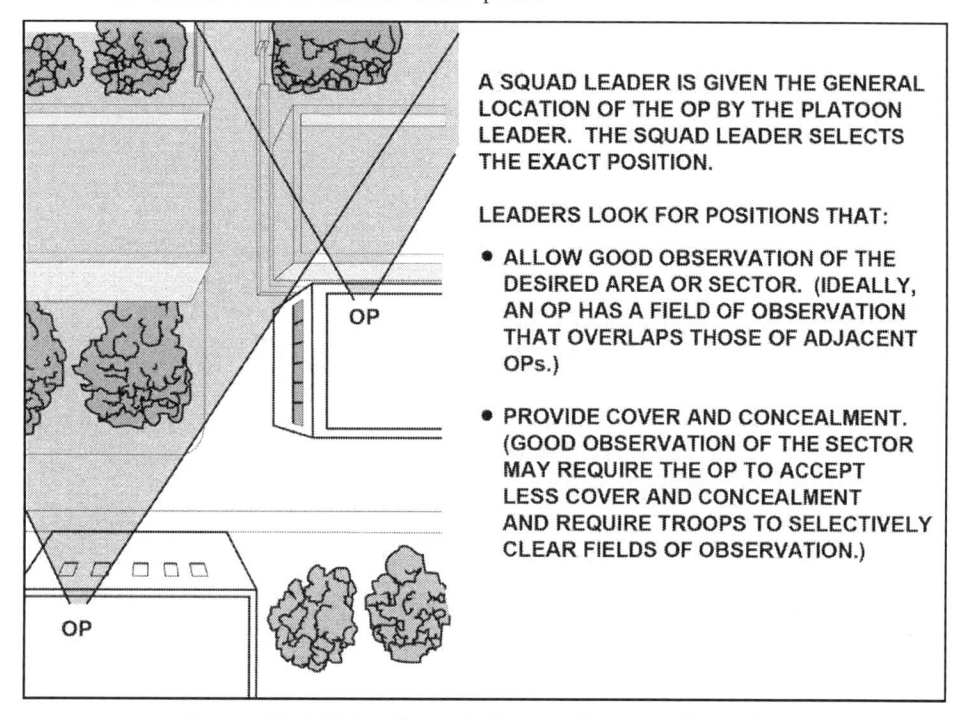

A SQUAD LEADER IS GIVEN THE GENERAL LOCATION OF THE OP BY THE PLATOON LEADER. THE SQUAD LEADER SELECTS THE EXACT POSITION.

LEADERS LOOK FOR POSITIONS THAT:

- ALLOW GOOD OBSERVATION OF THE DESIRED AREA OR SECTOR. (IDEALLY, AN OP HAS A FIELD OF OBSERVATION THAT OVERLAPS THOSE OF ADJACENT OPs.)

- PROVIDE COVER AND CONCEALMENT. (GOOD OBSERVATION OF THE SECTOR MAY REQUIRE THE OP TO ACCEPT LESS COVER AND CONCEALMENT AND REQUIRE TROOPS TO SELECTIVELY CLEAR FIELDS OF OBSERVATION.)

Figure D-4. Selection of observation post location

D-24. Small teams are extremely vulnerable in an observation post. Their best self-defense is not to be seen, heard, or otherwise detected by the enemy. They employ active and passive local security measures.

OCCUPYING THE OBSERVATION POST

D-25. The leader selects an appropriate technique to move to the observation post or screen line based on his mission analysis. (Infiltration, zone reconnaissance, movement to contact [mounted, dismounted, or air insertion], using traveling, traveling overwatch, or bounding overwatch.)

MANNING AND EQUIPMENT AT THE OBSERVATION POST

D-26. At least two Soldiers are required to operate an observation post. One man establishing security, recording information, and reporting to higher while the other observes. These men switch jobs every 20 to 30 minutes because the observer's efficiency

decreases with time. Three or more Soldiers are required to increase security. For extended periods (12 hours or more), the unit occupies long-duration observation post by squad-sized units. Essential equipment of the observation post includes the following:
- Map of the area.
- Compass/GPS.
- Communications equipment.
- Observation devices (binoculars, observation telescope, thermal sights, and night vision devices).
- Automated net control device essential information.
- Report formats contained in the SOP.
- Weapons.
- Protective obstacles and early warning devices.
- Camouflage, cover and concealment, and deception equipment as required.

DRAWING AN OBSERVATION POST SKETCH

D-27. Once the leader has established the observation post he prepares a sketch. This sketch is similar to a fighting position sketch but with some important differences. Figure D-5 (page D-12) shows an example observation post sketch. At a minimum, the sketch should include:
- A rough sketch of key and significant terrain.
- The location of the observation post and alternate observation post.
- The location of the hide position
- Routes to the observation post and fighting positions.
- Sectors of observation.
- Direct and indirect fire control measures.

Appendix D

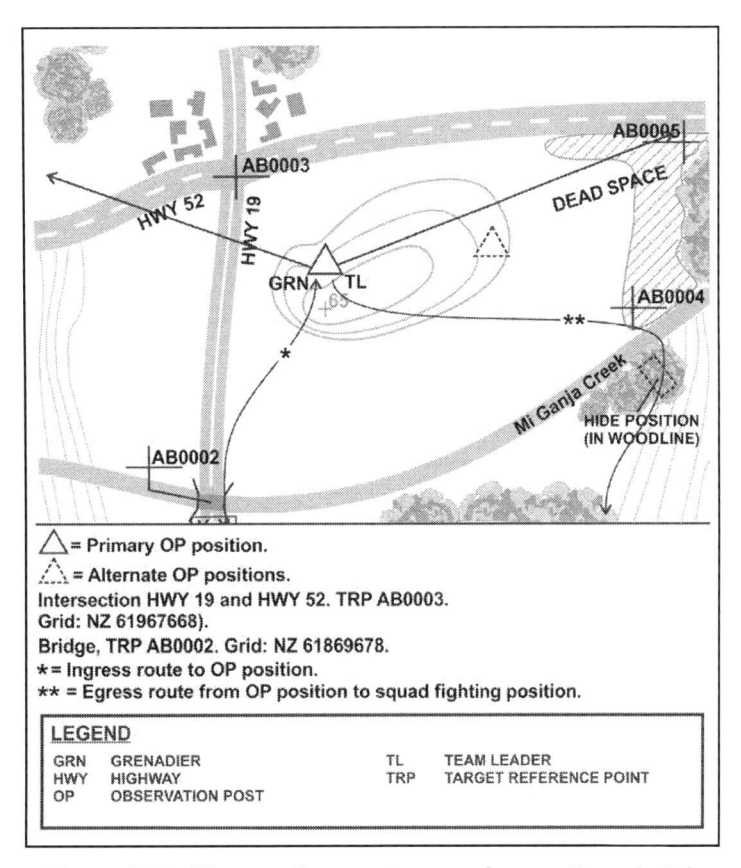

△ = Primary OP position.
⚠ = Alternate OP positions.
Intersection HWY 19 and HWY 52. TRP AB0003.
Grid: NZ 61967668).
Bridge, TRP AB0002. Grid: NZ 61869678.
* = Ingress route to OP position.
** = Egress route from OP position to squad fighting position.

LEGEND
GRN   GRENADIER   TL   TEAM LEADER
HWY   HIGHWAY   TRP   TARGET REFERENCE POINT
OP   OBSERVATION POST

Figure D-5. Observation post area of operation sketch

SECTION III – CHECKPOINTS AND TRAFFIC CONTROL POST

D-28. Checkpoint: As defined by ADRP 1-02 it is a predetermined point on the ground used to control movement, tactical maneuver, and orientation. Checkpoints are primarily a military police task; however, while conducting area security, platoons or squads are frequently employed to establish and operate checkpoints. (See figure D-6.)

D-29. Although similar, the checkpoint should not to be confused with a roadblock or blocking position. Roadblocks are designed to prevent all access to a certain area by both wheeled and pedestrian traffic for a variety of purposes. The checkpoint also should not be confused with an observation post which is established to collect information.

D-30. When conducting checkpoint operations, Soldiers need the following support:
- Linguists familiar with the local language and understand English.
- Host-nation police or a civil affairs officer.
- Wire/sandbags.
- Signs to reduce misunderstandings and confusion on the part of the local populace

Security

- Lighting.
- Communications equipment.
- Handheld translation devices.

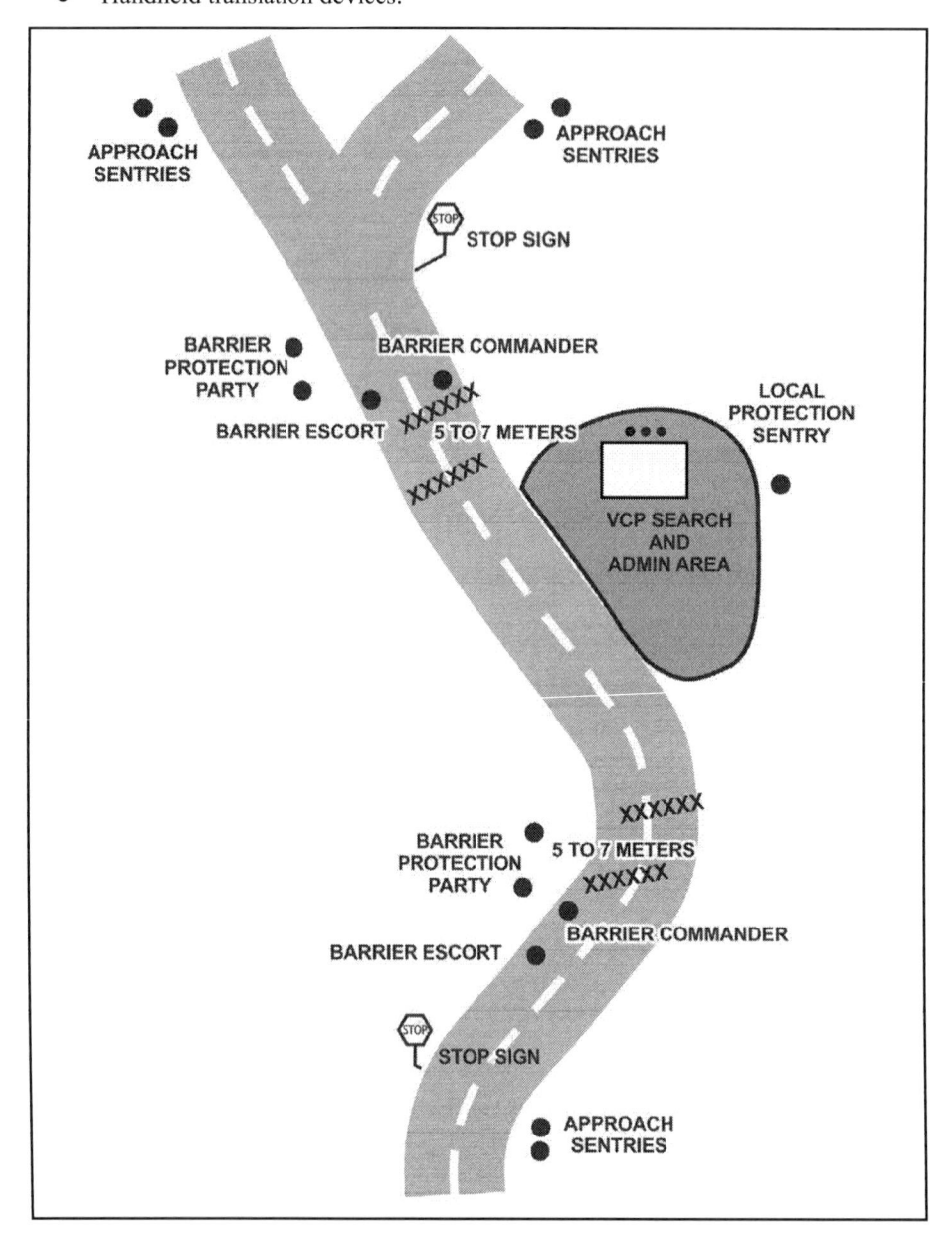

Figure D-6. Checkpoint sketch

Appendix D

TYPES OF CHECKPOINTS

D-31. There are two types of checkpoints: deliberate and hasty.

DELIBERATE CHECKPOINT

D-32. A deliberate checkpoint is permanent or semi-permanent. It is established to control the movement of vehicles and pedestrians, and to help maintain law and order. They typically are constructed and employed to protect an operating base or well-established roads. Like defensive positions, deliberate checkpoint should be improved continuously. Deliberate checkpoints—
- Control all vehicle and pedestrian traffic so crowds cannot assemble.
- Allow known offenders or suspected enemy personnel to be arrested.
- Enforce curfews.
- Deter illegal movement.
- Prevent the movement of supplies to the enemy.
- Deny the enemy contact with the local inhabitants.
- Dominate the area around the checkpoint. (This includes maintaining law and order by local patrolling to prevent damage to property or injury to persons.)
- Collect information.

HASTY CHECKPOINT

D-33. A hasty checkpoint differs from a deliberate checkpoint in it is not, in most cases, preplanned. A hasty checkpoint usually will be activated as part of a larger tactical plan or in reaction to hostile activities such as a bomb, mine incident, or sniper attack, and can be lifted on the command of the controlling headquarters. A hasty checkpoint always will have a specific task and purpose. Most often used to avoid predictability and targeting by the enemy. It should be set up to last from five minutes to up to two hours using an ambush mentality. The short duration reduces the risk of the enemy organizing an attack against the checkpoint. The maximum time suggested of the checkpoint to remain in place would be about eight hours, as this may be considered to be the limit of endurance of the units conducting the checkpoint and may invite the checkpoint to enemy attacks.

D-34. Characteristics of a hasty checkpoint (see figure D-7) include:
- Located along likely enemy avenues of approach.
- Achieve surprise.
- Temporary.
- Unit is able to carry and erect construction materiels without additional assistance.
- Uses vehicles as an obstacle between the vehicles and personnel, and reinforces them with concertina wire.
- Soldiers are positioned at each end of the checkpoint.
- Soldiers are covered by mounted or dismounted automatic weapons.
- Assault force/response force is concealed nearby to attack or assault in case the site is attacked.

Security

D-35. The hasty checkpoint's success is brought about by swift and decisive operations. In many cases, there may be no clear orders before the checkpoint is set up. Leaders must rely on common sense and instinct to determine which vehicles or pedestrians to stop for questioning or searching. They are moved quickly into position, thoroughly conducted, and just as swiftly withdrawn when lifted or once the threat has passed.

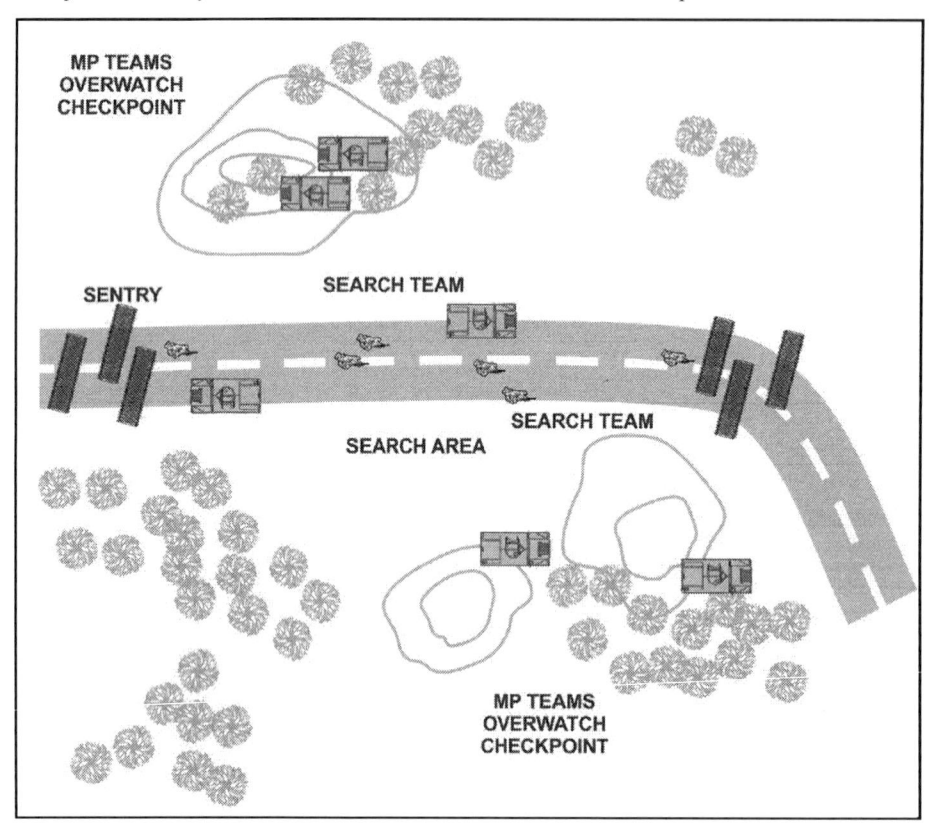

Figure D-7. Hasty checkpoint

PHYSICAL LAYOUT

D-36. A checkpoint should consist of four areas: canalization zone, turning or deceleration zone, search zone, and safe zone. (See figure D-8, page D-16.)

Appendix D

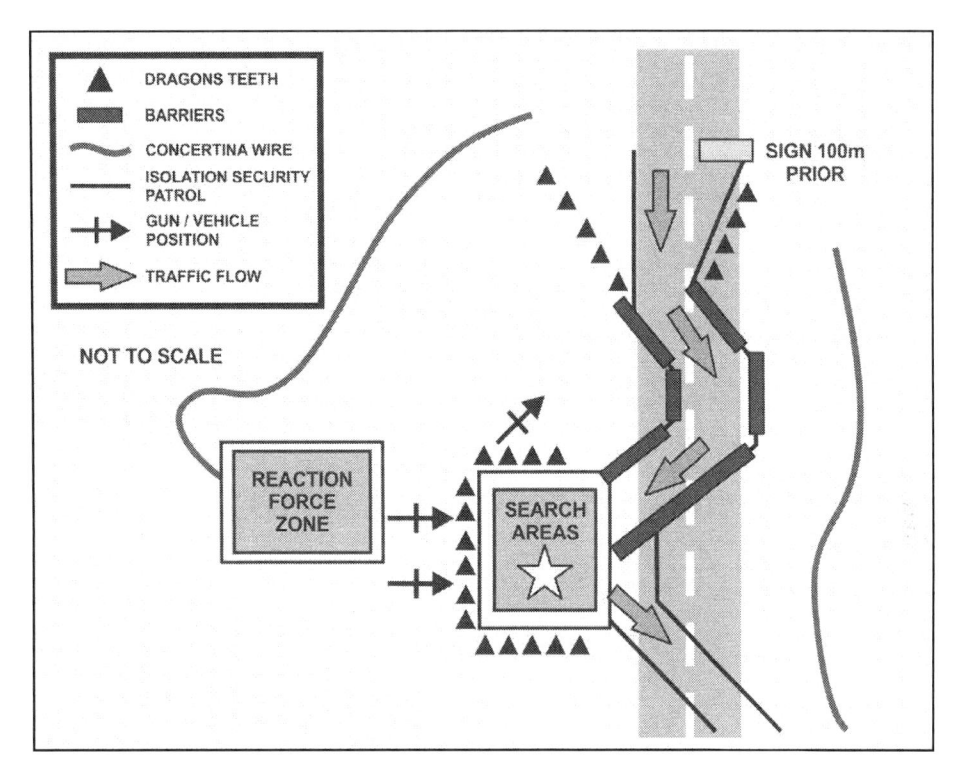

Figure D-8. Physical Layout

D-37. The checkpoint should be sited in such a position as to prevent persons approaching the site from bypassing it or turning away from the checkpoint without arousing suspicion. Ideal sites are where vehicles already have had to slow down. It should be remembered on country roads vehicles will need extra room to slow down and halt, (particularly large heavy vehicles). The sighting of the checkpoint must take into consideration the type and number of vehicles expected to be using part of the road where the checkpoint will be sited. Areas where there are few road networks enhance the checkpoint effectiveness.

D-38. The site should allow for a vehicle escape route and include plans to destroy a hostile element using such a route. If the checkpoint is completely sealed off, enemy forces may attempt to penetrate it by attempting to run over obstacles or personnel.

D-39. Location should make it difficult for a person to turn around or reverse without being detected. Soldiers establish hasty checkpoint where they cannot be seen by approaching traffic until it is too late for approaching traffic to unobtrusively withdraw. Locations on which to set up hasty checkpoint include:

- Bridges. (Near either or both ends, but not in the middle.)
- Defiles, culvert, or deep cuts. (Either end is better than in the middle.)
- Highway intersections. (These must be well-organized to reduce the inherent danger.)

- The reverse slope of a hill. (Hidden from the direction of the main flow of traffic.)
- Just beyond a sharp curve.

CANALIZATION ZONE

D-40. The canalization zone uses natural obstacles or artificial obstacles to canalize the vehicles into the checkpoint:
- Place warning signs out forward of the checkpoint to warn drivers of the checkpoint ahead (at least 100 meters).
- Canalize the vehicles so they have no way out until they have the consent of personnel controlling the checkpoint.
- This zone encompasses the area from maximum range to maximum effective range of your weapon systems. It usually consists of disrupting or turning obstacles.

TURNING OR DECELERATION ZONE

D-41. The search element establishes obstacles and an overwatch force to control each road or traffic lane being blocked. The turning or deceleration zone forces vehicles into making a rapid decision. The vehicle can decelerate, make slow hard turns, or maintain speed and crash into a series of obstacles. The road or traffic lanes should be blocked by means of obstacles positioned at either end of the checkpoint. (See appendix H of this publication for a discussion of obstacles.) These obstacles should be such as to be quickly and easily moved in case of emergencies. They should be sited so as to extend the full width of a traffic lane and staggered to force vehicles to slow to negotiate an 'S' turn. (See figure D-9, page D-18.) Stop signs also should be erected ahead of the obstacles and at night illuminated by means of a light or lantern.

D-42. Ensure vehicles are stopped facing an obstacle (berm, tank, or wall) capable of stopping a slow moving truck. Some obstacles will have to be improvised. Examples of these include:
- Downed trees.
- Beirut toothpick– nails driven through lumber.
- Caltrops placed across the road.
- Debris, rubble, large rocks.
- Abatis.
- Road cratering.
- Dragon's teeth, tetrahedrons, concrete blocks.
- Mines.
- Prepared demolitions.
- Concertina wire.

Appendix D

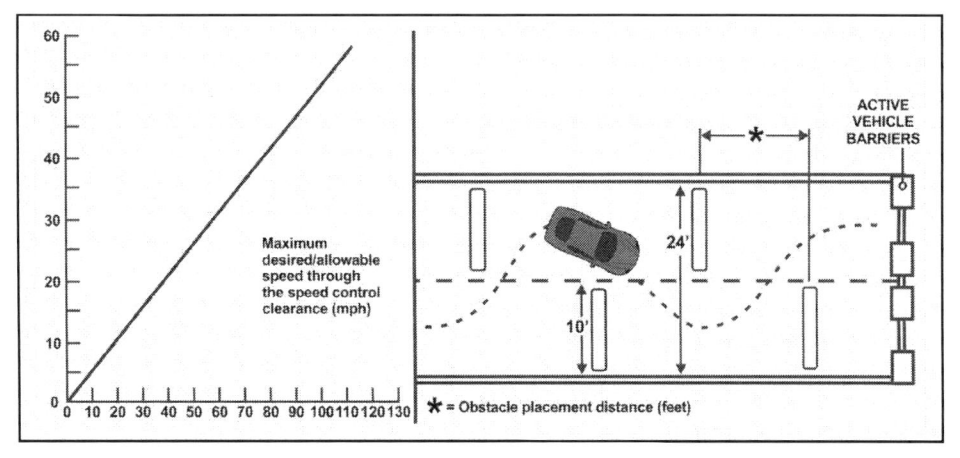

Figure D-9. Controlling vehicle speed through obstacle placement and serpentine placement

SEARCH ZONE

D-43. The search zone is a relatively secure area where personnel and vehicles are positively identified and searched. A decision is made to confiscate weapons and contraband, detain a vehicle, or allow it to pass. The area is set up with a blocking obstacle denying entry/exit without loss of life or equipment. When searching—

- Isolate the vehicle being checked from other cars by an obstacle of some type, which is controlled by a Soldier.
- Emplace an overwatch position with a crew-served weapon in an elevated position to cover the vehicle, particularly the driver. The crew-served weapon should be mounted on a T/E and tripod.

D-44. The search zone is further subdivided into three subordinate areas:

- Personnel search zone—is where personnel are positively identified, searched, or detained. This may include partitioned or screened areas to provide privacy, especially when searching women and children. Use female Soldiers to search women, if available.
- Vehicle search zone— is where vehicles are positively identified, and searched.
- Reaction force zone — is where a reaction force is located to reinforce the checkpoint and immediately provide assistance using lethal and nonlethal force. Additionally, engineers, and EOD personnel may be collocated here to assist in analyzing and diffusing/destroying ammunition, demolitions, or IED traps. This element is organized and equipped to conduct close combat. This element engages in accordance with the established engagement criteria and ROE. This element has a position which allows it to overwatch the checkpoint as well as block or detain vehicles trying to avoid the checkpoint.

D-45. When establishing these zones, consider the following:
- Weapons' surface danger zones, geometry.
- 360-degree security.
- Rapid removal of detainees and vehicles.
- Capabilities and skill level of all attachments.
- Potential suicide.

D-46. Placing the search area to the side of the road permits two-way traffic. If a vehicle is rejected, it is turned back. If vehicle is accepted for transit, it is permitted to travel through the position. If the vehicle is a threat, the checkpoint leader determines whether to attack or apprehend.

D-47. When confronted by a potentially threatening vehicle, —
- The search element alerts the checkpoint leader, moves to a safe/fortified position, and may engage or allow the vehicle to pass based on leader instructions and ROE.
- If the vehicle passes through the escape lane, the leader may direct the assault element to engage the vehicle based on ROE.

SAFE ZONE

D-48. The safe zone is the assembly area for the checkpoint, which allows personnel to eat, sleep, and recover in relative security.

TASK ORGANIZATION

D-49. The basic organization of a checkpoint includes a security element, a search element, an assault element, and a mission command element. The actual strength and composition of the force is determined by the nature of the threat, road layout, type of checkpoint required, and anticipated number of vehicles to be processed. Table D-3 details typical duties of these elements as well as a general list of do's and don'ts.

Table D-3. Task organization

MISSION COMMAND
Overall Responsibility
Exercises mission command.
Maintains communications with controlling HQ.
Maintains a log of all activities.
Coordinates relief in place as required.
Coordinates linkups as required.
Coordinates local patrols.
Integrates reserve / quick response force.
If available, the mission command element should have a vehicle for patrolling, for moving elements, or administrative actions.

Appendix D

Table D-3. Task organization (continued)

MISSION COMMAND
Security Element
Provides early warning to the checkpoint through local security measures.
Prevent ambush.
Able to reinforce position is necessary.
Observes and reports suspicious activity.
Monitors traffic flow up to and through the checkpoint.
Search Element
Halts vehicles at the checkpoint.
Guides vehicles to search area.
Conducts vehicle searches: passenger, cargo.
Conducts personnel searches: male, female.
Directs cleared vehicles out of the checkpoint.
Detains personnel as directed.
Assault Element
Destroys escaping vehicles and personnel.
Able to reinforce position as necessary.
Soldiers occupy support-by-fire positions beyond the actual checkpoint.
Do
Speak to driver – driver speaks to occupants.
Have the driver open all doors and compartments before Soldier conducts search of vehicle.
Ask politely to follow your instructions.
Speak naturally and no louder than necessary.
Allow driver to observe the search.
Be courteous when searching.
Use scanners and metal detectors when possible.
Stay calm and make a special effort to be polite.
Maintain a high standard of dress, military bearing, and stay in uniform.
Don't
Be disrespectful or give hints of dislikes.
Put your head or arm in vehicle or open the door without permission.
Shout or show impatience.
Frisk women or tell them to put their hands up.
Become involved in a heated argument.
Use force as directed by unit ROE.
Become careless or sloppy in appearance.

MISSION COMMAND ELEMENT

D-50. The mission command element controls the operation. The mission command element normally consists of a leader, his RTO and runner.

D-51. The leader normally establishes a headquarters administrative area to synchronize the efforts of the subordinate activities. The headquarters and security element should be sited centrally and in a position which facilitates control of the obstacles. The headquarters area should be secure and large enough to incorporate an administrative area and vehicle search area. Depending on the threat, this area should have sufficient cover or survivability positions should be built.

D-52. The checkpoint should have communication to their controlling headquarters by radio. A spare radio and batteries should be supplied to the checkpoint. Radio and telephone checks are carried out as per the unit's SOP using signal security measures. Communications within the site should be undertaken using whatever means is available.

CIVIL AUTHORITY ASSISTANCE

D-53. The closest liaison must be maintained between the checkpoint leader and senior policeman. Policemen at a checkpoint are employed to assist in the checking and searching of vehicles and personnel, to make arrests when necessary. Police ideally are employed on the scale of one officer for each lane of traffic. These civil authorities should attend rehearsals. As the degree of threat increases, police officers should be on standby to move with the patrol to the checkpoint site. Wherever possible, it should be the responsibility of the military to control the checkpoint while the police control the search aspects.

D-54. The leader must understand guidance from his chain of command on contingencies occurring outside of the checkpoint area that might require forces from the checkpoint. The checkpoint, unless otherwise ordered, is the primary task. If an incident occurs in the vicinity of the checkpoint most likely to require manpower and affect the efficient operation of the checkpoint, the leader should seek guidance from his higher headquarters.

D-55. Sequence of events for establishing the checkpoint include:
- Leader's reconnaissance.
- Establish support-by-fire positions (and fighting positions as required).
- Establish blocking positions (entrance and exit).
- Establish search area for personnel and vehicles.
- Establish holding area (if required).
- Establish an area for mission command and admin.

SECURITY ELEMENT

D-56. The nature of the checkpoint makes it particularly vulnerable to enemy attack. Protection should be provided for overall position as well as those of subordinate positions. Concealed sentries should also be positioned on the approaches to the checkpoint to observe and report approaching traffic, and to prevent persons or vehicles from evading the checkpoint. When available, early warning devices or radar may be used to aid guards on the approaches to the checkpoint.

D-57. The security element stays alert for changes of scenery around the checkpoint. Crowds gathering for no apparent reason or media representatives waiting for an event are all indicators something may happen.

Appendix D

ESCALATION OF FORCE

D-58. Escalation of force is a sequential action beginning with nonlethal force measures (visual signals to include flags, spotlights, lasers and pyrotechnics) which can escalate to lethal force measures to protect the force. Soldiers at the checkpoint must ensure they follow ROE and EOF guidance when reacting to situations.

D-59. An imminent hostile threat can be engaged at any time, but if not yet determined to be a threat, use reasonable non-deadly force or EOF as the situation dictates, to protect yourself and to develop the situation.

D-60. Soldiers at every level must understand EOF procedures – before, during, and after an EOF event; to include the possible Strategic Impacts of EOF incidents on Local Nationals' negative perceptions.
- Soldiers must train and rehearse EOF procedures.
- EOF never limits a Soldier's inherent right to self-defense.
- All Soldiers understand in order to prevent hesitation.
- Leaders must include EOF in planning and preparation for operations.
- Correct equipment reduces unnecessary casualties.

D-61. The use of nonlethal weapons and munitions provide a safer, less-than-lethal alternative to warn and deter individuals during potential EOF incidents. Units should use nonlethal munitions and tools whenever possible during EOF incidents. Soldiers should conduct proper training, familiarization, and certification with each type of nonlethal munitions and tools prior to their use.

D-62. When time and circumstances permit;
- Use audible warning (horn, loudspeaker, flash/bang device, or siren).
- Use visual aids (lights, laser pointers, flares, colored flags, signs).
- Show weapon and demonstrate intent to use it.
- Use other non-lethal means (stop strips, physical barrier, vehicle, visual/audio signal, signs).
- Fire disabling fire (tires, engine block, windows).

SEARCH ELEMENT

D-63. Soldiers may be required to conduct both vehicle and personnel searches at checkpoint.

Vehicle Searches

D-64. Two members of the search team position themselves at both rear flanks of the vehicle undergoing a search, putting the occupants at a disadvantage. These Soldiers maintain eye contact with the occupants once they exit the vehicle and react to threat attempts by the occupants during the vehicle search.

D-65. The actual search is conducted by two Soldiers. One Soldier conducts interior searches; the other performs exterior searches. They instruct the occupants (with interpreters if available) to exit the vehicle during the interior search and instruct the driver to watch the vehicle search. Once the interior search is complete, they escort the driver to the hood of the vehicle and instruct him to open it. After the engine compartment has been examined, they instruct the driver to open the other outside compartments (tool boxes, gas caps, trunks). The driver removes loose items not attached to the vehicle for inspection. Search team members rotate positions to allow for mental breaks.

D-66. Soldiers use mirrors and metal detectors to thoroughly search each vehicle for weapons, explosives, ammunition, and other contraband. Depending on the threat level, the vehicle search area provides blast protection of the surrounding area.

Personnel Searches

D-67. Every attempt should be made for host-nation authorities to conduct, or at least observe, searches of local nationals. Additionally, leaders must plan for same-gender searches. Personnel searches are conducted only when proper authorization has been obtained, usually from higher headquarters, according to the ROE, Status of Forces Agreement, or host nation agreements. This does not preclude units from searching individuals posing a threat to U.S. or other friendly forces.

D-68. Units may have to detain local nationals who become belligerent or uncooperative at checkpoint. The OPORD and ROE must address the handling of such personnel. In self-protection measures should be planned and implemented according to the orders from higher headquarters.

D-69. Searches of local nationals should be performed in a manner preserving the respect and dignity of the individual. Special consideration must be given to local customs and national cultural differences. In many cultures it is offensive for men to touch or even talk to women in public. Searchers must be polite, considerate, patient, and tactful. Leaders must make every effort not to unnecessarily offend the local population. Such situations can have a negative impact on peace operations and can quickly change popular opinion toward U.S. and other friendly forces.

D-70. Each captive is searched for weapons and ammunition, items of intelligence value, and other inappropriate items. Use of digital cameras will record detainees, weapons, ammunition, and evidence of contraband.

D-71. When possible, conduct same gender searches. However, this may not always be possible due to speed and security considerations. If females are not available, use medics or NCOs with witnesses. Perform mixed gender searches in a respectful manner using all possible measures to prevent actions interpreted as sexual molestation or assault. The onsite supervisor carefully controls Soldiers doing mixed-gender searches to prevent allegations of sexual misconduct.

D-72. Soldiers conduct individual searches in search teams consisting of the following:
- Searcher. A searcher is the Soldier actually conducting the search. He is in the highest-risk position.
- Security. Security includes at least one Soldier to provide security. He maintains eye contact with the individual being searched.

Appendix D

- Observer. The observer is a leader having supervisory control of the search operation. He also provides early warning to the other members of the team.

D-73. The two most common methods used to conduct individual searches are the frisk search, and wall search:
- Frisk search. This method is quick and adequate to detect weapons, evidence, or contraband. However, it is more dangerous because the searcher has less control of the individual being searched.
- Wall search. This method affords more safety for the searcher because the individual is searched in a strained, awkward position. Upright surfaces, such as a wall, vehicle, tree, or fence may be used.

D-74. If more control is needed to search an uncooperative individual, the search team places the subject in the kneeling or prone position.

SECTION IV – CONVOY AND SECURITY ROUTE

D-75. Convoy security missions are conducted when insufficient friendly forces are available to continuously secure lines of communication in an area of operation. They also may be conducted in conjunction with route security missions. A convoy security force operates to the front, flanks, and rear of a convoy element moving along a designated route. Convoy security missions are offensive in nature and orient on the force being protected.

D-76. To protect a convoy, the security force must accomplish the following critical tasks:
- Reconnoiter and determine the trafficability of the route the convoy will travel.
- Clear the route of obstacles or positions from where the threat could influence movement along the route.
- Provide early warning and prevent the threat from impeding, harassing, containing, seizing, or destroying the convoy.
- Protect the escorted force from enemy contact
- React decisively to enemy contact

D-77. Company-sized units utilizing its platoons and larger organizations usually perform convoy or route security missions. Convoy security provides protection for a specific convoy. Route security aims at securing a specific route for a designated period, during which multiple convoys may use the route. These missions include numerous tasks such as reconnaissance, security, escorting, and establishing a combat reaction force. These tasks become missions for subordinate units. The size of the unit performing the convoy or route security operation depends on many factors, including the size of the convoy, terrain, and length of the route. For example, a platoon or squad can escort convoys, perform route reconnaissance, and establish traffic control post along main supply routes.

ORGANIZATION OF FORCES

D-78. During convoy security operations, the convoy security commander and leaders must establish and maintain security in all directions and throughout the platoon. As noted, several factors, including convoy size affect this disposition. The vital consideration is whether the unit is operating as part of a larger escort force or is executing the escort mission independently. Additional considerations include the employment of rifle squads during the mission. (Fire teams ride in escorted vehicles.)

D-79. The unit also should be reinforced with engineers to reduce obstacles along the route. Higher headquarters should coordinate additional information collection assets to support the security mission. unmanned aircraft system s or aerial reconnaissance should reconnoiter the route in advance of the unit's lead elements.

D-80. When the platoon executes a convoy escort mission independently, the convoy commander and platoon leader disperse tactical vehicles throughout the convoy formation to provide forward, flank, and rear security. Engineer assets, if available, should be located near the front to respond to obstacles. At times, engineer assets may be required to move ahead of the convoy with scouts to proof the convoy route. In some independent escort missions, variations in terrain along the route may require the unit to operate using a modified traveling overwatch technique. In it, one section leads the convoy while the other trails the convoy. Dispersion between vehicles in each section is sufficient to provide flank security. The terrain may not allow the trail section to overwatch the movement of the lead section.

D-81. When sufficient forces are available, the convoy security should be organized into four elements: reconnaissance element; screen element; escort element; and a reaction element. (See figure D-10, page D-26.) The platoon or squad may be assigned one of the four tasks, but as a general rule, probably cannot be assigned all four.

Appendix D

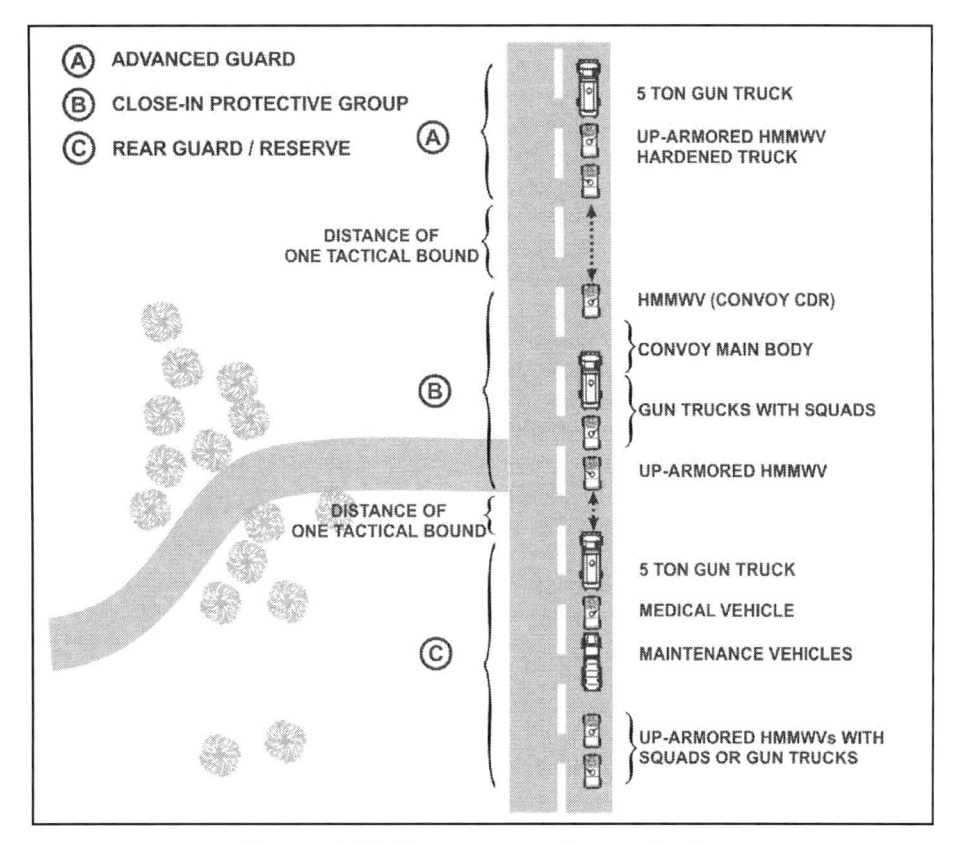

Figure D-10. Convoy escort organization

ADVANCED GUARD

D-82. The advance guard reconnoiters and proofs the convoy route. The advanced guard element performs tasks associated with movement to contact and zone or route reconnaissance forward of the convoy. It searches for signs of enemy activity such as ambushes and obstacles. This element focuses on identifying enemy forces able to influence the route, route trafficability, dislocated civilians or civilian traffic disrupting movement. Engineers are attached to the unit to assist reconnoitering and classifying bridges, fords, and obstacles along the route. The advanced guard normally operates from three to four kilometers ahead of the main body of the convoy. If available, unmanned aircraft system s or aerial reconnaissance should precede the reconnaissance element by five to eight kilometers dependent on the terrain and visibility conditions.

D-83. Within its capabilities, the advanced guard attempts to clear the route and provides the convoy commander with early warning before the arrival of the vehicle column. In some cases, an individual vehicle, a squad, or a platoon-sized element may be designated as part of the advanced guard and may receive additional combat vehicle support (tank with a mine plow, or mine roller). The leader plans for integrating engineer assets to aid

Security

in reducing point-type obstacles. Command-detonated devices and other IEDs pose a major threat during route reconnaissance.

FLANK AND REAR GUARD/SCREEN

D-84. This element performs a guard or screen, depending on the amount of combat power allocated, providing early warning and security to the convoy's flanks and rear. (Unit may utilize outposts.) The leader must develop graphic control measures to enable a moving flank screen centered on the convoy. The guard/screen's purpose is to prevent observation for employment of indirect fires and identify combat elements prior to a direct fire engagement against the convoy. These elements gain and maintain contact with threat reconnaissance and combat elements, employing fires (direct and indirect) to suppress and guiding reaction or escort elements to defeat or destroy the threat force. Units use a combination of observation posts or battle positions on terrain along the route.

D-85. The rear guard follows the convoy. (See figure D-11.) It provides security in the area behind the main body of the vehicle column, often moving with medical and recovery assets. Again, an individual vehicle or the entire unit may make up this element.

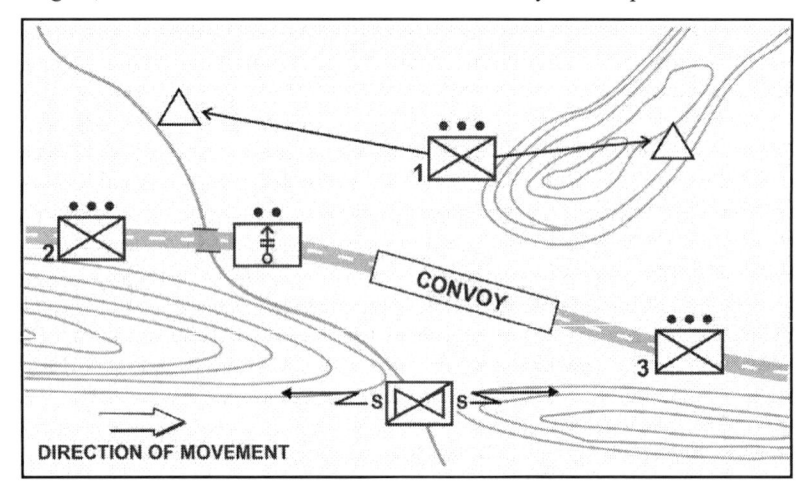

Figure D-11. Rear guard

ESCORT ELEMENT

D-86. The escort element provides close-in protection to the convoy. The convoy may be made of many types of vehicles, including military sustainment and mission command as well as civilian trucks and buses. The escort element also may provide a reaction force to assist in repelling or destroying threat contact. The unit assigned the escort mission to provide local security throughout the length of the convoy. The escort element defeats close ambushes and marks bypasses or breaches obstacles identified by reconnaissance as necessary. If the reaction force is not available in sufficient time, the escort element may be required to provide a reaction force to defeat far ambushes or block attacking threat forces. The platoon or squad may perform a convoy escort mission either independently

Appendix D

or as part of a larger unit's convoy security mission. Aviation units also may be a part of the escort force and leaders of both ground and air must be able to contact each other quickly.

RESPONSE FORCE

D-87. The response force provides firepower and support to the elements above in order to assist in developing the situation or conducting a hasty operation. It also may perform duties of the escort element. The reserve will move with the convoy or be located at a staging area close enough to provide immediate interdiction against the enemy.

MISSION COMMAND

D-88. Because of the task organization of the convoy escort mission, mission command is especially critical. The relationship between the platoon or squad and convoy commander must provide unity of command and effort if combat operations are required during the course of the mission. In most cases, the unit will execute the escort mission under the control of the security force commander, who is usually under operational control or attached to the convoy commander.

D-89. The leader should coordinate with the security force commander or the escorted unit to obtain or exchange the following information:
- Time and place of linkup and orders brief.
- Number and type of vehicles to be escorted.
- High value assets within the convoy.
- Available weapon systems, ammunition, and ordnance (crew-served, squad, and individual).
- Vehicle maintenance status and operating speeds.
- Convoy personnel roster.
- Unit's or escorted unit SOP, as necessary.
- Rehearsal time and location.

D-90. It is vital the convoy commander issues a complete movement OPORD to all convoy vehicle commanders before executing the mission. This is important because the convoy may itself be task-organized from a variety of units, and some vehicles may not have tactical radios or mission command systems. The order should follow the standard five-paragraph OPORD format (see table D-4, pages D-10 through D-11), but special emphasis should be placed on—
- Route of march (including a strip map for each vehicle commander).
- Order of march.
- Actions at halts.
- Actions in case of vehicle breakdown.
- Actions on contact.
- Chain of command.
- Communication and signal information.

Table D-4. Road movement order format example

ROAD MOVEMENT ORDER/ANNEX

ADMINISTRATIVE REMARKS (PERSONNEL ROLL CALL/INSTRUCTIONS)
1. March Commander
2. Assistant March Commander
3. Navigator/Pacesetter
4. Vehicle Commanders (If Applicable)
5. Drivers (If applicable) Primary/Alternate
6. Key Weapon System Operators
7. Escort/Security Element Leader
8. Snipers/Designated Marksmen
9. Medics/Corpsman/Combat Lifesavers
10. Guides/Interpreter
11. Higher Headquarters Representatives
12. Aid and Litter Team
13. Prisoner of War/Search Teams
14. Landing/Pick-up Zone Teams
15. Recovery Team (If Applicable)
16. Designated Close Air Support Control Personnel
17. Others not Mentioned

I. SITUATION:
  a. Enemy Forces: (Discuss Enemy)
   - Identification of Enemy (If Known)
   - Composition/Capabilities/Strength/Equipment
   - Location (Danger Areas Highlighted on Map)
   - Most Likely/Most Dangerous Course of Action (Defend, Reinforce, Attack, Withdraw, and Delay)
  b. Weather: General Forecast
  c. Light Data: (Beginning Morning/Early Evening, Nautical Twilight, Illumination %, Etc.)
  d. Friendly Forces:
   - Task Organization (Internal Organization of Unit)
   - Adjacent Units or Other Units Along the Route
   - Operational Support Provided by Higher Headquarters
   - Aviation Support
     - Air Support Operations Center
     - Direct Air Support Center
     - Joint Surveillance Target Attack Radar System
   - Security Forces/Quick Response Forces
   - Military Police Escort
   - Explosive Ordnance Disposal
   - Special Operations Forces
   - Fire Support Elements
   - Element Locations
   - Attachments (External)

II. MISSION:
  a. Who
  b. What
  c. When
  d. Where
  e. Why

III. EXECUTION:
  a. Concept of Operations:
   - March Executions and Tasks of Elements, Teams, and Individuals at the Objective or Mission Complete (Broad General Description from Beginning to End)
  b. Tasks to Subordinate Units: (Includes Attached or Operational Control Elements)
  c. Coordinating Instructions: (Instructions for ALL Units)
  d. Safety:
   - Overall Risk to Force: (Low, Medium, High, Extremely High)
   - Overall Risk to Mission Accomplishment: (Low, Medium, High, Extremely High)
   - Fratricide Reduction Measures
  1) Order of March (Spacing of Units/Location of Support Elements)
  2) Routes (Ensure Strip Map is Attached)
  3) Additional Movement Issues (Speed, Intervals, Stragglers, Lane, Reaction Units, and Accidents)
  4) March Execution

Appendix D

Table D-4. Road movement order format example (continued)

ROAD MOVEMENT ORDER/ANNEX (continuation)

5) Timeline:
    • Vehicle/Personnel Gear Preparation (Precombat Checks/Inspections Completed)
    • Briefing
    • Put on Equipment
    • Load Vehicles (If Applicable)
    • Rehearsals/Immediate Action Drills/Test Fires
    • Brief Back/Confirmation Brief from Key Leaders
    • Start Point/Departure/Checkpoints/Release Points Times
    • Return to Base (When Applicable)
    • Debrief
    • Recovery: Maintain Vehicles/Personnel Gear
6) Sectors-of-Fire: (Cover Assigned Sectors While Mounted/Dismounted; Cover Up/Down Bridges, Rooftops, Balconies, and Storefronts, Multi-Story Structures, and Cross Streets)
7) Scanning: (Scan Crowds, Vehicles, and Roadsides for Attack Indicators
   NOTE: Communicate Indicators Throughout the Unit)
    • Beware of Motorcycles, Vans with Side Doors, and Dump Trucks
    • Beware of Objects on the Road (Cars, Potholes, Objects, Fresh Asphalt/Concrete and Trash)
8) Unit Speed _____ Minimum/Maximum _____
    • Speed is Dictated by Either the Rear Unit's Ability to Keep Up or Placing Slower Individuals in the Lead
    • Highways/Open Roads
    • Urban/Canalized Areas: As Fast as Traffic Will Allow. For Vehicles Brief Evasive Maneuvers, Bumping and Blocking Technique, and use of Ramming
9) Units/Individuals Interval:
    • Highways/Open Roads
    • Urban/Canalized Areas: Close Interval, but Must Have Visual of Unit in Front of You. March on Wrong Side as Necessary (METT-TC)
10) Headlight Status (If Applicable) On/Off, Blackout, Use of Night Observation Devices
11) Reaction to Enemy Contact (Battle Drills)
12) Rules of Engagement for March Operations (Theater Specific)
 	
IV: SUSTAINMENT:
   a. Individual Equipment (Precombat Inspections in Accordance With Standard Operating Procedures)
   b. Vehicles (If Applicable) Preventive Maintenance Checks and Services
   c. Recovery/Wrecker Support (When Applicable)
   d. Class I thru Class IX Support (When Applicable)
   e. En-route Support
   f. Medical Support (Combat Lifesavers/Medics/Corpsmen/Aid and Litter Teams)
   g. Handling of Enemy Prisoner of War (Search, Segregate, Silence, Speed and Safeguard)
 	
V. COMMAND AND SIGNAL:
   a. Mission Command (Positioning in March Formation)
   b. Units Frequency: _____ Call Sign: _____
   c. Areas of Operations Communications/MEDEVAC/CASEVAC Plan
   d. Unit Primary/Alternate/Contingency/Emergency
   e. Counter Radio/Improvised Explosive Device Frequency Review, Communications (Extra Batteries)
   f. Unit Internal (Back to: _____)
   g. Arm and Hand/Visual Signals
   h. Unit to Unit:
    • Radio: _____ Primary/Alternate _____ / _____
   i. March Unit to Higher Headquarters:
    • Radio: _____ Primary/Alternate _____ / _____
   j. Other Support (External to March Unit)
    • Security Force/Quick Response Force: _____ Call Sign _____
    • Close Air Support: Frequency: _____ Call Sign _____
    • MEDEVAC/CASEVAC: Frequency: _____ Call Sign _____
    • Indirect Fire Support: Frequency: _____ Call Sign _____
   k. Crew Commands/Pro-Words/Brevity Codes
   l. FBCB2-BFT Serial Number (If Applicable)
   m. Pyrotechnics
   n. Special Instructions
   o. Reports (Individual and Higher Headquarters)
   f. Give Time Hack and Ask for Questions

REACTING TO ENEMY CONTACT

D-91. As the convoy moves to its new location, the enemy may attempt to harass or destroy it. This contact usually will occur in the form of an ambush, often with the use of a hastily-prepared obstacle. The safety of the convoy rests on the speed and effectiveness with which escort elements can execute appropriate actions on contact. Based on METT-TC, portions of the convoy security force such as the unit may be designated as a reaction force. The reaction force performs its escort duties, conducts tactical movement, or occupies an AA (as required) until enemy contact occurs and the convoy commander gives it a reaction mission.

ACTIONS AT AN AMBUSH

D-92. An ambush is one of the most effective ways to interdict a convoy. Reaction to an ambush must be immediate, overwhelming, and decisive. Actions on contact must be planned for and rehearsed so they can be executed quickly.

D-93. In almost all situations, the unit will take several specific, instantaneous actions when it reacts to an ambush. (See figures D-12 and D-13, page D-32.) However, if the convoy is moving fuel and other logistics, the best method might be to suppress the enemy, continue to move and report. These steps, illustrated in figure D-12 (page D-32) in include the following:

- As soon as they encounter an enemy force, the escort vehicles take action toward the enemy. They seek covered positions between the convoy and enemy; suppress the enemy with the highest volume of fire permitted by the ROE. Contact reports are submitted to higher headquarters as quickly as possible.
- The convoy commander retains control of the convoy vehicles and continues to move them along the route at the highest possible speed.
- Convoy vehicles, if armed, may return fire only if the escort has not positioned itself between the convoy and the enemy force.
- Leaders may request damaged or disabled vehicles be abandoned and pushed off the route.
- The escort leader uses SPOTREP to keep the convoy security commander informed. If necessary, the escort leader or the convoy commander requests support from the reaction force and or calls for and adjusts indirect fires.

Note. Indirect fire support for areas behind the forward line of troops is planned and coordinated on an area basis (such as a base operations center, base cluster operations center, or rear area operations center). This planning may provide direct and indirect fire support to main supply routes (MSRs) or other routes. Convoy commanders are responsible of direct and indirect fire support plans for their convoy and for ensuring escort security leaders are familiar with the plan.

Appendix D

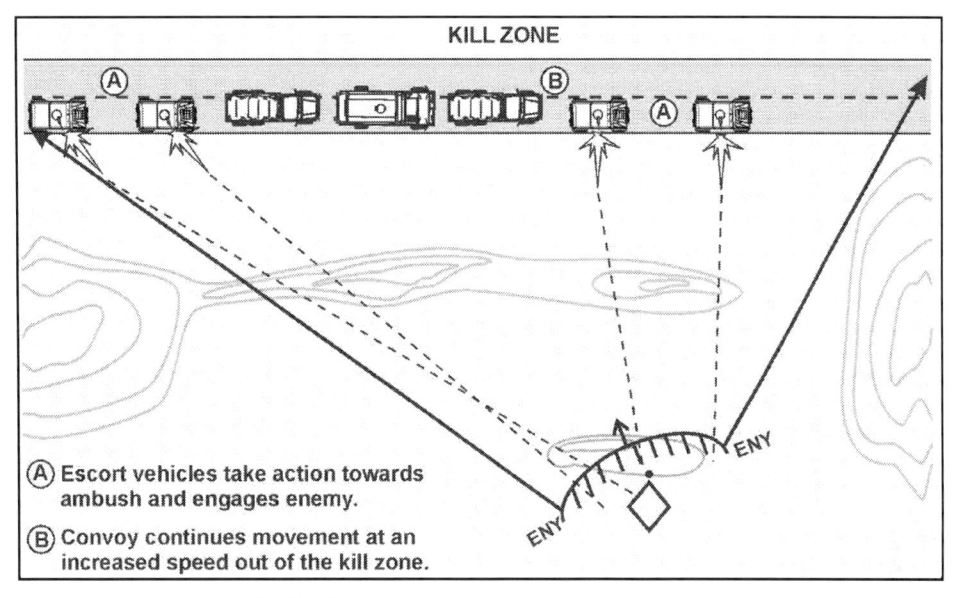

Ⓐ Escort vehicles take action towards ambush and engages enemy.
Ⓑ Convoy continues movement at an increased speed out of the kill zone.

Figure D-12. Convoy escort actions toward ambush

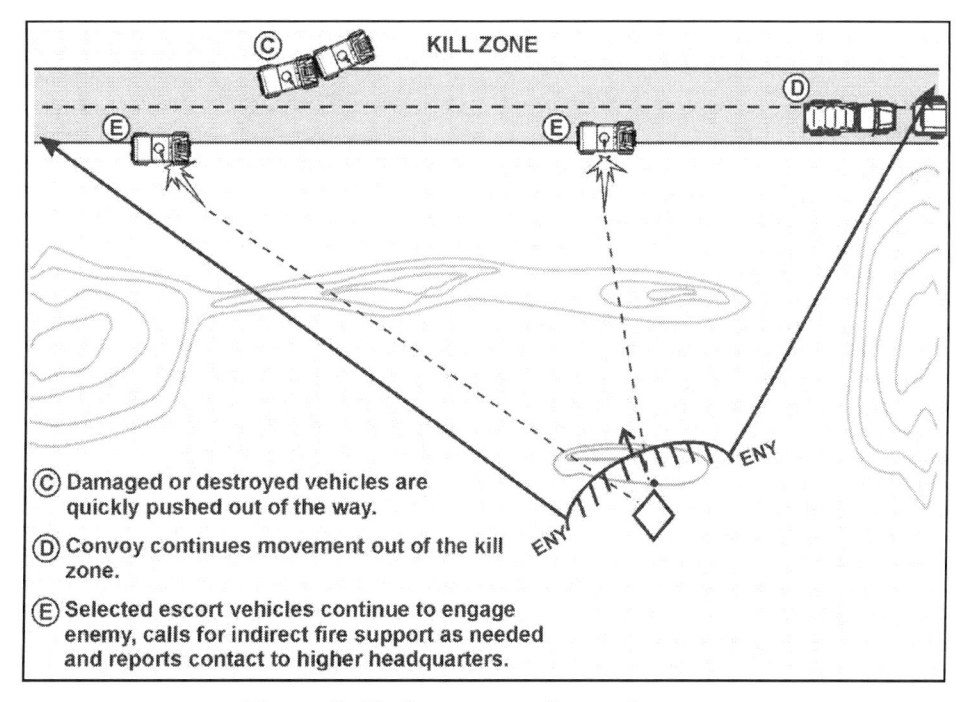

Ⓒ Damaged or destroyed vehicles are quickly pushed out of the way.
Ⓓ Convoy continues movement out of the kill zone.
Ⓔ Selected escort vehicles continue to engage enemy, calls for indirect fire support as needed and reports contact to higher headquarters.

Figure D-13. Convoy continues to move

D-94. Once the convoy is clear of the kill zone, the escort element executes one of the following COA:
- Continues to suppress the enemy as combat reaction forces move to support. (See figure D-14.)
- Uses the Infantry to assault the enemy. (See figure D-15, page D-34.)
- Breaks contact and moves out of the kill zone.
- Request immediate air support to cut off escape routes.

D-95. In most situations, platoons or squads will continue to suppress the enemy or execute an assault. Contact should be broken only with the approval of the controlling commander.

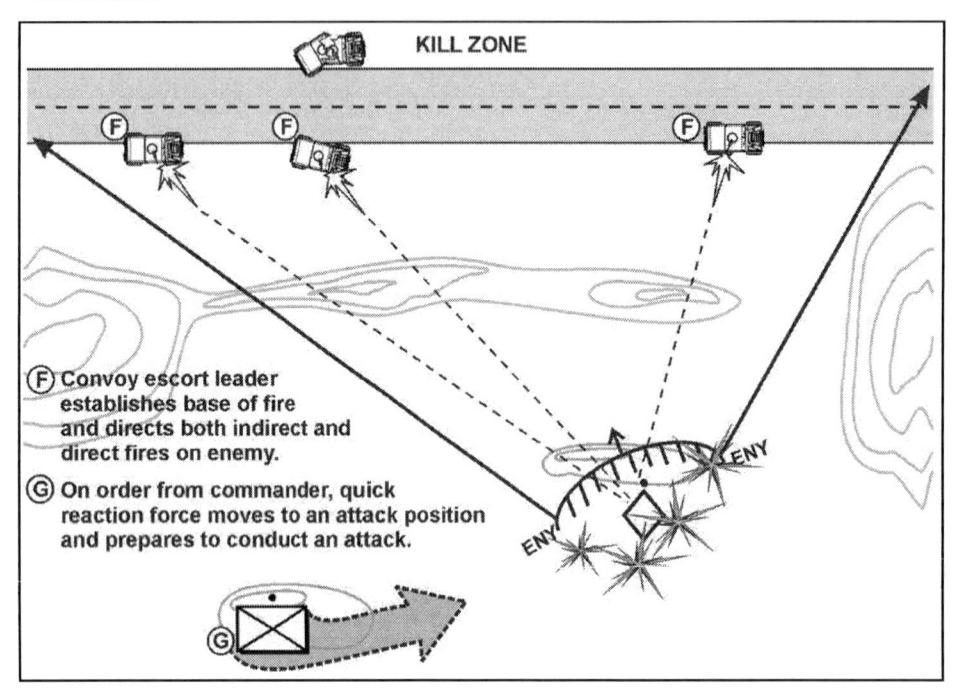

Figure D-14. Escort suppresses ambush for reaction force attack

Appendix D

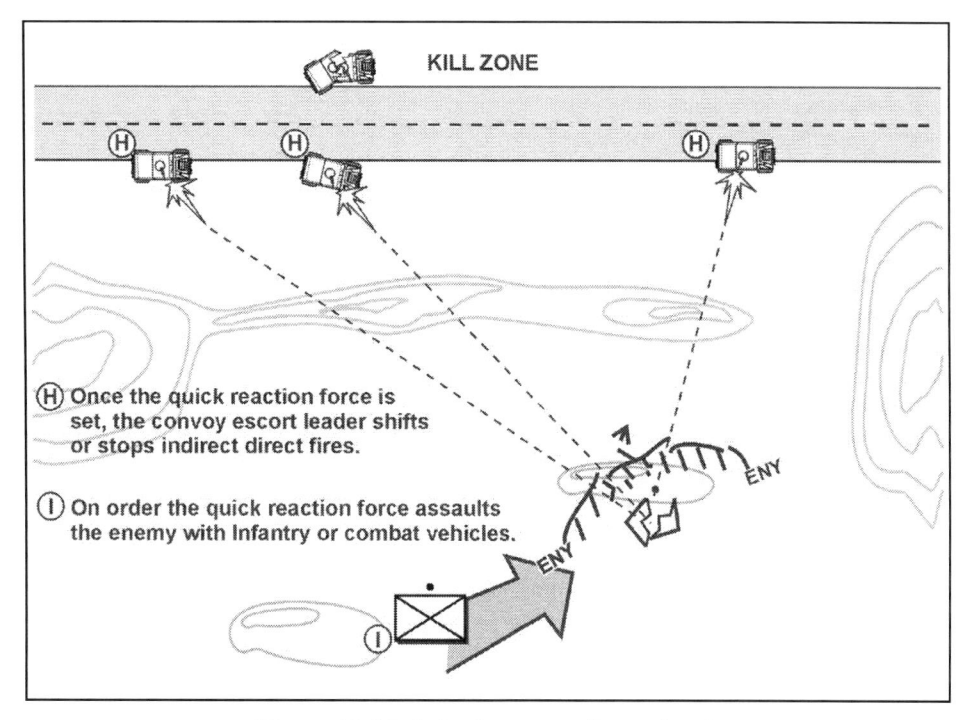

Figure D-15. Infantry assaults ambush

ACTIONS AT AN OBSTACLE

D-96. Obstacles are a major impediment to convoys. The purpose of reconnaissance ahead of a convoy is to identify obstacles and either breach or bypasses. In some cases the enemy or its obstacles may avoid detection by the reconnaissance element.

D-97. Obstacles can be used to harass the convoy by delaying it. If the terrain is favorable, the obstacle may stop the convoy altogether. Obstacles also may be used to canalize the convoy to set up an enemy ambush. When an obstacle is identified, the convoy escort faces two problems: reducing or bypassing the obstacle, and maintaining protection of the convoy. Security becomes critical, and actions at the obstacle must be accomplished quickly. The convoy commander must assume the enemy is covering the obstacle with direct- and indirect-fire weapons systems.

D-98. To reduce time the convoy is halted and to reduce its vulnerability, the following actions should occur when the convoy escort encounters a point-type obstacle:
- The lead element identifies the obstacle and directs the convoy to make a short halt to establish security. The convoy escort overwatches the obstacle and requests the breach element force to move forward. (See figure D-16.)
- The convoy escort maintains 360-degree security of the convoy and provides overwatch as the breach force reconnoiters the obstacle in search of a bypass.

D-99. Once all reconnaissance are complete, the convoy commander determines which of the following COA is suitable for mission accomplishment:
- Bypass the obstacle.
- Breach the obstacle with assets on hand.
- Breach the obstacle with reinforcing assets.

D-100. The convoy security commander relays a SPOTREP and requests support by combat reaction forces, engineer assets (if they are not part of the convoy), and aerial reconnaissance elements. Artillery units are alerted to prepare to provide indirect fire support.

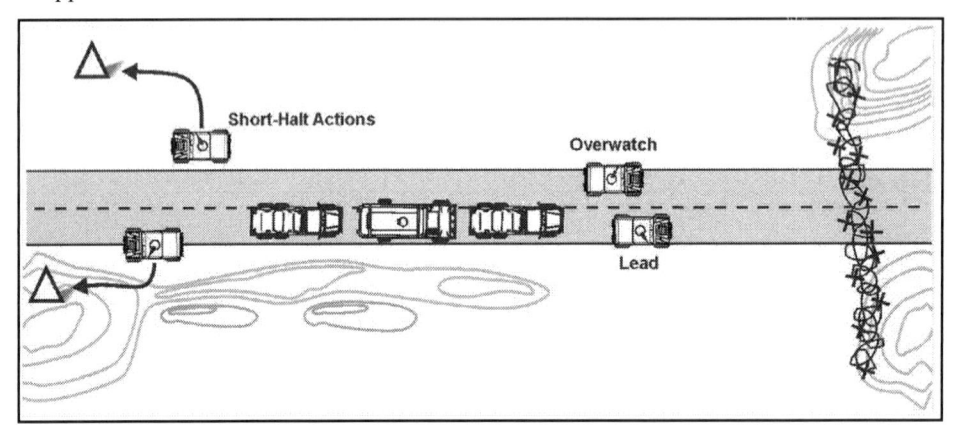

Figure D-16. Convoy escort overwatches an obstacle

D-101. Obstacles may be in the form of unexploded ordnance, or uncharted minefields. If the convoy encounters unexploded ordnance or mines, the convoy security commander should identify, mark, report, and bypass.

ACTIONS DURING HALTS

D-102. During a short halt, the convoy escort remains alert for possible enemy activity. If the halt is for reasons other than an obstacle, the following actions should be taken:
- The convoy commander signals the short halt and transmits the order via tactical radio. All vehicles in the convoy initially assume a herringbone formation.
- If possible, escort vehicles are positioned up to 100 meters beyond the convoy vehicles just clear of the route. Escort vehicles remain at the ready, dismount the rifles teams or squads as required, and establish local security. Security elements or escort vehicles must occupy terrain within small arms range dominating the convoy route during halts.
- When the order is given to move out, convoy vehicles reestablish movement formation, leaving space for escort vehicles. Once the convoy is in column, local security elements (if used) return to their vehicles, and escort vehicles rejoin the column.
- The convoy resumes movement.

Appendix D

SECTION V – ASSEMBLY AREA

D-103.   An AA is an area a unit occupies to prepare for a mission. Ideally, an AA provides—
- Concealment from air and ground observation.
- Adequate entrances, exits, and internal routes.
- Space for dispersion; each assembly area is separated by enough distance from other assembly areas to avoid mutual interference.
- Cover from direct fire.
- Good drainage and soil conditions sustaining the movement of the unit vehicles and individual Soldier.
- Terrain masking of electromagnetic signatures.
- Terrain allowing observation of ground and air avenues into the assembly area.
- Sanctuary from enemy medium-range artillery fires because it is located outside the enemy's range.

D-104.   The proper location of AA contributes significantly to both security and flexibility. It should facilitate future operations so movement to subsequent positions can take place smoothly and quickly by concealed routes. The tactical mobility of the Infantry platoon and squad allows it to occupy AA at greater distances from the LD.

QUARTERING PARTY

D-105.   Usually, the Infantry platoon and squad participates in the higher headquarters quartering party (also known as an advance party) to assist in the occupation of an AA. A quartering party is a group of unit representatives dispatched to a probable new site of operations in advance of the main body to secure, reconnoiter, and organize the site before the main body's arrival and occupation.

D-106.   The Infantry platoon and squad participates in the quartering party according to their SOP. For example, the quartering party could consist of one vehicle per platoon and a vehicle from the headquarters section. At company level the company executive officer, first sergeant or a senior NCO usually leads the quartering party. The quartering party's actions at the AA include the following:
- Reconnoiter for enemy forces and chemical, biological, radiological, and nuclear contamination.
- Evaluate the condition of the route leading into the assembly area and suitability of the area (drainage, space, internal routes).
- Organize the area based on the commander's guidance; designate and mark tentative locations for platoons' vehicles, command post vehicles, and trains.
- Improve and mark entrances, exits, and internal routes.
- Mark bypasses or removes obstacles (within the party's capabilities).
- Develop digital assembly area overlay and send overlays to Infantry company main body and Infantry battalion main command post.

OCCUPATION OF THE ASSEMBLY AREA

D-107. Once the quartering party finishes preparing the AA, the quartering party awaits the arrival of the main body, maintaining surveillance and providing security of the area within its capabilities. The main body is the principal part of a tactical command or formation. It does not include detached elements of the command, such as advance guards, flank guards, and covering force. SOPs and guides assist vehicle commanders to quickly find their positions, clear the route, and assume designated positions in the AA.

D-108. The Infantry platoon may occupy the AA as an independent element or as part of the company. In either situation, the platoon occupies its positions upon arrival using the procedures for hasty occupation of a battle position. The platoon leader establishes local security and coordinates with adjacent units. He assigns weapons orientation and sector for each squad and essential weapons systems in his area of operation. If the platoon occupies the AA alone, it establishes a perimeter defense. (See figure D-17, page D-38, and figure D-18, page D-39.)

Appendix D

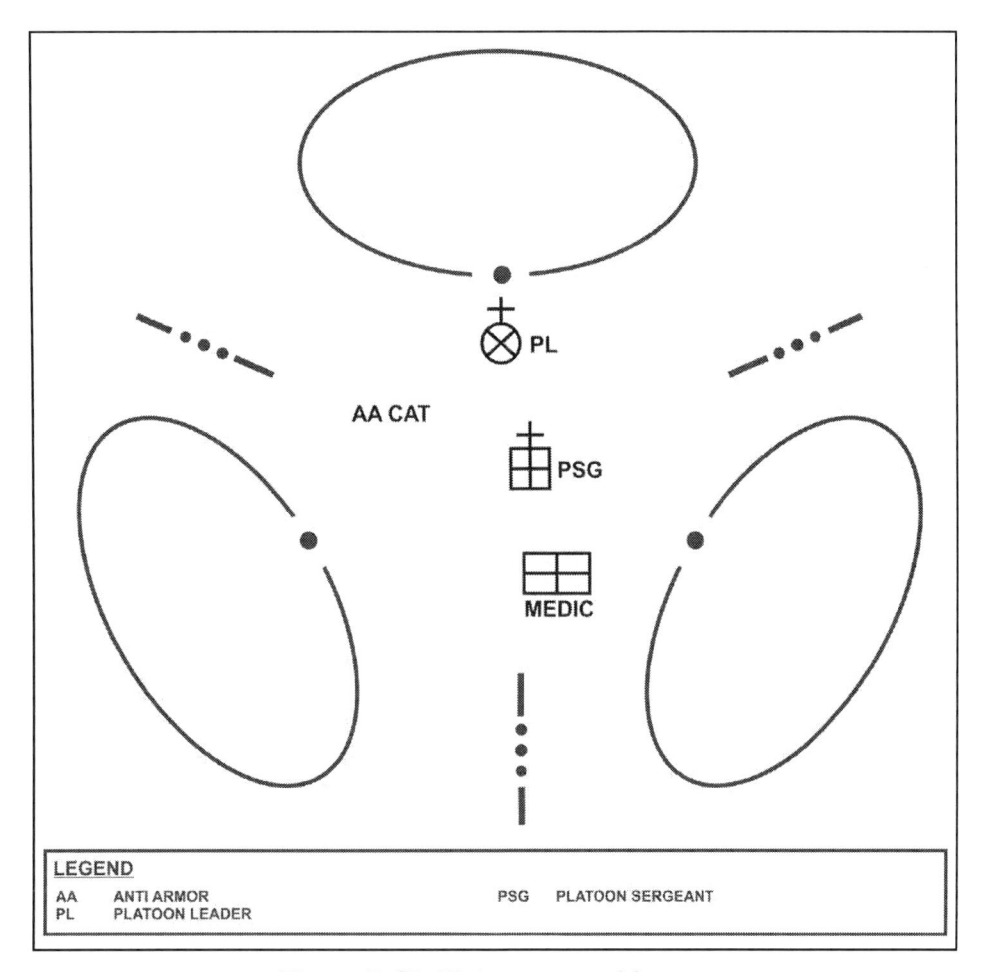

Figure D-17. Platoon assembly area

Security

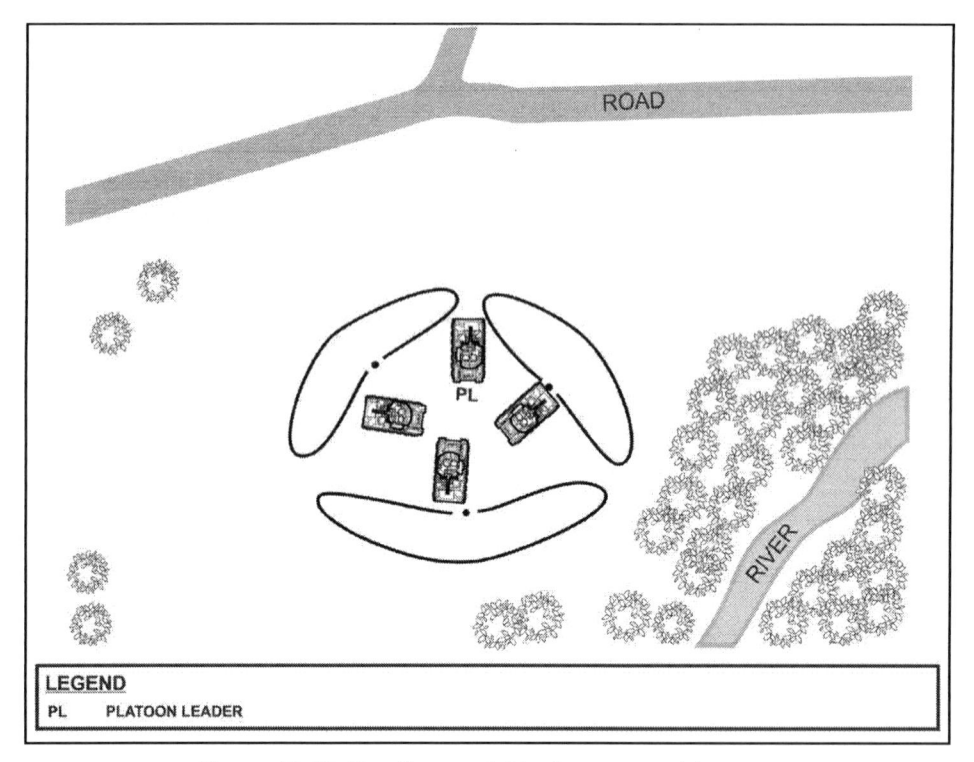

Figure D 18. Bradley and Stryker assembly area

ACTIONS IN THE ASSEMBLY AREA

D-109.   Following occupation of the AA, the platoon prepares for future operations by conducting TLP and priorities of work according to the company OPORD. These preparations include the following:
- Establish and maintain security (at the appropriate readiness level).
- Develop a defensive fire plan and forward to higher headquarters via Mission Command Systems if equipped.
- Conduct dismounted security patrols to clear dead space and restrictive terrain.
- Conduct troop leading procedures.
- Conduct precombat checks and a precombat inspection based on time available.
- Perform maintenance on vehicles and communications equipment.
- Verify weapons system status, conduct boresight adjustment, prepare-to-fire checks, test-firing, and other necessary preparations.

Note. The Infantry platoon and squad usually coordinates test-firing with its higher headquarters.

- Conduct resupply, refueling and rearming operations.

Appendix D

- Conduct rehearsals and other training for upcoming operations.
- Conduct personal care and hygiene activities.
- Adjust task organization as necessary.
- Account for Infantry platoon and squad personnel, to include attachments and sensitive items.
- Reestablish vehicle load plans as needed.

SECTION VI – ENEMY PRISONERS OF WAR AND RETAINED/DETAINED PERSONS

D-110. Detainees and captured enemy equipment or materiels often provide excellent combat information. This information is of tactical value only if the platoon processes and evacuates prisoners and materiel to the rear quickly. In tactical situations, the platoon will have specific procedures and guidelines for handling prisoners and captured materiel.

D-111. All persons captured, personnel detained or retained by U.S. Armed Forces during the course of military operations, are considered "detained" persons until their status is determined by higher military and civilian authorities. The BCT has an organic military police platoon organic to the brigade special troops battalion to take control of and evacuate detainees. (See figure D-19.) However, as a practical matter, when Infantry squads, platoons, companies, and battalions capture enemy personnel, they must provide the initial processing and holding for detainees. Detainee handling is a resource-intensive and politically sensitive operation requiring detailed training, guidance, and supervision.

Security

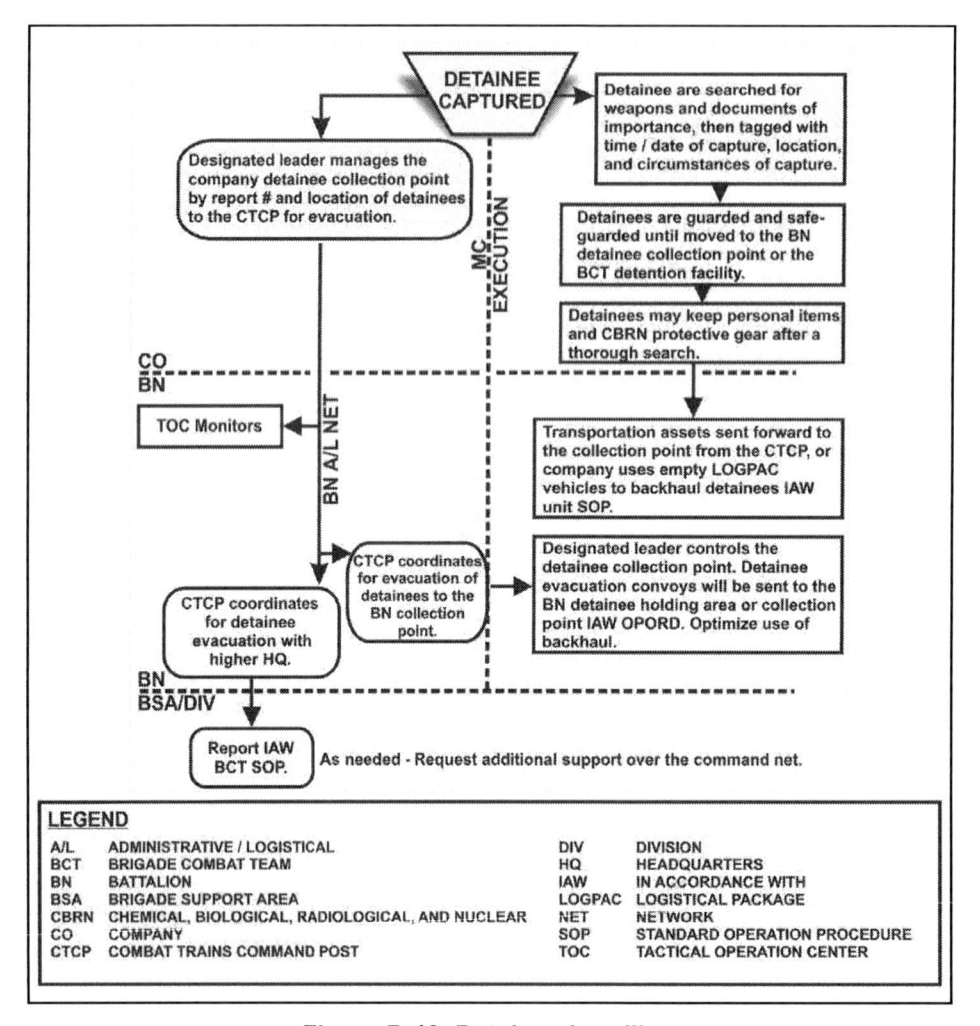

Figure D-19. Detainee handling

D-112. All detained persons immediately shall be given humanitarian care and treatment. U.S. Armed Forces never will torture, maltreat, or purposely place detained persons in positions of danger. There is never a military necessity exception to violate these principles.

D-113. Soldiers must process detainees using the "search, silence, segregate, speed, safeguard, and tag" (5 Ss and T) technique. The steps of this process are described as follows:

- *Search.* Neutralize a detainee and confiscate weapons, personal items, and items of potential intelligence or evidentiary value.
- *Silence.* Prevent detainees from communicating with one another or making audible clamor such as chanting, singing, or praying. Silence uncooperative detainees by muffling them with a soft, clean cloth tied around their mouths and fastened at the

Appendix D

backs of their heads. Do not use duct tape or other adhesives, place a cloth or either objects inside the mouth, or apply physical force to silence detainees.

- *Segregate.* Segregate detainees according to policy and SOPs. (Segregation requirements differ from operation to operation.) The ability to segregate detainees may be limited by the availability of manpower and resources at the POC. At a minimum, try to segregate detainees by grade, gender, age (keeping adults from juveniles and small children with mothers), and security risk. Military intelligence and military police personnel can provide additional guidance and support in determining the appropriate segregation criteria.
- *Safeguard.* Protect detainees and ensure the custody and integrity of all confiscated items. Soldiers must safeguard detainees from combat risk, harm caused by other detainees, and improper treatment or care. Report all injuries. Correct and report violations of U.S. military policy that occur while safeguarding detainees. Acts, omissions or both that constitute inhumane treatment are violations of the law of war and, as such, must be corrected immediately. Simply reporting violations is insufficient. If a violation is ongoing, a Soldier has an obligation to stop the violation and report it.
- *Speed to a safe area/rear.* Quickly move detainees from the continuing risks associated with other combatants or sympathizers who still may be in the area of capture. If there are more detainees than the Soldiers can control, call for additional support, search the detainees, and hold them in place until reinforcements arrive. Evacuate detainees from the battlefield to a holding area or facility as soon as possible. Transfer captured documents and other property to the forces assuming responsibility of the detainees.
- *Tag.* Ensure that each detainee is tagged using DD Form 2745. (See figure D-20a.) Confiscated equipment, personal items, and evidence will be linked to the detainee using the DD Form 2745 number. When a DA Form 4137, *Evidence/Property Custody Document,* is used to document confiscated items, it will be linked to the detainee by annotating the DD Form 2745 control number on the form or by field expedient means. Field expedient means should include tagging with date and time of capture, location of capture, capturing unit, and circumstances of capture. There are three parts to this form. DD Form 2745, *Unit Record Card, Part B*, is the unit record copy. (See figure D-20b, page D-44). DD Form 2745, *Document/Special Equipment Weapons Card, Part C*, is for detainee confiscated property. (See figure D-20c, page D-44). Tagging is critical. If it does not happen the ability of higher headquarters to obtain pertinent tactical information quickly is reduced greatly.

D-114. Detainees should be evacuated as soon as is practical to the BCT detainee collection point. Tactical questioning of detainees is allowed relative to collection of CCIRs. However, detainees must always be treated in accordance with the U.S. Law of War Policy as set forth in the Department of Defense Directive 2311.01E, *DoD Law of War Program*.

D-115. Soldiers capturing equipment, documents, and detainees should tag them (using the DD Form 2745, *Enemy Prisoner of War (EPW) Capture Tag, Part A* [see figures D-20a, D20b, and D20c on pages D-43 through D-44]), take digital pictures, and report the capture immediately. Detainees are allowed to keep protective equipment such as

Appendix D

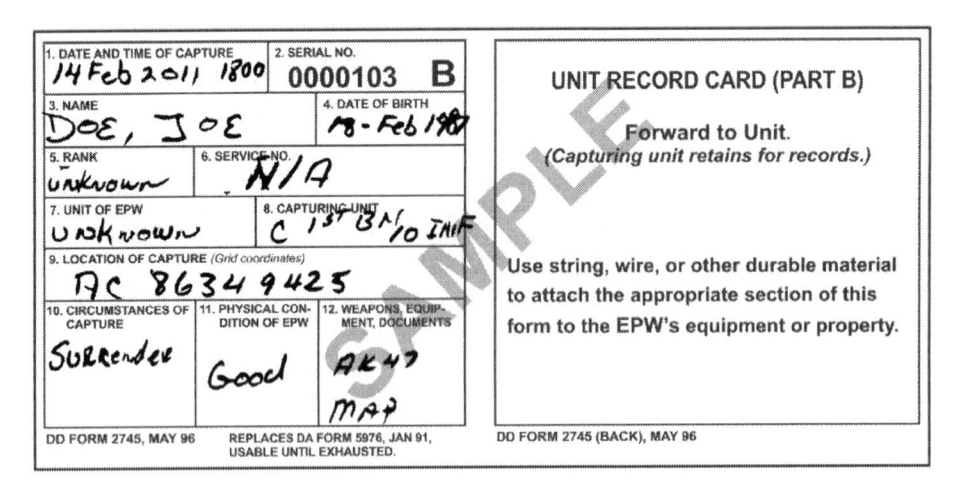

+Figure D-20b. DD Form 2745, Unit Record Card (Part B)

+Figure D-20c. DD Form 2745, Document/Special Equipment Weapons Card (Part C)

Appendix D

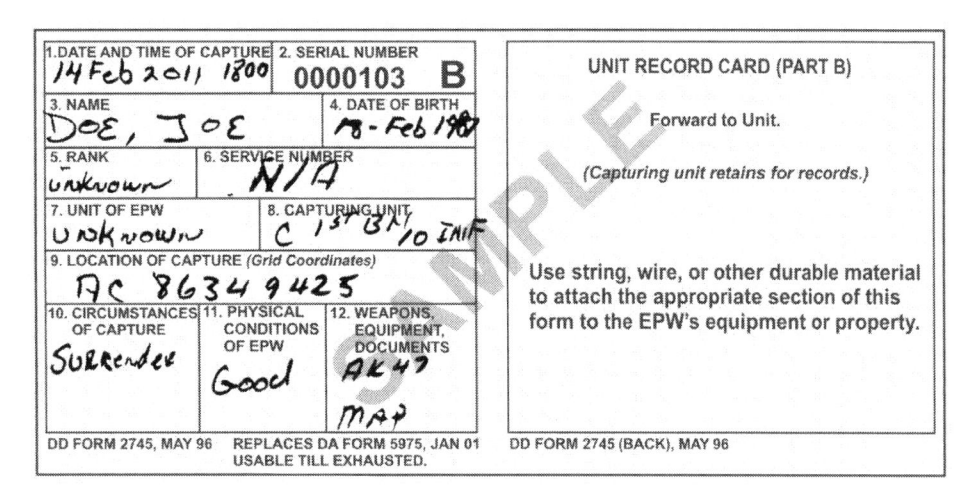

Figure D-20b. DD Form 2745, Unit Record Card (Part B)

Figure D-20c. DD Form 2745, Document/Special Equipment Weapons Card (Part C)

Appendix E
Vehicle Employment Considerations

Operations integrating Infantry forces and combat vehicles combine to create or produce greater effects. The principles for integrating combat vehicles with Infantry are similar regardless of the specific vehicle type. Combat vehicles that most often work with Infantry forces include the M1-series Abrams tank, the M2-series BFV, the Stryker ICV, multiple variants of the assault high-mobility multipurpose wheeled vehicle (HMMWV) and the MRAP. This appendix is written from the perspective of an Infantry platoon leader controlling a combat vehicle section or platoon. However, the technical and tactical information addressed in the following pages is generally valid for Infantry platoons and squads attached to armored units.

SECTION I – EMPLOYMENT AND CAPABILITIES

E-1. The primary roles of the combat vehicles discussed in this appendix are to provide Infantry platoons and squads with mobility, allowing them to maneuver. Combat vehicles also provide bases of fire; protection, breaching capabilities, enhanced communication platforms, and a variety of sustainment assets, including re-supply and medical evacuation capabilities. Integration of these forces provides complementary and reinforcing effects to Infantry and mounted forces.

PRINCIPLES OF EMPLOYMENT

E-2. The general principles for employing combat vehicles with Infantry Soldiers are—
- So the combat power capabilities of the vehicle can support the maneuver of the Infantry.
- So the combat power of the Infantry platoon or squad can support the maneuver of combat vehicle sections or platoons.
- The wingman concept. To achieve mutual support, combat vehicles almost always work in this concept. The wingman concept is similar to the buddy team concept that Infantry Soldiers employ (operating in two-vehicle sections). Just as Infantry Soldiers never fight alone, combat vehicles never operate without the mutual support and evacuation capability the combat vehicle wingman provides.

Appendix E

GENERAL EMPLOYMENT CONSIDERATIONS

E-3. Employment of combat vehicles requires thorough understanding and integration of vehicle and Infantry units. The following paragraphs focus on general employment considerations.

COMBAT VEHICLES SUPPORTING THE INFANTRY

E-4. Combat vehicles support Infantry units by leading Infantry Soldiers in open terrain and providing them with a protected, fast-moving assault weapons system. They suppress and destroy enemy weapons, bunkers, and tanks by fire and movement. They may provide transport when the enemy situation permits.

Mobility

E-5. The following is a list of the primary mobility functions combat vehicles provide an Infantry platoon and squads during combat operations:
- Assist opposed entry of Infantry Soldiers into buildings or bunkers.
- Breach or reduce obstacles by fire.
- Provide mobility to the dismounted force.
- Provide enhanced communication platforms and multiple communications systems.
- Sustainment, medical evacuation, and resupply.

Firepower

E-6. The following is a list of the primary firepower functions combat vehicles provide an Infantry platoon or squad during combat operations:
- Speed and shock effect to assist the Infantry in rapidly executing an assault.
- Lethal and accurate direct fire support.
- Suppression of identified sniper positions.
- Heavy volume of suppressive fires and a mobile base of fire of the Infantry.
- Employment of technical assets (thermal viewers and range finders) to assist in target acquisition and ranging.
- Neutralization or suppression of enemy positions with direct fire as Infantry closes with and destroys the enemy.
- Assaults by fire other targets designated by the Infantry.
- Accurate direct fires even while the vehicle is moving at high speeds with stabilized gun systems.
- Destruction of enemy tanks and armored personnel carriers.

Protection

E-7. The following are ways combat vehicles protect an Infantry platoon or squads during combat operations:

Vehicle Employment Considerations

- Dominate the objective during consolidation and reorganization to defeat a counterattack and protect Infantry forces.
- Protect the movement of advancing Infantry through open terrain with limited cover and concealment.
- Secure cleared portions of the objective by covering avenues of approach.
- Establish roadblocks or checkpoints.
- Provide limited obscuration with smoke grenades and smoke generators.
- Isolate objectives with direct fire to prevent enemy withdrawal, reinforcement, or counterattack.

INFANTRY SOLDIERS SUPPORTING COMBAT VEHICLES

E-8. Infantry Soldiers support vehicular forces by finding and reducing (or marking) antitank obstacles. They detect and destroy or suppress enemy antitank weapons. Infantry Soldiers may designate targets for armored vehicles and protect them in close terrain.

Mobility

E-9. Mobility functions Infantry provide to units with vehicles during combat operations include:
- Seize and retain terrain.
- Clear defiles and restrictive urban terrain ahead of vehicular forces.

Firepower

E-10. Firepower functions the Infantry provides to units with vehicles during combat operations include:
- Actions on the objective (such as clear trenches, knock out bunkers, enter and clear buildings).
- Employ antitank systems (Javelin) to destroy armored threats.

Protection

E-11. Ways the Infantry protects units with vehicles during combat operations include:
- Provide local security over dead space and blind spots that weapon systems on combat vehicles cannot cover.
- Consolidate and reorganize perform enemy prisoners of war procedures, and direct medical evacuation.

TECHNICAL CAPABILITIES

E-12. Infantry leaders must have a basic understanding of the technical capabilities of combat vehicles. These include vehicle characteristics, firepower and protection.

Appendix E

VEHICLE CHARACTERISTICS

E-13. To win in battle, leaders must have a clear understanding of the capabilities and limitations of their equipment. The Abrams tank, BFV, Stryker ICV, armament carrier HMMWV and the MRAP. Each has their own capabilities, limitations, characteristics, and logistical requirements. Even though their role to the Infantry is virtually the same, these vehicles provide support in different ways. To employ combat vehicles, leaders must understand specific capabilities and limitations of vehicles that are attached under operational control to their unit. The following information is a brief overview of the combat vehicles' characteristics as they apply to combat power. Table E-1 displays vehicle characteristics. (Specifics vary by vehicle and modifications.)

Table E-1. Mobility characteristics of combat vehicles

VARIABLES	ARMAMENT CARRIER HMMWV	ICV (STRYKER)	BFV (BRADLEY)	TANK (ABRAMS)	MRAP MAXXPRO DASH	M-ATV
Tracks or Wheels	Wheels	Wheels	Tracks	Tracks	Wheels	Wheels
Length	15'	22.9'	21.2'	32.04'	21.75'	20.67'
Width	7.08'	8.9'	11.83'	12.0'	10.75'	8.35'
Height	6.0' (without weapon)	8.6'	11.8'	8.0'	11.95' (with objective gunners protective kit)	10.95' (with objective gunners protective kit)
Weight	5200 lbs	38,000 lbs	50,000 lbs	136,800 lbs	46,500 lbs	34,400 lbs
Speed	65 mph	60 mph	42 mph	41.5 mph	68 mph	62 mph
LEGEND ATV – all-terrain vehicle; BFV – Bradley fighting vehicle; HMMWV – high-mobility multipurpose wheeled vehicle; ICV – Infantry carrier vehicle; lbs – pounds; mph – miles per hour; MRAP – mine resistant ambush protected							

Firepower

E-14. The weapons and ammunition of vehicular units are designed to defeat specific enemy targets, though many are multipurpose. An Infantry leader with a basic understanding of these weapons and ammunition types will be able to better employ vehicular units to defeat the enemy. Table E-2 (page E-6) lists the basic weapons and ammunition types offered by vehicular units that generally support Infantry platoons and squads. These weapons systems are organic to several vehicles while they are mounted on others. METT-TC driven.

> *Note.* When referring to the heavy machine gun in this manual, it refers to the M2 or M2A1 .50-caliber heavy machine gun. The M2A1 heavy machine gun is the next generation of heavy machine gun, currently being fielded and will be replacing the M2 heavy machine gun. (See appendix F for more information.)

Table E-2. Weapons, ammunition, and targets

	ARMAMENT CARRIER HMMWV		ICV (STRYKER)		BFV (BRADLEY)	
	Weapon Ammo	**Target**	**Weapon Ammo**	**Target**	**Weapon Ammo**	**Target**
Blast Munition	40 mm MK19 Max area: 2212 m Max point: 1500 m	Trucks, troops, bunkers, buildings	40 mm MK19 Max area: 2212 m Max point: 1500 m	Trucks, troops, bunker building	25 mm (HE) Max effective: 3000 m	Trucks, troops, bunkers, buildings
Cannon	None	None	None	None	25 mm (sabot) Max effective: 2500 m	APCs
Machine Gun	M249 5.56 mm Max area: 800 m Max point: 600 m M240B/L 7.62 mm (mounted) Max area: 1100 m Max point: 800 m M2 .50-caliber Max area: 1830 m Max point: 1200 m	Troops, trucks, equip	M2 .50-caliber Max area: 1830 m Max point: 1200 m M240B/L 7.62 mm (mounted) Max area: 1100 m Max point: 800 m	Troops, trucks, equip	M240C/L 7.62 mm Max effective: 900 m	Troops, trucks
TOW Missile	Max effective: 3750 m	Tanks	Max effective: 3750 m	Tanks, bunkers	Max effective: 3750 m	Tanks, bunkers

Vehicle Employment Considerations

Table E-2. Weapons, ammunition, and targets (continued)

	TANK (ABRAMS)		MRAP MAXXPRO DASH AND M-ATV	
	Weapon Ammo	Target	Weapon Ammo	Target
Blast Munition	120 mm High Explosive Antitank (HEAT) Max effective: 3000 m	Trucks, troops, bunker buildings, APCs	40 mm MK19 Max area: 2212 m Max point: 1500 m	Trucks, troops, bunker, building
Cannon	120 mm (sabot) Max effective: 3000 m	APCs, tanks	None	None
Machine Gun	M240C/L 7.62 mm Max effective: 900 m M2 .50-caliber Max area: 1830 m Max point: 1200 m	Troops, trucks, equip	M240C/L 7.62 mm Max effective: 900 m M2 .50-caliber Max area: 1830 m Max point: 1200 m	Troops, trucks, equip
TOW Missile	None	None	None	None
LEGEND ACP – armored personnel carrier; ammo – ammunition; equip – equipment; HE – high explosive; HEAT – high-explosive anti-tank; m – meter; mm – millimeter; max – maximum; TOW - tube-launched, optically-tracked, wire-guided			

Protection

E-15. All combat vehicles offer varying degrees of protection from direct and indirect fire. Figure E-1 (page E-8) illustrates the generally progressive degrees of protection offered by combat vehicles.

Appendix E

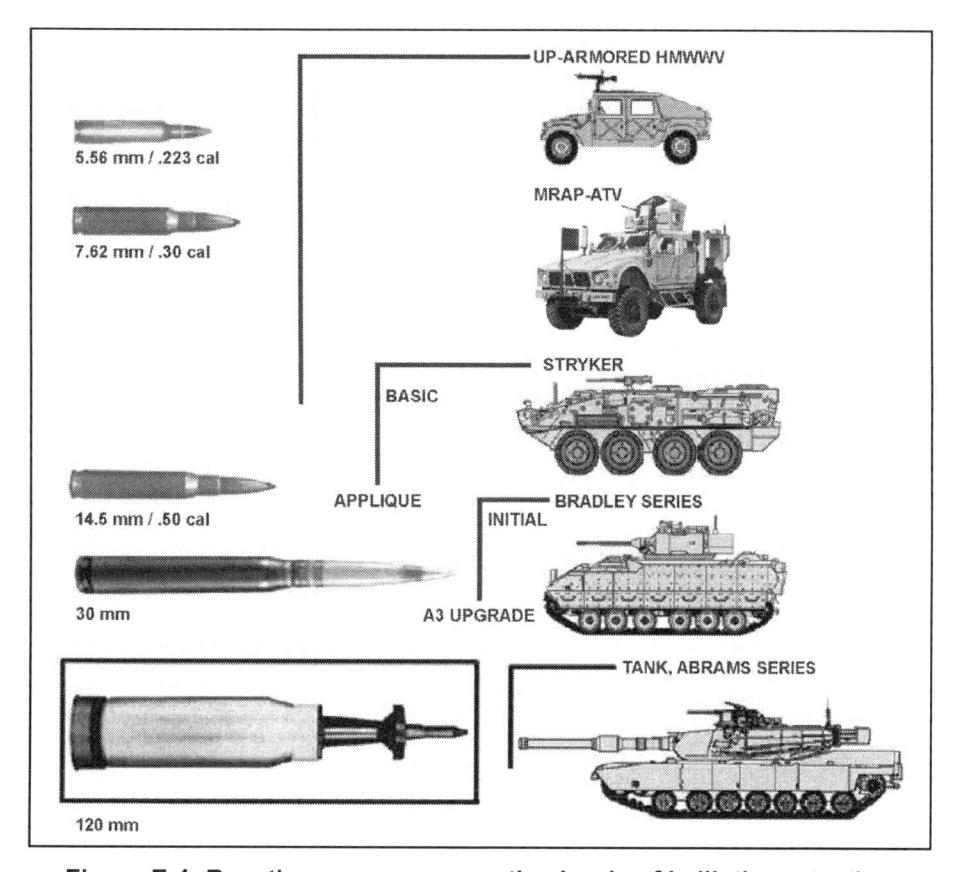

Figure E-1. Reactive armor comparative levels of ballistic protection

TANK

E-16. The M1-series Abrams tank provides rapid mobility combined with excellent protection and highly lethal, accurate fires. They are most effective in generally open terrain with extended fields of fire.

Mobility Advantages

E-17. The tank's mobility comes from its capability to move at high speed on and off road. The tank's ability to cross ditches; ford streams and shallow rivers; and push through small trees, vegetation, and limited obstructions allows movement in various types of terrain.

Mobility Disadvantages

E-18. Tanks consume large quantities of fuel. They are noisy and must be started periodically in cold weather, or when using thermal night sights and radios to ensure the batteries stay charged. The noise, obscurants, and dust generated by tanks make it difficult for the Infantry in their vicinity to capitalize on stealth to achieve surprise. Tanks cannot cross bodies of water deeper than four feet without deep water fording kits or bridging equipment. Due to the length of the tank main gun, the turret will not rotate if a solid object such as a wall, post, or tree is blocking it. Tracked vehicles also can "throw track." This occurs when the track loses tension on the sprockets, support arms, or both, and the track becomes disconnected from the tank. Repairing the track can be a lengthy process.

Firepower Advantages

E-19. The tank's main gun is extremely accurate and lethal at ranges out to 4000 meters. Tanks with stabilized main guns can fire even when moving at high speeds cross-country. The tank remains the best AT weapon on the battlefield. The various machine guns (M1-series Abrams tank's caliber .50 and 7.62-mm coax and loader's 7.62-mm machine gun) provide a high volume of supporting fires for the Infantry. The target acquisition capabilities of the tank exceed the capability of all systems in the Infantry battalion. The thermal sight provides a significant capability for observation and reconnaissance. It also can be used during daylight hours to identify heat sources (personnel and vehicles), even through vegetation. The laser range finder provides an increased capability for the Infantry force to establish fire control measures (such as trigger lines and TRP), and to determine exact locations.

Firepower Disadvantages

E-20. The normal, basic load of the tank's main gun is primarily armor piercing discarding sabots with tracer (APDS-T) antitank rounds. These rounds are not as effective against light-armored or wheeled vehicles, bunkers, trench lines, buildings, or enemy personnel. They also present a safety problem when fired over the heads of exposed Infantry Soldiers due to the discarded sabot pieces falling to the ground. HE ammunition provides better destructive effects on the above-mentioned targets, except enemy personnel, against which the tank's machine guns are most effective. The resupply of all tank ammunition is difficult and requires logistic support from the armored battalion. The main gun of an M1A2 only can elevate +20 degrees and depress -9 degrees. Figure E-2 (page E-10) illustrates M1A2 fields of fire on the urban terrain.

Appendix E

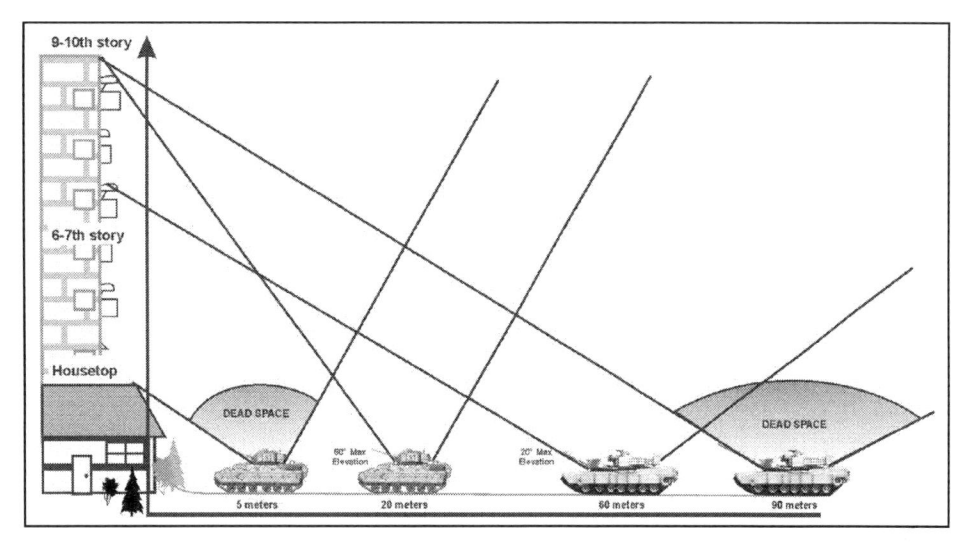

Figure E-2. M1A2 Abrams tank fields of fire on urban terrain

Protection Advantages

E-21. Generally, tank armor provides excellent protection to the crew. Across the frontal 60-degree arc, the tank is impenetrable to all weapons, except heavy antitank missiles or guns, and the main gun-on-enemy tanks. When fighting with the hatches closed, the crew is impenetrable to all small-arms fire, artillery rounds (except a direct hit), and antipersonnel mines. The tank's smoke grenade launcher and on-board smoke generator provide rapid concealment from all but thermal observation.

Protection Disadvantages

E-22. The tank is most vulnerable to lighter antitank weapons from the flanks, and especially the top and rear. The top is vulnerable to precision-guided munitions (artillery or air delivered). Antitank mines also can destroy or disable the vehicle. When fighting with hatches down, the tank crew's ability to see and engage targets (especially close-in Infantry) is reduced greatly.

Information Advantages

E-23. Mission Command Systems and inertial position navigation systems allow today's tanks the mobility to arrive at virtually any designated location with greater speed and accuracy than ever before. Use of visual signals and the single channel ground airborne radio system (SINCGARS) facilitates rapid and secure communication of orders and instructions. This capability allows tank crews to mass the effects of their weapon systems quickly while remaining dispersed to limit the effects of the tanks, armored vehicles, and fortifications using the main gun, and to suppress enemy positions, personnel, and light-armored targets with the tank's machine guns.

Information Disadvantages

E-24. Not all tanks are equipped with digitally enhanced Mission Command Systems. At present, the situational awareness and enemy situation acquired by the Mission Command Systems cannot be shared easily with Infantry units on the ground.

BRADLEY FIGHTING VEHICLE

E-25. The BFV provides good protection and mobility combined with excellent firepower to support Infantry units with direct fire.

Mobility Advantages

E-26. The mobility of the BFV is comparable to the tank. In addition to the three-man crew, the vehicle is designed to carry seven additional Infantry Soldiers with combat load.

Mobility Disadvantages

E-27. The BFV consumes significant quantities of fuel, but less than a M1-series Abrams tank. The BFV is louder than the M1-series Abrams tank, and like the M1-series Abrams tank, its engine must be started periodically in cold weather or when using the thermal night sight and radios to ensure the batteries stay charged. Like all heavy vehicles, the noise, obscurants, and dust generated by the BFV makes it difficult for the Infantry to capitalize on its ability to move with stealth and avoid detection when moving on the same approach. Improvised barricades, narrow streets and alleyways, or large amounts of rubble can block a BFV in an urban area, and heavy woods will restrict their movement in rural areas. The 25-mm cannon does not project out over the front of the Bradley like a tank, but protrudes over the sides when the gunner is aiming at 3 o'clock or 9 o'clock. This causes some problems for the Bradley when trying to negotiate narrow avenues of approach. Attaching and removing rucksacks to the exterior of the vehicle can be a lengthy process, and rucksacks are exposed to enemy fire.

Firepower Advantages

E-28. The primary weapon on the BFV is the 25-mm chain gun firing APDS-T, high explosive incendiary with tracer. This weapon is extremely accurate and lethal against light-armored vehicles, bunkers, trench lines, and personnel at ranges out to 2000 meters. The stabilized gun allows fires even when moving cross-country. The TOW provides a weapon for destroying enemy tanks or other point targets at extended ranges to 3750 meters. The 7.62-mm coax provides a high volume of suppressive fires for self-defense and supporting fires of the Infantry up to 800 meters. The combination of the stabilized turret, thermal sight, high volume of fire, and reinforcing effects of weapons and ammunition makes the BFV an excellent suppression asset supporting Infantry assaults. The thermal sight provides a significant capability for observation and reconnaissance. It can be used during the day to identify heat sources (personnel and vehicles) even through light vegetation. Figure E-3 (page E-12) shows the 25-mm supporting Infantry in an urban setting.

Appendix E

Figure E-3. BFV 25-mm Infantry support

Firepower Disadvantages

E-29. When operating the thermal sight with the BFV engine off, a "clicking" sound can be heard at a considerable distance from the vehicle. The resupply of ammunition is difficult and requires external logistic support.

Protection Advantages

E-30. Overall, the BFV provides good protection. When fighting with the hatches closed, the crew is well protected from small-arms fire, fragmentation munitions, and antipersonnel mines. The BFV smoke-grenade launcher and on-board smoke generator provide rapid concealment from all but thermal observation.

Protection Disadvantages

E-31. The vehicle is vulnerable from all directions to antitank weapons and especially enemy tanks. Antitank mines can destroy or disable the vehicle. When the crew is operating the vehicle with the hatches open, it is vulnerable to small-arms fire.

Information Advantages

E-32. The target acquisition capabilities of the BFV exceed the capability of the other systems in the Infantry battalion. The thermal sight provides a significant capability for observation and reconnaissance. It also can be used during the day to identify heat sources

Vehicle Employment Considerations

(personnel and vehicles) even through light vegetation. Many models of the BFV are equipped with the latest Mission Command Systems, while others are still equipped with the outdated systems.

Information Disadvantages

E-33. Bradley vehicle crewmembers have poor all-round vision through their vision blocks and are easily blinded by obscurants or dust. Therefore, the Bradley vehicle should not be approached while it is in contact because the crew may have difficulty seeing Infantry Soldiers outside of the vehicle. The Bradley commander must be informed where the dismounted Infantry Soldiers are located to prevent accidents on the battlefield.

STRYKER INFANTRY CARRIER VEHICLE

E-34. The Stryker vehicle is operated by a crew of two; a driver, and a vehicle commander and carries nine Infantry Soldiers and their equipment. The purpose of Stryker ICVs to provide protection for the Infantry to the dismount point prior to making contact with the enemy. The ICV carries the logistical load for the Infantry, with up to 72 hours of operation without resupply.

Mobility Advantages

E-35. The Stryker vehicle enables the team to maneuver in close and urban terrain, provide protection in open terrain, and transport Infantry quickly to critical battlefield positions. With a 4x8 and 8x8 wheel drive, the Stryker is designed for all-weather use over all types of terrain and can ford hard-bottomed bodies of water to a depth of 67 inches. Stryker vehicles have a maximum speed of 60 miles per hour and a range of 300 miles on a tank of fuel. The vehicles are swift, easily maintainable, and include features designed for Soldiers' safety. The Stryker's has run-flat tires inflated or deflated from inside the vehicle to adapt to surfaces ranging from deep mud to hardtop. It also has a built-in fire suppression system, and a self-recovery winch. The vehicles run quieter than current armored personnel carriers, increasing their stealth. Steel-belted tires with run-flat liners enable vehicle mobility for five miles (eight km) when all tires are flat.

Mobility Disadvantages

E-36. For vehicles weighing 10-20 tons, wheels are inferior to tracks in crossing sand, mud, and snow. Driving more than five miles on a flattened tire can cause a fire. Improvised barricades, narrow streets and alleyways, or large amounts of rubble can block Stryker vehicles in urban areas. Dense forests can block it in rural areas.

Firepower Advantages

E-37. The ICV has an RWS with a universal soft mount cradle mounting either a .50-caliber M2/M2A1 machine gun, an MK19 40-mm grenade launcher, or an M240-series 7.62-mm machine gun. It is also armed with four M6 smoke grenade launchers. Stowed ammunition includes:
- 32 66-mm smoke grenades.

Appendix E

- 3,200 7.62-mm rounds.
- 2,000 .50-cal rounds or 430 MK19 rounds.

E-38. Troops carry:
- 2,240 5.56-mm ball ammunition.
- 1,120 5.56-mm linked ammunition.

Firepower Disadvantages

E-39. The ICV loses some of the ammunition effects that tanks and BFV can provide the Infantry Soldier. For this reason the ICV can suppress light-skinned vehicles, bunkers, buildings, and enemy Infantry, but is not as effective as a BFV or tank against enemy light-armored or armored vehicles.

Protection Advantages

E-40. The basic ICV provides armored protection of the two-man crew and a squad of nine Infantry Soldiers. The ICV's armor protection stops .50-caliber bullets and protects against 152-mm airburst shells. The basic armor package on every Stryker vehicle is a steel hull protecting against 7.62-mm bullets; and a ceramic, added-on appliqué giving protection against 14.5-mm machine guns. Hull floor plate and fuel tank armor protect from blast and fragment effects of antipersonnel mine detonations. Low silhouette and noise output make the vehicle a difficult target to detect and to engage.

Protection Disadvantages

E-41. The ICV is vulnerable to all antitank fires and tanks. The effectiveness of RPG fire can be mitigated with a slat-armor application (cage) causing a premature detonation of the RPG warhead away from the hull of the ICV.

Information Advantages

E-42. Mission Command Systems provide real-time situational awareness of both enemy and friendly positions. It enables leaders and Soldiers to receive process and distribute information products in real time. Stryker platoons and squads have a variety of systems to communicate directly within and outside the platoon. These are mounted on the ICV and carried by Soldiers. The platoon can monitor and transmit on the company and platoon radio nets. The forward observer transmits on the fires net.

Information Disadvantages

E-43. The Stryker ICV vehicle crewmembers have limited vision when at name tape defilade in their vehicle commander's hatches. The addition of air guards stationed in the overhead hatches and a rearview camera provide more situational awareness around the vehicle, but does not mitigate all the blind spots.

Assault High-Mobility Multipurpose Wheeled Vehicle

E-44. The armament carrier HMMWV is a light, highly mobile, diesel-powered, four-wheel-drive vehicle equipped with an automatic transmission. Using components and kits common to the M998 chassis, the HMMWV can be configured as a troop carrier, armament carrier, TOW missile carrier, or a Scout vehicle.

Mobility Advantages

E-45. The HMMWV rests on a four-wheel chassis. Its four-wheel drive enables it to operate in a variety of terrain and climate conditions. It is capable of fording water up to 30 inches in depth, and can ford depths of up to 60 inches with the deep water fording kit. The HMMWV's size allows it to travel in the narrow streets of urban terrain with minimal damage to the infrastructure. Some models of the HMMWV (M1026, M1036, M1046, and M1114) employ a winch aiding in self-recovery and recovery of similar vehicles.

Mobility Disadvantages

E-46. Although generally equipped with run-flat tires, HMMWV tires are susceptible to enemy fire. HMMWVs have much less ability to breach obstacles than tracked vehicles. The HMMWV can be blocked by hasty and complex obstacles and can be easily rolled, especially with the armored M1114.

Firepower Advantages

E-47. The HMMWV can employ a variety of weapon systems offering excellent direct fire support to Infantry forces. The TOW, M2/M2A1, MK19, M240-series, and M249 can all be mounted in HMMWV models with turrets. The capabilities of these weapon systems are discussed in greater detail in table E-2 (page E-6).

Firepower Disadvantages

E-48. In almost all instances, the HMMWV can mount only one weapon system. This makes it less effective than tanks or BFVs that employ antitank and antipersonnel weapons simultaneously.

Protection Advantages

E-49. The M1114 is an up-armored HMMWV providing ballistic, artillery, and mine-blast protection to vehicle occupants. The M1114 can protect occupants from 7.62-mm assault rifle armor-piercing rounds and 155-mm artillery airbursts, and provides 12 pounds front and four pounds of rear antitank mine protection. Other protection features include complete perimeter ballistic protection, mine blast protection, and a turret shield for the gunner. Supplemental armor packages are available for many models of the HMMWV. This armor has been shown to be effective against IEDs.

Appendix E

Protection Disadvantages

E-50. All models other than the M1114 offer extremely limited protection from direct or indirect fire. Leaders should not plan or direct the use of these vehicles for cover from enemy small arms, indirect fire, or rocket-propelled grenades. Gunners are exposed while manning their weapon system to direct and indirect fire. The lack of internal space causes difficulties if transporting a casualty.

Information Advantages

E-51. The HMMWV has a variety of features making it excellent for gathering and managing information. The crew and passengers of the HMMWV generally have excellent situational awareness due to a large front windshield and large windows located on the door at each seat. HMMWVs can carry two SINCGARS-class radio systems. They also can employ a power amplifier to extend the communications range to 35 kilometers in open terrain. The HMMWV can be configured to carry the latest Mission Command Systems. The weapon systems of the HMMWV can employ sights with night vision, thermal, and range-finding capabilities with high resolution and magnification in some systems.

Information Disadvantages

E-52. Many of the digital and electronic devices of the HMMWV require constant power sources. The need to start the HMMWV to keep the batteries charged can present a tactical problem if stealth is desired during an operation.

MINE RESISTANT AMBUSH PROTECTED VEHICLE

E-53. The MRAP family of vehicles consist of three variants (MATV, MaxxPro Dash, and the MaxxPro long wheeled base ambulance). These variants are then arranged into seven configurations. (Refer to TC 7-31 for detailed information regarding the MRAP family of vehicles.) The variants are determined by the following broad mission profiles:
- *M-ATV.* A protected all-wheel drive combat vehicle used as a weapon/armament carrier in support of close combat maneuver, reconnaissance and surveillance, convoy protection, mission command and general battlefield circulation by maneuver, cavalry and support units. Inherent armor protects vehicle occupants from small arms fire, fragmenting munitions, and blast. It provides cargo space for Soldier equipment and supplies and can mount standard crew-served weapons.
- *MaxxPro Dash.* A protected all-wheel drive combat vehicle used as an armored personnel carrier, mobile command post, weapons/armaments carrier, and CBRNE reconnaissance in support of close combat in maneuver and support units. Delivers teams of Soldiers to decisive points. Inherent armor protects vehicle occupants from small arms fire, fragmenting munitions, and blasts. It provides cargo space for Soldier equipment and supplies and can mount standard crew-served weapons.
- *MaxxPro Long Wheel Bass (LWB) Ambulance.* A protected all-wheel drive vehicle used as an armored ambulance for medical evacuation from forward areas. Carries and powers medical equipment set to support enroute care. Inherent armor protects

vehicle occupants from small arms fire, fragmenting munitions, and blast. The objective gunner protective kit can mount an M249 5.56 squad automatic weapon for self-defense.

Mobility Advantages

E-54. MRAP vehicles have relatively quick acceleration and a high top speed for vehicles of their weight and size, 62 to 68 mph maximum speed. Most operations will not require use of all the speed the MRAP vehicle can deliver. Its dash speed permits rapid movement between covered and concealed positions or breaking contact. Ultimately, the commander determines and sets the rate of movement based on a thorough understanding of METT-TC. It's a 4x4 all terrain armored vehicle with the capacity to handle a maximum slope of 60 percent grade with a 30 percent side slope grade. Can ford water obstacles up to 36 inches deep. Can operate in excess of 300 miles without refueling. Operates on all terrain and in all-weather temperatures and conditions.

Mobility Disadvantages

E-55. Operating MRAP vehicles at high speed in a tactical environment can develop into a dangerous situation before the driver can counter or react. Traveling at high speeds (anything greater than 25 mph) significantly decreases the ability to accurately visually scan the road surface. MRAP vehicles are generally tall with a high center of gravity that greatly increases the chance of a roll or tip over. Slow speeds reduce the possibility of an accident, tip over, or rollover. MRAP vehicles will not accelerate or stop at the rate drivers may be accustomed to with other vehicles.

E-56. The overall size of the MRAP limits its mobility in urban and rough terrain conditions. Drivers and leaders consider the following information when operating in restricted terrain:
- Narrow streets and gates may make turns and turning around difficult.
- There is the potential for increased difficulty in navigating through traffic.
- Cross-country speeds are reduced significantly due to the high center of gravity. Tall vehicles pose a greater risk of tip or rollover when negotiating slopes, trenches, ditches, and other obstacles.
- Take special consideration for low-hanging wires. (Crews need to have a wire-strike plan. Leaders must account for antenna heights for counter radio-controlled IED electronic warfare (CREW) and radio antennas when operating in urban terrain.
- The MRAP will ascend longitudinal slopes of up to 60 percent; however, extreme caution must be exercised on slopes greater than 50 percent. The MRAP vehicle is capable of operating on side slopes of up to 30 percent. (Use extreme caution on side slopes greater than 25 percent.) The critical rollover angles vary among variants and will differ depending on the load plan used. Load heavier items as low in the vehicle as possible to decrease the possibility of rollovers or tip over when operating on side slopes.
- All drivers must be well-trained in judging terrain and negotiating various terrain conditions.

Appendix E

- Many operations and movements are at night. Driver training should focus on driver vision enhancer training along with training the vehicle commander and gunner using night vision devices.

Fire Power Advantages

E-57. Armament may include an M2/M2A1 .50-caliber heavy machine gun, an MK19 automatic grenade launcher, or an M240-series medium machine gun mounted on either an objective gunner's protection kit or operated from inside the vehicle using an M153-series common remote operated weapons station (CROWS). Ambulance variants are equipped with a M249 squad automatic machine gun for self-protection. (Refer to table E-2 (page E-6) for more information on weapons, ammunition, and targets pertaining to the MRAP.)

Fire Power Disadvantages

E-58. The gunner standing in the objective gunner protective kit or using the RWS is the only crewmember with 360-degree visibility. Vision restricted conditions require Soldiers to acquire situational awareness through thick transparent armor and video display screens allowing maneuver over and around unknown terrain day and night. Sequencing actions and timing can be critical during weapon system engagements, loading of ammunition, turret movements, and maneuvering the vehicle in combat. Not effective as a combat vehicle when fighting against enemy light armored or armored threat.

Protection Advantages

E-59. Designed from the ground-up to reduce casualties and increase crew and passenger survivability from mine explosions, IED detonations, and small-arms fire. Armored vehicles with blast-resistant body design (characterized by a V-shaped hull, integrated armor, raised chassis, and blow-off wheels). Blast forces are deflected away from the crew by the vehicles V-shaped hull. Equipped with automatic fire suppression system run-flat tires and antilock brakes. Equipped with blast-resistant suspension type seats, and ballistic windshield and windows.

Protection Disadvantages

E-60. While the MRAP vehicle provides a more stable firing platform than the HMMWV, it also significantly limits the gunner's field of fire (limited turret traversing due to antennas and limited capability to fully depress). There is significant dead space to the front, rear, and sides of the vehicle. Every MRAP vehicle crewmember should know the dead space their specific vehicle, which will assist in covering the dead space for other vehicles while on the move. This is especially important in an RKG-3 (anti-tank hand grenades) threat area.

E-61. While the MRAP vehicle appears large, the armor protection and V-shaped hull significantly reduce the interior space. When fully loaded with Soldiers and their combat gear, little space is left for additional mission equipment not directly designed into the vehicle.

E-62. Exiting the vehicle in response to an ambush and loading or unloading equipment and casualties are difficult due to the doors, steps, and back hatch on some MRAP variants. Soldiers and units must train and rehearse as individuals and teams to streamline the process for mounting and dismounting operations under various conditions. Experience has shown the heavy doors and hatches are causing serious injuries to Soldiers' fingers (amputation), elbows (shattering), ankles (sprains and breaks), and backs due to pinching in doors and hatches and from falling off vehicles.

Information Advantages

E-63. Includes accessories such as the, driver vision enhancer, AN/VRC 92 dual long-range radio system, Mission Command Systems, and CROWS II XM153.

Information Disadvantages

E-64. Due the different types of communication systems and accessories in the MRAP, Soldiers might not be familiar with the equipment, which will cause lack of usage. Leaders must consider how dismounted Soldiers will communicate with the mounted crew and other dismounted Soldiers. Communication with Mission Command Systems can be hampered in an urban area or even jammed by enemy forces. Antennas on the MRAP vehicle must be lowered or protected from contact with power lines since serious injury or death, as well as vehicle damage can occur. Know which antennas present the most hazards due to radio frequency burns, and keep out of the danger areas when transmitting.

SIZE AND WEIGHT CONSIDERATIONS

E-65. Infantry leaders must consider the size and weight of combat vehicles operating in units before conducting an operation. (See table E-1, page E-4.) Terrain supporting the movement of Infantry Soldiers may or may not support the movement of combat vehicles. Structures of particular concern are bridges, overpasses, and culverts. Structural failure could be deadly to the Soldiers in the vicinity. Many bridges in North America and Europe are marked with signs stating the load bearing capabilities of that structure. In other areas, Infantry Soldiers should rely on route reconnaissance overlays showing the carrying capabilities of the routes being used. In the absence of such information, Infantry leaders always should use the cautious approach and avoid suspect infrastructure.

SURFACE DANGER AREAS

E-66. Infantry leaders must consider the surface danger zones of combat vehicle weapon systems operating within their units. This information is crucial for leaders to develop safe direct fire control plans. Application of surface danger zones prevents fratricide and maximizes direct fire upon the enemy.

E-67. Each weapon system has a unique surface danger zone. Surface danger zones are the MSD and angles considered when operating in close proximity to weapon systems. Surface danger zones take into consideration a round's maximum distance, lateral dispersion, and back blast (if applicable). This information allows leaders to plan for safe and effective maneuver of forces.

Appendix E

TACTICAL CAPABILITIES

E-68. Infantry units may have combat vehicle sections attached for combat operations.

COMBAT VEHICLE TASKS

E-69. Table E-3 shows a list of tasks combat vehicle sections may perform while attached or under the operational control of Infantry units.

Table E-3. Tasks of combat vehicles in Infantry operations

INFANTRY OPERATIONS	COMBAT VEHICLE TASKS
Movement to Contact	Support by fire; attack by fire; assault; breach; follow and support; reserve; route clearance; convoy escort; checkpoint/roadblock operations.
Attack	Support by fire; attack by fire; assault; breach; isolate; isolation force; security force.
Site Exploitation	Serve as security force (screen); lead the site exploitation (assault or attack by fire).
Pursuit	Serve as enveloping force, reserve (attack by fire or assault), or security force (screen); lead direct pressure force (support by fire, attack by fire, or assault).
Security (Screen, Guard, Cover)	Screen; guard; defend; delay; attack by fire; assault.
Defend	Screen; guard; defend; delay; attack by fire (counterattack); assault (counterattack).
Retrograde (Delay, Withdraw, Retire)	Defend; delay; screen; guard; attack by fire (counterattack); withdraw.
Break out from Encirclement	Serve as rupture force (assault or attack by fire) or rear guard (delay).

INFANTRY TASKS

E-70. Infantry units may be attached to armored units during combat operations. Table E-4 shows a list of tasks Infantry units may perform while attached or under the operational control of combat vehicular units.

Table E-4. Tasks of the Infantry in combat vehicle operations

COMBAT VEHICLE OPERATIONS	INFANTRY TASKS
Attack by Fire	Secure an attack by fire position (reconnoiter an area or attack); provide local security or act as the blocking force (defend).
Support by Fire	Secure a support-by-fire position (reconnoiter an area or attack); provide local security; conduct overwatch/support by fire.
Bypass	Serve as the fixing force (defend); perform linkup with follow-on forces.
Assault	Attack; assault; breach; overwatch/support by fire; knock out a bunker; clear a trench line; clear a building.
Clearance in Restricted Terrain	Attack; assault; overwatch/support by fire; knock out a bunker; clear a trench line; clear a building; breach, clear AT teams.
Defend	Defend; defend in urban operations/building; construct an obstacle.
Screen/guard	Perform surveillance or screen.
Breach	Breach; overwatch/support by fire; assault.
Hasty Water/Gap Crossing	Cross water obstacles; assault; overwatch/support by fire.
Delay	Delay; break contact.
Withdrawal	Break contact; serve as advance party (AA procedures).

E-71. Leaders of combat vehicle units often fail to recognize the speed with which the Infantry can move when operating dismounted. Numerous factors can affect the rate of march the Infantry forces including, tactical considerations, weather, terrain, march discipline, acclimatization, availability of water and rations, morale, and individual loads. Table E-5 summarizes dismounted rates of march for normal terrain. The normal distance covered by an Infantry force in a 24-hour period is from 20 to 32 kilometers, marching from five to eight hours at a rate of 4 kilometers per hour (kph). A march in excess of 32 kilometers in 24 hours is considered a forced march. Forced marches increase the number of hours marched, not the rate of march. Absolute maximum distances for dismounted marches are 56 kilometers in 24 hours, 96 kilometers in 48 hours, or 128 kilometers in 72 hours.

Table E-5. Dismounted rates of march (ideal terrain)

TIME	ROADS	CROSS-COUNTRY
Day	4.0 kph	2.4 kph
Night	3.2 kph	1.6 kph

Appendix E

CARRYING CAPACITIES OF COMBAT VEHICLES

E-72. There may be times when combat vehicles and Infantry Soldiers must move quickly from one place to another to accomplish their mission. In such cases, and depending on the enemy threat and level of training, Infantry Soldiers should ride in or on combat vehicles.

E-73. Riding on the outside of the vehicles is hazardous. Therefore, Infantry Soldiers should ride only on vehicles when the need for speed is great. By riding on, not in, vehicles, the Infantry gives up its best protection, the ability to move with stealth and avoid detection. Infantry Soldiers riding on the outside of armored vehicles are vulnerable to all types of fire. Also, Infantry Soldiers must watch out for obstacles causing tanks to turn suddenly; tree limbs that may knock them off; and the traversing of the turret gun, which could knock them off as well.

E-74. The only advantages Infantry Soldiers gain from riding in or on combat vehicles are speed of movement and increased haul capability. In this case, the following apply:
- Avoid riding on the lead vehicle of a section or platoon. These vehicles are most likely to make contact and can react quicker without Infantry Soldiers on top.
- Position the Infantry leaders with the combat vehicle leaders. Discuss and prepare contingency plans for chance contact or danger areas. Infantry Soldiers should dismount and clear choke points or other danger areas.
- Assign air guards and sectors of responsibility for observation. Ensure all personnel remain alert and stay prepared to dismount immediately. In the event of contact, the armored vehicle will react immediately as required for its own protection. The Infantry on top are responsible of their own safety. Rehearse a rapid dismount of the vehicle.
- Consider putting rucksacks, ammunition, and other equipment on vehicles, and have Infantry Soldiers move on a separate avenue of approach. This can increase Infantry Soldiers mobility by allowing them to move through more suitable terrain.

Tanks

E-75. Riding on tanks reduces tank maneuverability and may restrict firepower. Infantry Soldiers may be injured if the tank slews its turret to return fire on a target. Consequently, Soldiers must dismount to clear danger areas or as soon as enemy contact is made.

E-76. Soldiers ride on tanks by exception and depending on the likelihood of contact. There are several tactical and safety considerations before Infantry Soldiers ride on a tank. The M1-series Abrams tank is not designed to carry riders easily. Riders must not move to the rear deck. Engine operating temperatures make this area unsafe for riders. (See figure E-4.)

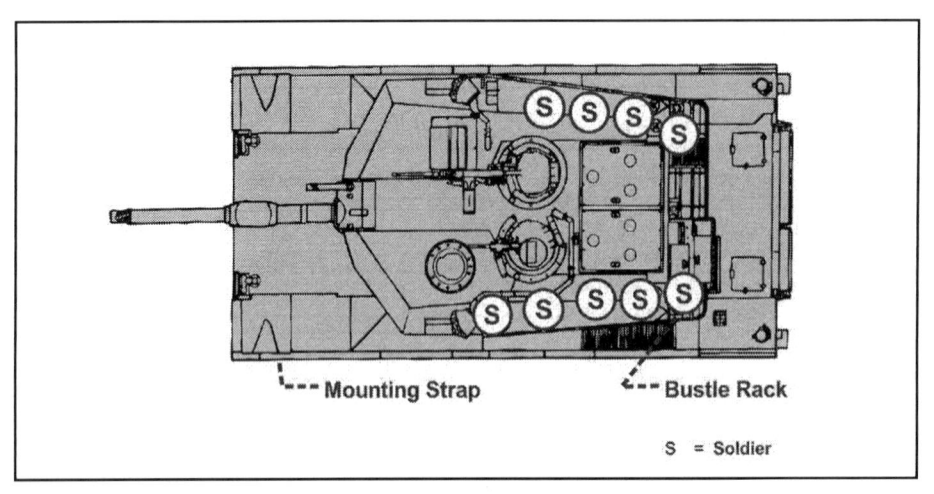

Figure E-4. Mounting and riding arrangements on the outside of an M1-series Abrams tank

> *Note.* If at all possible due to the danger of riding on an M1-series Abrams tank, it should be considered a last resort.

E-77. One Infantry squad can ride on the turret. Soldiers must mount in such a way their legs cannot become entangled between the turret and hull by an unexpected turret movement. Rope may be used as a field-expedient rail to provide secure handholds.

E-78. Everyone must ride to the rear of the smoke grenade launchers. This automatically keeps everyone clear of the coaxial machine gun and laser range finder.

E-79. Infantry Soldiers always must be prepared for sudden turret movement. Leaders should caution Soldiers about sitting on the turret blowout panels. This safety knowledge is critical because 250 pounds of pressure will prevent the panels from working properly. If there is an explosion in the ammunition rack, the panels blow outward to lessen the blast effect in the crew compartment.

E-80. If enemy contact is made, the tank should stop in a covered and concealed position and allow Infantry Soldiers time to dismount and move away from the tank. This action needs to be practiced before movement.

E-81. Infantry Soldiers should not ride with anything more than their battle gear. Personal gear should be transported elsewhere.

Bradley Fighting Vehicle

E-82. The BFV is designed to carry six Infantry Soldiers and a crew of three: a Bradley commander, gunner, and driver. The troop compartment of the BFV carries six Infantry Soldiers in combat gear. Rucksacks generally are carried on the outside of the vehicle. Prior to riding in the vehicle, Infantry Soldiers who are not familiar with the BFV should be thoroughly trained on its exit points, fire drills, and rollover drills. The major difference

Appendix E

in carrying capacity between the M2A1 and M2A2/ODS/M2A3 is the seating configuration. The M2A1 has six individual seats, while the M2A2/ODS/M2A3 has two benches on the left and right sides of the troop compartment. Figures E-5 and E-6 illustrate the carrying capacity of the BFV-series combat vehicles.

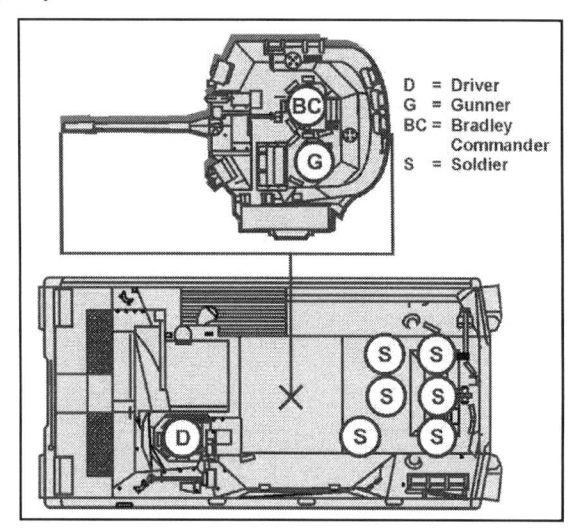

Figure E-5. Seating diagram inside the M2A1 BFV

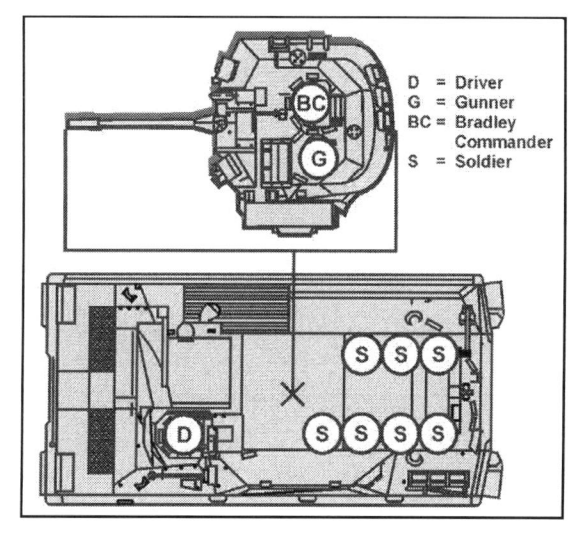

Figure E-6. Seating diagram inside the M2A2/ODS and M2A3 BFV

Infantry Carrier Vehicle

E-83. The Stryker ICV is designed to carry a nine-man Infantry squad in combat gear, a driver, and a vehicle commander. Rucksacks generally are carried on the outside of the

ICV. Infantry Soldiers who are not familiar with the ICV should be trained thoroughly on its exit points, fire drills, and rollover drills prior to riding in the vehicle. Figure E-7 illustrates the carrying capacity of the ICV.

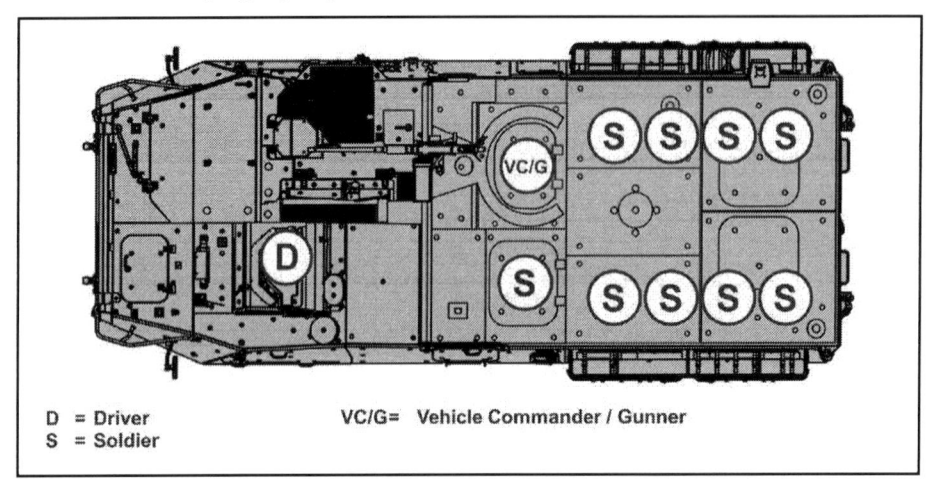

Figure E-7. Seating diagram inside the ICV

Armament Carrier HMMWV

E-84. The armament carrier HMMWV class of vehicles is designed to carry five Soldiers in combat gear, a truck commander, a gunner, a driver, and two Soldiers in the rear passenger seats. Rucksacks generally are carried on the outside or in the rear cargo storage area. Infantry Soldiers who are not familiar with the armament carrier HMMWV should be trained thoroughly on its exit points, fire drills, and rollover drills prior to riding in the vehicle. Figure E-8 illustrates the carrying capacity of the armament carrier HMMWV.

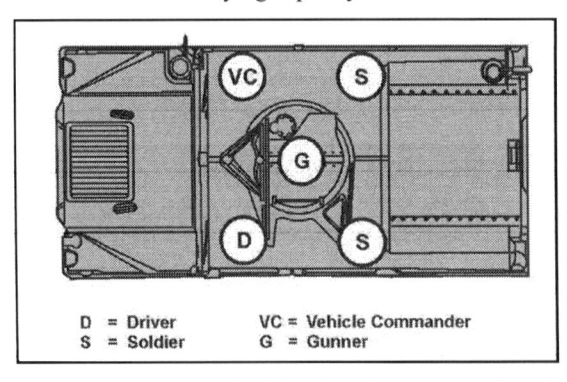

Figure E-8. Seating diagram inside the Armament Carrier HMMWV

Appendix E

Mine Resistant Ambush Protected (CAT) I

E-85. The seating capacity of the MRAP all-terrain vehicle (M-ATV) is five passengers, including the gunner. The seating capacity of the MaxxPro vehicle is seven passengers. (See figure E-9.)

Note. If MRAP is equipped with M153 CROWS, its troop-carrying capacity is reduced by one because the gunner is no longer occupying the objective gunners' protective kit and the CROWS gunner is in a seat normally used for a passenger.

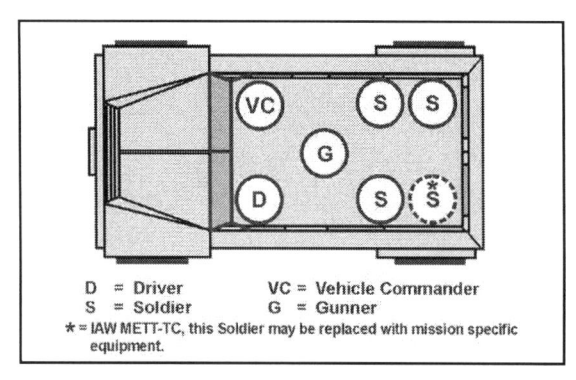

Figure E-9. Seating diagram inside the MRAP MaxxPro Dash

SECTION II – OPERATIONS

E-86. The intent of this section is to familiarize leaders conducting operations with combat vehicles. METT-TC and commander's intent always must be taken into consideration when executing these types of operations.

PLAN

E-87. Employment of combat vehicles requires thorough understanding and integration of the vehicle with the Infantry unit. The following paragraphs focus on planning considerations for combat vehicles and dismounted Infantry integration.

TASK ORGANIZATION OPTIONS

E-88. A combat vehicle platoon or section normally would be operational control to an Infantry company during combined arms operations at the company level. However, in the combat operation, Infantry platoons and squads may receive combat vehicle platoons or sections to conduct operations. There are four basic techniques of task-organizing the combat vehicle section into the Infantry company for combat operations: combat vehicle platoon as a maneuver element; combat vehicle sections under Infantry control; combat vehicle sections under company and platoon control; and Infantry squads under combat vehicle control. This concept holds true for all combat vehicle units.

Combat Vehicle Platoon as a Maneuver Element

E-89. The combat vehicle platoon leader is responsible for maneuvering the vehicles in accordance with the company commander's intent. Likely missions for combat vehicles with this task organization are support by fire, or overwatch of the Infantry's movement. The combat vehicle platoon leader can choose to maneuver the platoon by sections to execute the mission. This maneuver provides greater flexibility in supporting the Infantry during the close fight.

Combat Vehicle Sections Under Infantry Platoon Control

E-90. Combat vehicles are broken down into two sections. Each section is placed under the operational control of an Infantry platoon and maneuvered according to the company commander's intent. The commander relinquishes direct control of the combat vehicle maneuver to his subordinates. This technique is effective in maintaining the same rate of progress between the combat vehicles and Infantry Soldiers. Leaders have the additional responsibility of maneuvering combat vehicles. The general lack of experience with combat vehicles and overall battlefield focus of the leaders can affect this technique. This technique is best suited for when contact with the enemy is expected and close continuous support is required for movement or clearing buildings.

Combat Vehicle Sections Under Company and Platoon Control

E-91. Combat vehicle platoons can be broken down into two sections: one under company control and the other under platoon control. The selected maneuver Infantry platoon or squad would have a combat vehicle section available to support the close fight. With this technique, the company commander has a combat vehicle section to deploy. This task organization still allows support to the Infantry close fight while keeping additional support options in reserve for the commander to employ. The disadvantages to this technique are Infantry platoon leader instead of the combat vehicle platoon leaders are maneuvering vehicles, and the number of vehicles directly available to the company commander is cut in half. This technique requires detailed planning, coordination, and rehearsals between Infantry and combat vehicle sections.

Infantry Squads Under Combat Vehicle Platoon Control

E-92. The company commander has the option of placing one or more Infantry squads under the operational control of the combat vehicle platoon leader. He also may retain all combat vehicles under the control of the combat vehicle platoon leader, or place a combat vehicle section under the operational control of an Infantry platoon leader. This provides the company commander with a fourth maneuver platoon. It also involves the combat vehicle platoon leader in the fight. It can work well when a mobile reserve needs Infantry protection is required.

Appendix E

Guidelines

E-93. None of the techniques described are inherently better than another one. The task organization must be tailored to accomplish the mission. Regardless of the technique selected, the following guidelines should be followed.

E-94. It is preferable for combat vehicles to operate as sections. This is an integral component of how combat vehicle units train and fight. If the company commander is controlling the combat vehicles, he needs to move forward to a position where he can maneuver the combat vehicles in support of the Infantry.

E-95. Combat vehicles should be used to shield squads and teams (minus the unarmored versions of the armament carrier HMMWV) from building to building. As part of the maneuver plan, the leader of the forward element controls the combat vehicles.

E-96. The task organization should support the span of control. If the company commander is going to control the combat vehicles, there is no reason to task organize the tanks by section under Infantry platoons.

E-97. Combat vehicles need Infantry support when the two elements are working together. Do not leave combat vehicles alone because they are not well-suited to provide local security during the operation. Combat vehicles are extremely vulnerable to dismounted attack when operating in urban terrain. They are most vulnerable and need local security when Infantry Soldiers are in the process of clearing buildings.

RISK MANAGEMENT

E-98. Infantry leaders must identify and implement controls to mitigate risks associated with conducting operations with combat vehicles. These risks are divided into two categories: tactical and accidental risk. Table E-6 contains a basic list of risks and control measures leaders should consider when conducting operations with combat vehicles. Table E-7 (page E-30) contains a list of possible accidental hazards and control measures.

Table E-6. Risk management matrix for tactical hazards

TACTICAL HAZARDS	CONTROL MEASURES
Enemy Direct Fire	Wear IBA, reinforce vehicle (sand bags), use proper scanning techniques, and engage in marksmanship training.
Enemy Indirect Fire	Practice mounted react to indirect fire drills, vary speed and distance to avoid a trigger from an enemy indirect fire system.
Mines	Maintain situational awareness, maintain current obstacle overlay for area of operation, remain on cleared areas, and be proficient in minefield extraction.
IEDs	Scan, Use Counter-IED measures. Duke, Rhino, Mine rollers, use up-armor, and avoid predictability.
Sniper Attacks	Scan, maintain situational awareness, avoid predictability, use driver techniques, and engage in tactical movement training.
Media Exploitation	Train leaders, refer to public affairs officer, adhere to the ROE, Soldier's Creed, Law of War, and the Geneva Conventions.
VBIED	Gunner and Infantry Soldiers riding on vehicles use proper scanning techniques, maintain situational awareness, avoid predictability, use driver techniques, and engage in tactical movement training.
Ambush	Scan, maintain situational awareness, avoid predictability, use driver techniques, and engage in tactical movement training.
Sniper Attacks	Scan, maintain situational awareness, avoid predictability, use driver techniques, and engage in tactical movement training.
LEGEND IBA – individual body armor; IED – improvised explosive device; ROE – rules of engagement	

Appendix E

Table E-7. Risk management matrix for accidental hazards

ACCIDENTAL HAZARDS	CONTROL MEASURES
Vehicle Collision	Ensure driver is qualified and the truck commander is alert.
Vehicle Fire	Conduct fire drills, keep fire extinguishers present and serviceable, perform proper PMCS.
Vehicle Rollover	Stop, provide security, evaluate, attend, determine if medical evacuation is needed, and report to higher, Secure loads.
Vehicle Striking Dismount	Ensure driver/truck commander/dismount situational awareness, train and rehearse with vehicles, and know SOPs for communication between vehicle and dismounts.
Vehicle Malfunction	Perform proper PMCS, ensure BDR kit is available.
Hearing Damage	Train on high-decibel danger zones and wear hearing protection.
Eye Damage	Verify eye protection during PCI and leaders enforce it during execution.
Burns	Be aware of TOW backblast and high-heat exhaust zones, and wear gloves when riding or operating equipment and weapons (changing barrels).
Falling From Moving Vehicle	Have proper load plan, use tie downs with snap links (M1-series Abrams tank turret), wear seat belts (HMMWV, LMTV, 5-Ton), and ensure driver is qualified.
Drowning After Water Entry	Train on vehicle exits and ensure Soldiers have passed the Combat Water Survival Test.
Fratricide by Weapon Systems of Vehicle	Use day/night friendly recognition systems and proper fire control measures.
Disorientation	Ensure map is present, truck commander is briefed, and graphics are current, if equipped with latest Mission Command Systems.

LEGEND
BDR – battle damage repair ; HMMWV – high-mobility multipurpose wheeled vehicle; LMTV – light medium tactical vehicle ; PCI – precombat inspection; PMCS – preventive maintenance checks and services ; SOP – standard operating procedure; TOW – tube-launched, optically tracked, wire-guided

E-99. Many Infantry Soldiers are not familiar with the hazards arising during operations with combat vehicles. The most obvious of these include the dangers associated with main-gun fire, and inability of combat vehicle crews to see people and objects near their vehicles. Leaders of Armored and Infantry units alike must ensure their troops understand the following points of operational safety.

Discarding Sabot

E-100. Tank 120-mm sabot rounds and 25-mm BFV rounds discard stabilizing petals when fired, posing a downrange hazard for Infantry Soldiers. The aluminum petals of the tank rounds are discarded in an area extending 300 meters to the left and right of the gun-target line out to a range of 1300 meters. (See figure E-10.) Sabot petals create a hazard area extending 70 meters on each side of the gun target line, out to a range of 1 kilometer (See figure E-11, page E-32.) The danger zone for plastic debris from BFV rounds extends 60 degrees to the left and right of the gun-target line, and out to 100 meters from the vehicle. (See figure E-12, page E-33.) Infantry Soldiers should not be in or near the direct line of fire of the tank main gun or BFV cannon unless they are under adequate overhead cover.

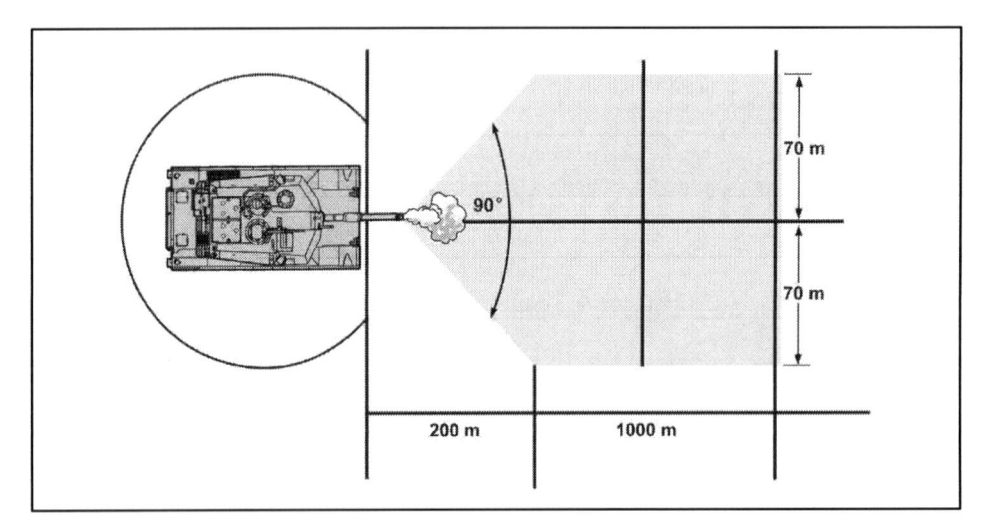

Figure E-10. M1-series Abrams tank danger zone

Appendix E

SABOT, HEAT, HEP, or canister rounds will not be fired over friendly troops, unless troops are provided proper protection.

Troops could be struck by discarding sabot petals, or fragments of the projectile body of HE rounds. Failure of the full frontal impact switch may cause premature detonation of a HEAT M456A2 round.

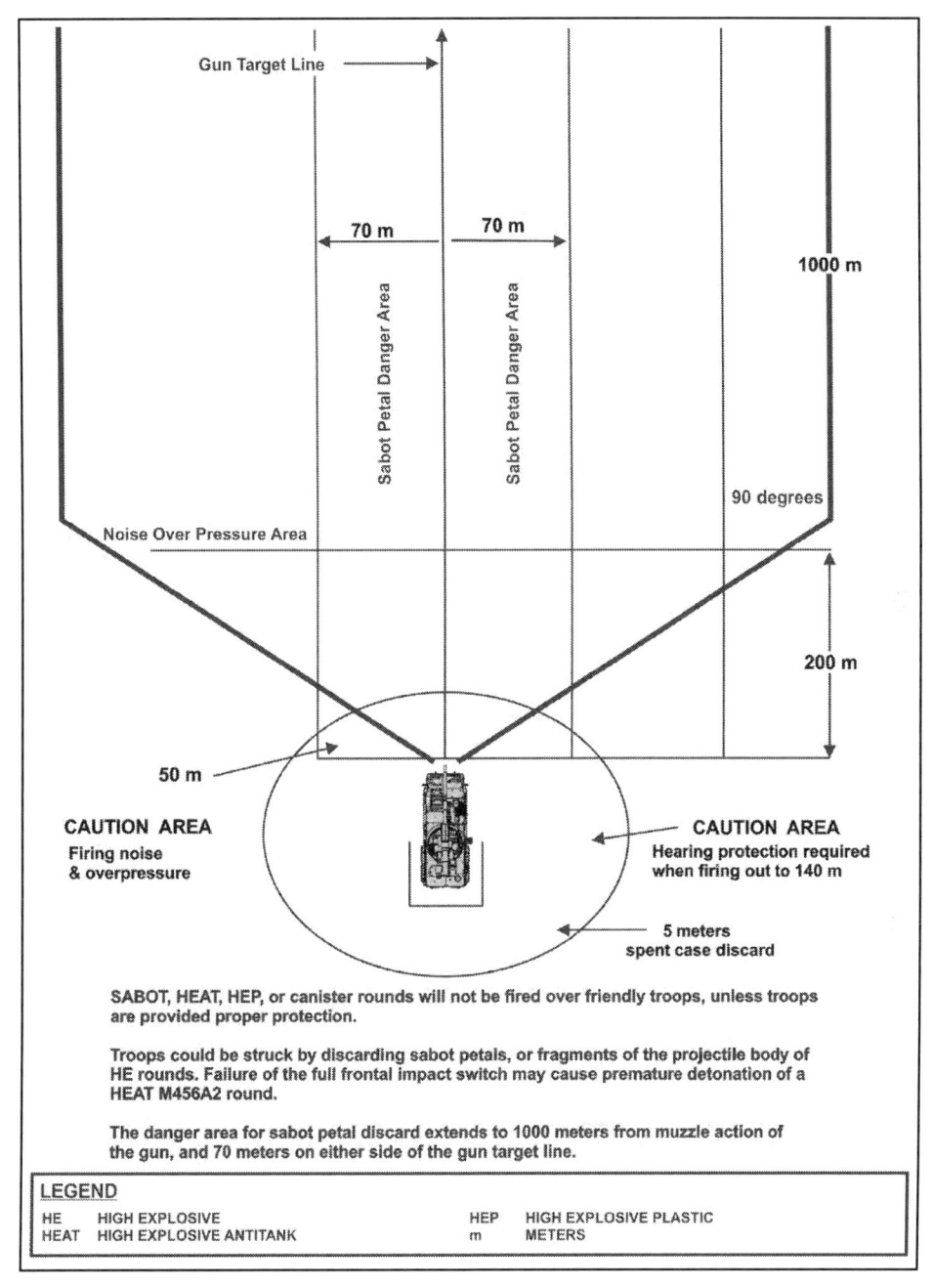

The danger area for sabot petal discard extends to 1000 meters from muzzle action of the gun, and 70 meters on either side of the gun target line.

LEGEND
HE   HIGH EXPLOSIVE   HEP   HIGH EXPLOSIVE PLASTIC
HEAT HIGH EXPLOSIVE ANTITANK   m   METERS

Figure E-11. MGS danger zone

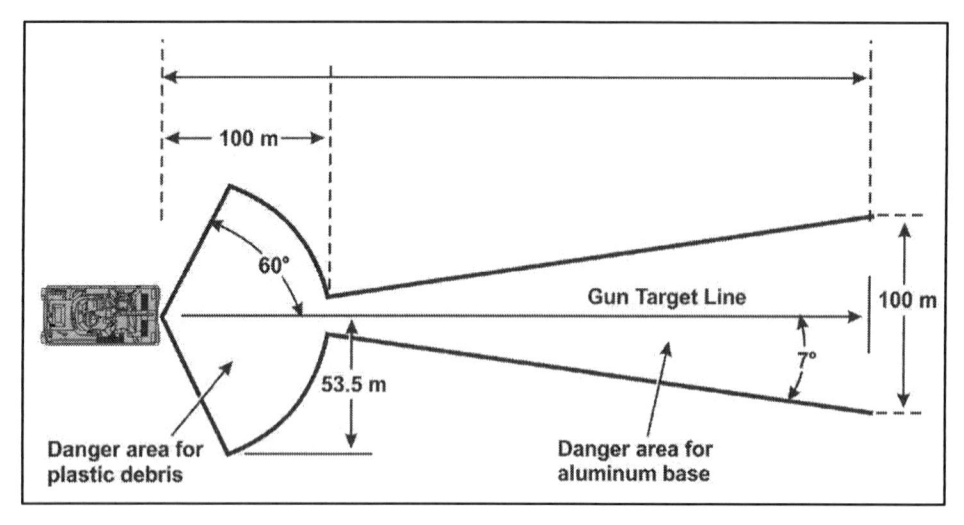

Figure E-12. BFV danger zone

Ground Movement Hazards

E-101. Crewmembers on combat vehicles have limited abilities to see anyone on the ground to the side or rear of the vehicle. As a result, vehicle crews and dismounted Infantry Soldiers share responsibility for avoiding the hazards this may create. Infantry Soldiers must maintain a safe distance from heavy vehicles at all times. In addition, when they work close to heavy vehicles, Infantry Soldiers must ensure the vehicle commander knows their location at all times, by establishing communication.

> *Note.* M1-series Abrams tanks are deceptively quiet and may be difficult for mounted Infantry Soldiers to hear as they approach. As noted, vehicle crews and Infantry Soldiers share the responsibility of eliminating potential dangers in this situation.

M1-Series Abrams Tank Exhaust Plume Hazard

E-102. M1-series Abrams tanks have an extremely hot exhaust plume exiting from the rear of the tank and angles downward. This exhaust is hot enough to burn skin and clothing. Infantry Soldiers should avoid the rear exhaust of the M1-series Abrams tank.

TOW Missile System

E-103. The TOW missile system can be employed on the BFV, the armament carrier HMMWV, and ICV. The system has a dangerous area extending 75 meters to the rear of the vehicle in a 90-degree "cone." The area is divided into a 50-meter danger zone and a 25-meter caution zone. (See figure E-13, page E-34.) In the 50-meter zone, serious casualties or fatalities are likely to occur from the blast and flying debris. Soldiers are safe in the 25-meter zone, provided they do not face the aft end of the launcher.

Appendix E

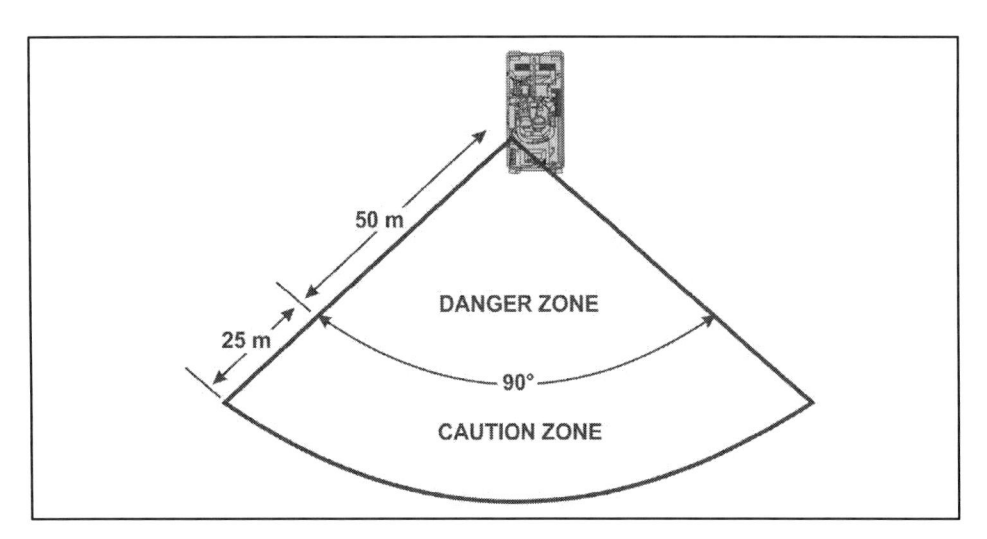

Figure E-13. BFV TOW backblast danger zone

PREPARE

E-104. The key to planning operations with combat vehicles is rehearsals that gain the trust and confidence of vehicle crews and Infantry Soldiers. Appendix A, section II of this publication describes rehearsal techniques. (Refer to FM 6-0 for more information regarding rehearsals.)

EXCHANGE INFORMATION

E-105. Task organizations of units are likely to change during combat operations. When this occurs, some basic exchange information must occur to ensure success. First, an area must be chosen providing security for the exchange to take place. The METT-TC may dictate the exchange must occur over radio or digital communications. However, when possible, leaders should meet and speak face-to-face. General exchange information includes:

- Number of personnel in the unit.
- Number of vehicles in the unit.
- Sensitive items list.
- Weapons capabilities.
- Logistical capability (particularly Class I, III, and V).
- Status/problems with logistics.
- Radio frequencies, call signs, and time hack.
- Graphics and overlays.
- Soldier uniform types.
- Day/night marking systems.
- Enemy situation updates.

Vehicle Employment Considerations

- Terrain/route information.

PRECOMBAT CHECKS AND INSPECTIONS

E-106. Infantry leaders may not always be proficient with the combat vehicles attached to their units for combat operations. Nevertheless, leaders still are responsible for ensuring combat vehicles and Soldiers in their unit are prepared to begin combat operations. Table E-8 contains a generic pre-execution checklist leaders can use to ensure combat vehicles in their unit are prepared for combat operations.

Table E-8. Vehicle pre-execution checklist

	VEHICLE PRE-EXECUTION CHECKLIST
Vehicle Preparations	<ul><li>Configured according to the secure load plan (personnel and equipment).</li><li>Vehicle refueled.</li><li>Water cans full, Class I stowed.</li><li>Equipment cleaned and stowed.</li><li>First-aid kit/combat-lifesaver bag complete and stowed.</li><li>Eye protection (sun, wind, dust goggles) stowed for exposed Soldiers.</li><li>Fire extinguisher secured and serviceable.</li><li>Slave cable secured and operational (at least one for each vehicle type).</li><li>One tow bar or recovery strap stowed for every two like-vehicle types.</li><li>Vehicle dispatched, technical manual present, vehicle tool kit stowed.</li><li>Basic load of ammunition stowed.</li><li>Rollover drill (water & land) complete.</li><li>Casualty evacuation drill complete.</li><li>Fire escape drill complete.</li><li>A basic Class IV load stowed (concertina wire, sandbags, and pickets).</li><li>Battle damage repair kit (BDR) stowed.</li><li>Map of area of operation with current graphic control measures stowed.</li></ul>

Table E-8. Vehicle pre-execution checklist (continued)

VEHICLE PRE-EXECUTION CHECKLIST	
Communication Equipment	• Radios operational, mounted, and secured; connections and receptacles cleaned and frequencies set. • Internal communication operational. • Extra hand microphones stowed. • Dismount kit for radios stowed. • Mission Command Systems and inertial navigational system are operational, loaded with current graphics (if applicable), and communicating with other digital systems. • Frequency modulation, integrated communications and communication checks are complete with higher, adjacent units, and subordinate units. • Vehicles' internal communication is operational. • Antennas present and operational, connections clean. • Communication security, automated net control device equipment operational. • Telephones operational and stowed. • OE-254 complete, operational, and stowed. • All required nets entered and monitored.
CBRN	• M100 Sorbent Decontamination System (SDS) mounted. • Automatic chemical, biological, radiological and nuclear alarm operational and mounted. • M256A1 kits stowed.
Optics	• Night-vision devices and binoculars cleaned, operational, and stowed for driver/truck commander/gunner (night vision goggles [NVGs]) and driver's night vision block (VVS2 for Bradley fighting vehicle). • Weapons' optics operational, zeroed, clean, with extra batteries (if needed).
Maintenance	• Preventive maintenance checks (-10) and services conducted on all equipment. • DA Form 2404 completed on all equipment.
Firepower	• Weapons' mounts and turrets are operational and move freely. • Boresight complete (if needed). • All weapons cleaned and test-fired.

Vehicle Employment Considerations

SECURITY

E-107. Security must be maintained at all times during combat operations. Combat vehicles and Infantry Soldiers provide complementary effects to one another with respect to security.

Combat Vehicles Securing Infantry

E-108. Combat vehicles can provide security to Infantry Soldiers in many ways. In patrol bases and AA, combat vehicles can use their weapon systems and night vision/thermal sights to provide early detection and a high volume of fire. During movement, combat vehicles can move to the front, rear, or flanks of the Infantry to provide protection from direct fire (tank, BFV, ICV, and M1114 armament carrier HMMWV) and antipersonnel mines. They also can use their sights and weapon systems to detect and engage the enemy. On the objective, combat vehicles can dominate the terrain, provide security, and defeat a counterattack while the Infantry Soldiers conduct actions on the objective.

Infantry Securing Combat Vehicles

E-109. Infantry Soldiers can provide security to combat vehicles throughout an operation. In patrol bases and AA, Infantry Soldiers can secure the perimeter while combat vehicles conduct maintenance. During movement, Infantry Soldiers can move to the front, rear, and flanks of combat vehicles to decrease close-in (such as RKG-3, handheld HEAT) antiarmor threats and detect antitank mines. Infantry Soldiers also clear defiles and other terrain restricting the movement of combat vehicles. On the objective, Infantry Soldiers can clear buildings, trenches, and bunkers while conducting EPW searches.

SUSTAINMENT

E-110. Infantry leaders should be aware of the robust logistical requirements of combat vehicles during combat operations. Normally, the leaders of attached vehicular units are responsible for bringing the majority of their logistical needs with them due to the austere and different logistical support system of Infantry units. Table E-9 (page E-38) provides leaders an overview of some logistical planning factors for combat operations.

Table E-9. Classes of supply considerations for combat vehicles

Class I	Class I food requirements are determined based on the vehicular unit's personnel strength reports. This process may be complicated by unique mission requirements imposed on the team. This could include rapid changes in task organization or dispersion of subordinate team elements over a wide area.
Class II	Many Class II items required by tank and BFV crews such as specialized tools and flame retardant clothing may be difficult to obtain in an Infantry organization. These items usually will come with the combat vehicles and should be checked by Infantry leaders.
Class III	The fuel and other POL products required by vehicular units are extremely bulky, so they present the greatest sustainment challenges in planning and preparing for armored and Infantry operations. Transportation support must be planned carefully. Planners must consider the placement of fuel heavy expanded mobility tactical trucks (HEMTTs) during all phases of the operation. Also, leaders must know their locations and resupply plan. They must focus on general-use POL products such as lubricants not ordinarily used by Infantry organizations. Vehicular units should stock their basic load of these items and make necessary resupply arrangements before attachment to the Infantry unit.
Class IV	Vehicular units do not have unique requirements for barrier or fortification materiel. The main consideration is Class IV materiel the vehicle commanders want may need loading and transport prior to attachment. Infantry leaders should be aware of the increased load capacity of combat vehicles and plan to utilize this asset to carry larger volumes of Class IV items such as sandbags, concertina wire, and pickets.
Class V	Along with POL products, ammunition for vehicular units presents the greatest transportation challenge in operations. Class V requirements may include TOW missiles, 120-mm main gun rounds, 25-mm rounds, 40-mm MK19 rounds, .50-cal rounds, 7.62-mm link, 5.56-mm loose, and smoke grenades for smoke grenade launchers. Planning for Class V resupply should parallel Class III. Key considerations include anticipated mission requirements, and availability of HEMTTs. Ammunition may be prestocked based on expected consumption rates.
Class VI	Vehicular unit operations create no unique requirements for personal demand items and sundries.

Table E-9. Classes of supply considerations for combat vehicles (continued)

Class VII	Class VII consists of major end items. This includes entire vehicles such as a "float" tanks or BFV units require as replacements for organic vehicles. The handling of these items requires thorough planning to determine transportation requirements and positioning in the scheme of the operation. Class VII items include smaller, but mission-essential items such as the boresight telescope of the BFV.
Class VIII	Vehicular units involved in operations have no unique requirements for medical supplies. However, vehicular units may be capable of carrying more Class VIII supplies and provide standard/nonstandard casualty evacuation for combat operations.
Class IX	Class IX products (repair parts) are crucial to the sustainment of combat vehicles attached to Infantry units. Repair parts are essential during combat operations. Requirements for items on the team's parts load list and ASL must be considered carefully before operations begin. The vehicular unit may find it advantageous to prestock selected items in anticipation of its operational needs.

E-111. Combat vehicle sections attached to Infantry units also may receive resupply through a LOGPAC (logistical resupply) from their parent unit. These LOGPACs generally occur in the tailgate or service station method.

E-112. As directed by the commander or executive officer, the first sergeant establishes the companies resupply point. He uses either the service station or tailgate method, and briefs each LOGPAC driver on which method to use. When he has the resupply point ready, the first sergeant informs the commander. The company commander then directs each unit or element to conduct resupply based on the tactical situation. (See chapter 7 of this publication for more information.)

MAINTAINANCE AND RECOVERY

E-113. Recovery operations and maintenance are crucial components of the leader's plan when working with combat vehicles.

MAINTENANCE

E-114. Leaders must plan for regular maintenance halts throughout extended operations. Combat vehicles require regular maintenance to perform consistently throughout combat operations. Combat vehicles can become non mission capable due to a number of variables including, direct and indirect enemy fire, mines and IEDs, vehicle accidents, and parts failure. Infantry leaders should enforce regular PMCS of all combat vehicles attached to their unit. PMCS is operator-level maintenance conducted before, during, and after equipment operations. Comprehensive PMCS identifies actual and potential problems and ensures repairs are made in a timely manner to minimize vehicle downtime. Early detection and correction of these faults can decrease the possibility of the combat vehicle breaking down during combat operations and prevent minor faults from deteriorating into

Appendix E

major faults. It is the vehicle crew's responsibility to conduct PMCS. It is the leader's job to ensure the PMCS is conducted regularly and to standard.

E-115. Leaders should plan vehicle security of the vehicle crews as they conduct PMCS, based on the enemy situation. Additionally, leaders should establish a maintenance rotation to ensure all their combat vehicles are not conducting maintenance at the same time. This will maximize the combat power of the unit. Leaders should also—

- Verify all current and updated technical manuals and references are available or requisitioned for unit assigned equipment.
- Verify all tools, POL, personnel, and other resources are available for PMCS.
- Observe operators performing PMCS at prescribed intervals.
- Review maintenance forms and reporting procedures for accuracy and completeness.
- Verify operators have correctly identified and corrected, or recorded, faults on DA Form 2404. (See figure E-14.)
- Confirm non mission capable faults are corrected before dispatch.

Vehicle Employment Considerations

Figure E-14. DA Form 2404 front page

E-116. Leaders also should plan the possibility of combat vehicles requiring maintenance at a level greater than the crew is equipped or trained to conduct. This often requires specially trained mechanics and equipment organic to the parent unit of the combat vehicle

Appendix E

attachment. Leaders should plan for two possibilities. One, the maintenance team moves to the combat vehicles. This may require additional security and or escorts from Infantry Soldiers. Two, the combat vehicles must move to the maintenance team. Maintenance teams often are located at the parent unit's maintenance collection point. Infantry leaders may have the responsibility of providing security or escort duties. Additionally, leaders should plan on the nonmission capable vehicles to be absent from their task organization if a major maintenance fault is discovered.

RECOVERY OPERATIONS

E-117. Leaders are responsible for recovery operations occurring within their units. However, leaders should consult the senior officer or noncommissioned officer of the attached vehicular unit for technical aspects of the recovery operation. Infantry leaders must have a thorough recovery plan ensuring their combat vehicles can be recovered throughout the operation. Recovery operations extricate damaged or disabled equipment and move it to locations where repairs can be made. Recovery is the primary responsibility of the using unit. The primary role of the Infantry during recovery operations is to provide security and assist with the recovery under supervision of the vehicle crew.

E-118. Recovery operations can be dangerous. Recovery should be conducted under the supervision of the Infantry leader, using the experience and technical competence of the combat vehicle crew. The general rule in recovering a vehicle simply non mission capable in simple terrain is like vehicles can recover each other. For example, tanks recover tanks, and BFV recover BFV. However, there are vehicles specifically designed for recovery operations. These vehicles should be used if vehicles become stuck, flipped over, or severely damaged. The M-936 medium wrecker can be used to recover some wheeled vehicles, to include the armament carrier HMMWV.

E-119. The M984A2 Heavy expanded mobility tactical truck (HEMTT) wrecker can be used to recover heavy or medium sized wheeled vehicle like all the variations of the ICV and MRAP. The MK36 MTVR wrecker can be used as well. One of the best recovery vehicles being utilized for wheeled vehicles is the Interim Stryker recovery system (ISRS). It can handle a towing payload of 60,000 lbs. The M88A1 medium recovery vehicle (MRV) is a full-tracked armored vehicle used to perform battlefield rescue and recovery missions. The M88A1 MRV performs hoisting, winching, and towing operations in support of recovery operations and evacuation of heavy tanks and other tracked combat vehicles. It has a fuel/defuel capability and is fully equipped to provide maintenance and recovery support of the main battle tank family and similar vehicles. These functions can be performed in all types of terrain during all weather conditions.

E-120. Leaders need to ensure every Soldier knows his specific job when it comes to vehicle recovery operations. It is vital every Soldier knows vehicle recovery battle drills. Every vehicle recovery may be different based on METT-TC and type of vehicle to be recovered. It is up to the leader to ensure rehearsals are conducted on a regular basis, METT-TC dependent.

Appendix F
Machine Gun Employment

Whether organic to the unit or attached, machine guns provide the heavy volume of close and continuous fire needed to achieve fire superiority. They are the Infantry platoon's most effective weapons against a dismounted enemy force. These formidable weapons can engage enemy targets beyond the capability of individual weapons with controlled and accurate fire. This appendix addresses the capabilities, limitations, and fundamental techniques of fire common to machine guns.

SECTION I – TECHNICAL AND DATA CONSIDERATIONS

F-1. Leaders must know the technical characteristics of their assigned weapon systems and associated ammunition to maximize their killing and suppressive fires while minimizing the risk to friendly forces. This section discusses machine gun technical data and considerations of the Infantry platoon and squad.

F-2. Machine gun fire has different effects on enemy targets depending on the type system, ammunition used, range to target, and nature of the target. It is important gunners and leaders understand technical aspects of each system and different ammunition available to ensure the machine guns are employed in accordance with their capabilities. Machine guns use several different types of standard military ammunition. Soldiers should use only authorized ammunition manufactured to U.S. and North Atlantic Treaty Organization (NATO) specifications.

F-3. The following paragraphs discuss weapons specification of the tactical employment of M249, M240-series, M2/M2A1, and MK19 machine guns. Refer to the specific FM of the machine guns listed in table F-1 (page F-2) for complete information regarding their technical specifications.

Appendix F

Table F-1. Machine gun specifications

WEAPON	M249	M240-SERIES	M2/M1A2	MK19
Field Manual	FM 3-22.68	FM 3-22.68	FM 3-22.65	FM 3-22.27
Description	5.56-mm gas-operated automatic weapon	7.62-mm gas-operated medium machine gun	.50-caliber recoil-operated heavy machine gun	40-mm air-cooled, blowback-operated automatic grenade launcher
Weight	16.41 lbs. (gun with barrel) 16 lbs. (tripod)	27.6 lbs. (gun with barrel) 20 lbs. (tripod)	128 lbs. (gun with barrel and tripod)	140.6 lbs. (gun with barrel and tripod)
Length	104 cm	110.5 cm	156 cm	109.5 cm
SUSTAINED RATE OF FIRE Rounds/Burst Interval Minutes to Barrel Change	50 RPM 6-9 rounds 4-5 seconds 10 minutes	100 RPM 6-9 rounds 4-5 seconds 10 minutes	40 RPM 6-9 rounds 10-15 seconds Change barrel end of day or if damaged	40 RPM
RAPID RATE OF FIRE Rounds/Burst Interval Minutes to Barrel Change	100 RPM 6-9 rounds 2-3 seconds 2 minutes	200 RPM 10-13 rounds 2-3 seconds 2 minutes	40 RPM 6-9 rounds 5-10 seconds Change barrel end of day or if damaged	60 RPM

Table F-1. Machine gun specifications (continued)

WEAPON	M249	M240-SERIES	M2/M1A2	MK19
Cyclic Rate of Fire	850 RPM in continuous burst Barrel change every 1 minute	650-950 RPM in continuous burst Barrel change every 1 minute	450-550 RPM in continuous burst	325-375 RPM in continuous burst
Maximum Effective Ranges	Bipod/point: 600 m Bipod/area: 800 m Tripod/area: 1,000 m Grazing: 600 m	Bipod/point: 600 m Tripod/point: 800 m Bipod/area: 800 m Tripod/area: 1,100 m Suppression: 1,800 m Grazing: 600 m	Point: 1,500 m (single shot) Area: 1,830 m Grazing: 700 m	Point: 1,500 m Area: 2,212 m
Maximum Range	3600 m	3725 m	6764 m	2212 m

M249 LIGHT MACHINE GUN

F-4. The M249 light machine gun is organic to the Infantry platoon and squads. It provides rifle squads with a light automatic weapon for employment during assault. (See figure F-1, page F-4.) The M249 also can be used in the medium machine gun role in defensive missions or support-by-fire position. The M249 fires from the bipod, the shoulder, the hip, or from the underarm position. The hip and underarm positions normally are used for close-in fire during an assault when the M249 gunner is on the move and does not have time to set the gun in the bipod position. It is best used when a high rate of fire is needed immediately. Accuracy of fire is decreased when firing from either the hip or shoulder.

Appendix F

Figure F-1. M249 light machine gun, bipod mode

F-5. Available M249 ammunition is classified as follows (see table F-2):
- M855 5.56-mm Ball. For use against light materiel and personnel, but not vehicles.
- M856 5.56-mm Tracer. Generally used for adjustments after observation, incendiary effects, and signaling. When tracer rounds are fired, they normally are mixed with ball ammunition in a ratio of four ball rounds to one tracer round.
- M193 5.56-mm Ball. M193 ball ammunition can be fired with the M249, but accuracy is degraded. For this reason, it only should be used in emergency situations when M855 ball is not available.
- M196 5.56-mm Tracer. M196 tracer ammunition can be fired with the M249, but accuracy is degraded. For this reason it only should be used in emergency situations when M856 ammunition is not available.

Table F-2. M249 light machine gun ballistic data

AVAILABLE M249 CARTRIDGES	MAXIMUM RANGE (METERS)	TRACER BURNOUT (METERS)	USES
Ball, M855	3600	—	Light materiel's, personnel
Tracer, M856	3600	900	Observation and adjustment of fire, incendiary effects, signaling

Note. The M249 SAW might be replaced by the MK48 light machine gun (LMG).

M240B MEDIUM MACHINE GUN

F-6. Two medium machine guns and crews are found in the weapons squad. (See figure F-2.) The M240B can be fired in the assault mode in emergencies, but normally is fired from the bipod or tripod platform. It also can be vehicle mounted. The platoon leader (through his weapons squad leader) employs his M240B medium machine guns with a rifle squad to provide long range, accurate, sustained fires against dismounted Infantry, apertures in fortifications, buildings, and lightly-armored vehicles. The M240B also provides a high volume of short-range fire in self-defense against aircraft. Machine gunners use point, traversing, searching, or searching and traversing fire to kill or suppress targets.

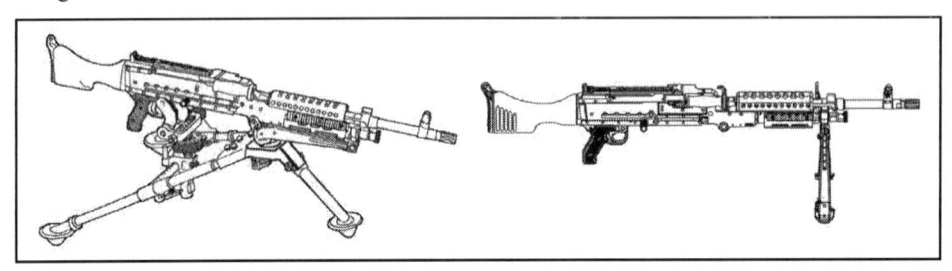

Figure F-2. M240B medium machine gun, bipod and tripod mounted

F-7. Available M240B medium machine gun ammunition is classified as follows (see table F-3):
- M80 7.62-mm Ball. For use against light materiel and personnel.
- M61 7.62-mm Armor Piercing. For use against lightly-armored targets.
- M62 7.62-mm Tracer. For observation of fire, incendiary effects, signaling, and for training. When tracer rounds are fired, they normally are mixed with ball ammunition in a ratio of four ball rounds to one tracer round.

Table F-3. M240B medium machine gun ammunition

AVAILABLE M240B CARTRIDGES	MAXIMUM RANGE (METERS)	TRACER BURNOUT (METERS)	USES
Ball, M80	3725	—	Light materiels, personnel
Armor Piercing, M61	3725	—	Lightly-armored targets
Tracer, M62	3725	900	Observation and adjustment of fire, incendiary effects, signaling

Appendix F

M240L MEDIUM MACHINE GUN

F-8. The M240L Short Barrel reduces the length of the standard barrel by four inches and the weight by .5 pounds, while maintaining accurate fire at extended ranges. The shorter barrel improves mobility in military operations in urban terrain environments. At 22.3 pounds, the M240L is 5.1 pounds lighter than the M240B and is 5.6 pounds lighter with the short barrel installed. (See figure F-3.)

Note. The M240L incorporates titanium construction and alternative manufacturing methods for fabricating major M240B components to achieve significant weight savings. These improvements reduce the Soldier's combat load while allowing easier handling and movement of the weapon. The M240L meets all of the reliability and operational characteristics of the M240B.

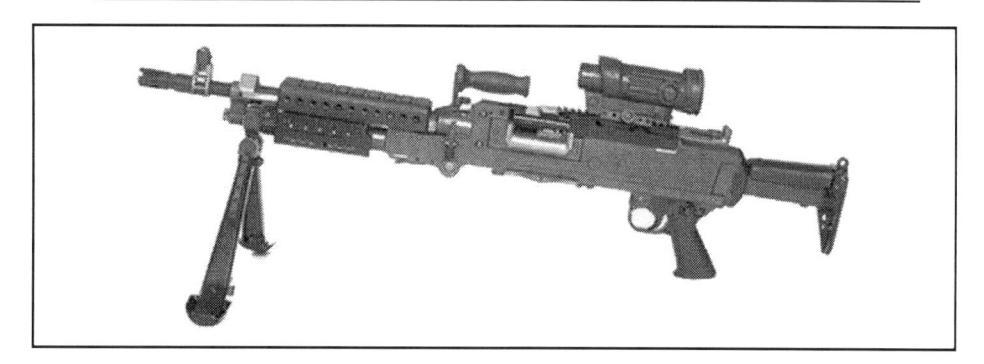

Figure F-3. M240L medium machine gun bipod mode

MK19 40-MM MACHINE GUN, MOD 3

F-9. The MK19 is not organic to the weapons company, not the Infantry platoon or squad, but because there are many times when Infantry Soldiers use it, it is described in this appendix. The MK19 supports the Soldier in both the offense and defense. It gives the unit the capability of laying down a heavy volume of close, accurate, and continuous fire. (See figure F-4.) The MK19 also can—

- Protect motor movements, assembly areas, and supply trains in a bivouac.
- Defend against hovering rotary aircraft.
- Destroy lightly-armored vehicles.
- Fire on enemy prepared positions.
- Provide high volumes of fire into an engagement area.
- Cover obstacles.
- Provide indirect fires from defilade positions.

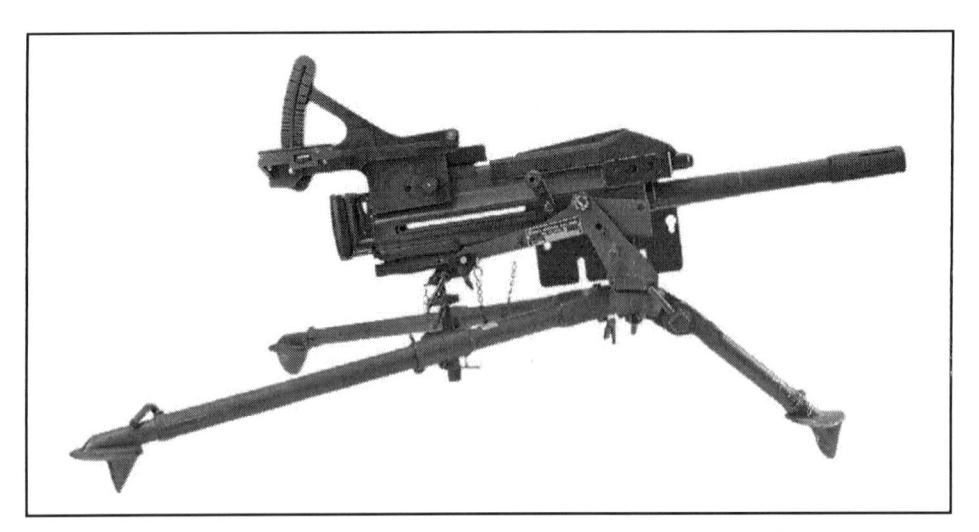

Figure F-4. MK19, 40-mm grenade machine gun, MOD 3

F-10. The MK19 is normally vehicle-mounted on a pedestal, ring, or weapon platform, but also can be fired from the M3 tripod. It fires HE and HEDP rounds. The HE round is effective against unarmored vehicles and personnel.

F-11. Available MK19 machine gun ammunition is classified as follows (see table F-4):
- M430 40-mm HEDP. This is the standard round of the MK19 and comes packed in either 48- or 32- round ammunition containers. It can penetrate two inches of steel armor at zero-degree obliquity and inflict casualties out to 15 meters from impact. It arms within 18 to 30 meters of the gun muzzle.
- M383 40-mm HE. Comes packed in a 48-round container. It has a wound radius of 15 meters, but lacks the armor-piercing capabilities of the HEDP round. It arms 18 to 36 meters from the muzzle.

Table F-4. MK19 40-mm grenade machine gun ballistic data

AVAILABLE MK19 CARTRIDGES	MAXIMUM RANGE (METERS)	PENETRATION/ CASUALTY RADIUS	USES
HEDP, M430	2212	2-inch armor 15-meter casualty radius	Lightly-armored targets, light materiel targets, personnel.
HE, M383	2212	15-meter casualty radius	Unarmored vehicles, light materiel targets, personnel

M2 .50-CALIBER HEAVY MACHINE GUN

F-12. The M2 .50-caliber heavy machine gun is not organic to the Infantry platoon or squad, but as there are many times when Infantry Soldiers use it, it is described in this appendix. (See figure F-5.)

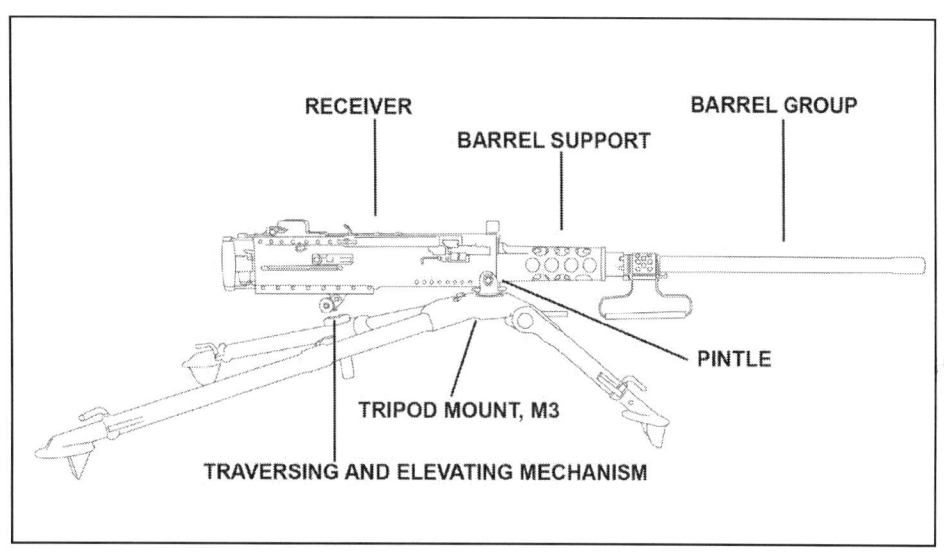

Figure F-5. M2 .50-caliber heavy machine gun

F-13. The available M2 .50-caliber heavy machine gun ammunition is classified as follows (see table F-5):

- M2 .50-Caliber Ball. For use against enemy personnel and light materiel targets.
- M1/M17 .50-Caliber Tracer. Aids in observing fire. Secondary purposes are for incendiary effect and for signaling.
- M1 .50-Caliber Incendiary. For incendiary effect, especially against aircraft.
- M2 .50-Caliber AP. For use against armored aircraft and lightly-armored vehicles, concrete shelters, and other bullet-resisting targets.
- M8 .50-Caliber API. For combined armor-piercing and incendiary effect.
- M20 .50-Caliber API Tracer. For combined armor-piercing and incendiary effect, with the additional tracer feature.

Machine Gun Employment

Table F-5. M2 .50-caliber heavy machine gun ballistic data

AVAILABLE M2 CARTRIDGES	MAXIMUM RANGE (METERS)	TRACER BURNOUT (METERS)	AVERAGE MUZZLE VELOCITY (FEET PER SECOND)
Ball, M2	7400	——	2930
Tracer, M1 (With Gilding Metal Jacket)	5575	1800	2860
Tracer, M1 (With Clad Steel Jacket)	5450	1800	3030
Tracer, M17	5450	2450	3030
Incendiary, M1	6050	——	3090
Armor-Piercing, M2	7400	——	2930
Armor-Piercing Incendiary, M8	6470	——	3050
Armor-Piercing Incendiary Tracer, M20	6470	*300-1750	3050
* This tracer is dim at near ranges but increases in brightness as it moves farther from the gun.			

M2A1 .50-CALIBER HEAVY MACHINE GUN

F-14. The M2A1 .50-caliber machine gun with *Quick Change Barrel* is an enhancement to the M2 .50-caliber machine gun offering Soldiers increased performance as well as new features and design improvements that make it easier and safer to use. The M2A1 provides a fixed headspace and timing configuration, flash hider, and removable carrying handle, which increase the performance of the battle-proven M2. The M2A1 speeds target engagement and improves survivability and safety by reducing the time required to change the barrel and eliminating the timely procedure of setting headspace. The flash hider reduces muzzle flash by 95 percent, making the M2A1 less detectable in limited visibility. (See figure F-6, page F-10.)

Appendix F

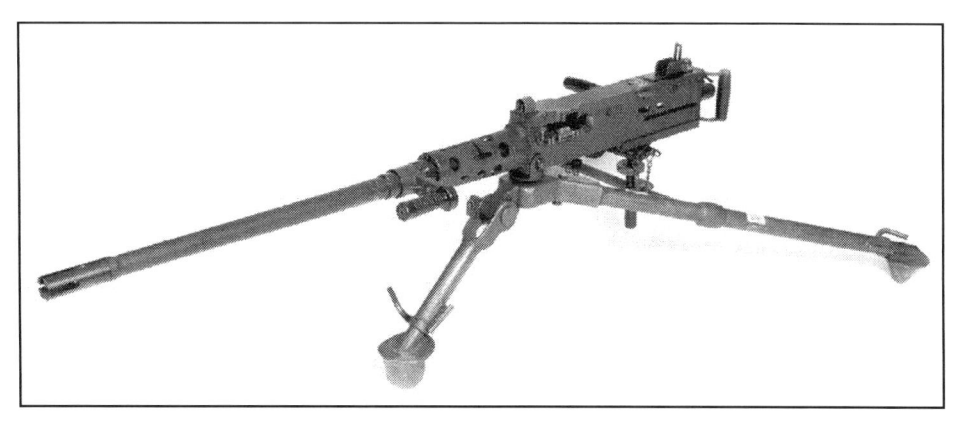

Figure F-6. M2A1 .50-caliber heavy machine gun

SECTION II – COMBAT TECHNIQUES OF FIRE

F-15. This section is designed to illustrate the characteristics of machine gun fire, the types of enemy targets engaged, and how to apply machine gun fire on those enemy targets.

F-16. Read the appropriate field manual as shown in table F-1 (page F-2) for more weapon-specific information on engaging enemy targets with a particular machine gun.

CHARACTERISTICS OF FIRE

F-17. The gunner's or leader's knowledge of the machine gun is not complete until he learns about the action and effect of the projectiles when fired. The following definitions will help the leader, gunner, and assistant gunner understand characteristics of fire of the platoon's weapon's squad machine guns.

LINE OF SIGHT

F-18. LOS is an imaginary line drawn from the firer's eye through the sights to the point of aim.

BURST OF FIRE

F-19. A burst of fire is a number of successive rounds fired with the same elevation and point of aim when the trigger is held to the rear. The number of rounds in a burst can vary depending on the type of fire employed.

TRAJECTORY

F-20. Trajectory is the curved path of the projectile in its flight from the muzzle of the weapon to its impact. The major factors influencing trajectory are the velocity of the round, gravity, rotation of the round, and air resistance. As the range to the target increases, so does the curve of trajectory. (See figure F-7.)

MAXIMUM ORDINATE

F-21. Maximum ordinate is the highest point above the LOS the trajectory reaches between the muzzle of the weapon and base of target. It always occurs at a point about two-thirds of the distance from weapon to target and increases with range. Like trajectory, maximum ordinate increases as the range increases. (See figure F-7.)

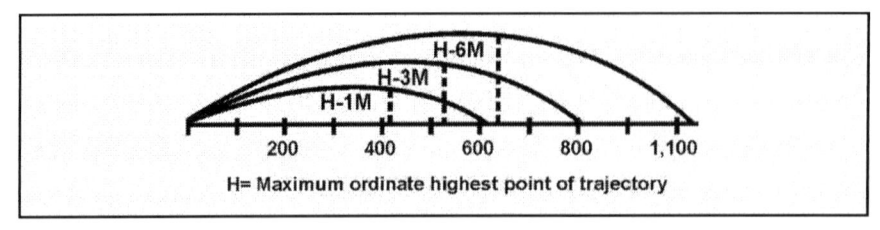

Figure F-7. Trajectory and maximum ordinate

CONE OF FIRE

F-22. The cone of fire is the pattern formed by the different trajectories in each burst as they travel downrange. Vibration of the weapon and variations in ammunition and atmospheric conditions all contribute to the trajectories making up the cone of fire. (See figure F-8, page F-12.)

BEATEN ZONE

F-23. The beaten zone is the elliptical pattern formed when the rounds within the cone of fire strike the ground or target. The size and shape of the beaten zone change as a function of the range to and slope of the target, but is normally oval or cigar shaped and density of rounds decreases toward the edges. Gunners and AR should engage targets to take maximum effect of the beaten zone. The simplest way to do this is to aim at the center base of the target. Most rounds will not fall over the target, and falling short creates ricochets into the target. (See figure F-8, page F-12.)

Effective Beaten Zone

F-24. Because of dispersion, only part of the beaten zone in which 85 percent of the rounds fall is considered the effective beaten zone.

Effect of Range on the Beaten Zone

F-25. As the range to the target increases, the beaten zone becomes shorter and wider. Conversely, as the range to the target decreases, the beaten zone becomes longer and narrower. (See table F-6, page F-12.)

Effect of Slope on the Beaten Zone

F-26. The length of the beaten zone for given ranges varies according to the slope of the ground. On rising ground, the beaten zone becomes shorter but remains the same width.

Appendix F

On ground sloping away from the gun, the beaten zone becomes longer but remains the same width.

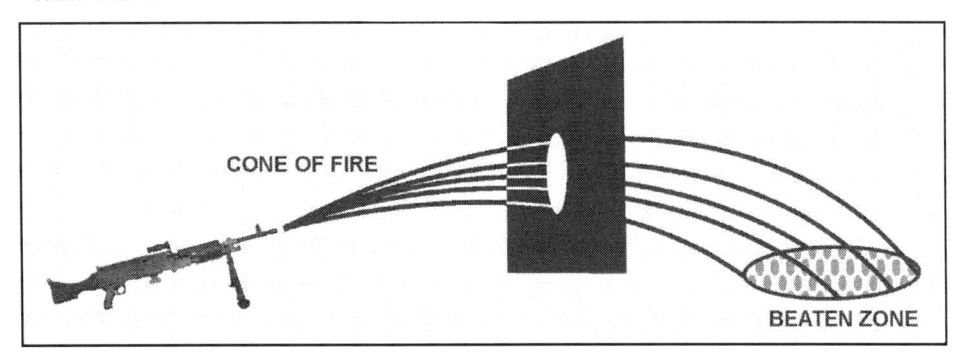

Figure F-8. Cone of fire and beaten zone

Table F-6. Beaten zones of the M240B

M240-SERIES MACHINE GUN
Range: 500 meters (1 meter wide x 110 meters long)
Range: 1000 meters (2 meters wide x 75 meters long)
Range: 1500 meters (3 meters wide x 55 meters long)
Range: 2000 meters (4 meters wide x 50 meters long)

DANGER SPACE

F-27. This is the space between the muzzle of the weapon and target where trajectory does not rise above 1.8 meters (the average height of a standing Soldier) including the beaten zone. Gunners should consider the danger space of weapons when planning overhead fires.

SURFACE DANGER ZONE

F-28. Surface danger zones were developed for each weapon and are defined as the area in front, back, or side of the muzzle of the weapon providing a danger to friendly forces when the weapon is fired. The surface danger zones is not just the area comprising the cone of fire as it moves downrange. It also involves the possible impact area on both sides of the gun target line and possible dispersion of materiel caused by the strike of the rounds, the possible ricochet area, and areas to the rear adversely affected by the effects of firing the weapon. (See figure F-9.)

F-29. Surface danger zones were developed primarily for ranges and must be complied with when training, but they also should be complied with in combat when possible to minimize risk to friendly forces. (Refer to DA Pamphlets 385-63 for more information.)

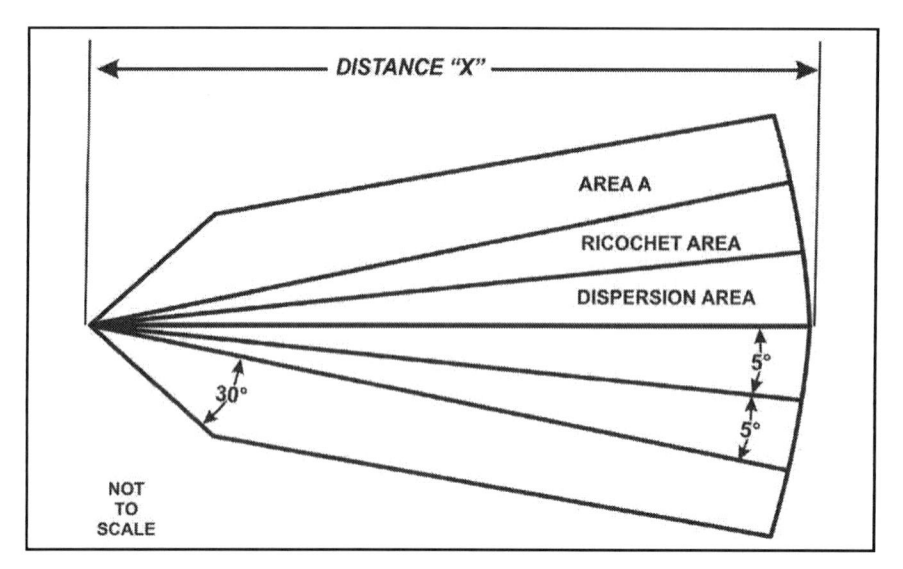

Figure F-9. Surface danger zones for machine guns

CLASSIFICATIONS OF AUTOMATIC WEAPONS FIRE

F-30. The U.S. Army classifies automatic weapons fires with respect to the ground, target, and weapon.

CLASSIFICATION OF FIRES WITH RESPECT TO THE GROUND

F-31. Fires with respect to the ground include grazing and plunging fire.

Dead Space

F-32. Folds or depressions in the ground preventing a target from being engaged from a fixed position are termed dead space. Paragraph F-80 discusses methods of determining dead space.

Grazing Fires

F-33. Automatic weapons achieve grazing fire when the center of the cone of fire does not rise more than one meter above the ground. Grazing fire is employed in the FPL in the defense and is only possible when the terrain is level or sloping uniformly. Dead space encountered along the FPL must be covered by indirect fire, such as from an M203/M320. When firing over level or uniformly sloping terrain, the machine gun M240-series and M249 can attain a maximum of 600 meters of grazing fire. The M2/M2A1 can attain a maximum of 700 meters. Paragraphs F-77 and F-78 discuss the FPL.

Plunging Fires

F-34. Plunging fire occurs when there is little or no danger space from the muzzle of the weapon to the beaten zone. It occurs when weapons fire at long range, when firing from high ground to low ground, when firing into abruptly rising ground, or when firing across uneven terrain, resulting in a loss of grazing fire at points along the trajectory. (See figure F-10.)

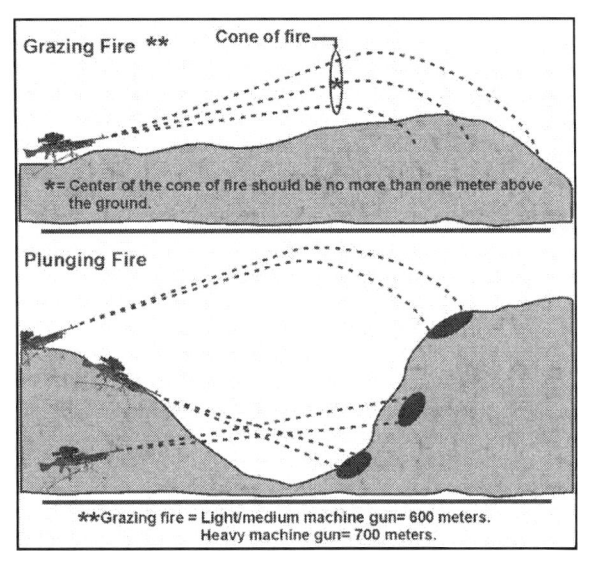

Figure F-10. Classes of fire with respect to the ground

CLASSIFICATION OF FIRES WITH RESPECT TO THE TARGET

F-35. Fires with respect to the target include enfilade, frontal, flanking, and oblique fire. (See figure F-11, page F-16, and figures F-12 and F-13, both on F-17.) These targets normally are presented to gun teams by the enemy and must be engaged as they are presented. For example, if the enemy presents its flank to the gun crew as it moves past their position from the left or right, the gun crew will have no choice but to employ flanking fire on the enemy.

F-36. Leaders and gunners should strive at all times to position their gun teams where they can best take advantage of the machine gun's beaten zone with respect to an enemy target. Channeling the enemy by use of terrain or obstacles so they approach a friendly machine gun position from the front in a column formation is one example. In this situation, the machine gun would employ enfilade fire on the enemy column, and effects of the machine gun's beaten zone would be much greater than if it engaged enemy column from the flank.

Enfilade Fire

F-37. Enfilade fire occurs when the long axis of the beaten zone coincides or nearly coincides with the long axis of the target. It can be frontal fire on an enemy column formation or flanking fire on an enemy line formation. This is the most desirable class of fire with respect to the target because it makes maximum use of the beaten zone. Leaders and gunners always should strive to position the guns to the extent possible engaging enemy targets with enfilade fire. (See figures F-11, page F-16, and F-13, page F-17.)

Frontal Fire

F-38. Frontal fire occurs when the long axis of the beaten zone is at a right angle to the front of the target. This type of fire is highly desirable when engaging a column formation. It then becomes enfilade fire as the beaten zone coincides with the long axis of the target. (See figures F-11, page F-16, and F-12, page F-17.) Frontal fire is not as desirable when engaging a line formation because the majority of the beaten zone normally falls below or after the enemy target.

Flanking Fire

F-39. Flanking fire is delivered directly against the flank of the target. Flanking fire is highly desirable when engaging an enemy line formation. It then becomes enfilade fire as the beaten zone will coincide with the long axis of the target. (See figures F-11, page F-16, and F-12, page F-17.) Flanking fire against an enemy column formation is least desirable because the majority of the beaten zone normally falls before or after the enemy target.

Oblique Fire

F-40. Gunners and automatic riflemen achieve oblique fire when the long axis of the beaten zone is at an angle other than a right angle to the front of the target. (See figures F-11, page F-16, and F-13, page F-17.)

Appendix F

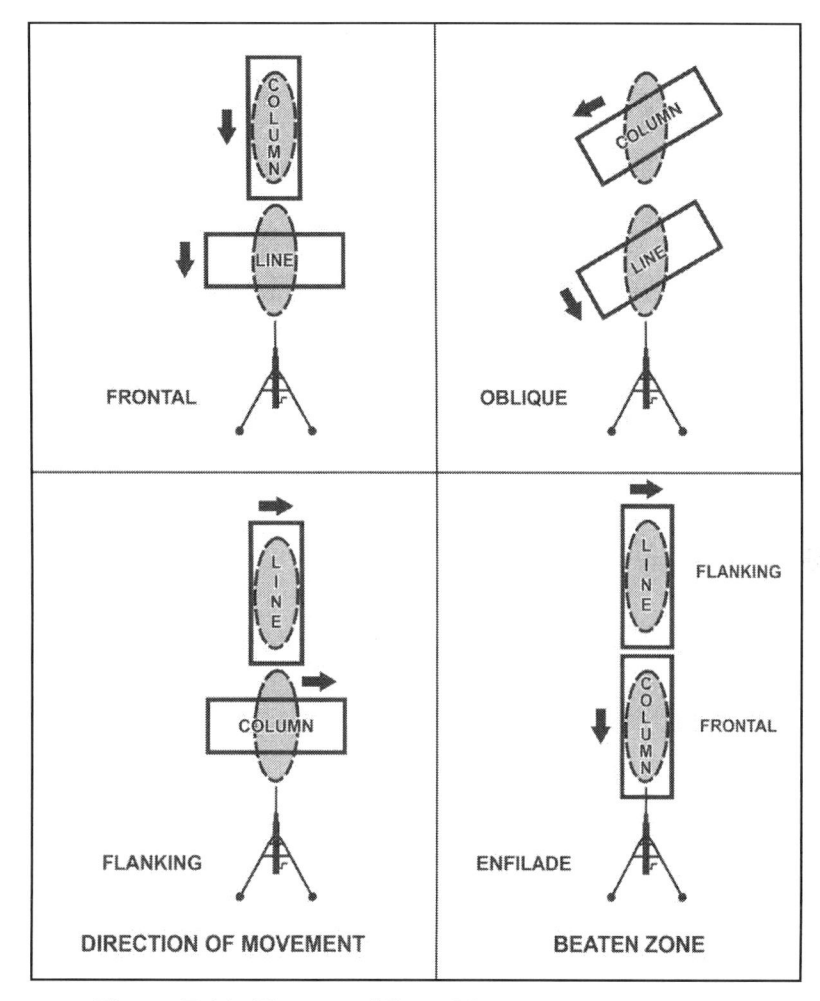

Figure F-11. Classes of fire with respect to the target

Machine Gun Employment

Figure F-12. Frontal fire and flanking fire

Figure F-13. Oblique fire and enfilade fire

CLASSIFICATION OF FIRES WITH RESPECT TO THE MACHINE GUN

F-41. Fires with respect to the weapon include fixed, traversing, searching, traversing and searching, swinging traverse, and free gun fires. (See figure F-14, page F-19.)

Appendix F

Fixed Fire

F-42. Fixed fire is delivered against a stationary point target when the depth and width of the beaten zone covers the target with little or no manipulation needed. After the initial burst, the gunners follow changes or movement of the target without command.

Traversing Fire

F-43. Traversing disperses fires in width by successive changes in direction, but not elevation. It is delivered against a wide target with minimal depth. When engaging a wide target requiring traversing fire, the gunner selects successive aiming points throughout the target area. These aiming points should be close enough together to ensure adequate target coverage. However, they do not need to be so close wasting ammunition by concentrating a heavy volume of fire in a small area.

Searching Fire

F-44. Searching distributes fires in-depth by successive changes in elevation. It is employed against a deep target or a target having depth and minimal width, requiring changes in only the elevation of the gun. The amount of elevation change depends upon the range and slope of the ground.

Traversing and Searching Fire

F-45. This class of fire is a combination in which successive changes in direction *and* elevation result in the distribution of fires both in width and depth. It is employed against a target whose long axis is oblique to the direction of fire.

Swinging Traverse

F-46. Swinging traverse fire is employed against targets requiring major changes in direction but little or no change in elevation. Targets may be dense, wide, in close formations moving slowly toward or away from the gun, or vehicles or mounted troops moving across the front. If tripod mounted, the traversing slide lock lever is loosened enough to permit the gunner to swing the gun laterally. When firing swinging traverse, the weapon normally is fired at the cyclic rate of fire. Swinging traverse consumes a lot of ammunition and does not have a beaten zone because each round seeks its own area of impact.

Free Gun

F-47. Free gun fire is delivered against moving targets rapidly engaging with fast changes in both direction and elevation. Examples are aerial targets, vehicles, mounted troops, or Infantry in relatively close formations moving rapidly toward or away from the gun position. When firing free gun, the weapon normally is fired at the cyclic rate of fire. Free gun fire consumes a lot of ammunition and does not have a beaten zone because each round seeks its own area of impact.

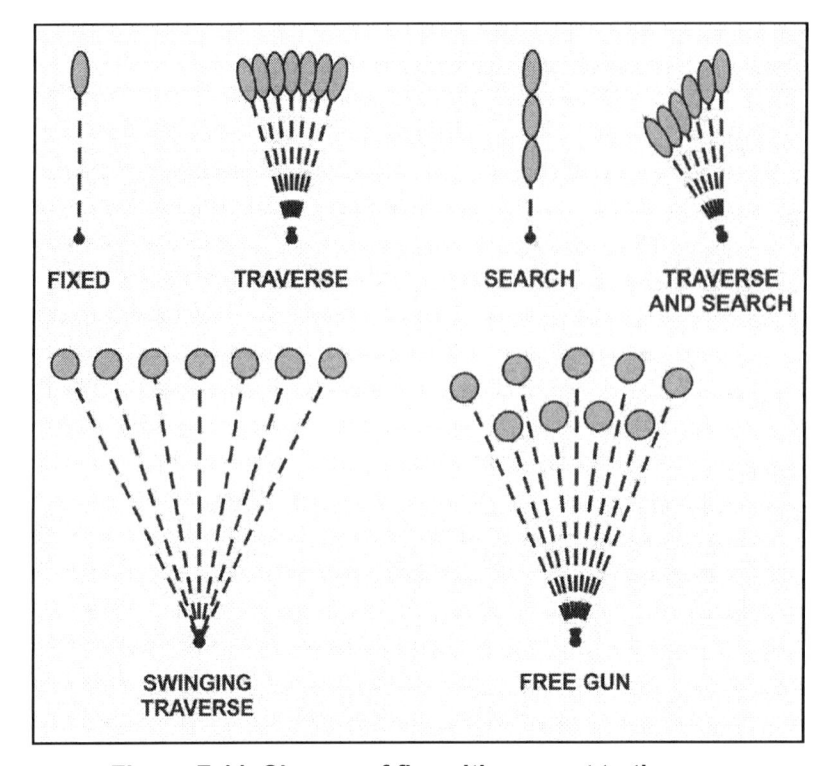

Figure F-14. Classes of fire with respect to the gun

APPLICATION OF FIRE

F-48. Application of fire consists of the methods the gunner uses to cover an enemy target area. Training these methods of applying fire can be accomplished only after the weapons squad leader and gunners have learned how to recognize the different types of targets they may find in combat. They also must know how to distribute and concentrate their fire, and how to maintain the proper rate of fire. Normally, the gunner is exposed to two types of targets in the squad or platoon area of operation: enemy soldiers and supporting automatic weapons. Leaders must ensure targets have priority and are engaged immediately.

F-49. Machine gun fire must be distributed over the entire target area. Improper distribution of fire results in gaps allowing the enemy to escape or use its weapons against friendly positions without opposition.

F-50. The method of applying fire to a target is generally the same for either a single gun or a pair of guns. Direct lay is pointing the gun for direction and elevation so the sights are aligned directly on the target. Fire is delivered in width, depth, or in a combination of the two. To distribute fire properly, gunners must know where to aim, how to adjust their fire, and direction to manipulate the gun. The gunner must aim, fire, and adjust on a certain point of the target. Binoculars may be used by the leader to facilitate fire adjustment.

Appendix F

SIGHT PICTURE

F-51. A correct sight picture has the target, front sight post, and rear sight aligned. The sight picture has sight alignment and placement of the aiming point on the target. The gunner aligns the front sight post in the center of the rear sight and aligns the sights with the target. The top of the front sight post is aligned on the center base of the target.

BEATEN ZONE

F-52. The gunner ensures throughout his firing the center of the beaten zone is maintained at the center base of the target for maximum effect from each burst of fire. When this is done, projectiles in the upper half of the cone of fire will pass through the target if it has height, and projectiles in the lower half of the beaten zone may ricochet into the target. (See figure F-15.)

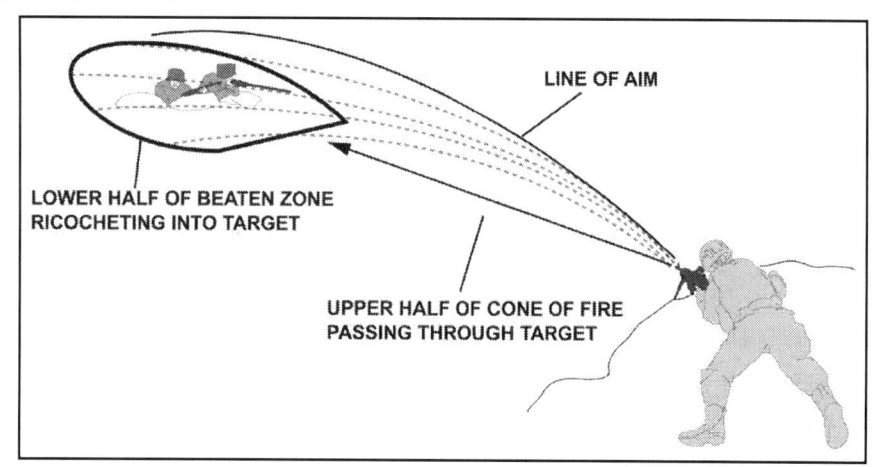

Figure F-15. Line of aim and placement of center of beaten zone on target

F-53. The gunner must move his beaten zone in a certain direction over the target. The direction depends on the type of target and whether the target is engaged with a pair of guns or a single gun. When engaging targets other than point targets with a pair of guns, the targets are divided so fire is distributed evenly throughout the target area. Fire delivered on point targets or a specific area of other target configurations is called concentrated fire.

TARGET ENGAGEMENTS BY TYPES OF TARGETS

F-54. Gunners engage targets throughout their respective sectors. They must know how to engage all types of targets, either individually or with other gunners.

F-55. Gunners' targets in combat are normally enemy troops in various formations or displacements, which require distribution and concentration of fire. These targets often have both width, depth, and application of machine gun fire is designed to completely cover the area in which the enemy is known or suspected to be. These targets may be easy to see or may be indistinct and difficult to locate. The size of the target, stated in terms of the number of aiming points required to engage it completely, determines its type.

F-56. When a single gunner is assigned targets he is responsible for covering the entire target. When a pair of gunners engage an enemy target, each gunner normally is responsible for covering one half of the target. The gunners must be prepared to engage the entire target should the other gun go down.

F-57. The machine gun can provide units with a self-defense capability against hostile low-flying, low-performance aircraft. These guns are employed in the air defense role as part of the unit's local defense. The machine guns are not components of an integrated and coordinated air defense system. Unless otherwise directed, hostile aircraft within range of the gun (about 800 meters maximum effective range) should be engaged. The decision will be made by the commander or leader. Typical targets are surveillance, reconnaissance, and liaison aircraft; troop carriers; helicopters; and drones.

ENGAGEMENT AND EMPLOYMENT

F-58. The mission is to impose maximum attrition upon the attacking enemy such as low-flying, low-performance aircraft. Employment of machine guns used for air defense is guided by the following defensive design factors:
- Defensive design should produce an equally balanced defense in all directions, unless a forced route of approach exists.
- Machine guns should be sited so the maximum number of targets can be engaged, continuous fire can be delivered, and likely routes of approach are covered.
- Machine guns used to defend march columns should be interspersed in the convoy, with emphasis on the lead and rear elements. (See figure F-16.)

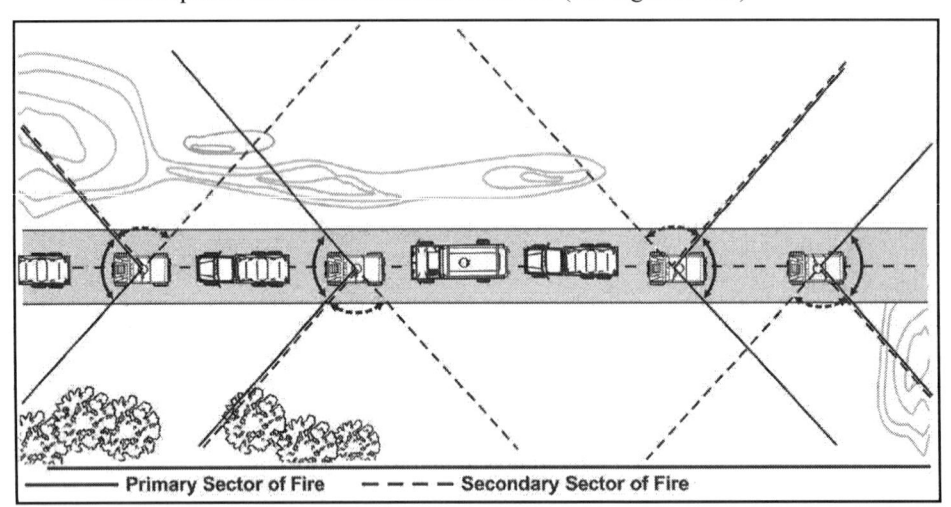

Figure F-16. March column with four machine guns

TARGET SELECTION AND ENGAGEMENT CONTROL

F-59. These actions depend upon visual means. The sites selected for guns must provide maximum observation and unobstructed sectors of fire. Units furnished machine guns in

Appendix F

sufficient numbers should site them within mutual support distances of 90 to 360 meters. Each gun is assigned a primary and secondary sector of fire. Weapon crews maintain constant vigilance in their primary sectors of fire, regardless of the sector in which the guns actually are engaged.

DISTRIBUTION, CONCENTRATION AND RATE OF FIRE

F-60. The size and nature of the enemy target determines how machine gun fire is applied. Automatic weapons fire in one of three rates: rapid, sustained, or cyclic. The rates of fire for each machine gun are shown in table F-1. The situation normally dictates the rate used, but the availability of ammunition and need for barrel changes play important roles as well. The rate of fire must be controlled to cover the target adequately, but not waste ammunition or destroy the barrel.

DISTRIBUTED AND CONCENTRATED FIRE

F-61. Distributed fire is delivered in width and depth such as at an enemy formation. Concentrated fire is delivered at a point target such as an automatic weapon or an enemy fighting position.

RAPID FIRE

F-62. Rapid rate of fire places an exceptionally high volume of fire on an enemy position. Machine gunners normally engage targets at the rapid rate to suppress the enemy quickly. Rapid fire requires more ammunition than sustained fire and requires frequent barrel changes.

SUSTAINED FIRE

F-63. Once the enemy has been suppressed, machine gunners fire at the sustained rate. Sustained fire conserves ammunition and requires only infrequent barrel changes, but it might not be enough volume of fire to suppress or destroy.

CYCLIC RATE OF FIRE

F-64. To fire the cyclic rate, the gunner holds the trigger to the rear while the assistant gunner feeds ammunition into the weapon. This normally is used only to engage aerial targets in self-defense or to fire the final protective fires in the defense to protect the perimeter. This produces the highest volume of fire the machine gun can fire, but can permanently damage the machine gun and barrel and should be used only in case of emergency.

TARGET ENGAGEMENT DURING LIMITED VISIBILITY

F-65. Gunners have difficulty detecting and identifying targets during limited visibility. The leader's ability to control the fires of his weapons also is reduced; therefore, he may instruct the gunners to fire without command when targets present themselves.

F-66. Gunners should engage targets only when they can identify the targets, unless ordered to do otherwise. For example, if one gunner detects a target and engages it, the other gunner observes the area fired upon and adds his fire only if he can identify the target or if ordered to fire.

F-67. Tracer ammunition helps a gunner engage targets during limited visibility and should be used if possible. It is important to note in certain circumstances the enemy will have an easy time identifying the machine gun's position if the gunner uses tracer ammunition. The need to engage targets must be balanced with the need to keep the guns safe before deciding to employ tracers. If firing unaided, gunners must be trained to fire low at first and adjust upward. This overcomes the tendency to fire high.

F-68. When two or more gunners are engaging linear targets, linear targets with depth, or deep targets, they do not engage these targets as they would when visibility is good. With limited visibility, the center and flanks of these targets may not be defined clearly. Therefore, each gunner observes his tracers and covers what he believes to be the entire target.

TECHNIQUES

F-69. Techniques of fire include assault fire; overhead fire; and fire from a defilade position. Only automatic rifles use assault fire.

ASSAULT FIRE

F-70. Automatic riflemen use assault fire when in close combat. Assault fire involves firing without the aid of sights using the hip, shoulder, and underarm positions. The underarm position is best when rapid movement is required. In all three positions, automatic riflemen adjust their fire by observing the tracer and impact of the bullets on the target area. Additional considerations for automatic riflemen using assault fire include:

- Maintaining alignment with the rest of the assault element.
- Reloading rapidly.
- Aiming low and adjusting the aim upward toward the target.
- Distributing fires across the objective when not engaging enemy automatic weapons.

OVERHEAD FIRE

F-71. Gunners can use overhead fire when there is sufficient low ground between the machine gun and target area of the maneuver friendly forces. A machine gun on a tripod is capable of delivering this type of fire because of the small and uniform dispersion of the cone of fire. Gunners must estimate accurately range to the target and establish a safety limit imaginary line parallel to the target where fire would cause casualties to friendly Soldiers. Gun crews and leaders must be aware of this safety limit. Leaders must designate signals for lifting or shifting fires. Gunners should not attempt overhead fires if the terrain is level or slopes uniformly, if the barrel is badly worn, or if visibility is poor.

Appendix F

Gunner's Rule

F-72. The gunner's rule can be applied when the friendly troops are at least 350 meters in front of the gun position and range to the target is 850 meters or less. (See figure F-17.) The rule follows:
- Lay the gun on the target with the correct sight setting to hit the target.
- Without disturbing the lay of the gun, set the rear sight at a range of 1600 meters.
- Look through the sights and notice where the new line of aim strikes the ground. This is the limit of troop safety. When the feet of the friendly troops reach this point, fire must be lifted or shifted.

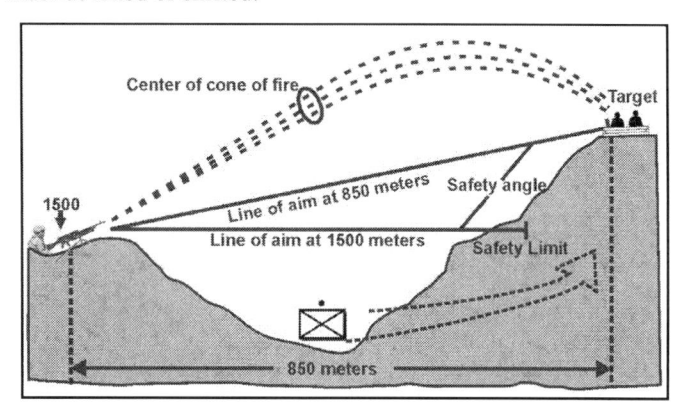

Figure F-17. Application of gunner's rule

Leader's Rule

F-73. When the range to the target is greater than 850 meters, overhead fire should be delivered only in an emergency. Even then, fire should extend only to a range at which the tracers or strike of the bullets can be seen by the gunner. In this situation the leader's rule applies. (See figure F-18.) The platoon or section leader uses the leader's rule only when the target is greater than 850 meters. The rule follows:
- Select a point on the ground where it is believed friendly troops can advance with safety.
- Determine the range to this point by the most accurate means available.
- Lay the gun on the target with the correct sight setting to hit the target.
- Without disturbing the lay of the gun, set the rear sight to 1600 meters or the range to the target plus 500 meters, whichever is the greater of the two ranges? Under no conditions should the sight setting be less than 1500 meters.
- Note the point where the new line of aim strikes the ground:
  - If it strikes at the selected point, that point marks the limit of safety.
  - If it strikes short of the selected point, it is safe for troops to advance to the point where the line of aim strikes the ground and to an unknown point beyond. If fire is called for after friendly troops advance farther than the point where the line of

aim strikes the ground, this farther point is determined by testing new selected points until the line of aim and selected point coincide.
- If it clears the selected point, it is safe for troops to advance to the selected point and to an unknown point beyond. If it is advantageous to have troops advance beyond the selected point, this farther point must be determined by testing new selected points until the line of aim and selected point coincide. This point marks the line of safety.

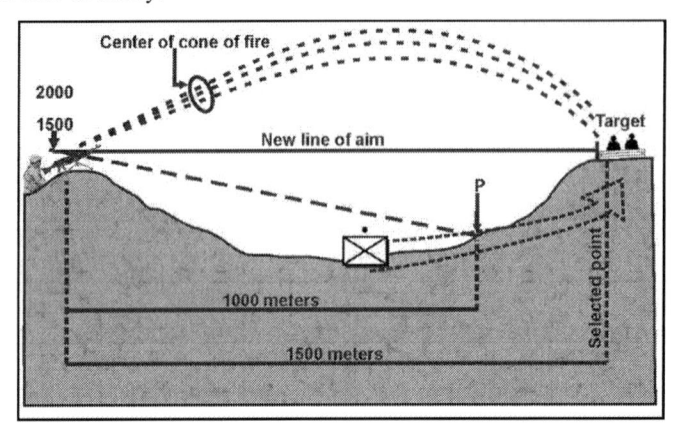

Figure F-18. Application of leader's rule

FIRE FROM A DEFILADE POSITION

F-74. Defilade positions protect gunners from frontal or enfilading fires. (See figure F-19, page F-26.) Cover and concealment may not provide the gunner a view of some or all of the target area. In this instance, some other member of the platoon or squad must observe the impact of the rounds and communicate adjustments to the gunner. (See figure F-20, page F-26.) Gunners and leaders must consider the complexity of laying on the target. They also must take into account the gunner's inability to make rapid adjustments to engage moving targets, the ease with which targets are masked, and difficulty in achieving grazing fires for an FPL.

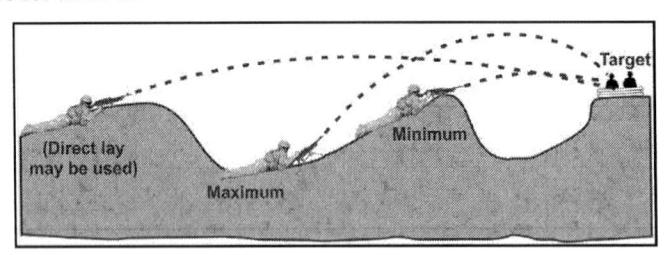

Figure F-19. Defilade positions

Appendix F

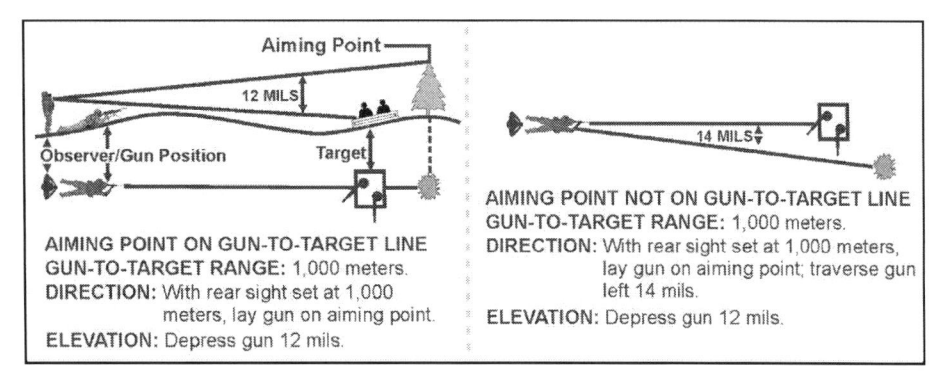

Figure F-20. Observer adjusting fire

SECTION III – PREDETERMINED FIRES

F-75. Predetermined fires organize the battlefield for gunners. They allow the leader and gunner to select potential targets or target areas most likely being engaged or have tactical significance. This includes dismounted enemy avenues of approach, likely positions for automatic weapons, and probable enemy assault positions. The gunners do this by using sectors of fire, FPL, or a PDF and selected target areas. This preparation maximizes the effectiveness of the machine gun during good as well as limited visibility. It enhances fire control by reducing the time required to identify targets, determine range, and manipulate the weapon onto the target. Abbreviated fire commands and previously recorded data enable the gunner to aim or adjust fire on the target quickly and accurately. Selected targets should be fired on in daylight whenever practical to confirm data. The range card identifies the targets and provides a record of firing data. DA Form 5517 provides a record of firing data and aids defensive fire planning.

TERMINOLOGY

F-76. Gunners need to know several terms associated with predetermined fire.

SECTOR OF FIRE

F-77. A sector of fire is an area to be covered by fire assigned to an individual, a weapon, or a unit. Gunners normally are assigned a primary and a secondary sector of fire.

FINAL PROTECTIVE FIRE

F-78. Final protective fires is an immediately-available, prearranged barrier of fire to stop enemy movement across defensive lines or areas.

FINAL PROTECTIVE LINE

F-79. An FPL is a predetermined line along which grazing fire is placed to stop an enemy assault. If an FPL is assigned, the machine gun is sighted along it except when other targets are being engaged. An FPL becomes the machine gun's part of the unit's FPFs. An FPL is fixed in direction and elevation. However, a small shift for search must be employed to prevent the enemy from crawling under the FPL and to compensate for irregularities in the terrain or the sinking of the tripod legs into soft soil during firing. Fire must be delivered during all conditions of visibility.

F-80. A good FPL covers the maximum area with grazing fire. Grazing fire can be obtained over various types of terrain out to a maximum of 600 meters. To obtain the maximum extent of grazing fire over level or uniformly sloping terrain, the gunner sets the rear sight at 600 meters. He then selects a point on the ground he estimates to be 600 meters from the machine gun, and he aims, fires, and adjusts on that point. To prevent enemy soldiers from crawling under grazing fire, he searches (downward) by lowering the muzzle of the weapon.

PRINCIPAL DIRECTION OF FIRE

F-81. PDF is assigned to a gunner to cover an area having good fields of fire or has a likely dismounted avenue of approach. It also provides mutual support to an adjacent unit. Machine guns are sited using the PDF if an FPL has not been assigned. If a PDF is assigned and other targets are not being engaged, machine guns remain on the PDF. A PDF has the following characteristics:

- It is used only if a final protective line is not assigned; it then becomes the machine gun's part of the unit's final protective fires.
- When the target has width, direction is determined by aiming on one edge of the target area and noting the amount of traverse necessary to cover the entire target.
- The gunner is responsible for the entire wedge-shaped area from the muzzle of the weapon to the target, but elevation may be fixed for a priority portion of the target.

DEAD SPACE AND GRAZING FIRE

F-82. The extent of grazing fire and dead space may be determined in two ways. In the preferred method, the machine gun is adjusted for elevation and direction. A squad member then walks along the FPL while the gunner aims through the sights. In places where the Soldier's waist (midsection) falls below the gunner's point of aim, dead space exists. Arm-and-hand signals must be used to control the Soldier who is walking and to obtain an accurate account of the dead space and its location. Another method is to observe the flight of tracer ammunition from a position behind and to the flank of the weapon.

PRIMARY SECTOR OF FIRE

F-83. The primary sector of fire is assigned to the gun team to cover the most likely avenue of enemy approach from all types of defensive positions.

SECONDARY SECTOR OF FIRE

F-84. The secondary sector of fire is assigned to the gun team to cover the second most likely avenue of enemy approach. It is fired from the same gun position as the primary sector of fire.

Appendix F

FIELD EXPEDIENT TECHNIQUES

F-85. When laying the machine gun for predetermined targets, the gunner can use field expedients as a means of engaging targets when other sources are not available.

BASE STAKE TECHNIQUE

F-86. A base stake is used to define sector limits and may provide the lay of the FPL or predetermined targets along a primary or secondary sector limit. This technique is effective in all visibility conditions. The gunner uses the following steps:

- Defines the sector limits by laying the gun for direction along one sector limit and by emplacing a stake along the outer edge of the folded bipod legs. Rotates the legs slightly on the receiver, so the gunner takes up the "play." Uses the same procedure for placing a stake along the opposite sector limit.
- Lays the machine gun along the FPL by moving the muzzle of the machine gun to a sector limit. Adjusts for elevation by driving a stake into the ground so the top of the stake is under the gas cylinder extension. This allows a few MILS of depression to cover irregularities in the terrain.
- Lays the machine gun to engage other targets within a sector limit. Done in a primary sector by using the procedure described previously, except he keeps the elevation fixed.

NOTCHED-STAKE OR TREE-CROTCH TECHNIQUE

F-87. The gunner uses the notched-stake or tree-crotch technique with the bipod mount to engage predetermined targets within a sector or to define sector limits. This technique is effective during all conditions of visibility and requires little additional materiel. The gunner uses the following steps:

- Drives either a notched stake or tree crotch into the ground where selected targets are anticipated. Places the stock of the machine gun in the nest of the stake or crotch and adjusts the weapon to hit the selected targets and to define his sector limits.
- Digs shallow, curved trenches or grooves of the bipod feet. (These trenches allow for rotation of the bipod feet as the gunner moves the stock from one crotch or stake to another.)

HORIZONTAL LOG OR BOARD TECHNIQUE

F-88. This technique is used with the bipod or tripod mount to mark sector limits and engage wide targets. It is good for all visibility conditions and is best suited for flat, level terrain. The gunner uses the following steps.

Bipod-Mounted Machine Gun

F-89. Using a bipod-mounted machine gun, the gunner places a log or board beneath the stock of the weapon so the stock can slide across it freely. He digs shallow, curved trenches or grooves for the bipod feet to allow rotation of the feet as he moves the stock along the log or board. (The gunner may mark the sector limits by notching or placing stops on the log or board. The gunner uses the bipod firing position and grip.)

Tripod-Mounted Machine Gun

F-90. Using a tripod-mounted machine gun, the gunner places a log or boards beneath the barrel, positioning it so the barrel, when resting on the log or board, is at the proper elevation to obtain grazing fire. When appropriate, he marks the sector limits as described of the bipod in the preceding paragraph. (This technique is used only if a T&E mechanism is not available.)

SECTION IV – FIRE CONTROL

F-91. Fire control includes all actions of the leader and Soldiers in planning, preparing, and applying fire on a target. The leader selects and designates targets. He also designates the midpoint and flanks or ends of a target, unless they are obvious to the gunner. The gunner fires at the instant desired. He then adjusts fire, regulates the rate of fire, shifts from one target to another, and ceases fire. When firing, the gunner should continue to fire until the target is neutralized or until signaled to do otherwise by the leader.

F-92. Predetermined targets, including the FPL or PDF, are engaged on order or by SOP. The signal for calling these fires normally is stated in the defensive order. Control these predetermined targets by using arm-and-hand signals, voice commands, or pyrotechnic devices. Gunners fire the FPL or PDF at the sustained rate of fire unless the situation calls for a higher rate. When engaging other predetermined targets, the sustained rate of fire also is used unless a different rate is ordered.

METHODS OF FIRE CONTROL

F-93. The noise and confusion of battle may limit the use of some of these methods. Therefore, the leader must select a method or combination of methods to accomplish the mission.

ORAL

F-94. The oral fire control method can be effective, but sometimes the leader may be too far away from the gunner, or the noise of the battle may make it impossible for him to hear. The primary means of the oral fire control method is the issuance of a fire command.

ARM-AND-HAND SIGNALS

F-95. Arm-and-hand signals are an effective fire control method when the gunner can see the leader. All gunners must know the standard arm-and-hand signals. The leader gets the gunner's attention and points to the target. When the gunner returns the READY signal, the leader commands FIRE.

Appendix F

PREARRANGED SIGNALS

F-96. Prearranged signals are either visual or sound signals such as casualty-producing devices (rifle or Claymore), pyrotechnics, whistle blasts, or tracers. These signals should be included in SOPs. If the leader wants to shift fire at a certain time, he gives a prearranged signal such as obscurants or pyrotechnics. Upon seeing the signal, the gunner shifts his fire to a prearranged point.

PERSONAL CONTACT

F-97. In many situations, the leader must issue orders directly to individual Soldiers. Personal contact is used more than other methods by Infantry leaders. The leader must use maximum cover and concealment to keep from disclosing the position or himself.

RANGE CARDS

F-98. When using the range card method of fire control, the leader must ensure all range cards are current and accurate. Once this is accomplished, the leader may designate certain targets for certain weapons with the use of limiting stakes or with fire commands. He also should designate no-fire zones or restricted fire areas to others. The vital factor in this method of fire control is gunners must be well-disciplined and pay attention to detail.

STANDARD OPERATING PROCEDURES

F-99. SOPs are actions to be executed without command developed during the training of the squads. Their use eliminates many commands and simplifies the leader's fire control. SOPs for certain actions and commands can be developed to make gunners effective. Some examples follow:
- Observation. The gunners continuously observe their sectors.
- Fire. Gunners open fire without command on appropriate targets appearing within their sectors.
- Check. While firing, the gunners periodically check with the leader for instructions.
- Return fire. The gunners return enemy fire without order, concentrating on enemy automatic weapons.
- Shift fire. Gunners shift their fires without command when more dangerous targets appear.
- Rate of fire. When gunners engage a target, they initially fire at the rate necessary to gain and maintain fire superiority.
- Mutual support. When two or more gunners are engaging the same target and one stops firing, the other increases the rate of fire and covers the entire target. When only one gunner is required to engage a target and the leader has alerted two or more, the gunner not firing aims on the target and follows the movements of the target. He does this to fire instantly in case the other machine gun malfunctions or ceases fire before the target has been eliminated.

FIRE COMMANDS

F-100. A fire command is given to deliver fire on a target quickly and without confusion. When the leader decides to engage a target not obvious to the squad, he must provide it with the information needed to engage the target. He must alert the Soldiers; give a target direction, description, and range; name the method of fire; and give the command to fire. There are initial fire commands and subsequent fire commands.

F-101. It is essential the commands delivered by the weapons squad leader are understood and echoed by the assistant gunner or gun team leader and gunner. Table F-7 provides an example of the weapons squad fire commands and actions used by the weapons squad leader, assistant gunner, gun team leader, and gunner.

Table F-7. Weapons squad fire commands and actions

ACTION	WSL COMMANDS	AG/GTL COMMANDS AND ACTIONS	GUNNER ACTIONS	GUNNER RESPONSES
WSL or GTL identifies TGT within gun team's sector.	"Light-skinned truck, 3 o'clock, 400 m, on my laser."	"Light-skinned truck, 3 o'clock, 400 m, on my laser, once on TGT, engage."	Gunner looks for laser and identifies TGT. Gunner traverses and gets on TGT. Gunner engages TGT with correct rate of fire.	"TGT identified." "TGT acquired."
Gun team (or weapons squad) go to bipod.	"Gun 1-Bipod."	Repeats "Gun 1-Bipod" and identifies location for gun.	Gets down beside AG/GTL.	"Gun 1 up" once ready to fire.

Appendix F

Table F-7. Weapons squad fire commands and actions (continued)

ACTION	WSL COMMANDS	AG/GTL COMMANDS AND ACTIONS	GUNNER ACTIONS	GUNNER RESPONSES
Gun team go to tripod.	"Gun 1-Tripod."	Repeats "Gun 1-Tripod" and lays down tripod (if not done) and prepares to lock gun on tripod.	Gunner picks up gun and places into tripod. He gets AG/GTL to lock it in. Once locked in, the AG/GTL collapses bipod legs.	"Gun 1 up" once ready to fire.
Barrel change.	NA	"Gun 1 prepare for barrel change." "Gun 1 barrel change."	Fires one more burst. Waits for barrel change.	Repeats AG/GTL command. Once done, "Gun 1 up."
Displace gun.	"Gun 1 out of action, prepare to move."	"Gun 1 out of action, prepare to move." Breaks down barrel bag, prepares to move.	Gunner takes gun off tripod, continues to orient towards target on bipod, and prepares to move.	"Gun 1, ready to move."
WSL identifies sector of fire for gun teams. Day-marks with tracer. Night-marks with PEQ/tracer.	"Gun 1, left, center, right sectors on my mark. Do you identify?" (Always marks left to right.)	Using binoculars identifies sectors and states, "Gun 1 identifies." Adjusts gunner onto target.	Gunner makes necessary adjustments, tells AG/GTL whether he identifies or not. Engages or makes further adjustments.	"Sector identified" to AG/GTL once he identifies.

Table F-7. Weapons squad fire commands and actions (continued)

ACTION	WSL COMMANDS	AG/GTL COMMANDS AND ACTIONS	GUNNER ACTIONS	GUNNER RESPONSES
WSL or AG/GTL gives or adjusts rate of fire.	"Gun 1, sustained __ seconds, engage."	Echoes command. Starts count. Tells gunner to fire. Keeps count between bursts and ensures gun does not fire out of turn.	Gunner echoes command. Also counts and fires when AG/GTL gives command to fire.	Echoes rate of fire "Sustained __ seconds."
WSL changes gun teams sector of fire or shift fire.	"Gun 1, shift fire, TGT # (or) right/left sector." Marks sector same as above.	Echoes command to shift; identifies new target/sector. Adjusts gunner, alerts WSL once the gunner has shifted.	Gunner echoes command, makes necessary adjustment, acquires new target. Confirms with AG/GTL all is OK. Engages new sector when told.	Echoes command with AG/GTL. "Shift fire to TGT #__." Once identified, "Sector/TGT identified."
Talking the gun teams (ensuring one gun fires during the other gun's interval and vice versa).	WSL gives gun teams the rate of fire. (As long as they are keeping correct interval, they should "talk" themselves.)	Repeats rate of fire and maintains proper count, telling gunner when to fire. Adjusts rate of fire off of lead gun.	Repeats rate of fire command, keeps own count. Fires when told to fire. Adjusts rate of fire off of lead gun.	"Sustained __ seconds."

Appendix F

Table F-7. Weapons squad fire commands and actions (continued)

ACTION	WSL COMMANDS	AG/GTL COMMANDS AND ACTIONS	GUNNER ACTIONS	GUNNER RESPONSES
Lift fire	"Lift fire, lift fire, lift fire." Or "Gun 1, lift fire."	Repeats command to gunner, ensures gunner lifts fire.	Repeats command. Ceases all fire onto the objective. Maintains overwatch and scans objective until told to reengage or go out of action.	Echoes "lift fire."
Round count	If need to know round count, prompt "Gun 1, round count."	AG/GTL continuously links rounds and gives WSL round count every 100. "Gun 1, 200 rounds."	Gunner echoes round count to ensure it is heard.	"Gun 1, 200 rounds."
"Watch and shoot" or "Traverse and search"	"Gun 1, watch and shoot." "Gun 1, traverse and search."	Repeats command, searches objective for targets of opportunity within sector.	Repeats command, searches objective for targets of opportunity in sector. Confirms target with AG/GTL before engaging.	"Gun 1, watch and shoot." "Gun 1, traverse and search."

LEGEND
AG – assistant gunner; GTL – gun team leader; TGT – target; WSL – weapons squad leader

INITIAL FIRE COMMANDS

F-102. Initial fire commands are given to adjust onto the target, change the rate of fire after a fire mission is in progress, interrupt fire, or terminate the alert.

ELEMENTS

F-103. Fire commands for all direct-fire weapons follow a pattern including similar elements. There are six elements in the fire command of the machine gun: alert; direction; description; range; method of fire; and command to open fire. The gunners repeat each element of fire command as it is given.

ALERT

F-104. This element prepares the gunners for more instructions. The leader may alert both gunners in the squad and may have only one fire, depending upon the situation. To alert and have both gunners fire, the leader announces FIRE MISSION. If he desires to alert both gunners but have only one fire, he announces GUN NUMBER ONE, FIRE MISSION. In all cases, upon receiving the alert, the gunners load their machine guns and place them on FIRE.

Direction

F-105. This element indicates the general direction to the target and may be given in one or a combination of the following methods.

Oral

F-106. The leader orally gives the direction to the target in relation to the position of the gunner example, FRONT, LEFT FRONT, RIGHT FRONT.

Pointing

F-107. The leader designates a small or obscure target by pointing with his finger or aiming with a weapon. When he points with his finger, a Soldier standing behind him should be able to look over his shoulder and sight along his arm and index finger to locate the target. When aiming his weapon at a target, a Soldier looking through the sights should be able to see the target. Leaders also may use lasers in conjunction with night vision devices to designate a target to the gunner.

Tracer Ammunition

F-108. Tracer ammunition is a quick and sure method of designating a target not clearly visible. When using this method, the leader first should give the general direction to direct the gunner's attention to the target area. To prevent the loss of surprise when using tracer ammunition, the leader does not fire until he has given all elements of the fire command except the command to fire. The leader may fire his individual weapon. The firing of the tracers then becomes the last element of the fire command, and it is the signal to open fire.

Appendix F

> **CAUTION**
> Soldiers must be aware night vision devices, temporary blindness ("white out") may occur when firing tracer ammunition at night or when exposed to other external light sources. Lens covers may reduce this effect.

Reference Points

F-109. Another way to designate obscure targets is to use easy-to-recognize reference points. All leaders and gunners must know terrain features and terminology used to describe them. (Refer to TC 3-25.26 for more information.) When using a reference point, the word "reference" precedes its description. This is done to avoid confusion. The general direction to the reference point should be given.

Description

F-110. The target description creates a picture of the target in the gunners' minds. To properly apply their fire, the Soldiers must know the type of target they are to engage. The leader should describe it briefly. If the target is obvious, no description is necessary.

Range

F-111. The leader always announces the estimated range to the target. The range is given, so the gunner knows how far to look for the target and what range setting to put on the rear sight. Range is announced in meters. However, since the meter is the standard unit of range measurement, the word "meters" is not used. With machine guns, the range is determined and announced to the nearest hundred or thousand example, THREE HUNDRED, or ONE THOUSAND.

Method of Fire

F-112. This element includes manipulation and rate of fire. Manipulation dictates the class of fire with respect to the weapon. It is announced as FIXED, TRAVERSE, SEARCH, or TRAVERSE AND SEARCH. Rate controls the volume of fire (sustained, rapid, and cyclic). Normally, the gunner uses the sustained rate of fire. The rate of fire is omitted from the fire command. The method of fire of the machine gun is usually 3- to 5-round bursts (M249) and 6- to 9-round bursts (M240-series).

Command to Open Fire

F-113. When fire is to be withheld so surprise fire can be delivered on a target or to ensure both gunners open fire at the same time, the leader may preface the command to commence firing with AT MY COMMAND or AT MY SIGNAL. When the gunners are ready to engage the target, they report READY to the leader. The leader then gives the command FIRE at the specific time desired. If immediate fire is required, the command FIRE is given without pause and gunners fire as soon as they are ready.

SUBSEQUENT FIRE COMMANDS

F-114. Subsequent fire commands are used to make adjustments in direction and elevation, to change rates of fire after a fire mission is in progress, to interrupt fires, or to terminate the alert. If the gunner fails to properly engage a target, the leader must correct him promptly by announcing or signaling the desired changes. When these changes are given, the gunner makes the corrections and resumes firing without further command.

F-115. Adjustments in direction and elevation with the machine gun always are given in meters; one finger is used to indicate one meter and so on. Adjustment for direction is given first. Example: RIGHT ONE ZERO METERS or LEFT FIVE METERS. Adjustment for elevation is given next. Example: ADD FIVE METERS or DROP ONE FIVE METERS. These changes may be given orally or with arm-and-hand signals:

- Changes in the rate of fire are given orally or by arm-and-hand signals.
- To interrupt firing, the leader announces CEASE FIRE, or he signals to cease fire. The gunners remain on the alert. They resume firing when given the command FIRE.
- To terminate the alert, the leader announces CEASE FIRE, END OF MISSION.

DOUBTFUL ELEMENTS AND CORRECTIONS

F-116. When the gunner is in doubt about elements of fire commands, he replies, SAY AGAIN RANGE, TARGET. The leader then announces THE COMMAND WAS, repeats the element in question, and continues with the fire command.

F-117. When the leader makes an error in the initial fire command, he corrects it by announcing CORRECTION, and gives the corrected element. When the leader makes an error in the subsequent fire command, he may correct it by announcing CORRECTION. He then repeats the entire subsequent fire command.

ABBREVIATED FIRE COMMANDS

F-118. Fire commands do not need be complete to be effective. In combat, the leader gives only the elements necessary to place fire on a target quickly and without confusion. During training, however, he should use all of the elements to get gunners in the habit of thinking and reacting properly when a target is to be engaged. After the gunner's initial training in fire commands, he should be taught to react to abbreviated fire commands, using one of the following methods.

Oral

F-119. The leader may want to place the fire of one machine gun on an enemy machine gun and quickly tells the gunner to fire on that gun.

Appendix F

Arm-and-Hand Signals

F-120. Battlefield noise and distance between the gunner and leader often make it necessary to use arm-and-hand signals to control fire. (See figure F-21.) When an action or movement is to be executed by only one of the gunners, a preliminary signal is given to the gunner only. The following are commonly used signals for fire control:

- Ready. The gunner indicates he is ready to fire by yelling UP or having the AG raise his hand above his head toward the leader.
- Commence firing or change rate of firing. The leader brings his hand (palm down) to the front of his body about waist level, and moves it horizontally in front of his body. To signal an increase in the rate of fire, he increases the speed of the hand movement. To signal slower fire, he decreases the speed of the hand movement.
- Change direction or elevation. The leader extends his arm and hand in the new direction and indicates the amount of change necessary by the number of fingers extended. The fingers must be spread so the gunner can easily see the number of fingers extended. Each finger indicates one meter of change of the weapon. If the desired change is more than five meters, the leader extends his hand the number of times necessary to indicate the total amount of change. For example, *right nine* would be indicated by extending the hand once with five fingers showing and a second time with four fingers showing for a total of nine fingers.
- Interrupt or cease firing. The leader raises his arm and hand (palm outward) in front of his forehead and brings it downward sharply.
- Other signals. The leader can devise other signals to control his weapons. A detailed description of arm-and-hand signals is given in FM 21-60.

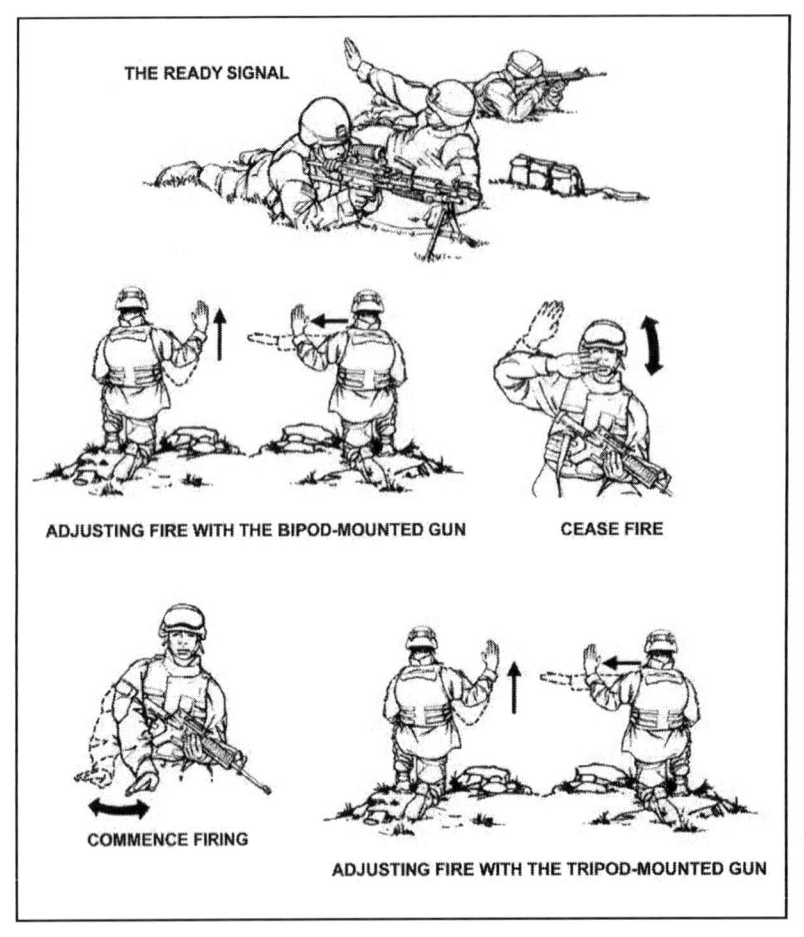

Figure F-21. Arm-and-hand signals

SECTION V – MACHINE GUN USE

F-121. Despite their post-Civil War development, modern machine guns did not exhibit their full potential in battle until World War I. Although the machine gun has changed, the role of the machine gun and machine gunner has not. The mission of machine guns in battle is to deliver fires when and where the leader wants them in both the offense and defense. Machine guns rarely, if ever, have independent missions. Instead, they provide their unit with accurate, heavy fires to accomplish the mission.

TACTICAL ORGANIZATION OF THE MACHINE GUN

F-122. The accomplishment of the platoon's or squad's mission demands efficient and effective machine gun crews. Leaders consider the mission and organize machine guns to deliver firepower and direct fire support to areas or point needed to accomplish the assigned mission.

Appendix F

F-123. Infantry platoons normally will have an organic weapons squad consisting of a weapons squad leader and two gun teams. Depending on the unit's organization or the platoon's and squad's mission, there could be additional machine gun teams attached or organic to the platoon or squad.

F-124. The weapon squad consists of a weapons squad leader and medium machine gun teams. Each medium machine gun team has a gunner, assistant gunner, and ammunition bearer. In some units the senior member of the gun team is the gunner. In other units the assistant gunner is the senior gun team member who also serves as the gun team leader. Table F-8 illustrates equipment carried by the weapons squad. Table F-9 (page F-42) illustrates the duty positions within the weapons squad and gives possible duty descriptions and responsibilities. The tables serve to show possible position and equipment use only. Individual unit SOPs and available equipment dictate the exact role each weapons squad member plays within his squad.

Table F-8. Weapons squad equipment by position example

	WSL	*AG/GTL*	*GUNNER*	*AMMUNITION BEARER*
Weapon	M4-series (w/ 7 magazines*)	M4-series (w/ 7 magazines*)	M240-series (50-100 rounds)	M4-series (w/ 7 magazines)
Day Optic	M68 or M150 Optics	M68 or M150 Optics	M145 Machine Gun Optic	M68 Optics
Laser	PEQ-2	PEQ-2	PEQ-2	PAQ-4/PEQ-2
Additional Equipment	3x magnifier**	3x magnifier** Spare barrels***	3x magnifier**	Tripod T&E

Table F-8. Weapons squad equipment by position example (continued)

	WSL	AG/ GTL	GUNNER	AMMUNITION BEARER
M240-Series Ammunition	100 rounds	300 rounds	100 rounds	300 rounds
Miscellaneous	Whistle Pen gun flare** Other shift signals** VS-17 panel Binoculars****	M9 pistol Cleaning kit Binoculars****	M9 pistol Cleaning kit CLP for 72 hours*****	NA
*WSL and AG/GTL load tracer rounds (4:1 mix) in magazines for marking targets.			
**3x magnifier, flares, and shift signals are readily accessible at all times.			
***Spare barrels marked by relative age with ¼ pieces of green tape on carrying handle. Oldest barrel=2 parallel strips Second newest barrel=1 strip Newest barrel=no tape			
****Binoculars carried in the assault pack or in suitable pouch on vest (mission dependent).			
*****Gunners always carry enough CLP for 72 hours of operations.			
LEGEND AG – assistant gunner; CLP – cleaner, lubricant, preservative; GTL – gun team leader; WSL – weapons squad leader			

Appendix F

Table F-9. Weapons squad duty positions and responsibilities

	WEAPONS SQUAD RESPONSIBILITIES
WSL	Senior squad leader within the platoon. Responsible for all training and employment of the medium machine guns. The WSL's knowledge, experience, and tactical proficiency influence the effectiveness of the squad.
AG/GTL	AG/GTL is a team leader with the responsibilities of a fire team leader. GTL is responsible for his team members and all the gun equipment. GTL and his team will be tactically proficient and knowledgeable on this FM and applicable FMs and TMs applying to the medium machine gun. GTL assists the WSL on the best way to employ the M240-series. GTL enforces field discipline while the gun team is employed. GTL leads by example in all areas. He sets the example in all things. GTL assists the WSL in all areas. He advises him of problems either tactical or administrative. AG is responsible for all action concerning the gun. AG/GTL calls the ammunition bearer if ammunition is needed or actively seeks it out if the ammunition bearer is not available. Constantly updates the WSL on the round count and serviceability of the M240-series. When the gun is firing, AG/GTL spots rounds and makes corrections to the gunner's fire. Also watches for friendly troops to the flanks of the target area or between the gun and target. If the gunner is hit by fire, AG/GTL immediately assumes the role of the gunner. AG/GTL is always prepared to change the gun's barrel (spare barrel is always out when the gun is firing). Ensures the hot barrel is not placed on live ammunition or directly on the ground when it comes out of the gun.

Machine Gun Employment

Table F-9. Weapons squad duty positions and responsibilities (continued)

	WEAPONS SQUAD RESPONSIBILITIES
Machine Gunner	If second in the gun team's chain of command, he is always fully capable of taking the GTL position. Primary responsibility is to the gun. Focused on its cleanliness and proper function. Immediately reports abnormalities to the GTL or WSL. If necessary for gunner to carry M240-series ammunition, carries it in on his back so the AG/GTL can access it without stopping the fire of the gun. Always carries the necessary tools of the gun to be properly cleaned, along with a sufficient amount of oil for the gun's proper function.
Ammunition Bearer	The Ammunition bearer is the RFLM/equipment bearer of the gun team. Normally the newest member of the gun team. Must quickly learn everything he can, exert maximum effort at all times, and attempt to outdo his gun team members in every situation. Follows the gunner without hesitation. During movement moves to the right side of the gunner and no more than one 3-5 meters rush away from the gun. During firing, pulls rear security and if the gunner comes under enemy fire, provides immediate suppression while the gun moves into new position. Responsible of the tripod and T&E mechanism. They always must be clean and ready for combat. Responsible for replacing them, if necessary.

LEGEND
AG – assistant gunner; CLP – cleaner, lubricant, preservative; FM – field manual; GTL – gun team leader; RFLM – rifleman; T&E – traversing and elevating; TM – training manual; WSL – weapons squad leader

SECURITY

F-125. Security includes all command measures to protect against surprise, observation, and annoyance by the enemy. The principal security measures against ground forces include employment of security patrols and detachments covering the front flanks and rear of the unit's most vulnerable areas. The composition and strength of these detachments depends on the size of the main body, its mission, and nature of the opposition expected. The presence of machine guns with security detachments augments their firepower to delay, attack, and defend, by virtue of inherent firepower.

Appendix F

F-126. The potential of air and ground attacks on the unit demands every possible precaution for maximum security while on the move. Where this situation exists, the machine gun crew must be thoroughly trained in the hasty delivery of antiaircraft fire and of counterfire against enemy ground forces. The distribution of the medium machine guns in the formation is critical. The medium machine gun crew is constantly on the alert, particularly at halts, ready to deliver fire as soon as possible. If the leader expects a halt to exceed a brief period, he carefully chooses medium machine gun positions to avoid unduly tiring the medium machine gun crew. If he expects the halt to extend for a long period, he can have the medium machine gun crew take up positions in support of the unit. The crew covers the direction from which he expects enemy activity as well as the direction from which the unit came. The leader selects positions permitting the delivery of fire in the most probable direction of enemy attack, such as valleys, draws, ridges, and spurs. He chooses positions offering obstructed fire from potential enemy locations.

MACHINE GUNS IN THE OFFENSE

F-127. Offensive missions result from the employment of fire and movement. Each is essential and greatly depends upon the other. Without the support of covering fires, maneuvering in the presence of enemy fire can result in disastrous losses. Covering fires, especially providing fire superiority, allow maneuvering in the offense. However, fire superiority alone rarely wins battles. The primary objective of the offense is to advance, occupy, and hold the enemy position.

MACHINE GUN AS A BASE OF FIRE

F-128. Machine gun fire from a support-by-fire position must be the minimum possible to keep the enemy from returning fire. Ammunition must be conserved so the guns do not run out of ammunition.

F-129. The weapons squad leader positions and controls the fires of all medium machine guns in the element. Machine gun targets include essential enemy weapons or groups of enemy targets either on the objective or attempting to reinforce or counterattack. In terms of engagement ranges, medium machine guns in the base-of-fire element may find themselves firing at targets within a range of 800 meters. The nature of the terrain, desire to achieve some standoff, and METT-TC prompts the leader to the correct tactical positioning of the base-of-fire element.

F-130. The medium machine gun delivers an accurate, high-volume rate of lethal fire on fairly large areas in a brief time. When accurately placed on the enemy position, medium machine gun fires secure the essential element of fire superiority for duration of the firing. Troops advancing in the attack should take full advantage of this period to maneuver to a favorable position from where they can facilitate the last push against the enemy. In addition to creating enemy casualties, medium machine gun fire destroys the enemy's confidence and neutralizes his ability to engage the friendly maneuver element.

F-131. There are distinct phases of rates of fire employed by the base-of-fire element:
- Initial heavy volume (rapid rate) to gain fire superiority.

- Slower rate to conserve ammunition (sustained rate) while still preventing return fire as the assault moves forward.
- Increased rate as the assault nears the objective.
- Lift and shift to targets of opportunity.

F-132. All vocal commands from the leaders to change the rates of fire are accompanied simultaneously by arm-and-hand signals.

F-133. Machine guns in the support by fire role should be set in and assigned a primary and alternate sector of fire as well as a primary and alternate position.

F-134. Machine guns are suppressive fire weapons used to suppress known and suspected enemy positions. Therefore, gunners cannot be allowed to empty all their ammunition into one bunker simply because it's all they can identify at the time.

F-135. The support-by-fire position, not the assault element, is responsible for ensuring there is no masking of fires. The assault element might have to mask the support-by-fire line because it has no choice on how to move. It is the support-by-fire gunner's job to shift fires continually, or move gun teams or the weapons squad to support the assault and prevent masking.

F-136. Shift and shut down the weapon squad gun teams one at a time, not all at once. M203/M320 and mortar or other indirect fire can be used to suppress while the medium machine guns are moved to where they can fire.

F-137. Leaders must take into account the surface danger zones of the machine guns when planning and executing the lift and or shift of the support-by-fire guns. The effectiveness of the enemy on the objective will play a large role in how much risk should be taken with respect to the lifting or shifting of fires.

F-138. Once the support-by-fire line is masked by the assault element, fires are shifted and or lifted to prevent enemy withdrawal or reinforcement.

MACHINE GUN WITH THE MANEUVER ELEMENT

F-139. Under certain terrain conditions, and for proper control, medium machine guns may join the maneuver or assault unit. When this is the case, they are assigned a cover fire zone or sector.

F-140. The medium machine guns seldom accompany the maneuver element. The gun's primary mission is to provide covering fire. The medium machine guns only are employed with the maneuver element when the area or zone of action assigned to the assault, platoon, squad or company is too narrow to permit proper control of the guns. The medium machine guns then are moved with the unit and readied to employ on order from the leader and in the direction needing the supporting fire.

F-141. When medium machine guns move with the element undertaking the assault, the maneuver element brings the medium machine guns to provide additional firepower. These weapons are fired from a bipod, in an assault mode, from the hip, or from the underarm position. They target enemy automatic weapons anywhere on the unit's objective. Once the enemy's automatic weapons have been destroyed (if any), the gunners distribute their

Appendix F

fire over their assigned zone or sector. In terms of engagement ranges, the medium machine gun in the assault engages within 300 meters of its target and frequently at point-blank ranges.

F-142. Where the area or zone of action is too wide to allow proper coverage by the platoon's or weapons squad organic medium machine guns, the platoon or squads can be assigned additional medium machine guns or personnel from within the company. This may permit the platoon or squads to accomplish its assigned mission. The medium machine guns are assigned a zone or a sector to cover and move with the maneuver element.

M249 LIGHT MACHINE GUN IN THE OFFENSE

F-143. In the offense, M249s target enemy-supporting weapons being fired from fixed positions anywhere on the squad's objective. When the enemy's supporting weapons have been destroyed, or if there are none, the machine gunners distribute their fire over portion of the objective corresponding to their team's position.

M240-SERIES MEDIUM MACHINE GUNS IN THE OFFENSE

F-144. In the offense the platoon leader has the option to establish his base-of-fire element with one or two machine guns, the M249 light machine gun, or a combination of the weapons. The platoon sergeant or weapons squad leader may position this element and control its fires when the platoon scheme of maneuver is to conduct the assault with the Infantry squads. The M240-series machine gun, when placed on a tripod, provides stability and accuracy at greater ranges than the bipod, but it takes more time to maneuver the machine gun should the need arise. The machine gunners target essential enemy weapons until the assault element masks their fires. They also can be used to suppress the enemy's ability to return accurate fire, or to hamper the maneuver of the enemy's assault element. They fix the enemy in position and isolate him by cutting off his avenues of reinforcement. They then shift their fires to the flank opposite the one being assaulted and continue to target automatic weapons providing enemy support, and engage enemy counterattack. M240-series fires also can be used to cover the gap created between the forward element of the friendly assaulting force and terrain covered by indirect fires when the indirect fires are lifted and shifted. On signal, the machine gunners and base-of-fire element displace to join the assault element on the objective.

MK19 AND M2/M2A1 IN THE OFFENSE

F-145. The MK19 and M2/M2A1 can be used as part of the base-of-fire element to assist the friendly assault element by suppressing enemy bunkers and lightly-armored vehicles. Even if ammunition fired from the guns is not powerful enough to destroy enemy vehicles, well-aimed suppressive fire can keep the enemy buttoned up and unable to place fire on friendly assault elements. The MK19 and M2/M2A1 are particularly effective in preventing lightly-armored enemy vehicles from escaping or reinforcing. Both vehicle mounted weapons can fire from a long range stand-off position, or be moved forward with the assault element.

MACHINE GUNS IN THE DEFENSE

F-146. The platoon's defense centers on its machine guns. The platoon leader sites the rifle squad to protect the machine guns against the assault of a dismounted enemy formation. The machine gun provides the necessary range and volume of fire to cover the squad's front in the defense.

F-147. The primary requirement of a suitable machine gun position in the defense is its effectiveness in accomplishing specific missions. The position should be accessible and afford cover and concealment. Machine guns are sited to protect the front, flanks, and rear of occupied portions of defensive positions, and to be mutually supporting. Attacking troops usually seek easily-traveled ground providing cover from fire. Every machine gun should have three positions: primary, alternate, and supplementary. Each of these positions should be chosen by the leader to ensure his sector is covered and machine guns are protected on their flanks.

F-148. The leader sites the machine gun to cover the entire sector or to overlap sectors with the other machine guns. The engagement range may extend from more than 1000 meters where the enemy begins his assault to point-blank range. Machine gun targets include enemy automatic weapons and command and control elements.

F-149. Machine gun fire is distributed in width and depth in a defensive position. The leader can use machine guns to subject the enemy to increasingly devastating fire from the initial phases of his attack, and to neutralize partial successes the enemy might attain by delivering intense fires in support of counterattacks. The machine gun's tremendous firepower enables the unit to hold ground. This is what makes it the backbone or framework of the defense.

M249 LIGHT MACHINE GUN IN THE DEFENSE

F-150. In the defense, the M249 adds increased firepower without the addition of manpower. Characteristically, M249s are light, fire rapidly, and have more ammunition than the rifles in the squad they support. Under certain circumstances, the platoon leader may designate the M249 machine gun as a platoon crew-served weapon.

M240-SERIES MEDIUM MACHINE GUNS IN THE DEFENSE

F-151. In the defense, the medium machine gun provides sustained direct fires covering the most likely or most dangerous enemy dismounted avenues of approach. It protects friendly units against the enemy's dismounted close assault. The platoon leader positions his machine guns to concentrate fires in locations where he wants to inflict the most damage to the enemy. He also places them where they can take advantage of grazing enfilade fires, stand-off or maximum engagement range, and best observation of the target area. Machine guns provide overlapping and interlocking fires with adjacent units and cover tactical and protective obstacles with traversing or searching fires. When FPFs are called for, machine guns (aided by M249 fires) place a barrier of fixed, direct fire across the platoon or squad front. Leaders position machine guns to—

- Concentrate fires where they want to kill the enemy.

Appendix F

- Fire across the platoon and squad front
- Cover obstacles by direct fire.
- Tie in with adjacent units.

MK19 AND M2/M2A1 IN THE DEFENSE

F-152. In the defense, MK19 and M2/M2A1 machine guns may be fired from the vehicle mount or dismounted from the vehicle and mounted on a tripod at a defensive fighting position designed for the weapon system.

F-153. These weapons provide sustained direct fires covering the most likely enemy mounted avenue of approach. Their maximum effective range enables them to engage enemy vehicles and equipment at far greater ranges than the platoon's or squads other direct fire weapons.

F-154. When mounted on the tripod, the M2/M2A1 and MK19 are highly accurate to their maximum effective range and predetermined fires can be planned for likely high pay off targets. The tradeoff is these weapon systems are relatively heavy, and take more time to move.

F-155. These guns are not as accurate when mounted on vehicles as they are when fired from the tripod-mounted system. However, they are\ maneuvered easily to alternate firing locations should the need arise.

AMMUNITION PLANNING

F-156. Leaders must carefully plan the rates of fire to be employed by machine guns as they relate to the mission and amount of ammunition available. The weapons squad leader must understand fully the mission the amount of available ammunition and application of machine gun fire needed to support fully all vital events of the mission. Planning ensures the guns do not run out of ammunition.

F-157. A mounted platoon or squad might have access to enough machine gun ammunition to support the guns throughout its operation. A dismounted platoon or squad with limited resupply capabilities has to plan for only the basic load to be available. In either case, leaders must take into account vital events the guns must support during the mission. They must plan the rate of machine gun fire needed to support the vital events, and amount of ammunition needed for scheduled rates of fire.

F-158. The leader must make an estimate of the total amount of ammunition needed to support all the machine guns. He then must adjust the amount of ammunition used for each event to ensure enough ammunition is available for all phases of the operation. Examples of planning rates of fire and ammunition requirements for a platoon's or weapons squad's machine guns in the attack follow.

KNOW RATES OF FIRE

F-159. Leaders and gunners must know how much ammunition is required to support the different rates of fire each platoon or weapons squad machine gun and assault weapon will require. Coupling this knowledge with an accurate estimate of the length of time and rates of fire their guns are scheduled to fire will ensure enough ammunition resources to cover the entire mission. As part of an example of the planning needed to use M240-series in support-by-fire roles, the rates of fire of the M240-series are listed in table F-10.

Table F-10. M240-series rates of fire

SUSTAINED	• 100 rounds per minute • Fired in 6- to 9-round bursts • 4-5 seconds between bursts (Barrel change every 10 minutes.)
RAPID	• 200 rounds per minute • Fired in 10- to 12-round bursts • 2-3 seconds between bursts (Barrel change every two minutes.)
CYCLIC	• 650-950 rounds per minute • Continuous burst (Barrel change every minute.)

AMMUNITION REQUIREMENT

F-160. Leaders must calculate the number of rounds needed to support every machine gun throughout all phases of the operation. Ammunition must be allocated for each vital event and to support movement with suppressive fires.

This page intentionally left blank.

Appendix G

Shoulder-Launched Munitions and Close Combat Missile Systems

SLM and CCMS are employed by the Infantry platoon squads and weapons squad to destroy enemy field fortifications or disable enemy vehicles at ranges from 15 to 3750 meters. They can engage targets in assault, support by fire, defensive roles, and are the Infantry platoon's highest casualty-producing organic weapons when used against armored enemy vehicles. This appendix addresses SLM and CCMS use by the Infantry platoon and discusses their capabilities and limitations.

SECTION I – MUNITIONS

G-1. SLM and CCMS are used against field fortifications, enemy vehicles, or other similar enemy targets. SLM are issued to Infantry Soldiers as rounds of ammunition in addition to their assigned weapons. While Javelins are organic to the Infantry weapons squad, TOW missile weapon systems are found in the assault platoons in the Infantry battalions weapon company. This section discusses the specific types of SLM and CCMS the Infantry platoon employs. Section II discusses their employment considerations. Section III discusses safety. For complete information refer to TM 3-23.25, *Shoulder-Launched Munitions*; TC 3-22.37, *Javelin-Close Combat Missile System, Medium*; FM 3-22.34, *TOW Weapon System*; and TC 3-22.32, *Improved Target Acquisition System, M41*.

SHOULDER-LAUNCHED MUNITIONS

G-2. SLM include the M136A1 AT4 combined space (AT4CS), M136 AT4; the M72A2/A3 light antitank weapon (LAW), improved M72A4/5/6/7 LAW; and M141 BDM. The M141 BDM also has been referred to as the shoulder-launched multipurpose assault weapon-disposable (SMAW-D). Table G-1 lists select SLM specifications.

G-3. All SLM are lightweight, self-contained, single-shot, disposable weapons consisting of unguided free flight, fin-stabilized, rocket-type cartridges packed in expendable, telescoping launchers (except the M 136 AT4/AT4CS which does not telescope) also serve as storage containers. The only requirement for their care is a visual inspection. SLM can withstand extreme weather and environmental conditions, including arctic, tropical, and desert climates.

G-4. SLM increase the lethality and survivability of the Infantryman and provide him a direct fire capability to defeat enemy personnel within armored platforms. BDM provides the Soldier a direct fire capability to defeat enemy personnel located within field

Appendix G

fortifications, bunkers, caves, masonry structures, and lightly armed vehicles and to suppress enemy personnel in lightly armored vehicles.

G-5. The individual Soldier will use SLM to engage threat combatants at close ranges, across the street or from one building to another. The Soldier may employ SLM as a member of a support-by-fire element to incapacitate threat forces threatening the assault element. When the assault element clears a building, the leader may reposition the SLM gunner inside to engage a potential counterattack force.

Note. Several numbers in table G-1 have been rounded off and might not represent exact numbers.

Table G-1. Shoulder-launched munitions

SHOULDER-LAUNCHED MUNITION	M136 AT4 DODIC C995	M136A1 (AT4CS) DODIC HA35	M72A2/A3 LAW DODIC H557
Field Manual	TM 3-23.25	TM 3-23.25	TM 3-23.25
Carry Weight	15.0 lbs.	17.0 lbs.	5.0 lbs.
Length: Carry Extended:	40 inches N/A	41 inches N/A	25 inches 35 inches
Caliber	84-mm	84-mm	66-mm
Muzzle Velocity	290 m/s 950 f/s	225 m/s 738 f/s	144.8 m/s 475 f/s
Operating Temperature	-40 to 60 C -40 to 140 F	-40 to 60 C -40 to 140 F	-40 to 60 C -40 to 140 F
Maximum Effective Range	300 m	300 m	Stationary – 200 m Moving - 165 m
Maximum Range	2100 m	2100 m	1000 m
Minimum Arming Range	10 m	10 m	10 m

Table G-1. Shoulder-launched munitions (continued)

SHOULDER-LAUNCHED MUNITION	M72A4/5/6/7 IMPROVED LAW DODIC HA29	M141 BDM DODIC HA08
Field Manual	TM 3-23.25	TM 3-23.25
Carry Weight	8.0 lbs.	16.0 lbs.
Length:	31 inches	32 inches
Carry Extended:	39 inches	55 inches
Caliber	60-mm	83-mm
Muzzle Velocity	200 m/s 656 f/s	217 m/s 712 f/s
Operating Temperature	-40 to 60 C -40 to 140 F	-32 to 49 C -20 to 120 F
Maximum Effective Range	220 m	500 m
Maximum Range	1400 m	2000 m
Minimum Arming Range	25 m	15 m

M136 AT4/M136A1 AT4CS

G-6. The M136 AT4 is a lightweight, self-contained, SLM designed for use against the improved armor of light-armored vehicles. It provides lethal fire against light-armored vehicles, and has some effect on most enemy field fortifications.

G-7. The M136A1 AT4CS is similar to the M136 AT4, but uses a different propulsion system. This system enables the M136A1 AT4CS to be fired from an enclosure.

G-8. The M136 AT4 and M136A1 AT4CS is a round of ammunition with an integral, rocket-type cartridge. The cartridge consists of a fin assembly with tracer element; a point detonating fuze; and a HEAT warhead (See figures G-1 and G-2, both page G-4.)

Appendix G

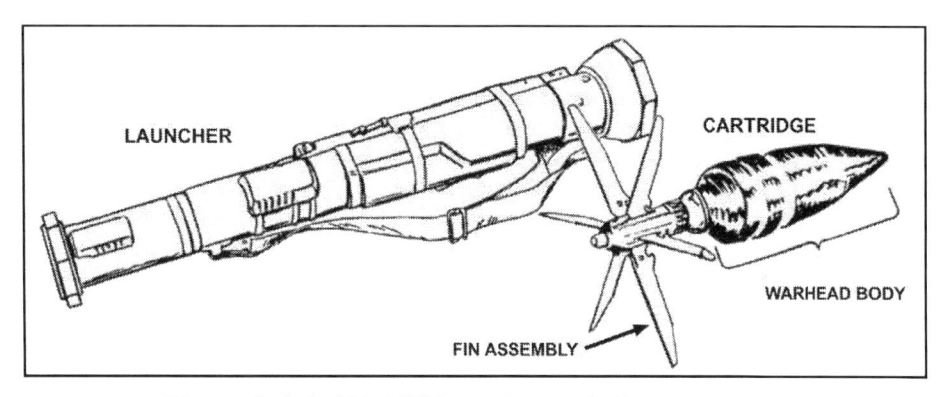

Figure G-1. M136 AT4 launcher and HEAT cartridge

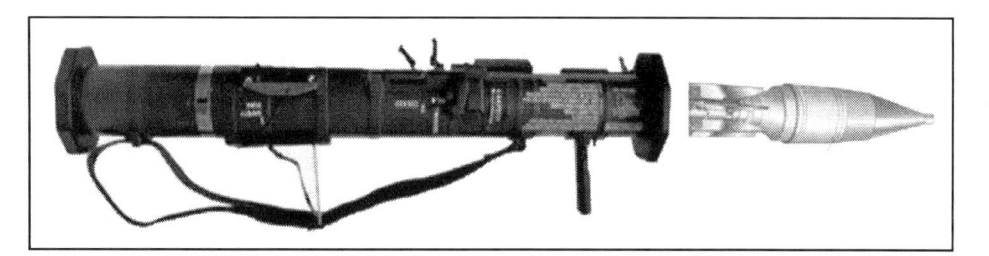

Figure G-2. M136A1 AT4CS launcher and HEAT cartridge

M72-SERIES LIGHT ANTITANK WEAPON

G-9. The M72 LAWs used by Infantry platoons and squads today are the M72A3 and M72A7. The M72 series are available as a contingency by request. They are lightweight and self-contained SLM consisting of a rocket packed in a launcher. (See figures G-3 through G-5, pages G-5 through G-7.) They are man-portable, and may be fired from either shoulder. The launcher, which consists of two tubes, one inside the other, serves as a watertight packing container of the rocket and houses a percussion-type firing mechanism activating the rocket.

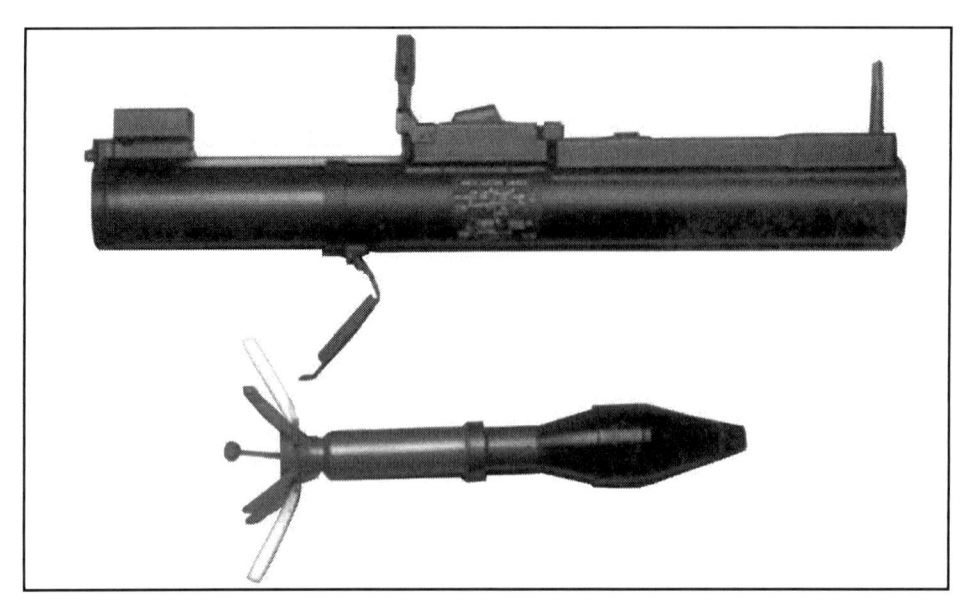

Figure G-3. M72A3 LAW

M72A3

G-10. The M72A3 contains a nonadjustable propelling charge and a 66-mm rocket. Every M72A3 has an integral HEAT warhead in the rocket's head (or body) section. (See figure G-4, page G-6.) Although the M72A3 mainly is employed as an antiarmor weapon, it may be used with limited success against secondary targets such as gun emplacements, pillboxes, buildings, or light vehicles.

Appendix G

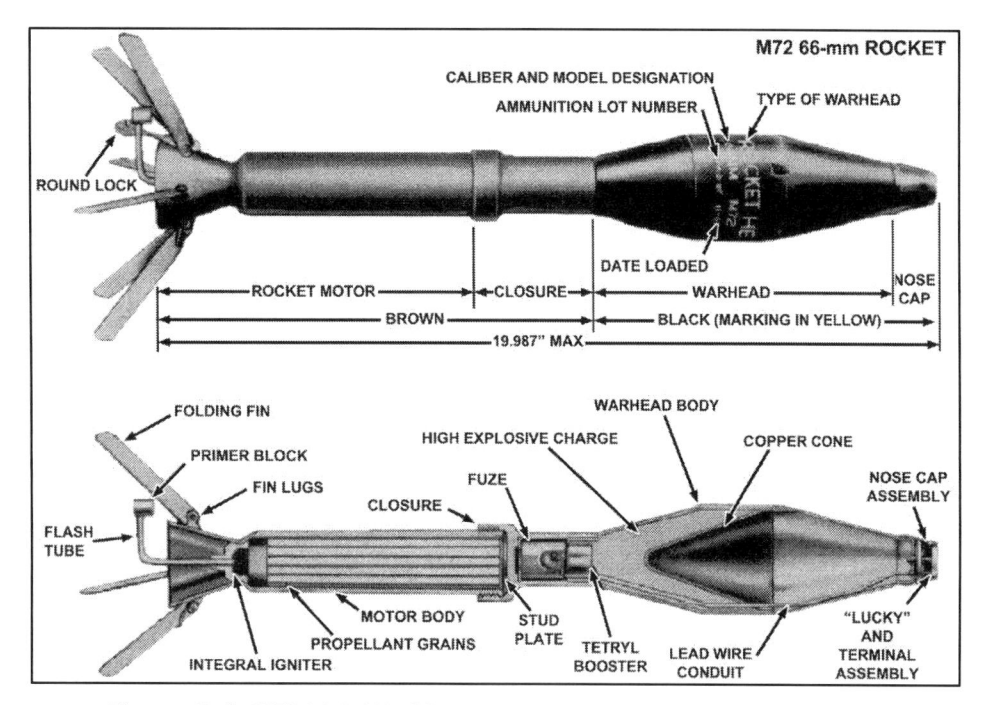

Figure G-4. M72A3 LAW 66-mm high-explosive antiarmor rocket

IMPROVED M72A7 LAW

G-11. The M72A7 is the improved LAW currently employed by Infantry platoons and squads. It is a compact, lightweight, single-shot, disposable weapon optimized to defeat lightly armored vehicles at close combat ranges. (See figure G-5.) The M72A7 offers enhanced capabilities beyond the original M72-series. The Improved M72 consists of a 66-mm unguided rocket prepackaged at the factory in a telescoping, throwaway launcher. The system performance improvements include a higher velocity rocket motor extending the weapon effective range, increased lethality warhead, lower and more consistent trigger release force, rifle-type sight system, and better overall system reliability and safety. The weapon contains a 66-mm rocket and an integral HEAT warhead. The warhead is designed to penetrate 150 millimeters of homogenous armor and is optimized for maximum fragmentation behind light armor, Infantry fighting vehicles (IFV), and urban walls.

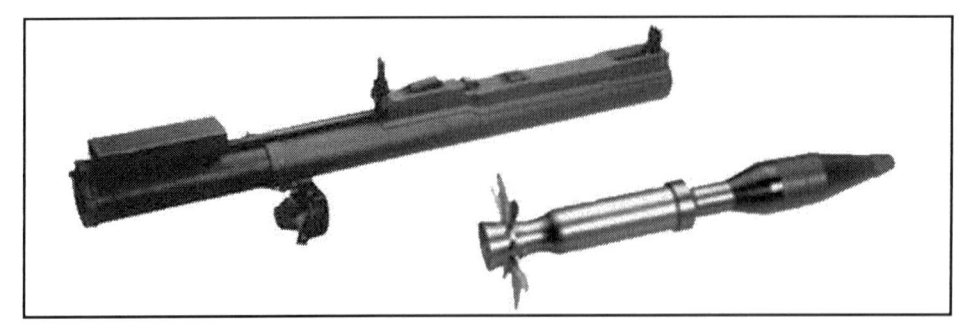

Figure G-5. Improved M72A7 LAW with rocket

M141 BUNKER DEFEAT MUNITIONS

G-12. The M141 BDM was developed to defeat enemy bunkers and field fortifications. (See figure G-6.) The M141 BDM is a disposable, lightweight, self-contained, man-portable, shoulder-fired, HE multipurpose munitions.

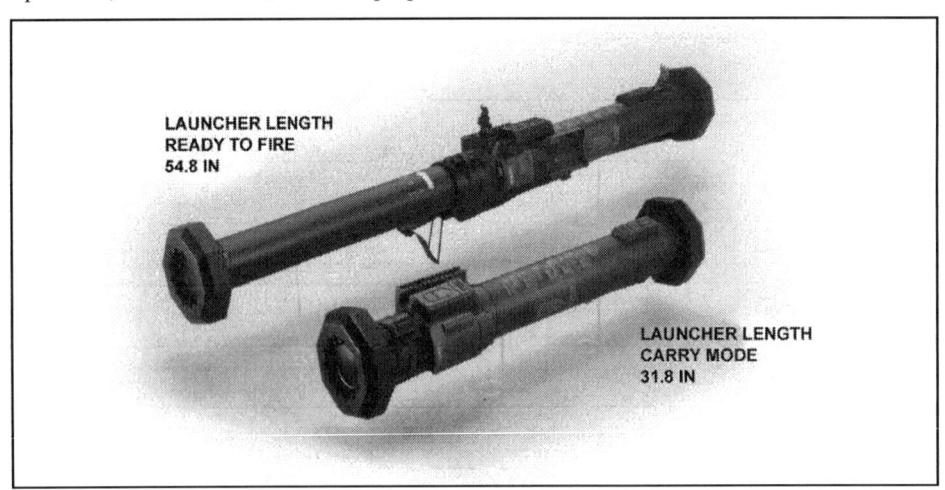

Figure G-6. M141 bunker defeat munitions

G-13. The M141 BDM utilizes the 83-mm HEDP assault rocket. (See figure G-7, page G-8.) The 83-mm HEDP assault rocket warhead consists of a dual mode fuze, and 2.38 pounds of A-3 explosive.

G-14. Warhead function, in quick or delay mode, is determined automatically by the fuze when the rocket impacts a target. The M141 BDM is fired at hard or soft targets without selection steps required by the gunner. This automatic feature assures the kill mechanism is employed. Warhead detonation is instantaneous when impacting a hard target, such as a brick or concrete wall or an armored vehicle. Impact with a softer target, such as a sandbagged bunker, results in a fuze time delay permitting the rocket to penetrate into the target before warhead detonation.

Appendix G

G-15. The M141 BDM can destroy bunkers, but is not optimized to kill the enemy soldiers within masonry structures in urban terrain or armored vehicles. The M141 BDM can penetrate masonry walls, but multiple rounds may be necessary to deliver sufficient lethality against enemy personnel behind the walls.

G-16. The M141 BDM has been used with great success in destroying personnel and equipment in enemy bunkers, field fortifications, and caves in recent operations.

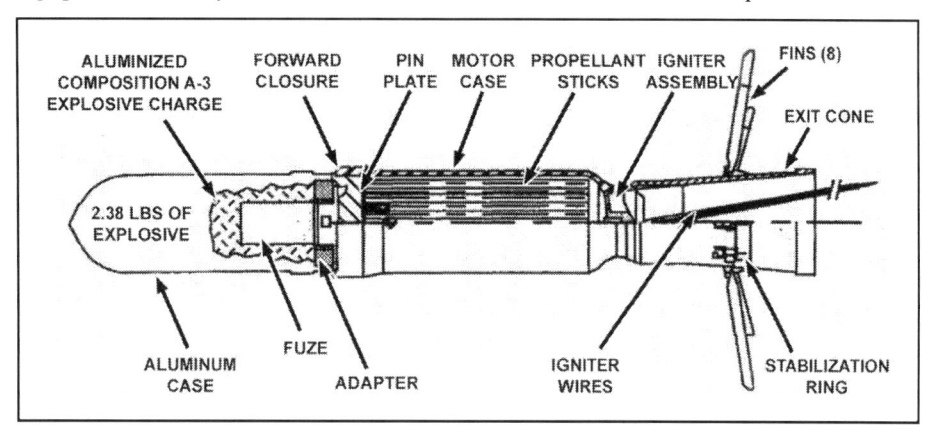

Figure G-7. M141 BDM high-explosive dual purpose assault rocket

CLOSE COMBAT MISSILE SYSTEMS

G-17. CCMS are used primarily to defeat main battle tanks and other armored combat vehicles. In the current force, this category of weapons includes the TOW and Javelin. The TOW and Javelin provide overmatch antitank fires during the assault and provide extended range capability for engaging armor during both offensive and defensive missions. These systems have a moderate capability against bunkers, buildings, and other fortified targets commonly found during combat in urban areas. The TOW's Bunker Buster (BB) round is capable of destroying the majority of urban targets.

JAVELIN

G-18. The Javelin is a fire-and-forget, shoulder-fired, man-portable CCMS consisting of a reusable M98A1 (Block 0) and the improved M98A2 (Block 1), CLU and a round. (See figure G-8.) The CLU houses the daysight, night vision sight (NVS), controls, and indicators. The round consists of the missile, the launch tube assembly (LTA), and battery coolant unit (BCU). The LTA serves as the launch platform and carrying container of the missile. (Refer to TC 3-22.37 for more information.)

G-19. The Javelin CCMS' primary role is to destroy enemy armored vehicles out to 2000 meters with the M98A1 and 2500 meters with the M98A2. The Javelin can be employed in a secondary role of providing FS against point targets such as bunkers and crew-served weapons positions. In addition, the Javelin CLU can be used alone as an aided vision device for reconnaissance, security operations, and surveillance. When BFV are part of a combined-arms team, the Javelin becomes a secondary antiarmor weapons system. It supports the fires of tanks and TOWs, covers secondary armor avenues of approach, and provides observation posts with an antiarmor capability. The Javelin gunner should be able to engage up to three targets in two minutes, making him effective against armor threat.

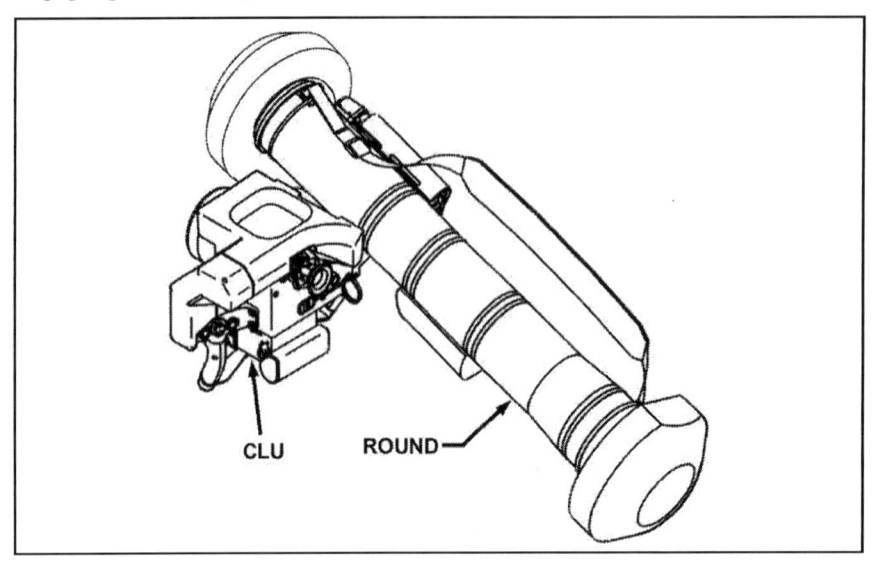

Figure G-8. Javelin close combat missile system

Command Launch Unit

G-20. The M98A1 and M98A2 CLU is the reusable portion of the Javelin system. It contains the controls and indicators. The CLU provides increased utility to the Infantry platoon and weapons squad by allowing accurate surveillance out to 2.5 plus kilometers in both day and night. CLUs have been used to spot and destroy enemy snipers in hidden positions more than 1000 meters away.

G-21. Tables G-2 through G-4 (pages G-9 through G-11) list the Javelin's capabilities and features, the physical characteristics of the CLU, and physical characteristics of the round.

Table G-2. Javelin capabilities and features

Javelin Missile System	Surface attack guided missile and M98A1 and M98A2 CLU
Type of System	Fire and forget
Crew	One- to three-Soldier teams based on TO&E
Missile modes	Top attack (default)
	Direct attack

Appendix G

Table G-2. Javelin capabilities and features (continued)

Ranges	Top attack mode minimum effective engagement: 150 meters
	Direct attack mode minimum effective engagement range: 65 meters
	Maximum effective engagement range (direct attack and top attack modes): 2000 meters for the M98A1 and 2500+ meters for the M98A2
Flight Time	About 14 seconds at 2000 meters with the M98A1 and 2500+ meters with the M98A2
Backblast Area	Primary danger zone extends out 25 meters at a 60-degree (cone-shaped) angle
	Caution zone extends the cone-shaped area out to 100 meters
Firing From Inside Enclosures	Minimum room length: 15 feet
	Minimum room width: 12 feet
	Minimum room height: 7 feet

Table G-3. Physical characteristics of the command launch unit

M98A1/M98A2 Command Launch Unit	With battery, carrying bag, and cleaning kit
	Weight: 14.16 lb. (6.42 kg)/14.99 lb. (6.80 kg)
	Length: 13.71 in (34.82 cm)/19.29 in (49.00 cm)
	Height: 13.34 in (33.88 cm) /13.00 in (33.02 cm)
	Width: 19.65 in (49.91 cm) /1650 in (41.91 cm)
Sights	Daysight
	Magnification: 4X
	Field-of-view (FOV): 4.80° x 6.40° /6.4°x 4.8°
	Night Vision Sight
	Wide field-of-view (WFOV) magnification: 4.2X
	WFOV: 4.58° x 6.11°
	Narrow field-of-view (NFOV) magnification: 9.2X/12X
	NFOV: 2.00° x 3.00° /2° x 1.5° (approximately)

Table G-3. Physical characteristics of the command launch unit (continued)

Battery Type	Lithium Sulfur Dioxide (LiSO2) BA-5590/U (Nonrechargeable)		
	Nickel metal hydride battery, BB-390A/U rechargeable (training use only)		
	Number required: 1		
	NSN: 6135-01-036-3495		
	Weight: 2.2 lbs. (1.00 kg)		
	Life:	4.0 hrs below 120°F (49°C)	
		3.0 hrs between 50°F to 120°F (10°C to 49°C)	
		1.0 hrs between -20°F to 50°F (-49°C to 10°C)	
		0.5 hrs above 120°F (49°C)	

Table G-4. Physical characteristics of the round

Complete Round (Launch tube assembly with missile and BCU)	Weight: 35.14 lb. (15.97 kg)
	Length: 47.60 in (120.90 cm)
	Diameter with end caps: 11.75 in (29.85 cm)
	Inside diameter: 5.52 in (14.00 cm)
Battery Coolant Unit	Weight: 2.91 lb. (1.32 kg)
	Length: 8.16 in (20.73 cm)
	Width: 4.63 in (11.75 cm)
	Battery type: lithium, nonrechargeable
	Battery life: 4 min of BCU time
	Battery coolant gas: argon

Missile

G-22. The Javelin missile consists of the guidance section; the midbody section, the warhead, the propulsion section, and control actuator section. A discussion of the guidance section and warhead follows.

Guidance Section

G-23. The guidance section provides target tracking and flight control signals. It is the forward section of the missile and includes the seeker head section and guidance electronics unit.

Appendix G

Warhead Section

G-24. The Javelin missile uses a dual-charged warhead (see figure G-9) containing a precursor charge and main charge:
- Precursor charge. The precursor charge is an HE AT shaped charge. Its purpose is to cause reactive armor on the target to detonate before the main charge reaches the armor. Once the reactive armor is penetrated, the target's main hull is exposed to the warhead's main charge. If the target is not equipped with reactive armor, the precursor provides additional explosives to penetrate the main armor.
- Main charge. The main charge is the second charge of a dual-charge warhead and is also an HE-shaped charge. The primary warhead charge is designed to penetrate the target's main armor to achieve a target kill.

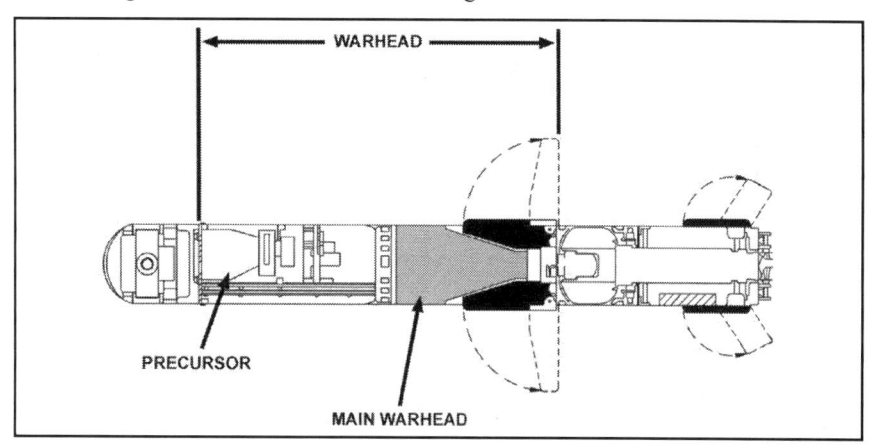

Figure G-9. Javelin missile warhead

Capabilities and Limitations

G-25. The Javelin has some unique capabilities providing the unit with an antiarmor weapon system. However, the Infantry leader also should understand system's limitations in order to employ this system. (See table G-5.)

Table G-5. Javelin capabilities and limitations

	CAPABILITIES	LIMITATIONS
FIREPOWER	• Maximum effective range is 2000 meters. • Fire-and-forget capability. Missile I2R system gives missile ability to guide itself to the target when launched by the gunner. • Two missile flight paths: • Top attack – impacts on top of target. • Direct attack – impacts on front, rear, or flank of target. • Gunner can fire up to three missiles within two minutes. • Dual-shaped charge warhead can defeat known enemy armor. • NVS sees little degradation of target image. • Countermeasures used by enemy are countered by the NVS filter.	• CLU sight cannot discriminate targets past 2000 meters. • NVS cool-down time is from 2.5 to 3.5 minutes. • Seeker's cool-down time is about 10 seconds. • BCU life, once activated, is only about 4 minutes. • FOV can be rendered useless during limited visibility conditions (rain, snow, sleet, fog, haze, obscurants, dust, and night). Visibility is limited by the following: • Day FOV relies on daylight to provide the gunner a suitable target image; limited visibility conditions may block sun. • NVS uses the infrared naturally emitted from objects. Infrared crossovers is the time at both dawn and dusk that terrain and targets are close enough in temperature to cause targets to blend in with their surroundings. • Natural clutter occurs when the sun heats objects to a temperature close enough to surrounding terrain that it causes a target to blend in with terrain. • Artificial clutter occurs when there are man-made objects that emit large amounts of infrared (example, burning vehicles). • Heavy fog reduces the capability of the gunner to detect and engage targets. • Flight path of missile is restricted in wooded, mountainous, and urban terrain. • Gunner must have LOS of the seeker to lock onto a target.

Appendix G

Table G-5. Javelin capabilities and limitations (continued)

MANEUVER	• Man-portable. • Fire-and-forget capability allows gunner to shoot and move before missile impact. • Soft launch capability allows it to be fired from inside buildings and bunkers. • Maneuverable over short distances of the gunners.	• Weight of Javelin makes maneuvering slow over long distances. • The Javelin round is bulky and restricts movement in heavily-wooded or vegetative terrain.
PROTECTION	• Passive infrared targeting system used to acquire lock-on cannot be detected. • Launch motor produces a small signature. • Fire-and-forget feature allows gunner to take cover immediately after missile is launched.	• Gunner must partially expose himself to engage the enemy. • CLU requires a LOS to acquire targets.
LEGEND BCU – battery coolant unit; CLU – command launch unit; FOV – field of view; I2R – Missile imaging infrared (I2R) system; LOS – line of sight; NVS – night vision system		

TUBE-LAUNCHED, OPTICALLY-TRACKED, WIRE-GUIDED MISSILE WEAPON SYSTEM

G-26. The TOW weapon system consists of the Improved Target Acquisition System (ITAS) launcher, which has tracking, control capabilities, and missile, which is encased in a launch container. The launcher is equipped with self-contained, replaceable units.

G-27. The TOW is designed to destroy enemy tanks, fortifications, and other materiel targets. Its LOS launcher initiates, tracks, and controls the missile's flight through command-link wire-transmitted guidance signals. It can be employed in all weather conditions as long as the gunner can see the target through the ITAS. The TOW also provides a long-range assault capability against heavily fortified bunkers, pillboxes, and gun emplacements.

G-28. The current versions of the TOW missile can destroy targets at a minimum range of 65 meters and a maximum range of 3750 meters. The TOW 2B missile can destroy targets at a minimum range of 200 meters and a maximum range of 3750 meters. TOW missiles in development are being produced to engage enemy targets out to 4500 meters.

Missile System Configurations and Types

G-29. The TOW CCMS consists of multiple configurations with numerous types of missiles. These configurations mainly consist of minor modified work orders transparent to the operator and are continually updated. All configurations use the same basic airframe, aerodynamic control system, command-link wire, and missile electronics designs. The current missile types are listed below:

- *Improved TOW (ITOW).* The ITOW missile has an improved five-inch warhead from the original TOW missile including extended probes for greater standoff and penetration. It can destroy targets at a minimum range of 65 meters and a maximum range of 3750 meters.
- *TOW 2.* The TOW 2 missile has a full-caliber six-inch warhead including an extended probe. In addition to the infrared radiator of the ITOW missile, TOW 2 has a second infrared radiator to provide hardened system performance against battlefield obscurants and countermeasures. The second radiator is called the thermal beacon and provides link compatibility with the electro-optical infrared nightsight, which is part of the TOW 2 launcher system.
- *TOW 2A.* The TOW 2A adds a small explosive charge in the tip of the extended probe causing enemy reactive armor to detonate prematurely, thus allowing the TOW 2A's warhead to penetrate the main armor.
- *TOW 2B.* The TOW 2B has an entirely different warhead and kill mechanism than the previous TOW missiles. It is a top-attack missile (fly over/shoot down) defeating enemy armor at its most vulnerable point the top deck of the turret and hull. The TOW 2B has a tandem warhead firing two explosively formed projectiles down through the thin upper deck armor of the enemy vehicle. The gunner tracks the target the same as other TOW missile with the crosshairs on center mass, but the missile automatically flies 2.25 meters above LOS. When the missile senses it's directly above the target (by means of the target's shape and magnetic field), it automatically fires its warhead. The TOW 2B missile can destroy targets at a minimum range of 288 meters when fired from the ground mount and 200 meters when fired from the HMMWV or BFV. The TOW 2B has a maximum range of 3750 meters whether ground- or vehicle-mounted.
- *TOW 2B GEN 1.* The TOW 2B GEN 1 is similar to the TOW 2B but includes the addition of the GEN 1 Counter Active Protection System (CAPS), which is used to defeat enemy active protection systems.
- TOW 2B Aero. The TOW 2B Aero is an extended range version of the TOW 2B missile with an aerodynamic nose and has an effective range of 4500 meters. (See figure G-10, page G-16.) This longer range (compared to the 3750 meter range of the previous TOW missiles) allows a TOW crew to fire well beyond the weapons range of its targeted vehicle.
- *TOW 2B Aero With GEN 1, 2, and 3A CAPS.* These versions of TOW 2B Aero have the addition of different generations of CAPS to defeat an enemy target's active protection system, allowing the TOW 2B missile to engage armored vehicles up to 4500 meters. (See figure G-10, page G-16.)
- TOW BB. The TOW BB replaces the TOW 2A warhead with a fragmenting bulk charge for nonarmor targets. (See figure G-11.) The TOW BB has a range of 3750

Appendix G

meters. Its missile is capable of defeating bunkers, creating a lane through masonry walls, and engaging targets in support of urban operations.

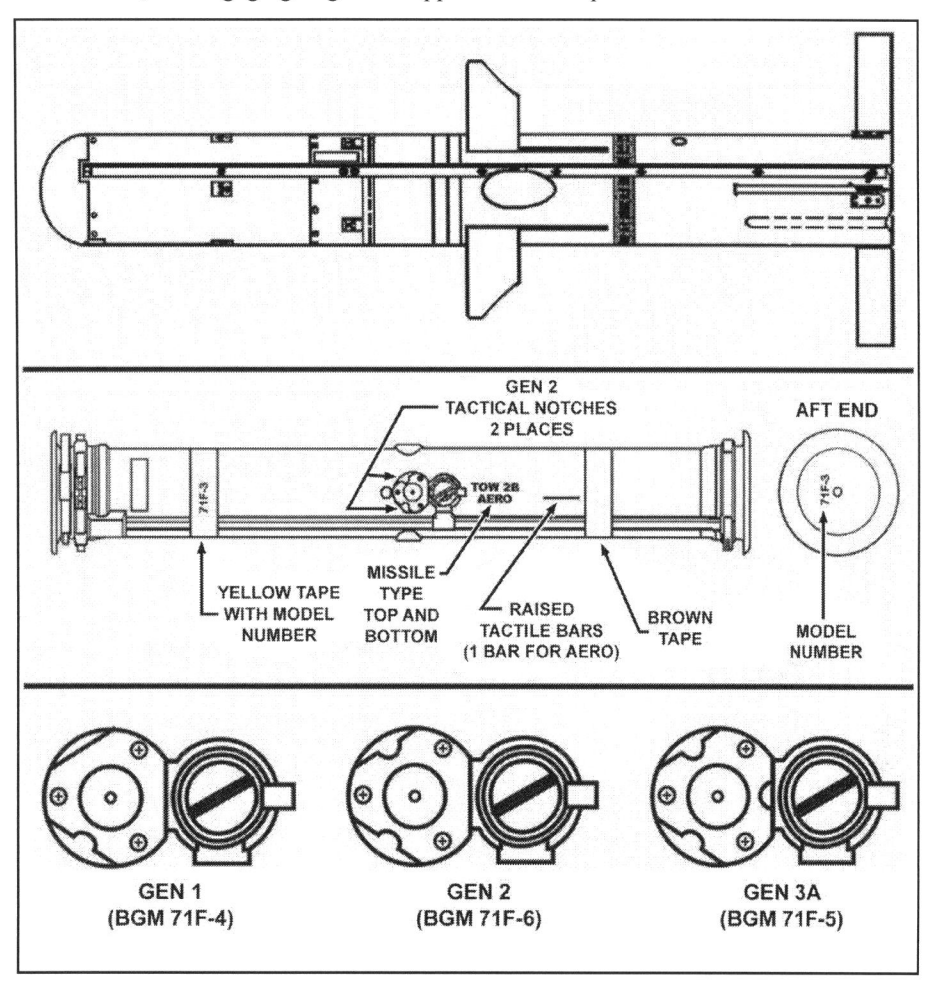

Figure G-10. TOW 2B aero missile with identification

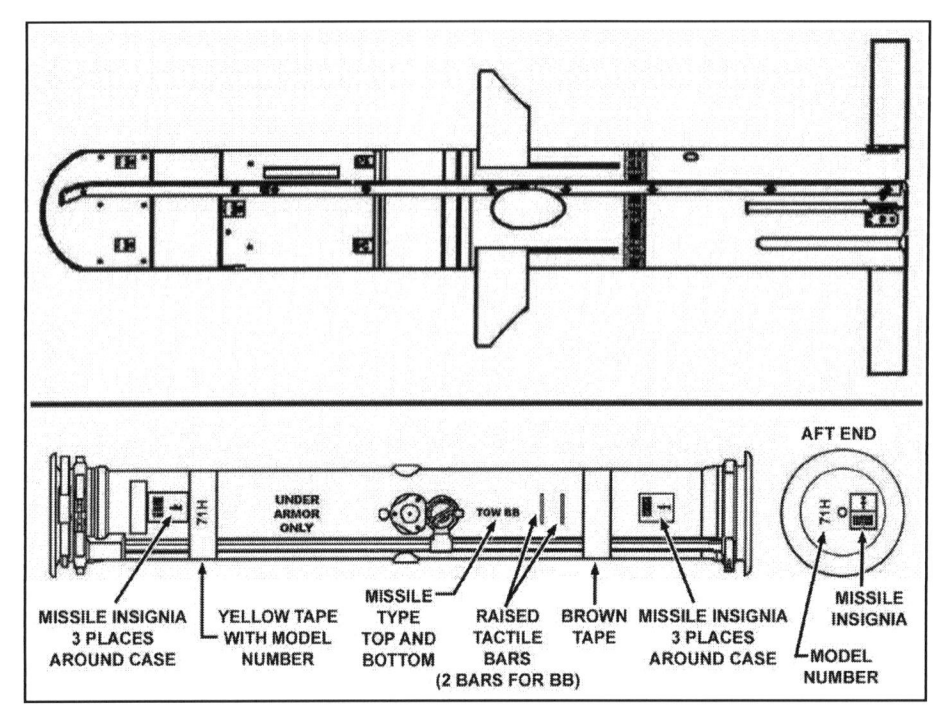

Shoulder-Launched Munitions and Close Combat Missile Systems

Figure G-11. TOW bunker buster missile and identification

M41 Improved Target Acquisition System

G-30. The ITAS is primarily a mounted system utilizing the M1121 HMMWV as the carrier vehicle. The M1121 HMMWV is a one-vehicle (1 1/4-ton truck) combat system air transportable, versatile, maintainable, and survivable. The vehicle carries one complete launcher system, seven encased missiles, and a three-man crew. The tactical or training situation may demand crew dismount the carrier and employ the ITAS in dismounted or tripod configuration.

G-31. The M41 ITAS fires all existing and future versions of the TOW family of missiles. The ITAS provides the integration of both the daysight and NVS into a single housing and for automatic boresighting. It has embedded training (for sustainment training) and advanced built-in test/built-in-test equipment (BIT/BITE), which provides fault detection and isolation.

G-32. The automatic missile tracking and control capabilities of the ITAS provide a high first-round-hit probability. To operate the system, the gunner places the track gates on the target, fires the missile, and centers the crosshairs on the target image until missile impact. The optical tracking and command functions within the system guide the missile to the target as long as the gunner keeps the crosshairs on target.

Appendix G

G-33. The ITAS provides the Infantry platoon and squads with advanced optics during daylight and limited visibility to aid in surveillance and target acquisition in both offensive and defensive missions.

G-34. The ITAS can be vehicle-mounted or ground-emplaced (tripod-mounted) for operation. Missiles can be launched from either operational mode. The entire system can be carried by a single crew for short distances. Moving it over long distances without the vehicle will require two crews, which causes two systems to be out of operation at the same time. The vehicle-mounted launcher is more mobile and can be prepared quickly for use. The launcher can be assembled and disassembled without the use of tools.

SECTION II – EMPLOYMENT CONSIDERATIONS

G-35. The objective of the Army's warfighting doctrine is to concentrate decisive combat power at the right time and place, by massing fires rather than by massing forces, and by presenting the enemy with multiple threats. This section discusses SLM and CCMS employment considerations. A lethal mix of CCMS and SLM provide the Infantry unit with the flexibility to employ multiple systems designed to deliver maximum direct fire lethality and destroy enemy formations at both long range and in close combat. At close combat range (15-300 meters), SLM provide Soldiers with the ability to deliver direct fire lethality at close proximity to the enemy. At extended range (300-4500 meters), a mix of Javelin and TOW provides the Infantry leader with overwhelming combat overmatch. These weapons serve as vital components by applying overlapping and interlocking fires to achieve synergy and mutual support for his maneuver force.

URBAN OPERATIONS AND FIELD FORTIFICATIONS

G-36. Operations in complex terrain and urban environments alter the basic nature of close combat. History tells us engagements are more frequent and occur more rapidly when engagement ranges are close. Studies and historical analyses have shown only five percent of all targets are more than 100 meters away. About 90 percent of all targets are located 50 meters or less from the identifying Soldier. Few personnel targets will be visible beyond 50 meters. Engagements usually occur at 35 meters or less.

G-37. Soldiers employ SLM in the short, direct fire, close-quarter engagement range of close combat. Their use is preferable in urban areas where other direct fire (M1-series Abrams tank and M2-series BFV) and indirect fire systems (artillery, mortars) and CAS are incapable of operating due to risks of fratricide and collateral damage. In close combat, Soldiers employ SLM against a wide variety of targets. These include: personnel armed with individual and crew-served weapons fighting from armored platforms (T-72s, BTRs, BRDMs); light armored personnel carriers and Infantry fighting vehicles (BMP1-3 and M113); modified personnel/Infantry vehicles; lightly armed vehicles; and enemy in fortified positions, behind walls, inside caves and masonry buildings, and within earthen bunkers.

G-38. CCMS teams provide overwatching antitank fires during the attack of a built-up area. They are best employed in these types of areas along major thoroughfares and in upper floors of buildings or roofs to attain long-range fields of fire. Because the minimum engagement distance limits firing opportunities in the confines of densely built-up areas, CCMS may not be the weapon of choice in the urban environment. Urban area hazards include, fires caused by both friendly and enemy forces may cause target acquisition and lock-on problems, clutter on the battlefield may cause lock-on problems, and LOS communications limited by structures. CCMS unique flight path forces the gunner to think in three dimensions. Other urban environment hazards include overhead obstacles such as street signs, light poles, and wires, which could impede the missile's flight path.

SHOULDER-LAUNCHED MUNITIONS IN THE BUNKER DEFEAT ROLE

G-39. The current inventory of the M141 BDM provides the Infantry platoon and squad the capability to incapacitate personnel within earth and timber bunkers, masonry buildings, and light armored vehicles. However, neither system is fully capable of fire-from-enclosure.

G-40. SLM can be fired safely from an enclosure to incapacitate personnel within earth and timber bunkers, masonry buildings, and light armored vehicles currently are being developed to increase the lethality, survivability, and mobility of the SLM gunner.

ENGAGEMENT OF FIELD FORTIFICATIONS AND BUILDING WITH SHOULDER-LAUNCHED MUNITIONS

G-41. The M141 BDM was designed to better enhance the destruction of field fortifications and buildings. (See table G-6, page G-20.) The M141 BDM contains a high-explosive dual purpose (HEDP) round with a dual-mode fuze that automatically adjusts for the type of target on impact. For soft targets, such as sandbagged bunkers, the M141 BDM warhead automatically adjusts to delayed mode and hits the target with high kinetic energy. This energy propels the warhead through the barrier and into the fortification or building, where the fuze detonates the warhead and causes greater damage.

Table G-6. Effects of the M141 BDM on field fortifications or bunkers

AIMPOINT		EFFECT WHEN MUNITION IS FIRED AT AIMPOINT	RECOMMENDED FIRING TECHNIQUE
Bunkers		Rounds fired into firing ports or apertures can destroy standard earth and timber bunkers, and hasty urban fighting positions (example, vehicles, and metal dumpsters). Rounds will detonate inside the rear of the position, causing major structural damage. Damage to enemy equipment may be minor unless it is hit directly. The round will cause injury or death to occupants.	Coordinate fire: Fire shoulder-launched munitions at and through firing ports.
Buildings	Windows/ Doorways	Rounds fired through windows and doorways can destroy the contents of the building. Destruction may not be contained within a single room. Rounds and debris from the round and materiel may pass through into other sections of the building, causing collateral damage. Damage to enemy equipment may be minor unless it is hit directly. The round will cause injury or death to occupants.	Coordinate fire: Fire an M141 BDM at the center of the visible part of a window or door.

Table G-6. Effects of the M141 BDM on field fortifications or bunkers (Continued)

AIMPOINT	EFFECT WHEN MUNITION IS FIRED AT AIMPOINT		RECOMMENDED FIRING TECHNIQUE
Buildings (continued)	**Walls**	Rounds fired at walls will penetrate double-reinforced concrete walls up to 8 inches thick, and triple-brick structures. The initial blast will open a hole in the wall, but may or may not completely penetrate the building.	Coordinate fire: Fire one or more M141 BDMs at the center of the desired location for the opening. Fire a second round through the opening to destroy targets within the structure. **Note.** It takes more than one round to create a man-size hole. Use pair or volley fire, placing the rounds about 12 to 18 inches apart.
Underground Openings	Rounds fired through underground openings can collapse the opening or destroy the contents within it. Destruction may not be contained within the opening. Rounds and debris may pass through into other sections of the opening, causing more damage. Damage to enemy equipment may be minor unless it is hit directly. The round will cause injury or death to occupants at the front entrance, and others farther into the opening may be incapacitated or die from the concussion, heat, and debris caused by the explosion.		Coordinate fire: Fire one or more M141 BDM.

CLOSE COMBAT MUNITION SYSTEM ENGAGEMENT CONSIDERATIONS

G-42. Urban engagement considerations for CCMS include engagement distance, thermal crossover, back blast, weapon penetration, and breaching structural walls. Details follow. TOW systems always should seek to engage at maximum range. If within 1000 meters of an enemy, the flight time of the TOW missile likely will be greater than the flight time of a main gun tank round:
- Engagement distance. The Javelin missile has a minimum engagement distance (150 meters in the attack mode and 65 meters in the direct attack mode), which

Appendix G

limits its use in built-up areas. The TOW 2B has a minimum range of 200 meters and a maximum range of 3750, which limits its use in built-up areas.
- Crossover. Sometimes the Javelin seeker or TOW round will not be able to distinguish between the background and target because the two have the same temperature (crossover).
- Time. When a gunner comes across a target of opportunity, he may not be able to take advantage of it. The cool down time of the Javelin's NVS is 2.5 to 3.5 minutes. Javelin seeker cool down takes about 10 seconds. Once the BCU is activated, the gunner has a maximum of four minutes to engage the target before the battery coolant unit is depleted.
- Back blast. The soft launch capability of the Javelin enables the gunner to fire from inside buildings because there is little overpressure or flying debris.
- Weapon penetration. The dual-charge Javelin warhead penetrates typical urban targets. The direct attack mode is selected when engaging targets in a building. Enemy positions or bunkers in the open closer than 150 meters are engaged using the direct attack mode. Positions in the open farther than 150 meters are engaged using either the top or direct attack mode, depending on the situation.
- Breaching structural walls. The Javelin and TOW (except the TOW BB) are not effective when breaching structural walls. ATGMs are not designed to breach structural walls. All CCMS are designed to produce a small hole, penetrate armor, and deliver the explosive charge. Breaching calls for the creation of a large hole. CCMS are better used against armored vehicles or the destruction of enemy-fortified fighting positions.

ANTIARMOR ROLE

G-43. In the past decade, there has been a revolution in armor technology. Research and new developments have come from Europe, the United States, and Israel. These improvements also are becoming much more common in Third World armies. In addition, many older tanks and other armored fighting vehicles are being retrofitted with improved armor protection. These advanced armor configurations improve the vehicles' survivability against all weapons. They are designed specifically to protect against HEAT warheads and essentially fall into four categories: reactive, laminated, composite, and appliqué. Improved armor types include the following:
- Reactive armor. Reactive armor comes in several varieties, but the principle is essentially the same for all. The armor consists of blocks of explosives sandwiched between two metal plates and bolted on the outside of the vehicle. Small-arms and artillery shrapnel will not set off the blocks. However, when a HEAT round strikes the block, the explosive ignites and blows outward. The blast and moving steel plates disperse and deflect the jet of the HEAT warhead, dramatically reducing its ability to penetrate armor.
- Laminated armor. Laminated armor consists of flat layers of steel armor plates with layers of ceramics, fiberglass, or other nonmetallic materiel's in between. This armor is highly effective against all types of weapons, but is difficult and expensive

to manufacture. Vehicles with laminated armor are characterized by flat, slab sides, such as on the M1-series Abrams tank and the German Leopard II.
- Composite armor. Composite armor consists of a nonmetallic core (usually some kind of ceramic) around which the rest of the steel of the hull or the turret is molded. This is much more effective than conventional steel armor against all types of weapons, but less so than laminated armor.
- Appliqué armor. Appliqué armor is essentially extra plates mounted or welded on top of the hull or turret of a vehicle. It can be made of any material, but is frequently made of ceramic or laminated materials. Like reactive armor, appliqué armor is an easy and cost-effective way of improving the protection of older vehicles.

EXPLOITING ARMORED VEHICLE WEAKNESSES

G-44. Because they are designed mainly for offense against other armored vehicles (see figure G-12), armored vehicles usually have their heaviest armor in front. All vehicles are vulnerable to repeated hits on their flanks and rear, though the flank offers the largest possible target. Shooters always should aim center of mass to increase the probability of a hit. The older the vehicle model, the less protection it has against SLM and CCMS. Newer versions of older vehicle models may use bolt-on (appliqué) armor to improve their survivability. Reactive armor usually covers the forward-facing portions and sides of the vehicle and can defeat shaped-charge weapons such as the SLM. When reactive armor detonates, it disperses metal fragments to 200 meters. SLM cause only a small entry hole in an armored vehicle target, though some fragmentation or spall may occur.

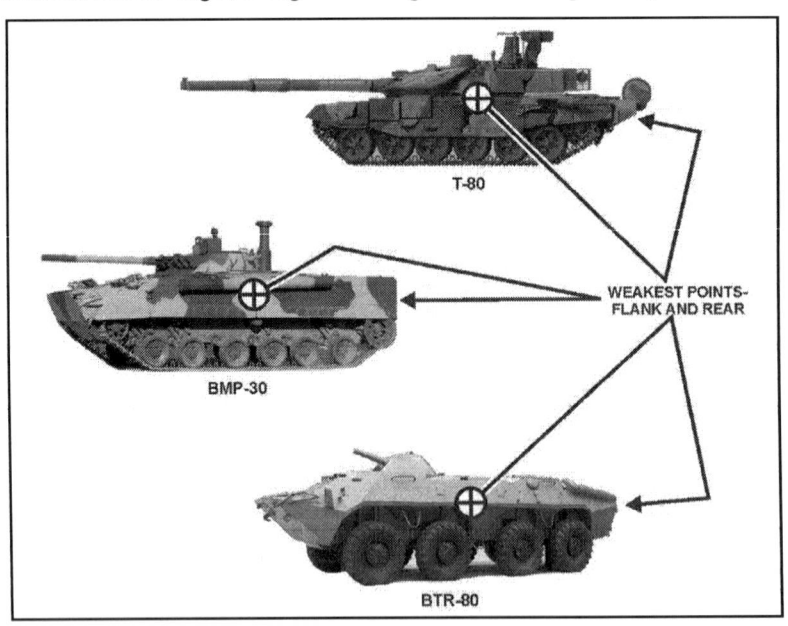

Figure G-12. Armored vehicle weak points

Appendix G

G-43. Natural or manmade obstacles can be used to force the armored vehicle to slow, stop, or change direction. This pause enables the shooter to achieve a first-round hit. If he does not achieve a catastrophic kill on the first round, he or another shooter must be ready to engage the target vehicle immediately with another round.

G-44. The white area in figure G-13 shows the most favorable direction of attack when the turret is facing to the front. The gray area shows the vehicle's PDF and observation when the turret is facing to the front). Volley fires can degrade the additional protection appliqué and reactive armors provide to the target vehicle greatly.

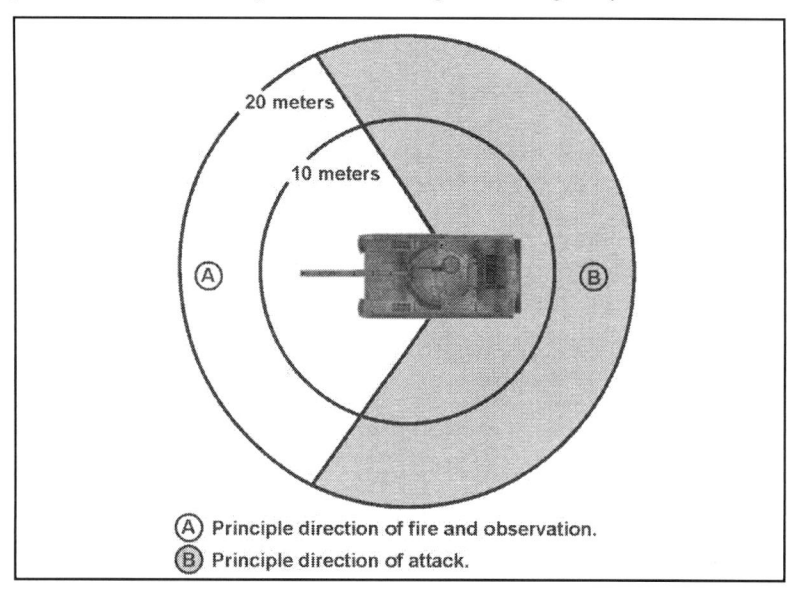

Figure G-13. Limited visibility of armored vehicles

G-45. Armored vehicle kills are classified according to the level of damage achieved. (See table G-7.)

Table G-7. Armored vehicle kills

TYPE OF KILL	PART OF VEHICLE DAMAGED OR DESTROYED	CAPABILITY AFTER KILL
Mobility Kill	Suspension (track, wheels, or road wheels) or power train (engine or transmission) has been damaged.	Vehicle cannot move, but it can still return fire.
Firepower Kill	Main armament has been disabled.	Vehicle still can move, so it can get away.
Catastrophic Kill	Ammunition or fuel storage section has been hit by more than one round.	Vehicle completely destroyed.

SHOULDER-LAUNCHED MUNITIONS IN THE ANTIARMOR ROLE

G-48. When Soldiers employ the M136 AT4, M136A1 AT4CS and M72-series LAW to defeat threat armored vehicles, it requires Soldiers to engage threat vehicles using single or paired shots. Gunners require positions allowing engagement against the flank or rear of the target vehicles. They must seek covered and concealed positions from where targets can be engaged. The M136A1 AT4CS is the only SLM that can be fired safely from within an enclosure because of its countermass propulsion system. TM 3-23.25 advises firing the M136 AT4 and M141 BDM from an enclosure under combat conditions only when no other tactical option exists due to the risk of both auditory and nonauditory injury.

Shoulder-Launched Munitions Warhead Effects on Armor

G-49. SLM warheads have excellent armor penetration ability and lethal after-armor effects (especially the M136 AT4, M136A1 AT4CS and M72A7). The extremely destructive shaped-charge explosives can penetrate more than 14 inches (35.6 centimeters) of rolled homogeneous armor. Types of warhead armor effects follow and are illustrated in figure G-14 (page G-26):

- Impact. The nose cone crushes; the impact sensor activates the fuze.
- Ignition. The fuze element activates the electric detonator. The booster detonates, initiating the main charge.
- Penetration. The main charge fires and forces the warhead body liner into a directional gas jet penetrating armor plate.
- Spalling (after-armor effects). The projectile fragments and incendiary effects produce blinding light and highly destructive results.

Appendix G

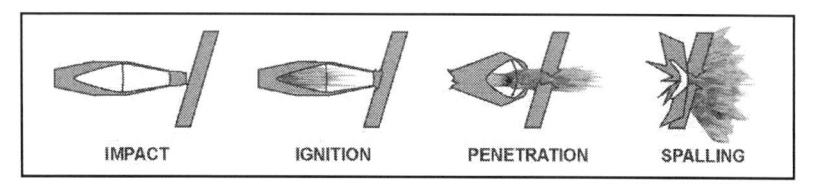

Figure G-14. Effects of SLM warheads on armor targets

Engagement of Other Vehicles

G-50. The M72-series LAW proves more effective against light-armored vehicles. The M136 AT4 proves more effective against armored vehicles. Nonarmored vehicles such as trucks, cars, and boats are considered soft targets. Firing along their length offers the greatest chance of a kill, because this type of shot is most likely to hit their engine block or fuel tank. Effects of different munitions on vehicle types are listed in table G-8.

Table G-8. Effects of different munitions on vehicle types

MUNITION	EFFECTS	REMARKS
Heavy-Armored Vehicle		
The older the vehicle model, the less protection it has against shoulder-launched munitions. Newer versions may use bolt-on (appliqué) armor to improve their survivability. Some vehicles are equipped with reactive armor, which consists of metal plates and plastic explosives.		
M141 BDM	Can cause mobility kills by disabling the vehicle's suspension system.	The M141 BDM should be a last resort when engaging armored vehicles.
M136-series	Causes only a small entry hole, though some fragmentation or spalling may occur.	Reactive armor usually covers the front and sides of the vehicle, and can defeat shaped-charge weapons; however, the munitions can restrict the vehicle's mobility and may destroy the vehicle if the round hits a vulnerable spot, such as the engine compartment area.
M72-series	Causes only a small entry hole, though some fragmentation or spalling may occur.	
Light-Armored Vehicle		
All current shoulder-launched munitions are capable of destroying most light-armored vehicles, if the round hits a vulnerable spot, such as the engine compartment area, or fuel tank. Unit leaders should provide squad and platoon supporting fires when engaging light-armored troop carriers. Any Infantry troops who survive the initial assault may dismount and return fire.		
M141 BDM	Can cause a catastrophic kill, if the round hits a vulnerable spot, such as the engine compartment area or fuel tank.	
M136-series	Can cause a catastrophic kill, if the round hits a vulnerable spot, such as the engine compartment area or fuel tank.	
M72-series	Can cause a catastrophic kill, if the round hits a vulnerable spot, such as the engine compartment area or fuel tank.	

Appendix G

Table G-8. Effects of different munitions on vehicle types (continued)

MUNITION	EFFECTS	REMARKS
Nonarmored Vehicles		
Nonarmored vehicles, such as trucks and cars, are considered soft targets. Firing along their length (flank) offers the greatest chance of a kill, because this type of shot is most likely to hit their engine block or fuel tank. Front and rear angles offer a much smaller target, reducing the chance of a first time hit.		
M141 BDM	Causes a catastrophic kill.	
M136-series	May penetrate, but will pass through the body with limited damage unless the rocket hits a vital part of the engine.	When engaging enemy-used privately-owned vehicles (POVs) with M136- or the M72-series munitions, do not fire at the main body. Instead, fire at the engine compartment area.
M72-series	May penetrate, but will pass through the body with limited damage unless the rocket hits a vital part of the engine.	

METHODS OF ENGAGEMENT

G-51. The four engagement methods for SLM include single, sequence, pair, and volley firing. The leader evaluates the situation on the ground to determine which of these methods to use. Regardless of whether they are used singly or in combination, communications are needed as well. The methods of engagement are rehearsed in accordance with unit SOP.

Single Firing

G-52. A single Soldier with one SLM may engage an armored vehicle, but this is not the preferred method of engagement. Several SLM normally are required to kill an armored vehicle. A single gunner firing one round must hit a vital part of the target in order to do damage. (See figure G-15.) A single shooter can engage targets out to 225 meters with the LAW, or 300 meters with the M136 AT4 (when he knows the actual range).

Shoulder-Launched Munitions and Close Combat Missile Systems

Figure G-15. SLM single firing

Sequence Firing

G-53. A single shooter, equipped with two or more SLM prepared for firing, engages the target. After engaging with the first round and observing the impact, the shooter adjusts his point of aim. He then engages with another round until he destroys the target or runs out of rounds. (See figure G-16.)

Figure G-16. SLM sequence firing

Pair Firing

G-54. Two or more shooters, equipped with two or more SLM prepared for firing, engage a single target. Before firing, the first shooter informs the others of the estimated speed and distance to the target. If the impact of his round proves his estimate to be correct, the other shooters engage the target until it is destroyed. If the impact of the round proves his estimate to be incorrect, the second shooter informs the others of his estimate, and he

Appendix G

engages the target. This continues until the target is destroyed or all rounds are expended. (See figure G-17.)

Figure G-17. SLM pair firing

Volley Firing

G-55. Two or more shooters can engage a single target when the range is known. These shooters engage the target at the same time on a prearranged signal such as a command, whistle, mine, or TRP. This can be the most effective means of engagement as it places the most possible rounds on one target at one time, increasing the possibility of a kill. (See figure G-18.)

Figure G-18. SLM volley firing

TOW COUNTERMEASURES TO IMPROVED ARMOR

G-56. TOW crews can expect to be issued a mix of TOW missile types on the battlefield, with widely varying capabilities. Gunners and leaders must be familiar with the different missile types and their respective capabilities. The proper type of missile must be chosen for each type of target. (See table G-9.)

G-57. TOW crews must strive harder than ever to find positions where they can engage enemy vehicles from the flank. Modern tanks with reactive armor have become increasingly difficult to kill from the front.

Table G-9. Missile selection priority chart

THREAT VEHICLE-TYPE TARGETS	SELECTION PRIORITY			
	FIRST	SECOND	THIRD	FOURTH
Tanks with appliqué armor	TOW 2B	TOW 2A	TOW 2	ITOW
Tanks with explosive reactive armor	TOW 2B	TOW 2A	TOW 2	ITOW
Tanks without appliqué/reactive armor	TOW 2B	TOW 2A	TOW 2	ITOW
Light armored personnel carriers	TOW 2	TOW 2A	TOW 2B	ITOW
Light armored wheeled vehicles	TOW 2	TOW 2A	TOW 2B	ITOW

Appendix G

Table G-9. Missile selection priority chart (continued)

THREAT VEHICLE-TYPE TARGETS	SELECTION PRIORITY			
	FIRST	SECOND	THIRD	FOURTH
Antiaircraft vehicles	TOW 2	TOW 2A	TOW 2B	ITOW
Armored vehicles in hull defilade positions	TOW 2B	TOW 2A	TOW 2	ITOW
Bunkers/fortifications	TOW BB	TOW 2	TOW 2A	ITOW

ANTIARMOR AMBUSH ROLE

G-58. Antiarmor ambushes usually are conducted to destroy small groups of armored vehicles, force the enemy to move slowly and cautiously, or force the enemy into a choke point. Units conducting an antiarmor ambush can use Javelins or TOWs for this purpose. The Javelin and TOW have a slow rate of fire, so other weapons systems must be prepared to engage the vehicles while the Javelin gunners attach the CLU to new rounds or the TOW gunners load new rounds. The Javelin's 2000-meter range and TOW's 3750-meter range allow flexibility in choosing ambush positions. In addition to fires into the kill zones, the Javelin and TOW can be employed in a security role to guard high-speed avenues of approach, to slow or stop enemy reinforcements, or to destroy vehicles attempting to flee the kill zone. (See figure G-19.)

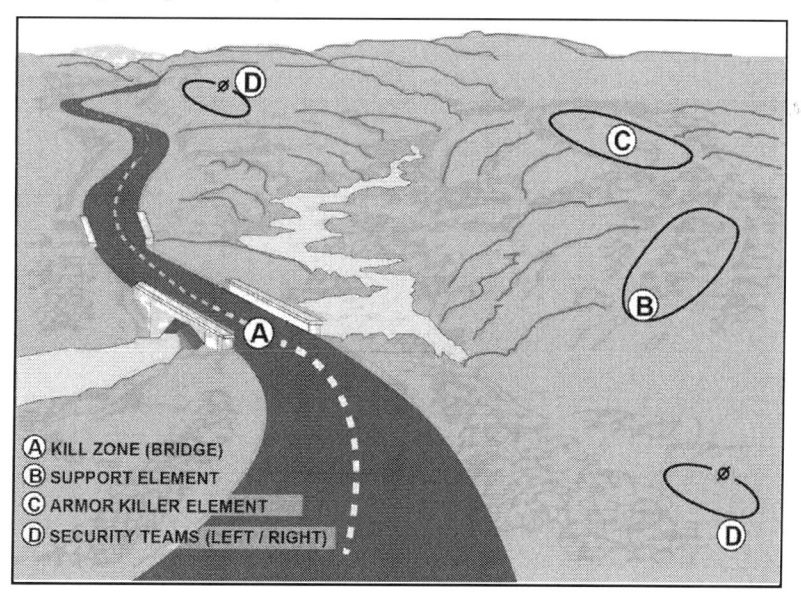

Figure G-19. Antiarmor ambush

OFFENSE

G-59. CCMS contribute to the offense by providing long-range fires destroying enemy armor and protect the force from armored counterattacks. In the absence of armored targets, CCMS can engage enemy fortifications and hovering helicopters. CCMS normally are used in a support-by-fire role during the offense. The primary consideration for such employment is the availability of appropriate fields of fire and armored threat. CCMS crews can protect flanks against armored threats and also can provide overwatch for unit movement. (See figure G-20.)

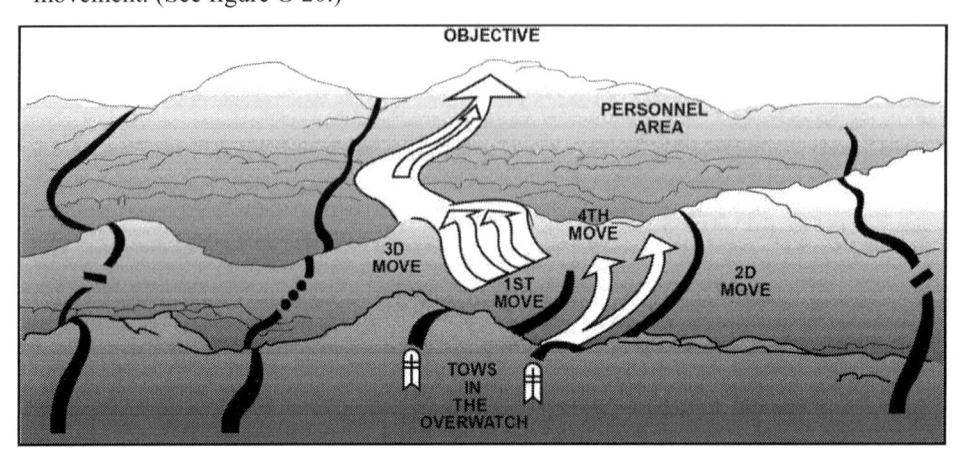

Figure G-20. TOW supporting offensive missions

DEFENSE

G-60. During planning, the leader considers the enemy armor threat, then positions antiarmor weapons accordingly to cover armor avenues of approach. He also considers the fields of fire, tracking time, and minimum engagement distance of each weapon. The section leader or squad leader selects a primary position and sector of fire for each antiarmor weapon. He also picks alternate and supplementary positions for them. Each position should allow flank fire and have cover and concealment. The leader should integrate the ITAS into his limited visibility security and observation plan. The squad leader selects the fighting position and assigns the sector of fire. Considering the fundamentals of antiarmor employment will improve the crew's survivability greatly. ITAS crews must coordinate with adjacent units to ensure security. The TOW's 3750-meter maximum range makes it difficult for the enemy to engage the crew with direct fire, which forces the enemy to deploy earlier than intended. The gunner prepares a range card for his primary position. If time permits, he also prepares them for his alternate and supplementary positions. (See table G-10, page G-34.)

G-61. Reserve forces armed with SLM may be employed to assist counterattacks to regain essential positions. They also are used to block enemy penetrations, to meet unexpected enemy thrusts, and to provide support by fire to endangered friendly units during disengagements and withdrawals. In the event defensive positions are in danger of being overrun by enemy armored vehicles, SLM may be used against armored vehicles and lightly armored vehicles posing an immediate threat, including light tanks. The maximum

Appendix G

range provides leaders with greater flexibility in positioning each round and provides a means of achieving overlapping sectors of fire for increased survivability.

Table G-10. Personnel duties

TASKS TO BE PERFORMED	SECTION SERGEANT	TL	GUNNER /AG
Integrate CCMS into the platoon tactical plan:			
• Select general weapons positions.	X		
• Assign sectors of fires.	X		
• Coordinate mutual support.	X		
• Coordinate with adjacent units.	X		
Positions (primary, alternate, and supplementary) and routes between positions.	X		
Supervise continual preparation and improvement of positions.	X	X	
Coordinate security of the CCMS teams.	X		
Confirm or make adjustments.	X	X	
Supervise preparation of range card.	X	X	
Control movement of gunners between positions.	X	X	
Issue fire commands to gunners.	X	X	
Coordinate resupply and collection of extra rounds carried in platoon.	X		
Identify enemy avenues of approach.	X		
Prepare fighting position (primary, alternate, supplementary).		X	
Prepare range card.		X	X
Designate TRP.	X		
Pre-stock rounds.		X	X
Prepare round for firing.			X
React to fire commands.			X
Engage targets.			X
LEGEND AG – assistant gunner; CCMS – close combat missile system ; TL – team leader; TRP – target reference point			

G-34 ATP 3-21.8 12 April 2016

SECTION III – SAFETY

G-62. Leaders must employ SLM and CCMS to minimize danger to friendly Soldiers caused by the surface danger zones or back blast danger zones. They must weigh the risk of firing the missile in close proximity to friendly assault forces against the need to suppress or destroy enemy fortifications or vehicles from the support by fire or assault position. This section discusses SLM and CCMS safety.

SHOULDER-LAUNCHED MUNITIONS

G-63. Figures G-21 through G-30 (pages G-35 through G-41) and table G-11 (page G-36) illustrate surface danger zones and back blast danger zone information for SLM. (Refer to DA Pamphlet 385-63 and TM 3-23.25 for more information.)

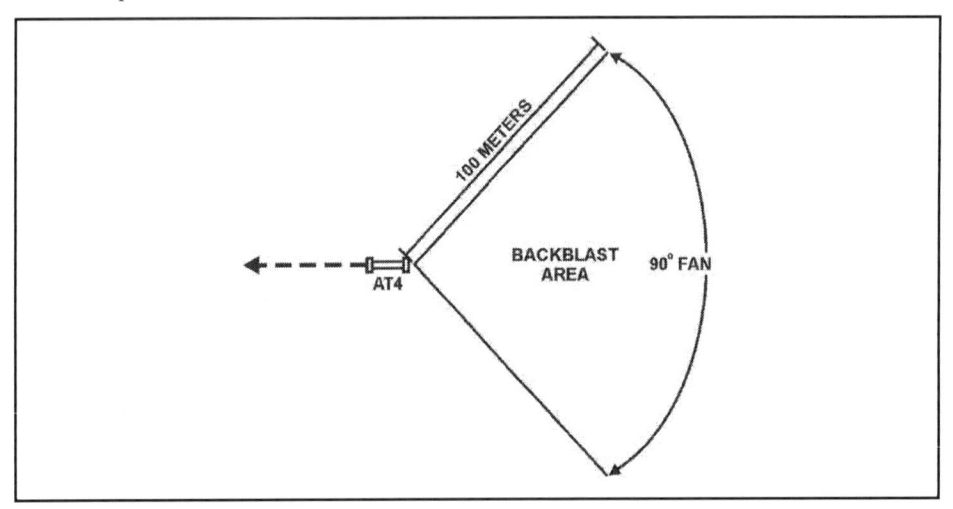

Figure G-21. M136 AT4 backblast danger area

Appendix G

Table G-11. AT4 Surface danger zones criteria in meters

TYPE	DISTANCE X	MINIMUM RANGE TO TARGET	AREA A	AREA B	AREA F2 DANGER ZONE DEPTH	AREA F2 CAUTION AREA DEPTH
84-mm HEAT M1361	2100	50	227	488	53	954
9-mm Trainer, M939	1600	N/A	N/A	N/A	N/A	N/A

NOTES:

1. Increased dud rates may occur when firing HE (M136) at impact angles of 10 degrees or less.
2. Area F is 90-degree angle (45 degrees left and right) of rearward extension of launcher target line.
3. Danger zone occupation could result in fatalities or serious casualties including, severe burns, eye damage, or permanent hearing loss. The hazards are base-plate fragments, debris, fireball, high noise levels, and overpressure.
4. Caution area is an extension of the primary danger area. Occupation of this area also could result in severe casualties due to back blast, debris, high noise levels, and possible base plate fragments. Primary danger area and caution area are conditions not to be modified.

LEGEND

HE – high explosive; mm – millimeter; N/A – not applicable

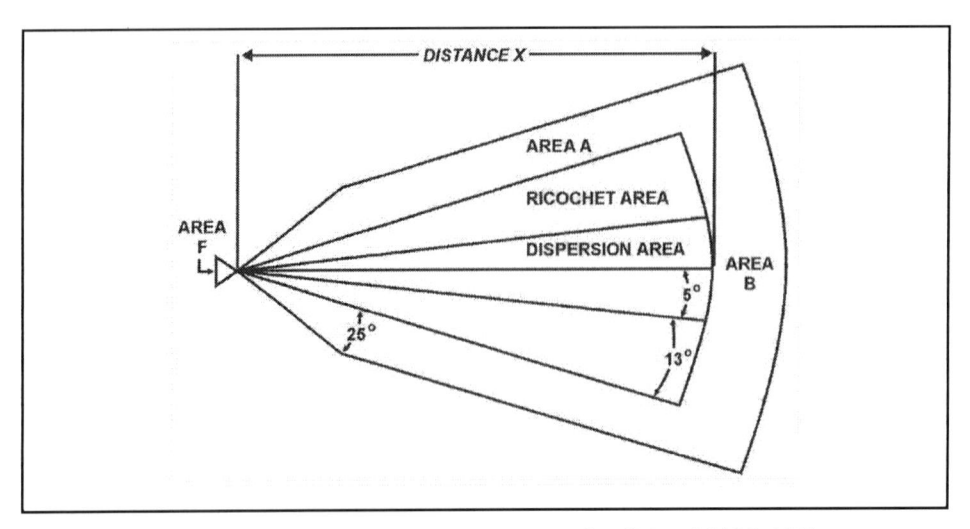

Figure G-22. Surface danger zones for firing M136 AT4

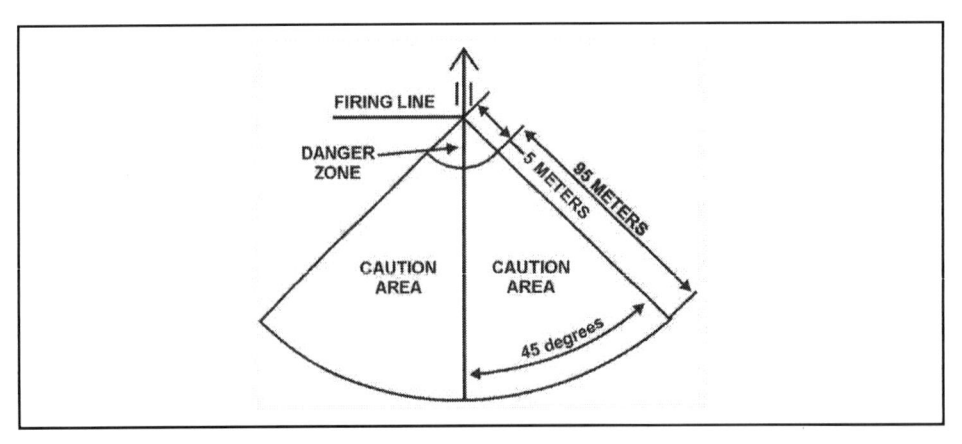

Figure G-23. Surface danger zones area F for firing M136 AT4

Appendix G

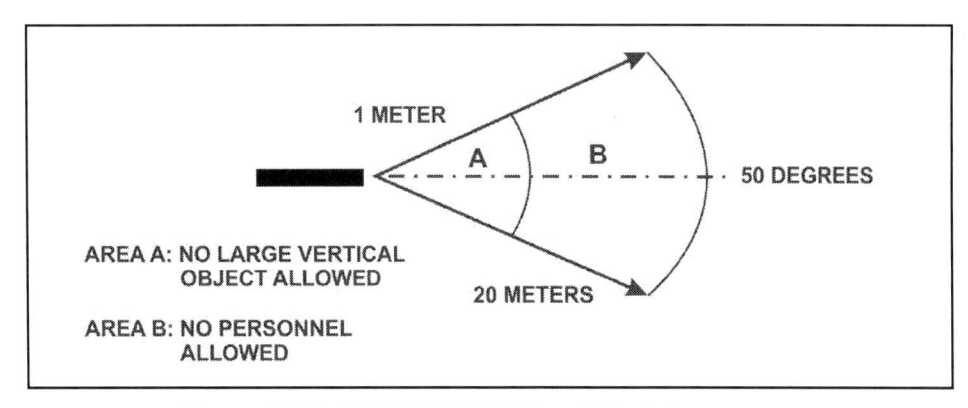

AREA A: NO LARGE VERTICAL OBJECT ALLOWED

AREA B: NO PERSONNEL ALLOWED

1 METER
20 METERS
50 DEGREES

Figure G-24. M136A1 AT4CS backblast danger area

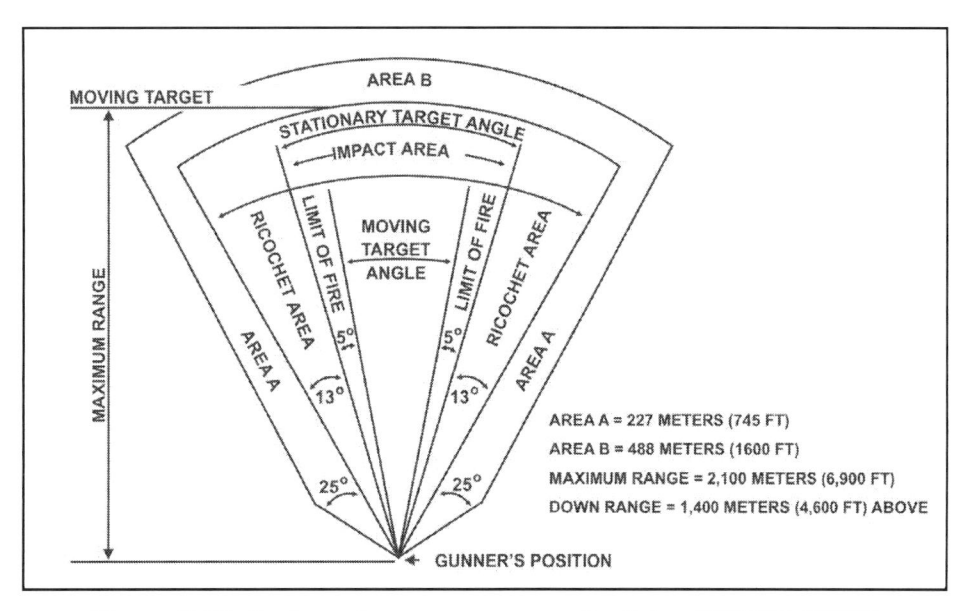

AREA A = 227 METERS (745 FT)
AREA B = 488 METERS (1600 FT)
MAXIMUM RANGE = 2,100 METERS (6,900 FT)
DOWN RANGE = 1,400 METERS (4,600 FT) ABOVE

Figure G-25. Surface danger zones area for firing M136A1 AT4CS

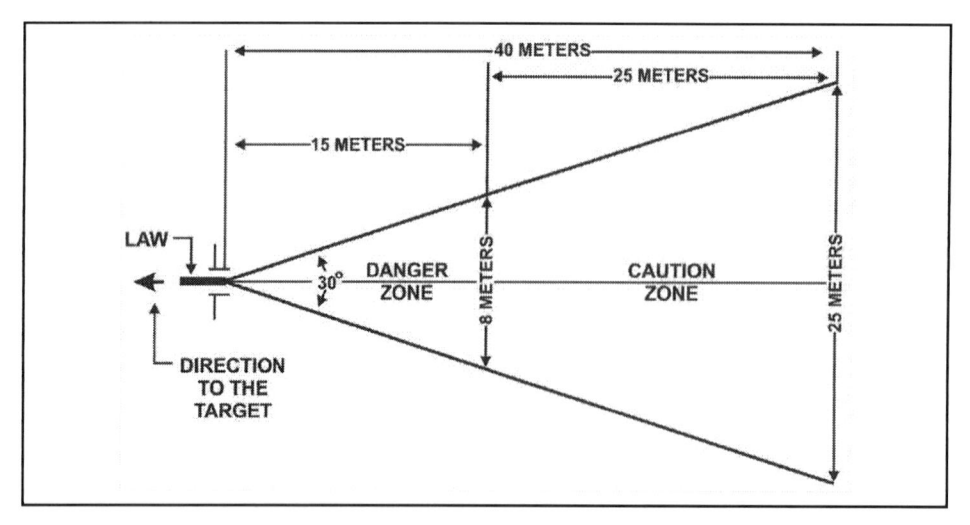

Figure G-26. M72A2/3 LAW backblast area

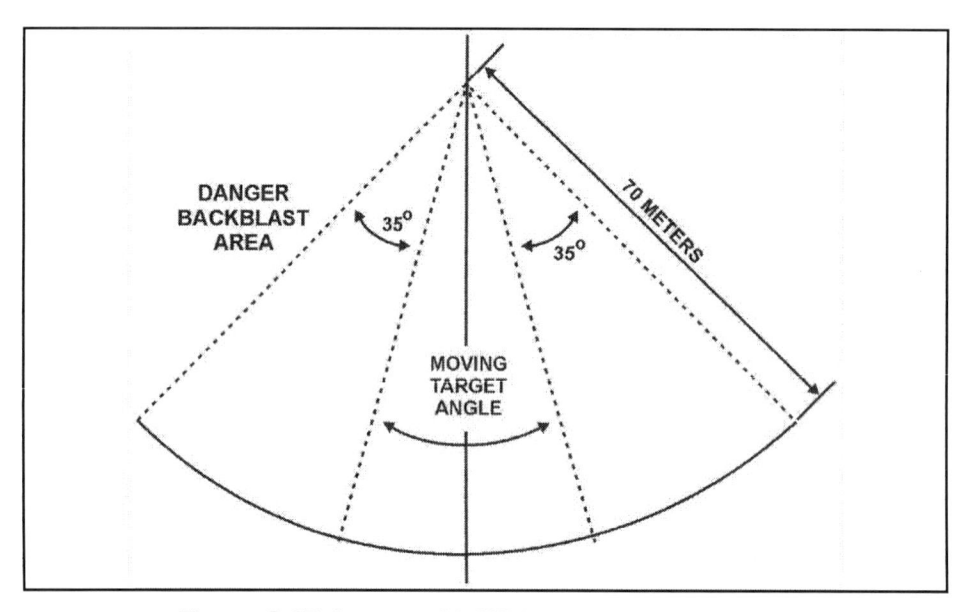

Figure G-27. Improved LAW backblast danger area

Appendix G

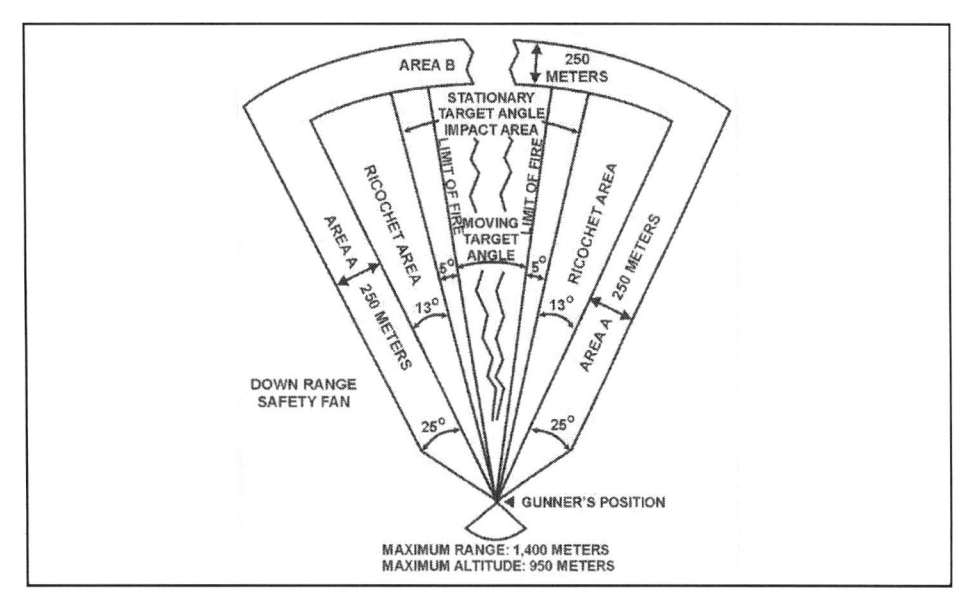

Figure G-28. Surface danger zones for firing Improved LAW

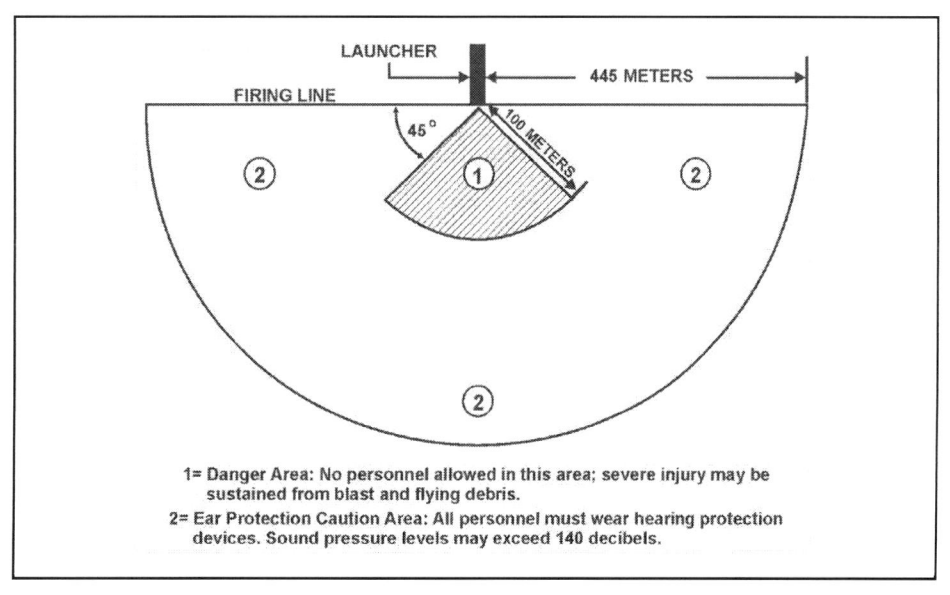

Figure G-29. M141 BDM backblast danger area

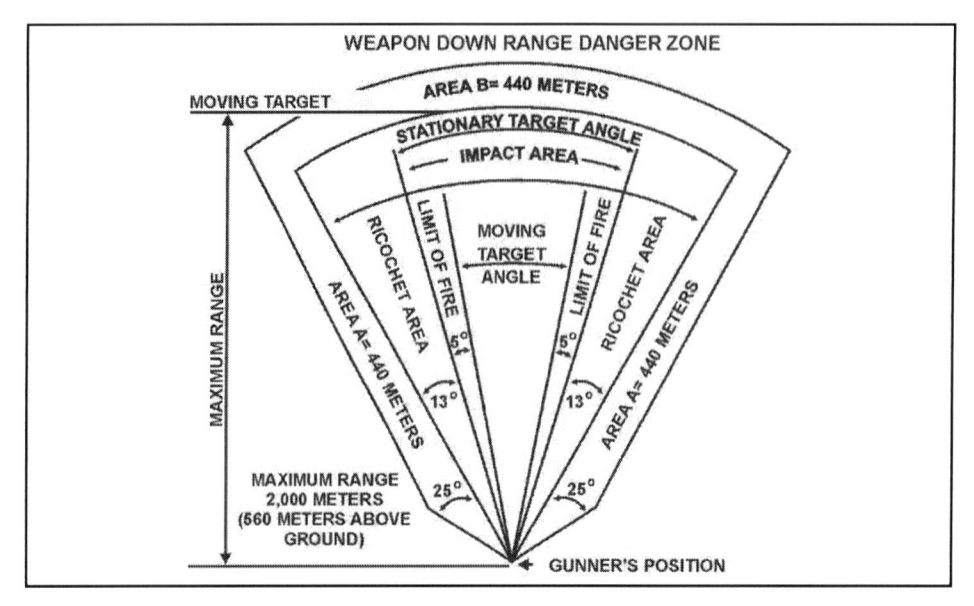

Figure G-30. Surface danger zones for firing M141 BDM

COMBAT SAFETY FOR ALL SHOULDER-LAUNCHED MUNITIONS

G-64. Combat safety rules and procedures include all those applying to training with the following modifications.

Engagement From an Enclosure

G-65. The M136A1 AT4CS is the only SLM proven safe for firing from enclosures; however, enclosures must meet the following specifications. (See figure G-31, page G-42.)

- The inside area must be a minimum of 12 feet wide and 15 feet long (about 3.5 meters wide and 4.5 meters long).
- The ceiling must be a minimum of seven feet (2.1 meters) high.
- The window opening must be a minimum of 36 inches wide and 36 inches long (one meter wide and one meter long).
- The door opening must be a minimum of 36 inches wide and 72 inches long (one meter wide and two meters long).
- The structure should be of significant construction to withstand the munitions back blast.

Appendix G

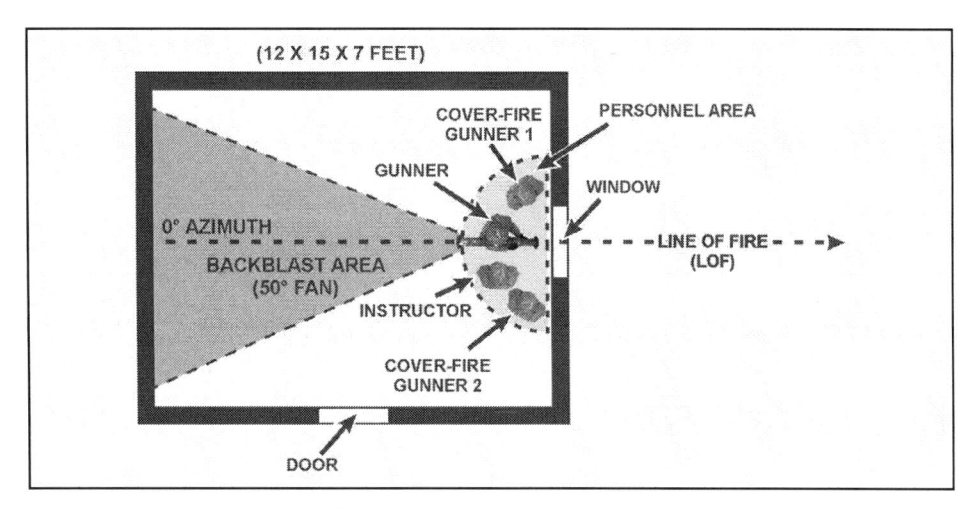

Figure G-31. Minimal dimensions of a confined space

G-66. The following requirements must be followed when firing indoors:
- Fire in the standing position only.
- Cover or protect all equipment (example, small arms, radio set) in the room.
- Remove any loose objects which might be thrown when firing from directly behind the launcher.
- Keep stuffed furniture (example mattresses, cushions, pillows), to absorb pressure.
- Hang a blanket 1.5 to two meters behind the launcher and 15 to 30 centimeters from the rear wall. This considerably reduces sound pressure.
- Open all windows and doors in room.
- Do not allow the angle of the launcher to exceed 20 degrees of depression from the horizontal plane. Do not fire the munitions at any angle of elevation. (See figure G-32.) Do not allow the angle of the launcher to exceed 45 degrees left or right of the vertical plane.
- Wear combat arms earplugs.
- Fire the munitions no more than 10 centimeters (four inches) from a door or window frame. (See figure G-32.)

Shoulder-Launched Munitions and Close Combat Missile Systems

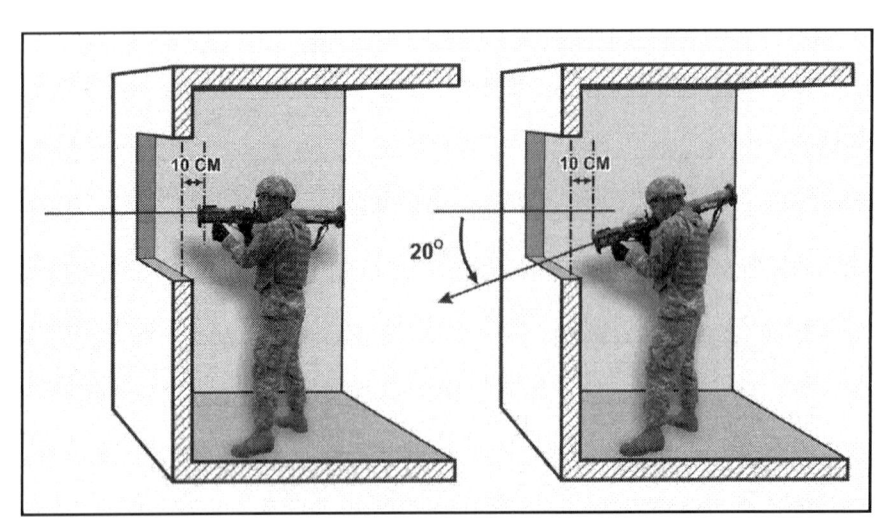

Figure G-32. Angle of launcher

Engagement From a Fighting Position

G-67. The M72-series LAW, M136 AT4, and M141 BDM can be fired from the standard Infantry fighting position. However, to increase accuracy and reduce danger to friendly Soldiers, the area to the rear of the firing position must have no walls, large trees, or other obstructions within five meters (5 1/2 yards). Ensuring the absence of such obstructions avoids deflection of weapon back blast onto the shooter or into the position:

- Individual Infantry fighting position. The Soldier must lean against the rear wall and ensure the venturi or the rear of the weapon protrudes past the rear of the position.
- Two-Soldier Infantry fighting position. Nonfiring personnel must remain clear of the back blast area. These positions should be constructed and sited so none are located in another position's back blast danger zone.
- Modified firing position. A modified firing position may be constructed to the side of the two-Soldier fighting position. Firing from a modified position reduces the possibility of injury to the shooter or the other Soldier in the fighting position, while still offering the shooter protection from enemy return fire.

Overhead Fire

G-68. SLM should not be fired over the heads of friendly Soldiers, unless the Soldiers have adequate protection against direct impact or other hazards.

JAVELIN

G-69. Figure G-33 (page G-44) shows the Javelin back blast danger area and surface danger zones. The primary danger area is a 60-degree sector, with the apex of the sector at the aft end of the missile launch motor.

Appendix G

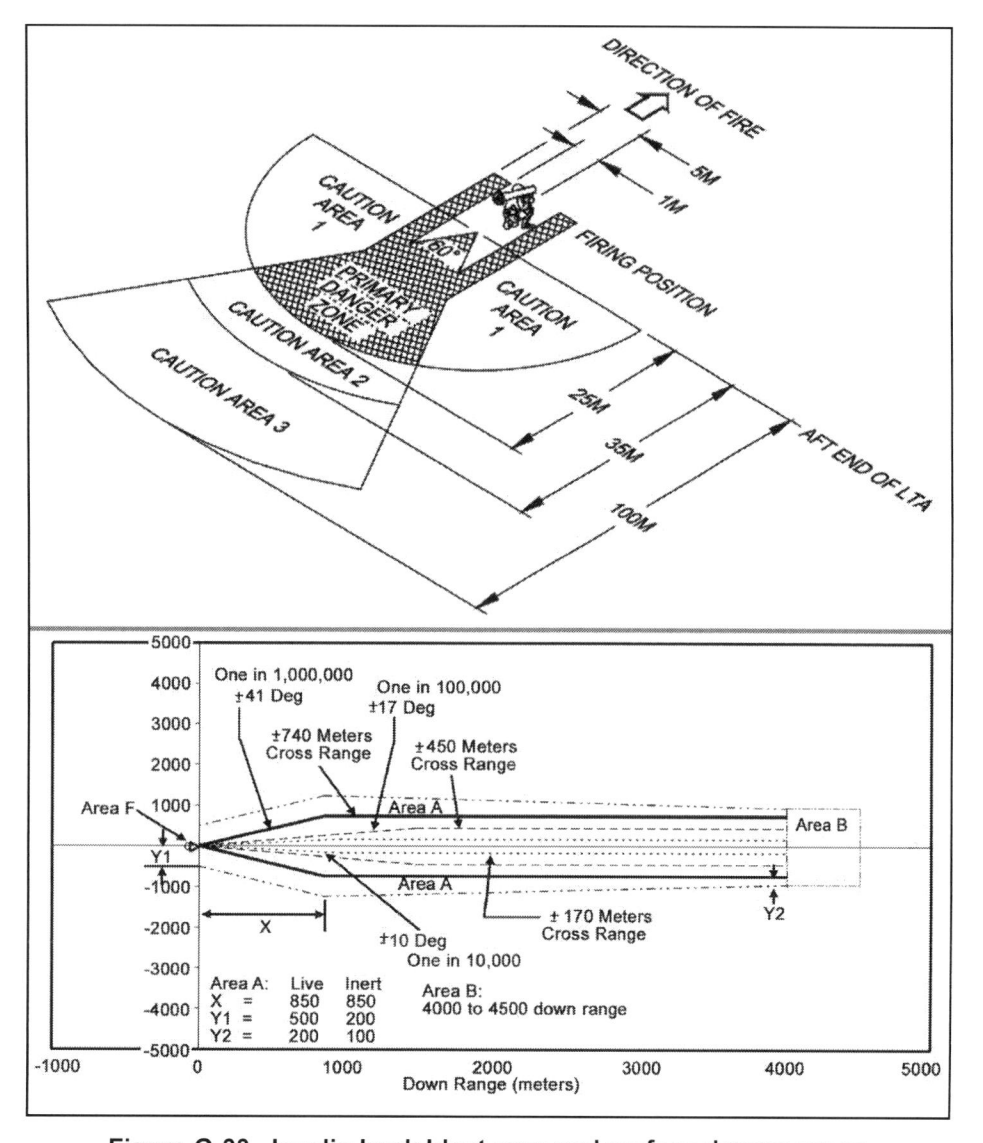

Figure G-33. Javelin back blast area and surface danger zones

FIRING FROM ENCLOSURES

G-70. The Javelin can be fired from inside a building. However, the room from which it is fired must be at least 7 feet high, 12 feet wide and 15 feet deep:
- Debris. Debris and loose objects are cleared from behind the launch site when firing within a confined area.
- Venting. When possible, doors and windows are opened to allow the back blast and overpressure to escape.

Shoulder-Launched Munitions and Close Combat Missile Systems

- Structural damage. Escaping gases from the missile's first-stage motor are hot and flammable. The materials that can catch fire easily are removed before firing. For example, some types of curtains and throw rugs.
- Hearing protection. All personnel within 25 meters of the Javelin must wear hearing protection.
- Face shield. The face shield protects the gunner's face. It is possible to damage the face shield absorber between the indentation and CLU main housing. If this part of the face shield is missing, the gunner must switch from firing the Javelin with the right eye to the left eye.

TUBE LAUNCHED, OPTICALLLY TRACKED, WIRE GUIDED MISSILE

G-71. When firing from either a hasty or improved fighting position, the gunner must take into consideration obstructions directly to his front, to his rear, and to the sides of the fighting position.

FIRING LIMITATIONS

G-72. Some conditions may limit the firing and engagement capabilities of the TOW. The following information should be considered before engaging targets:

- *Firing over bodies of water.* Maximum and limited range firing over water varies by missile type. If the range is less than 1100 meters, the missile's range is not affected. However, if it is wider than 1100 meters it can reduce the range of the TOW. A TOW position should be as high above and as far back from the water as the tactical situation allows. The squad or section leader should analyze his sector as soon as the position is occupied to determine if water will affect the employment of the TOW. Signals being sent through the command-link wires are shorted out when a large amount of wire is submerged in water.
- *Firing over electrical lines.* If the command-link wires make contact with a live high-voltage power line, personnel can be injured or control of the missile could be lost. The launcher electronics also may be damaged. In addition to power lines, other high-voltage sources include street cars, electric train ways, and some moving target trolleys on training ranges.
- *Firing in windy conditions.* Gusty, flanking, or quartering winds can cause the launch tube to vibrate and spoil the tracking performance. The effect is similar to driving in a strong crosswind. Strong winds can move the missile around during flight, but as long as the crosshairs are kept on the center mass of the target, the weapon system can compensate for wind effects.
- *Firing through obscurants and area fires.* Smoke can obscure the LOS and hide the target when using the daysight tracker. A smooth tracking rate should be maintained as the target disappears into an obscurant cloud so the missile will still be on target or close as the vehicle goes out the other side of the obscurants cloud. (This technique should be practiced during field tracking exercises.) A fire can burn through the command-link wire, causing loss of control of the missile.

Appendix G

- *Firing From bunkers and buildings.* In accordance with DA Pamphlet 385-63, TOWs will not be fired from buildings, bunkers, or within 100 meters of a vertical or nearly vertical backstop without the approval of the commanding general.
- *Clearance requirements.* The TOW muzzle must have at least nine inches of clearance at the end of the launch tube so the wings and control surfaces of the missile will not be damaged when they extend after clearing the launch tube. The muzzle of the launch tube must extend beyond enclosures, window sill, or aperture. It also must have at least 30 inches of clearance between the LOS and obstructions from 500 to 900 meters downrange. 30-inch LOS clearance ensures a high probability the missile will not strike the ground on the way to the target. (See figure G-34.)
- *Firing TOW BB missile.* The missile warhead arms after launcher is between 35 and 65 meters. There is a remote possibility of a TOW BB missile airburst 43 meters from launch platform. The probability of an inadvertent warhead detonation resulting in shrapnel injury to an exposed crewmember also is remote. The crew is protected from shrapnel during firing from Stryker ATGM vehicles. The TOW BB currently is not fired from a HMMWV.

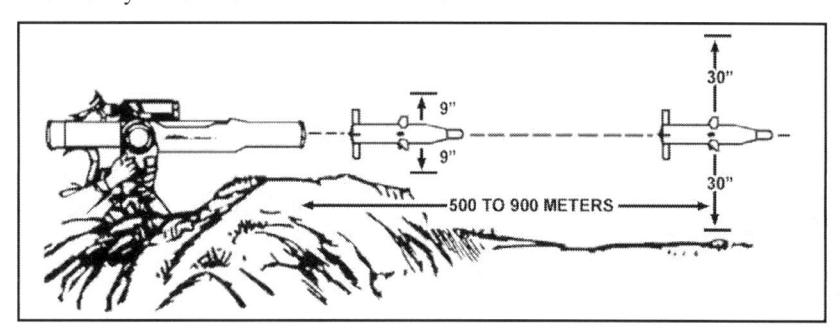

Figure G-34. TOW missile clearance requirements

SURFACE DANGER ZONE

G-73. The surface danger zones for firing ranges consists of a firing area, a target area, impact area, and danger areas surrounding these locations. (See figure G-35.) An additional area for occupation by personnel during firings also may be required. (Refer to DA Pamphlet 385-63 for more information.) The shape and size of the surface danger zones varies with the type of missile or rocket being fired:

- Primary danger area. The primary danger area is a 90-degree cone with a 50-meter radius. The apex of the cone is centered at the rear of the missile launcher. Serious casualties or fatalities are likely to occur to anyone in the area during firing. Hazards include launch motor blast, high noise levels, overpressure, and debris.
- Caution area 1. The caution area 1 extends in a radial pattern from each side of the primary danger area to the firing line with a radius of 50 meters. Permanent hearing damage could occur to personnel without adequate hearing protection in this area during firing. The hazards are high noise levels and overpressure.

- Caution area 2. The caution area 2 is an extension of the primary danger area with the same associated hazards and personnel protection required. The radius of this area is 75 meters.
- 200-meter zone. The 200-meter zone is the danger area for aerial firings 15.25 meters or more above ground level.

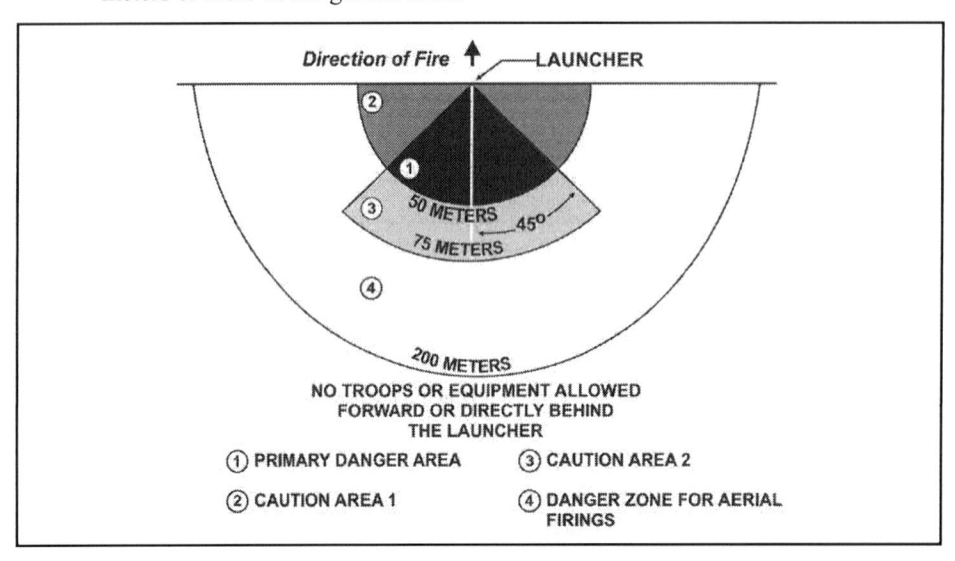

Figure G-35. Surface danger zones for firing basic TOW, TOW 2A, and TOW 2B missiles

FIRING ANGLE LIMITATIONS

G-74. Azimuth and elevation firing angles are limited by the traversing unit, the vehicle, and other external restrictions. All elevation angles are referenced to the horizontal plane of the traversing unit. Azimuth angles are referenced to the long axis of the vehicle and depend on whether the launch tube points over the front or rear of the vehicle. The other reference line is the LOS from the TOW to the target.

G-75. When the TOW is tripod-mounted, a 360-degree lateral track is possible, because the traversing unit is not restricted in azimuth. Mechanical stops limit the elevation angle coverage to 20 degrees below and 30 degrees above the horizontal plane. Before the missile is fired, the LOS angle should be estimated at the expected time of launch and throughout the expected missile flight time. The firing position should be changed or a different target selected if an expected LOS angle exceeds the firing limitation angle.

G-76. Firing angle limitations of TOW carriers are as illustrated in figure G-36 (page G-48).

Appendix G

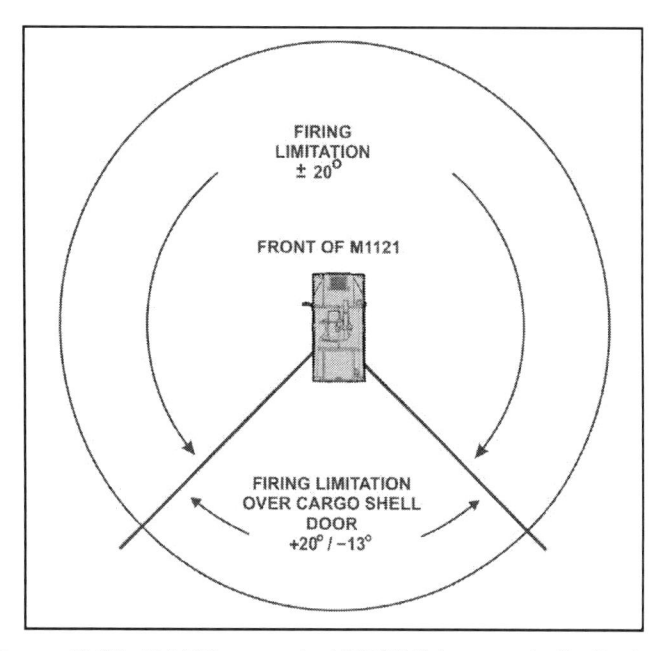

Figure G-36. M1121-mounted TOW firing angle limitations

Appendix H
Obstacle Reduction and Employment

The Army defines *mobility operations* as obstacle reduction by maneuver and engineer units to reduce or negate the effects of existing or reinforcing obstacles. (Refer to ADRP 3-90 for more information.) Mobility permits the Infantry platoon and squad to move from place to place while retaining the ability to fulfill its primary mission.

Countermobility operations help isolate the battlefield and protect attacking forces from enemy counterattack, even though force mobility in offensive actions normally has first priority. (Refer to ADRP 3-90 for more information.) Obstacle employment provides security for the Infantry platoon and squad as its fight progresses into the depth of the enemy's defenses.

This appendix provides information on the types of obstacles (see section I), reduction of enemy obstacles (see section II), and employment of friendly obstacles (see section III). (Refer to ATTP 3-90.4 and ATP 3-34.20 for more information.)

SECTION I – OBSTACLE TYPES AND CATEGORIES

H-1. An obstacle is an obstruction designed or employed by friendly or enemy forces to disrupt, fix, turn, or block the movement of the opposing force. Obstacles can impose additional losses in personnel, time, and equipment. It is e vital Infantry leaders and Soldiers are knowledgeable in the various types of obstacles; not only to employ them, but to reduce them when employed by enemy forces.

H-2. U.S. forces' employment of certain obstacles, mines, and anti-handling devices (AHDs) are governed by the Law of Land Warfare and applicable international laws. Rules governing their employment also are listed in the appropriate sections in this appendix.

H-3. There are four general types of obstacles. Each type is determined by its distinct battlefield purpose and overall concept of the operation:
- *Protective obstacles* are employed to protect Soldiers, equipment, supplies, and facilities from enemy attacks or other threats.
- *Tactical obstacles* directly affect the opponent's maneuver in a way giving the defending force a positional advantage.
- *Nuisance obstacles* impose caution on opposing forces. They disrupt, delay, and sometimes weaken or destroy follow-on echelons.

Appendix H

- *Phony obstacles* deceive the attacking force concerning the exact location of real obstacles. They cause the attacker to question his decision to breach and may cause him to expend his reduction assets wastefully.
    - Phony minefields are used to degrade enemy mobility and preserve-friendly mobility.
    - Intended to simulate live minefields and deceive the enemy, they are used when lack of time, personnel, or materiel prevents use of actual mines.
    - They also may be used as gaps in live minefields.
    - A phony minefield must look like a live minefield, so Soldiers must bury metallic objects or make the ground look as though objects are buried.

H-4. Obstacles are employed by both friendly and enemy forces. The main categories of obstacles are:
- Existing obstacles.
- Reinforcing obstacles.

EXISTING OBSTACLES

H-5. Existing obstacles are those natural or cultural restrictions to movement that are part of the terrain. Existing obstacles can be reinforced into more obstacles. They normally are in defilade from enemy observation (located where observation and fires can prevent the opposing force from breaching them), and are difficult to bypass. Existing obstacles include two types, natural and cultural. The following are examples: (Refer to ATP 3-34.22 for more information.)

- Natural.
    - Swamps.
    - Dense forests.
    - Deep, steep-sloped ravines.
    - Rivers.
    - Streams.
    - Hills or mountains with excessive slopes.
- Cultural.
    - Urban areas.
    - Quarries.
    - Railroad beds.
    - Built-up or elevated roads.
    - Potential storage sites.

REINFORCING OBSTACLES

H-6. Reinforcing obstacles are used by both friendly and enemy forces to tie together, anchor, strengthen, and extend existing obstacles. Careful evaluation of the terrain to determine its existing obstructing or canalizing effect is required to achieve maximum use

Obstacle Reduction and Employment

of reinforcing obstacles. Installation time and manpower usually are the two most important factors. The reinforcing obstacles are—
- Land mines.
- Constructed obstacles.
- Demolition obstacles.
- Improvised obstacles.

LAND MINES

H-7. Land mine is a munition on or near the ground or other surface area that is designed to be exploded by the presence, proximity, or contact of a person or vehicle. Land mines can be employed in quantities within a specific area to form a minefield, or they can be used individually to reinforce nonexplosive obstacles. Land mines fall into the following two general categories: persistent and nonpersistent. Persistent means they are not capable of self-destructing or self-deactivating. Nonpersistent means they are capable of self-destructing or self-deactivating. (See figure H-1.) (Refer to ATP 3-34.20 for more information.)

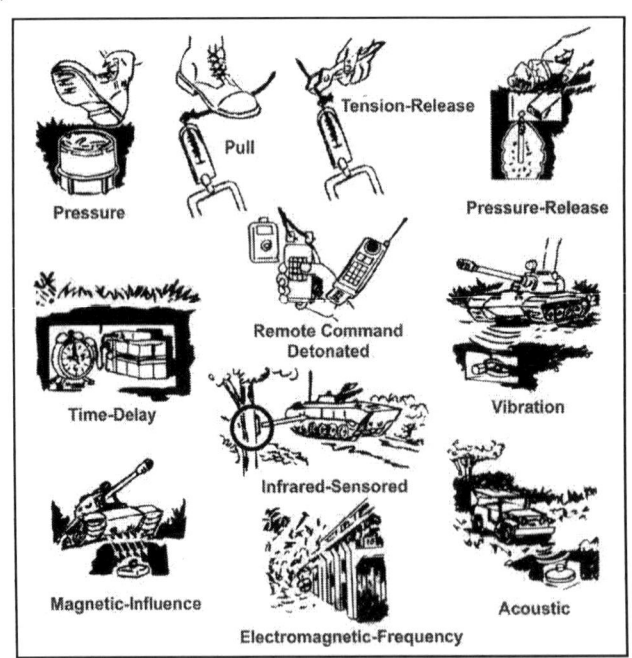

Figure H-1. Methods of activating mines

CONSTRUCTED OBSTACLES

H-8. Units create constructed obstacles with manpower or equipment without the use of explosives. Examples of constructed obstacles include:

Appendix H

- *Ditches.* Ditches across roads and trails are obstacles. Large ditches in open areas require engineer equipment.
- *Log hurdles.* Log hurdles act as "speed bumps" on roads. They are installed easily and are most effective when used in conjunction with other obstacles.
- *Log cribs.* A log crib is constructed of logs, dirt, and rocks. The logs are used to make rectangular or triangular cribs filled with dirt and rock.
  - *These are used to block narrow roads and defiles.* Unless substantially built, log cribs will not stop tanks.
- *Log posts.* Log posts embedded in the road and employed in-depth can stop tracked vehicles. If they are not high enough to be pushed out of the way, posts can cause a tracked vehicle to throw a track if it tries to climb over. If employed with wire and mines, they also can slow enemy Infantry.
- *Wire entanglements.* Wire entanglements impede the movement of dismounted enemy Infantry, and in some cases, tracked and wheeled vehicles.
  - Triple standard concertina is a common wire obstacle. However, there are other types, such as double apron, tanglefoot, and general-purpose barbed-tape obstacles.
  - Figures H-2a through H-2c (pages H-5 through H-6) illustrate examples of wire and log obstacles. The materials used in constructing wire entanglements are relatively lightweight (compared to other obstacles) and inexpensive, considering the protection they afford.

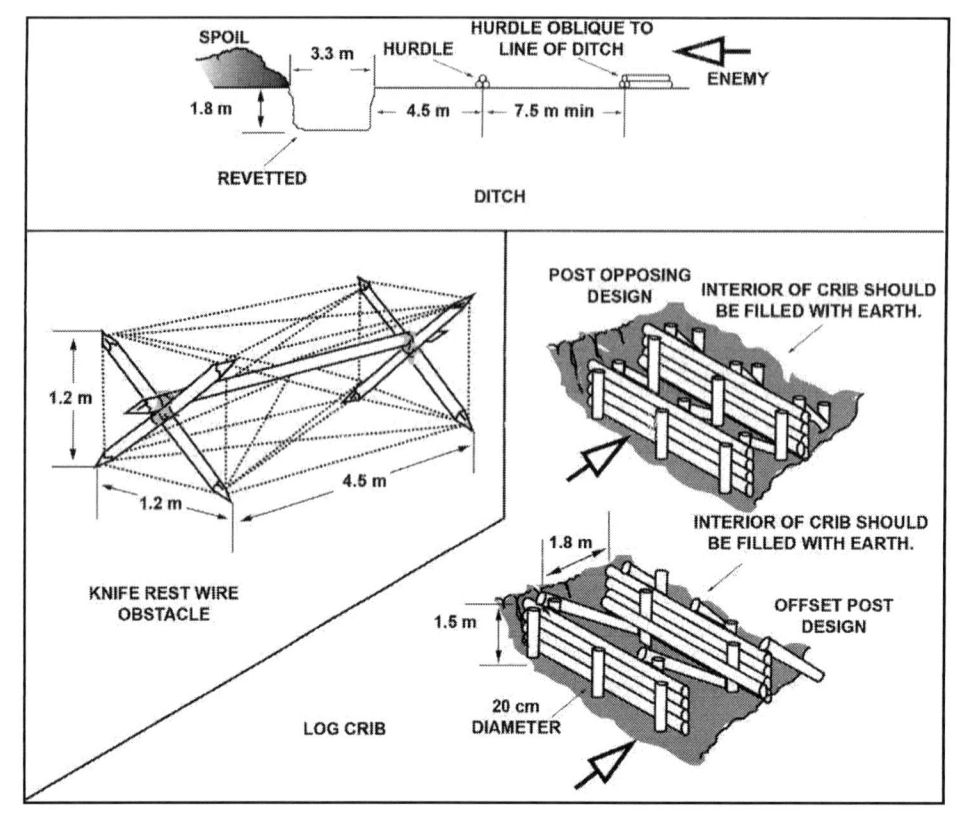

Figure H-2a. Constructed wire and log obstacles

Appendix H

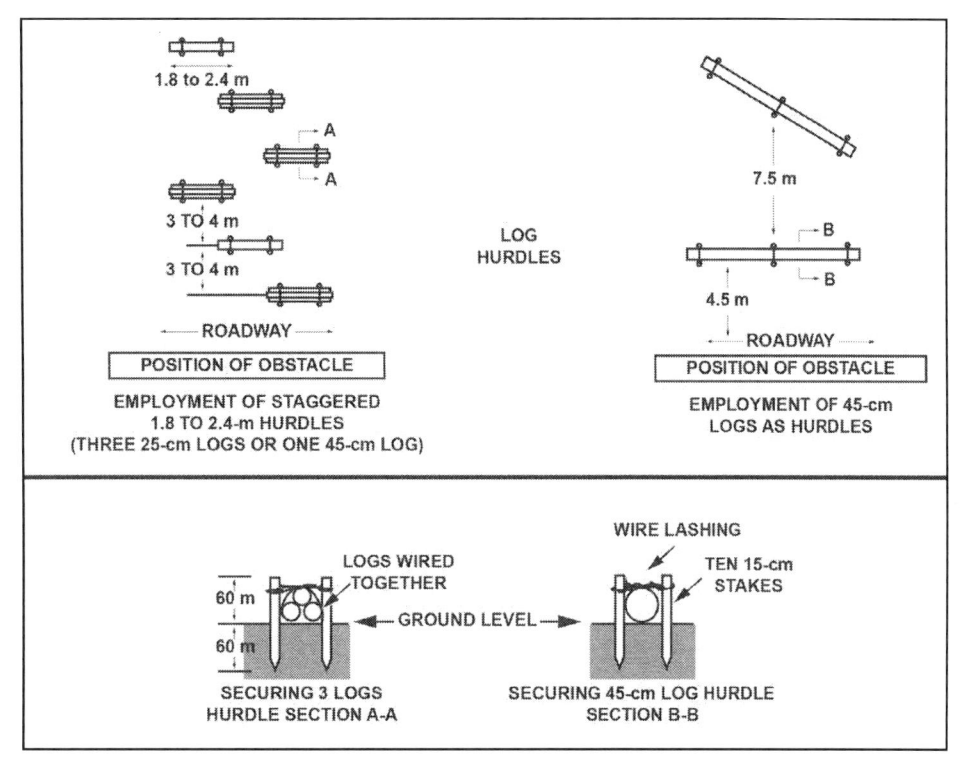

Figure H-2b. Constructed wire and log obstacles

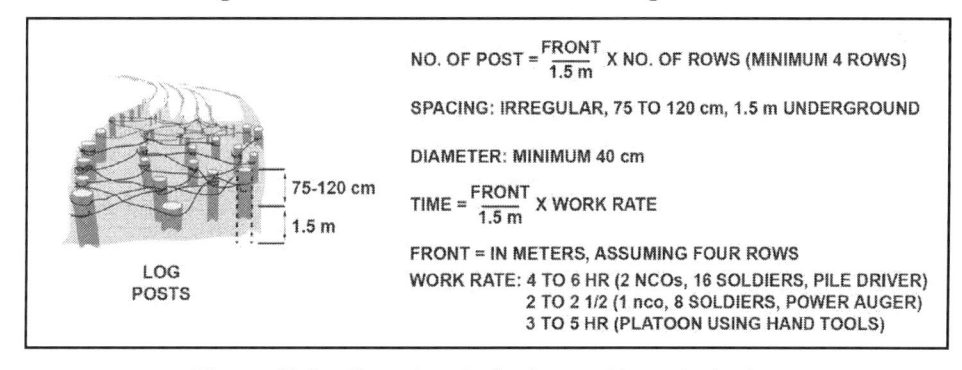

Figure H-2c. Constructed wire and log obstacles

DEMOLITION OBSTACLES

H-9. Units create demolition obstacles by detonating explosives. ATP 3-34.20 covers demolitions in detail. There are many uses for demolitions, but some examples are road craters and abatis.

Obstacle Reduction and Employment

H-10. Road craters are obstacles on roads or trails if the areas on the flanks of the crater are tied into steep slopes or mined areas. Road craters can compel the opposing force to use earthmoving equipment, blade tanks, or mechanical bridging assets.

H-11. Abatis are only effective if large enough trees, telephone poles, or other similar objects are available to stop the opposing force. An abatis is an obstacle created by cutting down trees so their tops are crisscrossed and pointing toward the expected enemy direction. It is most effective for stopping vehicles in a forest or narrow movement routes. This obstacle may be reinforced with claymore or non- persistent mines.

IMPROVISED OBSTACLES

H-12. Improvised obstacles are designed by Soldiers and leaders with imagination and ingenuity when using available materiel and other resources. An example of obstacles in urban terrain is shown in figure H-3. Improvised obstacles include the following:
- *Rubble.* Rubble from selected masonry structures and buildings in a built-up area will limit movement through an area and provide fortified fighting positions.
- *Battle damage.* Damaged vehicle hulks or other debris are used as roadblocks.
- *Flooding.* Flooded areas are created by opening floodgates or breaching levees.

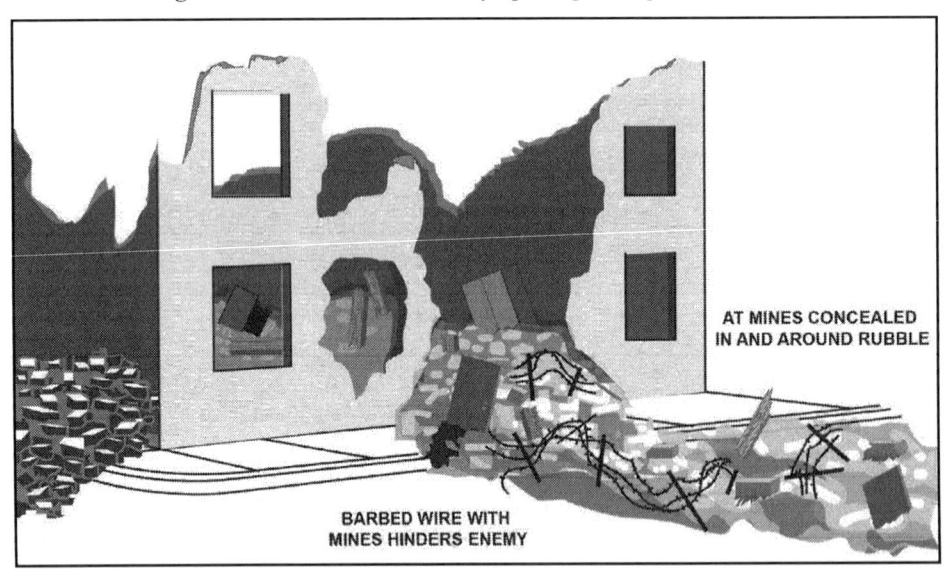

Figure H-3. Urban obstacles

SECTION II – OBSTACLE REDUCTION

H-13. Mobility operations involve obstacle reduction by maneuver and engineer units to reduce or negate the effects of existing or reinforcing obstacles. Infantry units must be proficient in the reduction of obstacles to enable the movement of combat power through obstacles while continuing to the objective.

Appendix H

BREACHING FUNDAMENTALS

H-14. Suppress, obscure, secure, reduce, and assault (SOSRA) are the breaching fundamentals being applied to ensure success when breaching against a defending enemy. These obstacle reduction fundamentals always will apply, but they may vary based on METT-TC.

SUPPRESS

H-15. Suppression is a tactical task used to employ direct or indirect fires or an electronic attack on enemy personnel, weapons, or equipment to prevent or degrade enemy fires and observation of friendly forces. The purpose of suppression during breaching operations is to protect forces reducing and maneuvering through an obstacle. Suppression is a mission-critical task performed during breaching operation. Suppression generally triggers the rest of the actions at the obstacle. Fire control measures ensure all fires are synchronized with other actions at the obstacle. Although suppressing the enemy overwatching the obstacle is the mission of the support force, the breach force should provide additional suppression against an enemy the supporting force cannot suppress.

OBSCURE

H-16. Obscuration must be employed to protect forces conducting obstacle reduction and passage of assault forces. Obscuration hampers enemy observation and target acquisition by concealing friendly activities and movement. Obscuration smoke deployed on or near the enemy's position minimizes its vision. Screening obscurants employed between the reduction area and the enemy conceals movement and reduction activities. It also degrades enemy ground and aerial observations. Obscuration must be planned carefully to provide maximum degradation of enemy observation and fires, but it must not degrade friendly fires and control significantly.

SECURE

H-17. Friendly forces secure reduction areas to prevent the enemy from interfering with obstacle reduction and passage of the assault force through lanes created during the reduction. Security must be effective against outposts and fighting positions near the obstacle and against overwatching units as necessary. The far side of the obstacle must be secured by fires or be occupied before attempting efforts to reduce the obstacle. The attacking unit's higher headquarters is responsible for isolating the breach area by fixing adjacent units, attacking enemy reserves in-depth, and providing counterfire support.

H-18. Identifying the extent of the enemy's defenses is critical before selecting the appropriate technique to secure the point of breach. If the enemy controls the point of breach and cannot be suppressed adequately, the force must secure the point of breach before it can reduce the obstacle.

H-19. The breach force must be resourced with enough maneuver assets to provide local security against the forces supporting force cannot engage sufficiently. Elements within the breach force securing the reduction area also may be used to suppress the enemy once reduction is complete. The breach force also may need to assault to the far side of the breach and provide local security so the assault element can seize its initial objective.

REDUCE

H-20. Reduction is the creation of lanes through or over an obstacle to allow an attacking force to pass. The number and width of lanes created varies with the enemy situation, the assault force's size, composition, and scheme of maneuver. The lanes must allow the assault force to rapidly pass through the obstacle. The breach force will reduce proof (if required), mark, and report lane locations and lane-marking method to higher command headquarters. Follow-on units will reduce or clear the obstacle when required. Reduction cannot be accomplished until suppression and obscuration are in place, the obstacle has been identified, and point of breach is secure.

ASSAULT

H-21. A breaching operation is not complete until:
- Friendly forces have assaulted to destroy the enemy on the far side of the obstacle as the enemy is capable of placing or observing direct and indirect fires on the reduction area.
- Battle handover with follow-on forces has occurred, unless no battle handover is planned.

BREACHING ORGANIZATION

H-22. A commander or platoon leader organizes friendly forces to accomplish breaching fundamentals quickly and effectively. This requires him to organize support, breach, and assault forces with the necessary assets to accomplish their roles. For tactical obstacle breaches, platoons and squads normally are assigned as either one or part of the following forces.

SUPPORT FORCE

H-23. The support force's primary responsibility is to eliminate the enemy's ability to place direct or indirect fire on friendly force and interfere with a breaching operation. It must—
- Isolate the reduction area with fires and establish a support-by-fire position to destroy, fix, or suppress the enemy. Depending on METT-TC, this may be the weapons squad or the entire platoon.
- Mass, control direct and indirect fires to suppress the enemy and to neutralize weapons able to bring fires on the breach force.
- Control obscuring smoke to prevent enemy-observed direct and indirect fires.

BREACH FORCE

H-24. The breach force assists in the passage of the assault force by detecting, creating, proofing (if necessary), marking and reporting lanes. The breach force is a combined-arms

Appendix H

force. It may include engineers, reduction assets, and enough maneuver forces to provide additional suppression and local security. The entire Infantry platoon or squad may be part of the breach force. The breach force may apply portions of the following breaching fundamentals as it reduces an obstacle.

Suppress

H-25. The breach force must be allocated enough maneuver forces to provide additional suppression against various threats, including:
- Enemy direct-fire systems that cannot be observed and suppressed by the support force due to the terrain or the masking of the support force's fires by the breach force as it moves forward to reduce the obstacle.
- Counterattacking and or repositioning forces that cannot be engaged by the support force.

Obscure

H-26. The breach force employs smoke pots, vehicle mounted smoke, handheld smoke or indirect fire obscurants if necessary, for self-defense and to cover lanes while the assault force is passing.

Secure

H-27. The breach force secures itself from threat forces providing close-in protection of the obstacle. The breach force also secures the lanes through the tactical obstacles once they are created to allow safe passage of the assault force.

Reduce

H-28. The breach force performs its primary mission by reducing the obstacle. To support the development of a plan to reduce the obstacle, the composition of the obstacle system must be an information requirement. If the obstacles are formidable, Infantry platoons and squads will be augmented with engineers to conduct reduction. Without engineers and special equipment such as Bangalore torpedoes and line charges, mine fields must be probed.

ASSAULT FORCE

H-29. The breach force assaults through the point of breach to the far side of an obstacle and seizes the foothold. The assault force's primary mission is to destroy the enemy and seize terrain on the far side of the obstacle to prevent the enemy from placing direct fires on the created lanes. The assault force may be tasked to assist the support force with suppression while the breach force reduces the obstacle.

H-30. The assault force must be sufficient in size to seize the point of penetration. Combat power is allocated to the assault force to achieve a minimum 3:1 ratio on the point of penetration. The breach and assault assets may maneuver as a single force when conducting breaching operations as an independent company team conducting an attack.

H-31. If the obstacle is defended by a small enemy force, assault and breach forces' missions may be combined. This simplifies mission command and provides more immediate combat power for security and suppression.

H-32. Fire control measures are essential because support and breach forces may be firing on the enemy when the assault force is committed. Suppression of overwatching enemy positions must continue and other enemy forces must remain fixed by fires until the enemy has been destroyed. The assault force must assume control for direct fires on the assault objective as support and breach force fires are ceased or shifted. Table H-1 illustrates the relationship between the breaching organization and breaching fundamentals.

Table H-1. Relationship between breaching organization and breaching fundamentals

BREACHING ORGANIZATION	BREACHING FUNDAMENTALS	RESPONSIBILITIES
Support force	Suppress Obscure	Suppress enemy direct fire systems covering the reduction area. Control obscuring smoke. Prevent enemy forces from repositioning or counterattacking to place direct fires on the breach force.
Breach force	Suppress (provides additional suppression) Obscure (provides additional obscuration in the reduction area) Secure (provides local security) Reduce	Create, proof and mark the necessary lanes in an obstacle. Secure the near side and far side of an obstacle. Defeat forces placing immediate direct fires on the reduction area. Report the lane status/location.
Assault force	Assault Suppress (if necessary)	Destroy the enemy on the far side of an obstacle if the enemy is capable of placing direct fires on the reduction area. Assist the support force with suppression if the enemy is not suppressed. Be prepared to breach follow-on and or protective obstacles after passing through the reduction area.

Appendix H

DETAILED REVERSE PLANNING

H-33. The platoon leader along with the platoon sergeant and squad leaders must develop the breaching plan using the following sequence when planning for a protective obstacle breach. The platoon leader can plan to breach wire, mine fields, trenches, and craters. (See figure H-4.) The following considerations must be made:

- Reverse planning begins with actions on the objective.
- Actions on the objective drive the size and composition of the assault force.
- The size of the assault force determines the number and location of lanes to be created.
- The ability of the enemy to interfere with the reduction of the obstacle determines the size and composition of the security element in the breach force.
- The ability of the enemy to mass fires on the point of breach determines the amount of suppression and size and composition of the support force.

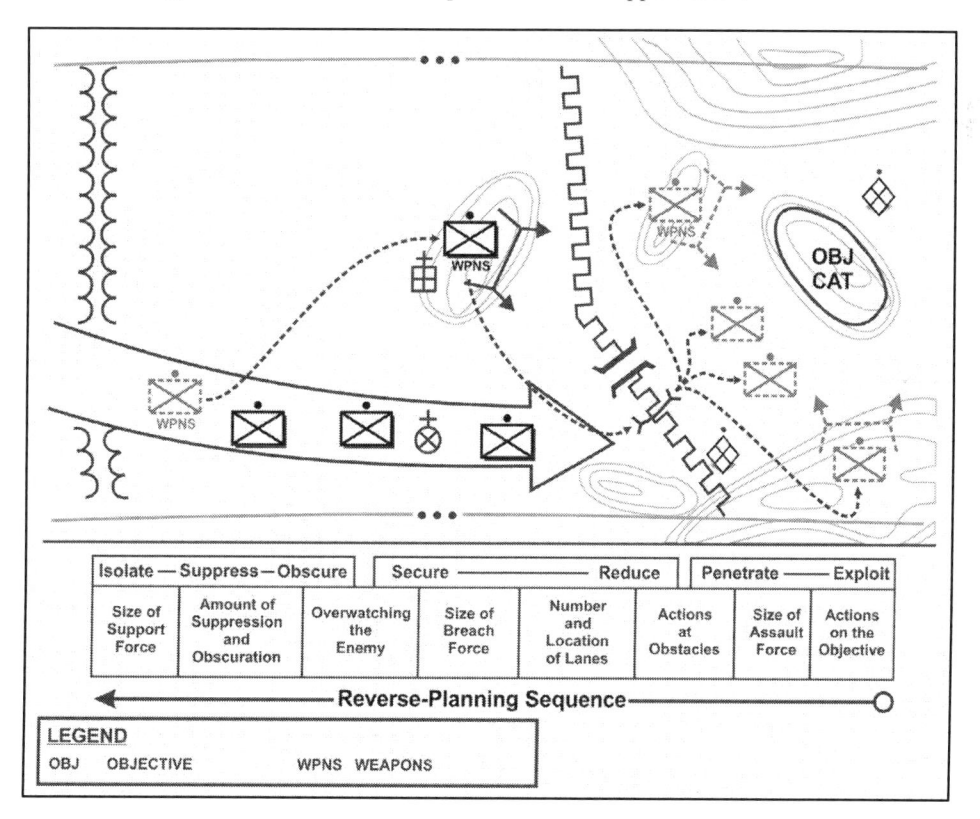

Figure H-4. Reverse planning

H-34. The approved technique for conducting obstacle breaching operations is SOSRA. The section focuses specifically on platoon and squad reduction techniques of land mines, construction obstacles, urban obstacles, IEDs and expedient devices.

H-35. As part of reducing obstacles, units also must detect, report, proof, and mark.

H-36. Detection is the actual confirmation of the location of obstacles. It may be accomplished through reconnaissance. It also can be unintentional (such as a vehicle running into a mine or wire). Detection is used in conjunction with information collection, bypass reconnaissance, and breaching/clearing operations. Specific detection methods for mines and IEDs are discussed more in this section.

H-37. Intelligence concerning enemy minefields is *reported* by the fastest means available. A SPOTREP should be sent to higher headquarters when Infantry platoons or squads have detected a minefield or other obstacle. This should be done whether they are sent on a specific minefield or obstacle reconnaissance mission, or if they encounter one in the course of normal operations. The SPOTREP should contain as much information possible including the type, location, size of the obstacle, and results of reduction efforts.

H-38. Proofing normally is done by engineers by passing a mine roller or another mine-resistant vehicle through the minefield to verify a lane is free of mines. If the risk of live mines remaining in the lane does not exceed the risk of loss to enemy fires while waiting, proofing may not be practical. Some mines are resistant to specific breaching techniques. For example, magnetically fused mines may be resistant to some explosive blasts. So proofing should be done when the time available, the threat, and mission allows. Proofing also involves verifying other obstacles (such as wire) are free of explosive or injurious devices.

H-39. Marking breach lanes and bypasses is critical to obstacle reduction.

REDUCE A MINEFIELD

H-40. Most types of obstacles do not cause casualties directly. Minefields do have this potential, and will cause direct casualties if not reduced. Buried mines usually are found in a highly prepared defense. When training the reduction of surface-laid and buried minefields, always assume the presence of AHDs and trip wires until proven otherwise.

MINEFIELD DETECTION

H-41. The three types of minefield detection methods the platoon or squad might employ visual, physical (probing), and electronic.

Visual Detection

H-42. Visual detection is part of all combat operations. Soldiers should constantly be alert for minefields and all types of enemy obstacles. Soldiers visually inspect the terrain for the following obstacle indicators:
- Trip wires and wires leading away from the side of the road. They may be firing wires that are partially buried.
- Signs of road repair (such as new fill or paving, road patches, ditching, and culvert work).
- Signs placed on trees, posts, or stakes. Threat forces may mark their minefields to protect their own forces.

Appendix H

- Dead animals or damaged vehicles.
- Disturbances in previous tire tracks or tracks stopping unexplainably.
- Odd features in the ground or patterns not present in nature. Plant growth may wilt or change color; rain may wash away some of the cover; the cover may sink or crack around the edges; or the materiel covering the mines may look like mounds of dirt.
- Civilians who may know where mines or IEDs are located in the residential area.
  - Civilians staying away from certain places or out of certain buildings are good indications of the presence of mines or IEDs.
  - Question civilians to determine the exact locations.
- Pieces of wood or other debris on a road. They may be indicative of pressure or pressure-release firing devices. These devices may be on the surface or partially buried.
- Patterns of objects being used as a sighting line. An enemy can use mines fired by command, so road shoulders and areas close to the objects should be searched.
- Berms may indicate the presence of an antitank ditch.

Physical (Probing) Detection

H-43. Physical detection (probing) is time-consuming and is used primarily for mine-clearing operations, self-extraction, and covert breaching operations. Detection of mines by visual or electronic methods should be confirmed by probing.

Electronic Detection

H-44. Electronic detection is effective for locating mines, but this method is time-consuming and exposes personnel to enemy fire. In addition, suspected mines must be confirmed by probing. As in probing, 20 to 30 minutes is the maximum amount of time an individual can use the detector.

H-45. The AN/PSS-14 uses ground penetrating radar (GPR) and metal detection sensing for the detection of AP and AT mines. (See figure H-5.) Both the metal detection and GPR are active search methods that transmit electronic signals into the ground and analyze the signals that return. The metal detection and GPR audio signal can be used separately and in combination as required by local conditions. (Refer to TC 3-34.14 for more information.)

Figure H-5. AN/PSS-14 mine detector in operation

H-46. The AN/PSS-12 mine detector (see figure H-6) is effective at finding metallic mines, but is less effective against low-metal mines. Employment and operation procedures of the AN/PSS-12 are discussed in ATP 3-34.20. The detector is handheld and identifies suspected mines by an audio signal in the headphones.

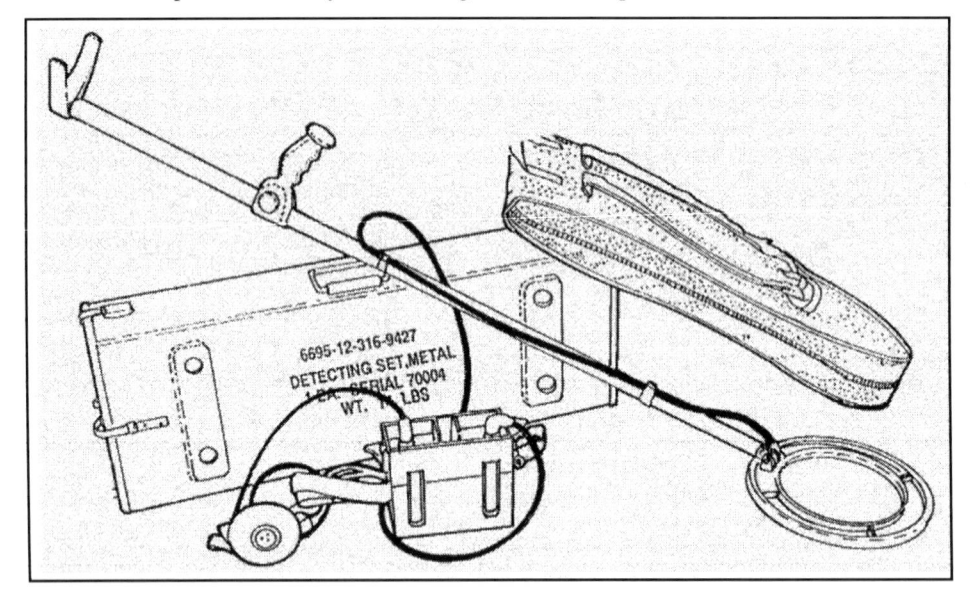

Figure H-6. AN/PSS-12 mine detector

Appendix H

MINEFIELD REDUCTION AND CLEARING EQUIPMENT

H-47. Minefield reduction and clearing equipment is broken down into explosive, manual, mechanical, and electronic. While chiefly an engineer task, the platoon or squad might need to reduce a minefield depending on the situation. The leader masses reduction assets to ensure they will create as many lanes as necessary to ensure the rapid passage of the assault force through the obstacle system. If necessary, the leader must carefully plan and synchronize the creation of additional lanes to reduce the potential for fratricide with assaulting troops. The distance between lanes depends on the enemy, the terrain, the need to minimize the effects of enemy artillery, the direct-fire plan of the support force, command control, and reduction-site congestion.

H-48. The breach force should be organized and equipped to use several different reduction techniques in case the primary technique fails. Additional reduction assets should be present to handle the unexpected. Normally, 50 percent more reduction assets than required for obstacle reduction are positioned with the breach force. Mechanical and electronic reduction techniques and equipment are employed by engineers and can be found in ATP 3-34.20.

Explosive Minefield Reduction

H-49. ATP 3-34.20 lists all explosive minefield reduction techniques and equipment. The different types of explosive minefield-reduction equipment the platoon or squad might use to breach obstacles are discussed below.

M1A1/M1A2 Bangalore Torpedo

H-50. The Bangalore torpedo (see figure H-7) is a manually emplaced, explosive-filled pipe designed to create a lane in wire obstacles and is also effective against simple pressure-activated AP mines. The M1A1 and M1A2 kits are issued as a demolition kit that consists of 10 1.5-meter tubes, 10 connecting sleeves, and one nose sleeve. Each tube contains four kilograms of HE and weighs six kilograms. The kit clears a 1-by 15-meter lane.

H-51. The M1A3 Bangalore torpedo demolition kit consists of eight charge assemblies, eight connecting sleeves, and two nose sleeves. The tube assemblies, or torpedoes, are steel tubes 2 1/2 feet long and 2 1/8 inches in diameter, grooved and capped at each end. The torpedoes have a 4-inch composition A3 booster (1/2 pound each) at both ends of each 2 1/2 foot section. The main explosive charge is five pounds of composition B4. The primary use of the torpedo is for clearing lanes through wire obstacles and heavy undergrowth. It will clear a 3- to 4-yard-wide path through wire obstacles.

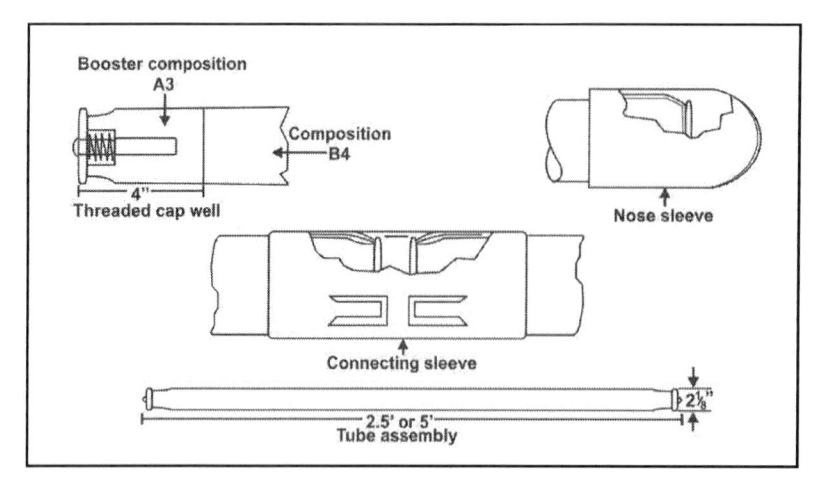

Figure H-7. Bangalore torpedo

H-52. All torpedo sections have a threaded cap well at each end so they can be assembled in any order. The connecting sleeves are used to connect the torpedo sections together. An individual or pair of Soldiers connect the number of sections needed, and push the torpedo through the antipersonnel minefield before priming the torpedo. A detailed reconnaissance is conducted before using the Bangalore torpedo to ensure trip wires have not been used. The Bangalore torpedo generates one short impulse. It is not effective against pronged, double-impulse, or pressure-resistant antipersonnel or antitank mines.

> **WARNING**
>
> Do not modify the Bangalore torpedo. Cutting the Bangalore in half or performing other modification could cause the device to explode.

Antipersonnel Obstacle Breaching System

H-53. The Antipersonnel Obstacle Breaching System (APOBS) (see figure H-8, page H-18) is a man-portable device capable of quickly creating a footpath through AP mines and wire entanglements. It provides a lightweight, self-contained, two-man, portable line charge rocket-propelled over AP obstacles away from the obstacle's edge from a standoff position

H-54. For dismounted operations, the APOBS is carried in 25-kilogram backpacks by no more than two Soldiers for a maximum of two kilometers. One backpack assembly consists of a rocket-motor launch mechanism containing a 25-meter line-charge segment and 60 attached grenades. The other backpack assembly contains a 20-meter line-charge segment and 48 attached grenades.

Appendix H

H-55. The total weight of the APOBS is about 54 kilograms. It is capable of creating a lane about 0.6 by 45 meters and is fired from a 25-meter standoff.

Figure H-8. Antipersonnel obstacle breaching system

Man Portable Line Charge

H-56. The man portable line charge (MPLC) is a lightweight, man-portable; rocket-launched explosive line charge system that assists in breaching through a complex mined or trip-wired environment. (See figure H-9.) The MPLC NSN No. 1375-01-593-8347, provides a precise, portable mine clearing weapon system at the small tactical unit level providing the ability to create a lane in urban and complex mined or trip-wired environments. Mobility and survivability is increased due to immediate precision fire from covered or concealed positions.

H-57. The system weighs about 35 pounds and can easily be carried, set up, and detonated by one Soldier. It is a rocket-launched explosive system designed to clear an area of other explosives. A Soldier proficient on the MPLC can set up and detonate an explosive in about one minute.

H-58. The MPLC provides small tactical units with the ability to conduct clearing operations in urban and complex, mined or trip-wired environments; in covered or concealed positions. It is designed to assist in the clearing of a narrow footpath to a target by exposing, disrupting or neutralizing IED trigger mechanisms, while minimizing collateral effects on noncombatant personnel, structures and property.

Obstacle Reduction and Employment

H-59. The MPLC system is self-contained in a backpack designed for carry and deployment by one Soldier. The system requires no additional special tools or equipment, however, a hammer, may be needed to secure the launch pad to the ground. Once the system is in place, a "shock tube" firing system will initiate the rocket and detonate the line charge.

H-60. MPLC offers a three-prong approach to optimal breaching effectiveness: It reduces time on target, improves information operations by reducing collateral damage during tactical operations and improves freedom of movement.

H-61. MPLC is composed of a plastic bonded explosive line charge, a small rocket motor used to deploy the line charge, an arresting strap, a launch rod, and dual shock tube housed in a SKIN-PACK detonator assembly. The shock tube is initiated by two M81 firing devices. The shock tubes are connected through an energetic transfer assembly that contains a PBXN-5 booster. All of these items are contained in a backpack.

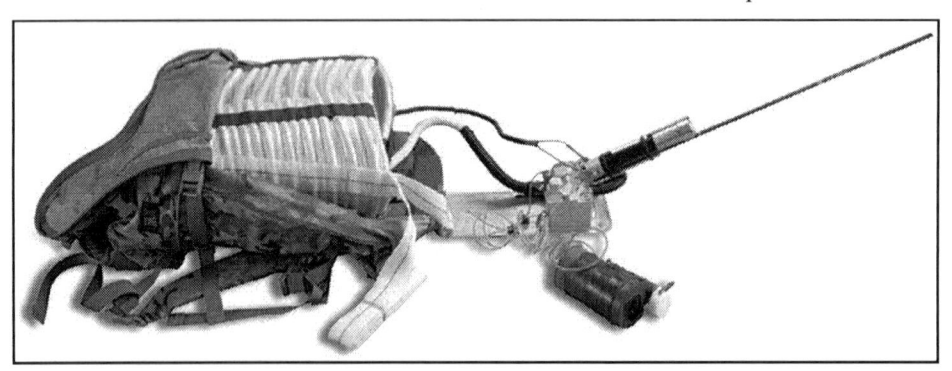

Figure H-9. Man portable line charge

Manual Minefield Reduction

H-62. Manual procedures normally are conducted by engineers (but also can be performed by Infantry units) and are effective against all obstacles under all conditions. Manual procedures involve dismounted Soldiers using simple explosives or other equipment to create a lane through an obstacle. These procedures expose the Soldier and may be manpower and time-intensive. While mechanical and explosive reduction procedures normally are preferred, Infantry platoons or squads may have to use manual procedures for the following reasons:

- Explosive, mechanical, and electronic reduction assets are unavailable or ineffective against the type of obstacle.
- Terrain limitations.
- Stealth is required.

H-63. Different manual reduction techniques for surface-laid and buried minefields are discussed below.

Surface-Laid Minefield

Appendix H

H-64. First use grappling hooks from covered positions to check for trip wires in the lane. The limited range of the tossed hook requires the procedure to be repeated through the estimated depth of the obstacle. A demolition team then moves through the lane. The team places a line main down the center of the lane, ties the line from the explosive into the line main, and places blocks of explosive next to surface laid mines. After the mines are detonated, the team makes a visual check to ensure all mines were cleared before directing a proofing roller and other traffic through the lane. Demolition team members are assigned special tasks such as grappler, detonating-cord man, and demolitions man. All members should be cross-trained on all procedures. Demolitions are prepared for use before arriving at the point of breach. The platoon and squad must rehearse reduction procedures until execution is flawless, quick, and technically safe. During reduction, the platoon or squad will be exposed in the lane for five minutes or more depending on the mission, the minefield depth, and Infantry platoon's or squad's level of training.

Buried Minefield

H-65. Manually reducing a buried minefield is extremely difficult to perform as part of a breaching operation. If mine burrows are not easily seen, mine detectors and probes must be used to locate mines. Mines then are destroyed by hand-emplaced charges. As an alternative, mines can be removed by using a grappling hook and, if necessary, a tripod. (See figure H-10.) Using a tripod provides vertical lift on a mine, making it easier to pull the mine out of the hole.

H-66. The leader organizes Soldiers into teams with distinct, rehearsed missions including grappling, detecting, marking, probing, and emplacing demolitions and detonating cord. Platoons or squads are exposed in the obstacle for long periods.

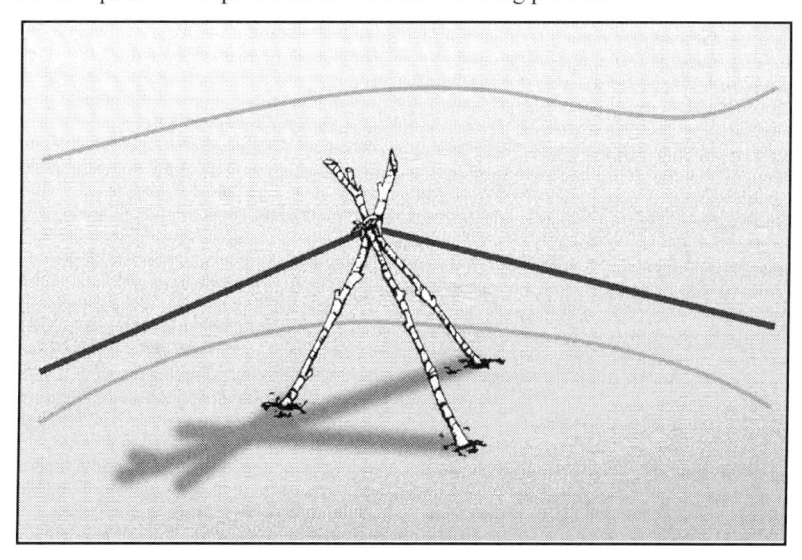

Figure H-10. Tripod

Grappling Hook

H-67. The grappling hook is a multipurpose tool used for manual obstacle reduction. Soldiers use it to detonate mines from a standoff position by activating trip wires and AHDs. After the grapnel is used to clear trip wires in a lane, dismounted Soldiers can move through the minefield, visually locate surface laid mines, and prepare mines for demolition. In buried minefields, Soldiers grapple and enter the minefield with mine detectors and probes.

H-68. Multiple grapplers can clear a lane of trip wires quickly and thoroughly, but they must time their efforts and follow procedures simultaneously. A hit on a trip wire or a pressure fuse can destroy the grappling hook and cord, so the platoon and squad should carry extras.

H-69. There are two types of grappling hooks: hand-thrown and weapon-launched.

H-70. Hand-thrown. A 60+-meter light rope is attached to the grappling hook for hand throwing. The throwing range is usually no more than 25 meters. The excess rope is used for standoff distance when the thrower begins grappling. The thrower tosses the grappling hook and seeks cover before the grappling hook and rope touch the ground in case their impact detonates a mine. He then moves backward, reaches the end of the excess rope, takes cover, and begins grappling. Once the grappling hook is recovered, the thrower moves forward to the original position, tosses the grapnel, and repeats the procedure at least twice. He then moves to the end of the grappled area and repeats this sequence through the depth of the minefield.

H-71. Weapon-launched. A 150-meter lightweight rope is attached to a lightweight grappling hook designed to be fired from an M16 or M4-series rifle using an M855 cartridge. The grappling hook is pushed onto the rifle muzzle with the opening of the retrieval-rope bag oriented toward the minefield. The shooter is located 25 meters from the minefield's leading edge and aims the rifle muzzle at a 30-to 40-degree angle for maximum range. Once fired, the grappling hook travels 75 to 100 meters from the firer's position. After the weapon-launched grappling hook (WLGH) has been fired, the firer secures the rope, moves 60 meters from the minefield, moves into a prone position, and begins to grapple. The WLGH can be used only once to clear a minefield, but it can be reused up to 20 times for training because blanks are used to fire it.

Demolitions

H-72. Different types of demolitions can be used for minefield obstacle reduction. (See table H-2, page H-22.) FM 3-34.214 covers each different type of demolition available to support all Infantry missions. Demolitions are used differently against certain types of mines:

- Pressure-Fused AP Mine. Place at least a one-pound charge within 15.2 centimeters of simple pressure-fused mines. Ensure the charge is placed within 2.54 centimeters of blast-hardened mines.
- Trip-Wire/Break-Wire-Fused AP Mine. Place at least a one-pound charge within 15.2 centimeters of the mine after the mine at the end of a trip wire has been located. Soldiers can use elevated charges if necessary against the Claymore and stake-type mines.

Appendix H

- Influence-Fused AP Mine. Do not use demolitions.
- Command-Detonated Blast Mine. Ensure the observer is neutralized before approaching. Elevated charges can be used if necessary against Claymores.

Table H-2. Demolitions

ITEM	DESCRIPTION
M183 Satchel Charge	Consists of 16 M112 (C4) charges and four priming assemblies. Total explosive weight of 20 pounds. Used primarily for breaching obstacles or demolishing structures when large charges are required. Is effective on smaller obstacles such as small dragon's teeth.
M112 Charge	Consists of 1.25 pounds of C4 packed in an olive drab Mylar film container with a pressure-sensitive adhesive tape on one surface. Primarily used for cutting and breaching. Because of its ability to cut and be shaped, the M112 is ideally suited for cutting irregularly-shaped targets such as steel. The adhesive backing allows you to place the charge on relatively flat surfaces.
Modernized Demolition Initiator (MDI)	MDI is a new family of nonelectric blasting caps and associated items. Components simplify initiation systems and improve reliability and safety. Components include the M11 high strength blasting cap, the M12 and M13 low strength blasting caps, and M14 high strength time delay cap.
Detonating Cord	Consists of a core of HE (6.4 pounds of PETN per 1,000 feet) wrapped in a reinforced and waterproof olive drab coating. Can be used to prime and detonate single or multiple explosive charges simultaneously. Can be used in conjunction with the MDI components.

MARKING AND CROSSING THE MINEFIELD

H-73. Lane marking allows the leader to project the platoon or squad through the obstacle quickly with combat power. It also gives Infantry platoons or squad's confidence in the safety of the lane and helps prevent unnecessary minefield casualties.

H-74. Once a footpath has been probed and mines marked or reduced, a security team should cross the minefield to secure the far side. After the far side is secure, the rest of the unit should cross. If mines and trip wires have been identified but not reduced, the mine and line of the trip wire are marked along the ground surface, 12 inches before the trip wire. (See figure H-11.)

Obstacle Reduction and Employment

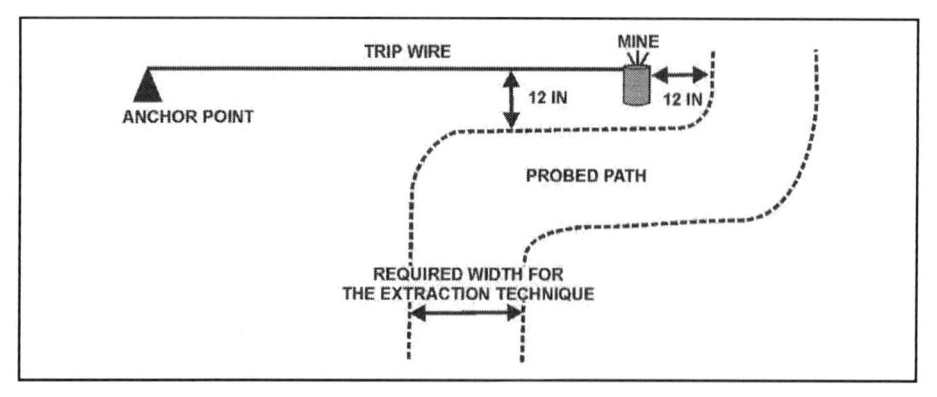

Figure H-11. Marking a footpath

REDUCE A CONSTRUCTED OBSTACLE

H-75. Reduction methods for enemy wire and tank ditch obstacles are as follows.

REDUCE A WIRE OBSTACLE

H-76. The enemy uses wire and concertina obstacles to separate Infantry from tanks and to slow or stop the Infantry movement. His wire obstacles are similar to ours. On patrol, reducing a wire obstacle may require stealth and is conducted using wire cutters or by crawling under or crossing over the wire. It may not require stealth during an attack and can be accomplished with Bangalore torpedoes and wire cutters.

Cut the Wire

H-77. To cut through a wire obstacle with stealth, —
- Cut only the lower strands and leave the top strand in place, making it less likely the enemy will discover the gap.
- Cut the wire near a picket. To reduce the noise of a cut, have another Soldier wrap cloth around the wire and hold the wire with both hands. Cut part of the way through the wire between the other Soldier's hands and have him bend the wire back and forth until it breaks. If you are alone, wrap cloth around the wire near a picket, partially cut the wire, and bend and break the wire.

H-78. To reduce an obstacle made of concertina, —
- Cut the wire and stake it back to keep the breach open.
- Stake the wire back far enough to allow room to crawl through or under the obstacle.

Bangalore Torpedo

H-79. After the Bangalore torpedo has been assembled and pushed through the wire obstacle, prime it with either an electric or nonelectric firing system. (See figure H-12, page H-24.) To prevent early detonation of the entire Bangalore torpedo if you hit a mine while pushing it through the obstacle, attach an improvised (wooden) torpedo section to

Appendix H

its end. The section can be made out of wooden poles or sticks the size of a real torpedo section. Attach the nose sleeve to the end of the wooden section. Once the Bangalore torpedo has been fired, use wire cutters to cut away wire not cut by the explosion.

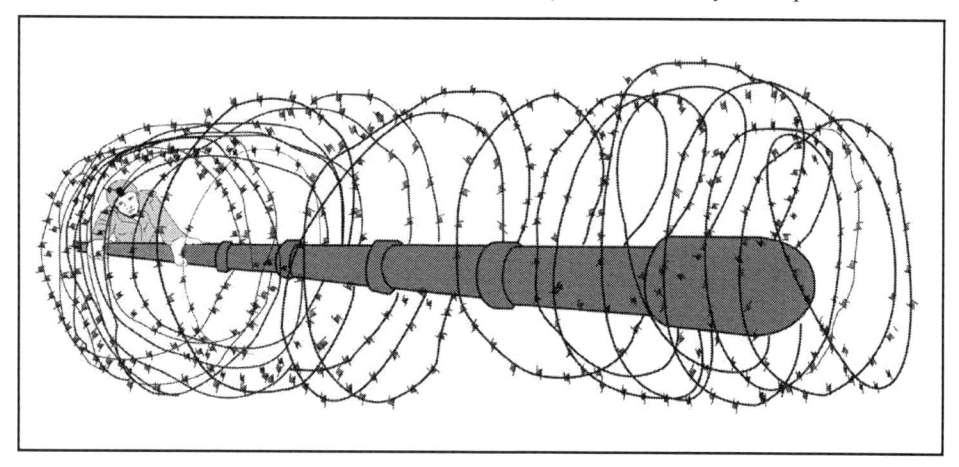

Figure H-12. Reducing wire obstacles with Bangalore torpedoes

REDUCE AN URBAN OBSTACLE

H-80. Understanding how to employ and incorporate reduction techniques is an important part of urban operations. Gaining quick access to targeted rooms is integral to room clearing. Reduction teams need to be supported by fires or obscurants. Reduction operations should be performed during hours of limited visibility whenever possible. Reduction techniques vary based on construction encountered and munitions available. The three urban reduction methods discussed in this appendix are mechanical, ballistic, and explosive.

H-81. The assault team's order of march to the breach point is determined by the method of reduction and its intended actions at the entry point. This preparation must be completed prior to or in the last covered and concealed location before reaching the entry point. Establishing an order of march aids the team leader with mission command and minimizes exposure time in open areas and at the entry point. One order of march technique is to number the assault team members one through four.

H-82. The No. 1 man always should be responsible for frontal and door security. If the reduction has been conducted prior to its arrival, the assault team quickly moves through the entry point. If a reduction has not been made prior to its arrival at the entry point, depending on the type of breach to be made, the team leader conducts the reduction himself or signals forward the breach man or element. One option is to designate the squad leader as the breach man. If the breach man is part of the assault team, he normally will be the last of the four men to enter the building or room. This allows him to transition from his reduction task to his combat role. (Refer to ATTP 3-06.11 for more information.)

BREACH LOCATIONS

H-83. The success of the assault element often depends on the speed with which it gains access into the building. It is important the breach location provide the assault element with covered or concealed access, fluid entry, and ability to be overwatched by the support element.

Creating Mouseholes

H-84. Mouse-holes provide a safe means of moving between rooms and floors. C4 plastic explosive can be used to create mouse-holes when lesser means of mechanical reduction fail. Because C4 comes packaged with an adhesive backing or can be emplaced using pressure-sensitive tape, it is ideal for this purpose. When using C4 to blow a mouse-hole in a lath and plaster wall, one block or a strip of blocks should be placed on the wall from neck-to-knee height. Charges should be primed with detonating cord or modernized demolition initiator (MDI) to obtain simultaneous detonation blowing a hole large enough for a man to fit through.

Expedient Reduction Methods

H-85. Because the internal walls of most buildings function as partitions rather than load-bearing members, smaller explosive charges can be used to reduce them. When C4 or other military explosives are not available, one or more fragmentation grenades or a Claymore can be used to reduce some internal walls. These field-expedient reduction devices should be tamped to increase their effectiveness and to reduce the amount of explosive force directed to the rear. Take extreme care when attempting to perform this type of reduction because fragments may penetrate walls and cause friendly casualties. If walls are made of plaster or dry wall, mechanical reduction may be more effective.

Windows and Restrictive Entrances

H-86. Regardless of the technique used to gain entry, if the breach location restricts fundamental movement into the room or building, local or immediate support must be used until the assault team can support itself. For example, as a Soldier moves through a window and into the room, he may not be in a position to engage an enemy. Therefore, another window having access to the same room may be used to overwatch the lead team's movement into the room. The overwatching element can come from the initial clearing team or from the team designated to enter the breach location second.

MECHANICAL REDUCTION

H-87. This method requires increased physical exertion by one or more Soldiers using hand tools such as axes, saws, crowbars, hooligan's tools, or sledgehammers to gain access. Although most Soldiers are familiar with these tools, practice on various techniques increases speed and effectiveness. The mechanical reduction is not the preferred primary method because it may be time-consuming and defeat the element of surprise. However, the ROE and situation may require the use of these tools, so Soldiers should be proficient in their use.

Appendix H

H-88. Typically, the order of movement for a mechanical breach is the initial assault team, followed by the breach man or element. At the breach point, the assault team leader brings the breach team forward while the assault team provides local security. After the reduction is conducted, the breach team moves aside and provides local security as the assault team enters the breach. (Refer to ATTP 3-06.11 for more information.)

H-89. When developing an urban operations mechanical breach kit SOP, Infantry units must consider their mission essential task list (METL) and unit tactical SOPs.

BALLISTIC REDUCTION

H-90. Ballistic reduction requires the use of a weapon firing a projectile at the breach point. Ballistic reduction is not a positive means of gaining entry and should not be considered the primary method for gaining initial entry into a structure. It may not supply the surprise, speed, and violence of action necessary to minimize friendly losses on initial entry. In certain situations, it may become necessary to use ballistic reduction as a back-up entry method. A misfire of an explosive charge or the compromise of the assault element during its approach to the target may necessitate the use of ballistic reduction as a means of initial entry into the structure. Ballistic reduction may have to be followed up with a fragmentation, concussion, or stun grenade before entry.

H-91. Once initial entry is gained, shotgun ballistic reduction may become the primary method for gaining access to subsequent rooms within the structure. Surprise is lost upon initial entry, and other reduction methods are often too slow, tending to slow the momentum of the assault team. If a door must be used for entry, several techniques can be used to open the door. Doors should be considered a fatal funnel because they usually are covered by fire, or may be booby-trapped. (Refer to ATTP 3-06.11 for more information.)

H-92. Unless a deliberate breach is planned, the platoon or squad can employ a series of progressive reductions. An example is an attempt to open a door by using the doorknob first, then shotgun reduction, then explosive reduction as a final option. Mechanical reduction can be used to clean up a failed attempt of a shotgun or explosive reduction, but also can be used as the primary reduction technique. Based on the multiple situations the complex urban environment presents, the leader needs latitude in his options.

Exterior Walls

H-93. For exterior walls, the use of a BFV or artillery piece in the direct fire role is ideal if the structure will support it and if the ROE will allow it. The BFV's 25-mm cannon is a reduction weapon when using HE rounds and firing a spiral firing pattern. (See figure H-13.) The main gun of an M1-series Abrams tank is effective when using the HEAT round. However, the APDS-T round rarely produces the desired effect because of its penetrating power.

Obstacle Reduction and Employment

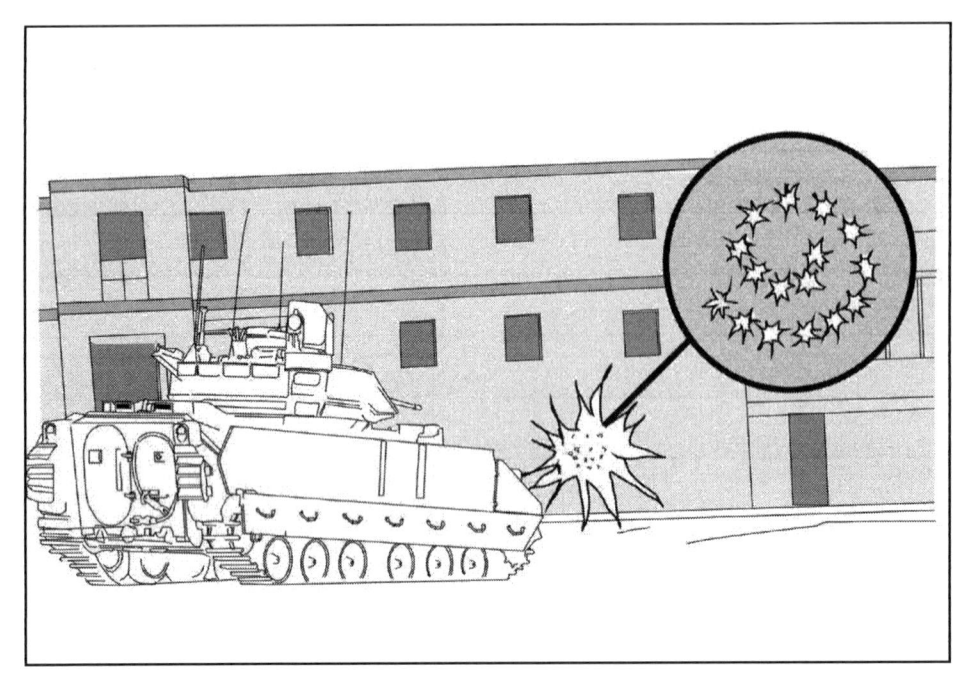

Figure H-13. Spiral firing pattern

Doors, Windows, and Interior Walls

H-94. The M500/M2612-gauge shotgun breaching round is effective on doorknobs and hinges, while standard small arms (5.56 mm and 7.62 mm) have proven to be virtually ineffective for reducing obstacles. These should not be used except as a last resort because of ricochet potential and shoot-through capability. Ballistic reduction of lightly-constructed interior walls by shotgun fire is normally an alternate means of gaining entry.

> **WARNING**
>
> Fragmentation and ricochet effects of standard small arms (5.56 mm and 7.62 mm) as breaching rounds is unpredictable and considered extremely dangerous. Do not attempt in training.

Rifle-Launched Entry Munitions

H-95. Rifle-launched entry munitions (RLEM) allow a remote ballistic reduction of an exterior door or window without having the assault or breaching element physically present at the entry point. This allows the assault element to assume a posture for entry in the last covered and concealed position before the breach. The RLEM shooter is not

Appendix H

normally part of the assault element but rather a part of the breaching or support element. This allows the RLEM to be fired from one position while the assault element waits in another position. In the event the first round does not affect the reduction, the firer should prepare a second round for reduction or a second firer should be prepared to engage the target.

> **WARNING**
>
> **The firer must be a minimum of 10 meters from the target to safely employ a 150-gram round.**

Note. Exact MSDs for firers and assault elements have not been established for the 150-gram round.

Shotgun Reduction

H-96. Various shotgun rounds can be used for ballistic reduction. Breaching and clearing teams need to be familiar with the advantages as well as the disadvantages of each type of round. Leaders must consider the potential for over penetration on walls and floors in multi-story buildings to avoid potential fratricide incidents or killing of noncombatants:

- Rifled slugs. Rifled slugs defeat most doors encountered, including some heavy steel doors. However, rifled slugs present a serious over penetration problem and could easily kill or injure anyone inside the room being attacked. Rifled slugs are excellent AP rounds and can be used accurately up to 100 meters.
- Bird shot. Bird shot (No. 6 through No. 9 shot) is used in close-range work up to 15 meters. A 2 ¾-inch shell of No. 9 shot typically contains an ounce of shot (though it can be loaded to 1 ½-ounce with an accompanied increase in recoil). The major advantage of bird shot is it does not over penetrate. Therefore, bird shot poses little hazard to fellow team members in adjoining rooms. When used at close range, bird shot offers the same killing potential as buckshot, especially in a full choke shotgun intended for dense shot patterns. Another advantage of bird shot is low recoil. This feature allows for faster recovery and quicker multi-target engagements. A disadvantage with bird shot is rapid-energy bleed-off reducing penetration at medium and long ranges. Moreover, the small size of the individual pellets requires hits be made with a majority of the shot charge to be effective. A hit with one-third of the No. 9 shot charge may not be fatal, unless the shot is at extremely close range. These disadvantages are negated when birdshot is fired from a full choke shotgun where it will produce a pattern quite small inside of 10 meters. Inside five meters, all of the shot will be clumped like a massive single projectile.
- Buckshot. Buckshot is used in close- to medium-range work, up to 30 meters. Because of its larger size, buckshot is more lethal than bird shot. A 2 ¾-inch shell of buckshot contains nine .30-caliber pellets. One .30-caliber ball of the 00 buckshot charge hit can prove fatal. Buckshot also retains its energy longer. Therefore, it is lethal at longer ranges than bird shot. A disadvantage of buckshot is over

Obstacle Reduction and Employment

penetration. Because buckshot typically is loaded with heavier shot charges, it also has heavy recoil. This problem becomes apparent when numerous shots have been taken and can result in fatigue.

- Ferret rounds. Ferret rounds contain a plastic slug filled with liquid chemical irritant (CS). When shot through a door or wall (drywall or plywood), the plastic slug breaks up and a fine mist of CS is sprayed into the room. The effectiveness of one round is determined by the size of the room on the other side of the door or the wall and also the ventilation in that room.
- When using the shotgun as an alternate reduction method to gain entry, shooters must consider the following target points on the door.
- Doorknob. Never target the doorknob itself because when the round impacts, the doorknob has a tendency to bend the locking mechanism into the doorframe. In most cases this causes the door to be bent in place and prevents entry into the room.
- Locking mechanism. When attacking the locking mechanism, focus the attack on the area immediately between the doorknob and doorframe. Place the muzzle of the shotgun no farther than one inch away from the face of the door directly over the locking mechanism. The angle of attack should be 45 degrees downward and at a 45-degree angle into the doorframe. After breaching the door, kick it swiftly. This way, if the door is not completely open, a strong kick usually will open it. When kicking the door open, focus the force of the kick at the locking mechanism and close to the doorjamb. After the locking mechanism has been reduced, this area becomes the weakest part of the door.
- Hinges. The hinge breach technique is performed much the same as the doorknob reduction, except the gunner aims at the hinges. He fires three shots per hinge, the first at the middle, then at the top and bottom. He fires all shots from less than an inch away from the hinge. Because the hinges are often hidden from view, the hinge reduction is more difficult. Hinges are generally 8 to 10 inches from the top and bottom of the door. The center hinge is generally 36 inches from the top, centered on the door. Regardless of technique used, immediately after the gunner fires, he kicks the door in or pulls it out. He then pulls the shotgun barrel sharply upward and quickly turns away from the doorway to signal the breach point has been reduced. This rapid clearing of the doorway allows the following man in the fire team a clear shot at enemy who may be blocking the immediate breach site. (Refer to ATTP 3-06.11 for more information.)

H-97. When the assault team members encounter a door to a "follow-on" room, they should line up on the side of the door giving them a path of least resistance upon entering. When the door is encountered, the first Soldier to see it calls out the status of the door, OPENED or CLOSED. If the door is open, Soldiers should never cross in front of it to give themselves a path of least resistance. If the door is closed, the No. 1 man maintains security on the door and waits on the No. 2 man to gain positive control of the No.1 man. The No. 1 man begins the progressive breaching process by taking his nonfiring hand and checking the doorknob to see if it is locked. If the door is unlocked, the No. 1 man (with his hand still on the door) pushes the door open as he enters the room. If the door is locked, the No. 1 man releases the doorknob (while maintaining security on the door) and calls out the breacher, BREACHER UP.

Appendix H

H-98. Once the breacher arrives at the door (with round chambered), he places the muzzle of the shotgun at the proper attack point, takes the weapon off safe, and signals the No. 2 man by nodding his head. At that time, the No. 2 man (with one hand maintaining positive control of the No. 1 man) takes his other hand (closest to the breacher) and forming a fist, places it within the periphery of the breacher and pumps his fist twice saying, READY BREACH. This action allows the breacher to see if a flash-bang or grenade is to be used. Once the breacher defeats the door, he steps aside and allows the assault team to enter. He then either assumes the position of the No. 4 man if he is acting as a member of the assault team or remains on-call as the breacher for follow-on doors. He should keep the shotgun magazine full at all times. There may be several doors, and stopping to reload will slow the momentum of the assault.

Note. The shotgun should not be used as a primary assault weapon because of its limited magazine capacity and difficulty of reloading.

Exterior Walls

H-99. One of the most difficult breaching operations of the assault team is reducing masonry and reinforced concrete walls. C4 normally is used for explosive reduction because it is safe, easy to use, and readily available. Engineers usually are attached to the platoon or squad if explosive reduction operations are expected. The attached engineers will conduct the reduction themselves or provide technical assistance to the Infantry Soldiers involved. The typical thickness of exterior walls is 15 inches or less, although some forms of wall construction are several feet thick. Assuming all outer walls are constructed of reinforced concrete, a rule of thumb for reduction is to place 10 pounds of C4 against the target between waist and chest height. When detonated, this charge normally blows a hole large enough for a man to go through. On substandard buildings, however, a charge of this size could level the building. When explosives are used to reduce windows or doors, the blast should eliminate IEDs in the vicinity of the window or doorframe. (Refer to ATTP 3-06.11 for more information.)

Note. Not all charges are mentioned in this manual, only the most commonly used by Infantry Soldiers. (Refer to ATP 3-34.20 for more information.)

Charge Placement

H-100. Place the charges (other than shape charges) directly against the surface to be reduced. When enemy fire prevents an approach to the wall, a potential technique is to attach the charge, untamped, to a pole and slide it into position for detonation at the base of the wall. Small-arms fire will not detonate C4 or TNT. Take cover before detonating the charge.

Tamping

H-101. Whenever possible, explosives should be tamped or surrounded with materiel to focus the blast to increase effectiveness. Tamping materiels could be sandbags, rubble, desks, chairs, and even intravenous bags. For many exterior walls, tamping may be impossible due to enemy fire. An untamped charge requires approximately twice the explosive charge of a tamped charge to produce the same effect.

Second Charges

H-102. Charges will not cut metal reinforcing rods inside concrete targets. If the ROE permit, hand grenades should be thrown into the opening to clear the area of enemy. Once the area has been cleared of enemy, the reinforcing rods can be removed using special steel-cutting explosive charges or mechanical means.

Door Charges

H-103. Various charges can be utilized for explosive reduction of doors. Leaders must conduct extensive training on the use of the charges to get proper target feedback.

H-104. The general-purpose charge, rubber band charge, and flexible linear charge are field-expedient charges that can be used to reduce interior and exterior doors. These charges give the breach element an advantage because they can be made ahead of time and are simple, compact, lightweight, and easy to emplace. (Refer to ATTP 3-06.11 for more information.)

General-Purpose Charge

H-105. This charge is the most useful ready charge for reducing a door or other barrier. It can cut mild steel chain and destroy captured enemy equipment. To construct the general purpose charge—
- Take a length of detonation cord about two feet long. Using another length of detonation cord, tie two uli knots around the 2-foot long cord.
- The uli knots need to have a minimum of six wraps and be loose enough for them to slide along the main line, referred to as an uli slider.
- Trim the excess cord from the uli knots and secure them with tape.
- Cut a block of C4 explosive to a two-inch square.
- Tape one slider knot to each side of the C4 block, leaving the length of detonation cord free to slide through the knots.

H-106. To place the charge, perform the following:
- To reduce a standard door, place the top loop of the charge over the doorknob. Slide the uli knots taped to the C4 so the charge is tight against the knob.
- Prime the loose ends of the detonation cord with an MDI firing system and detonate.

Note. To cut mild steel chain, place the loop completely around the chain link to form a girth hitch. Tighten the loop against the link by sliding the uli knots.

Appendix H

Rubber Band Charge

H-107. The rubber band charge is an easily fabricated lightweight device that can be used to remove the locking mechanism or doorknob from wooden/light metal doors, or to break a standard-size padlock at the shackle. To construct the rubber band charge, —
- Cut a 10-inch piece of detonation cord and tie an overhand knot in one end.
- Using another piece of detonation cord, tie an uli knot with at least eight wraps around the first length of cord.
- Slide the uli knot tightly up against the overhand knot. Secure it in place with either tape or string.
- Loop a strong rubber band around the base of the uli knot tied around the detonation cord.
- Tie an overhand knot in the other end of the cord to form a pigtail for priming the charge.

H-108. To place the charge, attach the charge to the doorknob (or locking mechanism) by putting the loose end of the rubber band around the knob. The charge must be placed between the knob and doorframe. This ensures the explosive is over the bolt securing the door to the frame.

Flexible Linear Charge

H-109. The simplest field-expedient charge for reducing wooden doors is the flexible linear charge. (See Tables H-3 and H-4 (page H-34) for charge use and system components.) It can be made in almost any length and is easily carried until needed. It is effective against hollow-core, particle-filled, and solid wood doors. When detonated, the flexible linear charge cuts through the door near the hinges

H-110. To construct the flexible linear charge, lay out a length of double-sided contact tape with the topside adhesive exposed. Place the necessary number of strands of detonation cord down the center of the double-sided tape, pressing them firmly in place. Military detonation cord has 50 grains of explosives per foot and 7,000 grains in a pound. Most residential doors are 80 inches tall. Commercial doors are 84 inches tall. This must be considered when calculating the quantities of explosives, overpressure, and MSDs. For hollow-core doors, use a single strand; for particle-filled doors, use two strands; and for solid wood doors, use three strands. If the door type is unknown, use three strands. One of the strands must be cut about a foot longer than the others and should extend past the end of the double-sided tape. This forms a pigtail where the initiating system is attached once the charge is in place. Cover the strands of detonation cord and all the exposed portions of the double-sided tape with either sturdy single-sided tape or another length of double-sided tape. Roll the charge, starting at the pigtail, with the double-sided tape surface to be placed against the door on the inside.

H-111. At the breach site, place the charge straight up and down against the door tightly. If it is too short, place it so it covers at least half of the door's height. Prime and fire the charge from the bottom.

Table H-3. Charges

CHARGE	OBSTACLE	EXPLOSIVES NEEDED	ADVANTAGES	DISADVANTAGES
Wall breach charge (satchel or U-shaped charge)	Wood, masonry, brick, and reinforced concrete walls	Detonation cord C4 or TNT	Easy and quick to make Quick to place on target	Does not destroy rebar High overpressure Appropriate attachment methods needed Fragmentation
Silhouette charge	Wooden doors (creates man-sized hole); selected walls (plywood, sheet-rock, CMU)	Detonation cord	Minimal shrapnel Easy to make Makes entry hole to exact specifications	Bulky; not easily carried
General purpose charge	Door knobs, mild steel chain, locks, and equipment	C4 Detonation cord	Small, lightweight Easy to make Very versatile	Other locking mechanisms may make charge ineffective
Rubber strip charge	Wood or metal doors (dislodges doors from the frame); windows with a physical security system	Sheet explosive Detonation cord	Small, lightweight Quick to place on target Uses small amounts of explosives	

Appendix H

Table H-3. Charges (continued)

CHARGE	OBSTACLE	EXPLOSIVES NEEDED	ADVANTAGES	DISADVANTAGES
Flexible linear charge	Wooden doors (widow cuts door along the length of the charge)	Detonation cord	Small, lightweight Quick to place on target One man can carry several charges Defeats most doors regardless of locking systems	Proper two-sided adhesive required
Doorknob charge	Doorknobs on wood or light metal doors	Detonation cord or flexible linear shaped charge	Small, lightweight Easily transported Quick to place on door	Other locking mechanisms may make charge ineffective
Charge	Chain link fence (rapidly creates a hole large enough to run through)	C4 Detonation cord	Cuts chain link quickly and effectively	Must stand to emplace it

Table H-4. Firing system components

FIRING SYSTEM	COMPONENTS
Time system	2 x M81 or M60; time fuze or M-14; 2 x M7 caps; detonation cord loop; red devil (detonation cord connector)
Command detonated	2 x M81; 2 x shock tube with caps (M11 or M12); detonation cord loop; red devil (desired length)
Delay system	1 x M81 or M60 (gutted); black adapter cap; direct shoot shock tube (NONEL); M11 MDI; detonation cord loop; red devil (STI may be used instead of a direct shoot with an M60.)

Explosive Safety Factors

H-112. When employing explosives during breaching operations, leaders must consider three major safety factors: overpressure; missile hazard; and MSD requirements.

Overpressure

H-113. Overpressure is the pressure per square inch (PSI) released from the concussion of the blast. Both outside and into the interior of the building or room, which can injure, incapacitate, or kill.

Missile Hazard

H-114. Missile hazards are fragmentation or projectiles sent at tremendous speed from the explosion area. This occurs from either the charge or target being breached.

Minimum Safe Distance Requirements

H-115. When using explosives in the urban environment, Soldiers must consider the presence of noncombatants and friendly forces. Additionally, there are many hazardous materiel's located in the urban environment, including CBRN and construction materiel's. There is always a risk of secondary explosions and fires when employing explosive breaching techniques.

CAUTION

Always handle explosives carefully. Never divide responsibility for preparing, placing, priming, and firing charges. Always use proper eye and ear protection and cover exposed skin to prevent injuries. Explosives may produce hazardous fumes, flames, fragments, and overpressure. Use AR 385-63, FM 3-34.214, and risk assessment to determine MSDs. Take into consideration whether the door is flush or receded when considering MSD.

REDUCE IMPROVISED EXPLOSIVE DEVICES

H-116. Soldiers must be aware of the threat presented by IEDs that can be found in an operational environment in which the platoon or squad might operate. The platoon and squad must receive sufficient training to recognize locations and items lending themselves to booby-trapping, striking a balance between what is possible and what is probable. (Refer to ATP 3-34.20 for more information.)

Note. Whenever mission variables allow call EOD or engineers for removal of IEDs.

Appendix H

H-117. When dealing with IEDs, the following rules and safety procedures can save lives:
- Suspect objects appearing to be out of place or artificial in its surroundings. Remember, what you see may well be what the enemy wants you to see. If you did not put it there, do not pick it up.
- Examine mines and IEDs from all angles, and check for alternative means of detonating before approaching them.
- Ensure only one man works on a booby trap.
- Do not use force. Stop if force becomes necessary.
- Do not touch a trip wire until both ends have been investigated and all devices are disarmed and neutralized.
- Trace trip wires and check for additional traps along and beneath them.
- Treat all parts of a trap with suspicion, because each part may be set to actuate the trap.
- Wait at least 30 seconds after pulling a booby trap or a mine. There might be a delay fuse.
- Mark all traps until they are cleared.
- Expect constant change in enemy techniques.
- Never attempt to clear IEDs by hand if pulling them or destroying them in place is possible and acceptable.

H-118. IEDs might be found in recently contested areas, so no items or areas that have not been cleared should be considered safe. By anticipating the presence of traps, it might be possible to isolate and bypass trapped areas. If this is not possible, employ countermeasures such as avoiding convenient and covered resting places along routes where mines or other explosive devices can be located. Collective training in booby-trap awareness and rapidly disseminating booby-trap incident reports to all levels is vital. This allows Soldiers to develop an understanding of the enemy's method of operation and a feel for what might or might not be targets.

INDICATIONS AND DETECTION

H-119. Detection depends on two things: being aware of what might be trapped and why, and being able to recognize the evidence of setting. The first requirement demands a well-developed sense of intuition; the second, a keen eye. Intuition is gained through experience and an understanding of the enemy's techniques and habits. A keen eye is the result of training and practice in the recognition of things indicating the presence of a trap.

H-120. Detection methods depend on the nature of the environment. In open areas, methods used to detect mines can usually detect IEDs. Look for trip wires and other signs suggesting the presence of an actuating mechanism. In urban areas, mine detectors are probably of little use. The platoon and squad will have to rely on manual search techniques and, if available, special equipment. The presence of IEDs or nuisance mines is indicated by—
- Disturbance of ground surface or scattered, loose soil.
- Wrappers, seals, loose shell caps, safety pins, nails, and pieces of wire or cord.

- Improvised methods of marking traps, such as piles of stones or marks on walls or trees.
- Evidence of camouflage, such as withered vegetation or signs of cutting.
- Breaks in the continuity of dust, paint, or vegetation.
- Trampled earth or vegetation; foot marks.
- Lumps or bulges under carpet or in furniture.

REDUCTION METHODS

H-121. Reducing IEDs and nuisance mines in area of operation is done primarily by engineers, especially in secured areas. However, some IEDs may have to be cleared by Infantry Soldiers to accomplish a mission during combat. The method used to disarm a trap depends on many things including, time constraints, personnel assets, and type of trap. A trap cannot be considered safe until the blasting cap or the detonation cord has been removed from the charge.

H-122. Use the safest method available to neutralize a trap. For example, if the firing device and detonation cord are accessible, it is usually safer to cut the detonation cord. This method does not actuate the trap, but inserting pins in the firing device might. Unit resources or locally-manufactured or acquired aids often are used to clear traps. In areas with a high incidence of IEDs, assemble and reserve special clearing kits. Mark all IEDs found.

H-123. Nonexplosive traps typically are used in tropical or rain forest regions. Ideal construction materiels abound and concealment in surrounding vegetation is relatively easy. No prescribed procedures exist for clearing nonexplosive traps. Each trap must be cleared according to its nature.

SECTION III – OBSTACLE EMPLOYMENT

H-124. Obstacles are used to reinforce the terrain. When combined with fires, they disrupt, fix, turn, or block an enemy force. Obstacles are used in all operations, but are most useful in defensive missions. Leaders must always consider what materiels are needed and how long the obstacle will take to construct. (Refer to ATTP 3-90.4 for more information.)

H-125. A primary concern of the platoon and squad in the defense is to supplement their fortified positions with extensive protective obstacles, both antipersonnel and antivehicular (particularly AP). AP obstacles, both explosive and nonexplosive, include all those mentioned in Section I of this chapter (such as wire entanglements, AP mines, and field expedient devices), and are used to prevent enemy troops from entering a friendly position. Antipersonnel obstacles usually are integrated with fires and are close enough to the fortification for adequate surveillance by day or night, but beyond effective hand grenade range. Obstacles also are used within the position to compartmentalize the area in the event outer protective barriers are breached.

H-126. In the offense, the platoon/squad uses obstacles to:
- Aid in flank security.

Appendix H

- Limit enemy counterattack.
- Isolate objectives.
- Cut off enemy reinforcement or routes of withdrawal.

H-127. In the defense, the platoon/squad uses obstacles to—
- Slow the enemy's advance to give Infantry platoons and squads more time to mass fires on them.
- Protect defending units.
- Canalize the enemy into places where he can be engaged more easily.
- Separate the enemy's tanks from its Infantry.
- Strengthen lightly defended areas.

MINES

H-128. A mine is an explosive device employed to kill, destroy, or incapacitate enemy personnel and equipment. Mines can be employed in quantities within a specific area to form a minefield, or they can be used individually to reinforce nonexplosive obstacles. Equipment targets include ground vehicles, boats, and aircraft. Land mines fall into the following two general categories:
- (U) Persistent
- (U) Non-Persistent

H-129. Within each of these categories, the mines and munitions can be more clearly defined as antitank or antipersonnel. Mines are one of the most effective tank killers on the battlefield. The type of minefield that a platoon or squad most commonly emplaces is the hasty protective. It is important to distinguish the difference between the types of minefield and means of emplacement. Volcano, MOPMS, standard-pattern, and row mining are not types of minefields; they are just some of the means used to emplace tactical, situational, nuisance, and protective minefields. They also may be the method of emplacement that is replicated by a phony minefield.

Note. U.S. forces are not authorized to employ persistent mines, except in Korea. Some countries employ AHDs on antipersonnel mines, but U.S. forces are not authorized to employ AHDs on antipersonnel mines, except in Korea.

H-130. The United States will—
- Not use APL outside the Korean Peninsula.
- Not assist, encourage, or induce anyone outside the Korean Peninsula to engage in activity prohibited by the Ottawa Convention; and undertake to destroy APL stockpiles not required for the defense of the Republic of Korea.

H-131. Land-based mines and munitions are hand-emplaced, remote-delivered, air-delivered, or ground-delivered. (See table H-5.) ATP 3-34.20 provides detailed instructions on the installation and removal of U.S. mines and firing devices.

Obstacle Reduction and Employment

Table H-5. Mine delivery methods

DELIVERY METHOD	CHARACTERISTICS
Hand-emplaced	Require manual arming and are labor-, resource-, and transport-intensive.
Remote- and Air-delivered	Require less time and labor; however, they are not as precisely placed as hand-emplaced mines and munitions.
Ground-delivered	Less resource-intensive than hand-emplaced mines. They are not precisely placed; however, the minefield boundaries are.

SCATTERABLE MINES

H-132. SCATMINEs are laid without regard to a classical pattern. They are designed to be delivered remotely by aircraft, artillery, missile, or a ground dispenser. All U.S. SCATMINEs have a limited active life and self-destruct after life has expired. The duration of the active life varies with the type of mine and delivery system.

H-133. SCATMINEs enable minefield emplacement in enemy-held territories, contaminated territories, and in most other areas where it is impossible for engineers, the platoon or squad to emplace countermobility obstacles. They may be used to support the platoon's and squad's mission by turning, fixing, disrupting, and blocking the enemy. However they are used, they must be planned and coordinated to fit into the overall obstacle plan. (Refer to ATP 3-90.8 for more information.)

Modular Pack Mine System, Man-Portable

H-134. The man-portable, 162-pound, suitcase-shaped MOPMS dispenses a total of 21 mines (17 AT mines and 4 AP mines). It propels them in a 35-meter, 180-degree semicircle from the container. Mines are dispensed on command using the M71 remote control unit (RCU) or an electronic initiating device such as the M34 blasting machine. When dispensed, an explosive propelling charge at the bottom of each tube expels mines through the container roof. (See figure H-14, page H-40.)

H-135. Infantry platoons and squads can use MOPMS to create a protective minefield or to close lanes in tactical obstacles. The safety zone around one container is 55 meters to the front and sides, and 20 meters to the rear. MOPMS has duration of four hours, which can be extended up to three times for a total of 16 hours. Once mines are dispensed, they cannot be recovered or reused. If mines are not dispensed, the container may be disarmed and recovered for later use. The RCU also can self-destruct mines on command, allowing a unit to counterattack or withdraw through the minefield. The RCU can control up to 15 MOPMS containers or groups of MOPMS containers from a distance of 300 to 1000 meters.

Appendix H

Figure H-14. Modular pack mine system

CONVENTIONAL MINES

H-136. Conventional mines are hand-emplaced mines requiring manual arming. This type of mine laying is labor, resource, and transport-intensive. Soldiers emplace conventional mines within a defined, marked boundary and lay them individually or in clusters. They record each mine location so the mines can be recovered. Soldiers can surface lay or bury conventional mines and may place AHDs on antitank mines.

Obstacle Reduction and Employment

> *Note.* The United States will—
> - Not use APL outside the Korean Peninsula;
> - Not assist, encourage, or induce anyone outside the Korean Peninsula to engage in activity prohibited by the Ottawa Convention; and
> - Undertake to destroy APL stockpiles not required for the defense of the Republic of Korea.

Antitank Mines

H-137. The M15 and M21 AT mines are used by U.S. forces. They are shown in figure H-15. Their characteristics are listed in table H-6 (page H-42).

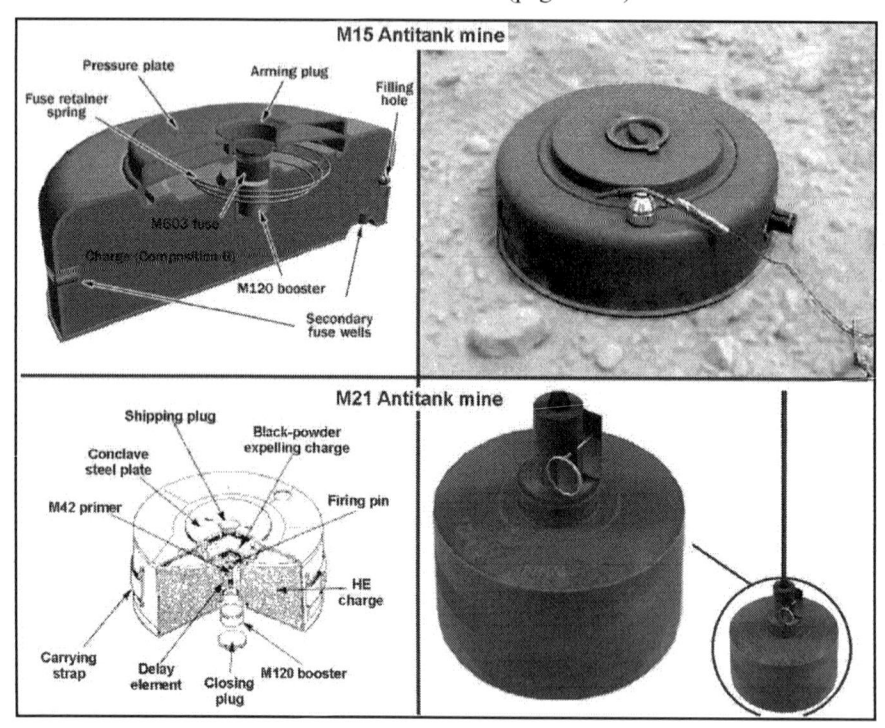

Figure H-15. Antitank mines

Appendix H

Table H-6. Characteristics of antitank mines

MINE	DODIC	FUSE	WARHEAD	AHD	EXPLOSIVE WEIGHT	MINE WEIGHT	MINES PER CONTAINER
M15 with M603 fuse	K180	pressure	blast	yes	9.9 kg	13.5 kg	1
M15 with M624 fuse	K180 (mine) K068 (fuse)	tilt rod	blast	yes	9.9 kg	13.5 kg	1
M21	K181	tilt rod or pressure	SFF	yes*	4.95 kg	7.6 kg	4
*Conventional AHDs will not couple with this mine. However, the M142 multipurpose firing device can be emplaced under this mine.							
LEGEND kg – kilogram; SFF – self-forging fragmentation							

Antipersonnel Mines

H-138. The M14 and M16 AP mines are used by U.S. forces on the Korean Peninsula. They also are used by many other countries. These mines are shown in figure H-16. Their characteristics are listed in table H-7.

Obstacle Reduction and Employment

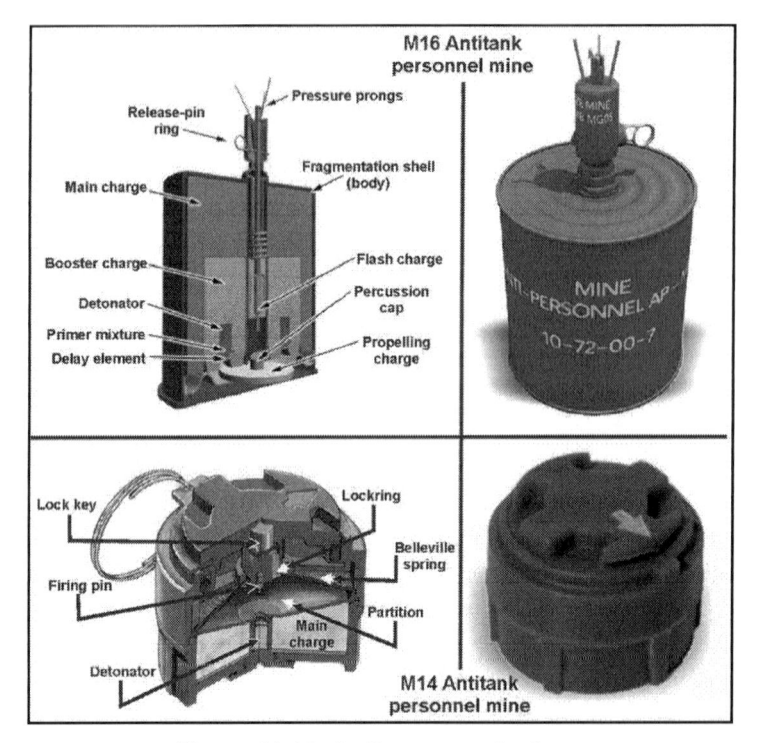

Figure H-16. Antipersonnel mines

Table H-7. Characteristics of antipersonnel mines

MINE	DODIC	FUSE	WARHEAD	AHD	EXPLOSIVE WEIGHT	MINE WEIGHT	MINES PER CONTAINER
M14	K121	pressure	blast	no	28.4 g	99.4 g	90
M16-series	K092	pressure or trip wire	bounding frag	no	450 g	3.5 kg	4
LEGEND g – gram; kg - kilogram							

SPECIAL-PURPOSE MUNITIONS

H-139. Special-purpose munitions the platoon or squad might employ include the M18A1 Claymore and selectable lightweight attack munitions (SLAM).

Appendix H

M18A1 CLAYMORE

H-140. The M18A1 Claymore (see figure H-17) is a fragmentation munitions containing 700 steel balls and 682 grams of composition C4 explosive. It weighs 1.6 kilograms and is command-detonated.

H-141. When employing the Claymore with other munitions or mines, separate the munitions by the following minimum distances:
- Fifty meters in front of or behind other Claymores.
- Three meters between Claymores placed side by side.
- Ten meters from antitank or fragmentation antipersonnel munitions.
- Two meters from blast antipersonnel munitions.

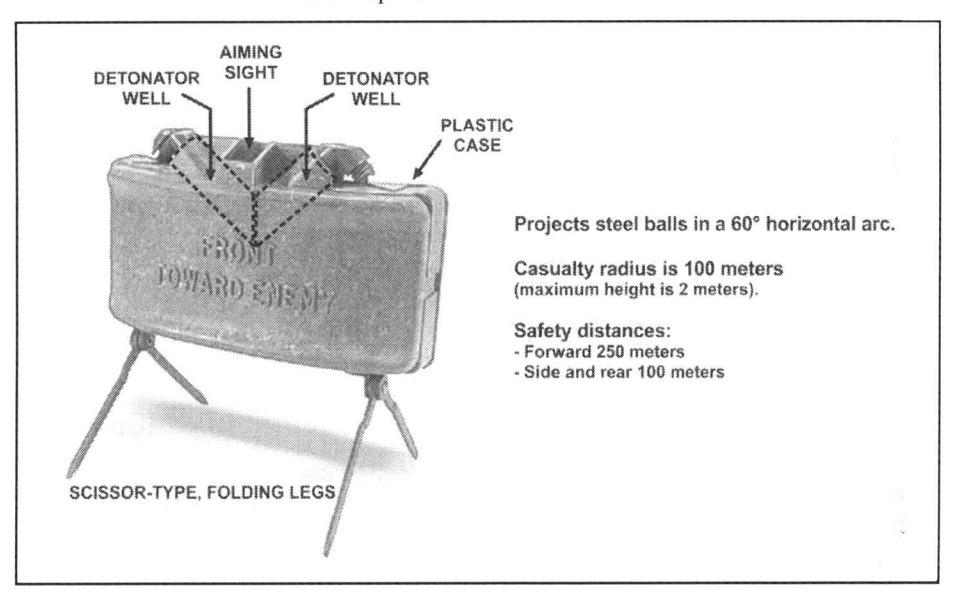

Figure H-17. M18A1 Claymore

SLAM

H-142. The M4 SLAM is a multipurpose munitions with an anti-tamper feature. (See figure H-18.) It is compact and weighs only a kilogram. It is easily portable and is intended for use against armored personnel carriers, parked aircraft, wheeled or tracked vehicles, stationary targets (such as electrical transformers), small (less than 10,000 gallon) fuel-storage tanks, and ammunition storage facilities. The explosive formed penetrator warhead can penetrate 40 millimeters of homogeneous steel. The SLAM has two models (the self-neutralizing [M2] and self-destructing [M4]). The SLAM's four possible employment methods include: bottom attack, side attack, timed demolition, and command detonation.

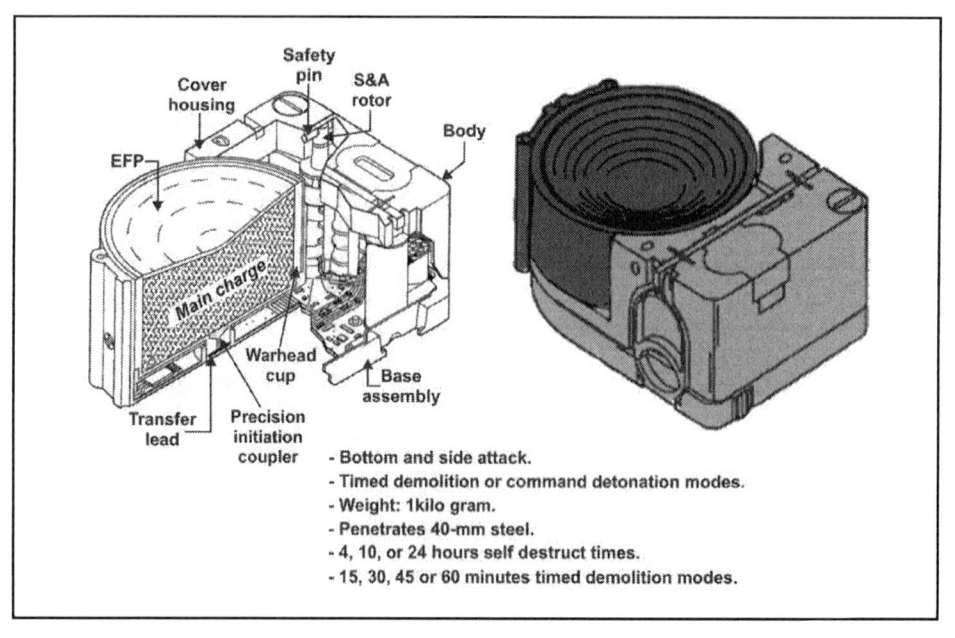

Figure H-18. Selectable lightweight attack munitions

M93 HORNET

H-143. The Hornet is a man-portable, nonrecoverable, AT/antivehicular, off-route munitions made of lightweight materiel (35 pounds) one person can carry and employ. It is capable of destroying vehicles by using sound and motion detection methods. It will automatically search, detect, recognize, and engage moving targets by using top attack at a standoff distance up to 100 meters. It can be a stand-alone tactical obstacle or can reinforce other conventional obstacles. (See figure H-19, page H-46.)

H-144. It disrupts and delays the enemy, allowing long-range, precision weapons to engage more effectively. This feature is particularly effective in non-LOS engagements. It normally is employed by combat engineers, Rangers, and SOF. The RCU is a handheld encoding unit interfacing with the Hornet when the remote mode is selected at the time of employment. After encoding, the RCU can be used to arm the Hornet, reset its self-destruct times, or destroy it. The maximum operating distance of the RCU is two kilometers.

Appendix H

Figure H-19. M93 Hornet

NETWORKED MUNITIONS

H-145. Networked munitions are designed to leverage our network centric fighting abilities. Ground-emplaced networked munitions are recoverable, reusable, and scalable. Existing fields may be reseeded and will accept added munitions into the network. Field sizes may vary from small, hasty protective fields to larger tactical fields. The network provides remote control, situational understanding, various attack modes, and various employment means. All networked munitions have self-destruct features.

FEATURES

H-146. Remote control, in barrier operations, is the ability of a user to actuate a charge or change the state of a mine from a distance. Remote control features include:
- ON-OFF-ON.
- Command destruct.
- Variable self-destruct features.
- Select lethal or nonlethal effects.
- Anti-tamper or anti-spoofing.
- Unmanned sentinel.

H-147. Situational-understanding features include:

- Field or munitions status.
- Field or munitions location.
- Alert to approaching friendly forces.
- Report battle damage information (intelligent munitions system).
- Cue other fire systems (intelligent munitions system).

H-148. Employment means include:
- Hand-emplaced (Spider system, intelligent munitions system).
- Mechanically dispensed (intelligent munitions system).
- Remotely delivered (out to 15 kilometers) (intelligent munitions system).

H-149. Networked munitions support assured mobility by providing the following capabilities:
- Detects and neutralizes the enemy force.
- Covers gaps and prevents enemy maneuver.
- Provides economy of force.
- Protects friendly forces.
- Provides immediate, selective engagement.

H-150. The capabilities of networked munitions will provide for unprecedented assured mobility. By leveraging the network and various employment means, networked munitions will support seamless transitions from the offense to stability. Given positive remote control, there is no longer the danger of impeding our own mobility. Hence, the authority for emplacement may be pushed down to lower tactical levels. (Refer to ATP 3-34.20 for more information.)

HASTY PROTECTIVE MINEFIELDS

H-151. Units report protective obstacles through their chain of command to their higher level headquarters. If the higher headquarters has authorized the use of protective obstacles in the ROE, tactical SOP, or OPORD, subordinate units are not required to submit a report of intention. Units establish SOPs for reporting initiation, progress, and completion of protective obstacles to the battalion level.

H-152. Individual units emplace and remove their own protective obstacles. Therefore, it is usually not necessary for the emplacing unit to turn over the obstacle to the overwatching force. If a nonorganic emplacing unit, such as an engineer platoon, emplaces the protective obstacle, the emplacing unit transfers the obstacle. Units mark protective minefields on all four sides. Units mark lanes and gaps according to ATTP 3-90.4. Commanders decide whether to mark other inherently dangerous obstacles based on the risk assessment. Protective munition fields are recorded using a +DD Form 3007 (*Hasty Protective Row Minefield Record*) as shown in figure H-20 (page H-48). Protective minefields are recorded using a scatterable minefield record. (Refer to JP 3-15 and ATP 3-34.20 for more information.)

Appendix H

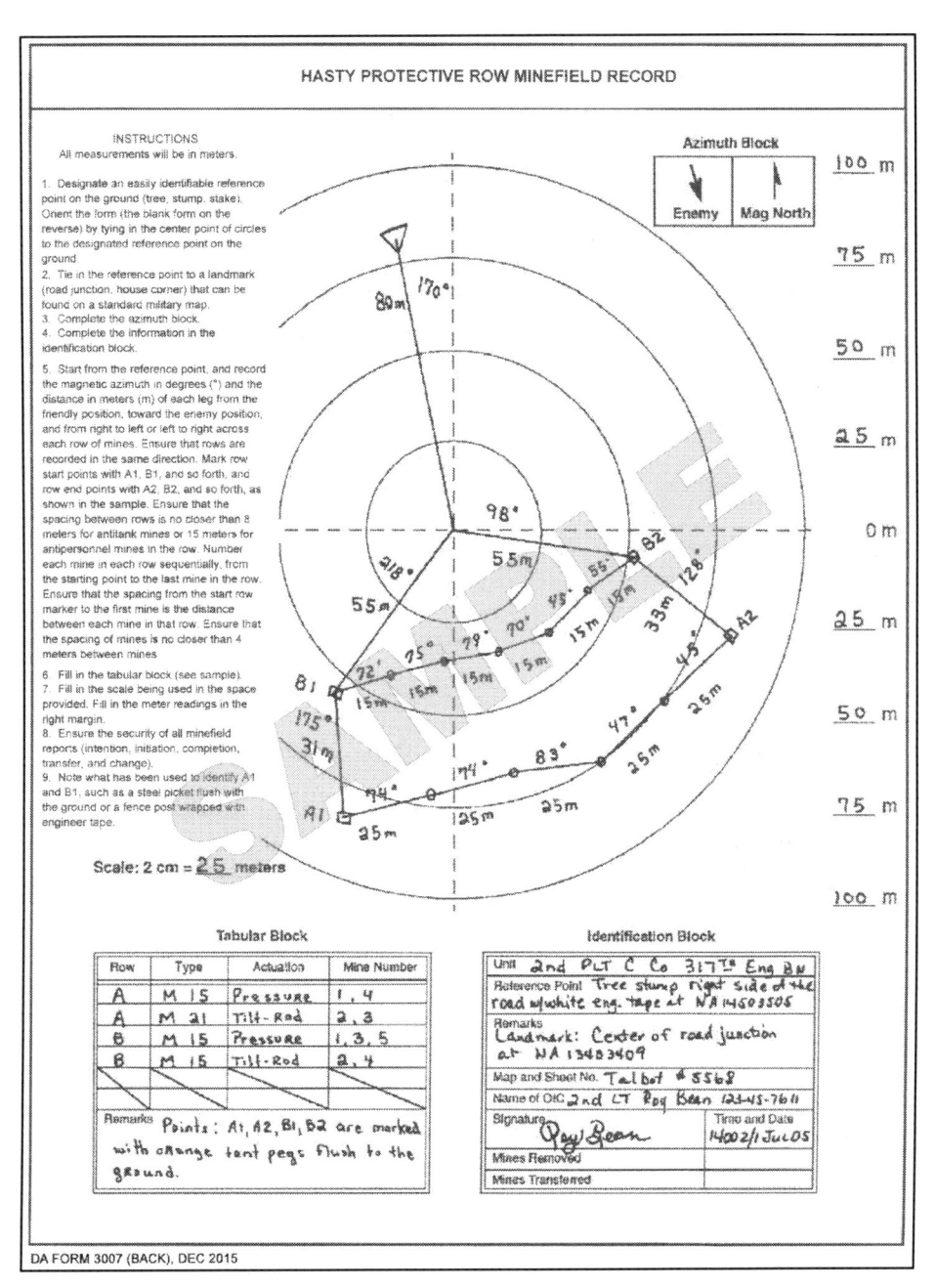

+Figure H-20. Example DD Form 3007 (Hasty Protective Row Minefield Record)

H-153. Units also depict protective minefields and munition fields on their sector sketches. If the minefield or munition field is transferred to another unit, the transferring

H-153. Units also depict protective minefields and munition fields on their sector sketches. If the minefield or munition field is transferred to another unit, the transferring unit leader briefs the receiving unit leader and provides the necessary obstacle records. If the minefield or munition field is abandoned unexpectedly, the unit forwards the record to higher headquarters. (Refer to ATP 3-90.8 for more information on protective obstacles.)

WIRE OBSTACLES

H-154. The platoon or squad normally employs wire obstacles as part of the protective obstacle plan in the defense. Wire obstacles include barbed-wire, triple-standard concertina, four-strand cattle fences, and tanglefoot. Construction methods for two of the more common wire obstacles the platoon or squad employs, triple standard concertina, and tanglefoot are shown in figures H-21 through H-25 (pages H-50 through H-52). (Refer to ATTP 3-90.4 for more information.)

TRIPLE STANDARD CONCERTINA FENCE

H-155. The most common wire entanglement a platoon or squad may build is the triple standard concertina fence. It is built of either barbed wire concertina or barbed tape concertina. There is no difference in building methods. The material and labor requirements for a 300-meter triple standard concertina fence are—

- Long pickets – 160.
- Short pickets – 4.
- Barbed wire, 400-meter reels – 3.
- Rolls of concertina – 59.
- Staples – 317.
- Man-hours to erect – 30.

H-156. First, lay out and install pickets from left to right (facing the enemy). Put the long picket's five paces apart and short (anchor) picket's two paces from the end of the long pickets. (See figure H-21, page H-50.) The enemy and friendly picket rows are offset and are placed three feet apart. Now lay out rolls of concertina. Place a roll in front of the third picket on the enemy side, and two rolls to the rear of the third picket on the friendly side. Repeat this step every fourth picket thereafter. Install the front row concertina and horizontal wire. (See figure H-22, page H-50.) Place the concertina over the pickets. Install the rear row of concertina and horizontal wire. Install the top row of concertina and join the rear horizontal wire. (See figure H-23, page H-50.)

Appendix H

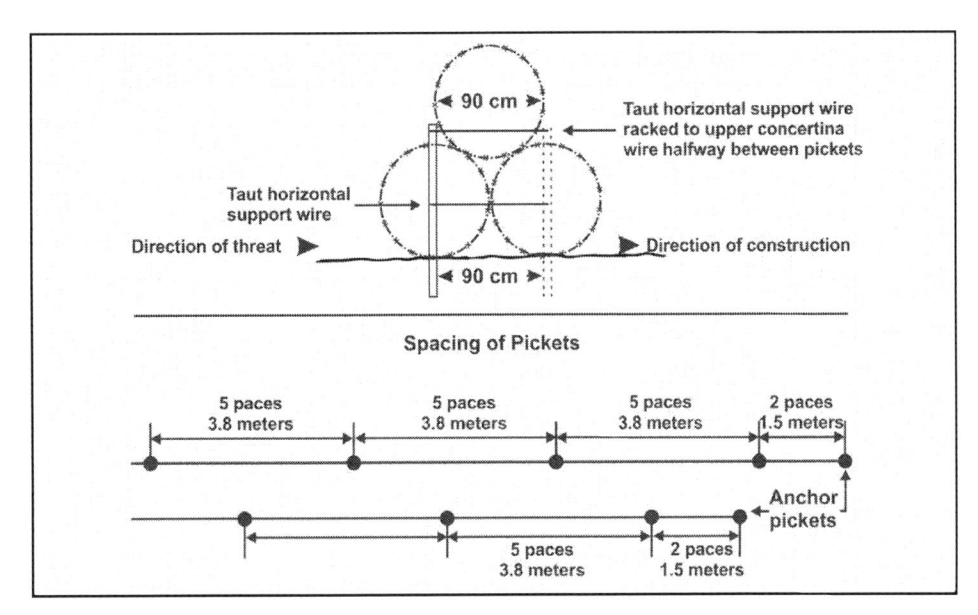

Figure H-21. Triple standard concertina fence

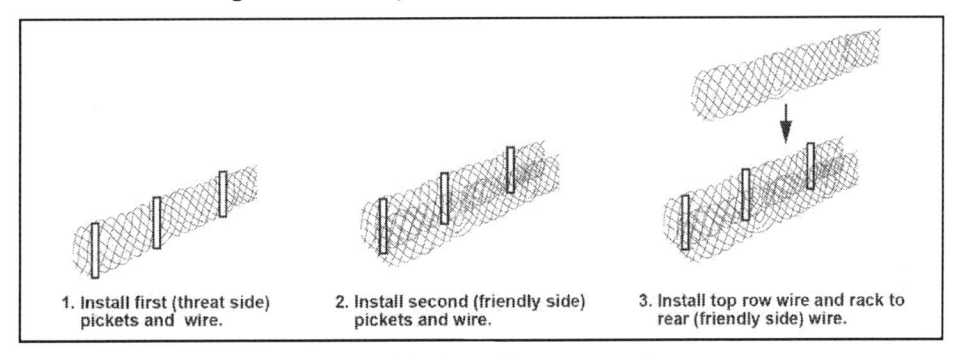

Figure H-22. Installing concertina

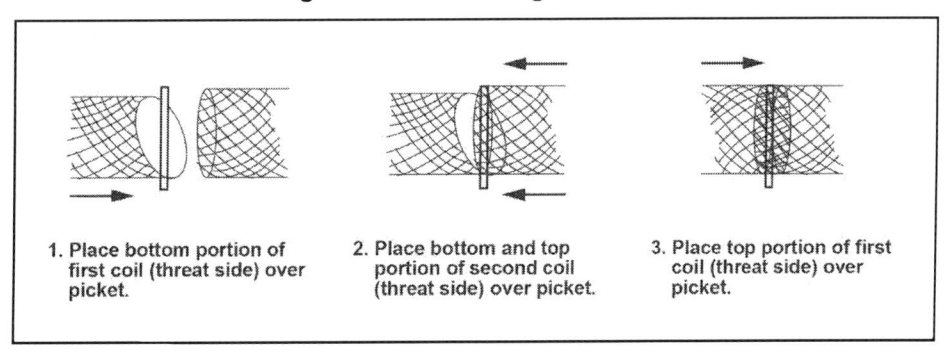

Figure H-23. Joining concertina

Obstacle Reduction and Employment

CONCERTINA ROADBLOCK

H-157. The concertina roadblock is placed across roadways and designed to block wheeled or tracked vehicles. The roadblock is constructed of 11 concertina rolls or coils placed together, about 10 meters in depth, reinforced with long pickets five paces apart. The rolls or coils should not be tautly bound allowing them to be dragged and tangled around axles, tank road wheels, and sprockets. Additionally, wire is placed horizontally on top of the concertina rolls or coils. (See figure H-24.)

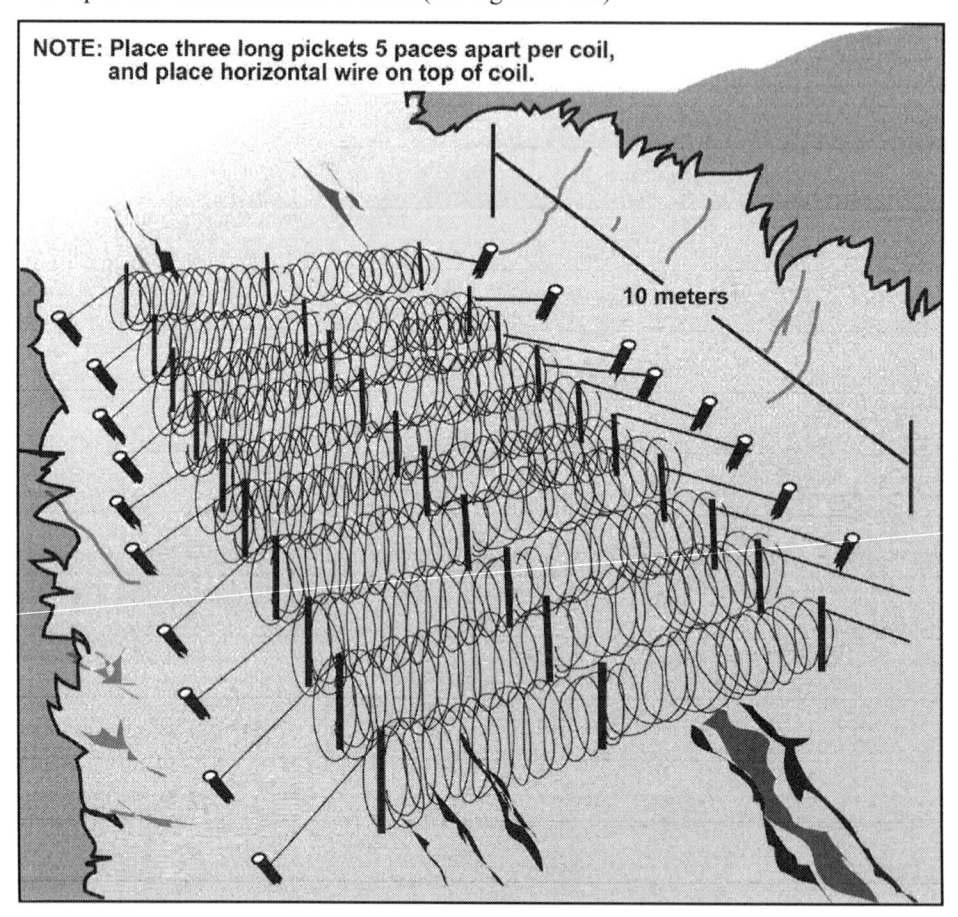

Figure H-24. Eleven-row anti-vehicular wire obstacle

TANGLEFOOT

H-158. Tanglefoot is used where concealment is essential and to prevent the enemy from crawling between fences and in front of emplacements. (See figure H-25, page H-52.) The obstacle should be employed in a minimum width of 32 feet. The pickets should be placed at irregular intervals of 2 ½ feet to 10 feet. The height of the barbed wire should vary

Appendix H

between 9 to 30 inches. Tanglefoot should be sited in scrub, if possible, using bushes as supports for part of the wire. On open ground, short pickets should be used.

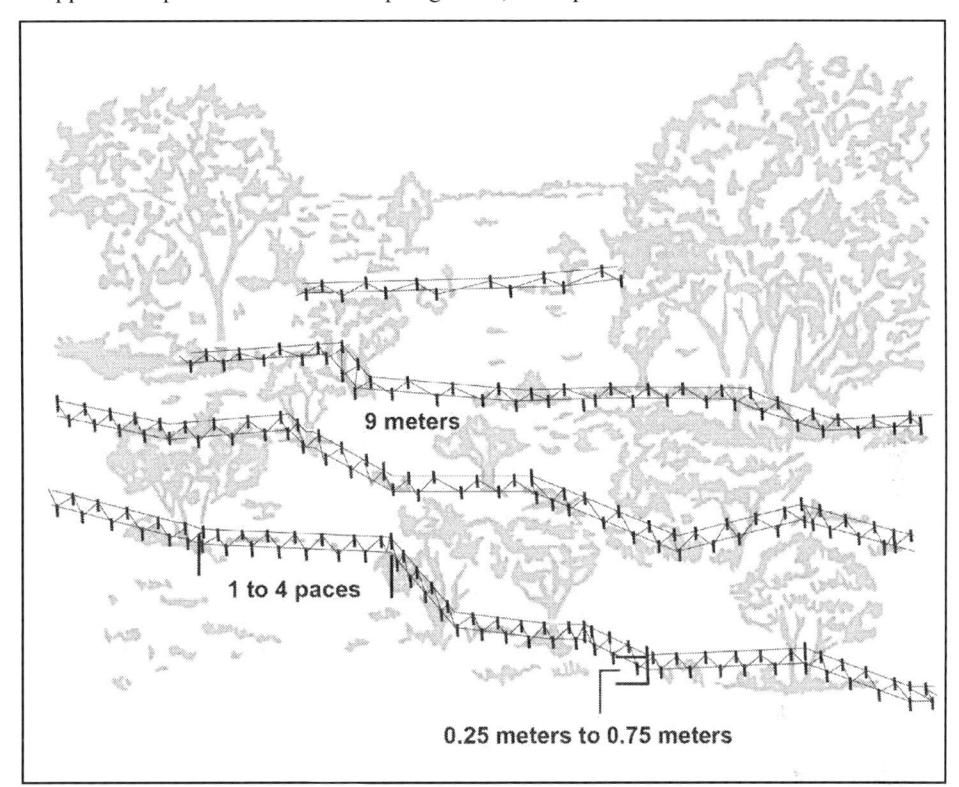

Figure H-25. Tanglefoot

Appendix I
CBRN Operations

CBRN operations are the employment of tactical capabilities that counter the entire range of CBRN threats and hazards. These are done through CBRN proliferation prevention, CBRN counterforce, CBRN defense, and CBRN consequence management activities in support of operational and strategic objectives to combat CBRN and operate safely in CBRN environments. Many state and nonstate actors (to include terrorists and criminals) possess or have the capability to possess, develop, or proliferate CBRN weapons. U.S. policy prohibits the use of chemical or biological weapons under any circumstances, but it reserves the right to employ nuclear weapons. Many potential enemies are under no such constraint. (Refer to FM 3-11 for more information.)

SECTION I – MISSION-ORIENTED PROTECTIVE POSTURE ANALYSIS

I-1. Protecting Soldiers from the harmful hazards associated with CBRN attacks in an area of operation is essential to preserving combat power. When the probability of CBRN threats exists, commanders and leaders must conduct a deliberate analysis to posture and equip forces for survival and mission effectiveness. CBRN and medical personnel consider mission variables and related information to provide recommendations on protection requirements that are reflected in the mission-oriented protective posture (MOPP) level.

I-2. Leader involvement is necessary to ensure safe and sustained operations under various climatic conditions. Leaders should develop standard responses and COAs for each projected mission. If the probability of CBRN threats exists all soldiers will carry a protective mask, and ensure that individual protective gear is available within two hours. Second set available in six hours. The standard MOPP are—

- **MOPP0.** Carry a protective mask, and ensure that individual protective gear is within arm's reach.
- **MOPP1.** Suit worn. Mask, gloves and boots carried.
- **MOPP2.** Suit and boots worn. Gloves and mask carried.
- **MOPP3.** Suit, boots and mask worn. Gloves carried.
- **MOPP4.** All protection worn.

I-3. Leaders know that they cannot expect the same work rates in MOPP4 as they achieved in MOPP0. They reevaluate the ability to meet mission requirements and

Appendix I

communicate changes to the force. MOPP reduction decisions are between the most difficult to make because of the many considerations that affect the final decision. Commanders must evaluate the situation from the Soldier and mission perspectives. Factors include the criticality of the current mission, potential effects of personnel exposure, and the impact on the casualty care system.

I-4. Leaders determine the appropriate MOPP level by assessing mission variables and weighing the impact of increased protection levels. Higher headquarters provide MOPP-level directives to subordinate elements.

I-5. When a CBRN attack is recognized, everyone in the company team must receive the warning and assume the appropriate MOPP level. Soldiers in immediate danger need warnings they can see or hear. The alarm or signal must be simple and unmistakable if it is to produce a quick and correct reaction.

I-6. If a CBRN hazard is located, the contaminated area should be marked. The CBRN warning and reporting system and standardized contamination markers contribute to orderly warning procedures. Warning methods include automatic alarms, vocal alarms (a shout of "GAS" is the most frequently used alarm), nonvocal alarms (horn blasts or banging of metal-to-metal objects), and visual alarms, most commonly the appropriate hand-and-arm signals.

SECTION II – UNMASKING PROCEDURES

I-7. Soldiers should unmask as soon as possible except when a live biological or toxin attack is expected. Use the procedures outlined in the following paragraphs to determine if unmasking is safe.

UNMASKING WITH M256/M256A1 DETECTOR KIT

I-8. If an M256/M256A1 detector kit is available, use it to supplement unmasking procedures. The kit does not detect all agents; therefore, proper unmasking procedures, which take approximately 15 minutes, must still be used. If all tests with the kit (to include a check for liquid contamination using M8 detector paper) have been performed and the results are negative, use the following procedures:

- The senior person should select one or two Soldiers to start the unmasking procedures. If possible, they move to a shady place; bright, direct sunlight can cause pupils in the eyes to constrict, giving a false symptom.
- Selected Soldiers unmask for 5 minutes, then clear and reseal masks.
- Observe the Soldiers for 10 minutes. If no symptoms appear, request permission from higher headquarters to signal "ALL CLEAR."
- Watch all Soldiers for possible delayed symptoms. Always have first-aid treatment immediately available in case it is needed.

UNMASKING WITHOUT M256/M256A1 DETECTOR KIT

I-9. If an M256/M256A1 kit is not available, the unmasking procedures take approximately 35 minutes. When a reasonable amount of time has passed after the attack, find a shady area; use M8 paper to check the area for possible liquid contamination. Conduct unmasking using these procedures:

- The senior person selects one or two Soldiers. They take a deep breath and break their mask seals, keeping their eyes wide open.
- After 15 seconds, the Soldiers clear and reseal their masks. Observe them for 10 minutes.
- If no symptoms appear, the same Soldiers break seals, take two or three breaths, and clear and reseal masks. Observe them for 10 minutes.
- If no symptoms appear, the same Soldiers unmask for 5 minutes, then remask.
- If no symptoms appear in 10 minutes, request permission from higher headquarters to signal "ALL CLEAR." Continue to observe all Soldiers in case delayed symptoms develop.

This page intentionally left blank.

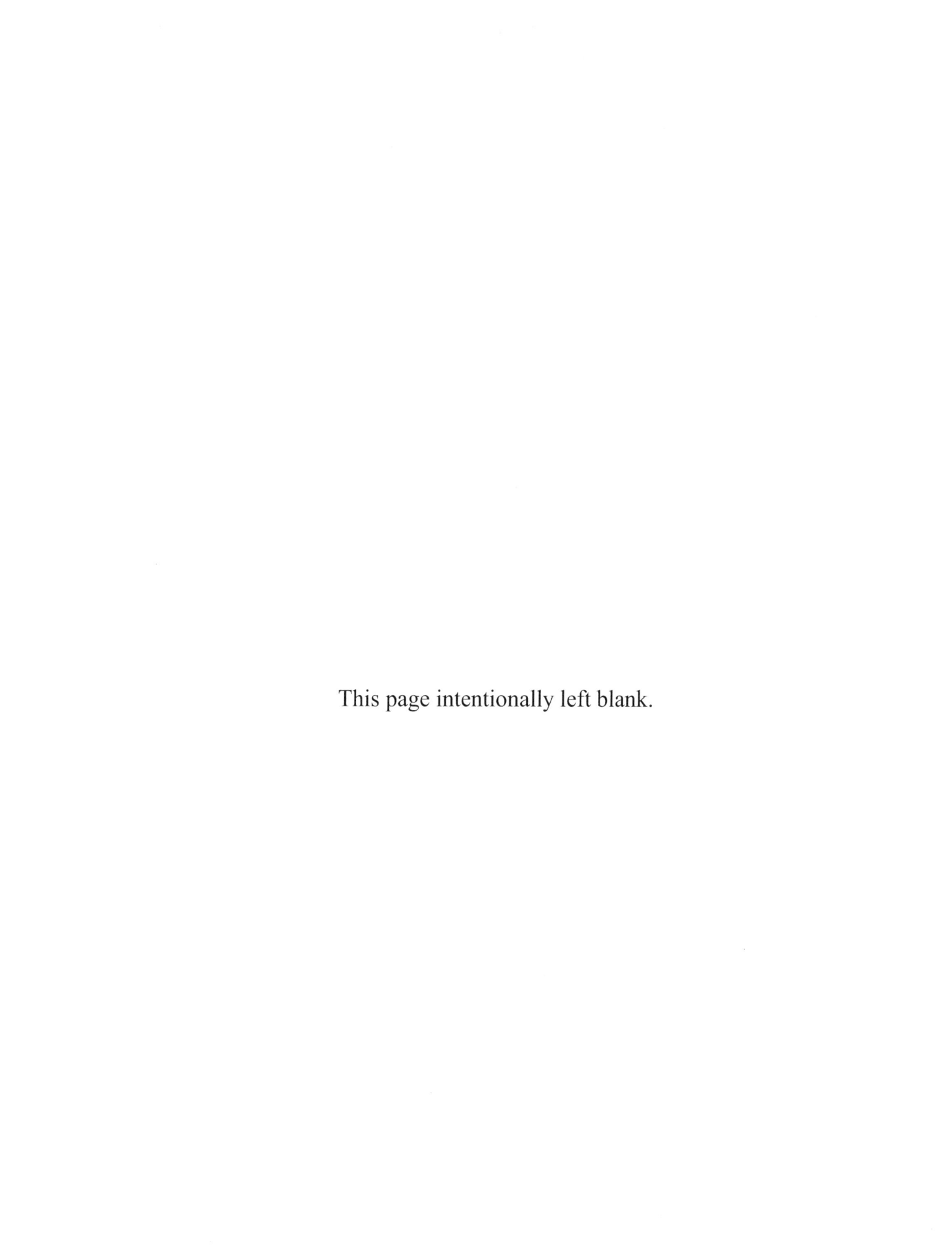

Appendix J
Selected Battle Drills

Infantry platoons and squads undergo extensive training to conduct combat operations in all operational evironments. In preparation for these operations battle drills are used to train and establish procedures to perform their mission. Battle drills are standardized collective actions made in response to common battle occurrences. They are designed for rapid reaction situations without the application of a deliberate decision-making process.

SELECTED BATTLE DRILLS

J-1. Battle drills are initiated on a cue, such as an enemy action or the leader's order, and are a trained response to that stimulus. They require minimal leader orders to accomplish, and are vital to success in combat and critical to preserving life.

J-2. This appendix identifies essential battle drills that an Infantry platoon and squad must train on to ensure success. They include:

- Battle Drill 1: React to Direct Fire Contact (07-3-D9501)
- Battle Drill 2: Conduct a Platoon Assault (07-3-D9514)
- Battle Drill 2A: Conduct a Squad Assault (07-4-D9515)
- Battle Drill 3: Break Contact (07-3-D9505)
- Battle Drill 4: React to Ambush (Near) (07-3-D9502)
- Battle Drill 5: Knock Out a Bunker (07-3-D9406)
- Battle Drill 6: Enter and Clear a Room (07-4-D9509)
- Battle Drill 7: Enter a Trench to Secure a Foothold (07-3-D9510)
- Battle Drill 8: Conduct the Initial Breach of a Mined Wire Obstacle (07-3-D9412)
- Battle Drill 9: React to Indirect Fire (07-3-D9504)
- Battle Drill 10: React to a Chemical Attack (03-3-D0001)
- Battle Drill 11: React to an IED (05-3-D1703)
- Battle Drill 12: Dismount a BFV and ICV (07-3-D9433)
- Battle Drill 13: Mount a BFV and ICV (07-3-D9434)
- Battle Drill 14: Execute Action Right or Left While Mounted (07-3-D9437)

Appendix J

BATTLE DRILL 1: React to Direct Fire Contact (07-3-D9501)

CONDITIONS: The unit is moving or halted. The enemy initiates direct fire contact on the unit.

CUE: This drill begins when the enemy initiates direct fire contact.

STANDARDS: The element in contact returns fire immediately and seeks cover. Element in contact locates the enemy and places well-aimed fire on known enemy position(s). The leader can point out at least one-half of the enemy positions and identify the types of weapons (such as small arms, and light machine guns). Unit leader reports the contact to higher headquarters.

TASK STEPS AND PERFORMANCE MEASURES

1. The element in contact immediately returns well-aimed fire on known enemy position(s). Vehicles move out of the beaten zone.

2. Soldiers and vehicles assume the nearest covered and concealed position. Mounted Soldiers dismount the vehicle, provide local security and add its suppressive fire against the enemy position. (See figure J-1.)

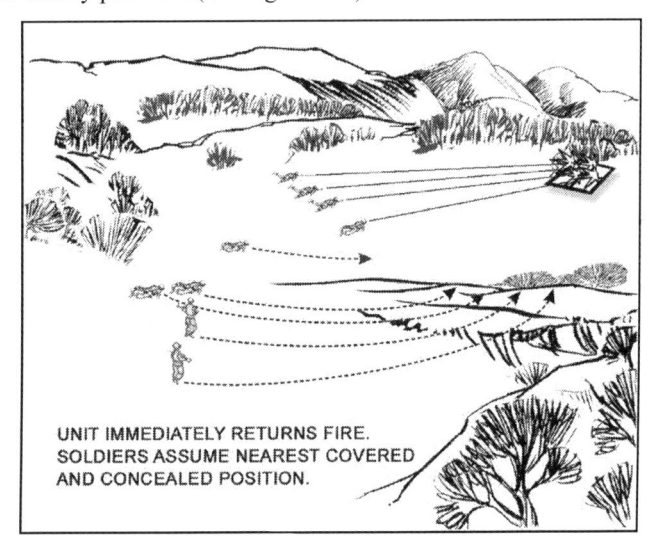

Figure J-1. Assuming nearest covered position

3. Element leaders locate and engage known enemy positions with well-aimed fire or battlesight fire command, and pass information to the unit leader and Soldiers.

4. Element leaders control the fire of their Soldiers by using standard fire commands (initial and supplemental) containing the following elements:
    a. Alert.
    b. Weapon or ammunition (optional).
    c. Target description.

d. Direction.
   e. Range.
   f. Method.
   g. Control (optional).
   h. Execution.
   g. Termination.

5. Soldiers and vehicle commanders maintain contact (visual or oral) with the leader, other Soldiers, and vehicles on their left or right.

6. Soldiers maintain contact with the team leader and indicate the location of the enemy positions. Vehicle commanders relay all commands to the mounted Infantry squads.

7. Unit leaders (visually or orally) check the status of their personnel.

8. Element leaders maintain visual contact with the unit leader.

9. The unit leader moves up to the element in contact and links up with its leader.
   a. Unit leader brings the radio-telephone operator, forward observer, element leader of the nearest element, one crew-served weapon team (machine gun team if available).
   b. Element leaders of the elements not in contact move to the front of their element.
   c. The platoon sergeant moves forward with the remaining crew-served weapons and links up with the unit leader and assumes control of the support element. (See figure J-2.)

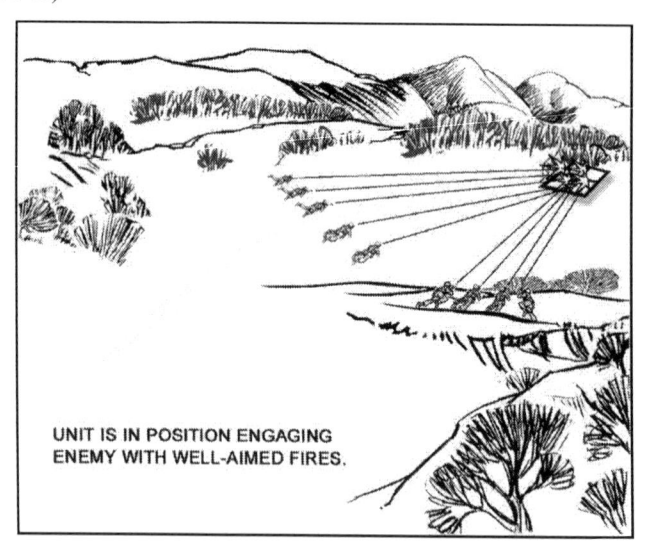

Figure J-2. Control of the support element

10. The unit leader determines whether or not the unit must move out of the engagement area.

Appendix J

11. The unit leader determines whether or not the unit can gain and maintain suppressive fires with the element already in contact (based on the volume and accuracy of enemy fires against the element in contact).

12. The unit leader makes an assessment of the situation identifies—
    a. The location of the enemy position and obstacles.
    b. The size of the enemy force engaging the unit in contact. (The number of enemy automatic weapons, the presence of any vehicles, and the employment of indirect fires are indicators of enemy strength.)
    c. Vulnerable flanks.
    d. Covered and concealed flanking routes to the enemy positions.

13. The unit leader decides whether to conduct an assault, bypass (if authorized by the company commander), or break contact.

14. The unit leader reports the situation to higher headquarters and begins to maneuver the unit.

BATTLE DRILL 2: Conduct a Platoon Assault (07-3-D9514)

CONDITIONS: The platoon is moving as part of a larger force conducting a movement to contact or an attack. The enemy initiates direct fire contact on the lead squad.

CUE: This drill begins when the enemy initiates direct fire contact.

STANDARDS: The platoon lead squad locates and suppresses the enemy, establishes supporting fire, and assaults the enemy position using fire and maneuver. The platoon destroys or causes the enemy to withdraw, and conducts consolidation and reorganize.

TASK STEPS AND PERFORMANCE MEASURES

1. The platoon conducts action on enemy contact. The squad or section in contact reacts to contact by immediately returning well-aimed fire on known enemy positions. Dismounted Soldiers assume the nearest covered positions. Vehicles move out of the beaten zone and Soldiers dismount the vehicle. The element in contact attempts to achieve suppressive fires. The element leader notifies the platoon leader of the action.

2. Platoon leader gives the command to dismount the vehicles. The platoon sergeant takes control of the vehicles.

3. The platoon leader, radio telephone operator, FO, squad leader of the next squad, and one machine gun team move forward to linkup with the squad leader of the squad in contact.

4. The squad leader of the trail squad moves to the front of the lead fire team.

5. The weapons squad leader and second machine gun team move forward and linkup with the platoon leader. If directed, the weapons squad leader assumes control of the base-of-fire element and positions the machine guns to add suppressive fires against the enemy.

Selected Battle Drills

6. Platoon sergeant repositions vehicles, as necessary, to provide observation and supporting fire against the enemy.

7. The platoon leader assesses the situation.

8. If the squad in contact cannot achieve suppressive fire, the squad leader reports to the platoon leader.
    a. The squad in contact establishes a base of fire. The squad leader deploys the squad to provide effective, sustained fires on the enemy position. The squad leader reports the final position to the platoon leader.
    b. The remaining squads (not in contact) take up covered and concealed positions in place, and observe to the flanks and rear of the platoon.
    c. The platoon leader moves forward with the radio-telephone operator, the platoon forward observer, squad leader of the nearest squad, and one machine gun team.

9. Lead squad locates the enemy.
    a. The squad leader of the squad in contact reports the enemy size and location, and any other information to the platoon leader. The platoon leader completes the squad leader's assessment of the situation.
    b. The squad continues to engage the enemy's position.
    c. The weapons squad leader moves forward with the second machine gun team and linksup with the platoon leader.
    d. The platoon sergeant repositions vehicles, as necessary, to provide observation and supporting fire against the enemy.

10. Lead squad suppresses the enemy:
    a. The platoon leader determines if the squad in contact can gain suppressive fire against the enemy based on the volume and accuracy of the enemy's return fire.
        (1) If the answer is **YES**, the platoon leader directs the squad (with one or both machine guns) and vehicle element in contact to continue suppressing the enemy:
            (a) The squad in contact destroys or suppresses enemy weapons that are firing most effectively against it; normally crew-served weapons.
            (b) The vehicle section in contact destroys or suppresses enemy weapons that were firing most effectively against them, including vehicles and crew-served weapons.
            (c) The squad in contact places screening smoke (M203/320) to prevent the enemy from seeing the maneuver element.
        (2) If the answer is **NO**, the platoon leader deploys another squad, second vehicle section, and the second machine gun team to suppress the enemy position. (The platoon leader may direct the trail leader to position this squad and vehicle section, and weapons squad leader to position one or both machine gun teams in a better support-by-fire position.)
    b. The platoon leader again determines if the platoon can gain suppressive fires against the enemy.
        (1) If the answer is **YES**, the platoon leader continues to suppress the enemy with the two squads, two machine guns, and vehicle-mounted weapons.

Appendix J

      (a) The trail squad leader assumes control of the base-of-fire element (squad in contact, machine gun teams, and any other squads designated by the platoon leader).
      (b) The platoon sergeant assumes control of the vehicle section and base-of-fire element (squad in contact and machine gun teams designated by the platoon leader).
      (c) The platoon FO calls for and adjusts fires based on the platoon leader's directions. (The platoon leader does not wait for indirect fires before continuing with his actions.)
   (2) If the answer is still **NO**, the platoon leader deploys the last squad to provide flank and rear security; guide the rest of the company forward, as necessary; and report the situation to the company commander. Normally, the platoon becomes the base-of-fire element for the company and may deploy the last squad to add suppressive fires. The platoon continues to suppress or fix the enemy with direct and indirect fire, and responds to orders from the company commander.

11. Platoon assaults the enemy position. If the squad(s) in contact together with the machine gun(s) and vehicle element can suppress the enemy, the platoon leader determines if the remaining squad(s) that are not in contact can maneuver.
   a. The platoon leader makes the following assessment:
     (1) Location of enemy positions and obstacles.
     (2) Size of enemy force. (The number of enemy automatic weapons, the presence of any vehicles, and the employment of indirect fires are indicators of enemy strength.)
     (3) Vulnerable flank.
     (4) Covered and concealed flanking route to the enemy position.
   b. If the answer is **YES**, the platoon leader maneuvers the squad(s) into the assault:
     (1) Once the platoon leader has ensured that the base-of-fire element is in position and providing suppressive fires, he leads the assaulting squad(s) to the assault position.
     (2) If the vehicle section can effectively suppress the enemy element, the platoon leader may reposition the weapons squad or machine gun to an intermediate or local support-by-fire position to provide additional suppression during the assault.
     (3) Once in position, the platoon leader gives the prearranged signal for the base-of-fire element to lift or shift direct fires to the opposite flank of the enemy position. (The assault element MUST pick up and maintain effective fires throughout the assault. Handover of responsibility for direct fires from the base-of-fire element to the assault element is critical.)
     (4) The platoon platoon forward observer shifts indirect fires to isolate the enemy position.
     (5) The assaulting squad(s) fight through enemy positions using fire and maneuver. The platoon leader controls the movement of the squads, assigns specific objectives for each squad, and designates the main effort or base maneuver element. The base-of-fire element must be able to identify the near flank of the assaulting squad(s).

(6) In the assault, the squad leader determines the way in which to move the elements of the squad based on the volume and accuracy of enemy fire against the squad and the amount of cover afforded by the terrain. In all cases, each Soldier uses individual movement techniques, as appropriate.
  (a) The squad leader designates one fire team to support the movement of the other team by fires.
  (b) The squad leader designates a distance or direction for the team to move and accompanies one of the fire teams.
  (c) Soldiers must maintain contact with team members and leaders.
  (d) Soldiers time their firing and reloading in order to sustain their rate of fire.
  (e) The moving fire team proceeds to the next covered position. Teams use the wedge formation when assaulting. Soldiers move in rushes or by crawling.
  (f) The squad leader directs the next team to move.
  (g) If necessary, the team leader directs Soldiers to bound forward as individuals within buddy teams. Soldiers coordinate their movement and fires with each other within the buddy team, and maintain contact with their team leader.
  (h) Soldiers fire from covered positions. They select the next covered position before moving and rush forward (no more than five seconds), or use high or low crawl techniques based on terrain and enemy fires.
 b. If the answer is **NO**, or the assaulting squad(s) cannot continue to move, the platoon leader deploys the squad(s) to suppress the enemy and reports to the company commander. The platoon continues suppressing enemy positions and responds to the orders of the company commander.

12. The platoon consolidates on the objective once the assaulting squad(s) has seized the enemy position.
 a. Establishes local security.
 b. The platoon leader signals for the base-of-fire element to move up into designated positions.
 c. The platoon leader assigns sectors of fire for each squad and vehicle.
 d. The platoon leader positions key weapons and vehicles to cover the most dangerous avenue(s) of approach.
 e. The platoon sergeant begins coordination for ammunition resupply.
 f. Soldiers take up hasty defensive positions.
 g. The platoon leader and FO develop a quick fire plan.
 h. The squads place out observation points to warn of enemy counterattacks.

13. Platoon organizes by:
 a. Reestablishing the chain of command.
 b. Redistributing and resupplying ammunition.
 c. Manning crew-served weapons first.
 d. Redistributing critical equipment such as radios; CBRN; and night vision devices.
 e. Treating casualties and evacuating wounded.
 f. Filling vacancies in key positions.

Appendix J

g. Searching, silencing, segregating, safeguarding, and speeding EPWs to collection points.
h. Collecting and reporting enemy information and materiel.

14. Platoon sends SITREP to the company commander.

BATTLE DRILL 2A. Conduct a Squad Assault (07-4-D9515)

CONDITIONS: The squad is moving as part of the platoon conducting a movement to contact or an attack. The enemy initiates direct fire contact.

CUE: This drill begins when the enemy initiates direct fire contact.

STANDARDS: The squad locates and suppresses the enemy, establishes supporting fire, and assaults the enemy position using fire and maneuver. The squad destroys or causes the enemy to withdraw, conducts consolidation and reorganizes.

TASK STEPS AND PERFORMANCE MEASURES

1. The team in contact immediately returns well-aimed fire on known enemy position(s) and assumes the nearest covered positions. Soldiers receiving fire take up nearest positions that afford protection from enemy fire (cover) and observation (concealment).

2. Soldiers in contact assume the nearest position that provides cover and concealment.
    a. Fire team Soldiers in contact move to positions (bound or crawl) where they can fire their weapons, position themselves to ensure that they have observation, fields of fire, cover, and concealment. They continue to fire and report known or suspected enemy positions to the fire team leader.
    b. The team leader directs fires using tracers or standard fire commands.
    c. The fire team not in contact takes covered and concealed positions in place, and observes to the flanks and rear of the squad.
    d. The squad leader reports contact to the platoon leader and moves toward the fire team in contact.

3. Lead team locates the enemy:
    a. Using sight and sound, the fire team in contact acquires known or suspected enemy positions.
    b. The fire team in contact begins to place well-aimed fire on suspected enemy positions.
    c. The squad leader moves to a position to observe the enemy and assess the situation.
    d. The squad leader requests, through the platoon leader, immediate suppression indirect fires (normally 60-mm mortars).
    e. The squad leader reports the enemy size and location, and any other information to the platoon leader. (As the platoon leader comes forward, he completes the squad leader's assessment of the situation.)

4. Team in contact suppresses the enemy.

Selected Battle Drills

    a. The squad leader determines if the fire team in contact can gain suppressive fire based on the volume and accuracy of the enemy fire.
    b. If the answer is **YES**, the fire team leader continues to suppress the enemy:
        (1) The fire team destroys or suppresses enemy crew-served weapons first.
        (2) The fire team places smoke (M203/320) on the enemy position to obscure it.
        (3) The fire team leader continues to control fires using tracers or standard fire commands. Fires must be well-aimed and continue at a sustained rate with no lulls.
        (4) Buddy teams fire their weapons so that both are not reloading their weapons at the same time.
    c. If the answer is **NO**, the squad leader then deploys the fire team not in contact to establish a support-by-fire position. The squad leader reports the situation to the platoon leader. Normally, the squad becomes the base-of-fire element for the platoon. The squad continues to suppress the enemy and responds to orders from the platoon leader. (The platoon leader, radio telephone operator, FO, one machine gun team, squad leader of the next squad, platoon sergeant, and the other machine gun team are already moving forward according to Battle Drill 2, Platoon Assault.)

5. The unit leader maneuvers the assault elements into the assault.
    a. Squad leader adjusts fires (both direct and indirect) based on the rate of the assault element movement and the minimum safe distances of weapons systems.
    b. Once in position, the squad leader gives the prearranged signal for the supporting fire team to shift direct fires to the opposite flank of the enemy position.
    c. The assaulting fire team assumes and maintains effective fires throughout the assault. Handover of responsibility for direct fires from support element to the assault element is critical to prevent fratricide.
    d. If available, unit leader directs the forward observer to shift indirect fire (including smoke) to isolate the enemy position.

6. The assaulting element(s) fight through enemy position(s) using fire and movement.
    a. Team leader controls the movement of the team.
    b. Team leader assigns specific objectives for each buddy team and designates a base maneuver element.
    c. Base-of-fire elements maintain visual contact of the near flank of the assaulting element.
    d. The assault element conducts fire and movement based on volume and accuracy of enemy fires against his element and the amount of cover afforded by the terrain.
        (1) Assault element leader designates a distance and direction for the assault element and moves with that element.
        (2) Soldiers maintain contact with team members and leaders.
        (3) Team leaders direct Soldiers to move as individuals or teams.
        (4) Soldiers fire from covered positions. Soldiers move using 3- to 5-second rushes or the low or high crawl techniques, taking advantage of available cover and concealment.
        (5) Soldiers time their firing and reloading in order to sustain their rate of fire.

Appendix J

(6) Team leaders maintain contact with the unit leader and pass signals to element members.
(7) If the assault element cannot continue to move, the unit leader deploys the element(s) to suppress the enemy and reports to higher headquarters.

7. The squad consolidates and reorganizes.
   a. Squad leaders establish local security.
   b. The squad leader signals for the base-of-fire element to move up into designated positions.
   c. The squad leader assigns sectors of fire for each element.
   d. The squad leader positions key weapons to cover the most dangerous avenue of approach.
   e. The squad leader begins coordination for ammunition resupply.
   f. Soldiers establish hasty fighting positions.
   g. Squad leader develops a quick fire plan.
   h. Squad leader place out observation posts to warn of enemy counterattacks.
   i. Reestablishes the chain of command.
   j. Redistributes and resupplies ammunition.
   k. Mans crew-served weapons, first.
   l. Redistributes critical equipment such as radios; CBRN; and night vision devices.
   m. Treats and evaluates wounded.
   n. Fills vacancies in key positions.
   o. Searches, silences, segregates, safeguards, speeds, and tags detainees.
   p. The unit leader consolidates ammunition, casualties' and equipment reports.

8. Squad leader reports situation to platoon leader.

BATTLE DRILL 3: Break Contact (07-3-D9505)

CONDITIONS: The unit is moving as part of a larger force, conducting a movement to contact or an attack. Following direct fire contact with the enemy, the unit leader decides to break contact.

CUE: This drill begins when the unit leader gives the command to break contact.

STANDARDS: The unit breaks contact using fire and movement, and continues to move until the enemy cannot observe or place fire on them. The unit leader reports the contact to higher headquarters.

TASK STEPS AND PERFORMANCE MEASURES

1. The unit leader directs an element to suppress the enemy.

2. The unit leader directs the vehicles to support the disengagement of the dismounted element. (If the vehicles cannot support the disengagement of the dismounted element, the platoon leader directs one squad or fire team to suppress by fire to support the disengagement of the remainder of the element.)

3. The unit leader orders a distance and direction, terrain feature, or last rally point of the movement of the element in contact.

4. The unit leader employs indirect fires to suppress enemy position(s). (See figure J-3.)

Figure J-3. Employing indirect fires to suppress enemy

5. The bounding element moves to occupy the overwatch position, employs smoke (M203, grenade launchers, indirect fires, and other options) to screen movement. If necessary, employs fragmentation and concussion grenades to facilitate breaking contact.

6. The base-of-fire element continues to suppress the enemy.

7. The moving element occupies their overwatch position and engages enemy position(s). (See figure J-4, page J-12.)

Appendix J

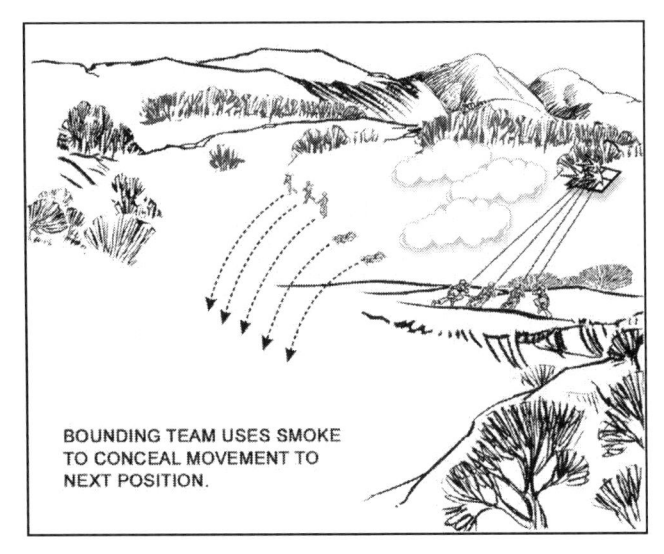

Figure J-4. Moving element occupies overwatch and engages enemy

8. The unit leader directs the base-of-fire element to move to its next covered and concealed position. Based on the terrain, and volume and accuracy of the enemy's fire, the moving element may need to use fire and movement techniques. (See figure J-5.)

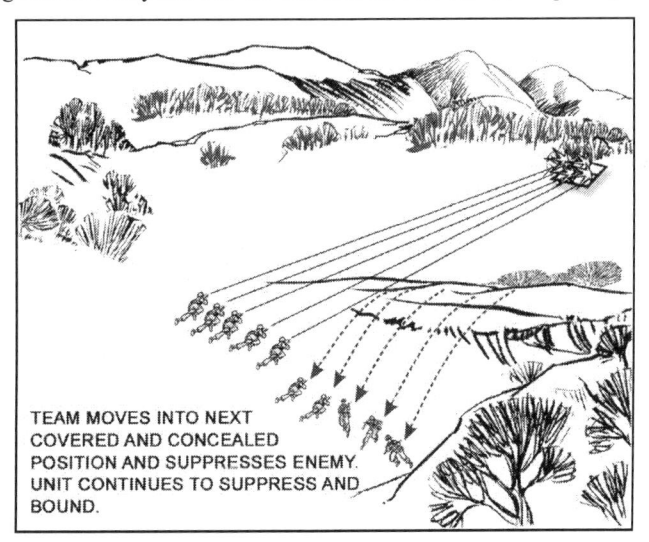

Figure J-5. Movement and fire technique

9. The unit continues to bound away from the enemy until:
   a. It breaks contact (the unit must continue to suppress the enemy as it breaks contact).
   b. It passes through a higher-level support-by-fire position.
   c. Its elements are in the assigned positions to conduct the next mission.

Selected Battle Drills

> *Note.* For a mounted element, the platoon leader directs the vehicles to move to a rally point and linkup with the dismounted element.

10. The leader should consider changing the unit's direction of movement once contact is broken. This reduces the ability of the enemy to place effective indirect fire on the unit.

11. Elements and Soldiers that become disrupted stay together and move to the last designated rally point.

12. Unit leaders account for Soldiers, reports the situation to higher leadership, reorganize as necessary, and continue the mission.

BATTLE DRILL 4: React to Ambush (Near) (07-3-D9502)

CONDITIONS: (Dismounted/mounted) The unit is moving tactically, conducting operations. The enemy initiates contact with direct fire within hand grenade range. All or part of the unit is receiving accurate enemy direct fire.

CUE: This drill begins when the enemy initiates ambush within hand grenade range.

STANDARDS: Dismounted, Soldiers in the kill zone immediately return fire on known or suspected enemy positions and assault through the kill zone. Soldiers not in the kill zone locate and place "well-aimed" suppressive fire on the enemy. The unit assaults through the kill zone and destroys the enemy.

Mounted, vehicle gunners immediately return fire on known or suspected enemy positions as the unit continues to move out of the kill zone. Soldiers on disabled vehicles in the kill zone dismount, occupy covered positions and engage the enemy with accurate fire. Vehicle gunners and Soldiers outside the kill zone suppress the enemy. The unit assaults through the kill zone and destroys the enemy. The unit leader reports the contact to higher headquarters

TASK STEPS AND PERFORMANCE MEASURES

1. Dismounted unit (see figure J-6, page J-14) takes the following actions:
    a. Soldiers in the kill zone execute one of the following two actions:
        (1) Return fire immediately. If cover is not available, immediately and without order or signal, assault through the kill zone.

Appendix J

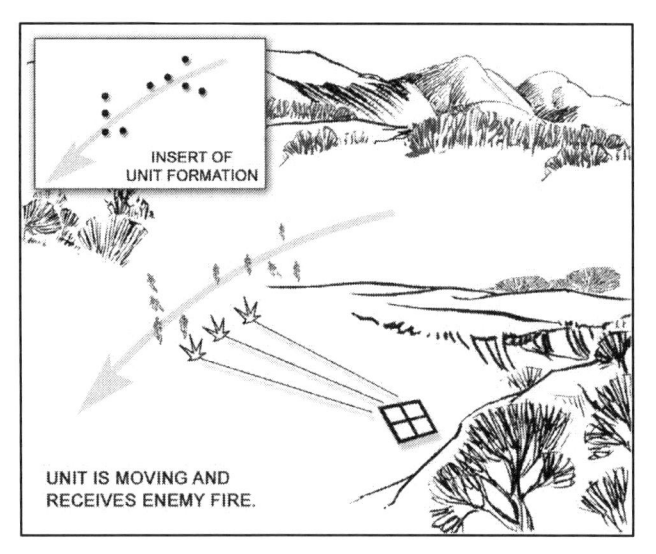

Figure J-6. React to ambush (near) (dismounted)

(2) Return fire immediately. If cover is not available, without order or signal, occupy the nearest covered position and throw smoke grenades. (See figure J-7.)

Figure J-7. Returning fire immediately

b. Soldiers in the kill zone assault through the ambush using fire and movement.
c. Soldiers not in the kill zone identify the enemy location, place "well-aimed" suppressive fire on the enemy's position and shift fire as Soldiers assault the objective.
d. Soldiers assault through and destroy the enemy position. (See figure J-8.)
e. The unit leader reports the contact to higher headquarters.

Figure J-8. Assaulting through enemy positions

2. Mounted unit takes the following actions:
    a. Vehicle gunners in the kill zone immediately return fire and deploy vehicle smoke, while moving out of the kill zone.
    b. Soldiers in disabled vehicles in the kill zone immediately obscure themselves from the enemy with smoke, dismount if possible, seek covered positions, and return fire.
    c. Vehicle gunners and Soldiers outside of the kill zone identify the enemy positions, place "well-aimed" suppressive fire on the enemy, and shift fire as Soldiers assault the objective.
    d. The unit leader calls for and adjusts indirect fire and request CAS according to METT-TC.
    e. Soldiers in the kill zone assault through the ambush and destroy the enemy.
    f. The unit leader reports the contact to higher headquarters.

BATTLE DRILL 5: Knock Out a Bunker (07-3-D9406)

CONDITIONS: The unit is moving tactically while conducting operations. The enemy initiates contact from a concealed bunker network. All or part of the unit is receiving accurate enemy direct fire.

CUE: The unit receives an order to knock out an enemy bunker from which it is receiving fire.

STANDARDS: The unit destroys the designated bunkers by killing, capturing, or forcing the withdrawal of enemy personnel. The unit maintains a sufficient fighting force to repel an enemy counterattack and continue operations.

Appendix J

TASK STEPS AND PERFORMANCE MEASURES

1. The unit deploys:
    a. The squad/team in contact establishes a base of fire. If mounted, the squad dismounts, establishes local security, and adds suppressive fires against the enemy. The platoon leader, radio telephone operator, and platoon FO dismount, and if not with the lead section, moves forward with the other squad leader and linkup with the squad leader of the lead squad.
    b. Weapons squad leader positions machine guns to reinforce rifle squad in contact.
    c. Platoon sergeant moves to support-by-fire position and assumes control of the position's fires and repositions vehicles if necessary, to provide additional observation and base of fire. The weapons squad leader repositions another machine gun, as needed, based on METT-TC.
    d. The squad in contact gains and maintains fire superiority by—
        (1) Destroying or suppressing enemy crew-served weapons.
        (2) Continuing suppressive fires at the lowest possible level.
        (3) Suppressing the bunker and supporting positions.
        (4) The squad employs SLMs, as required.
    e. The platoon FO calls for and adjusts indirect fires as directed by the platoon leader, including the use of smoke.
    f. Establishes security to rear and flanks of SBF position.
2. The unit reports:
    a. Submits contact reports.
    b. SALUTE report to commander.
    c. Submits SITREP, as needed.
3. Unit personnel evaluate and develop the situation:
    a. The platoon leader, radio telephone operator, and platoon FO move forward to linkup with the squad leader of the squad in contact.
    b. The platoon + leader evaluates the situation by identifying the enemy's composition, disposition, and capabilities:
        (1) Identifies enemy disposition: number and location of enemy bunkers, level of mutual support and overlapping fires between positions, and connecting trenches and protective obstacles.
        (2) Identifies enemy composition and strength: the number of enemy automatic weapons, the presence of vehicles, and employment of indirect fires are indicators of enemy strength.
        (3) Identifies enemy capability: to defend, reinforce, attack, and withdraw.
    c. Platoon leader develops the situation by determining where he can move to a position of advantage. These include—
        (1) A vulnerable flank or blind spot to at least one bunker.
        (2) A covered and concealed flanking route to the flank of the bunker.
4. Unit personnel develop a COA:
    a. The platoon + leader determines—
        (1) Which bunker poses the greatest threat.
        (2) Where the adjoining bunkers are located.
        (3) Requirement to breach protective obstacles.

Selected Battle Drills

      b. Platoon leader determines where support positions will be placed.
      c. Platoon leader determines size and make up of assault squad.
5. Unit personnel execute COA:
      a. Platoon leader directs the supporting element to suppress bunker:
          (1) Platoon sergeant repositions a squad, fire team, machine gun team, and mounted element to isolate the bunker and continue suppressive fires, as necessary.
          (2) FO shifts fires, as needed.
      b. Platoon leader directs the assault squad to attack the bunker:
          (1) The assaulting squad, platoon leader, and radio-telephone operator move along the covered and concealed route to an assault position and do not mask the fires of the support-by-fire element.
          (2) Soldiers constantly watch for other bunkers or enemy positions in support of bunkers.
          (3) On the platoon leader's signal, the supporting element shifts or ceases fire (direct fire and indirect fire).
          (4) Upon reaching the last covered and concealed position—
              (a) Buddy team #1 (team leader and automatic rifleman) remain where they can cover buddy team #2 grenadier and rifleman.
              (b) The squad leader positions himself where best to control the teams. On the squad leader's signal, the base-of-fire element lifts or shifts fires to the opposite side of the bunker from the assaulting fire team's approach.
          (5) Buddy team #2 moves to a blind spot near the bunker.
              (a) One Soldier takes up a covered position near the exit.
              (b) The other Soldier cooks off a grenade (two seconds, maximum), announces, "FRAG OUT," and throws it through an aperture.
              (c) After the grenade detonates, the Soldier covering the exit enters first and the team clears the bunker.
          (6) Buddy team #1 moves to join buddy team #2.
          (7) The team leader—
              (a) Inspects the bunker.
              (b) Marks the bunker according to unit SOP.
              (c) Signals the squad leader that the bunker is clear.
6. The platoon leader:
      a. Directs the supporting squad to move up and knock out the next bunker.
      OR directs the assaulting squad to continue and knock out the next bunker.
      b. Rotates squads, as necessary.
7. Unit leaders account for Soldiers, provide a SITREP to higher headquarters, consolidate and reorganize as necessary, and continue the mission.

BATTLE DRILL 6: Enter and Clear a Room (07-4-D9509)

CONDITIONS: The unit is conducting operations as part of a larger unit and has been given the mission to clear a room. Enemy personnel are believed to be in building. Noncombatants may be present in the building and are possibly intermixed with the enemy personnel. The

Appendix J

unit has support and security elements positioned at the initial foothold and outside the building.

CUE: This drill begins on the order of the unit leader or on the command of the clearing team leader.

STANDARDS: The unit clears and secures the room by killing or capturing the enemy while minimizing friendly casualties, noncombatant casualties, and collateral damage. The team complies with ROE, maintains a sufficient fighting force to repel an enemy counterattack, and continues operations.

TASK STEPS AND PERFORMANCE MEASURES

1. The unit leader occupies a position to best control the security and clearing teams.
    a. Unit leader directs a clearing team to secure corridors or hallways outside the room with appropriate firepower.
    b. The team leader (normally, the number two Soldier) takes a position to best control the clearing team outside the room.
    c. The unit leader gives the signal to clear the room.

Note. If the unit is conducting high-intensity combat operations and grenades are being used, the unit must comply with the ROE and consider the building structure. A Soldier of the clearing team cooks off at least one grenade (fragmentation, concussion, or stun grenade), throws the grenade into the room and announces, "FRAG OUT." The use of grenades should be consistent with the ROE and building structure. Soldiers can be injured from fragments if walls and floors are thin or damaged.

2. The clearing team enters and clears the room.
    a. The first two Soldiers enter the room almost simultaneously. (See figure J-9.)

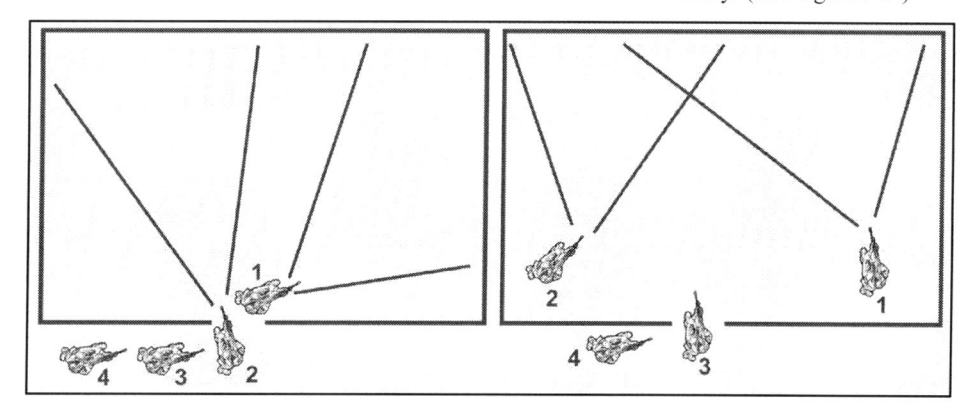

Figure J-9. Clear a room, first two Soldiers enter simultaneously

   b. The first Soldier enters the room, moves left or right along the path of least resistance to one of two corners, and assumes a position of domination facing into the room. During movement, the Soldier scans the sector and eliminates all immediate threats.

c. The second Soldier (normally the clearing team leader) enters the room immediately after the first Soldier and moves in the opposite direction of the first Soldier to his point of domination. During movement the Soldier eliminates all immediate threats in the sector.

Notes. During high intensity combat the Soldiers enter immediately after the grenade detonates. Both Soldiers enter firing aimed bursts into their sectors engaging all threats or hostile targets to cover their entry.

If the first or second Soldier discovers the room is small or a short room (such as a closet or bathroom), he announces, "SHORT ROOM or SHORT." The clearing team leader informs the third and fourth Soldiers whether or not to stay outside the room or to enter.

d. The third Soldier moves in the opposite direction of the second Soldier while scanning and clearing the sector and assuming the point of domination. (See figure J-10, page J-20.)

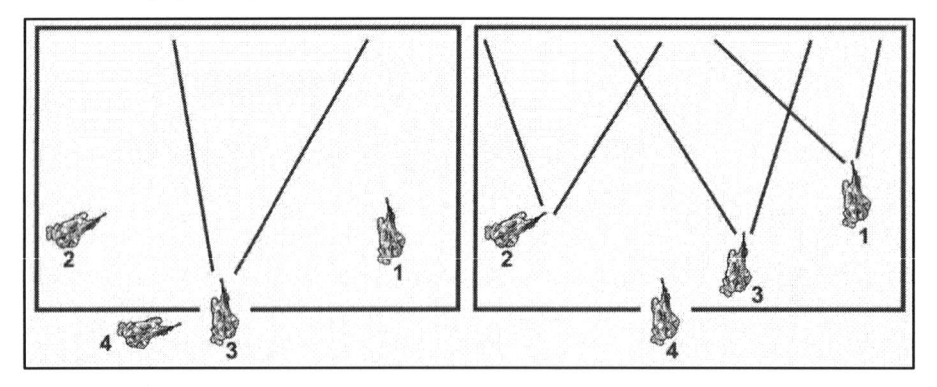

Figure J-10. Clear a room, third Soldier enters clearing his sector

e. The fourth Soldier moves opposite of the third Soldier to a position dominating his sector. (See Figure J-11.)

Appendix J

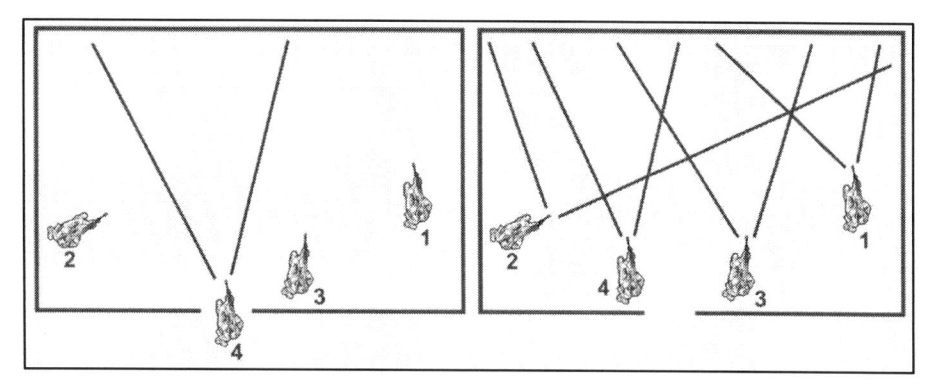

Figure J-11. Clear a room, third Soldier enters dominating his sector

   f. All Soldiers engage enemy combatants with precision aimed fire and identify noncombatants to avoid collateral damage.

   Note. If necessary or on order, number one and two Soldiers of the clearing team may move deeper into the room while overwatched by the other team members.

   g. The clearing team leader announces to the unit leader when the room is CLEAR.

3. Marks the entry point according to unit SOP.
   a. Makes a quick assessment of room and threat.
   b. Determines if unit has fire power to continue clearing their assigned sector.
   c. Reports to the higher unit leader the first room is clear.
   d. Requests needed sustainment to continue clearing his sector.
   e. Marks entry point according to unit SOP.

4. The unit consolidates and reorganizes, as needed.

BATTLE DRILL 7: Enter a Trench to Secure a Foothold (07-3-D9410)

CONDITIONS: The platoon is moving and receives fire from an enemy trench. The platoon is ordered to secure a foothold in the trench. Only organic weapons support is available.

CUE: The platoon leader initiates the drill by giving the order for the assault element to secure a foothold in the trench.

STANDARDS: The platoon leader quickly identifies the entry point. The platoon secures the entry point, enters the trench, and secures an area large enough for the follow-on unit. The platoon maintains a sufficient fighting force to repel enemy counterattack and continues the mission.

TASK STEPS AND PERFORMANCE MEASURES

1. A platoon executes Battle Drill 1, React to Direct Fire Contact.

Selected Battle Drills

2. The squad in contact takes the following actions:
    a. Deploys; takes the following actions:
        (1) Returns fire.
        (2) Seeks cover.
        (3) Establishes fire superiority.
        (4) Establishes local security.
    b. Unit leader's reports:
        (1) Squad leader reports location of hostile fire to platoon leader from base-of-fire position using the SALUTE format.
        (2) The platoon leader sends contact report followed by a SALUTE report to commander.

3. The platoon leader evaluates and develops the situation and takes the following actions:
    a. Evaluates the situation using the SITREPs from the squad in contact and his personal observations. At a minimum, the evaluation should include:
        (1) Number of enemy weapons or volume of fire.
        (2) Presence of vehicles.
        (3) Employment of indirect fires.
    b. Develops the situation by taking the following actions:
        (1) Conducts a quick reconnaissance to determine enemy flanks.
        (2) Locates mutually supporting positions.
        (3) Locates obstacles impeding the assault or provides some type of cover or concealment.
        (4) Determines whether the force is inferior or superior.
        (5) Analyzes reports from squad leader, teams in contact, or adjacent units.

4. The platoon leader chooses a COA and takes the following actions:
    a. Decides to enter the trench and selects the entry point.
    b. Selects a covered and concealed route to the entry point.
    c. Directs the maneuver element to secure the near side of the entry point and reduce the obstacle to gain a foothold.
    d. The platoon leader and platoon sergeant repositions the remaining squads and vehicles to provide additional observation and supporting fires.

5. The platoon executes the COA using SOSRA to set conditions for the assault. (See figure J-12.) The platoon takes the following actions:
    a. Suppresses and obscures. The platoon takes the following actions:
        (1) Platoon leader or FO calls for and adjusts indirect fire in support of assault.
        (2) Platoon sergeant directs base-of-fire squad to cover maneuvering squad.
        (3) Obscures maneuver element's movement with smoke (handheld/M203/320).

Appendix J

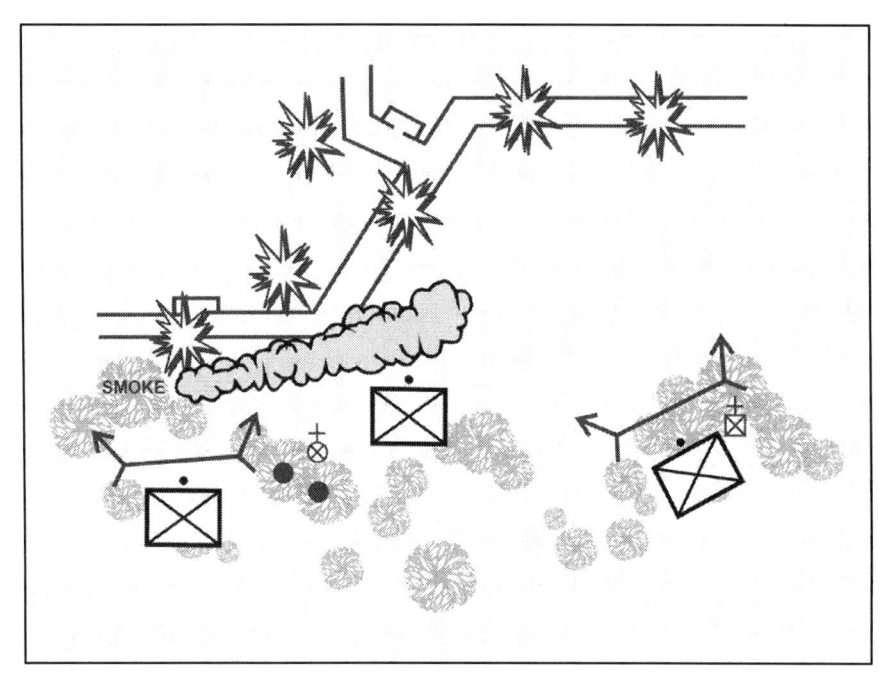

Figure J-12. Suppress, obscure, secure, reduce, and assault

b. Secures the near side and reduces the obstacle. The maneuver squad clears the entry point and take the following actions:
  (1) Squad leader moves the assaulting squad to last covered and concealed position short of the entry point.
  (2) Squad leader designates entry point.
  (3) Base-of-fire and vehicles squad shift fires away from entry point and continues to suppress adjacent enemy positions or isolate the trench, as required.
  (4) Squad leader uses one team to suppress the entry point and positions the assaulting team at the entry point.
c. The platoon leader directs FO to shift indirect fires to isolate the objective and the base-of-fire section/squads shifts fire as assault section/squad advances.
d. The platoon secures the far side and establishes a foothold. (See figure J-13.)

Selected Battle Drills

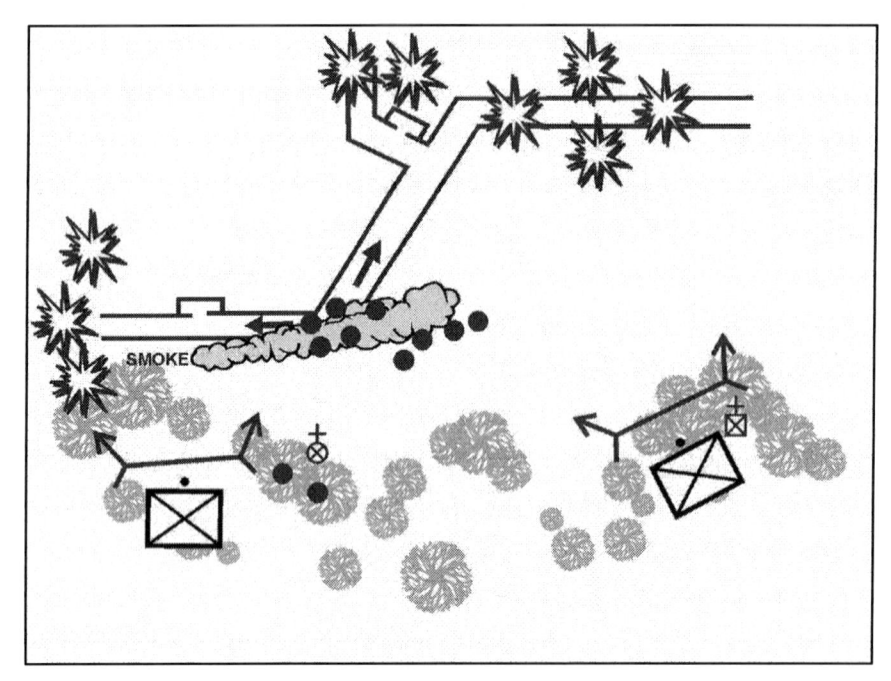

Figure J-13. Establishing a foothold

6. The first two soldiers of the assault fire team position themselves against the edge of the trench to roll right and left of the entry point to clear far side of obstacle and establish a foothold. On the squad leader's command, cook-off grenades (two seconds maximum), shout "FRAG OUT," and throw the grenades into the trench.

    a. After ensuring that both grenades detonate, the Soldiers roll into the trench back to back. Immediately, both Soldiers move in opposite directions down the trench clearing to the first corner or intersection.

    b. Both Soldiers halt and take up positions to block any enemy movement toward the entry point.

7. Upon detonation of the grenades, the remainder of the assault fire team enters the trench, moving to reinforce at the first secured corner or intersection.

8. The assault team clears enough room for the section/squad or to the first trench junction and announces, "CLEAR."

9. The squad leader marks the entry point according to the platoon SOP, then sends the next assault team in to increase the size of the foothold by announcing, "NEXT TEAM IN."

10. The next assault team moves into trench and secures assigned area. (See figure J-14, page J-24.)

Appendix J

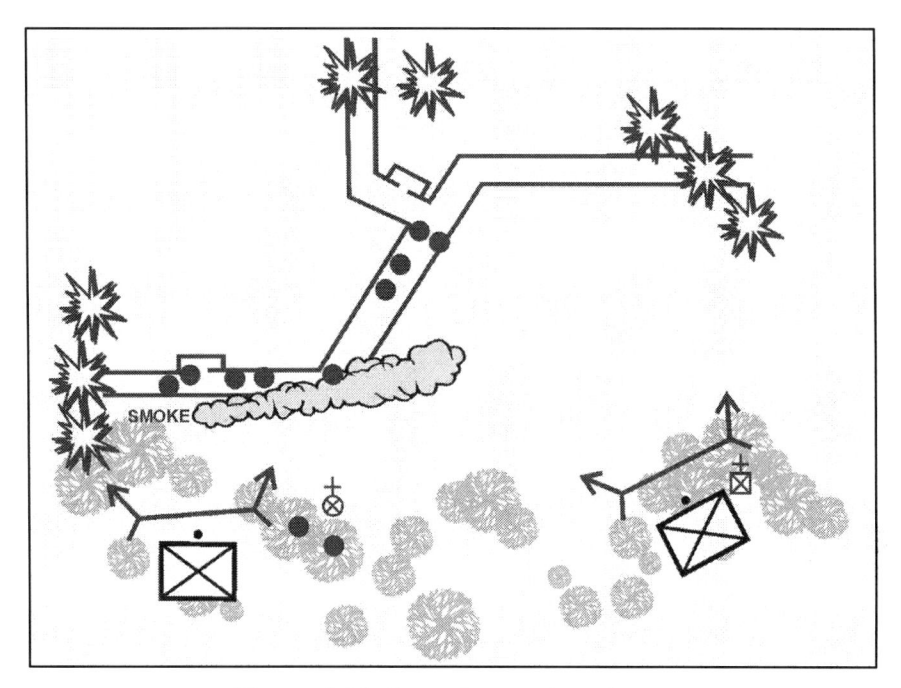

Figure J-14. Securing assigned area

11. The squad leader reports to the platoon leader the foothold is secure. The platoon follows the success of the seizure of the foothold with the remainder of the platoon, as part of the platoon actions to clear a trench line.

BATTLE DRILL 8: Breach a Mined Wire Obstacle (07-3-D9412)

CONDITIONS: The platoon encounters a mine wire obstacle preventing the company's movement. The platoon's forward movement is stopped by a wire obstacle reinforced with mines that cannot be bypassed. The enemy engages the platoon from positions on the far side of the obstacle.

CUE: This drill begins when the unit's lead element encounters a mine wire obstacle and the unit leader orders an element to breach the obstacle.

STANDARDS: The platoon breaches the obstacle and moves all personnel and equipment quickly through the breach. The platoon moves the support element and follow-on forces through the breach and maintains a sufficient fighting force to secure the far side of the breach.

TASK STEPS AND PERFORMANCE MEASURES

1. A platoon's squad executes actions on contact to reduce fires from the far side of the obstacle.

2. The squad in contact takes the following actions:

Selected Battle Drills

　　a. Deploys; taking the following actions:
　　　(1) Returns fire.
　　　(2) Seeks cover.
　　　(3) Establishes fire superiority.
　　　(4) Establishes local security.
　　b. The platoon sergeant repositions other squads to focus supporting fires and increase observation.
　　c. Unit leaders report:
　　　(1) Squad leader reports location of hostile fire to platoon leader from base-of-fire position using the SALUTE format.
　　　(2) Platoon leader sends a contact report followed by a SALUTE report to the commander.
3. The platoon leader evaluates and develops the situation and takes the following actions:
　　a. Quickly evaluates the situation using the SITREPs from the squad in contact and his personal observations. At a minimum, the evaluation should include:
　　　(1) Number of enemy weapons or volume of fire.
　　　(2) Presence of vehicles.
　　　(3) Employment of indirect fires.
　　b. Quickly develops the situation and takes the following actions:
　　　(1) Conducts a quick reconnaissance to determine enemy flanks.
　　　(2) Locates mutually supporting positions.
　　　(3) Locates obstacles impeding the assault or provides some type of cover or concealment.
　　　(4) Determines whether the force is inferior or superior.
　　　(5) Analyzes reports from squad leaders, teams in contact, or adjacent units.
4. The platoon leader directs the squad in contact, the lead vehicle, or both to support the movement of the squad to the breach point. The platoon leader takes the following actions:
　　a. Indicates the route to the base-of-fire position.
　　b. Indicates the enemy position to be suppressed.
　　c. Indicates the breach point and route the rest of the platoon will take.
　　d. Gives instructions for lifting and shifting fires.
5. On the platoon leader's signal, the support-by-fire squad, the lead vehicle section, or both take the following actions:
　　a. Destroys or suppresses enemy weapons firing against the platoon.
　　b. Obscures the enemy position with smoke.
　　c. Continues to maintain fire superiority while conserving ammunition and minimizing forces in contact.
6. The platoon leader designates one squad as the breach squad and remaining squad as assault squad, once the breach has been made. (The assault squad may add its fires to the support-by-fire squad. Normally, it follows the covered and concealed route of the breach squad and assaults through immediately after the breach is made.)

Appendix J

7. The base-of-fire squad moves to the breach point and establishes a base of fire.

8. The PSG moves forward to the base-of-fire squad with the second machine gun and assumes control of the squad.

9. The platoon leader leads the breach and assault squads along the covered and concealed route.

10. The platoon FO calls for and adjusts indirect fires, as directed by the platoon leader to support the breach and assault.

11. The breach squad executes actions to breach the obstacle (footpath). The squad leader takes the following actions:
    a. Directs one fire team to support the movement of the other fire team to the breach point.
    b. Designates the breach point.
    c. Ensures the support-by-fire team continues to provide suppressive fires and to isolate the breach point. (See figure J-15.)

Selected Battle Drills

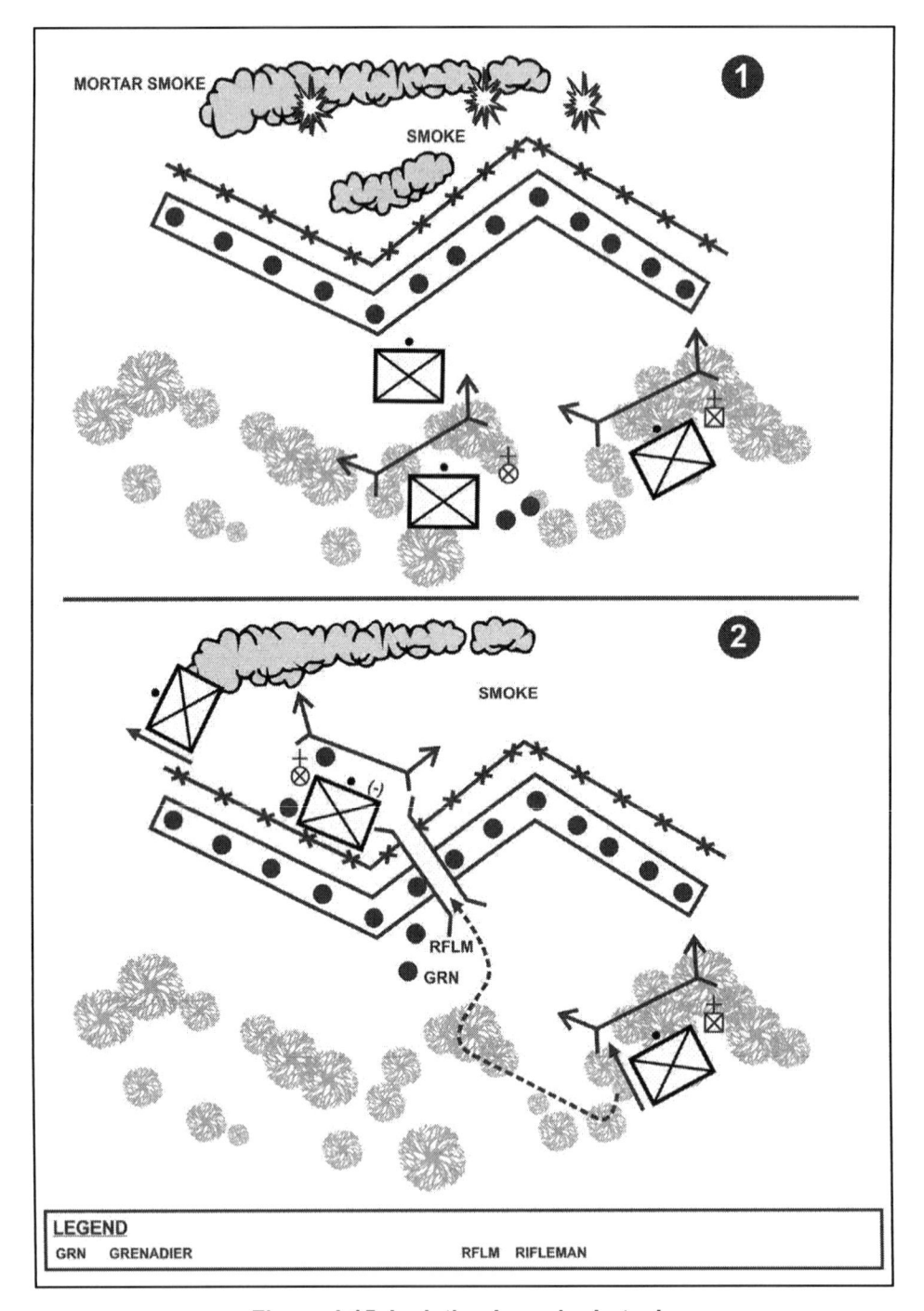

Figure J-15. Isolating breach obstacle

Appendix J

    d. The breaching fire team with the squad leader, moves to the breach point using the covered and concealed route.
        (1) The squad leader and breaching fire team leader employs smoke grenades to obscure the breach point. The platoon base-of-fire element shifts direct fires away from the breach point and continues to suppress adjacent enemy positions.
        (2) The breaching fire team leader positions himself and the automatic rifleman on one flank of the breach point to provide close-in security.
        (3) The grenadier and rifleman (or the antiarmor specialist and automatic rifleman) of the breaching fire team probe for mines and cut the wire obstacle, marking their path as they proceed. (Bangalore is preferred, if available.)
        (4) Once the obstacle is breached, the breaching fire team leader and automatic rifleman move to the far side of the obstacle using covered and concealed positions. They signal the squad leader when they are in position and ready to support.
    e. The squad leader signals the base-of-fire team leader to move the fire team up and through the breach. The fire team leader then moves through the obstacle and joins the breaching fire team, leaving the grenadier (or antiarmor specialist) and rifleman of the supporting fire team on the near side of the breach to guide the rest of the platoon through.
    f. Using the same covered and concealed route as the breaching fire team, the support-by-fire team moves through the breach and to a covered and concealed position on the far side.

12. The breach squad leader reports the situation to the platoon leader and posts guides at the breach point.

13. The platoon leader leads the assault squad through the breach in the obstacle and positions it on the far side.

14. The breaching squad continues to widen the breach to allow vehicle section to pass through and secure the far side.

15. The platoon leader provides a SITREP to the company commander and directs his breaching squad to move through the obstacle. The platoon leader appoints guides to guide the company through the breach point.

BATTLE DRILL 9: React to Indirect Fire (07-3-D9504)

CONDITIONS: Dismounted, the unit is moving, conducting operations. Any Soldier gives the alert, "INCOMING," or a round impacts nearby. Mounted, the unit is stationary or moving, conducting operations. The alert, "INCOMING," comes over the radio or intercom or rounds impact nearby.

CUE: This drill begins when any member alerts, "INCOMING," or a round impacts.

STANDARDS: Dismounted, Soldiers immediately seek the best available cover. The unit moves out of the area to the designated rally point after the impacts. Mounted, when moving, drivers immediately move their vehicles out of the impact area in the direction and distance ordered. If stationary, drivers start their vehicles and move in the direction and distance ordered. Unit leaders report the contact to higher headquarters.

TASK STEPS AND PERFORMANCE MEASURES

1. Dismounted. Unit personnel take the following actions:
    a. Any Soldier announces, "INCOMING!"
    b. Soldiers immediately assume the prone position or move to immediate available cover during initial impacts.
    c. The unit leader orders the unit to move to a rally point by giving a direction and distance.
    d. Soldiers move rapidly in the direction and distance to the designated rally point, after the impacts.
    e. The unit leaders report the contact to higher headquarters.

2. Mounted. Unit personnel take the following actions:
    a. Any Soldier announces, "INCOMING!"
    b. Vehicle commanders repeat the alert over the radio.
    c. The leaders give the direction and linkup location over the radio.
    d. Soldiers close all hatches, if applicable to the vehicle type; gunners stay below turret shields or get down into the vehicle.
    e. Drivers move rapidly out of the impact area in the direction ordered by the leader.
    f. Unit leaders report the contact to higher headquarters.

Appendix J

BATTLE DRILL 10: REACT TO A CHEMICAL ATTACK (03-3-D0001)

CONDITIONS: The element is moving or stationary, conducting operations. The unit is attacked with a chemical or biological agent. Soldiers hear a chemical alarm, observe an unknown gas or liquid, or are ordered to don their protective mask.

Note. The term MOPP on this drill equates to MOPP4.

CUE: Any Soldier gives an oral or visual signal for a chemical attack, or a chemical alarm activates. Standard MOPP conditions do not exist for this task. See the MOPP statement for specific conditions.

STANDARDS: All Soldiers don their protective mask within nine seconds (or fifteen seconds for masks with a hood). Soldiers assume MOPP4 within eight minutes. The element identifies the chemical agent using M8 chemical detector paper and the M256 kit. The squad or platoon leader reports that the unit is under a chemical attack and submits a CBRN 1 report to higher headquarters.

TASK STEPS AND PERFORMANCE MEASURES

1. Element dons their protective mask.

   Note. The mask gives immediate protection against traditional warfare agents. The mask may not completely protect you from certain toxic industrial chemicals, but it provides the best available protection to enable you to evacuate the hazard area. You may be required to evacuate to a minimum safe distance at least 300 meters upwind from the contamination (if possible), or as directed by the commander.

2. Element gives vocal or nonvocal alarm.

3. Element uses the appropriate skin decontamination kit within one minute for individual decontamination, as necessary.

4. Element assumes MOPP4 within 15 minutes.

5. Element initiates self-aid or buddy-aid, as necessary.

6. Element identifies the chemical agent using M8 chemical detector paper and the M256 detector kit.

7. Element leader reports the chemical attack to higher headquarters using the CBRN 1 report.

8. Element leader determines if decontamination is required and requests support, if necessary.

9. Element marks the contaminated area if contamination is present.

10. Element leader requests guidance for higher headquarters for follow-on mission(s).

Selected Battle Drills

BATTLE DRILL 11: REACT TO AN IED (05-3-D1703)

CONDITIONS: The element is performing a military operation when a suspected IED is found. Some iterations of this task should be performed in MOPP.

CUE: An element encounters a suspected IED.

STANDARDS: React to the suspected IED. Any Soldier reports the IED to the remainder of the element by using the 3-Ds (distance, direction, and description). The element performs the 5-Cs (check, confirm, clear, cordon and control).

TASK STEPS AND PERFORMANCE MEASURES

1. The first Soldier to realize there is a possible IED communicates the 3-Ds:
   a. Distance: the distance from the Soldier(s) that initially found the possible IED.
   b. Direction: the direction to which the possible IED is located from the Soldier(s) who initially found it.
   c. Description: the initial description of the possible IED. Soldiers should not move closer to the possible IED to retrieve a better description.

2. The element performs the 5-Cs.
   a. Check: all personnel should check their immediate area for secondary/tertiary devices by conducting 5/25/200 meter checks from their positions. If Soldiers suspect an IED while performing the 5/25/200 meter checks, they should assume it could detonate at any moment, even if the suspected IED turns out to be a false alarm.
   b. Confirm: the unit MUST confirm the existence of a suspected IED from a safe distance using any available standoff means (robot, Buffalo, optics, or other means). Once confirmed, the unit calls in an EOD 9-line explosive hazard spot report.
      (1) Line 1, date-time group: complete this line with the date and time the item was discovered.
      (2) Line 2, reporting activity and location: complete this line with the unit and the 8-digit grid location of the explosive hazard.
      (3) Line 3, contact method: enter the radio frequency, call sign, point of contact, and telephone number.
      (4) Line 4, type of ordnance: document whether it was dropped, projected, placed, or thrown; or whether it was a possible IED. Give the number of items, if more than one. Include as detailed of a description as possible of the item in question, to include the size, shape, and physical condition.
      (5) Line 5, CBRN contaminations: Be as specific as possible.
      (6) Line 6, resources threatened: document equipment, facilities, or other assets that were threatened.
      (7) Line 7, impact on mission: provide a short description of the current tactical situation and how the explosive hazard affected the status of the mission.
      (8) Line 8, protective measures: document any measures taken to protect personnel and equipment.
      (9) Line 9, recommended priority. indicate whether it was immediate, indirect, minor, or no threat:

Appendix J

(a) Immediate: stops the unit maneuver and mission capability, or threatens critical assets vital to the mission.
(b) Indirect: stops the unit maneuver and mission capability, or threatens critical assets important to the mission.
(c) Minor: reduces the unit maneuver and mission capability, or threatens noncritical assets.
(d) No threat: has little or no effect on the capabilities or assets of the unit.

> **WARNING**
>
> **Be alert for suspicious personnel exiting the cordon.**

c. Clear: the unit clears the area around the device of all personnel, working from the device outwards. If an IED has been confirmed, the unit must clear the area. The safe distance is determined by several factors: the tactical situation, avoiding predictability, and moving several hundred meters away from the IED.

Note. In the event of larger elements, personnel who are deemed nonessential for the purpose of cordoning the area can use an alternate route of movement and continue the mission or return to the nearest safe area. Theater-specific guidance or mission necessities may require the unit to react to the IED in a different manner, such as reporting and bypassing.

> **DANGER**
>
> **The element varies the minimum safe distance when moving away from the IED to avoid establishing predictability because of possible secondary/tertiary IEDs. Avoid using any communication or electronic equipment (other than crew devices) within the secured exclusion area.**

d. Cordon: establish a security cordon around the danger area by setting up blocking positions to prevent foot and vehicle traffic from approaching the IED. An effective cordon will deny the enemy observation of friendly TTPs, along with denying them IED effectiveness. Continue to check for secondary/tertiary IEDs, make use of available cover, and establish an incident command post.

Note. Minimum safe distance for exposed personnel is considered to be 300 meters.

Selected Battle Drills

> **WARNING**
>
> To reduce exposure of personnel, the patrol leader should minimize the number of dismounted soldiers used in performing the 25-meter search.

e. Control: the unit must control the area inside the cordon to ensure authorized access. Since the distance of all personnel from the IED directly affects their safety, Soldiers should control the site to prevent someone from straying dangerously close until the threat has been neutralized.

    (1) 5-meter check: identify a position to halt. Search five meters out from your vehicle through the window before opening the door. Conduct a systematic visual check using binoculars or other optics. Check for abnormalities such as disturbed earth, suspicious objects, or loose bricks in walls and security ties. Work from the ground up and continue above head height. Take your time, search methodically, and use a white flashlight during hours of reduced visibility.

    (2) 25-Meter check: once a 5-meter check is completed and if deemed necessary by the patrol leader; exit the vehicle and close the door in order to protect occupants from the potential blast and sniper threats. Immediately perform a visual search under the vehicle and continue visually clear the area out to 25 meters, while simultaneously checking for potential IED indicators or anything out of the ordinary. During the 5/25/200 meter checks, the patrol (including Soldiers remaining inside the vehicle), must remain outwardly focused while searching from far-to-near looking for suspected enemy activity such as a triggerman, cameraman, or sniper.

    (3) The driver and the gunner should remain inside the vehicle for security purposes.

Appendix J

BATTLE DRILL 12: DISMOUNT A BFV AND ICV (07-3-D9433)

CONDITIONS: The platoon is moving in a BFV or ICV while conducting operations. The platoon is ordered to DISMOUNT.

CUE: This drill begins when the order is given to prepare to dismount:

STANDARDS: BFV: the platoon moves to a covered and concealed position to provide protection to the dismounting squads. When the command, "DISMOUNT," is given, each fire team dismounts in the order specified, in 30 seconds if the ramp is used, or 45 seconds if the combat door is used. The platoon or squad leader establishes security and control of the squads and fire teams.

ICV: the platoon moves to a covered and concealed position to provide protection to the dismounting squads. When the command, "DISMOUNT," is given, each fire team dismounts following the seating numbers: first out are Soldiers sitting in seats 10 and 11, second is 8 and 9, third is 6 and 7, fourth is 4 and 5, and fifth is seat 3. The squad establishes security after dismounting the vehicle.

TASK STEPS AND PERFORMANCE MEASURES

1. The platoon leader selects the dismount point.

2. The platoon leader orders personnel to dismount:
    a. Gives the warning, "PREPARE TO DISMOUNT."
    b. Designates dismounted platoon's weapons composition; for example, "NO JAVELINS," "HEAVY ON AT4s," or "ALL M240B."
    c. Gives dismount instructions for each BFV; for example, "RIGHT (or left)," distance "FIFTY METERS," and identifying terrain feature "BACKSIDE OF HILL." The Bradley commander may give dismount instructions to the fire team aboard. The BC can identify the location to the squad/team leader through the squad leader's display (M2A3 only).

3. Squad/fire team leader(s) monitor commands: he then alerts the Soldiers in the troop compartment.

4. The drivers move the vehicles to the designated dismount point and orient the front of the vehicle toward the enemy.

5. The gunners orient the turret to provide overwatching support and supporting fire, if necessary.

6. The platoon leader gives the command, "DISMOUNT."

7. Fire team members take the M231 firing port weapons out of the ramp and secure them in the vehicle, if employed.

8. The drivers stop the vehicle and lower the ramp, or the BC orders the ramp access door opened.

9. The fire team members dismount in the specified order and then move to covered and concealed positions (see figures J-16 through J-19, pages J-35 through J-38):

Selected Battle Drills

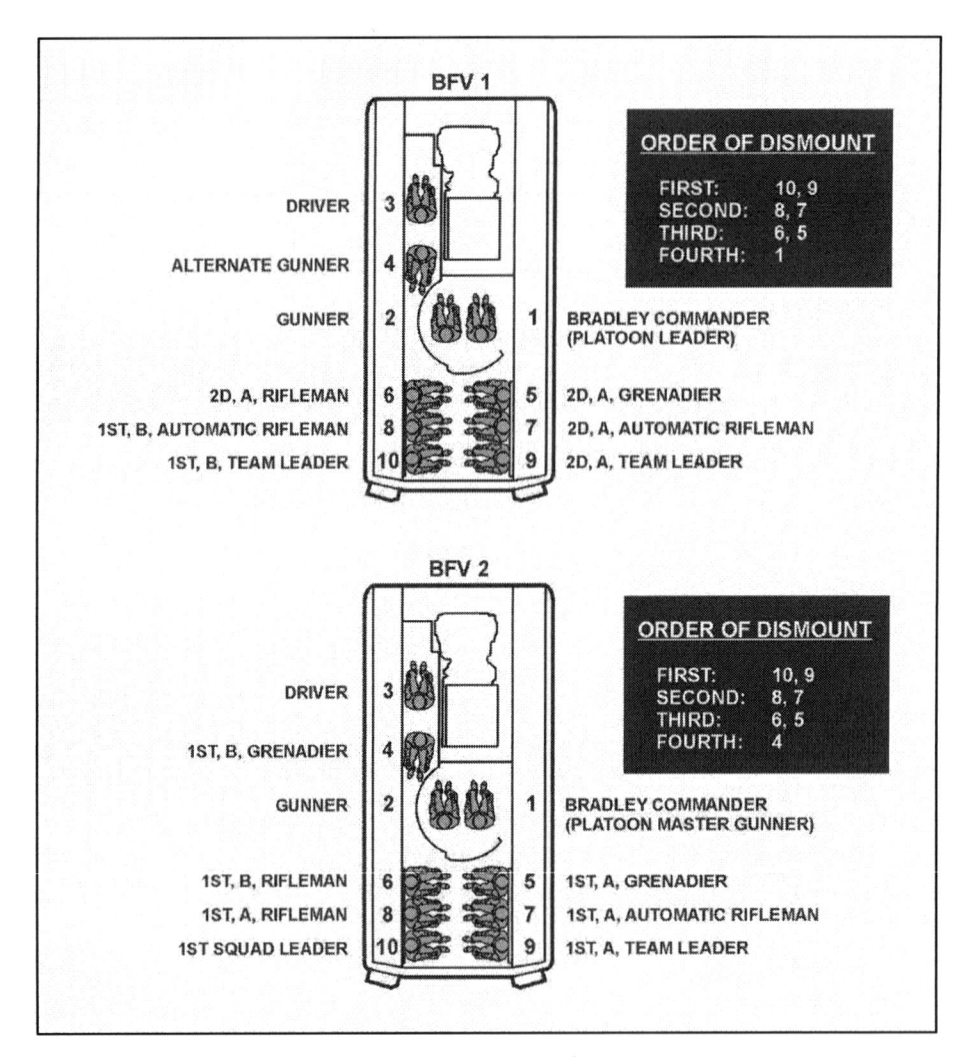

Figure J-16. BFV order of dismount

Appendix J

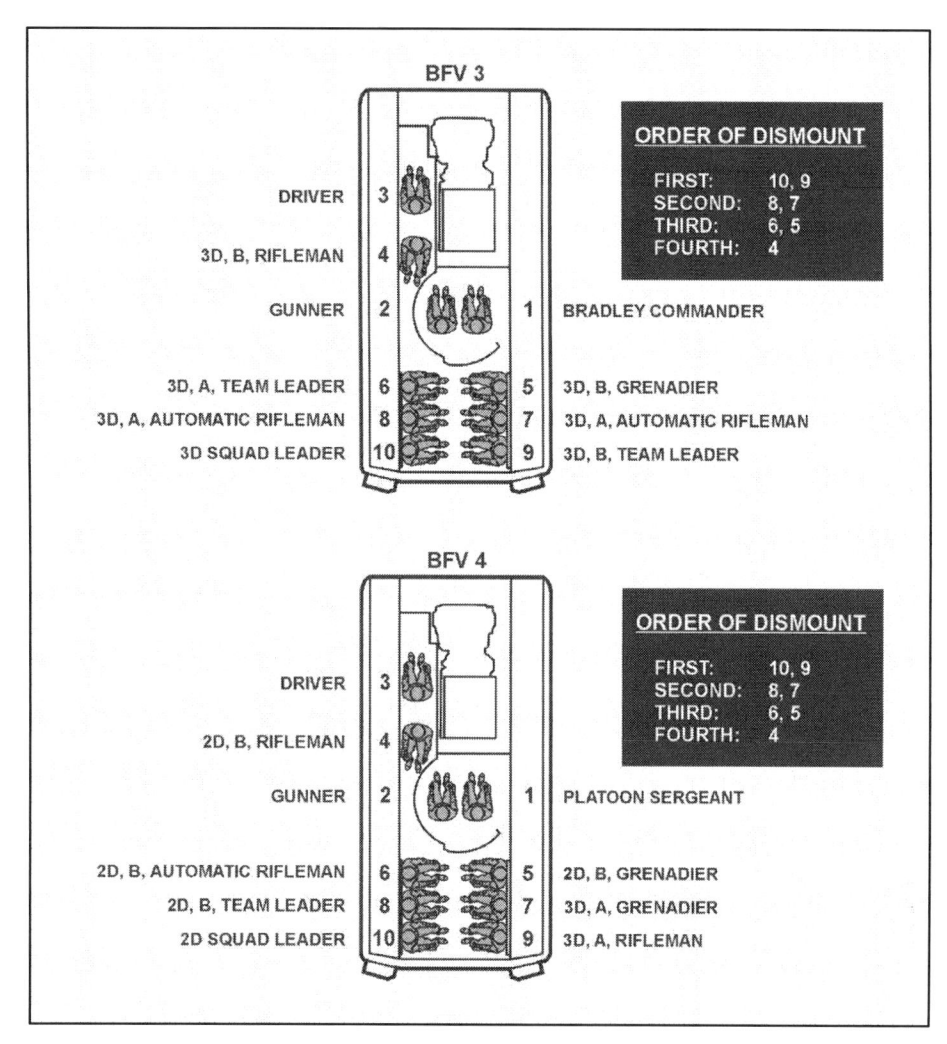

BFV 3

Position	#		#	Position
DRIVER	3			
3D, B, RIFLEMAN	4			
GUNNER	2		1	BRADLEY COMMANDER
3D, A, TEAM LEADER	6		5	3D, B, GRENADIER
3D, A, AUTOMATIC RIFLEMAN	8		7	3D, A, AUTOMATIC RIFLEMAN
3D SQUAD LEADER	10		9	3D, B, TEAM LEADER

ORDER OF DISMOUNT
FIRST: 10, 9
SECOND: 8, 7
THIRD: 6, 5
FOURTH: 4

BFV 4

Position	#		#	Position
DRIVER	3			
2D, B, RIFLEMAN	4			
GUNNER	2		1	PLATOON SERGEANT
2D, B, AUTOMATIC RIFLEMAN	6		5	2D, B, GRENADIER
2D, B, TEAM LEADER	8		7	3D, A, GRENADIER
2D SQUAD LEADER	10		9	3D, A, RIFLEMAN

ORDER OF DISMOUNT
FIRST: 10, 9
SECOND: 8, 7
THIRD: 6, 5
FOURTH: 4

Figure J-17. BFV order of dismount (continued)

Selected Battle Drills

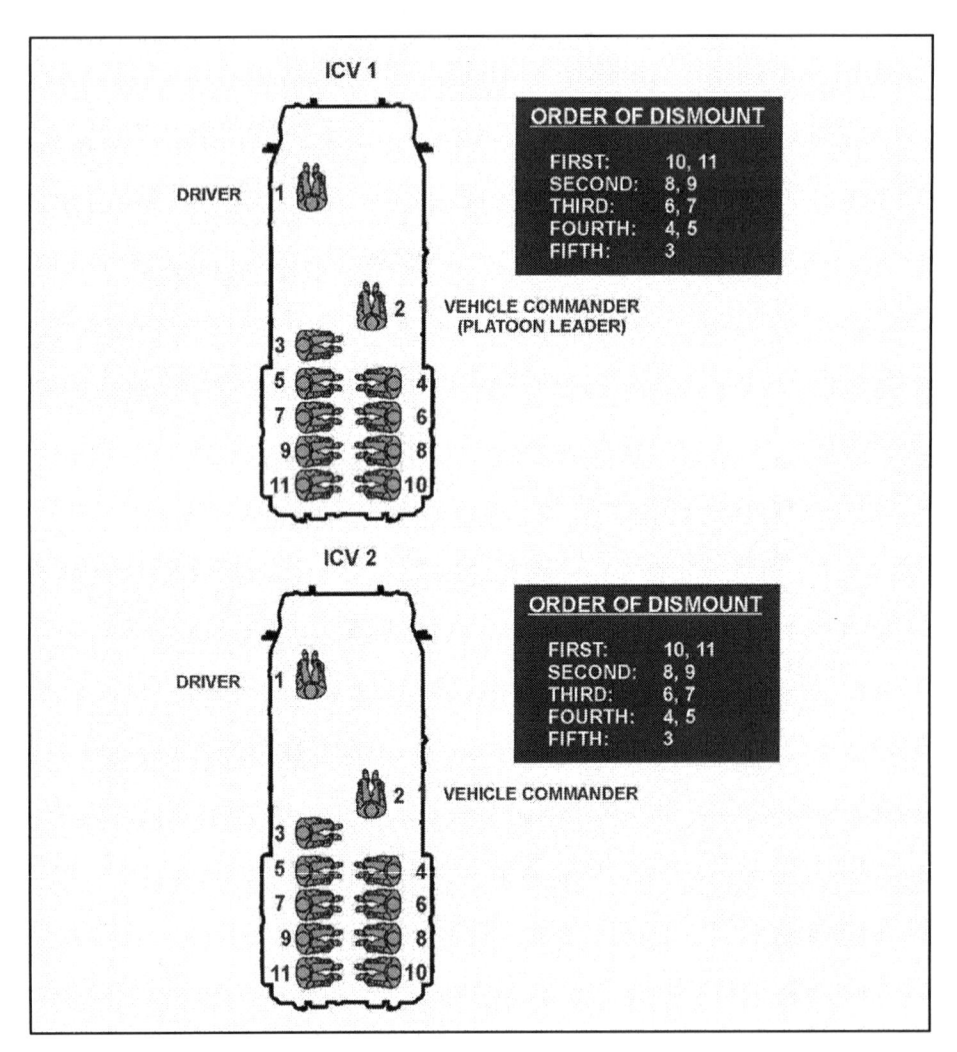

Figure J-18. ICV order of dismount

Appendix J

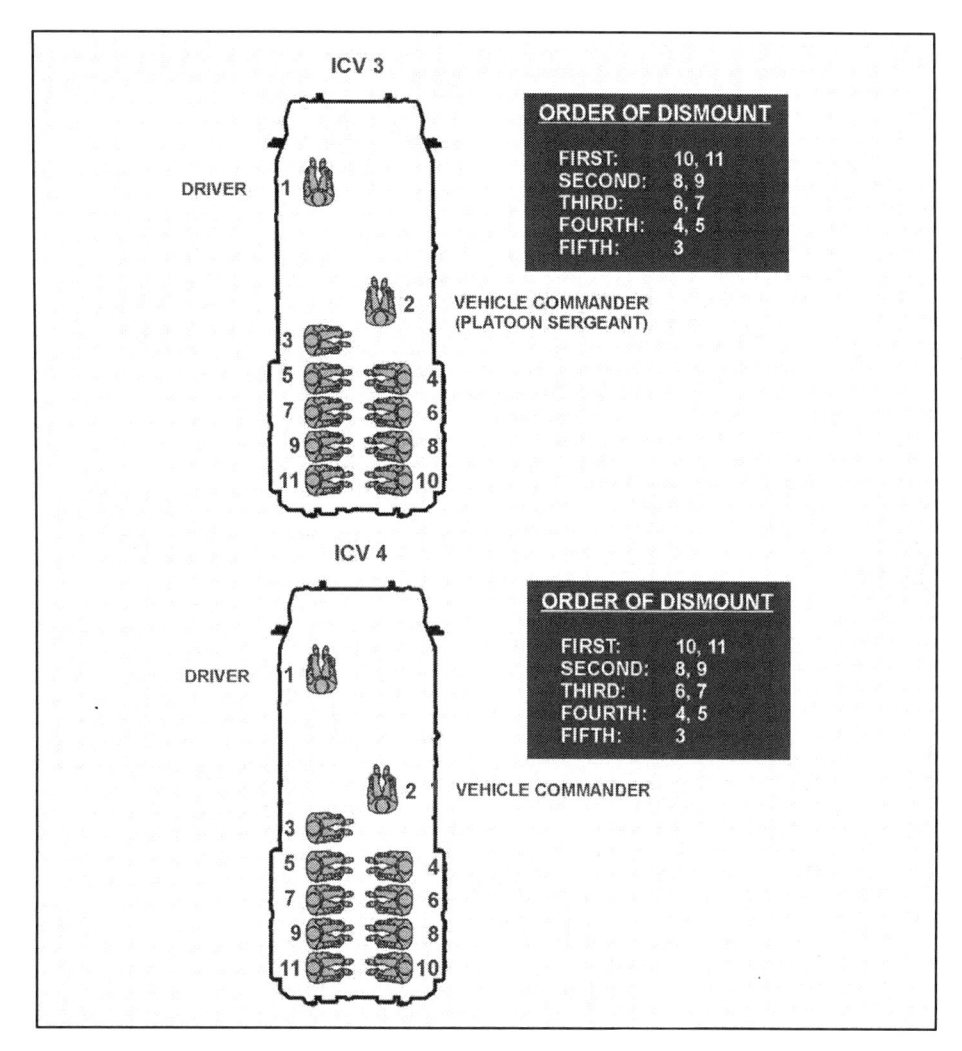

Figure J-19. ICV order of dismount (continued)

10. The fire teams linkup with the squads. The squad leaders establish contact with the platoon leader.

11. The mounted element occupies appropriate covered or concealed positions, and overwatches the dismounted element with primary weapons or maintains a hide position.

12. Squad and fire team leader's position or reposition squad members, if needed.

13. The platoon sergeant or section leader repositions vehicles according to METT-TC.

BATTLE DRILL 13: MOUNT A BFV AND ICV (07-3-D9434)

CONDITIONS: The platoon leader receives an order to move the platoon to a new location. The squads are dismounted and ordered to remount the vehicle.

CUE: The unit leader initiates the drill by giving the order to, "MOUNT UP."

STANDARDS: The vehicle moves to a covered and concealed position to provide protection to the remounting squads. Squads mount in the order specified.

TASK STEPS AND PERFORMANCE MEASURES

1. The platoon/squad leader gives an order to prepare to mount, then gives the order or signals to the squads to mount their vehicles, and designates a mount point.
2. Both elements (mounted and dismounted) move to the mount point using covered and concealed routes.
3. The crew, using the appropriate weapons, overwatches primary enemy avenues of approach and provides supporting fire and smoke, if necessary.
4. BFV or ICV, or both: the Bradley/vehicle commander orders the driver to lower the ramp or the squad to enter through the ramp access door.
5. The platoon/squad leader orders, "MOUNT." (The order to mount may come with clarifying instructions such as, "FIRST SQUAD, PROVIDE A BASE OF FIRE UNTIL SECOND SQUAD IS MOUNTED.")
6. Each squad mounts in the order specified. The squad leader designates which fire team mounts first--for example, Team A mounts first; Team B provides overwatching fires
7. Soldiers remount the vehicle in reverse sequence of dismount. (See figures J-20 through J-23, page J-40 through J-43.)

Appendix J

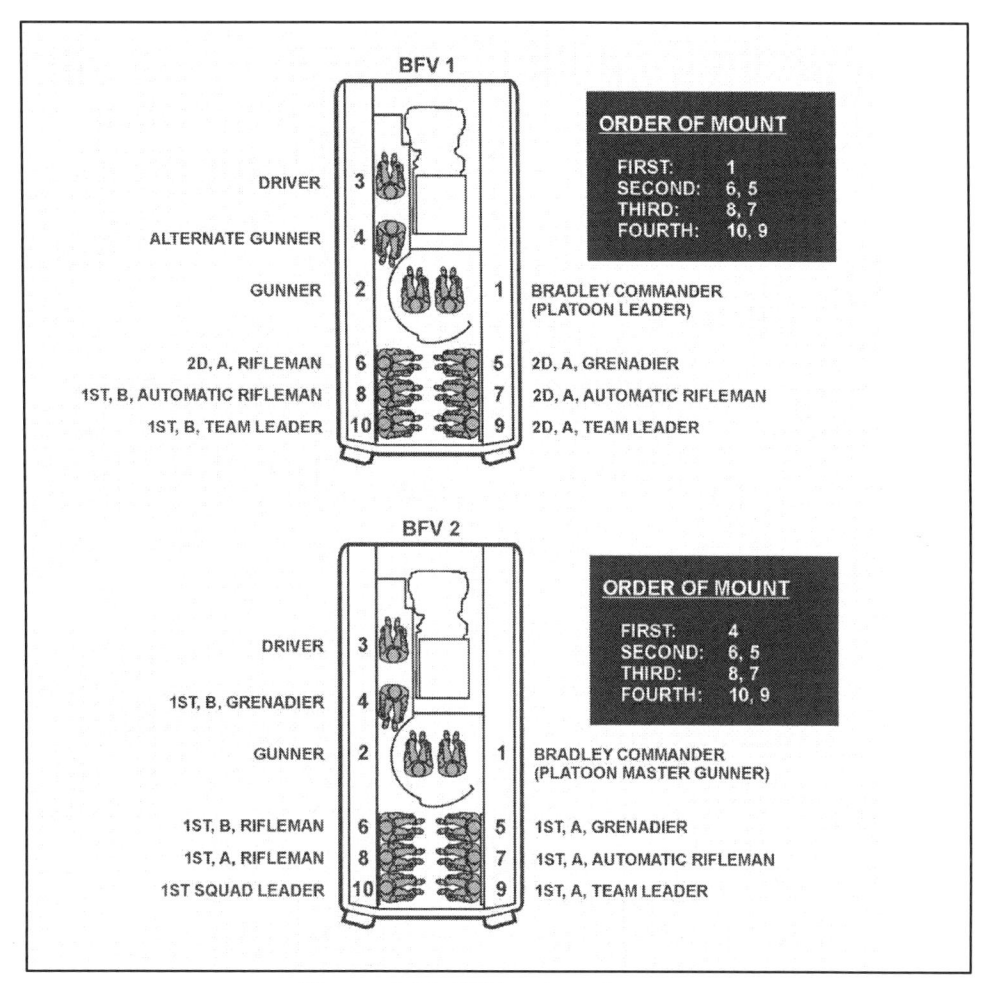

BFV 1

Position	Seat
DRIVER	3
ALTERNATE GUNNER	4
GUNNER	2
2D, A, RIFLEMAN	6
1ST, B, AUTOMATIC RIFLEMAN	8
1ST, B, TEAM LEADER	10

Seat	Position
1	BRADLEY COMMANDER (PLATOON LEADER)
5	2D, A, GRENADIER
7	2D, A, AUTOMATIC RIFLEMAN
9	2D, A, TEAM LEADER

ORDER OF MOUNT
FIRST: 1
SECOND: 6, 5
THIRD: 8, 7
FOURTH: 10, 9

BFV 2

Position	Seat
DRIVER	3
1ST, B, GRENADIER	4
GUNNER	2
1ST, B, RIFLEMAN	6
1ST, A, RIFLEMAN	8
1ST SQUAD LEADER	10

Seat	Position
1	BRADLEY COMMANDER (PLATOON MASTER GUNNER)
5	1ST, A, GRENADIER
7	1ST, A, AUTOMATIC RIFLEMAN
9	1ST, A, TEAM LEADER

ORDER OF MOUNT
FIRST: 4
SECOND: 6, 5
THIRD: 8, 7
FOURTH: 10, 9

Figure J-20. BFV order of mount

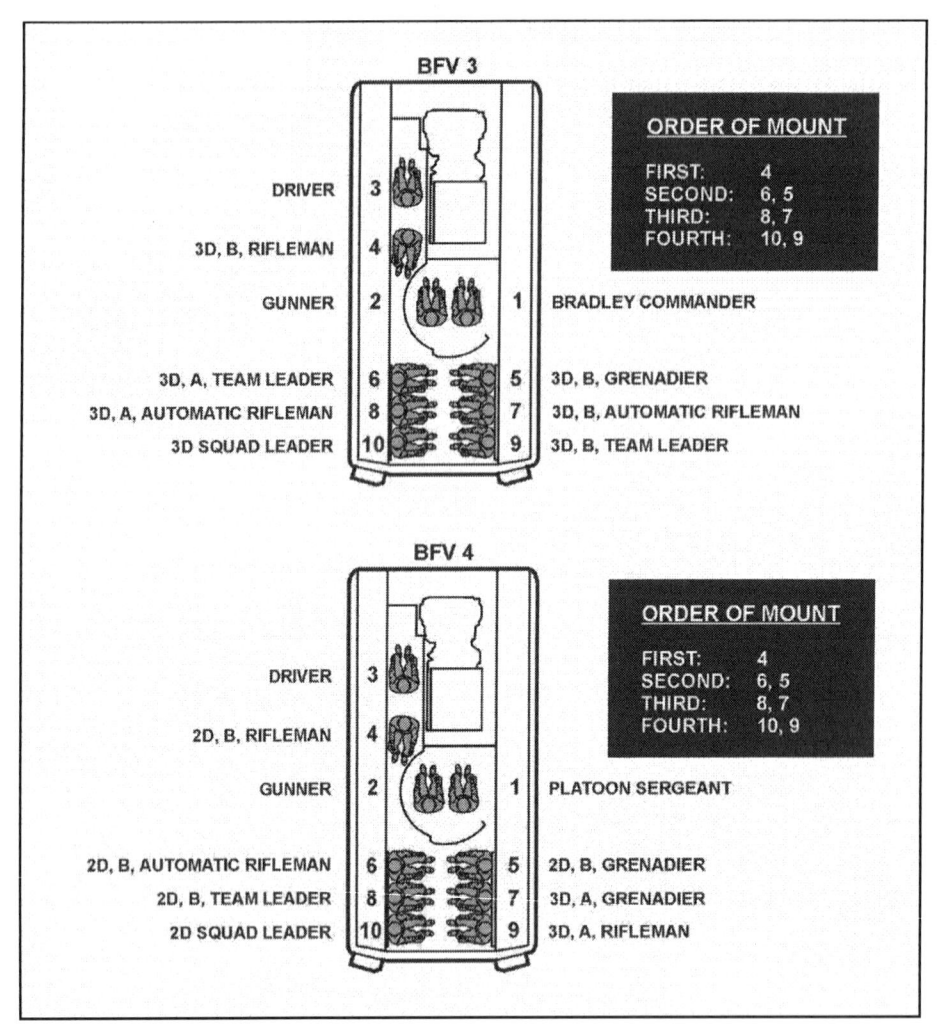

Figure J-21. BFV order of mount (continued)

Appendix J

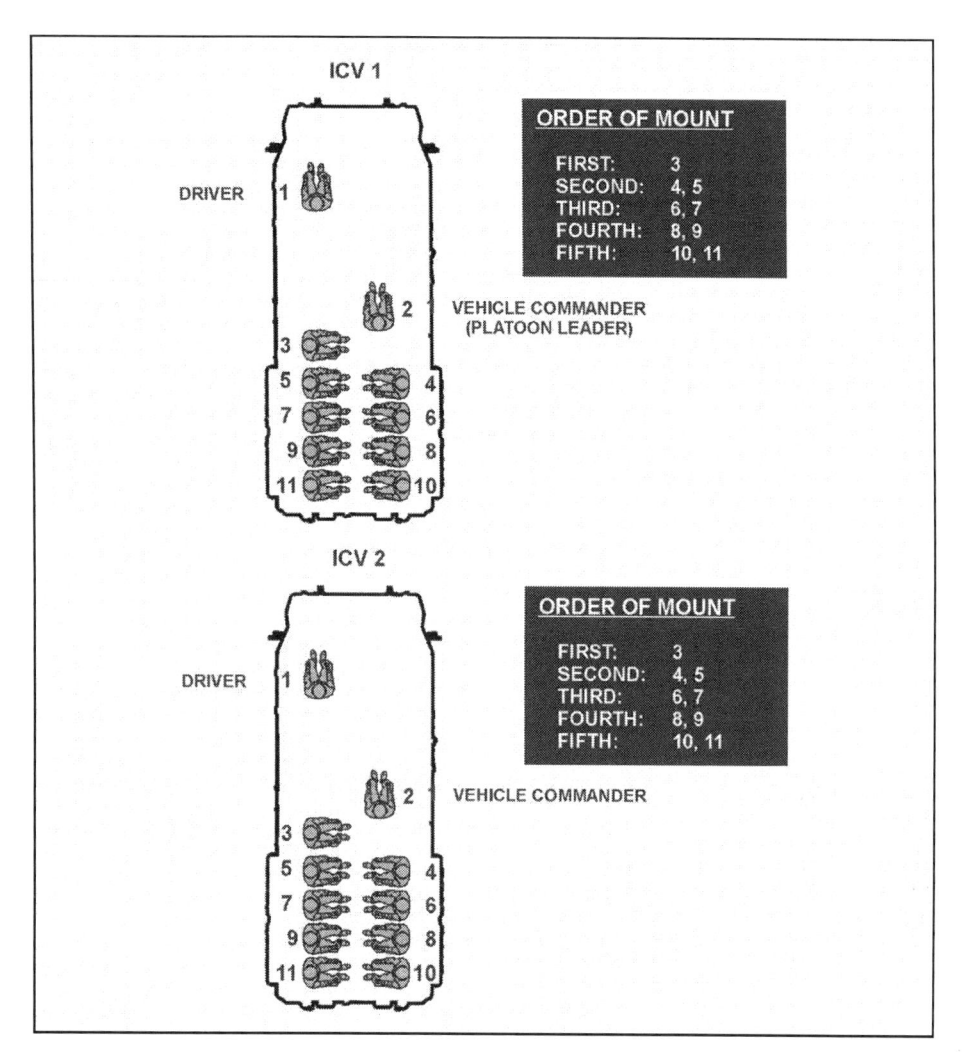

Figure J-22. ICV order of mount

Selected Battle Drills

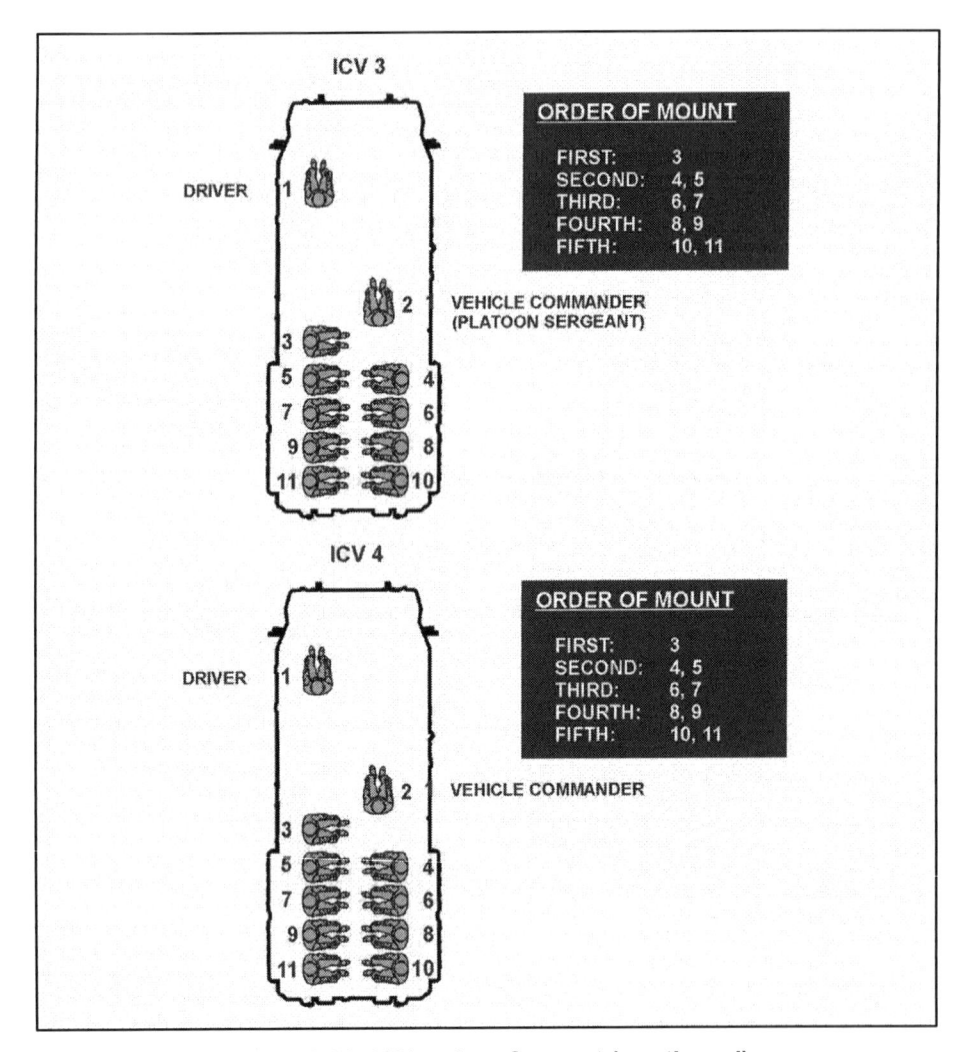

Figure J-23. ICV order of mount (continued)

8. The platoon/squad leader prepares to mount.
    a. Senior leader accounts for all personnel and equipment, ensures weapons are on SAFE in the vehicle, and reports to the Bradley/vehicle commander. The senior leader announces, "ALL UP."
    b. The Bradley/vehicle commander orders the driver to raise the ramp or the fire team to close the ramp access door.
    c. The platoon leader establishes visual or radio contact with the other Bradley/vehicle commander and designates a direction of movement, formation, and movement technique from the mount point.

Appendix J

BATTLE DRILL 14: EXECUTE ACTION RIGHT OR LEFT WHILE MOUNTED (07-3-D9437)

CONDITIONS: The platoon is moving, conducting operations, and must execute action right or left.

CUE: The unit leader initiates the drill by using arm-and-hand signals, flags, or radio to give the order, "EXECUTE ACTION RIGHT (or left)."

STANDARDS: The mounted platoon changes direction into a line formation, orienting weapons on the enemy force.

TASK STEPS AND PERFORMANCE MEASURES

1. The platoon leader signals action right or left using arm-and-hand, flags, or radio. (See figures J-24 through J-31, pages J-45 through J-52.)

2. The drivers immediately execute a turn in the direction indicated while moving into a line formation:
    a. The platoon sergeant orients his vehicle on the platoon leader's vehicle.
    b. Wingmen orient their vehicles on the platoon leader and platoon sergeant vehicles.

3. The platoon leader orders the vehicle commanders to seek covered positions for their vehicles or have them continue to move in the direction indicated.

4. The vehicle commanders orient the main weapons toward the enemy, and the vehicle commanders and gunners search for targets.

5. The platoon leader determines if it is necessary to dismount the rifle squads.

6. The platoon leader reports the situation to the company commander, if needed.

Selected Battle Drills

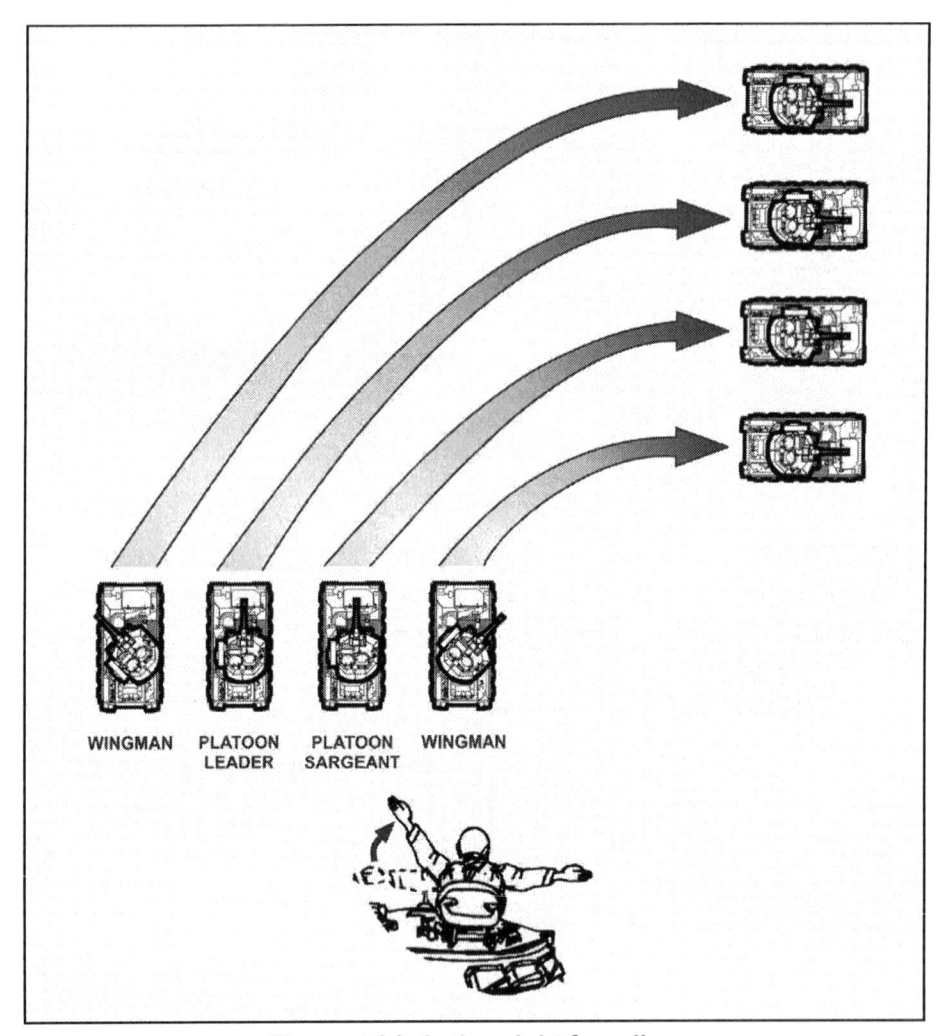

Figure J-24. Action right from line

Appendix J

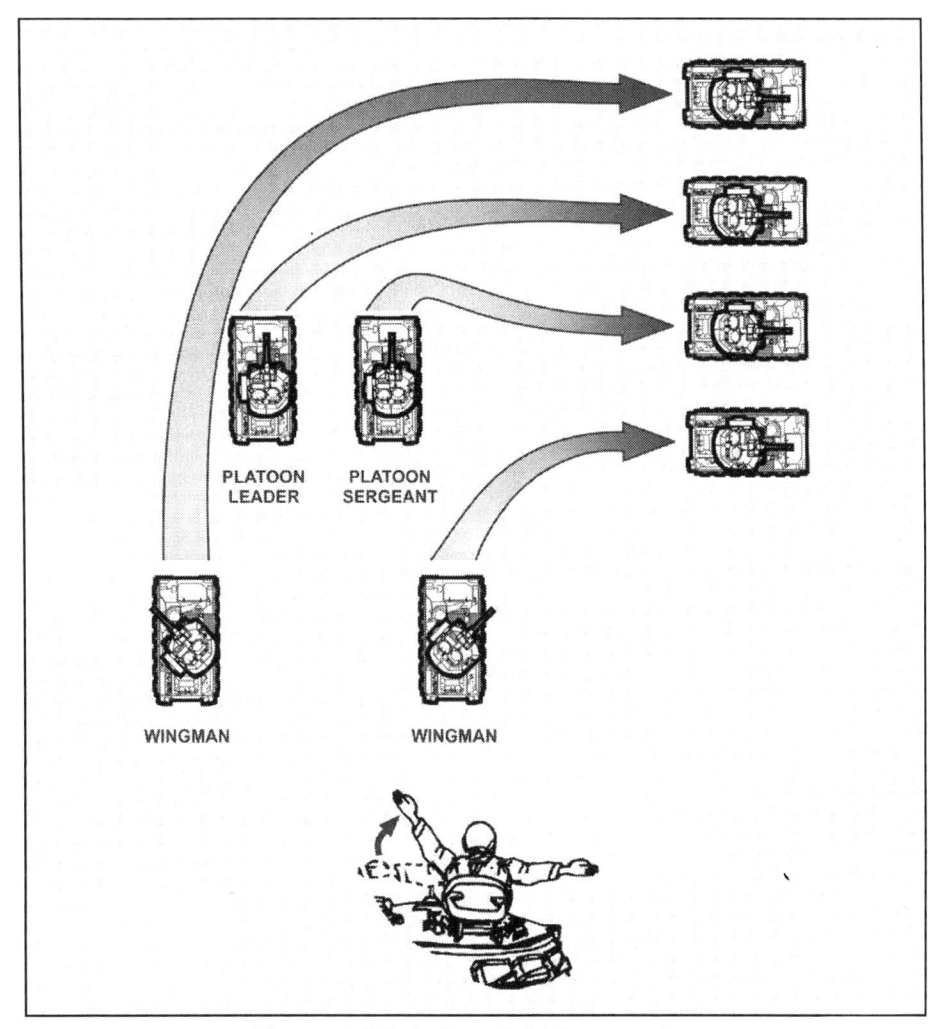

Figure J-25. Action right from wedge

Selected Battle Drills

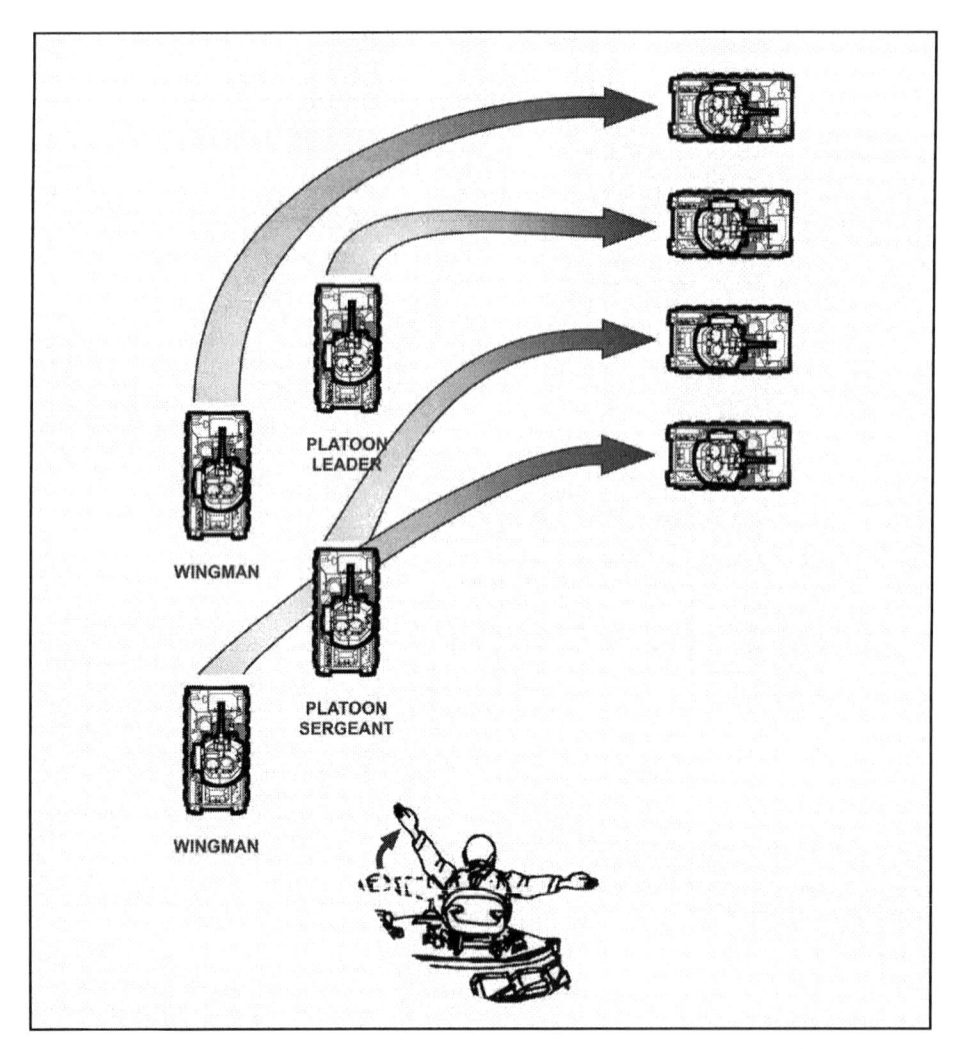

Figure J-26. Action right from column, wingman on left

Appendix J

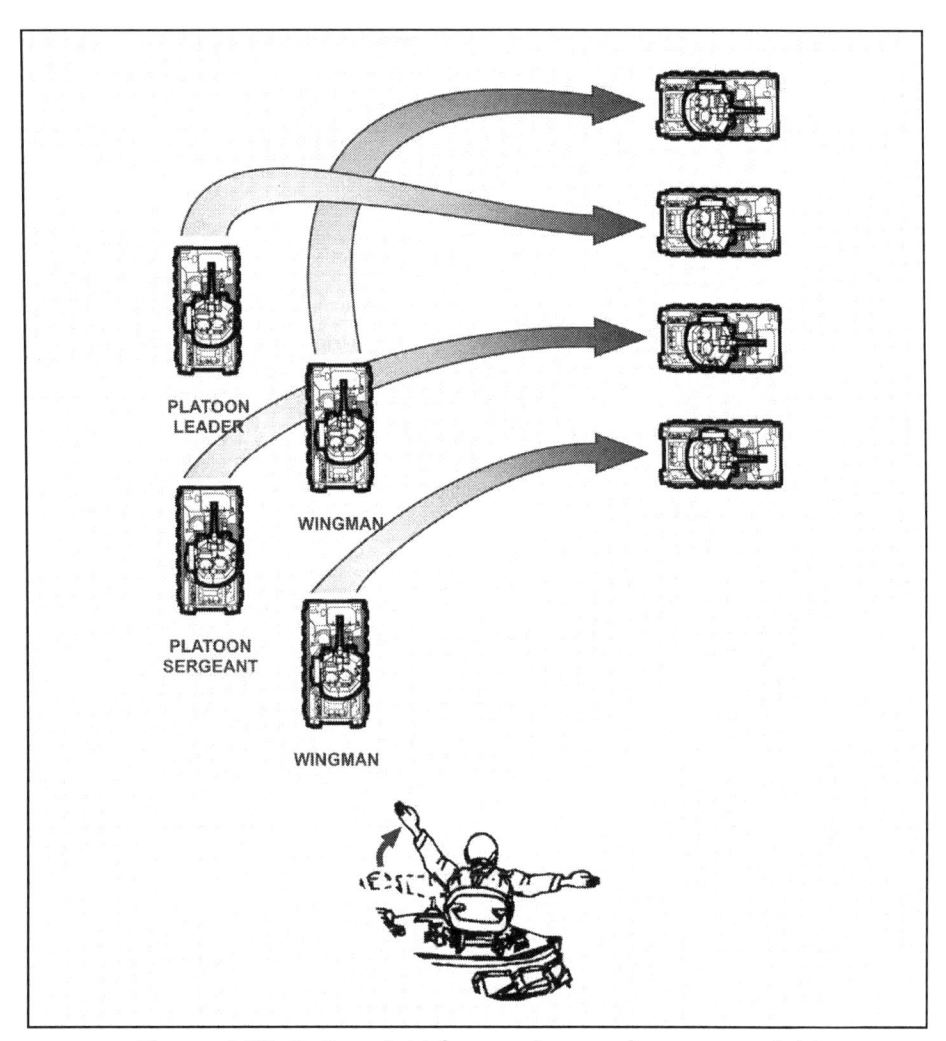

Figure J-27. Action right from column, wingman on right

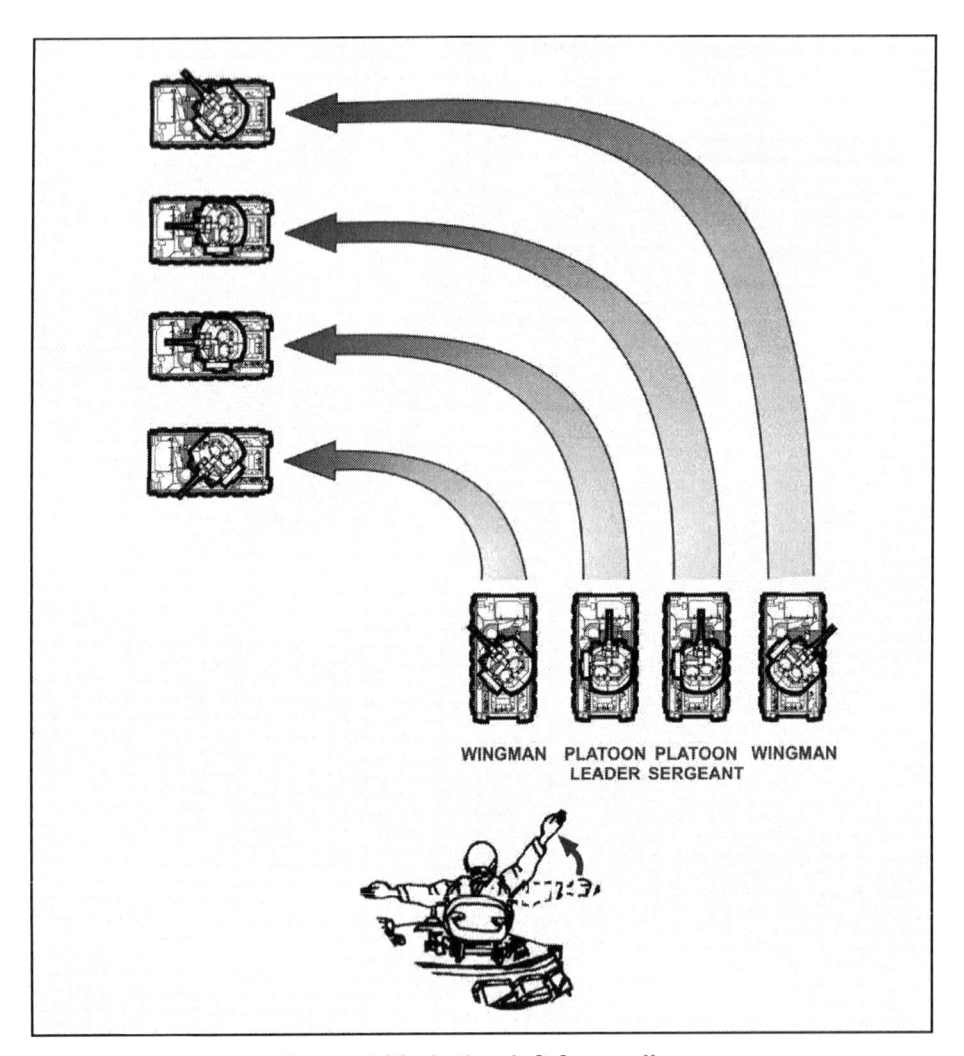

Figure J-28. Action left from a line

Appendix J

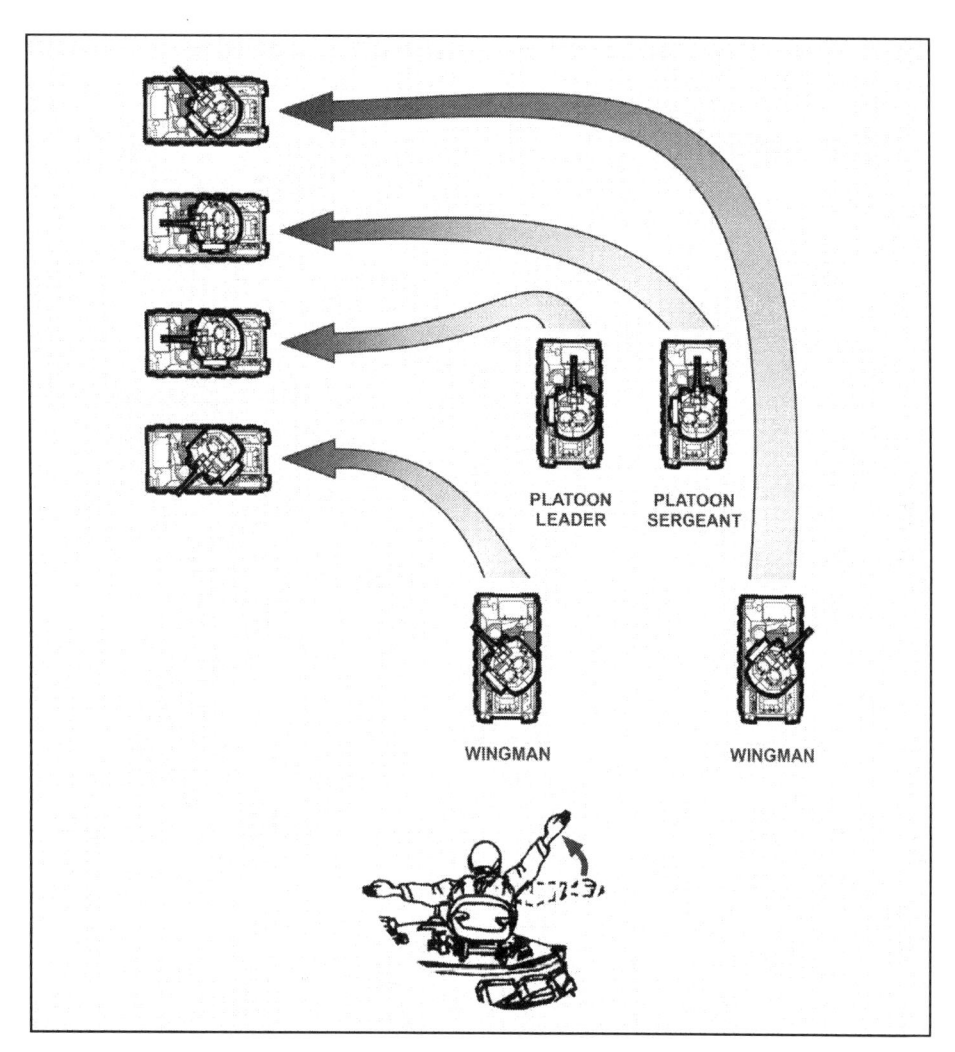

Figure J-29. Action left from a wedge

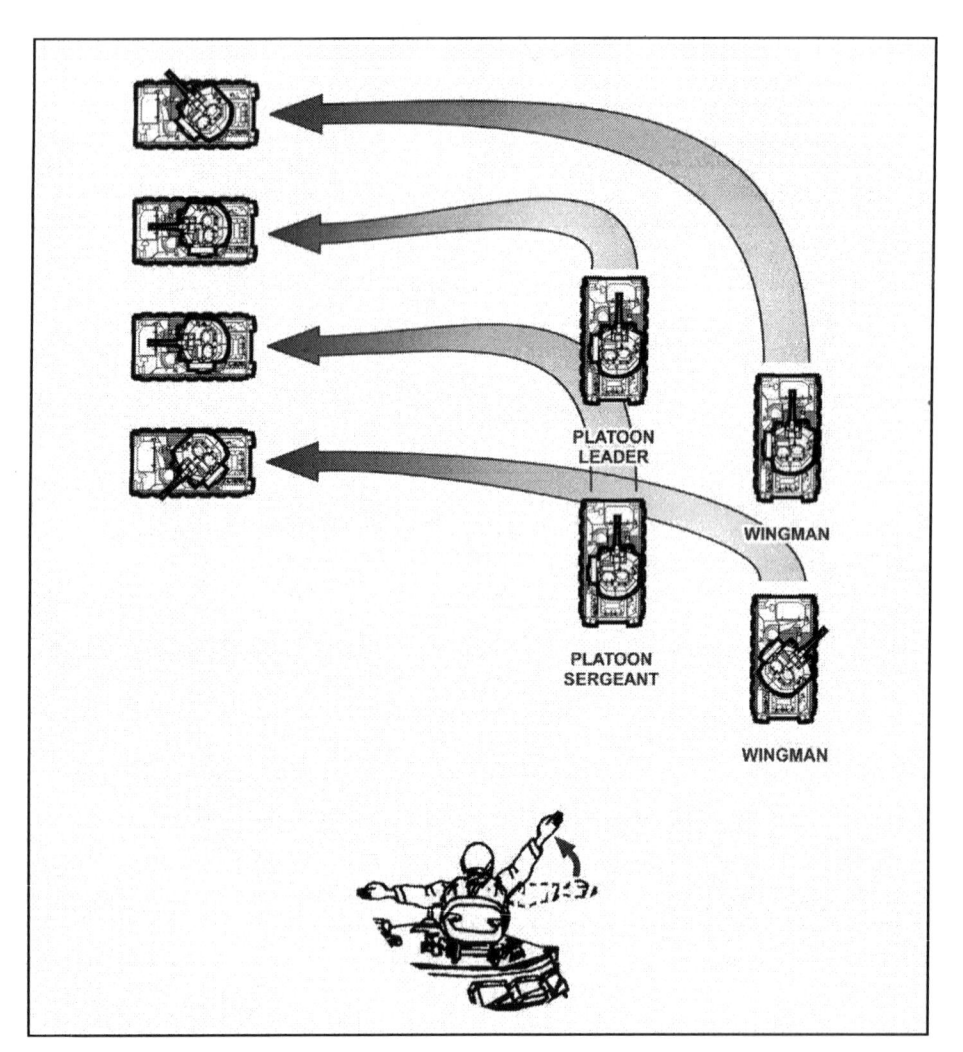

Figure J-30. Action left from a column, wingman on right

Appendix J

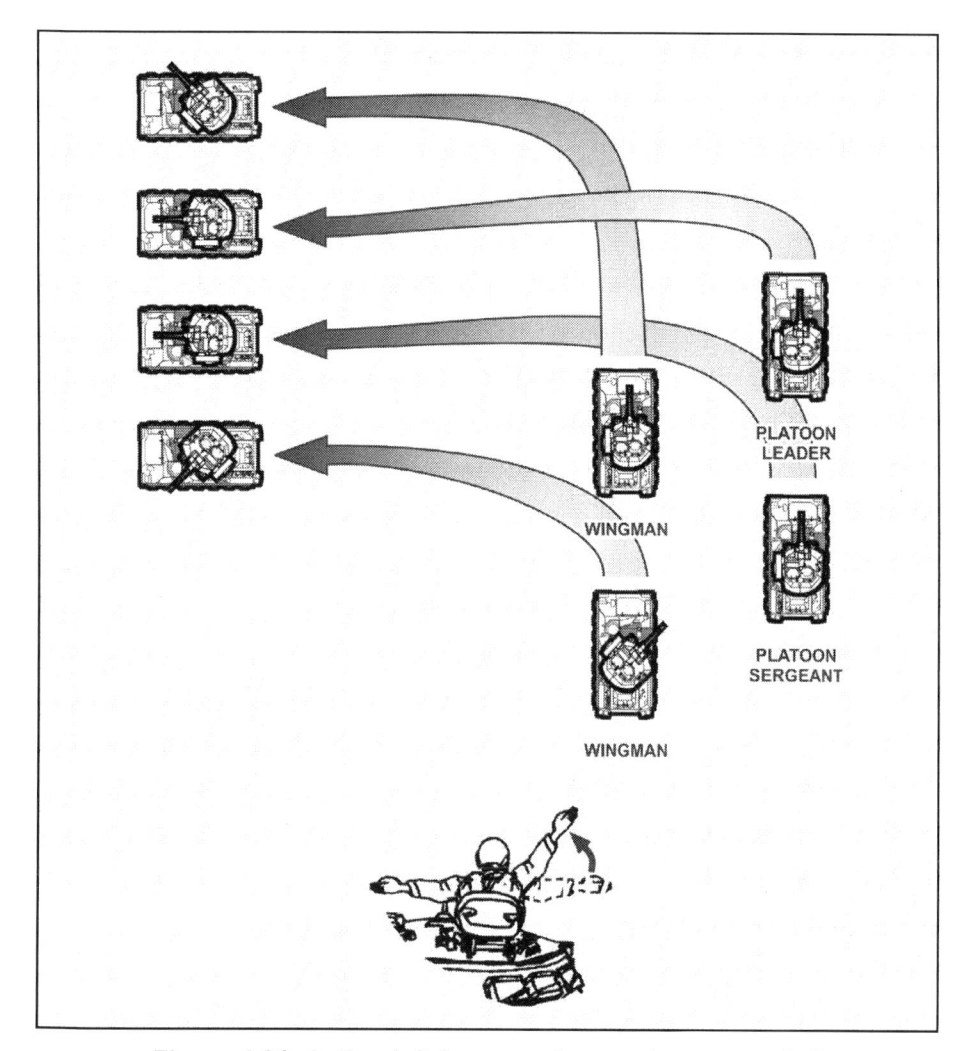

Figure J-31. Action left from a column, wingman on left

Made in the USA
Columbia, SC
15 April 2020